NTA UGC

NET / JRF / SET

Commerce

PAPER-2

Author

Neetu Singh *(MBA, B Ed, MA)*

Apeksha Agiwal *(CS, B Com, Diploma in Management and Business Basics)*

Satyabroto Roy *(MA, Economics)*

arihant

ARIHANT PUBLICATIONS (INDIA) LIMITED

arihant
ARIHANT PUBLICATIONS (INDIA) LIMITED

卐 **Administrative & Production Offices**

Regd. Office
'Ramchhaya' 4577/15, Agarwal Road, Darya Ganj, New Delhi -110002
Tele: 011- 47630600, 43518550

卐 **Head Office**
Kalindi, TP Nagar, Meerut (UP) - 250002
Tel: 0121-7156203, 7156204

卐 **Sales & Support Offices**
Agra, Ahmedabad, Bengaluru, Bareilly, Chennai, Delhi, Guwahati, Hyderabad, Jaipur, Jhansi, Kolkata, Lucknow, Nagpur & Pune.

卐 **ISBN** 978-93-25295-96-4
卐 **PRICE** ₹685.00

Published by Arihant Publications (India) Ltd.

For further information about the books published by Arihant, log on to www.arihantbooks.com or e-mail at info@arihantbooks.com

Follow us on

PREFACE

The National Eligibility Test also known as UGC NET or NTA-UGC-NET, is a test to determine the eligibility for college and University level lectureship and for the award of Junior Research Fellowship (JRF) for Indian Nationals. From December, 2018 onwards, National Testing Agency (NTA) is conducting this exam.

The key idea behind writing this book is to provide the aspiring candidates of UGC NET in Commerce, such a book that will be a complete package for this exam. The focus of this book is on providing exhaustive, crisp text resource and an enormous question bank with answers to help aspiring students of UGC NET to reach goal of passing this prestigious exam in the first attempt. The book has been prepared as per the latest syllabus applicable for June, 2019 Examination. The level of difficulty for this exam is kept in mind, while composing the text and questions.

Salient Features of the Book

- Theoretical aspect of the subject has been written in a very simple language.
- Main contents of the chapter are highlighted, so that brush-up can be done quickly before the exam.
- Units are divided in different number of chapters, according to the topic so as to synchronise the entire syllabus and helps student to correlate the topics.
- Solved examples are given to provide a better understanding of accounting issues.
- Question Bank of approx 4500 multiple choice questions are provided, which covers both conceptual issues and their practical applications that enables the student to pierce the topic and understand its depth.

We hope and believe that the book will cater to the requirements of the students and wish the readers a happy and enriching experience, while reading this book. However, in order to make the book more useful, suggestions from teaching fraternity and students are always welcome.

Authors

SYLLABUS

Applicabe from June 2019, Examination

UNIT 1 Business Environment and International Business

- Concepts and elements of business environment: Economic environment- Economic systems, Economic policies(Monetary and fiscal policies); Political environment- Role of government in business; Legal environment- Consumer Protection Act, FEMA; Socio-cultural factors and their influence on business; Corporate Social Responsibility (CSR)
- Scope and importance of international business; Globalization and its drivers; Modes of entry into international business
- Theories of international trade; Government intervention in international trade; Tariff and non-tariff barriers; India's foreign trade policy
- Foreign direct investment (FDI) and Foreign portfolio investment (FPI); Types of FDI, Costs and benefits of FDI to home and host countries; Trends in FDI; India's FDI policy
- Balance of payments (BOP): Importance and components of BOP
- Regional Economic Integration: Levels of Regional Economic Integration; Trade creation and diversion effects; Regional Trade Agreements: European Union (EU), ASEAN, SAARC, NAFTA
- International Economic institutions: IMF, World Bank, UNCTAD
- World Trade Organisation (WTO): Functions and objectives of WTO; Agriculture Agreement; GATS; TRIPS; TRIMS

UNIT 2 Accounting and Auditing

- Basic accounting principles; concepts and postulates
- Partnership Accounts: Admission, Retirement, Death, Dissolution and Insolvency of partnership firms
- Corporate Accounting: Issue, forfeiture and reissue of shares; Liquidation of companies; Acquisition, merger, amalgamation and reconstruction of companies
- Holding company accounts
- Cost and Management Accounting: Marginal costing and Break-even analysis; Standard costing; Budgetary control; Process costing; Activity Based Costing (ABC); Costing for decision-making; Life cycle costing, Target costing, Kaizen costing and JIT
- Financial Statements Analysis: Ratio analysis; Funds flow Analysis; Cash flow analysis
- Human Resources Accounting; Inflation Accounting; Environmental Accounting
- Indian Accounting Standards and IFRS
- Auditing: Independent financial audit; Vouching; Verification ad valuation of assets and liabilities; Audit of financial statements and audit report; Cost audit
- Recent Trends in Auditing: Management audit; Energy audit; Environment audit; Systems audit; Safety audit

UNIT 3 Business Economics

- Meaning and scope of business economics
- Objectives of business firms
- Demand analysis: Law of demand; Elasticity of demand and its measurement; Relationship between AR and MR
- Consumer behavior: Utility analysis; Indifference curve analysis
- Law of Variable Proportions: Law of Returns to Scale
- Theory of cost: Short-run and long-run cost curves
- Price determination under different market forms: Perfect competition; Monopolistic competition; Oligopoly- Price leadership model; Monopoly; Price discrimination
- Pricing strategies: Price skimming; Price penetration; Peak load pricing

UNIT 4 Business Finance

- Scope and sources of finance; Lease financing
- Cost of capital and time value of money
- Capital structure
- Capital budgeting decisions: Conventional and scientific techniques of capital budgeting analysis
- Working capital management; Dividend decision: Theories and policies
- Risk and return analysis; Asset securitization
- International monetary system
- Foreign exchange market; Exchange rate risk and hedging techniques
- International financial markets and instruments: Euro currency; GDRs; ADRs
- International arbitrage; Multinational capital budgeting

UNIT 5 Business Statistics and Research Methods

- Measures of central tendency
- Measures of dispersion
- Measures of skewness
- Correlation and regression of two variables
- Probability: Approaches to probability; Bayes' theorem
- Probability distributions: Binomial, poisson and normal distributions
- Research: Concept and types; Research designs
- Data: Collection and classification of data
- Sampling and estimation: Concepts; Methods of sampling - probability and non-probability methods; Sampling distribution; Central limit theorem; Standard error; Statistical estimation
- Hypothesis testing: z-test; t-test; ANOVA; Chi–square test; Mann-Whitney test (U-test); Kruskal-Wallis test (H-test); Rank correlation test
- Report writing

UNIT 6 Business Management and Human Resource Management

- Principles and functions of management
- Organization structure: Formal and informal organizations; Span of control
- Responsibility and authority: Delegation of authority and decentralization
- Motivation and leadership: Concept and theories
- Corporate governance and business ethics
- Human resource management: Concept, role and functions of HRM; Human resource planning; Recruitment and selection; Training and development; Succession planning
- Compensation management: Job evaluation; Incentives and fringe benefits
- Performance appraisal including 360 degree performance appraisal
- Collective bargaining and workers' participation in management
- Personality: Perception; Attitudes; Emotions; Group dynamics; Power and politics; Conflict and negotiation; Stress management
- Organizational Culture: Organizational development and organizational change

UNIT 7 Banking and Financial Institutions

- Overview of Indian financial system
- Types of banks: Commercial banks; Regional Rural Banks (RRBs); Foreign banks; Cooperative banks
- Reserve Bank of India: Functions; Role and monetary policy management
- Banking sector reforms in India: Basel norms; Risk management; NPA management
- Financial markets: Money market; Capital market; Government securities market
- Financial Institutions: Development Finance Institutions (DFIs); Non-Banking Financial Companies (NBFCs); Mutual Funds; Pension Funds
- Financial Regulators in India

- Financial sector reforms including financial inclusion
- Digitisation of banking and other financial services: Internet banking; mobile banking; Digital payments systems
- Insurance: Types of insurance- Life and Non-life insurance; Risk classification and management; Factors limiting the insurability of risk; Re-insurance; Regulatory framework of insurance- IRDA and its role

UNIT 8 Marketing Management

- Marketing: Concept and approaches; Marketing channels; Marketing mix; Strategic marketing planning; Market segmentation, targeting and positioning
- Product decisions: Concept; Product line; Product mix decisions; Product life cycle; New product development
- Pricing decisions: Factors affecting price determination; Pricing policies and strategies
- Promotion decisions: Role of promotion in marketing; Promotion methods - Advertising; Personal selling; Publicity; Sales promotion tools and techniques; Promotion mix
- Distribution decisions: Channels of distribution; Channel management
- Consumer Behaviour; Consumer buying process; factors influencing consumer buying decisions
- Service marketing
- Trends in marketing: Social marketing; Online marketing; Green marketing; Direct marketing; Rural marketing; CRM
- Logistics management

UNIT 9 Legal Aspects of Business

- Indian Contract Act, 1872: Elements of a valid contract; Capacity of parties; Free consent; Discharge of a contract; Breach of contract and remedies against breach; Quasi contracts
- Special contracts: Contracts of indemnity and guarantee; contracts of bailment and pledge; Contracts of agency
- Sale of Goods Act, 1930: Sale and agreement to sell; Doctrine of Caveat Emptor; Rights of unpaid seller and rights of buyer
- Negotiable Instruments Act, 1881: Types of negotiable instruments; Negotiation and assignment; Dishonour and discharge of negotiable instruments
- The Companies Act, 2013: Nature and kinds of companies; Company formation; Management, meetings and winding up of a joint stock company
- Limited Liability Partnership: Structure and procedure of formation of LLP in India
- The Competition Act, 2002: Objectives and main provisions
- The Information Technology Act, 2000: Objectives and main provisions; Cyber crimes and penalties
- The RTI Act, 2005: Objectives and main provisions
- Intellectual Property Rights (IPRs) : Patents, trademarks and copyrights; Emerging issues in intellectual property
- Goods and Services Tax (GST): Objectives and main provisions; Benefits of GST; Implementation mechanism; Working of dual GST

UNIT 10 Income-tax and Corporate Tax Planning

- Income-tax: Basic concepts; Residential status and tax incidence; Exempted incomes; Agricultural income; Computation of taxable income under various heads; Deductions from Gross total income; Assessment of Individuals; Clubbing of incomes
- International Taxation: Double taxation and its avoidance mechanism; Transfer pricing
- Corporate Tax Planning: Concepts and significance of corporate tax planning; Tax avoidance versus tax evasion; Techniques of corporate tax planning; Tax considerations in specific business situations: Make or buy decisions; Own or lease an asset; Retain; Renewal or replacement of asset; Shut down or continue operations
- Deduction and collection of tax at source; Advance payment of tax; E-filing of income-tax returns

CONTENTS

UGC NET/JRF/SET

Commerce (Paper-2)

Solved Paper, October 2020

General Instructions

1. There are total one hundred questions in this paper. Each question carries 2 marks.
2. All questions are compulsory.

1. As per Section 80G maximum deduction allowed for any cash donation is upto

(a) ₹ 1,000 (b) ₹ 2,000
(c) ₹ 5,000 (d) ₹ 10,000

2. In Leontief production function, L is considered as

(a) structural constraint in the production process.
(b) degree of homogeneity.
(c) binding constraint in the productions process.
(d) optimisation constraint in the production process.

3. EPRG frame work in International Business refers to

(a) ethno poly, regio, geo transformations
(b) ethnocentric, polycentric, regiocentric and geocentric orientations
(c) ethics, policies, regulations, guidelines orientations
(d) every Person refers Global Framework

4. Which one of the following is not a major direct selling company in India?

(a) Eureka Forbes
(b) Amway India Enterprises
(c) Modicare
(d) Hindustan Unilever Ltd

5. Which one of the following statements is 'True' in partnership?

(a) In the absence of any provision in the partnership deed, only a working partner is entitled to remuneration.
(b) Any firm which earns normal profits has no goodwill.
(c) The business of the firm must be carried on by all the partners.
(d) Interest on loan given by a partner to the firm shall be paid if there are profits.

6. Which of the following relationships is true in a model distribution?

(a) Mean − Mode = 3 (Mean − Median)
(b) Mode = 3 Median − 2 Mean
(c) 3 Median = 2 Mean + Mode
(d) 2 Median − 3 Quartile Deviation = 2 Mean

7. In continuous compounding, the time it takes to double the sum grossly follow 'Rule of 69'. If it is changed to discrete compounding, the relevant rule of thumb is ....

(a) rule of 69.3 (b) rule of 72
(c) rule of 84 (d) rule of 64

8. The 'going concern concept' is the underlying basis for

(a) disclosing the market value of securities.
(b) consolidating the accounts of subsidiary companies with those of parent company.
(c) depreciating fixed assets over their useful lives.
(d) disclosing the sales and other operating information in the income statement.

9. 'Constraint Optimisation' is closer to which of the following objectives of business firm?

(a) Sales maximisation
(b) Profit maximisation
(c) Satisfying behaviour
(d) Rent seeking behaviour

10. In a rising consumer income scenario, the preferred decision choice of business firms for low income elastic products will be ....

(a) product promotion (b) cost control
(c) product repositioning (d) product improvement

11. If an estimated Cobb-Douglas production function is $Q = 10K^{0.6}L^{0.8}$, what type of returns to scale does this production function indicate?
(a) Increasing returns (b) Decreasing returns
(c) Constant returns (d) Negative returns

12. Pricing strategy of setting a high price when a product is introduced and gradually lowering its price is known as
(a) skimming
(b) penetration pricing
(c) peak load pricing
(d) dumping

13. Which one of the following is not true for Mass Marketing?
(a) Provides very little scope for customisation.
(b) Deals with customers directly.
(c) Normally followed in case of FMCG and SMCG goods.
(d) Relies heavily on advertising.

14. A manufacturing enterprise monthly consumes 1,350 units of raw material at the cost of ₹ 20 per unit. Determine its economic order quantity given the ordering cost of ₹ 2,400 and carrying cost of inventory being 30 per cent of the price paid.
(a) 3,600 units (b) 2,400 units
(c) 4,800 units (d) 2,700 units

15. The portfolio theory articulates diversification to reduce which of the following risks?
(a) Market risk (b) Financial risk
(c) Unsystematic risk (d) Business risk

16. When foreign currency assets and liabilities match in terms of amount of exposure and timing of maturities, it is described as
(a) financial hedge (b) natural hedge
(c) perfect hedge (d) netting

17. What is the probability that a randomly choosen card from a deck of cards will either be a King or a Spade?
(a) 0.3077 (b) 0.3269
(c) 0.0384 (d) 0.3169

18. The standard deviation of the binomial distribution is
(a) np (b) $\sqrt{np}$
(c) npq (d) $\sqrt{npq}$

19. When sampling is done without replacement then standard error of mean is
(a) $SE_{\overline{X}} = \frac{\sigma}{\sqrt{n}}$ (b) $SE_{\overline{X}} = \frac{\sigma}{\sqrt{n}}\sqrt{\frac{N-n}{N-1}}$
(c) $SE_{\overline{X}} = \frac{\sigma}{\sqrt{n}}\sqrt{\frac{N-1}{N-n}}$ (d) $SE_{\overline{X}} = \frac{\sigma}{\sqrt{n}}\sqrt{1-\frac{n}{N}}$

20. Which of the following is not an example of compressed data?
(a) Data array (b) Frequency distribution
(c) Histogram (d) Ogive

21. The Human Relations Approach rejected the 'rabble hypothesis' by giving which of the following argument?
(a) The worker does not work money only.
(b) A worker operates in a techno-economic system with no room for emotions.
(c) Authoritarian style of leadership is more productive.
(d) Individual pays attention to self-achievement irrespective of informal group norms.

22. Which of the following is not correct with respect to matrix organisation?
(a) It is a combination of functional and product organisation.
(b) Functional departments are not permanent fixtures of matrix organisation.
(c) Product departments are created as the need for them arises.
(d) Team members have functional home when they are not needed on a project.

23. As per Carroll Model, the four levels of corporate social responsibility are
(a) physical, economic, social and legal.
(b) philanthropic, economic, legal and ethical.
(c) philanthropic, economic, legal and ethical.
(d) philanthropic, economic, social and ethical.

24. Who coined the term 'Collective Bargaining'?
(a) Reed Richardson
(b) Kurt Lewin
(c) WE Deming
(d) Sydney Webb and Beatrice Webb

25. The headquarters of the ASEAN is located in which of the following country?
(a) Indonesia (b) Vietnam
(c) Thailand (d) Singapore

26. What is the rate of tax deduction at source from insurance commission in case of 'Person'.
(a) 2 per cent (b) 5 per cent
(c) 10 per cent (d) 4 per cent

27. Which of the following is a long term source of finance?
(a) Commercial Paper (CP)
(b) External Commercial Borrowings (ECB)
(c) Factoring
(d) Line of Credit (LOC)

28. What is a 'Repo Rate'?
(a) Is the rate at which RBI lends to State Government.
(b) Is the rate at which International aid agencies lends to RBI.
(c) Is the rate at which the RBI lends to Banks in case of short maturity.
(d) Is the rate at which RBI borrows funds from the Commercial Banks in the country.

29. In Marketing, DSA stands for ....
(a) Delivery Staff Agency
(b) Direct Supplier Agent
(c) Direct Selling Agent
(d) Distribution and Supply Agency

30. In which of the following stages of product life cycle, a company reduces sale promotion to take advantage of heavy consumer demand?

(a) Introduction (b) Growth
(c) Maturity (d) Decline

31. In which of the following price adjustment strategies, a company reduces prices to reward customer responses such as volume purchases, paying early or promoting the products?

(a) Discount and allowance pricing
(b) Psychological pricing
(c) Promotional pricing
(d) Dynamic pricing

32. Some doctors charge patients for missed appointments because the service value existed only at the point disappeared when the patient did not show up, is an example of which one of the following four service characteristics?

(a) Inseparability (b) Intangibility
(c) Variability (d) Perishability

33. Which one is False as per the relevant provisions of the Indian Contract Act, 1872?

(a) A void agreement is one that is not enforceable by law.
(b) Assignment is the obvious mode of discharge of a contract.
(c) Where a party waives its rights under the contract, the other party is released of its obligations under the contract.
(d) Where the subject matter of a contract is destroyed for no fault of the promisor, the contract does not become void by impossibility of performance.

34. Which of the following is not an implied condition in a contract of sale?

(a) Condition as to quality or fitness
(b) Condition as to merchantable quality
(c) Condition as to wholesomeness
(d) Condition as to free from encumbrances

35. Which of the following does not come under the definition of 'Information' under RTI Act, 2005?

(a) Log Books
(b) Circulars
(c) File Notings in the process
(d) Data material held in any electronic form

36. Under which section of Information Technology Act of 2000, updated in 2008, stealing any digital asset or information is consider as cyber crime?

(a) 65 (b) 65-D (c) 67 (d) 70

37. Which one of the following statements is true for the set off and carry forward of loss under the head 'house property' in India?

(a) Can be carried forward for 8 years.
(b) Cannot be carried forward.
(c) Can be carried forward for 4 years.
(d) Can be carried forward infinitely.

38. Surcharge of 10% (per cent) is payable by an individual by an individual where the total income exceeds

(a) ₹ 7,50,000/- (b) ₹ 8,50,000/-
(c) ₹ 50,00,00/- (d) ₹ 20,00,000/-

39. Mohan, has rendered his services in India and retired in 2015. He then shifted and settled in Singapore. The pension received by him for such services would be .... ?

(a) deemed to accure or arise outside India
(b) deemed to accure or arise in India only when it is received in India
(c) deemed to accure or arise in India only when it is received outside India
(d) deemed to accure or arise in India

40. Sugam is also known as

(a) ITR-1 (b) ITR-2
(c) ITR-4 (d) ITR-6

41. Mercosur, a South American Trade block is a

(a) free trade area (b) common market
(c) custom union (d) economic cooperation

42.* Which of the following are possible negative impacts of FDI on domestic firms in host countries?

1. Market monopoly
2. Technology dependence
3. Increased competition
4. Profit outflow

Choose the correct answer from the options given below.

(a) 1, 2 only (b) 2, 3 only
(c) 1, 2, 4 only (d) 2, 3, 4 only

43. Charging different prices for the same product in different markets until the MR of last unit sold quals the MC of the product sold in each market is described by ....

1. price discrimination of first degree
2. price discrimination of second degree
3. price discrimination of third degree
4. equilibrium price
5. price discrimination

Choose the correct answer from the options given below.

(a) 1 and 2 only (b) 1 and 3 only
(c) 3 and 5 only (d) 1 and 4 only

44. Arrange the following steps in logical sequence of operation of the Arbitrage Pricing Theory (APT).

1. Estimate the factor sensitivities.
2. Estimate the risk premium for factor(s).
3. Identify the macroeconomic factors.

Choose the correct answer from the options given below.

(a) 1, 2, 3 (b) 2, 1, 3 (c) 3, 2, 1 (d) 3, 1, 2

* Answer not given in official answer key.

45. Cost audit for material covers

1. goods inward procedure.
2. methods of calculating standard cost variance.
3. classification of overhead.
4. accounting for scrap, wastage, materials transfers.
5. accounting treatment of under or over absorption.

Choose the correct answer from the options given below.

(a) 1, 4 only (b) 1, 5 only
(c) 1, 2 only (d) 5, 2 only

46. Which of the following explains the declining slope of indifference curves?

1. Diminishing marginal utility.
2. Diminishing Marginal Rate of substitutions between the commodities.
3. Diminishing marginal rate of technical substitution.
4. Ordinal measurement of utilities.
5. Diminishing marginal utility of money.

Choose the correct answer from the options given below.

(a) 1 and 4 only (b) 2 and 4 only
(c) 3 and 4 only (d) 1 and 5 only

47. Which of the following is/are conditions(s) for price discrimination of product?

1. Firm must have some monopoly power.
2. Price elasticities of demand for the product in different market must differ.
3. Market must be separable or able to be segmented.
4. Free entry and exit of firms.

Choose the correct answer from the options given below.

(a) 1 and 2 only
(b) 2, 3 and 4 only
(c) 1, 3 and 4 only
(d) 1, 2 and 3 only

48. Consumer rationality in business economics is collective manifestation of which of the following assumptions?

1. Non-Satiation
2. Clarity of preferences
3. Divisibility of goods and services
4. Economic selfish motive
5. Possession of information

Choose the correct answer from the options given below.

(a) 1, 2 and 4 only (b) 1, 3 and 5 only
(c) 1, 2, 3 and 4 only (d) 1, 2, 4 and 5 only

49. Net Present Value (NPV) and Internal Rate of Return (IRR) methods yield conflicting outcomes due to ....

1. unconventional cash flows
2. investment size disparity
3. investment life disparity
4. cash flow pattern disparity

Choose the correct answer from the options given below.

(a) 1 and 2 only (b) 1 and 3 only
(c) 1, 2 and 3 only (d) 2, 3 and 4 only

50. In which of the following situations, the Payback Period Method is advised for evaluation of investment opportunities?

1. Overleveraged business
2. Cash rich businesses
3. Uncertain market conditions
4. Stable market conditions

Choose the correct answer from the options given below

(a) 1 and 2 only (b) 1 and 3 only
(c) 2 and 3 only (d) 3 and 4 only

51. The regression Coefficient is independent of the change of

1. Scale only
2. Origin only
3. Both Scale and Origin
4. Neither Scale nor Origin

Choose the correct answer from the options given below.

(a) 1 only (b) 2 only
(c) 3 only (d) 4 only

52. Which of the following are positional averages?

1. Arithmetic Mean 2. Median
3. Mode 4. Geometric Mean
5. Harmonic Mean

Choose the correct answer from the options given below.

(a) 2, 3 only (b) 2, 3, 4 only
(c) 2, 3, 1 only (d) 1, 2, 3, 4 only

53. Which of following is not correct about properties of correlation coefficient?

1. Depends on the origin.
2. Depends on the scale.
3. Depends on both origin and scale.
4. Is independent with respect to origin.
5. Is independent with respect to unit of scale.

Choose the correct answer from the options given below.

(a) 1, 4, 5 only (b) 1, 2, 4 only
(c) 1, 2, 3 only (d) 4, 5, 2 only

54. What type of defense mechanism is used by a person when he gets angry at his child or spouse because he had a bad day at work?

1. Denial
2. Repression
3. Projection
4. Displacement
5. Regression

Choose the correct answer from the options given below.

(a) 1 and 2 only (b) 2 only
(c) 4 only (d) 5 only

55. Out of the following statements which of them explains the difference between enculturation and acculturation as a part of cross-cultural training?

1. Enculturation refer to the process of learning and adopting host cultural norms, and acculturation is the process of learning our own native culture.
2. Enculturation is a anthropological term used for socialisation like acculturation.
3. Both terms refers to the process of learning through social interaction.
4. Enculturation refers to the process of learning our own culture and acculturation refers to the process of learning host cultural norms.

Choose the correct answer from the options given below.

(a) 1, 2 3 only (b) 2, 4 only
(c) 2, 3, 4 only (d) 1, 2 3 and 4 only

56. Which of the following financial institution(s) got merged with their subsidiary?

1. UTI
2. IFCI
3. ICICI
4. IDBI
5. Global Trust Bank

Choose the correct answer from the options given below.

(a) 1, 2 only (b) 2, 3 only
(c) 3, 4 only (d) 3, 5 only

57. Objectives of IMPS (Immediate Payment Services) are

1. to enable bank customers to use mobile instruments as a channel for accessing their bank accounts and remit funds 24 × 7.
2. making payments simpler just with the mobile number of the beneficiary.
3. to build the foundation for a full range of mobile based banking services.
4. to create competition with NEFT and RTGS

Choose the correct answer from the options given below.

(a) 1, 2 3 only (b) 2, 3 4 only
(c) 1, 2 4 only (d) 2, 4 only

58. Which among the following are correct statements with regard to NBFC in India?

1. All NBFCs should be registered with RBI.
2. NBFCs cannot accept demand deposits.
3. NBFCs do not form part of the payment and settlement system and cannot issue cheques drawn on itself.
4. Deposit insurance facility of Deposit Insurance and Credit Guarantee Corporation is not available to depositors of NBFCs.

Choose the correct answer from the options given below.

(a) 1, 2 3 only (b) 1, 2, 3, 4 only
(c) 1, 2, 4 only (d) 1, 4 only

59. Which of the following are true about delivering customer value?

1. A company can go alone in creating customer value.
2. Company must work within a broader network of partners to accomplish customer value.
3. Individual companies and brands compete; their entire value delivery networks don't.
4. Individual companies and brands don't compete; their entire value delivery networks do.
5. Value = Contribution/cost (offer higher contribution through product or service to clients and lowers the cost).

Choose the correct answer from the options given below.

(a) 1 and 5 only (b) 1, 2 and 5 only
(c) 2, 3 and 5 only (d) 2, 4 and 5 only

60. Market for automobiles needs to be segmented on the basis of

1. buying behaviour
2. psychographics
3. geographics
4. demographics

Choose the correct answer from the options given below.

(a) 1, 4 only (b) 3, 4 only
(c) 1, 2, 4 only (d) 1, 2, 3, 4

61. The strategies of flanking defense, preemptive defense, mobile defense, contractor defense and counter offensive defense is used by which market player?

1. Market challenger
2. Market leader
3. Market follower
4. Market Nicher
5. Start up Marketer

Choose the correct answer from the options given below.

(a) 1 only (b) 2 only
(c) 3 only (d) 2, 5 only

62. Out of the following statements, which is not correct about the RTI Act, 2005?

1. The RTI Act came into force from 13th October, 2005.
2. Any citizen may request information from a Public Authority (Both Government and Private).
3. Reply for information asked can be given within 30 days.
4. There is a nominal application fee that are needs to pay to get information under the RTI application.
5. For getting information, applicant has to pay ₹ 10/- per page of information for Central Government Departments.

Choose the correct answer from the options given below.

(a) 1, 2, 5 only (b) 2, 5 on ly
(c) 3, 5 only (d) 2, 3, 4, 5 only

63. Out of the following, which are not the features of GST 2017 in India?

1. GST is applicable on 'supply' of Goods and Services.
2. GST is based on the principle of origin based taxation rather than principle of destination based consumption.
3. Import of Goods is treated as Inter-State supplies and would be subject to IGST in addition to applicable custom duties.
4. It is a dual taxation with Centre and State simultaneously levying it on a common base.
5. GST is applicable to all goods and services without any exemptions.

Choose the correct answer from the options given below.

(a) 1, 2 5 only (b) 2, 3, 5 only
(c) 2, 5 only (d) 3, 4, 5 only

64. Which of the following is correct about deduction available in respect of contribution to various provident funds in case of salaried employees?

1. Employer's contribution to recognised provident fund is exempted upto 12% of salary.
2. Employer's contribution to unrecognised provident fund is exempted from tax.
3. Employer does not contribute to Public Fund.
4. Deduction under Section 80C is available for employer's contribution in unrecognised provident fund.

Choose the correct answer from the options given below.

(a) 1, 2, 3 only (b) 1, 2 4 only
(c) 2, 3, 4 only (d) 1, 3, 4 only

65. Which of the following expenses debited to profit and loss A/c but disallowed while computing income from business?

1. General expenses
2. Personal expenses
3. Expenses of income which is taxable under the other heads of income
4. Charities and donations

Choose the correct answer from the options given below.

(a) 1, 2, 3 only (b) 2, 3, 4 only
(c) 3, 4 only (d) 1, 2, 3, 4 only

66. Match List I with List II.

List I (Authors of Trade Theory)	List II (Name of Theory)
A. Steffan Linder	1. Product Life Cycle Theory
B. Raymond Vernon	2. Country Similarity Theory
C. Heckshen-Ohlin	3. Absolute Advantage Theory
D. Adam Smith	4. Factor Proportion Theory

Choose the correct answer from the options given below.

	A	B	C	D		A	B	C	D
(a)	4	3	2	1	(b)	2	1	4	3
(c)	1	3	4	2	(d)	3	2	1	4

67. Match List I with List II.

List I	List II
A. Standard Costing	1. Financial forecasting and planning
B. Margin of Safety	2. Sales minus break-even sales
C. Ratio Analysis	3. Control of inventory
D. JIT System	4. Management by exception

Choose the correct answer from the options given below.

	A	B	C	D		A	B	C	D
(a)	4	2	1	3	(b)	3	1	2	4
(c)	2	3	1	4	(d)	1	2	4	3

68. Match the market forms in the List I and the role of the selling costs in the List II.

List I (Market Forms)	List II (Role of Selling Costs)
A. Perfect Competition	1. Sustained survival of firm
B. Monopoly	2. Influencing buying behaviour
C. Monopolistic Competition	3. Increasing market size
D. Oligopoly	4. Intimation of product or service

Choose the correct answer from the options given below.

	A	B	C	D		A	B	C	D
(a)	1	3	4	2	(b)	4	2	1	3
(c)	3	4	2	1	(d)	2	1	3	4

69. Match List I with List II.

	List I		List II
A.	Mezzanine Capital	1.	It is the speedy source of finance less regulated by the regulatory environment of debt and capital markets.
B.	Private Equity	2.	It is long term capital embraced by the high networth and high risk appetite investors.
C.	Global Depository Receipts	3.	It is an equity instrument issued in overseas market and is listed and traded on courses on an OTC basis.
D.	Venture Capital	4.	It refers to subordinated debt or preferred equity that allows firms to borrow additional capital beyond the levels lenders are willing to finance through the bank loans.

Choose the correct answer from the options given below.

	A	B	C	D		A	B	C	D
(a)	2	4	1	3	(b)	1	3	4	2
(c)	4	1	3	2	(d)	3	2	1	4

70. Match List I with List II.

	List I		List II
A.	Baye's Theorem	1.	$P(\bar{E}) = 1 - P(E)$
B.	Conditional Probability	2.	$P(E_1 \cup E_2) = P(E_1) + P(E_2)$
C.	Theorem of complementary events	3.	$P(E_2/E_1) = \frac{P(E_1 \cap E_2)}{P(E_1)}$
D.	Theorem of addition	4.	$P(H_i/E) = \frac{P(H_i \cap E)}{P(E)}$

Choose the correct answer from the options given below.

	A	B	C	D
(a)	1	4	3	2
(b)	3	4	2	1
(c)	3	4	1	2
(d)	4	3	1	2

71. Match List I with List II.

	List I		List II
A.	I am Not OK, you are Not OK	1.	Dependent
B.	I am OK, you are Not OK	2.	Confronting
C.	I am OK, you are OK	3.	Withdrawn
D.	I am Not OK, you are OK	4.	Task obsessive

Choose the correct answer from the options given below.

	A	B	C	D		A	B	C	D
(a)	3	4	2	1	(b)	3	2	4	1
(c)	1	2	3	4	(d)	2	1	3	4

72. Match List I with List II.

	List I (Capital Structure Preposition(s))		List II (Description(s))
A.	Target Capital Structure	1.	Expected yield on the equity capital is equal to the pure equity return plus a premium for financial risk.
B.	Optimum Capital Structure	2.	It refers to the perceived costs due to increased ratio of debt in the firm.
C.	Cost of Financial Distress	3.	It is the debt ratio of firm strive to achieve.
D.	MM Preposition-II	4.	It is the debt-equity ratio that maximises the value of the firm.

Choose the correct answer from the options given below.

	A	B	C	D		A	B	C	D
(a)	2	3	1	4	(b)	3	4	2	1
(c)	4	2	3	1	(d)	1	3	2	4

73. Match List I with List II.

	List I (Authors)		List II (Ideas)
A.	Bill Bishop	1.	Managing in the Market Space
B.	D. Bird	2.	Commonsense Direct Marketing
C.	Daniel S. Jonal	3.	Strategic Marketing for the Digital Age
D.	Jeffery F. Rayport	4.	On-line Marketing

Choose the correct answer from the options given below.

	A	B	C	D		A	B	C	D
(a)	3	2	4	1	(b)	1	2	3	4
(c)	2	1	4	3	(d)	4	3	2	1

74. Match List I with List II.

	List I		List II
A.	Limited Liability Partnership	1.	It can be formed with a minimum of two individuals or body corporate through their nominees.
B.	Particular Partnership	2.	It is formed for a specific venture or for a particular period.
C.	Partnership	3.	It is an association of two or more individuals.
D.	Mutual Agency	4.	A partner is both an agent and a principal in a partnership firm

Choose the correct answer from the options given below.

	A	B	C	D		A	B	C	D
(a)	1	2	3	4	(b)	2	3	1	4
(c)	2	1	3	4	(d)	4	2	1	3

75. Match List I with List II.

List I	List II
A. 80 GG	1. Deduction in respect of contribution given by companies to political parties.
B. 80 GGA	2. Deduction in respect of contribution given by any person to political parties.
C. 80 GGB	3. Deduction in respect of scientific research.
D. 80 GGC	4. Deduction in respect of rent paid.

Choose the correct answer from the options given below.

	A	B	C	D		A	B	C	D
(a)	4	3	1	2	(b)	3	4	2	1
(c)	4	3	2	1	(d)	4	2	1	3

76. Arrange the following following legal enactments in India in the chronological sequence from the first to the last.

1. The Mines Act
2. The Minimum Wages Act
3. The Payment of Gratuity Act
4. The Child Labour (Prohibition and Regulation) Act
5. The Apprentices Act

Choose the correct answer from the options given below.

(a) 2 4 3 1 5 (b) 2 1 5 3 4
(c) 1 5 2 3 4 (d) 5 2 1 3 4

77. Arrange in the sequence of decisions in manufacturing enterprises.

1. Making of forecasts
2. Determination of key factors
3. Consideration of alternative combination of forecasts
4. Preparation of budges
5. Combination of factors

Choose the correct answer from the options given below.

(a) 1 2 3 5 4 (b) 4 1 5 2 4
(c) 2 1 3 5 4 (d) 1 3 2 5 4

78. Arrange the following products in the increasing order of price elasticities.

1. Homogeneous products
2. Differentiated products
3. Necessities
4. Durable goods

Choose the correct answer from the options given below.

(a) 3, 2, 4 and 1 (b) 1, 2, 3 and 4
(c) 1, 3, 2 and 4 (d) 3, 1, 2 and 4

79. Arrange the following financing choices in order of preference suggested by the pecking order theory.

1. Reinvestment of earnings
2. New issue of equity
3. Issue of debt

Choose the correct answer from the options given below.

(a) 1, 2, 3 (b) 1, 3, 2
(c) 2, 3, 1 (d) 2, 1, 3

80. 80. Arrange the following stages of research in a proper sequence

1. Report Writing
2. Budgeting
3. Data Collection
4. Field Work
5. Research outcomes

Choose the correct answer from the options given below.

(a) 2, 4, 3, 5, 1
(b) 4, 1, 2, 3, 5
(c) 4, 3, 2, 5, 1
(d) 2, 5, 4, 3, 1

81. Arrange the following steps of creating a market-competitive pay plan in a sequence from the first to the last.

1. Choose benchmark jobs and select compensable factors.
2. Define each compensable factor and determine its degree in each job.
3. Establish rate changes.
4. Develop pay grades.
5. Compare and adjust current and market wage rates for jobs.

Choose the correct answer from the options given below.

(a) 2, 1, 5, 4, 3 (b) 1, 3, 2, 4, 5
(c) 1, 2, 5, 4, 3 (d) 1, 2, 3, 5, 4

82. Arrange the following initiatives taken by the Government of India to tackle the Non Performing assets in their ascending order of chronology.

1. Corporate Debt Restructuring
2. Compromise Settlement
3. The Debt Recovery Tribunals (DRTs)
4. Credit Information Bureau
5. SARFAESI Act

Choose the correct answer from the options given below.

(a) 3, 4, 1, 2, 5 (b) 1, 2, 5, 3, 4
(c) 3, 4, 2, 5, 1 (d) 4, 3, 2, 5, 1

83. Arrange the following steps of marketing process in proper sequence.

1. Construct an integrated marketing programme that delivers superior value.
2. Capture value from customers to create profits and customer equity.
3. Understand the market place and customer needs and wants.
4. Engage customers, build profitable relationships, and create customer delight.
5. Design a customer value-driven marketing strategy.

Choose the correct answer from the options given below.

(a) 3, 1, 5, 4, 2 (b) 2, 5, 1, 3, 4
(c) 4, 1, 2, 3, 5 (d) 3, 5, 1, 4, 2

84. Which one is the correct sequence implied in the Indian Contract Act 1872?

1. Offer of proposal 2. Contract
3. Promise 4. Agreement
5. Acceptance

Choose the correct answer from the options given below.

(a) 3, 5, 1, 4, 2 (b) 4, 2, 1, 3, 5
(c) 2, 4, 3, 5, 1 (d) 1, 5, 3, 4, 2

85. Arrange the following procedure of Income Tax return e-Filing in India.

1. Login
2. Register
3. Verification
4. Downloading utility and preparing return
5. e-Filing Income Tax Return

Choose the correct answer from the options given below.

(a) 1, 2, 3, 4, 5 (b) 1, 3, 2, 5, 4
(c) 2, 1, 5, 4, 3 (d) 2, 1, 4, 5, 3

86. Given below are two statements.

Statement I Monetary policy causes a deliberate change in government revenue and expenditure with a view to influencing the price level and the quantum of national output.

Statement II Fiscal policy regulates the money supply and the cost and availability of credit.

In the light of the above statements, choose the most appropriate answer from the options given below.

(a) Both Statement I and Statement II are correct
(b) Both Statement I and Statement II are incorrect
(c) Statement I is correct but Statement II is incorrect
(d) Statement I is incorrect but Statement II is correct

87. Given below are two statements, one is labelled as Assertion (A) and the other is labelled as Reason (R).

Assertion (A) Firms opt for buying an asset if the equivalent annual cost of ownership and operation is less than the best lease rate it can get.

Reason (R) Operating leases are attractive to equipment users if the lease payment is less than user's equivalent annual cost of buying the equipment.

In the light of the above statements, choose the most appropriate answer from the options given below.

(a) Both A and R are true and R is the correct explanation of A
(b) Both A and R are true, but R is not the correct explanation of A
(c) A is true, but R is false
(d) A is false, but R is true

88. Given below are two statements, one is labelled as Assertion (A) and the other is labelled as Reason (R).

Assertion (A) According to Herzberg, preventing or reducing dissatisfaction at work is not the same as providing satisfaction.

Reason (R) Under the 'Two Factor Theory', job satisfaction and dissatisfaction are the two different aspects of work motivation.

In the light of the above statements, choose the most appropriate answer from the options given below.

(a) Both A and R are true and R is the correct explanation of A
(b) Both A and R are true, but R is not the correct explanation of A
(c) A is true, but R is false
(d) A is false, but R is true

89. Given below are two statements, one is labelled as Assertion (A) and the other is labelled as Reason (R).

Assertion (A) Trade mark registration gives exclusive proprietary rights to the trademark owner.

Reason (R) A trademark is a recognisable sign, design or expression which identifies product or services of a particular source from those of others, and are used to claim exclusive proprietary rights of products or services.

In the light of the above statements, choose the correct answer from the options given below.

(a) Both A and R are true and R is the correct explanation of A
(b) Both A and R are true, but R is not the correct explanation of A
(c) A is true, but R is false
(d) A is false, but R is true

90. Given below are two statements.

Statement I Gratuity received by government employee is exempted from tax under Section 10(10)(i) of the Indian Income Tax Act, 1961.

Statement II Gratuity received by local authority employee is exempted from tax.

In the light of the above statements, choose the most appropriate answer from the options given below.

(a) Both Statement I and statement II are true
(b) Both Statement I and statement II are false
(c) Statement I is correct but statement II is false
(d) Statement I is incorrect but statement II is true

Directions *(Q. Nos. 91-95) Read the following paragraph and answer the five questions which as follows :*

Burnout is a psychological syndrome emerging as a prolonged response to chronic interpersonal stressors on the job. The three key dimensions of this response are an overwhelming exhaustion, feelings of cynicism and detachment from the job, and a sense of ineffectiveness and lack of accomplishment.

The significance of this three-dimensional model is that it clearly places the individual stress experience within a social context and involves the person's conception of both self and others. The exhaustion dimension was also described as wearing out, loss of energy, depletion, debilitation and fatigue. The cynicism dimension was originally called depersonalisation (given the nature of human services occupations), but was also described as negative or inappropriate attitudes towards clients, irritability, loss of idealism, and withdrawal. The inefficacy dimension was originally called reduced personal accomplishment and was also described as reduced productivity or capability, low morale, and an inability to cope.

There have been various conceptual models about the development of burnout and its subsequent impact. At first, the focus was on the relationship between the three dimensions of burnout which was often described in sequential stages. Exhaustion was assumed to develop first, in response to high demands and overload, and then this would precipitate detachment and negative reactions to people and the job (depersonalisation or cynicism). If this continued then the next stage would be feelings of inadequacy and failure (reduced personal accomplishment or professional inefficacy).

More recently, burnout models have been based on theories about job stress and the notion of imbalances leading to strain. Its three stages are : (a) Job stressors (b) Individual strain (c) Defensive coping. Subsequently, two developmental models of the demands-resources imbalance have emerged : The Job Demands-Resources (JD-R) Model and the Conservation of Resources (COR) Model. The JD-R model focuses on the notion that burnout arises when individuals experience incessant job demands and have inadequate resources available to address and to reduce those demands. The COR Model follows a basic motivational theory assuming that burnout arises as a result of persistent threats to available resources. A different variation of an imbalance model of burnout is the Areas of Worklife (AW) Model which frames job stressors in terms of person-job imbalances, or mismatches, but identifies six key areas in which these imbalances take place : workload, control, reward, community, fairness and values. Mismatches in these areas affect an individual's level of experienced burnout, which in turn determines various outcomes, such as job performance, social behaviours and personal well being.

91. Which of the following has the correct sequence of the stages of burnout?

(a) Fatigue due to excessive work, dislike for work, failure to achieve targets.
(b) Negative feelings about work, dislike for work, effort to quit work.
(c) Initial good interpersonal relations, depersonalisation, loss of idealism.
(d) Cynicism, inadequacy, inefficiency.

92. Given below are two statements.

Statement I Cynicism stage of burnout is often experienced by employees, engaged in production activity, due to excessive work pressure.

Statement II In Cynicism stage of burnout, person withdraws from others and shows lack of interest towards them.

In the light of the above statements, choose the correct answer from the options given below.

(a) Both Statement I and statement II are true
(b) Both Statement I and statement II are false
(c) Statement I is correct but statement II is false
(d) Statement I is incorrect but statement II is true

93. Match List I with List II.

List I	List II
A. Exhaustion	1. Not able to complete work
B. Cynicism	2. No energy for work
C. Inefficiency	3. No interest in customer

Choose the correct answer from the options given below.

	A	B	C		A	B	C
(a)	1	2	3	(b)	3	2	1
(c)	2	3	1	(d)	2	1	3

94. Which of the following is not a resource-imbalance model of Burnout?

(a) Job Demands-Resources Model
(b) Conservation of Resources Model
(c) Three Dimensional Model
(d) Areas of Worklife Model

95. Which of the following are caused by Burnout?

1. Concern for clients
2. Negative Social Behaviour
3. Physical and Mental Strain

Choose the most appropriate answer from the options given below.

(a) 1 only (b) 1 and 2 only
(c) 2 and 3 only (d) 1 and 3 only

Directions *(Q. Nos. 96-100) Read the following paragraph and answer the five questions which as follow :*

It is desirable for consumers to be aware of their rights, and to exercise those rights responsibility and intelligently. In these days of audio-video publicity on the public and private media. It is indeed very difficult, if not impossible, to verify the exaggerated or false claims made by producers, manufactures, distributors and dealers of various goods and services.

The all-pervasive, exaggerated and often false claims, made for services and goods, emphasise the imperative need for consumer protection legislation and creation of awareness about it among the general public.

In this connection, there are a number of enactments, in India such as the prevention of Food Adulteration Act., 1954, the Essential Commodities Act, 1955, the Hire Purchases Act 1972, the Standards Weight and Measure Act 1976 etc.

However, the remedies prescribed there under the time-consuming inadequate and expensive. As in other areas of Judicial processes, the offenders are hardly caught, proceeded against and rarely, if ever got convicted. When violators go scot-free, the victims have no remedy and gets frustated.

96. Which among the following is a correct statement based on the passage?
(a) Consumer' laws are not explained well in India.
(b) Indian Judiciary System needs a drastic reform to facilitate consumer' welfare.
(c) Indian manufacturers are clever.
(d) The Indian Consumers have no remedy and get frustrated.

97. Which among the following is a correct statement based on the passage?
(a) Consumer in India are aware of their rights.
(b) Consumers in India exercise their rights and responsibility.
(c) Consumers in India are unaware of their rights and hence, they do not exercise them.
(d) None of the above could be ascertained on the basis of paragraph given here above.

98. Which among the following is a correct statement based on the passage?
(a) The Government of India has enacted sufficient number of laws for protection of consumer interests.
(b) The paragraph does not give comprehensive list of laws in favour of consumers.
(c) Legal environment for consumers in India is not conducive.
(d) Legal environment for consumers in India is conducive.

99. Who among the following could be considered at the centre point in the passage?
(a) Consumers (b) Judicial Process
(c) Manufacturers (d) Government

100. Which among the following is a correct statement based on the passage?
(a) Producers and manufacturers are sensitive about consumers rights.
(b) Producers and manufacturers are insensitive about consumers rights.
(c) Producers and manufacturers are neutral about consumers rights.
(d) Producers and manufacturers are basically governed by ethics and values.

ANSWERS

1 (b)	2 (c)	3 (b)	4 (d)	5 (b)	6 (b)	7 (b)	8 (c)	9 (c)	10 (d)
11 (a)	12 (a)	13 (b)	14 (a)	15 (c)	16 (b)	17 (a)	18 (d)	19 (b)	20 (a)
21 (a)	22 (b)	23 (c)	24 (d)	25 (a)	26 (b)	27 (b)	28 (c)	29 (c)	30 (b)
31 (a)	32 (d)	33 (b)	34 (d)	35 (c)	36 (a)	37 (a)	38 (c)	39 (d)	40 (c)
41 (b)	42 (*)	43 (c)	44 (c)	45 (a)	46 (b)	47 (d)	48 (d)	49 (d)	50 (b)
51 (b)	52 (a)	53 (c)	54 (c)	55 (c)	56 (c)	57 (a)	58 (b)	59 (d)	60 (d)
61 (b)	62 (a)	63 (c)	64 (a)	65 (d)	66 (b)	67 (a)	68 (c)	69 (c)	70 (d)
71 (a)	72 (b)	73 (a)	74 (a)	75 (a)	76 (b)	77 (c)	78 (a)	79 (b)	80 (a)
81 (c)	82 (a)	83 (d)	84 (d)	85 (d)	86 (b)	87 (b)	88 (a)	89 (a)	90 (a)
91 (a)	92 (d)	93 (c)	94 (c)	95 (c)	96 (b)	97 (d)	98 (b)	99 (a)	100 (b)

UGC NET/JRF/SET

Commerce (Paper-2)

Solved Paper, December 2019

General Instructions

1. There are total one hundred questions in this paper. Each question carries 2 marks.
2. All questions are compulsory.

1. Which one of the following is not correct according to the Consumer Protection Act?

(a) District forum shall consist of a lady social worker.
(b) State Commission shall consist of person who is or has been a judge of a High Court.
(c) District forum shall consist of four members.
(d) National Consumer Disputes Redressal Commission shall consist of a person who is or has been a judge of the Supreme Court.

2. According to FEMA, Foreign exchange does not include

(a) deposits payable in any foreign currency.
(b) Bills of exchange drawn in Indian currency but payable in any foreign currency.
(c) travellers cheques drawn by institutions outside India but payable in Indian currency.
(d) drafts drawn by banks outside India and payable in foreign currency.

3. Which of the following laws affect business organisations?

(a) Incorporation and Bankruptcy Laws
(b) Environmental Protection Laws
(c) Occupational Health and Safety Laws
(d) Competition Laws

4. Which one is odd?

(a) Economic Policies
(b) Economic Planning
(c) Socio-cultural factors
(d) Macro-economic scenario

5. Which of the following is not a method for calculating or ascertaining the amount of purchase consideration?

(a) Net Payment Method (b) Net Assets Method
(c) Gross Receipts Methods (d) Share Exchange Method

6. Which of the following sections of Companies Act, 2013 facilitates amalgamation, absorption and reconstruction of companies?

(a) 319 (b) 320
(c) 410 (d) 502

7. Which of the following is not a part of the process of management audit?

(a) Identification of responsibility centre.
(b) Review of performance of each responsibility centre.
(c) Review of organisational structure.
(d) Investigating the depreciation method and its application on fixed assets in the company.

8. Which of the following statements is not correct regarding the duties of an auditor?

(a) Physical verification of fixed assets is primarily the responsibility of the auditor.
(b) Ownership of fixed assets should be verified by examining the title deed by auditor.
(c) Auditor should ascertain that the assets are in the possession of the client.
(d) The auditor should satisfy himself that the assets have been valued in the financial statements according to the accounting principles.

9. 'Maximisation of firm's growth rate subject to managerial and financial constraints' as one of the important alternative objectives of especially large business corporation was pleaded by

(a) Milton Friedman
(b) Robin Marris
(c) Cyert and March
(d) HA Simon

10. On which of the following assumptions, the theory of consumer behaviour on cardinal utility approach is not based?

(a) Consumer is rational.
(b) Limited money income of the consumer.
(c) Maximisation of total satisfaction.
(d) Diminishing marginal utility of money.

11. The following are the two statements regarding elasticity of demand and its measurement.

Statement I On every point on the straight line demand curve, the point elasticities are all equal.

Statement II On every point on the rectangular hyperbola shaped demand curve, the point elasticities are not equal.

Select the correct option for those below.

(a) Both the statements are correct.
(b) Both the statements are not correct.
(c) Statement I is correct, while Statement II is incorrect.
(d) Statement I is incorrect, while Statement II is correct.

12. A production function expressed as

$$Q = A[\alpha K^{-\beta} + (1-\alpha)L^{-\beta}]^{-\frac{1}{\beta}}$$

or $Q = A[\alpha L^{-\beta} + (1-\alpha)K^{-\beta}]^{-\frac{1}{\beta}}$

Where $A > 0$, $0 < \alpha < 1$ and $\beta > -1$

Where L – Labour, K = Capital and A, α and β are three parameters is called

(a) Constant elasticity substitution function
(b) Variable elasticity substitution function
(c) Leontief-type function
(d) Cobb-Douglas function

13. Under which of the following approaches, the cost of equity is assumed to increase linearly with leverage, i.e,the average cost of capital remains constant with increased use of leverage?

(a) Net Operating Income Approach
(b) Net Income Approach
(c) Traditional Approach
(d) Walter Approach

14. If the Risk-Free Return (Rf) is 6%, Beta value (β) is 1.5 and market rate of return (Km) is 10%, the expected rate of return would be

(a) 15% (b) 12%
(c) 17.5% (d) 16%

15. A company raises ₹ 1,00,000 by issue of 1000, 10% debentures of ₹ 100 each at a discount of 2% redeemable after 10 years. If the corporate tax rate is 40%, what would be the cost of capital?

(a) 6.82% (b) 5.98%
(c) 6.18% (d) 5.5%

16. In which of the following years, the Bretton Woods Agreement was signed by the delegates from 44 nations which led to the establishment of the IMF?

(a) 1940 (b) 1952
(c) 1944 (d) 1957

17. The sum total of the values of two variables 'X' and 'Y' is equal for all the observations. The value of the coefficient of correlation between 'X' and 'Y' is

(a) + 1 (Perfectly Positive)
(b) – 1(Perfectly Negative)
(c) Zero (No Correlation)
(d) > 0< 1(Imperfect Correlation)

18. Which of the following statements is false?

(a) When value of correlation coefficient is one, the two regression lines coincide.
(b) The regression coefficients are independent of the change of origin and of scale.
(c) The sign of the regression coefficient are always the same.
(d) The square of the coefficient of correlation is called coefficient of determination.

19. Which of the following is the non-random method of selecting samples from a given population?

(a) Stratified Sampling
(b) Systematic Sampling
(c) Quota Sampling
(d) Multi-Stage Sampling

20. Which of the following is an incomplete experimental research design?

(a) Before and after with control group design
(b) Factorial design
(c) One group before after design
(d) Latin Square design

21. Which of the following is not a factor contributing to MBO program failure?

(a) Altering goals to meet changes in circumstances
(b) Easy goals
(c) Lack of management support
(d) Setting of unrealistically difficult goals

22. Which of the following terms means the tendency of a supervisor to rate a subordinate lower than his performance?

(a) Horns Effect (b) Halo Effect
(c) Central Tendency (d) Pointing Tendency

23. The informal group's communication system is called

(a) group dynamics (b) grapevine
(c) exchange (d) interaction

24. Quality circle is a type of
(a) problem-solving team (b) cross-functional team
(c) self-directed team (d) project team

25. Choose incorrect statement from the following.
(a) 28 Days T-bills were introduced in 1998.
(b) 364 Days T-bills were introduced in 1992.
(c) 182 Days T-bills were introduced in 1986.
(d) 273 Days T-bills were introduced in 2006.

26. 14 Days intermediate T-bills were brought into effect from 1996-97 after the abolition of which of the following?
(a) 91 Days T-bills (b) 182 Days T-bills
(c) 273 Days T-bills (d) 364 Days T-bills

27. Which among the following is not a correct statement?
(a) The Reserve Bank of India worked as Central Bank of Burma till April 1947.
(b) The Reserve Bank of India worked as Central Bank of Pakistan till June 1948.
(c) The Reserve Bank of India worked as Central Bank of Bangladesh from January 1972 to December 1975.
(d) The Reserve Bank of India commenced its operations on 1st April, 1935.

28. National Housing Bank was established in 1987 as wholly owned subsidiary of which of the following?
(a) State Bank of India
(b) Life Insurance Corporation of India
(c) Reserve Bank of India
(d) Industrial Finance Corporation of India

29. In e-commerce,one of the key design elements of an effective website-community refers to
(a) its layout and design.
(b) the way site enables user to user communication.
(c) site's ability to tailor itself to different users or to allow users to personalise the site.
(d) degree that the site is linked to the other sites.

30. Which of the following is not true about web marketers?
(a) Web marketers usually try to attract prospects to their site through email, advertisements in newspapers.
(b) Use attractions like discounts, gifts and contests.
(c) Ask customers to give their personal data mandatorily.
(d) Give a lot of publicity to the discount schemes.

31. Companies that are becoming skilled in Customer Relationship Management (CRM) focus on
(a) understanding the perceived performance and buyer's expectations.
(b) giving benefits to the customers by reducing cost.
(c) developing programs to attract and retain the right customer and meeting the individual needs to valued customers.
(d) giving the quality in features and characteristics of a product or service that bear on its ability to satisfy stated or implied needs.

32. In the recent years-the major gain in logistical efficiency have come from which one of the following?
(a) Advances in Information Technology
(b) Reduction in petroleum pries
(c) Fast order processing
(d) Increase in production of commercial vehicles

33. Which of the following is not a presumption abut a negotiable instrument?
(a) Date
(b) Consideration
(c) Stamp
(d) Absolute and good title to the transferee

34. Which one of the following relates to warranty?
(a) It is of vital importance for completion of contract.
(b) If there is breach, the aggrieved party can repudiate the contact.
(c) It is essential to the main purpose of the contract.
(d) In case of breach, the aggrieved party can claim only damages.

35. Which of the following is the odd one out?
(a) Specific goods
(b) Un-ascertained goods
(c) Future goods
(d) Ascertained goods

36. The indemnity holder is not entitled to
(a) all damages which he may be compelled to pay in any suit in respect of any matter to which the promise applies.
(b) all costs that he may be compelled to bear in defending any such suit.
(c) all sums that he may have paid under the terms of any compromise of such suit.
(d) damages for liability incurred which is not absolute.

37. ADEN Rules, 1953 is related to which of the following?
(a) Tax exemption
(b) Residential status
(c) Double taxation relief
(d) Assessment of corporate entity

38. What percentage of income from compensation on disaster is exempted from tax liability?
(a) 100%
(b) 75%
(c) 50%
(d) 25%

39. Which among the following is a correct statement about residential status of a company?
(a) A company cab be classified as "not ordinarily resident".
(b) A company can never be classified as "not ordinarily resident".
(c) A company can be classified as "not ordinarily resident" with the permission from Ministry of Finance.
(d) A company can be classified as "not ordinarily resident" with the permission from Ministry of Commerce.

40. Under which of the following categories, a partner of partnership firm will be assessed?

(a) An individual (b) HUF
(c) Firm (d) Body of an Individual

41. What are drivers of globalisation?

1. Population mobility especially of labour
2. Financial flows
3. Exporting
4. Assembly operations

Choose the correct answer from the following.

(a) 1, and 4 (b) 2 and 4
(c) 1 and 2 (d) 3 and 4

42. Which of the following are part of Corporate Social Responsibility (CSR) to consumers?

1. Reasonable chances and proper system for accomplishment and promotion.
2. To supply goods at reasonable prices even when there is seller's market.
3. Improving the efficiency of the business operation.
4. To provide an opportunity for being heard and redress genuine grievances.

Choose the correct answer from the options given below.

(a) 1, and 2 (b) 2 and 4
(c) 2 and 3 (d) 1 and 3

43. Which among the following are not qualified to be appointed as auditor of a company?

1. An individual who is a Chartered Accountant and holds a Certificate of Practice as per CA Act, 1949.
2. A limited liability partnership firm, which has all partners as Chartered Accountants.
3. Officer or employee of a company who is qualified Chartered Accountant degree holder too
4. Any Chartered Accountant whose appointment will result in the person being the auditor of more than 10 companies.

Choose the most appropriate option.

(a) 1 and 2 (b) 2, 3 and 4
(c) 3 and 2 (d) 1, 2 and 4

44. Which of the following are the methods of determining cost behaviour?

1. High and low point method
2. Least square regression method
3. Accounting or analytical approach
4. Non-parametric method

Choose the correct answer from the options given below.

(a) 1, 2 and 4 (b) 1, 3 and 4
(c) 2, 3 and 4 (d) 1, 2 and 3

45. Which two of the following statements are correct?

1. In the short - run, Δ TFC = 0, therefore Δ TC = Δ TVC.
2. If decrease in AFC < increase in AVC, then AC decreases.
3. If decrease in AFC = increase in VC, AC remains constant.
4. If decrease in AFC > increase in AVC, then AC increases.

Choose the correct answer from the option given below.

(a) 1 and 3 (b) 2 and 3
(c) 2 and 4 (d) 1 and 4

46. Which two of the following statements are true?

1. A simple monopoly firm always earns super normal profit.
2. Sweezy's kinked demand curve model is the best known model explaining relatively more satisfactory behaviour of oligopoly firm for price rigidity.
3. A perfectly competitive firm is price-taker.
4. Firms under monopolistic competition earn only normal profits.

Choose the correct option from those below.

(a) 1 and 2 (b) 2 and 4
(c) 2 and 3 (d) 1 and 3

47. Which of the following statements are correct?

1. Dividend payout ratio refers to that portion of total earnings which is distributed among equity shareholders of the company.
2. 'Bird in hand' argument is given by Gordon's model.
3. MM model suggest that dividend payment is very relevant for value of the firm.
4. Walter's Model suggests that dividend payment does not affect the market price of the share.

(a) 1 and 2 (b) 1 and 3
(c) 2 and 3 (d) 3 and 4

48. Which of the following statements are true?

1. Pay-Back Period Method considers all cash flows of a project.
2. Pay-back Period Method concerns more with the recovery of cost than profitability.
3. Net Present Value represents net addition to the wealth of shareholders.
4. Accounting Rate of Return method incorporates risk as well as time value of money.

Choose the correct option from those given below.

(a) 1 and 2 (b) 1 and 4
(c) 2 and 3 (d) 2 and 4

49. Which of the following statements are true?

1. Transaction exposure is inherent in all foreign currencies denominated contractual transactions.
2. Translation exposure relates to the change in accounting income and balance sheet statements caused by change in exchange rate.
3. Economic exposure has an impact on the valuation of a firm.
4. Operating exposure does not have any impact on the firm's future operating revenues or future operating costs.

Choose the correct option from those given below.

(a) 1 and 2 only (b) 2 and 3 only
(c) 2 and 4 only (d) 1, 2 and 3 only

50. Which two of the following measures of central tendency are not capable of algebraic treatment?

1. Geometric Mean 2. Median
3. Arithmetic Mean 4. Mode
5. Harmonic Mean

Choose the correct answer from the option given below.

(a) 1 and 2 (b) 2 and 5
(c) 2 and 4 (d) 3 and 5

51. Which of the following statements are true?

1. The sum of the deviations from mean (ignoring algebraic signs) is greater than the sum of the deviations from median (ignoring algebraic signs).
2. Standard deviation is independent of change of origin and change of scale.
3. In a symmetrical distribution, mean deviation equals 4/5 of standard deviation.
4. In a symmetrical and bell shaped distribution, quartile deviation is 1/3 of standard deviation.

Choose the correct option from those given below.

(a) 2 and 4 (b) 1 and 3
(c) 3 and 4 (d) 1 and 2

52. Which of the following statements are true?

1. Skewness studies the flatness or peakedness of the distribution.
2. A positively skewed distribution curve is stretched more to the right than to the left.
3. On the basis of empirical relationship between mean, mode and median for moderately asymmetrical distribution, Karl Pearson's coefficient of skewness can be measured by 3 (Mean-Median) divided by Standard Deviation.
4. If mean < mode, the distribution is positively skewed.

Choose the correct option from those given below.

(a) 1 and 2 (b) 2 and 3
(c) 3 and 4 (d) 2 and 4

53. Which of the following types of authorities are found in most organisations?

1. Division Authority
2. Line Authority
3. Staff Authority
4. Functional Authority

Choose the correct option from those given below.

(a) 1 and 2 only (b) 2 and 3 only
(c) 1, 2 and 3 only (d) 2, 3 and 4 only

54. The theories that explain the formation of 'Informal Groups' are to include which of the following?

1. Propinquity Theory
2. Similarity (or) Balance Theory
3. Displacement Theory
4. Need for achievement Theory

Choose the correct option from those given below.

(a) 1 and 4 only (b) 1 and 2 only
(c) 1, 2 and 3 only (d) 1, 2, 3 and 4

55. Functions of a first-level or front line supervisors are to include which of the following?

1. To determine individual job assignment.
2. To attend to grievances and resolve conflicts.
3. To provide technical knowledge and guidance to workers.
4. To supply strategic information relating to production to management.

Choose the correct answer from the options given below.

(a) 1 and 2 only
(b) 1 and 3 only
(c) 1, 2 and 3 only
(d) All of them–1, 2, 3, and 4

56. Non-Banking Financial Companies can be classified as

1. Asset Finance Company (AFC)
2. Investment Company (IC)
3. Loan Company (LC)
4. Foreign Trade Company (FTC)

Choose the correct answer from the options given below.

(a) 1, 2, and 3 only (b) 2, 3 and 4 only
(c) 1, 3 and 4 only (d) 1, 2 and 4 only

57. Which three of the following types of cyber attacks may occur in the process of mobile banking?

1. Backdoor attack
2. Front door attack
3. Denial of service attack
4. Direct access attack

Choose the correct answer from the options given below.

(a) 1, 2 and 3 (b) 2, 3 and 4
(c) 1, 2 and 4 (d) 1, 3 and 4

58. Michael Porter proposed generic strategies that provide good starting points for strategic thinking. Identify them from the below mentioned strategies.

1. Overall cost leadership
2. Innovation
3. Focus
4. Differentiation

Choose the correct answer from the options given below.

(a) 1 and 2 only
(b) 1, 3 and 4 only
(c) 1, 2 and 4 only
(d) All of these–1, 2, 3 and 4

59. Given below are two statements, one labelled as Assertion (A) and the other labelled as Reason (R).

Assertion (A) Auto companies and other consumer goods companies offer cash rebates to encourage purchase of the manufacturer's products within a specified period.

Reason (R) The same product is priced differently at different times.

In the context of the two statements above related to pricing strategy, which one of the following options is correct?

(a) Both A and R are true and R is the correct explanation of A
(b) Both A and R are true, but R is not the correct explanation of A
(c) A is true, but R is false
(d) A is false, but R is true

60. According to Sale to Good Act, which two of the following are defined as 'goods'?

1. Moveable property 2. Growing crops
3. Actionable claims 4. Book debt

Choose the correct answer from the options given below.

(a) 1 and 4 (b) 2 and 3
(c) 1 and 2 (d) 4 and 2

61. Which of the following are true about the conditions according to the Sale of Goods Act?

1. Title 2. Description
3. Quite possession 4. Encumbrances

Choose the correct answer from the options given below.

(a) 1 and 4 only (b) 2 and 3 only
(c) 1, 3 and 4 only (d) 1 and 2 only

62. Who are the parties to a cheque?

1. Drawer 2. Payee
3. Acceptor 4. Holder

Choose the correct answer from the options given below.

(a) 1 and 2 only
(b) 1, 2 and 4 only
(c) 1 and 3 only
(d) All of these–1, 2, 3, and 4

63. Which of the following are correct about TDS Certificates?

1. TDS on non-salary payment–form 16.
2. TDS on salary payment–form 16A.
3. TDS on sale of property–form 16B.
4. TDS on rent–form 16C.

Choose the correct answer from the option given below.

(a) 1 and 2 (b) 3 and 4
(c) 1 and 4 (d) 2 and 3

64. Which two of the following are correct in terms of rate of Tax Deduction at Source (TDS)?

1. Income by way of winning from horse race : @ 30%.
2. Insurance commission : @ 10%.
3. Rent of plant and machinery : @ 5%.
4. Rent of furniture : @ 5%.

Choose the correct option from those given below.

(a) 1 and 2 (b) 1 and 3
(c) 1 and 4 (d) 2 and 3

65. Which two of the following are correct about the due date of issue of the TDS certificate?

1. Form no 16–Annual
2. Form no 16A–Quarterly
3. Form no 16B–Half-Yearly
4. Form no 16C–Monthly

Choose the correct option from those given below.

(a) 1 and 4 (b) 1 and 3
(c) 1 and 2 (d) 3 and 4

66. Match List I with List II.

	List I		List II
A.	Size of the market	1.	Globalisation of business
B.	Demographic environment	2.	Foreign trade policy
C.	Export–oriented units	3.	Macro-environment
D.	Multinational corporations	4.	Non-economic environment

Choose the correct option from those given below.

	A	B	C	D
(a)	4	2	3	1
(b)	2	3	1	4
(c)	3	2	1	4
(d)	3	4	2	1

67. Match List I with List II.

List I	List II
A. Qualified Report	1. Auditor Duty
B. Examine Valuation and Disclosure	2. Auditor Liabilities
C. Access to records of Company and its subsidiaries	3. Auditor Report
D. Mis-statement in prospectus in company issue of capital	4. Auditor Right

Choose the correct option from those given below.

	A	B	C	D
(a)	2	1	4	3
(b)	3	1	4	2
(c)	3	1	2	4
(d)	4	2	3	1

68. Match the following theories of profit with their propounders.

List I (Theory)	List II (Propounder)
A. Profit as Rent of Ability	1. FB Hawley
B. Dynamic Theory of Profit	2. Joseph A Schumpeter
C. Risk Theory of Profit	3. JB Clark
D. Innovation Theory of Profit	4. FA Walker

Choose the correct option from those given below.

	A	B	C	D
(a)	4	2	3	1
(b)	1	2	3	4
(c)	4	3	1	2
(d)	3	1	2	4

69. Match the following methods of capital budgeting with their respective formula.

Methods	Formula
A. ARR Methods	1. Present Value of Cash Inflows-Present Value of Cash Outflows
B. Pay Back Period Method	2. Present Value of Cash Inflows ÷ Present Value of Cash Outflows
C. NPV Method	3. Average Income ÷ Average Investment
D. Probability Index	4. Investment ÷ Annual Cash Inflows

Choose the correct option from those given below.

	A	B	C	D
(a)	3	1	4	2
(b)	3	4	1	2
(c)	1	2	3	4
(d)	1	4	2	3

70. Match the tests with suitable situations of their application for hypothesis-testing.

Test	Situation
A. Z-Test	1. Comparing the differences in the mean values of more than two sample groups (Parametric data)
B. ANOVA	2. Testing the significance of the difference between averages of two large sized sample groups (Parametric data)
C. Chi-Square Test	3. Comparing the differences in the mean values of more than two sample groups (Non-parametric data)
D. Kruskal-Wallis Test	4. Testing the significance of the association between the attributes

Choose the correct option from those given below.

	A	B	C	D
(a)	1	2	3	4
(b)	2	1	4	3
(c)	2	3	4	1
(d)	1	4	2	3

71. Match the 'Category of Compensation' with 'Compensation Plan'.

Category of Compensation	Compensation Plan
A. Pay for time not worked	1. Savings Plan
B. Services and Perquisites	2. Stock Option
C. Incentive Pay	3. Pension
D. Deferred Pay	4. Sick Leave

Choose the correct option from those given below.

	A	B	C	D	E
(a)	3	4	2	1	5
(b)	4	5	3	2	1
(c)	4	5	1	2	3
(d)	3	5	1	4	2

72. Match the following Banking Sector reform committees with their respective purposes.

List I	List II
A. YV Reddy Committee	1. Revised method of lending in place of cash credit system
B. Rashid Jilani Committee	2. Rationalisation of interest rate on small savings
C. SM Kelkar Committee	3. Working capital lending norms
D. IT Vaz Committee	4. Regional Rural Banks

Choose the correct option from those given below.

	A	B	C	D
(a)	1	2	3	4
(b)	2	1	4	3
(c)	4	3	2	1
(d)	2	3	4	1

73. Match the modes of communication in marketing and their communication platforms.

Mode of Communication	Communication Platform
A. Advertising	1. Blogs
B. Sales Promotion	2. Brochures and Bookers
C. Word of mouth marketing	3. Sales meetings
D. Personal selling	4. Contests

Choose the correct option from those given below.

	A	B	C	D		A	B	C	D
(a)	2	3	4	1	(b)	2	4	1	3
(c)	4	3	2	1	(d)	4	3	1	2

74. Match List I with List II.

List I	List II
A. Transfer of ownership	1. Negotiable instrument
B. Sale of goodwill after dissolution	2. Contract of sale of goods
C. Buy-back of securities	3. Dissolution of partnership firm
D. Promissory Note	4. Share capital of company

Choose the correct option from those given below.

	A	B	C	D		A	B	C	D
(a)	2	3	4	1	(b)	3	4	2	1
(c)	4	2	1	3	(d)	1	2	3	4

75. Match the following countries with the types of Double Taxation Avoidance Agreement signed by India with them.

Country	Type of Agreement
A. Austria	1. Limited Agreement
B. Bahamas	2. Comprehensive Agreements
C. Lebanon	3. Comprehensive Agreements/ Limited Multilateral Agreement
D. Sri Lanka	4. Tax Information Exchange Agreement

Choose the correct option from those given below.

	A	B	C	D		A	B	C	D
(a)	4	2	1	3	(b)	2	4	1	3
(c)	2	4	3	1	(d)	1	2	3	4

76. Which two of the following are the function of WTO?

1. To facilitate the implementation, administration and operation of trade agreement.
2. To carry out periodic reviews of the trade policies of its member countries.
3. To assist in the establishment of a multilateral system of payments.
4. To promote international monetary cooperation.

Choose the correct option from the following.

(a) 1 and 4 (b) 2 and 3
(c) 3 and 4 (d) 1 and 2

77. Following are the events which generally happen in the life of a public limited company.

1. Public Issue of shares (IPO)
2. Firm incorporation
3. Preliminary expenditures
4. Issue of equity shares to promoters of the company.

Choose the correct sequence (chronological order) of the events from the options given below.

(a) 1, 2, 3 and 4
(b) 2, 3, 4 and 1
(c) 3, 2, 1 and 4
(d) 3, 2, 4 and 1

78. In the case of consumers equilibrium to be explained through an ordinal approach, when there are commodities with their prices given and with limited income of the consumer, the following information is required.

1. Price line/budget line.
2. Indifference map.
3. Point of tangency between IC and budget line.
4. Equality of the slopes of IC budget line.

Arrange the information required in the correct sequence and choose the right option from those given below.

(a) 2, 4, 1 and 3 (b) 2, 1, 4 and 3
(c) 1, 4, 2 and 3 (d) 1, 2, 3 and 4

79. Which one of the following is the correct sequence of various stages of operating cycle of a manufacturing company?

(a) Raw material conversion period, work-in-progress conversion period, finished goods conversion period, receivables conversion period.
(b) Raw material conversion period, work-in-progress conversion period, yereditors payment period, receivable conversion period.
(c) Creditor payment period, raw material conversion period, receivables conversion period, work-in-progress conversion period.
(d) Raw material conversion period, finished goods conversion period, work-in-progress conversion period, receivables conversion period.

80. For calculating posterior probabilities (conditional probabilities under statistical dependence), the following information is available.

1. Conditional probabilities
2. Original probability estimates (prior-probabilities) of mutually exclusive and collectively exhaustive events.
3. Arbitrary event with probability # 0 and for which conditional probabilities are also known.
4. Joint probabilities of prior probability and conditional probability.

Given the information that the arbitrary event has occurred, arrange the above information in a sequence of their requirement as per Baye's Theorem.

Choose the correct option.

(a) 1, 2, 4 and 3 (b) 3, 2, 1 and 4
(c) 2, 3, 4 and 1 (d) 2, 1, 4 and 3

81. What is the typical sequence in which the following selection devices are used by the company?

1. Reference checks
2. Physical examination
3. Application Blank
4. Hire
5. Conditional Offers
6. More interviews
7. Screening interviews
8. Tests

Choose the correct answer from the options given below.

(a) 1, 7, 8, 6, 1, 5, 2 and 4
(b) 4, 7, 6, 8, 1, 5, 2 and 3
(c) 1, 8, 7, 1, 6, 5, 2 and 4
(d) 4, 7, 8, 6, 1, 5, 2 and 4

82. Arrange the following financial institutions in ascending order of their year of establishment.

1. National Housing Bank
2. Export-Import Bank of India
3. NABARD
4. Unit Trust of India

Choose the correct option from those given below.

(a) 2, 4, 3 and 1 (b) 4, 2, 1 and 3
(c) 4, 2, 3 and 1 (d) 4, 3, 2 and 1

83. Market Logistic planning has the following four steps. Arrange the steps in correct sequence.

1. Develop operational excellence in sales forecasting, warehouse management, transportation and material management.
2. Select the best channel design and network strategy for reaching the customers.
3. Implement the solution with the best information systems, equipment policies and procedures.
4. Decide on company's value proposition to its customers.

Select the correct option from those given below.

(a) 1, 2, 3 and 4 (b) 4, 2, 1 and 3
(c) 4, 2, 3 and 1 (d) 4, 3, 2 and 1

84. Which one of the following is a void contract?

(a) Unilateral contract
(b) A contract which ceases to be enforceable by law
(c) Implied contract
(d) Express contract

85. Arrange the steps to e-filing of Income Tax Return in correct sequence.

1. Register yourself
2. Verify ITR V
3. Select the requisite form
4. Fill form and upload

Choose the correct option from those given below.

(a) 1, 3, 4 and 2 (b) 1, 2, 3 and 4
(c) 1, 2, 4 and 3 (d) 3, 1, 4 and 2

86. Given below are two statements. One is labelled as Assertion (A) and the other is labelled as Reason (R).

Assertion (A) Indian Accounting Standards contain some 'carve outs' and for convergence with IFRS with some changes applied in India.

Reason (R) Financial statements prepared in India with Indian Accounting Standards will not be IFRS complaint.

In the light of the above two statements, choose the correct option.

(a) Both A and R are true and R is the correct explanation of A
(b) Both A and R are true, but R is not the correct explanation of A
(c) A is true, but R is false
(d) A is false, but R is true

87. Given below are two statements. One is labelled as Assertion (A) and the other is labelled as Reason (R).

Assertion (A) In the case of short run cost behaviour, MC curve intersects AC curve at its minimum.

Reason (R) While AC continues to decrease, MC begins to rise Also, when AC is at its minimum, it is neither increasing nor decreasing. It is constant when AC is constant, it is equal to MC at the point of intersection.

Choose the correct option from those given below.

(a) Both A and R are true and R is the correct explanation of A
(b) Both A and R are true, but R is not the correct explanation of A
(c) A is true, but R is false
(d) A is false, but R is true

88. Given below are two statements. One is labelled as Assertion (A) and the other is labelled as Reason (R).

Assertion (A) If the firm is prepared to incur increased cost on transportation, it may be in a position to reduce its inventory cost.

Reason (R) As in such a case, the firm can use the fastest mode of transport and rush the goods/stocks to the desired warehouse, unmindful of the cost of transportation.

In the context of the above two statements related to logistics management, which of the following options is correct.

(a) Both A and R are true and R is the correct explanation of A
(b) Both A and R are true, but R is not the correct explanation of A
(c) A is true, but R is false
(d) A is false, but R is true

89. Given below are two statements. One is labelled as Assertion (A) and the other is labelled as Reason (R).

Assertion (A) Tax should not be charged on dividend income from the shareholders.

Reason (R) Some economists are of the opinion that when tax has already been paid on the profit of the company and balance is distributed as dividend to the owners, tax need not be levied on them.

In the light of the above two statements, choose the correct answer from the options given below.

(a) Both A and R are true and R is the correct explanation of A
(b) Both A and R are true, but R is not the correct explanation of A
(c) A is true, but R is false
(d) A is false, but R is true

90. Given below are two statements. One is labelled as Assertion (A) and the other is labelled as Reason (R).

Assertion (A) Globalisation refers to the free cross-border movement of goods, services, capital, information and people.

Reason (R) Countries are consistently evolving innovative marketing barriers that are WTO compatible.

In the light of the above two statements, choose the correct answer from the options given below.

(a) Both A and R are true and R is the correct explanation of A
(b) Both A and R are true, but R is not the correct explanation of A
(c) A is true, but R is false
(d) A is false, but R is true

Directions *(Q. Nos. 91-95) Read the following paragraph and answer the five questions which as follows :*

Life insurance in its modern form came to India from England in the year 1818. The Oriental Life Insurance Company started by Europeans in Calcutta was the first life insurance company on Indian soil. All the insurance companies established during that period were brought up with the purpose of looking after the needs of the European community and Indian natives were not being insured by these companies.

However, later with the efforts of eminent people like Babu Muttylal Seal, foreign insurance companies started insuring Indian lives too. But Indian lives were being treated as sub standard lives and heavy extra premium were being charged upon them. The Bombay Mutual Life Assurance Society heralded the birth of the first Indian life insurance company in the year 1870 and covered Indian lives at normal rates.

Starting as an Indian enterprise with highly patriotic motives, insurance companies came into existence to carry the message of insurance and social security through insurance to various sectors of society. In 1907, the Hindustan Co-operative Insurance Company took birth in the rooms of 'The Jorsanko', house of the great poet Rabindranath Tagore in Calcutta.

The Indian Mercantile, General Assurance and Swadeshi Life (later Bombay Life) were some of the companies established during the same period. Prior to 1912, India had no legislation to regulate the insurance business. In the year 1912, Life Insurance Companies Act and Provident Fund Act were passed. The Life Insurance Companies Act, 1912 made it necessary that the premium rate tables and periodical valuations of companies should be certified by an actuary. But the Act discriminated between foreign and Indian Companies on many accounts, putting Indian Companies at a disadvantage.

91. The paragraph is about which of the following?

(a) Genesis of insurance in India
(b) Struggle of insurance business
(c) Conflict of insurance business
(d) Complications of insurance business

92. Identify the correct statement from the following

(a) Initially, insurance companies used to discriminate Indian and European clients.
(b) There was no discrimination in Indian and European clients by the insurance companies initially.
(c) Indian clients were charged lower premium by the insurance companies in the beginning.
(d) Indian insurance companies charged higher premium to Europeans at a later stage.

93. Which one among the following grew along with insurance business in India?

(a) Pension Fund (b) Provident Fund
(c) Gratuity (d) Arbitrage

94. The insurance business in India was started first by which one of the following?

(a) American (b) Indian merchants
(c) Europeans (d) Afro-Indians

95. **Which among the following was later renamed as Bombay Life?**

(a) The Indian Mercantile General Assurance
(b) The Oriental Life Insurance Company
(c) National Insurance
(d) Swadeshi Life

Directions *(Q. Nos. 96-100) Read the following paragraph and answer the five questions which as follows :*

Companies often define themselves in term of products. They are in the "auto business" or the "clothing business". 'Market definitions of a business, however, describe the business as a customer-satisfying process. Product are transient, basic needs and customer groups endure forever.

Transportation is a need : the horse and carriage, automobile, railroad, airline, ship and truck are products that meet the need. Viewing business in terms of customers can suggest additional growth opportunities.

There exists difference between a target market definition and a strategic market definition. To define its mission, a company should address Peter Drucker's classic question. What is our business?

96. **Pepsi could define its 'target market' as**

(a) everyone who drinks carbonated soft drinks and are competitors.
(b) anyone who drinks liquid.
(c) everyone who drinks non-milk drinks.
(d) anyone who drinks competitor's drinks.

97. **Which of the following is the correct market definition of 'BPCL'?**

(a) We distribute oil products.
(b) We are the largest oil supply company in India.
(c) We supply energy.
(d) Bharat's own oil distribution company.

98. **Which of the following is the correct product definition of 'Blue Star'?**

(a) We provide climate control in homes and offices.
(b) We supply air conditioners.
(c) We make air cooling systems.
(d) We make air conditioners.

99. **Which of the following is not a major characteristic of good mission statement?**

(a) They have very limited words.
(b) They focus on a limited number of goals.
(c) They stress the company's major competitive spheres in which company will operate.
(d) They have a long term view.

100. **Which of the following is the correct combination Product Definition and Market Definition of Xerox Company?**

(a) Product Definition–We sell photoelectric, Market Definition– We help improve office efficiency
(b) Product Definition–We make photo machines, Market Definition–We improve copy speeds
(c) Product Definition–We sell copying equipment, Market Definition–We make office more efficient
(d) Product Definition–We make copying equipment, Market Definition–We help improve office productivity

ANSWERS

1	(c)	2	(d)	3	(a)	4	(c)	5	(c)	6	(a)	7	(d)	8	(a)	9	(b)	10	(d)
11	(b)	12	(a)	13	(a)	14	(b)	15	(c)	16	(c)	17	(b)	18	(b)	19	(c)	20	(c)
21	(a)	22	(a)	23	(b)	24	(a)	25	(d)	26	(a)	27	(c)	28	(c)	29	(b)	30	(c)
31	(c)	32	(a)	33	(d)	34	(d)	35	(c)	36	(d)	37	(c)	38	(a)	39	(b)	40	(c)
41	(c)	42	(b)	43	(b)	44	(d)	45	(a)	46	(c)	47	(a)	48	(c)	49	(d)	50	(c)
51	(b)	52	(b)	53	(d)	54	(b)	55	(d)	56	(a)	57	(d)	58	(b)	59	(c)	60	(c)
61	(d)	62	(b)	63	(b)	64	(c)	65	(c)	66	(d)	67	(b)	68	(c)	69	(b)	70	(b)
71	(b)	72	(b)	73	(b)	74	(a)	75	(b)	76	(d)	77	(d)	78	(b)	79	(a)	80	(d)
81	(a)	82	(c)	83	(b)	84	(b)	85	(a)	86	(b)	87	(a)	88	(a)	89	(a)	90	(b)
91	(a)	92	(a)	93	(b)	94	(c)	95	(d)	96	(a)	97	(c)	98	(d)	99	(a)	100	(d)

NTA UGC

NET/JRF/SET

SOLVED PAPERS

UGC NET/JRF/SET

COMMERCE (Paper-2)

Solved Paper, December 2018

General Instructions

1. There are total one hundred questions in this paper. Each question carries 2 marks.
2. All questions are compulsory.

---

1 **Match the items of List I with the items of List II and choose the correct answer from the code given below.**

List I		List II	
A.	Rival firms	1.	External environment
B.	Technology	2.	Social and cultural environment
C.	Improving quality	3.	Internal environment
D.	Ethics in business	4.	Global environment

Codes

	A	B	C	D
(a)	1	2	3	4
(b)	2	3	1	4
(c)	2	3	4	1
(d)	4	1	2	3

2 **The companies having business in a large number of countries around the world at present are called**

(a) Transnational Corporations (TNCs)
(b) Multinational Corporations (MNCs)
(c) Global Corporations (GCs)
(d) Multinational Enterprises (MNEs)

3 **The Industrial Policy, 1956 has been prompted by which combination of the following developments?**

1. Adoption of the Constitution of India.
2. Implementation of economic planning.
3. Acceleration of economic growth and industrialisation.
4. Availability of sufficient funds for investment in public sector.

Choose the correct answer from the codes given below

Codes

(a) Both 1 and 2
(b) 1, 2 and 4
(c) 2, 3 and 4
(d) Both 2 and 4

4 **Indicate the most popular route to privatisation adopted by the Government of India in recent decades.**

(a) Management employees buyout
(b) Spontaneous privatisation
(c) Cross holdings
(d) Strategic sale

5 **Given below are two statements, one labelled as Assertion (A) and the other labelled as Reason (R). Read the statements and choose the correct answer using the codes given below.**

Assertion (A) Consumers need to be given legal protection against certain trade practices and business methods.

Reason (R) Protection as per market forces and 'Caveat Emptor' is not enough as perfectly competitive market is an economist's dream and consumer sovereignty is a myth.

Codes

(a) (A) is correct, but (R) is incorrect
(b) (A) in incorrect, but (R) is correct
(c) Both (A) and (R) are correct and (R) is the right explanation of (A)
(d) Both (A) and (R) are correct, but (R) is not the right explanation of (A)

6 Second generation reforms in our country do not comprise of which one of the following?

(a) Exploiting the knowledge based global economy
(b) Growing Indian transnational corporations
(c) Population control measures
(d) Clean environment

7 For the following two statements regarding infrastructural services in the country, choose the correct code for the statements being correct or incorrect.

Statement I Most infrastructure services are provided by public monopolies which generally suffer with severe problems like lack of accountability, low productivity, poor financial performance and over employment.

Statement II There is a need now to induce more private sector investment and participation in provision of social overheads as it may encourage better risk sharing, accountability, monitoring and management of infrastructure sector.

Codes

(a) Both statements are correct
(b) Both statements are incorrect
(c) Statement I is incorrect, but Statement II is correct
(d) Statement I is correct, but Statement II is incorrect

8 Choose the correct code for the following statements being correct or incorrect.

Statement I Punctuality and team spirit among employees of an organisation has great contribution in enhancing profits of the business but they do not appear as an assets in the balance sheet.

Statement II Financial statements do not reflect the correct financial position of a business.

Codes

(a) Both statements are correct
(b) Both statements are incorrect
(c) Statement I is correct, but Statement II is incorrect
(d) Statement I is incorrect, but Statement II is correct

9 X Ltd forfeited 40 shares of ₹ 10 each and on which ₹ 4 per share were paid. If the forfeited shares are re-issued as ₹ 8 per share paid-up, what is the minimum price the company must charge?

(a) ₹ 2 per share (b) ₹ 4 per share
(c) ₹ 8 per share (d) ₹ 10 per share

10 A and B partners in a firm sharing profits in the ratio of 3 : 2. They admit X as a partner for 1/3rd share in profits of the firm. The new profit sharing ratio of A, B and X is

(a) 3 : 2 : 1 (b) 3 : 2 : 2 (c) 3 : 2 : 3 (d) 6 : 4 : 5

11 Which one of the following statement is not true?

(a) Depreciation is a source of funds
(b) Major source of working capital in the long run, is profits from operations
(c) Any transaction that increases working capital is a source of funds
(d) Profits earned from non-operating activities is added to net profit while calculating profits from operations

12 Given below are two statements, one labelled as Assertion (A) and the other labelled as Reason (R). Read the statements and choose the correct answer using the codes given below.

Assertion (A) A low debt equity ratio is generally recommended for a newly started business.

Reason (R) During the initial years of the business, debt servicing will prove to be less burdensome.

(a) Both (A) and (R) are correct, but (R) is the correct explanation of (A)
(b) Both (A) and (R) are correct and (R) is not the correct explanation of (A)
(c) (A) is correct, but (R) is not correct
(d) (A) is not correct, but (R) is correct

13 Which of the following statement is not true?

(a) Conversion of debentures into preference shares will decrease debt equity ratio
(b) Long-term liabilities due for payment within a year should be treated as current liabilities
(c) Higher operating ratio indicates higher profits
(d) Cost of sales is a better numerator than sales while calculating stock turnover

14 A company proposes to introduce a new product in the market. The company wants to maintain P/V Ratio at 25%. If variable cost of the product is ₹ 300, what will be the selling price?

(a) ₹ 100 (b) ₹ 200 (c) ₹ 300 (d) ₹ 400

15 The inverse relationship between the variation in the price and the variation in the quantity demanded is not due to

(a) price effect
(b) entry and exit of buyers
(c) gossen's laws of consumption
(d) law of substitution

16 Cardinal utility analysis of consumer's behaviour is based on which combination of the following assumptions.

1. Utility is measurable in terms of cardinal numbers.
2. Constancy of the marginal utility of money.
3. Utilities of different goods are interdependent.

4. Gossen's first law of consumption.

Choose the correct answer from the codes given below

Codes

(a) Both 1 and 2 (b) 1, 2 and 4
(c) 2, 3 and 4 (d) Both 3 and 4

17 Match the items of List I with the items of List II and choose the correct answer from the code given below.

List I	List II
A. Income elasticity less than unity	1. Competitive goods
B. Cross elasticity less than unity	2. Inferior goods
C. Cross elasticity less than zero	3. Superior goods
D. Income elasticity less than zero	4. Complementary goods

Codes

	A	B	C	D		A	B	C	D
(a)	1	2	3	4	(b)	4	3	1	2
(c)	3	1	4	2	(d)	4	1	2	3

18 Production function is based on which combination of the main characteristics of the inputs from the following

1. substitutability 2. complementarity
3. flexibility 4. specificity

Choose the correct answer from the codes given below

Codes

(a) Both 1 and 2 (b) 2, 3 and 4
(c) 1, 2 and 4 (d) Both 3 and 4

19 Given below are two statements, one labelled as Assertion (A) and the other labelled as Reason (R). Read the statements and choose the correct answer using the codes given below.

Assertion (A) There exists excess capacity of the production for the firms if these incur losses.

Reason (R) Their production level has to remain below their economic capacity level.

(a) (A) is correct, but (R) is incorrect
(b) (A) is incorrect, but (R) is correct
(c) Both (A) and (R) are correct and (R) is the right explanation of (A)
(d) Both (A) and (R) are correct, but (R) is not the right explanation of (A)

20 The monopoly involves a social cost mainly due to its emphasis on which one of the following?

(a) Earning net profit in all possible situations
(b) Lower output at a higher cost in a normal profit situation
(c) Charging different pries from different categories of buyers of the same product
(d) Attempting to stall entry of other firms in the market

21 Cost plus pricing is considered appropriate for which combination of the following?

1. Product tailoring 2. Public utility pricing
3. Refusal pricing 4. Monopoly pricing

Choose the correct answer from the codes given below

Codes

(a) Both 1 and 2 (b) 1, 2 and 3
(c) 2, 3 and 4 (d) Both 3 and 4

22 If a perpendicular on X-axis from the point of intersection of both 'less than' and 'more than' frequency curves in drawn, it gives the value of

(a) arithmetic mean (b) third quartile
(c) mode (d) median

23 Choose the correct code for the following statements being correct or incorrect.

Statement I If the value of β_2, *i.e.* $\frac{\mu_4}{\sigma_4}$, of a distribution gives the value more than 3, its curve is platykurtic.

Statement II In a moderately asymmetrical distribution, the standard deviation is 1.25 times of mean deviation.

Codes

(a) Both statements are correct
(b) Both statements are incorrect
(c) Statement I is correct, but Statement II is incorrect
(d) Statement II is correct, but Statement I is incorrect

24 Which of the following statements relating to the sampling theory are correct?

1. The values of the statistical measures based on the sampled units are called values of statistic.
2. In the simple random sampling technique, the element of the population and the unit of the sample are different.
3. Snow-ball sampling technique is a probability based sampling technique.
4. The 'law of statistical regularity' and the 'law of inertia of large numbers' are the main bases of the sample to become representative of the population.

Choose the correct answer from the codes given below

Codes

(a) Both 1 and 3 (b) Both 1 and 4
(c) 1, 2 and 3 (d) 2, 3 and 4

25 Which of the following is not the correct property of normal distribution?

(a) Continuous distribution
(b) Equality of central values (mean, mode and median)
(c) Standard deviation is the sole parameter of the distribution
(d) Uni-modal distribution

26 The probable error of the coefficient of correlation (r) is calculated by which one of the following formulae?

(a) $0.6745\sqrt{\frac{1-r^2}{n}}$ (b) $0.6745\frac{(1-r^2)}{\sqrt{n}}$
(c) $0.6745\frac{1+r^2}{\sqrt{n}}$ (d) $0.6745\frac{(1+r^2)}{n}$

27 Choose the correct code for the following statements being correct or incorrect.

Statement I The geometric mean of the two regression coefficients of X and Y variables gives the value of the coefficient of correlation.

Statement II If the population distribution is not normal and a sampling distribution of mean is prepared by taking small sized samples, the sampling distribution of mean is not normal.

Codes

(a) Both statements are correct
(b) Both statements are incorrect
(c) Statement I is correct, but Statement II is incorrect
(d) Statement II is correct, but Statement I is incorrect

28 Which of the following is not the advantage of database management system?

(a) Centralised control
(b) High acquisition costs
(c) Improved data integrity
(d) Shared data

29 Choose the correct code for the following statements being correct or incorrect.

Statement I An identifiable group of people contributing their efforts towards attainment of goals is called organisation.

Statement II In its broadest sense, organisation refers to the relationship between the various factors present in a given endeavour.

Codes

(a) Both statements are correct
(b) Both statements are incorrect
(c) Statement I is correct, but Statement II is incorrect
(d) Statement II is correct, but Statement I is incorrect

30 Match the items of List I with the items of List II and choose the correct answer from the code given below.

List I (Propounder of Theory)	List II (Theory of Motivation)
A. Dr William Ouchi	1. X Theory
B. Douglas McGregor	2. Need Hierarchy Theory
C. Frederick Herzberg	3. Z Theory
D. AH Maslow	4. Hygiene Theory

Codes

	A	B	C	D		A	B	C	D
(a)	2	3	4	1	(b)	4	1	3	2
(c)	3	1	4	2	(d)	2	1	3	4

31 Arrange the following stages of staffing in correct sequence and indicate the code of correct sequence.

1. Performance appraisal
2. Recruitment
3. Transfers
4. Selection
5. Induction and orientation

Choose the correct answer from the codes given below

(a) 2, 1, 4, 5, 3
(b) 2, 4, 5, 1, 3
(c) 4, 2, 5, 3, 1
(d) 1, 2, 4, 5, 3

32 Given below are two statements, one labelled as Assertion (A) and the other labelled as Reason (R). Read the statements and choose the correct answer using the codes given below.

Assertion (A) Technological change and skill requirements have been made a subject of investigation in an organisation.

Reason (R) The neo-classical economic theory stated that technological changes require a broader variety of skills and higher average skills from the workers.

Codes

(a) Both (A) and (R) are correct and (R) is the right explanation of (A)
(b) Both (A) and (R) are correct, but (R) is not the right explanation of (A)
(c) Both (A) and (R) are incorrect
(d) (A) is correct, but (R) is incorrect

33 Corporations are controlled and directed by which one of the following?

(a) Corporate ethics
(b) Corporate codes
(c) Corporate governance
(d) Corporate mechanism

34 Critical path indicates which one of the following?

(a) Longest route of completing a task
(b) Shortest route of completing a task
(c) Average time of completing a task
(d) Recorded time of completing a task

35 Which one of the following is the oldest form of organisation?

(a) Committee organisation
(b) Project organisation
(c) Functional organisation
(d) Line organisation

36 Which one of the following demands states consumers are adequately buying all the products put into the marketplace?

(a) Overfull demand
(b) Full demand
(c) Irregular demand
(d) Latent demand

37 Which one of the following is not true for introducing multiple brands in a category?

(a) Increasing shelf presence and retailer dependence in the store
(b) Attracting consumers seeking variety who may otherwise have switched to another brand
(c) Decreasing internal competition within the firm
(d) Yielding economies of scale in advertising, sales, merchandising and physical distribution

38 Match the items of List I with the items of List II and choose the correct answer from the code given below.

List I	List II
A. Mobile defense	1. Occupying the most desirable position in consumers' minds, making the brand almost impregnable.
B. Contraction defense	2. The leader stretches its domain over new territories through market broadening and market diversification.
C. Position defense	3. Large companies give up weaker markets and reassign resources to stronger ones.

Codes

	A	B	C		A	B	C
(a)	2	1	3	(b)	1	2	3
(c)	2	3	1	(d)	1	3	2

39 Given below are two statements, one labelled as Assertion (A) and the other labelled as Reason (R). Read the statements and choose the correct answer using the code given below.

Assertion (A) Purchase decisions are not based on how customers perceive prices but on the marketer's stated price.

Reason (R) Customers nay have a lower price threshold, below which prices signal inferior or unacceptable quality and an upper price threshold where the product appears not worth the money.

Codes

(a) Both (A) and (R) are correct and (R) is the correct explanation of (A)
(b) Both (A) and (R) are correct, but (R) is not the correct explanation of (A)
(c) Both (A) and (R) are incorrect
(d) (A) is correct, but (R) is incorrect

40 In which one of the following modes of entry into foreign market are risk and profit potential the highest?

(a) Indirect exporting (b) Direct exporting
(c) Direct investment (d) Joint ventures

41 Which one of the following modes is not an example of direct and database marketing communication?

(a) Social media marketing (b) Catalogues
(c) Mailings (d) Telemarketing

42 To examine whether the company is pursuing its best opportunities with respect to markets, products and channels is the purpose of which one of the following types of marketing control?

(a) Annual plan control (b) Profitability control
(c) Efficiency control (d) Strategic control

43 Combined leverage can be used to measure the relationship between

(a) EBIT and EPS (b) Sales and EPS
(c) Sales and EBIT (d) PAT and EPS

44 Sales of a firm are ₹ 40 lakh; variable costs ₹ 10 lakh; fixed costs ₹ 15 lakh; interest ₹ 5 lakh. Combined leverage of the firm will be

(a) 2.5 (b) 3 (c) 2 (d) 8

45 A firm has inventory turnover of 3 and cost of goods sold is ₹ 2,70,000. With better inventory management, the inventory turnover is increased to 5. This would result in

(a) increase in inventory by ₹ 54,000
(b) decrease in inventory by ₹ 36,000
(c) increase in cost of goods sold by ₹ 20,000
(d) decrease in inventory by ₹ 90,000

46 Which of the following sources of finance has an implicit cost of capital?

(a) Equity share capital (b) Preference share capital
(c) Debentures (d) Retained earnings

47 Which of the following variables is not known in internal rate of return method of capital budgeting?

(a) Amount of cash inflows (b) Life of the project
(c) Amount of cash outflows (d) Discount rate

48 Which of the following statement(s) is/are false?

1. Capital profits can never be distributed as dividends to the shareholders.
2. Dividends are paid out of profits and therefore, do not affect the liquidity position of the firm.
3. Every company should follow the policy of low dividend payment.
4. Walter's model suggests that dividend payment does not affect the market price of the share.

Choose the correct answer from the codes give below

Code

(a) 1, 2 and 3 (b) Both 3 and 4
(c) 2, 3 and 4 (d) All of the above

49 Which of the following is not a method of preparation of cash budget?

(a) Proforma Balance Sheet method
(b) Adjusted Net Income method
(c) Receipts and Payments method
(d) Cash Cycle method

50 Match the items of List I with the items of List II and choose the correct answer from the code given below.

List I	List II
A. Behaviour referent	1. Wide ranging cultural, structural and personnel strategies
B. Focus of attention for interventions	2. Manage climate and culture
C. Conflict handling	3. Few
D. Job categories and grades	4. Values/Mission

Codes

	A	B	C	D		A	B	C	D
(a)	4	2	1	3	(b)	3	1	2	4
(c)	4	1	2	3	(d)	1	2	4	3

51 Which one of the following items is not a part of job specification?

(a) Location (b) Initiative
(c) Judgement (d) Emotional characteristics

52 Match the items of List I with the items of List II and choose the correct answer from the code given below

List I (Type of Interview)		List II (Usual Application)	
A.	Structured	1.	A realistic approach that yield comparable answers plus indepth insights
B.	Unstructured	2.	Useful to understand applicant's reasoning and analytical abilities under modest stress
C.	Mixed	3.	Useful for valid, results, especially when dealing with large number of applicants
D.	Behavioural	4.	Useful when the interviewer tries to probe personal details of the candidate to analyse whey they are not fit for the job.

Codes

	A	B	C	D
(a)	2	1	2	4
(b)	4	2	1	3
(c)	1	4	2	3
(d)	3	4	1	2

53 According to Donald Kirkpatrick, training programmes can be evaluated at four levels. Indicate the code of correct sequence from the following.

1. Result 2. Reaction
3. Learning 4. Behaviour

Choose the correct answer from the codes given below

(a) 1, 2, 3, 4 (b) 3, 4, 1, 2
(c) 2, 3, 4, 1 (d) 4, 3, 2, 1

54 Match the items of List I with the items of List II and choose the correct answer from the code given below

List I	List II
A. Claims	1. Company car, club membership, paid holidays, furnished house
B. Fringe benefits	2. Telephone/mobile allowance, internet allowance, medical allowance
C. Perquisites	3. Canteen, uniform, accident relief

Codes

	A	B	C
(a)	1	2	3
(b)	2	3	1
(c)	3	2	1
(d)	2	1	3

55 "Everyone benefits when the focus is on common interest and promotion of harmony" is the underlying assumption of which one of the following approaches to industrial relations?

(a) Unitary approach
(b) Pluralistic approach
(c) Marxist approach
(d) Human relations approach

56 Choose the correct code for the following statements being correct or incorrect.

Statement I Thousands of employees die everyday in factories due to accidents.

Statement II To make an accident free plant adds to cost and decreases productivity.

Codes

(a) Both statements are correct
(b) Both statements are incorrect
(c) Statement I is correct, but Statement II is incorrect
(d) Statement II is correct, but Statement I is incorrect

57 Which one of the following is not the fund based business of commercial banks?

(a) Overdraft facility
(b) Issuance of letters of credit
(c) Acceptance of deposits
(d) RTGS/NEFT transactions

58 Match the items of List I with the items of List II and choose the correct answer from the code given below.

List I	List II
A. NPA	1. The percentage of deposits to be kept with RBI in the form of cash
B. SLR	2. The rate at which RBI lends money to commercial banks
C. Repo rate	3. Loans and advances not paid for more than 90 days
D. CRR	4. The percentage of net demand and time liabilities to be kept in the form of liquid assets

Codes

	A	B	C	D
(a)	3	4	1	2
(b)	3	4	2	1
(c)	2	3	4	1
(d)	3	2	4	1

59 "Skimming" in e-banking is a method of

(a) converting Debit Card into Credit Card
(b) transferring cash from one account to another account
(c) stealing credit card information
(d) intimating the customer about his heavy withdrawals

60 When RBI reduces CRR, it results into

(a) increase in lendable resources
(b) decrease in lendable resources
(c) decrease in deposits
(d) increase in deposits

61 **Banking Ombudsman Scheme was introduced by RBI with effect from**

(a) 1998 (b) 1995
(c) 2001 (d) 2005

62 **Banks are required to classify non-performing assets into**

(a) sub-standard assets, doubtful assets and loss assets
(b) standard assets and sub-standard assets
(c) doubtful assets and bad debts
(d) doubtful assets, bad debts and loan assets

63 **Which one of the following is not the function of the Reserve Bank of India?**

(a) Issue of bank notes
(b) Custodian of cash reserves of commercial banks
(c) Accepting deposits and advancing loans to public
(d) Controller of credit

64 **The theory suggesting that the patterns of international trade are determined by factor endowment rather than productivity was propounded by which one of the following?**

(a) Adam Smith
(b) David Ricardo
(c) Heckscher and Bertil Ohlin
(d) Michael Porter

65 **Match the items of List I with the items of List II and choose the correct answer from the code given below.**

	List I		List II
A.	Balance of trade	1.	Imports and exports of goods and services and unilateral transfer of goods and services
B.	Current account	2.	Transactions leading to changes in the financial assets and liabilities of a country
C.	Balance of payments	3.	All economic transactions between a country's residents and residents of other countries
D.	Capital account	4.	Value of exports and imports of a country

Codes

	A	B	C	D		A	B	C	D
(a)	4	1	3	2	(b)	3	2	4	1
(c)	1	2	3	4	(d)	4	3	2	1

66 **Which of the following are included in the international liquidity? Indicate the correct code.**

1. Foreign exchange reserve
2. Borrowing capacity of the various countries
3. Gold reserves

Choose the correct answer from the codes given below

Code

(a) Both 1 and 2
(b) Both 1 and 3
(c) Both 2 and 3
(d) All of the above.

67 **Brettonwoods Conference resulted into the establishment of which of the following?**

(a) IMF and IDA
(b) IBRD and IFC
(c) IDA and ADB
(d) IMF and IBRD

68 **Which one of the following is not the basic function of WTO?**

(a) To facilitate the implementation, administration and operation of trade agreements
(b) To settle differences and disputes among its member countries
(c) To facilitate the expansion and balanced growth of international trade
(d) To carry out periodic reviews of the trade policies of its member countries

69 **'Finance for exporting companies' as part of major programmes of the Exim Bank of India does not include.**

(a) Working capital
(b) Post-shipment credit
(c) Overseas investment finance
(d) Term loans

70 **Which one of the following is the main government agency responsible for development and monitoring international trade in India?**

(a) Indian Institute of Foreign Trade
(b) Federation of Indian Export Organisations
(c) Department of Commerce
(d) Export Promotion Council

71 **Match the items of List I with the items of List II and choose the correct answer from the code given below.**

	List I		List II
A.	AS–1	1.	Accounting for fixed assets
B.	AS–3	2.	Disclosure of accounting policies
C.	AS–10	3.	Leases and its accounting
D.	AS–19	4.	Cash flow statements

Note : *For this question, discrepancy is found in question/answer. So, this question is ignored for all candidates.*

Codes

	A	B	C	D
(a)	3	4	2	1
(b)	1	2	3	4
(c)	3	2	1	4
(d)	3	1	4	2

72 **Which of the following statement(s) is/are true?**

1. Tax shield on depreciation and interest is an important variable for the lessor and the lessee
2. Lease transactions in India are governed by the Lease Act
3. A lessee should evaluate the lease options against the buying option

4. As per As-19, financial lease is shown in the balance sheet of the lessee as an asset

Choose the correct answer from the codes given below

Codes

(a) Both 1 and 4 (b) 1, 3 and 4
(c) 2, 3 and 4 (d) Only 2

73 Which one of the following statement is correct?

(a) SEBI has been constituted under the Securities (Contract and Regulation) Act, 1956
(b) SEBI is constituted from amongst the directors of various stock exchanges
(c) The purpose of issuing different types of rules and regulations by SEBI is to bring monetary gains to investors
(d) One of the objective of setting up SEBI is to protect the interests of investors

74 Merger of two companies under the Board for Industrial and Financial Reconstruction (BIFR) supervision is known as

(a) Reverse merger (b) Negotiated merger
(c) Offer for sale (d) Arranged merger

75 Choose the correct code for the following statements being correct or incorrect.

Statement I An option which gives its holder the privilege of selling to other party a fixed amount of some stock at a stated price on or before a pre-determined data is known as call option.

Statement II In an option, the holder has the privilege of purchasing from other party a fixed amount of some stock at a stated price on or before a pre-determined data is known as put option.

Codes

(a) Both statements are correct
(b) Both statements are incorrect
(c) Statement I is correct, but Statement II is incorrect
(d) Statement I is incorrect, but Statement II is correct

76 Choose the correct code for the following statements being correct or incorrect.

Statement I When the two securities returns are perfectly positively correlated, the risk of their portfolio is just a weighted average of the individual risks of the securities. In such case, diversification does not provide risk reduction but only risk averaging.

Statement II Total risk of a portfolio of two risk securities can be completely eliminated when their returns are perfectly negatively correlated and their proportionate holdings in the portfolio are inversely related to the relative individual risks of the securities.

Codes

(a) Both statements are correct
(b) Both statements are incorrect
(c) Statement I is correct, but Statement II is incorrect
(d) Statement I is incorrect, but Statement II is correct

77 Which among the following is not included in seven Ps of marketing mix given by Booms and Bitner?

(a) Process
(b) People
(c) Physical evidence
(d) Politics

78 Match the items of List I with the items of List II and choose the correct answer from the code given below

List I	List II
A. The economy was characterised by small regional suppliers who sold goods on a local basis	1. Mass marketing
B. Standardised, branded goods were sold at national level	2. Hyper segmentation
C. Era of market differentiation based on demographic, socio-economic and life style factors	3. Segmentation
D. Technological advancements, especially in the area of digital communication, allow marketers to communicate with individual consumers or very small groups	4. Fragmentation

Codes

	A	B	C	D
(a)	1	4	2	3
(b)	4	1	3	2
(c)	4	1	2	3
(d)	1	2	3	4

79 Which among the following is not an internal factor of pricing decision?

(a) Price elasticity as per sales of product
(b) Consumer's expectation from company by past pricing
(c) Position of product in product cycle
(d) Consumer behaviour for given product

80 Advertising method in which a commercial is broadcast simultaneously on several radio stations and/or television channels is known as

(a) exclusive drive (b) intensified campaign
(c) road side (d) road block

81 Choose the correct code for the following statements being correct or incorrect.

Statement I A well chosen marketing channel must be aligned to company's marketing strategy with respect to segmentation, targeting and positioning.

Statement II Marketing channels are set of interdependent organisations participating in the process of making the product available for the use of consumption.

Codes

(a) Both statements are correct
(b) Both statements are incorrect
(c) Statement I is correct, but Statement II is incorrect
(d) Statement II is correct, but Statement I is incorrect

82 Given below are two statements, one labelled as Assertion (A) and the other labelled as Reason (R). Read the statements and choose the correct answer using the codes given below.

Assertion (A) Database assist in market segmentation, especially behavioural segmentation such as developing loyalty segments.

Reason (R) Customer Relationship Management (CRM) databases have become an asset for the analysis of customer behaviour.

Codes

(a) Both (A) and (R) are correct and (R) is the correct explanation of (A)
(b) Both (A) and (R) are correct, but (R) is not the correct explanation of (A)
(c) Both (A) and (R) are incorrect
(d) (A) is correct, but (R) is not correct

83 Which one of the following initiatives is not the strategy for managing shortage of employees in an organisation?

(a) Attempt to reduce turnover
(b) Offer incentives to postpone retirement
(c) Hire temporary employees
(d) Employee training

84 Match the items of List I with the items of List II and choose the correct answer from the code given below.

List I	List II
A. Job context	1. Procedures used
B. Job related tangibles and intangibles	2. Work schedule
C. Work activities	3. Work standards
D. Work performance	4. Services rendered

Codes

	A	B	C	D		A	B	C	D
(a)	3	4	2	1	(b)	2	4	1	3
(c)	4	3	1	2	(d)	1	4	2	3

85 Which one of the following is not an advantage of external recruitment?

(a) Good performance is rewarded
(b) Scope of resentment, jealousies and heartburn are avoided
(c) Compliance with reservation policy becomes easy
(d) Benefits of new skills, new talents and new experiences to organisations are available

86 Given below are two statements, one labelled as Assertion (A) and the other labelled as Reason (R). Read the statements and choose the correct answer using the codes given below.

Assertion (A) Training aids in encouraging and achieving self-development and self-confidence.

Reason (R) It helps a person handle stress, tension, frustration and conflict.

Codes

(a) Both (A) and (R) are correct and (R) is the correct explanation of (A)
(b) Both (A) and (R) are correct, but (R) is not the correct explanation of (A)
(c) Both (A) and (R) are incorrect
(d) (A) is correct, but (R) is not correct

87 For performance assessment of employees, "helping to meet legal requirements" is the application of which one of the following?

(a) Developmental purpose
(b) Administrative purpose
(c) Organisational maintenance purpose
(d) Documentation purpose

88 In which one of the following forms of worker's participation in management is the role of the workers council not just advisory but the management is under a moral obligation to acknowledge, accept and implement the unanimous decision of the council?

(a) Consultative participation
(b) Associative participation
(c) Administrative participation
(d) Decisive participation

89 Match the items of List I with the items of List II and choose the correct answer from the code given below

List I	List II
A. Direct investment overseas aimed at manufacturing products not manufactured by tho firm in the home country	1. Inward FDI
B. Direct investment in a foreign country aimed to sell the output of the firm's domestic production	2. Backward Vertical FDI
C. Direct investment overseas aimed at providing inputs for the firms production process in the home country	3. Conglomerate FDI
D. Foreign firms investing overseas and taking control over foreign assets	4. Forward Vertical FDI

Codes

	A	B	C	D		A	B	C	D
(a)	4	3	2	1	(b)	1	4	2	3
(c)	3	4	2	1	(d)	3	2	1	4

90 Given below are two statements, one labelled as Assertion (A) and the other labelled as Reason (R). Read the statements and choose the correct answer using the codes given below.

Assertion (A) The multilateral trading system is an attempt by governments to make the business environment stable and predictable.

Reason (R) Promising not to raise trade barriers can be as important as lowering one, because the promise gives businesses a clearer view of their future market opportunities.

Codes

(a) Both (A) and (R) are correct and (R) is the right explanation of (A)
(b) Both (A) and (R) are correct, but (R) is not the right explanation of (A)
(c) Both (A) and (R) are incorrect
(d) (A) is correct, but (R) is incorrect

91 Who among the following is not an observer country of the SAARC?

(a) Iran (b) China
(c) USA (d) Canada

92 Foreign investment can be made through which of the following routes?

1. Foreign Direct Investment (FDI)
2. Foreign Portfolio Investment (FPI)
3. Private Equity Investment (PEI)
4. Foreign Venture Capital Investors (FVCI)

Choose the correct answer from the codes given below

(a) 1, 3 and 4 (b) Both 1 and 4
(c) 1, 2 and 4 (d) All of the above

93 Choose the correct code for the following statements being correct or incorrect.

Statement I Intellectual Property (IP) is a category of property that includes intangible creations of the human intellect.

Statement II IPR does not include trade secrets and moral rights.

Codes

(a) Both statements are correct
(b) Both statements are incorrect
(c) Statement I is correct, but Statement II is incorrect
(d) Statement II is correct, but Statement I is incorrect

94 Choose the correct code for the following statements being correct or incorrect.

Statement I FX Spot is an agreement between two parties to buy one currency against selling another currency at an agreed price for settlement on the spot date.

Statement II The date of maturity of a forward contract is more than two business days in future.

Codes

(a) Both statements are correct
(b) Both statements are incorrect
(c) Statement I is correct, but Statement II is incorrect
(d) Statement II is correct, but Statement I is incorrect

95 Given below are two statements, one labelled as Assertion (A) and the other labelled as Reason (R). Read the statements and choose the correct answer using the codes given below.

Assertion (A) Among all methods of charging depreciation of fixed assets, diminishing balance method is the best method.

Reason (R) Diminishing balance method of charging depreciation has been permitted under the Income Tax Act, 1961 for claiming deduction for depreciation.

Codes

(a) Both (A) and (R) are correct and (R) is the correct explanation of (A)
(b) Both (A) and (R) are correct, but (R) is not the correct explanation of (A)
(c) (A) is correct, but (R) is not correct
(d) (A) is not correct, but (R) is correct

96 Match the items of List I with the items of List II and choose the correct answer from the code given below.

List I	List II
A. Compensation received by an employee from his employer on termination of job	1. Exemption upto specified limit
B. Pension received by the widow of an employee	2. Profits in lieu of salary
C. Foreign allowance for rendering services abroad	3. Income from other sources
D. Children hostel allowance	4. Fully exempt from tax

Codes

	A	B	C	D		A	B	C	D
(a)	3	4	2	1	(b)	2	3	4	1
(c)	2	4	3	1	(d)	4	3	1	2

97 Under Section 194 IB of the Income Tax Act, 1961 an individual or HUF (who is not required to get his accounts audited under Section 44 AB) who is responsible for paying to a resident any rent, shall deduct income tax, for the use of any land and building or both, if the rent exceeds

(a) ₹ 50,000 per month (b) ₹ 40,000 per month
(c) ₹ 25,000 per month (d) ₹ 15,000 per month

98 Which one of the following is agricultural income under Income Tax Act?

(a) Income from the land used for storing agricultural produce
(b) Dividend from a company engaged in agriculture
(c) Income from dairy farm, poultry farm etc
(d) Income from the sale of replanted trees where denuded parts of the forest are replanted and subsequent operations in forestry are carried out

99 On fulfilling certain conditions, for an undertaking set up in special economic zones, deduction under Section 10 AA of the Income Tax Act is allowed for

(a) 5 years (b) 10 years
(c) 15 years (d) Unlimited period

100 Given is the information related to a house

Municipal Value (MV)	₹ 1,50,000
Fair Rent	₹ 1,80,000
Standard Rent	₹ 1,60,000
Actual Rent	₹ 20,000 p.m.

Municipal tax paid by owner is 20% of MV Unrealised rent ₹ 40,000 (conditions of Rule 4 satisfied). What is the annual value of the house?

(a) ₹ 1,50,000 (b) ₹ 1,60,000
(c) ₹ 1,70,000 (d) ₹ 2,10,000

ANSWERS

1 (c)	2 (c)	3 (b)	4 (d)	5 (d)	6 (c)	7 (c)	8 (a)	9 (b)	10 (d)
11 (*)	12 (d)	13 (c)	14 (d)	15 (*)	16 (b)	17 (c)	18 (c)	19 (c)	20 (b)
21 (b)	22 (d)	23 (d)	24 (b)	25 (c)	26 (b)	27 (a)	28 (b)	29 (a)	30 (c)
31 (b)	32 (a)	33 (c)	34 (a)	35 (d)	36 (b)	37 (c)	38 (c)	39 (d)	40 (c)
41 (a)	42 (d)	43 (b)	44 (b)	45 (b)	46 (d)	47 (d)	48 (d)	49 (d)	50 (c)
51 (a)	52 (d)	53 (c)	54 (b)	55 (a)	56 (c)	57 (b)	58 (b)	59 (c)	60 (a)
61 (b)	62 (a)	63 (c)	64 (c)	65 (a)	66 (d)	67 (d)	68 (c)	69 (b)	70 (c)
71 (*)	72 (b)	73 (d)	74 (d)	75 (b)	76 (a)	77 (d)	78 (b)	79 (d)	80 (d)
81 (a)	82 (a)	83 (d)	84 (b)	85 (a)	86 (b)	87 (d)	88 (b)	89 (c)	90 (a)
91 (d)	92 (d)	93 (c)	94 (a)	95 (d)	96 (b)	97 (a)	98 (d)	99 (c)	100 (c)

Note (*) All Options are incorrect.

UGC NET/JRF/SET

COMMERCE (Paper-2)

Solved Paper, July 2018

General Instructions

1. There are total one hundred questions in this paper. Each question carries 2 marks.
2. All questions are compulsory.

---

1. The central bank can significantly influence the savings, investments and consumer spending in the economy through which of the following policy?

(a) Fiscal policy
(b) Monetary policy
(c) Industrial policy
(d) Foreign exchange policy

2. Which one of the following is not the characteristic of capitalism?

(a) Individuals and associations behave with economic motive of maximising their profit with least sacrifice or cost
(b) The country's major means of production are either owned by the Government or their use is controlled by the Government
(c) Producers, consumers and employees compete among themselves, as the resources and opportunities are limited
(d) Price, the invisible hand, plays a predominant role in the flow of the factors of production and consumption

3. Which of the following is not the salient feature of the industrial policy developments since1991?

(a) The scope of the private sector has been enormously expanded
(b) Public sector has been withdrawing partially or fully from several of the enterprises by divestment
(c) The Indian industry is increasingly exposed to foreign competition
(d) Monopoly or dominant position for the public sector in most of the industries and control of the commanding heights of the economy by the public sector

4. Which of the following does not form the part of the important information to be incorporated in the Memorandum of Association as specified in the Companies Act, 2013?

(a) The name of the company and the state in which it is situated
(b) The objects for which the company is proposed to be incorporated
(c) The rules, regulations and bye-laws for the internal management of the company
(d) The liability of the members of the company, whether limited or unlimited

5. **Assertion** (A) The volume of imports tends to be very high when there is a conjecture of high rate of economic growth and a sharp fall in the relative price of imports and *vice-versa*.

Reason (R) High rate of growth, ceteris paribus, is associated with rise in imports and increase in the imports, ceteris paribus, is associated with a fall in the relative price of imports.

Codes

(a) Both (A) and (R) are correct and (R) is the right explanation of (A)

(b) Both (A) and (R) are correct, but (R) is not the right explanation of (A)

(c) (A) is correct, but (R) is not correct

(d) (R) is correct, but (A) is not correct

6. Which of the following statement is not correct relating to consumerism?

(a) Consumerism is a manifestation of the failure of the business to guarantee and ensure consumer legitimate rights

(b) The government does not have any role in consumer protection as it is the part of business organisations alone

(c) The consumers should accept consumerism as a means of asserting and enjoying their rights

(d) Consumerism evolution is not a set-back for marketing but rather points to the next stage in the evolution of enlightened marketing

7. Which one of the following is not covered in the approach adopted by "Niti Aayog" ?

(a) Five year planning approach

(b) Three year action agenda

(c) Seven year strategy

(d) Fifteen year vision

8. **Assertion** (A) Personal transactions of the owners of the business are not recorded in the books.

Reason (R) According to the business entity concept, each business enterprise is considered as an accounting unit separate from owners.

Codes

(a) Both (A) and (R) are correct and (R) is the correct explanation of (A)

(b) Both (A) and (R) are correct, but (R) is not the correct explanation of (A)

(c) (A) is correct, but (R) is not correct

(d) (A) is incorrect, but (R) is correct

9. Which one of the following is not an example of 'financing activities' with reference to cash flow statement?

(a) Repayment of bank loan

(b) Interest on debentures/dividend paid

(c) Cash proceeds from public deposits

(d) Sale of fixed assets

10. Which one of the following statement is true about estimated costs and standard costs?

(a) Standard costs are based on scientific analysis and engineering studies while estimated costs are based on historical basis

(b) Standard cost emphasis is on "what cost will be" while estimated cost emphasis is on "what cost should be"

(c) Standard costs are more frequently revised compared to estimated cost

(d) Estimated costs are more stable than standard costs

11. Which one of the following statements is not true?

(a) An expenditure intended to benefit current year is revenue expenditure

(b) Amount paid for acquiring goodwill is capital expenditure

(c) Wages paid for installation of a new machine is usually debited to wages account

(d) Revenue expenditure is not intended to benefit future period

12. X Ltd forfeited 20 shares of ₹ 10 each, ₹ 8 called up, on which John had paid application and allotment money of ₹ 5 per share, of these, 15 shares were re-issued to Parker as fully paid-up for ₹ 6 per share. What is the balance in the Share Forfeiture Account after the relevant amount has been transferred to Capital Reserve Account?

(a) Nil (b) ₹ 5 (c) ₹ 25 (d) ₹ 100

13. X and Y sharing profits in the ratio of 7 : 3, admit Z for 3/7 share in the new firm in which he takes 2/7 from X and 1/7 from Y. The new ratio of X, Y and Z will be

(a) 7 : 3 : 3

(b) 4 : 2 : 3

(c) 14 : 6 : 15

(d) 29 : 11 : 30

14. **Assertion** (A) A high operating ratio indicates a favourable position.

Reason (R) A high operating ratio leaves a high margin to meet non-operating expenses.

Codes

(a) Both (A) and (R) are correct and (R) correctly explains (A)

(b) Both (A) and (R) are correct, but (R) does not explain (A)

(c) Both (A) and (R) are incorrect

(d) (A) is correct, but (R) is incorrect

15. The following are the two statements regarding concept of profit. Indicate the correct code of the statements being correct or incorrect.

Statement I Accounting profit is a surplus of total revenue over and above all paid-out costs, including both manufacturing and overhead expenses.

Statement II Economic or pure profit is a residual left after all contractual costs have been met, including the transfer costs of management, insurable risks, depreciation and payments to shareholders sufficient to maintain investment at its current level.

Codes

(a) Both statements are correct

(b) Both statements are incorrect

(c) Statement I is correct while Statement II is incorrect

(d) Statement I is incorrect while Statement II is correct

16. Which one of the following sets is incorrect to show the inter-relationships among price elasticity coefficient, change in price and change in total revenue?

	Price elasticity coefficient	Change in price	Change in total revenue
(a)	Zero	Increase	Increase
		Decrease	Decrease
(b)	Less than 1	Increase	Decrease
		Decrease	Increase
(c)	Equal to 1	Increase	No change
		Decrease	No change
(d)	More than 1	Increase	Decrease
		Decrease	Increase

17. Which one of the following is not the basic property of indifference curves?

(a) Indifference curves have a negative slope
(b) Indifference curves of imperfect substitutes are concave to the origin
(c) Indifference curves do not intersect nor are they tangent to one another
(d) Upper indifference curves indicate higher level of satisfaction

18. When labour is plotted on X-axis and capital is plotted on Y-axis and an iso-quant is prepared, then which of the following statement(s) is/are false?

1. Marginal rate of technical substitution of labour for capital is equal to the slope of the iso-quant.
2. Marginal rate of technical substitution of labour for capital is equal to change in the units of capital divided by the change in the units of labour.
3. Marginal rate of technical substitution of labour for capital is the ratio of marginal productivity of capital to marginal productivity of labour.

Codes
(a) Both 1 and 2 (b) Only 3
(c) Only 1 (d) Only 2

19. Match the items of List II with the items of List I and indicate the code of correct matching. The items relate to economies of scale/scope.

List I	List II
A. Economies of scale	1. Arise with lower average costs of manufacturing a product when two complementary products are produced by a single firm
B. Internal economies	2. Mean lowering of costs of production by producing in bulk
C. External economies	3. Arise when cost per unit depends on size of the firm
D. Economies of scope	4. Arise when cost per unit depends on the size of the industry, not the firm

Codes

	A	B	C	D
(a)	2	4	1	3
(b)	1	2	3	4
(c)	2	3	4	1
(d)	4	3	2	1

20. A firm that produces highly substitute goods can adopt which one of the following pricing strategies?

(a) Transfer pricing (b) Going rate pricing
(c) Product bundling (d) Full cost pricing

21. In a perfectly competitive market, a firm in the long run operates at the level of output where

(a) AC = MC, when MC is lowest
(b) MC = AR = MR, when MC is lowest
(c) MR = MC
(d) AR = MR = AC = MC

22. Assignment of numerals to the objects to represent their attributes is known as

(a) nominal data (b) ordinal data
(c) interval data (d) ratio data

23. A graph of a cumulative frequency distribution is called

(a) frequency polygon (b) frequency curve
(c) ogive (d) pie diagram

24. In the case of classification of data, the class having its upper limit is treated as the lower limit of its next class is called

(a) open ended class (b) close ended class
(c) exclusive class (d) inclusive class

25. For a standard normal probability distribution, the mean (μ) and the standard deviation (σ) are

(a) $\mu = 0, \sigma = 1$ (b) $\mu = 16, \sigma = 4$
(c) $\mu = 25, \sigma = 5$ (d) $\mu = 100, \sigma = 10$

26. Match the items of List II with the items of List I and select the code of correct matching.

List I	List II
A. Standard error of mean	1. Ha : $\mu_2 \neq \mu_2$
B. Base of point estimate of	2. Values based on all the observations of the mean of the population the population
C. Non-specific hypothesis	3. Mean of the sampling distribution of mean
D. Parameter value of descriptive statistics	4. Standard deviation of the sampling distribution of mean

Codes

	A	B	C	D
(a)	4	3	1	2
(b)	1	2	3	4
(c)	4	3	2	1
(d)	3	4	1	2

27. There is a very high inverse relationship between measures of 'overweight' and 'life expectancy'. Which one of the following value of the coefficient of correlation is consistent with the statement?

(a) 0.80 (b) 0.20 (c) –0.20 (d) –0.80

28. Match the items of List II with the items of List I and select the code of correct matching.

List I	List II
A. Chi-square test	1. Testing the significance of the differences of the mean values among more than two sample groups
B. ANOVA (F-test)	2. Testing the goodness of fit of a distribution
C. Z - test	3. Testing the significance of the difference of the mean values between two large sized samples
D. t - test	4. Testing the significance of the difference of the mean values between two small sized samples when population standard deviation is not available

Codes

	A	B	C	D		A	B	C	D
(a)	1	2	3	4	(b)	4	3	2	1
(c)	1	2	4	3	(d)	2	1	3	4

29. Match the items of List II with List I and choose the correct code.

List I	List II
A. Sales Executive	1. Topmiddle Management
B. Branch Manager	2. Middle Management
C0 Foreman	3. Lower Management
D. Production Manager	4. Operating Force

Codes

	A	B	C	D		A	B	C	D
(a)	4	2	3	1	(b)	2	3	4	1
(c)	3	4	2	1	(d)	1	2	3	4

30. Select the correct code of the statements being correct or incorrect.

Statement I It is a significant feature of human that he plans.

Statement II A plan is a trap to capture the future.

Codes

(a) Statement I is correct, but Statement II is incorrect
(b) Statement II is correct, but Statement I is incorrect
(c) Both statements are correct
(d) Both statements are incorrect

31. **Assertion** (A) Management is a set of principles relating to its functions.

Reason (R) Management is essential to run all types of organisations.

Codes

(a) (A) and (R) both are correct and (R) is the right explanation of (A)
(b) (A) and (R) both are correct, but (R) is not the right explanation of (A)
(c) Both (A) and (R) are incorrect
(d) (A) is correct, but (R) is incorrect

32. Match the items of List II with List I and choose the correct code.

List I (Critical Control Standards)	List II (Critical Points)
A. Physical standards	1. Material cost per unit
B. Cost standards	2. Labour hours per unit of output
C. Revenue standards	3. Timing of production
D. Program standards	4. Average sales per customer

Codes

	A	B	C	D		A	B	C	D
(a)	2	1	4	3	(b)	2	1	3	4
(c)	1	2	4	3	(d)	4	1	3	2

33. Which among the following is not a correct statement with regard to Corporate Governance in India?

(a) Every company must appoint an individual or firm as auditor
(b) The independent directors must attend atleast three meetings a year
(c) One or more women directors are recommended for certain classes of companies
(d) The maximum number of permissible directors cannot exceed 15 in a public limited company

34. The popular statement, - "if all you have is a hammer, everything looks like a nail", is given by

(a) AH Maslow (Hierarchy of Needs)
(b) Henry Fayol (Industrial and General Administration)
(c) FW Taylor (Scientific Management)
(d) Fredrick Herzberg (Hygiene Theory)

35. Functional leadership Theory is associated with

(a) Hackman and Walton and McGrath
(b) Bernard and Ordway Tead
(c) Koontz and O'Donnell
(d) Alford and Beatty

36. When two separate companies or two divisions within the same company agree to place both of their respective brands on a particular product or enterprise, this arrangement is termed as

(a) differential branding (b) cobranding
(c) dual branding (d) Both (b) and (c)

37. The tangible goods for which a consumer wants to compare quality, price and perhaps style in several stores before making a purchase are called

(a) convenience goods (b) shopping goods
(c) speciality goods (d) unsought goods

38. When a company treats each single customer as a separate segment, this is called

(a) niche marketing
(b) nano marketing
(c) single marketing
(d) micro marketing

39. Under which of the following conditions, the level of consumer's involvement will not be high ?

(a) The consumer considers the amount of money involved to be large
(b) The product is seen as having low potential for providing significant benefits
(c) The consumer lacks information about alternatives for satisfying the need
(d) The product has considerable social importance

40. **Statement** I The mindset which is commonly associated with a long ago era when the demand for goods generally exceeded the supply and the primary focus in business was to effectively produce medium quantities of products ; finding the customers was viewed as a relatively major function.

Statement II The firms with product orientation typically focus on the quality and quantity of offerings while assuming that customers will seek out and buy reasonably priced, well made products.

From the above statements indicate the correct code of being statements correct or incorrect. The statements relate to concepts of marketing.

(a) Both statements are not correct
(b) Both statements are correct
(c) Statement I is correct, but Statement II is not correct
(d) Statement I is not correct, but Statement II is correct

41. Match the items of List II with List I to identify the correct code which are related to legal forces affecting international marketers.

List I	List II
A. Tariff	1. A regulation specifying the proportion of a finished product's components and labour that must be provided by importing country
B. Import quota	2. Tax imposed on product entering a country and used to protect domestic producers and/or raise revenue
C. Local-content law	3. A requirement that a product contain or exclude certain ingredients or that it be tested and certified as meeting certain restrictive standards
D. Local-operating law	4. Limiting amount of a particular product that can be brought into a country, to protect domestic industry or broadening access to its markets
E. Standards and certification	5. A refusal to buy products from a particular company or country
F. Boycott	6. A constraint on how, when or where retailing can be

Codes

	A	B	C	D	E	F
(a)	3	4	2	1	6	5
(b)	6	2	1	4	3	5
(c)	2	4	1	6	3	5
(d)	4	6	1	2	3	5

42. Match the items of List II with List I which are related to personal selling process and identify the correct code.

List I	List II
A. Prospecting	1. Attention, interest, desire, action
B. Preapproach	2. Identifying profiles, leads, records and qualifying capability and willingness
C. Presentation	3. Reduce dissonance, build goodwill
D. Post sales services	4. Information, habits, preferences

Codes

	A	B	C	D
(a)	1	3	4	2
(b)	3	4	2	1
(c)	2	4	1	3
(d)	4	3	2	1

43. Which of the following is not an approach to the capital structure?

(a) Gross Profit approach
(b) Net Operating Income approach
(c) Net Income approach
(d) Modigliani and Miller approach

44. Which one of the following methods of capital budgeting assumes that cash inflows are reinvested at the project's rate of return?

(a) Net Present Value
(b) Accounting Rate of Return
(c) Internal Rate of Return
(d) Discounted Payback Period

45. Cost of equity share capital is more than cost of debt because

(a) equity shares are not easily saleable
(b) equity shares do not provide the fixed dividend rate
(c) generally the face value of equity shares is less than the face value of debentures
(d) equity shares have high risk than debts

46. Negative net working capital implies that

(a) long-term funds have been used for fixed assets
(b) short-term funds have been used for fixed assets
(c) long-term funds have been used for current assets
(d) short-term funds have been used for current assets

47. Which of the following is an implicit cost of increasing proportion of debt of a company?

(a) PE ratio of the company would increase
(b) Rate of return of the company would decrease
(c) Tax-shield would not be available on new debts
(d) Equity shareholders would demand higher return

48. Profitability index of a project is the ratio of present value of cash inflows to

(a) total cash inflows
(b) total cash outflows
(c) present value of cash outflows
(d) initial cost minus depreciation

49. Which one of the following statement is false?

(a) Effective dividend policy is an important tool to achieve the goal of wealth maximisation

(b) According to Walter, the optimal payout ratio for a growth firm is 100%

(c) MM model asserts that the value of the firm is not affected whether the firm pays dividend or not

(d) 'Bird-in-the-hand theory' in reference to dividend decision has been developed by Myron Gordon

50. Which one of the following statements defines the correct meaning of the term 'boundary spanning'?

(a) It refers to an obligation of an individual, firm or institution to account for its activities and accept responsibility for them

(b) It refers to the process that helps the organisation and its employees to link with their external environment through specific activities/functions

(c) It refers to the science of morals, principles and rules of conduct

(d) It refers to multiculturism management

51. The VRIO framework, used in HR function in today's era, refers to four criteria. Identify the correct code which stands as correct explanation to VRIO as proposed by Barney.

(a) Valence - Recruiting - Industrial relations - Opportunities

(b) Vision - Rewards - Improvements - Options

(c) Value - Rarity - Imitability - Organisation

(d) Versatile - Resource - Information - Outsourcing

52. Assertion (A) Induction is an informal information sharing session on miscellaneous issues in an organisation.

Reason (R) The rationale of induction is to ensure effective integration of staff into or across the organisation for their mutual benefit.

Codes

(a) (A) and (R) both are correct and (R) is the correct explanation of (A)

(b) (A) and (R) both are correct, but (R) is not the correct explanation of (A)

(c) (A) is correct, but (R) is incorrect

(d) (A) is incorrect, but (R) is correct

53. Match the items of List II with the items of List I pertaining to the ranking methods used in performance management systems and select the code of correct matching.

List I (Ranking Methods)	List II (Methodology)
A. Simple ranking	1. Based on overall performance
B. Alternation ranking	2. Ends up with pre-determined number of people in each group
C. Paired comparison	3. Based on particular trait only for quantity/quality of work
D. Forced distribution	4. Based on a trait or a set of trait and avoids central tendency

Codes

	A	B	C	D
(a)	2	3	4	1
(b)	1	4	3	2
(c)	4	2	1	3
(d)	3	1	2	4

54. Assertion (A) Compensation has two vital domains economic concept and psychological concept.

Reason (R) Compensation basically represents an employment contract.

Codes

(a) (A) is correct and (R) is the right explanation of (A)

(b) (A) is correct, but (R) is not the right explanation of (A)

(c) (A) is correct, but (R) is incorrect

(d) (A) is incorrect, but (R) is correct

55. Which of the following is not the primary objective of industrial relations and labour laws?

(a) Maintaining social equity

(b) Providing credit facilities to industries

(c) International uniformity

(d) Promoting economic growth

56. Assertion (A) In real terms, workers' participation in management has failed in India.

Reason (R) There is lack of attitudinal change, multiplicity of unions and absence of a procedure to determine a sole bargaining agent in an organisation.

Codes

(a) (A) is correct and (R) is the correct explanation of (A)

(b) (A) is correct, but (R) is not the correct explanation of (A)

(c) (A) is correct, but (R) is incorrect

(d) (A) is incorrect, but (R) is correct

57. Which one of the following is not the function of NABARD?

(a) To provide refinance assistance by way of short-term credit to state cooperative banks and sectoral rural banks etc approved by the RBI for some specific purposes

(b) To undertake inspection of cooperative societies other than primary cooperative societies and RRBs

(c) To promote research in various aspects of the problems of urban development

(d) To subscribe to share capital or invest in securities of any institution concerned with agricultural and rural development

58. Which one of the following financial institutions coordinates the functions and operations of all the financial institutions into a single integrated financial structure so that each may contribute to the growth of the economy?

(a) IFCI (b) UTI

(c) IDBI (d) SIDBI

59. Assertion (A) The Reserve Bank of India is entrusted with the management of the public debt and issue of new loans and treasury bills on behalf of the Central and State Governments.

Reason (R) The Governor and the Deputy Governors of Reserve Bank of India are appointed by the central Government.

Codes

(a) (A) is correct, but (R) is not the correct

(b) (A) and (R) both are correct, but (R) is not the right explanation of (A)

(c) (A) and (R) both are correct and (R) is the right explanation of (A)

(d) (A) and (R) both are not correct

60. ...... **refers to the process of removing or stripping the legal status of a currency.**

(a) Digitisation (b) Financial inclusion

(c) Demonetisation (d) Micro finance

61. Which one of the following is not the objective of UTI ?

(a) To mobilise savings of the community by offering savers the triple benefits of safety, liquidity and profitability of investments

(b) To channelise the pooled savings into productive outlets

(c) To provide finance under hire purchase finance and housing finance to its members

(d) To give every one a chance to indirectly own shares and securities in a large number of select companies

62. Which one of the following is the main objective of IFCI ?

(a) To offer both small and large investors the means of acquiring shares in the widening prosperity resulting from the steady industrial growth of the country

(b) To upgrade technology, modernisation and to promote marketing of products of small scale sector

(c) To serve as the apex institution for term finance for industry with coordination, regulation and supervision of the working of other financial institution

(d) To provide medium and long-term financial assistance to industrial undertakings, particularly in those circumstances in which banking accommodation is in appropriate or resource to capital market is impracticable

63. Match the items of List II with the items of List I and indicate the correct code.

	List I		List II
A.	Term finance	1.	Providing finance to new or existing industrial units for encouraging commercial application of technology/ expansion
B.	Refinance	2.	Delivering of banking services at affordable cost to the vast sections of disadvantaged and low income groups
C.	Financial inclusion	3.	Providing replenishment finance to eligible institutions for their loans to industrial concerns
D.	Venture capital	4.	Providing finance to the borrowers for expansion and modernisation of plant and equipment

Codes

	A	B	C	D		A	B	C	D
(a)	1	2	3	4	(b)	1	2	4	3
(c)	4	3	2	1	(d)	4	3	1	2

64. Assertion (A) An export processing zone is different from free trade zone as it promotes units primarily devoted to exports.

Reason (R) Goods imported to a free trade zone may be re-exported without any processing, in the same form. But, goods exported by units in an EPZ are expected to have undergone some value addition by manufacturing/ processing.

Codes

(a) (A) is correct and (R) is the correct explanation of (A)

(b) (A) is correct, but (R) is not the correct explanation of (A)

(c) (A) is correct, but (R) is incorrect

(d) (A) is incorrect, but (R) is correct

65. Match the items of List II with the items of List I relating to liberalisation of agricultural trade.

	List I		List II
A.	Tariffication	1.	They have demonstrably adverse effects on other member countries
B.	Prohibited subsidies	2.	They act on goods which are contingent upon export performance
C.	Actionable subsidies	3.	Replacement of existing non-tariff restrictions
D.	Non-actionable subsidies	4.	For industrial research in disadvantaged regions

Codes

	A	B	C	D		A	B	C	D
(a)	2	3	1	4	(b)	4	1	2	3
(c)	3	2	1	4	(d)	2	4	3	1

66. Match the items of List II and with the items of List I relating to WTO impact.

	List I		List II
A.	NAMA	1.	Liberalisation of international investments
B.	GATTS	2.	Includes industrial goods, textile, jewellery, fish and fisheries product manufacturing industries
C.	TRIMs	3.	Liberalisation of trade in goods and services
D.	TRIPs	4.	Provides monopoly power to owners of intellectual property

Codes

	A	B	C	D
(a)	2	1	4	3
(b)	4	2	3	1
(c)	2	3	1	4
(d)	3	2	4	1

67. Indicate the correct code of the following statements being correct or incorrect. The statements relate to the type of transactions recorded in the current/capital accounts of the Balance of Payments.

Statement I The capital account consists of long-term capital transactions only.

Statement II The current account includes all transactions which give rise to or use up national income.

Codes

(a) Both statements are correct
(b) Both statements are incorrect
(c) Statement I is correct while Statement II is incorrect
(d) Statement I is incorrect while Statement II is correct

68. Select the correct code of the following statements being correct or incorrect.

Statement I International liquidity encompasses the international reserves only.

Statement II International liquidity covers only official holdings of gold, foreign exchange,

SDRs and reserve position in the IMF available for the settlement of the international transactions.

Codes

(a) Both statements are correct
(b) Both statements are incorrect
(c) Statement I is correct while Statement II is incorrect
(d) Statement I is incorrect while Statement II is correct

69. Match the items of List II with the items of List I and select the code of correct matching. The items relate to International Trade Theories.

List I	List II
A. Comparative Cost Theory	1. Adam Smith
B. Opportunity Cost Theory	2. Gottfried Haberler
C. Factor Endowment Theory	3. David Ricardo
D. Absolute Cost Theory	4. Eli Heckscher and Bertil Ohlin

Codes

	A	B	C	D
(a)	1	2	3	4
(b)	3	2	4	1
(c)	4	3	2	1
(d)	1	4	3	2

70. Which one of the following is not the guiding principle of the World Bank regarding it's lending operations ?

(a) Proper assessment of the repayment prospects of loans
(b) Lending should be only for specific projects which are economically and technically sound and of a high priority nature
(c) The lending should be to enable a country to meet foreign exchange content of the project cost
(d) The bank does expect the borrowing country to spend the loan in a particular country

71. Total return on a security is equal to the following :

(a) $\dfrac{\text{Periodic cash receipts + Capital gains}}{\text{Purchase price of the security}}$

(b) $\dfrac{\text{Periodic cash receipts + Capital gains}}{\text{Current market price of the security}}$

(c) $\dfrac{\text{Periodic cash receipts}}{\text{Current market price of the security}}$

(d) $\dfrac{\text{Periodic cash receipts − Capital gains}}{\text{Purchase price of the security}}$

72. Risk of a portfolio can be minimised by which one of the following ?

(a) Combining two securities having perfect positive correlation in their expected returns
(b) Combining two securities having perfect negative correlation in their expected returns
(c) Combining two securities having partially positive correlation in their expected returns
(d) Combining two securities having partially negative correlation in their expected returns

73. The certificate which evidences an unsecured corporate debt of short-term maturity, is known as

(a) certificate of deposit
(b) short-term loan certificate
(c) treasury bill
(d) commercial paper

74. Which of the following statements are false ? Indicate the correct code.

1. Grey market is a market for dealing in listed securities
2. OTCEI is mainly intended for big investors.
3. Insider trading is legally permitted in the capital market
4. The device adopted to make profit out of the differences in prices of a security in two different markets is called 'arbitrage'.

Codes

(a) 1, 2 and 3 (b) 1, 2 and 4
(c) 1, 2, 3 and 4 (d) 2, 3 and 4

75. Which of the following statements are false? Indicate the correct code.

1. Share capital issued by a company for the first time is known as venture capital.
2. All Venture Capital Funds in India are promoted by the Government.
3. In addition to capital, venture capitalists provide managerial and technical support also to the assisted firms.
4. Benefits from venture capital financing can be realised in long run only.

Codes

(a) 1, 2 and 4 (b) Both 1 and 2
(c) 2, 3 and 4 (d) Both 3 and 4

76. Match the items of List II with the items of List I and select the correct code.

	List I		List II
A.	Liquidity risk	1.	Risk related to purchasing power of income
B.	Business risk	2.	Risk related to firm's capital structure
C.	Financial risk	3.	Risk related to inability to pay its dues on time
D.	Inflation risk	4.	Risk related to fluctuation in profits

Codes

	A	B	C	D		A	B	C	D
(a)	2	3	4	1	(b)	1	4	3	2
(c)	3	2	4	1	(d)	3	4	2	1

77. Statement I Designing a distribution system for a service (for profit or non-business context) involves to select the parties only through which ownership will pass.

Statement II The ownership channel for most of the services is long and quite complex because of inseparability characteristic.

Statement III Short channels usually mean more control on the part of the seller.

Identify the correct code of being the statements correct or incorrect. These statements relate to channel strategies of products/services.

Codes

(a) Statements I and II are correct, but III is not correct
(b) Statements I and III are correct, but II is not correct
(c) Statements I and II are not correct, but III is correct
(d) Statements I, II and III all are not correct

78. An enormous collection of data on various topics from a variety of internal and external sources, compiled by a firm for its own use or for use by its clients, is called

(a) database (b) data warehouse
(c) data mining (d) MIS

79. Statement I A form of non-store retailing that uses advertising to contact consumers who, in turn, purchase products without visiting a retail store is called direct selling.

Statement II A form of non-store retailing in which personal contact between a sales person and a consumer occurs away from a retail store is called direct marketing.

In the light of above statements, identify the correct code of statements being correct or incorrect.

Codes

(a) Statement I is correct, but Statement II is not correct
(b) Statement I is not correct, but Statement II is correct
(c) Both statements are correct
(d) Both statements are not correct

80. 34% of the customers who fall in one of the categories of diffusion process who are deliberate customers to accept an innovation just before the average adopter in a social system. Such customers who are above average in social and economic measures, rely quite a bit on advertisements and salesmen are known as

(a) early adopters
(b) early majority
(c) late majority
(d) late adopters

81. The GE Business model is explained on which one of the following parameters ?

(a) Market attractiveness and business position
(b) Business attractiveness and market position
(c) Industry growth rate and company's market share
(d) Company's growth rate and industry's position

82. A reduction from the list price that is offered by a seller to buyers in payment for marketing functions the buyers will perform is known as

(a) trade discount
(b) functional discount
(c) cash discount
(d) Both (a) and (b)

83. Match the items of List II with the items of List I relating to Personnel Management (PM) and Human Resource Management (HRM) ; and select the code of correct matching.

	List I		List II
A.	Focus of PM	1.	Development attitude by making people contribute their best
B.	Focus of HRM	2.	Exercising it as a functional area of management
C.	Philosophy of PM	3.	Exercising it as humane management
D.	Philosophy of HRM3	4.	Profit maximisation by controlling people

Codes

	A	B	C	D		A	B	C	D
(a)	2	3	4	1	(b)	3	2	1	4
(c)	4	1	2	3	(d)	1	3	4	2

84. Select the correct code of the following statements being correct or incorrect.

1. Strategic HRM focuses on specific organisational intentions about what needs to be done while HR strategies focus on long-term issues only.
2. Strategic HRM focuses on macro concerns such as structure and culture while HR strategy focuses on specific issues assigned.
3. Human resource strategy decisions are derived from strategic HRM.

Codes

(a) Statements I and II are correct while Statement III is incorrect

(b) Statements II and III are correct while Statement I is incorrect
(c) Statements I and III are correct while Statement II is incorrect
(d) All the statements are correct

85. Which of the following code represents the full form of the term 'BARS' in performance management systems?
(a) Business Appraisal and Rating Systems
(b) Balanced Assessment Reviewing Scorecard
(c) Behaviourally Anchored Rating Scale
(d) Benchmarking Appraisal Reviewing Strategy

86. Match the items of List II with the items of List I relating to training and select the code of correct matching.

	List I		List II
A.	Andragogy	1.	Strategies or styles of instructions
B.	Pedagogy	2.	Ultimate knowledge level with which trainee leaves the training sessions
C.	Terminal behaviour	3.	Lack of commitment of management and scarcity of resources in training
D.	Training impediments	4.	Art and Science of training the adults

Codes

	A	B	C	D		A	B	C	D
(a)	1	4	3	2	(b)	2	3	1	4
(c)	4	1	2	3	(d)	3	2	4	1

87. Which of the following statements does not stand as a principle of compensation administration?
(a) An enterprise should have a clear cut plan to determine differential pay level in terms of divergent job requirements
(b) People and jobs should never be mingled
(c) The compensation system should be designed with subjectivity with respect to individual skill sets exercised from time to time
(d) There should be established wage grievance handling procedures

88. Match the items of List II with the items of List I relating to industrial relations and select the code of correct matching.

	List I		List II
A.	Healthy labour–management relations	1.	Industrial Disputes Act
B.	Industrial Peace Law	2.	Guiding principles for a grievance procedure
C.	Industrial Democracy	3.	Workers' participation in management
D.	National Commission on Labour, 1969	4.	Voluntary arbitration and responsible trade union

Codes

	A	B	C	D		A	B	C	D
(a)	4	1	3	2	(b)	2	3	4	1
(c)	3	1	4	2	(d)	2	4	1	3

89. In recent years, which among the following countries has been the largest source of foreign investment in India?
(a) Australia (b) Japan
(c) China (d) Mauritius

90. **Assertion** (A) The Government of India has been opening up domestic market to foreign players in baby steps.

Reason (R) Allowing foreign firms free play in India's retail sector has always been a political hot potato.

Codes
(a) (A) and (R) both are correct and (R) is the right explanation of (A)
(b) (A) and (R) both are correct, but (R) is not the right explanation of (A)
(c) (A) and (R) both are incorrect
(d) (A) is correct, but (R) is incorrect

91. Select the correct code of the following statements being correct or incorrect.

Statement I A Global Depository Receipt (GDR) is a bank certificate issued in more than one country for shares in a foreign company.

Statement II A GDR is very similar to American Depository Receipt (ADR).

Statement III GDRs are called EDRs when private markets are attempting to obtain Euros.

Codes
(a) Statements I, II and III are correct
(b) Statements I and II are correct, but Statement III is incorrect
(c) Statements I and III are correct, but Statement II is incorrect
(d) Statements II and III are correct, but Statement I is incorrect

92. In December 1999, European commission members signed a treaty that committed them to adopting a common currency known as Euro. This is better known as
(a) Treaty of Rome (b) Treaty of Maastricht
(c) Treaty of Lisbon (d) Treaty of London

93. Select the correct code of the following statements being correct or incorrect.

Statement I The 'law of one price' states that in competitive markets free of transportation costs and barriers to trade, identical products sold in different countries must sell for the same price when their price is expressed in terms of the same currency.

Statement II An 'Efficient market' has no impediments to the free flow of goods and services, such as trade barriers.

Codes

(a) Statement I is correct, but Statement II is incorrect
(b) Statement II is correct, but Statement I is incorrect
(c) Both statements are correct
(d) Both statements are incorrect

94. Which among the following is not a correct statement regarding patent ?

(a) A patent is a legal protection granted for an invention, i.e. new, non-obvious and useful
(b) The patent grants the patent holder the exclusive right to make use or sell the patented products or process
(c) The exclusive purpose of the patent system is to benefit the patent holder
(d) The Indian Patent Act, 1970, was amended and made effective from Ist January, 2005

95. Which one of the following is agricultural income under the Income Tax Act, 1961 ?

(a) Interest on arrears of rent in respect of agricultural land
(b) Interest received by a money-lender in the form of agricultural produce
(c) Income from sale of trees of forest which are of spontaneous growth and in relation to which forestry operations alone are performed
(d) Interest on capital received by a partner from the firm engaged in agricultural operations

96. Under the Income Tax Act, 1961 'block of assets' for the purpose of charging depreciation means

(a) value of all the assets after depreciation
(b) value of all tangible assets after charging depreciation
(c) value of all those assets to which one rate of depreciation is applicable
(d) gross value of machinery and plant less accumulated depreciation

97. The maximum amount of exemption of compensation received at the time of voluntary retirement U/S 10(10C) of the Income Tax Act, 1961, is

(a) ₹ 1,00,000 (b) ₹ 2,50,000 (c) ₹ 5,00,000 (d) ₹ 10,00,000

98. Which one of the following statement is not correct with reference to the assessment of firms ?

(a) All partnership firms formed under the Indian Partnership Act, 1932, are assessed as firms under the Income Tax Act, 1961
(b) Income of a firm is taxable at a flat rate of 30% without any exemption
(c) Partners' share in the income of a firm is not chargeable to tax in the hands of partners
(d) Remuneration paid to partners of a firm (assessed as such) is allowed as deduction subject to statutory limit

99. The due date of first instalment of advance tax by assessees other than companies is

(a) 15th April (b) 15th June
(c) 15th September (d) 15th December

100. Which one of the following items is not allowed as deduction while computing income from business and profession?

(a) Fees paid to the lawyer for drafting partnership deed
(b) Loss due to embezzlement by an employee
(c) Legal expenses paid to protect the building of the business
(d) Cost of installing a new telephone

ANSWERS

1 *(b)*	2 *(b)*	3 *(d)*	4 *(c)*	5 *(a)*	6 *(b)*	7 *(a)*	8 *(a)*	9 *(d)*	10 *(a)*
11 *(c)*	12 *(c)*	13 *(d)*	14 *(c)*	15 *(a)*	16 *(b)*	17 *(b)*	18 *(b)*	19 *(c)*	20 *(b)*
21 *(d)*	22 *(a)*	23 *(c)*	24 *(c)*	25 *(a)*	26 *(a)*	27 *(d)*	28 *(d)*	29 *(a)*	30 *(c)*
31 *(b)*	32 *(a)*	33 *(b)*	34 *(a)*	35 *(a)*	36 *(d)*	37 *(b)*	38 *(d)*	39 *(b)*	40 *(d)*
41 *(c)*	42 *(c)*	43 *(a)*	44 *(c)*	45 *(d)*	46 *(b)*	47 *(d)*	48 *(c)*	49 *(b)*	50 *(b)*
51 *(c)*	52 *(d)*	53 *(b)*	54 *(b)*	55 *(b)*	56 *(a)*	57 *(c)*	58 *(c)*	59 *(b)*	60 *(c)*
61 *(c)*	62 *(d)*	63 *(c)*	64 *(a)*	65 *(c)*	66 *(c)*	67 *(d)*	68 *(d)*	69 *(b)*	70 *(d)*
71 *(a)*	72 *(b)*	73 *(d)*	74 *(a)*	75 *(b)*	76 *(d)*	77 *(c)*	78 *(b)*	79 *(d)*	80 *(b)*
81 *(a)*	82 *(d)*	83 *(c)*	84 *(b)*	85 *(c)*	86 *(c)*	87 *(c)*	88 *(a)*	89 *(d)*	90 *(b)*
91 *(a)*	92 *(*)*	93 *(c)*	94 *(c)*	95 *(d)*	96 *(c)*	97 *(c)*	98 *(a)*	99 *(b)*	100 *(a)*

Note (*) All Options are incorrect.

NTA

UGC

NET/JRF/SET

COMMERCE

CHAPTER 01

Business Environment

Business is a process of production and distribution of goods and services. Business environment is a force that affects organisation's performance. It presents threats as well as opportunities for any business by various external and internal factors.

Concept of Business Environment

Business environment is a combination of two words, *i.e.* business and environment. So, for understanding the concept of business environment, we have to study 'business' and 'environment' individually.

Business is a very complex process. It does not operate in a vacuum. Business refers to all those human activities which are related with production and distribution of goods and services. All the profit earning activities are categorised in business.

According to **Davis**, "Business is combined efforts of people for production and distribution of goods and services."

According to **William S Lawrance**, "The environment includes factors outside the firm which can lead to opportunities for or threats to the firm. Although there are many factors, the most important of these factors are socio-economic, technological, supplier, competitors and government."

According to **Arthur M Weimer**, "Business environment encompasses the climate or set of conditions, economic, social, political or institutional in which business operations are conducted."

Thus, business environment encompasses all those factors (internal and external) that affect a company's operations and include strengths, weaknesses, internal power relationships, orientations of the organisation, nature of economy and economic conditions, socio-cultural factors, demographic trends, natural factors, global trends and cross border development, clients and suppliers, technological developments, laws and government activities.

In this Chapter

Nature of Business Environment

Dependence on Each Other *Entire* environment of a business is a combination of different factors like economic, social, political, legal and technological factors. All these factors are interdependent.

Mobility Business environment is flexible in nature. It means that environment of business changes according to time. In same way, due to continuous change in business factors, policies and strategies of business are also changed.

Multifarious Nature Business environment is multifarious in nature as it changes according to time, period and place. There are frequent changes in the environment which are followed by a chain of positive and negative reactions. This has been observed that when the same development is welcomed as an opportunity by one company while another company perceives it as a threat.

Ability to Understand Changing Scenario Understanding environment is a difficult task for business, as it changes from time-to-time. A business must be aware about these changes, as it helps them to formulate policies and strategies.

Knowledge of Danger by Accidental Changes Business management must be aware about accidental changes in business. It is seen that these changes may be controllable or non-controllable. These dangers are electricity crisis, high interest rate due to inflation etc. These changes must be known timely to overcome from them.

Importance of Business Environment

Business environment helps in economic development of country and also helps in understanding complexity of a business. At the time of cut-throat competition, it becomes more difficult to manage business activities. So, for successful management of business, analysis of business environment is compulsory. *We can understand the importance of business environment from the following points*

Helps in Knowledge of Internal Environment Study of business environment is necessary for knowledge of internal environment of a business. Internal environment which includes policies, objectives, sources and strategies are important for successful management of a business.

Helps in Long-term Planning Future of any business depends on its appropriate and long-term planning. Business environment plays an important role in planning of a business.

Analysis and Evaluation of Planning Formulation of policies and planning only is not sufficient for success of any business, its analysis and evaluation is also necessary. Successful planning is important for development of any business. For success of any planning, forecasting of future problems is necessary and policies should be made accordingly.

Helpful in Proper Utilisation of Resources Resources are of two types, *i.e.* natural and human resources. Natural resources of the country helps to decide nature of business, its success and development while human resources are helpful in deciding techniques of production, management capability etc to be adopted by any business.

Develops Competition Ability At present time, success of any business depends on its competition ability. It decides stability period of a business. Competition ability includes quality of goods, reduction of cost, delivery of goods to consumer etc. Apart from these, after sale services, attractive advertisement and high marketing strategies are also included in competition ability of a business.

General Elements of Business Environment

The main elements of business environment *are as follows*

Internal Environment

Internal environment refers to the factors internal to the firm, *i.e.* factors existing within a business firm. These factors are generally controllable because the company has control over them and determine the potential of a company to meet the environment challenges.

Important Internal Factors

Culture It is widely acknowledged fact that any business organisation is normally undertaken for profit maximisation. Nonetheless, persons holding top positions in certain modern corporate enterprises have some values which influence their policies, norms, working language, systems, symbols practices and overall internal environment. This may refer to as culture of the organisation which is the collective behaviour of humans that are part of an organisation. The extent to which the culture of the organisation is shared by all, leads to an important factor contributing to success.

Vision, Mission and Objectives Vision, mission and objectives of the company guide its priorities, philosophy, policies etc. *e.g.* Ranbaxy's mission 'to become a research based international pharmaceutical company' led it to enter foreign markets.

Top Management Structure The composition of the Board of Directors is very critical factor for the development and performance of company as they are highest decision maker authorities, extend of professionalism of management as it may be professionally managed or family controlled, nominee of financial institutions having large holdings in companies, the shareholding pattern could have important managerial implications. All these factors are of great importance from the point of view of the company's internal environment.

Power Structure The internal power relationship between the board of directors and senior executive officers highly effect the decision-making process of the organisation.

Human and other Resources The quality of human resources of a company depends largely on competence, commitment, attitude and motivation, which plays an important role in the success of the organisation.

Physical Resources and the Technology The production capacity, technology, R & D work, distribution logistics etc are the factors that influence functioning and competitiveness of the firm.

Company Image and Brand Equity The image and brand equity of the company matters a lot in raising finance, forming joint ventures and other alliance, choosing dealers and suppliers etc.

External Environment

External environment refers to external aspects of the surroundings of business enterprise, which have influence on the functioning of business. It can be categorised into two parts like micro and macro environment, *which are as follows*

Micro Environment

The micro environment or task environment comprises those forces in the immediate vicinity of an organisation that influence it's functioning. The micro forces need not necessarily affect all the firms in a particular industry in the same way. Some of the micro factors may be particular to a firm.

Important Performers in the Micro Environment

Suppliers Business enterprises requires a number of suppliers, who supply raw materials and components to the company. It is an important force of the micro environment of company.

Customers They are highly influential as they are the central point of every business. Success of business largely depends on identifying the need, desire, tastes liking etc of customers.

Market Intermediaries Every business enterprise is assisted with market intermediaries, which include agents, brokers, who help the company to find customers. These acts as a link between company and final consumer.

Competitors Activities of a business adjust according to the actions and reactions of a competitor. This factor should be known to a company as the upcoming profit or revenue will only be driven when this factor is in control.

Public Any group that has actual or potential interest in the business, has its impact on the business. *e.g.* Growth of consumer groups may effect the working of a newly developed business.

Macro Environment

Macro environment has major external and uncontrollable factors that influence an organisation's decision-making and affect its performance and strategies. When the macro environment is uncontrollable, the success of a company depends on its adaptability to the environment.

These factors include the following

Economic Environment

Business enterprises conduct its activities in the market system with the objective of profit maximisation. Since, business enterprise is essentially an economic institution, it is surrounded by an economic environment which consists of economic factors that influence the business in a country. These factors include gross national product, corporate profits, inflation rate, employment, balance of payments, interest rates, consumer income etc.

Political Environment

The economic and political systems of a country are mutually dependent, the one reflecting the ideologies of the other. It comprises political stability and the policies of the government. Ideological inclination of political parties, personal interest of politicians, influence of party forums etc create political environment.

Social-cultural Environment

Socio-cultural environment means the value attitudes, beliefs and customs of people in a given group or society. Socio-cultural dimensions complicate the environment in which entrepreneurs have to manage their ventures like literacy rate, customs, values, beliefs, lifestyle, demographic features and mobility of population which are part of the social environment. It is important for managers to notice the direction in which the society is moving and formulate progressive policies according to the changing social scenario.

Technological Environment

The progress of business depends on the level of technology available in a country which gives a massive impetus to the economic revival. It also indicates the pace of research and development and progress made in introducing modern technology in production. Technology provides capital intensive, but cost effective alternative to traditional labour intensive methods. In a competitive business environment, technology is the key to development.

Legal Environment

It has a great impact on the functioning of the organisation as it establishes codes and procedures for various types and aspects of business and deals with deviations or infringement law like product counterfeiting, gray markets, black markets, consumer deception and tax evasions.

The coverage, efficiency and efficacy of the legal system determine adequacy, cost and speed of economic justice and these factors are of great importance for the growth of business. In every country, there exist specific pieces of business legislation which together guide control and regulate business activity, such as in India Trademark Act, 1969, Essential Commodities Act, 1955, Standards of Weights and Measures Act, 1969 and Consumer Protection Act, 1986.

Natural Environment

No business can survive in climatically inhospitable conditions. Business has broadly two relationships with natural environment. First, the environment is the source of resource as raw material and second, it causes damage in the process of production.

Financial Environment

Business finance is concerned with making decisions about the investments in the business. It includes bond markets, forex markets, stock markets, commodity markets, OTC markets, real estate markets and cash or spot markets. All these markets play an important role in raising finances for the companies and at the same time give profits to the investors.

Global Environment

It includes rules and regulations of WTO, IMF, WB, SAARC, G20 and other international bodies which duly effect the business organisation operating their business in any particular country. Business has to exist in world market and then it should understand their effect and take action according to these rules and regulations.

Economic Environment

Business is affected by various environmental factors *viz*, economic, social, political, technological, demographic and international environment. Out of them, economic environment is the most important factor affecting the business. Economic environment refers to those factors, which have impact on the working of business. It is composed of various set of economic policies, economic system, strategy of economic growth and development, resource endowment, size of market, distribution of income and wealth, status of infrastructural facilities in a country etc. Economic environment is dynamic and complex in nature. It keeps on changing from time-to-time with the changes in an economy like change in government policies, political situations etc.

Characteristics of Economic Environment

- It analyse availability of capital.
- It symbolise a planned economy.
- It hepls in balanced distribution of income and wealth.
- It provide convenient direction of economic activities.
- It is effected by government policies.
- It depends on availability of basic resources.
- It can change from time-to-time.

Role of Government in Economic Environment

Role of Regulator

Role of government as a regulator is very broad. Basically, *this regulation is of two types*

Direct Regulation It is done with the help of existing laws.

Indirect Regulation It is implemented with the help of government policies.

Role of Enforcement or Promotion

Role of government as enforcement or promotion plays an important role in a any economy. With this type of role, generally the emphasis is on business promotion rather than regulation of Government plans to provide more assistance to industries in terms of development and promotion of industry and business.

Role of Entrepreneur

In different countries, the government fulfills the role of industrial adventurer in a variety of ways. Under this, the equipment is set-up and operated by the government.

Major Elements of Business Environment

Following two elements plays an important role in forming business environment of any country

Economic System

The way that each individual lives in a society is based on how the country handles problems and questions involving their economy. Each country operates under some economic system, which differs significantly and based on utilisation of their resources for the purpose of satisfying the needs and wants of people. The central problem of an economic system is the allocation of resources.

According to **WW Loucks**, "An economic system consists of those institutions, which is given nation or group of nations has chosen or accepted as the means through which their resources are utilised for the satisfaction of human wants."

To a great extent, economic system of a country determines its economic environment in which the organisation has to survive. Infact, business has no choice, but to adjust itself within the framework of the given economic system.

Types of economic system are as follows

Market Economy/Capitalism Economy

The economic system, in which business units or factors of production are privately owned and governed is called capitalism economy. The profit earning is the sole aim of the business units. Government of that country does not interfere in the economic activities of the country. It is also known as free market economy.

According to **GDH Cole**, "Capitalism is that profit-oriented system, which is characterised by private ownership of objects of labour, instruments of labour and means of labour. Production is mainly carried out with the help of labour services rendered by the working class in return for wages and the class of capitalists has the right to whatever output is produced within the system. e.g. US, Japan, Canada, Mexico etc."

Characteristics of the Capitalist Economy

Private Ownership In a capitalist economy, the factors of production, *i.e.* land, labour and capital are privately owned and production occurs at private initiative. Individuals have their property rights protected and are usually free to use their property in a way they like.

Free Enterprise The term 'free enterprise' implies that private firms are allowed to obtain resources to organise production and to sell the resultant product in any way they choose.

Consumers' Sovereignty Under this economy, consumers have complete freedom of choice of consumption. Market economy is based on the consumers' desire, which is reflected in the demand pattern.

Competition In a free market economy, there are a large number of buyers and sellers. Profit motive induces new firms to enter the market thereby increasing competition. Competition reduces market imperfections and related problems.

Price Mechanism The price system regulates the capitalist economy, all decisions concerning production, distribution and exchange are based on the price mechanism. Producers are free to fix up prices of their products and consumers are free to offer prices at which they want to buy.

Command Economy/Socialism Economy

Under socialism economic system, all the economic activities of the country are controlled and regulated by the government in the interest of the public. Under this economic system, government appoints a central planning authority that takes all economic decisions and formulates an exhaustive plan to achieve the set objectives.

According to **Paul M Sweezy**, "Socialism is a complete social system, which differs from capitalism not only in the absence of private ownership of means of production, but also in its basic structure and mode of functioning."

The first country to adopt this concept was Soviet Russia. Countries like China, Vietnam, Cuba etc have economies based on socialism.

The two main forms of socialism economy are as follows

Democratic Socialism All the economic activities are controlled and regulated by the government, but the people have the freedom of choice of occupation and consumption.

Totalitarian Socialism This form is also known as communism. Under this, people are obliged to work under the directions of government.

Characteristics of Socialism Economic System

Government Ownership In socialist countries, all important means of production are either owned by the government or their use is controlled by the government. Private ownership is nominal.

Social Welfare The socialist economic system works for the benefit of the whole society rather than merely for the private benefit of individuals. There is absence of profit motive and the ultimate objective is to maximise social welfare.

Fixation of Wages and Prices The wages and prices in a communist economy are fixed by the government and not by market forces. Non-communist socialist countries may also fix wages and prices by certain means.

Absence of Competition Since, the state owns all the major means of production, there is no competition between the different production units.

Abolition of Exploitation of Labour The working class collectively owns the means of production under a socialist set-up, which makes it possible for the people to use these means of production for their welfare.

Mixed Economy

It is the mixture of both capitalism and socialism feature, *i.e.* the economic system, in which both public and private sectors co-exist.

Some factors of production are privately owned and some are owned by government. There exists freedom of choice of occupation and consumption. Both private and public sectors play key roles in the development of the country.

Considering the limitations of both maximum role of government under socialism and minimum role of government under capitalism, the world political-economic order has moved towards mixed economy with optimum role of government. India is perhaps the best example of such economy and legitimately called as a mixed economy.

Characteristics of Mixed Economic System

Co-existence of Public and Private Sector In a mixed economy, both public sector and private sector are allowed to co-exist. The public sector is expected to provide necessary infrastructural facilities. The private sector is expected to undertake enterprises on the basis of the growth climate created by the public sector.

Classification of Industries All industries are classified into two or more categories. Industries of strategic importance are reserved for the public sector. The rest of the industries are left for the private sector.

Interventionist Role of the State The market mechanism in a mixed economy may not be entirely free from state control. Often legislative measures are undertaken to provide a regulatory system for industrial activity in the country.

Profit Motive-cum Social Welfare The private sector operates primarily with a profit motive. But in contrast, public sector seeks to achieve social welfare.

Economic Planning In developing countries, the state plays a very important role as planner. The modern state is the custodian of the welfare of society.

Economic Policies

Economic policies of a government play a significant role in determining the economic environment of business in a country. Economic policies may or may not have favourable effect on a business unit. The government may grant subsidies to one business or decrease the rates of excise or custom duty or the government may increase the rates of custom duty or excise duty for another business. All the business enterprises frame their policies keeping in view the prevailing economic policies.

The main economic policies are as follows

Fiscal Policy

This policy concerns itself with the aggregate effect of government expenditure and taxation on income, production and employment, deficit financing and management of public debts in an economy. It may be termed as budgetary policy. It is related with the income and expenditure of a country.

Fiscal policy works as an instrument in economic and social growth of a country. It is framed by the government of a country. Fiscal policy and monetary policy are closely interrelated and therefore should be pursued in coordination with each other. Fiscal policy brings about changes in money supply through budgetary deficit. An excessive fiscal deficit requires control of inflation through monetary policy. On the other hand, a fiscal policy of very low deficit enables a liberal monetary policy.

Objectives of Fiscal Policy

- Fiscal policy was implemented for promotion of import and export in trade.
- Fiscal policy was formulated to bring price stability and to control inflation.
- National income plays an important role in an economy. Fiscal policy helps in increasing national income of the country.
- Fiscal policy emphasises on equitable distribution of income and wealth.
- Fiscal policy reduces the deficit in the balance of payment.

Monetary Policy

This policy refers to the policy regarding money supply and bank credit in the country and in turn influences the savings, investment and consumer expenditure in the economy. Changes in monetary policy can be made at any time during the year. It is formulated and announced by the Central Bank of the country.

According to **C Rangarajan**, "Monetary policy, is an arm of macro economic policy and as such, its role and importance is determined in any economy by the overall policy framework and the various instruments available for implementing policy." Monetary policy may also be used to influence the exchange rate of the country's currency.

Objectives of Monetary Policy

Monetary policy is an important economic policy, its main objectives are as follows

- Accelerating economic growth so as to raise national income is one of the main objectives of monetary policy.
- Monetary policy provide stability in exchange rate.
- Price stability is a major objective of monetary policy. A high degree of inflation has adverse effects on the economy.
- It promotes skill payment system.
- Collection of saving of society and expansion of saving amount.

Political Environment

Politics plays an important role in shpaing business worldwide. Manager need to know how to interact between business and government and know-how to react in case of conflict. It includes all laws, government agencies and groups that influence or restrict individuals or organisations.

Role of Government in Business Activities

The government plays an important role in business activities in following ways

Permission to Form Most businesses need to register with a State Government to operate. The function of this registration is usually to define the financial liability the owners of the company have. It also allows the government to monitor companies to execute its other functions.

Contract Enforcement Business contract may be complex, such as mergers or they may be as simple as a warranty on supplies purchased. The government enforces these contracts.

Consumer Protection The government's role in business includes protecting the consumer. When a vendor fails to honor the guarantee, the purchaser has recourse in law.

Employee Protection Many state the federal agencies work to protect the rights of employees. The equal opportunity commission protects employees from discrimination.

Environmental Protection It is the government's role to regulate industry and thereby protect the public from environmental externalities. Whether the government is effective in this role is a matter of much discussion.

Legal Environment

Legal environment means the rules and regulations, which are framed to regulate the business. Laws are formulated to smoothen the working environment of the business. In every country, business can be started and operated within the framework of the legal system. Every nation has its own legal framework for the promotion and regulation of business and industry.

According to **Salmond**, "Legal environment may be defined as principles recognised and applied by the state in the administration of justice." In India, legal environment is studied after analysing the pre and post period of independence. If we are talking about the current scenario, India is marching fast to attain the economic development.

Consumerism

It can be defined as an organised efforts by individual, groups and governments to help protect consumers from policies and practices that infringe consumer rights to fair business practices. It helps to many organisations to improve quality of their services to the customers. It emphasis on consumption of goods and services. It also seeks to enforce laws against unfair trade practices and truthful product guarantees.

Effects of Consumerism

Positive Effects

- The real benefit of consumerism is to improve economy. When citizens buy goods and services in excess of their needs, they consume more and create a cycle of demand leading to greater production and to greater employment.
- It creates a boom in the consumer goods and services industries and for the retailers that serve these industries.
- It improves living standard of people.
- Due to increasing demand, producers improve quality of their goods and services to be in competition.
- It protects consumers rights.

Negative Impacts/Effects

- Over consuming of goods and services leads to obesity which in turn leads to further cultural and social problem.
- Consumerism is destroying our environment. As the demands for goods and services increases, the need to produce also increases, which leads to more pollutant emissions.
- Waste disposal is a problem created by consumerism. Our oceans are slowly but surely becoming a giant waste disposal pit.
- Consuming resources at an unsustainable rate is causing mass environmental destruction and social problems across the world.
- The huge rise in resource consumption has led to an ever widening gap between the rich and the poor.

Consumer Protection Act

Today, consumers depend upon hundreds of businesses to satisfy their needs and wants. In a free enterprise economy, consumer is said to be sovereign as the business produces what consumers want. But in the reality, consumer is at the mercy of business. They are often exploited by unscrupulous businessmen through misleading advertisement, adulteration, short weight, overcharging and other unfair practices. The Government of India had enacted several laws to protect the consumers.

Some of these laws are

- Agricultural Products Grading and Marketing Act, 1937.
- Indian Standards Institution Certification Act, 1952.
- The Prevention of Food Adulteration Act, 1954.
- The Essential Commodities Act, 1955.
- Trademarks and Merchandise Marks Act, 1958.
- Black Marketing and Maintenance of Supplies of Essential Commodities Act, 1980.

Inspite of these laws, consumers remained exploited. Therefore, the government enacted the Consumer Protection Act, 1986. The main aim is to protect consumers from immoral practice of business organisations.

When a company or business concern becomes monopolise in market, then that company starts to get benefits of his monopoly powers by illegal ways. This law is very helpful to secure consumers and customers from such cheating and market frauds.

Main Features of Consumer Protection Act, 1986

- The Consumer Protection Act, 1986 is one of the benevolent piece of legislation intended to protect a large body of consumer from exploitation.
- Under this act, consumers have right to get information of quality, quantity and price of products. It extends to the whole of India except the state of Jammu and Kashmir.
- Further, the act applies to all goods and services unless specially exempted by the Central Government and covers all sectors, whether private, public or cooperative.
- Under this act, consumer has power to sue in district forum and report or complaint against the cheating of businessmen to the authorities and get remedies for this.
- Its objective is to provide better protection to the consumers, which intends to be simple, speedy and inexpensive redressal to consumer grievances.

Main Authorities under Consumer Protection Act, 1986

Consumer Protection Councils

The consumer protection councils are established at the centre, state and district level.

The Central Consumer Protection Council

Section 4-6 Under the act, Consumer Protection Council was established to protect the specific rights of the consumers.

Establishment-Section 4 The Council Government known as Central Consumer Protection Council, referred to as Central Council.

The council shall consist the following members

- The minister incharge of consumer affairs in the Central Government, who shall be its Chairman.
- Such number of other official or non-official members representing such interests as may be prescribed.
- According to **Rule 3**, Central Council shall consist of 150 members.

Procedure for Meetings-Section 5

- The Central Council shall meet as and when necessary, but atleast one meeting of the council shall be held every year.
- The Central Council shall meet at such time and place as the Chairman may think fit.

Objects of the Central Council-Section 6

- The right to be protected against the marketing of goods and services, which are hazardous to life and property.
- The right to be informed about the quality, quantity, potency, purity, standard and price of goods and services, so as to protect the consumer against unfair trade practices.
- The right to be assured, wherever possible, access to a variety of goods and services at competitive prices.
- The right to be heard and assured that consumers' interest will receive due consideration at appropriate forums.
- The right to seek redressal against unfair trade practices or restrictive trade practice or unscrupulous exploitation of consumer.
- The right to consumer education.

The State Consumer Protection Council

Establishment-Section 7 The State Government shall, by notification, establish with effect from such date as it may specify in such notification, a council to be taken as Consumer Protection Council, referred to as the State Council.

Members *The State Council shall consist of the following members namely*

- The minister incharge of consumer affairs in the State Government who shall be its Chairman.
- Such number of other official or non-official members representing such interest as may be prescribed by the State Government.
- Such number of other official or non-official members, not exceeding 10, as may be nominated by the Central Government.

Procedure for Meetings

- The State Council shall meet as and when necessary, but not less than two meetings shall be held every year.
- The State Council shall meet at such time and place as the Chairman may think fit.

The District Consumer Protection Council

Establishment-Section 8(A) The provision for the establishment of the above council was made by the Consumer Protection (Amendment) Act, 2002. The State Government shall establish for every district, by notification, a council to be known as the District Consumer Protection Council with effect from such date as it may specify in such notification, referred to as District Council.

***Members** The District Council shall consist of the following members*

- The collector of the district, who shall be its Chairman.
- Such number of other official as may be prescribed by the State Government.

Procedure for Meetings

- The District Council shall meet as and when necessary, but not less than two meetings shall be held every year.
- The District Council shall meet at such time and place as the Chairman may think fit.

Consumer Disputes Redressal Agencies

- The District Forum (Section 10-15).
- The State Forum (Section 16-19).
- The National Forum (Section 20-23).

The District Forum

Composition-Section 10 A person who is or has been or is qualified to be a District Judge, who shall be its President. *Two other members, one of whom shall be a woman, who shall have the following qualifications*

- Be not less than thirty five years of age.
- Possess a bachelor's degree from recognised university.
- Person of ability, integrity and standing and have adequate knowledge and experience of atleast 10 years in dealing with problems relating to economics, law, commerce, accountancy, industry, public affairs or administration.

The State Forum

A state forum shall be established in each state by the respective State Government.

Each state forum shall consist of

- A person who is or has been, Judge of a High Court appointed by the State Government, who shall be its President.
- Two other members, one of whom shall be a woman, who shall be a persons of ability, integrity and standing and have adequate knowledge or experience of or have shown capacity in dealing with problems relating to economics, law, commerce, accountancy, industry, public affairs or administration.
- The State Commission can entertain complaints, where the value of goods or services and the compensation if any claimed, exceed ₹ 25 lakh, but does not exceed ₹ 1 crore.
- An appeal against the orders of a State Commission can be filed before the National Commission within 30 days from the date of the order.

The National Forum

The Central Government shall establish a National Consumer Disputes Redressal Forum which shall consist of

- A person who is, or has been a Judge of a Supreme Court who shall be its President.
- Two other members, one of whom shall be a woman, who shall be a person of ability, integrity and standing and have adequate knowledge or experience of or have shown capacity in dealing with problems relating to economics, law, commerce, accountancy, industry, public affairs or administration.
- The National Commission can entertain complaints where the value of goods or services and the compensation if any claimed, exceed ₹ 1 crore.
- An appeal against the orders of a National Commission can be filed in the Supreme Court within 30 days from the date of the order.

Foreign Exchange Management Act, 1999

The Foreign Exchange Management Act (FEMA) came into effect on 1st June, 2000 and has replaced the Foreign Exchange Regulation Act (FERA), 1973.

Objectives of FEMA

The object of FERA was to conserve the foreign exchange resources, whereas the objectives of FEMA are

- It facilitate external trade and payments.
- It promotes orderly maintenance of the foreign exchange market in India.
- It emphasises on transparency.
- It promotes foreign trade.
- It liberal the foreign policies for investment.

Foreign Exchange Regulation Act (FERA), 1973

FERA was enacted in 1973 and it came in force from 5th January, 1974. It was amended by FERA 1993 and replaced by FEMA in 2000. The idea was to regulate the foreign payments, regulate the dealing in foreign exchange securities and conservation of foreign exchange for the nation.

Socio-cultural Factors and their influence on Business

As society and culture change, business must adapt to stay ahead on their competitors and stay relevant in the minds of their consumers. *Some socio-cultural factors are as follows*

Changing Preferences A major socio-cultural factor influencing business and business decision is changing consumer preferences. Different styles and priorities can undermine long successful products and services.

Demographics Changes in demographics are also a significant factor in the business world. As population age, *e.g.* markets for popular music and fashions may shrink while markets for luxury goods and health products may increase.

Advertising Techniques In addition to a company's interactions with the market and its customers, socio-cultural factors also impact a company's internal decision-making process.

Internal Environment In addition to a company's interactions with the market and its customers, socio-cultural factors also impact a company's internal decision-making process. Attitudes towards social discrimination and sexual harassment have changed drastically over the years as a result of socio-cultural change.

Corporate Social Responsibility (CSR)

CSR in an extended model of corporate governance based on the fiduciary duties owed to all the firm's shareholders. It is about how companies manage the business proceses to produce on overall positive impact on the society. It is the responsibility of corporations to go above and beyond what the law requires them to do. It is the responsibility of corporations to contribute to a better society and cleaner environment.

Goals of CSR

- Eradicate extreme poverty.
- Achieve universal primary education.
- Promote gender equality and women empowerment.
- Reduce child morality.
- Ensure environmental sustainability.
- Develop a global partnership.

Benefits of CSR

- It increases employee loyalty and retention in the organisation.
- It increases quality of products and services.
- It also attracts customers and hence make them loyal.
- It increases reputation and brand image of the organisation.
- It reduces regulatory oversight.
- It makes access to capital and market.
- It makes safe products and reduced liability.
- It has less volatile stock value.

Corporate Social Responsibility in India

India is the first country in the world to make corporate social responsibility (CSR) mandatory, following an amendment to the Company Act, 2013 in April 2014. Businesses can invest their profits in areas such as education, poverty, gender equality, and hunger. Section 135(1) of the Companies Act, 2013 provides for the trigger point for the applicability of CSR provisions and constitution of CSR committee. *The constitution of CSR committee is mandatory in company having*

- Net Worth of ₹ 500 Crore
- Turnover of ₹ 1,000 Crore
- Net Profit of ₹ 5 Crore

EXAM BASED QUESTIONS

Business Environment

1 **An human being takes birth in which situation, period and country and survive for his life, is known as its**
(a) society (b) environment
(c) family (d) None of these

2 **Business environment is formed by those institutions and power on which business have .... control.**
(a) complete (b) very less
(c) No (d) None of these

3 **.......... of business activities is done in business environment.**
(a) Management (b) Planning
(c) Coordination (d) None of these

4 **Which of the following is not studied in business environment?**
(a) National income
(b) Cultural customs
(c) Management of business function
(d) All of the above

5 **Factors/Elements of business generally depends on which environment?**
(a) Social (b) Natural (c) Human (d) Physical

6 **Which of the following is not a form of business environment?**
(a) Partnership (b) Monopoly Trade
(c) Joint Capital Company (d) Employees

7 **Business environment is more descriptive and ....**
(a) simple (b) large
(c) complex (d) None of these

8 **................ is/are the main feature(s) of business environment.**
(a) Moving (b) Uncertainty
(c) Both (a) and (b) (d) None of these

9 **Result of technological environment in business environment is**
(a) e-commerce (b) e-banking
(c) Both (a) and (b) (d) None of these

10 **Which of the following statement is not true about business environment?**
(a) It affects working capacity of business
(b) Business environment always changes
(c) It affects operation of business
(d) A businessman had complete control over business environment

11 **Analysis of policies is done on the basis of**
(a) forecasting (b) change according to time
(c) Both (a) and (b) (d) None of these

12 **Which of the following is the part of development of competitive ability?**
(a) Product quality
(b) Ignorance of cost
(c) Least customer preference
(d) All of the above

13 **............. are a feature of the micro environment of an organisation.**
(a) Legal factors (b) Economic factors
(c) Social factors (d) Customers

14 **Characteristics such as age, income or gender are examples of**
(a) household patterns
(b) demographics
(c) income distribution
(d) Social-cultural environment

15 **Which of the following is a feature of the micro environment of an organisation?**
(a) Distribution channel factors
(b) Social factors
(c) Economic factors
(d) All of the abvoe

16 **Globalisation is an example of which macro environment factor?**
(a) Economic (b) Social
(c) Political (d) Technological

17 **Which of the following is not an environmental force, which must be monitored by marketers?**
(a) Demographic (b) Natural
(c) Political-legal (d) Mega trends

18 **.................. are features of macro environment.**
(a) Intermediaries
(b) Customers
(c) Competitors
(d) Legal framework

19 **Which of the following is not an element of the micro environment of business?**
(a) Suppliers (b) Competitors
(c) Trade policy (d) Public

20 **The external environment is composed of**
(a) the general and task environment
(b) the task environment and the cultural environment
(c) the global environment and the ecological environment
(d) it enhance vulnerability of political risk

21 Which of the following is element of internal environment?
(a) Financial institution (b) Customers
(c) Policies and objectives (d) All of these

Economic Environment

22 Which of the following is not a part of economic environment?
(a) Economic policy (b) Financial market
(c) Economic inequality (d) All of these

23 One of the characteristics of the economic environment is
(a) tradition (b) society
(c) life (d) public policies

24 Which of the following element determine economic environment of a country?
1. Economic system 2. Policies
3. Money and capital market
4. Social cost

Select the correct answer using the codes given bolow

Codes
(a) Both 1 and 2 (b) Both 2 and 3
(c) Only 3 (d) All of the above

25 China is an example of a .... system.
(a) mixed economy (b) socialist
(c) capitalism (d) None of these

26 Laissez faire policy is adopted in
(a) socialistic economic system
(b) capitalistic economic system
(c) mixed economic system
(d) communist economic system

27 Economic policy is the catalyst component of
(a) economic environment
(b) moral environment
(c) social environment
(d) legal environment

28 Relation between economic environment and policy is
(a) work and reason (b) ractor and analog
(c) analog and factor (d) None of these

29 Favourable investment on private investment in called
(a) effect of fiscal policy
(b) limits of fiscal policy
(c) effect on Public credit policy
(d) None of the above

30 Which policy helps in modifying investment structure of on economy?
(a) Monetary policy (b) Fiscal policy
(c) Budget (d) Foreign trade policy

31 Which of the following is not a equipment of monetary policy?
(a) Activities of open market (b) Cash reserve ratio
(c) Legal liquidity ratio (d) Deficit financing

32 Reason of decline of monetary policy is
(a) wide non-monetary region
(b) flow of black money
(c) measuring credit money
(d) All of the above

33 Which function is not performed by the government for promotion of economic environment?
(a) Nurture the mentality of country's development
(b) Exploitation of environment
(c) Effects proper utilisation of resources
(d) All of the above

34 Which among the following is an essential characteristic of mixed economy?
(a) Co-existence of small scale and large scale industries
(b) Co-existence of private and public sectors
(c) Assigning equal importance to both agriculture and heavy industries
(d) Co-existence of the rich and the poor

35 .... is the economic system whereby the state holds broad powers to serve the public interest, it decides what goods and services are produced and in what quantities and demand typically exceeds supply.
(a) Centrally-planned socialism
(b) Market socialism
(c) Centrally-planned capitalism
(d) Market capitalism

36 Which of the following statement is incorrect?
(a) Economic system is not the feature of mixed economy
(b) Price mechanism is not affective in socialist economy
(c) Classless society is a feature of socialist economy
(d) Socialism is an universal economic system

37 Which of the following is not the objective of fiscal policy in India?
(a) Enhances liquidity in economy
(b) Promote employment opportunities
(c) Promote price stability
(d) Remove income and asset unequality

38 The .... environment is composed of laws, government agencies and pressure groups.
(a) demographic (b) economic
(c) social-culture (d) political-legal

39 Which one of the following service is not covered under Consumer Protection Act?
(a) The service of a teacher
(b) The service of a lawyer
(c) The service of a doctor
(d) The service of a banker

40 A Central Consumer Protection Council established by the
(a) State Government
(b) Central Government
(c) Parliament
(d) President of India

41 Which of the following is not a part of machinery that settles industrial disputes?
(a) Wage Court
(b) Works Committee
(c) Conciliation Officers
(d) Board of Conciliation

42 The redressal forum of consumer consists of
(a) National Consumer Forum
(b) District Consumer Forum
(c) Both (a) and (b)
(d) None of the above

43 A district forum should not consist of
(a) a person who is qualified to be a district judge who shall be its President
(b) a lady social worker
(c) a person who is or has been judge of a High Court
(d) None of the above

44 Which of the following is not an way to implement CSR by organisation?
(a) Environmental sustainability
(b) Energy conservation
(c) Community involvement
(d) Ethical marketing process

45 In relation to the 'veil of incorporation' that is a feature of a limited company's separate legal personality, in which of the following circumstances will a court not lift the veil to identify the true nature of the relationship?
1. Where the company has been established to commit a fraud.
2. Where the company has been established to contractual agreements.
3. In the interests of Justice.
4. Where two separate legal entities are run as one economic undertaking.

Select the correct answer using the codes given below

Codes
(a) 1, 2 and 4
(b) Both 2 and 4
(c) Both 3 and 4
(d) All of the above

46 Arrange the following concepts/acts in the order in which they came into force.
1. Competitinon Act.
2. Foreign Exchange Management Act.
3. Consumer Protection Act.
4. Securities and Exchange Board of India Act.

Codes
(a) 3, 4, 2, 1
(b) 4, 3, 2, 1
(c) 1, 2, 4, 3
(d) 2, 1, 3, 4

47 Consumers have the right
1. to be protected against goods and services that are hazardous to life and property.
2. to be assured, wherever possible, access to a variety of goods and services at national prices.

Codes
(a) Both 1 and 2
(b) Only 2
(c) Only 1
(d) None of the above

48 If the amount claimed by a consumer as compensation is ₹ 89 lakh, the case under the Consumers Protection Act shall be filed with
(a) District Consumer Redressal Forum
(b) State Consumer Disputes Redressal Commission
(c) National Consumer Disputes Redressal Commission
(d) Supreme Court

49 Which of the following is not the responsibilities of the consumers?
(a) The consumer should make vague complaints
(b) The consumer should make a specific complaint with supporting exidence
(c) The consumer should, as a rule complain against a system and not attack individuals who are incumbents of post
(d) Consumers, in asserting their rights should not inconvenience or hurt other sections of the public

50 According to Charles Brady at Wellington, the main focus of corporate social responsibility should be
(a) providing employees with good jobs and the opportunity to develop
(b) giving part of the company's profits to worthy charities
(c) providing free training to local schools and universities
(d) making sure the company is as 'green' as possible

51 Which is one of an advantage to adopt shared value approach while practicing CSR for an organisation?
(a) Integrates the needs of both the business and the charitable cause
(b) Contributes to the firm by solving only environmental issues
(c) Contributes fastest way to form an alliance and increase engagement among the stakcholders
(d) Creates and interdependence of long-term business success on balanced social system

52 Which of the following general principle is not followed by corporation while practicing CSR?
(a) Managers are not responsible to follow and encourage ethical business practices among employees
(b) Companies should support the inclusion of the principles of United Nations Global Compact
(c) Companies should encourage and facilitate communication and dialogue with its shareholders, investors, employees, customers and suppliers
(d) Companies should indulge in free market practices rejecting any illegal practices and implement effective mechanism

53 What does CRS concern with?
(a) How an organisation meet the expectations of its stakeholders.
(b) External stakeholders relationship
(c) The behaviour of individual managers
(d) The ways in which an organisation exceeds its minimum required obligations to stakeholders

Political and Legal Environment

54 A stable and dynamic political environment is indispensable for
(a) business growth
(b) enhancing the export
(c) increasing participation
(d) Both (a) and (b)

55 Which of the following is not an element of social environment?
(a) Tendency of population
(b) Individual needs
(c) Cultural elements
(d) Policies of competition

56 Which of the following environmental factor is not the reason of political stability?
(a) Government policies
(b) Production cost of goods
(c) War
(d) Social grudge

57 Tax policy comes under which element of business environment?
(a) Economic (b) Legal
(c) Social (d) Political

58 Tax jurisdiction is an example of which environment factor?
(a) Social (b) Economic
(c) Political (d) Legal

59 Which of the following statement is true?
(a) Economic system affects economic environment of business
(b) It is possible to control business environment
(c) Both (a) and (b)
(d) None of the above

60 "The environment of business consists of all those external things to which it is exposed and by which it may be influenced, directly or indirectly". This statement was said by
(a) Wleer and Torch (b) Copen
(c) Reinecke and Schoell (d) Arthur M Weimer

61 Which of the following is not included in features of business environment?
(a) Business environment includes both types internal and external
(b) It is not in control of a businessman
(c) Business environment is movable/continuous
(d) Activities of business environment are complex in nature

62 Study of business environment is important because
(a) it gives information about complexicity of business
(b) it provides information about effects of business elements
(c) Both (a) and (b)
(d) Only (b)

63 Which of the following statement is not true?
(a) Mapping of business includes its localisation, results and progress
(b) Strategies of competitor, knowledge and financial problems are faced in a business
(c) Natural resources of a business affects it internally
(d) External environment does not affects a business

64 Adoption and promotion of e-commerce by government comes under which element of business environment?
(a) Social
(b) Political
(c) Legal
(d) Technological

65 Environment related elements which are closely related with business are known as
(a) special environment (b) macro environment
(c) general environment (d) All of these

66 Which of the following is not an element of micro environment?
(a) Technological factors
(b) Legal-political conditions
(c) Social-cultural factors
(d) Organisational customs

67 Which of the following statement is not true?
(a) Financial institutions are main elements of internal business environment
(b) Economic system affects economic environment of business
(c) If illegal buying and selling of goods does not comes under business
(d) Legal environment of business is the part of political environment

68 Which of the following is not included in economic policy of government?
(a) Import-export policy (b) Licensing policy
(c) Industrial policy (d) Monetary policy

69 Economic environment is affected by
(a) law and order
(b) domestic economic condition
(c) Both (a) and (b)
(d) None of the above

70 Economic elements of business environment are
(a) budget and investment condition
(b) income level
(c) price level
(d) All of the above

71 When was FEMA came into existence?
(a) 7th June, 2000
(b) 31st June, 2000
(c) 20th May, 1999
(d) None of the above

72 FEMA is implemented for
(a) to facilitate external trade and payment
(b) to emphasises on transparency
(c) Both (a) and (b)
(d) None of the above

73 Which of the following can not be included in socio-cultural factors of a business?
(a) Changing preferences (b) Demographics
(c) Poverty (d) Techniques

Miscellaneous

Directions (Q. Nos. 74-81) *In the questions given below are two statements labelled as Statement I and Statement II. You have to examine these two statements carefully, select the correct code.*

Codes
(a) Statement I is correct
(b) Statement II is correct
(c) Both statements are correct
(d) Both statements are incorrect

74 **Statement I** Business refers to all those human activities which are related with production and distribution of goods and services.
Statement II Environment refers to all external forces which have a bearing on the functioning of business.

75 **Statement I** Internal environment refers to the factors internal to the firm.
Statement II These factors are non-controllable.

76 **Statement I** External environment refers to external aspects of the sorroundings of business enterprises.
Statement II External environment can categorised into micro and macro environment.

77 **Statement I** Fiscal policy works as an instrument in economic and social growth of a country.
Statement II It is framed by the government of a country.

78 **Statement I** Monetary policy is used to influence the exchange rate of the country's currency.
Statement II Economic policy may or may not have favourable effect on a business unit.

79 **Statement I** The main aim is to protect consumers from immoral practice of business organisation.
Statement II This law is not helpful to secure consumers and customers from such cheating and market frauds.

80 **Statement I** Business environment always changes.
Statement II Society exchanges business for production.

81 **Statement I** Fiscal policy is decided under budgetary policy of the government.
Statement II Fiscal policy directly affects buying power of the citizens.

Directions (Q. Nos. 82-93) *In the questions given below are two statements labelled as Assertion (A) and Reason (R). In the context of the two statemetns, which one of the following is correct?*

Codes
(a) Both A and R are true, R is the correct explanation of A
(b) Both A and R are true, but R is not the correct explanation of A
(c) A is correct, but R is incorrect
(d) A is incorrect, but R is correct

82 **Assertion** (A) Business in responsible for whole society rather than businessman.
Reason (R) As business converts into independent from its responsibility maximise.

83 **Assertion** (A) The internal factors are generally regarded as controllable factors.
Reason (R) Since, the company has control over internal factors.

84 **Assertion** (A) Micro environment is also known as operating environment of business.
Reason (R) Micro environment forces have a direct bearing on the operations of the firm.

85 **Assertion** (A) Environmental understanding provide enough information regarding the need of consumers.
Reason (R) Environmental understanding is not a early warning system.

86 **Assertion** (A) Business environment is of two types external and internal environment.
Reason (R) Micro environment is related to external environment of the organisation.

87 **Assertion** (A) Business environment does not affect much the decision-making of the companies.
Reason (R) Business environment is related to all external forces outside the organisation.

88 Assertion (A) High intensity of competitive rivalry can make an industry more competitive and decrease profit potential for the existing firms.

Reason (R) Industry with excess production capacity will have greater rivalry among competitors.

89 Assertion (A) The private proprietorship is replaced by social ownership as and when we move from a capitalist system to a socialist system.

Reason (R) Under socialism, properties are managed by the state.

90 Assertion (A) Desire competition is generally very high in countries characterised by limited disposable incomes.

Reason (R) In competitive world the firms has to compete, not only the other firms which market the same or similar products, but also all those who compete for the discretionary income of the consumer

91 Assertion (A) In the totalitarian socialism, people are free to choose their occupations.

Reason (R) In the totalitarian socialism, all important means of productions are controlled or owned by the government.

92 Assertion (A) Budget surplus in frequently regarded as an index of fiscal policy actions.

Reason (R) A decrease in deficit is looked up as indicating restrictive fiscal policy and *vice versa*.

93 Assertion (A) Small scale industries have an important place in the national economy.

Reason (R) State has reserved production of some goods exclusively for the small scale industries.

94 Match the following.

List I	List II
A. Internal environment	1. Skilled labour
B. External environment	2. Financial and physical resources
C. Financial resources	3. Customer and competitor
D. human resources	4. Financial and profitable use of funds

Codes

	A	B	C	D
(a)	2	3	4	1
(b)	2	4	1	3
(c)	3	1	2	4
(d)	4	3	2	1

95 Match the following.

List I	List II
A. Micro environment	1. Interest rate
B. Macro environment	2. Restrictions of WTO
C. Political environment	3. Suppliers
D. Globalisation environment	4. Planning Commission

Codes

	A	B	C	D
(a)	3	1	4	2
(b)	2	4	1	3
(c)	1	3	2	4
(d)	3	2	4	1

96 Match the following.

List I	List II
A. Social factors	1. Increment and reduction in price of fuel
B. Political factors	2. Primary function of business
C. Economic factors	3. Customs, traditions and assumptions
D. Analysis of needs and interest of customers	4. Industrial policy of government

Codes

	A	B	C	D
(a)	4	2	1	3
(b)	3	4	1	2
(c)	1	2	3	4
(d)	4	3	2	1

97 Match the following.

List I	List II
A. Natural environment	1. High research and development budget
B. Technological environment	2. People's view on nature
C. Political environment	3. Increase cost of energy
D. Cultural environment	4. Increase in public interest group

Codes

	A	B	C	D
(a)	3	1	4	2
(b)	2	4	3	1
(c)	2	4	1	3
(d)	3	2	4	1

98 Match the following.

List I (Economic Systems)	List II (Features)
A. Traditional economy	1. Produces only those goods and services, which are required for the survival or which they want to consume
B. Capitalism	2. The freedom of occupation is absent or restricted
C. Socialism	3. Consumers have complete freedom of choice of consumption
D. Mixed economy	4. The private sector operates primarily with a profit motive and public sector seeks to achieve social welfare.

Codes

	A	B	C	D
(a)	3	1	4	2
(b)	1	4	3	2
(c)	1	3	2	4
(d)	3	2	4	1

99 Match the following.

List I	List II
A. Capitalist economy is the economy in which	1. condition of complete employment
B. Main feature of capitalist economy	2. mixed economy
C. Main feature of socialist economy is	3. skilled production
D. Capitalist and socialist economy includes	4. Individual ownership own main sources of production and distribution

Codes

	A	B	C	D
(a)	4	3	1	2
(b)	4	3	2	1
(c)	1	2	3	4
(d)	4	1	2	3

100 Match the following.

List I	List II
A. The Essential Commodities Act	1. 1937
B. Agricultural Products Grading and Marketing Act	2. 1958
C. The Prevention of Food Adulteration Act	3. 1955
D. Trademarks and Merchandise Marks Act	4. 1954

Code

	A	B	C	D
(a)	1	3	2	4
(b)	2	4	1	3
(c)	3	1	2	4
(d)	1	2	3	4

PREVIOUS YEARS' QUESTIONS

December 2018

1 Match the items of List I with the items of List II and choose the correct answer from the code given below.

List I	List II
A. Rival firms	1. External environment
B. Technology	2. Social and cultural Environment
C. Improving quality	3. Internal environment
D. Ethics in business	4. Global environment

Codes

	A	B	C	D
(a)	1	2	3	4
(b)	2	3	4	1
(c)	3	1	4	2
(d)	4	1	2	3

July 2018

2 The Central Bank can significantly influence the savings, investments and consumer spending in the economy through which of the following policy?

(a) Fiscal policy
(b) Monetary policy
(c) Industrial policy
(d) Foreign Exchange policy

3 Which of the following is not the characteristic of capitalism?

(a) Individuals and associations behave with economic motive of maximising their profit with least sacrifice or cost
(b) The country's major means of production are either owned by the government or their use is controlled by the government
(c) Producers, consumers and employees compete among themselves, as the resources and opportunities are limited
(d) Price, the invisible hand, plays a predominant role in the flow of the factors of production and consumption

4 Which of the following statement is not correct relating to consumerism?

(a) Consumerism is a manifestation of the failure of the business to guarantee and ensure cosumer legitimate rights
(b) The government does not have any role in consumer protection as it is the part of business organisation alone
(c) The consumers should accept consumerism as a means of asserting and enjoying their rights
(d) Consumerism evolution is not a setback for marketing but rather points to the next stage in the evolution of enlightened marketing

5 Which of the following is not the salient feature of the industrial policy developments since 1991?

(a) The scope of the private sector has been enormously expanded
(b) Public sector has been withdrawing partially or fully from several of the enterprises by divestment
(c) The Indian industry is increasingly exposed to foreign competition
(d) Monopoly or dominant position for public sector in most of the industries and control of the commanding heights of the economy by the public sector

November 2017

6 Which one of the following is not correct relating to competition policy and law?

(a) Collusion and dominance have potential for unfair competition
(b) The appeal against decisions of competition commission of India can be made to the Competition Appellate Tribunal
(c) State monopolies, government's business policies and functioning of Regulatory Authorities cannot be scrutinised under this law
(d) Abuse of dominance rather than dominance should be the key for competition policy law

7 Match items of List I with List II relating to macro environment of business and indicate the code of correct matching.

List I	List II
A. Economic environment	1. Ethical issues
B. Political and government	2. Trade and transport policies environment
C. Socio-cultural environment	3. Economic stratification of population
D. Demographic environment	4. Judiciary powers

Codes

	A	B	C	D
(a)	2	4	1	3
(b)	1	3	2	4
(c)	4	2	3	1
(d)	3	1	4	2

8 Match the items of List I with List II and indicate the correct code of matching.

List I	List II
A. Micro external environment	1. Economic and political factors
B. Macro external environment	2. Competition among diverse products targetting disposable income of consumers
C. Non-price competition	3. Input suppliers
D. Desire competition	4. Sponsoring of events like sports

Codes

	A	B	C	D
(a)	3	1	4	2
(b)	2	3	4	1
(c)	4	2	3	1
(d)	4	1	2	3

January 2017

9 Which of the following is not the objective of the Competition Act, 2002?

(a) Prohibition of restrictive trade practices
(b) Prohibition of dominant position
(c) Prohibition of anti-competitive agreements
(d) Regulation of combinations

July 2016

10 Which of the following is not a forum of Consumer Dispute Redressal System?

(a) Local forum
(b) District forum
(c) State forum (State commission)
(d) National commission

11 **Assertion** (A) Under FEMA, the receiver of laundered money is to be made culpable, instead of sender/distributor.

Reason (R) FEMA differs from the earlier Exchange Regulation Act FERA with regard to penalties and punishment in case of violation of the act.

Codes

(a) (A) is correct, but (R) is not correct
(b) Both (A) and (R) are correct, but (R) is not the correct explanation of (A)
(c) Both (A) and (R) are correct and (R) is the correct explanation of (A)
(d) Both A and R are incorrect

12 Match the items of List I with List II

List I	List II
A. Fiscal policy	1. Mitigation of national hazards
B. Technology policy	2. Balance of payment
C. Macro-economic policy	3. Fiscal federalism
D. Monetary policy	4. Inflation

Codes

	A	B	C	D
(a)	1	2	3	4
(b)	3	1	2	4
(c)	4	3	1	2
(d)	2	1	4	3

December 2015

13 Environmental degeneration does not consist of

(a) land degeneration and soil erosion
(b) problem of overgrazing and ecological degeneration
(c) floods
(d) None of the above

14 Which of the following is not the main objective of 'Fiscal Policy of India'?

(a) To increase liquidity in economy
(b) To promote price stability
(c) To minimise the inequality in income and wealth
(d) To promote employment opportunities

June 2015

15 From the following, identify the tools of fiscal policy.

1. Public expenditure
2. Open market operations
3. Deficit financing
4. Taxation
5. Reserve requirements

Select the correct answer using the codes given below

Codes

(a) 1, 3, 4 and 5 (b) 1, 2, 4 and 5
(c) Both 2 and 5 (d) 1, 3 and 4

December 2014

16 Match the following.

List I	List II
A. Industries Development Regulation Act	1. 1947
B. Import and Export Control Act	2. 1948
C. Foreign Exchange Management Act	3. 1951
D. Factories Act	4. 1999

Codes

	A	B	C	D		A	B	C	D
(a)	1	3	4	2	(b)	3	1	2	4
(c)	3	1	4	2	(d)	3	4	2	1

17 Which among the following is not a correct sequential combination?

(a) Macro Environment → Economic Environment → National Income → Pattern of Income Distribution
(b) Business Environment → Internal Environment → Business Ethics → Payment of Fair Wages
(c) Business Environment → External Environment → Micro Environment → Suppliers
(d) Macro Environment → External Environment → Customers → Prospects of Business Development

18 Internal environment of a business includes

1. business ethics and moral standards.
2. business and managerial policies.
3. prospects of business development.
4. government rules and regulations.
5. industrial relations.

Select the correct answer using the codes given below

Codes

(a) 1, 2, 4 and 5 (b) 2, 3, 4 and 5
(c) 1, 2, 3 and 4 (d) 1, 2, 3 and 5

June 2014

19 There is acute shortage of electricity in some of the states in India. This reflects a problem in which type of business environment?

(a) Economic
(b) Demographic
(c) Politico-legal
(d) Socio-cultural

20 The time limit for filing a complaints before the district forum under the, Consumer Protection Act, 1986 is

(a) 1 year
(b) 2 years
(c) 3 years
(d) There is no such time limit

21 The Competition Act, 2002 seeks to regulate

(a) anti-competitive agreements
(b) mergers and amalgamation
(c) unfair trade practices
(d) Both (a) and (b)

22 Which of the legislation do not from part of the legal environment of business in India?

(a) The Drugs and Cosmetics Act, 1940
(b) The prevention of Food Adulteration Act, 1954
(c) The Monopolies and Restrictive Trade Practices Act, 1969
(d) Both (b) and (c)

23 Which of the following in true?

(a) A consumer court set-up under the consumer protection act, does not have the power to punish for its contempt
(b) Professional services are outside the purview of the CPA
(c) A consumer court can not force a person indulging in misleading advertising to confess his quit
(d) None of the above

December 2013

24 Indicate what is incorrect in respect of the Consumer Protection Act, 1986?

(a) No complaint can be entertained in respect of a product purchased more than 2 years back
(b) A complaint against medical negligence can be filed by legal heir or representative of the deceased
(c) A complaint involving a claim of ₹ 15 lakh is to be filed before the state commission
(d) Both (a) and (c)

25 Which of the following are outside the scope of the Consumer Protection Act, 1986?

(a) Newspaper industry
(b) Services provided under contract of personal service
(c) Banking industry
(d) Both (a) and (b)

26 Strategies and policies

(a) are not closely related
(b) given direction
(c) are the framework for performance appraisal
(d) Both (a) and (b)

27 The Flagship Project of Government of India launched for generating guaranteed employment in rural areas is known as

(a) PMRY (b) MNREGA
(c) JRY (d) NREP

June 2013

28 Which of the following are sources of ethics?

1. Religion
2. Legal system
3. Economic system
4. Culture
5. Family system

Select the correct answer using the codes given below

Codes

(a) 1, 2, 3 and 5 (b) 1, 2 and 4
(c) 1, 4 and 5 (d) All of the above

29 Match the following.

List I	List II
A. Political and legal environment	1. Important for industries directly depending on imports or exports
B. Demographic environment	2. Close relationship with the economic system and economic policy
C. Economic environment	3. Related to natural resources
D. Geographical and ecological environment	4. Occupational and spatial mobilities of population having implications for business

Codes

	A	B	C	D		A	B	C	D
(a)	2	4	3	1	(b)	2	4	1	3
(c)	1	2	3	4	(d)	1	2	4	3

30 Consumer attitudes and beliefs about diet, health and nutrition are infuenced by
(a) economic environment
(b) cultural environment
(c) social environment
(d) natural environment

31 Indicate the ground on which a complaint under the Consumer Protection Act, 1936 shall be invalid?
(a) A product having short weight
(b) A service provided free of cost
(c) A misleading advertisement given in newspaper
(d) None of the above

32 The apex consumer court in India is refered to as
(a) the consumer education and research centre
(b) the consumer unity and trust society
(c) national consumer disputes redressal commission
(d) None of the above

December 2012

33 Which one is not an element of internal environment?
(a) Marketing capability
(b) Operational capability
(c) Money and capital market
(d) Personnel capability

34 Which one of the following is not an element of internal environment?
(a) Mission/Objectives (b) Human resources
(c) Customers (d) Shareholders values

June 2012

35 **Assertion** (A) Internal factors of business environment are controllable factors.

Reason (R) The company can alter or modify such factors to suit the environment.

Codes
(a) Both (A) and (R) are true
(b) (A) is correct, but (R) is false
(c) Both (A) and (R) are false
(d) (A) is false, but (R) is true

36 Which one is not an element of legal environment?
(a) Act of Parliamentarians in Lok Sabha
(b) Indian Contract Act, 1872
(c) Indian Partnership Act, 1932
(d) Negotiable Instruments Act, 1881

ANSWERS

Objective Questions

1 (b)	2 (b)	3 (a)	4 (a)	5 (b)	6 (d)	7 (c)	8 (c)	9. (c)	10 (d)
11 (c)	12 (d)	13 (d)	14 (b)	15 (a)	16 (d)	17 (d)	18 (d)	19. (c)	20 (a)
21 (c)	22 (b)	23 (d)	24 (a)	25 (c)	26 (b)	27 (a)	28 (c)	29. (c)	30 (b)
31 (d)	32 (b)	33 (b)	34 (b)	35 (a)	36 (a)	37 (a)	38 (d)	39. (a)	40 (b)
41 (a)	42 (c)	43 (c)	44 (c)	45 (a)	46 (a)	47 (a)	48 (b)	49. (a)	50 (a)
51 (d)	52 (a)	53 (d)	54 (a)	55 (d)	56 (b)	57 (b)	58 (d)	59. (a)	60 (c)
61 (d)	62 (c)	63 (d)	64 (b)	65 (a)	66 (d)	67 (a)	68 (c)	69. (c)	70 (a)
71 (a)	72 (c)	73 (c)	74 (c)	75 (a)	76 (c)	77 (c)	78 (c)	79. (a)	80 (c)
81 (d)	82 (a)	83 (a)	84 (a)	85 (c)	86 (a)	87 (d)	88 (b)	89. (b)	90 (b)
91 (d)	92 (c)	93 (a)	94 (a)	95 (a)	96 (b)	97 (d)	98 (c)	99. (a)	100 (b)

Previous Years' Questions

1 (c)	2 (b)	3 (b)	4 (d)	5 (b)	6 (c)	7 (a)	8 (a)	9 (a)	10 (a)
11 (c)	12 (b)	13 (d)	14 (a)	15 (d)	16 (c)	17 (d)	18 (d)	19 (a)	20 (b)
21 (d)	22 (d)	23 (a)	24 (c)	25 (d)	26 (b)	27 (b)	28 (c)	29 (b)	30 (b)
31 (b)	32 (c)	33 (c)	34 (c)	35 (a)	36 (a)				

CHAPTER 02

Concept of International Business

International business encompasses all commercial activities that take place to promote the transfer of goods, services, resources, people, ideas and technology across the national borders at a global or transnational level. Every country frames its own foreign trade policy according to their needs and availability of resources and plans accordingly.

International Business

International business refers to the business activities or transactions carried out beyond the national borders of a country. It is a much wider term comprising of all the commercial transactions taking place between two countries.

International business can occur in different modes, which can be exporting, licensing, contract, manufacturing, foreign assembly, foreign production, joint venturing and others. For a study of international business or trade, it is necessary to understand the nature and extent of economic inter-dependence among countries.

Countries depend on each other for a variety of economic transactions, *i.e.* transactions in goods, services and capital. Being a part of the world economy, no country can live in economic isolation or afford to keep out of a global economy. No country is self-sufficient in regard to its requirement nor can it consume all that it produces. In other words, inter-dependence of countries is reflected in the whole range of international transactions.

Objectives of International Business

Profit Advantage An important objective for international business is the profit advantage. International business could be more profitable than the domestic.

Growth Opportunities International business provide enormous growth potential of many foreign markets, which is a very strong attraction for foreign companies.

In this Chapter

Helps in Removing Domestic Market Constraints International business helps in removing domestic market constraints like constraints arising from the scale economies. Technological advances have increased the size of the optimum scale of operation substantially in many industries.

To Earn Foreign Exchange International business exports its goods and services all over the world. This helps to earn valuable foreign exchange, which to make the business more profitable and to strengthen the economy of its country.

To Make Optimum Utilisation of Resources International business makes optimum utilisation of resources. This is because it produces goods on a very large scale for the international market. It utilises resources from all over the world.

To Spread Business Risks International business spreads its business risk because it does business all over the world. So, a loss in one country can be balanced by a profit in another country. The surplus goods in one country can be exported to another country.

To Get Benefits from Government International business brings a lot of foreign exchange for the country. Therefore, it gets many benefits, facilities and concessions from the government. It gets many financial and tax benefits from the government.

Scope of International Business

Merchandise Exports and Imports Merchandise exports means sending tangible goods abroad and merchandise imports means bringing tangible goods belonging to a foreign country to a one's own country. These are included in international business.

Service Exports and Imports Service exports and imports comprise trade in intangibles. It is because of its intangible feature of services. Tourism, travel, training etc are its examples.

Licensing and Franchising Licensing is a process of permitting a new party in a foreign country in order to produce and sell goods under trademarks, patents or copyrights in lieu of some fee.

Franchising is similar to licensing, but it is a term used in connection with the provision of services.

Foreign Investment It is another important form of international business. It involves investments of funds abroad in exchange for financial return. It can be of two types direct and portfolio investments.

Importance of International Business

Earn Foreign Exchange International business exports its goods and services all over the world. It helps to earn valuable foreign exchange which makes the business more profitable and strengthen the economy.

Optimum Utilisation of Resources International business makes optimum utilisation of resources because it produces goods on very large scale for the international market.

To Spread Business Risks It spreads its business risk. This is because it does business all over the world. So, a loss in one country can be balanced by a profit in another country.

Improve Organisation's Efficiency It has very high organisation efficiency. This is because without efficiency they will not be able to face the competition in the international market. So, they use all the modern management techniques to improve their efficiency.

Get Benefits from Government It brings lot of foreign exchange for the country. Therefore, it gets many benefits, facilities and concessions from the government. It gets many financial and tax benefits from the government.

Advantages of International Business

A Country may Import Things which it cannot Produce International trade enables a country to consume things, which either cannot be produced within its borders or production may cost very high. Therefore, it becomes cost cheaper to import from other countries through foreign trade.

Maximum Utilisation of Resources International trade helps a country to utilise its resources to the maximum limit. If the country does not take up imports and exports, then its resources remain unexploited. Thus, it helps to eliminate the wastage of resources.

Benefit to Consumer Imports and exports of different countries provide opportunities to the consumer to buy and consume those goods, which cannot be produced in their own country. They therefore get a diversity in choices.

Reduces Trade Fluctuations By making the size of the market large with large supplies and extensive demand, international trade reduces trade fluctuations. The prices of goods tend to remain more stable.

Utilisation of Surplus Produce International trade enables different countries to sell their surplus produce to other countries and earn foreign exchange.

Fosters International Trade International trade fosters peace, goodwill and mutual understanding among nations. Economic inter-dependence of countries often leads to close cultural relationship and thus, avoid war between them.

Disadvantages of International Business

Import of Harmful Goods Foreign trade may lead to import harmful goods like cigarettes, drugs etc which may ruin the health of the residents of the country. *e.g.* The people of China suffered greatly through optimum imports.

It may Exhaust Resources International trade leads to intensive cultivation of land. Thus, it has the operations of law of diminishing returns in agricultural countries. It also makes a poor nation by giving too much burden over the resources.

Over Specialisation Over specialisation may be disasterous for a country. A substitute may appear and ruin the economic lives of millions.

Danger of Starvation A country might depend for her food mainly on foreign countries. In times of war, there is a serious danger of starvation for such countries.

One Country may Gain at the Expense of Another One of the serious drawbacks of foreign trade is that one country may gain at the expense of other due to certain accidental advantages. The industrial revolution in Great Britain ruined Indian handicrafts during the 19th century.

It may Lead to War Foreign trade may lead to war in different countries competing with each other in finding out new markets and sources of raw material for their industries and frequently come into clash. This was one of the causes of first and second world war.

Modes of Entry into International Business

The decision to enter forcign markets must be based on strong economic factors. Temperamental decision to export is transient in character and totally unsuitable for export marketing. Success in exporting requires total involvement and determination, which can come out of basic economic necessity as perceived by the corporate unit.

They grouped as

Exporting

It is a mode of entry into international business. *It comprises*

(a) ***Indirect Exporting*** It means that the firm participates in international business through an intermediary and does not deal with foreign markets.

(b) ***Direct Exporting*** It means that the firm works with foreign customers or markets with the apportunity to develop a relationship.

Advantages of Exporting

- It comprises relatively low financial exposure.
- It permit gradual market entry.
- It acquire knowledge about local market.
- It avoid restrictions on foreign investment.

Disadvantages of Exporting

- It provides vulnerability to tariffs and Non Tariff Barriers (NTBs).
- It creates logistical complexities.
- It causes potential conflicts with distributors.

Licensing

It is when a firm, called the licensor leases the right to use its intellectual property-technology, work methods, patents, copyrights, brand names to another firm, called the licensee, in return for a fee.

Advantages of Licensing

- It has low financial risks.
- It has low cost way to assess market potential
- It avoid tariffs, NTBs, restrictions on foreign investment.
- Licensee provides knowledge of local market.

Disadvantages of Licensing

- It has limited market opportunities.
- It depends on licensee.
- It causes potential conflict with licensee.
- It has possibility of creating future competitor.

Franchising

Under franchising, an independent organisation called the franchisee operates the business under the name of another company called the franchisor. It is a form of licensing but the franchisor can exercise more control over the franchisee as compared to that in licensing.

Advantages of Franchising

- It has low financial risks.
- Market potential cost way is low.
- It avoid tariffs.

Disadvantages of Franchising

- It comprises limited market profits.
- It has dependence on franchisee.

Theories of International Business

There are various famous theories of international business, which are as follows

Theory of Absolute Advantage

Adam Smith criticised theory of mercantilism by saying that wealth of nation does not lie in building huge stock piles of gold and silver in its treasure, but the real wealth of a nation is measured by the level of improvement in the quality of living of its citizens, as reflected by the per capita income.

An absolute advantage refers to the ability of a country to produce a good more efficiently and cost effectively than any other country. Thus, instead of producing all products, each country should specialise in producing those goods that it can produce more efficiently. A country's advantage may be either natural or acquired. Natural factors such as country's geographical and agro climatic conditions, mineral or other natural resources or specialised manpower contribute to a country's natural advantage in certain products, *e.g.* availability of relatively cheap labour contributes to India's edge in export of labour intensive products. Although, each country is assumed to possess equal resources, the production possibilities for each country would vary, depending upon their production efficiency and utilisation of available resources. This is called acquired advantage.

To illustrate the concept of absolute advantage, let us take example of two countries say India and UK, which employs resources to produce either tea or rice. Production efficiency is assumed to vary between countries because to produce a tonne of tea UK requires 10 units or resources, whereas India requires only 5 units of resources. On the other hand, for producing one tonne of rice, UK requires only 4 units of resources, whereas India needs 10 units of resources. Since, India require lower resources compared to UK for producing tea, it is relatively more efficient in tea production. On the other hand, since UK requires fewer resources compared to India for producing rice, it is relatively more efficient in producing rice.

Units Required	UK	India
Units required to produce one tonne of tea	10	5
Units required to produce one tonne of rice	4	10

Theory of Comparative Cost

The basic contention of the theory is that each country will produce those goods for the production, of which is specially suited and import those goods, which is less suited to produce or which it cannot produce at all. By how much a country is better suited than another to produce a given commodity is obtained by the differences in the cost of producing a unit of that commodity in the two countries. Since, the classical economists used labour costs, the difference in the cost of producing a commodity is measured in terms of the number of days of labour spent in the production of that commodity.

Thus, according to 'theory of comparative cost' what each country will export and what it will import is determined by comparative differences in labour costs.

In other words, it makes sense for a country to specialise in the production of those goods that it produces more efficiently and to buy the goods that it produces less efficiently from other countries, even if this seems buying goods from other countries that it could produce more efficiently itself.

Theory of Factor Endowment

Heckscher and Ohlin developed a theory to explain the reasons for differences in relative commodity prices and competitive advantage between two nations. According to this theory, a nation will export the commodity whose production requires intensive use of the nation's relatively abundant and cheap factors and import those commodities, whose production requires intensive use of nation's scarce and expensive factors.

Thus, the theory explains the basis of international trade in three stages

- The basis of trade lies in the difference in the final price of a commodity.
- The difference in final price of a commodity is due to difference in the comparative cost of producing that commodity.
- Finally, it examines the root cause, which produces this difference in the comparative cost.

It is difference in factor intensities in the production function of goods alongwith actual difference in relative factor endowments that explains the international differences in comparative cost of production.

A country can produce a commodity more cheaply by matching its abundant factor with the factor intensity of the commodity because, when a nation has relatively more of a particular factor, the cost of that factor will be comparatively lower.

The lower the price of the major input, the greater is the price advantage the producer will have in trade. *We can explain it with the help of following example*

Let us take two Countries A and B. In Country A, capital is abundant and labour is scarce. In Country B, labour is abundant and capital is scarce. In Country A, production of capital intensive goods will be comparatively cheaper while in Country B, production of labour intensive goods will be cheaper. Country A possess a comparative advantage in the production of capital intensive goods, Country B has a comparative advantage in the production of labour intensive goods. When a Country like A exports capital intensive goods in return for labour intensive goods from B, it means that Country A is indirectly exporting her abundant and cheap factor embodied in the form of goods. Thus, indirectly factors in abundant supply are exported in the form of goods produced by them and factors in scarce supply are imported by the country.

Assumptions of Factor Endowment Theory

- Perfect competition exists in both the product and factor markets in each country.
- Factor mobility within a country is complete.
- Factors are identical and homogenous, qualitatively in both the countries.
- Factor supplies are fixed, fully employed and constant return to scale.
- Trade is free and costless.
- The physical amount of each productive factor possessed by countries are different and can be measured.
- Techniques of producing identical goods are same in both the countries.
- Goods can be classified according to their factor intensity.

Government Intervention in International Trade

Government intervene in trade and investment to achieve political, social or economic objectives. Barriers are often created to benefit specific interest groups. A key rationale is to create jobs by protecting industries from foreign competition.

Objectives for Government Intervention

There are many different objectives that governments might persue by way of intervention in private markets.

These are as follows

Miximise Social Welfare Among the most common set of objectives for government, regulatory policy is the maximisation of social welfare through the remediation of various types of market failure.

Macro-economic Objectives A second set of objectives that are pursued primarily by national governments revolve around macro-economic performance. It include efforts to control inflation and counteract the effects of economic cycles.

Socio-economic Objectives Government may also intervene in order to promote a range of socio-economic objectives. These objectives may be motivated by concerns over fairness. Other interventions may be designed to promote safety where it is thought that market participants are unable to account for certain types of risk.

Other Objectives Apart from above categories, government may intervene for other reasons broadly related to national interests. Some intervention are undertaken to promote national unity and national prestige.

Trade Barriers

Trade barriers are restrictions imposed on the movement of goods between countries. The major purpose of trade barriers is to promote domestic goods than exported goods and there by safeguard the domestic industries.

Trade barriers can be broadly divided into the following

Tariff Barriers

The term 'tariff' means 'tax' or 'duty'. Tariff barriers are the tax barriers or the monetary barriers imposed on internationally traded goods when they cross the national borders.

Major tariff barriers includes

Specific Duty It is based on the physical characteristics of the good. A fixed amount of money can be levied on each unit of imported goods regardless on its price.

Ad Valorem Tariffs The latin phrase 'ad valorem' means 'according to the value'. This tax is flexible and depends upon the value or the price of the commodity.

Combined Duty It is a combination of specific and ad valorem duty on a single product.

Sliding Scale Duty The duty which varies alongwith the price of the commodity is known as sliding scale duty. These duties are confined to agricultural products, as their prices frequently vary because of natural and other factors.

Protective Tariff In order to protect domestic industries from stiff competition of imported goods, protective tariff is levied on imports.

Non-tariff Barriers

Any barriers other than tariff are known as non-tariff barriers. (NTBs) It is meant for constructing barriers for the free flow of the goods. It do not affect the price of the imported goods. It affects the quality and quantity of the goods.

Major non-tariff barriers includes

Licenses License is granted by the government and allows the importing of certain goods to the country.

Voluntary Export Restrains These type of barriers are created by the exporting country rather than the importing one. These restrains are usually levied on the request of the importing company.

Quotas Under this system, a country may fix in advance, the limit of import quantity of commodity that would be permitted for import from various countries during a given period.

Product Standards Here, the importing country imposes standards for goods. If the standard are not met, the goods are rejected.

Foreign Exchange Regulations The importer has to ensure that adequate foreign exchange is available for import of goods by obtaining a clearance from exchange control authorities prior to the concluding of contract with the supplier.

Foreign Trade Policy

Foreign trade policy refers to the policy concerning exports and imports. Therefore, it is also known as Export-Import Policy. They trade policy significantly affects the different business units differently. *e.g.* If restrictive import policy has been adopted by the government, then it will prevent the domestic business units from foreign competition and if the liberal import policy has been adopted by the government, then it will affect the domestic products in other way.

Objectives of Foreign Trade Policy

- The primary purpose is not the mere earning of foreign exchange, but the stimulation of greater economic activity. *The foreign trade policy of India is based on two major objectives*
  - (a) It emphasise to double the percentage share of global merchandise trade within the next five years.
  - (b) It act as an effective instrument of economic growth by giving a thrust to employment generation.
- Technological development was promoted in this policy for strengthening industrial infrastructure.

India's Foreign Trade Policy (2015-20)

FTP 2015-20 was unveiled by MS Nirmala Sitharaman, Minister of State for Commerce and Industry, Government of India on 1st April, 2015. *Following are the highlights of FTP*

- It provides a framework for increasing exports of goods and services as well as generation of employment and increasing value addition in the country, in time with the 'Make in India' programme.
- The policy aims to enable India to respond to the challenges of the external environment, keeping in step with a rapidly evolving international trading architecture and make trade a major contributor to the country's economic growth and development.
- Duty credit scrips issued under MEIS (Merchandise Exports from India Scheme) and SEIS (Service Exports from India Scheme) and the goods imported against these scrips are fully transferable.
- Measures have been taken to give a boost to exports of defense and hi-tech items.
- Trade facilitation and enhancing the ease of doing business are the other major focus area of this FTP.
- E-commerce exports of handloom products, books, leather footwear, toys and customised fashion garments through courier or foreign post office would also be able to get benefit of MEIS (for value upto INR 25,000).

Globalisation

The IMF defines globalisation as, "The growing economic inter-dependence of countries worldwide through increasing volume and variety of cross border transaction in goods and services and of international capital cash flows and through the more rapid and widespread diffusion of technology." Globalisation implies integration of the economy of the country with the rest of the world economy. In simple economic terms, globalisation refers to the process of integration of the world into one huge market. Such unification calls for the removal of all trade barriers among countries.

Objectives of Globalisation

- Its main objective is integration of the economy of country with the rest of the world economy.
- It focused on industrialisation.
- It emphasised on free flow of capital.
- It also considered total capital employment.
- It spread production facilities throughout the globe.

Features of Globalisation

- Opening and planning to expand business throughout the world.
- New global consumer market emerges with global brand.
- Erase the difference between domestic market and foreign market.
- Rapid growth in international financial transactions.
- Locate the production and other physical facilities on a consideration of the global business dynamics, irrespective of national consideration.

Globalisation of Indian Business

Globalisation in India is generally taken to mean integrating, the economy of the country with the world economy and it was limited because of the restrictive economic policies followed until 1991. Indian firm confined themselves, by and large, to the home market. Foreign investment by Indian firms was very insignificant. But with the new economic policy ushered in 1991, there has, however, been a change. Globalisation has in fact become a buzzword with Indian firms now.

The main policy measures initiated towards globalisation by the government of India are as under

Exchange Rate Adjustment and Rupee Convertibility

To integrate the economy of the country with the global economy, the country should make its currency fully convertible. The Government of India makes a two step downward adjustment of 18-19% in the exchange rate of the rupee on 1st and 3rd July, 1991. The 1992-93 budget introduced a dual exchange rate system implying partial convertibility of rupee. The 1993-94 budget introduced full convertibility of the rupee on trade account and switched over to a unified exchange rate system. India achieved full convertibility on current account on 19th August, 1994.

Import Liberalisation

In 1992-97, export-import policy of the country allowed the free import of all items including capital goods, except a negative (restricted) list. The supplementary trade policy announced in 13th August, 1991 decanalised the import of 20 items. In addition, import duties on a wide range of commodities were drastically cut down. For instance, custom duties on 35 items were bring down to 150% ad valorem from 255% ad valorem on 9th February, 1993. This was followed by substantial reduction of import duties in the 1993-94.

In addition, India, as a member of World Trade Organisation (WTO), had also committed itself to the phasing out of quantitative restrictions over a 6 years period beginning 1997. This period was further reduced following the ruling of the Disputes Settlement Body of the WTO against India on an appeal made by USA. In terms of the agreement arrived at with USA, the quantitative restrictions have now been totally removed. Trade Related Intellectual Property Rights (TRIPs), The Patent (Amendment) Act, 1999 was passed in March 1999 to provide Exclusive Marketing Rights (EMRs).

Opening upto Foreign Capital

To integrate Indian economy with the global economy, the Government of India open the doors to foreign investors. In 1991, the government announced a specified list of high technology and high investment priority industries wherein automatic permission was granted for direct foreign investment upto 51% foreign equity. This limit was raised from 51% to 74% for many of these industries. Presently, FDI is permitted upto 100% on the automatic route in most of the sectors subject to sectoral rules/regulation, applicable.

Drivers of Globalisation

A driver is a contributing factor of change. *The main drivers of globalisation are as follows*

Technological Advancement It drives globalisation by making it easier for people, goods and ideas to move across borders.

International Trade It encourages and strengthens inter-dependence between countries. Every country must import goods, services and capital to maintain a certain standard of living for their citizens. As a result, many countries and international organisations have enacted economic policies that fuel globalisation.

International Investment It drives globalisation by increasing economic integration. Many countries reap the benefits of international investment, which include the creation of productive enterprise, jobs and new source of income.

EXAM BASED QUESTIONS

International Business and Modes of Entry

1 What are the objectives of international trade?
(a) Sales expansion
(b) Diversification
(c) Maximise competitive risk
(d) Both (a) and (b)

2 A global company is sometimes called
(a) a joint stock company
(b) a corporation
(c) a globally integrated company
(d) None of the above

3 Which of the following are engaged in external influence?
(a) Political policies (b) Legal practices
(c) Both (a) and (b) (d) Neither (a) nor (b)

4 International trade brings developing countries in contact with
(a) developed nations
(b) underdeveloped countries
(c) low developed countries
(d) All of the above

5 Foreign exchange reserves include
(a) Gold Stock
(b) US Dollar
(c) Both (a) and (b)
(d) Neither (a) nor (b)

6 Foreign trade helps each country to make .... use of its natural resources.
(a) optimal (b) loss
(c) better (d) None of these

7 Which of the following are major objectives that engage companies in international business?
(a) To expand sales
(b) To acquire resources
(c) To diversify sources of sales and supplies
(d) All of the above

8 More companies operate internationally because
(a) new products take time to become known globally
(b) domestic companies competitors, suppliers and customers have become international
(c) Both (a) and (b)
(d) None of the above

9 Additional risk that have to be taken care of, while trading across nations are
(a) exchange risk
(b) country risk
(c) Both (a) and (b)
(d) Neither (a) nor (b)

10 Enjoying comparative advantage for a country means having a .... opportunity cost of domestically producing a commodity than the other country.
(a) lesser (b) greater
(c) no (d) None of these

11 Which of the following statement(s) is/are incorrect?
(a) Entrepot trade means sale of goods to a foreign country
(b) Import trade means sale of goods to a foreign country
(c) Both (a) and (b)
(d) None of the above

12 Which combination of the following factors has driven globalisation in the recent past?
1. Growth of multinational corporations.
2. Internationalisation of finance.
3. Increased international trade.
Select the correct answer using the codes given below
Codes
(a) Both 1 and 2 (b) Both 1 and 3
(c) Both 2 and 3 (d) All of these

13 Which of the following is/are the type of exporting?
(a) Direct exporting
(b) Indirect exporting
(c) Both (a) and (b)
(d) None of the above

14 Which of the following cannot be advantage of licensing?
(a) It has low financial risks
(b) It avoid tariffs
(c) It has possibility of creating future competitor
(d) None of the above

15 Which of the following statement is incorrect?
(a) Franchising is a part of licensing
(b) Licensing is a mode of entry into international business
(c) Both (a) and (b)
(d) None of the above

16 Which of the following are not included in modes of entry into an international business?
(a) Exporting (b) Licensing
(c) Importing (d) Franchising

Theories of International Business, Government Intervention and Foreign Trade Policy

17 Theory of comparative advantage is propounded by
(a) Adam Smith (b) David Ricardo
(c) Marshall (d) Robbins

18 The theory of comparative advantage assumes single factor of production, *i.e.*

(a) land (b) labour
(c) capital (d) All of these

19 What are the assumptions of Heckscher-Ohlin Model?

(a) No obstruction to trade
(b) Commodities and factor are perfectly competitive
(c) Both countries operate at same level of efficiency
(d) All of the above

20 Who has shown how international trade leads to equalisation of factor prices?

(a) JM Keynes (b) Bertil Ohlin
(c) David Ricardo (d) None of these

21 The comparative cost theory of international trade was developed by

(a) David Ricardo (b) Haberler
(c) Adam Smith (d) Alfred Marshal

22 The trade theory of absolute advantage was developed by

(a) Haberler (b) David Ricardo
(c) Adam Smith (d) Alfred Marshall

23 The theory of reciprocal demand is developed by.........

(a) Yeron (b) John Stuart Mill
(c) Ohlin (d) None of these

24 Factor endowment theory of international trade was propounded by

(a) David Ricardo (b) Bertil Ohlin
(c) JS Mill (d) CP Kindleberger

25 Heckscher-Ohlin theory explains international trade in terms of

(a) demand differences
(b) differences in factor endowments
(c) differences in labour productivity
(d) None of the above

26 Important factors considered in international product life cycle theory are

(a) technological innovation (b) market structure
(c) Both (a) and (b) (d) Neither (a) nor (b)

27 Theories of international trade can be broadly grouped into

(a) classical theory (b) modern theory
(c) Both (a) and (b) (d) Neither (a) nor (b)

28 Who was shown, how international trade leads to equalisation of factor prices?

(a) Prof Horst Kohaler (b) Prof Bertil Ohlin
(c) Prof IM Keynes (d) Prof PU Ouglus

29 The purpose of protectionism in to protect

(a) domestic industries from foreign competition
(b) foreign firms from foreign competitors
(c) domestic exports from high production cost
(d) foreign and domestic firms from labor unions

30 Anti-dumping duties are used to

(a) offset the margin of dumping
(b) punish domestic consumers for buying high priced imported goods
(c) discourage foreign governments from subsidising their exporters
(d) reduce the tariff revenue of the domestic government

31 A tariff rate quota

(a) is a limit on the number of tariff that a country can place on imports
(b) uses a single tariff alongwith import quotas to restrict import
(c) is designed to avoid the price increases caused by simple tariffs
(d) is a two-tier tariff system intended to restrict imports

32 According to which theory, one country may be more efficient in producing a particular goods than another country and that another country may be capable of producing some other goods more efficiently than the first one?

(a) Thoery of comparative advantage
(b) Theory of absolute advantage
(c) Theory of international product life cycle
(d) None of the above

33 Which theory explores the possibility of two nation operating at the same level of efficiency, benefiting by trading with each other?

(a) Theory of comparative advantage
(b) Heckscher-Ohlin Model
(c) Both (a) and (b)
(d) None of the above

34 Which of the following pair(s) is/are correct?

(a) Countries should export more than they import as per the theory of mercantilism
(b) Theory of comparative advantage is propounded by Adam Smith
(c) Both (a) and (b)
(d) None of the above

35 Who has demonstrated how prosperity of one country brings prosperity to other countries participating in international trade?

(a) Keynes (b) Adam Smith
(c) Ohlin (d) None of these

36 Which of the following statement(s) is/are correct?

(a) Mercantilism supported Autarky
(b) Mercantilism originated in Britain
(c) Mercantilism was based on the ideology of globalisation
(d) All of the above

37 Which of the following pair(s) is/are not correct?

(a) Endowment theory assumes that factor modility within a country is complete
(b) Imitation gap theory assumes that new products are initially developed in capital rich countries
(c) Both (a) and (b)
(d) None of the above

38 Difference between the time of introduction of the product in one country and the time, when the producers in other country start producing it

(a) imitation gap (b) demand gap
(c) Both (a) and (b) (d) Neither (a) nor (b)

39 Arrange the following steps of 'international product life cycle theory' in a correct order.

1. Maturity stage 2. Introductory stage
3. Decline stage 4. Growth stage

Codes

(a) 2, 4, 1, 3 (b) 3, 1, 4, 2
(c) 4, 3, 2, 1 (d) 4, 2, 3, 1

40 Which of the following is a rationale for governments imposing offensive trade and investment barriers?

(a) The protection of domestic industries
(b) The promotion of national security
(c) The pursuit of public policy objectives
(d) The support of special interest

41 If a tariff and import quota lead to equivalent increases in the domestic price of steel, then

(a) the quota results in efficiency reductions, but the tariff does not
(b) the tariff results in efficiency reductions, but the quota does not
(c) they have different impacts on how much is produced and consumed
(d) they have different impacts on how income is distributed

42 During periods of growing domestic demand an import quota,

(a) is less restrictive on a country's imports than a tariff
(b) is more restrictive on a country's imports than a tariff
(c) has the same restrictive effect on a country's imports as a tariff
(d) will always generate increased tax revenue for the government

43 Import quotas tend to result in all of the following except,

(a) domestic producers of the imported good being harmed
(b) domestic consumers of the imported good being harmed
(c) prices increasing in the importing country
(d) prices falling in the exporting country

44 Consider the following statements and identify the right ones.

1. A double entry system of record of all economic transactions between the residents of a country and rest of the world is called balance of trade.
2. All transactions related to goods, services or income are classified as capital account.

Codes

(a) Only 1
(b) Only 2
(c) Both of the above
(d) None of the above

45 The investment in productive assets and participation in management as stakeholders in business enterprise is

(a) FDI (b) FII
(c) balance of payment (d) SDR

46 Consider the following statement and identify the right ones.

1. India adopted LERMS in 1992.
2. In 1993, dual exchange rate system was replaced by a unified floating exchange rate.

Codes

(a) Only 1
(b) Only 3
(c) Both of the above
(d) None ot the above

Globalisation

47 Globalisation is beneficial for firms because

(a) it opens up new market opportunities
(b) it protects them against foreign competition
(c) it cushions them from the effects of events in other countries
(d) it increases the risk and uncertainty of operating in a globalising world economy

48 The following factors are key drivers of globalisation.

(a) Government action, exchange rates, competition and socio-demographic factors
(b) Market convergence, competition, exchange rates and cost advantages
(c) Cost advantages, government action, economic cycles and competition
(d) Market, cost, competition and government policies

49 What is the importance of globalisation for multinational firms?

(a) Home demand, home factor conditions and domestic rivalry are no longer important to multinational firms
(b) A multinational firm can gain a competitive advantage in a foreign country
(c) The home base is no longer important to multinational firms
(d) Regions are no longer important in global competition

50 Globalisation is term used to describe the process of removal of restriction on which of the following?

(a) Foreign trade
(b) Investment
(c) Both (a) and (b)
(d) None of the above

51 Globalisation can create problems for business because

(a) it increases vulnerability to political risk and uncertainty when operating abroad
(b) it means that they can increase prices
(c) it can result in more competition
(d) All of the above

52 Globalisation is a process of integration of world economics to realise the benefits of geography, demography, cost and efficiency. Which three characteristics represent globalisation?

1. Increasing space
2. Shrinking space
3. Strengthened borders
4. Shrinking time
5. Disappearing borders

Select the correct answer using the codes given below

Codes

(a) 2, 3 and 4
(b) 1, 2 and 4
(c) 1, 3 and 4
(d) 2, 4 and 5

53 In an economist's view, which of the following perspectives of globalisation is most suitable?

(a) The rise of global media and global culture
(b) The emergence of global institutions and global conflicts
(c) The development of communication technologies
(d) The growth of international trade and increase in international trade flows

54 Which of the following statement is/are correct

(a) Globalisation implies integration of the economy of the country with rest of the world economy
(b) Globalisation focussed on industrialisation
(c) Both (a) and (b)
(d) None of the above

55 Which of the following cannot be included in objectives of globalisation?

(a) It focused on industrialisation
(b) It emphasised on free flow of capital
(c) It enhance unemployment
(d) None of the above

56 Which of the following can be included in measures initiated towards globalisation by Government of India?

(a) Exchange rate adjustment and rupee convertibility
(b) Import liberalisation
(c) Both (a) and (b)
(d) None of the above

Miscellaneous

Directions (Q. Nos. 57-59) *In the questions, given below two statements are labelled as Statement I and Statement II. In the context, which of the following is correct?*

Codes

(a) Both statements are correct
(b) Both statements are incorrect
(c) Statement I is correct, but Statement II is incorrect
(d) Statement I is incorrect, but Statement II is correct

57 **Statement** I Foreign trade is subject to greater risk as compared to home trade.

Statement II Internal trade is known as foreign trade.

58 **Statement** I Imitation gap theory is given by Posner.

Statement II In the accounting sense, debit and credit will always balance each other.

59 **Statement** I International business does not spread business risks.

Statement II International business helps in removing domestic market constraints.

60 **Statement** I International business can imports harmful goods.

Statement II International business renew resources.

61 Which of the following statement(s) is/are correct?

1. Profit advantage is objective of international business.
2. International business helps in removing domestic market constraints.
3. International business shrink business risk.

Codes

(a) Only 1
(b) Only 2
(c) Both 1 and 2
(d) All of the above

Directions (Q. Nos. 62-65) *In the questions given below are two statements labelled as Assertion (A) and Reason (R). In the context of the two statements, which one of the following is correct*

Codes

(a) Both (A) and (R) are correct and (R) is the correct explanation of (A)
(b) (R) is correct, but (A) is incorrect
(c) (A) is correct, but (R) is incorrect
(d) Both (A) and (R) are incorrect

62 **Assertion** (A) International trade enables a country to consume things which it cannot produce.

Reason (R) International trade fosters trade.

63 **Assertion** (A) Removal of trade barriers may result in the growth of industries.

Reason (R) Economy does not depends on global market.

64 **Assertion** (A) Perfect competition only exist in product market in each country.

Reason (R) Barriers are often created to benefit specific interest group.

65 Assertion (A) Trade barriers are restrictions imposed on the movement of goods between countries.

Reason (R) The major purpose of trade barriers is to promote domestic goods than exported goods.

66 Match the following.

List I	List II
A. Importing	1. Modes of international business
B. Marketing	2. Functions of international business
C. Sales expansion	3. Objectives of international business
D. Economic forces	4. External influence

Codes

	A	B	C	D		A	B	C	D
(a)	1	2	3	4	(b)	3	1	4	2
(c)	4	1	3	4	(d)	4	3	2	1

67 Match the following.

List I (Theories of International Trade)	List II (Features)
A. Theory of reciprocal demand	1. Through specialisation, countries could increase their efficiency.
B. Theory of absolute advantage	2. It emphasises the demand side as well.
C. Theory of mercantilism	3. It assume that there is only one factor of production.
D. Theory of comparative costs	4. Countries should export more than they import.

Codes

	A	B	C	D		A	B	C	D
(a)	4	3	2	1	(b)	2	1	4	3
(c)	3	4	1	2	(d)	2	3	4	1

68 Match the following.

List I (Theories of International Trade)	List II (Founders)
A. Theory of reciprocal demand	1. David Ricardo
B. Theory of absolute advantage	2. Adam Smith
C. Theory of comparative advantage	3. Raymond Vernon
D. Product life cycle theory of trade	4. John Stuart Mill

Codes

	A	B	C	D
(a)	4	3	1	2
(b)	3	1	4	2
(c)	2	3	4	1
(d)	2	4	1	3

69 Match the following.

List I (Theories of International Trade)	List II (Features)
A. Theory of mercantilism	1. It is developed by John Stuart Mill.
B. Theory of absolute advantage	2. What each country will export and what it will import is determined by comparative differences in labour costs.
C. Theory of comparative costs	3. It refers to the ability of a country to produce a good more.
D. Theory of reciprocal demand	4. It attributes and measures the wealth of a nation by the size of its accumulated treasures.

Codes

	A	B	C	D
(a)	4	3	2	1
(b)	3	1	4	2
(c)	1	4	2	3
(d)	1	2	3	4

70 Match the following.

List I	List II
A. Adam Smith	1. Availability
B. David Ricardo	2. Endowment
C. Ohlin	3. Absolute advantage
D. IB Kravis	4. Comparative advantage

Codes

	A	B	C	D
(a)	1	2	3	4
(b)	2	4	3	1
(c)	3	4	2	1
(d)	4	3	1	2

PREVIOUS YEARS' QUESTIONS

December 2018

1 Which one of the following is the main government agency responsible for development and monitoring international trade in India?
(a) Indian Institute of Foreign Trade
(b) Federation of Indian Export Organisations
(c) Department of Commerce
(d) Export Promotion Council

2 The theory suggesting that the patterns of international trade are determined by factor endowment rather than productivity was propounded by which one of the following?
(a) Adam Smith
(b) David Ricardo
(c) Heckscher and Bertil Ohlin
(d) Michael Porter

3 In which one of the following modes of entry into foreign market are risk and profit potential the highest?
(a) Indirect exporting (b) Direct exporting
(c) Direct investment (d) Joint venture

November 2017

4 Which one among the following has the largest share of exports from India ?
(a) Agriculture and allied commodity
(b) Gems and jewellery
(c) Handicrafts
(d) Electronic goods

July 2016

5 **Assertion** (A) Comparative cost theory is static in character.
Reason (R) Comparative cost theory is based on fixed supplies of factors of production.
Codes
(a) (A) is correct, but (R) is incorrect
(b) (R) is correct, but (A) is incorrect
(c) Both (A) and (R) are correct, but (R) is not the correct explanation of (A)
(d) Both (A) and (R) are correct and (R) is the correct explanation of (A)

December 2015

6 **Assertion** (A) In 1991, government decided to allow all foreign investments to any industry without any restrictions.
Reason (R) Government has enhanced the investment limit of small scale industrial units.
Codes
(a) Both (A) and (R) are true and (R) is the correct explanation of (A)
(b) Both (A) and (R) are true, but (R) is not the correct explanation of (A)
(c) (A) is true, but (R) is false
(d) (A) is false, but (R) is true

7 Globalisation is the term used to describe process of removal of restriction on which of the following?
(a) Foreign trade (b) Investment
(c) Both (a) and (b) (d) None of these

June 2015

8 In respect of international business, a project is called a turnkey project because
(a) the licensee agree to construct an entire plant in his home country and hands over the key
(b) the licensor starts the operation and hands over the key of the operating plant to the licensee
(c) the licensor starts the operation and then invites the licensee and hands over the key to complete the remaining work
(d) the licensor and the licensee jointly carry out the project and agree to share profit equally

9 The highest percentage of export from India went to which of the following regions in 2013-14?
(a) OECD countries (b) USA
(c) SAARC (d) Latin America

December 2014

10 Which of the following is not ensured to the consumer in the globalisation?
(a) Lower prices
(b) Better selection
(c) Clear origin of goods and services
(d) Improved services

June 2014

11 From the following modes of international business, identify the mode which strategic alliance?
(a) Franchising (b) Leasing
(c) Turnkey project (d) Joint venture

12 In the context of globalisation, 'Levitt Thesis' means
(a) standardisation strategy to respond to the worldwide homogenised market and expand the market through aggressive low pricing
(b) customise products to regional markets
(c) customise products to meet the national markets
(d) None of the above

December 2013

13 Match the following.

List I	List II
A. Comparative cost theory of international trade	1. Gottfried Haberfer
B. International trade theory of opportunity cost	2. JS Mill
C. Factor endownment theory of international trade	3. David Ricardo
D. Doctrine of reciprocal demand	4. Hecksher Ohlin

Codes

	A	B	C	D		A	B	C	D
(a)	3	2	4	1	(b)	1	3	2	4
(c)	3	1	4	2	(d)	2	1	4	3

June 2013

14 The forces that lend momentum to the process of globalisation have been identified by Michael Porter include the following

1. Fluid global capital market
2. Technological restructuring
3. Decreasing religious command
4. Ethnic decontrol
5. New global competitors
6. End of the cold war in 1990s

Codes

(a) 6, 5, 4 and 3
(b) 6, 3, 2 and 1
(c) 6, 4, 2 and 1
(d) 4, 3, 2 and 1

December 2012

15 **Assertion** (A) Operating style of the international business can be spread to the entire globe.

Reason (R) The style is limited to the internal economy only.

Codes

(a) Both (A) and (R) are true and (R) is the correct explanation of (A)
(b) Both (A) and (R) are true and (R) is not the correct explanation of (A)
(c) (A) is true, but (R) is false
(d) (A) is false, but (R) is true

16 The comparative cost advantage theory was given by

(a) David Ricardo
(b) Adam Smith
(c) Raymond Vernon
(d) Michael E Porter

17 The companies globalise their operations through different means

(a) exporting directly
(b) licensing/franchising
(c) joint ventures
(d) All of these

18 In international trade, which of the following is a non-tariff trade barrier?

(a) Quotas
(b) Import bans
(c) Export controls
(d) Anti dumping laws

19 Franchising is a practice of

(a) leasing for a prescribed period of time, the right to use firm's successful business model and brand
(b) selling out a successful business model and brand
(c) hiring a firm's successful business model and brand
(d) None of the above

ANSWERS

Objective Questions

1 (d)	2 (b)	3 (c)	4 (c)	5 (c)	6 (a)	7 (d)	8 (b)	9 (d)	10 (a)
11 (c)	12 (b)	13 (c)	14 (c)	15 (a)	16 (c)	17 (b)	18 (b)	19 (d)	20 (b)
21 (a)	22 (c)	23 (b)	24 (b)	25 (b)	26 (c)	27 (c)	28 (b)	29 (a)	30 (a)
31 (d)	32 (b)	33 (b)	34 (a)	35 (a)	36 (b)	37 (b)	38 (a)	39 (a)	40 (a)
41 (d)	42 (b)	43 (a)	44 (d)	45 (a)	46 (a)	47 (b)	48 (a)	49 (d)	50 (c)
51 (a)	52 (d)	53 (d)	54 (c)	55 (c)	56 (c)	57 (c)	58 (a)	59 (d)	60 (c)
61 (d)	62 (a)	63 (c)	64 (b)	65 (a)	66 (a)	67 (b)	68 (d)	69 (a)	70 (b)

Previous Years' Questions

1 (c)	2 (c)	3 (c)	4 (b)	5 (d)	6 (d)	7 (c)	8 (d)	9 (a)	10 (c)
11 (d)	12 (a)	13 (c)	14 (c)	15 (b)	16 (a)	17 (d)	18 (b)	19 (a)	

CHAPTER 03

Foreign Direct Investment and Balance of Payment

FDI is a modern technique which is adopted for globalisation. It plays an important role in growth of a business and also maintains a balanced inflow and outflow of finance. Every country has its own FDI policy. BoP is also an important factor of business which maintains records of transactions of a country with other countries.

Foreign Direct Investment (FDI)

FDI simply refers to the act of investing capital in a business enterprise that operates overseas and in a foreign country. The investor is usually a multinational corporation. The control over the enterprise, in which the investment is made does not merely involve the control of the invested capital. It control in terms of actual power of management and effective decision-making in the major areas of working. The minimum voting rights or shares of an enterprise, that a foreign investor is supposed to control is 10%. This holds relevant in cases where a foreign investor opens up a whole new business operation in another country or it, simply merges with a local enterprise for the same purpose.

In effect, this is like any regular enterprise that invites investments and then grants the donor of that investment a certain degree of control in the enterprise, alongwith a share of profits as well, even though this depends on the policy of profit repatriation in that country.

The only difference here is that the investor is actually a foreign party. As a result of this, different rules, policies and governing factors came into play in such a scenario.

In this Chapter

- Foreign Direct Investment
- Foreign Portfolio Investment
- Balance of Payment

Importance of FDI

Easy International Trade It helps in smooth working of international trade. As country has its own import traiff, this makes trade difficult, but with the help of FDI it becomes more easier.

Employment and Economic Boost It creats new jobs, as investors build new companies in the target country and create new opportunities which increase income and buying power of people and finally economic boost prevails.

Development of Human Capital Resources Human capital is the competence and knowledge of those able to perform labour. A country with FDI can benefit greatly by developing its human resources while maintaining ownership.

Resource Transfer It allow resource transfer and other exchanges of knowledge, where various countries are given access to new technologies and skills.

Increased Productivity The facilities and equipment provided by foreign investors can increase a workforce's productivity in the target country.

Types of FDI

Inward FDI It is a particular form of inward investment when foreign capital is invested in local resources. It is encouraged by tax breaks, subsidies, low interest loans, long-term gain is worth more than the short-term loss.

Outward FDI It is called as direct investment abroad. Local capital is invested in foreign resources. It is encouraged by government backed insurance to cover risk.

Greenfield Investment These are the primary target of a host nation's promotional efforts. It create new production capacity and jobs.

Merger and Acquisitions Cross border acquisition occur when the control of assets an operations is transferred from a local to a foreign company, with that local company becoming an affiliate of the foreign company.

Horizontal FDI It occurs when a company investment is made for conducting the similar business operations in another country.

Vertical FDI Vertical integrate is the expansion of a firm into a stage of the production process other than that of the original business.

Resource Seeking Investment which seek to acquire factors of production, i.e. more efficient than those obtainable in the home economy of the firm.

Market Seeking It is the investment which aim at either penetrating new markets or maintaining existing ones.

Efficiency Seeking These are the investments by which firms hope will increase their efficiency by exploiting the benefits of economics of scale and scope and also those of common ownership.

Strategic Asset Seeking It is a tactical investment to prevent the gain of resource to a competitor.

Methods of FDI

- By acquiring shares in an associated enterprise.
- Through a merger or an acquisition of an unrelated enterprise.
- Low corporate tax and individual income tax rates.
- Tax holidays.
- Research and development support.
- Investment financial subsidies.

Advantages of FDI

The party making the investment is usually, known as the parent enterprise and the party invested is can be referred to as the foreign affiliate. Together, these enterprises form what is known as a Trams National Corporation (TNC) and *here some of the advantages of such an arrangement depicted*

- Many countries still have several import tariffs in place, so reaching these countries through international trade is difficult. There are certain industries that require to be present in international markets in order to succeed and they are the ones, who then provide FDI to industries in such countries, so that they can increase their sales presence.
- Many parent enterprises provide FDI because of the tax incentives that they get. Governments of certain countries invite FDI because they get additional expertise, technology and products, so to welcome these benefits they provide great tax incentives for foreign investors, which ultimately suits all parties.
- Foreign investment reduces the disparity that exists between costs and revenues, especially, when they are calculated in different currencies.
- Though, this is not such a big factor, some markets prefer locally produced goods due to a strong sense of patriotism and nationalism, making it very hard for international enterprises to penetrate such a market. FDI helps enterprises to enter such markets and gain a foothold there.
- From the foreign affiliate's point of view, FDI is beneficial because they get advanced resources and additional capital at their disposal. It also helps to strengthen the political relationships between various nations.

Disadvantages of FDI

- Foreign investments are always risky because the political situation in some countries can change in an instant.

- In certain cases, political changes could lead to a situation of 'expropriation'. This refers to a scenario, where the government can take control of a firm's property and assets, if it feels that the enterprise is a threat to national security.
- Investing in foreign countries is infinitely more expensive than exporting goods.
- From the point of view of foreign affiliates, FDI is ill-advised because they loss their national identity.

Cost Benefit Analysis

It is a process by which business decisions are analysed. The benefits of a given situation or business related action are summed and then the costs associated with taking that action are subtracted.

Cost and benefits of FDI can be classified as two, which are as follows

Cost and Benefits of FDI to Host Country

Cost to Host Countries

- Cultural and political interference
- Unhealthy competition to domestic players
- Over utilisation of local resources
- Threat to indigenous technology
- Threat to local products

Benefits to Host Countries

- Improving the balance of payments
- Providing employment
- Sources of tax revenue
- Technology transfer
- Building of economic and social infrastructure

Cost and Benefits of FDI to Home Countries

Cost to Home Countries

- Risk from political changes
- Hindrance to domestic investment
- Economic non-viability
- Expropriation
- Investment abroad takes away employment opportunity

Benefits to Home Countries

- Access to markets
- Access to resources
- Reduce cost of production
- Investment incentives

FDI Policy of India

Government of India has taken various effective steps to simplify the foreign direct investment policy. The foreign direct investment policy of India prescribes the foreign investment cap in specified industrial sectors. But in recent times, many activities have been transferred to unrestricted sectors in which 100%, FDI is permitted.

Broadly the industrial sectors are categorised as

Restricted Sectors

- Banking public sector and defense industry
- Broadcasting content service, print media and cable networks
- Petroleum and natural gas
- Scheduled air transport service, insurance, private security agencies, multi brand retail trading

Prohibited Sectors

- Lottery business including government/private lottery, online lotteries etc.
- Gambling and betting including casinos etc.
- Chit funds, Nidhi company, trading in transferrable development rights, real estate business
- Manufacturing of cigars, cheroots, tobacoo etc.
- Activities/Sectors not open to private sector investment are atomic energy and railway operations.

Unrestricted Sectors All the sectors other than those mentioned below, subject to terms and conditions in the FDI policy, come under unrestricted sectors. *It covers the following*

- Mining (except mining and mineral separation of titanium bearing mineral and uses).
- Manufacturing related commercial activities.
- Information technology related activities.
- E-commerce (permitted in marketplace model and not the inventory based model. Also, it applies only to Business-to-Business e-commerce and not business to commerce-e-commerce).

Trends of FDI in India

Foreign direct investment in India is the most influential financial resource, especially for the emerging sectors. Foreign direct investment helps in exploiting a wide range of opportunities and utilizing the same to attain the desired level of development in the nation. The world economy including both the developed countries and other emerging countries are facing some varying trends of foreign direct investment in recent years.

Analyzing the trend of foreign direct investment in India shows that it is rising and the main reasons for such an increase are due to new government policies and various initiatives such as Make in India. The country has faced elevated trends of the foreign direct investment due to building investor-friendly climate in the country, thereby enabling the ease to doing business.

Foreign Portfolio Investment

It is the passive holdings of securities such as foreign stocks, bonds or other financial assets, none of which entails active management or control of the securities issues by the investor.

In 1992, India opened up its economy and allowed foreign portfolio investment in its domestic stock market. It has emerged as a major source of private capital inflow in this country.

Advantages of Foreign Portfolio Investment

- It gives investors an opportunity to engage in international diversification of portfolio assets, which in turn helps to achieve a higher risk adjusted return. This means that an investor who has stocks in different countries will experience less volatility over the entire portfolio.
- Investors who have foreign investment portfolios have a broader credit base because they can access credit in foreign countries, where they have significant investments.
- International currency exchange rates keep changing. Sometimes the currency of the investor's home country may be strong and sometimes it may weak.

Disadvantages of FPI

- Political risk represented by the possibility of change in the political environment resulting in change in investment norms and repatriation regulation.
- Emerging markets which are the beneficiaries of most FPI traditionally suffer from low retail participation which results in inadequate liquidity which results in price volatility.
- Due to unpredictable nature of such funds there is a tendency to shift from one market to another at short intervals.
- Emerging economics tend to have depreciation prove currencies. These exposes the foreign investor to exchange rate risk on both principal and returns.

Difference between FDI and FPI

Basis	FDI	FPI
Meaning	It refers to the investment made by the foreign investors to obtain a substantial interest in the enterprise located in different country.	When an international investor, invests in the passive holdings of an enterprise of another country it is known as FPI.
Role of Investors	Investors are active.	Investors are passive.
Degree of Control	It is highly controlled.	It is not highly controlled.
Term	It is a long-term process.	It is a short-term process.
Investment	Investment is made in physical assets.	Investment is made in financial assets.

Balance of Payment (BoP)

The Balance of Payment (BoP) is a comprehensive record of economic transactions of the residents of a country with the rest of the world during a given period of time usually one year.

According to **Kindleberger**, "Balance of payment as a systematic record of all economic transactions between the residents of the reporting country and residents of foreign countries during a given period of time."

A consistently positive BoP reflects more foreign investment and money coming into the country and not much of its currency being exported. On the other hand, adverse or negative BoP indicates more outflows of money compared to inflows. Theoretical records of balance of payment is kept in standard double entry book keeping under which each transaction undertaken by residents of a country results in a debit and a credit of equal size. In the BoP sheet, currency inflows are recorded as credits(+), whereas outflows are recorded as debits(–).

Characteristics of Balance of Payment

- It is a way of listing receipts and payments in international transactions of a country.
- It adopts a double entry book keeping system. It has two sides, debit and credit. Payments are recorded on the debit side and receipts on the credit side.
- In the accounting sense, debit and credit will always balance each other.
- *It contains two sets of account*
  (a) Current account (b) Capital account.
- Real and short-term transactions are recorded under current account. Capital account records all financial and long-term transactions.

Importance of Balance of Payment

- It analyses the business transactions of any economy into exports or imports of goods and services for a particular financial year.
- The government can adopt some protective measures such as higher tariff and duties on imports, so as to discourage imports of non-essential items and eneourage the domestic industries to be self-sufficient.
- If the economy needs support in the form of imports the government can formulate appropriate policies to divert the critical sectors of the economy that can drive future growth.
- If the country has a flourishing export trade, the government can adopt measures such as devaluation of its currency to make its goods and services available in the international market at cheaper rates and bolster exports.
- The government can also use the indications from balance of payments to discuss the state of the economy and formulate its policies of inflation control, monetary and fiscal policies based on that.

Components of Balance of Payment

Current Account

Current account or income account of BoP includes the flow of all goods and services between one country and the rest of the world.

It includes

- Commodity imports and exports
- Service imports and exports

The current account is usually subdivided into visible and invisibles. Visible items refer to goods, *i.e.* those we can see and touch when they cross international borders invisible items refer to all those services, which we cannot see or touch like insurance and banking services.

Current account consists of

Merchandise Exports and Imports Merchandise exports include the sale of goods to foreign countries. Most of these transactions are on credit basis. All these transactions give rise to monetary claims on foreign importing companies. These claims are credits. While, merchandise imports include purchase of goods from foreign countries.

Travel The credit item under travel covers expenditure incurred by non-residents travellers during their stay in the country. It excludes international passenger services, which are included in transportation.

Transportations This item covers all receipts and payments attributable to international transportation services on freight and shipping account except for the freight on imports invoiced CIF, which is included under imports. These data are derived from transportation transactions reported in exchange control records.

Insurance The entries against this item cover all receipts and payments on life and general insurance and reinsurance excepting payments for marine insurance in respect of imports invoiced CIF, which are booked under import payments.

Investment Income Credits represent income received by Indian residents from the ownership of foreign financial assets while debit represent income paid to non-residents acquiring from their ownership of financial assets in India.

Government not Included Elsewhere Official transactions in goods and services, which are not classified in the current account transactions elsewhere, are included here.

Transfer Payments The entries represent all receipts and payments without a quid pro quo.

The basic significance of the current account in BoP is that on the credit side, it represents the current international income from goods and services and on the debit side, it represents the current international expenditure on goods and services. In current account, most important item is visible trade. Balance of trade is the difference between merchandise exports and imports.

Capital Account

Capital account covers debts and the claims payable in money or those constituting money. It contains all changes in claims on or of a country owed by or owed to the rest of the world. Thus, if a resident invests or loans money abroad, then the rest of the world owes a claim to that resident, who in turn, has an equivalent asset. In other words, capital account is concerned with changes in claim of residents on overseas residents and changes in the liabilities of residents to overseas residents. All capital inflows are classified as credits and all capital outflows as debits.

Capital account may be divided into official and private account on the basis that private capital flows normally takes place in order to make profit or avoid loss. Official capital account are flows that are taking elsewhere in the BoP. *Capital account consists of*

Private Capital This item includes capital transactions of resident individuals, firms, privately owned non-financial corporate enterprises and non-bank financial enterprises, with non-residents including international institutions. Private capital is sub-divided into long-term and short-term.

Banking Capital This item covers changes in the foreign financial assets and liabilities of deposit money banks, comprising commercial banks, whether privately owned or state owned and such cooperative banks, which are authorised to deal in foreign exchange.

Official Capital It comprises transactions affecting foreign financial assets and liabilities of the Government of India and the Reserve Bank of India. *The capital transactions, thus covered under this item are classified into*

- Loans
- Amortisation
- Reserve
- Miscellaneous

Meaning of Deficit and Surplus in BoP

Autonomous transactions are those transactions, which are undertaken for their own sake, for the profits they give. Induced transactions are movement of reserves. International reserves serve the purpose of filling up gaps in BoP and we can measure the size of surplus or deficit by the volume of reserve payments.

A deficit appears in country's BoP when autonomous transactions requiring payments exceed autonomous transaction involving receipts. A surplus is said to arise when receipt from exports of goods and services exceed autonomous payments for similar items.

Any imbalance in the current account must be offset by appropriate action under the capital account. A deficit in the current account must be covered by surplus in the capital account, by borrowing from foreign countries, sale of gold and drawing down foreign exchange from the official reserves.

Similarly, a surplus in the current account must be eliminated by a deficit in the capital account by lending to foreigners, purchasing gold and adding to official reserves. The current account and capital account together will remain in balance.

BoP Equilibrium

It is that state of BoP over the relevant time period which makes it possible to sustain an open economy without severe unemployment on a continuing basis.

There are two kinds of equilibrium

Static Equilibrium It is the state in which exports equal imports including exports and imports of services as well as goods and other items on the BoP. Besides, the BoP equilibrium, there should also be an equilibrium in national money incomes. The foreign exchange rate must also be in equilibrium.

Dynamic Equilibrium The condition of dynamic equilibrium for short periods of time is that exports and imports differ by the amount of short-term capital movements and gold (net) and there are no large destabilising short-term capital movements.

The condition for dynamic equilibrium in the long-run is that exports and import differ by the amount of long-term autonomous capital movements made in a normal direction, *i.e.* from the low interest rate country to those with high rates.

BoP Disequilibrium

Cyclical Disequilibrium This is caused by countries having cyclical patterns of income or the same income pattern with different income elasticities or identical income patterns and income elasticities with different price elasticities.

Structural Disequilibrium It occurs on account of structural changes in some sectors of economy at home or abroad, which may alter the demand or supply relations of exports or imports or both. Structural disequilibrium at the factor level results from factor prices, which fail to reflect accurately factor endowments, *i.e.* when factor prices distort the structure of production.

Autonomous Capital Flows These are capital flow, which has no connection with the country's balance of payment situation. Autonomous capital flow takes place regardless of other items in the balance of payment. These are planned capital movements and depend on the rate of return available in the country, where capital is being invested. It is influenced by rate of interest in the economy, taxation policy and political climate of the country.

Accommodating Capital Flows These are capital flows that take place specially to equalise, the balance of payment in the book keeping. They are unplanned and unforeseen capital flows. These are ex-post in nature. Only at the end of the period can one discover whether accommodating capital inflow or outflow is needed.

Economic Policy In order to balance the BoP, country can not concentrate on current account or capital account. To reduce deficit on current account, government may devalue its currency, which will increase price of imports and decrease price of exports. Government can increase capital flow by increasing the rate of interest.

Measures for Correcting Disequilibrium in BoP

Expenditure Reducing Policies Such measures aim at reducing the domestic demand and income levels in order to curtail the demand for imports, depressing prices and encouraging exports in order to correct a disequilibrium in the form of deficit. In the case of a surplus in the BoP, there will be a rise in the level of domestic aggregate demand.

Expenditure Switching Policies These policies aim at shifting expenditure to goods produced at home and away from foreign goods. *Following are the expenditure switching policies*

- ***Devaluation*** It is reduction in the value of the domestic currency in relation to foreign currencies will make domestic goods cheaper to foreigner and raise the prices of foreign goods. So, exports will be encouraged and imports discouraged.
- ***Protection*** Imposition of tariffs, restriction of imports quotas and liberalisation of export subsidies etc may reduce imports and boost exports.

Balance of Trade

Balance of payment is different from balance of trade. Balance of trade means the balance of visible trade that is trade in goods on merchandise account over a given period. Thus, if exports exceed imports, the trade balance is said to be favourable, whereas an excess of imports over exports yields an unfavourable trade balance.

Thus, the BoP of a country is an economic barometer, which measures the country's economic life. It reveals to the government a true picture of the international economic position of the country. Although, BoP accounts is an economic indicator of the nation's international health, yet it is not appropriate to draw any conclusion concerning the property or poverty of a country merely on the basis of BoP.

Thus, surplus in BoP is no proof of country's prosperity and similarly a deficit is no indication of its economic degradation. The main purpose of keeping BoP records is to inform the government of the international economic position of the country and to help it in reaching decisions on monetary and fiscal policy on one hand and trade and payment on another.

EXAM BASED QUESTIONS

Foreign Direct Investment

1 Foreign direct investment involves
(a) intangible goods (b) tangible goods
(c) human resource (d) intellectual property

2 Foreign policy decision makers, for spreading their information, rely on
(a) public (b) media
(c) politician (d) bureaucrats

3 International trade brings developing countries in contact with
(a) developed nations (b) modern ideas
(c) developing countries (d) substainable growth

4 The spot rate of exchange is quoted for the immediate delivery of
(a) foreign treasury
(b) foreign exchange
(c) foreign rate
(d) foreign transactions

5 Which of the following statement is incorrect?
(a) In foreign direct investment, foreign companies develop new companies in home country
(b) Foreign companies open their subsidiaries in the country in FDI.
(c) FDI does not create capital in the domestic country
(d) FDI has favorable impact on production and employment in the state

6 Which of the following pairs is not correct?
(a) Items in the negative list of imports and exports are prohibited goods
(b) Permit issued by custom authorities to export goods is dock warrant
(c) Items which require license for export and import are restricted goods
(d) None of the above

7 Arrange the following steps of export procedure in chronological order.
1. Order acceptance
2. Order placement
3. Goods removal from works
4. Goods readiness and documentation goods

Codes
(a) 4, 3, 2, 1 (b) 2, 1, 4, 3
(c) 3, 1, 4, 2 (d) 3, 4, 1, 2

8 Which statement is true in relation to the way of the arrival of foreign direct investment in India?
(a) Automatic route in called Delhi route
(b) FIPB works under the ministry of industry
(c) In relationship to FDI coming through automatic route, no prior approval in required from the government or the Reserve Bank
(d) FIPB is authorised to approve the investment of upto 1,200 crore

9 Currently, in which areas is FDI in India prohibited?
1. Atomic energy
2. Lottery business
3. Gambling and betting
4. Chit fund trade
5. Nidhi company
6. Home and real estate business
7. Construction of cigars and business
8. Metro rail

Codes
(a) 1, 2, 3, 6, 7 and 8 (b) 1, 2, 3, 4, 7 and 8
(c) 1, 2, 3, 4, 5 and 8 (d) All of the above

10 In order to overcome the ambiguity of foreign direct investment and foreign institutional investment in India, four member committee has been appointed under the chairmanship of
(a) Manmohan Singh
(b) P Chidambaram
(c) Raghuram Rajan
(d) Arvind Mayaram

11 Which of the following can not be included in methods of FDI?
(a) Tax holidays
(b) Investment financial subsidies
(c) Horizontal FDI
(d) None of the above

12 Investors of FDI are
(a) active (b) non-active
(c) Both (a) and (b) (d) None of these

13 Which of the following statement is not correct?
(a) Many parent enterprise provide FDI because of the tax incentives that they got
(b) Acquiring shares are disintegrated from FDI
(c) Both (a) and (b)
(d) None of the above

14 Which of the following can be cost of home countries?
(a) Risk from political change
(b) Access to market
(c) Reduce cost of production
(d) None of the above

Balance of Payment

15 Mercantilism was known as .... in France.

(a) colbertism
(b) physiocratism
(c) cameralism
(d) None of the above

16 Which of the following is not balance of payment?

(a) Capital A/c (b) Loss A/c
(c) Current A/c (d) None of these

17 A debit balance of payment occurs due to

1. low imports and high exports.
2. high imports and low exports.

Select the correct answer using the codes given below

Codes

(a) Both 1 and 2 (b) Neither 1 nor 2
(c) Only 1 (d) Only 2

18 The balance of payment of a country on current account is equal to

(a) Balance of trade + Short-term capital flows
(b) Balance of trade + Net invisible exports
(c) Balance of payment – Capital flows
(d) Balance of invisible trade + Imports

19 The current account is made up of visibles and ....

(a) invisible (b) constraint
(c) expert (d) None of these

20 The effects of foreign trade on the domestic economy may be at

(a) micro level
(b) macro level
(c) Both (a) and (b)
(d) Neither (a) nor (b)

21 Rapid economic development or economic growth requires most efficient use of the

(a) country's resources
(b) foreign investment
(c) Both (a) and (b)
(d) None of the above

22 In balance of payment accounts, all goods exported and imported are recorded in

(a) Capital A/c (b) Visible A/c
(c) Invisible A/c (d) Merchandise A/c

23 The balance of payment is an .... system.

(a) social (b) accounting
(c) Both (a) and (b) (d) None of these

24 Which of the following are not components of BoP account?

(a) Current A/c
(b) Capital A/c
(c) Official reserves
(d) Profit and Loss A/c

25 Which of the following is part of current account?

(a) Merchandise exports
(b) Merchandise imports
(c) Both (a) and (b)
(d) Neither (a) nor (b)

26 Official reserves are comprised of gold, SDRs and .... foreign exchange.

(a) non-convertible (b) convertible
(c) semi-convertible (d) All of these

27 The capital account consists of

(a) loans
(b) investments
(c) other transfer financial assets
(d) All of the above

28 Which of the following is not the item of capital account?

(a) NRI deposits
(b) Official transfers
(c) Disbursement
(d) External assistance

29 Which of the following is not a type of disequilibrium in the balance of payment?

(a) Structural disequilibrium
(b) Secular disequilibrium
(c) Transactional disequilibrium
(d) Cyclical disequilibrium

30 The current account is made up of

(a) visibles
(b) invisibles
(c) Both (a) and (b)
(d) All of the above

31 The BoP is composed of two accounts. They are

(a) Capital A/c (b) Current A/c
(c) Company A/c (d) Both (a) and (b)

32 Physical delivery of foreign exchange has to take place in case of

(a) spot market (b) forward market
(c) future market (d) All of these

33 If a country has deficit in balance of current account, balance of capital account will be

(a) zero (b) surplus
(c) deficit (d) None of these

34 The BoP is a fund statement that reflects changes in assets, liabilities and net worth during a .... period.

(a) given (b) specified
(c) financial (d) None of these

35 The .... include the value of merchandise exports and the value of merchandise imports.

(a) goods account (b) service account
(c) liquidity account (d) None of these

36 The difference between the value of goods and services exported and imported by a country is the measure of

(a) balance of payment (b) balance of trade
(c) services account (d) None of the above

37 Which items are included in the negative list of imports?

(a) Canalised items (b) Banned items
(c) Restricted items (d) All of the above

38 The balance of payments account is conventionally divided into

(a) current account and capital account
(b) visible account and invisible account
(c) long-term capital account and short-term capital account
(d) None of the above

39 The devaluation of currency of a country is done when

1. it has adverse balance of payment.
2. it has favourable balance of payment.

Select the correct answer using the codes given below

Codes

(a) Both 1 and 2 (b) Neither 1 nor 2
(c) Only 1 (d) Only 2

40 Which of the following are items of invisible transaction?

(a) International transportation of goods including warehouse
(b) Travel for reasons of business, education, health etc
(c) Insurance premium and payment of claims
(d) All of the above

41 Which of the following is/are principles of valuation for BoP account?

(a) The transaction should be valued at market price
(b) Both imports and exports should be valued at FOB basis
(c) Both (a) and (b)
(d) None of the above

42 Which of the following statements is/are incorrect?

(a) Listing receipts and payments in international transaction for a country is called balance of trade
(b) In the balance of payment, gifts from foreigners is unrequited receipts
(c) Both (a) and (b)
(d) None of the above

43 Which of the following is not correct?

(a) The absorption approach to BoP explains changes in national income and their impact on BoP
(b) Monetary approach to BoP emphasises the role played by money supply in country's BoP
(c) Traditional approach to BoP explains the volumes of exports and imports of a country is determined by relative prices
(d) None of the above

44 Which of the following statements is incorrect?

(a) In the balance of payment, indemnities paid by foreigners is unrequited receipts
(b) In the balance of payment, gifts from foreigners is/are capital in flow
(c) Both (a) and (b)
(d) None of the above

45 The following table shows cost per unit of production of two goods, wheat and cloth in 2 countries X and Y with no transportation cost and free trade

	X (₹)	Y (₹)
Wheat	50	350
Cloth	100	500

Which one of the following will take place?

(a) No trade will take place
(b) X will export wheat and import cloth
(c) X will export cloth and import wheat
(d) There is no enough information to comment

Miscellaneous

Directions (Q. No. 46-49) *The following two questions consist of two statements, statement I and Statement II. You have to examine these two statements carefully, select the correct code.*

Codes

(a) Both statements are correct
(b) Both statements are incorrect
(c) Statement I is correct, but Statement II is incorrect
(d) Statement I is incorrect, but Statement II is correct

46 **Statement** I A bill of lading is a document of title to the goods.

Statement II A bill of lading contains all the terms and conditions agreed upon between the ship owner and the charterer.

47 **Statement** I Easy international trade is helps in smooth working of international trade.

Statement II Many parent enterprises provide FDI because of the tax incentives that get.

48 **Statement** I In 1992, India opened up its economy and allowed foreign portfolio investment in its domestic stock market.

Statement II It is a part of international trade.

49 **Statement** I The balance of payment is a comprehensive record of economic transactions of the residents of a country.

Statement II Balance of payment is different from balance of trade.

Directions (Q. No. 50-53) *In the questions given below are two statements labelled as Assertion (A) and Reason (R). In the context of the two statements, which one of the following is correct?*

Codes

(a) Both (A) and (R) are true, (R) is the correct explanation of (A).

(b) Both (A) and (R) true, but (R) is not correct explanation of (A).
(c) (A) is correct, but (R) is incorrect
(d) (A) is incorrect, but (R) is Correct.

50 Assertion (A) In BoP, every transaction has two aspects.
Reason (R) Since, for every credit there is corresponding debit and for every debit there is corresponding debit is explanatory.

51 Assertion (A) FDI simply refers to the act of investment capital in a business enterprise that operates overseas and in a foreign country.
Reason (R) It control in term of actual power of management and effective decision-making in the major areas of working.

52 Assertion (A) Current account or income account of BoP includes the flow of all goods and services.
Reason (R) The current account is usually sub-divided into visible and invisibles.

53 Assertion (A) Capital account covers debts and the claims payable in money or those.
Reason (R) Capital account may be divided into official and private account on the basis that private capital flows normally takes place in order to make profit or avoid loss.

54 Match the following.

List I	List II
A. Foreign trade	1. It is in undertaking by its issue that the bills of exchange drawn by the foreign dealer on the importer will be honoured on presentation upon a specified amount
B. Bill of lading	2. It is a document of title to the goods
C. Quotation	3. Trade between two or more nations
D. Letter of credit	4. It is reply by the seller to the prospective buyer

Codes

	A	B	C	D
(a)	4	1	2	3
(b)	3	2	4	1
(c)	2	3	4	1
(d)	4	3	2	1

55 Match the following.

List I	List II
A. Merchandise exports	1. Purchase of foreign goods
B. Merchandise imports	2. Sales of goods abroad
C. Investment income	3. Largely caused by excess of imports over exports in merchandise
D. Balance of payment deficits	4. Dividends, interest etc received from abroad

Codes

	A	B	C	D		A	B	C	D
(a)	1	2	3	4	(b)	2	3	4	1
(c)	2	1	4	3	(d)	3	4	2	1

56 Match the following.

List I (Concepts)	List II (Features)
A. Absolute advantage	1. State, in which exports equal imports
B. Balance of trade	2. Ability of a country to produce a good more efficiently
C. Static equilibrium	3. It is a long-term phenomenon
D. Secular disequilibrium	4. Difference between merchandise exports and imports

Codes

	A	B	C	D		A	B	C	D
(a)	3	2	4	1	(b)	3	4	1	2
(c)	2	4	1	3	(d)	4	3	2	1

57 Match the following.

List I	List II
A. FOB basis	1. Means of international payment
B. Official reserves	2. Price paid for insurance and shipment of goods should not be included as part of value of goods either by exporter or importer
C. Balance of payment manual	3. Principles or concepts to be followed by countries while compiling BoP data to ensure consistency
D. Bill of lading	4. Document of title of sale of goods

Codes

	A	B	C	D		A	B	C	D
(a)	2	1	3	4	(b)	1	2	3	4
(c)	3	2	1	4	(d)	4	3	2	1

PREVIOUS YEARS' QUESTIONS

December 2018

1 Foreign investment can be made through which of the following routes?

1. Foreign Direct Investment (FDI)
2. Foreign Portfolio Investment (FPI)
3. Private Equity Investment (PEI)
4. Foreign Venture Capital Investors (FVCI)

Choose the correct answer from the codes given below

Codes

(a) 1, 3 and 4 (b) Both 1 and 4
(c) 1, 2 and 4 (d) All of the above

2 Match the items of List I with the items of List II and choose the correct answer from the code given below.

List I	List II
A. Balance of trade	1. Imports and exports of goods and services and unilateral transfer of goods and services
B. Current account	2. Transactions leading to changes in the financial assets and liabilities of a country
C. Balance of payments	3. All economic transactions between a country's residents and residents of other countries
D. Capital account	4. Value of exports and imports of a country

Codes

	A	B	C	D
(a)	4	1	3	2
(b)	3	2	4	1
(c)	1	2	3	4
(d)	4	3	2	1

3 Match the items of List I with the items of List II and choose the correct answer from the code given below.

List I	List II
A. Direct investment overseas aimed at manufacturing products not manufactured by the firm in the home country	1. Inward FDI
B. Direct investment in a foreign country aimed to sell the output of the firm's domestic production	2. Backward Vertical FDI
C. Direct investment overseas aimed at providing inputs for the firms production process in the home country	3. Conglomerate FDI
D. Foreign firms investing overseas and taking control over foreign assets	4. Forward Vertical FDI

Codes

	A	B	C	D
(a)	4	3	2	1
(b)	1	4	2	3
(c)	3	4	2	1
(d)	3	2	1	4

December 2015

4 **Statement** I Companies with low cash reserves normally prefer licensing mode rather than foreign direct investment.

Statement II Cash rich firms normally prefer foreign direct investment.

Codes

(a) Both statements are true
(b) Both statements are false
(c) Statement I is true, but Statement II is false
(d) Statement I is not true, but Statement II is true

June 2014

5 The Foreign Investment Promotion Board (FIPB) revamps the rules and regulations pertaining to

(a) accounting of foreign investment
(b) investment by NRIs
(c) foreign investments
(d) All of the above

June 2012

6 Which one is not the form of FDI?

(a) Purchases of existing assets in foreign currency
(b) New investment in property, plant, equipment
(c) Making investment in the mutual funds
(d) Transfer of many types of assets

ANSWERS

Objective Questions

1 (b)	2 (b)	3 (a)	4 (b)	5 (c)	6 (b)	7 (b)	8 (c)	9 (d)	10 (d)
11 (c)	12 (a)	13 (b)	14 (a)	15 (a)	16 (b)	17 (c)	18 (a)	19 (a)	20 (c)
21 (a)	22 (b)	23 (b)	24 (d)	25 (c)	26 (b)	27 (a)	28 (b)	29 (c)	30 (c)
31 (d)	32 (a)	33 (b)	34 (b)	35 (a)	36 (b)	37 (d)	38 (b)	39 (a)	40 (d)
41 (c)	42 (a)	43 (d)	44 (b)	45 (d)	46 (c)	47 (a)	48 (a)	49 (d)	50 (a)
51 (b)	52 (a)	53 (b)	54 (b)	55 (c)	56 (c)	57 (a)			

Previous Years' Questions

1 (a)	2 (a)	3 (c)	4 (c)	5 (c)	6 (c)

CHAPTER

04

Regional Economic Integration and WTO

As different countries of the world are engaged in international business, they formed different regional groups like ASEAN, NAFTA etc. International trade is managed and controlled by different international organisations such as World Bank, WTO.

Regional Economic Integration

Regional economic integration is a process, in which states enter into a regional agreement in order to enhance regional cooperation through regional institutions and rules. In other words, it is an agreement among countries in a geographic region to reduce and ultimately remove tariff and non-tariff barriers to the free flow of goods or services and factors of production among each other.

The objectives of the agreement could range from economic to political to environmental factors, although it has typically taken the form of a political economy initiative, where commercial interests have been the focus for achieving broader socio-political and security objects, as defined by National Governments. Regional integration has been organised either *via* supranational institutional structures or through inter-governmental decision-making or a combination of both.

In this Chapter

- *Regional Economic Integration*
- *Regional Trade Agreements*
- *International Economic Institutions*
- *World Trade Organisation (WTO)*
- *Multinational Corporations*

Levels of Regional Economic Integration

Customs Union A customs union occurs when a group of countries agree to eliminate tariffs between themselves and a set of common external tariff on imports from the rest of the world.

Common Market It establishes free trade in goods and services, sets common external tariffs among members and also allows for the free mobility of capital and labour across countries.

Economic Union An economic union typically will maintain free trade in goods and services, set common external tariffs among members, allow the free mobility of capital and labour and will also relegate some fiscal spending responsibilities to a supranational agency.

Free Trade Area It occurs when a group of countries agree to eliminate tariffs between themselves, but maintain their own external tariff on imports from the rest of the world. The North American Free Trade Area is an example of a FTA.

Benefits of Regional Economic Integration

- Since, a regional common market obviously provides a much larger market that than offered by the domestic market of a single country, economies of scale, both internal and external, become possible with the widened size of the market.
- Secondly, the large market so created would permit a high degree of sophistication and specialisation of products conducive to furtherance of modern industrial development.
- Apart from an increase in the volume of total trade as a result of such an integration, a favourable change in the cost and price structure may also be effected alongwith, the desirable change in the structure and composition of foreign trade.
- Further more, this may facilitate the realisation of the optimum allocation of resources and thus, lead to an increase in efficiency in production.

Trade Creation and Diversion Effects

Trade Creation

Trade creation is the increased trade that occurs between member countries of trading blocs, following the formation or expansion of trading bloc. This comes about as the removal of trade barriers and allows greater specialisation according to comparative advantage.

Trade Diversion

Trade diversion is the decrease in trade, following the formation of a trading bloc as trade with low cost non-trading bloc members are replaced by trade with relatively high cost trading bloc members.

Trade creation and diversion are important direct effects of the formation of a customs union. Trade creation will mean that consumption shifts from a high cost producer to a low-cost producer and trade therefore expands. Trade diversion on the other hand means that trade shifts from a lower cost producer outside the union to a higher cost producer inside the union. This will not benefit consumers within the union as they are not getting access to cheaper international goods.

Regional Trade Agreements

A regional trade agreement is a treaty between two or more governments that define the rules of trade for all signatories. *The regional trade agreements are discussed ahead.*

European Union

The European Union is based on the rule of law and democracy. It is neither a new state replacing existing ones nor is it comparable to other international organisations. All decisions and procedures are derived from the basic traties ratified by the member's state.

The EU is a political and economic community of 27 member states, located primarily in Europe. It was established in 1993 by 'Treaty of Maastricht' adding new areas of policy to the existing European community.

Goals of European Union

- To continue to improve Europe's economy by regulating trade and commerce.
- To form a single market for Europe's economic resources.
- Environmental movements.
- Regulatory acts.
- Human rights concern.

European Communities (EC)

The European Communities (ECs) were three international organisations that were governed by the same set of institutions. These were the European Coal and Steel Community (ECSC), the European Economic Community (EEC) and the European Atomic Energy Community (EAEC or Euratom).

The European Communities operated as the largest of the EU's three pillars until the EEC (renamed the European Community in 1993) was absorbed when the pillar system was abolished and the European Union was designated as its legal successor.

Association of South-East Asian Nations (ASEAN)

ASEAN was established on 8th August, 1947 in Bangkok by the 5 original member countries. Indonesia, Malaysia, Philippines, Singapore and Thailand. Brunei Darussalam joined on 8th January, 1984, Vietnam on 28th July, 1995 Laos and Myanmar on 23rd July, 1997 and Cambodia on 30th April, 1999.

Objectives of ASEAN

- The ASEAN Declaration states that the aims and purposes of the association are to accelerate the economic growth, social progress and cultural development in the region through joint endeavours in the spirit of equality and partnership in order to strengthen the foundation for a prosperous and peaceful community of South-East Asian Nations.
- To promote regional peace and stability through abiding respect for justice and the rule of law in the relationship among countries in the region and adherence to the principles of the united nations charter. In 1995, the ASEAN heads of State and Government re-affirmed that 'cooperative peace and shared prosperity shall be the fundamental goals of ASEAN'.

Fundamental Principles of ASEAN

The Treaty of Amity and Cooperation (TAC) in South-East Asia, signed at the first ASEAN summit on 24th February, 1976, declared that in their relations with one another, *the high contracting parties should be guided by the following fundamental principles*

- Mutual respect for the independence, sovereignty, equality, territorial integrity and national identity of all nations.
- The right of every state to lead its national existence free for external interference, subversion or coercion.
- Non-interference in the internal affairs of one another.
- Settlement of differences or disputes by peaceful manner.
- Renunciation of the threat or use of force.

South Asian Association for Regional Cooperation (SAARC)

SAARC is an organisation of South Asian nations, which was established on 8th December, 1985, when the government of Bangladesh, Bhutan, India, Maldives, Nepal, Pakistan and Sri Lanka formally adopted its charter providing for the promotion of economic and social progress, cultural development within the South Asia region and also for friendship and cooperation with other developing countries. It is dedicated to economic, technological, social and cultural development emphasising collective self-reliance. Afghanistan joined the organisation in 2007. Meetings of heads of state are usually scheduled annually and meetings of foreign secretaries are held twice in a year. It is headquartered in Kathmandu, Nepal.

Objectives of SAARC

- To promote the welfare of the people of South Asia and to improve their quality of life.
- To accelerate economic growth, social progress and cultural development in the region and to provide all individuals the opportunity to live in dignity and to realise their full potential.
- To promote and strengthen selective self-reliance among the countries of South Asia.
- To contribute to mutual trust, understanding and appreciation of one another's problems.
- To promote active collaboration and mutual assistance in the economic, social, cultural, technical and scientific fields.
- To strengthen cooperation with other developing countries.
- To strengthen cooperation among themselves in international forums on matters of common interest.
- To cooperate with international and regional organisations with similar aims and purposes.
- To maintain peace in the region.

Principles of SAARC

- Respect for sovereignty, territorial integrity, political equality and independence of all member states.
- Non-interference in the internal matters is one of its objectives.
- Cooperation for mutual benefit.
- All decisions to be taken unanimously and need a quorum of all 8 members. All bilateral issues to be kept aside and only multilateral issues to be discussed without being prejudiced by bilateral issues.

North American Free Trade Agreement (NAFTA)

Implementation of the North American Free Trade Agreement (NAFTA) began on 1st January, 1994. This agreement's objective is to remove most barriers to trade and investment among the United States, Canada and Mexico.

NAFTA covers Canada, the US and Mexico making it the world's largest free trade area (in terms of GDP). NAFTA was launched 20 years ago to reduce trading costs, increase business investment and help North America be more competitive in the global market 'place'. As on 1st January, 2008 all tariffs, between three countries were eliminated.

NAFTA was signed by President George HW Bush, Mexican President Salinas and Canadian Prime Minister Brian Mulroney in 1992. It was ratified by the legislatures of the three countries in 1993.

The US House of representatives approved it by 284 to 200 on 17th November, 1993. It was signed into law by President Bill Clinton on 8th December, 1993 and came into force on 1st January, 1994.

Purpose of NAFTA

Article 102 of the NAFTA agreement outlines its purpose

- Grant the signatories most favoured nation status.
- Eliminate barriers to trade and facilitate the cross border movement of goods and services.
- Promote conditions of fair competition.
- Increase investment opportunities.
- Provide protection and enforcement of intellectual property rights.
- Create procedures for the resolution of trade disputes.
- Establish a framework for further trilateral, regional and multilateral cooperation to expand NAFTA's benefits.

International Economic Institutions

Frequent changes in exchange rates introduce considerable uncertainty and make things difficult for the smooth conduct of international trade. Exchange rates should be reasonably stable for smooth conduct of international trade. This can be achieved if countries, particularly developed countries cooperate with each other. International cooperation is the basis of a sound international monetary system.

Cooperation in the monetary field refers to the joint efforts by a group of countries at regional or international level or both to resolve the problem of international payments either through bilateral or multilateral agreements among themselves or by setting-up an international organisations.

Some of these international organisations are

International Monetary Fund (IMF)

The IMF is an international monetary organisation, which came into existence in 27th December, 1945. The decision to set-up the IMF was taken at United Nations Monetary and Financial Conference of 45 countries held at the Bretton Woods in New Hampshire. Its headquarter is in Washington DC and is governed by and accountable to the government of countries that make-up its near global membership. The governments represented at that conference sought to build a framework for economic cooperation that would avoid a repetition of the disastrous economic policies that had contributed to the great depression of the 1930s.

The IMF was established to promote the health of the world economy, international monetary cooperation, exchange stability and orderly exchange arrangements to foster economic growth and high levels of employment and to provide financial assistance to countries to ease the Balance of payment adjustments. Currently, IMF has 188 members.

Objectives of IMF

Objectives of IMF according to 'Articles of Agreement' provide framework within which the fund function. *These are*

- To promote international monetary cooperation.
- To ensure exchange rate stability.
- To ensure balanced international trade.
- To eliminate or to minimise exchange restrictions by promoting the system of multilateral payments.
- To grant economic assistance to member countries for eliminating the adverse imbalance in BoP.
- To minimise imbalance in quantum and duration of international trade.

Constitution, Membership and Capital of IMF

Board of Governors controls and manages IMF. The Board of Governors is the group of Governors nominated by every country. Each country also nominates an alternate Governor, who his vote in the absence of the Governor. In the capital of IMF, each Governor is allotted a number of votes, which is determined by the quotta allotted to the respective country. On the basis of membership, each Governor has got the right of 250 votes and additional vote for each SDR 1,00,000. IMF allots quote to each country member, which has to be deposited portly in the member's own currency and the remainder in the form of foreign exchange.

Functions of IMF

The IMF operates in such a way as to fulfill its objectives as laid down in the Bretton Woods Articles of Agreement. It is the IMF's duty to see that these provisions are observed by member countries.

The functions are as follows

- The fund is regarded as the guardian of good conduct in sphere of BoP. It aims at reducing tariffs and other trade transaction by member countries.
- To have a surveillance of the policies being adopted by member countries. IMF should see that without its approval no member shall impose restrictions on making of payments or engage in discriminatory currency arrangements or multiple currency practices.

- To create a system of stable exchange rates with orderly cross rates. Change in exchange rate of ±1 will require IMF's permission.
- Besides performing regulatory and consultative functions, IMF acts as an important financial institution. The bulk of its financial resources comes from a quota subscription of member countries. Besides, it increases its funds by selling gold to its members.

India and IMF

India is one of the founder member of IMF. It signed the Fund Agreements on 27th December, 1945. Till 1970, India's quota in the fund was fifth and it had the power to appoint a permanent executive director. With the increase in fund quota after May 1970, the quota of Japan, Canada and Italy increased more than that of India.

Accordingly, India ceased to hold a permanent position as executive director of the fund. India is represented in IMF by an executive director, who also represents Bangladesh, Sri Lanka and Bhutan.

India has been one of the major beneficiaries of the fund assistance. It has been getting aid from the various fund agencies from time to time and has been regularly repaying its debts. Majorly, India has been borrowing to overcome BoP difficulties. India has also taken technical consultancy for solving its internal economic problem. The expert groups of the IMF have visited India on various occasions.

SDRs Allotment and Holding by India

India was allocated in million SDRs as part of India's allocation from SDRs created so far by IMF. The IMF members can either retain SDR, use them in payments etc or sell them to other members of countries. IMF remunerates the members holding SDRs by charging all the members for SDRs allocated to them .

Achievements of IMF

- The IMF has provided an excellent forum for the discussion and solution of the economic, fiscal and financial problems having an international aspect.
- Promoted expansion of international trade.
- Promoted exchange stability and at the same time proving an orderly adjustment of exchange rates.
- Simplified to some extent multiple exchange system.
- Liberalised the use of its resources by members in number of ways.
- It has accelerated the pace of economic development and economic growth of under developed countries.
- Further IMF has been instrumental in promoting steady progress towards the establishment of a multilateral system of payments in respect of current transactions.

World Bank

The International Bank for Reconstruction and Development (IBRD) known popularly as the World Bank was set-up at the same time as the IMF at the United Nations Monetary and Financial Conference held at Bretton Woods, New Hampshire in July, 1944. It began, its operation in June, 1946. It is an international agency owned by governments, which operated by Board of Governor making long-term loans to member countries and finance productive investment in member countries.

Since, the IMF was designed to provide temporary assistance in correcting balance of payments difficulties and institutions was also needed to assist long-term investment purpose. Thus, IBRD was established for promoting long-term investment loans on reasonable terms. The World Bank is an inter-governmental institution, corporate in form, the capital stock of which is entirely owned by its member governments. Initially, only nations that were members of the IMF could be members of the World Bank, this restriction on membership was subsequently relaxed.

Objectives of World Bank

- To help in the reconstruction and development of member countries by facilitating the investment of capital for the productive purposes including the restoration and reconstruction of economies devastated by war.
- To provide encouragement to the development of productive resources of less developed countries.
- To promote private foreign investment by means such as participation in loans or guarantee for loans made by private investors.
- To promote long-term balanced growth of international trade and the maintenance of equilibrium in the BoP of members countries by encouraging long-term international investments.
- To help in raising productivity, standard of living and conditions of labour in member countries.
- To make arrangements for loans or guarantees in respect of international loans.

The World Bank Group

In addition to IBRD and IDA, three other organisations make up the World Bank group which are

International Financial Corporation (*IFC*) It promotes private sector investment by supporting high risk sectors of the countries.

The Multilateral Investment Guarantee Agency (*MIGA*) It provides political risk insurance to investors and lenders in developing countries.

The International Centre for Settlement of Investment Disputes (ICSID) It settles investment disputes between foreign investors and their host countries.

Organisation of the World Bank

Board of Governors All the powers of the bank are vested in Board of Governors, which is the supreme policy making body of the bank. The board consists of one Governor and one alternate Governor appointed for 5 years by each member country. Each Governor has the voting power, which is related to the financial contribution of the government, which he represents. The Board of Governors meets annually to check out the general policy of the bank.

Board of Executive Directors The Board of Executive Directors consists of 21 members, 5 of them are appointed by permanent members like America, France, London, Japan and Germany for two years. The rest of 16 members are elected by the remaining countries. Each executive director holds voting power in proportion to the shares held by its government. The Board of Executive Directors meet regularly once a month to carry on the routine working of the bank.

Advisory Council The advisory council is appointed by the Board of Directors. It consists of 7 members from member countries who are expert in commerce, industry, banking, agriculture, labour, transportation and law.

Loan Committee This committee recommend loan required by member country.

President and Other Members of Staff The President of the bank is appointed by Board of Directors. He is the Chief Executive of the bank and is responsible for the conduct of the day-to-day business of the bank.

World Bank's Lending Operations

The World Bank advances loans to members in any of the following three ways

Loans Out of its Own Funds The bank collects contribution from its members and also raises money through bonds to advance loans to needy members. If the loan is to be given to a member country in terms of the national currency of other country, then it is obligatory for bank to obtain consent of that country.

Loans Out of Borrowed Capital Sometimes, bank grants loans by borrowing from other member countries. The bank pays interest to the member country from, which it has borrowed funds for specified period of time.

Loans through Bank's Guarantee Sometimes, the bank encourages the private investors of a country to lend their funds to another country by guaranteeing the repayment of loans and interest. But before the bank give guarantee, it has to secure the consent of both the countries involved in the transaction, the country to which the private investors belong and the country, to which loans is proposed to be given.

India and the World Bank

India is one of the founder member of the World Bank. It has been allotted a permanent place in the Board of Executive Directors of the bank. The bank has also appointed a Resident Representative in New Delhi to maintain close liaison with the Government of India in regard to the development plans and projects of the country.

India is the highest cumulative borrower of World Bank loan assistance was given for the improvement of transport, power projects, agriculture, technical assistance for effective implementation of its development plans. Recently, it has discontinues programme aid to India, which was extended to meet the foreign currencies requirements as India's foreign exchange reserves mounted.

United Nations Conference on Trade and Development (UNCTAD)

The UNCTAD is established as a principal organ of General Assembly of the United Nations. However, it has its own subsidiary bodies and also a full-time secretariat. It has a permanent organ called trade and development board as the main executive body. It meets twice anually.

It is composed of 195 members, elected by the conference from among its members on the basis of equitable geographical distribution.

Functions of UNCTAD

- To promote international trade all over the world between developed and developing countries with different socio-economic systems to accelerate economic development.
- To formulate principles and policies on international trade and related problems of economic development.
- To make proposals for putting the said principle and policies into effect.
- Generally, to review and facilitate the coordination of activities of other institutions within the UN system in the field of international trade.
- To be available as centre for harmonious trade and related documents in development policies of governments.

World Trade Organisation (WTO)

The World Trade Organisation (WTO) was established on 1st January, 1995. The World Trade Organisation is an international organisation that establishes rules for international trade thorough consensus among its member states. It also resolves disputes between the members, which are all signatories to its set of trade agreement. The WTO states that its aims are to increase International Trade by promoting power trade barriers and providing a platform for the negotiation of trade and to their business. The WTO is the embodiment of the Uruguay round results and the successor to GATT.

The administration of WTO is conducted by the secretariat, which is headed by the Director General appointed by the Ministerial Conference for the tenure of 4 years. He is assisted by the four Deputy Directors from different member countries. The annual budget estimates and financial statement of the WTO are presented by the Director General to the CBFA for review and recommendations for the final approval by the General Council.

Objectives of WTO

- To improve standard of living of people in the member countries.
- To ensure full employment and broad increase in effective demand.
- To enlarge production and trade of goods.
- To enlarge production and trade of services.
- To ensure optimum utilisation of world resources.
- To accept the concept of sustainable development.
- To protect the environment.

Functions of WTO

- To provide facilities for implementation administration, and operation of multilateral and bilateral agreements of the world trade.
- To provide a platform to member countries to decide future strategies related to trade and tariff.
- To administer the rules and processes related to dispute settlement.
- To implement rules and provisions related to trade policy review mechanism.
- To assist IMF and IBRD for establishing coherence in universal economic policy determination.
- To ensure the optimum use of world resource.
- To facilitate the expansion and balanced growth of international trade.

WTO Agreements

Agriculture Agreement

The WTO agreement on agriculture contains provisions in 3 broad areas of agriculture and trade policy, *which are as follows*

Market Access This include tariffication, tariff reduction and access opportunities. Tariffication means that all non-tariff barriers such as quotas, variable levies, minimum import prices, discretionary licensing need to be abolished and converted into an equivalent tariff.

Domestic Support For domestic support policies, subject to reduction commitments the total support given in 1986-88, measured by total aggregate measure of support should be reduced by 20% in developed countries.

Export Subsidies The agreement contains provisions regarding members commitment to reduce export subsidies. Developed countries are required to reduce their export subsidy expenditure by 36% and volume by 21% in 6 years in equal installments.

Agreement on Trade Related Aspects of Intellectual Property Rights (TRIPS)

The TRIPS agreement came into effect on 1st January, 1995. The areas of intellectual property that in covers are copyright and related rights performers, producers of sound recording etc. *The main features of the agreement are*

Standards The agreement sets out the minimum standards of protection to be provided by each member. Each of the main elements of protection is defined, namely the subject-matter to be protected, the rights to be conferred and permissible exceptions to those rights and the minimum duration of protection.

Enforcement The second main set of prouisions deal with domestic procedures and remedies for the enforcement of intellectual property rights. The agreement lays down certain general principles applicable to all IPR enforcement procedure.

Dispute Settlement The agreement makes disputes between WTO members about the respect of the TRIPS obligations subject to the WTO's dispute settlement procedures.

Agreement on Trade Related Investment Measures (TRIMs)

The agreement on TRIMs of the WTO is based on the belief that there is strong connection between trade and investment. Restrictive measures on investment are trade distorting. According to the TRIMs provision, countries should not adopt the investment measures which restrict and distort trade.

Investment measures are those steps used traditionally against foreign investment by host countries. Hence, the TRIMs instruct that WTO members may not apply any measure that discriminates against foreign investment that violates basic WTO principle.

The objective of TRIMs is to ensure fair treatment of investment in all member countries. As per the TRIMs agreement, members are required to notify the WTO council for trade in goods of their existing TRIMs that are inconsistent with the agreement.

General Agreement on Trade in Services (GATS)

The general agreement on trade in services is a treaty of the world trade organisation that entered into force in January 1995 as a result of the Uruguay Round Negotiations.

The treaty was created to extend the multilateral trading system to service sector, in the same way the general agreement or tariffs and trade provides such a system for merchandise trade. All members of the WTO are parties to the GATS.

The four modes of services supply

Mode 1 : Cross border services which themselves cross frontiers from one country to another.

Mode 2 : Consumption abroad services, which are made available within a country for foreign consumers.

Mode 3 : Commercial presence services supplied by an entity of one country, which is commercially pressed in another.

Mode 4 : Movements of natural persons This is a foreign national services, i.e. doctor, nurse, IT engineer etc.

Multinational Corporations (MNCs)

Multinational Corporations (MNCs) are the corporations that operate in more than one country. The model of a MNCs is dynamic offering both benefits and detriment factors to our society. In other words, "A corporation that has its facilities and other assets in at least one country other than its home country". Such companies have offices and for factories in different countries and usually have a certralised head office where they co-ordinate global management. Very large multinationals have budgets that exceed those of many countries. It is sometimes referred to as a 'transnational corporation'. Multinational Corporations (MNCs) are also known as Transnational Corporations (TNCs), super national enterprises, global companies and so on.

According to Professor **John H Dunning**, "A multinational enterprise is one, which undertakes foreign direct investment, *i.e.* which owns or controls income gathering assets in more than one country; and in so doing produces goods or services outside its country of origin, *i.e.* engages in international production."

Advantages of MNCs for the Host Country

- The investment level, employment level and income level of the host country increases.
- The industries of host country get latest technology from foreign countries through MNCs.
- The host country business also gets management expertise from MNCs.
- The domestic traders and market intermediaries of the host country gets increased business.
- Level of industrial and economic development increases due to the growth of MNCs in the host country.

Disadvantages of MNCs for the Host Country

- MNCs may transfer technology, which has become outdated in the home country.
- As MNCs do not operate within the national autonomy, they may pose a threat to the economic and political sovereignty of host countries.
- MNCs may kill the domestic industry by monopolising the host country's market.
- In order make profit, MNCs may use natural resources of the home country indiscriminately and cause depletion of the resources.
- A large sum of money flows to foreign countries in terms of payments towards profits, dividends and royalty.

Advantages of MNCs for the Home Country

- MNCs create opportunities for marketing the products produced in the home country throughout the world.
- They create employment opportunities to the people of home country both at home and abroad.
- It gives a boost to the industrial activities of home country.
- MNCs help to maintain favourable balance of payment of the home country in the long run.

Disadvantages of MNCs for the Home Country

- MNCs transfer the capital from the home country to various host countries causing unfavourable Balance of Payment.
- MNCs may not create employment opportunities to the people of home country if it adopts geocentric approach.
- As investments in foreign countries is more profitable, MNCs may neglect the home country's industrial and economic development.

EXAM BASED QUESTIONS

Regional Economic Integration and Regional Trade Agreements

1 Which article of the NAFTA agreement outlines its purpose?

(a) Article 103 (b) Article 101
(c) Article 102 (d) Article 104

2 Brunei Darussalam joined ASEAN on

(a) 23rd July, 1997 (b) 8th January, 1984
(c) 30th April, 1999 (d) None of these

3 SAARC helps to strengthen cooperation with other

(a) developed countries (b) developing countries
(c) underdeveloped countries (d) None of these

4 SAARC was established on

(a) 8th December, 1985 (b) 4th December, 1985
(c) 8th December, 1993 (d) None of these

5 Which of the following statements is correct?

(a) ASEAN was established in Bangkok
(b) Originally, ASEAN had 7 members countries
(c) Both (a) and (b)
(d) All of the above

6 NAFTA was signed by

(a) George HW Bush
(b) Mexican President Salinas
(c) Canadian Prime Minister Brian Mulroney
(d) All of the above

7 Which of the following statements is/are incorrect?

(a) ASEAN was established in Bangkok
(b) ASEAN had originally 6 members countries
(c) Combodia joined ASEAN on 23rd July, 1997
(d) None of the above

8 Which of the following is/are not correct?

(a) SAARC helps to promote the welfare of the people of South Asia
(b) NAFTA helps to promote conditions of fair competition
(c) ASEAN helps to promote regional peace and stability
(d) None of the above

9 Which of the following statements is/are incorrect?

(a) NAFTA grant the signatories most favoured nation status
(b) Cooperation for mutual benefit is the principle of ASEAN
(c) Both (a) and (b)
(d) All of the above

10 Which of the following statements is incorrect?

(a) NAFTA began on 1st January, 1994
(b) NAFTA was launched 20 years ago
(c) NAFTA will remove most barriers to trade and investment among US, Canada and Mexico
(d) None of the above

11 Which of the following statements is incorrect?

(a) NAFTA began on 1st January,1994
(b) NAFTA covers Canada, the US and Mexico
(c) NAFTA was launched 25 years ago to reduce trading costs
(d) None of the above

12 Which of the following statements is/are incorrect?

(a) Regional economic integration facilitate the realisation of the optimum allocation of resources
(b) Regional common market provides a largest market to all
(c) Regional integration facilitates desirable change in composition of foreign trade
(d) All of the above

13 Arrange the following organisations in the increasing order of their establishment years.

1. SAARC 2. NAFTA 3. ASEAN

Codes

(a) 3, 2, 1 (b) 3, 1, 2 (c) 2, 3, 1 (d) 1, 2, 3

14 Which conference gave birth to the IMF?

(a) Bretton Woods Conference
(b) Agency of United Nations
(c) Uruguay Round Conference
(d) None of the above

15 Which of the following is/are not the objective of IMF?

(a) Removal of disparities in international payment
(b) Imposition of trade tariff
(c) Imposition of exchange control
(d) Both (b) and (c)

16 Which country can take the membership of IMF?

(a) A developed country
(b) A developing country
(c) Under developed countries
(d) Any country who follow the rule of IMF

17 Which of the following is not an international financial institution?

(a) ICICI (b) IMF
(c) IDA (d) World Bank

18 India is the .... member of IMF.

(a) progressive
(b) founder
(c) additional
(d) active

19 Who may be Governor of IMF?
(a) Governor of Central Bank of private country
(b) President of a particular country
(c) Both (a) and (b)
(d) Neither (a) nor (b)

20 Board of executive director of IMF may be appointed for
(a) 6 years (b) 2 years
(c) 8 years (d) None of these

21 The quotas of all the member countries with IMF are valued in terms of
(a) SDR (b) Dollar
(c) Both (a) and (b) (d) None of these

22 Which of the following bodies are of IMF?
(a) Board of Governors (b) Executive Board
(c) Managing Director (d) All of these

23 The quotas of all the member countries with the IMF are valued in terms of
(a) SDR (b) GDR (c) Dollar (d) Swaps

24 In which of the following year, the Articles of Agreement of IMF were changed for the first time
(a) 1967 (b) 1968
(c) 1969 (d) None of these

25 Which of the following statement(s) is/are incorrect?
(a) Currently, IMF has 187 members
(b) Each member country of IMF nominates a Governor
(c) Both (a) and (b)
(d) None of the above

26 India has the power to appoint a permanent executive director in the .... on the Board of Directors.
(a) IMF (b) IBRD
(c) ADB (d) None of these

27 World Bank provides loan to the member country
(a) from own funds (b) from borrowings
(c) by guarantee (d) All of these

28 The World Bank is formed as .... body of IMF.
(a) supplementary (b) complementary
(c) legal (d) None of these

29 The World Bank began its operation in
(a) June, 1950
(b) June, 1946
(c) July, 1944
(d) August, 1950

30 Associate institutions of World Bank are
(a) IDA (b) IFC
(c) IMF (d) Both (a) and (b)

31 World Bank grant loans from
(a) own funds
(b) borrowed funds
(c) by guaranteeing in whole or part loans made by private investors through the investment channels
(d) All of the above

32 Which of the following countries are 'Blend Borrowers'?
(a) India (b) Indonesia
(c) Both (a) and (b) (d) Neither (a) nor (b)

33 The World Bank gives financial assistance only to its
(a) member countries (b) Managing Director
(c) staff. (d) Governor

34 Companies benefit from direct investment by
(a) access to foreign markets
(b) access to foreign resources
(c) Both (a) and (b)
(d) Neither (a) nor (b)

35 One Governor and one Substitute Governor of World Bank is appointed for
(a) 2 years (b) 5 years
(c) 7 years (d) None of these

36 The World Bank is owned by
(a) member countries (b) United States of America
(c) Both (a) and (b) (d) Neither (a) nor (b)

37 The SDRs can be used .... by the participating countries.
(a) freely (b) unconditionally
(c) conditionally (d) All of these

38 Countries joining World Bank after 31st December, 1945 come under category of
(a) founder member (b) general member
(c) temporary member (d) permanent member

39 The World Bank and the IDA are .... International Financial Institutions.
(a) private (b) complementary
(c) different (d) same

40 Long-term financial assistance for development purpose is provided by
(a) IMF (b) World Bank
(c) ADB (d) WTO

41 Which institution is known as the 'soft loan window' of World Bank?
(a) IMF (b) IFC
(c) IDA (d) None of these

42 In 1958, bank established .... for providing specific economic assistance to India.
(a) India Aid Club
(b) India Development Forum
(c) Both (a) and (b)
(d) None of the above

International Economic Institutions

43 Countries who are eligible for both IDA assistance due to low per capita income and credit worthy for some IBRD borrowing are called
(a) conditional borrower (b) blend borrowers
(c) participating borrowers (d) None of these

44 Each country in IMF nominates a (an) .... Governor who casts vote in the absence of the Governor.
(a) additional
(b) casual
(c) alternate
(d) None of the above

45 Each Governor of IMF has got the right of
(a) 250 votes + One additional vote for each SDR 1,00,000 of Quota
(b) 253 votes + One additional vote for each SDR 2,00,000 of Quota
(c) 244 votes
(d) 267 votes

46 Which of the following is/are correct in context to Exim Bank?
1. Non-banking financial company
2. Commercial bank
3. Non-financial company
Select the correct answer using the codes given below
(a) Both 1 and 2
(b) Only 1
(c) Only 2
(d) Both 1 and 3

47 IMF has raised the quota and voting share of India, which places India at the .... place among 184 members of the organisation.
(a) 10th (b) 11th
(c) 12th (d) 13th

48 Which of the following statements is/are incorrect?
(a) IMF make the balance of payments deficits
(b) IMF provide loans to governments or to any of their political subdivisions
(c) Both (a) and (b)
(d) All of the above

49 Which of the following statements is/are correct?
(a) The IMF financial years ends on 30th April
(b) Currently, IMF has 197 members upto 30th June, 2011
(c) Both (a) and (b)
(d) None of the above

50 Objective of World Bank does not include
(a) assistance in the reconstruction of member countries
(b) supplement private investment by its own loans and finances
(c) short-term assistance to member countries
(d) encourage long-term balanced growth of international trade

51 Member countries repay the share amount to the World Bank in following ways.
(a) 2% of allotted share are repaid in gold, US Dollar or SDR
(b) 18% of its capital share in its own currency
(c) 80% on demand by the bank
(d) All of the above

52 Before a loan is made or guaranteed the bank ensures that the
(a) borrower has reasonable prospects for repayment of loans
(b) loan is meant for reconstruction and development
(c) loan is meant for productive purpose
(d) All of the above

53 The World Bank provides long-term loans for various development projects of .... duration.
(a) 5-20 years (b) 10-30 years
(c) 3-15 years (d) None of these

54 For providing various technical services to member countries bank has established
(a) the economic development institute
(b) staff college
(c) Both (a) and (b)
(d) None of the above

55 A country leaving the membership of IMF can continue its membership with World Bank, if .... members of bank give their votes in its favour.
(a) 65% (b) 75% (c) 67% (d) 79%

56 Any member can be debarred from membership of World Bank if
(a) it gives written notice to the bank
(b) it work against the guidelines of bank
(c) it quits membership of IMF
(d) All of the above

57 Which of the following statements is/are incorrect?
(a) The initial authorised capital of the World Bank was $ 10,000 billion
(b) The World Bank has 40 founder members
(c) On 30th June, 2011, 187 countries were members of the World Bank
(d) All of the above

WTO and MNCs

58 .... is a negotiating, committing and controlling organisation.
(a) GATT (b) IDA (c) UNCTAD (d) ADB

59 The WTO covers
(a) intellectual property (b) services
(c) goods (d) Both (a) and (b)

60 Globalisation of financial services is being promoted by
(a) World Trade Organisation
(b) International Finance Corporation
(c) International Bank for Reconstruction and Development
(d) International Monetary Fund

61 Which of the following statements is/are incorrect?
(a) WTO helps to protect environment
(b) WTO applied to trade in merchandise goods
(c) Both (a) and (b)
(d) None of the above

62 Which of the following statements is/are incorrect ?
(a) The WTO is the embodiment of the Uruguay Round Result
(b) WTO was established on 1st January, 1995
(c) WTO cannot be described as a 'free trade' institution
(d) All of the above

63 Which of the following statements is incorrecet?
(a) IFC is headquartered in Washington DC
(b) India joined MIGA in 1994
(c) Multinational corporations are also known as global companies
(d) None of the above

64 Which of the following statements is/are incorrect ?
(a) Copyrights lie with the owner cum holder for a certain period
(b) Patents are rights related to literary or artistic work
(c) Industrial design rights can be an industrial commodity or a handicraft
(d) All of the above

65 Reasons for non-expansion of exports of Less Developed Countries (LDCs) are
(a) low tariff
(b) barriers imposed by the developed countries
(c) Both (a) and (b)
(d) None of the above

66 Majority of developed countries have .... in their BoP.
(a) deficit (b) equality
(c) surplus (d) None of these

67 Key currencies acceptable internationally are
(a) US dollar
(b) UK pound sterling
(c) Both (a) and (b)
(d) Neither (a) nor (b)

68 Consider the following statements in context of WTO.
1. WTO is a permanent body with its over dispute settlement machanism.
2. Scope of WTO has been broadened by inclusion of services, intellectual property rights and investment measures.
3. WTO promote international trade.
4. WTO banned the foreign currency.
5. WTO managed the hybrid system of clean floating, currency block etc.

Which of the statements given above are correct?
(a) Both 1 and 2
(b) Both 2 and 5
(c) 1, 2 and 3
(d) Both 3 and 4

69 Which of the following is the objective of WTO?
(a) To introduce new world trade policy
(b) Companies can produce in different countries
(c) Contraction to the trade and production
(d) None of the above

70 A company that has a worldwide approach to markets and production is known as
(a) Multinational enterprise (b) Multinational efficiency
(c) Multinational company (d) None of these

71 Which of the following is not the function of WTO?
(a) To optimum use of world resource
(b) To create dispute between IMF and IBRD for formulating the economic policy
(c) To introduce the rule and provision relating to the procedure of business policy
(d) None of the above

72 Which of the following are modes of service supply of GATS?
(a) Consumption abroad (b) Cross border services
(c) Both (a) and (b) (d) None of these

Miscellaneous

Directions (Q. Nos. 73-83) *The following questions consist of two statements, Statement I and Statement II, you have to examine these two statements carefully and select the answer by using the codes given below.*

Codes
(a) Both statements are correct
(b) Both statements are incorrect
(c) Statement I is correct, but Statement II is incorrect
(d) Statement I is incorrect, but Statement II is correct

73 **Statement** I Due to NAFTA, Canada's farmers were past out of business by US subsidised form product.
Statement II NAFTA created the world's smallest free trade area.

74 **Statement** I International liquidity does not include official holdings of International liquidity assets.
Statement II Only borrowed reserves are the source of international liquidity.

75 **Statement** I SDR constitute a temporary part of the reserves of each country.
Statement II Each country is free to decide as to how and when to use its SDRs.

76 **Statement** I Principles of ASEAN include renunciation of the threat or use of force.
Statement II NAFTA decrease investment apportunities.

77 **Statement** I There are many different levels of integration.
Statement II Regional integration has been organised only *via* inter-governmental decision-making.

78 **Statement** I Through Free Trade Policy, there will be free access to markets.
Statement II Regional economic integration lead an increase in efficiency in production.

79 **Statement** I WTO treats foreigners and locals equally.

Statement II The WTO dispute settlement system is faster.

80 **Statement** I Each Governor of IMF has got the right of 350 votes.

Statement II Each member country of IMF nominates a Governor.

81 **Statement** I World Bank offers long-term loans to developing countries.

Statement II World Bank provides loan for reconstruction and development.

82 **Statement** I The President is the highest policy making body of the bank.

Statement II All the powers of the bank are vested in the Board of Directors.

83 **Statement** I FDI is ill-advised because they loss their national identity.

Statement II FDI is cheaper than exporting goods.

Directions (Q. Nos. 84-95) *In the questions given below are two statements lablelled as Assertion (A) and Reason (R). In the context of the two statements, which one of the following is correct?*

Codes

(a) Both (A) and (R) are correct and (R) is the correct explanation of (A)
(b) (R) is correct, but (A) is incorrect
(c) (A) is correct, but (R) is incorrect
(d) Both (A) and (R) are incorrect

84 **Assertion** (A) SDRs are the right to draw on the IMF and are called paper gold.

Reason (R) Since, the value of SDRs is fixed in gold, so it is called paper gold.

85 **Assertion** (A) North American Free Trade Area is an example of FTA.

Reason (R) NAFTA permits trade of goods without taxes and other trade barriers.

86 **Assertion** (A) Cooperative peace and shared prosperity shall be the fundamental goals of ASEAN.

Reason (R) ASEAN helps to promote regional peace and stability.

87 **Assertion** (A) Problem of international liquidity is due to surplus in the BoP of developed countries.

Reason (R) Developed countries are creditors of LDCs and do not take interest in getting rid of their surpluses.

88 **Assertion** (A) The fund is regarded as the guardian of good conduct in sphere of BoP.

Reason (R) Fund aims at reducing tariffs and other trade transaction by member countries.

89 **Assertion** (A) Every member country of IMF automatically becomes the member of World Bank.

Reason (R) Any country, which quits IMF cannot expelled from the World Bank's membership.

90 **Assertion** (A) UNCTAD does not facilitate economic developments.

Reason (R) UNCTAD promote international trade with different socio-economic systems.

91 **Assertion** (A) IFC promotes sustainable public sector investment in developing countries.

Reason (R) IFC helps to reduce poverty and improve people lives.

92 **Assertion** (A) Trade development authority serves as a exchange of trade information between India and overseas.

Reason (R) This authority conducted surveys in several countries for the promotion of export.

93 **Assertion** (A) IMF is accountable to the governments of its member countries.

Reason (R) It is controlled and managed by Board of Governors.

94 **Assertion** (A) ADB suffers from serious shortage of investible resources.

Reason (R) ADB is not in a position to meet the loan requirements of the member countries completely.

95 **Assertion** (A) IBRD and IDA run on the same lines.

Reason (R) IBRD and IDA share the same staff and headquarters.

96 Match the following.

List I (Organisations)	List II (Features)
A. SAARC	1. It creates procedures for the resolution of trade disputes
B. ASEAN	2. It is dedicated to economic, technological, social and cultural development
C. NAFTA	3. Non-interference in the internal affairs of one another

Codes

	A	B	C		A	B	C
(a)	3	2	1	(b)	2	1	3
(c)	1	2	3	(d)	2	3	1

97 Match the following.

List I (Levels of Integration)	List II (Features)
A. Customs union	1. It allows for the free mobility of capital and labour across countries
B. Common market	2. Its example is NAFTA
C. Free trade area	3. It occurs when a group of countries agree to eliminate a set of common external tariffs on imports

Codes

	A	B	C		A	B	C
(a)	3	2	1	(b)	3	1	2
(c)	2	3	1	(d)	1	2	3

98 Match the following.

List I (Concepts)	List II (Features)
A. Free trade	1. Its value is fixed in gold
B. International liquidity	2. Removes tariffs and non-tariff barriers
C. Regional economic integration	3. Aggregate stock of internationally acceptable assets
D. Special drawing rights	4. It permits trading partner's mutual gains from trade of goods and services

Codes

	A	B	C	D
(a)	4	3	2	1
(b)	3	1	4	2
(c)	2	1	4	3
(d)	3	4	1	2

99 Match the following.

List I (Organisations)	List II (Objectives)
A. SAARC	1. To promote cooperative peace and shared prosperity
B. NAFTA	2. To provide protection and enforcement of intellectual property rights
C. ASEAN	3. To promote the welfare of the people of South Asia and to improve their quality of life

Codes

	A	B	C
(a)	3	2	1
(b)	2	1	3
(c)	2	3	1
(d)	1	2	3

100 Match the following.

List I (Concepts)	List II (Advantages)
A. International Monetary Fund	1. Risk factor is always extremely high
B. International Finance Corporation	2. It has failed to achieve of eliminating foreign exchange restrictions
C. Foreign Direct Investment	3. It may transfer technology, which has become outdated in other country
D. MNCs for the host country	4. It charges very high interest rates

Codes

	A	B	C	D		A	B	C	D
(a)	4	1	2	3	(b)	2	4	1	3
(c)	3	1	4	2	(d)	4	1	3	2

101 Match the following.

List I (IMF Facilities)	List II (Features)
A. Stand by arrangements	1. Overcoming BoP difficulties
B. Extended fund facility	2. To provide short-term BoP assistance for deficit of a temporary and cyclical nature.
C. Poverty, reduction and growth facility	3. It is aimed at preventing the spread of crisis
D. Contingent credit lines facility	4. To support programmes to strength substantially and in suitable manner BoP positions

Codes

	A	B	C	D		A	B	C	D
(a)	4	3	1	2	(b)	3	2	4	1
(c)	2	1	4	3	(d)	3	1	4	2

102 Match the following.

List I (Organisations of World Bank)	List II (Features)
A. Board of Governors	1. Responsible for the conduct of the day to day business of the bank
B. Board of Executive Directors	2. It meets annually to cheak out the general policy of the bank.
C. Advisory Council	3. It meet regularly once a month to carry on the routine working of the bank
D. President and other members of staff	4. It is appointed by the Board of Directors

Codes

	A	B	C	D		A	B	C	D
(a)	4	3	2	1	(b)	2	3	4	1
(c)	3	1	4	2	(d)	2	1	4	3

103 Match the following.

List I (Types of Intellectual Property Rights)	List II (Features)
A. Trademarks	1. It may refer to the creation of a shape colour, pattern or a combination of all these things.
B. Patents	2. It is a symbol generally used to identify a particular product, which indicates its source.
C. Industrial Design Rights	3. These are the designs, practices, formulas etc.
D. Trade Secrets	4. The invention must new and should be useful or can be applied in industries.

Codes

	A	B	C	D		A	B	C	D
(a)	4	3	2	1	(b)	2	3	4	1
(c)	3	1	4	2	(d)	2	4	1	3

104 Match the following.

List I (Concepts)	List II (Advantages)
A. Foreign direct investment	1. It gives a boost to the industrial activities of home country
B. Multinational corporations	2. It enables the owners or creators to protect their work
C. Intellectual property rights	3. It helps strengthen the political relationships between various nations

Codes

	A	B	C		A	B	C
(a)	3	1	2	(b)	2	3	1
(c)	3	2	1	(d)	1	2	3

PREVIOUS YEARS' QUESTIONS

December 2018

1 The companies having business in a large number of countries around the world at present are called

(a) Transnational Corporations (TNCs)
(b) Multinational Corporations (MNCs)
(c) Global Corporations (GCs)
(d) Multinational Enterprises (MNEs)

2 Which one of the following is not the basic function of WTO?

(a) To facilitate the implementation, administration and operation of trade agreements
(b) To settle differences and disputes among its member countries
(c) To facilitate the expansion and balanced growth of international trade
(d) The carry out periodic reviews of the trade policies of its member countries

3 Bretton Woods Conference resulted into the establishment of which of the following?

(a) IMF and IDA (b) IBRD and IFC
(c) IDA and ADB (d) IMF and IBRD

July 2018

4 Match the items of List II and with the items of List I relating to WTO impact

List I	List II
A. NAMA	1. Liberalisation of international investments.
B. GATTS	2. Includes industrial goods, textile, jewellery, fish and fisheries product manufacturing industries.
C. TRIMs	3. Liberalisation of trade in goods and services.
D. TRIPs	4. Provides monopoly power to owners of intellectual property.

Codes

	A	B	C	D		A	B	C	D
(a)	2	1	4	3	(b)	4	2	3	1
(c)	2	3	1	4	(d)	3	2	4	1

November 2017

5 Which among the following is not an international economic institution?

(a) IMF (b) IBRD
(c) ADB (d) IFRS

July 2016

6 **Statement I** WTO is only international organisation which deals with the rules of trade between organisations.

Statement II The limit of holding by individual foreign institutional investors in a company has been raised from 5 to 10% of company's share while the aggregate limit has been increased from 24 to 34%.

Codes

(a) Statement I is correct, but Statement II is incorrect
(b) Statement II is correct, but Statement I is incorrect
(c) Both the Statements I and II are correct
(d) Both the Statements I and II are incorrect

7 Which combination of the following is correct with regard to World Trade Organisation (WTO)?

1. WTO initiates peace process among the member countries to enhance international trade.
2. WTO avoids the task of 'Settlement of Disputes' among the member countries.
3. WTO administers the 'Trade Review Mechanism'.
4. WTO cooperates in an appropriate manner with the IMF and the World Bank.

Codes

(a) 2, 3 and 4
(b) Both 1 and 3
(c) Both 3 and 4
(d) 1, 2 and 3

December 2015

8 The major outcome of the Bretton Woods Conference was

(a) establishment of IMF and IFC
(b) establishment of IBRD and IFC
(c) establishment of IBRD and ADB
(d) establishment of IMF and IBRD

June 2015

9 **Assertion** (A) Amended Patent Act, in compliance with WTO, provides for grant of product patent as well as a process patent for a period of 20 years from the date of application.

Reason (R) Under the Act, patent may be granted to an invention which means a new product or process involving an inventive step and capable of industrial application, a technical advance over existing knowledge.

Codes

(a) Both A and R are true, but R is not the correct explanation of A
(b) A is false, but R is true
(c) Both A and R are true and R is the correct explanation of A
(d) A is true, but R is false

10 Which of the following have been recognised under the intellectual property eligible for creation of rights as per WTO mandate?

1. Computer software, music disc, performing art
2. Geographical indicator
3. Global positioning system
4. Journals, books, seeds, design, brand

Select the correct answer using the codes given below

(a) 1, 2 and 3
(b) 1, 3 and 4
(c) 1, 2 and 4
(d) 1, 2 and 3

11 NAFTA came into force from January, 1994 embracing

(a) USA, Canada, Cuba, Trinidad and Tobago
(b) USA, Canada, Mexico
(c) Cuba, Mexico, USA, Havana
(d) Trinidad, The USA, Mexico

December 2014

12 Which of the following are the outcomes of the Sixth Ministerial Conference of WTO which was held at Hong Kong in December 2005?

1. Resolve to complete the Doha Work Programme fully and to conclude negotiations in 2006.
2. Amendments to TRIPS agreement reaffirmed to address public health concerns of developing countries.
3. To continue export subsidies in agriculture upto 2018.
4. Duty free, quota free market access for all LDC's products to all developed countries.

Codes

(a) 1, 2 and 4
(b) 1, 2, 3 and 4
(c) Both 1 and 3
(d) Both 2 and 4

13 The important objectives of WTO are

1. to improve the quality of technology in the member countries.
2. to improve the standard of living of people in the member countries.
3. to ensure full employment and broad increase in effective demand.
4. to enlarge production and trade of goods.
5. to increase trade of services.

Select the correct answer using the codes given below

Codes

(a) 1, 2, 3 and 4
(b) 2, 3, 4 and 5
(c) 1, 2, 3 and 5
(d) 1, 3, 4 and 5

December 2013

14 Out of the following, which are the important objectives of IMF?

1. To promote exchange rate stability.
2. To create standby reserves.
3. To print international currency notes.
4. To establish a multilateral system of payments.
5. To maintain orderly exchange rate stability.
6. To create employment

Select the correct answer using the codes given below

Codes

(a) 2, 4, 5 and 6
(b) 3, 5 and 6
(c) 1, 2, 4 and 5
(d) 1, 2, 5 and 6

15 Possible impact of WTO on various aspects of the Indian economy.

1. Quantitative restriction will be allowed.
2. Secondhand cars will be imported.
3. There will be dumping of Chinese goods.
4. Increase in population.
5. Child labour exploitation.
6. Unemployment will increase.

Which of the combination is correct?

Codes

(a) 1, 2 and 3
(b) 3, 4 and 5
(c) 2, 3 and 6
(d) 4, 5 and 6

December 2012

16 The components of WTO are

(a) ministerial conference (b) disputes settlement body
(c) Director General (d) All of these

17 Which one of the following matches correspond to the member and observer countries of the SAARC?

1. India, Pakistan, Bangladesh, Bhutan, Nepal, Sri Lanka, Afghanistan, Maldive
2. Iran, China, Japan, USA, South Korea, European Union
3. Pakistan, Nepal, India, Bangladesh, Iran
4. UK, USA, North Korea, South Africa

Select the correct answer using the codes given below

Codes

(a) Both 3 and 4 (b) Both 2 and 4
(c) Both 1 and 2 (d) Both 2 and 3

18 Which one is not an international organisation?

(a) SAARC
(b) ASEM
(c) ASEAN
(d) CBDT

19 Which one is not an objective of IMF?

(a) To promote international monetary cooperation
(b) To ensure balanced international trade
(c) To finance productive efforts according to peace-time requirement
(d) To ensure exchange rate stability

20 Out of the following which one is not related with WTO?

(a) TRIPS
(b) Ministerial conference
(c) TRIMS
(d) TRAI

ANSWERS

Objective Questions

1 (a)	2 (c)	3 (b)	4 (a)	5 (a)	6 (d)	7 (a)	8 (d)	9 (b)	10 (d)
11 (c)	12 (b)	13 (b)	14 (a)	15 (d)	16 (d)	17 (a)	18 (b)	19 (a)	20 (b)
21 (a)	22 (a)	23 (a)	24 (c)	25 (d)	26 (a)	27 (d)	28 (b)	29 (b)	30 (d)
31 (d)	32 (c)	33 (a)	34 (c)	35 (b)	36 (a)	37 (a)	38 (b)	39 (b)	40 (b)
41 (c)	42 (c)	43 (b)	44 (c)	45 (a)	46 (b)	47 (c)	48 (b)	49 (a)	50 (c)
51 (d)	52 (d)	53 (a)	54 (b)	55 (b)	56 (d)	57 (c)	58 (a)	59 (d)	60 (d)
61 (b)	62 (c)	63 (b)	64 (b)	65 (d)	66 (c)	67 (a)	68 (b)	69 (a)	70 (c)
71 (b)	72 (c)	73 (b)	74 (b)	75 (d)	76 (c)	77 (c)	78 (a)	79 (a)	80 (d)
81 (a)	82 (c)	83 (c)	84 (c)	85 (a)	86 (a)	87 (a)	88 (d)	89 (a)	90 (c)
91 (d)	92 (a)	93 (a)	94 (b)	95 (a)	96 (d)	97 (b)	98 (a)	99 (a)	100 (b)
101 (c)	102 (b)	103 (d)	104 (a)						

Previous Years' Questions

1 (c)	2 (c)	3 (d)	4 (c)	5 (d)	6 (c)	7 (c)	8 (d)	9 (d)	10 (c)
11 (b)	12 (a)	13 (c)	14 (c)	15 (d)	16 (d)	17 (c)	18 (d)	19 (c)	20 (d)

CHAPTER 05

Accounting and Its Concepts

Accounting is often called the language of business because the purpose of accounting is to communicate or report the results of business operations and its various aspects to various users of accounting information. In view of the utility of accounting reports to various interested parties, it becomes imperative to make this language capable of commonly understood by all.

Accounting

Accounting is a very dynamic profession, which is constantly adapting itself to varying needs of its users. Accounting is the analysis and interpretation of book-keeping records. It includes not only the maintenance of accounting records, but also the preparation of financial and economic information, which involves the measurement of transactions and other events relating to the entity. We can also say that accounting is a science of keeping the business records in a regular and most systematic manner, so as to know the business results with minimum trouble. Therefore, it is said to be statistical procedure for the collection, classification and summarisation of financial information.

According to **RN Anthony**, "Nearly every business enterprise has accounting system. It is a means of collecting, summarising, analysing and reporting in monetary terms, information about business."

According to **American Accounting Association** (AAA), "Accounting is the process of identifying, measuring and communicating information to permit judgement and decisions by the users of accounts."

According to **American Institute of Certified Public Accountants** (AICPA), "Accounting is the art of recording, classifying and summarising in a significant manner and in terms of money, transactions and events which are, in part at least, of a financial character and interpreting the result thereof."

In this Chapter

Characteristics of Accounting

Identifying the Transactions and Events Accounting identifies transactions and events of a specific entity. A transaction is an exchange, in which each participant receives or sacrifice value. An event is a happening of consequence to an entity.

Recording All business transactions of a financial character, as evidenced by some documents such as sales bills, pass book, salary slip etc are recorded in the books of accounts.

Classifying It is concerned with the systematic analysis of the recorded data, with a view to group transactions or entries of one nature at one place, so as to put information in compatible usable form.

Summarising This function involves the preparation of financial statement such as income statement, balance sheet, statement of changes in financial position, statement of cash flow and statement of value added.

Analysis It means methodical classification of the data given in the financial statements. It provides the basis for interpretation.

Interpreting It is concerned with explaining the meaning and significance of the relationship, so established by the analysis. The recorded financial data is analysed and interpreted in a manner that it will enable the end user to make a meaningful judgement about the financial condition and profitability of business operations.

Communicating It is concerned with the transmission of summarised, analysed and interpreted information to the users to enable them to make reasonable decisions. This is done through preparation and distribution of accounting reports.

Branches of Accounting

Financial Accounting It is the process of identifying, measuring, recording, classifying, submarining, analysing, interpreting and communicating the financial transactions and events. Financial accounting is primarily concerned with providing of financial information of the business enterprise to all its stakeholders.

Cost Accounting It is that part of accounting which is concerned with the process of accounting and controlling the cost of units produced or services rendered by the business enterprise. It also estimates the cost in advance and helps the management in exercising strict control over cost.

Management Accounting It is that part of accounting which is concerned with the decision-making process of the management. The management accountant uses various techniques and concepts to make the accounting data more useful for managerial decision-making.

Social Responsibility Accounting It is that part of accounting which is concerned with the process of identification, measurement and communicating the contribution made by the business enterprise to the society in which business enterprise is born and thereafter grows.

Accounting Principles

Accounting statement discloses the profitability and solvency of the business to various parties like proprietors, investors, creditors, government and many more. It is therefore, necessary that such statements should be prepared according to some standard language and set rules. These rules are generally called Generally Accepted Accounting Principles (GAAP).

GAAP may be defined as those rules of action or conduct, which are derived from experience and practice and when they prove useful, they become accepted as principles of accounting.

Characteristics of Accounting Principles

Relevance A principle is relevant, if it results in information that is useful to the user of the accounting information.

Objectivity A principle is objective if it is free from personal bias or judgements of those, who furnish the information. Objectivity also implies verifiability, which means that there is some way of finding out the truthfulness or correctness of the information reported.

Feasibility A principle is feasible, if it can be applied without undue complexity or cost.

Kinds of Accounting Principles or Postulates

Accounting principles are described by various terms such as assumptions, conventions, concepts, doctrines, postulates etc. *These principles can be classified mainly into two categories*

Accounting Concepts or Assumptions

Concepts are ideas or notion about the desirability and applicability of a particular method. These concepts guide how transactions should be recorded and reported.

Following may be treated as basic concepts or assumptions

Business Entity Concept

According to this assumption, a business is treated as a separate entity *i.e.* distinct from its owner(s) and all other economic proprietors. Business unit should have a completely separate sets of book and we have to record business transaction from firm's point of view and not from the point of view of the proprietor. The proprietor is treated as a creditor of the business to the extent of capital invested by him in the business.

Business entity assumption is applicable to all types of business organisations *viz.* sole proprietorship, partnership firm, companies etc. It should be noted that in case of companies, the legal relationship of company and its shareholder is also separate as against a sole proprietorship and partnership firms.

Money Measurement Assumption

Only those transactions and events are recorded in accounting which are capable of being expressed in terms of money. In other words, the information which cannot be expressed in terms of money is not included in accounting records. Since, money is the medium of exchange and the standard of economic value, this concept requires that those transactions alone, that are capable of being measured in terms of money, be only recorded in the books of accounts.

Going Concern Assumption

The financial statements are normally prepared on the assumption that an enterprise is a going concern and will continue in operation for the foreseeable future. It is also known as continuity assumption. It is assumed that the enterprise has neither the intention nor the necessity of liquidation of curtailing materiality the scale of its operations. It is on this concept that we record fixed assets at their original cost and depreciation is charged on these assets without reference to their market value.

Accounting Period Assumption

It is also known as periodicity concept or time period assumption. As per 'going concern' assumption, an indefinite life of the entity is assumed, so the economic life of an enterprise is artificially split into periodic intervals which are known as accounting periods, at the end of which an income statement and position statement are prepared to show the performance and financial position.

Cost Concept or Historical Cost Concept

The value of an asset is to be determined on the basis of historical cost, in other words, acquisition cost. Although, there are various measurement bases, accountants traditionally prefer this concept in the interests of objectivity. This cost is the basis of valuation of the assets in the financial statements. It is highly objective and free from all bias. Other measurement bases are not so objective.

Dual Aspect Concept (Duality)

As the name suggests, duality deals with double effect. This aspect provides the basis for recording all business transactions in the books of account, so it is regarded as one of the basic principles of accounting. According to this principle, every business transaction has a two fold effects. In other words, every transaction affect atleast two accounts. If one account is debited, any other account must be credited.

Revenue Recognition Concept (Realisation Concept)

This period is mainly concerned with the revenue being recognised in the income statement of enterprise. Recognising the revenue means recording the income in the income statement, prepared for the particular period. Revenue means the amount, which is added to the capital as a result of business operations. Revenue is earned by sales of goods or by providing a service.

Matching Concept

The matching principle facilitates to ascertain the amount of profit or loss incurred in a particular period by deducting the related expenses from the revenue recognised during the period. Accordingly, the expenses incurred in an accounting period should be matched with the revenue recognised in that period. For matching costs with revenue, first revenues should be recognised and then cost incurred for generating that revenue should be recognised.

Accrual Concept

In accounting, accrual basis is used for recording of transactions. It provides more appropriate information about the performance of business enterprise as compared to cash basis. Accrual concept is applied equally to revenue and expenses. In this concept, the effects of transactions and other events are recognised on mercantile basis, *i.e.* when they occur and they are recorded in the accounting records and reported in the financial statements of the period to which they relate.

Objectivity Concept

This concept requires that accounting transaction should be recorded in a financial manner, free from the person bias of either the management or the accountant, who prepare the account. In other words, this principle requires that each recorded transaction/event in the books of accounts should have an adequate evidence to support it.

Accounting Conventions

It may be defined as a custom or generally accepted practice, which is adopted either by general agreement or common consent among accountants. But the remembering point is that accounting concepts and accounting conventions both differ from each other, *i.e.* accounting concepts are established by law while accounting conventions are guidelines based upon custom or usage or general agreement.

Convention of Full Disclosure

This principle requires that all significant information relating to the economic affairs of the enterprise should be completely disclosed. There should be a sufficient disclosure of information, which is of material interest to the users of the financial statement. The principle is so important that the Companies Act, make ample provisions for the disclosure of essential information in the financial statement of a company.

Convention of Consistency

This convention states that accounting principles and methods should remain consistent from one year to another. These should not be changed from year-to-year, in order to enable the management to compare the profit and loss account and balance sheet of the different period and draw important conclusions about the working of the enterprise. The concept of consistency is applied particularly, when alternative method of accounting are equally acceptable.

Convention of Conservation or Prudence

According to this convention, all anticipated losses should be recorded in the books of accounts, but all anticipated profit or unrealised gains should be ignored. In other words, we can say that conservation is a policy of playing safe. Provisions is made for all known liabilities and losses even though the amount cannot be determined with certainity.

Convention of Materiality

Materiality principle permits other concepts to be ignored, if the effect of transaction/ event is not considered material. This principle is the exception of full disclosure principle. According to this convention, items having an insignificant effect or being irrelevant to the user need not be disclosed. According to **American Accounting Association** (AAA), "An item should be regarded as material, if there is reason to believe that knowledge of it would influence decision of informed investor."

Capital and Revenue Items

It is important to make a clear distinction between items of capital nature and revenue nature for the preparation of trading and profit and loss account and the balance sheet. If any item is wrongly classified, *i.e.* if any item of revenue nature is treated as capital item or *vice-versa*, the ascertainment of profit or loss will be incorrect.

The various capital and revenue items are as follows

Capital Expenditure

It is money spent on the purchase of permanent or fixed asset for use in the business and not for immediate resale or on the permanent improvement of or addition to or extension of an existing asset with a view to increase the earning capacity of the business enterprise. *e.g.* Purchase of plant and machinery etc.

Capital expenditure as opposed to revenue expenditure, is generally of a one-off kind and its benefit is derived over several accounting periods. Capital expenditure may include purchase cost, delivery costs, legal charges, installation costs, upgradation costs and replacement costs.

As capital expenditure results in increase in the fixed asset of the entity, *the accounting entry is as follows*

Debit	Fixed Assets
Credit	To Cash/Payable

Revenue Expenditure

It is money spent on materials and services, which are consumed by a business enterprise in carrying out normal business activities and maintenance of fixed assets. The direct benefit of such expenditure is exhausted in the accounting period itself. *e.g.* cost of finished goods or establishment cost etc. Revenue expenditures comprise of repair costs, maintenance charges, repainting costs, renewal expenses. As revenue costs do not form part of the fixed asset cost, they are expensed in the income statement in the period in which they are incurred.

The accounting entry to record revenue expenditure is as follows

Debit	Revenue Expense
Credit	To Cash/Payable

Deferred Revenue Expenditure

There are certain expenditure, which are primarily of revenue nature, but the benefit from which is not consumed or exhausted in the year in which the expenditure is incurred, *i.e.* its benefit extends beyond that accounting period. Such expenditure are called as deferred revenue expenditure. *e.g.* Advertisement campaign to launch a new product.

Capital Income

An income which does not arise out of operating profit of the business firm. *e.g.* If a machinery costing ₹ 55,000 purchased by a business for its use is sold for ₹ 70,000, ₹ 15,000 will be taken as capital income.

Revenue Income

An income which is earned during a regular business transaction of a firm. *e.g.* Profit made on sale of goods or services.

Revenue Loss

A loss which arises during a regular business transaction of a firm. *e.g.* Loss made on sale of goods or services.

Capital Receipts

An amount received in the form of capital from the owner and as loan from outsiders is known as capital receipts. Besides, cash received by selling shares, debentures and permanent assets is also capital receipt. It is non-recurring type of receipt. It is treated as obligation of the business and shown on liabilities side of the balance sheet.

Items relating to capital receipts

- Amount received from the owner as capital.
- Amount received through the sale of shares and debentures.
- Amount of loan received.
- Amount received from the sale of old assets.
- Other receipts of non-recurring nature.

Revenue Receipts

It is an amount, which is received from the regular transaction of a business. It is the amount received from the sale of goods and services. It is the main source of income. It is a regular type of income. It is shown on the credit side of the trading and profit and loss accounts.

Items relating to revenue receipts

- Amount received from the sale of goods and services.
- Amount received by way of discount, commission, rent, interest and dividend.
- Amount received from the sale of waste paper and packing cases.

Financial Statements

Financial statements are the end product of an accounting process. Financial statements are historical in nature and are prepared following the accounting concepts and principles.

These statements present in an organised and summarised form, detailed information about the financial performance of an entity for an accounting period and also discloses its financial position at the end of the period.

The legal requirements related to financial statements are

- These statements should be based on accrual basis and double entry system of accounting.
- The statement of profit and loss should be annexed with the balance sheet.

John N Myer defines financial statements as, "Financial statements provide a summary of accounts of a business enterprise, the balance sheet reflecting the assets, liabilities and capital as on a certain date and income statement showing the results and operations during a certain period."

A set of financial statements as per Section 2(40) of the Companies Act, 2013 includes

Balance Sheet It is a statement of assets and liabilities, showing the financial position of an enterprise at a given date. It is also known as position statement.

Statement of Profit and Loss It shows the net result of business operations during an accounting period. It is also known as income statement.

Cash Flow Statement It is a statement prepared in accordance with AS-3, to show inflow and outflow of cash and cash equivalents.

Statement of Changes in Equity It shows changes in equity during a year.

Notes to Accounts It is any explanatory note annexed to any document referred above.

➡ **Note** *Section 129 of the Companies Act, 2013 requires every company to prepare its financial statements every year in the form prescribed, i.e. Schedule III of the Companies Act, 2013.*

Balance Sheet

Balance sheet may be defined as a statement of assets and liabilities of the company at a particular date. Balance sheet is prepared and presented in the form prescribed in Schedule III, Part I of the Companies Act, 2013. The form prescribed is vertical. Balance sheet must exhibit a true and fair view of the financial position of the company at the close of the year.

Format of Balance Sheet

The form prescribed under Schedule III, Part I of the Companies Act, 2013 is as follows

Name of the Company ...
Balance Sheet
as at ...

Particulars	Note No.	Figures as at the End of the Current Reporting Period (₹)	Figures as at the End of the Previous Reporting Period (₹)
I. **EQUITY AND LIABILITIES**			
1. **Shareholders' Funds**			
(a) Share Capital		...	...
(b) Reserves and Surplus		...	...
(c) Money Received against Share Warrants		...	...
2. **Share Application Money Pending Allotment**		...	...
3. **Non-current Liabilities**			
(a) Long-term Borrowings		...	...
(b) Deferred Tax Liabilities (Net)		...	...
(c) Other Long-term Liabilities		...	...
(d) Long-term Provisions		...	...
4. **Current Liabilities**			
(a) Short-term Borrowings		...	...
(b) Trade Payables		...	...
(c) Other Current Liabilities		...	...
(d) Short-term Provisions		...	...
Total			
II. **ASSETS**			
1. **Non-current Assets**			
(a) Fixed Assets			
(i) Tangible Assets		...	...
(ii) Intangible Assets		...	...
(iii) Capital Work-in-progress		...	...
(iv) Intangible Assets under Development		...	...
(b) Non-current Investments		...	...
(c) Deferred Tax Assets (Net)		...	...
(d) Long-term Loans and Advances		...	...
(e) Other Non-current Assets		...	...
2. **Current Assets**			
(a) Current Investments		...	...
(b) Inventories		...	...
(c) Trade Receivables		...	...
(d) Cash and Cash Equivalents		...	...
(e) Short-term Loans and Advances		...	...
(f) Other Current Assets		...	...
Total		...	...

Statement of Profit and Loss

Statement of profit and loss shows the net result of business operations i.e. financial performance (profit earned or loss suffered) during an accounting period. The vertical form for preparing statement of profit and loss is prescribed under Schedule III, Part II of the Companies Act, 2013.

Format of Statement of Profit and Loss

The format of statement of profit and loss as specified in Schedule III is as follows

Particulars	Note No.	Figures for the Current Reporting Period (₹)	Figures for the Previous Reporting Period (₹)
I. Revenue from Operations		...	...
II. Other Income		...	...
III. Total Revenue (I – II)		...	...
IV. **Expenses**			
Cost of Materials Consumed		...	...
Purchases of Stock-in-trade			
Changes in Inventories of Finished Goods			
Work-in-progress and Stock-in-trade			
Employees Benefits Expenses			
Finance Costs		...	...
Depreciation and Amortisation Expenses		...	
Other Expenses		...	
Total Expenses			
V. Profit before Tax (III – IV)		...	...
VI. (–) Tax		(...)	(...)
VII. Profit after Tax (V – VI)		...	...

Accounting Standards

Accounting Standards are formulated with a view to harmonise different accounting policies and practices in use in a country. The objective of Accounting Standards is to reduce the accounting alternatives in the preparation of financial statements within the bounds of rationality, thereby ensuring comparability of financial statements of different enterprises with a view to provide meaningful information to various users of financial statements to enable them to make informed economic decisions.

Objective of accounting standards is to standarise the diverse accounting policies and practices with a view to eliminate, to the extent possible, the non-comparability of financial statements and the reliability of the financial statements.

Indian Accounting Standards (Ind AS)

Indian Accounting Standards (Ind AS) are a set of accounting standards notified by the Ministry of Corporate Affairs (MCA), which are converged with International Financial Reporting Standards (IFRS). These accounting standards are formulated by Accounting Standards Board of Institute of Chartered Accountants of India.

The Ministry of Corporate Affairs (MCA) by way of notification dated February 16, 2015 notified the companies (Ind AS) Rules, 2015 effective 1st of April, 2015 in pursuance of the provisions of Section 133 read with Section 469 of the Companies Act, 2013 and Section 210 A (1) of the Companies Act, 1956 providing roadmap for implementation of Ind-AS, which stipulates the implementation of Ind-AS in a phased manner beginning from the Accounting Period 2016-17 (MCA roadmap).

The Indian accounting standards are as follows

Ind AS-101 First Time Adoption of Indian Accounting Standards

This standard ensures that an entity's first Ind AS financial statements and its interim financial reports for part of the period covered by those financial statements, contain high quality information that is transparent for users and comparable over all periods presented. An entity shall prepare and present an opening Ind AS Balance Sheet at the date of transition to Ind AS. This is the starting point for its accounting in accordance with Ind AS.

Ind AS-102 Share Based Payments

This standard specifies the financial reporting by an entity when it undertakers a share-based payment transaction. An entity shall recognise the goods or services acquired or received in a share based payment transaction when it obtains the goods or as the services are received. For cash-settled share-based payment transactions, the entity shall measure the goods or services acquired and the liability incurred at the fair value of the liability.

Ind AS-103 Business Combinations

A business combination is a transaction or other event in which a reporting entity, *i.e.* the acquires obtains control of one or more businesses, *i.e.* the acquire.

Ind AS 103 does not apply to the following

- The formation of a joint arrangement.
- The acquisition of an asset or group of assets that is not a business.

Ind AS-104 Insurance Contracts

This standard specifies the financial reporting for insurance contracts by an entity that issues, such contracts. It requires limited improvements to accounting by insurers for insurance contracts. An insurance contract is a contract under which one party, *i.e.* the insurer accepts significant insurance risk from another party by agreeing to compensate the policyholder if a specified uncertain future event adversely affects the policyholder.

Ind AS-105 Non-current Assets held for Sale and Discontinued Operations

This standard specifies the accounting for assets held for sale and the presentation and disclosure of discontinued operations. It requires assets that meet the criteria to be classified or held for sale, to be measured at the lower of carrying amount and fair value less costs to sell and depreciation on such assets to cease.

Here, a discontinued operation is a component of an entity that either has been disposed of or is classified as held for sale and represents a separate (major) line of business or geographical area of operations.

Ind AS-106 Exploration for and Evaluation of Mineral Resources

This standard specifies the financial reporting for the exploration for and evaluation of mineral resources. Here, exploration and evaluation expenditure refers to those, which are incurred by an entity in connection with the exploration for and evaluation of mineral resources before the technical feasibility. An entity shall disclose information that identifies and explains the amounts recognised in its financial statements arising from the exploration for and evaluation of mineral resources.

Ind AS-107 Financial Instruments Disclosures

This standard requires entities to provide disclosures in their financial statements that enable users to evaluate the significance of financial instruments for the financial position and performance of an entity. This standard applies to all entities, including entities that have few financial instruments and those that have many financial instruments.

Ind AS-108 Operating Segments

This standard requires an entity to report financial and descriptive information about its reportable segments. Reportable segments are operating segments or aggregations of operating segments that meet specified criteria. This standard requires an entity to report a measure of operating segment profit or loss and of segment assets.

Ind AS-109 Financial Instruments

This standard establishes principles for the financial reporting of financial assets and liabilities that will present relevant and useful information to users of financial statements for their assessment of the amounts, timing and uncertainty of an entity's future cash flow.

Ind AS-110 Consolidated Financial Statements

The objective of this statement is to present financial statements of a parent and its subsidiary(ies) as a single economic entity. In other words, the holding company and its subsidiary(ies) are treated as one entity for the preparation of these consolidated financial statements.

Consolidated profit/loss account and consolidated balance sheet are prepared for disclosing the total profit/loss of the group and total assets and liabilities of the group. As per this Accounting Standard, the consolidated balance sheet, if prepared, should be prepared in the manner prescribed by this statement. A holding company has to prepare its financial statement consolidated with its all subsidiary companies as per AS-21. Both balance sheet and profit and loss account has to be consolidated for the holding and subsidiary companies.

Ind AS 111 Joint Arrangements

This standard establishes principles for financial reporting by entities that have an interest in (joint) arrangements. This standard shall be applied by all entities that are a party to a joint arrangement. Joint arrangement is an arrangement of which two or more parties have joint control. It is either a joint operation or a joint venture.

Ind AS-112 Disclosure of Interests in other Entities

This standard requires an entity to disclose information that enables users of its financial statements to evaluate the nature of and risks associated with, its interests in other entities and the effects of those interests on its financial position and performance.

Ind AS-113 Fair Value Measurement

This standard applies when another Ind AS requires or permits fair value measurements or disclosures about fair value measurements. Here, fair value refers to the price that would be received to sell an asset or paid to transfer a liability in an orderly transaction between market participants at the measurement date.

Ind AS-114 Regulatory Deferral Accounts

This standard specifies the financial reporting requirements for regulatory deferral account balances that arise when an entity provides goods or services to customers at a price or rate that is subject to rate regulation.

Ind AS-115 Revenue from Contracts with Customers

This standard establishes the principles that an entity shall apply to report useful information to users of financial statements about the nature, amount, timing of revenue etc.

This standard applies to all contracts with customers, except

- The lease contracts (within the scope of Ind AS 17).
- Insurance contracts (within the scope of AS 104).

Ind AS-1 Presentation of Financial Statements

This standard prescribes the basis for preparation of financial statements to ensure comparability both with the entity's financial statements of previous period and with the financial statements of other entities. It requires an entity to present a complete set of financial statements (at least annually) with comparative amounts for the preceding year.

A complete set of financial statements includes

- A balance sheet as at the end of the period.
- A statement of profit and loss for the period.
- A statement of changes in equity for the period.
- A statement of cash flow for the period.
- Notes and other explanatory information.

Ind AS-2 Inventories Accounting

The objective of this standard is to formulate the method of computation of cost of inventories / stock, determine the value of closing stock / inventory, at which the inventory is to be shown in balance sheet till it is not sold and recognised as revenue. Stock, to be valued at cost or market value, whichever is lower. Quantity of the stock should be verified physically.

Ind AS-7 Statement of Cash Flow

Cash flow statement is additional information to user of financial statement. This statement exhibits the flow of incoming and outgoing cash. This statement assesses the ability of the enterprise to generate cash and to utilise the cash. This statement is one of the tools for assessing the liquidity and solvency of the enterprise.

Cash flow is divided into three activities which are as follows

***Operating Activity** It includes*

- Current year profit
- Changes in working capital
- Non-cash expenses
- Extraordinary cash inflows or outflows

***Financing Activity** It includes*

- Issue of equity or preference shares or debentures
- Loan taken
- Repayment of loan
- Redemption of shares and debentures

***Investing Activity** It includes*

- Purchase of fixed assets or investments
- Sales of fixed assets or investment
- Dividend, interest or rental recieved on fixed assets or investments.

Ind AS-8 Accounting Policies, Changes in Accounting Estimate and Errors

This standard prescribes the criteria for selecting and changing accounting policies, together with the accounting treatment and disclosure of changes in accounting policies, changes in accounting estimates and corrections of errors. Accounting policies are the specific principles, bases, conventions, rules and practices applied by an entity in preparing and presenting financial statements. This standard is intended to enhance the relevancy and reliability of an entity's financial statements.

Ind AS-10 Events after the Reporting Period

This standard states that an entity should adjust its financial statements for events after the reporting period. Here 'events after the reporting period' are those events, that occur between the end of the reporting period and the date when the financial statements are approved by the BOD (in case of company) or by the corresponding approving authority (in other case). This standard requires that an entity should not prepare its financial statements on a going concern basis if events after the reporting period indicate that the going concern assumption is not appropriate.

Ind AS-11 Construction Contracts

Accounting for long-term construction contracts involves question as to, when revenue should be recognised and how to measure the revenue in the books of contractor. As the period of construction contract is long, work of construction starts in 1 year and is completed in another year or after 4-5 years or so. Therefore, question arises how the profit or loss of construction contract by contractor should be determined. There may be following two ways to determine profit or loss-On year-to-year basis based on percentage of completion or on completion of the contract.

Ind AS-12 Income Taxes

This Accounting Standard prescribes the accounting treatment for taxes on income. Traditionally, amount of tax payable is determined on the profit/loss computed as per Income Tax Laws. According to this Accounting Standard, tax on income is determined on the principle of accrual concept. According to this concept, tax should be accounted in the period, in which corresponding revenue and expenses are accounted. In simple words, tax shall be accounted on accrual basis, not on liability to pay basis.

Ind AS-16 Property, Plant and Equipment

The objective of this standard is to prescribe the accounting treatment for property, plant and equipment, so that users of the financial statements can discern information about investment made by an enterprise in its property, plant and equipment and the changes in such investment.

Ind AS-17 Leases

Lease is an arrangement, by which the lessor gives the right to use an asset for given period of time to the lessee on rent. It involves two parties, a lessor and a lessee and an asset, which is to be leased. The lessor who owns the asset, agrees to allow the lessee to use it for a specified period of time in return of periodic rent payments.

There are two types of lease agreements

- Operating lease
- Finance lease

AS-18 Revenue

It explains as to, when the revenue should be recognised in profit and loss account and also states the circumstances, in which revenue recognition can be postponed. Revenue means gross inflow of cash receivable or other consideration arising in the course of ordinary activities of an enterprise such as the sale of goods, rendering of services and use of enterprises resources by other yielding interest, dividend and royalties. In other words, revenue is a charge made to customers/clients for goods supplied and services rendered.

Ind AS-19 Employee Benefits

This Accounting Standard has been revised by ICAI and is applicable in respect of accounting period commencing on or after 1st April, 2006. The scope of the Accounting Standard has been enlarged, to include accounting for short-term employee benefits and termination benefits.

Ind AS-20 Accounting for Government Grants and Disclosure of Government Assistance

Government grants are assistance by the government in the form of cash or kind to an enterprise in return for past or future compliance with certain conditions. Government assistance, which cannot be valued reasonably, is excluded from government grants. Those transactions with government, which cannot be distinguished from the normal trading transactions of the enterprise, are not considered as government grants.

Government assistance is action by government designed to provide an economic benefit specific to an entity or range of entities qualifying under certain criteria.

Ind AS-21 The Effects of Changes in Foreign Exchange Rates

Effect of changes in foreign exchange rate shall be applicable in respect of accounting period commencing on or after 1st April, 2004 and is mandatory in nature. This Accounting Standard is applicable to accounting for transactions in foreign currencies in translating in the financial statement of foreign operation, integral as well as non-integral and also accounting for forward exchange.

Effects of changes in Foreign Exchange Rate, an enterprises should disclose following aspects

- Amount exchange difference included in net profit or loss.
- Amount accumulated in foreign exchange translation reserve.
- Reconciliation of opening and closing balance of Foreign Exchange Translation Reserve.

Ind AS-23 Borrowing Costs

Enterprises are borrowing the funds to acquire, build and install the fixed assets and other assets, these assets take time to make them useable or saleable, therefore the enterprises incur the interest (cost on borrowing) to acquire and build these assets. The objective of the Accounting Standard is to prescribe the treatment of borrowing cost (interest + other cost) in accounting, whether the interest and other cost *i.e.* borrowing cost related to a qualifying assets must be capitalised into the cost of that assets rather than transferring it into the profit and loss account.

Qualifying asset is an asset, which takes a period of 12 months or more to be constructed or manufactured longer or shorter period may be considered as per the conditions.

Ind AS-24 Related Party Disclosure

Sometimes business transactions between related parties lose the feature and character of the arms length transactions. Related party relationship affects the volume and decision of business of one enterprise for the benefit of the other enterprise. Hence, disclosure of related party transaction is essential for proper understanding of financial performance and financial position of enterprise.

Ind AS-27 Separate Financial Statements

This standard prescribes the accounting and disclosure requirement for investments in joint ventures, subdiaries etc. When an entity prepares separate financial statements, it shall account for investments in subsidiaries, joint ventures and associates either at cost or, in accordance with Ind AS 109, *i.e.* financial instruments.

Ind AS-28 Investments in Associates and Joint Ventures

This standard prescribes the accounting for investments in associates and joint ventures. This standard shall be applied by all entities that are investors with joint control of or significant influence over an investee.

If an entity holds, directly or indirectly, 20% or more of the voting power of the investee, it is presumed that the entity has significant influence. An associate is an entity over which the investor has significant influence.

Joint venture is defined as a contractual arrangement, whereby two or more parties carry on an economic activity under 'joint control'. Control is the power to govern the financial and operating policies of an economic activity so as to obtain benefit from it. Joint control is the contractually agreed sharing of control over economic activity.

Ind AS-29 Financial Reporting in Hyperinflationary Economies

This standard is applied to the financial statements, including the consolidated financial statements, if any entity whose functional currency is the currency of a hyperinflationary economy. Appendix of Ind AS-29 prescribes that in the reporting period in which an entity identifies the existence of hyperinflation in the economy of its functional currency, not having been hyperinflationary in the prior period, the entity shall apply the requirements of this standard, as if the economy had always been hyperinflationary.

Ind AS-32 Financial Instruments: Presentation

The objective of this standard is to establish principles for presenting financial instruments as liabilities or equity and for offsetting financial assets and financial liabilities. It applies to the classification of financial instruments, from the perspective of the issuer, into financial assets, financial liabilities and equity instruments; the classification of related interest, dividends, losses and gains and the circumstances, in which financial assets and financial liabilities should be offset. The principles in this standard complement the principles for recognising and measuring financial assets and financial liabilities in Accounting Standard financial instruments.

Ind AS-34 Interim Financial Reporting

Interim financial reporting is the reporting for periods of less than a year generally for a period of 3 months. As per clause 41 of listing agreement, the companies are required to publish the financial results on a quarterly basis.

Ind AS-36 Impairment of Assets

'Impairment of asset' means weakening in value of asset. In other words, when the value of asset decreases, it may be called impairment of an asset. As per this AS, asset is said to be impaired, when carrying amount of asset is more than its recoverable amount.

Ind AS-37 Provisions, Contingent Liabilities and Contingent Assets

This standard prescribes the accounting for provisions, contingent liabilities, contingent assets, provision for restructuring cost.

Provision It is a liability, which can be measured only by using a substantial degree of estimation.

Contingent Liability A liability is present obligation of the enterprise arising from past events, the settlement of which is expected to result in an outflow from the enterprise of resources embodying economic benefits.

Ind AS-38 Intangible Assets

An intangible asset is an identifiable non-monetary asset without physical substance, held for use in the production or supplying of goods or services for rentals to others or for administrative purpose. A self generated intangible asset can not be recognised into the balance sheet.

Ind AS-40 Investment Property

This standard prescribes the accounting treatment for investment property and related disclosure requirements. An investment property is a property (either land or building), which is held by the owner or lessee to earn rentals or for capital appreciation, or both. However, investment property shall be recognised as an asset when it is probable that the future economic benefits that are associated with the investment property will flow to the entity and the cost of the investment property can be measured reliably.

Ind AS-41 Agriculture

This standard prescribes the accounting treatment and disclosures related to agricultural activity. Here, agriculture activity refers to the management by an entity of the biological transformation and harvest of biological assets for sale or for conversion into agricultural produce or into additional biological assets. A biological asset shall be measured on initial recognition and at the end of each reporting period at its fair value less costs to sell.

Existing Accounting Standards (AS)

Accounting standards are the existing accounting standards which are issued under Companies (accounting standard) Rules, 2006. *The list of AS is as follows*

AS No.	Title
AS 1	Disclosure of Accounting Policies
AS 2	Valuation of Inventories
AS 3	Cash Flow Statements
AS 4	Contingencies and Events occurring after the Balance Sheet date
AS 5	Net profit or loss for the period, prior period items and changes in Accounting Policies
AS 7	Construction Contracts
AS 9	Revenue Recognition
AS 10	Property, Plant and Equipment
AS 11	The Effects of Changes in Foreign Exchange Rates
AS 12	Accounting for Government Grants
AS 13	Accounting for Investment
AS 14	Accounting for Amalgamations
AS 15	Employee Benefits
AS 16	Borrowing Costs
AS 17	Segment Reporting
AS 18	Related Party Disclosures
AS 19	Leases
AS 20	Earnings per Share
AS 21	Consolidated Financial Statements
AS 22	Accounting for Taxes on Income
AS 23	Accounting for Investments in Associates
AS 24	Discontinuing Operations
AS 25	Interim Financial Reporting
AS 26	Intangible Assets
AS 27	Financial Reporting of Interests in Joint Venture
AS 28	Impairment of Assets
AS 29	Provisions, Contingent Liabilities and Contingent Assets

Now, India have two sets of accounting standards viz existing accounting standards under Companies (Accounting Standard) Rules, 2006 and IFRS converged Indian Accounting Standards (Ind AS).

International Financial Reporting Standards (IFRS)

These are issued by International Accounting Standard Board (IASB). IASB replaced International Accounting Standard Committee (IASC) in 2001. IASC was formed in 1973 to develop International Accounting Standards (IAS) which had global acceptance and made different accounting statements of different countries similar and comparable. These IAS are applicable up to date along with IFRS.

Objectives of IFRS

The IFRS foundation is an independent, not for profit private sector organisation working in public interest.

Its principal objectives are

- To develop a single set of high quality, understandable, enforceable and globally accepted international financial reporting standards, through its standard body, the IASB.
- To promote the use and application of those standards.
- To take account of the financial reporting needs of emerging economies and small and medium-sized entities.
- To bring about convergence of national accounting standards and International Financial Reporting Standards to high quality solutions.

IFRS issued by the IASB

IFRS-1 First-time Adoption of International Financial Reporting Standards

This standard sets out the procedures that an entity must follow when it adopts IFRSs for the first time as the basis for preparing its general purpose financial statements.

Here, first time adoption means making an explicit and unreserved statement, for the first time, that its general purpose financial statements comply with IFRSs.

IFRS-2 Share Based Payment

This standard requires an entity to recognise share based payment transactions (such as granted shares, share options, or share appreciation rights) in its financial statements, including transactions with employees or other parties to be settled in cash, other assets, or equity instruments of the entity. Specific requirements are included for equity settled and cash settled share based payment transactions, as well as those where the entity or supplier has a choice of cash or equity instruments.

IFRS-2 was originally issued in February, 2004 and first applied to annual periods beginning on or after 1st January, 2005.

IFRS-3 Business Combinations

This standard outlines the accounting when an acquirer obtains control of a business, *i.e.* an acquisition or merger. Such business combinations are accounted for using the 'acquisition method', which generally requires assets acquired and liabilities assumed to be measured at their fair values at the acquisition date.

A revised version of IFRS-3 was issued in January, 2008 and applies to business combinations occurring in an entity's first annual period beginning on or after 1st July, 2009.

IFRS-4 Insurance Contracts

This standard applies, with limited exceptions, to all insurance contracts that an entity issues and to reinsurance contracts that it holds. *This standard requires disclosure of information that helps users*

- to understand the amounts in the insurer's financial statements that arise from insurance contracts.
- to evaluate the nature and extent of risks arising from insurance contracts.

IFRS-4 was issued in March, 2004 and applies to annual periods beginning on or after 1st January, 2005.

IFRS-5 Non-current Assets held for Sale and Discontinued Operations

This standard outlines how to account for non-current assets held for sale (or for distribution to owner). In general terms, assets (or disposal groups) held for sale are not depreciated but are measured at the lower of carrying amount and fair value less costs to sell and are presented separately in the statement of financial position. Specific disclosures are also required for discontinued operations and disposals of non-current assets.

IFRS-5 was issued in March, 2004 and applies to annual periods beginning on or after 1st January, 2005.

IFRS-6 Exploration for an Evaluation of Mineral Resources

This standard has the effect of allowing entities adopting the standard for the first time to use accounting policies for exploration and evaluation assets that were applied before adopting IFRS. It also modifies impairment testing of exploration and evaluation assets by introducing different impairment indicators and allowing the carrying amount to be tested at an aggregate level.

IFRS-6 was issued in December, 2004 and applies to annual periods beginning on or after 1st January, 2006.

IFRS-7 Financial Instruments: Disclosures

This standard requires disclosure of information about the significance of financial instruments to an entity and the nature and extent of risks arising from those financial instruments both in qualitative and quantitative terms. Specific disclosures are required in relation to transferred financial assets and a number of other matters.

IFRS-7 was originally issued in August, 2005 and applies to annual periods beginning on or after 1st January, 2007.

IFRS-8 Operating Segments

This standard requires particular classes of entities (essentially those with publicly traded securities) to disclose information about their operating segments, products and services, the geographical areas in which they operate and their major customers. Information is based on internal management reports both in the identification of operating segments and measurement of disclosed segment information.

IFRS-8 was issued in November, 2006 and applies to annual periods beginning on or after 1st January, 2009.

IFRS-9 Financial Instruments

This standard includes requirements for recognition and measurement, impairment, derecognition and general hedge accounting. The IASB completed its project to replace IAS 39 in phases, adding to the standard as it completed each phase. This standard does not replace the requirements for portfolio fair value hedge accounting for interest rate risk.

IFRS-10 Consolidated Financial Statements

This standard outlines the requirements for the preparation and presentation of consolidated financial statements, requiring entities to consolidate entities, it controls. Control requires exposure or rights to variable returns and the ability to affect those returns through power over an investee.

IFRS-10 was issued in May, 2011 and applies to annual periods beginning on or after 1st January, 2013.

IFRS-11 Joint Arrangements

This standard outlines the accounting by entities that jointly control an arrangement. Joint control involves the contractually agreed sharing of control and arrangement subject to joint control which are classified as either a joint venture (representing a share of net assets and equity accounted) or a joint operation (representing rights to assets and obligations for liabilities, accounted for accordingly).

IFRS-11 was issued in May, 2011 and applies to annual reporting periods beginning on or after 1st January, 2013.

IFRS-12 Disclosure of Interest in other Entities

This standard requires a wide range of disclosures about an entity's interests in subsidiaries, joint arrangements, associates and unconsolidated 'structured entities'. Disclosures are presented as a series of objectives, with detailed guidance on satisfying those objectives.

IFRS-12 was issued in May, 2011 and applies to annual periods beginning on or after 1st January, 2013.

IFRS-13 Fair Value Measurement

This standard requires or permits fair value measurements or disclosures and provides a single IFRS framework for measuring fair value and requires disclosures about fair value measurement. The standard defines fair value on the basis of an 'exit price' notion and uses a 'fair value hierarchy', which results in a market based rather than entity specific measurement.

IFRS-13 was issued in May, 2011 and applies to annual periods beginning on or after 1st January, 2013.

IFRS-14 Regulatory Deferral Accounts

This standard permits an entity which is a first time adopter of International Financial Reporting Standards (IFRS) to continue to account, with some limited changes 'for regulatory deferral account balances' in accordance with its previous GAAP, both on initial adoption of IFRS and in subsequent financial statements.

IFRS-14 was originally issued in January, 2014 and applies to an entity's first annual IFRS financial statements for a period beginning on or after 1st January, 2016.

IFRS-15 Revenue from Contracts with Customers

This standard specifies how and when an IFRS reporter will recognise revenue as well as requiring such entities to provide users of financial statements with more informative, relevant disclosures. This standard provides a single, principles based five step model to be applied to all contracts with customers.

IFRS-15 was issued in May, 2014 and applies to an annual reporting period beginning on or after 1st January, 2018.

IFRS-16 Leases

This standard specifies how an IFRS reporter will recognise, measure, present and disclose leases. The standard provides a single lessee accounting model, requiring lessees to recognise assets and liabilities for all leases unless the lease term is 12 months or less or the underlying asset has a low value. Lessors continue to classify leases as operating or finance, with IFRS 16's approach to lessor accounting substantially unchanged from its predecessor, IAS 17.

IFRS-16 was issued in January, 2016 and applies to annual reporting periods beginning on or after 1st January, 2019.

IFRS-17 Insurance Contracts

This standard establishes the principles for the recognition, measurement, presentation and disclosure of insurance contracts within the scope of the standard. The objective of this standard is to ensure that an entity provides relevant information that faithfully represents those contracts. This information gives a basis for users of financial statements to assess the effect that insurance contracts have on the entity's financial position, financial performance and cash flows.

IFRS-17 was issued in May, 2017 and applies to annual reporting periods beginning on or after 1st January, 2020.

Human Resource Accounting

The American Accounting Association's Committee on Human Resource Accounting (1973) has defined Human Resource Accounting as "the process of identifying and measuring data about human resources and communicating this information to interested parties".

Flamholtz (1971) too has offered a similar definition for Human Resource Accounting. He defines HRA as "the measurement and reporting of the cost and value of people in organisational resources."

The concept of human resource accounting can be basically examined from two dimensions

- The investment in human resources.
- The value of human resources.

Basically, Human Resource Accounting (HRA) is an information system that tells management what changes are occuring over the time to the human resource of the business. HRA also involves accounting for investment in people and their replacement cost, it also involves economic value of people in the organisation. It is a process of identifying and reporting the investment made in human resource of the organisation that is not accounted for in current conventional accounting system.

Objectives of Human Resource Accounting

- To furnish cost value information for making proper and effective management decisions about acquiring, allocating, developing and maintaining human resources in order to achieve cost effective organisational objectives.
- To monitor effectively the use of human resources by the management.
- To have an analysis of the human asset *i.e.* whether such assets are conserved, depleted or appreciated.
- To aid in the development of management principles and proper decision-making for the future by classifying financial consequences of various practices.
- In all, it facilitates valuation of human resources, recording the valuation in the books of account and disclosure of the information in the financial statement.
- Further, *it is to help the organisation in decision-making in the following areas*
    (a) Direct Recruitment V/s Promotion.
    (b) Transfer V/s Retention.
    (c) Retrenchment V/s Retention.
    (d) Impact on budgetary controls of human relations and organisational behaviour.
    (e) Decision on reallocation of plants, closing down existing units and developing overseas subsidiaries etc.

Need for Human Resource Accounting

The adoption of system of Human Resource Accounting discloses the value of human resources. It helps the management in employment and utilisation of human resource. It helps in deciding transfer, training and retrenchment of human resource.

The Human Resource Accounting is focused on return on knowledge rather than return on investment about which most of the companies are concerned.

There are a few organisations, that do recognise the value of their human resources and furnish the related information in their annual reports.

In India, some of these companies are

- Infosys, Bharat Heavy Electricals Ltd (BHEL), The Steel Authority of India Ltd (SAIL).
- The Minerals and Metals Trading Corporation of India Ltd (MMTC).
- The Southern Petrochemicals Industries Corporation of India (SPIC).
- The Associated Cement Companies Ltd.

Limitations of Human Resource Accounting

- The valuation of human assets is based on the assumption that the employees are going to remain with the organisation for a specified period. However, this assumption is wrong because employee mobility is very high.
- The human resource accounting may lead to the de-humanisation in the organisation. If the valuation is not done correctly or the results of the valuation are not used properly.
- In the case of financial accounting, there are certain specified accounting standards, which every organisation must follow. However, there are no standards for HRA. Each organisation has its own standards for HRA. So, there are no uniform standards for human resource accounting. Therefore, the HRA of two organisations cannot be compared.
- There are no specific and clear cut guidelines for cost and value of human resources of an organisation. The present valuation systems have many limitations.

Methods of Human Resource Accounting

Quite a few models have been suggested in the past for the human resource accounting and these can be classified into two parts each having various models.

Some of important ones are

Cost Based Models

Capitalisation of Historical Costs Model

Under this method, the sum of all costs *i.e.* recruitment, acquisition, formal training, informal training, informal familiarisation, experience and development is taken together to indicate the value of the human resources.

The value is amortised annually over the expected length of the service of individual employees and the unamortised cost is shown as investments in the human assets. If an employee leaves the firm (*i.e.* human assets expire) before the expected service life period, then the net value to that extent is charged to the current revenue.

Limitations of Capitalisation of Historical Cost Model

- This method ignores the aggregate value of the employees potential services, as it takes into account a part of the employees acquisition cost.
- The number of years over which the capitalised expenditure is to be amortised, is difficult to estimate.
- Difficulty in determining the rate of amortisation, whether it should be increasing, decreasing or constant.
- As per this approach, the capital cost decreases through amortisation, but in reality the economic value of human resources increases over time as the people gain experience.

Replacement Cost Model

As the historical cost method only takes into account the sunk costs, which are irrelevant for decision-making, a new model for human resource accounting was conceptualised, which took into account, the costs that would be incurred to replace its existing human resources by an identical one. *It consists of two types*

Individual Replacement Costs It refers to the cost, which is to be incurred in replacing an individual by a substitute, who can provide the same set of services as that of the individual being replaced.

Positional Replacement Costs It refers to the cost of replacing the set of services referred by an official in a defined position, the positional replacement cost takes into account the position in the organisation currently held by the employee and also the future positions expected to be held by him.

Limitations of Replacement Cost Model

- The determination of replacement cost of an employees as per this method is highly subjective and often impossible.
- This method is at variance with the conventional accounting practice of valuing assets.
- There can be no similar replacement for a similar certain existing assets. It is really difficult to find identical replacement of the existing human resource.
- The determination of a replacement value is affected by the subjective considerations to a marked extent and therefore, the value is likely to differ from person to person.
- The exit of a top management person may substantially change the human assets value.

Opportunity Cost Model

This model was advocated by **Hekiman and Jones** in the year 1967 and is also known as the market value method. This model is based on the concept of opportunity cost *i.e.* the value of an employee in its alternative best use, as a basis of estimating the value of human resources.

This method was advocated for a company with several divisional heads bidding for the services of various people, the need among themselves and then include the bid price in the investment cost.

There is no opportunity cost for those employees that are not scarce and also those at the top will not be available for auction. As such, only scarce people should comprise the value of human resources.

Limitations of Opportunity Cost Model

- This method excludes employees of the type, which can be hired readily from outside the firm.
- This method is concerned with only one section of a firm's human resources, having special skills within the firm or in the labour market.
- This methodis specifically excluded from its preview the employees scarce or not being 'bid' by the other departments. This is likely to result in lowering the morale and productivity of the employees, who are not covered by the competitive process.
- The total valuation of human resources on the competitive bid price may be misleading or inaccurate.
- Under this method, valuation on the basis of opportunity cost is restricted to alternative use within the organisation. In real life such alternative use may not be identifiable on account of the constraints in an organisational environment.

Value Based Models

Present Value of Future Earnings Model

This model of human resource accounting was developed by Lev and Schwartz in the year 1971 and involves determining the value of human resources as per the present value of estimated future earnings discounted by the Rate of Return on Investment (Cost of Capital). This method helps in determining what an employee's future contribution worth's today.

As per this method, valuation model of human resource accounting, the value of human capital embodied is a person, who is '*y*' years old, is the present value of his/her future from employment and can be calculated by using the following formula

$$V_x = \Sigma \frac{I(t)}{(I+r)} T - x$$

Where,

V_x = the value of an individual x years old.

$I(t)$ = the individuals annual earnings upto retirement

r = a discount rate specific to a person

T = retirement age

Limitations of Present Value of Future Earnings Model

This model is the most commonly used model across the globe for the purpose of human resource accounting, *which are as follows*

- This model ignores the possibility and probability that an individual may leave an organisation for reasons other than death or retirement.
- This model also ignores the probability that people may make role changes during their careers. *e.g.* A junior executive will not remain in the same position throughout the expected service life in the organisation.

Reward Valuation Model/Flamholtz Model

This model was advocated by Flamholtz. It says that an individual's value to an organisation is determined by the services, he is expected to render. This model of human resource accounting is an improvement to the 'Present Value of Future Earnings Model' as it takes into account the probability that an individual is expected to move through a set of mutually exclusive organisational roles or service states during a time interval.

Such movement can be estimated by using the following formula

$$E(S) = \sum_{i=1}^{n} S_i P(S_i)$$

Where, S_i is the services that are expected from the individual in each service state and $P(S_i)$ is the probability that the individual will occupy a particular service state.

Limitations of Reward Valuation Model

- In this model, estimation of the probabilities of likely service states of each employee is difficult.
- Determining the monetary equivalent of service states is a andols.
- It ignores the value added element of individuals working as groups.

Valuation on Group Basis

The proper valuation as per human resources accounting is not possible unless the contributions of the individuals as a group are taken into consideration. An individual's expected service tenure in the organisation is difficult to estimate, but on a group basis it is relatively easier to estimate the percentage of people in a group likely to leave the organisation in the future.

This model of human resource accounting attempted to calculate the present value of all existing employees in such rank.

Such present value is ascertained with the help of the following steps

- Ascertain the number of employees in each rank.
- Estimate the probability that an employee will be in his rank within the organisation or will be terminated in the next period. This probability will be estimated for a specified time period.
- Ascertain the economic value of an employee in a specified rank during each time period.
- The present value of existing employees in each rank is obtained by multiplying the above three factors and applying an appropriate discount rate.

Limitations of Valuation on Group Basis

- This method of human resource accounting ignores the exceptional qualities of certain skilled employees.
- As this method ignores the exceptional qualities of skilled employees the performance of a group may be affected is the events of a single individual, leaving the organisation.

  Despite of these limitations, this method simplifies the process valuation of human resources accounting by considerating a group of employees as a valuation base.

Inflation Accounting

Inflation normally refers to the increasing trend in general price level. In other words, it is a state in which the purchasing power of money goes down.

Prices are continuously rising in the commodities/goods, while the accounts are maintained at historical cost only. Thus, impact of inflation on financial position of a business is increasingly felt in view of the fact that the accounts are prepared on the basis of historical cost only. In such circumstances, accounts are required to be maintained on present value basis.

Inflation accounting is a system of accounting, which shows the effect of changing costs and prices on affairs of a business unit during an accounting year. While the cost in the traditional accounting refers to the historical cost, in inflation accounting, it represents the cost that prevails at the time of reporting. The different ways, through which financial accounts can be adjusted for changing prices is studied under the subject 'Inflation Accounting'. Given that price changes can also be downward, it is more appropriately called 'accounting for price level changes'.

Inflation Effects on Financial Statements

These are as follows

Implied Assumption The value of money will remain stable, but the value of money has been fluctuating violently in most of the parts of the world.

Revenue Statements Some expenditures are shown at current price level *e.g.* wages, rent, lighting charges, etc. Some expenditures are shown at historical price level *e.g.* depreciation, amortisation, depletion, etc.

Balance Sheet Acquisition cost of various assets purchased at different time intervals are added together. Some assets are shown at current price level, *e.g.* current assets, some assets are shown at historical price level *e.g.* fixed assets.

Effects of Price Level Changes on Accounts

- Profit and loss statement will show more profit than actual as depreciation is inadequate and closing stock is valued at higher amount.
- More amount of income tax and dividend. So, acute shortage of working capital.
- Balance sheet would not show true and fair view.

Evaluation of Change in Price Level

- General indexes/indices
- Price index of gross domestic product
- Cost of living index
- Consumer price index
- Wholesale price index
- Production price index
- Special indexes/indices
- Industry indexes
- Commodity group indexes
- Commodity indexes

Needs of Inflation Accounting

In the traditional accounting, assets are shown at historical cost, year after year.

Also during the inflationary period, historical cost based depreciation would be highly insufficient to replace the existing assets at current cost. Moreover, current revenues for the period are not properly matched with the current cost of operation.

Therefore, the problems created by price changes in the historical cost based accounts necessitates some methods to take care of inflation into the accounting system.

The significance of inflation accounting emerges from the inherent limitations of the historical cost accounting system.

Following are the limitations of historical accounting

- Historical accounts do not consider the unrealised holding gains arising from the rise in the monetary value of the assets due to inflation.
- The objective of charging depreciation is to spread the cost of the asset over its useful life and make reserve for its replacement in the future. But it does not take into account the impact of inflation over the replacement cost, which may result into the inadequate charge of depreciation.
- Under historical accounting, inventories acquired at old prices are matched against revenues expressed at current prices. In the period of inflation, this may lead to the overstatement of profits due to mixing-up of holding gains and operating gains.
- Future earnings are not easily projected from historical earnings.

Techniques of Inflation Accounting

There is no agreement on the method to be adopted for adjusting the financial statements for price level changes. Price level changes can be broadly classified into general price level changes and specific price level changes.

Specific price refer to changes in the price of a specific asset. It is important to note that the price of a particular asset may not follow the same trend as WPI or CPI.

On the basis or price level changes, techniques are as follows

- Current Purchasing Power (CPP) Method, based on changes in general price level changes.
- Current Cost Accounting (CCA) Method, based on changes in prices of specific assets.

Current Purchasing Power (CPP) Method

In this method, all items in the financial statements are restated in terms of a constant unit of money *i.e.* in terms of general purchasing power. In order to measure changes in the price level and incorporate changes in the financial statements, we use general price index which is considered to be a barometer for this purpose. The index is used to convert the values of various items in the Financial Statements. This method takes into account the changes in the general purchasing power of money and ignores the actual rise or fall in the price of the given item.

CPP method involves the refurnishing of historical figures at current purchasing power. For this, historical figures are converted into value of purchasing power at the end of the period. Two index numbers are required: one showing the general price level at the end of the period and the other reflecting the same at the date of the transaction. Profit under this method is an increase in the value of the net asset over a period, all valuations being made in terms of current purchasing power.

Current Cost Accounting (CCA) Method

This method is an alternative to the current purchasing power method. The current cost accounting method matches current revenues with the current cost of the resources, which are consumed in earning them. Changes in the general price level are measured by index numbers.

Specific price change occurs, if price of a particular asset changes without any general price change. Under this method, assets are valued at current cost, which is the cost at which asset can be replaced on a date.

While the Current Purchasing Power (CPP) method is known as the General Price Level Approach, the Current Cost Accounting (CCA) method is known as Specific Price Level Approach or Replacement Cost Accounting.

Other Techniques of Inflation Accounting

Only Putting a Note in Accounts

Accounts will be prepared on historical cost basis only on the assumption that value of money remains stable. A note should be appended to show changing price level in accounts presented. Thus, no changes are made in the accounts. So, profit is in excess and enough amount is not available for replacement of the assets.

Replacement Reserve Method

Accounts are prepared on historical basis only. Depreciation is calculated on historical cost. But replacement amount is inadequate, when the asset is discarded. So, additional amount required for replacement purpose should be transferred to Replacement Reserve Account every year. Replacement cost is estimated and will be spread over future period.

Partial Change Method

Fixed assets are generally written-up and stock is valued on the basis of LIFO method. Link-up fixed assets in accordance with a legally established index. Thereafter, charge depreciation on written-up value. Stock and issue of material priced on LIFO basis which resembles the current price of goods. As a result, profit won't be higher, it will reflect true profit or loss on price level change.

Limitations of Inflation Accounting

- Change in the price level is a continuous process.
- This system makes the calculations a tedious task because of too many conversions and calculations.
- This system has not been preferred by tax authorities.

Use of Inflation Accounting

The inflation accounting solution allows to adjust the accounts for inflation. All the functions described in the following documentation are for high-inflation countries, in which such adjustments are required to be made at regular intervals.

The solution affects three application components

***Financial Accounting** (FI)* The functions allows to restate the G/L accounts and open payables and receivables for inflation (general and specific price-level changes).

***Asset Accounting** (FI-AA)* This component enables to revalue the assets to take into account the effects of inflation.

***Materials Management** (MM)* In this component, you can revaluate your materials according to various principles.

Environmental Accounting

Environmental accounting is an attempt to broaden the scope of the accounting frameworks used to assess economic performance, to take stock of element that are not recorded in public or private accounting books. These gaps occur because the various costs of using nature are not captured, being considered in many cases as externalities that can be forwarded to others or postponed.

Environmental accounting is an important tool to understand the role played by natural environment in the development of an economy. It provides data related to contribution of natural resources to economic well being as well as the costs imposed by environmental pollution and resource degradation.

Thus, environmental accounting refers to the identification measurement and communication of the data on environmentally responsible performance of a business entity to facilitate economic decision-making.

The environmental accounting was first implied by Norway in the early 1970s. In India, this concept is limited to certain industries only such as cement, power and electronics, oil and petroleum, natural gas, steel and textile industries.

Objectives of Environmental Accounting

- To support the development and operation of environmental management system.
- To minimise and control the total expenditure on protection and enhancement of environment.
- To segregate and collaborate environmental flows and natural resources.
- To help managers in decision-making that will reduce or eliminate their environmental costs.

Advantages of Environmental Accounting

- It set outs the opportunity to find ways to eliminate or reduce the environmental costs.
- It improves the safety of the workers which in turn will help increasing productivity.
- Better knowledge of environmental cost can facilitate more accurate costing and pricing of products.

- It helps to build up confidence and trust in the society.
- It promotes more accurate costing and pricing of products.

Limitations of Environmental Accounting

- There is no standard method for environmental accounting.
- It is a long-term and difficult process.
- If method of this accounting is different, then comparison between two firms is impossible.
- It mainly considers the cost internal to the company and excludes cost to society.
- This accounting method cannot work independently as it depends on financial accounting.

Forms of Environmental Accounting

Environmental Management Accounting It focuses on environmental cost information as well as material and every flow information.

It can be classified into three sub-classes

- Segment environmental accounting.
- Eco-balance environmental accounting.
- Corporate environmental accounting.

Environmental Financial Accounting It refers to the financial accounting practice. It includes the reporting of environmental liability costs and other significant environmental costs too.

Environmental National Accounting It focuses on stocks of natural resources, environmental costs etc. It is a national level accounting.

EXAM BASED QUESTIONS

Accounting, its Principles and Financial Statements

1 If accounting information is based on facts and it is verifiable by documents, it has the quality of

(a) relevance (b) understandability
(c) reliability (d) comparability

2 Which of the following practices is not in consonance with the convention of conservatism?

(a) Creating provision for bad debts
(b) Creating provision for discount on creditors
(c) Creating provision for discount on debtors
(d) Creating provision for tax

3 Which of the following statement is correct?

(a) Accounting principles represent laws fixed by the respective governments
(b) Accounting principles represent laws fixed by accounting expert
(c) Accounting principles represent inviolable laws fixed by a legal board
(d) Accounting principles represent a consensuses at a particular time to the recording of accounting transactions

4 Consider the following statements.

1. The entity concept of accounting is not applicable to sole trading concerns and partnership concerns.
2. Assets are to be shown in the balance sheet at their rcplacement cost on liquidation.
3. Money measurement concept takes into account changes in the value of monetary unit.
4. When a creditor is paid, this results in decrease of one asset and a corresponding increase in other asset.

Which of the statements given above are correct?

(a) Both 1 and 2 (b) Both 2 and 3
(c) Both 3 and 4 (d) None of the above

5 As per Revenue Recognition Concept, revenue is deemed to be realised

(a) when purchase order is received from the purchaser
(b) when goods are delivered to the purchaser
(c) when the title of the goods has been transferred to the purchaser
(d) when cash is received from the purchaser

6 Which of the following is not an accounting concept?

(a) Matching Concepts (b) Dual Aspect Concepts
(c) True and Fair Concepts (d) Going Concern Concept

7 Everything a firm owns, it also owes out to somebody. This co-incidence is explained by the .... concept.

(a) dual aspect (b) prudence
(c) money measurement (d) revenue recognition

8 The basic concept related to profit and loss account is/are

(a) realisation concept (b) matching concept
(c) cost concept (d) Both (a) and (b)

9 Which of the following accounting equations is not correct?

(a) Assets – Liabilities = Equity
(b) Assets – Equity = Liability
(c) Asset + Liability = Equity
(d) Liability + Equity = Assets

10 The term 'financial assets' includes all of the following except

(a) technical knowledge (b) bank loan
(c) lease obligations
(d) shares, bonds and debentures

11 Assets which have a fixed content and the value of asset goes down as the contents are taken out are called

(a) intangible assets (b) fictitious assets
(c) wasting assets (d) floating assets

12 Under statement of closing work-in-progress in the period will

(a) understate cost of goods manufactured in that period
(b) overstate current assets
(c) overstate gross profit from sales in that period
(d) understate net income in that period

13 In case of a news agent, which of the following is a revenue receipt?

(a) The proceeds of the sale of plant and equipment
(b) Money received from insurance company as a result of crashing a delivery vehicle
(c) A refund received from a supplier as compensation for damaged stock supplied
(d) None of the above

14 Present liability of uncertain amount, which can be measured reliably by using a substantial degree of estimation is termed as

(a) liability (b) contingent liability
(c) provision (d) None of these

15 Expenditure, which result increase in the earning capacity of a business is

(a) capital expenditure
(b) revenue expenditure
(c) deferred revenue expenditure
(d) All of the above

16 Which of the following equation is correct?

(a) Gross profit = Net sales – Cost of goods sold
(b) Gross profit = Sales + Closing stock – Opening stock – Purchase
(c) Cost of goods sold + Gross profit = Sales
(d) All of the above

17 Fees paid to lawyer for drawing a purchase deed of land is which type of expenditure?

(a) Capital expenditure
(b) Revenue expenditure
(c) Deferred revenue expenditure
(d) None of the above

18 Sale of an asset on credit at a price higher than written down value of the asset, would

(a) leave owner's equity unaffected
(b) increase owner's equity to the extent of less value
(c) increase owner's equity by the amount of sale
(d) increase owner's equity to the extent of profit on sale

19 Out of the following, which four expenditures would be recorded in the motor van account?

1. Cost ₹ 2,00,000 2. Registration ₹ 5,000
3. Petrol ₹ 2,000 4. Salary to driver ₹ 4,000
5. Writing the company name ₹ 3,500
6. Road tax paid (one time) ₹ 4,500

Select the correct answer using codes given below

Codes

(a) 1, 2, 3 and 4 (b) 1, 2, 5 and 6
(c) 1, 3, 5 and 6 (d) 1, 2, 3 and 5

20 Where is the depreciation account appearing in the trial balance is shown?

(a) Profit and Loss A/c
(b) Liabilities side
(c) Deducted from the concerned assets
(d) All of the above

21 Arrange the following in chronological order about assets as per liquidity order.

1. Debtors 2. Building
3. Cash 4. Stock

Codes

(a) 2, 3, 1, 4 (b) 3, 4, 1, 2
(c) 1, 4, 2, 3 (d) 3, 1, 4, 2

22 Consider the following statements.

1. Inventory includes raw material, finished goods and goods in process.
2. Inventory is the part of working capital.
3. Inventory includes goods likely to be purchased in the coming months.

Which of the statements given above are correct?

(a) Both 1 and 2 (b) Both 2 and 3
(c) Both 1 and 3 (d) All of the above

23 Arrange the following items in the order of their appearance in the preparation of financial statements.

1. Net profit 2. Gross profit
3. Cash at bank

Codes

(a) 1, 2, 3 (b) 3, 2, 1 (c) 2, 1, 3 (d) 2, 3, 1

24 Financial activities in a cash flow statement as per AS-7 do not include

(a) issue of shares (b) buy back of shares
(c) purchase of building (d) dividend paid

IAS and IFRS

25 AS-37 does not apply to contingent liabilities of

(a) listed companies (b) unlisted companies
(c) small business (d) insurance companies

26 Which one of the following is an investment activity as per AS-7?

(a) Redemption of debentures (b) Cash in hand
(c) Purchase of fixed assets (d) Interest paid

27 Which of the following are examples of cash flow from operating activities as per AS-7?

1. Cash receipts from the sale of goods and the rendering of services.
2. Cash receipts from disposal of intangible assets.
3. Cash receipts from royalties, fees, commissions and other revenue.
4. Cash payments to suppliers for goods and services.
5. Cash proceeds from issuing shares or other similar instruments.
6. Cash payments to and on behalf of employees.

Select the correct answer using the codes given below

Codes

(a) 1, 3, 4 and 6 (b) 2, 5 and 6
(c) 1, 2, 3 and 4 (d) 2, 3, 4 and 6

28 Which of the following loan commitments are within the scope of IFRS-9?

(a) Loan commitments that can be settled net in cash or by delivering or issuing another financial instrument
(b) Commitment to provide a loan at a below market interest rate
(c) Loan commitment that the entity designates as financial liabilities at fair value through profit or loss
(d) All of the above

29 An entity issues shares as consideration for the purchase of inventory. The shares were issued on 1st January, 2017. The inventory is eventually sold on 31st December, 2018. The value of the inventory on 1st January, 2017, was ₹ 8,00,000. This value was unchanged upto the date of sale. The sale proceed was ₹ 12,00,000. The shares issued have a market value of ₹ 9,00,000. Which of the following statement correctly describes the accounting treatment of this share based payment transaction?

(a) Equity is increased by ₹ 8,00,000 and inventory is increased by ₹ 8,00,000. The inventory value is expensed on sale on 31st December, 2018.
(b) Equity is increased by ₹ 9,00,000, inventory is increased by ₹ 9,00,000, the inventory value is expensed on sale on 31st December, 2018.
(c) Equity is increased by ₹ 8,00,000 and inventory is increased by ₹ 8,00,000, the inventory value is expensed over the two years to 31st December, 2018.
(d) Equity is increased by ₹ 9,00,000, inventory is increased by ₹ 9,00,000, the inventory value is expensed over the two years to 31st December, 2018.

30 A company XYZ (parent co.) is required to present consolidated financial statements, except if it meets certain conditions. You need to identify those conditions from the following.

1. It is a subsidiary of another entity and all its other owners, including those not otherwise entitled to vote, have been informed about and do not object to, the parent not presenting consolidated financial statements.
2. Its debt or equity instruments are not treaded in a public market.
3. Its ultimate or any intermediate parent produces Ind AS complaint consolidated financial statements available for public use.

(a) Both 1 and 3 (b) Both 2 and 3
(c) Both 1 and 2 (d) All of these

31 A complete set of financial statements under Ind AS includes the following.

1. Balance sheet at the end of the period.
2. Statement of profit and loss for the period.
3. Statement of changes in equity for the period.
4. Statement of cash flow for the period.
5. Balance sheet at the beginning of the preceding period.

Which statements given above are correct?

(a) 1, 2 and 4 (b) Both 3 and 5
(c) 2, 3 and 5 (d) All of the above

32 Which of the following parties cannot be granted shares or share options by the entity?

(a) Executive director
(b) Supplier of goods and services
(c) Chief Accountant
(d) None of the above

33 IFRS-2 applies to share-based payment transactions in which an entity ..... goods or services.

(a) acquires (b) receives
(c) transfers (d) Both (a) and (b)

34 Does IFRS-8 allow an entity to combine information about operating segments into one reportable segment?

(a) Yes, if the operating segments do not meet the quantitative thresholds
(b) Yes, if the operating segments share the majority of the aggregation criteria listed in this IFRS
(c) Yes, if the operating segments have similar economic characteristics
(d) All of the above

35 After recognition, an entity applies

(a) revaluation model to the exploration and evaluation assets
(b) cost model to the exploration and evaluation assets
(c) Either (a) or (b)
(d) Both (a) and (b)

36 Which of the following types of information does Ind AS-107 not require to be disclosed about the significance of financial instruments?

(a) Fair value of financial instruments
(b) Carrying amounts of categories of financial instruments
(c) Information about the use of hedge accounting
(d) Information about financial instruments, contracts and obligations under share based payment transactions

37 All the following are benefits of Accounting Standards except

(a) AS cannot override the statute
(b) AS reduce to a reasonable extent confusing variations in the accounting treatments used to prepare financial statements
(c) AS facilitates comparison of financial statements of companies
(d) AS may call for disclosure beyond that required by law

38 Which of the following transactions involving the issuance of shares does not come within the definition of a 'share based payment' under Ind AS- 102?

(a) Employee share purchase plans
(b) Employee share option plans
(c) Share based payment relating to an acquisition of a subsidiary
(d) Share appreciation rights

39 The objective of hedge accounting is to represent, in the financial statements, the effect of an entity's .... that use financial instruments to manage .... arising from particular risks that could affect profit or loss.

(a) risk management activities, exposures
(b) risk mitigation activities, credit losses
(c) risk diversification activities, credit concentration
(d) risk mitigation activities, credit exposures

40 For equity-settled share-based payment transactions, the entity shall measure the goods or services received and the corresponding increase in equity, directly at the .... of the goods or services received, unless that it cannot be estimated reliably.

(a) amortised cost (b) net book value
(c) fair value (d) historical cost

41 As per AS-11 construction contracts, costs that may be attributable to contract activity in general and can be allocated to specific contracts include

1. insurance
2. freight
3. costs of design and technical assistance that is not directly related to a specific contract
4. manufacturing overheads
5. construction overheads

Select the correct answer using the codes given below
Codes
(a) 1, 3 and 5 (b) 2, 3 and 4
(c) 3, 4 and 5 (d) 1, 2 and 3

42 **What items of inventories are outside the scope of AS-2?**
1. Work-in-progress arising under construction contracts.
2. Raw materials including maintenance supplies.
3. Share, debentures held as stock-in-trade.
4. Machinery spares exclusively used with fixed assets.

Select the correct answer using the codes given below
(a) 1, 3 and 4 (b) 1, 2 and 4
(c) 2, 3 and 4 (d) All of these

43 **As per AS-2 valuation of inventories, inventories are assets**
1. held for sale in the ordinary course of business.
2. held for sale in the special course of business.
3. in the process of production for such sale.
4. in the form of materials or supplies to be consumed in the production processor or in the rendering of services.
5. in the process of services for such sale.

Select the correct answer using the codes given below
(a) 1, 2, 3 and 4 (b) 1, 4 and 5
(c) 1, 3 and 4 (d) 2, 4 and 5

44 **As per AS-2 this standard should be applied in accounting for inventories other than**
1. work-in-progress arising under constrution contracts, including directly related service contracts (see Accounting Standard (AS)-7, construction contracts).
2. work-in-progress arising in the ordinary course of business of service providers.
3. shares, debentures and other financial instruments held as stock-in-trade.
4. producer's inventories of livestock, agricultural and forest products and mineral oils, ores and gases to the extent that they are measured at net realisable value in accordance with established practices in those industries.
5. work-in-progress arising in the special course of business of service providers.

Select the correct answer using the codes given below
Codes
(a) 1, 2 and 3 (b) 1, 2, 3 and 4
(c) 2, 3, 4 and 5 (d) 3, 4 and 5

45 **If an entity owns directly or indirectly more than 50% of voting rights, control is presumed unless clearly proven that it is not control. Sometimes control exists, even if there is less than 50% of voting rightes exist. State which of the followings is/are example(s) of control even if voting power is less than 50%.**
(a) Power to govern financial and operating policies under statute
(b) Power to remove/appoint majority members of BOD that controls the entity
(c) Power to cost majority of votes at meetings of BOD that controls the entity
(d) All of the above

46 **When the sale is expected to occur beyond one year, the entity shall measure the costs to sell at their present value. Any increase in the present value of the costs to sell that arises from the passage of time shall be presented in**
(a) Capital Reserve A/c
(b) Profit or loss as a financing cost
(c) General Reserve A/c
(d) None of the above

47 **Human Resource Accounting is the measurement and reporting .... and .... of people in organisational resources.**
(a) benefit, opportunities (b) cost, value
(c) contract, agreement (d) None of these

48 **When the cost incurred on recruiting, training and developing the employees is considered for determining the value of employees, it is called**
(a) the opportunity cost approach
(b) the historical cost approach
(c) the replacement cost approach
(d) the marginal cost approach

HR, Inflation and Environmental Accounting

49 **The value of HR is the function of the average salary of the employees and their average employment tenure in the organisation. This is the essence of**
(a) five-dimensional model
(b) unpurchased goodwill model
(c) aggregate payment model
(d) casual, intervening and end-result model

50 **A .... is used to reflect the changes in purchasing power of money or a whole.**
(a) general price index
(b) special price index
(c) monetary value index
(d) discount factor index

51 **Current Cost Accounting method attempted to match the current income against which cost?**
(a) Past cost (b) Current cost
(c) General cost (d) Individual cost

52 **Under CCA method, surplus or deficit due to change in value of assets and adjustment in profit and loss statement should be adjusted to**
(a) General Reserve A/c
(b) Profit and Loss statement
(c) Revaluation Reserve A/c
(d) None of the above

53 When there is change in the value of rupee, it is said to be change in
(a) over all price level (b) general price level
(c) individual price level (d) discounting price level

54 Environmental accounting concept is applied on
(a) cement industries (b) steel industries
(c) textile industries (d) All of these

55 Which of the following is/are the form(s) of environmental accounting?
(a) Environmental Management accounting
(b) Environmental Financial accounting
(c) Environmental National accounting
(d) All of the above

56 Environmental management accounting focuses on
(a) natural resources stock
(b) environmental cost information
(c) environmental liability costs
(d) None of the above

57 Segment Environmental accounting is the part of
(a) environmental management accounting
(b) environmental financial accounting
(c) environmental national accounting
(d) None of the above

58 Which of the following statements is/are correct?
(a) The main purpose of any business is to earn profit
(b) If expenses exceed revenue then business is running loss
(c) Both (a) and (b)
(d) None of the above

59 Which of the following statements is/are correct?
(a) Dual aspect concept assumes an indefinite life of the entity
(b) In accounting, accrual basis is used for recording of transactions
(c) Both (a) and (b)
(d) None of the above

60 Which of the following is/are the method(s) of Human Resource Accounting?
(a) Capitalisation of historical cost model
(b) Replacement cost model
(c) Present value of future earning model
(d) All of the above

61 Which method of HR Accounting was developed by Lev and Schwartz?
(a) Capitalisation of historical cost model
(b) Opportunity cost model
(c) Present value of future earning model
(d) Replacement cost model

62 Increasing trend in general price level is known as
(a) depreciation (b) inflation
(c) profit (d) pricing

Miscellaneous

63 **Statement** I If the going concern concept is no longer valid, then all prepaid assets would be completely written-off immediately.

Statement II Also land held as an investment would be valued at its realisable value.

Codes
(a) Both statements are correct
(b) Both statements are incorrect
(c) Statement I is correct, but Statement II is incorrect
(d) Statement I is incorrect, but Statement II is correct

64 **Statement** I If an entity holds directly/indirectly 50% or more of the voting power of the investee, it is presumed thus such entity has significant influence.

Statement II AS-24 deals with related party disclosures.

Which of the following is/are correct?
(a) Only statement I is true
(b) Only statement II is true
(c) Both statements are true
(d) Both statements are false

65 **Statement** I IFRS are issued by International Accounting Standard Board (IASB).

Statement II IFRS-16, i.e. 'leases' applies to annual reporting periods beginning on or after 1st January, 2019.
(a) Only statement I is true
(b) Only statement II is true
(c) Both statements are true
(d) Both statements are false

66 **Statement** I In the traditional accounting, assets are shown at cost, year after year.

Statement II The cost in inflation accounting represent the cost that prevails at the time of reporting.

Which of the following is/are correct?

Codes
(a) Both statements are correct
(b) Both statements are incorrect
(c) Statement I is correct, but statement II is incorrect
(d) Statement II is correct, but statement I is incorrect

67 **Statement** I These is no standard method for environmental accounting.

Statement II Environmental accounting is applied to textile industries.

Which of the following is/are correct?
(a) Statement I is true, but Statement II is false
(b) Statement I is false, but Statement II is true
(c) Both statements are true
(d) Both statements are false

68 Statement I Capital expenditure benefits the current accounting period.

Statement II Capital expenditure will also benefit the next accounting period.

Codes
(a) Both statements are correct
(b) Both statements are incorrect
(c) Statement I is correct, but statement II is incorrect
(d) Statement I is incorrect, but statement II is correct

69 Statement I The profit and loss account shows the financial results of the concern for a period.

Statement II In profit and loss account, indirect expenses are charged against the gross profit.

Codes
(a) Both statements are correct
(b) Both statements are incorrect
(c) Statement I is correct, but statement II is incorrect
(d) Statement I is incorrect, but statement II is correct

Directions (Q. Nos. 70-81) *In the questions given are two statements labelled as Assertion (A) and Reason (R). In two context of two statements, which one of the following is correct?*

Codes
(a) Both (A) and (R) are true and (R) is the correct explanation of (A)
(b) Both (A) and (R) are true, but (R) is not the correct explanation of (A)
(c) (A) is true, but (R) is false
(d) (A) is false, but (R) is true

70 Assertion (A) Accounting principles are not feasible.

Reason (R) Accounting principles can be applied without undue complexity or cost.

71 Assertion (A) Accounting helps to provide information to various parties.

Reason (R) Accounting aims to meet the information needs of the decision-makers.

72 Assertion (A) Legal fee paid to acquire any property is part of the cost of that property.

Reason (R) Legal fee is incurred to possess the ownership right of that property and hence, a capital expenditure.

73 Assertion (A) General reserve is created by appropriation of profits without any specific or particular purpose.

Reason (R) The aim of general reserve is to provide additional working capital or to strengthen the cash resources of the business.

74 Assertion (A) Assets are to be shown in the balance sheet at the realisable value.

Reason (R) Balance sheet discloses financial position of the business.

75 Assertion (A) Fixed asset is an asset held with the intention of being used for the purpose of producing or providing goods or services.

Reason (R) Bank balance implies balance of funds held by bank on behalf of the company.

76 Assertion (A) Deferred revenue expenditure's benefit lasts for more than one accounting period.

Reason (R) It is therefore written off during the periods over which the benefits lasts.

77 Assertion (A) A contingent asset is a possible asset that arises from past event.

Reason (R) The existence of it will be confirmed only by the occurrence or non-occurrence of one or more certain future events wholly within the control of the enterprise.

78 Assertion (A) Computers taken on hire by a business for a period of twelve months is not an assets.

Reason (R) Computers are not owned by the business to be classified as an asset.

79 Assertion (A) Human resource accounting provides valuable information for persons interested in making long-term investment in firm.

Reason (R) Human resource accounting is "the process of identifying and measuring data about human resources and communicating this information to interested parties".

80 Assertion (A) Human resource accounting may lead to dehumanisation in the organisation.

Reason (R) It is affected in case the valuation is not done correctly or the results of the valuation are not used properly.

81 Assertion (A) The human resource accounting is focused on return on knowledge rather than return on investment.

Reason (R) It is focused on the measurement of abilities of all the employees of the company, at every level, to produce value from their knowledge and capabilities.

82 Match the following.

	List I		List II
A.	Capital is the difference between	1.	Cost of goods sold from sales
B.	Gross profit is ascertained by deducting	2.	To find out cost of production
C.	Wages paid for erecting machines are	3.	Assets and liabilities
D.	The manufacturing account is prepared	4.	Debited to machinery account

Codes

	A	B	C	D		A	B	C	D
(a)	4	3	2	1	(b)	4	3	1	2
(c)	3	4	1	2	(d)	3	1	4	2

83 Match the following.

List I	List II
A. Revenue means the income of a .... nature.	1. Fixed assets
B. Premium paid on the life insurance policy of the proprietor will be debited to .... account.	2. Regular
C. Going concern concept is relevant for	3. Matching
D. Recognition of cost in the same period as associated revenues is called .... principle.	4. Drawings

Codes

	A	B	C	D
(a)	4	3	2	1
(b)	2	3	4	1
(c)	2	1	4	3
(d)	2	4	1	3

84 Match the following.

List I	List II
A. .... concept is related to recognition of income.	1. Rent
B. Trading account and profit and loss account are .... statements.	2. Realisation
C. .... is a tangible fixed assets.	3. Periodic
D. Outstanding rent will be debited to .... account.	4. Land

Codes

	A	B	C	D		A	B	C	D
(a)	2	3	4	1	(b)	4	3	2	1
(c)	2	1	4	3	(d)	2	4	1	3

85 Match the following.

List I	List II
A. The document from which the returns to suppliers are recorded is known as	1. Assets
B. Wages paid on erection of a new machinery should be debited to	2. Debit note
C. Prepaid expense is an item of	3. Credit note
D. The receiver of goods returned will send a .... to the person, who return the goods.	4. Machinery account

Codes

	A	B	C	D
(a)	2	1	4	3
(b)	4	1	2	3
(c)	2	4	1	3
(d)	4	3	1	2

86 Match the following.

List I	List II
A. The document related to sales return is .... note.	1. Business
B Bank reconciliation statement is prepared by the .... enterprise.	2. Credit
C. Purchases account will always have a .... balance.	3. Cash
D. When the word 'paid' occurs, it means a reduction of	4 Debit

Codes

	A	B	C	D		A	B	C	D
(a)	4	3	2	1	(b)	2	1	4	3
(c)	2	4	1	3	(d)	3	4	1	2

87 Match the following.

List I	List II
A. Income is measured and financial position is assessed	1. Consistency concept
B. Anticipate no profit and provide for all possible losses	2. Going concern concept
C. Assets are depreciated on the basis of expected life rather than on the basis of market value	3. Conservatism concept
D. The comparison of one accounting period with that in the past is possible	4. Matching concept

Codes

	A	B	C	D		A	B	C	D
(a)	4	3	2	1	(b)	2	1	4	3
(c)	4	3	1	2	(d)	3	4	2	1

88 Match the following.

List I	List II
A. Ind AS- 223	1. Impairment of assets
B. Ind AS- 27	2. Borrowing costs
C. Ind AS- 36	3. Agriculture
D. Ind AS- 41	4. Separate financial statements

Codes

	A	B	C	D		A	B	C	D
(a)	3	2	1	4	(b)	2	4	1	3
(c)	4	2	3	1	(d)	1	2	3	4

89 Match the following.

List I	List II
A. IFRS-3	1. Operating segments
B. IFRS-8	2. leases
C. IFRS-9	3. Business combinations
D. IFRS-16	4. Financial Instruments

Codes

	A	B	C	D		A	B	C	D
(a)	1	2	3	4	(b)	2	4	1	3
(c)	3	1	4	2	(d)	4	3	2	1

PREVIOUS YEARS' QUESTIONS

December 2018

1 Match the item list I with the items of list II and choose the correct answer from the code given below.

List I	List II
A. AS-01	1. Accounting for fixed assets
B. AS-3	2. Disclosure of accounting policies
C. AS-10	3. Leases and its accounting
D. AS-19	4. Cash flow statements

Codes

	A	B	C	D		A	B	C	D
(a)	3	4	2	1	(b)	1	2	3	4
(c)	3	2	1	4	(d)	3	1	4	2

2 Which of the following statement is/are true?

1. Tax shield on depreciation and interest is an important variable both for the lessor and the lessee.
2. Lease transactions in India are governed by the lease act.
3. A lessee should evaluate the lease options against the buying option.
4. As per AS-19, financial lease is shown in the balance sheet of the lessee as an asset.

(a) Both 1 and 4 (b) 1, 3 and 4
(c) 2, 3 and 4 (d) Only 2

July 2018

3 Assertion (A) Personal transactions of the owners of the business are not recorded in the books.

Reason (R) According to the business entity concept, each business enterprise is considered as an accounting unit separate from owners.

Codes

(a) Both (A) and (R) are correct and (R) is the correct explanation of (A)
(b) Both (A) and (R) are correct, but (R) is not the correct explanation of (A)
(c) (A) is correct, but (R) is not correct
(d) (A) is wrong, but (R) is correct

4 Which one of the following statement is not true?

(a) An expenditure intended to benefit current year is revenue expenditure
(b) Amount paid for acquiring goodwill is capital expenditure
(c) Wages paid for installation of a new machine is usually debited to wages account
(d) Revenue expenditure is not intended to benefit future period

November 2017

5 The balance of property at cost has been ₹ 20,000 and ₹ 17,000 in 2015 and 2016, respectively. The profit on the sale of property of ₹ 2,000 is credited to Capital Reserve Account. New property costing ₹ 5,000 was bought in 2016. Determine the sale proceeds from property.

(a) ₹ 3,000 (b) ₹ 7,000
(c) ₹ 10,000 (d) ₹ 15,000

6 Which one of the following receipts is of revenue nature?

(a) Amount realised from the sale of investments
(b) Dividend received on investment
(c) Amount borrowed from a bank
(d) Compensation received from municipal corporation for the acquisition of land for the construction of road.

7 Schedule III Part II of the Companies Act, 2013 deals with which one of the following?

(a) Format of Balance Sheet
(b) Format of Profit and Loss Account
(c) Format of Trading Account
(d) Format of Cash Flow

8 Match the items of List - I with those of List - II and indicate the correct code.

List I (Accounting Standard)	List II (Relationship)
A. AS-6	1. Accounting for Consolidated Financial Statements
B. AS-3	2. Accounting For Fixed Assets
C. AS-10	3. Depreciation Accounting
D. AS-21	4. Accounting For Cash Flow Statement

Codes

	A	B	C	D
(a)	2	4	3	1
(b)	3	4	2	1
(c)	4	3	1	2
(d)	1	2	3	4

9 Which of the following are the benefits of responsibility accounting?

1. It facilitates the centralisation of decision taking.
2. It provides a system of closer control.
3. It measures the performance of individuals in an objective manner.
4. It develops a sense of cost consciousness among managers and their subordinates.

Codes

(a) 1, 2 and 3 (b) 2, 3 and 4
(c) 1, 2 and 4 (d) 1, 3 and 4

10 Which one of the following methods of Inflation Accounting has been proposed by Sandilands Committee of UK?

(a) General Price Level Method
(b) Specific Price Level Method
(c) Current Cost Accounting Method
(d) Generally Accepted Accounting Principles

January 2017

11 Which of the following activities should be shown separately in the cash flow statement prepared as per Accounting Standard-3?

1. Cash flow from borrowing activities
2. Cash flow from operating activities
3. Cash flow from financing activities
4. Cash flow from investing activities
5. Cash flow from miscellaneous activities

Codes
(a) 1, 2 and 3
(b) 1, 3 and 5
(c) 1, 3 and 4
(d) 1, 2 and 5

July 2016

12 Which of the following is a deferred revenue expenditure?

(a) Legal expense incurred on the purchase of land
(b) Expenses on a mega advertisement campaign while launching a new product
(c) Expenses incurred on installation of a new machine
(d) Wages paid for construction of an additional room in the building

13 The amount of depreciation charged to Profit and Loss Account varies every year under

(a) fixed installment method
(b) annuity method
(c) diminishing balance method
(d) insurance policy method

December 2015

14 Interest on loan taken for the purchase of fixed assets is a

(a) revenue expenditure
(b) capital expenditure
(c) deferred revenue expenditure
(d) capital loss

15 Dual aspect concept results in which of the following accounting equation?

(a) Revenue = Expenses
(b) Capital + Profits = Assets + Expenses
(c) Capital + Liabilities = Assets
(d) Capital + Drawings = Owner's Equity

16 Match the following.

	List I		List II
A.	Materiality concept	1.	The same accounting method used by a firm from one period to another
B.	Going concern concept	2.	An inappropriate assumption of a firm being bankrupt
C.	Historical cost concept	3.	A normal basis used for accounting assets
D.	Consistency concept	4.	Relates to the importance of an item or event

Codes

	A	B	C	D		A	B	C	D
(a)	4	2	3	1	(b)	1	2	3	4
(c)	2	3	4	1	(d)	4	2	1	3

17 Which of the following statements are correct?

1. Analysis and interpretation of financial statements is a function of accounting.
2. Profit and loss account is prepared for ascertaining financial position of a firm.
3. Goodwill is a wasting asset.
4. Balance sheet is prepared for ascertaining financial position of a firm.

Select the correct answer using the codes given below

(a) Both 1 and 2
(b) Both 1 and 3
(c) Both 1 and 4
(d) Both 2 and 3

18 Match the following.

	List I		List II
A.	Intangible assets	1.	Ind AS- 31
B.	Impairment of assets	2.	Ind AS- 34
C.	Interim financial reporting	3.	Ind AS- 36
D.	Interests in joint ventures	4.	Ind AS- 38

Codes

	A	B	C	D		A	B	C	D
(a)	1	2	3	4	(b)	4	3	2	1
(c)	4	1	2	3	(d)	4	2	1	3

19 **Assertion** (A) Human resource accounting is the measurement of the cost and value of people to the organisation.

Reason (R) Human resource accounting involves measuring costs incurred by the organisations to recruit, select, hire, train and develop employees and judge their economic value to the organisation.

Codes
(a) (A) and (R) are true and (R) is the correct explanation of (A)
(b) (A) and (R) are true and (R) is not the correct explanation of (A)
(c) (A) is true, but (R) is false
(d) Both (A) and (R) are false

June 2015

20 In what order, the following assets are shown in the balance sheet of a company?

1. Trade receivables 2. Cash
3. Furniture and fittings
4. Investment in shares and debentures

Select the correct answer using the codes given below

(a) 2, 1, 4 and 3 (b) 1, 2, 3 and 4
(c) 3, 4, 1 and 2 (d) 4, 3, 2 and 1

December 2014

21 'Make sufficient provisions for future losses, but do not anticipate future profits'. This statement is in accordance to the concept of

(a) matching (b) objectivity
(c) conservatism (d) materiality

June 2014

22 What is the underlying concept that support the immediate recognition of an estimated loss?

(a) Substance over form
(b) Consistency
(c) Matching
(d) Prudence

23 Subsequent expenditures that extend the useful life, improve the quality of output or reduce operating costs of an existing asset beyond their originally estimated levels are

(a) capital expenditures
(b) revenue expenditures
(c) deferred revenue expenditures
(d) None of the above

December 2013

24 Which of the following is a non-operating expense?

(a) Salary of managing director
(b) Depreciation
(c) Advertisement expenditure
(d) Interest on loan

25 The present value of the future contributions of employees is one of the methods of

(a) HR accounting
(b) inflation accounting
(c) social accounting
(d) responsibility accounting

June 2013

26 Insurance expenses paid to bring an equipment from the place of purchase to the place of installation is a type of

(a) revenue expenditure
(b) capital expenditure
(c) deferred revenue expenditure
(d) operating expense

December 2012

27 In accounting, profit prior to incorporation is treated as

(a) revenue reserve (b) secret reserve
(c) capital reserve (d) general reserve

28 Receipts and payments account is prepared by

(a) manufacturing concerns
(b) non-trading concerns
(c) trading concerns
(d) companies registered under Companies Act, 1956

29 Owners equity stands for

(a) Fixed assets – Flood liabilities
(b) Fixed assets – Current liabilities
(c) Current assets – Fixed liabilities
(d) Total assets – Total outside liabilities

30 The funds available with a company after paying all claims including tax and dividend is called

(a) net profit (b) net operating profit
(c) capital profit (d) retained earnings

31 **Assertion** (A) Accounting information refers to only events which are concerned with business firm.

Reason (R) Accounting information is presented infinancial statements.

Codes

(a) Both (A) and (R) are true and (R) is the correct explanation of (A)
(b) Both (A) and (R) are true and R is not the correct explanation of (A)
(c) (A) is true, but (R) is false
(d) (A) is false, but (R) is true

32 The main objective of Accounting Standards is

(a) to prepare the accounting reports which is easily understood by common man
(b) to comply with the legal formalities
(c) to harmonise the diversified accounting practices
(d) To comply with the requirements of the International Accounting Standards (IAS)

33 Income and expenditure account of non-profit organisation is a

(a) Real account
(b) Nominal account
(c) Personal account
(d) Representative Personal account

34 Consider the following statements.

1. Inventory includes raw materials, finished goods and work-in-progress.
2. Inventory is a part of the working capital.
3. Inventory includes goods likely to be purchased.

Which of the statement given above is/are correct?

(a) Both 1 and 2
(b) Both 2 and 3
(c) Both 1 and 3
(d) All of the above

35 Window dressing is prohibited due to

(a) conservative convention
(b) convention of disclosure
(c) convention of materiality
(d) arrear of book accounts

June 2012

36 Match the following.

	List I		List II
A.	Measurement of income	1.	Accrues to the equility of curves
B.	Recognition of expense	2.	Recognition of revenue
C.	Basis of realisation	3.	Matching revenue with expenses
D.	Identification of revenue	4.	Accounting period

Codes

	A	B	C	D		A	B	C	D
(a)	1	2	3	4	(b)	2	1	3	4
(c)	3	4	1	2	(d)	3	4	2	1

37 Which of them are current liabilities?

1. Debentures
2. Prepaid rent
3. Interest accrued
4. Bank overdraft

Select the correct answer using the codes given below

(a) 1, 2, 3 and 4
(b) Only 4
(c) 2, 3, and 4
(d) 1, 2 and 3

38 If Opening Stock is ₹ 10,000, Net Purchase ₹ 70,000, Wages ₹ 2,500, Carriage Inward ₹ 500 and Closing Stock ₹ 15,000. What is the Manufacturing Cost?

(a) ₹ 65,000
(b) ₹ 83,000
(c) ₹ 68,000
(d) ₹ 73,000

39 Which one of the following statement is true?

(a) Capital expenditure does not affect the profitability of a concern, but revenue expenditure does
(b) Capital expenditure affects the profitability of a concern directly, but revenue expenditure does not
(c) Capital expenditure affects the profitability of a concern indirectly, but revenue expenditure affects directly
(d) Both capital expenditure and revenue expenditure affect the profitability of a concern directly

40 Identify the true statement of the following.

1. Balance sheet is always prepared from the point of view of the business,but not from, that of the owners.
2. The financial relationship of the business to its owners is shown in the balance sheet.
3. Balance sheet is always related to a period of time.

Codes

(a) Both 1 and 2
(b) Both 2 and 3
(c) Both 1 and 3
(d) All of the above

41 Which one of the following will not affect the working capital?

(a) Realisation of cash from debtors
(b) Sale of plant and machinery in cash
(c) Issue of equity shares
(d) Redemption of debentures

42 Match the following.

	List I		List II
A.	Goodwill of a company	1.	Current liability
B.	Overdraft	2.	Fixed assets
C.	Preliminary expenses	3.	Reserves surplus
D.	Premium on issue of shares	4.	Fictitious assets

Codes

	A	B	C	D		A	B	C	D
(a)	2	1	4	3	(b)	1	2	4	3
(c)	1	2	3	4	(d)	2	1	3	4

43 In India, Which one of the following is prepared on the guidelines of AS-3 (Accounting Standard-3)?

(a) Balance sheet of a company
(b) Funds flow statement
(c) Cash flow statement
(d) Consolidated financial statement

44 What is the correct sequence of the following actions required for the preparationof financial accounts?

1. Trading account
2. Making adjusting entries
3. Balance sheet
4. Profit and Loss account

Select the correct answer using the codes given below

Codes

(a) 4, 2, 1 and 3
(b) 2, 4, 3 and 1
(c) 2, 1, 4 and 3
(d) 4, 2, 3 and 1

ANSWERS

Objective Questions

1 (c)	2 (b)	3 (d)	4 (d)	5 (c)	6 (c)	7 (a)	8 (d)	9 (c)	10 (a)
11 (c)	12 (d)	13 (c)	14 (c)	15 (a)	16 (d)	17 (a)	18 (d)	19 (b)	20 (c)
21 (b)	22 (a)	23 (c)	24 (c)	25 (d)	26 (c)	27 (a)	28 (d)	29 (a)	30 (d)
31 (d)	32 (d)	33 (d)	34 (d)	35 (c)	36 (d)	37 (a)	38 (c)	39 (a)	40 (c)
41 (a)	42 (a)	43 (c)	44 (b)	45 (d)	46 (b)	47 (b)	48 (b)	49 (c)	50 (a)
51 (b)	52 (c)	53 (b)	54 (d)	55 (d)	56 (b)	57 (a)	58 (a)	59 (a)	60 (d)
61 (c)	62 (b)	63 (d)	64 (b)	65 (c)	66 (a)	67 (c)	68 (a)	69 (b)	70 (a)
71 (b)	72 (a)	73 (a)	74 (b)	75 (b)	76 (a)	77 (c)	78 (d)	79 (a)	80 (a)
81 (a)	82 (d)	83 (d)	84 (a)	85 (c)	86 (b)	87 (a)	88 (b)	89 (c)	

Previous Years' Questions

1 (*)	2 (c)	3 (d)	4 (b)	5 (a)	6 (b)	7 (b)	8 (b)	9 (c)	10 (c)
11 (d)	12 (b)	13 (b)	14 (d)	15 (d)	16 (c)	17 (a)	18 (a)	19 (c)	20 (d)
21 (c)	22 (a)	23 (b)	24 (d)	25 (c)	26 (d)	27 (a)	28 (c)	29 (b)	30 (a)
31 (c)	32 (a)	33 (c)	34 (a)	35 (a)	36 (b)	37 (d)	38 (b)	39 (c)	40 (d)
41 (a)	42 (d)	43 (b)	44 (a)						

Note (*) All options are incorrect

CHAPTER

06

Partnership Accounts

Accounting for partnership is just as important as accounting for any other business. Like how every business should account its activities and transactions, so should the partnership firm. But accounting for partnership firms vary from accounting the transactions of any other business form. Before understanding the treatment of accounting for partnership firms, it is important to know all the fundamentals.

In this Chapter

- Introduction of Partnership
- Admission of a Partner
- Retirement of a Partner
- Death of a Partner
- Dissolution
- Insolvency of Partners

Introduction of Partnership

A sole trader has certain limitations. He may not have the requisite capital, skill or experience to run a particular business. Even, if he has all these, he may not have the initiative to undertake the risk involved in starting a new business. These limitations on the part of a sole trader drive to enter into partnership with others. The partnership agreements in India are governed by the Indian Partnership Act, 1932. Partnership is an association of persons, who agree to contribute the financial and human resources for carrying legal business to earn profit and share the profit of that business in an agreed ratio.

The following are the essential elements of partnership

- There must be an agreement entered into by all the persons concerned.
- The agreement must be to share the profits of a business.
- The business must be carried on by all or any of them acting for all.

All these elements must be present, then only a partnership can come into existence. If any of them is not present, then a partnership cannot be formed.

According to Section 4 of the Indian Partnership Act, 1932, "Partnership is the relation between persons, who have to share the profits of a business carried on by all or any of them acting for all."

The persons entering into a partnership with another person are individually called 'partners' and collectively a 'firm'.

Partnership Deed

The partnership deed is a document containing the agreement among partners in writing. It is stamped according to the provisions of the Stamp Act. Partnership is an agreement between persons to carry on a business. The agreement entered into between partners may be either oral or written. But, it is always desirable to have a written agreement, so as to avoid unnecessary litigations in future. When the agreement is in written form, it is called 'partnership deed'. It must be duly signed by all the partners, stamped and registered.

It contains the following particulars

- Description of the partners
- Capital contribution
- Description of the firm
- Principal place of business
- Interest on capital
- Interest on drawings
- Nature of business8.Profit sharing ratio
- Interest on loan 10.Valuation of assets
- Accounting period
- Bank operations
- Duration of partnership
- Salary
- Settlement of disputes

All of above particulars are discussed in partnership deed. It should be comprehensive to avoid disputes later on it.

Provisions affecting Accounting Treatment in Absence of a Partnership Deed

Profit Sharing Profit or loss should be shared equally among all partners.

Right to Remuneration No remuneration is allowed to any partner.

Interest on Capital No interest on capital is allowed to any partner.

Interest on Drawings No interest on drawings is charged by any partner.

Interest on Loans or Advances Interest on loans and advances are allowed to partners @ 6% per annum.

Features of Partnership

Association of Two or More Persons Partnership is an association of two or more persons agreeing to carry on business on sharing of profit or loss. Minimum number of partners must be 2 and maximum number of partners that a firm can have is 50 [as per Rule 10 of Companies (miscellaneous) Rules, 2014].

Agreement Partnership comes into an existence on account of an agreement among the partners and not from status or by operation of law. This agreement may be verbal or written and may be for a fixed period or for particular venture or at will.

Lawful Business Partnership is formed to carrying some lawful business. So long as the business does not come into an existence or something is not done, which may be taken as a commencement of the business, there can be no partnership.

Profit Sharing To constitute a partnership, the parties must have agreed to carry on the business and to share the profit in common. An agreement to share losses is not essential since, the agreement to share profit also implies an agreement to share losses.

Business can be Carried on by All or any of them Acting for All Partnership is a mutual agency. Each partner is an agent of the firm as well as of the other partners. Moreover, it is not necessary that every partner should actively participate in the conduct of business, what is an essential is that the business must be carried on behalf of all the partners.

Kinds of Partners

Active Partner

A partner, who takes an active part in the management of the business is called active partner. He may also be called actual or ostensible partner. He is an agent of the other partners in the ordinary course of business of the firm and considered a full fledged partner in the real sense of the term.

Sleeping or Dormant Partner

A sleeping or dormant partner is one, who does not take any active part in the management of the business. He contributes capital and shares the profit, which is usually less than that of the active partners. He is liable for all the dues of the firm, but his relationship with the firm is not disclosed to the general public.

Nominal Partner

A partner, who simply lends his name to the firm is called nominal partner. He neither contributes any capital nor shares in the profits or take part the management of the business. But, he is liable to third party like other partners. A nominal partner must be distinguished from the sleeping partner. While the nominal partner is known to the outsiders and does not share in the profits, the sleeping partner shares in the profit as his relationship is kept secret.

Partners in Profits Only

A partner, who shares in the profit only without being liable of the losses is known as partner in profits. He does not take part in the management of the business, but he is liable to third party for all debts of the firm.

Minor Partner

Partnership arises from contract and a minor is not competent to enter into contract. Therefore, strictly speaking, a minor cannot be a full fledged partner. But with the consent of all the partners, he can be admitted into partnership for benefits only. He is not personally liable to third party for all the debts of the firm, on attaining majority, if he continues as a party, his liabilities will become unlimited with effect from the date of his original admission into the firm.

Partners by Estoppel or Holding Out

If a person holds out to another that he is a partner of the firm, either by his words, actions or conduct then such a partner cannot deny that he is not a partner. The person who thus becomes liable to third party to pay the debts of the firm is known as a holding out partner.

Rights of Partners

To Participate in Management Every partner has a right to take part in the conduct of the business of the firm.

To Inspect Books of Accounts Every partner has a right to inspect the books of account and have a copy of the same.

To Share Profit or Loss Every partner has a right to share the profit or losses with other partners in the agreed ratio.

To Receive Interest on Loans and Advances On amounts advanced by a partner to the firm in excess of his agreed share of capital, the partner is entitled to receive interest on such excess at the rate of 6% per annum. Such interest is payable even if there is a loss.

To not Allow the Admission of New Partners A partner has the right not to allow the admission of a new partner.

To Concern about the Affairs of Firm Every partner has a right to concern about the affairs of the partnership business.

Duties of Partners

- To carry on the business with the greatest common advantage.
- To hold and use the property of the firm only for the official use.
- To devote time and attention to the business of the partnership.
- To act within the authority.
- To identify the loss caused by his wilful neglect or any breach of agreement.

Power of Partners

The act of a partner, which is done to carry on the business of the kind, carried on by the firm, binds the firm. The authority of the partners to bind the firm is known as the implied authority.

Every partner within the scope of his implied authority may bind the firm by the following acts

- Buying and selling of goods.
- Engaging servants to perform the business of the firm.
- Receiving payments of the debts due to the firm and issuing receipts for the same.
- Borrowing money for the purposes of the business on the credit of the firm. However, in a non-trading firm, no partner can borrow or pledge the partnership property.
- Drawing cheques and endorsing bills of exchange and promissory notes in the name of the firm.

The implied authority of a partner does not extend to the following acts

- Acquisition of immovable property belonging to the firm.
- Opening a banking account on behalf of the firm in his own name.
- Entering into partnership on behalf of the firm.
- Submitting a dispute relating to the business of the firm to arbitration.
- Withdrawal of suit or proceeding filed on behalf of the firm.
- Compromising or relinquishing any claim or portion of a claim by the firm.
- Admission of a liability in a suit or proceeding against the firm.
- Transfer of immovable property belonging to the firm.

Types of Partnership Accounts

Partnership accounts are almost similar to that of a proprietorship business. However, there are some points, which are peculiar to the partnership accounts, *they are described below*

Profit and Loss Appropriation Account

Profit and loss appropriation is a nominal account. It is prepared by partnership firm and it is an extension of the profit and loss account.

Appropriation of profit is a distribution of net profit to partners under different heads and appropriation of profit arise only, when there is profit. In other words, we can say that, any amount payable to a partner is an appropriation, not a charge. *e.g.* interest on capit. l etc.

Format of Profit and Loss Appropriation Account

Profit and Loss Appropriation A/c

Dr For the Year ended ...... Cr

Particulars	Amt (₹)		Particulars	Amt (₹)
To Interest on Capital A/c			By Profit and Loss A/c (Net profit transferred)	......
A	......			
B	......		By Interest on Drawings A/c	
To Partner's Commission A/c		......	A	......
			B	......
To Partner's Salary A/c		......	*By Loss Transferred to	
			A's Capital/Current A/c	......
			B's Capital/Current A/c	......
To Reserve A/c		......		
*To Profit Transferred to				
A's Capital/Current A/c	......			
B's Capital/Current A/c	......	......		
		......		......

** Either loss or profit occur at one time.*

Partners' Capital Accounts

In a partnership firm, there are two methods by which partners' capital accounts may be maintained. *These are*

Fixed Capital Method

Under this method, the capitals of the partners shall remain fixed, unless additional capital is introduced or a part of the capital is withdrawn as per the agreement among the partners.

Two accounts are maintained under this method, which are as follows

Capital Account Transactions related to introduction and withdrawal of capital are recorded in capital accounts. It will always have a credit balance.

Current Account All the other transactions (like interest on capital, drawings, salary etc), are recorded in this account. Current account may have credit or debit balance.

Format of Fixed Capital Account

Partner's Capital A/c

Dr Cr

Particulars	Amt (₹)	Particulars	Amt (₹)
To Cash/Bank A/c (If capital is withdrawn)	......	By Balance b/d (If there is old credit balance of capital account)	......
To Balance c/d (Closing Balance) (Difference between the two sides)	......		
		By Cash/Bank A/c (Additional capital introduced)	......
	......		......

Dr **Partner's Current A/c** Cr

Particulars	Amt (₹)	Particulars	Amt (₹)
*To Balance b/d (Opening Balance)	......	*By Balance b/d (Opening Balance)	......
To Drawings A/c	......	By Interest on Capital A/c	......
To Interest on Drawings A/c	......	By Salary A/c	......
To Profit and Loss A/c (Share in loss)	......	By Commission/Bonus A/c	......
*To Balance c/d (Closing Balance)	......	By Profit and Loss Appropriation A/c (Share in profit)	......
		*By Balance c/d	......
	......		......

* *Any one will appear.*

Fluctuating Capital Method

Under this method, only one account, *i.e.* capital account of each partner is maintained. All transactions are recorded in capital accounts. Generally, capital account have a credit balance but in exceptional cases, it may have debit balance due to heavy losses.

Format of Fluctuating Capital Account

Dr **Partner's Capital A/c** Cr

Particulars	Amt (₹)	Particulars	Amt (₹)
*To Balance b/d (Opening Balance)		*By Balance b/d (Opening Balance)	......
To Drawings A/c	......	By Cash A/c (If capital is contributed initially)	......
To Interest on Drawings A/c		By Interest on Capital A/c	......
To Profit and Loss A/c (Share in loss)		By Salary A/c	......
To Cash A/c (Withdrawal of capital)	......	By Commission/Bonus A/c	......
*To Balance c/d (Closing Balance)	......	By Profit and Loss Appropriation A/c (Share in profit)	......
		*By Balance c/d	......
	......		

* *Any one will appear.*

Interest on Capital

It is allowed to partners for investing their money into the firm. It is an expe... n the debit side of profit and loss appropriation account.

Interest on capital is to be allowed to the partners, if the same has b... nership deed. *It can be calculated as interest on capital*

$$= \text{Amount of capital} \times \frac{\text{Rate}}{100} \times \text{Time}$$

When closing capital is given, then calculation of opening capital is as following

Particulars		Amt (₹)
Capital at the End		....
(+) Loss During the Year	....	
Interest on Drawings	....	....
(–) Drawings	(.....)	
Share of Profit	(.....)	
Additional Capital	(.....)	
Interest on Capital	(.....)	(.......)
Capital at the Beginning of the Year		......

Points to Remember

- Interest on capital is allowed only, if partnership deed provides clause for it.
- When partnership deed provides clause for interest on capital, but silent about treatment of it, then it is treated as
  - (i) Interest on capital is allowed only, if there is profit.
  - (ii) Interest on capital is allowed, if profit before interest is equal to interest.
  - (iii) If profit before interest is less than interest, then interest on capital is allowed to the extent of profit in the ratio of their capital.
- When the partnership agreement provides interest on capital as charge, that interest is allowed whether there is profit or loss.
- Interest on capital is always calculated on opening capital.

Interest on Drawings

nterest on drawings is the interest charged by the firm from Partners. Sometimes, partners may withdraw amount for rsonal use. Therefore, firm charges interest from them on drawings. The interest charged is transferred to the de of profit and loss appropriation account. It is in of income to the firm.

awings is to be charged specifically provided in deed. *It can be calculated as*

s = Amount of drawings

$$\times \frac{\text{Rate of interest}}{100} \times \frac{\text{Months}}{12}$$

or Inter

ount of drawings

$$\times \frac{\text{Rate of interest}}{100} \times \frac{\text{Days}}{365}$$

Value of time under different circumstances will be as under

	Monthly Drawings for 12 Months	Quarterly Drawings for 12 Months	Half-yearly Drawings for 12 Months	Monthly Drawings for 9 Months	Monthly Drawings for 6 Months
When drawings are made in the beginning of each period	6.5	7.5	9	5	3.5
When drawings are made in the middle of each period	6	6	6	4.5	3
When drawings are made at the end of each period	5.5	4.5	3	4	2.5

Salary/Commission to Partners

According to Partnership Act, 1932, salary or commission is allowed to partners, if deed permits.

Salary/Commission can be calculated as follows

Percentage of Net Profit before Charging Commission

$$\text{Net profit (before commission)} \times \frac{\text{Rate of commission}}{100}$$

Percentage of Net Profit after Charging Commission

$$\text{Net profit (before commission)} \times \frac{\text{Rate of commission}}{100 + \text{Rate of commission}}$$

Past Adjustments

Sometimes, after the final accounts of a firm have been closed, certain matters come to light, which were left out by mistake. *e.g.* interest on partners' capital or drawings or remuneration may have been omitted completely or allowed/charged at a high or low rate, profit or losses have been distributed in 1 year or in several years among the partners in a wrong proportion etc. In such cases, instead of altering the final accounts which have already been closed, an adjustment for such mistake may have to be made in the capital accounts at the beginning of new year.

➡ **Note** *In order to make adjustment, it is better that firstly an adjustment table is prepared to find out the net effect of errors then debit the capital account of the partner, who had been credited in excess and credit the capital account of the partner, who had been debited in excess.*

Guarantee of Profit

Sometimes, a new partner is admitted into the firm with a guarantee that he shall get a minimum amount by way of his share in the profits of the firm. The guarantee to an incoming partner may be given by all the old partners in a certain ratio or by one of the old partners. When the profit of new partner is less than the guaranteed amount then the new partner is entitled to recover it from the partner(s), who has/have given the guarantee.

Goodwill

Goodwill means the good name or wide business connections or reputations earned by a businessman through his hard work and honesty. This helps the business to earn more profit. This means good profit is the result of the reputation that the business has built-up. In accounting, the monetary value of such asset is known as goodwill.

According to **Lord Eldon**, "Goodwill is nothing more than the profitability, that the old customers will resort to the old place."

According to **Lord Lindley**, "The term goodwill is generally used to denote benefit arising from connections and reputations."

Characteristics of Goodwill

- It is an intangible asset and not a fictitious asset.
- It is the extra earning capacity of the business.
- It is an attractive force which bring customers to old place.
- It have a definite value.
- Goodwill cannot be sold separately because it does not have separate existence.
- Due to changing circumstances, goodwill value may fluctuate from time to time that's why the valuation of goodwill is a difficult task.

Factors Affecting Value of Goodwill

Location of Business If the business is at centrally located place having customer traffic, it results in high sales, thus increase in goodwill.

Types of the Business In case, it is a monopoly business, where it is difficult for other firms to enter, the business will definitely have excellent goodwill.

Efficiency of Management A well managed and efficient business generally enjoys the advantage of high productivity and cost efficiency, therefore has more goodwill.

Good Quality of Product A business which produce best quality of products is likely to earn more profit and therefore the firms enjoy good reputation.

Impressive Publicity Effective and impressive publicity and advertisement by the firm will create demand for its products resulting an increased goodwill.

Favourable Contracts If the contracts of the firm have been with other reputed firms and business houses or the firm has received bulk orders from highly reputed firms, its goodwill increase tremendously.

Trend of Profit If the market conditions are favourable, the profits of the business are increasing continuously, the value of its goodwill will be more.

Personal Popularity If the owners of the firm are honest, sincere, customers friendly, diligent, hard working and socially cautious, the business will earn higher profits due to their popularity.

Methods of Valuation of Goodwill

Average Profit Method

This is a very simple and widely followed method of valuation of goodwill. In this method, goodwill is valued taking into consideration the average profits of last few years.

Value of goodwill = Average profit × Number of years' purchase

Super Profit Method

The term super profit means the profit over and above the normal or average profit earned by similar firms.

Super profit = Average profit − Normal profit

Where, Normal profit = Capital invested $\times \dfrac{\text{Normal rate of return}}{100}$

So, goodwill is valued by the following formula

Goodwill = Super profit × Number of years' purchase

Weighted Average Profit Method

This method is a modified version of average profit method.

Weighted average profit $= \dfrac{\text{Total of the product of profits}}{\text{Total of weights}}$

and Goodwill = Weighted average profit × Agreed number of years' purchase

Capitalisation Method

Under capitalisation method, capital value of business profit is to be found out. Capital value means to find out the capital needed to earn a fixed profit and on the basis of this capital, goodwill is valued. There are two methods for calculation of goodwill under capitalisation method. *These are*

Capitalisation of Average Profit

Goodwill = Total value of the business − Net assets

and, total value of business/capitalised value of business

$= \text{Average profit} \times \dfrac{100}{\text{Normal rate of return}}$

Capitalisation of Super Profit

Goodwill = Total value of business – Net assets

and, Total value of business/capitalised value of business

$$= \text{Super profit} \times \frac{100}{\text{Normal rate of return}}$$

Reconstitution of a Firm

Whenever there is a change in relation between the partners, it is called reconstitution of a firm.

Firm can be reconstituted in the following cases

- When, there is a change in profit sharing ratio among the existing partners.
- Admission of new partner.
- Retirement of an existing partner.
- Death of a partner.
- Amalgamation of two partnership firm.

When there is a change in profit sharing ratio, some partner(s) will gain or other partner(s) will lose their share.

The partner, whose share of profit increases is called gaining partner and the partner, whose share of profit decreases is called sacrificing partner.

Revaluation of Assets and Reassessment of Liabilities

When there is a change in the profit sharing ratio of an existing partners, assets and liabilities of a firm may also be revalued, since realisable or actual value of assets and liabilities may be different from those shown in balance sheet.

It may happen that with the passage of time, some assets might have appreciated in value, while the value of certain other assets might have decreased.

Revaluation of assets and liabilities becomes necessary because the change in the value of assets and liabilities belongs to the period prior to change in their profit sharing ratio.

Hence, any gain or loss on revaluation must be shared in their old profit sharing ratio by partners.

Dr **Revaluation A/c** Cr

Particulars	Amt (₹)	Particulars	Amt (₹)
To Assets (Decrease in the value) A/c	....	By Assets (Increase in the value) A/c	....
To Liabilities (Increase on reassessment)	.....	By Liabilities (Decrease on reassessment) A/c	.....
To Partner's Capital A/c (Gain on revaluation)	.....	By Partner's Capital A/c (Loss on revaluation)	.....
	.....		.....

Accounting Treatment of Accumulated Profits and Reserves

At the time of change in the profit sharing ratio, reserves or accumulated profits/losses exists in the books of a firm, they are transferred to partner's capital account or current account in their old profit sharing ratio.

These are as

For transfer of reserve and accumulated profit

Reserve/Profit and Loss A/c	Dr	....
Workmens Compensation Reserve A/c	Dr	....
Investments Fluctuation Reserve A/c	Dr	....
To Partner's Capital or Current A/c		....

For transfer of accumulated losses

All Partner's Capital or Current A/c	Dr	....
To Profit and Loss A/c		....
To Deferred Revenue Expenditure A/c		....

Adjustment of Capitals

Reconstitution of firm may also recognise the capital of the partners in the reconstituted firm to be in accordance with their profit sharing ratio.

The steps involved are

Step 1 Calculate the adjusted old capitals of partners.

Step 2 Calculate the total capital of new firm.

Total capital = Aggregate of adjusted old capital of partners.

Step 3 Find out the new capitals of partners by dividing the total capital in the new profit sharing ratio.

Step 4 Find out the surplus/deficiency in each of partner's capital account by comparing the new capital with adjusted old capital.

Step 5 At last, adjust the surplus by paying off or by transfer to the credit of his current account and adjust the deficiency by asking the concerned partner to bring the required amount or by transfer to the debit of his current account.

Admission of a Partner

Admission of a partner is one of the modes of reconstituting the firm under which existing partnership comes to an end and a new one between all partners (including incoming partner) is formed.

This incoming partner or newly admitted partner will receive the share equal to the sacrifice made by the existing partners and this new partner will compensate for that to the existing partners by bringing goodwill or premium for goodwill.

Adjustments to be Made on Admission

- Calculation of new profit sharing ratio.
- Accounting treatment of goodwill.
- Adjustment for revaluation of assets and reassessment of liabilities.
- Adjustment for accumulating profits and reserves.
- Adjustment of capital.

New Profit Sharing Ratio

New profit sharing ratio is the ratio in which all the partners including the new partner will share the future profits or losses of the firm.

Computation of New Profit Sharing Ratio

New partner acquires his share in following ways

In Old Profit Sharing Ratio In such a case, new partner's share and old profit sharing ratio is given. Here, we assume that the total profit is 1 and after deducting the new partner's share from total profit, the balanced profit will be shared by old partners in old ratio.

In a Particular Ratio Sometime, a new partner acquires a part of his share in a particular ratio from other partners. In such a case, the acquired share will be added to compute total share of incoming partner and the sacrificed share will be deducted from existing partners' share.

In Particular Fraction of their Share of Old Partners In this case, the surrendered share of old partners will be added to get the new share of incoming partner and old partners' share shall be derived by deducting their surrendered share from their old share.

Sacrificing Ratio

Whenever a new partner is admitted into a partnership firm, old partners have to surrender some of their old shares in favour of the incoming partner.

The ratio in which the old partners agree to sacrifice their share of profit in favour of the incoming partner is called sacrificing ratio.

Goodwill is paid to the old partners in their sacrificing ratio.

Accounting Treatment of Goodwill

Goodwill is a way for compensating old partners for the sacrifice made by them on the admission of a new partner. *From accounting point of view, there may be different situations, related to treatment of a goodwill, which are discussed as follows*

When Goodwill** (or Premium) **is Paid Privately When the amount of goodwill is paid to the old partner privately or directly or outside the business by new partner, then 'no journal entry' is required in the books of the firm.

When Goodwill** (or Premium) **is Brought in Cash When new partner brings his share of goodwill in cash, *the following required journal entries will be made*

- *For amount of goodwill brought in cash*

Cash/Bank A/c Dr
To Premium A/c

- *Distribution of goodwill amongst sacrificing old partners in their sacrificing ratio*

Premium A/c Dr
To Sacrificing (old) Partners' Capital/Current A/c

- *Goodwill withdrawn by sacrificing (old) partners (if any)*

Sacrificing (old) Partners' Capital/Current A/c Dr
To Cash/Bank A/c

When Goodwill (or Premium) is Brought in Kind The incoming partner may bring his share of goodwill (or premium) in form of assets instead of bringing in cash. In such a situation, the amount of assets brought in will be debited in place of cash/bank in above entry (i) and other entries (ii), (iii) will be recorded in the same manner.

When Goodwill (or Premium) is not Brought in Cash Whenever, the new partner is not able to bring his share of goodwill (or premium) in cash. In such a situation, goodwill should be adjusted through partners' capital account.

The following journal entry will be recorded

New Partner's Capital/Current A/c Dr
To Sacrificing (old) Partner's Capital/Current A/c
(Being new partner's share of goodwill transferred to old partners in their sacrificing ratio).

Note *If goodwill appears in the balance sheet of the firm. It would be desirable to close the goodwill account by making the following entry*

Old Partners' Capital/Current A/c Dr
To Goodwill (or Premium) A/c

When Partly Amount of Goodwill is Brought in Cash When new partners bring only a part of their share of goodwill in cash.

In such a situation, following journal entries will be passed

- *For bringing portion of share of goodwill (or premium)*

Cash/Bank A/c Dr
To Premium A/c

- *For transferring goodwill to partner's accounts in their sacrificing ratio*

Premium A/c Dr (cash goodwill)
New Partner's Capital A/c Dr (unpaid goodwill)
To Sacrificing (Old) Partner's Capital/Current A/c

Hidden or Inferred Goodwill Sometimes, the value of goodwill is not given at the time of admission of a new partner. In such a situation, it has to be inferred from the arrangement of the capital and profit sharing ratio.

The following steps will be taken into account for calculating hidden goodwill

To Find out the Total Capital of the New Firm For finding out the total capital of the new firm, new partner's capital for this will be taken as the basis.

To Ascertain the Existing Total Capital of the New Firm We will have to ascertain the existing total capital of the new firm by adding the capital (of all partners, including new partner's capital after adjustments, if any excluding goodwill).

➠ **Note** *If items of assets and liabilities are given, capital of old partners will be the difference between assets and liabilities.*
i.e. Capital = Assets at revalued figures
– Liabilities at revalued figures

Determination of Goodwill Goodwill is assumed to be the excess of the total capital of the new firm on the basis of new partners over the existing total capital of the partners. Generally, this method is used when the new partner does not bring amount of goodwill in cash.

Adjustment for Revaluation of Assets and Reassessment of Liabilities

When a new partner is admitted it is to be checked that neither he is not benefited by appreciation of value in the assets or reduction in liabilities. Nor should he suffers because of depreciation in the value of assets or increase in the value of liabilities. Keeping this aspect in mind, the assets and liabilities are revalued at the real value on the day of admission.

The adjustments on account of revaluation is done through 'revaluation or profit and loss adjustment account'.

Revaluation account is a nominal account, therefore, if the credit balance is in excess of the debit balance of this account, it means profit.
On the other hand, if debit balance happens to be more than the credit balance, it would means loss.

This profit or loss (as the case may be) is transferred to capital accounts to the old partners in their profit sharing ratio.

Dr **Revaluation A/c** Cr

Particulars	Amt (₹)	Particulars	Amt (₹)
To Decrease in the Value of Assets	......	By Increase in the Value of Assets	......
To Increase in the Value of Liabilities	......	By Decrease in the Value of Liabilities	......
To Unrecorded Liabilities	......	By Unrecorded Assets and Investments	......
To Profit Transferred to Old Partners' Capital Accounts (in old ratio)	......	By Loss Transferred to Old Partners' Capital Accounts (in old ratio)	......
	.....		.....

Adjustments for Reserves and Accumulated Profits (or Losses)

At the time of admission of a new partner, if there is any general reserve, reserve and surplus or the balance of profit and loss account appearing in the balance sheet, it should be transferred to capital accounts of old partners in their old profit sharing ratio.

The new partner is not entitled to any share of such reserves or accumulated profits, as these are undistributed profit earned by the old partners.

The following journal entries are passed

- *For distributing reserves and accumulated profits*

  Reserve Fund A/c Dr
  Profit and Loss A/c Dr
  To Old Partners' Capital A/c
  (In their old profit sharing ratio)

- *For distributing accumulated losses*

  Old Partners' Capital A/c Dr
  To Profit and Loss A/c
  (In their profit sharing ratio)

Sometimes, the firm may have created some specific reserves like 'Workmen's Compensation Fund' or 'Investment Fluctuation Fund' to meet certain future obligation. At the time of admission of a new partner, such funds must be transferred to the capital accounts of old partners in their old profit sharing ratio.

For this purpose, the following journal entry is passed

Investment Fluctuation Fund A/c Dr
Workmen's Compensation Fund A/c Dr
To Old Partners' Capital A/c

Determination/Adjustment of Capital

Sometimes, at the time of admission of a new partner, the partners may agree that their capital should also be adjusted, so as to be proportionate to their profit sharing ratio. In some case, a capital of a new partner is not given in the question and it is expected from him to bring proportionate capital.

Thus, the adjustment for capital may be on any of the following two ways

Adjustment of Capital

- Adjustment of old partners' capital on the basis of incoming partner's capital
- Calculating the capital of incoming partner on the basis of old partners' capital

The following steps are included in adjustment of old partners' capital on the basis of incoming partner's capital

Step 1 Calculate total capital of a firm on the basis of new partner capital.

$$\text{Total capital of firm} = \text{Capital of new partner} \times \frac{1}{\text{Share of new partner}}$$

Step 2 Determine the new capital of each partner, by dividing the capital computed in step 1, in new profit sharing ratio.

Step 3 As certain the present capital of the old partners.

Step 4 Find the surplus/deficit capital by comparing step 2 and step 3.

Surplus = Present capital > Proportionate capital

Deficit = Present capital < Proportionate capital

Computing the capital of incoming partner on the basis of old partners' capital

Step 1 Determine the total adjusted capital of the old partners.

Step 2 Determine the new capital of the new firm as Total adjusted capital of old partners × Reciprocal of total share of old partner.

Step 3 Determine the capital of the incoming partners as Total capital (as computed in step 2) × Share of incoming partner.

Retirement of a Partner

When one or more partner(s) leave the firm and the remaining partners continue to do the business of the firm, it is known as retirement of a partner. Thus, due to some reasons like old age, poor health, strained relations etc, an existing partner may decide to retire from the partnership. Due to retirement, the existing partnership comes to an end and the remaining partners form a new agreement and the partnership firm is reconstituted with new terms and conditions. At the time of retirement, the retiring partner's claim is settled.

The amount payable to the retiring partner includes

- Balance in his capital/current account.
- Share of accumulated profits (losses) and reserves.
- Share in the gain/loss on revaluation of assets and reassessment of liabilities.
- Share of goodwill.
- Share in the profit of the current year.
- Share in the Joint Life Policy.
- Interest on capital, salary etc from the date of last balance sheet to the date of retirement (if applicable) will be credited to him, drawings and interest on drawings will also be debited for that period to the concerned partner's capital account.

A Partner Retires Either

- with the consent of all partners or
- as per rules of the agreement or
- at his or her own will

The terms and conditions of retirement of a partner are normally provided in the partnership deed. If not, they are agreed upon by the partners at the time of retirement.

At the time of retirement, the following accounting issues are dealt

- New profit sharing ratio and gaining ratio of continuing partners.
- Goodwill.
- Adjustment of changes in the value of assets and liabilities.
- Treatment of reserve and accumulated profits.
- Settlement of retiring partners' dues.
- New capital of the continuing partners.

New Profit Sharing Ratio and Gaining Ratio

As soon as partner retires, the profit sharing ratio of the continuing partners get changed. The share of the retiring partner is distributed amongst the continuing partners.

In the absence of information, the continuing partners take the retiring partner's share in their profit sharing ratio or in an agreed ratio. The ratio, in which retiring partner's share is distributed amongst continuing partners is known as gaining ratio. *It is*

Gaining ratio = New ratio – Existing ratio

Various cases of new ratio and gaining ratio are illustrated as follows

Retiring Partner's Share Distributed in Existing Ratio In this case, retiring partner's share is distributed in existing ratio amongst the remaining partners. The remaining partners continue to share profits and losses in the existing ratio.

➠ **Note** *In absence of any information in the question, it will be presumed that retiring partner's share has been distributed in existing ratio.*

Retiring Partner's Share Distributed in Specified Proportions Sometimes, the remaining partners purchase the share of the retiring partner in specified ratio. The share purchased by them is added to their old share and the new ratio is arrived at.

Retiring Partner's Share is taken by One of the Partners The retiring partner's share is taken-up by one of the remaining partners. In this case, the retiring partner's share is added to that of partner's existing share and only his/her share changes. The other partners continue to share profit in the existing ratio.

Treatment of Goodwill

The retiring partner is entitled to his/her share of goodwill at the time of retirement because the goodwill is the result of the efforts of all partners including the retiring one in the past. The retiring partner is compensated for his/her share of goodwill.

As per Accounting Standard 10 (AS-10), goodwill is recorded in the books only when some consideration in money is paid for it. Therefore, goodwill is recorded in the books only when it is purchased and the goodwill account cannot be raised on its own.

Therefore, in case of retirement of a partner, the goodwill is adjusted through partner's capital accounts. The retiring partner's capital account is credited with his/her share of goodwill and remaining partner's capital accounts are debited in their gaining ratio. *The journal entry is made as under*

Remaining Partners' Capital A/c Dr (individually)
To Retiring Partner's Capital A/c
(Retiring partner's share of goodwill adjusted to remaining partners in the gaining ratio).

When the Goodwill Account Already Appears in the Books

Normally, the goodwill is not shown in the books of the firm. If at the time of retirement/death of a partner, goodwill appears in the balance sheet of the firm, it will be written-off by debiting all the partners' capital accounts in their existing profit sharing ratio and crediting the goodwill account.

In such a case, the following journal entry is made

Partners' Capital A/c Dr
(Including retiring partner's capital account)
To Goodwill A/c
(Existing goodwill written-off)

Revaluation of Assets and Liabilities

At the time of retirement of a partner, the assets and liabilities of the firm are revalued and revaluation account is prepared in the same way as in case of admission of a partner. This is done to adjust the change in the value of assets and liabilities at the time of retirement/death of a partner. Any profit or loss due to revaluation is divided amongst all the partners including retiring /deceased partner in their existing profit sharing ratio.

Following journal entries are made for this purpose.

- *For increase in the value of assets*

Assets A/c Dr
To Revaluation A/c (Individually)
(Increase in the value of assets)

- *For decrease in the value of assets*

Revaluation A/c Dr
To Assets A/c (Individually)
(Decrease in the value of asset)

- *For increase in the value of liabilities*

Revaluation A/c Dr
To Liabilities A/c (Individually)
(Increase in the value of liabilities)

- *For decrease in the value of liabilities*

Liabilities A/c Dr
To Revaluation A/c (Individually)
(Decrease in the value of liabilities)

Revaluation account is prepared to record the change in the value of assets or liabilities. It will reveal profit or loss on revaluation. This profit or loss is divided amongst all partners including the retiring/deceased partner in their existing profit sharing ratio.

- *For profit on revaluation*

Revaluation A/c Dr
To Partners' Capital A/c (Individually)
(Profit on revaluation divided amongst all partners in their existing profit sharing ratio).

- *For loss on revaluation*

Partners' Capital A/c Dr
To Revaluation A/c (Individually)
(Loss on revaluation borne by all partners in their existing profit sharing profit).

Treatment of Accumulated Reserves and Undistributed Profit

All the balances of accumulated reserves, funds and undistributed amount of profit and loss appearing in the balance sheet of the firm on the date of retirement /death is distributed amongst all partners including retiring /deceased partner in their old profit sharing ratio.

The following entries are made

- *For distribution of undistributed profit and reserve*

Reserves A/c Dr
Profit and Loss A/c (Profit) Dr
To Partner's Capital A/c (Individually)
(Being reserves and profit and loss (profit) transferred to all partners' capital account in their existing profit sharing ratio)

- *For distribution of undistributed loss*

Partner's Capital A/c Dr (Individually)
To Profit and Loss A/c (Loss)
(Being profit and loss transferred to all partners capitals account in their old profit sharing ratio)

Accounting Treatment of Outgoing Partner's Share in Profits

The outgoing partner's share in the profits may be readjusted in either of the following ways

Through Profit and Loss Suspense Account This method is used only when the new profit sharing ratio of continuing partners does not differ from their old profit sharing ratio.

In this case, the following entries will be passed

- *In case of profit*

 Profit and Loss Suspense A/c Dr
 To Outgoing Partner's Capital A/c

- *In case of loss*

 Outgoing Partner's Capital A/c Dr
 To Profit and Loss Suspense A/c

Through Capital Transfer This method is used only when the new profit sharing ratio of continuing partners differ from their old sharing ratio.

In this case, the following entries will be passed

- *In case of profit*

 Gaining Partner's Capital A/c Dr
 To Outgoing Partner's Capital A/c
 (Gaining ratio)

- *In case of loss*

 Outgoing Partner's Capital A/c Dr
 To Gaining Partner's Capital A/c
 (Gaining ratio)

It should be remembered that, if partner is retired during the year, the above rules will also be applicable for calculating his share of profit.

Adjustment of Remaining Partner's Capital Accounts after Retirement

After retirement of a partner, the remaining partners may decide to adjust their capital. Often the remaining partners determine the total amount of capital of the reconstituted firm and decide to keep their respective capital accounts in proportion to the new profit sharing ratio.

The total capital of the firm may be more or less than the total of their capital at the time of retirement. The new capitals of the partners are compared with the balance standing to the credit of respective partner's capital account.

If there is a surplus in the capital account, the amount is withdrawn by the concerned partner. The partner brings cash when the balance in the capital account is less than the calculated amount.

Adjustment of Remaining Partner's Capital in their Profit Sharing Ratio, when the Total Capital of the New Firm is not Predetermined

In this case, the total amount of adjusted capital of the remaining partners is rearranged as per agreed proportion, in which they share profit of the reconstituted firm.

The following steps may be adopted

- Add the balance standing to the credit of the remaining partners' capital account.
- The total so obtained is the total capital of the firm.
- This capital is divided according to the new profit sharing ratio.

Death of a Partner

On the death of a partner, the accounting treatment regarding goodwill, revaluation of assets and reassessment of liabilities, accumulated reserves and undistributed profits are similar to that of the retirement of a partner. When the partner dies, the amount payable to him/her is paid to his/her legal representatives.

The representatives are entitled to the following

- The amount standing to the credit of the capital account of the deceased partner.
- Interest on capital, if provided in the partnership deed upto the date of death.
- Share of goodwill of the firm.
- Share of undistributed profits or reserves.
- Share of profit on revaluation of assets and liabilities.
- Share of profit upto the date of death.
- Share of Joint Life Policy.

The following amounts are debited to the account of the deceased partner's legal representatives

- Drawings
- Interest on drawings.
- Share of loss on revaluation of assets and liabilities.
- Share of loss that have occurred till the date of his/her death.

The above adjustments are made in the capital account of the deceased partner and then the balance in the capital account is transferred to an account opened in the name of his/her executor. The payment of the amount of the deceased partner depends on the agreement. In the absence of agreement, the legal representative of a deceased partner is entitled to interest @ 6% per annum on the amount due from the date of death till the date of final payment.

Calculation of Profit upto the Date of a Partner's Death

If the death of a partner occurs during the year, the representatives of the deceased partner are entitled to his/her share of profits earned till the date of his/her death.

Such profit is ascertained by any of the following methods

Time Basis In this case, it is assumed that the profit has been earned uniformly throughout the year.

Turnover or Sales Basis In this method, we have to take into account the consideration of the profit and the total sales of the last year. Thereafter, the profit upto the date of death is estimated on the basis of the sale of the last year. Profit is assumed to be earned uniformly at the same rate.

Ascertainment of Amount due to Deceased Partner

The share of the deceased partner can be ascertained by preparing his capital account. *In preparing, the deceased partner's capital account, the following items have to be taken into account*

Dr Partner's Capital A/c Cr

Particulars	Amt (₹)	Particulars	Amt (₹)
To Undistributed Losses (Share in such losses)	....	By Balance b/d	....
To Revaluation A/c (Share of loss)	....	By Interest on Capital A/c	....
To Goodwill A/c (Share of reduction in goodwill)	....	By Salary and Commission A/c	....
To Drawings A/c	....	By Undistributed Profits A/c (Share in such profits)	....
To Interest on Drawings A/c	....	By Goodwill A/c (Share of goodwill)	....
To Executor's A/c (Balancing figure)	....	By Joint Life Policy A/c (Share of JLP)	....
		By Profit and Loss Suspense A/c (Share in profits till the death)	....
	....		....

Payment of Amount due to the Deceased Partner

On the death of a partner, the accounts of such partners in the books of the firm are maintained in the same way as on the retirement of a partner. But the only difference is that the amount due to a deceased partner shown by his capital account is transferred to his executor's account.

The entry will be

Deceased Partner's Capital A/c Dr
    To Deceased Partner Executor's A/c
  (For amount due to partner transferred to his executor's account)

The amount due to executor of deceased partner is either paid off immediately or is paid in installments with or without interest as per agreement. In the absence of an agreement in this regard, the executor at his option receives either interest @ 6% per annum till the amount is paid off or a share of the profit, which has been earned by using the amount due to him.

In this case, the following entries will be passed

- *If amount is paid in cash*

  Partner's Executor's A/c Dr
      To Cash/Bank A/c

- *For transferring the balance/unpaid amount of executor's account to his loan account*

  Deceased Partner's Executor's A/c Dr
      To Deceased Partner's Executor Loan A/c

Joint Life Policy

A partnership firm may decide to take a Joint Life Policy on the lives of all partners. The firm pays the premium and the amount of policy is payable to the firm on the death of any partner or on the maturity of policy, whichever is earlier. The objective of taking such a policy is to minimise the financial hardships to the event of payment of a large sum to the legal representatives of deceased partner or to the retiring partner.

The accounting treatment for the premium paid and the joint life policy may be on any of the following ways

When Premium Paid is Treated as an Expense

When premium paid is treated as an expense, then it is closed every year by transferring to profit and loss account. In this case, complete amount received from the insurance company either on a surrender of policy or on the death of the partner becomes a gain.

Accounting entries are

- *On payment of premium*

  Joint Life Policy Insurance Premium A/c Dr
      To Bank A/c

- *On charging to profit and loss account*

  Profit and Loss A/c Dr
      To Joint Life Policy Insurance Premium A/c

- *On the maturity of the policy*

  Insurance Company/Bank A/c Dr
  To Partner's Capital A/c (individually)
  (Including the account of representative of deceased partner)

In this case, the amount received from the company in excess of the surrender value results in a gain at the time of receipt of such amount, which is transferred to capital accounts of the partners in the profit sharing ratio.

Creation of Joint Life Policy

Under this method, premium paid is debited to policy account and credited to bank account. At the end of the year, amount equal to premium is transferred from profit and loss appropriation account to policy reserve account. After this, policy account is brought down to its surrender value by debiting the life policy reserve account with amount which exceeds the surrender value of the policy.

Thus, in this method, policy account appears on the asset side and policy reserve account appears on the liabilities side of the balance sheet until it is realised.

This method is different from the method discussed earlier only in respect of reserve account. On the death of a partner, joint life policy reserve account is transferred to joint life policy account and then the balance is transferred to partner's capital accounts.

Dissolution

Dissolution means discontinuance of relationship among the partners. Section 39 of the Partnership Act, 1932 provides that " The dissolution of partnership between all the partners of a firm is called dissolution of the firm." It implies complete breakdown of the relation of partnership between all the partners. Business activity comes to an end. Firm's books of accounts are closed. Assets are realised, liabilities are paid off or settled and partner's claims are also settled.

Dissolution of a Partnership

It is the act of ending the old partnership agreement and a reconstruction of the firm due to admission, retirement and death of a partner. It may or may not close the business.

Cases of Dissolution of Partnership

- In case of change in profit sharing ratio of the existing partners.
- In case of admission of a new partner.
- In case of retirement of a partner.
- In case of expulsion of a partner.
- In case of death of a partner.
- In case of insolvency of a partner.
- In case of expiry of the period of partnership.

Dissolution of Partnership Firm

In this situation, the firm closes its business then the assets of the firm are sold and liabilities are paid off and remaining amount is distributed among the partners.

There is a difference between dissolution of partnership and dissolution of firm. This may be explained with the help of an example. Suppose A and B are partners in a firm. They admit a new partner C. The partnership between A and B comes to an end and a new partnership between A, B and C comes into an existence. This is dissolution of partnership. In this case, the firm continues. If, however, A and B decide to close the business of the firm permanently, there takes place dissolution of firm. This means complete breakdown of partnership relation between all the partners. In such a case, the assets are disposed of, liabilities are paid off and whatever remains is paid to the partners in settlement of their accounts.

Cases of Dissolution of Partnership Firm

Dissolution without the Intervention of Court

***By Consent** (Section 40)* A partnership firm can be dissolved any time with the consent of all the partners whether the partnership is at will or for a fixed duration.

***By Agreement** (Section 40)* A partnership can be dissolved in accordance with the terms of the partnership deed or of the separate agreement.

***Compulsory Dissolution** (Section 41)* In case, any of the following events take place then, it becomes compulsory for the firm to dissolute. *These are as follows*

- ***Insolvency of Partners*** In case, all the partners or all the partners except one become insolvent.
- ***Unlawful Business*** In case, the firm's business become unlawful on the happening of a subsequent event. *e.g.* trading with alien country.

***Dissolution on the Happening of Contingent Event** (Section 42)*

- ***Expiry of Fixed Period*** If the firm is constituted for fixed period, then the firm is dissolved automatically.
- ***On Achievement of Specific Task*** If the firm has been constituted for the achievement of specific task, on achievement of that task, firm ceases to exist.
- ***Death of Partner*** Death of any of the partners dissolves the partnership.
- ***Insolvency of Partner*** The insolvency of any of the partners may dissolve the firm.

- ***Resignation of Partner*** Resignation by any of the partners dissolve the partnership.

***Dissolution by Notice** (Section 43)* In case of partnership at will, a partner can dissolve it by giving written notice of dissolution to other partners duly signed by him.

Dissolution by Court (Section 44)

Insanity of Partner On the application of any of the partner, court may order for the dissolution of the firm, if a partner has become of an unsound mind.

Incapacity of Partner If a partner has become permanent incapable of discharging his duties and obligations, then court may order for the dissolution of firm on the application of any of the partner.

Misconduct of Partner If any partner other than partner suing is responsible for any loss to the firm, then the court may order for the dissolution of the firm.

Constant Breach of Agreement by Partner The court may order for the dissolution of the firm, if the partner other than the suing partner is found guilty for constant breach of agreement and it becomes impossible to continue the business with such partner.

Transfer of Interest When any of the partner other than the suing partner, transfers whole of its share to the third party permanently.

Continuous Losses The court may order for dissolution, if the firm is continuously suffering losses and there is no more capital available for the future growth of the firm.

Just and Equitable The court may order for dissolution on any other ground, which court think is just fair and equitable. *e.g.* loss of total confidence between the partners.

Settlement of Accounts (Section 48)

Treatment of Losses *Losses including deficiency of capital are to be paid in the following order*

- First out of profit.
- Then, out of capital of the partners.
- Lastly by partner's individually in their profit sharing ratio. [Section 48 (a)]

Application of Assets *The assets of the firm, including any sum contributed by the partners to make up deficiencies of capital shall be applied in the following manners*

- In paying firms debts to the third party.
- In paying to each partner what is due on account of loans and advances.
- In paying to each partner what is due on account of capital.
- The surplus, if any, shall be distributed among the partner in their profit sharing ratio. [Section 48 (b)]

Distribution of Cash

In all the problems of dissolution, it was assumed that assets were realised immediately on the date of dissolution or partners waited for the distribution of cash until the realisation of all assets of the firm. Both the above assumptions are to some extent imaginary. In actual practice, there is a gap of even a few month between the realisation of two assets and realisation of all assets. It is therefore, urgently felt that distribution of cash, after the payment to outside and internal liabilities should be done with the realisation of assets and should not be held up in waiting for other realisations. There are some different techniques for distribution of cash.

The method applied for distribution of cash are

Proportionate Capital Method According to this method, the partner, who has the higher relative capital *i.e.* whose capital is highest in proportion to this profit sharing ratio is first paid off. This method is also called as highest relative capital method.

Maximum Loss Method In this method, each installment realised from assets realisation is considered to be the final payment *i.e.* outstanding assets and claims are considered worthless and partners' accounts are adjusted on that basis each time when a deposit is made following either Garner *Vs* Murray rule or the profit sharing ratio rule.

Treatment of Firm's Debts and Private Debts (Section 49)

- Firm's property is applied first towards the payment of firm's debts, then the surplus, if any, is applied towards the payment of partner's private debts to the extent, to which the concerned partner is entitled to share in the surplus.
- Partner's private property is applied first in payment off his private debts and the surplus, if any, in payment of firm's debts, if the firm's liabilities exceed the firm's assets.

Accounts in the Firm's Book at the Time of Dissolution

Following accounts are opened in the firm's book at the time of dissolution

Realisation Account

It is opened at the time of dissolution. It is of nominal nature. The main objective of this account is to ascertain the profit or loss on realisation of assets and payment of liabilities.

The steps involved are

Step 1 First of all, the assets account except cash in hand or at bank is transferred to realisation account.

Realisation A/c Dr ...
  To Various Assets A/c ...

Step 2 Then, all the liabilities account are transferred

Sundry Creditors A/c Dr
Other Liabilities A/c Dr ...
  To Realisation A/c ...

Step 3 Then, the assets are realised

Cash/Bank A/c Dr ...
  To Realisation A/c ...

Or

If asset taken over by partner

Partner's Capital A/c Dr ...
  To Realisation A/c ...

Step 4 For settlement of liabilities

On Payment

Realisation A/c Dr ...
  To Cash/Bank A/c ...

Or

If partner agree to settle the liabilities

Realisation A/c Dr ...
  To Partner's Capital A/c ...

Step 5 For realisation expenses

- *When expenses are paid by firm*

Realisation A/c Dr ...
  To Cash/Bank A/c ...

- *When realisation expenses are paid by partner*

Realisation A/c Dr ...
  To Partner's Capital A/c ...

- *When firm agree to pay fixed amount to the partner towards realisation expenses irrespective of the actual expenses*

(a) For fixed amount payable to partner

Realisation A/c Dr ...
  To Partners' Capital A/c ...

(b) For payment of actual expenses, if paid by firm on behalf of the partner

Partners' Capital A/c Dr ...
  To Cash/Book A/c ...

Step 6 For closing of realisation account

- *If there is profit, then*

Realisation A/c Dr ...
  To Partners' Capital A/c (In old ratio)...

- *If there is loss, then*

Partners' Capital A/c Dr ...
  To Realisation A/c (In old ratio) ...

Specimen of the Realisation Account

Dr | | | Cr

Particulars	Amt (₹)	Particulars	Amt (₹)
To Land and Building A/c	....	By Provision for Doubtful Debts A/c	....
To Plant and Machinery A/c	....	By Sundry Creditors A/c	....
To Furniture A/c	....	By Bills Payable A/c	....
To Stock A/c	....	By Outstanding Expenses A/c	....
To Debtors A/c	....	By Bank Loan A/c	....
To Bank A/c (Liabilities paid) Sundry Creditors, Bills Payable, Outstanding Expenses, Bank Loan	....	By Bank A/c (Assets realised) Land and Building, Plants and Machinery, Furniture, Stock, Debtors	....
To Cash/Bank (Expenses)	....	By Partner's Capital A/c (Assets taken over)	....
*To Partner's Capital A/c (Profit on realisation) X .... Y .... Z		*By Partner's Capital A/c (Loss on realisation) X Y Z	....
	....		....

* *Any one will appear.*

Partner's Loan Account

A loan from any partner is not an external liability. It's payment can be made only after payment of outsider's liability. *Following entry is passed at the time of payment*

Partner's Loan A/c Dr
  To Cash/Bank A/c ...

Partners' Capital Account

Balance of partners' capital account and current accounts are recorded in this account. *Following entries are passed*

On Transfer of Undistributed Profits and Reserves

Profit and Loss A/c Dr
General Reserve A/c Dr
  To Partners' Capital A/c ...
  (In profit sharing ratio)

On Accumulated Losses

Partners' Capital A/c Dr
  To Profit and Loss A/c ...

For Final Settlement with Partners

- ***On bringing of cash equal to the deficiency in capital***

Cash/Bank A/c Dr ...
  To Partners' Capital A/c ...

- ***On payment of amount due to him***

Partners' Capital A/c Dr ...
  To Cash/Bank A/c ...

Bank or Cash Account

On the debit side, entries for opening balance, amount received from sale of assets and amount brought in by the partners and on the credit side, entries for payment by various liabilities, expenses and amount paid to partners are shown.

Insolvency of Partners

Insolvency of partner is a situation, in which the partner is unable to pay the amount due to him.

When all the adjustments have been made in respect of realisation profit or loss and accumulated profits or losses etc, the capital account of a partner may show a debit balance. Such a partner, then is a debtor to the firm to that extent and he has to bring in the necessary cash to clear debit balance in his capital account. But, if the partner with a debit balance, in his capital account is unable to bring the necessary cash, he is said to be insolvent. Then, the irrecoverable debit balance is a further loss, which will have to be borne by the solvent partners in addition to the loss on realisation. The reason is that the liability of the partners in a partnership firm is unlimited.

Decision in Garner *VS* Murray

- Sometimes, partnership deed is silent about the treatment of deficiency of insolvent partner. In such a situation, the leading case of Garner vs Murray, (1903) is followed.
- In case of Garner Vs Murray, it was held that the deficiency of insolvent partner must be borne by the other solvent partners in proportion to their capital, after each solvent partner has brought in cash equal to his own share of loss on realisation.
- To apply the decision, three conditions must be fulfilled
  - (a) There are two or more than two solvent partners.
  - (b) One or more of partners are insolvent.
  - (c) The capitals are not in profit sharing ratio.

Fixed Vs Fluctuation Capitals

Where the Capitals are Fixed

When the capitals of the partners have been maintained on the fixed capital system, the deficiency of the insolvent partners would be borne by the solvent partners in proportion to their original contribution subject of course, to any agreed additions or withdrawal of the capitals during the period.

Accounting Treatment

- At the time of transfer of accumulated profits, if any, to each partner's current account in the profit sharing ratio.

  Profit and Loss A/c Dr ...
  Reserve Fund A/c Dr ...
  Any Other Fund A/c Dr ...
  To Partners' Current A/c ...

- Profit on realisation in the profit sharing ratio will be transferred with the help of following entry.

  Realisation A/c Dr ...
  To Partners' Current A/c ...

- Loss on realisation in the profit sharing ratio will be transferred to current account.

  Partners' Current A/c Dr ...
  To Realisation A/c ...

- For bringing in cash equal to realisation loss respectively by the solvent partners.

  Bank A/c Dr ...
  To Solvent Partners' Current A/c ...

- Debit or credit balance of the current account of the insolvent partner would be transferred to his capital account to determine the total deficiency.
  - (a) *For debit current account balance*

    Insolvent Partners' Capital A/c Dr ...
    To Insolvent Partner's Current A/c ...

  - (b) *For credit current account balance*

    Insolvent Partners' Current A/c Dr ...
    To Insolvent Partner's Capital A/c ...

- For distributing the deficiency of insolvent partner among the solvent partners.

  Solvent Partners' Current A/c Dr ...
  To Insolvent Partners' Capital A/c ...

- For closing current account of solvent partner
  - (a) *For debit balance of current account*

    Solvent Partners' Capital A/c Dr ...
    To Solvent Partners' Current A/c ...

  - (b) *For credit balance of current account*

    Solvent Partners' Current A/c Dr ...
    To Solvent Partners' Capital A/c ...

Where the Capitals are Fluctuating

Where the capitals are maintained on the fluctuating method, the actual capital of each partner at the date of dissolution is determined by adjustment of the balances of reserve fund, debit or credit balance of profit and loss account etc given in the balance sheet.

When all Partners are Insolvent

When the firm cannot meet the claims of its creditors in full because of insufficiency of firm's assets as well as private estates of the partners. All the partners are said to be insolvent, in fact, it is case of insolvency of the firm as such.

All the cash available will be paid to creditors in proportion to their respective claims after the expenses on realisation have been paid. The realisation account should be prepared without transferring liabilities. The loss on realisation account will be debited to capital accounts of a partners in their profit sharing ratio. The available cash then should be used to pay the liabilities and the balance representing unpaid amount should be transferred to a newly opened account called deficiency account. The capital accounts of the partners are closed by transferring the balance to the deficiency account.

EXAM BASED QUESTIONS

Partnership and its Firm

1 An ordinary partnership firm can have maximum
(a) 5 partners (b) 10 partners
(c) 150 partners (d) 20 partners

2 After the new partnership agreement, assets and liabilities in a balance sheet are recorded at ....
(a) original value (b) revalued figure
(c) realisable value (d) None of these

3 When a partner is given guarantee lay the other partner, loss on such guarantee will be borne by............ .
(a) partner giving guarantee
(b) partner with highest ratio
(c) partnership firm
(d) all the other partners

4 Liability of a partner in a partnership firm
(a) limited (b) unlimited
(c) restricted (d) undefined

5 As per Partnership Act, which of these rights are available to a partner?
(a) Bonus (b) Salary
(c) Commission (d) Equal profit

6 Consider the following statements.
1. Atleast three persons are necessary for forming a partnership.
2. The right to share a profit is full proof of one being a partner.
3. The business of the firm can be conducted even by one partner.

Which of the statement(s) given above is/are correct?
(a) Both 1 and 3 (b) Only 3
(c) All of the above (d) None of the above

7 Which of the following is conclusive evidence of partnership?
(a) Sharing of profits
(b) Mutual agency
(c) Carrying of some business
(d) All of the above

8 In the absence of any provision in the partnership agreement, partners are paid interest on partners loan @
(a) 5% per annum (b) 6% per annum
(c) 8% per annum (d)10% per annum

9 Under capitalisation method, goodwill is calculated by
(a) Number of years purchase × Average profit
(b) Number of years purchase × Super profit
(c) Average profit ÷ Expected rate of return
(d) Super profit ÷ Expected rate of return

10 Which of these is not an essential feature of a partnership firm?
(a) Mutual agency
(b) Compulsory registration
(c) Association of two or more persons
(d) Existence of business

11 Identify, which of the following partnership's characteristic is a disadvantage?
(a) Voluntary association
(b) Minimal legal restrictions
(c) Limited liability
(d) None of the above

12 Arrange the following steps of adjustment of capital (reconstitution of firm) in correct order.
1. Calculation of total capital of new firm.
2. Finding out the surplus/deficiency in each of partner's capital account.
3. Calculation of adjusted old capitals of partners.
4. Finding out the new capitals of partners.

Select the correct answer using the codes given below
Codes
(a) 3, 4, 2, 1 (b) 4, 3, 2, 1
(c) 3, 1, 4, 2 (d) 3, 2, 4, 1

13 Which of the following are correct regarding rights of partners?
1. A partner has the right to allow the admission of a new partner.
2. Every partner has a right to take part in the management of business.
3. Every partner has a joint ownership of partnership property.
4. Every partner has a right to share the profit not the losses with other partners.
5. Every partner has a right to inspect the books of account and have a copy of the same.
6. In case of emergency, a partner has a right to act as a man of prudence.

Select the correct answer using the codes given below
(a) 1, 2, 3, 4
(b) 2, 3, 4, 6
(c) 3, 4, 5, 6
(d) 2, 3, 5, 6

14 Choose the odd one out. The court has the option to order dissolution of a firm, where
1. a partner is of sound mind.
2. a partner do not suffer from permanent in capacity.
3. a partner is not guilty of misconduct of the business.
4. a partner transfers his interest or share to a third party.

Select the correct answer using the codes given below

Codes

(a) Both 1 and 2 (b) Both 2 and 3
(c) Only 3 (d) Only 4

15 The inter-se-relations of the partners between themselves is that of
(a) family friends
(b) business associates
(c) agents of each other
(d) close relatives

16 In the absence of an agreement to the contrary, all partners sleeping or working share profits and losses in the
(a) capital ratio (b) equal ratio
(c) Both (a) and (b) (d) None of these

17 The current account of a partner
(a) may have a debit or a credit balance
(b) will always have a debit balance
(c) will always have a credit balance
(d) will never have a balance

18 Which of the following account's balance will not be transferred to realisation account?
(a) Provision for bad debts
(b) Debtors
(c) Goodwill
(d) Cash and Bank

19 What type of account is revaluation account?
(a) Personal account
(b) Nominal account
(c) Real account
(d) None of the above

20 Goodwill in a partnership firm can be valued at the time of
(a) admission (b) retirement
(c) death (d) All of these

21 Firm has earned exceptionally high profits from a contract, which will not be renewed. In such a case, this profit will not be included in ....
(a) profit share of the partners
(b) calculation of the goodwill
(c) Both (a) and (b)
(d) None of these

22 In which of the following account(s), accounting entries are made at the book value of assets and liabilities?
(a) Revaluation (b) Realisation
(c) Capital (d) Suspense

23 Sometimes all the partners including the new partner may agree not to alter the book value of assets and liabilities even when they agree to revalue them. In order to record this, ... is opened.
(a) Revaluation A/c
(b) Goodwill A/c
(c) Suspense A/c
(d) Memorandum Revaluation A/c

24 Which of the following are methods of calculating goodwill?
1. Average profit method
2. Super profit method
3. Log method
4. Sum of years digit method
5. Capitalisation of average profit method
6. Capitalisation of super profit method
7. FIFO method

Select the correct answer using the codes given below

Codes

(a) 1, 2, 5 and 6 (b) 1, 2, 4 and 5
(c) 1, 2, 4 and 6 (d) 1, 2, 6 and 7

25 In partnership, which of the following account(s) is/are opened under fixed capital account method?
(a) Partner's Capital A/c (b) Partner's Current A/c
(c) Both (a) and (b) (d) None of these

26 Arrange the following steps of 'adjustment of old partners' capital on the basis of incoming partner's capital in a correct order.
1. Ascertain the present capital of the old partners.
2. Calculation of total capital of firm on the basis of new partner's capital.
3. Finding the surplus/deficit capital.
4. Determining the new capital of each partner.

Select the correct answer using the codes given below

Codes

(a) 2, 4, 1, 3 (b) 3, 2, 1, 4
(c) 4, 3, 2, 1 (d) 1, 4, 2, 3

27 Which of the following factors generally contribute to the value of goodwill of a firm?
(a) Quality of goods sold by the firm
(b) Reputation of the owners
(c) Risk involved in the business
(d) All of the above

28 Which of the following are shown is profit and loss appropriation account?
1. Salary to staff
2. Salary to partners
3. Interest on capital
4. Fresh capital introduced
5. Share of profit
6. Amount of drawings
7. Interest on drawings

Select the correct answer using the codes given below
Codes
(a) 1, 4, 5, 6 (b) 2, 3, 5, 7
(c) 1, 2, 6, 7 (d) 2, 3, 6, 7

29 Profit or loss on revaluation is shared among the partners in .... ratio.
(a) old profit sharing (b) new profit sharing
(c) sacrificing (d) equal

30 Consider the following statements.
1. Realisation account and revaluation account are the same.
2. While preparing cash account or bank account (dissolution), the debit and credit side are same.
3. Items appearing in the balance sheet are posted at one place only.

Which of the statements given above is/are correct?
(a) Only 1 (b) Both 2 and 3
(c) All of the above (d) None of the above

31 When a partner draws a fixed sum at the beginning of each month, interest on total drawings will be equal to interest of .... at an agreed rate.
(a) 5 months (b) 5.5 months
(c) 6 months (d) 6.5 months

32 X and Y are partners in a firm. They withdrew @ ₹ 1,500 and ₹ 1,000 respectively on 15th day of every month for all the twelve months during 2009. Interest on drawings is chargable @ 10% per annum. What would be the interest on drawings respectively?
(a) ₹ 1,800 and ₹ 1,200 (b) ₹ 900 and ₹ 600
(c) ₹ 18,000 and ₹ 12,000 (d) ₹ 150 and ₹ 100

Admisssion, Retirement and Death

33 Goodwill brought in by new partner in cash is called
(a) capital (b) loan
(c) drawings (d) premium

34 The amount of goodwill brought in by new partner is transferred to old partners in ....
(a) old ratio (b) new ratio
(c) sacrificing ratio (d) gaining ratio

35 If nothing otherwise mentioned, on admission of a new partner, the sacrificing ratio is same as the
(a) old ratio (b) new ratio
(c) gaining ratio (d) capital ratio

36 Which of the following is not the purpose of admission of a partner?
(a) For procuring additional capital
(b) For acquiring additional managerial skill
(c) For progress of the firm
(d) For increasing competition

37 Arrange the steps of adjustment of partner's capital on the admission of a new partner in sequence.
1. Calculate the adjusted capital of old partners.
2. Calculate the proportionate capital of a new partner.
3. All adjustments should be made.
4. Calculate the total capital of new firm.

Select the correct answer using the codes given below
Codes
(a) 3, 1, 4, 2 (b) 3, 4, 1, 2
(c) 4, 3, 2, 1 (d) 3, 4, 2, 1

38 A, B and C are three equal partners. D is admitted for, $\frac{1}{4}$th share. What is the sacrificing ratio?
(a) 1 : 1 : 1 (b) 1 : 2 : 1
(c) 2 : 1 : 1 (d) 1 : 1 : 2

39 X and Y are partners in a firm sharing profits in the ratio of 3 : 1. They admit Z as a partner with new profit sharing ratio of 2 : 1 : 1. The amount of goodwill brought in by new partner will be credited to
(a) X and Y equally (b) Only X
(c) Only Y (d) None of these

40 A and B are partners sharing profit in the ratio of 2 : 3. They admit C for $\frac{1}{4}$th share in the business. The sacrificing ratio of A and B is
(a) 3 : 1 (b) 1 : 4
(c) 2 : 3 (d) 1 : 1

41 A and B are partners in a firm sharing profit and loss in the ratio of 3 : 2. They admit C into partnership for $\frac{1}{4}$th share and the new ratio between A and B is 2 : 1. The sacrificing ratio is
(a) 1 : 1 (b) 2 : 1
(c) 3 : 1 (d) 2 : 3

42 At the time of death of a partner, firm gets ....
(a) policy amount (b) surrender value
(c) Both (a) and (b) (d) None of these

43 Retirement of a partner leads to .... of remaining partners.
(a) gain in profit sharing ratio
(b) loss in profit sharing ratio
(c) no change in profit sharing ratio
(d) None of the above

44 At the time of retirement of a partner, the existing profit and loss balance is transferred to which account?
(a) Realisation (b) Revaluation
(c) Goodwill (d) Existing partners capital

45 At the time of retirement of a partner, the adjustment of goodwill is done, in which ratio?
(a) Old profit sharing ratio
(b) Gaining ratio
(c) Sacrificing ratio
(d) New profit sharing ratio

46 To provide funds to pay to the retiring partner or to the representatives of a partner, generally .... is created by partners.
(a) sinking fund (b) joint life policy
(c) reserve fund (d) None of these

47 As per Section 37 of the Indian Partnership Act 1932, the executors of a deceased partner would be entitled at their choice to the interest calculated from the date of death till the date of payment on the final amount due to the partner at .... per annum.
(a) 12% (b) 10%
(c) 6% (d) 5%

48 Joint life policy is taken by the firm on the life of
(a) all the partners severally (b) all the partners jointly
(c) Both (a) and (b) (d) None of these

49 On the death of a partner, the amount received from Joint life policy should be credited to the capital accounts of
(a) only continuing partners (b) only deceased partners
(c) all the partners (d) None of these

50 A, B and C enter into a partnership investing ₹ 35,000, ₹ 45,000 and ₹ 55,000 respectively. Find their respective shares in annual profit of ₹ 40,500.
(a) ₹ 10,500, ₹ 13,500, ₹ 19,500
(b) ₹ 10,500, ₹ 10,500, ₹ 21,500
(c) ₹ 10,500, ₹ 13,500, ₹ 17,500
(d) ₹ 10,500, ₹ 13,500, ₹ 16,500

51 X and Y are partners sharing profits and losses in the ratio of 3 : 2 (X's capital is ₹ 30,000 and Y's capital is ₹ 15,000). They admitted Z agreed to give 1/5th share of profits to him. How much Z should bring in towards his capital?
(a) ₹ 9,000 (b) ₹ 11,250
(c) ₹ 12,000 (d) ₹ 14,500

52 X and Y are partners sharing the profit in the ratio of 3 : 2. They take Z as the new partner who is supposed to bring ₹ 25,000 against capital and ₹ 10,000 against goodwill. New profit sharing ratio is1 : 1 : 1. Z is able to bring only his share of capital. How this will be treated in the books of the firm?
(a) X and Y will share goodwill bought by Z as ₹ 4,000 : ₹ 1,000
(b) Goodwill be raised to ₹ 30,000 in old profit sharing ratio
(c) Both (a) and (b)
(d) No treatment in the books of the firm

Dissolution and Insolvency

53 The private property of a partner should be used to ....
(a) pay his private debts first
(b) if there is any surplus it can be used to pay firm's liabilities
(c) Both (a) and (b)
(d) None of the above

54 .... rule is applicable at the time of any partner becoming insolvent.
(a) Garner *vs* Murray
(b) Derry *vs* Peek
(c) Salomon *vs* A Salomon and Corporation Limited
(d) Mohiri Bibi *vs* Dharamdas Ghosh

55 Dissolution of partnership between all partners of firm is called ....
(a) dissolution of firm
(b) dissolution of partnership
(c) dissolution of firm name
(d) None of the above

56 As per the decision in the Garner *vs* Murray case, when the partner's capital accounts are fixed, any loss arising due to the capital deficiency in the insolvent partner's capital account is to be borne by solvent partners in the ratio of ....
(a) profit sharing ratio (b) last agreed capital ratio
(c) sacrificing ratio (d) gaining ratio

57 Garner *vs* Murray rule requires
(a) that the solvent partners should bear the loss arising due to insolvency of a partner in their last agreed capital ratio
(b) that the solvent partners should bring in cash equal to their respective shares of the loss on realisation
(c) Both (a) and (b)
(d) None of the above

58 A firm stands dissolve in the following cases
1. the partners agree that the firm should be dissolved.
2. the business becomes legal.
3. in case of partnership at will, a partner gives notice of dissolution.
4. the court orders dissolution.

Select the correct answer using the codes given below

Codes
(a) 1, 2 and 4 (b) Both 2 and 3
(c) Only 3 (d) Only 2

59 In which of the following cases Garner *vs* Murray rule is not applicable?
(a) Only one partner is solvent
(b) All partners are insolvent
(c) Partnership deed provides for a specific method to be followed in case of insolvency of a partner
(d) All of the above

60 In case of dissolution, prior to final distribution to partners, the balance of cash should be equal to

(a) the sale of assets plus the beginning balance of cash after payment of liabilities
(b) the balance of cash prior to the sale of assets plus or minus a gain or loss from realisation
(c) the sale of assets minus the beginning balance of cash prior to payment of liabilities
(d) the total capital balances

61 In settling the accounts of a firm after dissolution losses including deficiencies of capital, shall be paid in which sequence?

1. By the partners individually in profit sharing ratio.
2. Out of profit.
3. Out of capital.

Select the correct answer using the codes given below

Codes

(a) 1, 2 and 3 (b) 3, 2 and 1
(c) 2, 1 and 3 (d) 2, 3 and 1

62 Arrange the following in correct sequence in the event of dissolution of a partnership firm.

1. Residue, if any, divided among the partners.
2. Paying to each partner for his capital.
3. Paying the debts of third party.
4. Paying to each partner for advances made by him.

Select the correct answer using the codes given below

Codes

(a) 4, 3, 2, 1 (b) 3, 4, 2, 1
(c) 2, 1, 4, 3 (d) 3, 1, 4, 2

63 Which of the following are the consequences in case of insolvency of partner?

1. The partner adjudicated as insolvent ceases to be a partner.
2. He ceases on the date on which the order of adjudication is made.
3. The firm is dissolved on the date of the order.
4. The estate of the insolvent partner is liable for any act of the firm after the date of the order of adjudication.
5. The firm can be held liable for any acts of the insolvent partners after the date of the order of adjudication.

Select the correct answer using the codes given below

Codes

(a) Only 5
(b) Both 4 and 5
(c) 3, 4 and 5
(d) 1, 2 and 3

64 Upon dissolution, which is the proper order for application of the firm's assets?

1. Payment of partner's loan.
2. In paying, the debts of the firm to third partiy.
3. Distribution of surplus to partners in profit sharing ratio.
4. Payment of partners' capital.

Select the correct answer using the codes given below

Codes

(a) 1, 4, 3 and 2 (b) 2, 1, 4 and 3
(c) 2, 1, 3 and 4 (d) 1, 2, 3 and 4

65 Arrange the following in correct sequence in the event of dissolution of a partnership firm.

1. If surplus, it is distributed among the partners.
2. The assets of the firm are realised.
3. Amount realised is applied towards repayment of liabilities to outsiders and loan taken from partners.
4. Capital contributed by partners is repaid.

Select the correct answer using the codes given below

Codes

(a) 4, 3, 2, 1 (b) 2, 4, 1, 3
(c) 2, 3, 4, 1 (d) 2, 1, 4, 3

66 What will be the treatment, if assets are taken over by a creditor of the firm at the time of dissolution?

(a) Realisation A/c will be debited
(b) Realisation A/c will be credited
(c) No entry should be passed
(d) None of the above

Miscellaneous

Directions (Q. Nos. 67-73) *The following three items consist of two statements, Statement (I) and Statement (II). You have to examine these two statements carefully and select the answers to these items using the codes given below.*

Codes

(a) Both statements are correct
(b) Both statements are incorrect
(c) Statement I is correct, but Statement II is incorrect
(d) Statement I is incorrect, but Statement II is correct

67 According to Garner *vs* Murray

Statement I The normal loss on realisation is to be borne by all partners in the profit sharing ratio.

Statement II Loss due to insolvency of a partner has to be borne by the solvent partners in the capital ratio.

68 Statement I Profit or loss on revaluation is shared among the partners in old profit ratio.

Statement II Current accounts of the partners should be opened when the capitals are fixed.

69 Statement I Investment in partnership is made by introducing goodwill.

Statement II Partnership is formed by partners either by written or oral agreement.

70 Statement I Liability of partners in a partnership is unlimited.

Statement II All the time of admission of a new partner general reserve is credited to capital account of old partners.

71 Statement I Drawings against capital is debited in capital account.

Statement II Drawings against profit is debited in drawings account.

72 Statement I As per Section 69, if a partnership firm is not registered then no partner can sue his co-partners or firm in any court.

Statement II The firm cannot file a suit against third party or breach of contract etc.

73 Statement I Revaluation account assets and liabilities are to appear at their revalued figures.

Statement II Memorandum revaluation account assets and liabilities are to appear at their old figures.

Directions (Q. Nos. 74-80) *In the questions given below are two statements labelled as Assertion (A) and Reason (R). In the context of two statements, which one of the following is correct?*

Codes

(a) Both (A) and (R) are true and (R) is the correct explanation of (A)
(b) Both (A) and (R) are true, but R is not the correct explanation of (A)
(c) (A) is true, but (R) is false
(d) (A) is false, but (R) is true

74 Assertion (A) On the incoming of a new partner, assets and liabilities of the firm are revalued.

Reason (R) This is for the benefit of the new as well as the old partners.

75 Assertion (A) When a partner is unable to pay his debt, he is said to be insolvent.

Reason (R) The share of his loss is to be borne by other solvent partners in accordance with the decision in English case of Garner *vs* Murray.

76 Assertion (A) New partner acquires his share in profits from the old partners.

Reason (R) There is no need to calculate future profit sharing ratio among all the partners at the time of admission.

77 Assertion (A) Outgoing partner is compensated for parting with firm's future profit in favour of partners.

Reason (R) Therefore, the remaining partners contribute to such compensation in sacrificing ratio.

78 Assertion (A) A new partner is admitted, with a stipulation that the firm will not be dissolved before the expiry of a certain term.

Reason (R) He will be entitled to a suitable refund, if the firm is dissolved before the term has expired.

79 Assertion (A) The court has the option to order dissolution of a firm.

Reason (R) Where the business cannot be carried on except at a loss.

80 Assertion (A) In case of dissolution, open a realisation account and transfer assets (except cash and bank) and liabilities.

Reason (R) Accounts denoting accumulated losses or profits should not be transferred to the realisation account.

81 Assertion (A) The Partnership Act does not make it obligatory that a firm must a deed in writing.

Reason (R) It is better to have it in writing to avoid confusion.

Codes

(a) (A) is true, but (R) is false
(b) (A) is false, but (R) is true
(c) Both (A) and (R) are true
(d) Both (A) and (R) are false

82 Match the following.

List I	List II
A. Admission	1. Gaining ratio
B. Retirement	2. Equal ratio
C. Revaluation	3. Sacrificing ratio
D. No partnership deed	4. Old ratio

Codes

	A	B	C	D		A	B	C	D
(a)	4	3	2	1	(b)	2	1	4	3
(c)	3	4	1	2	(d)	3	1	4	2

83 Match the following.

List I	List II
A. Interest on partner's capital is chargeable to the extent of available	1. competing
B. The amount due to the retiring partner can be made by ...... payment method.	2. mutual
C. A partner must not carry on a ...... business.	3. profit
D. Partners are ...... for each other.	4. lumpsum

Codes

	A	B	C	D		A	B	C	D
(a)	4	3	1	2	(b)	3	4	1	2
(c)	3	4	2	1	(d)	4	3	2	1

84 Match the following.

	List I	List II
A.	A new partner can be admitted with the consent of ...... existing partners.	1. current
B.	Increase in liability at the time of retirement is debited to ...... account.	2. all
C.	Buying and selling is ...... power of partners.	3. revaluation
D.	The ...... account of partner may have a debit or credit balance.	4. implied

Codes

	A	B	C	D		A	B	C	D
(a)	4	1	2	3	(b)	2	3	4	1
(c)	2	4	1	3	(d)	2	3	4	1

85 Match the following.

	List I	List II
A.	Partnership can be formed for the purpose of carrying	1. incoming partner
B.	Guaranteed profit is generally given to	2. business
C.	Every partner is a joint ...... of the partnership property.	3. nominal
D.	Partners, who do not contribute any capital and have no interest in the business are known as ...... partners.	4. owner

Codes

	A	B	C	D		A	B	C	D
(a)	2	1	4	3	(b)	2	4	1	3
(c)	4	3	2	1	(d)	4	1	2	3

86 Match the following.

	List I	List II
A.	New share (Admission)	1. Old share + Gaining share
B.	Gaining ratio	2. Old ratio – New ratio
C.	Sacrificing ratio	3. New ratio – Old ratio
D.	New share (Retirement)	4. Old share – Sacrifice share

Codes

	A	B	C	D		A	B	C	D
(a)	2	1	4	3	(b)	3	4	2	1
(c)	4	3	2	1	(d)	4	3	1	2

87 Match the following in respect of interest on drawings.

	List I	List II
A.	At the beginning of each month	1. 5 and 1/2 month
B.	At the end of each month quarter	2. 6 and 1/2 month
C.	At the beginning of each quarter	3. 4 and 1/2 month
D.	At the end of each	4. 7 and 1/2 month

Codes

	A	B	C	D		A	B	C	D
(a)	2	1	4	3	(b)	4	3	2	1
(c)	4	3	1	2	(d)	3	4	1	2

88 Match the following.

	List I	List II
A.	Revaluation account is prepared at the time of	1. may or may not be surrendered at the time of retirement of a partner.
B.	Joint Life Policy	2. to settle the claim of the outgoing partner
C.	Premium on Joint Life Policy taken up on the lives of all partners is paid by	3. admission of a partner
D.	The objective of taking Joint Life Policy by a partnership firm is	4. partnership firm

Codes

	A	B	C	D
(a)	4	3	2	1
(b)	3	1	4	2
(c)	2	1	4	3
(d)	2	4	1	3

89 Match the following.

	List I	List II
A.	Compulsory Dissolution	1. Section 44
B	Dissolution by Court	2. Section 41
C.	Dissolution by Notice	3. Section 42
D.	Contingent Dissolution	4. Section 43

Codes

	A	B	C	D
(a)	4	3	2	1
(b)	3	4	2	1
(c)	2	1	4	3
(d)	2	4	1	3

90 Match the following.

	List I	List II
A.	...... is difference between old ratio and new ratio.	1. Dissolution
B.	Dissolution of partnership all the partners of firm is called ...... of firm.	2. Admitted
C.	A minor can be ...... to the benefits.	3. Duties
D.	Every partner is bound to attend diligently to his	4. Sacrificing ratio

Codes

	A	B	C	D		A	B	C	D
(a)	4	3	1	2	(b)	4	1	2	3
(c)	4	3	2	1	(d)	3	4	1	2

PREVIOUS YEARS' QUESTIONS

December 2018

1 A and B are partners in a firm sharing profits in the ratio of 3 : 2. They admit X as a partner for 1/3rd share in profits of the firm. The new profit sharing ratio of A,B and X is

(a) 3 : 2 : 1 (b) 3 : 2 : 2 (c) 3 : 2 : 3 (d) 6 : 4 : 5

July 2018

2 X and Y sharing profits in the ratio of 7 : 3, admit Z for 3/7th share in the new firm in which he takes 2/7th from X and 1/7th firm Y. The new ratio of X, Y and Z will be

(a) 7 : 3 : 3 (b) 4 : 2 : 3
(c) 14 : 6 : 15 (d) 29 : 11 : 30

November 2017

3 Goodwill of a firm of X and Y is valued at ₹ 30,000. It is appearing in the books at ₹ 12,000. Z is admitted for 1/4th share. What amount he is supposed to bring for goodwill ?

(a) ₹ 3,000 (b) ₹ 4,500 (c) ₹ 7,500 (d) ₹ 10,500

January 2017

4 Amount due to outgoing partner is shown in the balance sheet as his

(a) liability (b) asset
(c) capital (d) loan

July 2016

5 Ram and Shyam are partners in a firm with capital of ₹ 4,80,000 and ₹ 3,10,000 respectively. They admitted Ganesh as a partner with $\frac{1}{4}$th share of profit. Ganesh brings ₹ 3,00,000 as his capital. Ganesh's share of goodwill will be

(a) ₹ 1,10,000 (b) ₹ 27,500
(c) ₹ 17,500 (d) ₹ 70,000

6 A, B and C are partners in a firm sharing profits and losses in the ratio of 4 : 3 : 2. They agreed to take D into partnership and gave him $\frac{1}{8}$th share. What will be their new profit sharing ratio?

(a) 4 : 3 : 2 : 1 (b) 28 : 21 : 14 : 9
(c) 28 : 21 : 14 : 8 (d) 4 : 1 : 2 : 1

June 2015

7 A retiring partner continues to be liable for obligations incurred after his retirement

(a) if unpaid amount is transferred to his loan account
(b) if he does not give public notice
(c) if he starts a similar business elsewhere
(d) in all the situations till he survives

December 2014

8 X, Y and Z are sharing profits in the ratio of 6 : 5 : 3. A is admitted into partnership for 1/8th share. The sacrificing ratio of X, Y and Z is

(a) equal (b) 6 : 5 : 3
(c) 5/14, 4/14, 5/14 (d) 4 : 5 : 5

9 When a firm is dissolved, profit or loss on realisation is shared by the partners

(a) equally
(b) in the ratio of their capital balances
(c) in the profit sharing ratio
(d) in the ratio laid down in Garner *vs* Murray

June 2014

10 A, a partner in firm, is drawing ₹ 500 regularly on the 16th of every month. He will have to pay interest at the given rate in a year on ₹ 6,000 for the total period of

(a) 5 months (b) 6 months (c) 7 months (d) 12 months

December 2013

11 A and B are partners sharing profits in the ratio of 3 : 2. Their books showed goodwill at ₹ 3,000. C is admitted with $\frac{1}{4}$th share of profit and brings ₹ 10,000 as his capital. But, he is not able to bring in cash for his share of goodwill ₹ 3,000. How will you treat this?

(a) Goodwill is raised by ₹ 12,000
(b) C will remain as debtor for ₹ 3,000
(c) C's A/c is debited for ₹ 3,000
(d) Goodwill is raised by ₹ 9,000

December 2012

12 Arrange the following parties in the event of dissolution of a firm.

1. Secured creditors
2. Unsecured creditors
3. Partners who have granted loans
4. Partners who have contributed over and above profit sharing ratio

Select the correct answer using the codes given below

Codes

(a) 2, 1, 3, 4 (b) 1, 2, 3, 4 (c) 1, 2, 4, 3 (d) 2, 1, 4, 3

June 2012

13 X and Y are partners in a firm sharing profits in the ratios of 2 : 1. Z is admitted with a 1/3rd profit sharing. What will be the new profit sharing ratio of X, Y and Z?

(a) 3 : 3 : 3 (b) 4 : 3 : 2 (c) 4 : 2 : 3 (d) 2 : 3 : 4

ANSWERS

Objective Questions

1 (d)	2 (b)	3 (a)	4 (b)	5 (d)	6 (c)	7 (b)	8 (b)	9 (d)	10 (b)
11 (d)	12 (c)	13 (d)	14 (b)	15 (c)	16 (b)	17 (a)	18 (d)	19 (b)	20 (d)
21 (b)	22 (b)	23 (d)	24 (a)	25 (c)	26 (a)	27 (d)	28 (b)	29 (a)	30 (b)
31 (d)	32 (b)	33 (d)	34 (c)	35 (a)	36 (d)	37 (a)	38 (b)	39 (b)	40 (c)
41 (d)	42 (c)	43 (a)	44 (d)	45 (b)	46 (b)	47 (c)	48 (c)	49 (c)	50 (d)
51 (b)	52 (b)	53 (c)	54 (a)	55 (a)	56 (b)	57 (c)	58 (d)	59 (d)	60 (d)
61 (d)	62 (b)	63 (d)	64 (c)	65 (c)	66 (c)	67 (d)	68 (a)	69 (d)	70 (a)
71 (a)	72 (b)	73 (c)	74 (a)	75 (b)	76 (c)	77 (c)	78 (a)	79 (a)	80 (b)
81 (a)	82 (d)	83 (b)	84 (d)	85 (a)	86 (c)	87 (a)	88 (b)	89 (c)	90 (b)

Previous Years' Questions

1 (d)	2 (d)	3 (c)	4 (d)	5 (b)	6 (b)	7 (c)	8 (b)	9 (c)	10 (b)
11 (c)	12 (b)	13 (c)							

CHAPTER 07

Corporate Accounting

Every company must perform some accounting. This is so as to identify its financial state. Corporate accounting is especially suited for compaines. It deals with processes such as the preparation of cash flow statements, financial statements, shares and debentures and more.

Company

The word 'company' is derived from the Latin word 'com', *i.e.* with or together and 'panis', *i.e.* bread. Originally, the word referred to an association of persons or merchant men discussing matters and taking food together. However, in law 'Company' is termed as company, which is formed and registered under the Companies Act, 2013 or an existing company formed and registered under any of the previous company laws.

A company is an association of person, who contribute money or money's worth to a common stock and use it for a common purpose. It is created by law and effected by law. It is a legal person as much as an individual, but with no physical existence.

According to **Indian Companies Act, 2013**, "Company means a company formed and registered under this act." The Company Act has defined a company without giving a straight meaning.

According to **Justice Marshal**, "A corporation is an artificial being, invisible, intangible and existing only in the contemplation of law." It is not affected by the death, insanely and insolvency of an individual member.

In simple words, the company can be described as an organisation consisting of individuals called shareholders by virtue of holding the shares of a company, who are authorised by law to elect a Board of Directors and through it, to act as a separate legal entity as regards its activities.

In this Chapter

Share

The capital of a company is divided into a number of equal units. Each unit is called a share. The word share implies a unit of share capital having property rights. Section 2 (84) of the Companies Act, 2013 defines a share as "A share in the share capital of the company and includes stock except where a distinction between stock and shares is expressed or implied." A company may divide its capital into share of ₹ 10, ₹ 50 and ₹ 100 or any suitable denomination. A share is proportionate part of the share capital and forms the basis of ownership interest in a company. The persons, who contribute money through shares are known as 'shareholders'. A share is not a sum of money but is an interest measured by a sum of money. Share is a bundle of rights and obligations contained in the contract, *i.e.* Articles of Association.

Share Capital

Total capital of company is divided into a number of small indivisible units of a fixed amount and each such unit is called a share. The fixed value of a share, printed on the share certificate, is called nominal/par/face value of a share. The liability of holder of shares (called shareholders) is limited to the issue price of shares acquired by them. As the total capital of the company is divided into shares, the capital of the company is called 'share capital'.

Kinds of Shares

Under the Companies Act, 2013, shares can be of two classes only

Preference Shares *Preference shares are those shares which satisfy the following two conditions*

- As regards dividend, they carry a preferential right to fixed amount of dividend.
- As regards capital, they carry a preferential right over other shareholders to be paid first in case of winding-up of the company.

Equity Shares Those shares which are not preference shares are equity shares. It is the risk capital of business. They don't enjoy any preferential right in the matter of dividend or repayment of capital. Rate of dividend on equity shares is recommended by Board of Directors and may vary from year to year. These shares carry voting rights.

Special points in respect of issue of such shares and minimum subscription are as follows

- Application money cannot be less than 5% of face value of shares.
- A company cannot allot shares unless minimum subscription stated in prospectus is received by the company. Such minimum subscription is the amount which according to the directors must be raised in cash by issue of shares. Such amount is required for preliminary expenses, commission payable on issue of shares, for purchase of fixed assets and for working capital etc.
- As per SEBI, minimum 90% subscription must be received by the company out of entire issue.

  If the company does not receive minimum subscription of 90% then entire subscription shall be refunded to the applicants within 10 days from the date of closer of issue.
- Shares issued are to be made fully paid-up within 12 months of the date of allotment. If the size of issue is upto ₹ 500 crore.

Issue of Shares

When a public company desires to raise capital by issuing its shares to the public, it has to invite the public to subscribe for its shares. The invitation is made through a document called the prospectus. The person, who intends to subscribe to those shares should make an application for the desired number of shares to the company.

First installment, paid alongwith application is called application money. Then, the company will allot shares to the applicant.

Allotment means the appropriation of a certain number of shares to an applicant in response to his application. The company cannot allot more than the number of shares offered to the public for subscription through the prospectus. Moreover, the company cannot make allotment unless the amount stated in the prospectus as the minimum subscription has been subscribed and the sum payable on application for the stated amount has been received by the company.

If the number of shares applied is less than the number of shares offered, the allotment can be made only for the shares applied, provided minimum subscription is raised *i.e.* 90% of the issued amount.

A company may issue shares either

For Cash When the company receives cash against the issued shares, shares are said to have been issued for cash.

For Consideration other than Cash When a company issues shares in consideration against purchase of fixed assets, it is said to have been issued for consideration other than cash.

Terms of Issue of Shares

A company may issue shares

At Par When shares are issued at their face value, the shares are said to have been issued at par, *i.e.* issue price and face value are same. *e.g.* Share with a face value of ₹ 10 is issued at ₹ 10.

At Premium When shares are issued at a value that is higher than the face value of shares, the shares are said to have been issued at premium *i.e.* issue price is more than face value. *e.g.* Share with a face value of ₹ 10 is issued at ₹ 15, premium being ₹ 5.

Accounting Treatment of Issue of Shares for Cash

Accounting treatment for shares issued can be discussed under two heads, *i.e.* when amount is payable in lumpsum and when amount is payable in instalments. *These are as*

Shares Payable in Lumpsum Shares are said to have been issued against lumpsum payment when amount is payable in one instalment.

Journal Entries

For receiving share application money	Bank A/c To Share Application and Allotment A/c (Being application money received)	Dr
For allotment of shares	**At Par** Share Application and Allotment A/c To Share Capital A/c (Being the shares allotted and application money transferred to share capital account)	Dr
	At Premium Share Application and Allotment A/c To Share Capital A/c (With the face value of shares) To Securities Premium Reserve A/c (With the amount of premium) (Being shares allotted and application money transferred to share capital account and securities premium reserve account)	Dr

Shares Payable in Instalments The amount against the shares may be received in instalments. First instalment is called **application money** (it is paid alongwith the application). Second instalment is called **allotment money** (it is collected by the company at the time of allotment).

After allotment of shares, the remaining part of share money, when called-up, is known as **call money**. It may be collected in one or more instalments. If only one call is made, then it is called first and final call in place of first call, otherwise the word 'final' will be added to the last instalment.

The issue price of shares can be received by the company in instalments and these instalments are referred to as

First instalment	⟶	Application money payable alongwith application
Second instalment	⟶	Allotment money payable at the time of allotment
Third instalment	⟶	First call
Fourth, fifth and sixth instalment	⟶	Second call, third call and so on
Last instalment	⟶	Final call

The journal entries required to be passed are

Journal Entries for Issue of Shares for Cash

On receipt of application money	Bank A/c To Share Application A/c	Dr	[With application money received] [Number of shares applied × Application money per share]
On allotment of shares	Share Application A/c To Share Capital A/c	Dr	[With application money on shares allotted] [Number of shares allotted × Application money per share]
On making allotment due	(a) **At Par** Share Allotment A/c To Share Capital A/c	Dr	[With allotment money due] [Number of shares allotted × Allotment money per share]
	(b) **At Premium** Share Allotment A/c To Share Capital A/c To Securities Premium Reserve A/c	Dr	[With the total money] [With allotment money due] [With premium money due]
On receipt of allotment money	Bank A/c To Share Allotment A/c	Dr	[With allotment money received]
On making the first call due	Share First Call A/c To Share Capital A/c	Dr	[With first call money due] [Number of shares allotted × First call money per share]
On receipt of the first call	Bank A/c To Share First Call A/c	Dr	[With first call money received]

Subscription of Shares

Accounting for issue of shares depends upon the type of subscription. Whenever a company decides to issue shares to public, it invites applications for subscription by issuing a prospectus. It is not necessary that company receives full applications for the number of shares to be issued by it.

There are three possibilities for subscription of shares

Full Subscription

When applications are received for the shares offered by the company, the issue is called fully subscribed. Issue is fully subscribed, if the number of shares offered for subscription and the number of shares actually subscribed by the public are same.

Under Subscription

It means the number of shares offered for subscription is more than the number of shares subscribed by the public. In this case, the journal entries are passed with one change, *i.e.* calculation of application, allotment and for that matter, the call money is based on number of shares actually applied and allotted. It must be remembered that shares can be allotted only when the minimum subscription is received.

Over Subscription

When the number of shares applied for is more than the number of shares offered for subscription, the issue is said to be our subscribed. If an issue is over subscribed, some applications may be rejected and application money is refunded and in respect of others, only a part of the shares applied for may be allotted and the excess amount received can be utilised towards allotment or call money, which has fallen or will soon fall due for payment.

Pro-rata Allotment When the shares are oversubscribed, the company cannot satisfy all the applicants. It means that a decision is to be made on how the shares are going to be allotted. In such situation, the directors allot shares on some reasonable basis because the company can allot only that number of shares actually offered for subscription. Moreover, as per the guidelines issued by SEBI, the company cannot reject outrightly any application for share, unless it has incomplete information or absence of signature(s) or insufficient application money and so on.

In short, the following procedure is adopted

- Total rejection of some applications.
- Acceptance of some applications in full.
- Allotment to the remaining applicants on pro-rata basis.

The shares should be issued in tradable lot. In case of pro-rata allotment, no applicant for shares is refused and no applicant is allotted the shares in full. Each applicant receives the share in some proportion. In such cases, the excess amount of application money (*i.e.* overpaid amount) is not refunded but retained and treated as a payment towards allotment money.

The following journal entry is made to transfer excess application money to allotment account

Share Application A/c Dr
(With the excess application money)
To Share Allotment A/c
(Being the surplus application money transferred to share allotment account)

Surplus money exceeding that due on allotment should be refunded to the allottees. *However, the company may transfer this to calls-in-advance account if*

- Acceptance of calls-in-advance is permitted by the company's articles.
- The consent of the applicant has been taken either by a separate letter or by inserting a clause in the company's prospectus.

The company can retain the calls-in-advance at the most so much amount as is sufficient to make the allotted shares fully paid-up ultimately.

The journal entry will be as follows

Share Application A/c Dr
(With the excess application money left over the amount due on application and allotment)
To Calls-in-advance A/c
(Being the surplus application money transferred to calls-in-advance account)

Accounting Treatment of Issue of Shares for Consideration other than Cash

It is not necessary to issue shares for cash only. *It can be issued for a consideration other than cash viz*

Issue of Shares to Vendors

If a company purchases some assets from vendors, in exchange it can issue fully paid shares to them whereby, the later agrees to accept it. Thus, no cash is received for the issue of shares and normal procedure of application and allotment is also dispensed with.

In such a case, the following journal entries are required for this purpose

On Purchase of Assets

Assets A/c Dr
To Vendor's Personal A/c
(Being assets purchased)

On Issue of Shares

Shares can be issued to vendors in any manner out of the following

- ***At Par***

Vendor's Personal A/c Dr
To Share Capital A/c
(Being payment made by shares)

- ***At Premium***

Vendor's personal A/c Dr
To Share Capital A/c
To Securities Premium A/c
(Being payment made by shares)

Issue of Shares to Promoters

A company may issue shares without cash to the promoters for the services rendered by them.

The following journal entry is made

Formation Expenses/Goodwill A/c Dr
To Share Capital A/c
(For shares issued to promoters for their services)

Issue of Shares to Underwriter

A company may issue shares without cash to underwriter for the service rendered by him.

In this case, the following journal entries are passed

For Commission Due

Underwriting Commission A/c Dr
To Underwriter's Personal A/c
(Being underwriting commission due)

For Commission Paid in the form of Shares

Underwriter's Personal A/c Dr
To Share Capital A/c
(Being underwriting commission paid in shares)

For Transferring Underwriting Commission

Statement of Profit and Loss Dr
To Underwriting Commission A/c
(Being underwriting commission transferred)

Note

- *Goodwill account is debited on the assumption that promoter's function has resulted in forming the company into profitable unit.*
- *These shares are disclosed separately under the head share capital (sub-head, subscribed capital) in the balance sheet of a company.*
- *Within 1 month of allotment, the company must produce before the registrar a written contract of sale of service in respect of which shares have been allotted.*

Calls-in-Arrears

Sometimes, some of the shareholders may fail to pay the amount due from them on allotment or on call. The amount remaining unpaid on allotment or on calls is called calls-in-arrears or unpaid calls. It is shown by way of deduction from 'called-up capital' to arrive at paid-up value of the share capital to be shown in the balance sheet.

The Articles of Association of a company usually empower the directors to charge interest at a stipulated rate on calls-in-arrear. According to Table 'F' of Companies Act, 2013, interest at the rate of 10% per annum is to be charged on unpaid calls for the period intervening between the due date of the call and the time of actual payment.

Calls-in-Advance

When a company accepts money from the allottees against the calls not yet made, the amount received in advance is known as calls-in advance. A company may, if authorised by its articles, accept calls-in-advance from its shareholders. The balance of calls-in-advance account is shown separately on the liabilities side of balance sheet, but is not added to the amount of paid-up capital. The board must pay interest on calls-in-advance at a rate specified in the articles from the date of its receipt to the date when the calls become due. But, if the Articles are silent, Table 'F' of Companies Act, 2013 shall be applicable, which allows to pay the interest at a rate not exceeding 12% per annum on any calls-in-advance received by the company.

Forfeiture of Shares

The company demands the share money in instalments from the shareholders from time to time. If a shareholder fails to pay allotment money and/or call money on his shares as called upon by the company, his shares may be forfeited by giving due notice and following the procedure specified in the Articles of Association.

Shares once forfeited, become the property of the company and may be sold on such terms as directors think fit. Upon forfeiture, the original shareholder ceases to be a member and his name must be removed from the register of members.

Accounting Treatment

As discussed earlier, the effect of the forfeiture is to cancel allotment. Therefore, all entries relating to the shares forfeited, except those relating to premium, already passed in the accounting books must be reversed. *These are*

Forfeiture of Shares, Issued at Par

Share Capital A/c	Dr	(Amount called-up so far)
To Share Allotment A/c		(Amount not received on allotment)
To Share Call/Calls A/c		(Amount not received on calls)
To Share Forfeiture A/c		(Amount received so far)

Forfeiture of Shares, Issued at Premium

If Premium Amount has not been paid by the Shareholders

Share Capital A/c	Dr	(Amount called-up so far)
Securities Premium A/c	Dr	(Premium amount called-up)
To Share Allotment A/c		(Amount not received on allotment)
To Share Call(s) A/c		(Amount not received on calls)
To Share Forfeiture A/c		(Amount received so far (for shares forfeited)

If Premium Amount has been paid by the Shareholders

Share Capital A/c	Dr	(Amount called up-premium)
To Share Allotment A/c		(Amount not received on allotment)
To Share Call(s) A/c		(Amount not received on calls)
To Share Forfeiture A/c		(Amount received so far for shares forfeited)

Disclosure The balance of share forfeiture account is shown on the liabilities side of the balance sheet.

Reissue of Forfeited Shares

A forfeited share is merely a share available to the company for sale and remains vested in the company for that purpose only. Reissue of forfeited shares is not allotment of shares but only a sale. The directors of a company have an authority to reissue the shares once forfeited by them due to non-payment of calls. They can reissue the forfeited shares at par, at premium or at discount. However, if the forfeited shares are reissued at a discount, the amount of the discount does not exceed the amount paid on such shares by the original shareholder.

Accounting Treatment

For Forfeited Shares Reissued at Par

Bank A/c	Dr	
To Share Capital A/c		

For Forfeited Shares Reissued at Premium

Bank A/c	Dr	
To Share Capital A/c		
To Securities Premium Reserve A/c		

For Forfeited Shares Reissued at Discount

Bank A/c	Dr	
Share Forfeiture A/c	Dr	(Discount allowed)
To Share Capital A/c		

When all forfeited shares have been reissued, the credit balance left on the share forfeiture account is transferred to capital reserve account. *Entry will be*

Share Forfeiture A/c	Dr
To Capital Reserve A/c	

Important Terms related to Shares

Rights Issue

Rights issue of shares means an issue of shares in which existing shareholders have an option to subscribe for the new shares at a specified price (much below the market price). Companies Act provides that a public company is under legal obligation to offer its new shares to the existing shareholders. However, shareholders have a right to accept or reject the offer. Rights issue of shares is beneficial to the company as well as to the existing shareholders.

Since, fresh issues are made, the market price of the share may be above the previous issue price, the difference is known as value of right *i.e.*

Value of right

= Market price of share – average price of a share

Sweat Equity Shares

Sweat equity shares are basically given to a company's employees on favourable terms in recognition of their work. It usually takes the form of giving options to employees to buy shares of the company, so they become part as owners and participate in the profits, apart from salary. Basically when a startup company forms, it engages the best talent/employees, who bring in their IPR and knowhow, skills and expertise with them, which eventually makes value addition for the company. Such employees are awarded with sweat equity as an incentive to join and stick to the company.

Following are the conditions to be fulfilled for the issue of sweat equity

- The company must have been in business for not less than 1 year. Sweat equity shares should belong to a class of shares already issued. Issue of sweat equity share should be authorised by special resolution passed by shareholders.
- SEBI regulations should be followed where the shares are listed in a stock exchange.

Unclaimed Dividend

Unclaimed dividend is that dividend which have been declared and paid by the company, but it has not been taken or claimed by the shareholder. The reason for dividend being not claimed may be ignorance or shareholder may have shifted to other place and therefore missed the dividend cheque. Unclaimed dividends are shown under current liability and provisions in the balance sheet of the company, since shareholders can claim these dividends any time.

Proposed Dividend

The proposed dividend of a company is the amount of dividends that the company's directors have agreed to pay to its shareholders. This amount has not been paid yet at the time of being proposed.

It is a dividend which is paid by the company at the end of the financial year.

Valuation of Shares

The shares of the Private Limited Company are never quoted on stock exchange. Also not all the public companies shares are quoted on the stock exchange. A public company may either be widely held or closely held. A closely held company means a company having very few shareholders.

Each shareholder is flowing a substantial part of the share capital. A widely held public company means a company having large number of shareholders spread over the entire country. Thus, it has innumerable shareholders, share of only such companies are quoted on one or more stock exchanges. The prices of such shares depend upon various factors like demand and supply, market sentiments etc.

Need for Valuation of Shares

- When shares of one class are to be converted into shares of another class.
- When shareholders wants to take loan from financial institution against the security of shares hold by him.
- When shares are to be transferred, bought or sold.
- When the companies are amalgamated, absorbed, merged or reconstructed.
- When the government wants to compensate the shareholders on the nationalisation of the company.
- Whenever there is a death of a shareholder and the distribution of shares held by him is to be made among the legal heir officers.

Methods of Valuation of Shares

Net Assets Method

Net assets method is also known as Asset Backing, Intrinsic Value and Break-up Value Method.

In this method, the value of net assets is divided by the total number of equity shares to arrive at value of each equity share.

It is calculated as follows

Calculation of Net Assets *There are two methods of calculation of Net Assets*

First Method

	Particulars	(₹)
	Market or Book Value of Assets	...
(–)	Estimated Liabilites	(...)
(–)	Paid-up Preference Share Capital (including arrears of preference dividend)	(...)
	Net Assets available to equity shareholders	...

Second Method

	Particulars	(₹)
	Equity Share Capital	...
(+)	Reserves and surplus	...
(+)/(–)	Profit and Loss on Sale of Revaluation of Assets	.../(...)
(–)	Accumulated Losses	(...)
(–)	Fictitious Assets	(...)
	Net Assets	...

Ascertainment of Liabilities

- Contingent liabilities not shown in the balance sheet, should be recorded.
- All liabilities shown in the balance sheet should be recorded.
- Proposed dividend can be considered as liability, if ex-dividend price is desired, but if cum-dividend price is desired then it can't be considered as liabilities.
- Arrears of dividend to preference shareholder have to be included as liabilities.

Fixation of Value of Equity Shares

- When the company has issued one type of equity share, fully paid-up or partly paid-up, then there is no problem in dividing the amount between one category of person.
- When the company has issued shares belonging to different category, then proportionate amount for each category should be computed.

$$\text{Value per equity share} = \frac{\text{Net Assets}}{\text{Number of equity shares}}$$

Merits of Net Assets Method

- Asset basis valuation of shares is very useful when the firm is liquidated since, the very first foundation of this method is net realisation of the value of asset.
- This method takes into account both types of assets *i.e.* tangible and intangible.
- This method creates no problem in calculating different value of equity shares.

Demerits of Net Assets Method

- It is difficult to estimate realisable value of asset.
- As the company is treated as going concern and where there is no possibility of liquidation in near future, this method of share valuation is most hypothetical.

Earning Basis Mehod

Yield Method or Dividend Yield Method

Under yield method, the value of shares is arrived at by comparing the expected rate of return with the normal rate of return. If the expected rate of return is more than the normal rate of return, the paid-up value of share is increased proportionately. *It is calculated as follows*

Market value of share or security

$$= \frac{\text{Rate of dividend expected}}{\text{Normal rate of dividend}} \times \text{Paid-up value of shares}$$

Or

$$\text{Market value of share} = \frac{\text{Dividend per share}}{\text{Normal rate of dividend}} \times 100$$

Earning Capacity Method

The primary consideration of the Shrewd Investor, who intend to acquire the controlling interest in the company is to base their valuation of shares not on the actual dividend declared by a company but on the earning capacity of the company. *It is calculated as follows*

Value of shares under earning capacity method

$$= \frac{\text{Rate of earning}}{\text{Normal rate of return}} \times \text{Paid-up value of the shares}$$

$$\text{Rate of earning} = \frac{\text{Total actual profits earned}}{\text{Capital employed}} \times 100$$

Or

$$\text{Rate of earning} = \text{Capitalisation factor} \times \text{Paid-up value of shares}$$

Merits of Earning Basis Method

- The buyers and sellers in the open market would be more directly influenced by the apparent earning power and not by the complex calculations based on net assets.
- The value of shares is primarily based on what the investor will earn.

Demerits of Earning Basis Mehod

- In practice, it is difficult to predict the future maintainable profits.
- It is difficult to select normal rate of earning or rate of capitalisation representing the element of risk involved in a particular business.

Dual Method

(Fair Value Method) In accounting literature, neither the earning basis nor the net assets basis considered correctly. The suggestion is that valuation of shares may be done by comparing the above said methods. This is popularly known as dual method or fair value method.

Value per share

$$= \frac{\text{Value of share on earning basis} + \text{Value of share on net assets basis}}{2}$$

Winding-up/Liquidation

Liquidation or 'winding-up' is a process by which a company's existence is brought to an end. First, a liquidator is appointed, either by the shareholders or the court. The liquidator represents the interests of all creditors. The liquidator supervises the liquidation, which involves collecting and realising the company's assets (turning them into cash), discharging the company's liabilities and distributing any funds left over among the shareholders in accordance with the company's constitution (or the Companies Act, 1993, if there is no Constitution). After these steps, the company is formally dissolved.

Liquidator

A liquidator is a person who is appointed when a company is in the process of winding-up. A liquidator is responsible for collecting all the assets of a company and settling all claims against the company. A liquidator can be appointed by unsecured creditors, shareholders or on a court order.

Modes of Winding-up/Liquidation

Compulsory Winding-up by Tribunals

A winding-up by tribunal or compulsory winding-up, as it is often called, is initiated by an application by way of petition presented to the tribunal for a winding-up order.

***Grounds for Compulsory Winding-up** Section 271 provides that the company may be wound-up by the tribunal*

- If the company does not commence its business within an year from its incorporation or suspends its business for a whole year.
- If default is made in delivering the statutory report to the registers or in holding the statutory meeting.
- If the company is unable to pay its debts.
- If the court is of an opinion that it is just and equitable that the company should be wound-up.
- If the number of members falls below seven and in case of a private company, below two.

Voluntarily Winding-up

- When the period, if any fixed for the duration of the company by the Articles has expired or the event, if any, has occurred, on the occurrence of, which the articles provides that the company is to be dissolved and the company in general meeting passes a resolution reacquiring the company to be wound-up voluntarily.
- If the company passes the special resolution that the company should be wound-up voluntary.
- Winding-up under the supervision of the court.

Consequences of Liquidating a Company

- The company no longer has the power to dispose of its property.
- The company may carry on its business only for the limited purpose of completing the liquidation process.
- The power of the company directors come to an end, when a liquidator is appointed.
- A liquidation order operates as a notice of dismissal to all of the company's employees.
- When an application is made for a court-ordered liquidation, the court may stay or restrain any proceedings against the company as the court sees fit.

Purchase of Business/Acquisition

If someone wants to start the business, he can start on its own or by acquiring the business of other. When somebody acquires the business of other, the process is known as acquisition process.

Purchase Consideration

Purchase consideration is the amount paid by purchaser to vendor against purchase or acquisition of business. Sometimes, purchase consideration is given in the question but if purchase consideration is not given in the question, then we have to compute the same.

How to compute Purchase Consideration

Assets taken over	...
(—) Liabilities	(...)
Net Assets	...

➠ **Note** • *The following items are not considered as assets*

(i) Debit Balance of Statement of Profit and Loss
(ii) Underwriting Commission
(iii) Preliminary Expenses
(iv) Discount on Issue of Shares or Debentures
(v) Commission on Issue of Shares or Debentures

• *The following items are not considered as liabilities*

(i) Share Capital
(ii) General Reserve
(iii) Credit Balance of Statement of Profit and Loss
(iv) Securities Premium
(v) Profit and Loss Appropriation
(vi) Sinking Fund
(vii) Any other Reserve or Fund

Accounting Treatment

When Purchase Price due to Vendor

Business Purchase A/c	Dr	...	
To Vendor's Personal A/c			...
(Being puchase price is due to vendor)			

At the Time of Recording of Assets and Liabilities

Land and Building A/c	Dr	...	
Plant and Machinery A/c	Dr	...	
Furniture A/c	Dr	...	
Debtors A/c	Dr	...	
Stock A/c	Dr	...	
Any other Assets A/c	Dr	...	
Goodwill A/c*	Dr	...	
To Business Purchase A/c (Purchase consideration)			...
To Creditors A/c			...
To Bank Loan A/c			...
To Bills Payable A/c			...
To Any Other Liabilities A/c			...
To Capital Reserves A/c**			...
(Being assets and liabilities are recorded for acquisition of business)			

➠ **Note** • **Goodwill exists when purchase consideration exceeds the net assets.*

• *** Capital Reserve comes into existence when purchase consideration is lower than net assets.*

On Payment to the Vendor

Vendor's Personal A/c (Purchase consideration)	Dr	...	
To Cash A/c (To the extent paid in cash)			...
To Share Capital A/c			...
To Securities Premium A/c			...
To % Debenture A/c			...
(Being amount of purchase consideration is paid to vendor)			

If Purchasing Company Makes Delay in Payment of Purchase Consideration

• ***At the Time of Due of Interest***

Interest A/c	Dr	...	
To Vendors' Personal A/c			...

• ***At the Time of Making Payment***

Vendors' Personal A/c	Dr	...	
To Bank A/c			...

• ***At the Time of Transferring of Expenses***

Statement of Profit and Loss	Dr	...	
To Interest A/c			...

Amalgamation of Companies

"Amalgamation is a union of two or more companies, made with an intention to form a new company." Thus, amalgamation of companies means to form one company by merging two or more companies. It may also means that one company has acquired another company. In India, accounting problems regarding amalgamations are dealt within accordance with the Accounting Standard (AS)-14 issued by the Institute of Chartered Accountants of India. In case of amalgamation, as the transferor company is dissolved, its assets and liabilities find place in the financial statements of the transferee company, prepared subsequent to the date of amalgamation.

In terms of finance, "Amalgamation is an agreement (deal) between two or more companies to consolidate (strengthen) their business activities by establishing a new company having a separate legal existence."

It will be worthwhile here to explain certain terms used in amalgamation

Amalgamating Companies are those two or more companies, which willingly unite (combine) to carry on their business activities jointly.

Amalgamated Company is a newly formed union (alliance) of two or more amalgamating companies. It has a separate legal existence with a new unique name.

Transferor Company means the company, which is amalgamated into another company.

Transferee Company means the company into which a transferor company is amalgamated.

Illustration of Amalgamation

Consider the illustration of amalgamation shown in the following diagram

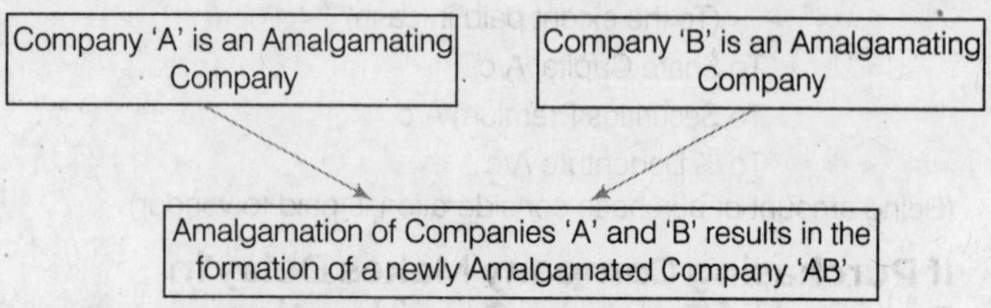

In this illustration of amalgamation, Company 'A' and Company 'B' will surrender all their equity shares to the newly formed amalgamated Company 'AB'. The assets and liabilities of amalgamating Companies 'A' and 'B' will be transferred to Company 'AB'. The amalgamating Companies 'A' and 'B' will lose their individual existence (identity) and continue to operate jointly under the name of Company 'AB'.

Types of Amalgamation

The Companies Act, 2013 has not specifically defined the term 'Amalgamation'. However from several legal decisions, the definition of amalgamation may be inferred. The Institute of Chartered Accountants has introduced Accounting Standard 14 (AS-14) on Accounting for Amalgamations. *The standard recognises two types of amalgamations*

In the Nature of Merger

Amalgamation in the nature of merger is the one which satisfies all the following conditions

- All the assets and liabilities of the transferor company are taken over by the transferee company.
- Shareholders holding not less than 90% of the face value of equity shares of the transferor company (other than the equity shares already held therein, immediately before the amalgamation, by the transferee company or its subsidiaries of their nominees become equity shareholders of the transferee company by virtue of the amalgamation.
- The consideration for the amalgamation receivable by those equity shareholders of the transferor company, who agree to become equity shareholders of the transferee company wholly by the issue of equity shares in the transferee company, except that cash may be paid in respect of any fractional shares.
- The business of the transferor company is intended to be carried on after the amalgamation, by the transferee company.
- No adjustment is intended to be made to the book values of the assets and liabilities of the transferor company when they are incorporated in the financial statements of the transferee company except to ensure uniformity of accounting policies.

In the Nature of Purchase

Amalgamation in the nature of purchase, if amalgamation does not satisfy any one of the above 5 conditions then it will be regarded as amalgamation in the nature of purchase.

Purchase Consideration

For the purpose of accounting for amalgamations, we are essentially guided by AS-14 'Accounting for Amalgamations'. Para 3(g) of AS-14 defines the term purchase consideration as the "aggregate of the shares and other securities issued and the payment made in the form of cash or other assets by the transferee company to the shareholders of the transferor company."

In simple words, it is the price payable by the transferee company to the transferor company for taking over the business of the transferor company.

It is notable that purchase consideration does not include the sum which the transferee company will directly pay to the creditors of the transferor company.

Sometimes adjustments may have to be made in the purchase consideration in the light of one or more future events. When the additional payment is probable and can be reasonably estimated, it is to be included in the calculation of purchase consideration.

Methods of Calculating Purchase Consideration

Lumpsum Method The problem may give the amount of purchase consideration directly and hence, there will not be any need to calculate the purchase consideration.

Net Payment Method If the purchase consideration is not given lumpsum then, this method should be adopted. Here, the purchase consideration is arrived at by adding up cash paid and the agreed values of shares, securities issued by the transferee company to shareholders of transferor company in discharge of the purchase consideration.

Net Assets Method If the purchase consideration cannot be calculated by above two methods, then this method should be adopted. It is the aggregate of the assets taken over at agreed values less liabilities taken over at agreed values.

Calculation of Purchase Consideration

Particulars	Amt (₹)	Amt (₹)
Assets taken over at agreed value (excluding fictitious assets)		
Goodwill	...	
Land and Buildings	...	
Plant and Machinery	...	
Furniture and Fittings	...	
Motor Vehicles	...	
Investments	...	
Stock	...	
Debtors	...	
Cash and Bank Balances	...	...
(–) **Liabilities taken over at agreed value**		
Creditors	(...)	
Bills Payable	(...)	
Bank Overdraft	(...)	
Debentures	(...)	(...)
Purchase Consideration		...

Note *Assets and liabilities will be taken over at revised figure, if given otherwise at book value.*

Exchange of Shares Method/Intrinsic Value Method Under this method, intrinsic value of the shares of both the companies are calculated and then the transferor company issue the shares to the transferee company on the basis of these values.

Methods of Accounting for Amalgamation

- The pooling of interest method
- The purchase method

The first method is used in case of amalgamation in the nature of merger and the second method is used in case of amalgamation in the nature of purchase.

These are as follows

Pooling of Interest Method

- Assets and liabilities of the transferor company should be recorded at their existing carrying amounts, *i.e.* they are to be taken at their book values.
- Reserves (whether capital or revenue or arising on revaluation) of the transferor company should be recorded at their existing carrying amounts and in the same form *i.e.* balance of general reserve should be carried as revaluation reserve and balance of revaluation reserve is carried as revaluation reserve etc.
- Difference of the share capital issued and other consideration paid to the transferor company over and above its own share capital should be adjusted in reserves.
- Balance of the profit and loss account of the transferor company should be aggregated with that of the transferor company or transferred to the general reserve.

Purchase Method

- The assets and liabilities of the transferor company should be incorporated at their existing carrying amounts or the purchase consideration should be allocated to individual identifiable assets and liabilities on the basis of their fair values at the date of amalgamation.
- No reserves, other than statutory reserves, of the transferor company should be incorporated in the financial statements of transferee company. Statutory reserves of the transferor company should be incorporated in the balance sheet of transferee company by way of the following journal entry

Amalgamation Adjustment A/c	Dr
To Statutory Reserves A/c	

When the above statutory reserves will no longer be required to be maintained by transferee company, such reserves will be eliminated by reversing the above entry. The balance of profit and loss account of the transferor company is not recorded at all.

Note *Any excess of the amount of purchase consideration over the value of the net assets of the transferor company acquired by the transferee company should be recognised as goodwill in the financial statement of the transferee company. Any short fall should be shown as capital reserve. Goodwill should be amortised over period of 5 years unless a some what longer period can be justified.*

In the Book of Transferor Company

Journal Entries

Date	Particulars	LF	Amt (Dr)	Amt (Cr)
1.	When assets are transferred to realisation account			
	Realisation A/c Dr		...	
	To Sundry Assets A/c (Write individually)			...
	Note			
	(i) Fictitious assets should not be transferred to realisation account.			
	(ii) Cash and bank balances should be transferred to realisation account only, if it taken over by the transferee company.			
	(iii) Debtors and RDD should be treated as separate account. Debtors should be transferred at their gross value on debit side and RDD should be transferred on the credit side of realisation account.			
	(iv) This entry closes all assets account.			
2.	When liabilities are transferred to realisation account			
	Sundry Liabilities A/c (Write individually) Dr		...	
	To Realisation A/c			...
3.	When purchase consideration becomes due			
	Transferee Company A/c Dr		...	
	To Realisation A/c			...
	Note *To making transferee company as our debtors because purchase consideration will be get later.*			
4.	When any asset sold in the market by transferor company			
	Bank A/c Dr		...	
	To Realisation A/c			...
	Note *Only, if amalgamation in the nature of purchase*			
5.	When any liability is paid off by transferor company itself			
	Realisation A/c Dr		...	
	To Bank A/c			...
	Note *Only, if amalgamation in the nature of purchase*			
6.	When preference shareholders are discharged at premium or discount			
	At Premium			
	Realisation A/c Dr		...	
	To Preference Shareholders A/c			...
	At Discount			
	Preference Shareholders A/c Dr		...	
	To Realisation A/c			...
7.	For recording of dissolution/realisation expenses			
	(i) When realisation expenses are paid by the transferor company itself			
	Realisation A/c Dr		...	
	To Bank A/c			...
	(ii) When realisation expenses are paid by the transferee company			
	No entry will be passed			
	(iii) When realisation expenses are paid by transferor company and they are reimbursed by the transferee company.			
	(a) Transferee Company A/c Dr		...	
	To Bank A/c			...
	(b) Bank A/c Dr		...	
	To Transferee Company A/c			...

Date	Particulars		LF	Amt (Dr)	Amt (Cr)
8.	For recording of profit/loss on realisation				
	(i) **In case of Profit**				
	Realisation A/c	Dr		…	
	To Equity Shareholders A/c				…
	(ii) **In case of Loss**				
	Equity Shareholders A/c	Dr		…	
	To Realisation A/c				…
9.	When purchase consideration is received				
	Equity Share in Transferee Company A/c	Dr		…	
	Preference Share in Transferee Company A/c	Dr		…	
	Debenture in Transferee Company A/c	Dr		…	
	Other Securities in Transferee Company A/c	Dr		…	
	Cash A/c	Dr		…	
	To Transferee Company A/c				…
	Note *Purchase consideration can be discharged by any one or more than one or by all which are mentioned above.*				
10.	When preference share capital being transferred to preference shareholders account				
	Preference Share Capital A/c	Dr		…	
	To Preference Shareholders A/c				…
11.	When purchase consideration is discharged to preference shareholders Accounts				
	Preference Shareholders A/c	Dr		…	
	To Equity Share in Transferee Company A/c.				…
	To Preference Share in Transferee Company A/c				…
	To Debentures in Transferee Company A/c				…
	To Other Securities in Transferee Company A/c				…
	To Cash A/c				…
12.	When equity share capital and reserve and surplus are transferred to equity shareholders account				
	Equity Share Capital A/c	Dr		…	
	Securities Premium A/c	Dr		…	
	Capital Reserve A/c	Dr		…	
	Capital Redemption Reserve A/c	Dr		…	
	General Reserve A/c	Dr		…	
	Profit and Loss statement	Dr		…	
	Reserve and Surplus A/c	Dr		…	
	To Equity Shareholders A/c				…
13.	When miscellaneous expenditure and profit and loss account (Dr) balance is adjusted in equity shareholders' account				
	Equity Shareholders' A/c	Dr		…	
	To Miscellaneous Expenditure A/c				…
	To Profit and Loss A/c				…
14.	When the amount of purchase consideration is discharged to equity shareholders account				
	Equity Shareholders A/c	Dr		…	
	To Equity Share in Transferee Company A/c				…
	To Preference Share in Transferee Company A/c				…
	To Debentures in Transferee Company A/c				…
	To Other Securities in Transferee Company A/c				…
	To Cash A/c				…

In the Books of Transferor Company

Ledger Accounts

- Realisation Account
- Preference Shareholders Account
- Transferee's Account
- Equity Shareholders Account

➟ **Note** *Generally, we prepare only four accounts in practical questions*

- Cash/Bank Account
- Equity Shares in Transferee Company Account
- Liabilities not taken over Account
- Preference Shares in Transferee Company Account

Dr **Realisation A/c** Cr

Particulars	JF	Amt (₹)	Particulars	JF	Amt (₹)
To Sundry Assets (Write individually)		...	By Sundry Liabilities (Write individually)		...
To Bank A/c (Any liabilities paid off)		...	By Transferee Co A/c (Purchase consideration)		...
To Preference Shareholders A/c (Loss due to premium)		...	By Bank A/c (Any assets sold)		...
To Bank A/c (Realisation expenses paid by company)		...	By Preference Shareholders A/c (Profit due to discount)		...
To Equity Shareholders A/c [Profit (Balancing figure)]		...	By Equity Shareholders A/c [Loss (Balancing figure)]		...
		...			...

Dr **Transferee Company A/c** Cr

Particulars	JF	Amt (₹)	Particulars	JF	Amt (₹)
To Realisation A/c (Purchase consideration)			By Equity Shares in Transferee Co A/c		...
			By Preference Shares in Transferee Co A/c		...
			By Debentures in Transferee Co A/c		...
			By Other Securities in Transferee Co A/c		...
			By Cash A/c		...
		...			...

➟ **Note** *Items will be varying in amalgamation in the nature of merger or purchase as case may be. The "*" items will not be entertained in amalgamation in the nature of merger.*

Dr **Preference Shareholders A/c** Cr

Particulars	JF	Amt (₹)	Particulars	JF	Amt (₹)
To Equity Shares in Transferee Co A/c		...	By Preference Share Capital A/c		...
To Preference Shares in Transferee Co A/c		...	By Realisation A/c (Premium)		...
To Debentures in Transferee Co A/c		...			
To Other Securities in Transferee Co A/c		...			
To Cash A/c		...			
To Realisation A/c (Discount)					
		...			...

Dr **Equity Shareholders A/c** Cr

Particulars	JF	Amt (₹)	Particulars	JF	Amt (₹)
To Miscellaneous Expenditure A/c		...	By Equity Share Capital A/c		...
To Profit and Loss A/c (Loss/Dr Bal)		...	By Reserve and Surplus A/c		...
To Realisation A/c (If loss)		...	By Realisation A/c (If profit)		...
To Equity Shares in Transferee Co A/c		...			
To Equity Shares in Transferee Co A/c		...			
To Preference Shares in Transferee Co A/c		...			
To Debentures in Transferee Co A/c		...			
To Other Securities in Transferee Co A/c		...			
To Cash A/c		...			
		...			...

In the Books of Transferee Company

In the Nature of Merger

Date	Particulars		LF	Amt (Dr)	Amt (Cr)
1.	When business of transferor company is taken over				
	Business Purchase A/c	Dr		...	
	To Liquidator of Transferor Co A/c				...
2.	When assets and liabilities taken over are recorded				
	Sundry Assets A/c (Individually)	Dr		...	
	Reserve and Surplus A/c (Balancing figure)	Dr			
	To Sundry Liabilities (Individually)				...
	To Business Purchase				...
	To Reserve and Surplus (Balancing figure)				...
	Note *Any one balancing figure will be come either in Dr or Cr.*				
3.	When purchase consideration is discharged				
	Liquidator of Transferor Co A/c	Dr		...	
	To Equity Share Capital A/c				...
	To Securities Premium A/c				...
	To Preference Share Capital A/c				...
	To Cash A/c				...
4.	When discharge of liabilities of transferor company				
	Debentures of Transferor Company A/c	Dr		...	
	Discount on Issue of Debentures A/c	Dr		...	
	To New Debentures A/c				...
	To Securities Premium A/c				...
5.	When realisation/dissolution expenses of transferor company paid by transferee company				
	Reserve and Surplus (GR or P/L)	Dr		...	
	To Bank A/c				...
	[GR—General Reserve P/L—Profit and Loss A/c]				
6.	When formation expenses of transferee company are recorded				
	Formation Expenses /Preliminary Expenses A/c	Dr		...	
	To Bank A/c				...
7.	When inter company transaction are recorded				
	Sundry Creditors A/c	Dr		...	
	To Sundry Debtors A/c				...
	Or				
	Bills Payable A/c	Dr		...	
	To Bills Receivable A/c				...
	Or				
	Loan Taken A/c	Dr		...	
	To Loan Given A/c				...
8.	When unrealised profit is recorded				
	Reserve and Surplus/Profit A/c	Dr		...	
	To Stock/Current Assets A/c				...
	Note *When there is no profit in balance sheet then debit the goodwill* account.				

In the Books of Transferee Company

In the Nature of Purchase

Date	Particulars		LF	Amt (Dr)	Amt (Cr)
1.	When business of transferor company is taken over				
	Business Purchase A/c	Dr		...	
	To Liquidator of Transferor Co A/c				...
2.	When assets and liabilities taken over are recorded				
	Sundry Assets A/c (Individually)	Dr		...	
	Goodwill A/c (Balancing figure)	Dr		...	
	To Sundry Liabilities A/c (Individually)				...
	To Business Purchase A/c				...
	To Capital Reserve A/c (Balancing figure)				...
	Note (*i*) *Any one balancing figure will be come either in Dr or Cr.*				
	(*ii*) *If purchase consideration is calculated by net assets method there will no difference, but, if calculated by net payment method, difference will be come either in Dr or Cr.*				
3.	When purchase consideration is discharged				
	Liquidator of Transferor Co A/c	Dr		...	
	To Equity Share Capital A/c				...
	To Securities Premium A/c				...
	To Preference Share Capital A/c				...
	To Debentures A/c				...
	To Other Securities A/c				...
	To Cash A/c				...
4.	When discharge of liabilities of transferor company				
	Debentures of Transferor Company A/c	Dr		...	
	Discount on Issue of Debentures A/c	Dr		...	
	To New Debenture A/c				...
	To Securities Premium A/c				...
5.	When realisation/dissolution expenses of transferor company paid by transferee company				
	Goodwill/Capital Reserve A/c	Dr		...	
	To Bank A/c				...
	Note *It is a capital loss, so that goodwill account is debited.*				
6.	When formation expenses of transferee company are recorded				
	Formation Expenses/Preliminary Expenses A/c	Dr		...	
	To Bank A/c				...
7.	When Inter company transactions are recorded				
	Sundry Creditors A/c	Dr		...	
	To Sundry Debtors A/c				...
	Or				
	Bills Payable A/c	Dr		...	
	To Bills Receivable A/c				...
	Or				
	Loan Taken A/c	Dr		...	
	To Loan Given A/c				...
8.	When unrealised profit is recorded				
	Reserve and Surplus/ Profit and Loss A/c	Dr		...	
	To Stock/Current Assets A/c				...
	Note *When there is no profit in balance sheet then debit the goodwill account*				
9.	When statutory reserve of transferor company are transferred to transferee company				
	Amalgamation Adjustment A/c	Dr		...	
	To Statutory Reserve A/c				...
	Note *At the time of merge the balance sheet, amalgamation adjustment account will be shown in miscellaneous expenditure account.*				

Reconstruction of Company

The term reconstruction means reorganising the capital structure of a company including the reduction of the claim of both the classes of shareholders and the creditors against the company. Sick companies (loss making companies) may be taken over by the profit making companies. However, in case of c/f of huge losses, assets are overvalued or undervalued, in such cases company may go for reconstruction. It may be external or internal reconstruction.

Types of Reconstruction

The company can be reconstructed internally or externally. *It means two types of reconstruction is possible*

External Reconstruction In case of external reconstruction, a new company is formed to take over the business of an existing company which has suffered huge losses and which is in bad financial position. The vendor company goes into liquidation and its business is taken over by the new company.

Internal Reconstruction In case of internal reconstruction, the capital structure of the company is recognised to infuse new life in the company. It includes alteration, reduction and reorganisation of share capital of the company.

Amalgamation Vs *External Reconstruction*

	Old Company	New Company
Amalgamation	2 or more company	1 newly formed company
External Reconstruction	1 loss making company	1 newly formed company

Holding Companies

An important development of recent times in the business units into a group or an economic unit has emerged. A company may acquire either the whole or majority of shares of another company, so as to have a controlling interest in such a company or companies. The controlling company is also known as holding or parent company and the company controlled is known as subsidiary company.

Meaning of Holding Company

Section 2(46) of the Companies Act, 2013 defines a holding company. According to this section, *one company can become the holding company of another in any of the following three ways*

- By holding more than 50% of the nominal value of equity shares of the other company, *i.e.* the holding company holds the majority of voting power in the subsidiary company.
- By controlling the composition of the Board of Directors of the other company, so that the holding company is able to appoint or remove the directors of the subsidiary company.
- By controlling a holding company which controls another subsidiary or subsidiaries. *e.g.* If B Ltd is a subsidiary of C Ltd and C Ltd is a subsidiary of A Ltd then B Ltd is also deemed to be a subsidiary of A Ltd.

Advantages of Holding Company

- Subsidiary company maintains their separate identity.
- The public may not be aware of the existence of combination among the various companies.
- Holding company need not to invest entire amount in the share capital in subsidiary company, still enjoy controlling power in such company.
- It would be possible to carry forward losses for income tax purposes.
- Each subsidiary company prepares its own accounts and therefore, financial position and profitability of each undertaking is known.

Disadvantages of Holding Company

- There is a possibility of fraudulent manipulation of accounts.
- Inter company transactions may not be at a fair prices.
- Minority shareholders' interest may not be properly protected.
- The accounts of various companies may be made upon different dates to manipulate profit or financial position of group companies.
- The shareholders in the holding company may not be aware of true financial position of subsidiary company.
- The subsidiary companies may be forced to appoint person of the choice of holding company such as auditors, directors, other officers etc at high remuneration.

Purpose of Holding Company

The purpose of getting the control over another company may be to gain advantages such as

- To eliminate competition.
- To enjoy the economies of large scale of production.
- To ensure a smooth supply of raw materials.

Presentation of Accounts of Holding Company

Under Indian Companies Act, there is no need to prepare combined or consolidated final accounts of holding and subsidiary company in the books of holding company, but holding company attaches the copy of balance sheet, one copy of profit and loss statement and one copy of audit report of subsidiary company with its final accounts. But for showing true financial position, often holding company prepares consolidated balance sheet.

Accounting Entries in the Books of Holding Company

On Purchase of Shares

Shares in Subsidiary Company A/c Dr
  To Bank A/c
  To Debenture A/c
  To Share Capital A/c

On Transfer of Dividend to Profit and Loss Statement

Dividend A/c Dr
  To Statements of Profit and Loss

On Assets and Liabilities Shown in Consolidated Balance Sheet

Sundry Assets A/c Dr
  To Sundry Liabilities A/c
  To Investment in Subsidiary Company A/c

For Share of Profit of Holding Company in the Pre-acquisition Profit of Subsidiary Company

Consolidated Profit and Loss A/c Dr
  To Capital Reserve A/c

For Share of Loss of Holding Company in the Pre-acquistion Loss of Subsidiary Company

Capital Reserve A/c Dr
  To Consolidated Profit and Loss A/c

On Sale of Shares of Subsidiary Company by the Holding Company

Cash A/c Dr
  To Shares in the Subsidiary Company A/c

Steps for Preparing Consolidated Balance Sheet of the Holding Company and its Subsidiary Company

Step 1 Add all the assets of subsidiary company with the assets of holding company. But investment of holding company in subsidiary company will not be shown in consolidated balance sheet because investment in subsidiary company will automatically adjust with the amount of share capital of subsidiary company in holding company.

Step 2 Add all the liabilities of subsidiary company with the liabilities of holding company. But, share capital of subsidiary company in holding company will not be shown in consolidated balance sheet because this share capital automatically adjust with the amount of the investment of holding company into subsidiary company.

Step 3 ***Calculation of Minority Interest*** (MI) First of all, we should know that when some of the shares in the subsidiary company are held by outside shareholders, they will be entitled to a proportionate share in the assets and liabilities of that company. The share of the outsiders in the subsidiary is called minority interest.

Calculation

Total share capital of subsidiary company	.....
Invest(m)ent of holding company into subsidiary company	(.....)
(+) Proportionate share of the subsidiary company's profit and reserves or increase in the value of assets	.....
(–) Proportionate share of the subsidiary company's loss and decrease in the value of total assets	(.....)
Value of Minority Interest	.....

Step 4 ***Calculation of Cost of Capital/Goodwill or Capital Reserve*** If holding company purchases shares of subsidiary company at premium, then the value of premium will be deemed as goodwill or cost of capital and shows as goodwill on the assets side of consolidated balance sheet. But, if holding company purchases the shares at discount, then this value of discount will be capital reserve and shown in the liability side of consolidated balance sheet.

Step 5 ***Pre-acquisition Profit and Reserve*** Subsidiary company will be shown as capital reserve in consolidated balance sheet, but the value of minority interest's profit or reserves deducts from it and add in minority interest value.

Step 6 ***Calculation of Post-acquisition Profits*** After the date of purchasing the shares of subsidiary company, profit of subsidiary company will also be deemed to be of holding company and is included in the profit of holding company and we also separate the part of profit of minority interest and add in minority interest's value and it is shown in liability side.

Step 7 ***Elimination of Common Transactions***

- Goods sold or goods purchased on credit and the value of debtor or creditor (either subsidiary company or holding company) will not be shown in consolidated balance sheet.

- Value of bill payable or bill receivable of holding company or subsidiary company will also not shown, but, if some bills' value is discounted from third party then either of both company's payable value is shown as liability in the consolidated balance sheet.

Step 8 ***Treatment of Unrealised Profit*** If subsidiary company sells the goods to holding company or *vice-versa* at profit and if such goods will not be sold to third party, then the profit will not be realised, so such unrealised profit will not be credited to profit and loss account. At this time, a stock reserve account is opened and all amounts of unrealised profit transfers to this account and this accounts' total amount is deducted from closing stock of consolidated balance sheet.

Step 9 ***Treatment of Dividends*** If holding company gets the dividends from subsidiary company, then this will be divided into two parts. If subsidiary company declares dividend out of capital profits, then this will added in capital reserves in consolidated balance sheet. But, if subsidiary company has declared the profit out of revenue gains, then this dividend will added in general profit and loss statements anded will be shown in the liability side of consolidated balance sheet.

Subsidiary Company

A company is a 'subsidiary' of another company or its 'holding company', if that other company

- holds a majority of the voting rights in it.
- is a member of it and has the right to appoint or remove a majority of its Board of Directors.
- is a member of it and controls alone, pursuant to an agreement with other members, a majority of voting rights in it, or if it is a subsidiary of a company that is itself a subsidiary of that other company.

Wholly Owned Subsidiary Company

When all the shares of a subsidiary company are held or owned by the holding company, the subsidiary company is known as a wholly owned subsidiary company.

Partly Owned Subsidiary Company

When a majority of shares, but not all the shares of a subsidiary company are owned by the holding company, the subsidiary company is known as a partly owned subsidiary company.

Consolidation of Financial Statement

AS-21 came into effect in respect of accounting periods commencing on or after 1st April, *i.e.* for year ending 31st March, 2002. The AS-21 is applicable to all the enterprises that prepare consolidated financial statement. It is mandatory for listed companies and banking companies.

As per AS- 21, the consolidated financial statements include

- Consolidated Statement of Profit and Loss
- Consolidated Balance Sheet
- Consolidated Cash Flow Statement
- Notes of Accounts except typical notes
- Segment reporting

EXAM BASED QUESTIONS

Company and Share Capital

1 The company's nationality is decided by its

(a) shareholders
(b) registered office
(c) place at books of accounts are kept
(d) None of the above

2 The statutory meeting of a company is convened

(a) once in a year
(b) once in the life time of the company
(c) once in 6 months
(d) once in 3 months

3 And reduced words are to be shown in balance sheet as per the requirement of

(a) Company Law
(b) Income Tax
(c) Accounting Standard
(d) SEBI

4 Liability of a member in case of a private company can be

(a) limited (b) unlimited
(c) Both (a) and (b) (d) None of these

5 Minimum number of members in case of public company is

(a) 7 (b) 5
(c) 2 (d) 1

6 A concern should select an accounting policy which enables it to

(a) pay the proper amount of income tax
(b) calculate the correct amount of cash in hand
(c) present a true and fair view of its state of affairs and profit or loss
(d) Both (a) and (b)

7 Which one of the following statement is correct?

(a) A company consists of heterogeneous members
(b) A body corporate includes a cooperative society
(c) The expression 'corporation' or 'body corporate' are same
(d) A partner cannot contract with his firm, whereas a member of a company can

8 Which of the following reports have to be submitted before the company's annual general meeting as per the Companies Act?

(a) Director's Report
(b) Auditor's Report
(c) Statement of Profit and Loss and Balance Sheet
(d) All of the above

9 Ploughing back of profit means

(a) dividend declared, but not claimed by shareholders
(b) non-declaration of dividend in any year
(c) profits earned from illegal sources and employed in business
(d) retaining the earnings of business for future expansion programme

10 That portion of the share capital which can be called up only on the winding-up of the company is the

(a) reserve capital (b) subscribed capital
(c) issued capital (d) authorised capital

11 Read the following statements.

1. Financial statements are only interim reports.
2. Financial statements are prepared on the basis of realisable values.
3. The preparation of financial statements is not an ultimate aim.
4. Certain assumptions are necessary to prepare financial statements.

Which of the following combinations consists of all true statements?

Codes

(a) 1, 2 and 3 (b) 2, 3 and 4 (c) 1, 3 and 4 (d) 1, 2 and 4

12 The amount received over and above the par value is credited to which account?

(a) Share Capital A/c (b) Calls-in-advance A/c
(c) Securities Premium A/c (d) Share Forfeiture A/c

13 Arrange the following liabilities in the order of company's balance sheet.

1. Bank Overdraft 2. Bank Loan
3. Share Capital 4. Provision for Taxation

Codes

(a) 1, 2, 3, 4 (b) 4, 3, 2, 1 (c) 3, 2, 1, 4 (d) 3, 2, 4, 1

14 Which of the following should be deducted from the share capital to find out paid-up capital?

(a) Calls-in-advance (b) Calls-in-arrear
(c) Securities premium (d) Bonus

15 Redeemable preference shares can be redeemed

(a) if they are paid not less than 50% of the nominal value of shares
(b) only if they are fully paid
(c) even if they are partly paid
(d) only if they are issued at premium

16 Which of the following conditions have to be met to receive calls-in-advance?

(a) It should be authorised by a special resolution of the company
(b) It should be authorised by an ordinary resolution of the company
(c) It should be approved by the Company Law Board
(d) It should be authorised by the articles

17 **Which type of company's shares are freely transferable?**

(a) Private company (b) Public company
(c) Both (a) and (b) (d) None of these

18 **Share can be issued at a discount only after .... year from the commencement of business.**

(a) shares can not be issued at discount
(b) one
(c) two
(d) two and a half

19 **If minimum subscription is not received, application money should be refunded within how many days?**

(a) 7 (b) 10 (c) 15 (d) 30

20 **A company can buy back**

(a) partly paid share (b) fully paid share
(c) partly called up (d) None of these

21 **Minimum number of members in case of private company is**

(a) 1 (b) 2 (c) 5 (d) 10

22 **Capital redemption reserve is created due to**

(a) volunta (b) legal requirements
(c) Both (a) and (b) (d) None of these

23 **Within how many days minimum subscription should be received?**

(a) 60 (b) 100 (c) 120 (d) 150

24 **A company can redeem preference shares**

(a) at par (b) at premium
(c) out of free reserves (d) All of these

25 **The following relate to the shares of a company. What is the correct order?**

(a) Issue, Application, Call and Forfeiture
(b) Application, Call, Forfeiture and Issue
(c) Call, Issue, Application and Forfeiture
(d) Forfeiture, Application, Issue and Call

26 **Which of the following statement is incorrect?**

(a) Calls-in-arrear do not form part of paid-up capital
(b) Preference shareholders get dividend at flexible rate
(c) Share application account is a personal account
(d) None of the above

27 **Which of the following items cannot be shown as reserves?**

(a) Capital Reserve
(b) Capital Redemption Reserve
(c) Securities Premium
(d) None of the above

28 **Secret reserves may be created by**

(a) under valuation of liabilities only
(b) under valuation of assets only
(c) over valuation of assets only
(d) over valuation of liabilities and under valuation of assets

29 **Buy back of equity shares in any financial year shall not exceed**

(a) 5% of its total capital
(b) 25% of nominal share capital
(c) 25% of fully paid equity share capital
(d) None of the above

30 **The balance in share forfeiture account, after the reissue of all forfeited shares, should be**

(a) transferred to Goodwill A/c
(b) transferred to Capital Reserve A/c
(c) shown as Share Forfeiture A/c
(d) added to paid-up capital

31 **Which of the following pairs is/are correctly matched?**

(a) When a company issues its securities at a price more than the face value – Shares issued at discount
(b) When shares issued at an amount less than par value of shares – Shares issued at premium
(c) When shares are issued at their face value– Shares issued at par
(d) All of the above

32 **Rights shares are the shares**

(a) that have a right of redemption
(b) offerred to the existing equity shareholders
(c) legally issued to the public at large
(d) issued by a newly formed company

33 **The sub-division of shares does not result in .... of capital.**

(a) reduction (b) increase
(c) sub-division (d) None of these

34 **Arrange the following categories of share capital of a company in the correct order.**

1. Paid-up capital 2. Issued capital
3. Called-up capital 4. Subscribed share capital

Codes

(a) 2, 4, 3, 1 (b) 1, 2, 3, 4 (c) 3, 2, 4, 1 (d) 3, 2, 1, 4

35 **Which of the following statement is correct?**

(a) Rights shares are first offered to employees
(b) Rights shares are offered in lieu of dividends
(c) Rights shares are offered to the existing shareholders in proportion to the equity shares held by them
(d) Rights shares are those shares which are offered to the promoters

36 **Preference shares can be redeemed**

(a) partly out of issue of shares and balance out of free reserves
(b) out of proceed of issue of shares
(c) out of profits
(d) All of the above

37 **For what, a company may utilise the securities premium amount?**

(a) Writing off the discount on the issue of debentures
(b) Writing off any loss of revenue nature
(c) Writing off any loss on sale of fixed assets
(d) Payment of dividends

38 **Profit on sale of sinking fund investment will be debited to**
(a) Profit and Loss A/c
(b) Sinking Fund A/c
(c) Sinking Fund Investment A/c
(d) Revaluation A/c

39 **On issue of shares, the application money should not be less than**
(a) 2.5% of the nominal value of shares
(b) 2.5% of the issue price of shares
(c) 5.0% of the nominal value of shares
(d) 5.0% of the issue price of shares

40 **The discount allowed on reissue of forfeited shares is debited to**
(a) Share Capital A/c
(b) Profit and Loss A/c
(c) Capital Redemption Reserve A/c
(d) Forfeited Shares A/c

41 **Which one of the following statement is incorrect?**
(a) Bonus shares are issued without payment
(b) Only revenue reserves should be used when bonus is declared in order to make partly paid shares into fully paid shares
(c) Fully paid bonus shares are issued only out of capital reserves
(d) The process of issue of bonus shares is also known as capitalisation of reserves

42 **When dividend is actually received on due date**
(a) the pro-rata amount relating the period before the date of acquisition is entered in the income column (Cr) of the following investment account
(b) the pro-rata amount relating to the period after the date of acquisition is entered in the income column (Cr) of the investment account
(c) the entire amount is entered in the income column (Dr) of the investment account
(d) the entire amount is entered in the capital column (Cr) of the investment account

43 **Dividend declared and paid by a company is**
(a) an expense of the company
(b) an income of the company
(c) the distribution of profit earned by the company
(d) the source of fund for the company

44 **Which of the following statements is incorrect?**
(a) When proposed dividend does not exceed 10%. It is not obligatory on the company to transfer any profit to its reserve
(b) Capital redemption reserve can be utilised for writing off miscellaneous expenses and losses
(c) Dividends is not payable on the calls paid in advance by shareholders
(d) Reserves created by revaluation of fixed assets are not permitted to be capitalised

45 **A company can buy back equity shares out of**
(a) its securities premium account
(b) the proceeds of preference shares
(c) its free reserves
(d) All of the above

46 **For purpose of redemption of preference share company can issue**
(a) debentures at premium
(b) equity shares
(c) bonds
(d) fixed deposits certificates

47 **The cost of right shares is**
(a) subtracted from the cost of investments
(b) added to the cost of investments
(c) no treatment is required
(d) None of the above

48 **Dividend policy of a company mainly concerns with**
1. Dividend payout
2. Stability of dividend

Select the correct answer using the codes given below

Codes
(a) Only 1
(b) Only 2
(c) Both 1 and 2
(d) Neither 1 nor 2

49 **When shares are forfeited, the share capital account is debited with ..... and the share forfeiture account is credited with ....**
(a) calls-in-arrear of shares forfeited, amount received on shares forfeited
(b) called-up capital of shares forfeited, amount received on shares forfeited
(c) called-up capital of shares forfeited, calls-in-arrear of shares forfeited
(d) paid-up capital of shares forfeited, called-up capital of shares forfeited

50 **50,000 equity shares of ₹ 10 each, issued at ₹ 20, for the purpose of redemption of preference share capital amounting ₹ 7,50,000. How much amount will be transferred to capital redemption reserve?**
(a) ₹ 2,00,000
(b) ₹ 2,50,000
(c) ₹ 5,00,000
(d) ₹ 10,00,000

51 **Raj industires limited offers equity shares to its existing shareholders at the rate of 2 shares for every 5 shares held by them. If the right issue price is ₹ 180 per share and the market value is ₹ 200 per share, then the value of a right is**
(a) ₹ 20
(b) ₹ 180
(c) ₹ 200
(d) ₹ 40

52 **A limited company issued equity shares of ₹ 100 each. It has called-up ₹ 75 on each share, but received only ₹ 60 per share. The share capital account will be credited with**
(a) ₹ 75 per share
(b) ₹ 60 per share
(c) ₹ 100 per share
(d) None of the above

53 When shares are forfeited, the share capital account is debited by
(a) nominal value of forfeited shares
(b) paid-up amount of forfeited shares
(c) called-up amount on forfeited shares
(d) forfeited amount of shares

54 A Ltd has allotted 10,000 shares to the applicants of 14,000 shares on pro-rata basis. The amount payable an application is ₹ 2. Mr X applied for 420 shares. The number of shares allotted and the amount carried forward for adjustment against allotment money due from X is
(a) 60 shares, ₹ 120 (b) 320 shares, ₹ 200
(c) 340 shares, ₹ 160 (d) 300 shares, ₹ 240

55 X Ltd allotted 25,000 equity shares to the applicants of 36,000 shares for ₹ 10 each on pro-rata basis. A applied for 1800 equity shares. Shares allotted to him are ...... and he had paid an application money of ₹ 5 per share ...... is the excess amount received that can be utilised towards allotment money.
(a) 1500 shares, ₹ 1,500
(b) 1250 shares, ₹ 2,750
(c) 1350 shares, ₹ 2,250
(d) 1050 shares, ₹ 3,750

56 The directors of Murfi Ltd made a final call of ₹ 50 per share on 1st August, indicating the last date of payment of call money to be 31st August. Mr. Akshit holding 5,000 shares paid the call money on 15th October, if the company adopts Table A, the amount of interest on calls-in-arrears to be paid
(a) ₹ 3125 (b) ₹ 1,562.50
(c) ₹ 1875 (d) ₹ 1500

57 The directors of company forfeited 1,000 shares of ₹ 10 each, ₹ 7.5 paid-up for non-payment of call money @ ₹ 2.5 per share, 700 of this shares are re-issued @ ₹ 7 per share. The amount transfer to Capital Reserve A/c would be
(a) ₹ 2,500 (b) ₹ 3,150
(c) ₹ 3,500 (d) ₹ 5,400

Valuation of Shares and Winding-up

58 Interest is always calculated on the
(a) market value
(b) cost of purchase
(c) nominal/face value
(d) higher of cost and fair value

59 Which account will be debited with the nominal value of shares, when shares are issued to promoters for the service offered by them?
(a) Preliminary expenses
(b) Assets
(c) Goodwill
(d) Share capital

60 Which of the following is not an example of contingent liability?
(a) Liability under guarantee
(b) Interim dividend
(c) Liability in respect of bills discounted
(d) None of the above

61 Intrinsic value of a share is given by
(a) $\frac{\text{Total net assets}}{\text{Number of shares}}$ (b) $\frac{\text{Total assets}}{\text{Number of shares}}$
(c) $\frac{\text{Share capital}}{\text{Number of shares}}$ (d) $\frac{\text{Market capitalisation}}{\text{Number of shares}}$

62 If vendors are issued fully paid shares of ₹ 12,000 in consideration of net assets of ₹ 9,000, then the balance of ₹ 3,000 will be
(a) credited to Securities Premium A/c
(b) credited to Capital Reserve A/c
(c) debited to Goodwill A/c
(d) debited to Profit and Loss A/c

63 Under purchase method, any excess of the amount of purchase consideration over the acquired assets of the transferor company should be recognised as
(a) statutory reserve
(b) amalgamation adjustment
(c) equity shares
(d) goodwill

64 For allocation of income and expenses, the date of .... is not considered.
(a) take over (b) commencement
(c) year end (d) All of these

65 A contributory is
(a) a creditor
(b) a shareholder
(c) a debentureholder
(d) a convertible debentureholder

66 Liquidator's statement of receipts and payment is known as
(a) cash flow statement
(b) cash book
(c) liquidator's final statement of account
(d) deficiency account

67 Deficiency Surplus Account in liquidation of a company is called
(a) List-C (b) List-D (c) List-G (d) List-H

Purchase of Business

68 What is the excess of net assets over consideration paid called?
(a) Capital reserve (b) Reserve capital
(c) Security premium (d) Goodwill

69 As per AS-14, purchase consideration is payable to
(a) debentureholders and creditors
(b) shareholders and creditors
(c) shareholders and debentureholders
(d) shareholders

70 If the purchase consideration is calculated by adding the various payments to be made, the method is called
(a) Lumpsum method (b) Networth method
(c) Net payment method (d) Value of share method

71 To account profit on sale of investment should be debited to?
(a) Profit and Loss A/c (b) Capital Reserve A/c
(c) Investment A/c (d) Sinking Fund A/c

72 When the purchasing company makes payment of the purchase consideration, it debits
(a) Business Purchase A/c (b) Assets A/c
(c) Cash A/c (d) Vendor Company's A/c

73 For paying liabilities not taken over by the purchasing company, the vendor company credits
(a) Realisation A/c (b) Bank A/c
(c) Liabilities A/c (d) Assets A/c

74 In case of inter-company holdings, the purchasing company, at the time of payment of the purchase consideration surrenders the shares in the vendor company by crediting
(a) Vendor Company's A/c
(b) Shares in the Vendor Company's A/c
(c) Share Capital A/c
(d) None of the above

Amalgamation and Reconstruction

75 When two or more companies liquidate to form a new company, it is called
(a) amalgamation (b) absorption
(c) reconstruction (d) purchase of business

76 Pooling of interest is a method of
(a) valuation of inventory
(b) calculation of purchase consideration
(c) accounting of amalgamation
(d) valuing goodwill

77 Method/methods of accounting for amalgamation
(a) The Pooling of Interest Method
(b) The Purchase Method
(c) Both (a) and (b)
(d) None of the above

78 When a company takes over another one and clearly becomes a new owner, the action is called
(a) merger (b) acquisition
(c) strategic alliance (d) None of these

79 The adjustment entry passed to eliminate the inter company owing is
(a) Debit Amalgamation Adjustment A/c, Credit Sundry Debtors A/c
(b) Debit Sundry Debtors A/c, Credit Statutory Reserve A/c
(c) Debit Sundry Creditors A/c, Credit Sundry Debtors A/c
(d) Debit Amalgamation Adjustment A/c, Credit Statutory Reserve A/c

80 Under the 'purchase method of accounting', the transferee company incorporates in its books
(a) The assets, liabilities and reserves of the transferor company
(b) The assets, liabilities and not statutory reserves of the transferor company
(c) The assets, liabilities and statutory reserves of the transferor company
(d) The assets and liabilities of the transferor company

81 How many companies are involved in the scheme of internal reconstruction?
(a) One (b) Two
(c) Three (d) Unlimited

82 When amalgamation is in the nature of merger, the accounting method to be followed is
(a) equity method
(b) purchase method
(c) pooling of interest method
(d) consolidated method

83 Amalgamate adjustment account is opened in the books of transferee company to incorporate
(a) the assets of the transferor company
(b) the liabilities of the transferor company
(c) the statutory reserves of the transferor company
(d) the non-statutory reserves of the transferor company

84 Goodwill arising on amalgamation is to be
(a) retained in the books of the transferee company
(b) amortised to income on a systematic basis normally five years
(c) adjusted against reserves or profit and loss account balance
(d) All of the above

85 Under pooling interest method, the difference between the purchase consideration and share capital of the transferee company should be adjusted to
(a) General Reserve A/c
(b) Amalgamation Adjustment A/c
(c) Goodwill or Capital Reserve A/c
(d) None of the above

86 For amalgamation in the nature of merger, the shareholders holding atleast ...... or more of the equity shares of the transferor company becomes the equity shareholders of transferee company.
(a) 51% (b) 90%
(c) 99% (d) 100%

87 X Ltd goes into liquidation and a new company Z Ltd is formed to take over the business of X Ltd. It is a case of
(a) amalgamation
(b) absorption
(c) reconstruction
(d) acquisition

Holding Company

88 The share of outsiders in the net assets of subsidiary company is known as
(a) assets
(b) outsiders liability
(c) subsidiary company's liability
(d) minority interest

89 Arrange the following steps of preparation of consolidated balance sheet correctly.
1. Calculation of pre-acquisition profits.
2. Calculation of minority interest.
3. Calculation of post-acquisition profits.
4. Calculation of cost of capital.

Codes
(a) 4, 3, 2, 1 (b) 2, 4, 1, 3
(c) 3, 1, 4, 2 (d) 3, 4, 1, 2

90 Which of the following items is not taken in profit and loss appropriation account?
(a) Transfer to dividend equalisation reserve
(b) Transfer to general reserve
(c) Provision for taxation
(d) Proposed dividend

91 Pre-acquisition profit in subsidiary company is considered as
(a) revenue profit (b) capital profit
(c) goodwill (d) outsiders liability

92 Excess of cost of investment over paid-up value of the shares is considered as
(a) goodwill (b) capital reserve
(c) minority interest (d) None of the above

93 Profit earned before acquisition of share is treated as
(a) capital profit (b) revenue profit
(c) general reserve (d) revaluation loss

94 Preparation of consolidated statement as per AS-21 is
(a) optional
(b) mandatory for listed companies
(c) mandatory for Pvt. Ltd
(d) partnership firm

95 Minority interest includes
(a) share in share capital (b) share in capital profit
(c) share in revenue profit (d) All of the above

Miscellaneous

Directions (Q. Nos. 96-100) *In the questions given below are two statemens labelled as Statement I and Statement II. You have to examine these two statements carefully, select the correct code.*

Codes
(a) Statement I is true, but Statement II is false
(b) Statement II is true, but Statement I is false
(c) Both statements are true
(d) Both statements are false

96 **Statement** I A company which is merged into another company is called a transferor company or a vendor company.
Statement II A company into which the vendor company is merged is called transferee company or vendee company or purchasing company.

97 **Statement** I Under purchase method, the assets and liabilities of the transferor company should be incorporated at their existing carrying amounts.
Statement II The purchase consideration should be allocated to individual identifiable assets and liabilities on the basis of their fair values at the date of amalgamation.

98 **Statement** I In internal reconstruction, there is no reduction of capital.
Statement II In external reconstruction, there is certain reduction of capital.

99 **Statement** I The process of two or more companies combining to form a new company is called amalgamation.
Statement II Under the pooling of interest method, shares are issued by the tranferee company at par.

100 **Statement** I When there is one or more liquidation and no formation, it is known as acquisition.
Statement II When there is one liquidation and one formation it is known as reconstruction.

Directions (Q. Nos. 101-106) *In the questions given below are two statements are labelled as Assertion (A) and Reason (R). In the context of the two statements, which one of the following is correct?*

Codes
(a) Both (A) and (R) are true and (R) is the correct explanation of (A)
(b) Both (A) and (R) are true, but (R) is not the correct explanation of (A)
(c) (A) is true, but (R) is false
(d) (A) is false, but (R) is true

101 **Assertion** (A) Dividends paid out of pre-acquisition profits must be credited to investment in shares of the subsidiary account.
Reason (R) Dividends paid out of post-acquisition profits must be credited to profit and loss account.

102 **Assertion** (A) A company has to acquire more than 50% shares of another company in order to become a holding company.
Reason (R) No company can become the subsidiary of another company.

103 Assertion (A) In absorption, an existing company takes over the business of another existing company.

Reason (R) Thus, there is liquidation of both the companies.

104 Assertion (A) Amalgamation means joining of two or more existing companies into one company.

Reason (R) The joined companies lose their identity and form themselves into a new company.

105 Assertion (A) In amalgamation in the nature of purchase, one company acquires the business of another company.

Reason (R) Purchase consideration can be defined as the aggregate of the shares and securities issued and the payment made in form of cash or other assets by the transferee company to the shareholders of the transferor company.

106 Assertion (A) The pooling of interest method is one of the methods of accounting for amalgamation.

Reason (R) The assets, liabilities and reserves of the transferee company will be taken over by transferor company at existing carrying amounts.

107 Match the following.

	List I		List II
A.	Absorption	1.	Profit on reissue of shares is to be transferred to ....
B.	Accumulated losses and fictitious assets	2.	When there are one or more liquidation and no formation, it is known as ....
C.	Consolidated revenue profits	3.	Internal reconstruction is generally resorted to write off ....
D.	Capital reserve	4.	The group share of proposed dividends by the subsidiary is added to ....

Codes

	A	B	C	D
(a)	4	3	2	1
(b)	3	4	2	1
(c)	2	3	4	1
(d)	3	4	1	2

108 Match the following.

	List I		List II
A.	Buy-back of equity shares must be authorised by	1.	Not allowed
B.	Buy-back of partly paid equity shares	2.	Governs buy back of shares
C.	Redemption of preference shares	3.	Article of Association
D.	Section 68 of the Companies Act	4.	Only fully paid

Codes

	A	B	C	D		A	B	C	D
(a)	3	4	2	1	(b)	3	1	4	2
(c)	4	3	2	1	(d)	2	1	4	3

109 Match the following.

	List I		List II
A.	Partly paid preference share	1.	Premium on redemption of preference shares
B.	Capital redemption reserve	2.	Current liabilities
C.	Security premium	3.	Redemption out of free reserve
D.	Unclaimed dividend	4.	Can not be redeem

Codes

	A	B	C	D		A	B	C	D
(a)	4	3	2	1	(b)	2	1	4	3
(c)	4	3	1	2	(d)	4	1	2	3

110 Match the following.

	List I		List II
A.	After reissue of forfeited shares the balance of share forfeiture account is transferred to	1.	Assets
B.	Bonus issue is made out of	2.	Free reserve
C.	Debentures secured by a charge on ...... are termed as secured debentures.	3.	Accumulated profits
D.	Workmen's compensation fund is .... to extent there is no compensation payable.	4.	Capital Reserve A/c

Codes

	A	B	C	D		A	B	C	D
(a)	4	3	2	1	(b)	4	3	1	2
(c)	2	1	4	3	(d)	2	4	1	3

111 Match the following.

	List I		List II
A.	Expenses of scheme	1.	Not transferable to capital reduction
B.	Statutory reserve	2.	Indicate 'and reduced'
C.	Balance sheet after reduction	3.	Transfer difference to capital reserve
D.	Reduction in paid-up value of shares	4.	Debit capital reduction account

Codes

	A	B	C	D
(a)	4	3	2	1
(b)	2	4	1	3
(c)	4	2	1	3
(d)	4	1	2	3

112 Match the following.

List I	List II
A. The formula for calculating the profit on reissue is	1. Article of Association
B. Right shares must be first offerred to existing	2. Security premium
C. Premium received on issue of debenture is credited to .... account	3. Amount forfeited less discount on reissue
D. Redeemable preference shares can be issued only when it is authorised by its	4. Equity shareholders

Codes

	A	B	C	D
(a)	3	4	1	2
(b)	3	1	4	2
(c)	3	4	2	1
(d)	4	3	2	1

PREVIOUS YEARS' QUESTIONS

December 2018

1 X Ltd forfeited 40 shares of ₹ 10 each and on which ₹ 4 per share were paid. If the forfeited shares are reissued as ₹ 8 per share paid-up. What is the minimum price the company must charge?

(a) ₹ 2 per share (b) ₹ 1 per share
(c) ₹ 8 per share (d) ₹ 10 per share

July

2 X Ltd forfeited 20 shares of ₹ 10 each, ₹ 8 called up, on which John had paid application and allotment money of ₹ 5 per share, of these, 15 shares were reissued to Parker as fully paid-up for ₹ 6 per share. What is the balance in the share Forfeiture Account after the relevant amount has been transferred to Capital Reserve Account?

(a) NIL (b) ₹ 5 (c) ₹ 25 (d) ₹ 100

November 2017

3 Which one of the following statements is not true?

(a) When there is one liquidation and one formation it is known as external construction
(b) Goodwill or Capital reserve arises only when the amalgamation is in the nature of merger
(c) Under the pooling of interest method, the transferee company incorporates the assets and liabilities of the transferor company at book value
(d) The vendor company transfers preliminary expenses (at the time of absorption) to equity shareholders' account

4 A Ltd issued a prospectus inviting applications for 2,000 shares. Applications were received for 3,000 shares and pro-rata allotment was made on the applications of 2,400 shares. If A has been allotted 40 shares, how many shares he must have applied for?

(a) 40 (c) 44
(c) 48 (d) 52

5 Consolidated financial statements are prepared on the principle

(a) In form the companies are one entity, in substance they are separate
(b) In form companies are separate, in substance they are one
(c) In form and substance the companies are one entity
(d) In form and substance the companies are separate

6 Under the yield method of valuation of equity share capital, if for an equity share of ₹ 50 the normal rate of return is 10% and expected rate of return is 5%, then the value of an equity share will be

(a) ₹ 25 (b) ₹ 40
(c) ₹ 50 (d) ₹ 100

January 2017

7 Which of the following is not true?

(a) When all the forfeited shares are not reissued, the forfeited shares account will also show as credit balance equal to gain on forfeiture of shares not yet reissued
(b) Loss on reissue of shares cannot be more than gain on forfeiture of those shares
(c) At the time of forfeiture of shares, securities premium is debited along with share capital when premium has not been received
(d) When forfeited shares are issued at premium, the premium amount is credited to Capital Reserve Account

8 Preparation of consolidated balance sheet of holding company and its subsidiary company is done as per

(a) AS-11 (b) AS-21
(c) AS-22 (d) AS-23

July 2016

9 X Ltd. purchased 70% of the shares of Y Ltd. at a price of ₹ 1,00,000. Share capital of Y Ltd. was of ₹ 70,000 and its accumulated profits amounted to ₹ 90,000. What would be the amount of Minority Interest in the consolidated balance sheet?

(a) ₹ 25,000
(b) ₹ 70,000
(c) ₹ 1,00,000
(d) ₹ 40,000

December 2015

10 When a business is purchased, any amount paid in excess of the total of assets, minus the liabilities taken, is called

(a) share premium
(b) goodwill
(c) capital employed
(d) working capital

June 2015

11 Preparation of consolidated statement of accounts as per AS-21 is

(a) optional
(b) mandatory for private limited companies
(c) mandatory for listed companies
(d) mandatory for all companies

12 Study the following transactions.

1. Raising of short-term loans.
2. Goods purchased for cash.
3. Payment of bonus in the form of shares.
4. Issue of shares in lieu of raw materials.

Select the correct answer using the codes given below

Codes

(a) Only 4
(b) 2, 3 and 4
(c) Both 3 and 4
(d) All of the above

December 2014

13 Pre-acquisition profit in subsidiary company is considered as

(a) revenue profit
(b) capital profit
(c) goodwill
(d) minority interest

December 2013

14 If there is mutual indebtedness between the transferor company and the transferee company in business combination, which of the following is correct?

(a) No adjustment is required in the books of the transferor company
(b) Adjustment is required in the books of the transferor company
(c) No adjustment is required in the books of the transferee company
(d) None of the above

June 2013

15 ABC Ltd was incorporated with an authorised share capital of ₹ 1,00,000 equity shares of ₹ 10 each. The Board of Directors of the company decided to allot 10,000 shares credited as fully paid to the promoters of the company for their services. Which account should be debited in the books of ABC Ltd?

(a) Promoters' A/c
(b) Services' A/c
(c) Goodwill A/c
(d) Share Capital A/c

16 In a reconstruction scheme, the reduction of capital may take the form of

(a) reducing the liability of the shareholders in respect of any unpaid amount on the shares held by them
(b) paying off any paid-up share capital which is in excess of its requirement
(c) cancelling any paid-up share capital, which is lost or unrepresented by available assets
(d) All of the above

17 While determining the normal rate of return for the valuation of shares in market value method, which of the following should be taken into consideration?

(a) The degree of risk involved
(b) The current rate of interest on gilt-edged securities
(c) Weighted average cost of capital
(d) All of the above

December 2012

18 ABC Ltd has declared 40% dividend. Which one of the following does it means?

(a) The company has declared 40% of net profit as dividend
(b) The company has declared 40% of profits after tax as dividend
(c) The company will provide dividend 40% on issued capital
(d) The company will provide dividend 40% on paid-up capital

June 2012

19 **Assertion** (A) When a company earns profit prior to its incorporation, it is called capital profit.
Reason (R) Capital profit cannot be used for distribution as dividend to the shareholders.

Codes

(a) (A) is true, but (R) is false
(b) Both (A) and (R) are false
(c) (A) is false, but (R) is true
(d) Both (A) and (R) are true

20 Reconstruction of a company takes place when

1. the company is undercapitalised.
2. company has incurred heavy losses which must be written off.
3. the company is overcapitalised.

Select the correct answoer using the codes given below

Codes

(a) Both 1 and 2
(b) Both 1 and 3
(c) Both 2 and 3
(d) All of the above

21 Assertion (A) Premium received on issue of shares is credited to share premium account, but not to profit and loss account.

Reason (R) Since, share premium is not a trading profit, it is not distributed to shareholders.

Codes

(a) Both (A) and (R) are true and (R) is the correct explanation of (A)
(b) Both (A) and (R) are true, but (R) is not the correct explanation of (A)
(c) (A) is true, but (R) is false
(d) (A) is false, but (R) is true

22 Assertion (A) Sinking fund is a charge against profit and loss account.

Reason (R) Sinking fund is created for repayment of a long-term liability.

Codes

(a) (A) is true, but (R) false
(b) Both (A) and (R) are true
(c) (A) is false, but (R) true
(d) Both (A) and (R) are false

ANSWERS

Objective Questions

1 *(b)*	2 *(b)*	3 *(a)*	4 *(c)*	5 *(a)*	6 *(c)*	7 *(d)*	8 *(d)*	9 *(d)*	10 *(a)*
11 *(c)*	12 *(c)*	13 *(c)*	14 *(b)*	15 *(b)*	16 *(d)*	17 *(c)*	18 *(a)*	19 *(b)*	20 *(b)*
21 *(b)*	22 *(b)*	23 *(c)*	24 *(d)*	25 *(a)*	26 *(b)*	27 *(d)*	28 *(d)*	29 *(c)*	30 *(b)*
31 *(c)*	32 *(b)*	33 *(a)*	34 *(a)*	35 *(c)*	36 *(d)*	37 *(a)*	38 *(c)*	39 *(c)*	40 *(d)*
41 *(c)*	42 *(b)*	43 *(c)*	44 *(b)*	45 *(d)*	46 *(b)*	47 *(b)*	48 *(c)*	49 *(b)*	50 *(b)*
51 *(a)*	52 *(a)*	53 *(c)*	54 *(d)*	55 *(b)*	56 *(b)*	57 *(b)*	58 *(c)*	59 *(c)*	60 *(b)*
61 *(a)*	62 *(c)*	63 *(d)*	64 *(b)*	65 *(b)*	66 *(c)*	67 *(d)*	68 *(a)*	69 *(d)*	70 *(c)*
71 *(c)*	72 *(d)*	73 *(b)*	74 *(b)*	75 *(a)*	76 *(c)*	77 *(c)*	78 *(b)*	79 *(c)*	80 *(c)*
81 *(a)*	82 *(c)*	83 *(c)*	84 *(b)*	85 *(c)*	86 *(b)*	87 *(c)*	88 *(d)*	89 *(b)*	90 *(c)*
91 *(b)*	92 *(a)*	93 *(a)*	94 *(b)*	95 *(d)*	96 *(c)*	97 *(c)*	98 *(d)*	99 *(b)*	100 *(c)*
101 *(b)*	102 *(c)*	103 *(c)*	104 *(a)*	105 *(a)*	106 *(c)*	107 *(c)*	108 *(b)*	109 *(c)*	110 *(b)*
111 *(d)*	112 *(c)*								

Previous Years' Questions

1 *(b)*	2 *(b)*	3 *(b)*	4 *(c)*	5 *(c)*	6 *(a)*	7 *(d)*	8 *(b)*	9 *(b)*	10 *(b)*
11 *(c)*	12 *(a)*	13 *(b)*	14 *(a)*	15 *(c)*	16 *(d)*	17 *(d)*	18 *(d)*	19 *(b)*	20 *(c)*
21 *(a)*	22 *(b)*								

CHAPTER 08

Cost and Management Accounting

Cost management is the process of planning and controlling the budget of a business. Various techniques are used by cost accounting *viz.* standard costing, marginal costing, budgetary control, inter-firm comparison etc. Management accounting also uses all these techniques used in cost accounting but in addition, it also uses techniques like ratio analysis, fund flow statement etc.

Cost Accounting

Cost accounting is the classifying, recording and appropriate allocation of expenditure for the determination of the costs of products or services and for the presentation of suitably arranged data for the purpose of control and guidance of management.

According to **Wheldon**, "Cost accounting is the application of accounting and costing principles, methods and techniques in the ascertainment of costs and the analysis of saving or excess cost incurred as compared with previous experience or with standards." It is a branch of accounting and has been developed due to limitations of financial accounting.

Features of Cost Accounting

- It is a process of accounting for costs.
- It records income and expenditure relating to production of goods and services.
- It provides statistical data on the basis of which future estimates are prepared and quotations are submitted.
- It is concerned with cost ascertainment and cost control.
- It establishes budgets and standards, so that actual cost may be compared to find out deviations or variances.

In this Chapter

- *Cost and Management Accounting*
- *Marginal Costing*
- *Break-even Analysis*
- *Standard Costing*
- *Process Costing*
- *Activity Based Costing*
- *Costing for Decision-making*
- *Life Cycle Costing*
- *Target and Kaizen Costing*
- *Budgetary Control*
- *Financial Statement Analysis*

Management Accounting

The origin of management accounting can be traced to overcome the limitations of financial accounting and cost accounting. Management accounting is the presentation of accounting information in such a way as to assist management in the creation of policy and the day-to-day operation of an undertaking.

According to **RN Anthony**, "Management accounting is concerned with accounting information that is useful to management."

Marginal Costing

The term 'marginal cost' is defined as "the amount at any given volume of output, by which aggregate costs are charged, if the volume of output is increased or decreased by one unit. It is a variable cost of one unit of a product or a service, *i.e.* a cost, which would be avoided is that unit was not produced or provided."

According to CIMA terminology, "Marginal costing is the ascertainment of marginal costs and of the effect on profit of changes in volume or type of output by differentiating between fixed costs and variable costs."

It is a technique of decision-making, which involves

- Ascertainment of total costs.
- Classification of costs into one fixed and variable.
- Use of such information for analysis and decision-making.

Thus, marginal costing is defined as the ascertainment of marginal cost and of the effect on profit of changes in volume or type of output by differentiating between fixed costs and variable costs.

Marginal costing is mainly concerned with providing information to management to assist in decision-making and to exercise control. Marginal costing is also known as 'variable costing' or 'out of pocket costing'.

Important Factors to be Considered in Marginal Costing Decisions

In all recommendations of marginal costing decisions, the following factors are to be considered

Contribution Whether the product or production line in question makes a contribution.

Specific Fixed Cost Where a choice is to be made between two course of action, the additional fixed overhead, if any, should be taken into account.

Cost Volume Profit Relationship The effect of increase in volume on profits and the rate of earning, additional profits should be analysed.

Incremental Contribution Where additional quantities can be sold only at reduced prices, incremental contribution will be more effective in decision-making, as it takes into account the additional sale quantity and additional contribution per unit.

Capacity Whether acceptance of the incremental order or additional product line is within the firms capacity or whether key factor comes into play, should be analysed.

Non-cost Factors Non-cost factor should also be considered, wherever applicable.

Advantages of Marginal Costing

Pricing Decisions Since, marginal cost per unit is constant from period to period within a short span of time, firms decisions on pricing policy can be taken. If fixed cost is included, the unit cost will change from period to period depending upon the volume of output. This will make decision-making difficult.

Overhead Variance Overheads are recovered in costing based on predetermined rates, this creates the problem for treatment of under-recovery or over-recovery of overheads, if fixed overheads were included. Marginal costing avoids such, under-recovery or over-recovery of fixed overheads, since, these costs are recognised as period costs.

True Profit Under the marginal costing technique, the stock of finished goods and work-in-progress are carried on marginal cost basis and the fixed expenses are written-off to profit and loss account as period cost. This shows the true profit of the period.

Break-even Analysis Marginal costing helps in break-even analysis, which shows the effect of increasing or decreasing production activity on the profitability of the company.

Control Over Expenditure Segregation of expenses as fixed and variable helps the management to exercise control over expenditure. The management can compare the actual variable expenses with the budgeted variable expenses and take corrective action through variance analysis.

Business Decision-making Marginal costing helps managemen in taking a number of business decisions like make or buy, discontinuance of a particular product, acceptance of export offers etc.

Limitations of Marginal Costing

Difficult to Classify It is difficult to classify exactly the expenses into fixed and variable category, as most of the expenses are neither totally variable nor wholly fixed.

Wrong Pricing Decisions Sales staff may mistake marginal cost for total cost and sell at a price, which will result in loss or low profits. Hence, sales staff should be cautioned against incorrect pricing decisions, while giving them information on marginal cost.

Stock Valuation Overheads of fixed nature cannot altogether be excluded particularly in large contracts, while valuing the work-in-progress. In order to show the correct position, fixed overheads may also have to be included in work-in-progress. This aspect is not considered in marginal costing.

Naive Assumptions Some assumptions regarding the behaviour of revenues and costs are not necessarily true in realistic situation, *e.g.* additional output can be sold only by reducing sale prices.

Ignores Time Value Marginal costing ignores time factor and investment. *e.g.* the marginal cost of two jobs may be the same, but the time taken for their completion and the cost of machines used may differ. The true cost of a job, which takes longer time and uses costlier machine, would be higher. The effect of time value of money is not analysed by marginal costing.

Proforma of Cost Sheet Under Marginal Costing Approach

	Particulars	Amt (₹)	Amt (₹)
A.	Sales		...
	Direct Material	...	
	Direct Labour	...	
	Direct Expense	...	
	Prime Cost	...	
	Variable Factory Overhead	...	
	Variable Administrative Overhead		
	Variable Selling and Distribution Overheads	...	
B.	Total Variable Cost		...
C.	Contribution (A – B)		...
	Fixed Factory Overheads	...	
	Fixed Administrative Overheads	...	
	Fixed Selling and Distribution Overheads	...	
D.	Total Fixed Cost		...
E.	Profits/Loss (C – D)		...

Contribution

Contribution is the excess of sales revenue over the variable cost, *i.e.*

Contribution = Sales – Variable cost

It is called, so since it initially contributes towards recovery of fixed costs and thereafter towards profit of the business. The contribution forms a fund for fixed expenses and profit.

The contribution concept is based on the theory that the profit and fixed expenses of a business is a 'joint cost', which cannot be equitably apportioned to different segments of the business. Hence, contribution serves as a measure of efficiency of operations of various segments of the business.

Profit Volume Ratio (P/V Ratio)

This ratio is a very useful as it indicates profitability of the concern. It indicates the relation of contribution to sales. This ratio shows a percentage relationship between profits and sales volume only after fixed costs have been recorded and the break-even point has been reached. This ratio is usually expressed in percentage.

This ratio is calculated by using the following formulae

- $$\text{P/V Ratio} = \frac{\text{Sales} - \text{Total variable cost}}{\text{Sales}} \times 100$$

  Or

  $$\text{P/V Ratio} = \frac{\text{Total contribution}}{\text{Sales}} \times 100$$
- $$\text{P/V Ratio} = \frac{\text{Net profit}}{\text{Margin of safety}} \times 100$$
- $$\text{P/V Ratio} = \frac{\text{Change in profits}}{\text{Change in sales}} \times 100$$

Significance of P/V Ratio

- P/V ratio is considered as the basic indicator of the profitability of the business.
- The higher the P/V ratio, the better it is for the business. In case, a firm is enjoying steady business conditions over a period of years, P/V ratio will also remain stable and steady.
- If P/V ratio is improved, it will result in better profits.

Uses of P/V Ratio

- To compute the variable costs for any volume of sales
- To measure the efficiency or to choose a most profitable time. The overall profitability of the firm can be improved by increasing the sales/output of a product giving a higher P/V ratio.
- To determine break-even point and the level of output required to earn a desired profit.
- To decide more profitable sales mix.

Improvement of P/V Ratio

P/V ratio can be improved by the following means

- By reducing the variable cost.
- By increasing the selling price.
- By increasing the share of products with higher P/V ratio in the overall sales mix.

(Where a firm produces a number of products)

Break-even Analysis

Break-even analysis is a useful technique of profit planning and prediction. This analysis is principally concerned with the study of revenues and costs of a firm in relation to profit at different levels of sales. In fact, break-even analysis is cost volume profit relationship analysis. It magnifies a set of inter-relationship of fixed cost, the level of activity and sales mix to the profitability of the concern.

Assumptions Underlying Break-even Analysis

- Selling price per unit remains constant, irrespective of quantity sold.
- The total amount of fixed costs will remain constant at each output level and variable costs will fluctuate in direct proportion of output.
- Productivity of the factors of production will remain the same.
- There will be no change in technological methods and efficiency of men and machines.
- There will be no significant change in the level of opening and closing inventory.
- Either there is only one product of the enterprise and if more than one product are being produced and sold, their sales mix will remains unchanged, *i.e.* all products are sold in a predetermined ratio.
- Both revenue and cost functions are linear over the range of activity under consideration, *i.e.* there will be a straight line, if cost date are shown on a graph.
- Cost control will be neither strengthened nor weakend.

Break-even Point

Break-even point may be described as that point of output and sales volume, at which total sales revenue equals the total cost to make and sell the product and no profit or loss is reported. This is why this point is also called as 'no profit, no loss point'. At this point, the amount of contribution is equal to fixed costs.

The significance of break-even point may be summarised as

Condition	Impact
Sales < BEP	Firms incur losses, *i.e.* Contribution < Fixed cost
Sales = BEP	No profit and no loss, *i.e.* Contribution = Fixed cost
Sales > BEP	Firms earn profits, *i.e.* Contribution > Fixed cost

Formulae to compute break-even point

$$\text{Break-even point (in units)} = \frac{\text{Total fixed costs}}{\text{Contribution per unit}}$$

$$\text{Break-even point (in units)} = \frac{\text{Total fixed costs}}{\text{P/V ratio}}$$

Types of Break-even Point

Cash Break-even Point This is the point at which cash receipts of the firm are equal to its cash costs. It is that sales volume where cash realisation through sales will be just sufficient to meet firm's immediate cash liabilities.

Cash break-even point

$$= \frac{\text{Cash fixed cost} + \text{Loan installment}}{\text{Contribution per unit}}$$

Income Break-even Point This is that level of activity at which payment of certain fixed amount of dividend together with the recovery of total cash costs plus loan installment is possible.

Income break-even point

$$= \frac{\text{Cash fixed cost} + \text{Loan installment} + \text{Cash earnings required for dividend}}{\text{Contribution per unit}}$$

Margin of Safety

Margin of safety represents the difference between the actual total sales and sales at break-even point. It can be expressed as a percentage of total sales or in value or in terms of quantity.

On the break-even chart and profit volume graph, this is represented as the distance between the break-even point and the present product sales.

$$\text{Margin of safety} = \frac{\text{Profit}}{\text{P/V ratio}}$$

$$Or \quad \frac{\text{Profit} \times \text{Sales}}{\text{Contribution}}$$

$$Or \quad \frac{\text{Profit percentage}}{\text{P/V ratio}} \times 100$$

Improvement in Margin of Safety

- Increase in the selling price, provided the inelastic demand so as to absorb the increased price.
- Reduction in fixed expenses.
- Reduction in variable expenses.
- Increasing the sales volume.
- Substitution or introduction of a product mix such that more profitable lines are introduced.

Standard Costing

Standard costing is a system of accounting, in which all expenses (fixed and variable) are considered for the determination of standard cost for a prescribed set of working conditions. In other words, standard costing is the preparation of standard cost and applying them to measure the variations from actual costs and analysing the causes and variations with a view to maintain maximum efficiency in production. It is a technique, which uses standards for costs and revenues for the purpose of control through variance analysis.

Standard costing is defined by the ICMA, London as the preparation and use of standard costs their comparison with actual costs and the analysis of variances to their causes and points of incidence.

The three components of standard costing are

- Standard cost, which provide a standard or predetermined performance level.
- A measure of actual performance.
- A measure of the variance between standard and actual performance.

Objectives of Standard Costing

- To provide a formal basis for assessing performance and efficiency.
- To control cost by establishing standards and analysis of variance.
- To enable the principle of 'management by exception' to be practised at the detailed operational level.
- To assist in setting budgets.
- The standard cost are reality available substitutes for actual average unit costs and can be used for stock and work-in-process valuations, profit planning and decision-making and as a basis of pricing where cost plus systems are used.
- To assist in assigning responsibility for non-standard performance in order to correct deficiencies or to anticipate benefits.
- To motivate staff and management.
- To provide a basic of estimating.
- To provide guidance on possible ways of improving performance.

Features of Standard Costing

- Predetermined estimates.
- Established for inputs and outputs.
- Applicable to all routine aspects of an organisation operations.
- Accounting for standard costs and obtaining variance.
- Reporting to management for taking appropriate action, wherever necessary.

Process of Standard Costing

The following preliminaries should be gone through before a standard costing system is established

Establishment of Cost Centres It is necessary for fixing responsibilities for unfavourable variances.

Types of Standard There are three types of standards, *i.e.* (current, basic, normal).

Setting the Standards Of all the persons, the cost accountant plays a very important role in setting the standards because he is to supply the necessary cost figures and coordinate the activities of the committee, so that standards set are as accurate as possible.

Standard Cost

Standard cost is defined as a predetermined cost, which is calculated from management standards of efficient operation and the relevant necessary expenditure. It may be used as a basis for price fixing and for cost control through variance analysis.

Types of Standard

The accuracy and relevance of an established standard cost depends upon the reliability of the standard set-up. In order to compute the standards, we must know what degree of accuracy is necessary.

There are four different bases or standard, which should be considered. *These standard have been discussed below*

Ideal Standards

These standards represent the level of performance attainable, when prices for material and labour are most favourable, when the highest output is achieved with the best equipment and layout and when the maximum efficiency in utilisation of resources results in maximum output with minimum costs.

These types of standards are criticised on three grounds

- Since, such standards would be unattainable, no one would take them seriously.
- The variance disclosed would be variance from the ideal standard. These would not therefore, indicate the extent to which they are practically and reasonable avoided.
- There would be no logical method of disposing of these variances.

Normal Standards

Normal standards are the standard, which may be achieved under normal operating conditions. The normal activity has been defined as "the number of standard hours, which will produce, at normal efficiency, sufficient goods to meet the average sales demand over a term of years".

These standards are difficult to set, because they require a degree of forecasting. The variances thrown out under this system are deviation from normal efficiency, normal sales volumes or normal productive volumes. If the actual performance is found to be abnormal, large variances may result and necessitate revision of standard.

Basic Standards

These standards are used only when they are likely to remain constant of unaltered over a long period. According to this standard, a base year is chosen for comparison purpose in the same way as statisticians use price indices. Since, basic standard do not represent, what should be attained in the present period, current standard should also be prepaid, if basic standards are used.

Current Standards

These standards reflects the management anticipation of what actual costs will be for the current period. These are the costs, which the business will incure, if the anticipated prices are paid for the goods and services and the usage correspond to that believed to be necessary to produce the planned output. The variances arising from expected standard represent the degree of efficiency in usage of the factors of production.

Need for Standard Costs

Standard costs are predetermined costs computed before the production takes place, they are preferable to actual costs. In the situation of mass production, the computation of standard costs are strongly advisable, *these situations are*

- Historical costs may be too expensive to compute.
- The units costs computed on historical data may vary from day-to-day and they are of no use to the sales department in setting selling prices.
- Historical costs are not known until after the competition of a month or even a longer period. But in many cases, to take a decision, the cost of product has to be calculated even before the production begins.
- Historical costs may not be adequate for the measurement of efficiency. Standard costs are well suited for measuring operating efficiency because they represent what the costs should be.

Uses of Standard Costs

- Standard cost is an effective way for planning and controlling costs.
- Pricing decisions and decisions involving submission of questions, answering tenders etc are also facilitated by the use of standard costs.
- It facilitates management by exception.
- Identification and measurement of variances from standards has been made possible with the use of standard cost, with a view to improve performance or to correct loose standard, if any.

It can be established that standard costing is a notion of accounting to determine of standard for each constituent of costs. These fixed costs are compared with actual costs to realise the deviations known as 'variances'.

Variance Analysis

Variance analysis is the procedure of computing the differences between standard costs and actual costs and recognising the causes of those differences.

Calculation of Variance

Variances can be computed under the following cost heads

Material

In the manufacturing industry, the main expenditure head is the material.

There are two types of variances which are calculated as follows

Material Usage Variance

$$= \text{Standard price} \times \text{Standard quantity} - \text{Standard price} \times \text{Actual quantity}$$

$$= \text{Standard price (Standard quantity} - \text{Actual quantity)}$$

Material Price Variance

$$= \text{Actual quantity} \times \text{Standard price} - \text{Actual quantity} \times \text{Actual price}$$

$$= \text{Actual quantity} \times \text{(Standard price} - \text{Actual price)}$$

Note *How to learn the above formulae*

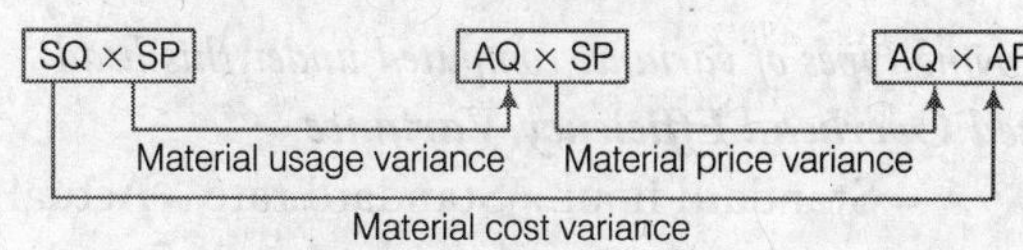

Here, **SQ** Standard Quantity, **AQ** Actual Quantity
SP Standard Price, **AP** Actual Price

Labour

Second important component in manufacturing expenses is amount spent on labour.

The variances computed under this head are as under

Labour Efficiency Variance

$$\text{Standard rate} \times \text{Standard hours} - \text{Standard rate} \times \text{Actual hours}$$

$$= \text{Standard rate} \times \text{(Standard hours} - \text{Actual hours)}$$

Labour Rate Variance

$$= \text{Actual hours} \times \text{Standard rate} - \text{Actual hours} \times \text{Actual rate}$$

$$= \text{Actual hours} \times \text{(Standard rate} - \text{Actual rate)}$$

Note *How to learn the above formulae*

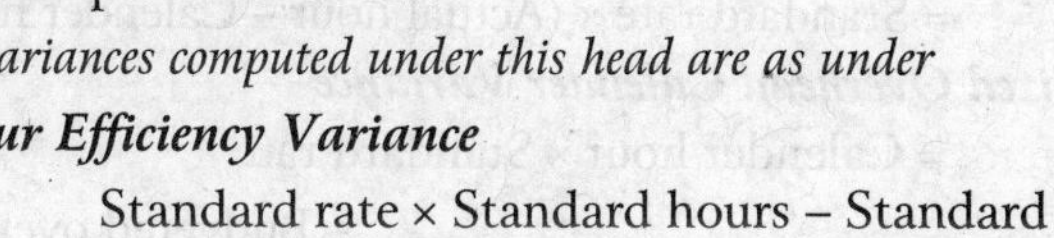

Here, **SH** Standard Hour, **SR** Standard Rate
AH Actual Hour, **AR** Actual Rate

Overheads

These can be divided as variable overhead and fixed overhead which are as follows

Variable Overhead They represents the other manufacturing expenses. It depends upon working hours.

The following are the variances computed

- ***Variable Overhead Efficiency Variance***
  = Standard hours × Standard rate – Actual hours × Standard rate
  = Standard rate (Standard hours – Actual hours)
- ***Variable Overhead Expenditure Variance***
  = Actual hours × Standard rate – Actual overhead

➡ **Note** *How to learn the above formulae*

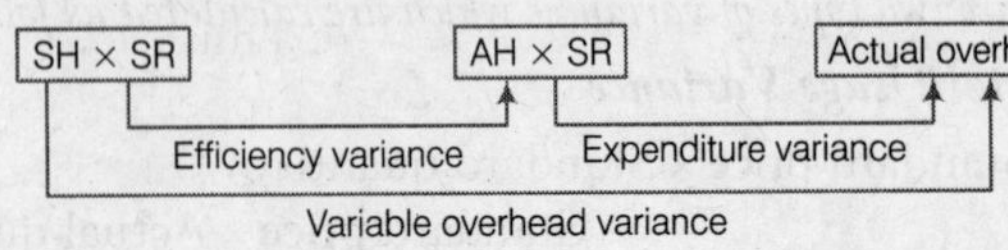

Here, **SH** Standard Hours, **SR** Standard Rate
AH Actual Hours

Fixed Overhead

These are the type of manufacturing expenses, which remains fixed over a period of time. It does not depends upon working hour.

The following types of variance computed under this head

- ***Fixed Overhead Efficiency Variance***
  = Standard hour × Standard rate – Actual hour × Standard rate
  = Standard rate × Standard hour – Actual hour
- ***Fixed Overhead Capacity Variance***
  = Actual hour × Standard rate – Calender hour × Standard rate
  = Standard rate × (Actual hour – Calender hour)
- ***Fixed Overhead Calender Variance***
  = Calender hour × Standard rate – Budgeted overhead
- ***Fixed Overhead Volume Variance***
  = Standard hour × Standard rate – Budgeted overhead

  Or

  = Can be derived as efficiency variance + Capacity variance + Calender variance

Hence, Standard hour × Standard rate – Budgeted overhead

- ***Fixed Overhead Expenditure Overhead***
  = Budgeted overhead – Actual overhead

➡ **Note** *How to learn the above formulae*

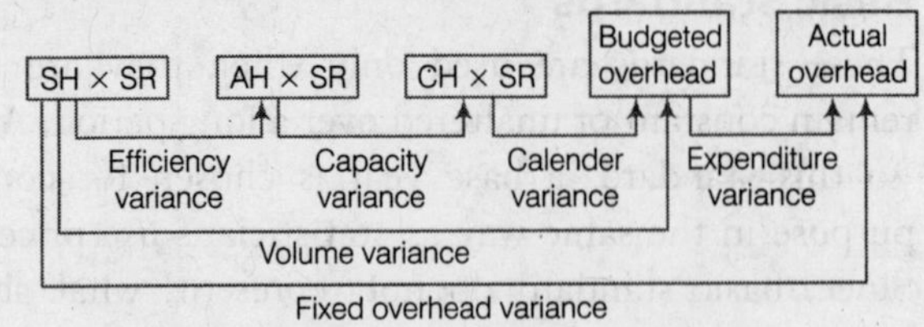

Here, **SH** Standard Hour, **SR** Standard Rate
AH Actual Hour, **CH** Calender Hour

Calender hours are the maximum possible hours worked in actual number of days. Standard hours are the hours for actual production.

If the computation give positive results, it means we got favourable variance represented by 'F' and whereas the negative results denotes adverse variance represented by 'A'.

Reporting of Variances

Computation of variance and their reporting is not the final steps towards the control of various elements of costs. It demands an analysis of variances from the side of the executive to ascertain the correct reasons for their occurrence. After knowing the exact reasons, it becomes their responsibility to take necessary steps, so as to stop the reoccurrence of adverse variance in future. To enhance the utility of such a reporting system, it is necessary that such a system of reporting should not only be prompt, but should also facilitates. The concerned managerial level to take the necessary steps.

The variance reports should give due regards the following points

- The concerned executive should be informed about what the cost performance should have been.
- How close the actual cost performance is with reference to standard cost performance.
- The analysis and causes of variances.
- Reporting should be based on the principle of management by exception.
- The magnitude of variances should be stated.

Criticism of Standard Costing

Variation in Price One of the chief problem faced in the operation of the standard costing is the system of precise estimation of likely price or rates to be paid. But the use of sophisticated forecasting technique should be able to cover the price fluctuation to some extent.

Varying Level of Output If the standard level of output set for predetermination of standard cost is not achieved, the standard costs are said to be not realised. In vast majority of industries, uses of forecasting technique etc helps to estimate the output with reasonable accuracy and thus, variation is unlikely to be very large.

Changing Standard of Technology In case of industries, that have frequent technological changes affecting the condition of production, standard costing may not be suitable. This criticism does not affect the system of standard costing.

Mix of Products Standard costing presupposes a predetermined combination of products both in variety and quantity. The mixture of material used to manufacture the products may vary in the long run, but since standard costs are set normally for a short period, such changes can be taken by revision of standard.

Process Costing

Process costing is a method of costing used to ascertain the cost of a product which passes through various processes before completion. In this method of costing, goods are produced continuously and output of one process is transferred to next process as input of next process. Finished product of last process is transferred to finished stock account.

This method of costing is used in those industries where uniform or standard type of goods is produced in large quantity, i.e.

- Manufacturing industries for cement, leather, cosmetic goods, oil, paint, iron, steel etc.
- Mining industries for gold, coal, minerals etc.

Accounting of Process Costing

Ascertainment of Cost by Preparing a Statement Generally, process accounts are maintained by preparing process accounts. But, in process accounts, information of cost of all process is not available at a single place so to provide results in a comparative manner, a statement of cost is also prepared. Statement of cost is generally prepared in unit costing method only as product is produced in a single process.

Ascertainment of Cost by Preparing a Process Account It is better to prepare process account on double entry system as in that case, accounts are maintained in a systematic manner. But, some accountants are preparing a statement also for reporting purposes.

Format of process account is as follows

Process Account

Particulars	Units	Amt (₹)	Particulars	Units	Amt (₹)
To Direct Material	—	—	By Wastage	—	—
To Direct Wages	—	—	By Next Process A/c	—	—
To Direct Expenses	—	—	(Transfer)		
To Indirect Expenses	—	—	Cost per Unit		
To Other Expenses (if any)	—	—	$= \frac{\text{Cost}}{\text{Total Production}}$		
	—	—		—	—

Merits of Process Costing

- The calculation of average cost is quite easy since the homogeneous products are produced.
- The cost is calculated periodically.
- In this method, less clerical efforts and costs are enough to calculate cost.
- Effective control can be exercised on production very easily.

Demerits of Process Costing

- This system does not disclose the weaknesses and inefficiencies of any process. Hence, the accurate cost per unit cannot be calculated.
- The calculated cost per unit may be a misleading, if the apportionment of joint costs is not properly done.
- It has all the weaknesses of historical costing since it is based on historical costs.
- The use of excessive materials and labour are not disclosed until the end of the period.

Thus, life cycle costing is defined as the total cost throughout its life including planning, design, acquisition and support costs and any other costs directly attributable to owning/using the asset.

Activity Based Costing

The activity based costing is a costing system, which focuses on activities performed to produce products. In this method, costs are first traced to activities and then to products.

According to CIMA, "Activity based costing is the cost attribution to cost units on the basis of benefit received from indirect activities, *e.g.* ordering, setting-up, assuring quality."

ABC aims at identifying as many costs possible to be subsequently accounted as direct cost of production. Any cost that is traced to a particular product via its consumption of activity becomes direct cost of the product. ABC is generally used as a tool for understanding product and customer cost and profitability.

Objectives of Activity Based Costing

- To improve product costing.
- To provide required information for decision-making.
- To encourage managers to evaluate the efficiency of internally provided services.
- To reduce the non-essential use of common resources.

Merits of Activity Based Costing

- It helps to eradicate the problem of over costing and under costing.
- It is the more accurate costing of product/services, customers, SKVs and distribution channel.

- It utilises unit cost rather than just total cost.
- It integrates well with six sigma and other continuous improvement programs.
- It enables costing of process, supply chains and value streams.

Demerits of Activity Based Costing

- In this costing, it is difficult to identify the overall activities that influence costs.
- This costing system is not suitable for small manufacturing concerns.
- It is difficult to evaluate cost on the basis of activities.
- This costing is more complex and expensive than traditional product costing system.

Process of Activity Based Costing

Step 1 To identify costs that is to be allocated.

Step 2 Create cost pools for those costs incurred to provide services to other parts of the company.

Step 3 Create a set of cost pools for those costs more closely aligned with the production of goods or services.

Step 4 Use a data collection system to collect information about the activity drivers that are used to allocate the costs in secondary cost pools to primary cost pools.

Step 5 Allocate costs in secondary pools to primary pools.

Step 6 Use an activity driver to allocate the contents of each primary cost pool to cost objects.

Step 7 Convert the results of the ABC system into reports for management consumption.

Costing for Decision-Making

There are some techniques in costing, which helps management in managerial decision-making. It helps in profit planning, cost control and making policy decisions.

The following techniques are as follows

Key Factor or Limiting Factor

Key factor is that factor, which is most important one for taking decisions about profitability of a product. A key factor or limiting factor is a factor which limits production or sales and thus, prevent the company from making unlimited profits. The limiting factor may be raw material, labour, plant capacity, capital etc. The extent of its influence must be assumed first so as to maximise the profits. On the basis of contribution, the decision regarding the product mix is taken.

Fixation of Selling Price

Marginal cost of a product represents the minimum price for that product and any sale below the marginal cost would entail a cash loss. The price for the product should be fixed at a level which not only covers the marginal cost, but also makes a reasonable contribution towards the common fund to cover fixed overheads. The fixation of such price for a product would be easier, if its marginal cost and overall profitability of the concern is known.

Maintaining a Desired Level of Profit

The industry has to cut prices of its products from time to time on account of competition, government regulations and other compelling reasons. The contribution per unit on account of such cutting is reduced, while the industry is interested in maintaining a minimum level of its profits. In case, the demand for the company's product is elastic, the minimum level of profits can be maintained by pushing-up the sales.

Determination of Sales Mix

When an organisation manufactures more than one product, then a problem often arises as to the product mix or sales mix which will yield the maximum profits. In determining the profitable sales mix, the product, which gives the maximum contribution are to be retained and their production should be increased. A product giving a negative contribution should be discontinued or given-up, unless there are other reasons to continue production.

Exploring New Markets

Decision regarding selling goods in a new market whether Indian or foreign should be taken after considering the following factors

- Whether the firm has surplus capacity to meet the new demand?
- What price is being offered by new market?
- Whether the sale of goods in new market will affect the present market for the goods? It is particularly true in case of sale of goods in a foreign market at a price lower than the domestic market at a price. Before accepting such an order from a foreign buyer, it must be seen that the goods sold are not dumped in the domestic market itself.

Discontinuance of a Product Line

The following factors should be considered before taking a decision about the discontinuance of a product line

- The contribution given by the product.
- The capacity utilisation.

- The availability of product to replace the product which the firm wants to discontinue and which is already accounting for a significant proportion of total capacity.
- The long-term prospects in the market for the product.
- The effect on sale of other products.

Make or Buy Decision

Whether a particular part of a finished product is to be manufactured within the industry or it has to be bought from outside will depend on the consideration of marginal costs. The marginal cost of manufacturing is to be compared with the purchase price of the relevant material and if the marginal cost is more than the purchase price, a decision as to buying it from the market can be taken. However, there are certain non-cost factors also which must be taken into an account before making a final decision.

The factors are as under

- The part to be bought should be available whenever it is needed and at the same price at which we are considering to buy it at present.
- If there is difference in quality, specification etc of the component to be bought, it must be workable.
- If production is not carried out, labour problems should not occur up. The surplus labour force should be absorbed in other productive work.

Profit Planning

Marginal costing techniques can be applied for profit planning as well. Profit planning involves the planning of future operations to achieve maximum profits or to maintain a desired level of profits. *With the help of marginal costing, the required value of sales for maintaining or attaining a desired level of profit may be ascertained as follows*

$$\text{Desired sales} = \frac{\text{Fixed cost} + \text{Desired profit}}{\text{P/V ratio}}$$

Life Cycle Costing

Life cycle costing is a management technique which is used to identify and monitor the costs of a product throughout the life cycle. Product life cycle is a pattern of expenditure, sales level revenue and profit over the period from new idea generation to the deletion of product from product range. Thus, life cycle costing is defined as the total cost throughout its life including planning, design, acquisition and support costs and any other costs directly attributable to owning/using the asset.

Objectives of Life Cycle Costing

- To assist management to smartly manage total cost throughout products life cycle.
- To identify areas in which cost reduction efforts are likely to more effective.
- To estimate the cost impact of various designs and support options.

Stages of Life Cycle Costing

It consists of four phases- introduction, growth, maturity and decline. *The costs included in different stages of the product life cycle are*

- Introduction–Production cost, high advertising cost, set-up cost etc.
- Growth–Manufacturing cost, marketing cost etc.
- Maturity–Increase in profit, competition etc.
- Decline–Plants reused/sold/scrapped related cost, replacement cost etc.

According to **Horngreen, Foster and Datar**, "Life cycle cost tracks and accumulates the actual costs attributable to each product from start to finish".

Target Costing

Target costing is based on the concept that there are three C's which affect demand and supply of a product, *i.e.* customer, competitor and cost. Target costing is a management technique which determines total cost at which a proposed product is produced with the aim of desired profit margin.

According to CIMA, "Target cost is a product cost estimate derived from a competitive market price".

In short, target costing is a structured approach for determining the cost at which a proposed product with specified functionality and quality must be produced to generate a desired level of profitability at its anticipated selling price.

Thus, we can say that

Target price = Sale price – Desired profit

Objectives of Target Costing

- To lower the cost of new products.
- To enhance the product development and design.
- To recognise the necessity to balance the trade-offs.
- To plan, manage and reduce costs to get desired profit margin.
- To motivate the employees.

Process of Target Costing

- Development of a product.
- Fixation of target price.
- Fixation of target cost.
- Value engineering.
- Reduce indirect cost allocation.
- Maintain the focus of the management.

Advantages of Target Costing

- It helps in minimising the cost of new products so that desired profit margin can be achieved.
- It focus on customer orientation, *i.e.* matching of products with customer's needs.
- It helps in creating market driven management.
- It reduces the development cycle of a product that saves the time.
- It increases the teamwork and team sprit among employees.

Kaizen Costing

Kaizen costing is originated in Japan. Kaizen is a Japanese word, comprising of two words 'Kai' means change and 'Zen' means good or improvement. Thus, Kaizen means that you need to change something for good or improvement.

Kaizen costing is developed by Yashuhiro Monden in Japan. He defines Kaizen costing as the maintenance of present cost levels for products currently being manufactured *via* systematic efforts to achieve the desired cost level. *Monden describes two types of Kaizen costing*

- Asset and organisation-specific Kaizen costing activities planned according to the exigencies of each deal.
- Product-model-specific costing activities carried out in special projects with added emphasis on value analysis.

Kaizen is small incremental changes made for improving productivity. It is used in manufacturing stage of the existing products as cost reduction process. This technique is applied to product that is already under production for cost reduction.

According to this, cost of a product can be reduced through estimation of seven types of waste, *i.e.* over processing, over production, defective, waiting, transportation, inventory and motion.

Steps of Kaizen Costing

- When planning, a cost target is set and a gap occurs.
- Establish why the goal was set and what are the possibilities of reaching the target.
- Cost reductions are broken down into smaller reductions.
- New cost applies on the day of activity.
- Each activity bears its own investment estimate prepared in advance.
- Finally resources are allocated.

Merits of Kaizen Costing

- It reduces waste-like inventory waste, time waste, workers motion etc.
- It improves space utilisation, product quality results in higher employee moral and job satisfaction and lower turnover.
- It minimises non-value added activities.
- It encourages selection of lowest cost value added activities.
- It breaks down barriers between departments.

Demerits of Kaizen Costing

- Lack of proper procedure to implement.
- Too much suggestions may lead to confusion and time waste.
- Effective implementation and use requires the development of detailed resource data.

JIT or Just In Time Approach

Over the period, sufficient efforts are made to reduce size of inventory to reduce cost of working capital. For this purpose, Just In Time (JIT) approach was developed in Japan for assembling of different products where no inventory of raw material, work-in-progress or finished goods was required or maintained.

In this approach, production for the next day is planned earlier and order for raw material required for next day is placed. In the early morning, supplier supplies all the raw material required and by the evening all the units are produced and supplied to the customers. Thus, inventory is reduced to zero so it is also known as zero inventory production system.

Budgetary Control

Budget

According to **CIMA, England,** "A financial and/or quantitative statement, prepared and approved prior to a defined period of time of the policy to be pursued during that period for the purpose of attaining a given objective. It may include income, expenditure and employment of capital".

In case of budgetary control, the entire exercise starts with the setting-up of budgets or targets and ends with the taking of an action, in case, the actual figures differed with the budgetary ones.

Budgetary control can be defined as "the establishment of budgets relating the responsibilities of executives to the requirements of a policy and the continuous comparison of actual with budgeted results either to secure the objective of that policy by individual action or to provide a base for its revision."

Procedure of Budgetary Control

- Determining the objectives to be achieved.
- Activities for achievement of objectives.
- Drawing up a plan.
- Laying out a system for comparing of actual performance.
- Corrective action.

Objectives of Budgetary Control System

- Determining targets of performance for each section of the business.
- Laying down the responsibilities of each of the executives, so that every one known what is expected of him and how will be judged.
- Providing a basis for the comparison of actual performance with the predetermined targets and investigation of deviation, if any.
- Ensuring the best use of all available resources to maximise profit or production subject to the limiting factors.
- Providing a basis for revision of current and future policies.
- Coordinating the various activities of business.

Essentials of Budgetary Control

- Establishment of budgets are for each function given below and section of the organisation.
- Continuous comparison of the actual performance with that of the budget, so as to know the variations from budget and placing the responsibility of executives for failure to achieve the desired result as given in the budget.
- Taking suitable remedial action to achieve the desired objective, if there is a variation of the actual performance from the budgeted performance.
- Revision budgets in the light of changed circumstances.

Preliminaries for the Adoption of a System of Budgetary Control

The following are the prerequisites or steps for the successful implementation of a sound system of budgetary control

- A concern must have an organisation chart. This necessary order to have a clear idea of authority and responsibility of each executive, so that here may be conflict among functional executives for shirking responsibilities and blaming others for poor performance.
- The business objectives, plans and policies should be clearly defined and stated in unambiguous terms. The scope of budgetary control should also be clearly laid down.
- The budgeted output should be stated in clear terms.
- The budget or key factor, if any, must be indicated before starting the preparation of budgets.
- There must be efficient system of accounting in order to record and must provide necessary accounting information to the management for successful system of budgetary control.
- To make budgetary control successful, there should be a proper system of communication and reporting between the various levels of management. A two-way system of communication should be adopted. The top management should be able to communicate the budgeted plan to the lower levels in clear terms, who in turn should feedback by reporting the deviations from the targets to the higher levels. On the basis of feedback, the top management may again communicate instructions to the lower management for taking corrective action.
- Budget centres should be established for cost control and all budgets should be related to cost centres. Budget centres will disclose the sections of the organisations, where planned performance is not achieved.
- There should be a budget manual to indicate charter of programme. It contains all details regarding the plan and procedures for its execution and specify the length of the budget period.
- To motivate the workers, the budget must be prepared by those who are responsible for its performance.
- The budget should cover all phases, attainable and on continuous basis.
- Top management approval is necessary in order to get full cooperation and acceptance of the system of budgetary control. The system may fail in future due to disagreements, which may arise later on without approval of the top management.

Working of a Budgetary Control System

The responsibility for successfully introducing and implementing a budgetary control system rests with the budget committee acting through the budget officer. The budget committee would be composed of all functional heads and a member from the board to preside over and guide the deliberation.

Advantages of Budgetary Control System

- The use of budgetary control system enables the management of a business concern to conduct its business activities in efficient manner.
- It is a powerful instrument used by business houses for the control of their expenditure.
- It reveals the deviations to management, from the budgeted figures after making a performance of individuals and their departments.
- It helps in effective utilisation of various resources.
- It helps in the review of current trends and framing of future inculcates policies.
- It creates suitable conditions for the implementation of standard costing system in a business organisation.
- It inculcates the feeling of cost consciousness among workers.

Limitations of Budgetary Control System

- Budgets may or may not be true, as they are based on estimates.
- Budgets are considered as rigid document.
- Budgets can not be executed automatically.
- Staff cooperation is usually not available during budgetary control exercise.
- Its implementation is quite expensive.

Components of Budgetary Control System

The policy of a business for a defined period is represented by the master budget, the details of which are given in a number of individual budgets called functional budgets.

The functional budgets are broadly grouped under the following heads

Physical Budget The budget which contains information in terms of physical units about sales, production etc.

Cost Budget The budget, which provides cost information in respect of manufacturing, selling, administration etc.

Profit Budget A budget, which enables in the ascertainment of profits.

Essentials of an Effective Budgetary Control System

Cooperation of Top Management Budgeting must have complete cooperation of the top management.

Maximum Profit The ultimate object of releasing maximum profit should always be kept upper most.

Budget Committee A budget committee should be established constituting of the budget director, chief executive officer and executive of various departments of the organisation.

Constant Vigilance Effective system of budgeting requires that periodic reports comparing budget and the actual results should be prepared monthly.

Reasonably Attainable Goals Budget figures should be realistic and represent reasonably attainable goals.

Budget Report

Establishing budgets in itself is of no use unless there is a continuous flow of budget reports showing comparison of actual and budgeted figures. Budget reports should be prepared at regular intervals showing the reasons for the difference between actual and budget figures. The reports should be prepared in such a way that they establish the responsibility for the variance.

Essentials of a Budget Period

- The budget reports should be simple and suitable for the level of understanding of the user.
- Reports should be presented promptly.
- Reports should be accurate.
- The reports should contain only essential information according to the needs of the user.

Conventional Budgeting

Conventional budgeting is done in any organisation to compute the maximum amount given to each department for a year. The main disadvantage of this budgeting is that the inefficiencies of the previous year creep into this year's budget. In such a budget, justification is to be given only for now or additional funds required.

Financial Statement Analysis

Financial statements are the only source of information about the position of a business entity. It gives the true and fair view of affairs of an entity which is available to the public, shareholders, investors and creditors and the government but these groups are interested to know the progress and prospects of such entity in various ways. For this purpose, financial statements are analysed. Analysis of financial statement refers to the treatment of information contained in the financial statement in a way so as to afford a full diagnosis of the profitability and financial position of the firm concerned.

According to **Myers**, "Financial statement analysis is largely a study of relationship among the various financial factors in business as disclosed by a single set of statements and a study of the trend of these factors as shown in a series of statements."

Methods of Analysing Financial Statements

Following methods are used to analyse financial statements

- Comparative statement
- Common size statements
- Trend ratios
- Ratio analysis
- Cash flow analysis
- Fund flow analysis

➠ **Note** *We will be discussing point 4, 5 and 6 at broad level ahead in this chapter.*

Ratio Analysis

It is one of the powerful tools of the financial analysis. A ratio can be defined as "the indicated quotient of two mathematical expressions" and as "the relationship between two or more things." Ratio is, thus, the numerical or an arithmetical relationship between two figures. A ratio can be used as a yardstick for evaluating the financial position and performance of a concern, because the absolute accounting data cannot provide meaningful understanding and interpretation. Ratio analysis helps the analyst to make quantitative judgement with regard to concern's financial position and performance.

Accounting ratios show inter-relationships, which exist among various accounting data. When relationships among various accounting data supplied by financial statements are worked out, they are known as accounting ratios.

Accounting ratios can be expressed in various ways, such as

- A pure ratio, *i.e.* ratio of current assets to current liabilities is 2 : 1.
- A rate, *i.e.* current assets are two times of current liabilities.
- A percentage, *i.e.* current assets are 200% of current liabilities.

Advantages of Ratio Analysis

Ratio analysis serves the purpose of various users, who are interested in financial statements. *The advantages of ratio analysis are as follows*

Useful in Simplifying Accounting Figures Accounting ratio simplifies, summarises and systematises accounting figures to make them understandable.

Useful in Analysis of Financial Statement Accounting ratios are useful for understanding the financial position of enterprise.

Useful for Forecasting Accounting ratios are helpful in business planning and forecasting.

Useful for Locating the Weak Spots Accounting ratios are of great assistance in locating the weak spots in the business even though the overall performance may be avite good.

Useful in Inter-firm and Intra-firm Comparison A firm would like to compare in performance with that of other firm and of industry in general. This comparison is called inter-firm comparison. If the performance of different units belonging to the same firm is to be compared, it is called intra-firm comparison.

Limitations of Ratio Analysis

False Result Ratios are calculated by using the accounting information, hence, the ratio analysis depends upon the accuracy of financial statement. If financial statements are not true, the analysis will give a false picture.

Lack of Standard Ratio There is no single standard ratio against, which the ratio may be measured and compared.

Window Dressing It means manipulation of accounts in a way to conceal vital facts and present the statement better than, what they actually are in such a situation, ratios are affected.

Personal Bias While preparing the financial statement, personal judgement or decision play a very important role hence, it affects the ratio analysis also.

Classification of Ratio

Liquidity Ratios (Short-term Solvency)

These ratios are used to measure the firm's ability to meet short-term obligations. They compare short-term obligations to short-term (or current) resources available to meet these obligations. For instance, if it is decided to study the liquidity position of the concerns, in order to highlight the relative strength of the concerns in meeting their current obligations to maintain sound liquidity and to pinpoint the difficulties, if any in it, then liquidity ratios are calculated.

Some of the important liquidity ratios are

Current Ratio or Working Capital Ratio

Current ratio signifies a relationship of current assets to current liabilities and it is computed to assess the short-term financial position of the enterprise.

It is calculated as

$$\text{Current ratio} = \frac{\text{Current asset}^{*}}{\text{Current liabilities}^{**}}$$

As per the standard norms, the current assets should be twice of current liabilities, *i.e.* 2 : 1.

Current Asset*

- Cash and cash equivalents and bank balance
- Trade receivable or debtors (after deducting provisions)
- Bills receivable
- Inventory
- Marketable securities
- Prepaid expenses
- Advance payments
- Income due, but not received

Current Liabilities**

- Trade payables or creditors
- Bills payable
- Bank overdraft
- Short-term loans and advances
- Outstanding expenses
- Provision for taxation
- Unclaimed dividend
- Income received in advance

➠ **Note** *Working capital = Current assets − Current liabilities*

Liquidity Ratio or Quick Ratio or Acid Test Ratio

Liquidity ratio expresses the relationship of liquid assets with current liabilities and it is computed to assess the short-term liquidity of the enterprise.

This is computed as under

$$\text{Liquidity ratio} = \frac{\text{Liquid assets or Quick assets*}}{\text{Current liabilities}}$$

* Liquid or Quick assets = Current assets − Stock − Prepaid expenses

The standard norms for quick ratio is 1:1.

$$\text{Liquidity ratio} = \frac{\text{Liquid assets*}}{\text{Current liabilities}}$$

Solvency Ratios (Long-term Solvency)

Solvency ratios indicate the ability of enterprise to meet its long-term liabilities. *Some of the solvency ratios are as follows*

Debt equity Ratio

It is computed to ascertain the long-term financial position of the firm.

It is calculated as

$$\text{Debt equity ratio} = \frac{\text{Debt (Long-term loans) *}}{\text{Equity (Shareholder's fund)**}}$$

The ideal ratio is 2 : 1.

* Debt includes debentures, loans etc.

** Equity shareholders fund
= Preference share capital + Equity share capital
+ Reserves − Accumulated losses − Fictitious assets

Or = Total assets − Total debts

Total Assets to Debt Ratio

Total assets to debt ratio signifies a relationship between total assets and total long-term debts.

It is calculated as

$$\text{Total assets to debt ratio} = \frac{\text{Total assets *}}{\text{Long-term debts **}}$$

It is computed to measure the safety margin available to the lender of long-term loan. It is expressed as pure ratio.

* Total assets include fixed assets as well as current assets.

** Long-term debts include the debts, which are payable after 1 year.

Proprietary Ratio

This ratio shows the relationship between proprietor's fund and total assets.

It is calculated as

$$\text{Proprietary ratio} = \frac{\text{Proprietor's fund or Shareholder's fund}}{\text{Total assets (excluding fictitious asset)}}$$

The objective of computing the proprietary ratio is to measure the proportion of total assets financed by equity or proprietor's fund.

Interest Coverage Ratio

The ratio expresses the relationship between the net profit before interest and tax and interest payable on long-term debts.

This is determined as follows

$$\text{Interest coverage ratio} = \frac{\text{Net profit before interest and tax}}{\text{Fixed interest charges}}$$

This ratio is computed with the objective to ascertain the amount of profit available to cover the interest charge.

Activity Ratios

Activity ratios are also known as performance or turnover ratio. These ratios express the operational capabilities of enterprise. This ratio are expressed as number of times. Higher the ratio, better the utilisation of resources.

These are as follows

Stock Turnover Ratio or Inventory Turnover Ratio

It express relationship between the cost of goods sold during the year and the average amount of inventory carried during that period.

It is calculated as under

$$\text{Stock turnover ratio} = \frac{\text{Cost of goods sold}}{\text{Average stock or Inventory}}$$

Cost of goods sold = Opening stock + Net purchases
+ Direct expenses − Closing stock

Or

Cost of goods sold = Net sales – Gross profit

$$\text{Average stock} = \frac{\text{Opening stock} + \text{Closing stock}}{2}$$

This ratio is computed to know whether the required amount is invested in the security or not.

Debtor's Turnover Ratio or Trade Receivable Turnover Ratio

Debtor's turnover ratio establishes the relationship between net credit sales and average debtors of the year.

This ratio is ascertained as follows

$$\text{Debtor's turnover ratio} = \frac{\text{Net credit sales}}{\text{Average debtors}}$$

It is expressed in 'times'.

Net credit sales = Credit sales – Sales return

Average debtors

$$= \frac{\text{Opening debtors} + \text{Opening bills receivable} + \text{Closing debtors} + \text{Closing bills receivable}}{2}$$

In case, the opening and closing debtors are not given and information about the sales are not available, *then compute the ratio as*

$$\text{Debtor's turnover ratio} = \frac{\text{Total sales}}{\text{Debtors}}$$

Debt Collection Period or Average Collection Period (ACP) It calculates the approximate time that it takes to collect debts.

$$\text{Debt collection period} = \frac{\text{365 Days}}{\text{Debtor's turnover ratio}}$$

= .... Days

Or

$$= \frac{\text{12 Months}}{\text{Debtor's turnover ratio}}$$

= .... Months

Creditor's Turnover Ratio

Creditor's turnover ratio expresses the relationship between net credit purchases and average payables.

It is calculated as under

$$\text{Creditor's turnover ratio} = \frac{\text{Net credit purchases}}{\text{Average payable}}$$

Average payable

$$= \frac{\text{Opening creditors} + \text{Opening bills payable} + \text{Closing creditors} + \text{Closing bills payable}}{2}$$

Net credit purchase

= Credit purchase – Purchase return

$$\text{Average payment period} = \frac{\text{12 Months}}{\text{Creditor's turnover ratio}}$$

= .... Months

Or

$$= \frac{\text{365 Days}}{\text{Creditor's turnover ratio}}$$

= ....Days

Capital Turnover Ratio

This ratio shows the efficiency of capital employed in the business by computing how many times capital employed is turned -over in a stated period.

This ratio is ascertained as follows

$$\frac{\text{Sales}}{\text{Capital employed (}\textit{i.e.,}\text{ Shareholder's fund + Long-term liabilities)}}$$

Fixed Assets Turnover Ratio

This ratio measures the efficiency of the usage of assets. The efficient use of assets will generate greater sales per rupee invested in all the assets of a concern.

It is calculated as under

$$\frac{\text{Sales}}{\text{Net fixed assets (}\textit{i.e.,}\text{ Fixed assets} - \text{Depreciation)}}$$

Working Capital Turnover Ratio

This ratio shows the number of times working capital is turned over in a stated period.

$$\frac{\text{Sales}}{\text{Net working capital (Current assets} - \text{Current liabilities)}}$$

This ratio is computed to ascertain whether the working capital is utilised effectively for making sales or not.

Profitability Ratios

The profitability ratio refers to ability of the firm to earn profit. *Some of the profitability ratios are as follows*

Gross Profit Ratio

The gross profit ratio establishes the relationship of gross profit on sales to net sales of a firm.

It is calculated as follows

$$\text{Gross profit ratio} = \frac{\text{Gross profit}}{\text{Net sales}} \times 100$$

Net sales = Cash sales + Credit sales – Sales return

Gross profit = Net sales – Cost of goods sold *

* Cost of goods sold

= Opening Stock + Purchases + Direct expenses – Closing stock

The gross profit ratio is a reliable guide for fixing selling prices and efficiency of trading activities.

Operating Ratio

Operating ratio is computed to express the relationship between operating costs and net sales.

It is calculated as under

Operating ratio

$$= \frac{\text{Cost of goods sold} + \text{Operating expenses}}{\text{Net sales}} \times 100$$

Or $$= \frac{\text{Operating cost}}{\text{Net sales}} \times 100$$

Cost of goods sold

$$= \text{Opening stock} + \text{Purchases} + \text{Direct expenses} - \text{Closing stock}$$

Or $= \text{S} - \text{Gross profit}$

Operating expenses = Administrative expenses + Selling and distribution expenses + Interest on short-term loans + Discount allowed and bad debts

It tests the operational efficiency of the business.

Operating Profit Ratio

Operating profit ratio expresses the relationship between operating profit and net sales.

It is calculated as under

$$\text{Operating profit ratio} = \frac{\text{Operating profit}}{\text{Net sales}} \times 100$$

Operating profit = Net profit + Non-operating expenses – Non-operating income

Net sales = Cash sales + Credit sales – Sales return

This ratio is computed to determine the operational efficiency of the business. This ratio judges the profitability of the concern.

Net Profit Ratio

Net profit ratio establishes the relationship between net profit and sales.

$$\text{Net profit ratio} = \frac{\text{Net profit}}{\text{Net sales}} \times 100$$

Net Profit Can be Taken

Before tax | After tax

- $$\text{Net profit ratio} = \frac{\text{Net profit before tax}}{\text{Net sales}} \times 100$$

Or $$= \frac{\text{Net profit after tax}}{\text{Net sales}} \times 100$$

The net profit ratio is an indicator of overall efficiency of the business. The higher the ratio, better it is for the business.

Return on Investment (RoI) or Return on Capital Employed Ratio

Return on capital employed ratio establish the relationship of profit before interest and tax with capital employed.

It is calculated as under

Return on capital employed

$$= \frac{\text{Net Profit before interest, tax and dividend}}{\text{Capital employed}} \times 100$$

Capital employed

= Equity share capital + Preference share capital + Reserve and surplus + Long-term loans – Miscellaneous expenditure – Non-operating assets

Or

Capital employed = Fixed assets + Working capital

It judges the overall performance of enterprise. It measures how efficiently the resources are used in the business.

Expenses Ratio

These are calculated to ascertain the relationship that exists between operating expenses and volume of sales.

The following ratios will help in analysing operating ratio

- $$\text{Material consumed ratio} = \frac{\text{Material consumed}}{\text{Net sales}} \times 100$$
- Conversion cost ratio
$$= \frac{\text{Labour expenses} + \text{Manufacturing expenses}}{\text{Net sales}} \times 100$$
- Administrative expenses ratio
$$= \frac{\text{Administrative expenses}}{\text{Net sales}} \times 100$$

Earning Ratios

These ratios are calculated in respect of those companies, whose shares are treated on the stock exchanges. Shareholders are not only interested in the profits of the company, but also in the appreciation of the value of their shares in the stock exchange market. *The following ratios reflect the effect of dividend declared, the payment policy etc on the market value of the shares*

Earning Per Share

This helps in determining the market price of the equity shares of the company and in estimating the company's capacity to pay dividend to its equity shareholders.

It is calculated as

Earning per share

$$= \frac{\text{Net profit after tax and preference dividend}}{\text{Number of equity shares}}$$

Price Earning Ratio

This ratio indicates the market value of every earning in the firm and is compared with industry average.

It is computed by the following formula

$$\text{Price earning ratio} = \frac{\text{Market price per equity share}}{\text{Earning per share}}$$

Dividend Yield Ratio

This ratio is important for those investors, who are interested in the dividend income.

This is computed as under

$$\text{Dividend yield ratio} = \frac{\text{Dividend per share}}{\text{Market price per share}} \times 100$$

Pay-out Ratio

This ratio indicates as to what proportion of earning per share has been used for paying dividend and what has been retained for ploughing back.

This is determined as follows

$$\text{Payout ratio} = \frac{\text{Dividend per equity share}}{\text{Earning per share}}$$

Earning Yield Ratio

The earning yield which is the inverse of the P/E ratio. This yield is used by many investment managers to determine optional asset allocations. *It is calculated as*

$$\frac{\text{Earning per share}}{\text{Market price per share}} \times 100$$

Leverage Ratios

These ratios explain the extent to which the debt is employed in the capital structure of the concerns.

Leverage ratios can be of two types

Operating Leverage

It occurs, when with fixed costs the percentage change in profits due to change in sales volume. It shows the extent of the change in earnings before interest and tax as a result of change in sales volume.

It is calculated as

$$\text{Operating leverage} = \frac{\text{Marginal contribution}}{\text{Earning before interest and tax}}$$

Financial Leverage

It tells the extent of the change in earnings before tax due to change in operating income.

It is calculated with the help of the following formula

$$\text{Financial leverage} = \frac{\text{Earnings before interest and tax}}{\text{Earning before tax}}$$

Fund Flow Analysis

Meaning of Funds

In the broader sense, it includes all resources used in the business whether in the form of men, material, money, machinery, methods etc. In the narrow sense, funds include only cash resources of the business. But with reference to the preparation of the funds flow statement, it is referred to working capital, *i.e.* the difference between the current assets and current liabilities.

Meaning of Flow of Funds

Whenever, there is change in the funds, it is presumed that flow of funds has taken place. Transactions that increase working capital into the enterprise are application of funds. On the other hand, if the working capital decreases, it is a source of funds.

Change in Working Capital

The following transactions will bring the change in the working capital

Current Assets and Non-current Assets Whenever in any transaction one aspect affects the current assets and the other non-current assets, there will be flow in the working capital. *e.g.* when machinery is purchased for cash, non-current assets will increase and current assets will reduce without any corresponding change in current liabilities. So, working capital will decrease.

Current Assets and Non-current Liabilities If in any transaction, one aspect affects the current assets and the other non-current liabilities, there will be flow in the working capital. *e.g.* if equity shares are issued for cash, it will increase current assets (cash) without any corresponding increase in current liabilities (equity share capital), there is increase in working capital.

Current Liabilities and Non-current Liabilities If in any transaction, one aspect affects the current liabilities and the other non-current liabilities, there will be flow in the working capital. *e.g.* if debentures are issued to the creditors, it will increase the non-current liabilities and decrease the current liabilities without any change in current assets; so there will be increase in the working capital.

Current Liabilities and Non-current Assets If in any transaction, one aspect the current liabilities and the other non-current assets, there will be flow in the working capital. *e.g.* if building is purchased on credit, it will increase the non-current assets and also current liabilities; so there will be decrease in the working capital.

Features of Fund Flow Analysis

- The fund flow analysis reflect the movement of funds and is report of the financial operations of the business undertaking . This statement reflects the sources and application of funds.
- Under cash flow statement, only cash transactions are gets recorded, but under fund flow statement sources and application of fund got recorded in whatever form they exists.
- Accordingly, "Fund flow statement is a either prospective or retrospective setting out the sources and application of the funds of an enterprise. The purpose of the statement is to indicate clearly the requirement of funds and how they are proposed to be raised and the efficient utilisation and application of the same."

Procedure for Preparing the Fund Flow Statement

In fund flow analysis, we can study about the change, which is affected between the two balance sheet dates.

Hence, the preparation of fund flow consists of two parts

- Schedule of changes in working capital .
- Statement of sources and application of funds.

Schedule of Changes in Working Capital

Particulars	Previous Year	Current Year	Effect on Working Capital	
			Increase	Decrease
Current Assets				
Cash in Hand	...	...	...	...
Cash at Bank	...	...	...	...
Bills Receivable	...	...	...	...
Sundry Debtors	...	...	...	...
Marketable Investments	...	...	...	...
Stock/Inventory	...	...	...	...
Prepaid Expenses	...	...	...	...
Accrued Income	...	...	...	...
A. **Total Current Assets**	...	...	...	...
Current Liabilities				
Bills Payable	...	...	...	...
Sundry Creditors	...	...	...	...
Outstanding Expenses	...	...	...	...
Bank Overdraft	...	...	...	...
Short-term Advances	...	...	...	...
Dividend Payable	...	...	...	...
Proposed Dividend	...	...	...	...
Provision for Taxation	...	...	...	...
B. **Total Current Liabilities**	...	...	...	...
C. **Working Capital** (A– B) (Current assets – Current liabilities)	...	...		
D. **Net Increase or Decrease in Working Capital**	...	...		

Statement of Sources and Application of Funds

Fund flow statement is a statement, which reflect the sources, from where fund is obtained and the uses of these funds.

It can be prepared in two formats

Statement Form

Fund Flow Statement

Particulars	Amt (₹)
Sources of Funds	...
Funds from Operation	...
Issue of Share Capital	...
Raising of Long-term Loans	...
Sale of Fixed Assets	...
Sale of Investments	...
Receipts from Partly Paid-up Shares	...
Non-operating Income (*i.e.* dividend, interest received)	...
Decrease in Working Capital	...
Total	...
Application of Funds	
Funds Lost in Operations	...
Redemption of Debenture	...
Redemption of Preference Shares	...
Repayment of Long-term Loans	...
Purchase of Fixed Assets	...
Purchase of an Investment	...
Non-operating Expenses	...
Payment of Dividends	...
Payment of Tax	...
Increase in Working Capital	...
Total	...

Account Form

Fund Flow Statement
(for the year ended on ....)

Sources	Amt (₹)	Applications	Amt (₹)
Funds from Operation	...	Funds Lost in Operation	...
Issue of Share Capital	...	Redemption of Preference Share Capital	...

Sources	Amt (₹)	Applications	Amt (₹)
Issue of Debentures	...	Redemption of Debenture	...
Raising of Long-term Loans	...	Repayment of Long-term Loan	...
Receipts from Partly Paid-up Shares	...	Purchase of Fixed Assets	...
Sale of Fixed Assets	...	Purchase of an Investment	...
		Non-operating Expenses	...
Non-operating Income	...	Payment of Dividends	...
Sale of Investments	...	Payment of Tax	...
Net Decrease in Working Capital	...	Net Increase in Working Capital	...
	...		...

Computation of Funds from Operations

Particulars	Amt (₹)
Closing Balance of Profit and Loss A/c (As per balance sheet)	...
(+) **Non-cash and Non-operating Item, which is Debited to Profit and Loss A/c**	
(i) Depreciation and Depletion	...
(ii) Amortisation of Intangible Assets and Fictitious Assets, *such as*	
(a) Preliminary Expenses	...
(b) Goodwill	...
(c) Patents	...
(d) Trademarks	...
(e) Copyright	...
(f) Discount on Issue of Debentures etc.	...
(iii) Appropriation of Retained Earning, *such as*	
(a) Transfer to General Reserves	...
(b) Dividend Equalisation Fund	...
(c) Transfer to Sinking Fund	...
(d) Contingency Reserves etc.	...
(iv) Loss on Sale of Fixed Assets, *such as*	
(a) Sale of Land and Building	...
(b) Sale of Machinery	...
(c) Sale of Furniture	...
(d) Sale of Long-term Investments etc	...
(v) Dividend, *such as*	
(a) Interim Dividend	...
(b) Proposed Dividend (if it is an appropriation of profit and not current liability)	...
(vi) Provision for Taxation (if it is not taken as current liabilities)	...
(vii) Other Item of Non-cash and Non-operating Item	...
Total (A)	...
(–) **Non-cash and Non-operating Item, which are Credited to Profit and Loss A/c**	
(i) Profit on Sale of Fixed Assets, *such as*	
(a) Sale of Land and Building	...
(b) Sale of Machinery	...
(c) Sale of Long-term Investments	...
(ii) Dividends Received	...
(iii) Excess Provision retransferred to Profit and Loss A/c or Written-off	...
(iv) Any other Non-operating Item	...
(v) Opening Balance of Profit and Loss A/c (as given in the balance sheet)	...
Total (B)	...
3. Total (A) – Total (B) Funds from Operation*	...

* *If the difference is positive, then it is classified as funds from operation, but if the difference is negative, it is classified as funds lost in operation.*

Computation of Issue of Share Capital When the company issues their shares, then it can be at par or premium and discount. As issue of share capital classified under the heading of sources of funds, hence the actual realisation will be as considered as amount against the issue of shares.

Issue of Debenture or Raising of Long-term Loans Proceeds from issue of debenture will be taken into consideration and raising of loan against the current asset should be taken as generation of funds.

Sale of Fixed Assets On the sale of fixed assets, the amount received as consideration is the source of funds.

Non-operating Income The income generates from the non-operating source like rent from property, interest from investment, dividend from investment etc.

Decrease in Working Capital Decrease in working capital of current year as compared to previous year means the amount blocked in working capital is released.

Funds Lost in Operation When the business suffers losses from their trading operations.

Redemption of Preference Share Capital The amount paid on the redemption of preference share capital is considered as outflow of funds or application of fund. It can be at premium or discount, hence amount should be taken into consideration.

Purchase of Fixed Assets The amount paid on purchase of fixed assets, such as land and building, plant and machinery etc will be considered as location of funds.

Payment of Dividend and Tax Actual payment of dividend and tax will be deemed as application of funds.

Notes

- *Issue of bonus share will not be considered under the heading of sources of funds.*

- *Shares issued for consideration other than cash will not be considered as sources of funds.*
- *Conversion of debenture into shares will not be considered as inflow of funds.*
- *Loan raised for purchase of fixed asset should not be considered as sources of fund.*
- *Sale of fixed asset as exchange for other should not be taken into account as sources of funds.*
- *If preference shares are redeemed in exchange of some other type of shares or debentures as it does not constitutes outflow of funds, hence not taken as application of funds.*
- *Here, declaration of dividends or creating of a provision for taxation will not be considered as application of funds.*
- *In case of sole proprietor, drawings considered as application of funds.*

Cash Flow Statement

Cash is the basic input needed to keep the operations of the business going on a continuing basis; it is also the final output expected to be realised by selling the product manufactured by the manufacturing unit. Cash is both the beginning and the end of the business operations. It is difficult to predict cash inflows and outflows accurately and there is not perfect coincidence between the inflows and outflows of cash giving rise to either cash outflows exceeding inflows or cash inflows exceeding cash outflows thus, cash flow statement is one of the important tool of cash management because it throws light on cash inflows and cash outflows of a particular period.

Meaning of Cash Flow Statement

A cash statements can be defined as a statement, which summarises sources of cash inflows and uses of cash outflows of a firm during a particular period of time, say a month or a year. Such a statement can be prepared from the data made available from comparative balance sheets, profit and loss statement and additional information.

Some features of cash flow statements are

- Cash flow statement highlights the factors that bring changes in cash position of an enterprise.
- *Cash flow statement are prepared under three heads*

(a) Cash Flow from Operating Activities

(b) Cash Flow from Investing Activities

(c) Cash Flow from Financing Activities

Uses of Cash Flow Statement

These are as follows

Helps in Understanding Liquidity and Solvency Cashflow statement helps to know whether the company is able to meet his liabilities or not.

Short-term Planning Cash flow statement provides information about sources and application of cash and cash equivalent for a specific period.

Efficient Cash Management Cash flow statement provides the information about the surplus or deficit of cash. If there is surplus, then it can be invested in some short-term investment and in case of deficit, it can be arrange from short-term credit.

Reasons for Cash Position Cash flow statement explains the reasons for lower and higher cash balances.

Limitations of Cash Flow Statement

- Non-cash transactions are ignored.
- It is historical in nature.
- It is not a substitute for income statement.
- Fundamental accounting concepts are ignored.

➡ **Note** *Cash equivalents are short-term liquid investment that are readily convertible into cash.*

Computation of Cash Flow from Operating Activities

Following are the computation of cash flow from operating activities

Step 1 Determine net profit before tax and extraordinary item

Net Profit before Tax and Extraordinary Item

	Difference in the closing and opening balance of statement of profit and loss account	...
(+)	Proposed dividend for the current year	...
	Interim dividend paid during the year	...
	Transfer to reserves	...
	Provision for tax made during the year	...
(–)	Refund of tax credited	...
	Extraordinary items, if any credited to the statement of profit and loss account	...
	Net profit before tax and extraordinary items	...

Step 2 Adjust net profit before tax and extraordinary item for non-cash and non-operating items.

Non-cash and Non-operating Expenses Depreciation, interest on long-term borrowing, discount on issue of debentures written-off, goodwill/patent/copyright, loss on sale of fixed assets or investment, premium payable on redemption of preference shares or debentures are added back.

Non-operating Income and Gains Profit on sale of fixed assets and investments, interest, rent or dividend received are deducted.

Step 3 Adjust operating profit before working capital for changes in working capital
↓ Current assets and ↑ Current liabilities are added.
↑ Current assets and ↓ Current liabilities are deducted.

Step 4 Deduct the income tax paid or add refund of income tax.

Step 5 Add or deduct extraordinary items.

Computation of Cash Flow from Investing Activities

Investing activities of an enterprise are acquisition and disposal of long-term assets and other investments not included in cash equivalent. *It can be calculated as under*

Dr **Fixed Assets Account** (At written down value) Cr

Particulars	Amt (₹)	Particulars	Amt (₹)
To Balance b/d	...	By Bank A/c (Sale of fixed assets)	...
To Bank A/c (Purchases)	...	By Profit and Loss A/c (Loss on sale)	...
To Profit and Loss A/c (Profit on sale)	...	By Depreciation A/c	...
		By Balance c/d	...

Dr **Fixed Assets at Cost** Cr

Particulars	Amt (₹)	Particulars	Amt (₹)
To Balance b/d	...	By Bank A/c (Sale of fixed assets)	...
To Bank A/c (Purchases)	...	By Accumulated Depreciation A/c (Accumulated depreciation on fixed assets sold)	...
To Profit and Loss A/c (Profit on sale)	...	By Profit and Loss A/c (Loss on sale)	...
		By Balance c/d	
			...

Dr **Accumulated Depreciation Account** Cr

Particulars	Amt (₹)	Particulars	Amt (₹)
To Fixed Assets A/c (Accumulated depreciations on fixed assets sold)	...	By Balance b/d	...
To Balance c/d	...	By Profit and Loss A/c (Depreciation charged for current year)	...
	...		...

Computation of Cash Flow from Financing Activities

Financing activities of an enterprise includes those activities which results into change in the size and composition of owner's capital and borrowing of the enterprise. It includes proceeds from issue of shares or other similar instruments, issue of debenture, loans, bonds, other short-term or long-term borrowing and repayment of amounts borrowed. *These are as follows*

Proposed Dividend

Of current year → Add back to current year profit

Of previous year → Deduct net dividend paid

Interim Dividend

Add to current year profits

Show as cash outflow from financing activities

Format of Cash Flow Statement (Indirect Method)
(for the year ended on........)
As per AS-3

	Particulars	Amt (₹)
I.	**Cash Flow from Operating Activities**	
	Net Profit as per Statement of Profit and Loss or difference between Closing Balance and Opening Balance of Statement of Profit and Loss Account	...
(+)	Transfer to Reserves	...
	Proposed Dividend for Current Year	...
	Interim Dividend paid during the year	...
	Provision for Tax made during the Current Year	...
	Extraordinary item, if any, Debited to the Statcment of Profit and Loss	...
(–)	Extraordinary item,if any, Credited to the Statement of Profit and Loss	(...)
	Refund of Tax, Credited to the Statement of Profit and Loss	(...)
(A)	Net Profit before Taxation and Extraordinary Item	...
	Adjustment for Non-cash and Non-operating Items	...
(B)		
(+)	**Items to be Added**	
	Depreciation	...
	Preliminary Expenses/ Discount on issue of Shares and Debenture written-off	...
	Interest or Borrowings and Debentures	...
	Goodwill, Patents and Trademarks Amortised	...
	Loss on Sale of Fixed Assets	...
(C)		
(–)	**Items to Deducted**	
	Interest Income	(...)
	Dividend Income	(...)
	Rental Income	(...)
	Profiting Sale of Fixed Assets	(...)

	Particulars	Amt (₹)
(D)	Operating Profit before Working Capital Changes (A + B – C)	
(E)		
(+)	Decrease in Current Assets and	...
	Increase in Current Liabilities	...
(F)		
(–)	Increase in Current Assets and	(...)
	Decrease in Current Liabilities	(...)
(G)	Cash generated from operation (D + E – F)	
(–) (H)	Income Tax Paid (Net of tax refund received)	(...)
(I)	Cash Flow before extraordinary Items(+/–)	.../(...)
(J)	Net Cash from (or used in) Operating Activities	...
II.	**Cash Flow Investing Activities**	
	Proceeds from Sale of Fixed Assets	...
	Proceeds from Sale of Investments	...
	Proceeds from Sale of Intangible Assets	...
	Interest and Dividend Received (for non-financial companies only)	...
	Rent Income	...
	Purchases of Fixed Assets	...
	Purchases of Investments	...
	Purchases of Intangible Assets like goodwill	...
	Extraordinary Item (+/–) Net Cash from (or used in) Investing Activities	...
III.	**Cash Flow from Financing Activities**	
	Proceeds from Issue of Shares and Debentures	...
	Proceeds from other Long-term Borrowings	...
	Final Dividend paid	...
	Interim Dividend paid	...
	Interest on Debentures and Loans paid	...
	Repayment of Loans	...
	Redemption of Debentures/ Preference Shares	...
	Extraordinary Item (+/–)	.../(...)
	Net Cash from (or used in) Financing Activities	...
IV.	**Net Increases/Decreases in Cash and Cash Equivalent** (I+II+III)	
(+)	Cash and Cash equivalents in the beginning of the year	...
	Cash in Hand	...
	Cash at Bank	...
	Short-term Deposits	...
	Marketable Securities	...
V.	**Cash and Cash Equivalent at the End of the Year**	
	Cash in Hand	...
	Cash at Bank	...
	(–) Bank Overdraft	(...)
	Short-term Deposits	...
	Marketable Securities	...

Difference between Fund Flow Statement and Cash Flow Statement

Concept

Fund flow statement is based on the concept of working capital, whereas cash flow statement is based on the concept of cash.

Term

Fund flow analysis is more relevant and useful in long-term financial strategy, while cash flow analysis is useful in short-term phenomena.

Operating Profit

In a fund flow statement, operating net profit are shown separately as sources of funds, whereas in cash flow statements, it is included in cash flow from operating activities.

View Points

The fund flow statement shows the causes of the changes in net working capital, whereas the cash flow statement shows the causes for the change in cash.

Basis of Accounting

Fund flow statement is related with the accrual basis of accounting, while in the cash flow statement, data obtained on accrual basis are converted into the cash basis. *e.g.* cash flow.

Illustration From the following balance sheet of Reeta Ltd. Prepare cash flow statement.

Balance sheet
as at ......

Liabilities	2017	2018	Assets	2017	2018
Equity Share Capital	4,50,000	5,00,000	Goodwill	1,10,000	90,000
Profit and Loss A/c	70,000	1,20,000	Building	1,50,000	2,00,000
Proposed Dividend	40,000	50,000	Plant	1,30,000	2,00,000
Creditors	70,000	95,000	Current Assets	2,50,000	3,07,000
Tax Provision	40,000	50,000	Cash	30,000	18,000
	6,70,000	8,15,000		6,7,0000	8,15,000

Additional Information

- Income tax ₹ 38,000 was paid during the year.
- Depreciation provided on plant during the year ₹ 30,000.

Solution

Cash Flow Statement

	Particulars		Amt (₹)
A.	**Cash Flow from Operating Activities**		
	Net Profit before Tax		1,48,000
(+)	Non-cash and Non-operating Expenses		
	Depreciation on Plant	30,000	
	Goodwill written-off	20,000	50,000
	Operating Profit of before Working Capital Changes		1,98,000
(+)	Increase in Creditors	25,000	
(–)	Increase in Current Assets	(57,000)	
(–)	Payment of Tax	(38,000)	(70,000)
	Cash Inflow from Operating Activities		1,28,000
B.	**Cash Flow from Investing Activities**		
(–)	Purchase of Building	(50,000)	
(–)	Purchase of Plant	(1,00,000)	
	Cash Outflow from Investing Activities		(1,50,000)
C.	**Cash Flow from Financing Activities**		
(+)	Issue of Equity Shares	50,000	
(–)	Payment of Proposed Dividend	(40,000)	
	Cash Outflow from Financing Activities		10,000
	Net Decrease in Cash and Cash Equivalents (A+B+C)		(12,000)
(+)	Opening balance of Cash and Cash Equivalents		30,000
	Closing Balance of Cash and Cash Equivalents		18,000

Working Notes

1. Calculation of Net Profit before Tax

	Particulars	Amt (₹)
	Increase in Profit and Loss A/c	50,000
(+)	Proposed Dividend	50,000
(+)	Provision for Tax	48,000
	Net Profit before Tax	1,48,000

2. Dr Plant Account Cr

Particulars	Amt (₹)	Particulars	Amt (₹)
To Balance b/d	1,30,000	By Depreciation A/c	30,000
To Bank A/c (Purchase)	1,00,000	By Balance c/d	2,00,000
	2,30,000		2,30,000

3. Dr Provision for Tax Account Cr

Particulars	Amt (₹)	Particulars	Amt (₹)
To Bank A/c (Tax paid)	38,000	By Balance b/d	40,000
To Balance c/d	50,000	By Profit and Loss A/c	48,000
	88,000		88,000

EXAM BASED QUESTIONS

Marginal Costing, Standard Costing and Process Costing

1 **Which one of the following cost would not be termed as product costs?**
(a) Administrative salaries
(b) Direct labour
(c) Indirect material
(d) Plant supervisor's salary

2 **Under marginal costing, only ...... costs are charged to products.**
(a) fixed (b) variable
(c) Both (a) and (b) (d) None of these

3 **Which is the best measurement by the centre's for the contribution of a profit centre to the overall profitability of the business in the long-run?**
(a) Taxable income
(b) Contribution margin
(c) Performance margin
(d) Responsibility margin

4 **Why is profit volume ratio used?**
1. To compute the variable cost for any volume of sales.
2. To determine break-even point and the level of output required to earn a desired profit.
3. To decide most profitable sales mix.

Select the correct answer using the codes given below
(a) Both 1 and 2 (b) Both 2 and 3
(c) Both 1 and 3 (d) All of these

5 **What is the effect of increase in fixed cost?**
(a) Reduces profit volume ratio
(b) Raises break-even point
(c) Increases margin of safety
(d) Reduces contribution

6 **Which of the following is correct at break-even point?**
(a) Contribution = Fixed assets
(b) Sales revenue = Total cost – Variable cost
(c) Profit = Fixed cost + Variable cost
(d) Sales revenue = Variable cost

7 **Break-even point is also known as ...... point.**
(a) total cost
(b) total revenue
(c) no profit no loss
(d) contribution

8 **The margin of safety may be defined as**
(a) the point at which break-even point sales are achieved
(b) the excess of planned sales over the current actual sales
(c) the extent to which sales revenue exceeds fixed costs
(d) the difference between planned sales and break-even point sales

9 **The break-even point in units is calculated using**
(a) fixed expenses and the contribution margin ratio
(b) variable expenses and the contribution margin ratio
(c) fixed expenses and the unit contribution margin
(d) variable expenses and the unit contribution margin

10 **An increase in fixed costs will result, in which of the following?**
(a) A decrease in the contribution sales ratio
(b) A decrease in the contribution per point
(c) An increase in the break-even point sales level
(d) An increase in the margin of safety

11 **In the context of standard costing; basic standard is established for**
(a) short period (b) current period
(c) indefinite period (d) predefined period

12 **A variable such as activity that causes cost over a given time is**
(a) cost driver (b) cost behaviour
(c) cost centre (d) None of these

13 **Process costing is used in which industry?**
(a) Manufacturing industries
(b) Mining industries
(c) Both (a) and (b)
(d) None of the above

14 **Which of the following system applies when standardised goods are produced under a series of operations?**
(a) Job order costing (b) Process costing
(c) Standard costing (d) Kaizen costing

15 **The statement prepared under process costing is called**
(a) cost of goods sold statement
(b) income statement
(c) cost of production report
(d) variance statement

16 **A process costing system is used by a company that**
(a) produces heterogeneous products
(b) produces items by special request of customers
(c) produces homogeneous products
(d) accumulates costs by job

17 **When partially completed units are converted to a comparable number of completed units, they are referred to as**
(a) split-off units (b) equivalent units
(c) converted units (d) equitable units

18 **In increasing production volume situation, the behaviour of fixed cost will be ...... and variable cost will ..... .**
(a) decreases, increases (b) increase, decreasing
(c) constant, increase (d) increase, constant

19 Under the marginal costing concept, unit product cost would most likely be increased by

(a) a decrease in the number of units produced
(b) an increase in the number of units produced
(c) an increase in the commission paid to salesman for each units sold
(d) a decrease in the commission paid to salesman for each units sold

20 Which inventory costing method is based on the assumption that costs should be charged against revenue in the order, in which they were incurred?

(a) Perpetual inventory (b) LIFO
(c) FIFO (d) Average cost

21 Profits can be increased by

1. decreasing the selling price per unit.
2. increasing the selling price per unit.
3. decreasing the volume of sales.
4. increasing the volume of sales.
5. decreasing the fixed or variable expenses.
6. increasing the fixed or variable expenses.
7. giving more weightage for products having higher P/V ratio.
8. giving less weightage for products having higher P/V ratio.

Select the correct answer using the codes given below

Codes

(a) 1, 3, 5 and 7 (b) 2, 4, 6 and 8
(c) 2, 4, 5 and 7 (d) 1, 3, 6 and 8

22 What is the most useful information derived from a break-even chart?

(a) Relationship between revenue and costs at various levels of output
(b) Volume or output level at which the enterprises break-even
(c) Amount of sales revenue needed to cover enterprise variable costs
(d) Amount of sales revenue needed to cover enterprise fixed costs

23 Portion of labour cost variance which is due to the difference between predetermined working days and actual working days is

(a) labour idle time variance (b) labour calender variance
(c) labour rate variance (d) labour efficiency variance

24 Which of the following accounts is similar to the inventory account of a merchandising company?

(a) Raw materials inventory
(b) Work-in-process inventory
(c) Finished goods inventory
(d) Manufacturing inventory

25 Consider the following statements.

1. Marginal costing and absorption costing are the same.
2. For decision-making, absorption costing is more suitable than marginal costing.
3. Marginal costing is based on the distinction between fixed and variable costs.

Which of the statement(s) given above is/are correct?

Codes

(a) Both 1 and 2 (b) Both 2 and 3
(c) Both 1 and 3 (d) None of these

26 If sales revenue at 60% capacity is ₹ 4,50,000, sales revenue at 70% capacity on a fall in selling price by 5% would be?

(a) ₹ 4,98,750 (b) ₹ 7,50,000
(c) ₹ 5,25,000 (d) ₹ 7,12,500

27 Which of the following are possible causes of material price variance?

1. Change in market price.
2. Use of poor quality of material.
3. Inefficient buying.
4. Untimely buying.
5. Paying overtime for urgent work.
6. Use of substitute material of different prices.

Select the correct answer using the codes given below

Codes

(a) 1, 3, 4 and 6 (b) 2, 3, 5 and 6
(c) 3, 4, 5 and 6 (d) 1, 3, 5 and 6

28 If beginning work-in-process equivalent units are 2500 units, work done in current period equivalent units are 3800 units and ending work-in-process equivalent units are 5000 units, then complete equivalent units 8 in current period are

(a) 1800 units (b) 1500 units
(c) 1300 units (d) 1000 units

29 The cost of material that is not completely processed, would be found in which of the following inventory account on the balance sheet?

(a) Direct material inventory
(b) Work in-process inventory
(c) Finished goods inventory
(d) Supplier inventory

30 If the beginning balance in the raw materials inventory account for the month was ₹ 25,000, the ending balance was ₹ 22,000 and material used during the month was ₹ 1,30,000. What is the amount of materials purchased during the month?

(a) ₹ 1,77,000 (b) ₹ 1,30,000
(c) ₹ 1,27,000 (d) ₹ 1,33,000

31 If the beginning balance in raw materials inventory is ₹ 5,000, the ending balance is ₹ 3,500 and material of ₹ 60,000 was purchased, what is the amount of materials transferred to work-in-process inventory during the period?

(a) ₹ 58,500 (b) ₹ 60,000
(c) ₹ 61,500 (d) ₹ 68,500

ABC, Life Cycle Costing, Target Costing, JIT and Budgetary Control

32 In an activity based costing implementation, product's diverse demand is based on
(a) batch size (b) complexity
(c) process steps (d) All of these

33 The costing method in which fixed factory overheads are added to inventory is
(a) process costing (b) activity based costing
(c) marginal costing (d) standard costing

34 Target price is subtracted from per unit target operating income to calculate
(a) total current full cost
(b) total cost per unit
(c) target operating income per unit
(d) target cost per unit

35 The origin of Kaizen costing in
(a) India (b) Japan (c) China (d) France

36 Kaizen costing is applied to a product that is
(a) produced (b) under production
(c) targeted to produce (d) sold to customer

37 Life cycle costing
(a) is sometimes used as a basis for cost planning and product pricing
(b) includes only manufacturing costs incurred over the life of the product
(c) includes only manufacturing cost, selling expenses and distribution expense
(d) emphasises cost savings opportunities during the manufacturing cycle

38 Which aspect of business is affected the most by implementing JIT?
(a) Sales (b) Inventory
(c) Manpower requirement (d) Total maintenance

39 Why is cash budget prepared?
(a) It helps in cash management
(b) It helps in preparing balance sheet
(c) It is legally compulsory
(d) Both (a) and (c)

40 Which budget is prepared first of all?
(a) Cash budget (b) Master budget
(c) Budget for the key factor (d) Flexible budget

41 Which of the following is usually as long-term budget?
(a) Capital expenditure budget (b) Cash budget
(c) Sales budget (d) None of these

42 Cash budget is based on
(a) past performance (b) future estimates
(c) Both (a) and (b) (d) None of these

43 In proper capital budgeting analysis, we evaluate incremental
(a) cash flow (b) accounting income
(c) earnings (d) operating profit

44 Which of the following would be included in a cash budget?
(a) Patent amortisation
(b) Goodwill
(c) Dividends
(d) Depreciation charges

45 What may be the principle budget factor in case of plant?
(a) General shortage of power
(b) Shortage of experienced salesman
(c) Insufficient capacity
(d) All of the above

46 The concept of budget that requires all levels to work from scratch is
(a) flexible budget (b) total budget
(c) master budget (d) zero base budget

47 In an activity based cost system, an activity/unit of work or task with differentiated purpose will be classified as
(a) different task
(b) purpose cost
(c) an activity
(d) an allocation cost

48 An estimated price, which is expected to be paid by customers for particular market offering is classified as
(a) target price (b) target cost
(c) outsource price (d) offshore price

49 A technique, which accumulates and tracks costs of business function in value chain attributed to each market, offering from R and D to final customer support, is called
(a) product life cycle (b) life cycle budgeting
(c) life cycle costing (d) target costing

50 Which of the following involves receiving a required inventory item at the exact time needed?
(a) PERT (b) FOB
(c) JIT (d) ABC

51 The difference between fixed and variable cost has a special significance in the preparation of
(a) flexible budget (b) master budget
(c) cash budget (d) All of these

52 What is the basic difference between a static budget and a flexible budget?
(a) A static budget is based on one specific level of production and a flexible budget can be prepared for any production level within a relevant range
(b) A static budget is for an entire production, but a flexible budget is applicable only to a single department
(c) Flexible budget allow management latitude in meeting goals, whereas a static budget is based on a fixed standard
(d) A flexible budget considers only variable costs, but a static budget considers all costs

53 When is a business unit known to be a profit centre?
(a) If its operations or departments are not directly involved in revenue generating activities, but instead focus on elements of cost control
(b) If its management is evaluated not only on revenues and expenses, but also on asset investment
(c) If its management is compensated based on the level of profitability
(d) If its management is held accountable for both revenues and expenses and has the authority to make decision regarding its products, markets and source of supply

Financial Statement Analysis

54 What is a serious limitation of financial ratio?
(a) Ratios are not predictive
(b) Ratios indicate weakness only
(c) Ratios can be used only by themselves
(d) Ratios are screening devices

55 What does a low proprietary ratio indicates?
(a) Sound financial position (b) Weak financial position
(c) Both (a) and (b) (d) None of these

56 Debt equity ratio is a test of
(a) liquidity (b) profitability (c) solvency (d) turnover

57 What does a low stock turnover indicates?
(a) Managerial efficiency (b) Solvency
(c) Over-investment in stock (d) All of these

58 What is the ideal quick ratio?
(a) 1 : 1 (b) 2 : 1 (c) 3 : 1 (d) 4 : 1

59 Increase in the amount of creditors result in
(a) decrease in cash (b) increase in cash
(c) no changes in cash (d) None of these

60 What is not included in quick assets?
(a) Cash
(b) Gold
(c) Inventories
(d) Advance for supply of raw materials

61 Price earning ratio is useful to whom?
(a) Short-term creditors (b) Long-term creditors
(c) Shareholders (d) Both (a) and (b)

62 The ratio for testing immediate solvency is
(a) current ratio (b) liquidity ratio
(c) debt equity ratio (d) proprietary ratio

63 Working capital requirement of a sugar mill is assessed as per
(a) traditional method of lending
(b) turnover method
(c) cash budget method
(d) None of the above

64 A capital investment is one that
(a) has the prospect of long-term benefits
(b) has the prospect of short-term benefits
(c) applies only to investment in fixed assets
(d) All of the above

65 Fund flow refers to changes in
(a) application (b) sources
(c) Both (a) and (b) (d) working capital

66 An examination of the sources and uses of funds is a part of
(a) ratio analysis
(b) fund flow analysis
(c) forecasting technique
(d) calculation for preparing the balance sheet

67 Sale of investment in marketable securities implies
(a) a sources of funds (b) an application of funds
(c) no flow of funds (d) None of these

68 Depreciation on fixed assets implies
(a) an application of funds (b) a sources of fund
(c) no flow of funds (d) None of these

69 The purchase of machinery by issuing long-term notes payable should be reported as a
(a) non-cash investing and financing activity
(b) cash outflow in the operating activity
(c) cash outflow in the investing activity
(d) cash outflow in the financing activity

70 Which of the following is not an activity listed in the statement of cash flows?
(a) Financing activities (b) Operating activities
(c) Funding activities (d) Investing activities

71 Significant non-cash transactions are included in
(a) cash flow from operating activities
(b) cash flow from investing activities
(c) cash flow from financing activities
(d) None of the above

72 Which of the following is not a cash outflow?
(a) Increase in creditors
(b) Increase in debtors
(c) Increase in stock
(d) Increase in bills receivable

73 Cash from operation is equal to
(a) net profit plus decrease in current assets
(b) net profit plus increase in current assets
(c) net profit minus decrease in current assets
(d) None of the above

74 Cash flow statement is prepared from
(a) Balance Sheet (b) Profit and Loss A/c
(c) Additional information (d) All of these

75 Which of the following is an investing activity?
(a) Cash inflow from interest income
(b) Cash inflow from dividend income
(c) Cash outflow to acquire fixed assets
(d) All of the above

76 Which of the following is not a cash outflow for the firm?
(a) Taxes (b) Interest payments
(c) Dividends (d) Depreciation

77 Which category of ratios is useful in assessing the capital structure and long-term solvency of a firm?

(a) Activity ratio (b) Profitability ratio
(c) Leverage ratio (d) Liquidity ratio

78 What is the capital structure referred to as when equity shareholder's funds exceed the total of debentures and preference share capital?

(a) High geared (b) Low geared
(c) Evenly geared (d) None of these

79 Which of the following measures the best operating performance?

(a) Ratio of return on total assets
(b) Ratio of return of fixed assets
(c) Ratio of return on shareholder's equity
(d) All of the above

80 In a profitable firm, total sources of funds will always .... total uses of funds.

(a) be less than (b) be greater than
(c) be equal to (d) None of these

81 Which of the following affects the flow of funds?

(a) A transaction affecting both current account
(b) A transaction affecting both non-current account
(c) A transaction affecting current and non-current account
(d) None of the above

82 If provision for taxation is treated as a current liability, then payment of tax is

(a) an application of funds (b) a sources of funds
(c) no flow of funds (d) None of these

83 Which of the following is not included in estimating after tax incremental operating cash flows, for a project?

(a) Effects of inflation (b) Opportunity cost
(c) Sunk cost (d) None of these

84 Which of the following would increase the cash flow of a firm?

(a) A decrease in inventory
(b) An increase in debtors
(c) An increase in the prepaid expenses
(d) A decrease in income in advance

85 Cash flow statement is useful for financial planning.

(a) short-term
(b) long-term
(c) short-term as well as long-term
(d) None of the above

86 An inflow of cash would result from which of the following?

(a) The increase in an assets account other than cash
(b) The decrease in an assets account other than cash
(c) The decrease in an equity account
(d) The decrease in a liability account

87 In ratio analysis, 'proforma analysis' implies

(a) making a list of all the present ratios of the firm
(b) comparison of liquidity ratios with other kind of ratio of the firm
(c) comparison of the ratio of the firm relating to the performance of the firm
(d) comparison of the firm's past and current ratios with future ratios to ascertain the relative strengths and weakness in the past and future

88 In ratio analysis, 'time series analysis' refers to

(a) making a time series of various ratio to assess the firm's profitability
(b) a graphical comparison of the firm's sources of finance
(c) the comparison of financial ratios over a period of time to access the direction of change and the financial performance of the firm
(d) a comparison of time values for various ratios of the firm

89 When is the net present value negative,

(a) the present value of cash outflows is greater than the future value of cash outflows
(b) the future value of cash inflows is greater than the present value of cash outflows
(c) the present value of cash outflows is greater than the present value of cash inflows
(d) the present value of cash inflows is greater than the present value of cash outflows

90 Calculating ratio for industry analysis implies all of the following except,

(a) it is difficult to assess and rely on the average of ratios of the strong and weak firms in the industry
(b) it helps to assess the financial standing of the firm as compared to other firms in the same industry
(c) it is not possible to standardise the accounting data of various firms following varied accounting policies
(d) comparison of average of the industry with those of the firm

91 Why are the estimated benefits from a project are expressed as cash flows instead of income flows?

(a) It is cash, not accounting income, that is central to the firm's capital budgeting decision
(b) It is simple to calculate cash flows than income flows
(c) Both (a) and (b)
(d) None of the above

92 Arrange the following categories of cash inflows and cash outflows in a correct order.

1. Cash flows from investing activities.
2. Cash flows from financing activities.
3. Cash flows from operating activities.

Codes

(a) 3, 1, 2
(b) 1, 3, 2
(c) 3, 2, 1
(d) 2, 1, 3

Miscellaneous

Directions (Q. Nos. 93-102) *The following four items consist of two statements, Statement I and Statement II. You have to examine these two statements carefully and select the answer to these items using the codes given below.*

Codes

(a) Both statements are correct
(b) Both statements are incorrect
(c) Statement I is correct, but Statement II is incorrect
(d) Statement I is incorrect, but Statement II is correct

93 **Statement** I The stock of finished goods and work-in- progress are carried on marginal cost basis.

Statement II The fixed expenses are written-off to profit and loss account as period cost.

94 **Statement** I The contribution concept is based on the theory that the fixed expenses of a business is not a joint cost.

Statement II Fixed expenses are those expenses which can be equitably apportioned to different segment of the business.

95 **Statement** I The activities or operations of every cost centre should be homogeneous so as to ensure uniform basis of charging expenses within the center.

Statement II The activities or operations of each cost centres must not be well defined and clearly identifiable.

96 **Statement** I Margin of safety represents the difference between the sales at break-even point and the total sales.

Statement II Margin of safety can be expressed as a percentage of total sales or in value or in terms of quantity.

97 **Statement** I Segregation of expenses as fixed and variable helps the management to exercise control over expenditure.

Statement II The management can be compare the actual variable expenses with the budgeted variable expenses and take corrective action through variance analysis.

98 **Statement** I In fund flow analysis, current assets and current liabilities are shown separately in a statement known as statement of changes in working capital.

Statement II In cash flow analysis, increases and decreases of all current accounts are adjusted in the calculation of cash flow from operating activities.

99 **Statement** I At the time of replacement of plant, according to marginal cost technique, the proposal which yield lowest contribution is to be selected.

Statement II According to total cost technique, the proposal which involves the highest costs is to be selected.

100 **Statement** I If any fixed asset remains idle due to abnormal or unusual events, it should be included in capital employed.

Statement II But, idle machines and tools required for normal operation of plant would not be included in capital employed.

101 **Statement** I Target costing helps in minimising the cost of new products.

Statement II Target price = Sale price + Desired profit

102 **Statement** I JIT approach was developed in Japan.

Statement II JIT stands for just in time approach which is an inventory control system.

Directions (Q. Nos. 103-113) *In the questions given below are two statements labelled as Assertion (A) and Reason (R). In the context of the two statements, which one of the following is correct?*

Codes

(a) Both (A) and (R) are true and (R) is the correct explanation of (A)
(b) Both (A) and (R) are true, but (R) is not the correct explanation of (A)
(c) (A) is true, but (R) is false
(d) (A) is false, but (R) is true

103 **Assertion** (A) In management accounting, firm decisions on pricing policy can be taken.

Reason (R) As marginal cost per unit is constant from period to period within a short span of time.

104 **Assertion** (A) The business earns a surplus of sale revenue over variable costs, which is called contribution.

Reason (R) Once fixed costs are fully recovered such excess contribution is termed as profits.

105 **Assertion** (A) Profit volume ratio is considered to be the best indicator of the profitability of the business.

Reason (R) If profit volume ratio improved, it will result in better profits.

106 Assertion (A) Material cost variance is the difference between the standard cost of material allowed for the actual output and the actual cost of material used.

Reason (R) A favourable variance would result, if actual cost is less than standard cost.

107 Assertion (A) Acceptance of the special order at a low price should be kept secret.

Reason (R) The other customers may also demand a similar price cut or else threaten to cancel their orders.

108 Assertion (A) A current ratio of 2 : 1 is considered satisfactory as a rule of thumb, but it should not be followed blindly.

Reason (R) The greatest weakness of current ratio is the possibility of window dressing and manipulation.

109 Assertion (A) Cash flow statement enhances the comparability of report.

Reason (R) CFS eliminates the effect of using different treatments for same transactions.

110 Assertion (A) Cost accounting hides the relative efficiencies of different workers.

Reason (R) Cost accounting does not disclose profitable and unprofitable activities.

111 Assertion (A) Accounting ratios reveal the financial position of the concern.

Reason (R) Accounting ratios are not useful in assessing the operational efficiency.

112 Assertion (A) Higher the gross profit ratio, the better it is.

Reason (R) A low gross profit ratio indicates unfavourable trend in the form of reduction in selling prices.

113 Assertion (A) Funds are not related to working capital.

Reason (R) Flow of funds has taken place whenever there is change in the funds.

Directions (Q. Nos. 114-116) *In the questions given below are two statements labelled as Assertion (A) and Reason (R). In the context of the two statements, which one of the following in correct?*

Codes

(a) Both (A) and (R) are true
(b) Both (A) and (R) are false
(c) (A) is true, but (R) is false
(d) (A) is false, but (R) is true

114 Assertion (A) Overheads are recovered in costing based on predetermined rates.

Reason (R) This solves the problem of treatment of under recovery or over recovery of overhead.

115 Assertion (A) In the case of financial enterprise, interest paid and received should be classified as cash flow arising from investing activities.

Reason (R) In the case of other enterprise it should be classified as cash flow from operating activities.

116 Assertion (A) If the working capital at the end of the current year is more than the working capital at the end of previous year, the excess is called as 'Increase in working capital.'

Reason (R) Increase in working capital is shown as application of funds in the fund flow statement.

117 Assertion (A) Break-even point can be determined both mathematically as well as graphically.

Reason (R) When it is determined on a graph paper, the graph drawn is named as 'break-even chart'.

Codes

(a) (A) is true, but (R) is false
(b) (A) is false, but (R) is true
(c) Both (A) and (R) are true and (R) is the correct explanation of (A)
(d) Bothe (A) and (R) are true, but (R) is not the correct explanation of (A)

118 Match the following.

List I (Variances)	List II (Formulae)
A. MCV	1. SP (RSQ – AQ)
B. MPV	2. SP (SQ – AQ)
C. MUV	3. AQ consumed (SP – AP)
D. MMV	4. SC – AC

Codes

	A	B	C	D		A	B	C	D
(a)	4	3	2	1	(b)	2	1	4	3
(c)	4	1	2	3	(d)	3	4	2	1

119 Match the following.

List I (Variances)	List II (Causes)
A. Overhead efficiency variance	1. Power failure
B. Overhead volume variance	2. Appointing low grade employees
C. Labour idle time variance	3. Poor working condition
D. Labour efficiency variance	4. Working days being more or less than budgeted

Codes

	A	B	C	D
(a)	4	3	2	1
(b)	3	4	1	2
(c)	3	1	4	2
(d)	2	1	4	3

120 Match the following.

List I	List II
A. Labour cost variance	1. Actual hours paid (Standard rate – Actual rate)
B. Labour rate variance	2. Standard cost – Actual cost
C. Efficiency variance	3. Idle hours × Standard rate per hour
D. Idle time variance	4. Standard rate (Standard hours – Actual hours worked)

Codes

	A	B	C	D
(a)	4	3	2	1
(b)	2	3	4	1
(c)	4	1	2	3
(d)	2	1	4	3

121 Match the following.

List I	List II
A. Performance budgeting	1. Fixed budget
B. Zero base budgeting	2. Production oriented
C. Summary of all functional budgets	3. Jimmy Carter
D. Remain unchanged irrespective of level of activity actually attained	4. Master budget

Codes

	A	B	C	D
(a)	3	4	1	2
(b)	3	4	2	1
(c)	2	4	1	3
(d)	2	3	4	1

122 Match the following.

List I	List II
A. Prepaid expenses	1. Solvency ratio
B. Sales ratio	2. Net profit margin x Investment turnover
C. Return on investments	3. Turnover ratio
D. 100-Proprietary ratio	4. Current asset

Codes

	A	B	C	D
(a)	4	3	1	2
(b)	4	3	2	1
(c)	2	1	4	3
(d)	2	4	1	3

123 Match the following.

List I	List II
A. Increase in fund	1. Application of funds
B. Goods purchased on credit	2. Drain in working capital
C. Commission outstanding	3. Sources of funds
D. Net loss	4. No flow of funds

Codes

	A	B	C	D
(a)	4	3	2	1
(b)	4	3	1	2
(c)	3	4	1	2
(d)	3	4	2	1

124 Match the following.

List I	List II
A. Variable costing	1. Absorption costing
B. Valuation of stock is higher	2. Fixed cost is excluded from inventory valuation
C. Marginal and differential costs are same	3. Marginal costing
D. Marginal costing	4. No change in fixed cost

Codes

	A	B	C	D
(a)	3	4	1	2
(b)	3	1	4	2
(c)	4	3	1	2
(d)	4	3	2	1

125 Match the following.

List I	List II
A. Classification of costs into fixed and variable costs	1. Contribution
B. Difference between sales and variable costs	2. P/V ratio
C. Both fixed and variable costs are charged to product	3. Marginal costing
D. Relative profitability	4. Absorption costing

Codes

	A	B	C	D
(a)	4	3	1	2
(b)	3	4	1	2
(c)	3	1	4	2
(d)	4	3	2	1

126 Match the following.

List I	List II
A. Excess of actual sales over the break-even sales volume	1. Contribution
B. Sum of fixed cost and profit	2. Cost volume profit analysis
C. Break-even chart	3. Unaffected by change in output
D. Break-even point	4. Margin of safety

Codes

	A	B	C	D
(a)	4	1	2	3
(b)	4	3	2	1
(c)	4	3	1	2
(d)	3	1	4	2

127 Match the following.

List I	List II
A. Short-term	1. ......is a financing activity.
B. Current liabilities	2. Cash flow statement is useful for......financial planning.
C. Amount of creditors	3. Increase in......is´a source of cash.
D. Payment of dividends	4. Increase in the......results in increase in cash.

Codes

	A	B	C	D
(a)	4	3	2	1
(b)	2	3	4	1
(c)	3	2	4	1
(d)	3	4	1	2

128 Match the following.

List I	List II
A. Cost control purposes	1. .....is a predetermined cost
B. Standard cost	2. Responsibility accounting fixes responsibility for....
C. Integrates	3. Cost accounting guides future.......
D. Production policies	4. Budgeting system......key managerial functions

Codes

	A	B	C	D
(a)	4	3	2	1
(b)	2	1	4	3
(c)	2	3	4	1
(d)	3	2	4	1

129 Match the following.

List I	List II
A. Cost accounting	1. ....is usually prepared every month.
B. Funds flow statement	2. .....deals with the cost of production, selling and distribution.
C. Cash flow statement	3. .....is an important technique financial analysis.
D. Ratio analysis	4. .....depicts the profit or loss made during a specified period.

Codes

	A	B	C	D
(a)	4	3	2	1
(b)	2	1	4	3
(c)	4	3	1	2
(d)	3	4	2	1

130 Match the following.

List I	List II
A. Operating profit	1. Capital employed = ...+ Preference share capital
B. Liquid liabilities	2. ....= Gross profit − Operating expenses
C. Capital employed	3. Quick assets = Quick ratio × ......
D. Equity share capital	4. Fixed assets ratio = Fixed assets ÷ ....

Codes

	A	B	C	D
(a)	2	3	4	1
(b)	3	4	1	2
(c)	4	3	2	1
(d)	2	1	4	3

131 Match the following.

List I	List II
A. Absorption costing	1. .....is a logical extension of marginal costing.
B. Fixed expenses	2. .....is a valuable adjust to standard costing and budgetary costing.
C. Marginal costing	3. Contribution = ...+ Profit.
D. Break-even analysis	4. ....is not very helpful in taking managerial decisions.

Codes

	A	B	C	D
(a)	4	3	2	1
(b)	2	1	4	3
(c)	3	2	4	1
(d)	4	3	1	2

132 Match the following.

List I	List II
A. Marginal cost	1. .....= Contribution ÷ Sales
B. P/V ratio	2. Contribution = Selling price − ....
C. Profit	3. .... = Sales (1 − P/ V ratio)
D. Variable costs	4. Margin of safety = ... ÷ P/ V ratio

Codes

	A	B	C	D
(a)	4	3	2	1
(b)	3	1	4	2
(c)	2	1	4	3
(d)	2	3	4	1

PREVIOUS YEARS' QUESTIONS

December 2018

1 A company proposes to introduce a new product in the market. The company wants to maintain P/V ratio at 25%. If variable cost of the product is ₹ 300, then what will be the selling price?

(a) ₹ 100
(b) ₹ 200
(c) ₹ 300
(d) ₹ 400

July 2018

2 Which one of the following is not an example of 'financing activities' with reference to cash flow statement?

(a) Repayment of bank loan
(b) Interest on debentures/Dividend paid
(c) Cash proceeds from public deposits
(d) Sale of fixed assets

3 Which one of the following statements is true about estimated costs and standard costs ?

(a) Standard costs are based on scientific analysis and engineering studies, while estimated costs are based on historical basis
(b) Standard cost emphasis is on "what cost will be", while estimated cost emphasis is on "what cost should be"
(c) Standard costs are more frequently revised compared to estimated cost
(d) Estimated costs are more stable than standard costs

4 **Assertion** (A) A high operating ratio indicates a favourable position.

Reason (R) A high operating ratio leaves a high margin to meet non-operating expenses.

Codes

(a) (A) and (R) both are correct and (R) correctly explains (A)
(b) Both (A) and (R) are correct, but (R) does not explain (A)
(c) Both (A) and (R) are incorrect
(d) (A) is correct, but (R) is incorrect

November 2017

5 **Assertion** (A) Debt equity ratio indicates the long-term solvency of a company.

Reason (R) It measures the ability of the company to pay-off its long-term liabilities.

Codes

(a) Both (A) and (R) are correct and (R) is the correct reason for (A)
(b) Both (A) and (R) are correct, but (R) does not explain (A) correctly
(c) (A) is correct, but (R) is wrong
(d) (A) is wrong, but (R) is correct

6 Which one of the following is not correct with reference to standard costing?

(a) Standard costing is a system where predetermined costs are used for control of entire organisation
(b) Standard may be expressed in quantitative and monetary measures
(c) Only adverse variances are investigated intensively
(d) Standard is determined for each element of cost

7 Which one of the following is not correct?

(a) Margin of safety profit = $\dfrac{\text{Profit}}{\text{P / V ratio}}$

(b) P/V Ratio = $\dfrac{\text{Change in Contribution}}{\text{Change in sales}} \times 100$

(c) Break-even point in units = $\dfrac{\text{Fixed cost}}{\text{Contribution per unit}}$

(d) Required sales to earn desired profits = $\dfrac{\text{Desired profit}}{\text{P/V ratio}}$

January 2017

8 Match the items of List I with those of List II.

List I	List II
A. Acid test ratio	1. Profitability analysis
B. Debt service coverage ratio	2. Activity analysis
C. Debt equity ratio	3. Liquidity analysis
D. Stock turnover ratio	4. Long-term solvency analysis

Codes

	A	B	C	D		A	B	C	D
(a)	2	1	3	4	(b)	2	3	4	1
(c)	3	4	1	2	(d)	3	1	4	2

9 From the following two statements of Assertion (A) and Reason (R). Indicate the correct code.

Assertion (A) From the marginal costing approach point of view, the marginal cost is compared with the purchase price.

Reason (R) If the marginal cost is less than the purchase price, it should be purchased rather than manufactured.

Codes

(a) Both (A) and (R) are correct
(b) (A) is correct, but (R) is not correct
(c) (A) is not correct, but (R) is correct
(d) Both (A) and (R) are incorrect

10 Which one of the following statement is true about standard labour time?

(a) Standard labour time indicates the time in hours needed for a specific process
(b) It is standardised on the basis of past experience
(c) In fixing standard, time due allowance should not be given to fatigue and tool setting
(d) The production manager does not provide any input in setting the labour time standards

July 2016

11 Match the items in List I with the items in List II.

List I	List II
A. Debt equity ratio	1. $\frac{\text{Net Profit before Interest and Tax}}{\text{Interest on Long-term Loans}}$
B. Proprietary ratio	2. $\frac{\text{Equity Share Capital + Reserves}}{\text{Preference Share Capital + Interest Bearing Finance}}$
C. Interest coverage ratio	3. $\frac{\text{Long-term Debts}}{\text{Shareholder's Funds}}$
D. Capital gearing ratio	4. $\frac{\text{Shareholder's Funds}}{\text{Total Assets}}$

Codes

	A	B	C	D		A	B	C	D
(a)	1	2	3	4	(b)	3	4	1	2
(c)	3	4	2	1	(d)	2	3	4	1

12 From the following information, find out the number of units that must be sold by the firm to earn profit of ₹ 80,000 per year.

Sales price ₹ 25 per unit

Variable manufacturing costs = ₹ 12 per unit

Variable selling costs = ₹ 3 per unit

Fixed factory overheads = ₹ 5,00,000

Fixed selling costs = ₹ 3,00,000

(a) 60000 units (b) 88000 units
(c) 98000 units (d) 100000 units

13 Which of the following is not a cash inflow?

(a) Decrease in creditors (b) Decrease in debtors
(c) Issue of shares (d) Sale of a fixed asset

December 2015

14 X Ltd has a liquid ratio of 2 : 1. If its stock is ₹ 40,000 and its current liabilities are of ₹ 1,00,000, its current ratio will be

(a) 1.4 times (b) 2.4 times (c) 1.2 times (d) 3.4 times

15 'Comparison of the financial statements of the current year with the performance of previous years of the same firm' is known as

(a) trend analysis (b) horizontal analysis
(c) intra-firm comparison (d) All of these

16 Indicate the correct code as regards the sources of funds for a funds flow statement from the following

1. Increase in working capital.
2. Decrease in working capital.
3. Writing-off the intangible/fictitious assets.
4. Issuing equity shares for acquisition of a building for office.
5. Charging depreciation on fixed assets.

Select the correct answer using the codes given below

Codes

(a) 1, 3 and 4 (b) 2, 3 and 5
(c) 1, 4 and 5 (d) 2, 3 and 4

17 Match the following.

List I	List II
A. Debtor's turnover ratio	1. Solvency ratio
B. Proprietary ratio	2. Liquidity ratio
C. Operating ratio	3. Activity ratio
D. Acid test ratio	4. Profitability ratio

Codes

	A	B	C	D		A	B	C	D
(a)	2	4	3	1	(b)	3	2	1	4
(c)	3	1	4	2	(d)	4	3	2	1

18 **Assertion** (A) Cash flow statement as per the financial statements as well is incapable in revealing the overall financial position of a firm.

Reason (R) Cash is an important constituent of the working capital based on the recorded facts only.

Codes

(a) Both (A) and (R) are true and (R) is the correct explanation of (A)
(b) (A) is true, but (R) is not true
(c) (A) is not true, but (R) is true
(d) Both (A) and (R) are false

June 2015

19 The basic difference between a static budget and flexible budget is that

(a) a flexible budget considers only variable costs but a static budget considers all costs
(b) a flexible budgets allows management latitude in meeting goals, whereas static budget is based on fixed standards
(c) a flexible budget is applicable for a single department only but a static budget for entire production facility
(d) a flexible budget can be prepared for any production level within a relevant range but a static budget is based on one specific level of production

20 When opening stock is ₹ 50,000, closing stock is ₹ 60,000 and the cost of goods sold is ₹ 2,20,000, the stock turnover ratio is

(a) 2 times (b) 3 times
(c) 4 times (d) 5 times

21 If stock turnover ratio is 6 times

Average stock = ₹ 8,000

Selling price = 25% above cost

What is the amount of gross profit?

(a) ₹ 2,000 (b) ₹ 4,000
(c) ₹ 10,000 (d) ₹ 12,000

22 Labour rate of pay variance can be calculated by which one of the following equations?
(a) Budgeted labour costs – Actual labour costs
(b) Standard hours – Actual hours) × Actual wage rate
(c) Standard wage rate – Actual wage rate × Actual hours worked
(d) Standard wage rate – Actual wage rate × Standard hours worked

23 Given

Margin of Safety	₹ 80,000
Profit	₹ 20,000
Sales	₹ 3,00,000

What is the amount of fixed cost?
(a) ₹ 1,00,000 (b) ₹ 75,000
(c) ₹ 55,000 (d) ₹ 20,000

24 Which one of the following is not true of cash budget?
(a) The shortage or excess of cash would appear in a particular period
(b) All inflows would arise before outflows for those periods
(c) Only revenue nature cash flows are shown
(d) Proceeds from issue of share capital is shown as an inflow

25 What is economic order quantity?
(a) Cost of an order (b) Cost of stock
(c) Reorder level (d) Optimum order size

December 2014

26 Current ratio 2.5, liquid ratio 1.5 and working capital ₹ 60,000. What is current assets?
(a) ₹ 60,000 (b) ₹ 80,000 (c) ₹ 1,00,000 (d) ₹ 1,20,000

27 Accounting information given by a company is

Total assets turnover	3 times
Net profit margin	10%
Total assets	₹ 1,00,000

The net profit is
(a) ₹ 10,000 (b) ₹ 15,000 (c) ₹ 25,000 (d) ₹ 30,000

28 A flexible budget requires careful study and classification of expenses into
(a) product expenses and period expenses
(b) past and current expenses
(c) administrative, selling and factory expenses
(d) fixed, semi-variable and variable expenses

29 Return on Investment (RoI) is computed as
(a) Net profit ratio × Capital turnover ratio
(b) Operating net profit ratio × Shareholder's fund
(c) Net profit/Sales
(d) Cost of sales / Capital employed

30 Margin of safety is calculated by using
(a) $\frac{\text{Profit}}{\text{P / V ratio}}$ (b) $\frac{\text{Fixed cost}}{\text{Contribution}}$
(c) $\frac{\text{Break-even sales}}{\text{Sales}}$ (d) $\frac{\text{Profit}}{\text{Sales}}$

June 2014

31 Marginal costing technique is useful for
(a) make or buy decisions (b) profit planning
(c) shut-down decisions (d) All of these

32 Which one is not a feature of budgetary control?
(a) A tool for management control
(b) An instrument of delegation and authority
(c) An instrument for evaluating the over all performance
(d) A statement of budget and forecasts

33 The debt-equity Ratio of a company is 2:1. In this relation, match the following.

List I	List II
A. Issue of equity shares	1. No change on the ratio
B. Cash received from debtors	2. Reduce the ratio
C. Redemption of debentures	3. No change on the ratio
D. Purchased goods on credit	4. Reduce the ratio

Codes

	A	B	C	D		A	B	C	D
(a)	1	2	3	4	(b)	2	3	4	1
(c)	1	3	4	2	(d)	2	4	1	3

34 Which is not the limitation of budgetary control?
(a) Budgets are based on forecasts which may not be true
(b) Installation and operation of a system of budgetary control is costly
(c) Budget is a tool of management and not a substitute of management
(d) Budgets do not pinpoint the lack of efficiency or the presence of it

35 Profit volume ratio of an enterprise is 40%. To offset 10% decrease in selling price, how much sales must be increased?
(a) 10% (b) 20%
(c) 25% (d) 40%

36 If debt is ₹ 220, cash balance is ₹ 20 and equity is ₹ 300, then the gearing ratio is
(a) 20% (b) 40%
(c) 50% (d) 30%

December 2013

37 Improvement of profit volume ratio can be done by
(a) increasing selling price (b) altering sales mixture
(c) reducing variable cost (d) All of these

38 **Assertion** (A) Increasing the value of closing inventory increases profit.
Reason (R) Increasing the value of closing inventory reduces cost of goods sold.
Codes
(a) Both (A) and (R) are true
(b) (A) is true, but (R) is false
(c) (A) is false, but (R) is true
(d) Both (A) and (R) are false

June 2013

39 Master budget is a
(a) functional budget (b) operating budget
(c) summary budget (d) financial budget

40 Which of the following comes under efficiency ratios ?
(a) Average collection period
(b) Inventory turnover ratio
(c) Fixed assets turnover ratio
(d) All of the above

41 Match the following.

List I	List II
A. Statement of changes in working capital	1. Cash flow statement
B. Deferred tax	2. Fixed assets
C. Three activities	3. Fund flow statement
D. Impairment loss	4. Balance sheet

Codes

	A	B	C	D		A	B	C	D
(a)	1	2	3	4	(b)	3	4	2	1
(c)	3	4	1	2	(d)	4	3	1	2

42 Match the following.

List I	List II
A. Earning ability of firm	1. Basis of accounting
B. Conservatism	2. P/V ratio
C. Cash profit	3. Cash flow statement
D. Cash and accrual	4. Prudence

Codes

	A	B	C	D		A	B	C	D
(a)	2	4	3	1	(b)	2	1	4	3
(c)	3	4	1	2	(d)	3	4	2	1

Directions (Q. Nos. 43 and 44) *In the following questions given below are two statements labelled as Assertion (A) and Reason (R). In the context of two statements, which one of the following is correct?*

Codes
(a) Both (A) and are true and (R) is the correct explanation of (A)
(b) Both (A) and (R) are true, but (R) is not the correct explanation of (A)
(c) (A) is true, but (R) is false
(d) (R) is true, but (A) is false

43 **Assertion** (A) Only the relevant costs should be taken into consideration for decision-making.
Reason (R) All variable costs are relevant costs and all fixed costs are irrelevant costs.

44 **Assertion** (A) Variance analysis is undertaken for planning and control of costs.
Reason (R) Future costs are taken into consideration in budgeting and standard costing.

December 2012

45 Which one of the following concepts is used as fund in the preparation of funds flow statement?
(a) Current Assets
(b) Working Capital
(c) Cash
(d) All Financial Resources

46 **Assertion** (A) Ratio analysis is one of the tools employed to know the financial health of a concern.
Reason (R) Ratio analysis is not the only technique available to take investment decision.
Codes
(a) Both (A) and (R) are true and (R) is the correct explanation of (A)
(b) Both (A) and (R) are true, but (R) is not the correct explanation of (A)
(c) (A) is true, but (R) is false
(d) (A) is false, but (R) is true

47 Which of the following relate to measures of non-financial performance of a concern ?
1. Customer satisfaction
2. Business process improvement
3. Economic value added
4. Learning organisation
Select the correct answer using the codes given below
Codes
(a) 1, 2 and 4 (b) 2, 4 and 3
(c) 4, 1 and 3 (d) All of these

48 **Assertion** (A) Marginal cost and differential cost do not convey the same meaning in all the circumstances.
Reason (R) Differential cost increases or decreases due to change in fixed cost.
Codes
(a) Both (A) and (R) are true and (R) is the correct explanation of (A)
(b) Both (A) and (R) are true, but (R) is not the correct explanation of (A)
(c) (A) is true, but (R) is false
(d) (A) is false, but (R) is true

49 When the debt turnover ratio is 4, what is the average collection period?
(a) 5 months (b) 4 months (c) 3 months (d) 2 months

50 In marginal costing, contribution is equal to
(a) Sales – Fixed cost
(b) Sales – Variable cost
(c) Sales – Profit
(d) Sales – Variable cost + Fixed cost

51 If the current ratio is 2 :1 and working capital is ₹ 60,000. What is the value of the current assets?
(a) ₹ 60,000 (b) ₹ 1,00,000
(c) ₹ 1,20,000 (d) ₹ 1,80,000

June 2012

52 Consider the following.

1. Basic defensive and interval ratio
2. Current ratio
3. Super quick ratio
4. Quick ratio

Arrange these ratios in sequence to reflect the liquidity in descending order.

Codes

(a) 2, 4, 3 and 1 (b) 1, 2, 4 and 3
(c) 4, 2, 3 and 1 (d) 3, 4, 1 and 2

53 What does a high payout ratio indicate?

(a) A high Earning Per Share (EPS)
(b) The management is not ploughing back enough profit
(c) The management is ploughing back profit
(d) The company is earning high profit

54 Match the following.

List I	List II
A. Leverage ratio	1. Short-term solvency
B. Liquidity ratio	2. Earning capacity
C. Turnover ratio	3. Relationship between debt and equity
D. Profitability ratio	4. Efficiency of asset management

Codes

	A	B	C	D
(a)	2	1	4	3
(b)	3	2	1	4
(c)	4	3	1	2
(d)	3	1	4	2

ANSWERS

Objective Questions

1 (a)	2 (b)	3 (d)	4 (d)	5 (b)	6 (a)	7 (c)	8 (d)	9 (c)	10 (c)
11 (b)	12 (b)	13 (c)	14 (b)	15 (c)	16 (c)	17 (b)	18 (c)	19 (c)	20 (c)
21 (c)	22 (b)	23 (b)	24 (c)	25 (c)	26 (a)	27 (a)	28 (c)	29 (b)	30 (c)
31 (c)	32 (d)	33 (b)	34 (d)	35 (b)	36 (b)	37 (a)	38 (b)	39 (a)	40 (c)
41 (a)	42 (b)	43 (a)	44 (c)	45 (c)	46 (d)	47 (c)	48 (a)	49 (c)	50 (c)
51 (a)	52 (a)	53 (d)	54 (a)	55 (b)	56 (c)	57 (c)	58 (a)	59 (b)	60 (c)
61 (c)	62 (b)	63 (c)	64 (a)	65 (d)	66 (b)	67 (c)	68 (c)	69 (a)	70 (c)
71 (d)	72 (a)	73 (a)	74 (d)	75 (c)	76 (d)	77 (c)	78 (b)	79 (a)	80 (c)
81 (c)	82 (a)	83 (c)	84 (a)	85 (a)	86 (b)	87 (d)	88 (c)	89 (c)	90 (c)
91 (a)	92 (a)	93 (b)	94 (a)	95 (a)	96 (a)	97 (a)	98 (a)	99 (b)	100 (b)
101 (a)	102 (c)	103 (a)	104 (c)	105 (a)	106 (a)	107 (a)	108 (a)	109 (a)	110 (b)
111 (c)	112 (a)	113 (d)	114 (c)	115 (b)	116 (b)	117 (c)	118 (a)	119 (b)	120 (d)
121 (d)	122 (b)	123 (c)	124 (b)	125 (c)	126 (a)	127 (b)	128 (b)	129 (b)	130 (a)
131 (a)	132 (c)								

Previous Years' Questions

1 (d)	2 (d)	3 (a)	4 (c)	5 (a)	6 (c)	7 (d)	8 (d)	9 (b)	10 (a)
11 (b)	12 (b)	13 (a)	14 (b)	15 (d)	16 (b)	17 (c)	18 (a)	19 (d)	20 (a)
21 (c)	22 (c)	23 (c)	24 (c)	25 (d)	26 (c)	27 (d)	28 (d)	29 (a)	30 (a)
31 (d)	32 (d)	33 (b)	34 (d)	35 (b)	36 (b)	37 (d)	38 (a)	39 (c)	40 (d)
41 (c)	42 (a)	43 (c)	44 (b)	45 (d)	46 (a)	47 (a)	48 (c)	49 (c)	50 (b)
51 (c)	52 (a)	53 (b)	54 (d)						

CHAPTER 09

Auditing and Its Recent Trends

Economic decisions in every society must be based upon the information available at the time, the decision is made. If decisions are to be consistent with the intention of the decision makers, the information used in the decision process must be reliable. A common way to obtain such reliable information is to have some type of verifications (audit) performed by independent persons.

Auditing

The word 'audit' has been derived from the latin word 'audire' which means 'to hear'. Audit is an official examination and verification of accounts and records, especially of financial accounts. Thus, its ultimate aim is to verify the financial position as disclosed by the balance sheet and profit and loss statement of business.

According to **AW Hanson**, "An audit is an examination of such records to establish their reliability and authenticity of statements drawn from them."

According to **Taylor** and **Perry**, "Audit is defined as an investigation of some statements of figures involving examination of certain evidence, so as to enable an auditor to make a report on the statement".

Objectives of Auditing

- To ascertain, through an examination, the true picture of financial position of the company.
- To discover errors and detect frauds and rectify them.
- To create a moral pressure on employees to act honestly and truthfully.
- To meet the statutory requirements.

In this Chapter

Merits of Auditing

- Auditing acts as a watchdog of investors.
- It presents the correct position of business.
- It helps in prevention of fraud and errors.
- It ensures credibility of audited accounts.

Demerits of Auditing

- There is no guarantee of 100% correctness.
- There is a lack of practical independence.
- It focus on clerical errors only.
- It provides no certification of the commercial prudence of transactions.

Independent Financial Audit

Independent financial audit is the examination of truthness and fairness of financial records. The word 'independent' here refers to the fact that the auditor is not an employee of the organisation but instead he is retained through a contract for services and hence is independent. It is compulsory to conduct every year and is done by Chartered Accountant. Financial audit involves a focus on financial control as they relate to reporting conducted by external auditors. Financial auditor submits his report to the shareholders in board meetings.

Need of Financial Audit

- To ensure that the company has followed true and fair business practices.
- To ensure that accounting transactions give true and fair view.
- To ensure that the funds of the company has been utilised only for the purpose of business.
- To ensure that the concern has followed the basic concepts, *i.e.* going concern concept, accrual method, consistency concept etc and if not, a proper disclosure to that effect has been made.

Vouching

While examining the book of original entries, it is to be checked that the preliminary accounting in these books is authentic. It has been done on the basis of documentary evidence and no voucher has been left unentered. This activity of examining is called 'vouching' in audit. It is the act of checking evidential documents to find out errors and frauds and to know the authenticity, accuracy and reliability of the books of accounts.

According to **JR Batliboi**, "Vouching means testing the truth of the items appearing in the books of original entry".

Objectives of Vouching

- The main objective of vouching is authentication of accuracy and truth of book entries.
- Vouching is to satisfy the auditor that all the transactions are carefully authorised because proper and authorised evidence is present.
- Vouching is to satisfy auditor that all related transactions are recorded in the books.
- Knowledge of the transactions unrelated to business to ensure that no transaction related to business has been recorded in the books.

Voucher

A voucher is a written document to be used in support of an entry made in the account books. It is a documentary evidence. Vouching is done with the help of vouchers.

According to **Ronald A Irish**, "A voucher may be a receipt, an invoice, an agreement, a requisition slip or in short, any suitable evidence, which confirms a written transaction."

Types of Voucher

Primary Voucher An original written evidence supporting a transaction. *e.g.* Invoice for a purchase is termed as primary voucher.

Collateral Voucher It is a part from the original voucher of a transaction. It is prepared in the procedure of the transaction. It is termed as collateral voucher. *e.g.* Copy of invoice as an original voucher in respect of credit sales and the order received for sale, copy of bill of lading, copy of packing notes etc are collateral vouchers.

Duties of an Auditor in Vouching

- The auditor must check that all the vouchers are properly filed separately and in serial order for each of the book of original entry.
- While checking, the auditor should check that all the dates and year in the records are same as on the voucher. Besides, the amount and particulars are same as on the voucher. If there is any difference, then it must be investigated.

Verification of Assets and Liabilities

Verification is a process that is normally carried out at the end of the year, to conform the ownership, valuation and existence of items at the balance sheet date. The auditor is required to mention in his audit report whether the balance sheet of the business, prepared at a certain date, presents a true and fair picture of the financial position of the business or not.

The verification of assets implies an inquiry into the value, ownership and title, existence, possession and presence of any charge on the assets.

The verification of liabilities aims at ascertaining whether all the liabilities of the business are properly disclosed, valued, classified and shown in the balance sheet.

Objectives of Verification

- To ascertain whether the balance sheet presents a true picture of the company's financial position or not.
- To see that the assets and liabilities are valued properly on the basis of generally accepted principles.
- To ascertain that the assets shown in the balance sheet are actually existing in the business and all of them are in its possession.
- To assure that there is no fraud or irregularity with regard to assets and liabilities.
- To verify that all the records of assets and liabilities are free from any error from arithmetical view.

Duties of an Auditor with Regard to Verification

- Verifying that no such assets and liabilities have been shown which do not belong to the organisation.
- Verifying whether all the assets are shown in the balance sheet or not.
- Examining any change in asset which is not shown in the balance sheet.
- Whether mortgage or charge on assets is shown in the balance sheet or there is any other charge.

Valuation of Assets and Liabilities

Valuation is an essential feature or element of verification. Valuation means an inquiry into the true and fair value of assets as presented in the balance sheet, without proper valuation. Balance sheet will not show true and fair picture of financial position of a business entity.

Valuation is basically the act of determining the value of assets and critical examination of these values on the basis of normally accepted accounting standards. Valuation of assets is to be made by the authorised officer and the duty of auditor is to see whether they have been properly valued or not. For ensuring the proper valuation, auditor should obtain the certificates of professionals, approved values and other competent persons. Auditor can rely upon the valuation of concerned officer, but it must be clearly stated in the report because an auditor is not a technical person.

Objectives of Valuation

- To show the actual financial position of a business.
- To check the correctness of value of assets and liabilities.
- To assure the shareholders.

Audit of Financial Statements

Companies prepare their financial statements in accordance with the framework of Generally Accepted Accounting Principles (GAAP). A financial statement audit comprises the examination of an entity's financial statements by an independent auditor. The result of this examination is a report by the auditor. In preparing financial statements, company's management makes implicit or explicit claims, *i.e.* assertions, regarding the existence, valuation, rights, obligations and disclosure of assets, liabilities, equity, income, expenses etc. The auditor then needs to draw an audit programme to verify and obtain sufficient and appropriate audit evidence for each of the assertions made by the management.

Checklist for Financial Statement's Audit

***In Respect of Income Statement** These are as follows*

- Check that transactions recognised in the financial statements have occurred and related to the entity.
- Check that all transactions regarding income and expenses have been recognised in the financial statements.
- Check that all transactions have been recorded accurately at their appropriate amounts.

***In Respect of Balance Sheet** These are as follows*

- Check that all assets, liabilities and equity balances exist as at the period end.
- Check that all assets, liabilities and equity balances have been recognised in the financial statements.
- Check that all assets, liabilities and equity balances have been valued appropriately.

Audit Assertions related to Financial Statements

Income Statement Assertions

Occurrence Transactions and events that have been recorded have occurred and pertains to the entity.

Completeness All transactions and events that should have been recorded, have been recorded.

Accuracy Amounts and other data relating to recorded transactions and events have been recorded appropriately.

Cut-off Transactions and events have been recorded in the correct accounting period.

Classification Transactions and events have been recorded in the proper accounts.

Balance Sheet Assertions

Existence Assets, liabilities and equity interests exist.

Rights and Obligations The entity holds or controls the rights to assets and liabilities are the obligations of the entity.

Completeness All assets, liabilities and equity interests that should have been recorded, have been recorded.

Valuation and Allocation Assets, liabilities and equity interests are included in the financial report at appropriate amounts and any resulting valuation or allocation adjustments are appropriately recorded.

Presentations and Disclosure Assertions

Occurrence, Rights and Obligations Disclosed events, transactions and other matters have occurred and pertains to the entity.

Completeness All disclosures that should have been included in the financial report, have been included.

Classification and Understandability Financial information is appropriately presented, described and disclosures are clearly expressed.

Accuracy and Valuation Financial and other informations are disclosed fairly and at appropriate amounts.

Audit Report

Audit report is the end product of every audit. It is the medium through which an auditor expresses his opinion on the financial statements. Auditor has to furnish this report after completion of audit work in which he gives the results and conclusion of audit work, thus it is called audit report.

According to **Companies Act, 2013**, "An auditor has to furnish a report about accounts, profit and loss and balance sheet and statements related to them after completion of audit work."

Importance of Audit Report

- It is an extremely significant document as it will acquaint the shareholders with the true and fair view of the company's affairs.
- It increases the faith of the investors and accordingly they take decisions for investment.
- Tax authorities also rely on the audited accounts and take their decisions without depth examination of accounts.
- With the help of auditor's report, directors analyse upto what extent employees fulfil their duties with honesty and reliability.

Types of Audit Report

Clean Report If the auditor is fully satisfied on facts to be incorporated in his report, he shall submit a clean or unqualified report on the final account. Such a report shall be given on the accounts regarding which the auditor does not find any irregularity or fallacy and about which there are no complaint and the auditor has no suspicious about their being true and fair.

Qualified Report If the auditor is not satisfied regarding the facts to be mentioned in his report, he must mention his dissatisfaction in his report, such a report is called qualified report.

Content of Auditor's Report

- Details regarding statement of profit and loss account and balance sheet.
- Descriptions related to necessary account books.
- Information and clarification regarding audit work.
- Description related to branch audit.

Cost Audit

Cost audit deals with the examination of adequacy of cost accounts and activation of planning related with cost accounts. It helps management in various ways, *i.e.* determination of price, control in dissipation and finding the facts of sales and purchase. It also controls cost and quality of product of business.

According to **Institute of Cost and Works Accountants of India**, "Cost audit can be defined as verification of the correctness of cost accounts and adherence to the cost accounting principles, plans and procedures."

According to **Smith** and **Day**, "Cost audit means the detailed checking of the costing system, technique and accounts to verify their correctness and to ensure adherence of the objectives of cost accounting."

Characteristics/Elements of Cost Audit

- Cost audit controls cost related to production and services.
- Cost audit is necessary for manufacturing units.
- Cost audit determines personal responsibilities.
- Cost audit is conducted for the businesses which are engaged in production, manufacturing and mining activities.

Significance of Cost Audit

Important for Managers Audited cost accounts help in comparative study of organisation that leads to improvement of mistakes and identify the fraud in business.

Important for Business Unit Cost audit verify the cost records that make easier for business to fix adequate sale price of commodity and if any content found expenses according to business, then plans are made for its implement.

Important for Shareholders Cost audit increases the profit making capacity of business by detecting error in cost accounts and extra costing in production that directly effects on the profits of shareholders.

Important for Labours Audited cost accounts make labours believe that accounts are true and adequate and salary is provided to them adequately and they also get platform for their demands.

Important for Government Audited cost accounts sometimes helps authorities in deciding the amount of tax. Government can use price fixing plan for deciding adequate selling price of commodity etc.

Important for Consumers By the control on cost and quality and because of their proper examination, consumers gets the commodity on adequate price.

Important for Investors Audited cost accounts enables investors to know the true and fairness of accounts by which investors get knowledge of reason of change in nature of sale price and cost price and its impact on future profit and loss capacity.

Advantages of Cost Audit

- It increases the reliability of cost report that helps managers in taking important decisions.
- It controls extra expenses incurred in the production process.
- It increases the profitability of business by detecting error in cost accounts.
- It helps authorities in deciding the amount of tax.
- It enables the investors to know the true and fair position of the business.

Cost Audit Procedure

Review

The cost auditor should familiarise himself with the memorandum and Articles of Association, past audit reports, annual reports issued by the board etc. He should have detailed knowledge of the flow of production process and documents that arise or received in that course. A list of cost account books maintained by client should also be obtained. Before audit work is taken up, all books and records should be posted up to date, vouchers for the various transactions filed serially and all working sheets made available to the auditors.

Verification

A suitable programme for cost audit is made. The procedure and programme to be adopted for audit and the various forms and documents used for it, should be laid down in audit manual. The audit programme should be drawn out in detail, specifying each item of audit work to be carried out.

Reporting

With the help of working papers an audit report is issued on completion of audit. It should summarise the final result of audit. Certificate regarding correctness of the accounts should be included in the report. The report should consist of notes. Observations and comments on the cost accounting system, financial position, stores and spare parts, depreciation, sales etc. Suggestion regarding improvements and corrective measure to be taken.

Recent Trends in Auditing

Many trends have been emerged in the field of auditing. Changes in the economic environment and the market for audit services have impacted how the audit industry operates. It includes management audit, safety audit, environmental audit, energy audit, system audit, social audit, audit committees etc. Utilisation of emerging technologies may increase the value and efficiency of the audit. These audits have been discussed ahead.

Management Audit

Management audit is a new and different concept from traditional auditing. It is a critical review of all managerial performance. Its purpose is to examine effectiveness of management and to ensure that human resources are utilised optimally.

According to **William P Leonard**, "The management audit may be defined as a comprehensive and constructive examination of an organisational structure of a company, institution or branch of government or any component thereof, such as division or department and its plans and objectives, its methods of control, its means of operations and its use of human and physical facilities."

Objectives of Management Audit

- To review the efficiency of management performance.
- To increase the efficiency of managerial work.
- To review the organisational structure and identify its weaknesses.
- To prepare the best management process for successful operation of business.
- To help in establishing a sound relationship between the management and employees of the enterprise.

Significance of Management Audit

- Management audit provides inspiration to managers.
- Management audit provides security to financial institution about the loan they grant to a company.

- Management audit helps government to invest in sick industries for their revival.
- By management audit, amount of incentive is decided that is given for good managerial work.
- Companies that depends on foreign investment and survive on basis of foreign investment did requires management audit to ensure performance level of management planning and progress of business.

Energy Audit

Energy audit is an in depth check that is carried out on a building or equipment to assess the amount of energy being utilised. It is an effective tool in defining and pursuing comprehensive energy management programmes.

In short, energy audit helps businesses understand the areas of improvement from an energy perspective and what needs to be done to bridge the gap.

Types of Energy Audit

Preliminary Audit In this audit, readily available data is used to analyse the performance.

General Audit In this audit, more detailed data and information is analysed which is recorded using specific sensors and meters.

Stages of Energy Audit

Preparation Information gathering stage.

Survey Review and analysis on the information gathered.

Report Analyse the data.

Environmental Audit

Environmental auditing is an environmental tool which measures the impacts of industrial activities on the environment against set standards and criteria.

It includes the examination or investigation of the effects of air emission, water and soil pollution, landscapes. It helps to improve environment by the regulation or reduction of existing industrial/human activities which harm the environment.

According to **The International Chamber of Commerce** (1989), "Environmental audit is a way of management consisting of a systematic, documented, periodical and objective evaluation of performance of the management system and the proceedings drafted for environmental protection aiming at facilitating the control of practices with a possible impact on the environment and evaluating the respect of environmental policies, including the achievement of environmental aims."

In short, environmental audit is the audit of whether the environmental report produced by the company is in true and fair view. It assess on how well the company's control systems are safeguarding the environment, mitigating environmental risk.

Objectives of Environmental Audit

- Environmental audit needs for an industry are of internal as well as external value.
- External needs serve to achieve compliance standards and establish a report with regulatory bodies for implementation of environment management policies.
- Internal need serves the industry as well as self- evaluation tool for the process and technology.
- It helps in pollution control, improves production safety and health conservations of nocturnal resources by the way of ensuring waste prevention and reduction, assessing compliance with regulatory requirement, placing environmental information to the public.

Advantages of Environmental Audit

- Audit report provides the necessary information on how well the management systems are performing to keep place with sustainable level of development.
- It provides performance evaluation of industrial working facilities and its possible effect in the surrounding.
- It refers to compliance with local, regional and national laws and regulation.
- Potential areas for reduction in raw material consumption leads to cost saving.
- It provides an upto-date environmental data to the inspecting authority.

System Audit

System audit is the process of collecting and evaluating evidence to determine whether a computer system safeguards assets, maintains data integrity, allows organisational goals to be achieved effectively and uses resources efficiently.

Objectives of System Audit

- Validation of the controls of the system development cycle.
- Validation of the organisational aspects.
- Administration of the information service function.
- To provide training to members of the information service function department.

Steps Involved in Conducting System Audit

Purviewing the Environment The auditor must understand which applications are running on which machines etc. In case the auditor decides to use any audit software, he must decide whether the given environment would support it.

Understanding the Information System The auditor should go through the system documention to understand the overall framework and individual sub-system.

Indentifying the Audit Risk The next step is to see which of the risks can have serious adverse outcomes and assign higher priority to them.

Identifying Audit Evidence The auditor has to make an exhaustive list of evidence to be gathered from the flow chart and the risk analysis.

Identifying Key Control Points Based on the risk prioritisation, the auditor looks for those control points that control maximum risks.

Identifying Control Weaknesses It is quite possible that the controls may be leaving the door open for some loss to occur. The auditor should identify that control weaknesses.

Verifying Veracity of Computer Files The auditor has to start with the user output that was corrected and come back to the computer files. He should also look out for corrections directly made on the databox without correcting the transaction files.

Conduct Audit Test The auditor calculates the correct result for a correct data and passes the same through system. Then, the results are compared and conclusions drawn.

Conducting the Audit The last step is to have a meeting with the management representation who have to implement the findings and record the action points for the next audit review.

Safety Audit

Safety audit is an essential tool to ensure the safety of the workplace and workers in an organisation. It is a critical systematic inspection of an organisation's activities so that losses can be minimised. These losses can be occurred due to accidents in a factory.

Thus, a safety audit is structured process whereby information is collected relating to the efficiency, effectiveness and reliability of a company's total health and safety management system. It is a risk management tool for any organisation.

Safety Audit Serves Two Broad Purposes

- They are routinely conducted in order to determine whether the company is in compliance with safety legislation.
- They are used to identify weakness in their safety programs and process. These audits are then used as a guide for designing safety plans or to identify corrective actions that should be undertaken.

Benefits of Safety Audit

- Safety audit promotes constant review of systems to ensure that they do not become weakened by habit.
- It facilitates planned improvement to programs, policies and procedures.
- It helps to identify weaknesses in human resources departments.
- It helps to demonstrate management's dedication to employees' health and safety.

As per IS 14489, (code of practice on occupational saftey and health audit) "Safety audit is mandatory for hazardous industries in India."

EXAM BASED QUESTIONS

Auditing, Vouching and Verification and Valuation of Assets and Liabilities

1 The person who conducts audit is called

(a) Chartered Accountant (b) Company Secretary
(c) Auditor (d) Accountant

2 The beneficiaries of auditing include(s)

(a) company (b) bankers
(c) sole proprietorship (d) All of these

3 The area of operations in auditing includes

(a) condition of appointment
(b) needs of related law
(c) Both (a) and (b)
(d) Either (a) or (b)

4 To be an auditor, a person must be an

(a) employee (b) employer
(c) accountant (d) independent person

5 The definite period of auditing is

(a) 1 financial year (b) 2 financial years
(c) 3 financial years (d) 5 financial years

6 .... is the backbone of auditing.

(a) Accounting (b) Vouching
(c) Revaluation (d) Reassessment

7 The objective(s) of vouching is/are

(a) no knowledge of entire business transactions
(b) authorisation of transactions
(c) partial knowledge of the transactions unrelated to business
(d) All of the above

8 Process of checking the evidence of the entries called ....

(a) verification (b) observation
(c) vouching (d) inspection

9 To verify cash transactions, what is necessary?

(a) System of internal control
(b) Check all transactions
(c) Documentary evidence for every transaction
(d) All of the above

10 Voucher should be addressed to the ....

(a) auditor (b) client
(c) employee (d) None of these

11 Which of the following can be accepted as a supporting document?

(a) Invoice/Challan
(b) Debit note/Credit note
(c) E-mails/letters
(d) All of the above

12 In order to audit petty cash expenses, the auditor has to check

(a) petty cash register
(b) internal controls
(c) reconciliation cash has been repaid to the client
(d) All of the above

13 The objective(s) of verification of assets is/are

(a) to examine the existence of assets
(b) to examine the ownership of assets
(c) proper explanation of mortgage or charge
(d) All of the above

14 The essential documents for verification of freehold land

(a) rights statement
(b) receipt of contractor
(c) lease receipt
(d) Both (a) and (b)

15 Valuation is the base of

(a) verification (b) marketing
(c) vouching (d) All of these

16 The value at which the assets are shown in the books of account is known as

(a) book value
(b) market value
(c) cost value
(d) replacement value

17 An auditor is a watchdog but not a bloodhound. This statement has been given in decision of which case?

(a) Kingston cotton mills case
(b) Garner *vs* Murray case
(c) Paglar cotton mills case
(d) None of the above

18 Which of the following statement(s) is/are true?

1. Audit can be done by any person.
2. Auditing is guarantee of 100% correctness.
3. Errors can be detected and prevented from auditing.
4. Auditing is the examination of books and statements.

Codes

(a) Both 1 and 2
(b) Both 2 and 3
(c) Both 3 and 4
(d) 1, 2 and 4

19 In order to vouch, which of the expenses the auditor will examine in bill of entry?

(a) Customs (b) Income tax
(c) GST (d) VAT

20 While vouching, how will the auditor ensure himself that all credit sales transactions have been recorded by the entity?
(a) Examining cut-off points
(b) Matching entries in the sales book against renumbered sales invoices and goods outward notes
(c) Counting the number of invoices and matching the number with entries on sales book
(d) Both (a) and (b)

21 In case of sales return, the auditor should examine which documents?
(a) Credit notes, advice notes and inward return notes
(b) Debit notes, advice notes and inward return notes
(c) Purchase invoices, advice notes and inward return notes
(d) Credit notes, inspection report and inward return notes

22 Vouching helps the auditors to ascertain whether the entries in the book ...., this is the basic objective of auditing.
(a) true and fair (b) Only true
(c) Only fair (d) None of these

23 Checking the head of account debited or credited during vouching helps the auditor to
(a) detect errors of principle
(b) check whether accounting is proper
(c) find errors of commission
(d) All of the above

24 Which of the point is not to be considered while checking, a voucher?
(a) Name of party
(b) Serial number of voucher
(c) Credit period of payment
(d) Accounting entry

25 Checking the date of voucher on the voucher during vouching, mainly helps the auditor to obtain evidence that
(a) the transaction relates to current year
(b) the transaction has taken place
(c) the transaction is genuine
(d) the transaction is legal

26 The auditor does not have to check the following while auditing salaries/wages,
(a) calculation of the salary
(b) whether the calculation was verified by department heads
(c) whether dues like PF, PT, TDS have been deducted and deposited
(d) payment has been made to all the employees on first of the month

27 In case of sales return, the auditor should check
(a) credit notes and delivery challans
(b) whether cash has been repaid to the client
(c) purchase invoices and goods received notes
(d) credit notes and goods received notes

Audit of Financial Statements, Audit Report and Cost Audit

28 Auditors accumulate evidence to
(a) defend themselves in the event of a law suit
(b) justify the conclusion they have, otherwise reached
(c) satisfy the requirements of the act
(d) unable them to reach conclusions about the fairness of the financial statements

29 The report through which an auditor expresses his opinion on the financial statement is known as
(a) cost report (b) audit report
(c) statutory report (d) management report

30 The beneficiary(s) of audit report is/are
1. creditor 2. income tax authority
3. director 4. government
Select the correct answer using the codes given below
Codes
(a) Only 1 (b) Both 2 and 4
(c) Both 3 and 4 (d) All of the above

31 To whom special audit report is addressed?
(a) Manager (b) Director
(c) Central Government (d) Shareholders

32 The reason(s) of qualified report is/are
(a) violation of generally accepted principles of auditing
(b) violation of accounting principles
(c) lack of adequate information and explanations
(d) All of the above

33 The examination of cost accounts and statements is called
(a) complete audit (b) interim audit
(c) cost audit (d) internal audit

34 The cost auditor gives his report to the
(a) directors (b) shareholders
(c) managers (d) company law board

35 Which of the following is/are the object(s) of cost audit for organisations?
(a) Examination of new plans
(b) Increase in work efficiency
(c) Determination of policies
(d) All of these

36 Which of the following can not be appointed as cost auditor?
(a) Employee of company
(b) A company
(c) Financial audit of company
(d) All of the above

37 The objective of the ordinary audit of financial statements is the expression of an opinion on
(a) the fairness of the financial statements
(b) the accuracy of the financial statements
(c) the accuracy of the annual report
(d) the balance sheet and income statement

38 If the auditor believes that the financial statements are fairly stated or is unable to reach and conclusion because of insufficient evidence, the auditor
(a) should withdraw from the engagement
(b) should request an increase in audit fees so that more resources can be used to conduct the audit
(c) has the responsibility of notifying financial statements, users through the auditor's report
(d) should notify regulators of the circumstances

39 During the audit of accounts receivable, an auditor obtains sufficient and appropriate evidence in support of the existence assertion this evidence can be used to support which of the following assertions in respect of sales?
(a) Existence (b) Cut-off
(c) Occurrence (d) Completeness

40 If auditor does not find any irregularity or fallacy and about which there are no complaint, then which report will be submitted by auditor?
(a) Qualified report (b) Clean report
(c) Management report (d) Cost report

41 Which report will be submitted by an auditor, if he is dissatisfied regarding the facts and informations?
(a) Qualified report (b) Clean report
(c) Management report (d) Cost report

42 Which of the following is/are beneficiary(s) of cost audit?
1. Manager
2. Shareholders and investors
3. Society and consumers
4. Government
Select the correct answer using the codes given below
Codes
(a) Both 2 and 3 (b) Both 1 and 4
(c) 2, 3 and 4 (d) All of the above

43 Which industries fall under strategic area?
1. Industries related to equipments for safety and power generation.
2. Electricity, road and steel industries.
3. Industries related to railway and mineral products.
4. Health and education related industry.
Select the correct answer using the codes given below
Codes
(a) Only 1 (b) Only 2
(c) Both 3 and 4 (d) All of the above

Recent Trends in Auditing

44 Management audit is done by
(a) Chartered Accountant
(b) Company Secretary
(c) Manager
(d) Any Qualified Person

45 The audit conducted to check and examine the efficiency and effectiveness of management is called
(a) management audit (b) cost audit
(c) energy audit (d) safety audit

46 The technique(s) of management audit is/are
1. co-relation of information
2. observation
3. ratio analysis
4. financial data analysis
Codes
(a) Only 2 (b) Both 2 and 3
(c) Both 1 and 4 (d) All of the above

47 What is the maximum time limit for submitting management audit report?
(a) 15 days (b) 20 days
(c) 30 days (d) No time limit

48 The practical aspects of management audit is/are
(a) changes in sales (b) changes in price
(c) organisational control (d) All of these

49 The management auditors work begins
(a) after the work of a statutory auditor ends
(b) before the work of a statutory auditor begins
(c) varies from firm to firm
(d) None of the above

50 The approach of management auditor should be
(a) brief (b) internal (c) analytical (d) configured

51 What is the first stage of energy audit?
(a) Survey (b) Report
(c) Checking (d) Preparation

52 The step(s) involved in conducting system audit is/are
(a) audit evidence (b) conduct audit tests
(c) concluding the audit (d) All of these

53 Safety audit is mandatory for
(a) manufacturing industries
(b) hazardous industries
(c) textile industries
(d) mining industries

54 The technique of management audit in which functions and achievements of two or more firms are compared, is called
(a) comparative analysis (b) inter-firm comparison
(c) routine check (d) ratio analysis

55 In which type of energy audit readily available data is used to analyse the performance?
(a) General audit (b) Preliminary audit
(c) Safety audit (d) System audit

56 In which audit, the examination of the effects of air emission, water and soil pollution, landscape etc is done?
(a) Management audit (b) Energy audit
(c) Environmental audit (d) Safety audit

Miscellaneous

57 **Statement** I The scope of valuation is wider than verification.

Statement II Valuation is done after vouching but before verification.

Codes

(a) Statement I is true, but statement II is false
(b) Statement II is true, but statement I is false
(c) Both statements are true
(d) Both statements are false

58 **Statement** I Management audit is a part of financial audit.

Statement II Management audit is not compulsory under any law.

Codes

(a) Only statement I is true (b) Only statement II is true
(c) Both statements are true (d) Both statements are false

59 **Statement** I Energy audit is an indepth check of the amount of energy being utilised.

Statement II Energy audit includes general and preliminary audit.

Codes

(a) Statement I is correct, but statement II is incorrect
(b) Statement II is correct, but statement I is incorrect
(c) Both statements are correct
(d) Both statements are incorrect

60 **Statement** I Safety audit is a risk management tools.

Statement II Management audit is a part of traditional auditing.

Codes

(a) Statement I is correct (b) Statement II is correct
(c) Both statements are correct
(d) Both statements are incorrect

Directions (Q.Nos. 61-65) *The following questions consists of two statements, one labelled as the Assertion (A) and the other as Reason (R). Examine these two statements carefully and select the answer to these items using the codes given below.*

Codes

(a) Both (A) and (R) are true and (R) is the correct explanation of (A)
(b) Both (A) and (R) are true, but (R) is not the correct explanation of (A)
(c) (A) is the true, but (R) is false
(d) (A) is false, but (R) is true

61 **Assertion** (A) Management audit should be conducted by a team of experts.

Reason (R) Management audit is a critical examination of policies and practices of management from the highest level to downward in order to ascertain that sound management prevails in the business concern.

62 **Assertion** (A) Financial audit is the examination of truthness and fairness of financial records.

Reason (R) Financial audit is done by Chartered Accountant.

63 **Assertion** (A) Valuation is an essential feature of verification.

Reason (R) Valuation includes the amount of energy being utilised.

64 **Assertion** (A) Auditing is not the guarantee of 100% correctness.

Reason (R) Audit report is the medium through which auditor expresses his opinion in respect of auditing procedure.

65 **Assertion** (A) Safety audit is not mandatory for hazardous industries in India.

Reason (R) Safety audit is a critical systematic inspection of an organisation's activities to minimise the losses due to accidents.

66 Match the following.

	List I (Assertions)		List II (Explanations)
A.	Cut-off	1.	Assets and liabilities exist
B.	Classification	2.	Transactions and events have been recorded in proper accounts
C.	Occurrence	3.	Transactions and events have been recorded in the correct accounting period
D.	Existence	4	Transactions and events that have been recorded, have occurred and pertain to the entity

Codes

	A	B	C	D		A	B	C	D
(a)	1	3	2	4	(b)	3	2	4	1
(c)	2	1	3	4	(d)	4	3	2	1

ANSWERS

Objective Questions

1 (c)	2 (d)	3 (c)	4 (d)	5 (a)	6 (b)	7 (b)	8 (c)	9 (d)	10 (b)
11 (d)	12 (d)	13 (d)	14 (d)	15 (a)	16 (a)	17 (a)	18 (c)	19 (a)	20 (d)
21 (d)	22 (a)	23 (a)	24 (c)	25 (a)	26 (d)	27 (d)	28 (d)	29 (b)	30 (d)
31 (c)	32 (d)	33 (c)	34 (a)	35 (d)	36 (d)	37 (a)	38 (c)	39 (c)	40 (b)
41 (a)	42 (d)	43 (b)	44 (d)	45 (a)	46 (d)	47 (b)	48 (d)	49 (a)	50 (c)
51 (d)	52 (d)	53 (b)	54 (b)	55 (b)	56 (c)	57 (b)	58 (b)	59 (c)	60 (a)
61 (a)	62 (b)	63 (c)	64 (a)	65 (d)	66 (b)				

CHAPTER 10

Business Economics and Demand Analysis

Business economics is a special branch of economics, which is applied in business decision-making. Study of demand comes under the scope of economics, which helps in understanding the demand for goods and services.

Business Economics

Business economics means the application of economic theory to the problems of management. Business economics lies on the border line of management and economics and serves as a bridge between the two disciplines. Therefore, the business economics formulates principles which provide a framework for evaluating whether resources are being allocated efficiently within a firm.

According to **McNair** and **Meriam**, "Business economics consists of the use of economic modes of thought to analyse business situations."

According to **Joseph L Messey**, "Business economics is the use of economic theories by the management in making business decisions."

After studying the above definitions, it can be concluded that business economics is that branch of knowledge in which theories of economic analysis are used for solving business management problems and determination of business policies.

Characteristics of Business Economics

Managerial Decision Business economics is an applied subject, which helps in taking managerial decision to formulate business policies. It helps in decision-making to maximise output with minimum cost.

Applied Nature of Economic Theory In economic theory, different laws are formulated but the applied part of economics is used in business economics. The nature of business economics is applied and not theoretical.

In this Chapter

- *Business Economics*
- *Demand Analysis*
- *Law of Demand*
- *Elasticity of Demand*

Problems and Solutions Business economics helps in studying the complicated and different types of problems related to business and suggests policy implications, so that the problems can be easily solved.

Economics of a Firm The aim of a firm is to get maximum profit, which is possible only by effective policy adoption and decision-making to minimise the cost of production.

Coordinating Nature Business economics coordinates between the theoretical and practical aspects necessarily required for running a firm. It uses micro as well as macro models.

Nature of Business Economics

Nature of business economics can be studied in two ways, i.e. economics as a science and as an art which are as follows

Economics as a Science

As a science, it can be further studied as

Normative Science It deals with things as 'what ought to be'. It has no objection to discuss the moral rightness or wrongness of things. Economics is not only explaining facts as they are but also justifies them.

Positive Science It deals with things as 'what is'. It explains their cause and effect, but it remains strictly neutral as regards ends, it refuses to pass moral judgements.

Economics as an Art

As an art, economics helps us in the solution of our practical problems. Its study enables us to know the best method of achieving economic objective.

In short, economics is both a science and an art. So, it can be summarised that business economics is the science. It is a fundamental economic discipline, the study which increases the ability of executives to understand and solve decision-making problems scientifically.

Scope of Business Economics

Business economics is a developing subject, hence it has no definite scope.

Yet the following topics fall under business economics

Demand Analysis Forecasting Business decision-making depends on accurate estimates of demand. Demand analysis in short, is necessary for two reasons, *i.e.* for forecasting of demand and for the manipulation of demand. The chief topics dealt within demand analysis are demand determinants, demand distinctions and demand forecasting.

Production and Cost Analysis It is essential for project planning. Cost analysis is required for cost control. Cost estimate help in the expansion of the production process.

Pricing Decisions, Policies and Practices Price is the basis for revenue of a firm. Some of the aspects of the pricing problem are price determination in various market forms, pricing methods, differential pricing, product line pricing and price forecasting.

Profit Management The main purpose of a business firm is to earn profit. But there is uncertainty about profits due to variation in costs and revenue. Under profit management, we study the nature and management of profit, planning and techniques of profit planning.

Capital Management It is the most troublesome problem. Capital management deals with planning and control of capital expenditure, cost of capital etc.

Product Policy, Sales Promotion and Market Strategy In modern days, the consumer wants new products and new services. A business should have a policy for promoting its products. Therefore, product policy, sales promotion and market strategy are important aspects of business economics.

Linear Programming and Theory of Games Recently, there is a trend towards integration of business economics and operation research. Hence, techniques such as linear programming inventory models are regarded as part of business economics.

Uses of Business Economics

Effective Utilisation of Business Resources Business economics is very helpful for effective utilisation of business resources. It determines every factor's price on supply and demand of such factor, so that the price becomes optimise by this supply and demand analysis.

Full Employment Keynesian's general theory of employment tells that full employment depends on investment and effective demand, if both will increase after this employment can increase. Government takes steps for increasing investment in self employment schemes and try to help to sell the products, through which full employment is generated.

Effective Use of Economic Policies for Business Development Business economics makes different economic policies under macro economics and these policies utilise for business and trade development.

Solving Economic Problems Business economics is an indispensable tool for the business people to make proper decision and with it they solve the economic problem.

Objectives of Business Firms

Profit Maximisation

It is the principle objective of any business firm, under the assumption of given tasks, technology and price of given output. It refers to pure profit which is a surplus above the average cost of production. In other words, it is the money left after making all payments to all factors of production, including his wages of management. *The profit maximising conditions are*

- Marginal revenue is equal to marginal cost.
- Marginal cost must cut marginal revenue from below.

Marris Growth Maximisation

Prof. Robin Marris stated about this objective of business firm in 1964. According to him, the managers aim at the maximisation of the growth rate of the firm and the shareholders aim at the maximisation of their dividends and share prices.

To establish a link between such a growth rate and the share prices of the firms, Marris developed a balanced growth model, in which the manager chooses a constant growth rate at which the firm's sales, profits, assets etc grow. If he chooses a higher growth rate, he will have to spend more on advertisement and on R and D in order to create more demand and new products.

As the managers are concerned more about their job security and growth of the firm, they will choose that growth rate which maximises the market value of shares, give satisfactory dividends to shareholders and avoid the takeover of the firm.

Multiple Objectives

The basic difference between the objectives of neo-classical and modern thinkers arises from the fact that the profit maximisation objectives relates to the entrepreneurial behaviour, while modern corporations are motivated by different objectives because of the separate roles of shareholders and managers.

Baumol's Sales Maximisation

According to Baumol's theory, with the separation of ownership and control in modern corporations, managers seek prestige and higher salaries by trying to expand company sales even at the expense of profits.

According to Baumol, revenue or sales maximisation rather than profit maximisation is consistent with the actual behaviour of firms.

Baumol cites evidence to suggest that short-run revenue maximisation may be consistent with long-run profit maximisation. But sales maximisation is regarded as the short-run and long-run goal of the management. Sales maximisation is not only a means but an end in itself. Also a firm attaches great importance to the magnitude of sales and is much concerned about declining sales.

Output Maximisation

According to **Prof. Milton Kafoglis**, "The performance of firms frequently is measured directly in terms of physical output with revenue occupying a secondary position." Thus, it is preferred that output maximisation both profit maximisation and revenue maximisation as the objective of a firm. Given some minimum level of profits, a firm wants to maximise its output.

Security Profits

Prof. Rothschild has put forward the view that the firm is motivated not by profit maximisation but by the desire for security profits.

According **Prof. Rothschild,** "There is another motive which is probably of a similar order of magnitude as the desire for maximum profit, the desire for security profit."

Rothschild also argued that the objective of profit maximisation cannot be persued perfect competition or in monopolistic competition. However under oligopoly firms persue this objective, but the desire to increase its security leads to the struggle for position and to the setting of a price which will not be so low that it provokes retaliation from its rivals.

According to Rothschild, security objective is nothing but profit maximisation objective from a different angle.

Satisfaction Maximisation

This objective was talked about by Prof. Scitovsky, he prefers maximisation of satisfaction in preference to the profit maximisation objective of the firm. He is concerned with managerial efforts and the distaste that managers have for work. According to him, an entrepreneur would maximise profits only if his choice between more income and more leisure is independent of his/her income.

Demand Analysis

Demand analysis means research into the desire of consumers for a particular product or service. Demand analysis is used to identify who wants to buy a given product, how much they are likely to pay for it, how many units they might purchase and other factors that can be used to determine product design, selling cost and advertising strategy for a product.

Demand

It is the quantity of a goods or services that consumers are willing and able to buy at a given price in a given time period. Demand is always related to price and time.

According to **Prof. Benham**, "The demand for anything at a given price is the amount of it which will be bought per unit of time at that price."

According to **Ferguson**, "Demand refers to the quantities of a commodity that the consumer is able and willing to buy at each possible price during a given period of time, other things being equal."

Thus, demand for a commodity should be expressed as

Demand = Desire + Ability to Pay + Willingness to Pay

Determinants of Demands/Factor Affecting Demand

Price of the Products

Price and commodity has close relation. Changes in the price of the commodity will lead to changes in quantity demanded.

Income of the Consumer

A change in real income means that there is a change in the quantity of goods and services money income can buy. For most goods, an increase in real income will lead to an increase in demand. Goods for which demand increases when income increases are called normal goods. Infact, there exists a direct relationship between income and quantity demanded for normal goods. However, there are some goods for which demand decreases as income increases and *vice-versa*. These are called inferior goods.

Tastes, Habits and Preferences

Demand depends on the individual's taste, habits and preferences which is controlled and influenced by advertising and sales promotion. A change in consumer tastes in favour of a good can increase the demand for that commodity. Similarly, if a commodity is in fashion, demand will rise. The demand goes on increasing or decreasing on their basis.

Relative Price of Other Goods: Substitutes and Complementary Goods

Demand for a commodity depends much on the price of its complementary goods. If the price of a complementary good falls, demand for the product will rise. Thus, there exists an inverse relationship between demand for a commodity and the price of its complements.

Demand for a commodity is also influenced by changes in the price of its substitutes. If the price of substitutes increases, demand for a commodity will also increase. Thus, there exists a direct relationship between demand for a commodity and the price of its substitutes.

Consumer Expectations

Change in consumer's expectations about commodities such as product price, product availability and future income is another factor affecting demand. There is generally a direct relationship between the expectation of rise in income and a demand of a commodity. Expectation of future rise in income leads to increase in demand and fear of future fall in income leads to decrease in demand.

Changes in Population

When the size of the total population changes, demand for goods and services would generally change. An increase in total population would generally lead to an increase in demand.

Changes in Distribution of Income

Demand is also affected by changes in the distribution of income within a society. Incomes could be redistributed to achieve greater equality of income by taxing the rich and subsidising the poor. This would leave the poor with more money, thus, increasing their demand for goods and services.

Government Policy (Income Tax)

If government imposes high income tax rate or lowers transfer payments, this would lead to a fall in disposable incomes, thus reducing demand for the commodities.

Saving and Rate of Interest

An individual's desire to save would influence his demand for commodities. An increase in savings would lead to a fall in demand since the individual forgoes present consumption in order to save. But what encourages people to save is the rate of interest.

Demand Schedule

It is that schedule which shows various amount of a commodity that the consumer is ready to buy at different possible prices of that commodity at a given time.

It has two aspects which are as follows

Individual Demand Schedule It is a table showing various quantities of a commodity which an individual buyer is ready to buy at different possible prices of the commodity at a point of time.

Market Demand Schedule It is a table showing various quantities of a commodity which all the buyers are ready to buy at different possible prices of the commodity at a point of time.

Market Demand Schedule

Price of Commodity (X) (In ₹)	Demand by (P)	Demand by (Q)	Market Demand (Units)
1	4	5	4 + 5 = 9
2	3	4	3 + 4 = 7
3	2	3	2 + 3 = 5
4	1	2	1 + 2 = 3

Demand Curve

It is the curve which shows the relationship between the price of a good and the quantity demanded, holding constant all other factors that influence demand.

Like demand schedule, concept of demand curve include the following

Individual Demand Curve

This curve graphically shows different quantities of a particular commodity demanded by an individual consumer at different possible prices at a point of time. The figure given below shows graphical presentation of individual demand schedule. In the given figure, 1 unit of a commodity is demanded when price is ₹4 per unit and 4 units of a commodity are demanded when price is ₹ 1 per unit.

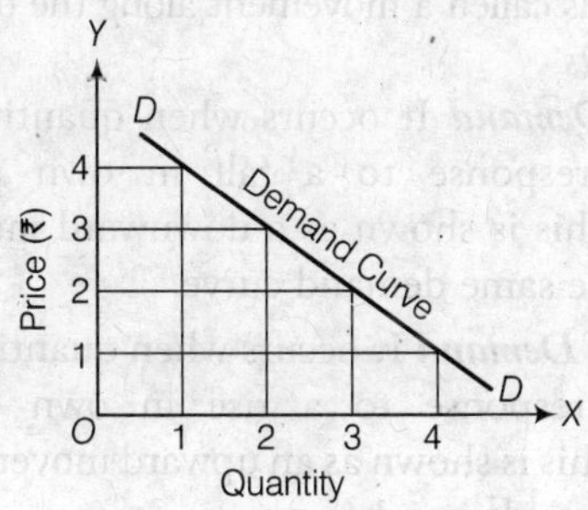

Individual Demand Curve

Market Demand Curve

This curve is the horizontal summation of the individual demand curves. This curve graphically shows different quantities of a particular commodity demanded by all the consumers at different possible prices at a point of time.

The figure given below shows graphical presentation of market demand schedule. *P* and *Q* are two consumers in the market.

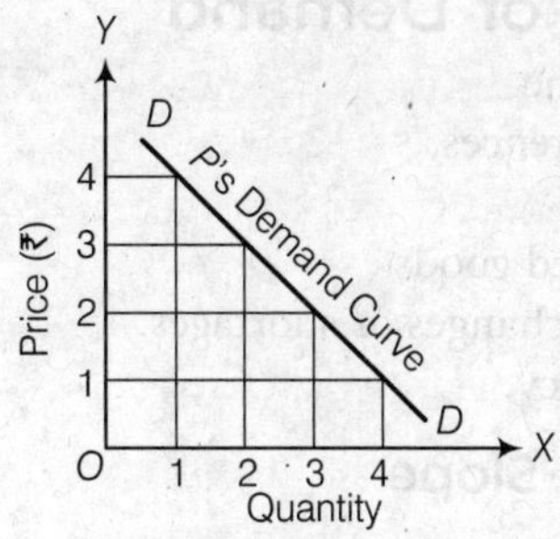

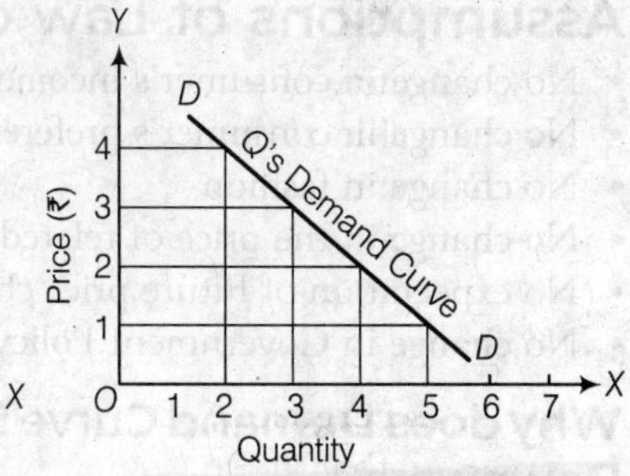

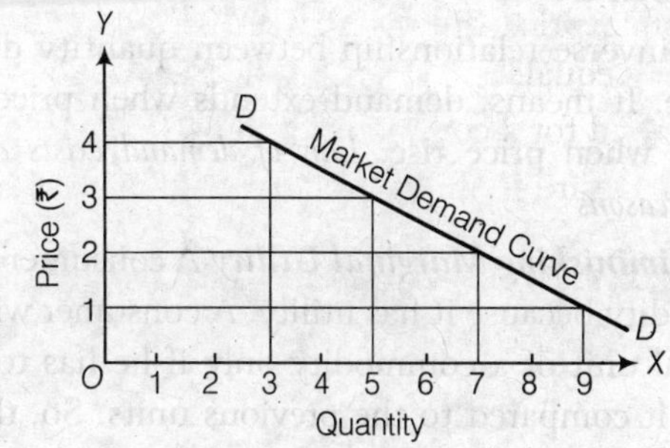

Market Demand Curve

Demand Function

Individual Demand

$$D_x = f\,(P_x, P_r, Y, T, E)$$

Where, D_x = Quantity demanded of a commodity-X

P_x = Own price of commodity-X

P_r = Price of related goods

Y = Consumer's income

T = Consumer's tastes and preferences

E = Consumer's expectations

Market Demand

$$D_x = f\,(P_x, P_r, Y, T, E, P, Y_d)$$

Where,

P = Size and composition of population

Y_d = Distribution of income

Law of Demand

The law of demand expresses the nature of functional relationship between two variables of the demand relation *viz* the price and the quantity demanded. It simply states that demand varies inversely to change in price.

The higher the price of a commodity the smaller is the quantity demanded and lower the price, larger the quantity demanded. So, there is inverse relationship between price of the commodity and its quantity demanded.

Assumptions of Law of Demand

- No change in consumer's income.
- No change in consumer's preferences.
- No change in fashion.
- No change in the price of related goods.
- No expectation of future price changes or shortages.
- No change in Government Policy.

Why does Demand Curve Slope Downward?

There is inverse relationship between quantity demanded and price. It means, demand extends when price fall and contracts when price rise. *Law of demand exists due to the following reasons*

Law of Diminishing Marginal Utility A consumer demands a commodity because it has utility. A consumer will buy an additional unit of a commodity only if he has to pay less price for it compared to the previous units. So, the law of diminishing marginal utility is the basis of the law of demand.

Income Effect When the price of a goods decreases, a person's income will increase and he will tend to purchase more quantity of same commodity. Thus, fall in price causes increase in real income and extension in demand. On the contrary, due to increase in price, the real income of the consumer goes down, as a result, the consumption of the commodity declines.

Substitution Effect The consumer substitutes cheaper commodities for those commodities whose price has no change. The demand for that commodity extends. On the contrary, when price of the substitute goods increases, its demand of other goods contracts due to substitution effects.

Different Uses Some commodities have more than one use. The demand for the commodities with alternative uses tends to extend consequent upon the fall in their prices.

New Consumer Group When the price of a commodity falls, then many consumers, who were unable to buy that commodity at its previous price come forward to buy it.

Exceptions to the Law of Demand

Articles of Distinction or Veblan Goods The demand for the articles of distinction like diamonds and jewellery is more when their price is high. Greater the price of the commodity, greater the utility. If their price falls, they will no longer be considered as article of distinction and so their demand will decrease.

Giffen Goods These are the goods, whose price effect is positive and income effect is negative. In case of price effect is positive, demand rise with the rise in price and falls with the falls in price.

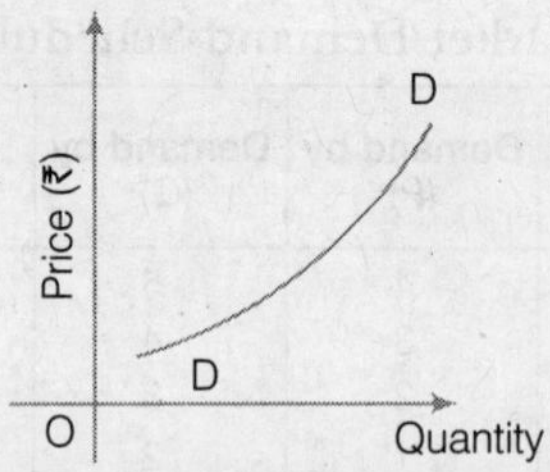

Demand Curve for Giffen Goods

Ignorance about Quality Usually, consumers judge the quality of a commodity from its price. A high priced commodity is thought to have higher value than that of a low priced commodity.

Movements along a Demand Curve and Shifts in Demand Curve

A movement along the demand curve occurs when quantity demanded changes because of a change in the price of the commodity alone, while other factors in conditions of demand (income, tastes, population, price of complements and substitutes etc) remain constant.

Infact, when a demand curve is drawn, only the price of the product is allowed to vary, while the conditions of demand do not change. Moving from one point to the other on the same demand curve is called a movement along the demand curve.

It has two aspects

Extension of Demand It occurs when quantity demanded increases in response to a fall in own price of the commodity. This is shown as a downward movement (left to right) on the same demand curve.

Contraction of Demand It occurs when quantity demanded decreases in response to a rise in own price of the commodity. This is shown as an upward movement (right to left) on the same demand curve.

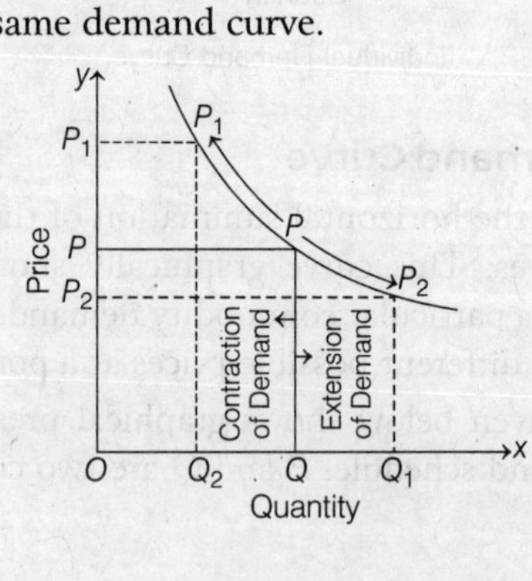

A Shift in the Demand Curve or a Change in Demand

It occurs when quantity demanded changes only because there are changes in conditions of demand, while the price of the commodity remains constant. The demand curve can shift either to the right or to the left, depending upon the changes in the conditions of demand.

It has two aspects, which are as follows

Increase in Demand It refers to increase in quantity demanded of a commodity at its existing prices and refers to a situation when demand curve shifts to the right or there is a forward shift in demand curve.

Decrease in Demand It refers to a decrease in quantity demanded of a commodity at its existing prices and refers to a situation when demand curve shifts to the left or there is a backward shift in demand curve.

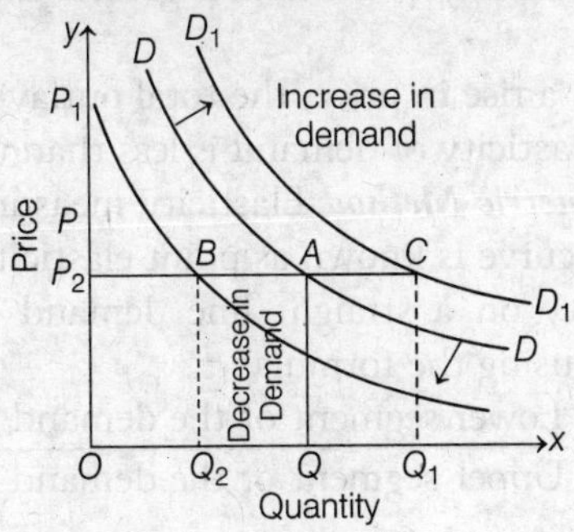

Elasticity of Demand

The responsiveness of demand to a change in any one of its determining factors is called the elasticity of demand.

Kinds of Elasticity of Demand

Price Elasticity of Demand

The price elasticity of demand refers to the percentage change in the quantity demanded of a commodity as a result of a percentage change in its price.

It refers to the degree of responsiveness of demand for commodity to a given change in its price

$$e_d = \frac{\text{\% Change in quantity demanded}}{\text{\% Change in price}}$$

$$e_d = \frac{\Delta Q}{\Delta P} \times \frac{P}{Q}$$

Where, e_d = Price elasticity of demand
ΔQ = Change in demand
ΔP = Change in price
P = Original price
Q = Original quantity

Types/Degrees of Price Elasticity of Demand

Perfectly Elastic Demand ($e = \infty$) When a negligible or no change in price brings about a very large or infinite change in quantity demanded, then demand for such a commodity is said to be perfectly elastic.

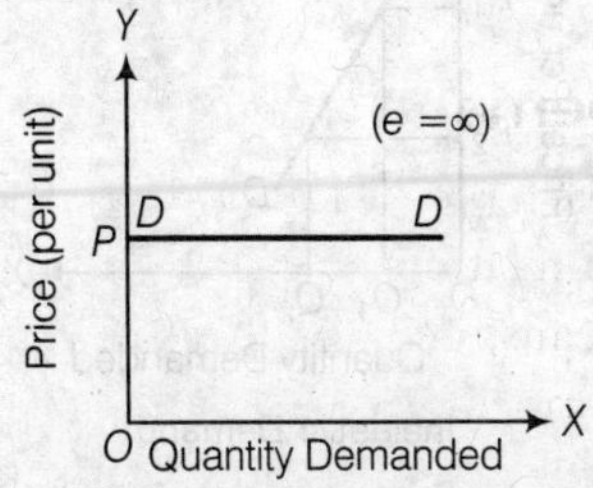

Perfectly Elastic Demand

Its mathematically expressed as $e = \infty$.
In this case, demand curve will be a horizontal straight line.

Perfectly Inelastic Demand ($e = 0$) In this, quantity demanded remain unaffected by the price movements.

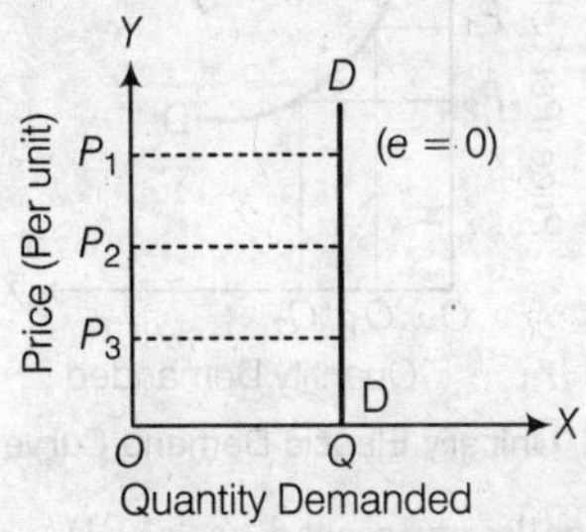

Perfectly Inelastic Demand

It is mathematically expressed as ($e = 0$).

In this case, demand curve would be a straight vertical line.

Elastic Demand ($e > 1$) When the change in the quantity demanded for a commodity is more than the proportionate change in its price, then the demand for a commodity is said to be elastic.

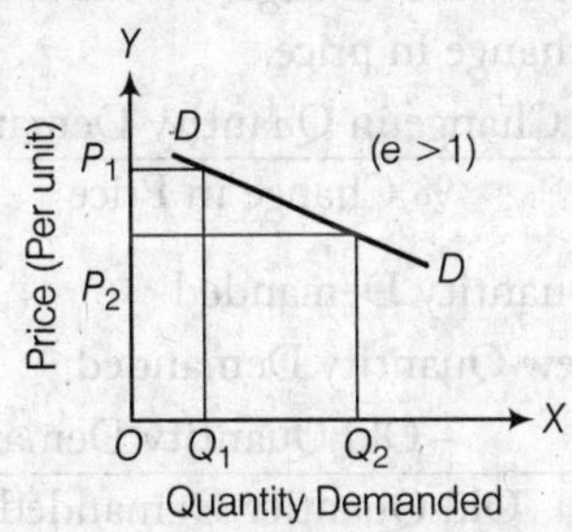

Elastic Demand

It is mathematically expressed as ($e > 1$).
It is shown by a flatter demand curve.

Inelastic Demand ($e < 1$) When the change in quantity demanded for a commodity is less than the proportionate change in its price, then the demand for a commodity is said to be inelastic. It is mathematically expressed as ($e < 1$).

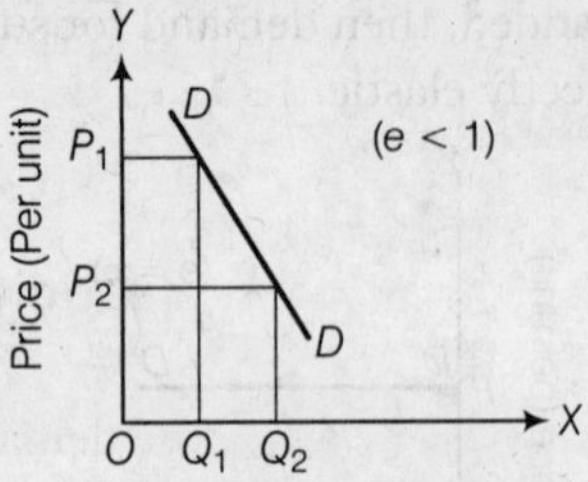

Inelastic Demand

It is shown by a steeper demand curve.

Unitary Elastic Demand ($e = 1$) When the proportion of change in quantity demanded is exactly the same as change in its price, the demand is said to be unitary elastic.

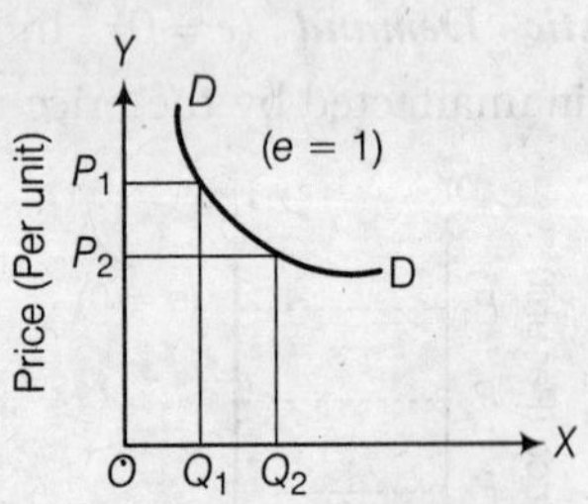

Unitary Elastic Demand Curve

It is mathematically expressed as ($e = 1$).

In this case, demand curve would be a rectangular hyperbola.

Measurement of Price Elasticity

There are different methods of measuring price elasticity of demand, which are as follows

Percentage Method or Proportionate Method As per this method, proportionate change in demand is divided by proportionate change in price.

$$e = \frac{\text{\% Change in Quantity Demanded}}{\text{\% Change in Price}}$$

% Change in Quantity Demanded

$$= \frac{\text{New Quantity Demanded} - \text{Old Quantity Demanded}}{\text{Old Quantity Demanded}} \times 100$$

$$\text{\% Change in Price} = \frac{\text{New Price} - \text{Old Price}}{\text{Old Price}} \times 100$$

Proportionate method formula

$$e = \frac{\Delta Q}{Q} \div \frac{\Delta P}{P}$$

$$\therefore \quad e = \frac{\Delta Q}{Q} \times \frac{P}{\Delta P}$$

$$\text{or} \quad e = \frac{\Delta Q}{\Delta P} \times \frac{P}{Q}$$

Total Outlay Expenditure Method When price of a commodity rises or falls, the expenditure incurred on this commodity also change. This method is called total expenditure method. This is given by Dr. Alfred Marshall.

According to this method,

- When with a change in price, the total outlay remains unchanged, demand is unitary elastic ($e = 1$).
- When with a rise in price, the total outlay falls and *vice-versa*, elasticity of demand is greater than unity ($e > 1$).
- When with a rise in price, the total outlay also rises and *vice-versa*, elasticity of demand is less than unity ($e < 1$).

Point or Geometric Method Elasticity measured at a point on a demand curve is known as point elasticity of demand. Point elasticity on a straight line demand curve can be calculated by using the formula.

$$e = \frac{\text{Lower segment of the demand curve}}{\text{Upper segment of the demand curve}}$$

Arc Elasticity Method This method is used to measure elasticity of demand on an arc of the demand curve. When elasticity is computed between two separate points on a demand curve, this is known as arc elasticity.

The formula is

$$e = \frac{(Q_1 - Q_0)}{(Q_1 + Q_0)} \div \frac{(P_1 - P_0)}{(P_1 + P_0)}$$

Here, Q_0 = Original quantity
Q_1 = New quantity
P_0 = Original price
P_1 = New price

Factors Affecting Price Elasticity of Demand

Nature of Commodity *It can be*

- ***Necessities*** The demand for necessities is inelastic because when their prices rise, the consumers' demand will fall very slightly.
- ***Luxuries*** Demand for luxuries is elastic. If their prices fall, demand will increase by a much greater percentage, but if their prices rise, consumers will reduce their demand considerably.

Availability of Substitutes The more close and numerous availability of substitutes a commodity has, the more will be its price elasticity of demand, *i.e.* demand is price elastic. This is because if the price of a commodity rises, consumers would then shift to other substitutes.

Thus, the demand for the commodity will fall by a greater proportion. But fewer substitutes a commodity has, the lower is the price elasticity of demand (inelastic). However, demand for a group of commodity as a whole has an inelastic demand.

Proportion of Income Spent on a Commodity Commodities on which a very low proportion of income is spent, the demand for the such commodity is inelastic. On the other hand, commodities on which a large proportion of income is spent, the demand is elastic.

Number of Uses of a Product A product, which has several uses, has an elastic demand. *e.g.* people use electricity for many purposes. A slight fall in the price of electricity will cause quantity demanded to increase by a larger extent. Consumers will be in a position to afford its use even for less important purposes. On the other hand, a product, which has a single use, has an inelastic demand, *e.g.* Toothpaste.

Habit There are certain goods which people consume because they have developed a habit, *e.g.* cigarettes for a chain-smoker. Once consumers develop a habit for a particular commodity, they will continue to demand even if the price increases. Thus, the demand for these commodities is inelastic since quantity demanded will change very slightly to a change in price.

Time Period Demand tends to be more elastic in the long run than in the short-run. This is because it takes time for consumers to develop satisfactory substitutes. *e.g.* if the price of petrol rises, consumers will find it very difficult to switch from petrol to diesel immediately. Thus, in the short-run, demand for petrol will fall by a smaller percentage.

Income Elasticity of Demand

It refers to the degree of responsiveness of demand for a commodity to a given change in the income of a consumer.

$$E_y = \frac{\text{Proportionate change in quantity demanded}}{\text{Proportionate change in consumer's income}}$$

$$E_y = \frac{y}{Q} \times \frac{\Delta Q}{\Delta y}$$

Types/Degrees of Income Elasticity of Demand

Negative Income Elasticity When the demand for a product decreases as income increases and *vice-versa*, the income elasticity of demand is negative. The demand for inferior goods is of this type.

Zero Income Elasticity When a change in income has no effect upon the quantity demanded of a product, the income elasticity of demand would be zero. *e.g.* demand for salt.

Unit Income Elasticity When demand for a product increases in the same proportion in which income increases, income elasticity of demand will be equal to unity.

Income elasticity of demand for necessities will be less than unity and for comforts will be more than unity.

Cross Elasticity of Demand

Cross elasticity of demand refers to the degree of responsiveness of demand for one good to the change in the price of the other good.

It can be calculated as follows

e_c (Cross Elasticity of Demand)

$$= \frac{\text{Percentage change in the demand of } x}{\text{Percentage change in the price of } y} = \frac{\Delta Q_x}{\Delta P_y} \times \frac{P_y}{Q_x}$$

Where, ΔQ_x = Change in quantity of x

ΔP_y = Change in price of y

P_y = Original price of y

Q_x = Original quantity of x

EXAM BASED QUESTIONS

Business Economics

1 Marginal cost curve cuts the average cost curve from below at
(a) its lowest point
(b) the left of the lowest point
(c) right of the lowest point
(d) All of the above

2 Which of the following is the best general definition of the study of economics?
(a) Inflation and unemployment in a growing economy
(b) The best way to invest in the stock market
(c) Business decision-making under foreign competition
(d) Individual and social choice in the face of scarcity

3 Consider the following statements.
1. Business economics is a special branch of economics applied in business decision-making.
2. The nature of business economics is applied not theoretical.
3. The nature of business economics is based on micro economics.

Which of the statement(s) given above is/are correct?
Codes
(a) Only 1 (b) Both 1 and 3
(c) Both 2 and 3 (d) All of the above

4 Which of the following is a reason for economic problem?
(a) Unlimited ends or wants
(b) Scarce resources
(c) Alternative uses of scarce resources
(d) All of the above

5 Which of the following is the best general definition of the study of business economics?
(a) The best way to invest in the stock market
(b) Behaviour of the firm in theory and practices
(c) Individual choice in the face of scarcity
(d) Use of economic theories for making business decisions

6 For profit maximisation of a firm following conditions should be fulfilled.
1. MC = MR.
2. Marginal cost curve cuts the average cost curve from below.

Which of the above said condition(s) is/are correct?
Codes
(a) Only 1
(b) Only 2
(c) Both 1 and 2
(d) Neither 1 nor 2

7 What is the fundamental premise of economics?
(a) Individuals are capable of establishing goals and acting in a manner consistent with achievement of those goals
(b) Natural resources will always be scarce
(c) Individuals choose the alternative for which they believe the net gains to be the greatest
(d) No matter what the circumstances, individuals choice always involve a trade-off

8 According to Lionel Robbins definition of economics, "Economics is a science which
(a) studies human behaviour
(b) relationship between ends and scares resources
(c) scarce means have alternate uses
(d) All of the above

9 Consider the following statements.
1. The main purpose of a business firm is to earn profit.
2. Capital management(s) is dealt within business economic.
3. Cost analysis is required for cost control.

Which of the statement(s) given above is/are correct?
Codes
(a) Only 3 (b) Only 2
(c) Only 1 (d) All of the above

Demand Analysis

10 In the case of giffen goods like bajra, a fall in its price tends to
(a) reduce the demand
(b) increase the demand
(c) demand will remain constant
(d) None of the above

11 Which of the following pairs of commodities is an example of substitutes?
(a) Coffee and milk
(b) Diamond and cow
(c) Pen and ink
(d) Mustard oil and coconut oil

12 In a demand schedule, quantity demanded
(a) varies directly with price
(b) varies inversely with price
(c) varies proportionately with price
(d) None of the above

13 A good, whose demand by a consumer falls with the rise in income of that consumer is called
(a) normal goods
(b) inferior goods
(c) substitute goods
(d) complementary goods

14 Which of the following does not influence the individual demand for a product?

(a) Price of product
(b) Price of close substitute
(c) State of production technology
(d) Change in climatic condition

15 Which is a cross demand curve?

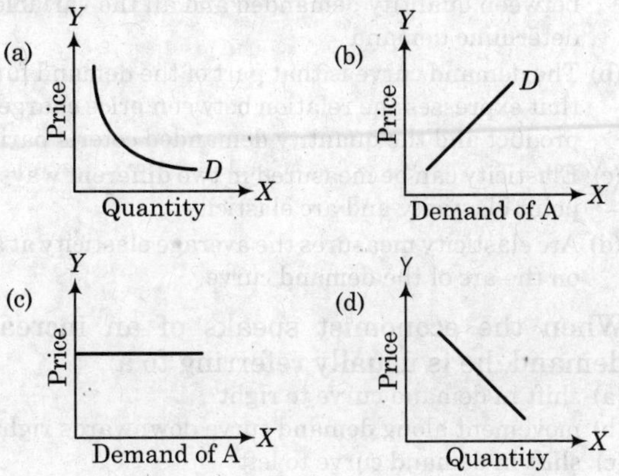

16 Shifts in demand curve as shown in the figure below represents

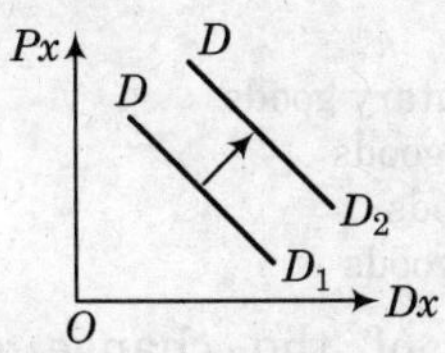

(a) extension of demand (b) increment of demand
(c) increase of demand (d) expansion of demand

17 Which one of these is an exception to the law of demand?

(a) Demonstration effect goods
(b) Giffen goods
(c) Future scarcity of goods
(d) All of the above

18 If the demand curve is a rectangular hyperbola, elasticity is

(a) 1 (b) 0
(c) ∞ (d) less than 1

19 Reasons for change in demand (increase or decrease in demand) are

(a) change income of consumer
(b) change in population
(c) change in fashion and customs
(d) All of the above

20 Demand for a commodity depends on the relative price of its

(a) substitute goods
(b) abnormal goods
(c) inferior goods
(d) None of the above

21 Demand curve of a normal goods is

(a) graphical presentation of law of demand
(b) slopes downward
(c) explain the relation between price and demand
(d) All of the above

22 The demand curve is .... representation of a demand schedule, demand curve slopes .... ward from left to right.

(a) graphical, down (b) down, graphical
(c) graphical, up (d) schedule, up

23 For inferior commodities, income effect is

(a) zero (b) negative (c) infinite (d) positive

24 When the decrease in the price of one good causes the demand for another good to decrease, the goods are

(a) complements (b) normal
(c) inferior (d) substitutes

25 Which of the following shapes of demand curve shows elasticity equal to unity at all points?

(a) a rectangular hyperbola (b) a perpendicular
(c) a parabola (d) a straight line

26 An income demand curve for an inferior commodity slopes

(a) horizontal (b) vertical
(c) upwards to the right (d) downwards to the right

27 When the demand curve is a rectangular hyperbola, a fall in the price of a commodity causes total expenditures on the commodity to

(a) increase (b) decrease
(c) remain unchanged (d) None of these

28 Which one is not a type of demand?

(a) Price demand (b) Derived demand
(c) Joint demand (d) All of these

29 The total effect of a price change of a commodity is

(a) Substitution effect + Price effect
(b) Substitution effect – Income effect
(c) Substitution effect + Income effect
(d) Substitution effect – Price effect

30 Individual demand schedule shows

(a) tabular presentation of law of demand
(b) the prices of goods
(c) the quantities of a commodity purchased
(d) All of the above

31 Goods which are paradoxical to the law of demand are

(a) giffen goods
(b) substitute goods
(c) complementary goods
(d) None of the above

32 Baumol has suggested as an alternative objective for profit maximisation, the maximisation of

(a) sales (b) profit
(c) income (d) None of these

33 According to law of demand,
(a) price of commodity is an independent variable
(b) quantity demanded is a dependent variable
(c) reciprocal relationship is found between price and quantity demanded
(d) All of the above

34 According to the law of diminishing marginal utility,
(a) utility is at a maximum with the first unit
(b) increasing units of consumption increase the marginal utility
(c) marginal product will fall as more units are consumed
(d) total utility will rise at a falling rate as more units are consumed

35 Market demand for any goods is a function of the
1. price per unit of the goods
2. price per unit of other goods
3. incomes of consumers
4. tastes of consumers

Select the correct answer using the codes given below
Codes
(a) Only 1 (b) Both 1 and 3
(c) Both 3 and 4 (d) All of the above

36 Which of the following is a correct statement?
(a) Decrease in input prices causes a leftward shift in the supply curve
(b) The demand for a commodity is inversely related to the price of its substitutes
(c) The desire for a commodity backed by ability and willingness to pay is demanded
(d) When income increases demand for essential goods increases more than proportionately

37 Which of the following statement(s) is/are not correctly?
(a) Decrease in own price of the commodity means extension of demand
(b) Increase in own price of the commodity means increase in demand
(c) Both (a) and (b)
(d) None of the above

38 The demand function is a statement of the relationship between
(a) quantity of factors of production
(b) quantity of product demanded and all the factors that affect this quantity
(c) quantity demanded and profit
(d) product demand and cost of output

39 Movement along a demand curve as a result of change in price is known as
(a) change in quantity demanded
(b) change in demand
(c) increase or decrease in demand
(d) None of the above

40 Ceteris paribus, a change in the price of a commodity causes the quantity purchased of its complements to move
(a) in the same direction (b) in the opposite direction
(c) in an improper manner (d) cannot be determined

41 Which of the following statement is incorrect?
(a) The demand function specifies the relationship between quantity demanded and all the variables that determine demand
(b) The demand curve is that part of the demand function, that expresses the relation between price charged for a product and the quantity demanded ceteris paribus
(c) Elasticity can be measured in two different ways called point elasticity and arc elasticity
(d) Arc elasticity measures the average elasticity at a point on the arc of the demand curve

42 When the economist speaks of an increase in demand, he is usually referring to a
(a) shift in demand curve to right
(b) movement along demand curve downwards right
(c) shift in demand curve to left
(d) movement along demand curve upwards

43 When in order to satisfy a given want, two or more goods are needed in combination, these goods are called
(a) complementary goods
(b) substitute goods
(c) inferior goods
(d) abnormal goods

44 The extent of the change of demand for a commodity to a given change in .... , other demand determinants remaining constant, is termed as the .... of demand.
(a) price, price elasticity (b) price, cross elasticity
(c) income, price (d) None of these

45 Assume in a competitive market that price is initially above the equilibrium level. We can predict that price will
(a) decrease, quantity demanded will decrease and quantity supplied will increase
(b) decrease and quantity demanded and quantity supplied will both decrease
(c) decrease, quantity demanded will increase and quantity supplied will decrease
(d) increase, quantity demanded will decrease and quantity supplied will increase

46 Which of the following statement is incorrect?
(a) If demand increases and supply decreases, equilibrium price will rise
(b) If supply increases and demand decreases, equilibrium price will fall
(c) If demand decreases and supply increases, equilibrium price will rise
(d) If supply declines and demand remains constant, equilibrium price will rise

47 The demand for a product would be more inelastic
(a) the greater is the time under consideration
(b) the greater is the number of substitutes available to buyers
(c) the less expensive is the product in relation to incomes
(d) All of the above

48 Giffen goods may be defined as those goods whose price effect is ...... and income effect is ..... .
(a) positive, negative
(b) negative, positive
(c) positive, elastic
(d) negative, elastic

49 Put these concepts in chronological order of their development.
1. Law of demand
2. Law of indifference
3. Law of diminishing MU
4. Revealed preference theory
5. Indifference curve

Codes
(a) 1,3,2,4,5 (b) 1,2,3,4,5
(c) 1,3,2,5,4 (d) 1,5,2,4,3

50 Good Y is substitute for good X, if
1. a fall in price of good X leads to the fall in the marginal utility of good Y.
2. a fall in price of good X leads to the fall in the quantity purchased of good Y.

Select the correct answer using the codes given below

Codes
(a) Only 1 (b) Only 2
(c) Both 1 and 2 (d) Neither 1 nor 2

51 Consider the following statements.
1. Demand is always related to price and time.
2. Individual demand is the sum total of individual demand function.
3. Demand is desire/want back of money.

Which of the statement(s) given above is/are correct?

Codes
(a) Both 1 and 2
(b) Only 1
(c) Only 2
(d) All of the above

52 Which of the following statement(s) is/are correct?
(a) Degree of responsiveness of demand to a given change in its price is price elasticity of demand
(b) Degree of responsiveness of demand for one good to change in price of other good is income elasticity of demand
(c) Both (a) and (b)
(d) None of the above

53 Which of the following statement(s) is/are incorrect?
(a) There exists an inverse relationship between demand for commodity and its price in case of complementary goods
(b) There exists direct relationship between demand for commodity and its price in case of substitute goods
(c) Both (a) and (b)
(d) None of the above

54 Consider the following statements
1. Decrease in demand is caused by change in factors other than own price of the commodity.
2. Contraction of demand is caused by decrease in own price of the same commodity.
3. Extension of demand is caused by increase in own price of the same commodity.

Which of the statement(s) given above is/are correct?

Codes
(a) Only 1 (b) Both 1 and 2
(c) Both 2 and 3 (d) None of these

55 Which of the following statement is true?
(a) In inferior goods, the income and substitution effects are negative
(b) In inferior goods, the income and substitution effects are positive
(c) In case of inferior goods, the income effect is negative although the substitution effect is positive
(d) In case of inferior goods, the income effect is positive although the substitution effect is negative

Elasticity of Demand

56 Demand for safety pins is
(a) elastic (b) inelastic
(c) unity (d) None of these

57 In general, the demand for necessities is relatively
(a) inelastic (b) elastic
(c) unity (d) None of these

58 Unitary elasticity of demand refers to
(a) proportionate change in price and quantity
(b) more than proportionate change in price
(c) less than proportionate change in price
(d) None of the above

59 The elasticity of demand for luxury good is
(a) infinite
(b) more than one
(c) less than one
(d) equal to one

60 Formula for price elasticity of demand is
(a) $\frac{Q_1 - Q_0}{P_1 - P_0} \times \frac{P_1 + P_0}{Q_1 + Q_0}$ (b) $\frac{\Delta Q}{\Delta P} \times \frac{P}{Q}$
(c) $\frac{dQ}{dP} \times \frac{P}{Q}$ (d) $\frac{\Delta P / P}{\Delta Q / Q}$

61 Which one is the technique of measuring elasticity of demand?
(a) Total outlay method (b) Arc method
(c) Point method (d) All of these

62 The demand for life saving drugs
(a) elastic (b) inelastic
(c) infinity (d) None of these

63 When demand for the product increases in the same proportion in which income increases, income elasticity of demand will be equal to
(a) unity (b) elastic
(c) inelastic (d) None of these

64 The price elasticity of demand is the
(a) ratio of the percentage change in quantity demanded to the percentage change in price
(b) ratio of the change in price to the change in quantity demanded
(c) ratio of the change in quantity demanded to the change in price
(d) ratio of the percentage change in price to the percentage change in quantity demanded

65 Elasticity of demand measures the
(a) volume of product
(b) sensitivity of sales to change in a particular causal factor
(c) value of price and cost
(d) sensitivity of production to change in a particular cost

66 When demand is inelastic, an increase in the price of a commodity causes the total expenditures of a consumers of the commodity to
(a) increase (b) decrease
(c) remain unchanged (d) None of these

67 Demand is elastic when
(a) change in price does not change the demand
(b) change in fashion causes a great change in demand
(c) change in income causes a change in demand
(d) small change in price causes big changes in demand

68 Demand for electricity is elastic because
(a) it is very expensive
(b) it has alternative uses
(c) it has a number of close substitutes
(d) None of the above

69 $\dfrac{\text{\% Change in quantity demanded of good } x}{\text{\% Change in the price of good } y}$

This formula indicates to
(a) cross price elasticity of demand
(b) income elasticity of demand
(c) price elasticity of supply
(d) cost elasticity of supply

70 The nature of cross price elasticity of demand in case of complementary products will be
(a) positive (b) negative
(c) Both (a) and (b) (d) zero

71 What is the nature of elasticity of demand for luxury item like high class furnitures?
(a) Unit elastic
(b) Highly elastic
(c) Fairly elastic
(d) Zero elastic

72 Elasticity of demand is based on which of the following factors?
(a) Range of substitutes available
(b) Joint demand
(c) Proportion of income spent on the commodity
(d) All of the above

73 The responsiveness of changes in quantity demanded to change in price of other commodity is known as
(a) price elasticity of demand
(b) income elasticity of demand
(c) cross elasticity of demand
(d) None of the above

74 The responsiveness of changes in quantity demanded to change in price is known as
(a) price elasticity of demand
(b) income elasticity of demand
(c) cross elasticity of demand
(d) None of the above

75 Type(s) of income elasticity of demand is/are
(a) negative income elasticity
(b) zero income elasticity
(c) unit income elasticity
(d) All of the above

76 The concept of price elasticity of demand measures
(a) the slope of the demand curve
(b) the number of buyers in a market
(c) the extent to which the demand curve shifts as the result of a price decline
(d) the sensitivity of consumers to price change

77 If a demand for a product is said to be 'elastic', the value of the elasticity coefficient is
(a) zero (b) greater than one
(c) equal to one (d) less than one

78 The various degrees of price elasticity of demand can be shown on a single demand curve as per which one of the following?
(a) Total outlay method
(b) Proportional method
(c) Arc method
(d) Geometrical method

79 Which of the following statement(s) is/are incorrect?
(a) Elastic demand curve is shown by letter demand curve
(b) Perfectly inelastic demand curve will be a horizontal straight line
(c) Both (a) and (b)
(d) None of the above

80 Calculate elasticity of demand when a 60% increase in the price of rice causes the amount of rice you buy to fall by 120%.
(a) 2 (b) 4
(c) 6 (d) 8

81 When the income elasticity of demand is greater than unity, the commodity is
(a) a necessity
(b) a luxury
(c) inferior good
(d) non-related good

82 Income elasticity is computed by the formula
(a) $e_i = \dfrac{Q_1 - Q_2}{P_1}$ (b) $e_i = \dfrac{\frac{Q_2 - Q_1}{Q_1}}{\frac{Y_2 - Y_1}{Y_1}}$
(c) $e_i = \dfrac{Q_2 - Q_1}{Q_1} \times \dfrac{Y_1}{Y_2 - y} \times 100$ (d) $e_1 = \dfrac{Y_1 - Q_1}{Y_2 - Q_2}$

83 The formula for calculating arc elasticity is
(a) $e_a = \dfrac{Q_1 - Q_2}{Q_1 + Q_2} \div \dfrac{P_1 - P_2}{P_1 + P_2}$ (b) $e_a = \dfrac{Q_1 + Q_2}{Q_1 - Q_2} \div \dfrac{P_1 + P_2}{P_1 - P_2}$
(c) $e_a = \dfrac{Q_1 - Q_2}{P_1 - P_2} \div \dfrac{Q_1 - Q_2}{P_1 + P_2}$ (d) None of these

84 Elasticity of demand measures the
(a) responsiveness of sales to change in advertisement expenditure
(b) responsiveness of demand to change in supply of goods
(c) change in price due to change in demand
(d) change in demand due to change in tastes of consumer

85 Cross elasticity of complementary goods is
(a) negative (b) zero
(c) infinite (d) unitary

86 The larger the co-efficient of price elasticity of demand for a product, the
(a) larger the resulting price change for a given increase in supply
(b) more rapid the rate at which the marginal utility of that product diminishes
(c) less competitive will be the industry supplying that product
(d) smaller the resulting price change for a given increase in supply

87 Elasticity is commonly stated in the form of
(a) 1% change
(b) 5% change
(c) 5% change
(d) All of the above

88 If the cross price elasticity of demand between two goods is negative, then the two goods are
(a) unrelated goods (b) substitutes
(c) complements (d) normal goods

89 Income elasticity of demand is the percentage change in quantity demanded divided by the percentage change in income. Which type of goods have negative income elasticity of demand?
(a) Inferior goods (b) Normal goods
(c) Substitute goods (d) Complementary goods

90 Price discrimination is profitable and possible if the two markets have
(a) equal elasticity of demand
(b) different elasticity of demand
(c) inelastic demand
(d) highly elastic demand

91 Consider the following statements.
1. The demand for necessities in inelastic.
2. Demand for luxuries is elastic.
3. A product which has several uses has an elastic demand.

Which of the statement(s) given above is/are correct?
(a) Only 3
(b) Both 2 and 3
(c) Both 1 and 2
(d) All of the above

Miscellaneous

92 **Statement** I The objective of finance function is wealth maximisation.
Statement II The objective of finance function is profit maximisation.
Codes
(a) Both statements are correct
(b) Both statements are incorrect
(c) Statement I is correct, Statement II is incorrect
(d) Statement I is incorrect, Statement II is correct

Directions (Q. Nos. 93-98) *In the questions given below are two statements labelled as Assertion (A) and Reason (R). In the context of these two statements, which one of the following is correct?*
Codes
(a) Both (A) and (R) are true
(b) Both (A) and (R) are false
(c) (A) is true, but (R) is false
(d) (R) is true, but (A) is false

93 **Assertion** (A) Business economics is tool centric facilitating decision-making in business.
Reason (R) It provides an analytical understanding of economic activities.

94 **Assertion** (A) Demand curve shows that price and quantity demanded are inversely related.
Reason (R) Demand curve illustrates the inverse relationship between the rate of change of demand and price.

95 Assertion (A) The law of demand states that when price falls demand rises and *vice-versa.*
Reason (R) The law of demand indicates the relationship between the price of a commodity and the quantity demanded.

96 Assertion (A) Demand for a commodity refers to quantity of the commodity demanded at a certain price during any particular period of time.
Reason (R) Contraction of demand is the result of increase in the price of the good concerned.

97 Assertion (A) Baumol's theory found that short run revenue maximisation may be consistent with long-run as well.
Reason (R) Sales maximisation is a long-run goal of management.

98 Assertion (A) The demand for inferior goods has negative income elasticity.
Reason (R) Negative income elasticity refers to decrease in income owing to increase in price of a commodity.

Directions (Q. Nos. 99-103) *In the questions given below are two statements labelled as Assertion (A) and Reason (R). In the context of these two statements, which one of the following is correct?*

Codes

(a) Both (A) and (R) are true and (R) is the correct explanation of (A)
(b) Both (A) and (R) are true, but (R) is not the correct explanation of (A)
(c) (A) is true, but (R) is false
(d) (A) is false, but (R) is true

99 Assertion (A) Giffen goods face negative price effect.
Reason (R) Giffen goods has a low demand with rise in its price.

100 Assertion (A) Extension of demand is shown as a downward movement on same demand curve.
Reason (R) Extension of demand is caused due to change in other factors affecting demand.

101 Assertion (A) Inferior goods face positive income effect.
Reason (R) Demand of inferior goods decreases as income of buyer rises.

102 Assertion (A) Demand curve for perfectly elastic demand is a vertical straight line.
Reason (R) Perfectly elastic demand is expressed as $e = 0$.

103 Assertion (A) Elastic demand curve is shown by rectangular hyperbola.
Reason (R) Elastic demand shows no change in demand due to price movement.

104 Match the following.

List I	List II
A. Graphical presentation of demand for a consumer	1. Individual demand
B. Horizontal summation of quantity	2. Market demand

Codes

	A	B		A	B
(a)	1	2	(b)	2	1
(c) Both are incorrect			(d)	1	1

105 Match the following.

List I	List II
A. Normal demand curve	1. Vertical straight line
B. Income consumption curve	2. Downwards to the right
C. Inelastic demand curve	3. Upwards to the right

Codes

	A	B	C		A	B	C
(a)	2	3	1	(b)	1	3	2
(c)	2	1	3	(d)	1	2	3

106 Match the following.

List I	List II
A. Substitute goods	1. Income effect is positive
B. Complementary goods	2. Tea and coffee
C. Normal goods	3. Car and petrol
D. Inferior goods	4. Income effect is negative

Codes

	A	B	C	D		A	B	C	D
(a)	2	3	1	4	(b)	1	2	3	4
(c)	1	4	3	2	(d)	4	3	2	1

107 Match the following.

List I (Economist)	List II (Statement)
A. Robinson	1. The elasticity of demand at any price or at any output is the proportional change of amount purchased in response to a small change in price divided by the proportional change in price
B. Boulding	2. The elasticity of demand may be defined as the percentage change in quantity demanded, which would result from 1% change in price
C. Cairn Cross	3. The elasticity of demand for a commodity is the rate at which the quantity bought changes as the price changes
D. Marshall	4. The elasticity for demand in a market is large or small according to how the amount of demand increases for a given fall in price and diminishes more or less for a given rise in price

Codes

	A	B	C	D		A	B	C	D
(a)	1	3	4	2	(b)	1	2	4	3
(c)	1	3	2	4	(d)	1	2	3	4

108 Match the following.

List I	List II
A. Cross demand is the change in the quantity demanded of a given commodity in response to the	1. Relationship between the price of a commodity and the quantity demanded
B. The elasticity of demand for product will be higher	2. Change in the price of another commodity
C. The law of demand indicates	3. When price falls demand rises
D. The law of demand states	4. The more available are substitutes for that product

Codes

	A	B	C	D		A	B	C	D
(a)	2	4	1	3	(b)	1	2	3	4
(c)	4	1	3	2	(d)	3	2	1	4

109 Match the following.

List I	List II
A. Equilibrium price is the price where the	1. Complimentary goods
B. Excess supply can be defined as	2. Quantity demanded = Quantity supplied
C. Tea and sugar	3. Quantity demanded – Quantity supplied
D. Excess demand can be defined as	4. Quantity supplied – Quantity demanded

Codes

	A	B	C	D		A	B	C	D
(a)	2	4	1	3	(b)	1	2	3	4
(c)	4	1	3	2	(d)	3	2	1	4

110 Match the following.

List I	List II
A. Increase in demand	1. Leftward shift of the demand curve
B. Extension of demand	2. Upward shift of the demand curve
C. Decrease in demand	3. Upward movement on the demand curve
D. Contraction of demand	4. Downward movement on the demand curve

Codes

	A	B	C	D		A	B	C	D
(a)	2	4	1	3	(b)	1	2	3	4
(c)	4	1	3	2	(d)	3	2	1	4

111 Match the following.

List I	List II
A. Normal demand curve	1. Vertical straight line
B. Income consumption curve	2. Downwards to right
C. Inelastic demand curve	3. Infinity
D. Cross elasticity of demand between two perfect substitute will be	4. Upwards to the right

Codes

	A	B	C	D		A	B	C	D
(a)	2	4	1	3	(b)	1	2	3	4
(c)	4	1	3	2	(d)	3	2	1	4

112 Match the following.

List I (Consumer Goods)	List II (Effect on Sale)
A. Essential goods	1. Less than proportionate change in sale
B. Comforts	2. Almost proportionate change in sale
C. Luxuries	3. More than proportionate increase in sale
D. Prestige goods	4. Increase in sale

Codes

	A	B	C	D		A	B	C	D
(a)	1	2	3	4	(b)	2	1	3	4
(c)	2	4	1	3	(d)	3	1	2	4

113 Match the following.

List I	List II
A. Law of demand is fully applicable	1. Giffen goods not applicable
B. Law of demand is not applicable at all	2. Veblon goods partly applicable
C. Law of demand is partly applicable	3. Normal goods fully applicable

Codes

	A	B	C		A	B	C
(a)	1	2	3	(b)	2	3	1
(c)	3	1	2	(d)	2	1	3

114 Match the following.

List I	List II
A. Perfectly elastic demand	1. $e_D = 1$
B. Elastic demand	2. $e_D > 1$
C. Inelastic demand	3. $e_D = 0$
D. Perfectly inelastic demand	4. $e_D = \infty$
E. Unitary elastic demand	5. $e_D < 1$

Codes

	A	B	C	D	E
(a)	2	5	3	1	4
(b)	4	2	5	3	1
(c)	3	1	5	2	4
(d)	1	2	3	4	5

115 Match the following.

List I (Elasticity of Demand)	List II (Curve)
A. Perfectly elastic	1. 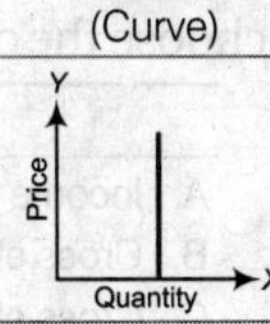
B. Perfectly inelastic	2. 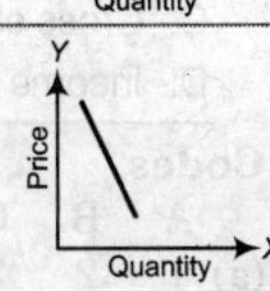

List I (Elasticity of Demand)	List II (Curve)
C. Unitary elastic	3. 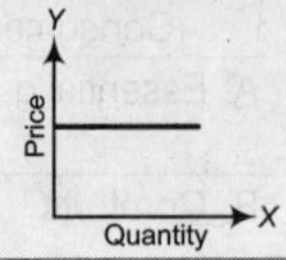
D. Relatively inelastic	4. 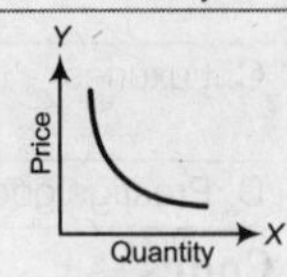

Codes

	A	B	C	D
(a)	1	2	3	4
(b)	3	1	4	2
(c)	1	4	3	2
(d)	2	1	4	3

116 Match the following.

List I (Elasticity Coefficient)	List II (Change in Total Revenue)
A. $e = 0$	1. Increase
B. $e < 1$	2. Decrease
C. $e = 1$	3. No change
D. $e = \infty$	4. Decrease to zero

Codes

	A	B	C	D		A	B	C	D
(a)	1	2	3	4	(b)	1	3	4	2
(c)	2	1	3	4	(d)	4	3	1	2

117 Match the following.

List I	List II
A. Prof Robin	1. Security profits
B. Prof Milton Kafoglis	2. Marris growth maximisation
C. Prof Rothschild	3. Output maximisation

Codes

	A	B	C		A	B	C
(a)	1	2	3	(b)	2	3	1
(c)	3	1	2	(d)	2	1	3

118 Match the following.

List I	List II
A. Decrease in own price	1. Contraction in demand
B. Unfavourable change in taste	2. Extension in demand
C. Increase in own price	3. Decrease in demand

Codes

	A	B	C		A	B	C
(a)	2	1	3	(b)	2	3	1
(c)	1	2	3	(d)	3	2	1

PREVIOUS YEARS' QUESTIONS

December 2018

1 Cardinal utility analysis of consumer's behaviour is based on which combination of the following assumptions.

1. Utility is measurable in terms of cardinal number.
2. Constancy of the marginal utility of money.
3. Utilities of different goods are interdependent.
4. Gossen's first law of consumption.

Choose the correct answer from the codes given below

(a) Both 1 and 2 (b) 1, 2 and 4
(c) 2, 3 and 4 (d) Both 3 and 4

2 Match the items of List I with items of List II and choose the correct answer from the code given below.

List I	List II
A. Income elasticity less than unity	1. Competitive goods
B. Cross elasticity less than unity	2. Inferior goods
C. Cross elasticity less than zero	3. Superior goods
D. Income elasticity less than zero	4. Complementary goods

Codes

	A	B	C	D		A	B	C	D
(a)	1	2	3	4	(b)	4	3	1	2
(c)	3	1	4	2	(d)	4	1	2	3

3 The inverse relationship between the variation in the price and the variation in the quantity demanded in not due to

(a) price effect (b) entry and exit of buyers
(c) Gossen's laws of consumption
(d) law of substitution

July 2018

4 A firm that produces highly substitute goods can adopt which one of the following pricing strategies?

(a) Transfer pricing (b) Going rate pricing
(c) Product bundling (d) Full cost pricing

November 2017

5 **Statement** I Business decision makers deal with the complex, rather chaotic, business conditions of the real world and have to find the way to their destination, *i.e.* achieving the goal that they set for themselves.

Statement II Even without application of economic logic and tools of analysis, business decisions are always rational and real and are not counter productive.

Codes
(a) Both the statements are correct
(b) Both the statements are incorrect
(c) Statement I is correct, while Statement II is incorrect
(d) Statement I is incorrect, while Statement II is correct

6 **Statement** I Point price elasticity of demand in terms of marginal and average revenues can be measured with the following formula $\frac{AR}{AR - MR}$.

Statement II The point price elasticity of demand is the product of the slope of the demand function and the ratio between corresponding price and quantity.

Codes
(a) Both the statements are correct
(b) Both the statements are incorrect
(c) Statement I is correct, while Statement II is incorrect
(d) Statement I is incorrect, while Statement II is correct

January 2017

7 Match the items of List I with items of List II and indicate the code of their correct matching.

List I	List II
A. Non-price quantity relationships of demand	1. Extension and contraction of demand
B. Income effect of a price rise greater than its substitution effect	2. Ordinal utility approach
C. Transitivity and consistency of choices	3. Increase and decrease in demand
D. Price quantity relationships of demand	4. Giffen goods

Codes

	A	B	C	D
(a)	4	2	3	1
(b)	2	1	4	3
(c)	3	4	2	1
(d)	1	2	3	4

December 2015

8 Match the following.

List I	List II
A. Substitute goods	1. Negative cross elasticity
B. Complementary goods	2. Low price elasticity
C. Giffen goods	3. Positive cross elasticity
D. High income group, consumption goods	4. Positive price elasticity

Codes

	A	B	C	D
(a)	3	4	2	1
(b)	3	1	4	2
(c)	2	3	1	4
(d)	1	2	3	4

9 **Assertion** (A) The quantity of a commodity demanded invariably changes inversely to changes in its price.

Reason (R) The price effect is the net result of the positive substitution effect and negative income effect.

Codes
(a) Both (A) and (R) are true (b) (A) is true, but (R) is false
(c) (A) is false, but (R) is true (d) Both (A) and (R) are false

June 2015

10 A rectangular hyperbola shaped demand curve on all its points has
(a) equal slopes of the price demand curve
(b) price elasticity equal to unit
(c) varying price elasticity
(d) both slope and price elasticity equal

11 The following is the demand function in the small market.
= 50 – 5
Where, '*Q*' denotes quantity in physical units and '*P*' denotes price of the commodity. At price ₹ 5, the point price elasticity of demand would be
(a) zero (b) equal to unity
(c) highly elastic (d) highly inelastic

December 2014

12 The inverse relationship variations in the price and quantity demanded is not due to
(a) income effects
(b) substitution effects
(c) future expectations
(d) law of diminishing marginal utility

13 Match the following.

List I	List II
A. Zero income elasticity	1. Substitute goods
B. Unit cross elasticity	2. Complementary goods
C. Positive cross elasticity	3. Indifferent goods
D. Negative cross elasticity	4. Independent goods

Codes

	A	B	C	D
(a)	3	2	1	4
(b)	2	3	4	1
(c)	3	4	1	2
(d)	4	1	2	3

June 2014

14 Which one of the following does not explain the basic nature of business economics?
(a) Behaviour of firms in theory and practice
(b) Distribution theories like rent, wages and interest alongwith the theory of profit
(c) Use of the tools of economic analysis in clarifying problems in organising and evaluating information and in comparing alternative courses of action
(d) Integration of economic theory with business practices for the purpose of facilitating decision-making

15 A rectangular hyperbola shaped demand curve on all its points has
(a) equal slopes and equal point elasticities
(b) unequal slopes and unequal point elasticities
(c) unequal slopes and equal point elasticities
(d) equal slopes and unequal point elasticities

December 2013

16 A measure of the responsiveness of quantity demanded to changes in the price of a related good is known as
(a) cross elasticity of demand
(b) substitution elasticity of demand
(c) complementary elasticity of demand
(d) price elasticity of demand

17 There is no exceptions to the law of demand in the case of
(a) giffen goods
(b) normal goods
(c) articles of conspicuous consumption
(d) ignorance of the buyer

18 What is the degree of elasticity of demand in case the demand is represented by a straight line parallel to the *x*-axis?
(a) $e > 1$ (b) $e = 0$ (c) $e = \infty$ (d) $e < 1$

June 2013

19 Match the following.

List I	List II
A. Contraction of demand	1. Non-price change effect
B. Decrease in demand	2. Demand curve remains the same
C. Increase in demand	3. Price change effect
D. Expansion of demand	4. Shifts the demand curve

Codes

	A	B	C	D		A	B	C	D
(a)	3	1	4	2	(b)	4	3	2	1
(c)	1	2	3	4	(d)	2	4	1	3

20 Demand must have the elements
(a) desire (b) want
(c) quantity, price and time (d) All of these

21 Business economics is a subject which
(a) studies economic relationships
(b) studies economic activities at the aggregate level
(c) deals with the tools of economics used for decision-making in business
(d) studies optimum allocation of limited resources

22 **Assertion** (A) The demand curve has negative slope showing inverse relationship between price and the quantity demanded.
Reason (R) It applies only to giffen goods.
Codes
(a) Both (A) and (R) are true
(b) (A) is true, but (R) is false
(c) (A) is false, but (R) is true
(d) Both (A) and (R) are false

December 2012

23 Which kind of economics explains the phenomenon of cause and effect relationship?
(a) Normative
(b) Positive
(c) Micro
(d) Macro

24 If price of any commodity decrease by 20% and the demand for that commodity increases by 40%, then elasticity of demand would be
(a) perfectly elastic
(b) perfectly inelastic
(c) unit elastic
(d) highly elastic

25 Which one of the following statement is true?
(a) In case of inferior goods, the income effect is negative, although the substitution effect is positive
(b) In inferior goods, the income and substitution effect is positive
(c) In inferior goods, the income and substitution effect are negative
(d) In case of inferior goods, the income effect is positive, although the substitution effect is negative

June 2012

26 Normal demand drives slopes
(a) upward (b) downward
(c) horizontal (d) vertical

ANSWERS

Objective Questions

1 *(a)*	2 *(d)*	3 *(d)*	4 *(d)*	5 *(d)*	6 *(c)*	7 *(c)*	8 *(d)*	9 *(d)*	10 *(a)*
11 *(d)*	12 *(b)*	13 *(b)*	14 *(c)*	15 *(b)*	16 *(c)*	17 *(d)*	18 *(a)*	19 *(d)*	20 *(a)*
21 *(d)*	22 *(a)*	23 *(b)*	24 *(d)*	25 *(a)*	26 *(c)*	27 *(c)*	28 *(c)*	29 *(c)*	30 *(d)*
31 *(a)*	32 *(a)*	33 *(c)*	34 *(d)*	35 *(d)*	36 *(c)*	37 *(b)*	38 *(b)*	39 *(a)*	40 *(b)*
41 *(d)*	42 *(a)*	43 *(a)*	44 *(a)*	45 *(c)*	46 *(b)*	47 *(c)*	48 *(a)*	49 *(c)*	50 *(c)*
51 *(a)*	52 *(a)*	53 *(a)*	54 *(a)*	55 *(c)*	56 *(b)*	57 *(a)*	58 *(a)*	59 *(a)*	60 *(b)*
61 *(d)*	62 *(b)*	63 *(a)*	64 *(a)*	65 *(a)*	66 *(a)*	67 *(d)*	68 *(b)*	69 *(a)*	70 *(b)*
71 *(b)*	72 *(d)*	73 *(c)*	74 *(a)*	75 *(d)*	76 *(d)*	77 *(b)*	78 *(d)*	79 *(b)*	80 *(a)*
81 *(b)*	82 *(b)*	83 *(a)*	84 *(a)*	85 *(a)*	86 *(d)*	87 *(a)*	88 *(c)*	89 *(a)*	90 *(b)*
91 *(d)*	92 *(a)*	93 *(a)*	94 *(a)*	95 *(a)*	96 *(a)*	97 *(c)*	98 *(c)*	99 *(b)*	100 *(c)*
101 *(d)*	102 *(b)*	103 *(b)*	104 *(b)*	105 *(a)*	106 *(a)*	107 *(d)*	108 *(a)*	109 *(a)*	110 *(a)*
111 *(a)*	112 *(a)*	113 *(c)*	114 *(b)*	115 *(b)*	116 *(a)*	117 *(b)*	118 *(b)*		

Previous Years' Questions

1 *(b)*	2 *(c)*	3 *(b)*	4 *(b)*	5 *(c)*	6 *(a)*	7 *(c)*	8 *(b)*	9 *(a)*	10 *(d)*
11 *(b)*	12 *(c)*	13 *(c)*	14 *(b)*	15 *(c)*	16 *(a)*	17 *(b)*	18 *(c)*	19 *(a)*	20 *(d)*
21 *(c)*	22 *(b)*	23 *(b)*	24 *(d)*	25 *(a)*	26 *(b)*				

CHAPTER 11

Consumer's Behaviour and Producer's Behaviour

The theory of microeconomics primarily deals with economic concerns associated with an individual consumer and producer. This chapter will discuss about the behaviour of both consumers and producers in the presence of market forces of demand and supply.

Consumer's Behaviour

Consumer's behaviour refers to the study of how consumers buy or use goods and services to satisfy their needs and wants. In other words, It is the study of how a consumer behaves in the marketplace to maximise his/her satisfaction given their limited income. In other words, we can say that a consumer's behaviour is guided by his intention to maximise the utility derived from the consumption of goods and services.

Utility

In economics, the term 'utility' refers to the quality of a commodity by virtue of which it satisfies consumer's wants or want satisfying power of a good is called utility. It is measured in terms of 'utils' or 'units of utility'. In other words, it is the satisfaction (value for money) derived by a person from the consumption of a good or service or from being in a particular place and for the maximisation of which all economic actions are motivated.

Utility has following characteristics

- Utility is subjective in nature, *i.e.* it varies from person to person.
- Utility depends upon urgency of wants, *i.e.* how urgently one needs a good or service will determine its utility.

In this Chapter

- *Utility*
- *Consumer Equilibrium*
- *Law of Variable Proportion*
- *Law of Returns to Scale*
- *Concept of Cost*
- *Concept of Revenue*

- Utility should not be confused with 'usefullness', *i.e.* one commodity may give utility but it may or may not be useful like liquor, tobacco etc.

Approaches to Utility

There are following two approaches to utility

Cardinal Approach

Under cardinal approach, utility is measured in terms of units like 2, 4, 6, 8 and 10, etc. It is called cardinal measurement of utility. It is measured in terms of 'utils'. This approach was given by **Marshall**.

Ordinal Approach

Under ordinal approach, utility is measured in terms of psychological satisfaction on consuming one good in comparison to other. This approach was given by **Hicks** and **Allen**.

Measures of Utility

Utility has the following measures

Marginal Utility

It refers to additional utility from consumption of an additional unit of a commodity. It is calculated as the change in total utility, which results from a unit increase in consumption.

Or $MU = TU_n - TU_{n-1}$

Or $\dfrac{\text{Change in Total Utility}}{\text{Change in Quantity Consumed}}$

Here, MU = Marginal Utility

TU_n = Total Utility from n units of a commodity

TU_{n-1} = Total Utility from $(n-1)$ units of a commodity

Suppose, the total utility from the consumption of 6 units of a commodity is equal to 30 units and from 7 units we get 35 utils as the total utility, then the marginal utility of 7th unit is equal to 5 utils (35 – 30).

Total Utility

It refers to sum total of utilities from consumption of different units of a good. It is calculated as the sum of marginal utilities obtained from the consumption of different units of a commodity.

Or $TU = \Sigma MU$

Here, TU = Total Utility

ΣMU = Sum total of Marginal Utilities

Suppose, the marginal utilities of 3 units of a commodity are 3, 2 and 1 utils, respectively. Hence, total utility will be equal to 6 utils (3 + 2 + 1).

Relationship between Marginal Utility and Total Utility

It can be explained with the help of following schedule and diagram

Units of a Commodity	MU (Utils)	TU (Utils)
1	6	6
2	4	6 + 4 = 10
3	2	10 + 2 = 12
4	0	12 + 0 = 12
5	–2	12 – 2 = 10
6	–4	10 – 4 = 6

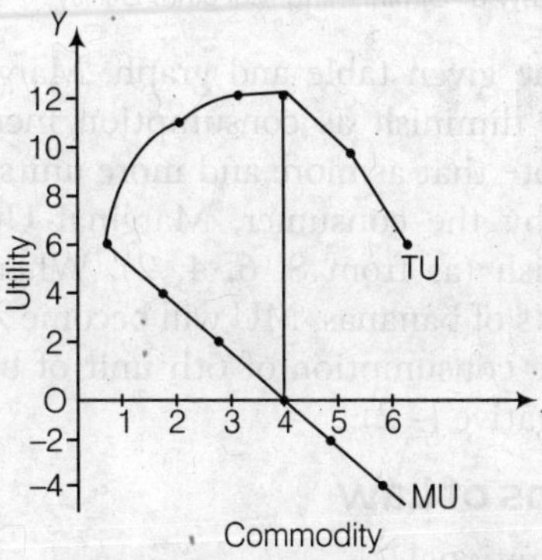

Relationship between Marginal Utility and Total Utility

As long as MU remains positive, TU increases at a diminishing rate, when MU becomes zero, TU is maximum and constant, when MU is negative, TU begins to fall. In short,

(+) MU — TU increases at diminishing rate
(0) MU — Maximum and constant TU
(–) MU — TU falls

MU can be positive, zero or negative. But TU is always positive. In the beginning, TU increases then after reaching its maximum point it starts to decline. At the first unit of consumption TU and MU are the same.

Law of Diminishing Marginal Utility

It states that keeping other things constant marginal utility tends to decline as more and more units of a commodity are consumed by a consumer. In other words, as more and more units of a commodity are consumed by the consumer, the intensity of desire for a commodity tends to decrease. This is called law of diminishing marginal utility. This law was given by Gossen and is also referred to as Gossen's first law of consumption.

This can be explained with the help of following schedule and diagram

Units of a Commodity (Bananas)	MU (Utils)
1	8
2	6
3	4
4	2
5	0
6	– 2

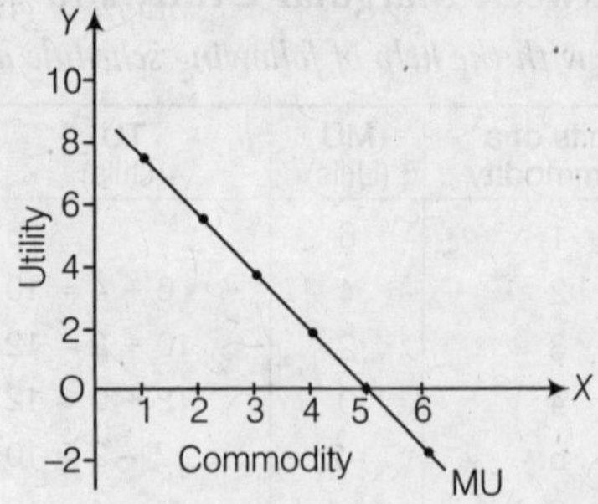

Law of Diminishing Marginal Utility

According to the given table and graph, Marginal Utility (MU) tends to diminish as consumption increases. It is important to note that as more and more units of bananas are consumed by the consumer, Marginal Utility (MU) tends to diminish (as from 8, 6, 4, 2). When consumer consumes 5 units of bananas, MU will become zero (0) and after that at the consumption of 6th unit of banana, MU will become negative (– 2).

Assumptions of Law

- Consumer is rational.
- Only standard units of the commodity are consumed, like, a cup of tea not its spoon.
- Consumption of the commodity should be continuous.
- Price and income remains constant.
- Marginal utility of money remains constant.

Consumer's Equilibrium

Consumer's equilibrium refers to a state where a consumer attains maximum satisfaction with his given income. *It can be understood with the help of the following approaches*

Under Cardinal Approach

Cardinal approach has two situations, when consumer consumes only one good/commodity and when he consumes two or more commodities.

One Good/Commodity Case In this case, it is assumed that consumer is consuming only good *X*. Condition of equilibrium (in one commodity case).

$$\frac{MU_x}{P_x} = MU_m$$

Taking $MU_m = 1$, then $MU_x = P_x$

Here, MU_x = Marginal Utility of Good *X*,
P_x = Price of Good *X*,
MU_m = Marginal Utility of money

This can be understood with the help of the following schedule and diagram

Q	MU_x	P_x
1	10	4
2	8	4
3	6	4
4	4	4
5	2	4

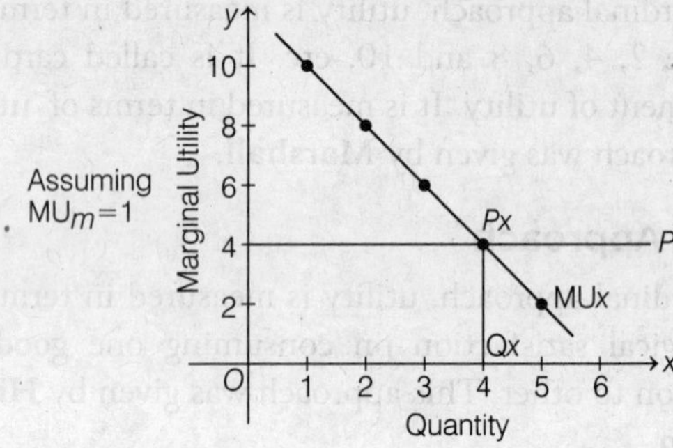

From the above schedule and graph, we can infer that the consumer is at equilibrium when he is consuming 4 units of Good *X* because at this level of consumption MU_x is 4 and P_x is also 4. Below this level of consumption, MU_x exceeds its price, therefore consumer will be tempted to increase his consumption. Beyond this level, MU_x is less than its price. So, the consumer will be at equilibrium only when he consumes 4 units.

Two Goods/More Than Two Goods It is based on the law of equi-marginal utility also given by Prof Gossen. This law states that consumers, in order to maximise their satisfaction should spend their money income on two goods in such a manner that the ratio of marginal utility of a good to its price becomes equal to the marginal utility of other good to its price. This law is also referred to as Gossen's second law of consumption.

Symbolically, *the conditions of equilibrium can be written as follows*

- $\frac{MU_x}{P_x} = \frac{MU_y}{P_y} = MU_m$

  taking $MU_m = 1$, then $\frac{MU_x}{P_x} = \frac{MU_y}{P_y}$

  Here, MU_x = MU of Good *X*
  MU_y = MU of Good *Y*
  P_x = Price of Good *X*
  P_y = Price of Good *Y*

- $P_xQ_x + P_yQ_y = M$

  Here, Q_x = Quantity of Good *X*
  Q_y = Quantity of Good *Y*
  M = Money income of consumer

This can be understood with the help of the following schedule and diagram

Q	MU_x	MU_y
1	10	8
2	8	7
3	6	6
4	4	5
5	2	4

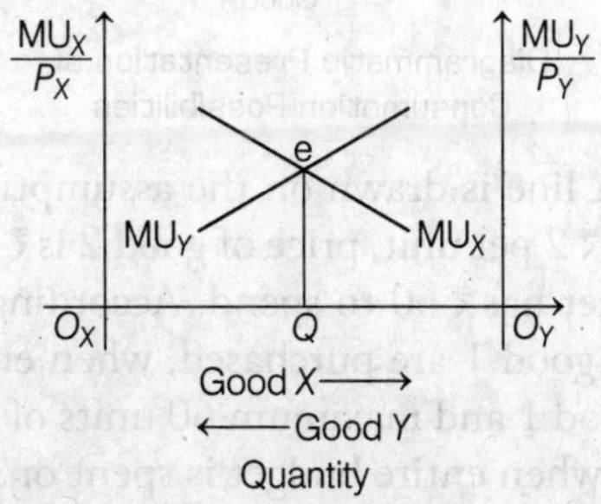

Taking $MU_m = 1$

Assuming consumer's income is ₹ 6 and $P_x = P_y =$ ₹ 1

According to above situation, consumer is in equilibrium when $\frac{MU_x}{P_x} = \frac{MU_y}{P_y}$ in the above example this condition is satisfied at

$(Q_x, Q_4) = (2, 1), (3, 3), (4, 5)$

However, combination (2, 1) is less than consumer's income and (4, 5) is greater, hence he will be in equilibrium at (3, 3).

Many Goods Case

- $\frac{MU_x}{P_x} = \frac{MU_y}{MU_y} = \frac{MU_z}{P_z} \ldots\ldots \frac{MU_n}{P_n}$
- $P_xQ_x + P_yQ_y + \ldots\ldots P_nQ_n = M$

Under Ordinal Approach

Indifference curve analysis assumes that the consumer behaviour is governed by monotonic preferences. It refers to a situation when more of a good offers higher level of satisfaction to the consumers.

The equilibrium of a consumer is struck at a point, where indifference curve and price line are tangent to each other or where,

Slope of Indifference Curve = Slope of Price Line

The conditions of consumer's equilibrium under this approach can be summed up as follows

- Marginal Rate of Substitution $(MRS_{xy}) = \frac{P_x}{P_y}$
- At the point of equilibrium, IC (Indifference Curve) should be convex to the origin, *i.e.* MRS must be diminishing.

- *This can be understood with the help of graph given below*

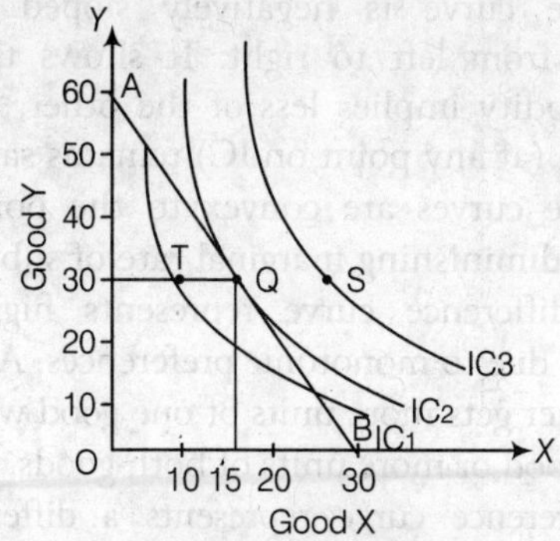

Consumer Equilibrium

Equilibrium is struck at point *Q*. At the point of equilibrium, price line and IC are tangent to each other. Implying that the slope of price line $\left(\frac{P_X}{P_Y}\right)$ = Slope of IC $\left(\frac{\Delta Y}{\Delta X}\right)$, called marginal rate of substitution.

Indifference Curve Analysis

Some of the important terms related to indifference curve analysis are explained below

Indifference Curve

It is a curve showing different combinations of two goods, each combination offering the same level of satisfaction to the consumer.

This concept can be understood with the help of following indifference set and indifference curve

Different Combination of Apples and Oranges

Combination	Number of apples	Number of oranges
A	1	10
B	2	7
C	3	5
D	4	4

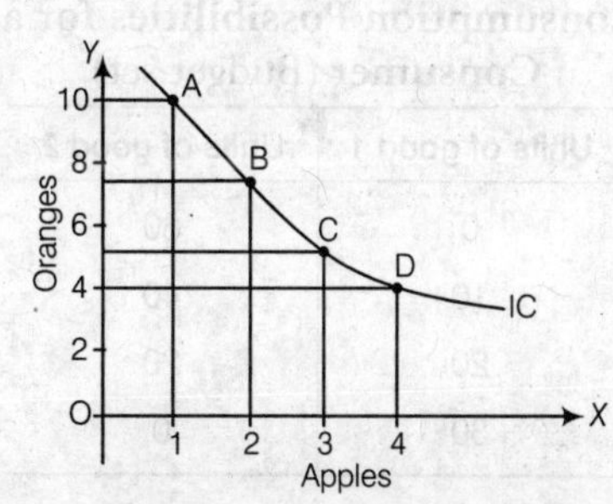

Indifference Curve (diagrammatic presentation of indifference set)

It has the following characteristics

- Indifference curve is negatively sloped or it slope downward from left to right. It shows that more of one commodity implies less of the other, so that total satisfaction (at any point on IC) remains same.
- Indifference curves are convex to the point of origin because of diminishing marginal rate of substitution.
- Higher indifference curve represents higher level of satisfaction due to monotonic preferences. As on a higher IC, consumer gets more units of one good with no less of the other good or more units of both goods.
- Each indifference curve represents a different level of satisfaction, so they never touch or intersect each other.
- Indifference curve touches neither X-axis nor Y-axis because it is assumed that a consumer buys a combination of two economic goods.

Indifference Map

It is a set of those combinations of two goods which offer same level of satisfaction to a consumer pertaining to different income levels. An indifference curve, which is to the right and above another indifference curve correspond to higher level of income and therefore, represents higher level of satisfaction.

Budget Set and Budget Line

- Budget set refers to attainable combinations of a set of two goods, given prices of goods and income of consumer, which a consumer afford to buy.
- A budget line or price line represents the different combinations of two goods that the consumer can purchase by spending all his money-income, given the price of the goods, which is equal to income of the consumer.
- Budget line is a straight line.
- Slope of budget line shows the rate at which market price allows the consumer to substitute Good-X for Good-Y. It is expressed as $\frac{P_X}{P_Y}$.

Budget set and line can be understood as follows

Consumption Possibilities for a Consumer (Budget set)

Units of good 1	Units of good 2
0	60
10	40
20	20
30	0

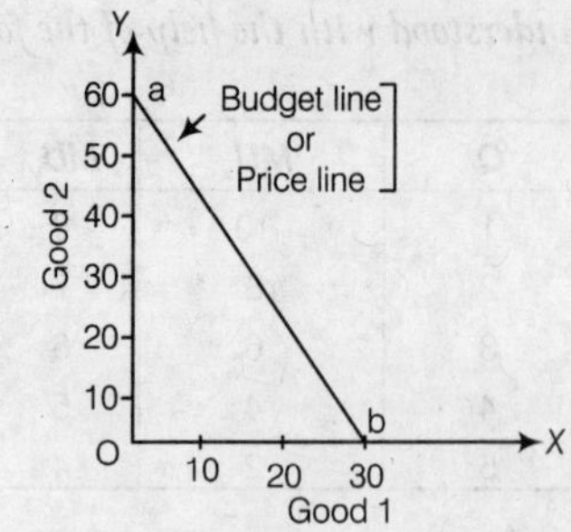

Diagrammatic Presentation of Consumption Possibilities

- This budget line is drawn on the assumptions that price of good 1 is ₹ 2 per unit, price of good 2 is ₹ 1 per unit and the consumer has ₹ 60 to spend. Accordingly, maximum 30 units of good 1 are purchased, when entire budget is spent on good 1 and maximum 60 units of good 2 can be purchased, when entire budget is spent on good 2. Slope of budget line is Market Rate of Exchange (MRE) or price ratio (Px/Py).
- Slope of Indifference Curve (IC) shows the rate at which a consumer is willing to substitute Good-X for Good-Y. It is known as Marginal Rate of Substitution (MRS) and is expressed as $\frac{\Delta Y}{\Delta X}$. This is determined by the consumer, depending on his taste and preferences.

Producer's Behaviour

Producer's behaviour refers to the study of how an individual producer decides the quantity to be produced to maximise his/her profit or minimise losses. In other words, it is the study of how a producer behaves in the marketplace to minisse the cost in order to maximise the gap between total revenue and total cost. A producer's behaviour is guided by law of variable proportion and law of returns to scale.

Law of Variable Proportion

It states that in short-run as more and more of the variable factor is used (along with the fixed factor), a stage must ultimately come when Total Product (TP) of the variable factor starts declining or Marginal Product (MP) becomes negative. *It has three stages which are as follows*

- When MP is increasing (from 2 to 3 to 4), TP is increasing at increasing rate. This is the stage of **increasing returns to a factor.**

- When MP is decreasing (from 4 to 3 to 2 to 1), TP is increasing at diminishing rate. This is called **diminishing returns to a factor.**
- When MP is negative, TP starts declining. This is the stage of negative returns to a factor.

This can be understood with the help of following schedule and graph

Units of Land	Units of Labour	Total Product (TP)	Marginal Product (MP)	
1	1	2	2	← Increasing MP implying increasing returns to a factor
1	2	5	3	
1	3	9	4	
1	4	12	3	← Diminishing MP implying diminishing returns to a factor
1	5	14	2	
1	6	15	1	
1	7	15	0	← Negative MP implying negative returns to a factor
1	8	14	– 1	

➠ **Note** *Where MP stops increasing, from that very point it starts diminishing. Thus, overlapping is indicated in the above table when MP = 4.*

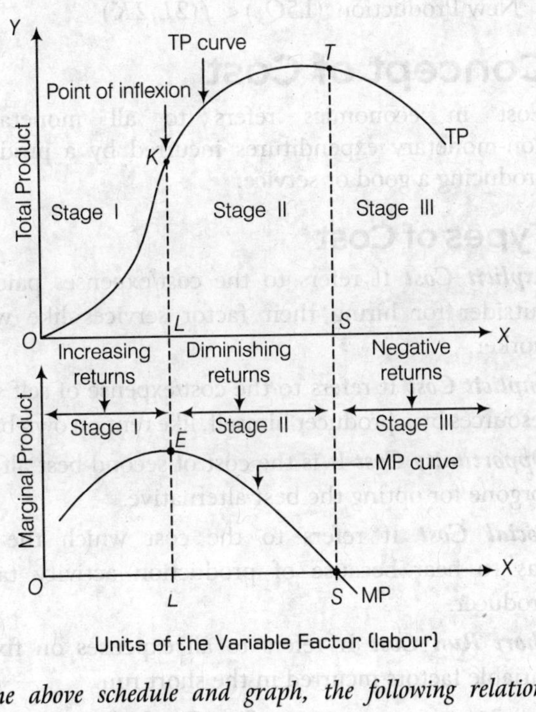

From the above schedule and graph, the following relationship is observed between MP and TP

- When MP is increasing. TP increases at an increasing rate.
- When MP is decreasing but positive, TP increases at a diminishing rate.
- When MP is zero, TP is maximum and constant.
- When MP becomes negative, TP falls.

Relationship between Average Product and Marginal Product

The following relationship is also observed between AP and MP

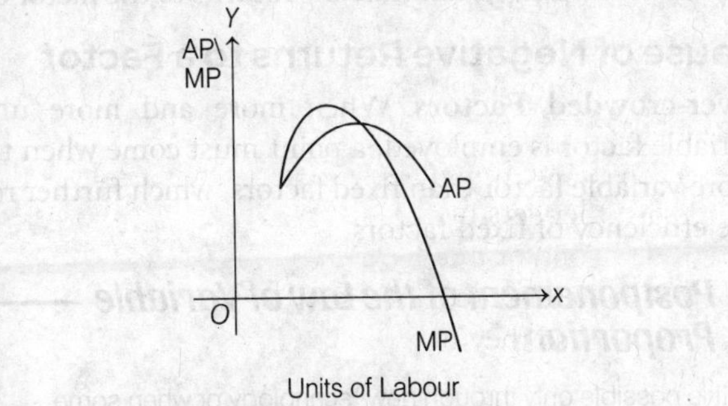

- When MP> AP, AP increases.
- When MP= AP, AP is maximum.
- When MP< AP, AP decreases.
- MP can become zero or negative but AP always remains positive.

Causes of Increasing Returns to a Factor

Fuller Utilisation of the Fixed Factor and Variable Factors In the initial stages, fixed factor (such as machine) remains underutilised. Its fuller utilisation needs greater application of the variable factor. Hence, initially additional units of the variable factor add more and more to total output or marginal product of the variable factor tends to increase.

Increased Efficiency of the Variable Factor Additional application of the variable factor causes process based division of labour that raises efficiency of the variable factor. Accordingly, marginal productivity of the factor tends to rise.

Better Coordination between the Factors So long as fixed factor remains underutilised, additional application of the variable factor tends to improve the degree of coordination between the fixed and variable factor. As a result, total output increases at the increasing rate.

Causes of Diminishing Returns to a Factor

Fixity of the Factor As more and more units of the variable factor are combined with the fixed factor, the latter gets excessively utilised. It suffers greater wear and tear and loses its efficiency. Hence, the diminishing returns to a factor occur.

Imperfect Factor Substitutability Factors of production are imperfect substitutes of each other. For instance, more and more of labour cannot be continuously used in place of capital. Accordingly, diminishing returns to the variable factor occur.

Poor Coordination between the Factors Continuous increasing application of the variable factor alongwith fixed factor beyond a point crosses the limit of ideal factor ratio. This leads to poor coordination between the fixed and variable factors. Accordingly, diminishing returns to the factor occur.

Cause of Negative Returns to a Factor

Over-crowded Factors When more and more units of variable factor is employed, a point must come when there is more variable factor than fixed factors, which further reduces the efficiency of fixed factors.

> **Postponement of the Law of Variable Proportion**
>
> It is possible only through new technology or when some substitute of the fixed factor is discovered in no situation, occurrence of the law can be avoided for the time being when the technology is used repeatatively, the law becomes inconsistant.

Returns to Scale or Law of Returns to Scale

It is a long run law that studies the changes in output, when all the factors of production or inputs are increased together. The study of changes in output as a result of changes in the scale forms the subject matter of 'returns to scale'.

The law of return to scale has certain assumptions

- Technique of production is unchanged.
- All units of factors are homogenous.
- Returns are measured in physical terms.

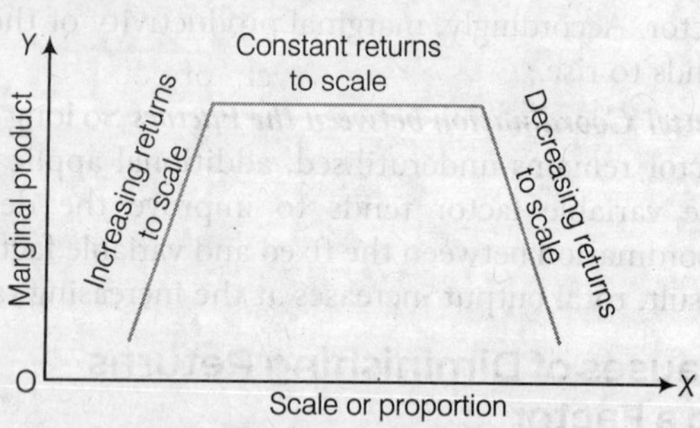

The Laws of Returns to Scale

It also has the following three stages

Stage of Increasing Returns to Scale (IRS)

If the increase in all the factors leads to more than proportionate increase in output, returns to scale are said to be increasing.

Mathematically,

Initial Production $(Q_x) = f(L,K)$

New Production, $(3Q_x) > f(2L,2K)$

Here, f = Functional relationship

L = Units of labour

K = Units of capital

Q_x = Quantity of good X

Stage of Constant Returns to Scale (CRS)

If all the factors of production are increased in a given proportion and the output increases in the same proportion, returns to scale are said to be constant. Mathematically,

Initial Production $(Q_x) = f(L, K)$

New Production $(2Q_x) = f(2L, 2K)$

Stage of Diminishing or Decreasing Returns to Scale (DRS)

If the increase in all the factors leads to a less than proportionate increase in output, returns to scale are decreasing.

Mathematically,

Initial Production $(Q_x) = f(L,K)$ {DRS}

New Production $(1.5Q_x) < f(2L,2K)$

Concept of Cost

Cost in economics refers to all monetary and non-monetary expenditures incurred by a producer for producing a good or service.

Types of Cost

Explicit Cost It refers to the cost/expenses paid to the outsider for hiring their factor services like wages of worker.

Implicit Cost It refers to the cost/expense of self supplied resources by a producer himself, like rent on own building.

Opportunity Cost It is the cost of second best alternative forgone for opting the best alternative.

Social Cost It refers to the cost which the society has to bear because of production activity taken by producer.

Short Run Cost It refers to all expenses on fixed and variable factors incurred in the short run.

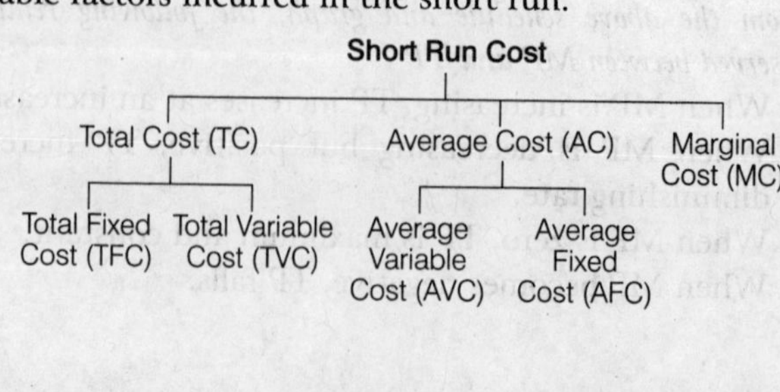

These are as follows

- TC refers to sum total of TFC and TVC.

$$TC = TFC + TVC$$

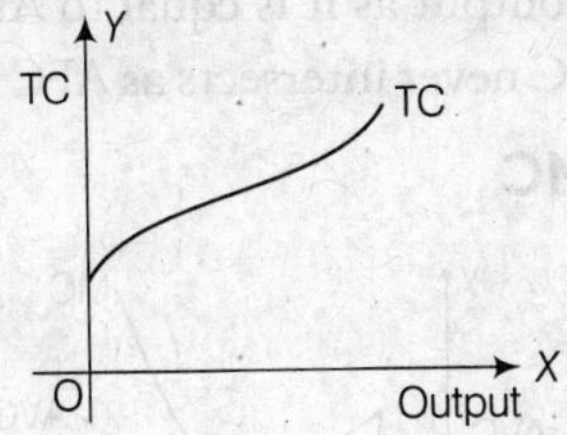

- TFC refers to total cost incurred on fixed factors. This cost does not changes as the level of output changes.

$$TFC = TC - TVC$$

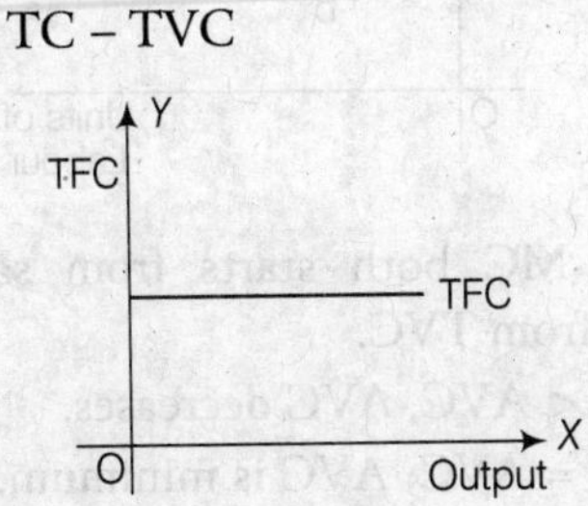

- TVC refers to total cost incurred on variable factors. This cost changes with change in level of output.

$$TVC = TC - TFC$$

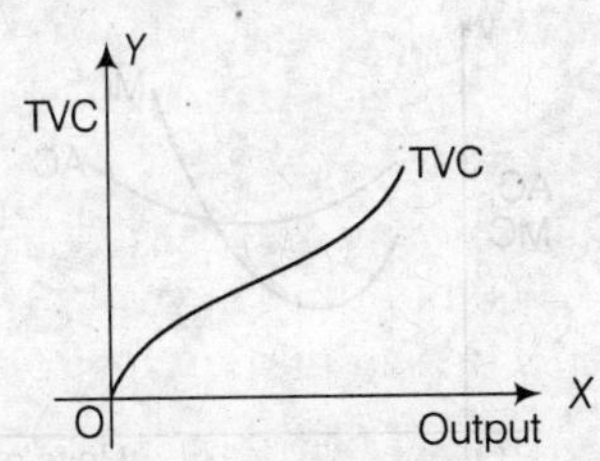

- AC refers to per unit of TC.

$$AC = \frac{TC}{Q} \text{ or } AC = AFC + AVC$$

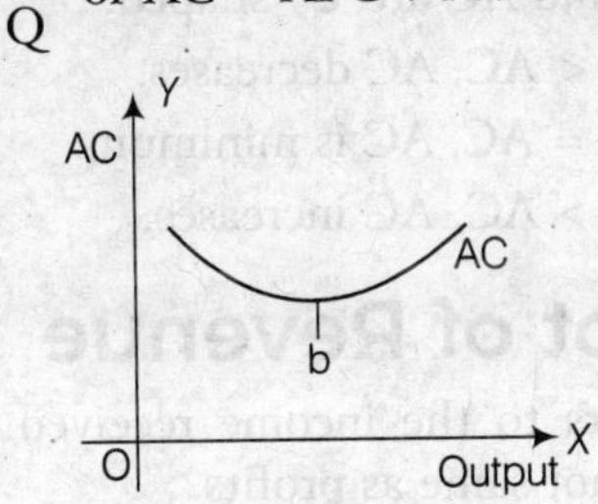

- FC refers to per unit of TFC.

$$AFC = \frac{TFC}{Q} \text{ or } AFC = AC - AVC$$

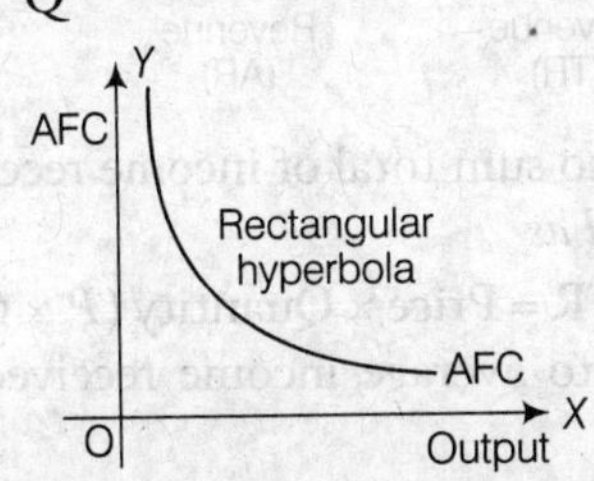

- AVC refers to per unit of TVC.

$$AVC = \frac{TVC}{Q}$$

Or $AVC = AC - AFC$

Q = Output

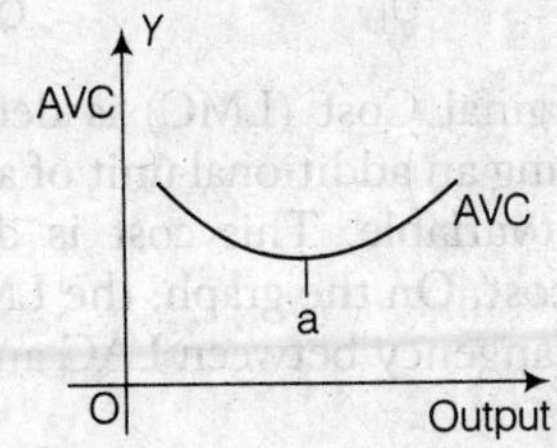

- **Marginal Cost** (MC) It refers to additional cost of employing additional unit of variable factor.

$$MC = \frac{\Delta TVC}{\Delta L} \text{ or } TVC_n - TVC_{n-1}$$

$$= \frac{\Delta TC}{\Delta L} \text{ or } TC_n - TC_{n-1}$$

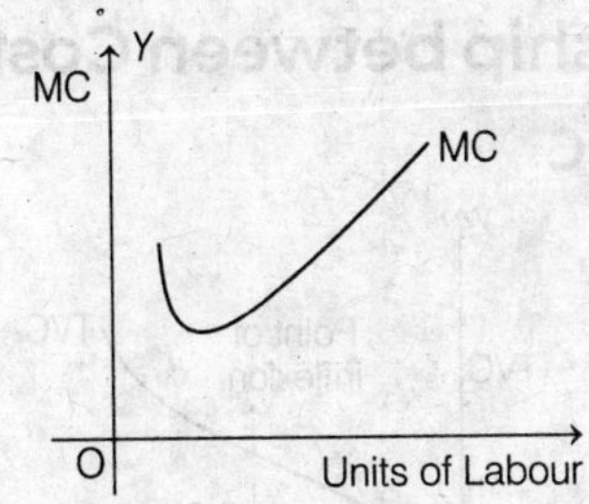

Long Run Cost In long run, all factors become variable, *i.e.* a producer can change any of its factors to change the level of output. *It can be classified as follows*

- Long-run Total Cost (LTC) refers to the minimum cost at which given level of output can be produced. LTC is always less than or equal to short run total cost, but it is never more than short run cost.

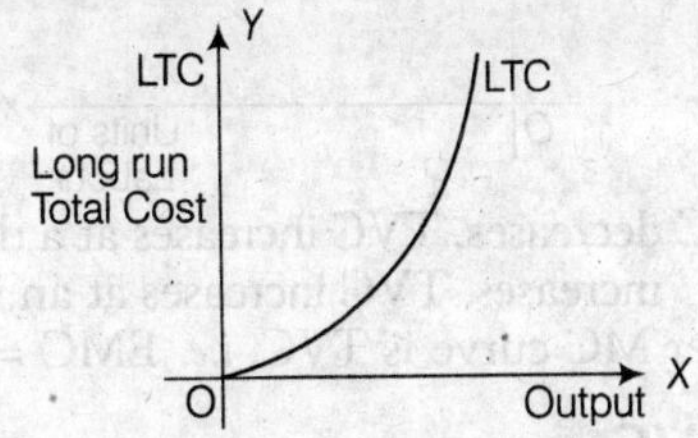

- Long-run Average Cost (LAC) is equal to LTC divided by the level of output. The derivation of LAC is done from short run average cost. In the short run, plant is fixed and each short run curve corresponds to a particular plant. The long-run average cost is also called as planning curve or envelope curve.

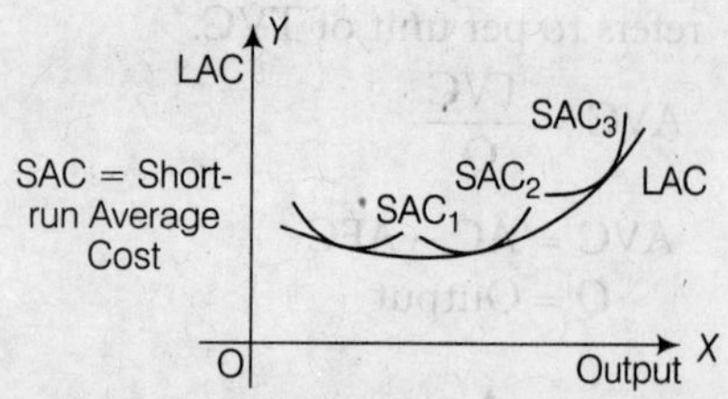

- Long-run Marginal Cost (LMC) is defined as additional cost of producing an additional unit of a commodity, when all inputs are variable. This cost is derived from short run marginal cost. On the graph, the LMC is derived from the points of tangency between LAC and SAC.

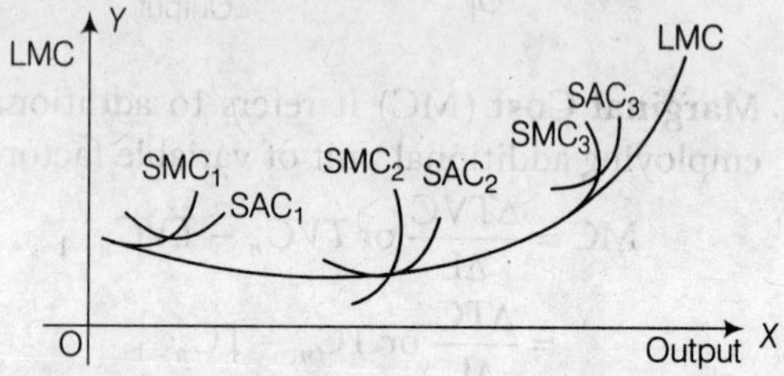

Relationship between Cost Curves

TVC and MC

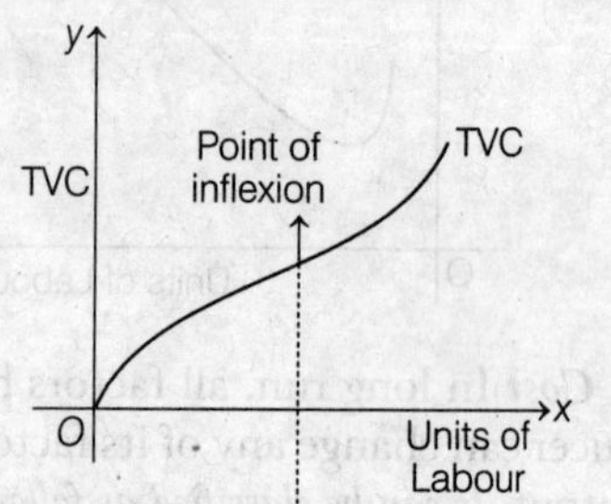

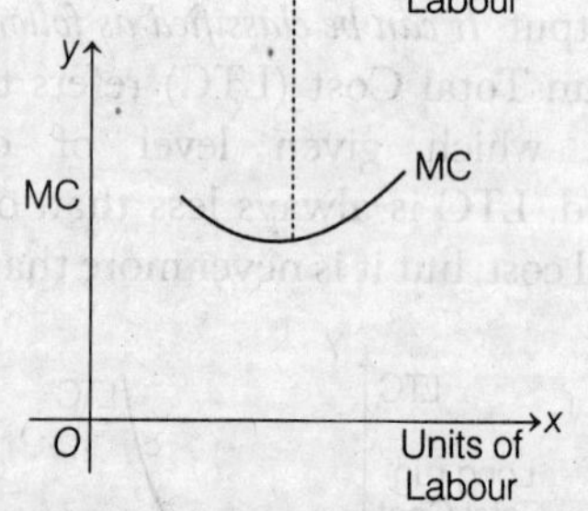

- When MC decreases, TVC increases at a diminishing rate.
- When MC increases, TVC increases at an increasing rate.
- Area under MC curve is TVC, *i.e.* EMC = TVC.

AC and AVC

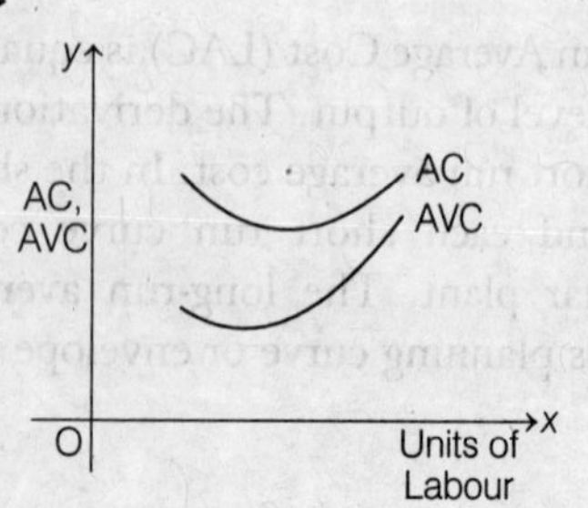

- Both AC and AVC are *'U'* shaped.
- Vertical distance between AC and AVC falls with increase in output as it is equal to AFC.
- AC and AVC never intersects as AFC is always positive.

AVC and MC

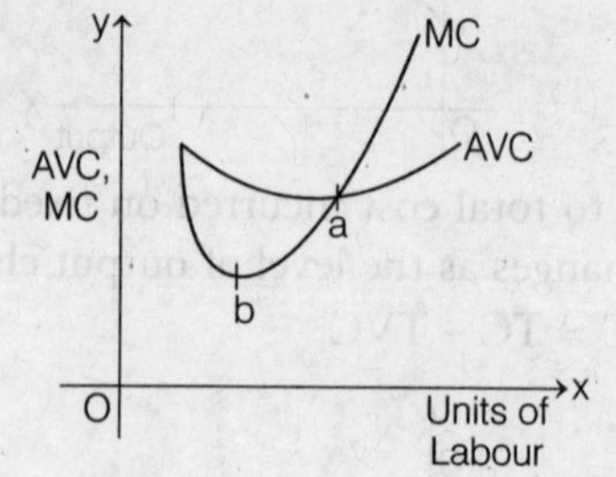

- AVC and MC both starts from same points and calculated from TVC.
- When MC < AVC, AVC decreases.
- When MC = AVC, AVC is minimum.
- When MC > AVC, AVC increases.

AC and MC

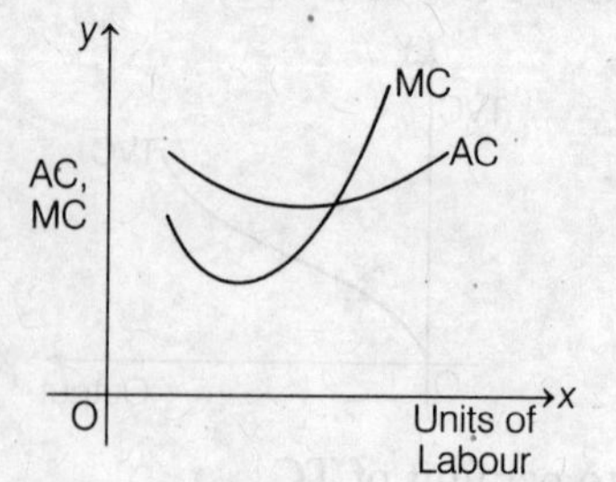

- Both MC and AC are *'U'* shaped.
- When MC < AC, AC decreases.
- When MC = AC, AC is minimum.
- When MC > AC, AC increases.

Concept of Revenue

Revenue refers to the income received from sale of an output. It is not same as profits.

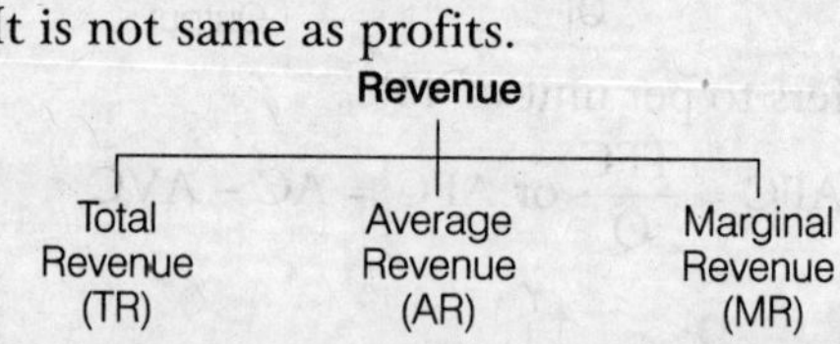

- TR refers to sum total of income received from sales. *It is calculated as*

$$TR = \text{Price} \times \text{Quantity}\ (P \times Q)$$

- AR refers to average income received from sale of an output.

It is calculated as

$$AR = \frac{TR}{Q} = \text{Price}$$

- MR refers to additional income received from sale of an additional unit of output. *It is calculated as*

$$MR = \frac{\Delta TR}{\Delta Q}$$

Or $TR_n - TR_{n-1}$

Shape of revenue curves depends upon form of market which are as follows

Under Perfect Competition (when price remains constant)

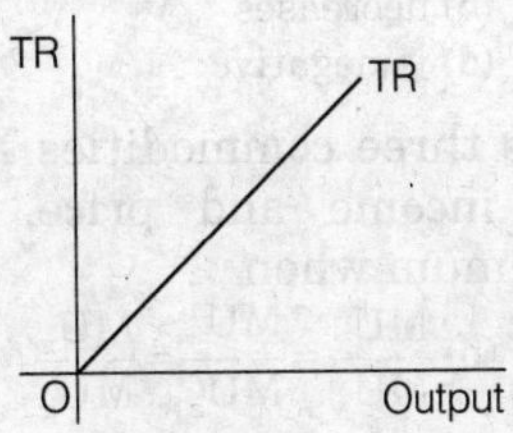

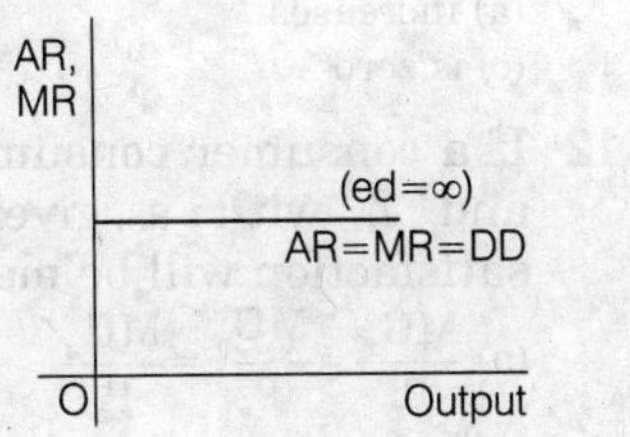

Under Imperfect Competition (when price falls with increase in output)

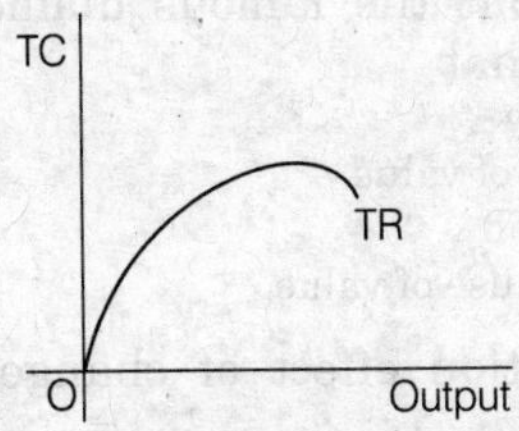

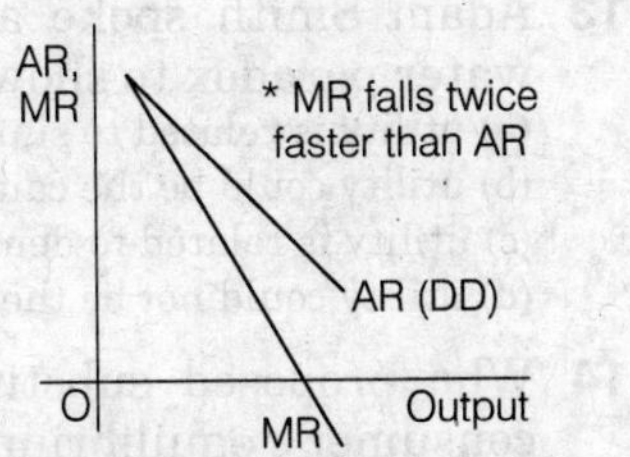

Under monopoly, AR(DD) is inelastic due to absence of substitute goods where as under monopolistic competition, AR(DD) is elastic due to availability of substitute goods.

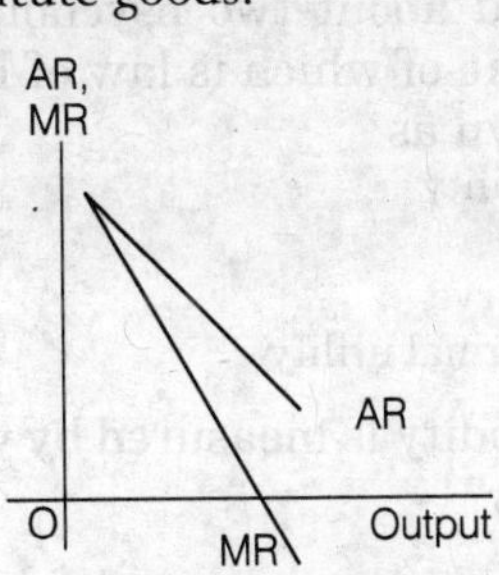

(Monopoly)

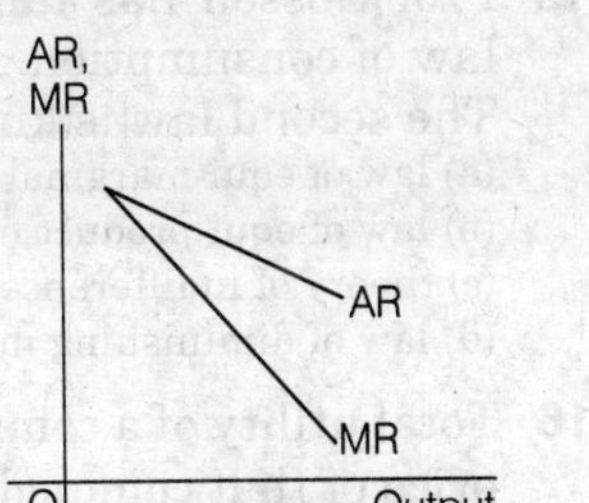

(Monopolistic competition)

Relation between TR and MR

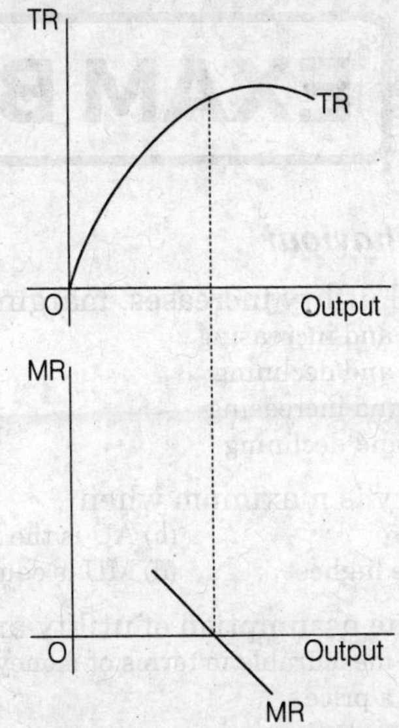

- When MR is decreasing but positive, TR increases at a diminishing rate.
- When MR is zero, TR is maximum and constant.
- When MR is negative, TR decreases.

Relation between AR and MR

- Both AR and MR start from same point and downward sloping.
- AR and MR both falls continuously.

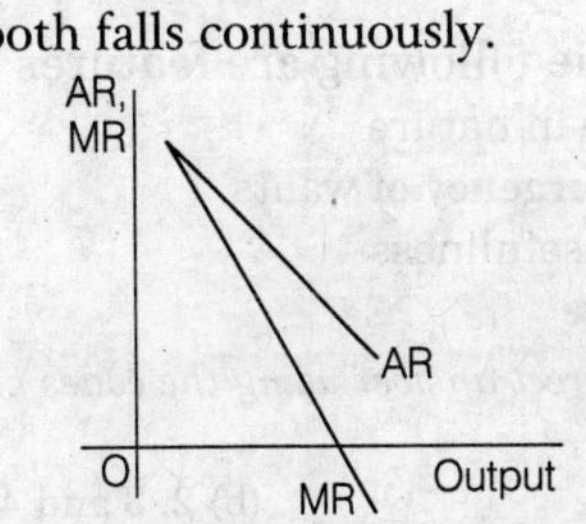

- MR can be zero or negative, but AR is always positive.
- MR falls twice faster than AR.

Relation between AR and MR based on Elasticity of Demand

$$MR = AR\left(1 - \frac{1}{e}\right) \quad \text{[Where, } e = \text{elasticity]}$$

when $e = 1$, MR = 0

$e > 1$, MR > 0 (Positive); $e < 1$, MR < 0 (Negative)

EXAM BASED QUESTIONS

Consumer's Behaviour

1 **When total utility increases, marginal utility is**
(a) negative and increasing
(b) negative and declining
(c) positive and increasing
(d) positive and declining

2 **Total utility is maximum when**
(a) MU is zero (b) AU is the highest
(c) MU is the highest (d) MU is equal to AU

3 **Which is the assumption of utility analysis?**
(a) Utility is measurable in terms of money
(b) Utility is a price
(c) There are substitute
(d) None of the above

4 **MU curve will intersect x-axis when**
(a) MU is negative (b) TU is maximum
(c) Both (a) and (b) (d) None of these

5 **The area which lies under the demand curve for a given good measures**
(a) marginal utility (b) marginal cost
(c) marginal profit (d) total utility

6 **Which of the following are features of utility?**
1. Subjective in nature
2. Based on urgency of wants
3. Same as usefullness
4. Qualitative

Select the correct answer using the codes given below
Codes
(a) 1, 2 and 4 (b) 2, 3 and 4
(c) 1, 3 and 4 (d) All of the above

7 **Ordinal approach is based on**
(a) law of maximum satisfaction
(b) utility cannot be measured in cardinal numbers
(c) utility could not be measured in ordinal numbers
(d) utility can be measured

8 **A consumer get maximum satisfaction where the .... are same.**
(a) total utility and marginal utility
(b) price of commodity and marginal utility
(c) price of commodity and total utility
(d) Both (b) and (c)

9 **Which of the following is one of the basis for the indifference curve analysis?**
(a) Independent utility
(b) Ordinal utility
(c) Cardinal utility
(d) Diminishing utility

10 **Cardinal utility measurement is required in**
(a) indifference curve analysis
(b) utility theory
(c) revealed preference theory
(d) consumption analysis

11 **When marginal utility is negative, then total utility**
(a) increases (b) decreases
(c) is zero (d) is negative

12 **If a consumer consumes three commodities X, Y and Z with a given income and price, his satisfaction will be maximum when**
(a) $\frac{MU_x}{P_x}=\frac{MU_y}{P_y}=\frac{MU_z}{P_z}$ (b) $\frac{MU_x}{MU_y}=\frac{MU_y}{MU_z}=\frac{MU_z}{MU_x}$
(c) $\frac{MU_x}{MU_y}=\frac{P_x}{P_y}=\frac{MU_x}{P_z}$ (d) $\frac{MU_x}{P_y}=\frac{MU_y}{P_z}=\frac{MU_z}{P_x}$

13 **Adam Smith spoke about the famous diamond water paradox to show that**
(a) utility is related to supply
(b) utility could be the cause of value
(c) utility is related to demand
(d) utility could not be the cause of value

14 **Who proposed substitution effect of change in consumer's equilibrium?**
(a) Hicks and Allen
(b) Boulding
(c) Marshall
(d) Schumpeter

15 **Prof Gossen has talked about two psychological law of consumption. One of which is law of DMU. The second law is known as**
(a) law of equi-marginal utility
(b) law of equi-product
(c) theory of indifference curve
(d) law of diminishing marginal utility

16 **Total utility of a commodity is measured by which price of that commodity?**
(a) Value in use
(b) Value in exchange
(c) Both (a) and (b)
(d) None of the above

17 **According to Marshall, the basis of consumer surplus is**
(a) law of diminishing marginal utility
(b) law of equi-marginal utility
(c) law of proportions
(d) All of the above

18 Marginal rate of substitution of x and y can be shown in the curve by formula

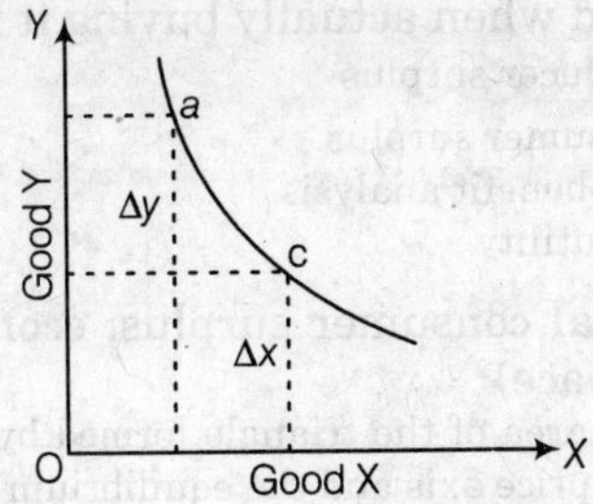

(a) $MRS_{xy} = \frac{-\Delta y}{\Delta x}$ (b) $MRS_{xy} = \frac{\Delta x}{\Delta y}$

(c) $MRS_{xy} = \frac{\Delta y}{\Delta x}$ (d) $MRS_{xy} = \frac{-\Delta x}{\Delta y}$

19 In case of two goods, following utility approach, a consumer is in equilibrium when

(a) $MU_x/P_x = MU_y/P_y$ (b) $MU_x/P_x < MU_y/P_y$

(c) $MU_x/M_x > MU_y/P_y$ (d) Both (b) and (c)

20 The law of equi-marginal utility states the condition of equilibrium as

(a) $MU_x, P_x = MU_y, P_y = MU_Z, P_Z$

(b) $\frac{MU_x}{P_x} = \frac{MU_y}{P_y} = \frac{MU_z}{P_z} = MU_m$

(c) $\frac{MU_x}{P_y} = \frac{MU_y}{P_x} = MU_m$

(d) $\frac{MU_x}{P_x} < \frac{MU_y}{P_y} < \frac{MU_z}{P_z}$

21 Put these concepts in chronological order of their development.

1. Law of demand
2. Law of indifference
3. Law of DMU
4. Revealed preference theory
5. Indifference curve

Codes

(a) 1, 3, 2, 4, 5 (b) 1, 2, 3, 4, 5

(c) 1, 3, 2, 5, 4 (d) 1, 5, 2, 4, 3

22 If $P_x = P_y$, then when the consumer maximises utility,

(a) X must be equal to Y

(b) MU(X) must be equal to MU(Y)

(c) MU(X) may equal MU(Y), but it is necessarily so

(d) X and Y must be substitutes

23 The law of diminishing marginal utility states that

(a) total satisfaction will decrease as more units of the good are consumed

(b) the satisfaction derived from each additional unit of a good consumed will decrease

(c) total utility will become negative

(d) Both (a) and (c)

24 The MU_x / MU_y ratio is 10 and the P_x / P_y ratio is 8, so the consumer should buy

(a) less X and more Y (b) more X and less Y

(c) more X and more Y (d) less X and less Y

25 A consumer attains equilibrium at a point on the indifference curve where

(a) $MRX_{xy} = \frac{P_x}{P_y}$ (b) $MRX_{xy} > \frac{P_x}{P_y}$

(c) $MRX_{xy} < \frac{P_x}{P_y}$ (d) $MRS_{xy} = P_x P_y$

26 A consumer consuming two goods will be in equilibrium, when the marginal utilities from both goods are

(a) maximum possible positive

(b) minimum possible positive

(c) equal

(d) zero

27 Which of the following conditions is necessary for the utility to be maximum?

1. $_{xy} = \frac{x}{y} = \frac{x}{y}$

2. Convexity of the indifference curve

3. $_{x} = {}_{y}$

Which of the statement(s) given above is/are correct?

Codes

(a) Only 1 (b) Only 2

(c) Only 3 (d) All of the above

28 Which of the following statement(s) is/are not correct?

(a) As per law of Diminishing Marginal Utility, MU tends to decline as consumption of the commodity increase

(b) As per law of diminishing returns to a factor, when MP is decreasing, TP is increasing at diminishing rate

(c) Both (a) and (b)

(d) None of the above

29 The term optimum allocation on consumer's expenditure on various goods and services is used in

(a) Giffen paradox

(b) law of demand

(c) law of diminishing MU

(d) law of equi-marginal utility

30 Consumer attains equilibrium when he maximises his utility, given his income and market price of two products for which

1. marginal rate of substitution be equal to the ratio of commodity prices *i.e.*,

$$MRS_{xy} = MU_x / MU_y = P_x / P_y$$

2. indifference curve is convex to the origin.

Select the correct answer using the codes given below

Codes

(a) Only 1 (b) Both 1 and 2

(c) Only 2 (d) Neither 1 nor 2

31 Gossen's second law states that
(a) consumer maximises his total pleasure, when satisfaction gained from marginal units of all commodities is the same
(b) consumers gain satisfaction only when $\frac{P_x}{P_y} = \frac{MU_x}{MU_y}$
(c) when more units are consumed, marginal utility diminishes
(d) All of the above

32 Which of the following best expresses the law of diminishing marginal utility?
(a) The more a person consumes a product, the smaller becomes the utility, which he receives from its consumption
(b) The more a person consumes a product, the smaller becomes the additional utility, which he receives as a result of consuming an additional unit of the product
(c) The less a person consumes a product, the smaller becomes the utility, which he receives from its consumption
(d) The less a person consumes a product, the smaller becomes the additional utility which he receives as a result of consuming an additional unit of the product

33 Consider the following statements.
1. TU increases so long as MU is positive.
2. TU = ΣAU
3. When MU is negative, TU starts increasing.
Which of the statement(s) given above is/are correct?
Codes
(a) Only 1 (b) Both 1 and 3
(c) Both 2 and 3 (d) None of these

34 As a consumer increases his consumption of a commodity, the total utility he derives from its consumption increases but at a diminishing rate. This is
(a) a statement of fact (b) an economic law
(c) a hypothesis (d) None of these

35 Of the following goods, the one where the law of diminishing marginal utility is least likely to apply is
(a) water (b) cigarettes (c) toothpaste (d) rap music.

36 In the following diagram, consumer's surplus is shown by

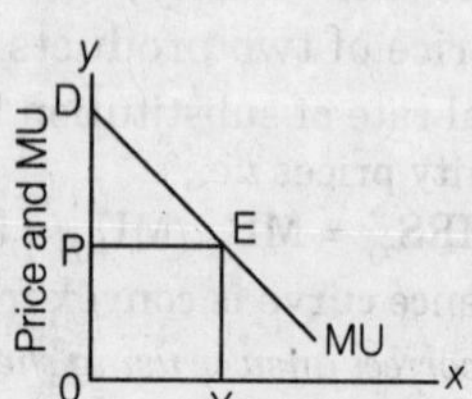

(a) OPEX (b) ODEX
(c) PDE (d) None of these

37 The difference between what a consumer is willing to pay for a unit of a good and what must be paid when actually buying it is called
(a) producer surplus
(b) consumer surplus
(c) cost-benefit analysis
(d) net utility

38 By total consumer surplus, economists mean (in P-Q space)
(a) the area of the triangle formed by the demand curve, the price axis and the equilibrium price line
(b) the area between the average revenue and marginal revenue curves
(c) the difference between the maximum price the consumer is willing to pay for a good (vertical intercept of demand curve) and the minimum price the producer is willing to sell at (vertical intercept of supply curve)
(d) Both (a) and (c)

Producer's Behaviour

39 The equilibrium level of output for the pure monopolist is where
(a) MR = MC (b) P < AC
(c) MR < MC (d) MR > MC

40 The point at which the total product stops increasing at increasing rate and starts increasing at decreasing rate is called
(a) break even point (b) shutdown point
(c) inflexion point (d) None of these

41 Law of increasing and constant returns are temporary phases of
(a) law of variable proportion
(b) law of diminishing return
(c) law of diminishing utility
(d) law of proportionality

42 Total production will be maximum when
(a) marginal production is maximum
(b) average production is maximum
(c) marginal production is zero
(d) average production is equal to the marginal production

43 When AR is constant, MR is
(a) equal to AR
(b) less than AR
(c) more than AR
(d) equal to zero

44 Marginal revenue will be zero, if the elasticity of demand is
(a) zero (b) greater than one
(c) equal to one (d) less than one

45 A concept, which has importance in the equilibrium analysis and thus, economic analysis is
(a) opportunity cost
(b) average variable cost
(c) marginal cost
(d) total cost

46 Marginal revenue, at the quantity that generates maximum total revenue and negative beyond that point, has the value of

(a) zero (b) +1
(c) −1 (d) infinite

47 The basic nature of average fixed cost is that it

(a) increases as output increases
(b) remain same at all levels of output
(c) decreases with increase in output
(d) All of the above

48 The normal LAC curve is influenced by

(a) principle of constant returns to scale
(b) economies and diseconomies of large scale production
(c) principle of diminishing returns
(d) All of the above

49 In the following figure, marginal product reaches its maximum at a level of labour, which as compared to that for average product is

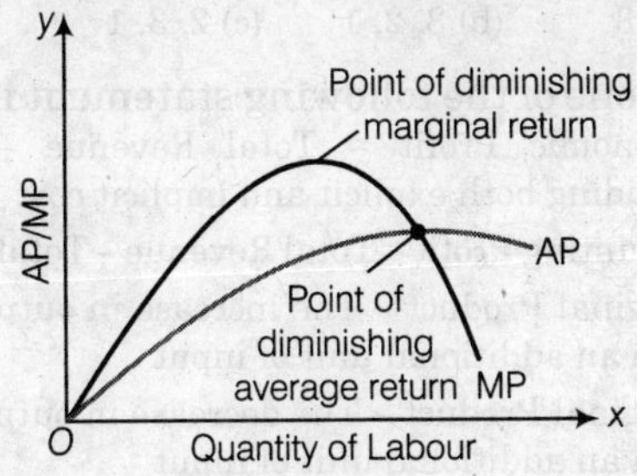

(a) higher
(b) lower
(c) same
(d) not comparable

50 Which one of the following is curve for law of increasing returns?

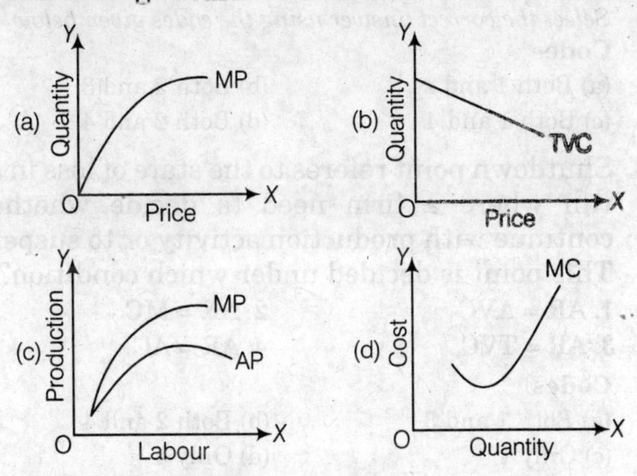

51 The Cobb-Douglas production function $Q = 4$ K = 0.6, L = 0.3 exhibits

(a) constant returns to scale
(b) increasing returns to scale
(c) decreasing returns to scale
(d) None of the above

52 In case, law of constant returns is applicable,

(a) marginal product will be more than average product
(b) marginal product will be lesser than average product
(c) marginal and average product will be equal
(d) total, marginal and average product will be equal

53 Which of the following is not the reason for increasing returns to scale?

(a) Indivisibility of the factors
(b) Fuller utilisation of fixed factors
(c) Greater specialisation of factors
(d) Dimensional economies

54 In Cobb-Douglas production function, elasticity of factor substitution is equal to

(a) zero (b) infinity
(c) one (d) less than 1

55 Consider the following statements.

1. Point of inflexion exists where Ist stage of law of variable proportions ends.
2. TP increases even when MP is decreasing.
3. Producer will stop only at IInd stage of variable proportions.

Which of the statement(s) given above is/are correct?

Codes

(a) Both 1 and 2 (b) 1, 2 and 3
(c) Only 1 (d) None of the above

56 Consider the following statements.

1. MP is also called MPP.
2. Physical product refers to production as measured in terms of physical units of the commodity.
3. TP increases even when MP is decreasing.

Which of the statement(s) given above is/are correct?

(a) Only 1 (b) Both 2 and 3
(c) Both 1 and 2 (d) All of the above

57 The Cobb-Douglas production function $Q = 4K^{0.6} L^{0.3}$ exhibits .... returns to scale.

(a) constant (b) increasing
(c) decreasing (d) None of these

58 Returns to scale involve variations in the quantities of the various factors of production

1. Simultaneously 2. Proportionately

Codes

(a) Both 1 and 2 are correct
(b) 1 is correct, but 2 is incorrect
(c) 1 is incorrect, but 2 is correct
(d) Neither 1 nor 2

59 Relation between AR, MR and elasticity of demand can be established by the formula

(a) $MR = AR\left(1 - \frac{1}{e}\right)$ (b) $AR = MR\left(\frac{e-1}{e}\right)$
(c) $MR = AR\left(\frac{1}{e-1}\right)$ (d) $AR = \left(\frac{MR}{e}\right)$

60 **If ATC curve is a rising straight line, then as output expands, MC curve will**
(a) lie above the ATC curve (b) lie below the ATC curve
(c) Both coincide (d) None of these

61 **The MC curve cuts AVC and ATC curves at**
(a) falling parts of each (b) different points
(c) rising parts of each (d) their minimum level

62 **Which is a long-run average cost curve?**

(a) 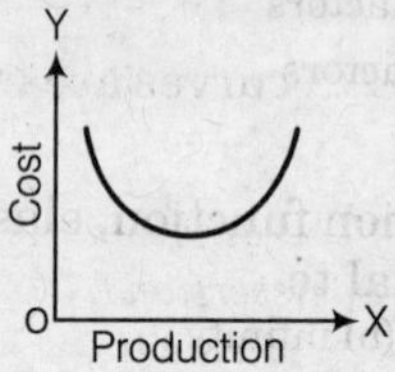

(b) 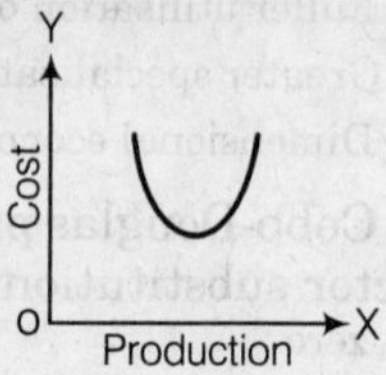

(c) 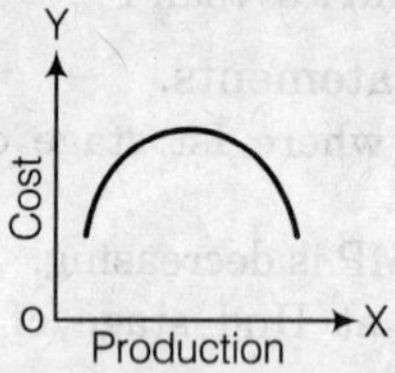

(d) 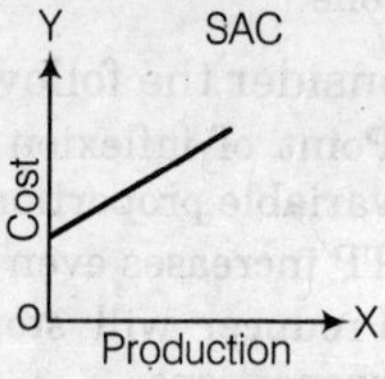

63 **On a less than perfectly elastic demand curve, the MR for a given price and output is equal to price multiplied by**
(a) $[1-e]$ (b) $\left[e-\frac{1}{e}\right]$
(c) $\left[1-\frac{1}{e}\right]$ (d) $\left[\frac{1}{e}-1\right]$

64 **Normal profits refers to the no profit no loss state. This is equal to which type of the cost?**
(a) explicit costs (b) implicit costs
(c) social costs (d) private costs

65 **If MC is above AC at a time when output is rising, then**
(a) ATC is falling (b) AVC is rising
(c) AVC is falling (d) ATR is rising

66 **MC curve always cuts the AC curve from below**
(a) on the falling portion of AC curve
(b) on the rising portion of AC curve
(c) at any point on the AC curve
(d) at the minimum point of the AC curve

67 **Which of the following is an implicit cost of production?**
(a) Wages to the labour
(b) Rent on building
(c) Interest on owned money capital
(d) Payment for machine

68 **Break-even point in units is given by**
(a) $\frac{\text{TFC}}{\text{SP}-\text{MC}}$ (b) $\frac{\text{P/V Ratio}}{\text{Fixed cost}}$
(c) $\frac{\text{TFC} \times \text{SP}}{\text{SP}-\text{VC}}$ (d) None of these

69 **When the TR curve and TC curve moves in parallel and TR exceeds TC**
(a) normal profit is maximised
(b) abnormal profit is maximised
(c) total profit is maximised
(d) total profit is minimised

70 **Which of the following statement is correct?**
(a) Law of variable proportion will not apply, if there is an improvement in the technology.
(b) Product obtained from the additional factor of production is termed as average product
(c) If marginal product goes on increasing it should be understood that the law of constant returns is applying
(d) Modern economies have propounded the law of increasing return

71 **Arrange the following in chronological order.**
1. Diminishing returns 2. Negative returns
3. Increasing returns
Codes
(a) 1, 2, 3 (b) 3, 2, 1 (c) 2, 3, 1 (d) 3, 1, 2

72 **Which one of the following statement is incorrect?**
(a) Economic Profit = Total Revenue – Total Cost, including both explicit and implicit cost
(b) Accounting Profit = Total Revenue – Total Explicit Cost
(c) Marginal Product – The increase in output that arises from an additional unit of input
(d) Marginal Product – The decrease in output that arises from an additional unit of input

73 **If all inputs are increased in the same proportion, than it is the case of**
1. short-run production function
2. long-run production function
3. laws of variable proportion
4. laws of returns to scale
Select the correct answer using the codes given below
Codes
(a) Both 1 and 2 (b) Both 2 and 3
(c) Both 1 and 4 (d) Both 2 and 4

74 **Shutdown point referes to the state of loss in short run where a firm need to decide whether to continue with production activity or to suspend it. This point is decided under which condition?**
1. AR = AVC 2. AR = MC
3. AR = TVC 4. AR = AC
Codes
(a) Both 1 and 3 (b) Both 2 and 4
(c) Only 1 (d) Only 4

75 **The fixed costs of a firm**
1. are fixed only in the short period.
2. when expressed as an average, do not change with output.
3. do not reflect diminishing marginal returns.

Select the correct answer using the codes given below

Codes

(a) Both 1 and 2 (b) Both 1 and 3
(c) Only 2 (d) Both 2 and 3

76 Consider the following.

1. Output × Price = Total Revenue
2. MR cannot be zero
3. TR = MR × Q

Select the correct answer using the codes given below

Codes

(a) Only 1 (b) Both 1 and 2
(c) Only 3 (d) All of the above

77 "The law of diminishing returns is merely a matter of logical necessity, but the law of increasing return is a matter of empirical fact." This statement comes from

(a) George Stigler (b) Samuelson
(c) Joan Robinson (d) Alfred Marshall

Miscellaneous

Directions (Q. Nos. 78-84) *In the questions given below are two statements labelled as Assertion (A) and Reason (R). In the context of the two statements, which one of the following is correct?*

Codes

(a) Both (A) and (R) are true and (R) is the correct explanation of (A)
(b) Both (A) and (R) are true, but (R) is not correct explanation of (A)
(c) (A) is true, but (R) is false
(d) (A) is false, but (R) is true

78 **Assertion** (A) MU tends to decline as consumption of the commodity increases.

Reason (R) Every successive unit of the commodity offers less and less satisfaction.

79 **Assertion** (A) Consumer behaviour is not governed by monotonic preferences.

Reason (R) Greater consumption of the commodity gives less satisfaction.

80 **Assertion** (A) Indifference curves are concave to the point of origin.

Reason (R) Shape of indifference curve is due to diminishing MRS.

81 **Assertion** (A) TU is maximum when MU is maximum.

Reason (R) TU starts increasing when MU is negative.

82 **Assertion** (A) An indifference curve touches neither X axis nor Y axis.

Reason (R) A consumer buys a combination of two goods.

83 **Assertion** (A) Equilibrium is struck when $\frac{MU_x}{P_x} = MU_m$

Reason (R) Equilibrium is due to law of diminishing marginal utility.

84 **Assertion** (A) The rate of fall of Marginal Revenue (MR) curve is more than twice the rate of fall of Average Revenue (AR) curve.

Reason (R) The MR and AR curves are linear and negatively sloped.

Directions (Q. Nos. 85-90) *In the questions given below are two statements labelled as Assertion (A) and Reason (R). In the context of the two statements, which one of the following is correct?*

Codes

(a) (A) is true, (R) is false
(b) (A) is false, (R) is true
(c) Both are true
(d) Both are false

85 **Assertion** (A) According to law of monotonic preferences, higher indifference curve gives higher satisaction as it contains more units of either goods.

Reason (R) Indifference curve is convex due to operation of law of diminishing marginal utility.

86 **Assertion** (A) In two indifference curves intersects each, it will give same level of staisfaction on both the curves.

Reason (R) Law of diminishing marginal rate of substitution is reason why two indifference curve intersects.

87 **Assertion** (A) Law of increasing returns to scale is indicated of economies of scale in production.

Reason (R) Economies of scale indicates fall in long run average cost.

88 **Assertion** (A) Under imperfect competition, marginal revenue will be positive, if price elasticity of demand is inelastic.

Reason (R) At the mid-point of demand curve, marginal revenue becomes equal to zero.

89 **Assertion** (A) Incrimental utility tends to decline with increase in consumption of a good.

Reason (R) A consumer is a rational one, his need gets satisfied for the time being but not always.

90 **Assertion** (A) Total utility will be maximum, when marginal utility to price of respective products are equal.

Reason (R) Deviation from this situation leads to reduction in maximum utility.

91 Match the following.

List I (Concepts)	List II (Features)
A. Utility	1. MU tends to decline as consumption of the commodity increases
B. Total utility	2. It is a want satisfying power of a good
C. Marginal utility	3. Sum total of utility derived from the consumption of all the units of a commodity
D. Law of diminishing marginal utility	4. Additional utility an account of the consumption of an additional unit of a commodity

Codes

	A	B	C	D		A	B	C	D
(a)	4	1	2	3	(b)	2	4	1	3
(c)	2	3	4	1	(d)	1	2	3	4

92 Match the following.

List I (Curves)	List II (Costs)
A. 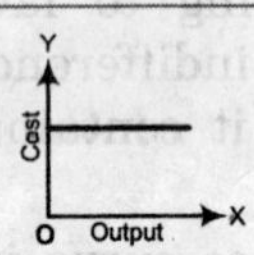	1. TFC
B. 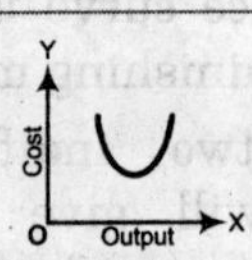	2. ATC
C. 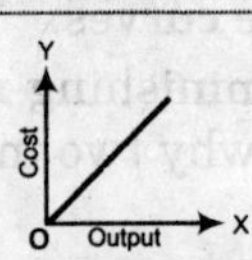	3. AVC
D. 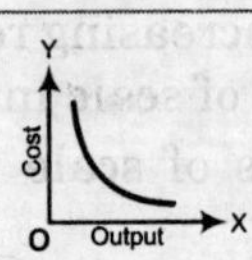	4. LAC

Codes

	A	B	C	D		A	B	C	D
(a)	1	4	2	3	(b)	1	2	3	4
(c)	4	3	2	1	(d)	2	1	4	3

93 Match the following.

List I	List II
A. Consumer surplus	1. Loniet
B. Concept of compensating variation	2. Newman Morgensterm
C. Utility index number	3. Hick
D. Input-output model	4. Marshall

Codes

	A	B	C	D		A	B	C	D
(a)	1	2	3	4	(b)	4	3	2	1
(c)	4	2	3	1	(d)	1	4	3	2

94 Match the following.

List I	List II
A. Total cost	1. TR ÷ Q
B. Average revenue	2. ΔTC ÷ ΔQ
C. Marginal cost	3. AR × Q
D. Total revenue	4. TFC + TVC

Codes

	A	B	C	D		A	B	C	D
(a)	4	3	2	1	(b)	3	1	4	2
(c)	2	3	4	1	(d)	4	1	2	3

95 Match the following.

List I	List II
A. Fixed costs	1. Fall at first and then rise as the firm approaches full capacity
B. Variable costs	2. Continue to fall at rate proportionate with the increase in output
C. Total costs	3. Are those costs which do not increase as output increases
D. Average total costs	4. Are the amount paid to all the factors employed in producing the output
E. Average fixed costs	5. Are those costs which increase as output increases

Codes

	A	B	C	D	E
(a)	3	5	4	1	2
(b)	4	5	1	2	3
(c)	5	4	3	1	2
(d)	1	2	3	4	5

96 Match the following.

List I	List II
A. Input-output isoquant	1. Arrow and Chenery
B. CES production function	2. Loniet
C. Duopoly model	3. P Sweezy
D. Kinked demand curve	4. Cournot

Codes

	A	B	C	D		A	B	C	D
(a)	1	3	2	4	(b)	2	1	4	3
(c)	1	2	3	4	(d)	2	1	3	4

97 Match the following.

List I	List II
A. Law of increasing returns	1. TP starts declining
B. Law of diminishing returns	2. TP is increasing at the decreasing rate
C. Law of negative returns	3. MP is increasing

Codes

	A	B	C		A	B	C
(a)	3	2	1	(b)	1	2	3
(c)	2	3	1	(d)	1	3	2

98 Match the following.

List I	List II
A. Cardinal approach	1. Marginal utility
B. Ordinal approach	2. Revealed preference theory
C. Hicks-Allen approach	3. Indifference curve
D. Consumer's surplus	4. Alfred Marshall

Codes

	A	B	C	D
(a)	1	3	2	4
(b)	1	2	3	4
(c)	4	3	2	1
(d)	4	2	3	1

99 Match the following.

List I	List II
A. Marginal utility	1. Hick and Allen
B. Indifference curve analysis	2. Alfred Marshall
C. Revealed preference hypothesis	3. Paul A Samuelson

Codes

	A	B	C		A	B	C
(a)	2	1	3	(b)	2	3	1
(c)	3	1	2	(d)	1	2	3

100 Match the following.

List I	List II
A. Law of equi-marginal utility	1. Gossen
B. Ordinal utility	2. Hicks
C. Monopolistic competition	3. Mrs Robinson
D. Marginal productivity theory of distribution	4. Clark

Codes

	A	B	C	D		A	B	C	D
(a)	2	1	4	3	(b)	3	4	2	1
(c)	1	2	3	4	(d)	4	2	3	1

101 Match the following.

List I	List II
A. $AP \times L$	1. Marginal product
B. $TU_n - TU_{n-1}$	2. Marginal utility
C. $TP_n - TP_{n-1}$	3. Total product

Codes

	A	B	C		A	B	C
(a)	1	2	3	(b)	3	2	1
(c)	2	3	1	(d)	2	1	3

PREVIOUS YEARS' QUESTIONS

December 2018

1 Production function is based on which combination of the main characteristics of the inputs from the following.

1. Substitutability **2. Complementarity**

3. Flexibility **4. Specificity**

Choose the correct answer from the codes given below

Codes

(a) Both 1 and 2 (b) 1, 3 and 4

(c) 1, 2 and 4 (d) Both 3 and 1

July 2018

2 The following are the two statements regarding concept of profit. Indicate the correct code of the statements being correct or incorrect.

Statement I Accounting profit is a surplus of total revenue over and above all paid-out costs, including both manufacturing and overhead expenses.

Statement II Economic or pure profit is a residual left after all contractual costs have been met, including the transfer costs of management, insurable risks, depreciation and payments to shareholders sufficient to maintain investment at its current level.

Codes

(a) Both the statements are correct

(b) Both the statements are incorrect

(c) Statement I is correct while Statement II is incorrect

(d) Statement I is incorrect while Statement II is correct

3 Which one of the following sets is incorrect to show the inter-relationships among price elasticity coefficient, change in price and change in total revenue?

Price Elasticity Coefficient	Change in Price	Change in Total Revenue
(a) Zero	Increase Decrease	Increase Decrease
(b) Less than 1	Increase Decrease	Decrease Increase
(c) Equal to 1	Increase Decrease	No change No change
(d) More than 1	Increase Decrease	Decrease Increase

4 Which one of the following is not the basic property of indifference curves ?

(a) Indifference curves have a negative slope
(b) Indifference curves of imperfect substitutes are concave to the origin
(c) Indifference curves do not intersect nor are they tangent to one another
(d) Upper indifference curves indicate higher level of satisfaction

5 Match the items of List - II with the items of List - I and indicate the code of correct matching. The items relate to economies of scale/scope.

List I	List II
A. Economies of scale	1. Arise with lower average costs of manufacturing a product when two complementary products are produced by a single firm
B. Internal economies	2. Mean lowering of costs of production by producing in bulk
C. External economies	3. Arise when cost per unit depends on size of the firm
D. Economies of scope	4. Arise when cost per unit depends on the size of the industry, not the firm

Codes

	A	B	C	D		A	B	C	D
(a)	2	4	1	3	(b)	1	2	3	4
(c)	2	3	4	1	(d)	4	3	2	1

November 2017

6 Which one of the following statements is true ?

(a) Pure profit is the return in excess of the opportunity cost
(b) Accounting profit is the excess of total revenue over and above the explicit and implicit costs
(c) Profit maximisation is the sole objective of the modern firms
(d) Profit is maximum when the difference between marginal revenue and marginal cost is maximum

7 Which one of the following is not the basic property of indifference curves ?

(a) Negative slope
(b) Indifference curves of two imperfect substitutes are concave to the point of origin
(c) The indifference curves do not intersect nor are they tangent to one another
(d) Upper indifference curves indicate a higher level of satisfaction

8 **Statement** I The least-cost or optimal input combination of labour capital requires that the marginal revenue productivity ratio of the two inputs should be equal to their price ration.

Statement II In a hypothetical production function of the following from $Q = L^3 + 15L^2 + 10$

Where Q = Quantity of the product and L = No. of variable input (labour) the marginal physical productivity of labour is $L^2 + 15L + 10$

Codes

(a) Both, statements are true
(b) Both, statements are false
(c) Statement I is true while Statement II is false
(d) Statement I is false, while Statement II is true

January 2017

9 From the following two statements of Assertion (A) and Reason (R), indicate the correct code.

Assertion (A) From the marginal costing approach point of view, the marginal cost is compared with the purchase price.

Reason (R) If the marginal cost is less than the purchase price it should be purchased rather than manufactured.

Codes

(a) Both (A) and (R) are correct
(b) (A) is correct, but (R) is not correct
(c) (A) is not correct, but (R) is correct
(d) Both (A) and (R) are incorrect

10 The short-run production function for a firm is as follows

$Q = -L^3 + 15L^2 + 10L$

Where Q denotes total output in physical units and L denotes units of labour which are homogeneous, but are not perfectly divisible and change in labour does not tend to become zero.

Statement I In this production function, the marginal product of 5th unit of labour is 85.

Statement II Similarly, in this production function, the average product of the 5th unit of labour is 60.

Codes

(a) Both the statements are true
(b) Both the statements are false
(c) Statement I is true, while Statement II is false
(d) Statement I is false, but Statement II is true

July 2016

11 Ordinal utility analysis of the consumer's behaviour is considered superior to the cardinal utility analysis mainly due to

(a) assumption of the rationality of the consumer's behaviour
(b) possibility of the derivation of the consumer's demand
(c) bifurcation of price effects into income and substitution effects
(d) consideration of the available limited resources for satisfying consumer's demand

12 The minimum Long Run Average Cost (LAC) can be determined on a
1. LAC curve for a normal production function
2. LAC curve for a linear production function
3. planning curve
4. envelope curve

Select the correct answer using the codes given below

Codes
(a) 1, 2 and 3 (b) 2, 3 and 4
(c) 1, 3 and 4 (d) 1, 2 and 4

13 When labour is plotted on X-axis and capital is plotted on Y-axis and an isoquant is prepared, then which of the following statement(s) is/are false?
1. Marginal rate of technical substitution of labour for capital is equal to the slope of the iso-quant.
2. Marginal rate of technical substitution of labour for capital is equal to change in the units of capital divided by the change in the units of labour.
3. Marginal rate of technical substitution of labour for capital is the ratio of marginal productivity of capital to marginal productivity of labour.

Codes
(a) Both 1 and 2 (b) Only 3
(c) Only 1 (d) Only 2

December 2015

14 Match the following.

List I	List II
A. Convexity of the indifference curve to origin	1. Indifference curve analysis
B. Quantity of certain goods sacrificed for a large quantity of other goods	2. Consumer's equilibrium
C. Equality of the ratio of the marginal utilities with that of the prices of the two goods	3. Substitutability / Complementarity of the two goods
D. Separation of substitution and income effects from the total price effect	4. Marginal rate of substitution

Codes

	A	B	C	D		A	B	C	D
(a)	4	2	1	3	(b)	3	4	2	1
(c)	3	1	4	2	(d)	1	3	2	4

15 In case, the elasticity of demand on an average revenue curve is equal to unity, the marginal revenue will be
(a) more than unity (b) equal to unity
(c) equal to a fraction of unity (d) equal to zero

16 The Marshallian utility analysis is based on a less valid assumption of
(a) cardinal measurability of the utility
(b) given marginal utility of money
(c) diminishing marginal utility of the goods
(d) additivity of the utility

June 2015

17 Match the following.

List I (Production functions)	List II (Name of the shapes of returns to scale)
A. $Q = 10.2\ K^{0.19} L^{0.88}$	1. Constant returns to scale
B. $Q = 1.01\ L^{0.75} K^{0.25}$	2. Diminishing returns to scale
C. $Q = 0.84\ L^{0.63} K^{0.3}$	3. Increasing returns to scale

Codes

	A	B	C		A	B	C
(a)	1	2	3	(b)	2	1	3
(c)	2	3	1	(d)	1	3	2

18 Which one of the following statement is false?
(a) Normally, a price demand curve slopes downward from left to right
(b) Economies of scale and economies of scope are the same
(c) For optimisation, equality between marginal cost and marginal revenue is a necessary condition but it is not a sufficient one
(d) Law of variable proportions denotes input-output relationship during short run

19 Match the following.

List I	List II
A. Law of diminishing marginal utility	1. Cross demand
B. Relationship between price of one commodity and demand for other commodity	2. Oligopoly
C. Skimming the cream policy	3. Cardinal approach
D. Price rigidity	4. Pioneer pricing

Codes

	A	B	C	D		A	B	C	D
(a)	1	2	3	4	(b)	3	1	2	4
(c)	2	4	1	3	(d)	4	3	2	1

December 2014

20 Consumer is said to be in equilibrium, maximising his total utility, when
(a) the marginal utilities of the two goods consumed are equal
(b) the proportions of the marginal utilities and respective prices are equal
(c) the consumer gets full satisfaction from the consumption
(d) the consumer feels satisfied with his expenditure on the various goods

21 **Statement** I The isoquant curves are drawn convex to the origin due to diminishing technical rate of substitution.

Statement II The lesser the convexity of the isoquant curve, the greater the possibility of the complementarity of the two inputs.

Codes
(a) Both statements are true
(b) Statement I is true, but Statement I is false
(c) Statement I is false, but Statement II is true
(d) Both statements are false

June 2014

22 **Marginal costing technique is useful for**
(a) make or buy decisions
(b) profit planning
(c) shutdown decisions
(d) All of the above

23 **At a point of satiety for a commodity the marginal utility is**
(a) negative (b) positive
(c) zero (d) highly positive

24 **Match the following.**

List I	List II
A. Excess of profit total revenue over total explicit cost	1. Normal Profit
B. Total profit revenue equals total economic cost	2. Economic Profit
C. Excess of total revenue over total of explicit and implicit costs and a normal rate of return	3. Accounting Profit

Codes

	A	B	C		A	B	C
(a)	3	1	2	(b)	2	1	3
(c)	1	2	3	(d)	1	3	2

25 **Assertion** (A) A monopoly firm's revenue curve is downward sloping from left to right.

Reason (R) The monopoly firm does not simultaneously enjoy the freedom to determine both price and quantity to be sold according to its whims and fancy.

Codes
(a) Both (A) and (R) are true
(b) Both (A) and (R) are false
(c) (A) is true, but (R) is false
(d) (A) is false, but (R) is true

December 2013

26 **Match the following.**

List I	List II
A. Cross elasticity is zero	1. Price = AVC
B. Shut down point	2. Two commodities are independent
C. Slutskey theorem	3. Transformation line
D. Production possibility	4. Substitution effect

Codes

	A	B	C	D		A	B	C	D
(a)	2	4	1	3	(b)	3	2	1	4
(c)	1	3	2	4	(d)	2	1	4	3

27 **The consumer is said to be in equilibrium when he plans his expenditure on x, y and z commodities in such a way that he ultimately attains**
(a) $MU_X = MU_Y = M_Z$
(b) $\frac{MU_X}{P_X} = \frac{MU_Y}{P_Y} = \frac{M_Z}{P_Z}$
(c) $\frac{MU_X}{P_X} = \frac{MU_Y}{P_Y} = \frac{MU_Z}{P_Z} = MU_m$
(d) $\frac{MU_X}{P_X} < \frac{MU_Y}{P_Y} < \frac{MU_Z}{P_Z} < MU_m$

28 **Match the following.**

List I	List II
A. Monopoly	1. Price taker
B. Monopolistic competition	2. Homogeneous product's price maker
C. Perfect competition	3. Heterogeneous product
D. Oligopoly	4. Price rigidity

Codes

	A	B	C	D		A	B	C	D
(a)	2	3	1	4	(b)	1	2	4	3
(c)	3	4	2	1	(d)	4	1	3	2

29 **Optimal input combination to minimise the cost for a given output will be at the point where**
(a) Isocost is tangent to isoquant
(b) MRTS between inputs is equal
(c) Any movement from optimum point will lead to low level of output
(d) All of the above conditions are fulfilled

June 2013

30 **Match the following.**

List I	List II
A. Indifference curve	1. Slopes downward to the right
B. Demand curve	2. $P = AR = MR = d$
C. Perfect competition	3. Oligopoly
D. Price leadership	4. Convex to the origin

Codes

	A	B	C	D
(a)	2	3	4	1
(b)	3	4	1	2
(c)	4	1	2	3
(d)	1	2	3	4

31 **Assertion** (A) Want satisfying power of a commodity is called its utility.

Reason (R) Utility may not have the characteristic of morality.

Codes
(a) Both (A) and (R) are correct
(b) (A) is correct, but (R) is not correct
(c) Both (A) and R are not correct
(d) (R) is correct, but (A) is not correct

32 Assertion (A) As the proportion of one variable factor in a combination with fixed factor is increased, after a point the marginal product of the factor will diminish.

Reason (R) Beyond the level of optimum combination of inputs leads to this.

Codes

(a) (R) is appropriate reason of (A)
(b) (R) is not appropriate reason of (A)
(c) (A) and (R) are not related with each other
(d) (A) is independent of (R)

33 Price, marginal revenue and elasticity are related to each other. When e = 1, then

(a) MR > 0 (b) MR < 0
(c) MR = 0 (d) MR = 1

34 Match the following.

List I	List II
A. Utilitarian approach	1. Marginal rate of substitution
B. Ordinal approach	2. Budget line and indifference curve
C. Price consumption curve	3. U = f (x, y)
D. Consumer equilibrium	4. $MRS_{xy} = MRs_{yx}$

Codes

	A	B	C	D
(a)	1	4	3	2
(b)	2	3	4	1
(c)	3	1	2	4
(d)	4	2	1	3

December 2012

35 Assertion (A) Marginal cost and differential cost do not convey the same meaning in all the circumstances.

Reason (R) Differential cost increases or decreases due to change in fixed cost.

Codes

(a) Both (A) and (R) are true and (R) is the correct explanation of (A)
(b) Both (A) and (R) are true, but (R) is not the correct explanation of (A)
(c) (A) is true, but (R) is false
(d) (A) is false, but (R) is true

36 When average cost is declining

(a) marginal cost must be declining
(b) marginal cost must be above average cost
(c) marginal cost must be below average cost
(d) marginal cost must be rising

June 2012

37 Assertion (A) Total utility will be maximum, when marginal utility to price of respective products are equal.

Reason (R) Deviation from this situation leads to reduction in maximum utility.

Codes

(a) Both (A) and (R) are true
(b) Both (A) and (R) are false
(c) (A) is true, but (R) is false
(d) (A) is false, but (R) is true

ANSWERS

Objective Questions

1 (d)	2 (a)	3 (a)	4 (c)	5 (d)	6 (a)	7 (b)	8 (b)	9 (b)	10 (b)
11 (b)	12 (a)	13 (a)	14 (a)	15 (a)	16 (a)	17 (a)	18 (a)	19 (a)	20 (b)
21 (c)	22 (b)	23 (b)	24 (b)	25 (a)	26 (c)	27 (a)	28 (d)	29 (d)	30 ()
31 (a)	32 (b)	33 (a)	34 (c)	35 (b)	36 (c)	37 (b)	38 (a)	39 (a)	40 (c)
41 (a)	42 (c)	43 (a)	44 (c)	45 (c)	46 (a)	47 (c)	48 (b)	49 (b)	50 (c)
51 (c)	52 (c)	53 (b)	54 (c)	55 (b)	56 (d)	57 (c)	58 (c)	59 (a)	60 (a)
61 (d)	62 (a)	63 (c)	64 (b)	65 (b)	66 (d)	67 (c)	68 (a)	69 (c)	70 (a)
71 (d)	72 (d)	73 (d)	74 (c)	75 (b)	76 (a)	77 (c)	78 (a)	79 (b)	80 (d)
81 (b)	82 (a)	83 (a)	84 (b)	85 (c)	86 (d)	87 (c)	88 (b)	89 (c)	90 (c)
91 (c)	92 (b)	93 (b)	94 (d)	95 (a)	96 (b)	97 (a)	98 (b)	99 (a)	100 (c)
101 (b)									

Previous Years' Questions

1 (c)	2 (a)	3 (b)	4 (b)	5 (c)	6 (a)	7 (b)	8 (d)	9 (d)	10 (b)
11 (c)	12 (d)	13 (c)	14 (b)	15 (d)	16 (a)	17 (b)	18 (b)	19 (b)	20 (b)
21 (b)	22 (c)	23 (c)	24 (a)	25 (c)	26 (d)	27 (c)	28 (a)	29 (a)	30 (c)
31 (a)	32 (a)	33 (c)	34 (c)	35 (c)	36 (c)	37 (c)			

CHAPTER 12

Market Structure and Price Determination

In this chapter, we will study about market and its different forms. Forms of market can be divided on the basis of competition faced by the existing firms *i.e.* perfect competition and imperfect competition.

In this Chapter

- *Market*
- *Perfect Competition*
- *Monopoly*
- *Monopolistic Competition*
- *Oligopoly*
- *Pricing Strategies*

Market

It refers to a place where buyers and sellers of a good/commodity meet and exchange goods at a particular price during a time period. In other words, market is to be viewed in terms of the volume or value of sale and purchase of goods and services. *Depending on the degree of competition, a market is often described as one of the following forms*

Forms of Market based on Competition

- Perfect Competition
- Imperfect Competition
  - Monopoly
  - Monopolistic Competition
  - Oligopoly

Perfect Competition

Perfect competition refers to the form of market where there are very large number of buyers and sellers of a commodity. Sellers sell homogenous (identical) products at a price determined by the market.

Features of Perfect Competition

Very Large Number of Buyers and Sellers There are very large number of buyers and sellers in the market. Each seller produces only a small portion of the market supply of the commodity and each buyer also purchase only a small portion of the commodity according to market. Therefore, an individual seller or buyer cannot influence the price of the commodity by his or her individual efforts.

Homogeneous Products The products produced and sold by all the sellers are perfectly identical or having no difference, *i.e.* the products produced and sold by all the sellers are homogeneous products or perfect substitutes of each other.

Free Entry and Exit of Firms Under perfect competition, new firms are free to enter the industry, if they expect to earn profits and existing firms are free to leave the industry, if they suffer losses. There is no restriction on entry or exit of firms in perfect competition market. Because of this feature, firms in this market form earn only normal profit in the long run.

➠ **Note** *Because of freedom of entry and exit of firms under perfect competition, no firm can either earn super normal profits or losses in the long-run.*

Perfect Knowledge of the Market Condition In perfect competition market, the buyers and sellers have perfect or complete knowledge about the market situation. Buyers and sellers have very close contact with each other, which enable them to know the prices at which goods are being bought and sold.

Uniform Price In perfect competition market, products are bought and sold at a uniform price, *i.e.* only one price prevails in the whole market at a particular point of time and an individual firm can sell any number of units of the commodity at the prevailing price.

Perfect Mobility of Factors of Production The factors of production are perfectly mobile between places in perfect competition market. They can easily move from one line of production to another, *i.e.* different factors of production are free to seek employment in any industry as they like.

Firms are Price-takers In perfect competition market, firms are price-takers not price-makers, because the price is determined by the industry and is taken by the firms. Firms follow the price given by the industry and they sell their commodity at that price in the market. No individual firm can influence the price of the commodity by changing its activity.

No Transportation Cost It is assumed that the transportation cost is nil in perfect competition market, *i.e.* a firm can sell at any place without any addition of cost.

Demand Curve Under Perfect Competition

The demand curve of the firm is perfectly elastic under perfect competition.

It can be understood with the help of following graphs

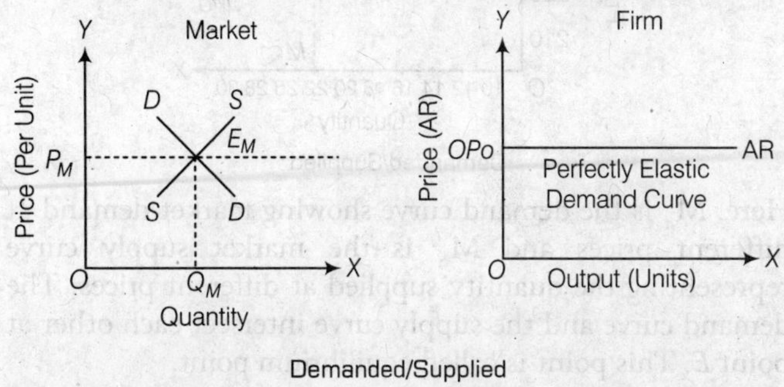

In the above figure, DD is the market demand curve and SS is the market supply curve, E_M is the point of market equilibrium, where market demand and a market supply are equal to OQ_M. This gives the equilibrium price in the market (OP_M). This price is accepted by every firm (OP_O) under perfect competition.

Working of Price Mechanism Under Perfect Competition

General Rule of Price Determination

Under perfect competition, demand and supply play an equally important role in determining the price. This is called market mechanism.

Under perfect competition, price is determined by the interaction of the market demand and market supply. Price is determined at a point, where the market forces of demand and supply interact. The price at which demand is equal to supply and exchange take place is called equilibrium price and the quantity is called equilibrium quantity.

Determination of equilibrium price can be explained with the help of the following demand and supply schedule and their curves

Price (₹ per metre)	Quantity Demanded (million metres)	Quantity Supplied (million metres)
250	19	28
240	20	26
230	22	22
220	25	17
210	30	10

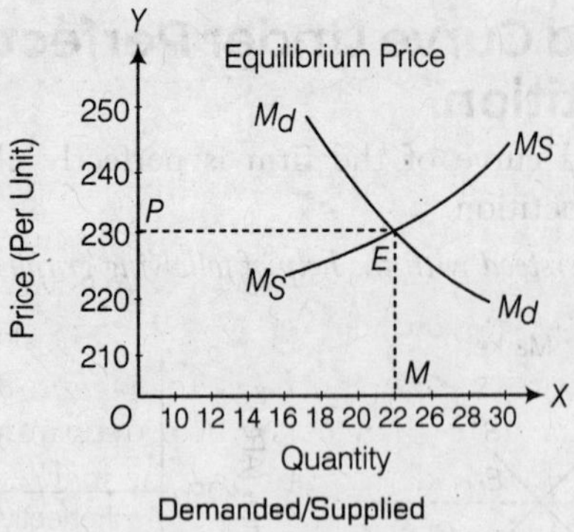

Here, M_d is the demand curve showing market demand at different prices and M_S is the market supply curve representing the quantity supplied at different prices. The demand curve and the supply curve intersect each other at point *E*. This point is called equilibrium point.

Under perfect competition, the equilibrium price would, therefore, be ₹ 230 per metre and quantity would be 22 units, as per given schedule.

Change in Equilibrium

Due to Change in Demand

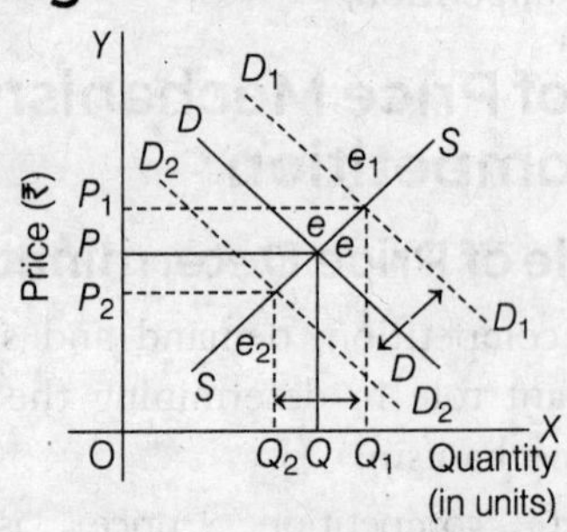

- When demand increases to D_1D_1, new equilibrium shifts to e_1, as a result equilibrium price increases to OP_1 and quantity increases to OQ_1.
- When demand decreases to D_2D_2, new equilibrium shifts to e_2, as a result equilibrium price decreases to OP_2 and quantity decreases to OQ_2.

Due to Change in Supply

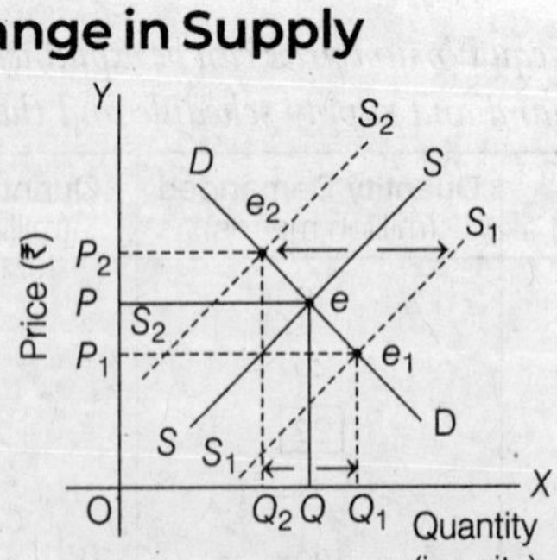

- When supply increases to S_1S_1, new equilibrium shifts to e_1, as a result equilibrium price decreases to OP_1 and quantity increases to OQ_1.
- When supply decreases to S_2S_2, new equilibrium shifts to e_2, as a result equilibrium price increases to OP_2 and quantity decreases to OQ_2.

Change in Equilibrium Price and Quantity when both Demand and Supply Changes

When both Demand and Supply Increases

- Increase in Demand > Increase in Supply
  Effect : Equilibrium Price Increases
  Equilibrium Quantity Increases
- Increase in Demand < Increase in Supply
  Effect : Equilibrium Price Decreases
  Equilibrium Quantity Increases
- Increase in Demand = Increase in Supply
  Effect : Equilibrium Price remains Constant
  Equilibrium Quantity Increases

When both Demand and Supply Decreases

- Decrease in Demand > Decrease in Supply
  Effect : Equilibrium Price Decrease
  Equilibrium Quantity Decrease
- Decrease in Demand < Decrease in Supply
  Effect : Equilibrium Price Increases
  Equilibrium Quantity Decreases
- Decreases in Demand = Decrease in Supply
  Effect : Equilibrium Price remains Constant
  Equilibrium Quantity Decreases

When Demand Increases and Supply Decreases

- Increase in Demand > Decrease in Supply
  Effect : Equilibrium Price Increases
  Equilibrium Quantity Increases
- Increase in Demand < Decrease in Supply
  Effect : Equilibrium Price Increases
  Equilibrium Quantity Decreases
- Increase in Demand = Decrease in Supply
  Effect : Equilibrium Price Increases
  Equilibrium Quantity remains Constant

When Demand Decreases and Supply Increases

- Decreases in Demand > Increase in Supply
  Effect : Equilibrium Price Decreases
  Equilibrium Quantity Increases
- Decrease in Demand = Increase in Supply
  Effect : Equilibrium Price Decreases
  Equilibrium Quantity remains Constant

When Demand is Perfectly Elastic and Supply Changes

- When Supply Increases
  Effect : Equilibrium Price remains Constant
  Equilibrium Quantity Increases
- When Supply Decreases
  Effect : Equilibrium Price remains Constant
  Equilibrium Quantity Decreases

When Demand is Perfectly Inelastic and Supply Changes

- When Supply Increases
  Effect : Equilibrium Price Decreases
  Equilibrium Quantity remains Constant
- When Supply Decreases
  Effect : Equilibrium Price Increases
  Equilibrium Quantity remains Constant

When Supply is Perfectly Elastic and Demand Changes

- When Demand Increases
  Effect : Equilibrium Price remains Constant
  Equilibrium Quantity Increases
- When Demand Decreases
  Effect : Equilibrium Price remains Constant
  Equilibrium Quantity Decreases

When Supply is Perfectly Inelastic and Demand Changes

- When Demand Increases
  Effect : Equilibrium Price Increases
  Equilibrium Quantity remains Constant
- When Demand Decreases
  Effect : Equilibrium Price Decreases
  Equilibrium Quantity remains Constant

Monopoly

Monopoly is a form of market in which there is a single seller or producer of a commodity. There are no substitutes of the monopoly's product and there are legal, technical or natural barriers to the entry of new firms in the monopoly market.

Features of Monopoly Market

Single Seller and Large Number of Buyers In monopoly market, there is only one seller or producer of the commodity, but there are a large number of buyers of the commodity produced in the market.

No Substitutes In monopoly market, the commodity produced by the producer has no substitutes available in the market, *i.e.* the goods produced are unique.

Restrictions on the Entry of New Firms There are either natural or artificial restrictions on the entry of new firms into the monopoly market.

The Monopoly Firm is also an Industry Under monopoly market, there is only one firm which constitutes the industry. Therefore, there is no difference between firm and industry in a monopoly market.

Price-maker In a monopoly market, the monopolist is the price-maker of his product. The firm determines its price and sells the quantity of output that the market will buy at that price.

Full Control Over the Supply The monopolist has full control over the supply of his product, *i.e.* he can increase or decrease the supply of his product in the market.

Inelastic Demand A monopolist has to face downward sloping inelastic demand of his product. This means that the monopolist can sell additional units only by reducing the price of the commodity but demand remains inelastic.

Imperfect Knowledge Under monopoly, knowledge of the buyers is imperfect, *i.e.* seller is more aware than buyers.

Price and Output Determination in Monopoly Market

Price and output determination under monopoly market can be studied under two different time periods which are as follows

Price and Output Determination in the Short Period

Short period is the time period in which there are two types of factors of production, namely fixed factors and variable factors. In the short period, production can be changed only by changing the variable factors of production. Fixed factors of production cannot be changed in the short period.

In other words, in the short period, supply can be changed but only to some extent.

In this period, volume of production can be changed, but capacity of the plant cannot be changed. The producer can increase the supply only with the help of existing machines and plants. New factories and plant equipment cannot be installed.

In short period, the monopoly firm attains equilibrium when

- Marginal Cost (MC) is equal to Marginal Revenue (MR) of the firm, *i.e.*
  $$MC = MR$$
- MC curve must intersects the MR curve from below, *i.e.* MC > MR, beyond the point of equilibrium.

In the short period, the monopoly firm may earn super normal profit, normal profit and it may also suffer losses in the short run equilibrium.

These are explained as follows

Super Normal Profits The monopoly firm earns super normal profit in the short run equilibrium when the Average Revenue (AR) or price is more than the Average Cost (AC) of the firm, *i.e.* AR > AC at the point of equilibrium.

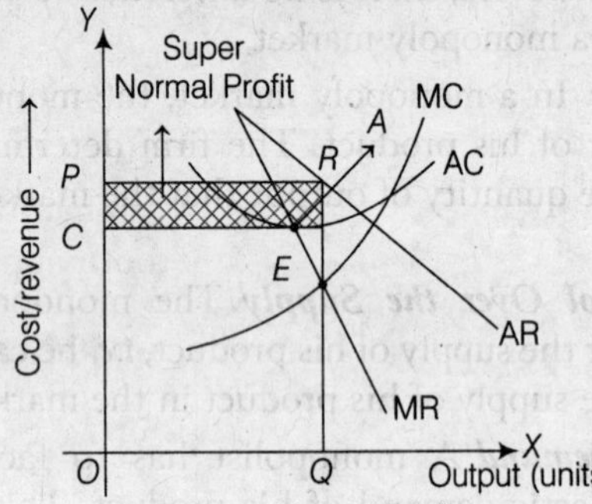

Super Normal Profits

In the above figure, *E* is the point of equilibrium, *OQ* is the equilibrium output, *OP* is the equilibrium price. Corresponding to this point,

$$AC = AQ, AR = RQ$$

Since, AR > AC, the firm makes super normal profits equal to the area given by *PRAC*.

Normal Profits The monopoly firm earns only normal profits, if AR = AC in the short run equilibrium.

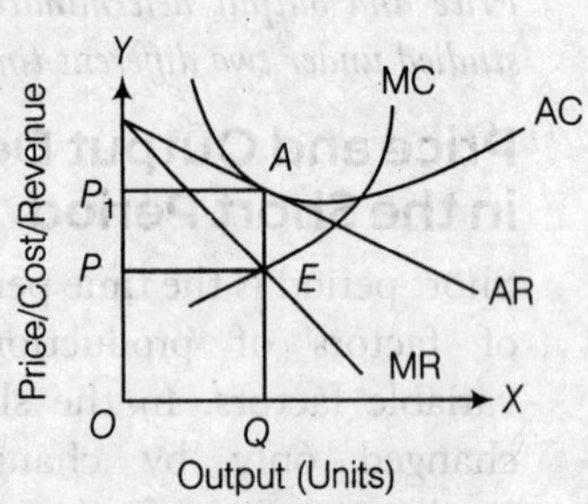

Normal Profits

In the above figure, *E* is the point of equilibrium, *OQ* is the equilibrium output and *OP* is the equilibrium price. Corresponding to this point,

$$AC = AQ, AR = AQ$$

Since, AC = AR, the firm makes normal profits.

Super Normal Loss The firm suffer losses, if AR < AC in the short run equilibrium.

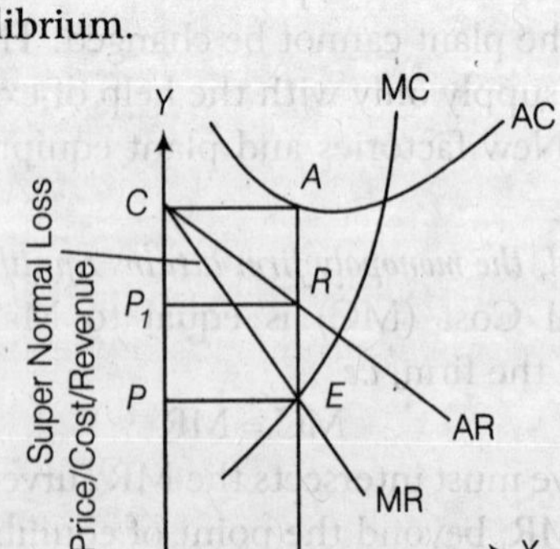

Super Normal Loss

In the above figure, *E* is the point of equilibrium, *OQ* is the equilibrium output, *OP* is the equilibrium price. Corresponding to this point,

$$AC = AQ$$
$$AR = RQ$$

Since, AR < AC, the firm makes super normal loss equal to *CARP*. Even though the firm makes losses, it continues to produce in the short run because AVC is covered.

Price Output Determination in the Long Period

Long run is the time period, which is enough to fully adjust the supply to the demand for a commodity. In this period, all factors of production are variable. Volume as well as capacity of production can be changed.

In the long period, the monopoly firm is in equilibrium, when firms Long run Marginal Cost (LMC) is equal to the Long run Marginal Revenue (LMR) and LMC curve cuts LMR curve from below.

At this equilibrium point, the monopoly firm could be earning super normal profit or normal profit, but in any condition could not be suffering a loss.

Normally, a monopoly firm earns super normal profit in the long run equilibrium. *The long run equilibrium or price output determination of a firm can be shown through the following figure*

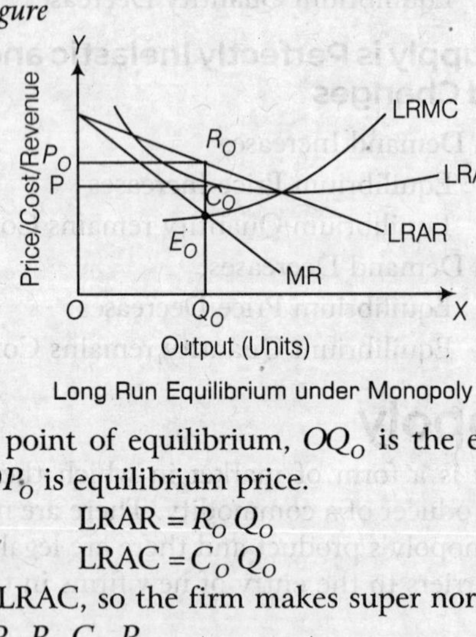

Long Run Equilibrium under Monopoly

E_O is the point of equilibrium, OQ_O is the equilibrium output, OP_O is equilibrium price.

$$LRAR = R_O Q_O$$
$$LRAC = C_O Q_O$$

LRAR > LRAC, so the firm makes super normal profits equal to $P_O R_O C_O P$.

Price Discrimination Under Monopoly

It occurs when a business charges a different price to different groups of consumers for the same good or service, for reasons not associated with costs. It is important to stress that charging different price for similar goods is not pure price discrimination.

Types of Price Discrimination

Perfect/First Degree Price Discrimination

Sometimes known as optimal pricing, with perfect price discrimination, the firm separates the market into each individual consumer and charges them the price they are willing and able to pay.

If successful, the firm can extract the entire consumer surplus that lies underneath the demand curve and turn it into extra revenue or producer surplus. This is hard to achieve unless a business has full information on every consumer's individual preferences and willingness to pay.

Second Degree Price Discrimination

This involves businesses selling off packages or blocks of a product deemed to be surplus capacity at lower prices than the previously published or advertised price. Price tends to fall as the quantity bought increases. Like electricity bill, water bill etc.

Third Degree Price Discrimination

This is the most frequently found form of price discrimination and involves charging different prices for the same product in different segments of the market. The key is that third degree discrimination is linked directly to consumer's willingness and ability to pay for a good or service. It means that the prices charged may bear little or no relation to the cost of production.

Conditions Necessary for Price Discrimination to Work

Essentially, there are two main conditions required for discriminatory pricing

Differences in Price Elasticity of Demand There must be a price elasticity of demand for each group of consumers. The firm is then able to charge a higher price to the group with a more price inelastic demand and a lower price to the group with a more elastic demand. By adopting such as strategy, the firm can increase total revenue and profits.

Barriers to Prevent Consumers Switching from One Supplier to Another The firm must be able to prevent 'consumer switching' a process whereby consumers, who have purchased a product at a lower price are able to re-sell it to those consumers, who would have otherwise paid the expensive price.

Consequences of Price Discrimination

Impact on Consumer Welfare *Following terms which impact on consumer welfare are*

- Consumer surplus is reduced in most cases representing a loss of welfare.
- For the majority of buyers, the price charged is well above the marginal cost of supply.
- Examples might include legal and medical services where charges are dependent on income levels.
- Greater access to these services may yield external benefits improving social welfare and equity.

Producer Surplus and the Use of Profit *It is as follows*

- Price discrimination benefits businesses through higher revenues and profits.
- Discriminating monopoly is extracting consumer surplus and turning it into supernormal profit.

Monopolistic Competition

Monopolistic competition refers to form of the market in which there are a large number of sellers, selling differentiated product which are close substitutes of each other.

Features of Monopolistic Competition

Large Number of Buyers and Sellers In monopolistic competition market, there are a large number of sellers or producers each selling a small share of the market demand for a product and there are large number of buyers.

Product Differentiation In monopolistic competition market, products produced by different sellers are not perfectly identical, but are slightly differentiated in quality, *i.e.* the product of one seller is slightly different from the product of another seller in a monopolistic competition market. In other words, the products of various firms working under monopolistic competition are differentiated products. The difference could be actual or imaginary. These differences can be of the quality of the product, size and colour, quality of packing, brand name, trademark, seller's behaviour or location of the shop. These commodities are close substitute of each other.

Free Entry and Exit of Firms This is another characteristic of monopolistic competition. Firms have the freedom of entry and exit in monopolistic competition. A new firm can easily enter into the industry and an old firm can also exit from the industry. There is no restriction on the entry and exit of firms in monopolistic competition market. Profit attracts new sellers and losses induces existing sellers to leave.

Selling Cost An important feature of monopolistic competition market is selling cost, by which every firm tries to promote its own product among the consumers through advertisement. The cost incurred for advertisement purposes is called selling cost. This cost is incurred as the commodities are heterogenous.

Some Influence Over the Price Each firm under monopolistic competition produces a product variety, which is close substitute to others. Therefore, if a firm lowers the price of its product, some customers of other product varieties will switch over to it. This means, as it lowers the price of its product variety, quantity demanded of it will increase. On the other hand, if it raises the price of its product, some of its customers will leave it and buy the similar products from its competing firms.

This implies that demand curve facing a firm working under monopolistic competition slopes downward but AR or demand curve is elastic in nature due to available substitutes and marginal revenue curve lies below it. This also means that under monopolistic competition, an individual firm is not a price-taker though price is set by market forces in the industry, but firms will have some influence over the price of its product.

Thus, under monopolistic competition, a firm has to choose a price-output combination, which will maximise its profits.

Imperfect Knowledge The consumers do not have complete knowledge about the product and the market in monopolistic competition. The existence of monopolistic competition depends upon imperfections in the knowledge of the buyers. Much of selling cost is simply meant to create imaginary superiority in the minds of consumers. The products may really be the same, but consumers may come to know a particular brand name more than the others. This divides the whole market into sub-markets, where individual firms have monopolistic competition.

Non-price Competition Another very important feature of monopolistic competition is the non-price competition through which firms in the market try to win over customers. There are definite methods of competing rivals other than in price.

It may be a guarantee for repairs within a particular time, after sales services, a gift scheme with particular purchases, a discount not declared in the price list or transport free of cost. All these methods are ways of attracting customers to particular brands.

Price and Output Determination Under Monopolistic Competition Market

Price and output determination under monopolistic competition market can be studied under two different time periods

Price and Output Determination in Short Run

The short period is so short that firms cannot increase their scale of production and new firms cannot enter in the production too. A firm can change the quantity of production in short period by changing the variable factors of production. In the short period, a firm can increase the demand by increasing advertisement and improving the quality and design. Firm's production and price decisions are based on the marginal revenue and cost analysis. A firm keeps on increasing production till the cost of producing an extra unit is equal to revenue received by selling one more unit of the product.

Conditions of producer's equilibrium

- MR = MC
- MC must cut MR from below, *i.e.* MC > MR.

In the short-run, a firm can earn profits or incur losses.

Super Normal Profits

In the short-run, a monopolistic competitive firm can earn super normal profits, if corresponding to the point of equilibrium, AR exceeds AC, *as is depicted in the graph below*

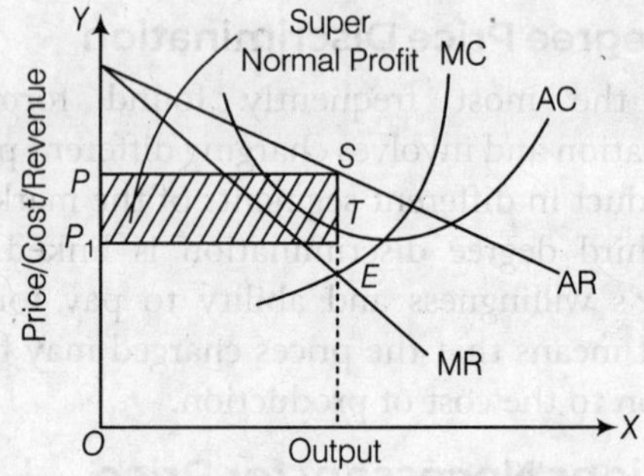

Short Run Equilibrium under Monopolistic Competition : Profit

In the figure, MR is the marginal revenue curve and AR is the average revenue curve. Similarly, AC is the average cost curve and MC is the marginal cost curve. Here, the price is OP and the total profit is $TSPP_1$. The profit is shown by the shaded area. This profit is super normal.

Super Normal Loss

An existing firm can also incur losses in the short run. If the position of demand and cost is unfavourable, *the firm may incur losses as shown below*

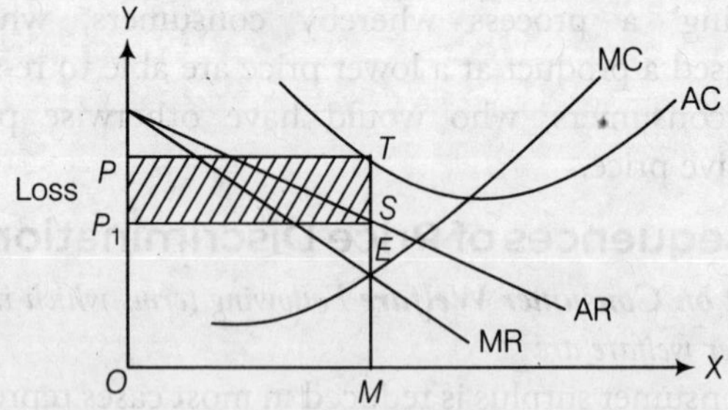

Losses under Monopolistic Competition

In the figure, AC is the average cost curve and it is higher than the average revenue curve AR. Here, the firm would incur a loss of $STPP_1$.

Thus, in the short run a firm working under monopolistic competition can earn super normal profit as well as incur a loss or may earn normal profits.

Price and Output Determination in Long Run

The super normal profit earned by a firm may not last long, because new firms may be attracted to the industry and the excess profits would be shared between existing and new firms. The super normal profits earned in the short run would, therefore, disappear in the long run.

Another characteristic of long term equilibrium is that a number of substitutes are available in the market. The marginal revenue curve is therefore elastic. *The following figure shows how the firm would earn normal profits under long run equilibrium*

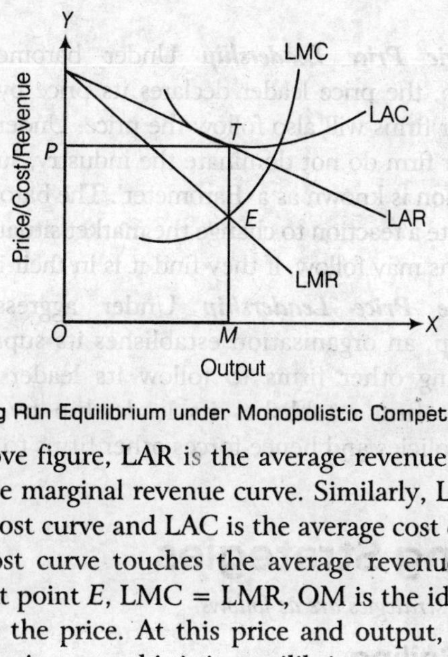

Long Run Equilibrium under Monopolistic Competition

In the above figure, LAR is the average revenue curve and LMR is the marginal revenue curve. Similarly, LMC is the marginal cost curve and LAC is the average cost curve. The average cost curve touches the average revenue curve at point *T*. At point *E*, LMC = LMR, OM is the ideal output and OP is the price. At this price and output, the firm's profit is maximum and it is in equilibrium.

Oligopoly

Oligopoly is a form of market in which there are a few large sellers/firms selling both homogenous and heterogenous goods.

Features of Oligopoly

Few Sellers and Large Number of Buyers Oligopoly form of market consists of few sellers. As against perfect market, the numbers in oligopoly is limited, usually it is generally not more than ten. In case, there are more sellers, few will be dominant firms, others being insignificant.

Nature of Product Oligopolists usually sells both homogenous and differentiated products. Differentiation is in the form of trademark, design or service. Developing brand equity has become important for oligopoly firms.

Entry is Possible but Difficult A new firm can enter the oligopoly market. In reality, however, it is highly difficult to enter due to financial, technological and other barriers to the entry. Whenever, the profits are high, the new firms do enter the market.

Interdependence Due to few firms in the market, an individual firm is neither dependent nor independent to take its own decision about the output and price.

Any decision resulting in a change in the price or output attracts reaction from the rival firms. There may be different reactions from different firms.

The situation makes a firm interdependent on each others for its own decision. It is essential for a firm to keep in mind the possible reaction of its competitors, while taking a decision.

Indeterminateness The demand curve faced by an oligopolist is indeterminate. Firms are interdependent, hence if one firm decreases its price, other firms may also do the same, which results in fall in output, instead of increase. This makes demand curve indeterminate.

Non-price Competition In an oligopoly market, price remains rigid. This is due to the fear about the reaction of their rivals. An increase in price would not be responded to but any decrease will be followed by similar or at times a larger reduction in price. Such fears make a firm stick to a particular price without further changes in order to avoid a possible price war. Oligopolists though avoid price war or competion, yet indulge in non-price competition. Such a competition usually takes the form of secret discounts, additional facilities or any other secret benefit to the retailer or the final consumer.

Forms of Oligopoly

Based on Nature of Commodity

Pure Oligopoly It refers to the form of market which sells homogenous goods/commodities which are perfect substitute of each other like cement, steel.

Impure Oligopoly It refers to the form of market which sells differentiated goods, which are substitute of each other like automobile.

Based on Competition

Collusive Oligopoly In collusive oligopoly, firm form a cartels to avoid competition. *e.g.* OPEC.

Non-collusive Oligopoly In non-collusive oligopoly, there is a cut throat competition and a high degree of interdependence between the firms. *e.g.* Telecom.

Kinked Demand Curve and Price Determination Under Oligopoly

An oligopoly firm do not have a demand (AR) curve. To deal with this situation, Prof Paul Sweezy introduced the concept of kinked demand curve, which has different elasticity on same demand (AR) curve.

Assuming that firms are attempting to maintain a high level of profits and their market share, it may be the case that

- Rivals will not follow a price increase by one firm therefore, demand will be relatively elastic and a rise in price would lead to a fall in the total revenue of the firm.
- Rivals are more likely to match a price fall by one firm to avoid a loss of market share. If this happens, demand will be more inelastic and a fall in price will also lead to a fall in total revenue.

The kink in the demand curve at price P_1 and output Q_1 means that there is a discontinuity in the firm's marginal revenue curve. If we assume that the marginal cost curve is cutting the MR curve, then the firm is maximising profits at this point.

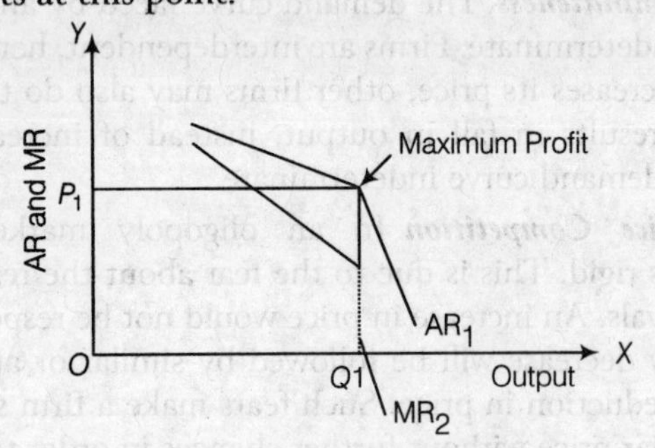

Curve Showing Maximum Profit Situation

In the diagram given below, we see that a rise in marginal costs will not necessarily lead to higher prices providing that the new MC curve (MC_2) cuts the MR curve at the same output.

The kinked demand curve theory suggests that there will be price stickness in these markets and that firms will rely more on non-price competition to boost sales, revenue and profits.

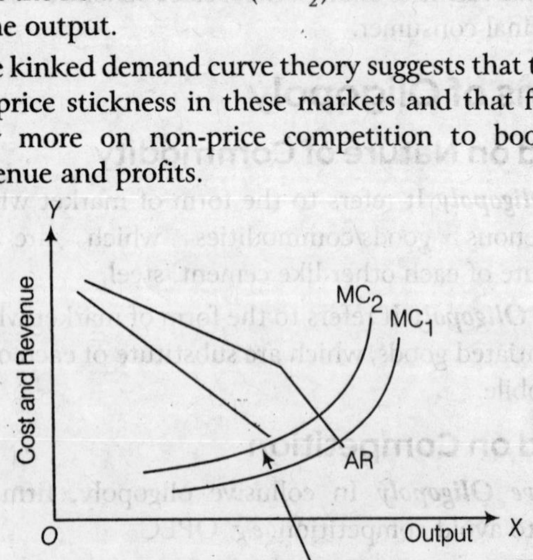

Curve Showing Firms Reliability on Non-price Competition

Price Leadership Model Under Oligopoly

Oligopolistic model is characterised by indeterminate demand curve, thus different strategies are used to set price and output.

Price leadership takes place where there is only one dominant firm, who sets the price and others are bound to follow the same. Sometimes, an agreement may be developed among organisations to assign a leadership to one of the firm. The leadership may be assigned under certain conditions like large market size, economies of scale, advance technique of production etc.

Price leadership can be of three types

Dominant Price Leadership Under dominant price leadership, a single firm dominates the entire market, while other firms cannot change the price. In other words, dominant firms creates its monopoly to maximise its own profits, while the interest of the other organisations are ignored.

Barometric Price Leadership Under barometric price leadership, the price leader declares its price by assuming that other firms will also follow the price. Under this type, the leader firm do not dominate the industry, such type of organisation is known as a 'Barometer'. The barometer firm just initiate a reaction to change the market situation, which other firms may follow, if they find it is in their interest.

Aggressive Price Leadership Under aggressive price leadership, an organisation establishes its supremacy by threatening other firms to follow its leadership, *i.e.* a dominant firm establishes its leadership by aggressive pricing policies and hence forces other firms to follow the same.

Pricing Strategies

Following strategies are as follows

Price Ceiling

When government intervenes in the market by setting a maximum price below market equilibrium, it is called price ceiling. This is done to protect the interest of the buyers.

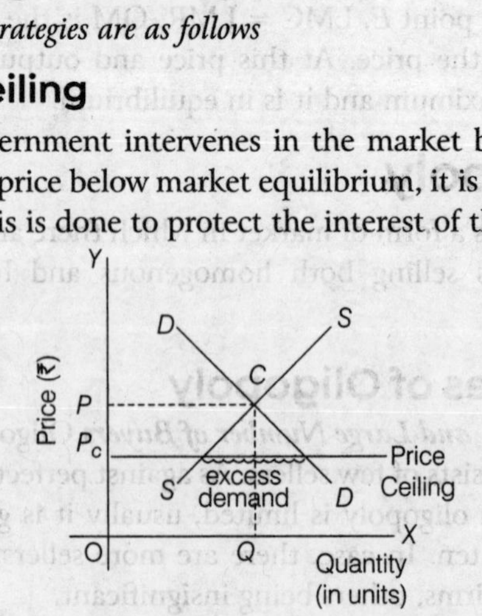

Consequences of Price Ceiling

- Excess demand
- Black marketing
- Rationing

Price Floor

When government intervenes in the market by setting a minimum price above the market equilibrium, it is called price floor. This is done to protect the interest of sellers.

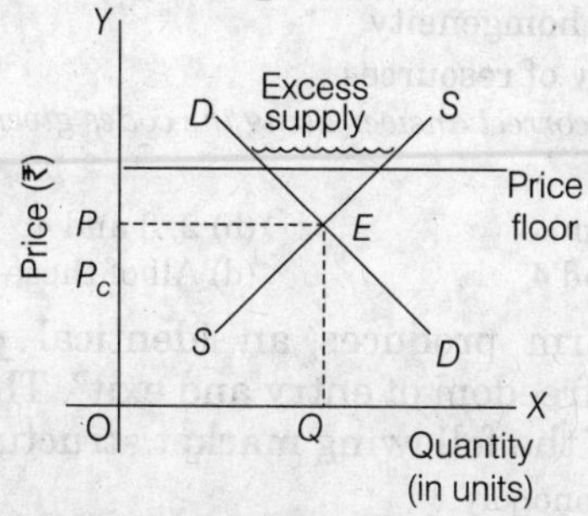

Consequences of Price Floor

- Excess supply
- Buffer stock

Price Skimming

It is a form of price discrimination under which a seller charges higher price for initial level of output and gradually reduces the price with increase in output sold. Generally, this strategy is adopted by 'First mover' under oligopoly market, who faces no competition at initial level. However, this strategy cannot be pursued for long as competitors tend to entre the market.

Price Penetration

Opposite to price skimming, under this pricing strategy a seller initially a low price to cover wide market or to increase sales. This strategy often leads to increase in market share. Generally, new firms which enters the market follows this strategy like Reliance Jio did before entering telecom industry. An extreme form of penetration is called predatory pricing.

Peak Load Pricing

This is a pricing strategy under which firms charges higher price during the period of higher demand and charges lower prices during the period when demand is low. This type of price discrimination is based on the efficiency, *i.e.* a firm discriminates on the basis of high usage and low usage. This pricing is widely used in case of non-storable goods such as electricity transport etc when the price are low due to low demand is known as off load pricing.

EXAM BASED QUESTIONS

Perfect Competition

1 The demand curve facing a perfectly competitive firm is

(a) upward sloping (b) downward sloping
(c) horizontal (d) vertical

2 Under perfect competition, the long run equilibrium of the firm is established at

(a) minimum point of LAC (b) highest point of LAC
(c) minimum point of SAC (d) highest point of SAC

3 Demand curve for a firm facing perfect competition is

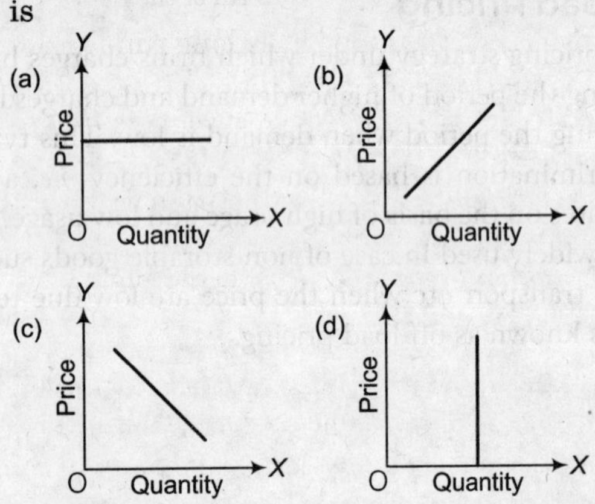

4 When a monopolist is able to sell each separate unit of the output at a different price according to the pocket of the customer, he is applying

(a) first degree price discrimination
(b) second degree price discrimination
(c) third degree price discrimination
(d) None of the above

5 The supply function will move downwards to the right, if the MC of all the firms in a perfectly competitive industry were to

(a) decrease (b) remain unchanged
(c) increase (d) None of these

6 Under perfect competition, a firm will be in equilibrium, when its AC is

(a) at minimum level
(b) equal to AR
(c) covering only prime cost of production
(d) None of the above

7 In which type of market do you have the largest number of firms?

(a) Perfect competition and oligopoly
(b) Perfect competition and differentiated competition
(c) Perfect competition and monopoly
(d) Differentiated competition and oligopoly

8 Which of the following are the features of pure competition?

1. Large number of buyers and sellers
2. Freedom of entry and exit
3. Perfect homgeneity
4. Mobility of resources

Select the correct answer using the codes given below

Codes

(a) 1, 2 and 3 (b) 2, 3 and 4
(c) 1, 3 and 4 (d) All of these

9 "Each firm produces an identical product and there is freedom of entry and exit". This is true for which of the following market structures?

(a) For monopoly
(b) For oligopoly
(c) For perfect competition
(d) For monopolistic competition

10 If a firm operates in a perfectly competitive market, then it will most likely

(a) advertise its product on television
(b) have difficult time obtaining information about the market price
(c) settle for whatever price is offered
(d) have an easy time keeping other firms out of the market

11 Which of the following refers to perfect competition?

1. There are restriction on buyers and sellers.
2. There are no restriction on movement of goods.
3. There are no restriction on factors of production.

Select the correct answer using the codes given below

Codes

(a) Both 1 and 2 (b) Both 2 and 3
(c) Both 1 and 3 (d) Only 1

12 Firms in perfect competition face a

(a) perfectly elastic demand curve
(b) perfectly inelastic demand curve
(c) perfectly elastic supply curve
(d) perfectly inelastic supply curve

13 A profit maximising firm in perfect competition produces where

(a) total revenue is maximised
(b) marginal revenue equals zero
(c) marginal revenue equals marginal cost
(d) marginal revenue equals average cost

14 Which of the following are true for perfect competition?

1. Very large number of buyers and sellers
2. Restriction on entry and exit of firms
3. Perferctly elastic demand

Select the correct answer using the codes given below
Codes
(a) Both 1 and 2 (b) Both 2 and 3
(c) Both 1 and 3 (d) All of the above

15 A perfectly competitive firm cannot earn super normal profit or incur losses in the long run due to which of the following reasons?
(a) Freedom of entry and exit of firms
(b) Perfect knowledge
(c) Perfect mobility of factors
(d) All of the above

16 In perfect competition,
(a) short run abnormal profits are competed away by firms leaving the industry
(b) short run abnormal profits are competed away by firms entering the industry
(c) short run abnormal profits are competed away by the government
(d) short run abnormal profits are competed away by greater advertising

17 In the short run, firms in perfect competition will still produce provided
(a) the price covers average variable cost
(b) the price covers variable cost
(c) the price covers average fixed cost
(d) the price covers fixed costs

18 In the long run, equilibrium in perfect competition is attained when
(a) Price = Average Cost = Marginal Cost
(b) Price = Average Cost = Total Cost
(c) Price = Marginal Revenue = Total Cost
(d) Total Revenue = Total Variable Cost

19 For a perfectly competitive firm
(a) total revenue is a straight line
(b) price is greater than marginal revenue
(c) price equals total revenue
(d) price equals total cost

20 The competitive equilibrium leads to
(a) the firms producing with excess capacity
(b) the firms producing at their minimum cost
(c) the firms producing at a cost higher than the minimum
(d) some firms produce under low cost and others under high cost

21 Long run equilibrium price of a perfectly competitive firm is always
(a) above the LAC (b) below the LAC
(c) equal to AFC (d) equal to LAC

22 Assume that a firm's total revenue curve takes the form of a straight line, which passes through the origin. We may conclude that
(a) price and marginal revenue are equal
(b) price exceeds MR
(c) TC equals TR
(d) elasticity demand is unity

23 In perfect competition, when a firm is in short period equilibrium
1. marginal cost must equal marginal revenue.
2. average cost must equal average revenue.
3. marginal revenue must equal average revenue.
4. marginal cost must equal average cost.
Select the correct answer using the codes given below
Codes
(a) 1, 2 and 4 (b) Both 1 and 3
(c) 2, 3 and 4 (d) Only 3

24 The conditions of long period equilibrium for a firm operating under perfect competition are
1. MC=MR 2. AC=AR 3. AR=MR 4. AC=MC
Select the correct answer using the codes given below
Codes
(a) Only 1 (b) Both 1 and 3
(c) 2, 3 and 4 (d) All of the above

25 In perfect competition in the long run there will be no
(a) normal profits (b) super normal profits
(c) production (d) costs

26 The firm under perfect competition will be in short run equilibrium when
(a) rising marginal cost is equal to the minimum average cost
(b) marginal revenue is equal to rising marginal cost
(c) average revenue is equal to average cost
(d) marginal revenue is equal to the falling marginal cost

Monopoly

27 Compared to the case of perfect competition, a monopolist is more likely to
(a) charge a higher price
(b) produce a lower quantity of the product
(c) make a greater amount of economic profit
(d) All of the above

28 The strategy of price discrimination is followed under which firm of market?
(a) Monopoly (b) Monopolistic
(c) Oligopoly (d) Both (a) and (c)

29 Price discrimination will always lead to
(a) increase in output (b) decrease in output
(c) no change in output (d) None of these

30 Discriminating monopoly is possible, if two markets have
(a) rising cost curves
(b) rising and declining cost curves
(c) different elasticities of demand
(d) equal elasticities of demand

31 Bilateral monopoly refers to the market situation of
(a) two sellers
(b) two buyers
(c) one seller and two buyers
(d) None of the above

32 A profit maximising monopolist in two separate markets will
(a) always charge a higher price in less selling market
(b) always charge higher price in more selling market
(c) charge same price in both markets
(d) adjust his sales in the two markets, so that his MR in each market just equals his marginal cost

33 Degree of monopoly power, according to Learner is
(a) $\frac{P}{e}$ (b) $\frac{P-MC}{P}$
(c) $\frac{AR-MR}{P}$ (d) $\frac{MC-P}{P}$

34 The profit seeking monopolist operates at a level of output, where
(a) P = MC
(b) MC = AC
(c) MR = MC
(d) All of the above

35 A monopolist has a downward sloping demand curve because
(a) it has an inelastic demand
(b) typically, it sells only to a few large buyers
(c) its demand curve is the same as the industry's demand curve
(d) consumers prefer that product

36 A natural monopoly is a market situation, in which
(a) all firms sell natural resources
(b) a single firm supplies natural resources to an entire industry
(c) a single firm can supply the market output more efficiently than many firms
(d) None of the above

37 A monopoly is a market structure, in which
(a) a single firm exercises its power over smaller firms
(b) a single firm produces a product with a wide variety of very close substitutes
(c) each firm is run by a small proprietor
(d) there is only one firm producing a product, which has no close substitutes

38 Price discrimination involves
(a) firms selling different products at different prices to different consumers
(b) firms selling the same product at different prices to different consumers
(c) consumers discriminating between different sellers on the basis of the different prices they quote for different products
(d) consumers discriminating between different sellers on the basis of the different prices they quote for the same product

39 Which of the following is necessary for a natural monopoly?
(a) Economies of scale
(b) A high proportion of the total cost is the cost of capital goods
(c) The market is very small
(d) All of the above

40 Which of the following best defines price discrimination?
(a) Charging different prices on the basis of race
(b) Charging different prices for goods with different costs of production
(c) Charging different prices based on cost of service differences
(d) Selling a certain product of given quality and cost per unit at different prices to different buyers

41 Which of the following is a characteristic of pure monopoly?
(a) One seller of the product
(b) Low barriers to entry
(c) Close substitute products
(d) Perfect information

42 In the short period, monopolist firm's equilibrium is at
(a) break-even point (b) AR > AC
(c) AR < AC (d) All of these

43 Price discrimination is profitable and possible, if the two markets have
(a) equal elasticity of demand
(b) different elasticity of demand
(c) inelastic demand
(d) highly elastic demand

44 The marginal revenue curve in monopoly
(a) equals the demand curve
(b) is parallel with the demand curve
(c) lies below and converges with the demand curve
(d) lies below and diverges from the demand curve

45 In monopoly, when abnormal profits are made
(a) the price set is greater than the average cost
(b) the price is less than the marginal cost
(c) the average revenue equals the marginal cost
(d) revenue equals total cost

46 Which of the following statements are true according to Prof Schumpeter about a monopolist?
1. Monopolies are inefficient.
2. Monopoly profits acts as an incentive for innovation.
3. AR is equal to MR.
Select the correct answer using the codes given below
Codes
(a) Both 1 and 2 (b) Both 2 and 3
(c) Only 2 (d) Only 1

47 A welfare loss occurs in monopoly where
(a) the price is greater than the marginal cost
(b) the price is greater than the marginal benefit
(c) the price is greater than the average revenue
(d) the price is greater than the marginal revenue

48 .... is also known as optimal pricing.
(a) Perfect price discrimination
(b) Second degree price discrimination
(c) Third degree price discrimination
(d) All of the above

49 Price discrimination policy helps in increasing profits in case of
(a) perfect competition
(b) monopolistic competition
(c) monopoly
(d) oligopoly

50 Which one of the following is not correct about the price discrimination by a monopolist, who intends to
(a) maximise the sales/profit
(b) share the consumer's surplus
(c) increase the welfare of masses
(d) reduce the welfare of masses

51 Which of the following is not a condition for successful price discrimination?
(a) Different elasticity of demand for different consumers
(b) Sellers should be an MNC
(c) Location of markets at distant places
(d) Consumers ignorance and prejudices

52 Marginal cost is equal to marginal revenue, average cost is equal to average revenue, average revenue is equal to marginal revenue and average cost is equal to marginal cost. This is the condition of
1. long period equilibrium for a firm under monopoly
2. short period equilibrium for a firm under oligopoly
3. long period equilibrium
4. long period equilibrium for a firm under perfect competitions

Select the correct answer using the codes given below
Codes
(a) Both 1 and 4 (b) Both 3 and 4
(c) Both 3 and 1 (d) Only 1

53 Under monopoly, the supply curve is absent because
(a) the monopolist always makes profit
(b) there is no entry for others
(c) equilibrium involves MC = MR and MC < P
(d) the monopolist controls the supply

54 Price discrimination will not be a good approach for
(a) railway company
(b) electric supply company
(c) FMCG company
(d) mobile company

55 Price discrimination policy helps in increasing profits in case of
(a) perfect competition
(b) monopolistic competition
(c) monopoly
(d) oligopoly

Monopolistic Competition

56 The monopolistic firm will be in equilibrium, where
(a) Price = Marginal cost
(b) Marginal revenue = Marginal cost
(c) Marginal revenue = Marginal cost = Price
(d) None of the above

57 In the long-run, for all monopolistic firms
(a) MR = AR (b) Price = MR = MC
(c) MR = MC = Price = AC (d) None of these

58 A firm under monopolistic competition advertises
(a) to lower the cost of production
(b) to increase sales and profits
(c) to compete successful with the rival firms
(d) because it cannot raise the price

59 The short run equilibrium level of output for monopolistic competitor is given by the point where
(a) P = SMC
(b) P = SAC
(c) the MR curve intersects the SMC curve
(d) the MR curve intersects the SMC curve from below and P = AVC

60 Consumers are likely to get maximum variety of goods under
(a) monopolistic competition
(b) monopoly
(c) perfect competition
(d) oligopoly

61 Monopolistic competition differs from perfect competition primarily because
(a) in perfect competition, firms can differentiate their products
(b) in monopolistic competition, firms can differentiate their products
(c) in monopolistic competition, there are relatively few firms
(d) in perfect competition, there are no barriers to entry

62 Consider the following statements.
1. One way the government can induce a monopolist to expand his output is by imposing a price ceiling that make the monopolist lower his price.
2. MC = MR = AC = AR shows the equilibrium position of the competitive firm.
3. One way the government can induce a monopolist to expand his output by imposing a price floor that makes the monopolist raise his price.
4. One way the government can induce a monopolist to expand his output by imposing a specific tax on the monopolist output.

Which of the statement(s) given above is/are correct?
(a) Both 1 and 2 (b) Both 3 and 4
(c) Only 2 (d) 1, 2 and 3

63 A firm may be considered to be of optimum size when
(a) its TC and TR curve coincide
(b) AC is at its minimum
(c) AC = TFC
(d) it is faced with a horizontal demand curve

64 In all forms of imperfect competition, the average revenue curve facing the individual slopes
(a) upward
(b) downward
(c) parallel to *X*-axis
(d) vertically

65 Due to which of the following reason/s monopolistic firms incur advertisement cost.
1. Differentiate goods
2. Large number of sellers
3. Avoid price war

Select the correct answer using the codes given below
Codes
(a) 1 and 2 (b) Both 1 and 3
(c) Both 2 and 3 (d) All of the above

66 Generally, the profits are maximised in the short-run at the point at which
(a) MC = MR (b) MR = 0
(c) MR is negative (d) MC = 0

67 Consider the following statements.
1. TR starts declining when MR is negative.
2. MR can be zero or even negative.
3. TR stops increasing when MR = 0.

Which of the statement(s) given above is/are correct?
Codes
(a) Both 1 and 3 (b) Both 1 and 2
(c) Only 1 (d) None of the above

68 Consider the following statements.
1. Monopolistic competition is characterised by full control over price.
2. In monopoly, the product may or may not be homogeneous.
3. Perfect mobility of the factors is the characteristic of oligoploy.

Which of the statement(s) given above is/are correct?
Codes
(a) Only 1 (b) Only 2
(c) Only 3 (d) None of the above

69 Which one of the following statement is correct?
(a) Monopolist charges the maximum possible price
(b) Monopolist always makes (economic) profit
(c) Monopolist operates on an inelastic demand curve
(d) None of the above

70 Which of the following is not the feature of monopolistic competition?
(a) Fairly large number of firms
(b) Co-existence of efficient and inefficient firms
(c) Product homogenity
(d) Independent price output policy

71 Which of the following statement is correct?
(a) Under perfect competition, a firm determines its price where AR = MR
(b) In perfect competitive industry, a firm is in equilibrium in the short run only when its AC = AR = MR = MC
(c) The short run supply curve has a negative slope
(d) A firm is price taken under perfect competition

72 Average revenue curve will not touch *X* axis because it cannot be
(a) positive
(b) zero
(c) negative
(d) None of the abvoe

73 For profit maximisation of a firm we must have
1. MC = MR
2. Marginal cost curve cuts the average cost

Select the correct answer using the codes given below
Codes
(a) Only 1
(b) Only 2
(c) Both 1 and 2
(d) Neither 1 nor 2

74 Which of the following is not the feature of monopolistic competition?
(a) Fairly large number of firms
(b) Coexistence of efficient and inefficient firms
(c) Product homogeneity
(d) Independent price output policy

Oligopoly Competition

75 Which one is not the characteristics of oligopoly firm?
(a) Conflicting attitude of firms
(b) Advertising and sales promotion
(c) One firm
(d) Few sellers

76 The lines ABCD represents which type of a curve?

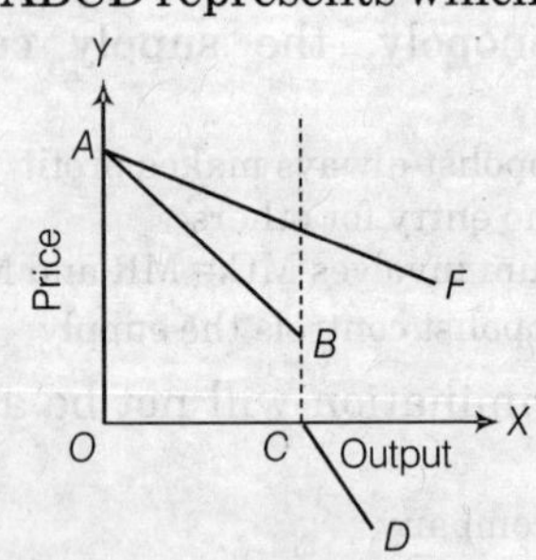

(a) Kinked curve of oligopoly
(b) Price rigidity curve
(c) Demand curve for duopoly
(d) None of the above

77 Barriers to entry are highest, in which two types of markets?
(a) Differentiated competition and oligopoly
(b) Perfect competition and differentiated competition
(c) Monopoly and differentiated competition
(d) Oligopoly and monopoly

78 **Oligopolistic firms making their price-output decisions keeping in view the current and possible future decisions of their rival firms, is an example of**
(a) strategic interaction (b) prisoner's dilemma
(c) price leadership (d) None of these

79 **A group of firms that gets together to make price and output decisions is called**
(a) a non-collusive oligopoly
(b) price leadership
(c) a cartel
(d) a concentrated industry

80 **A collusive oligopoly (with a dominant price leader) will produce a level of output**
(a) that would prevail under perfect competition
(b) between that which would prevail under perfect competition and that which a monopolistic competitor would choose in the same industry
(c) between that which would prevail under perfect competition and that which a monopolist would choose in the same industry
(d) equal to what a monopolist would choose in the same industry

81 **The kinked demand curve model of oligopoly assumes that the price elasticity of demand**
(a) in response to a price increase is more than the elasticity of demand in response to a price decrease
(b) is constant regardless of whether price increases or decreases
(c) is infinite, if price increases and zero, if price decreases
(d) in response to a price increase is less than the elasticity of demand in response to a price decrease

82 **In the kinked demand curve model, if one firm reduces its price**
(a) other firms will also reduce their price
(b) other firms will compete on a non-price basis
(c) other firms will raise their price
(d) All of the above

83 **Consider the following statements.**
1. Cartel is an informal agreement among the firms to avoid competition.
2. There is a free entry of firms in monopoly market.
3. There is a full control over price in perfect competition.

Which of the statement(s) given above is/are correct?
Codes
(a) Only 1 (b) Both 1 and 2
(c) Only 2 (d) All of the above

84 **Under kinked demand model, the demand curve for the firm's product is drawn on the assumption that**
(a) all rivals charge the same price which is charged by the oligopolist
(b) all rivals charge a price independent of the price charged by the oligopolist
(c) all rivals follow the oligopolist upto certain price, but beyond that they do not
(d) all oligopolist charge the price as independent sellers

85 **A firm producing a large number of products will follow the pricing strategy known as**
(a) cost plus pricing (b) differential pricing
(c) product line pricing (d) price leadership

86 **Cartels under oligopoly do not survive for long because of**
(a) inter-firm rivalry (b) low profits
(c) high cost of marketing (d) heavy losses

87 **In oligopoly market, kinked demand curve explains**
(a) collusion among rival firms
(b) average variable cost curves
(c) short run average cost curve
(d) long run average cost curve

88 **When goods in the domestic market are sold at a high price and in the foreign market at a low price, it is a situation of**
(a) dumping
(b) perfect competition
(c) oligopoly
(d) duopoly

89 **Which of the following statement is incorrect?**
(a) Even monopolistic can earn losses
(b) Firms in a perfectly competitive market are price takers
(c) It is always beneficial for a firm in a perfectly competitive market to discriminate prices
(d) Kinked demand curve is related to an oligopolistic market

Price Determination and Pricing Strategies

90 **Price determination often favours public interest because it**
(a) allows some products to be produced that would otherwise not be produced in the economy due to the fear of making losses
(b) opens consumption possibilities to consumers that would otherwise not be inaccessible (or unaffordable), if a single price prevailed in the market
(c) allows firms to make supernormal profits, which in turn allows them to sustain price wars when breaking into new markets
(d) All of the above

91 **If demand increases in a market, this will usually lead to**
(a) a higher equilibrium price and output
(b) a lower equilibrium price and higher output
(c) a lower equilibrium price and output
(d) a higher equilibrium price and lower output

92 **A shift in supply will have a bigger effect on price than output, if demand is**
(a) income elastic (b) income inelastic
(c) price elastic (d) price inelastic

93 If the price was fixed below the equilibrium price there would be

(a) excess supply
(b) excess demand
(c) equilibrium
(d) downward pressure on prices

94 Which of the following are consequences of price ceiling strategy by the government.

1. Black marketing
2. Hoarding
3. Rationing

Codes

(a) Both 1 and 2 (b) Both 1 and 2
(c) Both 2 and 3 (d) All of the above

95 Price floor is an important instrument of protecting sellers' interest however if has following implications.

(a) Hoarding and black marketing
(b) Rationing and buffer stock
(c) Illegal sales
(d) Buffer stock and minimum support price

96 Assuming a downward sloping demand curve and upward sloping supply curve, a higher equilibrium price may be caused by

(a) a fall in demand
(b) an increase in supply
(c) improvements in production technology
(d) an increase in demand

97 Which of the following pair(s) is/are incorrectly matched?

(a) Demand curve is indeterminate : Oligopoly
(b) Ed = ∞ : Monopoly
(c) Demand curve is relatively more elastic : Monopolistic competition
(d) All of the above

98 A particular price level, there are no forces tending to move it either up or down, it means

1. the firm is in equilibrium.
2. the price is in equilibrium.
3. the equilibrium price of the firm.
4. the equilibrium price and quantity of a firm.

Select the correct answer using the codes given below

Codes

(a) Both 1 and 4 (b) 1, 2 and 4
(c) Both 1 and 3 (d) Only 4

99 The market period supply curve for perishable commodities is

(a) relatively inelastic (b) perfectly inelastic
(c) relatively elastic (d) perfectly elastic

100 Using TR and TC a profit maximising firm will be in equilibrium at a point where the

(a) gap between the two is small
(b) gap between the two is greatest
(c) gap does not exist
(d) None of the above

101 Consider the following statements.

1. A profit maximising monopolist in different markets will adjust his sales in the two markets, so that his MR in each market just equals his MC.
2. A profit maximising monopolist in separate markets will not adjust his sales.
3. A profit maximising monopolist in separate markets will adjust his sales in the two markets, so that his MR in each market will greater than MC.
4. A profit maximising firm in separate markets will adjust his sales in each market so, that his MR is less than MC.

Which of the statement(s) given above is/are correct?

Codes

(a) Both 1 and 4
(b) Only 1
(c) Only 4
(d) Both 1 and 2

102 Which of the following pair(s) is/are not correct?

(a) Under perfect competition, demand curve is perfectly elastic
(b) Under monopoly, demand curve is relatively more elastic
(c) Both (a) and (b)
(d) All of the above

103 In the figure given below is shown the determination of price in the

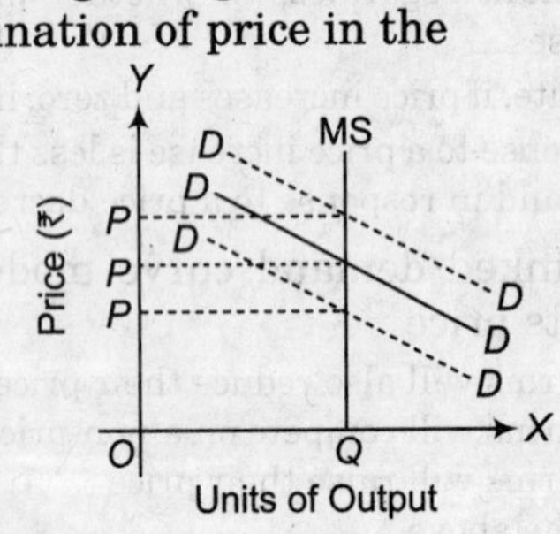

(a) short run
(b) market period
(c) long run
(d) secular run

Miscellaneous

104 **Statement I** The important difference between our assumptions for monopolistic competition and those for perfect competition is that monopolistic competitors sell similar, but not identical products.

Statement II In monopolistic competition, we have many firms selling a differentiated product.

Codes

(a) Both statements are correct
(b) Both statements are incorrect
(c) Statement I is correct, but Statement II is incorrect
(d) Statement I is incorrect, but Statement II is correct

Directions (Q. Nos. 105-111) *In the question given below are two statements labelled as Assertion (A) and Reason (R). In the context of these two statements, which one of the following is correct?*

Codes

(a) (A) is true, but (R) is false
(b) (A) is false, but (R) is true
(c) Both are true
(d) Both are false

105 Assertion (A) Under automatic mechanism of demand and supply any disturbance is setteled by the government.

Reason (R) Market mechanism sometimes proves to be ineffcient.

106 Assertion (A) A firm is a price-taker in a competitive market.

Reason (R) Price is determined by the intersection of the total demand curve with the supply curve of the industry.

107 Assertion (A) A monopolist enjoys considerable power to manipulate the price of his product.

Reason (R) The monopoly power of the monopolist is measured by the excess of price over marginal cost.

108 Assertion (A) A firm sets prices using the 'cost plus mark-up' methods.

Reason (R) The firm has no knowledge about the demand and marginal cost.

109 Assertion (A) Peak load price is possible when demand is inelastic.

Reason (R) Entre of new firms reduces the power to change high price for high demand.

110 Assertion (A) A firm under monopolistic produces reserve capacity to compete with the existing firms.

Reason (R) Reserve capacity leads increase in market price due to additional selling cost.

111 Assertion (A) A oligopoly firm do not have a demand curve to interdependence between the firms and price rigidity.

Reason (R) To deal with the problem of indeterminate demand curve, kinked demand is used.

112 Assertion (A) Negative MR is not possible in case of perfect competition.

Reason (R) Price remains constant for a perfectly competitive firm.

Codes

(a) Both (A) and (R) are true and (R) is the correct explanation of (A)
(b) Both (A) and R are true, but (R) is not the correct explanation of (A)
(c) (A) is true, but (R) is false
(d) (A) is false, but (R) is true

113 Match the following.

List I (Characteristics of Perfect Competition)	List II (Explanations)
A. Many small sellers	1. No seller is able to exert a significant influence over price
B. Many small buyers	2. No buyer's is able to exert a significant influence over price
C. Product undifferentiated	3. Decision to buy are made on the basis of price
D. Easy entry and exit	4. Resources are easily transferable among industries

Codes

	A	B	C	D
(a)	2	3	4	1
(b)	1	3	4	2
(c)	3	1	2	4
(d)	1	2	3	4

114 Match the following.

List I	List II
A. Monopoly	1. Single buyer, single seller
B. Oligopoly	2. Single seller, many buyers
C. Monopsony	3. Single buyer, many sellers
D. Duopoly	4. Few sellers, many buyers
E. Bilateral monopoly	5. Two sellers, many buyers

Codes

	A	B	C	D	E
(a)	1	2	3	4	5
(b)	1	3	5	2	4
(c)	2	4	3	5	1
(d)	2	4	1	3	5

115 Match the following.

List I	List II
A. Large number of seller with identical products	1. Monopolistic competition
B. Large number of seller with differentiated products	2. Oligopoly
C. Single seller with single buyer	3. Bilateral monopoly
D. Few sellers	4. Perfect competition

Codes

	A	B	C	D
(a)	1	2	3	4
(b)	4	1	3	2
(c)	4	2	3	1
(d)	1	4	3	2

116 Match the following.

List I	List II
A. Kinked demand curve	1. Prof Samuelson
B. Duopoly model	2. Paul M Sweezy
C. Managerial theory of firm	3. Cournot
D. Social welfare function	4. Williamson

Codes

	A	B	C	D
(a)	2	3	4	1
(b)	2	3	1	4
(c)	3	2	4	1
(d)	1	2	3	4

117 Match the following.

List I	List II
A. Perfect competition	1. Less elastic
B. Monopoly	2. Ed = ∞ (Straight line horizontal)
C. Monopolistic competition	3. Indeterminate
D. Oligopoly	4. More elastic

Codes

	A	B	C	D		A	B	C	D
(a)	4	3	2	1	(b)	2	1	4	3
(c)	3	1	4	2	(d)	2	3	4	1

118 Match the following.

List I (Forms of Market)	List II (Features)
A Perfect competition	1. High degree of interdependence
B. Monopolistic competition	2. Homogeneous product
C. Monopoly	3. Product differentiation
D. Oligopoly	4. One seller and large number of buyers

Codes

	A	B	C	D		A	B	C	D
(a)	4	3	2	1	(b)	2	3	4	1
(c)	3	1	4	2	(d)	2	4	1	3

119 Match the following.

List I	List II
A. Homogeneous product	1. Perfect competition
B. Barriers to entry	2. Monopoly
C. Differentiated product	3. Oligopoly
D. Absence of close substitutes	4. Monopolistic competition

Codes

	A	B	C	D		A	B	C	D
(a)	1	2	3	4	(b)	1	3	4	2
(c)	2	3	4	1	(d)	3	4	1	2

120 Match the following.

List I (Types of Market Structures)	List II (Methods of Marketing)
A. Perfect competition	1. Market exchange
B. Monopolistic competition	2. Competitive advertising
C. Oligopoly	3. Quality
D. Monopoly	4. Promotional advertising

Codes

	A	B	C	D
(a)	1	2	3	4
(b)	3	1	2	4
(c)	2	4	3	1
(d)	1	2	4	3

PREVIOUS YEARS' QUESTIONS

December 2018

1 Given below are two statements, one labelled as Assertion (A) and the other labelled as Reason (R). Read the statements and choose the correct answer using the codes given below.

Assertion (A) There exists excess capacity of the production for the firms if these incur losses.

Reason (R) Their production level has to remain below their economic capacity level.

Codes

(a) (A) is correct, but (R) is incorrect
(b) (A) is incorrect, but (R) is correct
(c) Both (A) and (R) are correct and (R) is the right explanation of (A)
(d) Both (A) and (R) are correct, but (R) is not the right explanation of (A)

2 The monopoly involves a social cost mainly due to its emphasise on which one of the following?

(a) Earning net profit in all possible situations
(b) Lower output at a higher cost in a normal profit situation
(c) Charging different prices from different categories of buyers of the same product
(d) Attempting to stall entry of other firms in the market

July 2018

3 In a perfectly competitive market, a firm in the long run operates at the level of output where

(a) AC = MC, when MC is lowest
(b) MC = AR = MR, when MC is lowest
(c) MR = MC
(d) AR = MR = AC = MC

November 2017

4 Manufacturing TV sets and refrigerators are their pricing in India belongs to which one of the following market structure?

(a) Monopolistic competition
(b) Perfect competition
(c) Monopoly
(d) Oligopoly

January 2017

5 **The kinked demand curve model of oligopoly was developed by**

(a) Augustin Cournot (b) Stackelberg
(c) Edgeworth (d) Sweezy

6 **Short run demand and total cost functions for a monopoly firm are as under**

Demand function Q = 100 – 0.2 P

Price function P = 500 – 5 Q

Cost function TC = 50 + 20 Q + Q2

Where,

Q = Total quantity of the product in physical units

P = Price of the product per unit

TC = Total cost

What is the profit maximising output of the pure monopoly firm?

(a) 20 (b) 35 (c) 40 (d) 50

7 **In which one of the following market situations, the pricing above the prevailing market price is used as a more common practice ?**

(a) Markets where the selling firms face perfect competitive situations
(b) Markets where the selling firms want to gain popularity of the products having high cross elasticity of their demand
(c) Markets where sellers rely on their customers' high propensity to consume a prestigious commodity
(d) Markets where the selling firms have entered into the stages of maturity and saturation

July 2016

8 **Monopoly is not considered desirable from the point of view of the society mainly because the monopolist endeavours to**

(a) earn net revenue on sale of all goods including those involving no cost of production
(b) earn net revenue on sale of good in short-run as well as long run
(c) charge different prices for the same product from the different categories of buyers
(d) produce below economic capacity level when he exhibits satisfaction with normal profit only

December 2015

9 **Assertion** (A) All firms under perfect competition in long run earn only normal profit.

Reason (R) All firms under perfect competition in long run operate at the minimum average cost level.

Codes

(a) Both (A) and (R) are true
(b) (A) is true, but (R) is not true
(c) (A) is not true, but (R) is true
(d) Both (A) and (R) are false

10 **Match the following.**

List I	List II
A. Trade channel discount	1. Oligopoly pricing
B. Loss leadership	2. Locational price differentials
C. Pricing being non-responsive to changes in the demand and the cost	3. Differential pricing
D. Basing point pricing	4. Product line pricing

Codes

	A	B	C	D
(a)	4	3	2	1
(b)	3	4	1	2
(c)	2	3	4	1
(d)	1	2	3	4

June 2015

11 **In the short run, when a simple monopoly firm attains equilibrium and earns only normal profit, its level of output will correspond to**

(a) lowest average cost
(b) average cost above optimum level of output
(c) average cost equals marginal cost
(d) marginal cost much below average cost

December 2014

12 **Monopolists prefer to sell the products in the markets with**

(a) elastic demand
(b) unitary elastic demand
(c) inelastic demand
(d) absence of elasticity of demand

13 **Assertion** (A) In long run under perfect competition, all firms invariably get only normal profit.

Reason (R) All firms incur minimum average cost and incur no selling cost due to absence of product differentiation.

Codes

(a) (A) and (R) both are true
(b) (A) is true, but (R) is false
(c) (A) is false, but (R) is true
(d) (A) and (R) both are false

June 2014

14 **Assertion** (A) A perfectly competitive firm is not a market but is a price taker.

Reason (R) The firm is intereshed in deciding the level of output only.

Codes

(a) Both (A) and (R) are true
(b) Both (A) and (R) are false
(c) (A) is false, but (R) is true
(d) (A) is true, but (R) is not a correct explanation of (A)

15 **Match the following.**

List I	List II
A. Dumping	1. Monopolistic competition
B. Kinked revenue curve	2. Oligopoly firm
C. Horizontal straight line revenue curve	3. Perfectively competitive firm
D. Large number of buyers and sellers with differentiated goods	4. Discriminatory monopoly

Codes

	A	B	C	D
(a)	1	4	3	2
(b)	2	4	1	3
(c)	4	2	3	1
(d)	1	2	3	4

June 2013

16 **Match the following.**

List I	List II
A. Economic profit	1. Total revenue explicit cost
B. Accounting profit	2. Buyers and sellers exchanging
C. Collusion/Cartel	3. Total revenue – Total cost
D. Market	4. Oligopoly

Codes

	A	B	C	D
(a)	3	1	4	2
(b)	1	2	3	4
(c)	4	3	2	1
(d)	2	4	1	3

17 **The Learner index measures**

(a) market power
(b) price
(c) price marginal cost
(d) None of the above

18 **Match the following.**

List I	List II
A. Perfect competition	1. Different prices for the same product
B. Monopolistic competition	2. Dominant strategy
C. Oligopoly	3. Product differentiation
D. Discriminating monopoly	4. Identical product

Codes

	A	B	C	D
(a)	4	3	2	1
(b)	1	2	3	4
(c)	2	4	1	3
(d)	3	1	4	2

19 **Match the following.**

List I	List II
A. Indifference curve	1. Slopes downward to the right
B. Demand curve	2. P = AR = MR = d
C. Perfect competition	3. Oligopoly
D. Price leadership	4. Convex to the origin

Codes

	A	B	C	D
(a)	2	3	4	1
(b)	3	4	1	2
(c)	4	1	2	3
(d)	1	2	3	4

December 2012

20 **Kinked demand curve is related with**

(a) monopoly
(b) discriminating monopoly
(c) oligopoly
(d) perfect competition

June 2012

21 **Which of the following refers to perfect competition?**

1. There are restrictions on buyers and sellers.
2. There are no restrictions on movement of goods.
3. There are no restrictions on factors of production.

Select the correct answer using the codes given below

Codes

(a) Both 1 and 2
(b) Both 2 and 3
(c) Both 1 and 3
(d) Only 1

ANSWERS

Objective Questions

1 (c)	2 (a)	3 (a)	4 (a)	5 (c)	6 (a)	7 (b)	8 (a)	9 (c)	10 (c)
11 (b)	12 (a)	13 (c)	14 (c)	15 (a)	16 (b)	17 (a)	18 (a)	19 (a)	20 (b)
21 (d)	22 (a)	23 (b)	24 (d)	25 (b)	26 (b)	27 (d)	28 (b)	29 (c)	30 (c)
31 (d)	32 (d)	33 (b)	34 (c)	35 (c)	36 (b)	37 (d)	38 (b)	39 (d)	40 (d)
41 (a)	42 (d)	43 (b)	44 (d)	45 (a)	46 (c)	47 (a)	48 (a)	49 (c)	50 (c)
51 (b)	52 (b)	53 (c)	54 (c)	55 (c)	56 (b)	57 (d)	58 (b)	59 (d)	60 (a)
61 (b)	62 (c)	63 (b)	64 (b)	65 (b)	66 (a)	67 (d)	68 (b)	69 (a)	70 (c)
71 (d)	72 (b)	73 (c)	74 (c)	75 (c)	76 (a)	77 (d)	78 (a)	79 (c)	80 (d)
81 (a)	82 (a)	83 (d)	84 (c)	85 (d)	86 (a)	87 (a)	88 (a)	89 (c)	90 (d)
91 (a)	92 (d)	93 (b)	94 (b)	95 (d)	96 (d)	97 (b)	98 (b)	99 (b)	100 (b)
101 (c)	102 (b)	103 (b)	104 (a)	105 (b)	106 (a)	107 (a)	108 (a)	109 (d)	110 (a)
111 (c)	112 (a)	113 (d)	114 (c)	115 (b)	116 (a)	117 (b)	118 (b)	119 (b)	120 (a)

Previous Years' Questions

1 (c)	2 (b)	3 (d)	4 (a)	5 (d)	6 (c)	7 (b)	8 (d)	9 (a)	10 (b)
11 (a)	12 (c)	13 (a)	14 (d)	15 (c)	16 (a)	17 (a)	18 (a)	19 (c)	20 (c)
21 (b)									

CHAPTER 13

Finance and Its Sources

Business is concerned with the production and distribution of goods and services for the satisfaction of needs of society. In order to produce and distribute goods and services, business needs money. Therefore, finance is called the soul of any business

Business Finance

Business finance refers to "the provision of money at the time when it is needed by a business." It includes the ways in which a company obtains and uses money, usually in reference to loans. In broader context, business finance is about strategies for earning, saving and investing revenue.

Nature of Business Finance

- The concept of business finance is very wide and is used in every type of business house whether it is small or large.
- It includes all types of funds and capital that are needed to start, run, expand and diversify the business.
- The primary goal of business finance is to increase the corporate value.

Scope of Business Finance

Necessary to Start Business Every new venture needs money to buy plant and machinery, land and building, raw material etc. So, finance is needed to start a business.

Necessary to Face Economic Cycle During recession and depression, the sales of the business go down and the profitability is adversely affected. To overcome problems during such times, a business needs finance.

Necessary for Growth Sometimes, in order to attain more or to achieve greater success, a company needs significant financial investment to acquire new capital, staff or inventory.

Necessary for the Payments of Debts It is necessary that a business firm meets its liabilities in time. Prompt payment of debts can be possible only because of adequate arrangement of finance.

In this Chapter

- *Business Finance*
- *Sources of Finance*
- *Lease Financing*
- *Risk and Return Analysis*
- *Asset Securitisation*

Necessary for Availing the Opportunities Business can take the advantage of upcoming opportunities and can earn more, only if it has adequate finance at its disposal.

Sources of Finance

Retained Earnings

It means that part of trading profits which are not distributed in the form of dividends, but retained by directors for future expansion of the company. This is also referred to as 'ploughing back of profits'. In other words, they are sacrifice made by equity shareholders, therefore, referred to as internal equity.

It is calculated as

Retained Earnings

(RE) = Net Income − Dividends

Trade Credit

Trade credit facilitates the purchase of supplies and raw material without immediate payment. Such credit appears in the accounts of the buyer of goods as sundry creditors or accounts payable. It is commonly used by business organisation as a source of short-term financing.

The amount and period of trade credit depends on the following factors

- Goodwill or reputation of the purchasing firm.
- The amount of purchases made.
- Past record of the buyer and his financial position.

Also, the terms to trade credit may vary from industry to industry and person to person.

Public Deposits

It refers to the deposits that are raised by business organisations directly from the public. Under it, a company directly raises loans from the public, in the form of deposits for a fixed period of time at a fixed rate of interest. This rate is generally higher than that offered on bank deposits. Companies generally invite public deposits for a period upto three years. Its acceptance is regulated by the Reserve Bank of India. Any person who is interested in depositing money with a company, can do so by filling a prescribed form. The company issues a deposit receipt as acknowledgement of debt.

Inter-corporate Deposits (ICDs)

It is a deposit made by one company with another company for a period of upto six months. These are generally unsecured.

Companies having surplus funds lend it to other companies who are in need of funds. This arrangement is mutually benefiting. The lending company earns interest on its idle funds and the borrowing company is able to fulfil its short-term financial needs.

Following are the types of inter-corporate deposits

Call Deposits Such deposits can be withdrawn by the lending company by giving a one day notice.

Three Months Deposits As the name suggests, these deposits are made for a period of three months. These are the most popular form of inter-corporate deposits.

Six Months Deposits These are made for a period of six-months, only with the companies which enjoy a high credit rating.

Issue of Shares

A company can raise necessary finance by issue of shares. The capital of a company is divided into small units called shares. Each share has a nominal value. The capital obtained by issue of shares is known as share capital and the person holding the shares is referred to as shareholder.

It includes

Equity Shares

The capital obtained by issue of equity shares is known as equity share capital.

It is considered as a permanent source of capital for a company, as it is not required to be returned during the life of the company. The return on equity shares is paid in the form of dividend. The company pays dividend only in case of profits. The rate of dividend is not fixed and depends upon the surplus profit left after paying dividend to preference shareholders. Because of these features, the equity shareholders are known as the 'residual owners' of the business. They are original risk bearers. Voting rights are conferred upon them, to enable them to participate in the affairs of the business.

➠ **Note** *Generally, dividend to equity shareholders is paid out of profits, but in certain conditions it can be paid out of reserves also.*

Preference Shares

The capital raised by issue of preference shares is called preference share capital. *Preference shares confer following two preferential rights to its holders*

- Preferential right to receive dividend at a predetermined rate, before dividend is paid to equity shareholders.
- Preferential right to receive repayment of capital at the time of dissolution of the company. This right authorises them to receive payment against capital before any amount is paid to equity shareholders.

Preference shares resemble debentures as they bear a fixed rate of return. Also, as the dividend is payable only at the discretion of the directors and only out of profit after tax, to that extent, they resemble equity shares.

Debentures and Bonds

Debentures It is an important instrument for raising long-term debt capital. Debenture is basically a written acknowledgement of the company, under its seal, that it has borrowed certain amount of money. In general, it refers to long-term loan to the company by the debenture holders on which they receive a fixed rate of interest.

Bonds These also loan instruments and resemble debentures in all aspects except one. No predetermined rate of interest is announced at the time of issuing bonds , but a specific rate of interest is announced while issuing debentures.

The above discussion brings forth the following features of debentures

- Debentures are basically borrowed funds. Because of this feature, the debenture holders are deemed to be the creditors of the company.
- Generally, companies pay half yearly interest, at a specified rate, to the debenture holders.
- Public issue of debentures requires that the issue be rated by a credit rating agency like Credit Rating and Information Services of India Ltd, (CRISIL) on aspects like track record of company, its profitability, debt servicing capacity, credit worthiness and the perceived risk of lending.

Commercial Banks

Commercial banks such as State Bank of India (SBI), Canara Bank etc, advance money to the business firms for different purposes and different time periods. Banks extend credit in many ways, like cash credits, overdrafts, discounting of bills of exchange and issue of letter of credit.

The repayment is made by the borrower in instalments as per the agreement between the bank and the borrower. Interest charged by banks depends upon a number of factors, such as nature of advance, period for which the loan is taken etc. Loan is generally offered by banks on the basis of security of assets. The loan can be repaid either in instalments or in lumpsum.

Loans from Financial Institutions

The government has established a number of financial institutions all over the country to provide finance to business organisations. These institutions are established by the Central as well as State Governments.

These institutions provide loan for medium and long-term needs of a business. These institutions also provide technical assistance and managerial services to business units. These institutions provide for specialised finance, keeping in view, the diverse requirements of business units. Since, these institutions facilitate industrial development in the country, they are called development banks.

Special Financial Institutions

Industrial Finance Corporation of India (IFCI) It was established in July 1948, as a statutory corporation under the Industrial Finance Corporation Act, 1948. Its objectives include assistance towards balanced regional development and encouraging new entrepreneurs to enter into the priority sectors of the economy.

State Financial Corporations (SFCs) It was established under the State Financial Corporations Act, 1951. This act empowered the State Government to establish State Financial Corporations in their respective regions for providing medium and short-term finance to industries, which are outside the scope of the IFCI.

Industrial Credit and Investment Corporation of India (ICICI) It was established in 1955 as a public limited company under the Companies Act. It assists the creation, expansion and modernisation of industrial enterprises exclusively in the private sector.

Industrial Development Bank of India (IDBI) It was established in 1964 under the Industrial Development Bank of India Act, 1964 . Its objective is to coordinate the activities of other financial institutions including commercial banks.

State Industrial Development Corporations (SIDCs) These have been set up by many State Governments for the purpose of promoting industrial development in their respective states. The objectives of the SIDCs differ from one state to other.

Unit Trust of India (UTI) It was established by the Government of India in 1964 under the Unit Trust of India Act, 1963. The basic objective of UTI is to mobilise the community's savings and channelise them into productive ventures.

Industrial Investment Bank of India Ltd (IIBI) It was set-up as a primary agency for rehabilitation of sick units and was known as Industrial Reconstruction Corporation of India. It was again reconstituted and renamed as the Industrial Reconstruction Bank of India in 1985 and again in 1997 its name was changed to Industrial Investment Bank of India.

The bank assists sick units in the reorganisation of their share capital, improvement in management system and provision of finance at liberal terms.

Life Insurance Corporation of India (LIC) It was set-up in 1956 under the LIC Act, 1956 after nationalising 245 existing insurance companies.

It mobilises the community's savings in the form of insurance premiums and makes it available to industrial concerns, both public as well as private, in the form of direct loans and underwriting of subscription of shares and debentures.

International Finance

Apart from raising finance through domestic sources such as equity shares, preference shares, loans from Indian commercial banks etc there are various avenues present internationally, from which a company can raise funds.

The various sources of international finance are discussed below

International Commercial Banks

Commercial banks all over the world extend foreign currency loans for business purposes. These banks are an important source of financing non-trade international operations. The types of loans and services provided by banks vary from country to country. *e.g.* Standard Chartered Bank is a major source of foreign currency loans for the Indian industries.

International Agencies and Development Banks

A number of international agencies and development banks have emerged over the years to finance international trade and business. These bodies provide long and medium term loans and grants to promote the development of economically backward areas of the world. These bodies were set-up by the governments of developed countries at national, regional and international levels for funding various projects.

International Finance Corporation (IFC), EXIM Bank and Asian Development Bank are the examples of such institutions.

International Capital Markets

Domestic companies can also raise finance from international capital markets by issuing American Depository Receipts (ADRs) and Global Depository Receipts (GDRs). *These instruments are as follows*

American Depository Receipt (ADR) As we have already discussed that a company can raise owned funds by issuing equity shares in the domestic market. But, if the company wants to raise finance from the American capital market, then it can issue equity shares specially targeted for the American investors by issuing American Depository Receipts (ADRs). These receipts are basically shares of an Indian company denominated in US dollars.

The stock of many non-US companies trade on US stock exchanges through the use of ADRs. Dividend on ADRs is also paid in US dollars and may be traded like shares of US domiciled companies. However, ADRs do not carry voting rights.

Global Depository Receipt (GDR)/ International Depository Receipt (IDR) Global Depository Receipts (GDRs) are similar to American Depository Receipts, except that they are issued in some other foreign country, except America.

In the Indian context, a GDR is an instrument issued abroad by an Indian company to raise funds in some foreign currency and is listed and traded on a foreign stock exchange.

Classification of Sources of Finance

Classification on the Basis of Period

Long-term Sources These sources provide finance to business firms for a period exceeding five years. *e.g.* Equity shares, retained earnings etc.

Medium-term Sources These sources provide finance to business firms for a period exceeding one year but less than five years. *e.g.* Loan from banks, public deposits etc.

Short-term Sources These sources provide finance to business firms for less than one year. *e.g.* Trade credit, factoring etc.

Classification on the Basis of Ownership

Owner's Funds Funds or finance provided by the owners of the business is referred to as owner's funds. Being the recipient of the profit earned by the business, they have the incentive to invest in the business. The funds provided by the owners are not required to be paid back during the life of the business, therefore they are a permanent source of finance. *e.g.* Equity shares, GDR/ADR etc.

Borrowed Funds The funds that are raised by way of loans and credit from the public, banks and financial institutions are termed as borrowed funds. These funds are raised from external source and are required to be paid back after a stipulated period. A fixed rate of interest is also required to be paid on amount raised from these sources. *e.g.* Debentures, lease financing etc.

Classification on the Basis of Source of Generation

Internal Sources These include all those funds which are generated from within a business, such as, from collection of receivables, disposing off surplus inventories and ploughing back of profit. These sources can however, fulfil only limited needs. *e.g.* Equity shares, retained earnings etc.

External Sources These include all those funds which are generated from outside a business. These sources carry a cost, but large amounts can be raised through these sources. Also, in some cases, business is required to mortgage its assets for raising finance from these sources. *e.g.* Debentures, public deposits etc.

Lease Financing

A lease transaction is a commercial arrangement, whereby an equipment owner or manufacturer conveys to the equipment user the right to use the equipment in return for a rent. In other words, lease is a contract between the owner of an asset (the lessor) and its user (the lessee) for the right to use the asset during a specified period in return for a mutually agreed periodic payment (the lease rentals). The important feature of a lease contract is separation of the ownership of the asset from its usage.

Importance of Lease Financing

- Leasing industry plays an important role in the economic development of a country by providing money incentives to lessee.
- The lessee does not have to pay the cost of asset at the time of signing the contract of lease.
- Leasing contracts are more flexible so, lessees can structure the leasing contracts according to their needs for finance.
- The lessee can also pass on the risk of obsolescence to the lessor by acquiring those appliances, which have high technological obsolescence.
- Leasing of houses, apartments, offices etc are familiar to most of us.

Advantages of Lease Financing

- Leasing covers the full cost of the equipment used in the business by providing 100% finance. The lessee is not to provide or pay any margin money as there is no down payment. Thus, the saving in capital or financial resources can be used for other productive purposes.
- The lease agreement can be tailor made in respect of lease period and lease rentals according to the convenience and requirements of all lessees.
- Leasing enables the lessee to plan its cash flows properly. The rentals can be paid out of the cash coming into the business from the use of the same assets.
- Leasing enables the lessee to improve their liquidity position by adopting the sale and lease back technique.

Types of Lease Agreements

Operating Lease

Operating lease, also called service lease, generally provide both financing and maintenance. IBM was one of the pioneers of operating lease contracts and computers and office copying machines, together with automobiles, trucks and medical diagnostic equipment are the primary types of equipment involved in operating leases.

Operating leases typically require the lessor to maintain and service the leased equipment, the cost of maintenance is built into the lease payments. Additionally, operating leases are not fully amortised, in that the payments required under the lease contract are not sufficient for the lessor to recover the full cost of the equipment. However, the lease contract is written for a period considerably shorter than the expected useful life of the leased asset and the lessor expects to recover all costs eventually either by lease renewal payments or by sale of the equipment.

A final feature of operating lease is that they frequently contain a cancellation clause that gives the lessee the right to cancel the lease and return the equipment to the lessee or before the lease expires. This clause is important to the lessee because it allows the equipment to be returned, if it is rendered obsolete by technological developments or is no longer needed because of a decline in the lessee's business.

Financial Lease

Financial lease, also called as capital lease, are different from operating lease as they

- typically do not provide for maintenance.
- typically are not cancelable.
- are generally for a period that approximates the useful life of the asset.
- are fully amortised.

In a financial lease, the lessee selects the item it requires and negotiates the price and delivery terms with the manufacturer. The lessee then arranges to have a leasing firm (lessor) to buy the equipment from the manufacturer and the lessee simultaneously, executes a lease agreement with the lessor.

Under a financial lease, the lease payments are set-up exactly the same way, the payments are just sufficient to return the full purchase price to the lessor plus a stated return on the lessor's investment. At the end of a financial lease, the ownership of the leased asset is transferred from the lessor to the lessee.

Sale and Lease Back

It is a sub-part of financial lease, which are as follows

- Under this, the owner of an asset sells the asset to a party (the buyer), who in turn leases back the same asset to the owner in consideration of lease rentals. However, under this arrangement, the assets are not physically exchanged, but it all happens in records only. This is nothing, but a paper transaction.
- Sale and lease back transaction is suitable for those assets, which are not subjected to depreciation, but appreciation, say land.
- The advantage of this method is that the lessee can satisfy himself completely regarding the quality of the asset and after possession of the asset convert the sale into a lease arrangement.
- Under this transaction, the seller assumes the role of a lessee and the buyer assumes the role of a lessor. The seller gets the agreed selling price and the buyer gets the lease rentals. It is possible to structure the sale at agreed value (below or above the fair market price) and to adjust difference in the lease rentals. Thus, the effect of profit /loss on sale of assets can be deferred.

Risk and Return Analysis

Risk

In investment analysis, risk refers to the likelihood that the actual return on an investment received is different from the expected return. In other words, risk can be referred as the volatility in the return with respect to expected return.

Types of Risk

Systematic Risk

Risks, which are caused due to uncontrollable factors that tend to affect all sectors of business, government and any other entity and leads to unavoidable affects for the investor, are systematic risk. These risks are practically impossible to protect and influences large number of assets.

Systematic risk
= Market risk + Purchasing power risk + Interest rate risk

Market Risk Risk caused due to market cycles, *i.e.* demand and supply pressures, sudden movements in the market and change in public fashions among investment alternatives leading to uncertainty of return is market risk. Factors that lead to market risks are recessions, wars and structural changes in the economy, tax law changes, even changes in consumer preferences.

Purchasing Power Risk/Inflation Risk The purchasing power risk is also called as inflation risk. It refers to exchange in real value of return as a result of inflation. Inflation leads to rise in cost of production, lower margins, lesser profits, etc. These risks are inherent in all the investments and are beyond the control of an investor.

Interest Rate Risk The interest rate risk refers to uncertain returns caused by the uncertain market rates of interest. The return on an investment depends upon the interest rates promised on it and changes in market rate of interest from time to time adversely affects the investor's return. Interest rate risk affects bonds more directly than common stocks and is a major risk faced by all bondholders. As interest rates change, bond prices change in the opposite direction.

Non-systematic Risk

Risk are firm specific risks, caused due to known or controllable factors and can be eliminated or reduced through diversification.

Non-systematic risk = Business risk + Financial risk

Business Risk The risk of doing business in a particular industry or environment is called business risk. This risk refers to uncertain return to the investor caused due to uncertain business environment, in which it operates. These risks may arise due to both internal and external factors. Business risk caused due to internal factors leads to poor performance of the company, but can be reduced or avoided by some changes in the company's policies.

Financial Risk Risk caused due to inability of the organisation to meet its financial obligations is referred to as financial risk. *e.g.* Obligations such as interest and principal payment of the funds borrowed. Investment in organisation that is heavily into debt may leads to greater uncertainty of return because of financial risk to their owners. *Types of financial risk are as follows*

Credit Risk It is also called as insolvency risk or default risk. This is the risk that a company or individual will be unable to pay the contractual interest or principal on its debt obligations. This type of risk is particularly a concern to investors, who hold bonds within their portfolio. Government bonds, especially those issued by the Federal Government, have the least amount of default risk and least amount of returns, while corporate bonds tend to have the highest amount of default risk, but also the higher interest rates.

Liquidity Risk It refers to the risk of liquidating the assets as and when required. Liquidity here means both ability of converting asset into cash and doing it without compromising on price levels.

The more uncertainty about the time element and the price concession, the greater is the liquidity risk. A treasury bill has little or no liquidity risk, whereas a small OTC stock may have substantial liquidity risk.

Measurement of Risk

Variance or standard deviation is a measure of dispersion of distribution. The spread of the actual returns around the expected return is measured by the variance or standard deviation of the distribution. The greater the deviation of the actual returns from the expected return, the greater the variance.

The probability distributions of returns of investments exhibiting different variances, these would be as follows

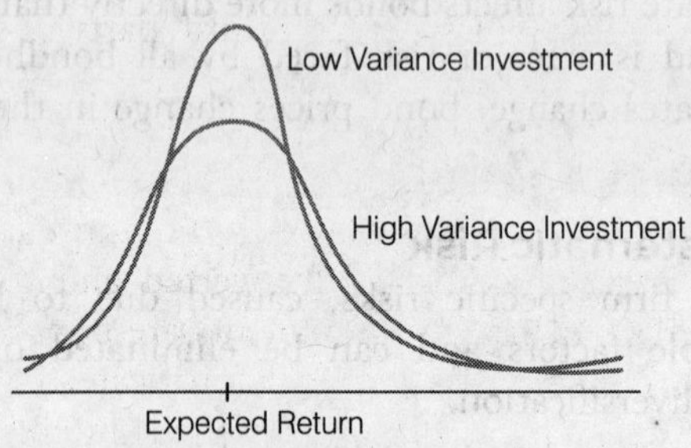

Relation Between Variance and Expected Return

If the actual return of an investment is always equal to the expected return, then such an investment is a risk free investment. Therefore, the probability of actual return being equal to expected return will be 1 and the variance of return will be zero.

Total risk of any investment can be measured by the concept of variance, standard deviation, covariance etc.

Return

Returns are always calculated as annual rates of return or the percentage of return created for each unit of original value, Returns are the value created by an investment, though either income or gains.

Measurement of Return

It is the weighted average of possible outcomes, where the weights represents the outcome probabilities.

Total return is measured by taking the income plus the price change. Income is either in the form of dividend or interest and the price change of the security is capital gain or loss.

This can be put into formula as under

$$\text{Return during a period (in \%)} = \frac{I + (P_E - P_B)}{P_B}$$

Where, I = Income received during the period

P_E = Price at the end of the period

P_B = Price at the beginning of the period

The difference between price at the end of the period and price at the beginning of the period is called as price appreciation.

Similarly, for a fixed income bearing security the rate of return would be calculated as under

$$\text{Return} = \frac{\text{Interest received} + (\text{Principal repayment} - \text{Initial investment}) \times 100}{\text{Initial investment}}$$

The average return is calculated by using two methods, namely, arithmetic mean and geometric mean.

Risk and Return Relationship

Investment decision are important in portfolio management. The main motive of an investor behind any investment is maximum returns with minimum risk. Investors like returns, but dislikes risks but returns are directly proportional to risk. The returns depend upon the extent of risk taken by the investor. It is said higher the risk, higher is the return. *The risk and return relationship of various investment alternatives shown with the help of figure given below*

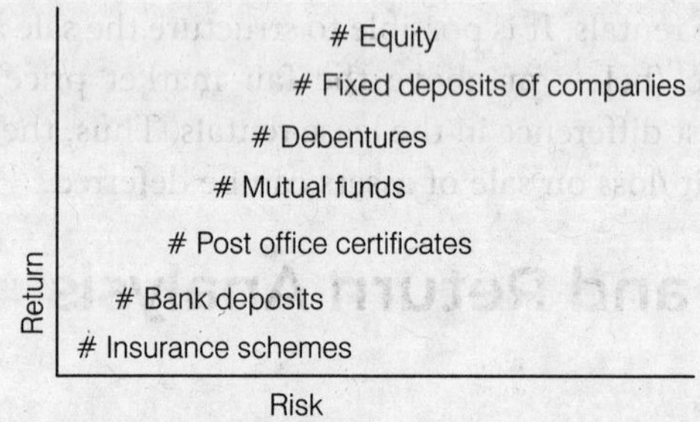

Relationship Between Risk and Return

Portfolio Risk

A portfolio is a combination of assets or investments. Investing in a portfolio helps us reduce the risk as compared to investing completely in one asset. When two or more securities are combined in a portfolio, their covariance or combined risk is to be considered. Thus, if the returns on two assets move together, their covariance is positive and risk increases on such portfolio. But, if the returns move in opposite direction, then the covariance is negative and risk is lesser.

Portfolio Returns

The return on a portfolio of assets is simply a weighted average of the return on the individual assets. The expected return on a portfolio is also a weighted average of the expected returns on the individual assets.

$$R_p = \sum_{i=1}^{n} X_i R_i$$

Where, R_p = Expected return on the portfolio

R_i = Expected return on the individual asset

N = Number of assets in the portfolio

X_i = Weight of assets in the portfolio

Portfolio Variance

The variance on a portfolio consisting of assets 1 and 2 is given by the following formula

$$\sigma p^2 = X_1^2\sigma_2^2 + X_2^2\sigma_2^2 + 2X_1X_2\sigma_{12}$$

Where, σp^2 = Portfolio variance

σp_1^2 = Variance of returns on assets 1

σ_2^2 = Variance of returns on assets 2

X_1 and X_2 = Weights of assets 1 and 2 in the portfolio

σ_{12} = Covariance

$$\text{Covariance} = \frac{\sum_{t=1}^{n}(r_{1t} - r_1)(r_{2t} - r_2)}{n-1}$$

The correlation coefficient between securities 1 and 2 and it is defined as

$$p_{12} = \frac{\sigma_{12}}{\sigma_1 \sigma_2}$$

Where, σ_{12} = Covariance between returns on securities 1 and 2

σ_1 = Standard deviation on returns on security 1

σ_2 = Standard deviation on returns on security 2

The possibility of reduction of risk through the construction of a portfolio thus, depends on the value of correlation coefficient between the two assets.

Asset Securitisation

Securitisation means the conversion of existing or future cash inflows into tradable security which then is sold in the market. The cash inflow from financial assets such as mortgage loans, automobile loans, trade receivables, credit card receivables, fare collections become the security against which borrowings are raised.

RBI in its circular on Securitisation of Standard assets, describes "Securitisation as a process by which assets are sold to a bankruptcy remote Special Purpose Vehicle (SPV) in return for an immediate cash payment."

Securitisation can be defined as "Acquisition of financial assets by any securitisation company or reconstruction company from any originator, whether by raising funds by such securitisation company or reconstruction company from qualified institutional buyers by issue of security receipts representing undivided interest in such financial assets or otherwise."

Let us try to understand it from a Layman's View

In the normal course assets like loans and securities held by banks/financial institutions are expected to yield a quantifiable stream of future income (*e.g.* EMIs etc). However, since this income is yet to be realised, it can not be brought onto their books immediately. Through the process of securitisation, banks try to encash these future flow of as yet unrealised income.

Securitisation thus follows a two stage process. In the first stage, there is a sale of single asset or pooling and sale of pool of assets to a 'bankruptcy remote' Special Purpose Vehicle (SPV) in return for an immediate cash payment and in the second stage, repackaging and selling the security interests representing claims on incoming cash flows from the asset or pool of assets to third party investor's by issuance of tradable debt securities.

Process of Securitisation

Securitisation is a process by which the future cash inflows of an entity (originator) are converted and sold as debt instruments. These debt instruments are popularly known as 'Pay through or Pass through Certificates', with a fixed rate of return to the holders of beneficial interest.

Under this process, the originator of a typical securitisation actually transfers a portfolio of financial assets to a 'Special Purpose Vehicle' (SPV). An SPV is an entity, specially created for doing the securitisation deal. It invites investment from investors, uses the invested funds to acquire to receivables of the originator. An SPV may be a trust, corporation or any other legal entity. As a consideration for the transfer of such a portfolio, the originator gets cash up front on the basis of a mutually agreed valuation of the receivables. The transfer value of the receivables is arrived in such a way so as to give the lenders a reasonable rate of return. In 'pass through' and 'pay through' securitisations, receivables are transferred to the SPV at the inception of the securitisation and no further transfers are made. All cash collections are paid to the holders of beneficial interests in the SPV.

Thus, we can say that a securitisation deal usually passes through the following stages

- First of all, the originator determines which assets they wants to securitise.
- At second stage, originator has to find out a SPV or new SPV is formed.
- The SPV collects the funds from investors and in return issues securities to them.
- The SPV acquires the receivables under an agreement at their discounted value.
- The servicer for the transaction is appointed, who is usually the originator.
- The debtors are/are not notified depending on the legal requirements.

- The servicer collects the receivables, usually in an escrow mechanism and pays off the collection to the SPV.
- The SPV either passes the collection to the investors or reinvests the same to pay off to investors at stated intervals.
- In case of default, the servicer takes action against the debtors as the SPV's agent.
- When only a small amount of outstanding receivables are left to be collected, the originator may clean up the transaction by buying back the outstanding receivables.
- At the end of the transaction, the originator's profit, if retained and subject to any losses to the extent agreed by the originator, in the transaction is paid off.

Merits of Securitisation

- Transfer of credit risk.
- Helps in raising fund.
- Helps in generating liquidity.
- Helpful for small investors as they can invest small amounts through SPV and acquire beneficial interest.
- Availability of more credit.

Demerits of Securitisation

- Originator may hide the true picture of its financial health.
- It is opaqueness.
- Limits investors to monitoring credit risk.

Securitisation in India

Securitisation in India has been in existence since early 1990s. The first securitisation deal took place in 1991 when citibank raised ₹ 16 crore from GIC Mutual Fund by securitising some of its auto loans. The major players in the asset securitisation market in India are expected to be commercial Financial Institutions (FIs), Public Sector Units (PSUs), Corporate Government Bodies, Mutual Funds, Pension Funds etc.

EXAM BASED QUESTIONS

Finance and Lease Financing

1 Finance is required for
(a) social development (b) economic development
(c) industrial development (d) All of these

2 Finance is related to
(a) monetary resources (b) tax planning
(c) borrowing (d) lending

3 Form of Government International of finance is
(a) technical assistance (b) debt
(c) grant (d) All of these

4 External source of finance do not include
(a) debentures (b) leasing
(c) overdrafts (d) retained earnings

5 Internal source of finance do not include
(a) ordinary shares
(b) better management of working capital
(c) retained earnings
(d) trade credit

6 Which of the following is an example of owner's fund?
(a) Debentures (b) Equity shares
(c) Public deposits (d) Commercial papers

7 Which of the following is/are an external source of finance?
(a) Lease financing (b) Equity shares
(c) Retained earnings (d) All of these

8 Which of the following is an internal source of finance?
(a) Factoring (b) Trade credit
(c) Retained earnings (d) Debentures

9 Funds required for purchasing current assets is an example of
(a) fixed capital requirement
(b) lease financing
(c) working capital requirement
(d) ploughing back of profits

10 Public deposits are the deposits, that are raised directly from
(a) the public (b) the directors
(c) the auditors (d) the owners

11 Equity shareholders are called
(a) guardian of the company
(b) owners of the company
(c) partners of the company
(d) executives of the company

12 Which of the following is not a source of long-term finance?
(a) Trade credit (b) Debentures
(c) Retained earnings (d) Equity shares

13 Which of the following is not a source of short-term finance?
(a) Factoring (b) Commercial papers
(c) Trade credit (d) Retained earnings

14 Finance made available by specialised financial institutions is called
(a) institutional finance (b) business finance
(c) public finance (d) All of these

15 Debentures represent
(a) fixed capital of the company
(b) permanent capital of the company
(c) fluctuating capital of the company
(d) loan capital of the company

16 The maturity period of a commercial paper usually ranges from
(a) 20 to 40 days (b) 60 to 90 days
(c) 120 to 365 days (d) 90 to 364 days

17 Which is not a form of short-term spontaneous credit?
(a) Commercial paper
(b) Accrued wages
(c) Trade credit
(d) Accrued taxes

18 Short-term loans are for a period of
(a) one year (b) two years
(c) three years (d) six months

19 Medium term loans are for a period of
(a) three months (b) one year
(c) three years (d) five years

20 Long-term loans are for a period of
(a) one year (b) five years
(c) more than five years (d) None of these

21 In finance, working capital means the same thing as
(a) total assets (b) fixed assets
(c) current assets (d) None of these

22 Government grants are generally offered to businesses in
(a) prosperous areas
(b) cold areas
(c) economically deprived areas
(d) areas with high employment

23 Which is the source of mid-term finance?
(a) Micro credit
(b) Specialised financial institution
(c) Collect advances from purchasers
(d) Discounting the bills receivable

24 .... varies inversely with profitability.
(a) Liquidity (b) Risk
(c) Return (d) Loss

25 We should keep our savings with banks because
(a) it is safe
(b) earns interest
(c) can be withdrawn anytime
(d) All of the above

26 Bank pays interest on
(a) deposits
(b) loan
(c) Both (a) and (b)
(d) Neither (a) nor (b)

27 Personal saving
1. is that part of personal income, *i.e.* is not consumed.
2. equals income minus consumption.

Codes
(a) Only 1
(b) Only 2
(c) Both 1 and 2
(d) Neither 1 nor 2

28 Permanent working capital
(a) varies with seasonal needs
(b) includes fixed assets
(c) is the amount of current assets
(d) includes accounts payable

29 If a bank thinks lending money to a certain business is risky, it will
(a) charge a lower interest rate
(b) charge a higher interest rate
(c) send the business packing
(d) think about it

30 Share capital is
(a) money given to a company by shareholders in return for a stake in the business
(b) business borrowing capital from a financial institution
(c) capital shared amongst owners
(d) capital shared with shareholders

31 Under the factoring arrangement, the factor
(a) produces and distributes the goods or services
(b) makes the payment on behalf of the client
(c) collects the client's debt or account receivables
(d) transfer the goods from one place to another

32 Internal sources of capital are those that are
(a) generated through outsiders such as suppliers
(b) generated through loans from commercial banks
(c) generated through issue of shares
(d) generated within the business

33 Financing a long lived assets with short-term financing would be
(a) an example of 'moderate risk-moderate (potential) profitability' assets financing
(b) an example of 'low risk-low (potential) profitability' assets financing
(c) an example of 'high risk-high (potential) profitability' assets financing
(d) an example of the 'hedging approach' for financing

34 Net working capital refers to
(a) total assets minus fixed assets
(b) current assets minus current liabilities
(c) current assets minus inventories
(d) current assets

35 Factors that are considered to solve the financial problems of business organisations are
1. cost of capital supply.
2. importance and objectives of capital
3. different types of benefits

Select the correct answer by using the codes given below

Codes
(a) Both 1 and 2
(b) Both 1 and 3
(c) Both 2 and 3
(d) All of the above

36 Which of the following is the most appropriate form for financing a new capital investment in plant and equipment?
(a) Trade credit
(b) Six months bank notes
(c) Account payable
(d) Common stock equity

37 Which of the following is the most appropriate non-spontaneous form for financing the excess seasonal current assets needs?
(a) Trade credit
(b) Six months bank notes
(c) Account payable
(d) Common stock equity

38 Under the terms of finance lease
(a) the lessor is responsible for service and maintenance of the asset
(b) it is cancellable
(c) legal title to the assets with the lessee
(d) the asset is capitalised in the balance sheet of the lessee

39 The following is an example of the core principle 'information is the basis for decisions.'
(a) Wealthy depositors are the bank's best customers
(b) Payment made over time generally add upto more than the original loan amount
(c) lenders requires credit scores on individuals who want to take out loans
(d) Car insurance is often required by law

40 A company can improve (lower) its debts to total assets ratio by doing which of the following?
(a) Borrow more
(b) Sell common stock
(c) Shift short-term to long-term debts
(d) Shift long-term to short-term debts

41 Which of the following would be consistent with a more aggressive approach to financing working capital?
(a) Financing short-term needs with short-term funds
(b) Financing permanent inventory build up with long-term debt
(c) Financing seasonal needs with short-term funds
(d) Financing cost long-term needs with short-term funds

42 Which of the following statement is correct?
(a) For small companies, long-term debt is the principle source of external financing
(b) Current assets of the manufacturing firm account for over a half of its total assets
(c) Strict adherence to the maturity matching approach for financing would call for all current assets to be financed solely with current liabilities
(d) Similar to the capital structure management, working capital management requires the financial manager to make a decision and not address the issue again for several months

43 A leased asset should be depreciated over the
(a) shorter of the lease term and the asset's useful life
(b) longer of the lease term and the asset's useful life
(c) entire lease term
(d) useful life of the asset

44 Operating leases are mostly .... agreements.
(a) long-term (b) medium-term
(c) short-term (d) verbal

45 In a land lease, if title does not pass at the end of a lease to the lessee, it is normally treated as
(a) finance lease (b) operating lease
(c) mixed lease (d) accounting lease

46 The payments over the lease term the lessee can or must make, is called
(a) principal
(b) interest
(c) present value payments
(d) minimum lease payments

47 When a lease transfers substantially all the risks and rewards of ownership to lessee, this is called
(a) a finance least
(b) an operating lease
(c) a buy-to-let agreement
(d) a rental agreement

48 Finance leases are accounted for in a similar manner to
(a) credit transactions
(b) cash transactions
(c) sale and leaseback agreements
(d) loan forgiveness

49 Under the lease agreement, the lease gets the right to
(a) share profits earned by the lessor
(b) participate in the management of the organisation
(c) use the asset for a specified period
(d) sell the assets

50 How should the Minimum Lease Payment (MLP) of a land and building lease get apportioned?
(a) Treat entirely as building
(b) Treat entirely as land
(c) Apportion MLP between land and buildings based on fair value of leasehold interests
(d) Apportion MLP between land and buildings based on management's judgement

51 One difference between a financial lease and operating lease is that
(a) there is a often a call option in a financial lease
(b) there is often an option to buy in an operating lease
(c) an operating lease is often cancellable by the lessee
(d) a financial lease is often cancellable by the lessee

52 Which type of lease is presumed, when the present value of minimum lease payments is approximately equal to the fair value of the lease assets?
(a) Finance lease
(b) Operating lease
(c) Mixed lease
(d) All of the above

53 Which of the following is not a disclosure requirement for finance leases?
(a) Carrying amount of asset
(b) Market value of asset
(c) General description of significant leasing arrangements
(d) Reconciliation between total minimum lease payments and their present value

54 A lease is likely to be most beneficial to both parties when
(a) the lessor's tax rate is lower than the lessee's
(b) the lessor's tax rate is higher than the lessee's
(c) the lessor's tax rate is equal to the lessee's
(d) a lease can not be beneficial to both parties

55 Which of the following sets out concisely the information about the scheme that a prospective investor ought to know before investing?
(a) Scheme source document
(b) Scheme information book
(c) Scheme document
(d) Scheme information document

56 The principal reason for the existence of leasing is that
(a) intermediate term loans are difficult to obtain
(b) this is a type of financing unaffected by changes in tax law
(c) companies, financial institutions and individuals derive different benefits from owing assets
(d) leasing is a renewable source of intermediate term funds

57 Which of the following is not an indication a lease is a finance lease?
(a) The lease transfers ownership of the asset to the lessee at the end of the lease
(b) The lease term is for a short part of the economic life of the asset
(c) The leased assets are specialised in nature
(d) The present value of minimum lease payment amounts to substantially all of the fair value of the asset

58 Which of the following statements are true? Indicate the correct code.
1. Tax shield on depreciation and interest is an important valuable both for lessor and lessee.

2. A lessee may evaluate the lease options as against the buying option.
3. Sale and lease back and leveraged lease are types of financial lease.
4. Lease or financing is a type of capital budgeting decision from the point of view of the lessee

Select the correct answer by using the codes given below

Codes

(a) 1, 2 and 4 (b) 2, 3 and 4
(c) 1, 3 and 4 (d) 1, 2 and 3

Risk and Return Analysis and Asset Securitisation

59 Which risk arises, if a party discharges his obligations, but the counterparty defaults?

(a) Replacement cost risk (b) Principal risk
(c) Systematic risk (d) Unsystematic risk

60 Efficient frontier comprises of

(a) inefficient portfolios
(b) efficient portfolios
(c) portfolios that have negatively correlated securities
(d) portfolios that have positively correlated securities

61 Efficient portfolios can be defined as those portfolios which for a given level of risk provides

(a) maximum return (b) average return
(c) minimum return (d) None of these

62 Capital market line is

(a) Capital allocation line of a market portfolio
(b) Capital allocation line of a risk free asset
(c) Both (a) and (b)
(d) Neither (a) nor (b)

63 The point of tangency between risk return indifferences curves and efficient frontier highlights.

(a) Optimal portfolio
(b) Efficient portfolio
(c) Sub-optimal portfolio
(d) None of the above

64 Which of the following are the means of marketing new issues of securities?

1. By listing of securities.
2. Through jobbers and brokers.
3. By private placing of securities.
4. Through privileged subscription.

Select the correct answer by using the codes given below

Codes

(a) Both 1 and 2
(b) 1, 2 and 3
(c) Both 3 and 4
(d) All of the above

65 Riskness of investing in .... is more than the riskness of investing in ....

(a) debentures, equity shares
(b) Equity shares, debentures
(c) Both (a) and (b)
(d) None of the above

66 Which capital investors are long-term investors who are prepared to take the risk that the entrepreneurial project can fail?

(a) Mega (b) Progress (c) Multiple (d) Venture

67 Some equity schemes take opposite positions in different market segments, such that a return is earned while remaining risk neutral. They are called

(a) positional funds (b) arbitrage funds
(c) directional funds (d) speculative funds

68 How many Greeks used for hedging portfolios of options with underlying assets?

(a) Four (b) Five (c) Six (d) Ten

69 Risk of two securities with different expected return can be compared with

(a) coefficient of variation
(b) variance of securities
(c) standard deviation of securities
(d) None of the above

70 Which of the following is the systematic risk?

(a) Market risk (b) Purchasing power risk
(c) Interest rate risk (d) All of these

71 Securitised assets carry a unique form of risk called

(a) default risk (b) inflation risk
(c) interest rate risk (d) pre-payment risk

72 Securitisation and Reconstruction of Financial Assets and Enforcement of Security Interest (SARFAESI) Act was enacted in which year?

(a) 2000 (b) 2001 (c) 2002 (d) 2003

73 In SARFAESI Act, 'E' stands for

(a) Equity (b) Enhancement
(c) Empowerment (d) Enforcement

74 SPV stands for

(a) Securities Pool Vehicle
(b) Special Pool Vehicle
(c) Securities Purpose Vehicle
(d) Special Purpose Vehicle

75 Securitisation market in India includes.

(a) Mutual Funds (b) Pension Fund
(c) Public Sector Units (d) All of these

76 Since, investors can diversify away their .... risks, they have to be compensated only for .... risk.

(a) systematic, non-systematic
(b) Non-systematic, systematic
(c) Both (a) and (b)
(d) None of the above

77 A portfolio having two risky securities can be turned risk less, if

(a) the correlation ranges between zero and one
(b) the securities are completely positively correlated
(c) the securities are completely negatively correlated
(d) None of the above

78 A portfolio comprises two securities and the expected return on them is 12% and 16% respectively. Determine return of portfolio if first security constitutes 40% of total portfolio.
(a) 12.4% (b) 13.4% (c) 14.4% (d) 15.4%

79 Securitisation is a process in which assets are sold to a bankruptcy remote .... in return for an immediate cash payment.
(a) special purpose vehicle
(b) asset reconstruction corporation
(c) bank or NBFC
(d) mortgage company

80 In securitisation, which of the following is/are not a benefit to the issuer?
1. Off-balance sheet treatment.
2. Frees up regulatory capital.
3. Higher credit ratings and lower borrowing costs.
4. Provides Collateral security.
5. Transfer of Credit risk.

Select the correct answer by using the codes given below

Codes
(a) Only 1 (b) 2, 3 and 4
(c) Only 4 (d) All of the above

81 Regarding securitisation, which of the following is not correct?
(a) Derivatives are treated as on balance sheet items
(b) Granularity of securitised assets can mitigate the credit risk
(c) 'Credit enhancement' means credit quality is increased above from the originator's underlying asset pool
(d) Securitisation makes it possible to transfer risks from an entity that does not want to bear it, to one that does

82 Arrange the following stages of securitisation in series.
1. To find out a SPV or new SPV is formed.
2. To determine which assets are to be securitised.
3. To acquire the receivables under an agreement at their discounted value.
4. To collect the fund from investors and issue securities in return.

Codes
(a) 1, 2, 3, 4 (b) 2, 1, 4, 3 (c) 4, 2, 3, 1 (d) 3, 2, 1, 4

Miscellaneous

Directions (Q. Nos. 83-88) *In the questions given below are two statements labelled as Statement I and Statement II. In the context of the two statements, which one of the following is correct?*

Codes
(a) Only Statement I is true (b) Only Statement II is true
(c) Both statements are true (d) Both statements are false

83 **Statement** I The most common type of spontaneous financing is trade credit.
Statement II Two different firms get the same size short-term loans, for identical purposes and with identical.

84 **Statement** I An overdraft is where a business is permitted to overspend on its bank account upto an agreed limit.
Statement II A debenture is a long-term loan.

85 **Statement** I IAS 17 assumes a lessor will not recover their asset, which is leased under a finance lease.
Statement II Lease payments should be split into an interest component and expense component.

86 **Statement** I Trustees manage investor's money.
Statement II Fund managers of close-ended schemes are not allowed to churn portfolios as frequently as open-ended schemes.

87 **Statement** I Return on any financial asset consists of capital yield and current yield.
Statement II There is no difference between the capital market line and security market line as both the terms are same.

88 **Statement** I Securitisation is the conversion of existing or future cash in flow into tradable security.
Statement II Securitisation shows the true picture of financial position of a firm.

Directions (Q. Nos. 89-93) *In the questions given below are two statements labelled as Assertion (A) and Reason (R). In the context of two statements, which one of the following is correct?*

Codes
(a) Both (A) and (R) are true and (R) is the correct explanation of (A)
(b) Both (A) and (R) are true, but (R) is not the correct explanation of (A)
(c) (A) is true, but (R) is false
(d) (A) is false, but (R) is true

89 **Assertion** (A) Sale and lease back technique is a type of lease agreement.
Reason (R) It enables the lessee to improve their liquidity.

90 **Assertion** (A) ADR is not a US dollar denominated form of equity ownership in a non-US Company.
Reason (R) An ADR is a physical certificate evidencing ownership of American Depository Shares (ADSs).

91 **Assertion** (A) External sources of funds include debentures.
Reason (R) Debentures are basically borrowed funds from public.

92 **Assertion** (A) Lease is a contract between the lessor and the lessee for the right to use the asset during a specified period in return for a mutually agreed periodic payment.
Reason (R) The lessee does not have to pay the cost of asset at the time of signing the contract of lease.

93 Assertion (A) Variance or standard deviation is a measure of dispersion of distribution.

Reason (R) Average return can be measured by concept of variance or standard deviation.

94 Match the following.

List I (Term)	List II (Source)
A. Long-term	1. Factoring
B. Medium-term	2. Debentures
C. Short-term	3. Lease financing

Codes

	A	B	C		A	B	C
(a)	3	1	2	(b)	1	2	3
(c)	2	3	1	(d)	1	3	2

95 Match the following.

List I	List II
A. Equity shares	1. Deposits, raised by business directly from public
B. Inter-corporate Deposits	2. Deposit made by one company with another for a period upto six months
C. Trade Credit	3. Permanent source of capital for a company
D. Public Deposits	4. Facilitates the purchase of raw material without immediate payment

Codes

	A	B	C	D		A	B	C	D
(a)	1	2	3	4	(b)	3	2	4	1
(c)	2	3	1	4	(d)	4	3	2	1

96 Match the following.

List I (Source of Fund)	List II (Example)
A. Commercial Bank	1. IFCT
B. International Capital Market	2. SBI
C. International Commercial Bank	3. GDR
D. Financial Institution	4. Standard Chartered Bank (SCB)

Codes

	A	B	C	D		A	B	C	D
(a)	1	3	4	2	(b)	2	3	1	4
(c)	3	4	1	2	(d)	2	3	4	1

97 Match the following.

List I	List II
A. Market risk	1. It is known as insolvency risk
B. Inflation risk	2. Risk caused due to demand and supply pressure
C. Credit risk	3. Risk due to inability to meet firm's financial obligations
D. Financial risk	4. Exchange in real value of return as a result of rise in production cost

Codes

	A	B	C	D		A	B	C	D
(a)	4	3	1	2	(b)	1	3	2	4
(c)	2	4	1	3	(d)	3	2	1	4

PREVIOUS YEARS' QUESTIONS

July 2018

1 Risk of a portfolio can be minimised by which one of the following ?

(a) Combining two securities having perfect positive correlation in their expected returns
(b) Combining two securities having perfect negative correlation in their expected returns
(c) Combining two securities having partially positive correlation in their expected returns
(d) Combining two securities having partially negative correlation in their expected returns

2 Match the items of List II with the items of List I and select the correct code.

List I	List II
A. Liquidity risk	1. Risk related to purchasing power of income
B. Business risk	2. Risk related to firm's capital structure
C. Financial risk	3. Risk related to inability to pay its dues on time
D. Inflation risk	4. Risk related to fluctuation in profits

Codes

	A	B	C	D
(a)	2	3	4	1
(b)	1	4	3	2
(c)	3	2	4	1
(d)	3	4	2	1

November 2017

3 Which of the following are the examples of systematical risk. Indicate the correct code.

1. Elimination of Government Subsidy
2. Increase in bank rate
3. Labour problem
4. High levered fund

Select the correct answer using the codes given below

Codes

(a) 1, 2 and 3
(b) 1, 2 and 4
(c) Both 1 and 2
(d) Both 1 and 4

ANSWERS

Objective Questions

1 (d)	2 (a)	3 (d)	4 (d)	5 (d)	6 (b)	7 (a)	8 (c)	9 (c)	10 (a)
11 (b)	12 (a)	13 (d)	14 (a)	15 (d)	16 (d)	17 (a)	18 (a)	19 (d)	20 (c)
21 (c)	22 (c)	23 (b)	24 (b)	25 (d)	26 (c)	27 (c)	28 (c)	29 (b)	30 (a)
31 (c)	32 (d)	33 (c)	34 (b)	35 (a)	36 (d)	37 (b)	38 (d)	39 (c)	40 (b)
41 (d)	42 (b)	43 (a)	44 (c)	45 (b)	46 (d)	47 (a)	48 (a)	49 (c)	50 (c)
51 (c)	52 (a)	53 (b)	54 (b)	55 (d)	56 (c)	57 (b)	58 (d)	59 (b)	60 (b)
61 (a)	62 (c)	63 (a)	64 (d)	65 (d)	66 (d)	67 (b)	68 (b)	69 (a)	70 (d)
71 (d)	72 (c)	73 (d)	74 (d)	75 (d)	76 (b)	77 (c)	78 (c)	79 (a)	80 (c)
81 (a)	82 (b)	83 (c)	84 (c)	85 (a)	86 (b)	87 (a)	88 (a)	89 (b)	90 (d)
91 (a)	92 (b)	93 (c)	94 (c)	95 (b)	96 (d)	97 (c)			

Previous Years' Questions

1 (b)	2 (d)	3 (c)

CHAPTER 14

Capital Structure and Budgeting

In every business, there are two forms of capital, *i.e.* equity and debt, having their our benefits and drawbacks. The cost of capital is an ingredient in both investment decision-making by the company's management and the valuation of the company by investors. Capital budgeting is the process that companies use for decision-making on capital projects with a life of an year or more.

Capital Structure

It refers to the mix of a firm's capitalisation and includes long-term sources of funds such as debentures, preference share capital, equity share capital and retained earnings.

According to **Gerstenberg**, "Capital structure is the make-up of a firm's capitalisation."

In other words, "It refers to the proportion of debt preference capital and equity capital."

Choice of Capital

It is very difficult to choose the components (equity, debenture, preference capital etc) of capital for an organisation as there is no ideal capital structure. A company's capital structure depends upon its function and how risky the particular business is.

Patterns/Forms of Capital Structure

- Whole equity share capital.
- Different proportions of equity and preference share capital.
- Different proportions of equity and debenture capital.
- Different proportions of equity, preference and debenture capital.

Fundamental Principles should be kept in Mind, while Selecting the Financing Pattern

Financing pattern of an organisation is based on fundamental principles, *i.e.* cost principles and risk principles, *These are as follows*

In this Chapter

- *Capital Structure*
- *Cost of Capital*
- *Time Value of Money*
- *Capital Budgeting*

Fundamental Principles should be kept in Mind, while Selecting the Financing Pattern

Financing pattern of an organisation is based on fundamental principles, *i.e.* cost principles and risk principles, *These are as follows*

Cost Principles The best suited pattern of capital structure is one that minimises cost of capital and maximises Earning Per Shares (EPS).

Risk Principles According to this principle, reliance is placed more on equity for financing capital than excessive use of debt. *There are two associated risk*

- Business risk
- Financial risk

So while selecting the financing pattern, the following points should be kept in mind

- The risk less cost of the particular type of financing (rj)
- The business risk premium (b)
- The financial risk premium (f)

Symbolically, cost of capital may be represented as

$$Ko = rj + b + f$$

Optimum Capital Structure

One of the basic objective of financial management is to maximise the value or wealth of the firm. Capital structure is optimum, where the firm has a combination of equity and debt, so that the wealth of the firm is maximum. At this level, cost of capital is minimum and market price per share is maximum.

Features of an Appropriate Capital Structure or Factors affecting Capital Structure

While developing an appropriate capital structure for his company, the financial manager should aim at maximising the long-term market price of equity shares.

An appropriate capital structure should have the following features

Return The capital structure of the company should give maximum return to the shareholders. Within the constraints, maximum use of the leverage at a minimum cost should be made, so as to obtain maximum advantage of trading on equity at minimum cost.

Risk The capital structure should involve minimum risk of financial insolvency. The use of excessive debt threatens the solvency of the company. Since, use of debt adds to the risk of the company and shareholders, it should be used cautiously with equity.

Flexibility The company should be able to change the proportion of debt and equity in the capital structure, if required depending on changing conditions. The capital structure should be flexible to meet the changing conditions. It should also be possible for the company to provide funds whenever needed to finance its profitable activities.

Capacity The company should have capacity to pay the fixed periodic charges and the installments of principal sum. The debt capacity of the company should not be exceeded. The debt capacity of a company depends on its ability to generate cash flows.

Control The capital structure should not involve loss of control of the shareholders. If there is too much debt, then shareholders are likely to loss control to debenture holders.

Major Consideration in Capital Structure Planning

Type of Fund	Risk	Cost	Control
Equity Capital	**Low Risk** As no question for repayment of capital except, when the company is under liquidation. Hence, best from point of view of risk.	**Most Expensive** As the dividend expectation of shareholders are higher than interest rates. Also, dividends are not tax deductible.	**Dilution of Control** As the capital base might be expanded and new shareholders are involved.
Preference Capital	**Slightly Higher Risk** It is redeemable after certain period of time.	**Slightly Cheaper** It is cheaper than equity share capital, but higher cost than loan fund.	**No Dilution of Control** Since, voting rights are restricted.
Loan Funds	**High Risk** Capital should be repaid as per agreement.	**Comparatively Cheaper** Prevailing interest rates are considered only to the extent of after tax impact.	**No Dilution of Control**

Theories of Capital Structure

General Assumptions in Capital Structure Theories

- There are only two sources of funds, *i.e.* debts and equity (no preference share capital).
- The total assets of a firm and its capital employed are fixed.
- All earnings are distributed to equity shareholders.
- The firm earns operating profits and it is expected to grow.
- The business risk assumed to be constant and is not affected by the financing mix decision. (no change in fixed cost).
- There are no corporate or personal taxes. (no taxation)
- The investors have the same subjective profitability distribution of expected earnings.

Theories of capital structure are as follows

Net Income Approach

Assumptions

Apart from the general assumptions, additional assumptions are as follows

- There are no corporate taxes
- K_d = Debt Capitalisation Rate
- K_e = Equity Capitalisation Rate
- The cost of debt (K_d) is always less than cost of equity (K_e).
- K_d and K_e remains constant at all levels of debt equity mix.

Theory

- Debt is a cheaper source of finance than equity due to tax saving effect and investor's risk expectation.
- Use of cheaper debt funds in total capital structure will reduce the overall or weighted average cost of capital.
- Hence, as the degree of financial leverage increases, the weighted average cost of capital will decline with every increase in the debt content in total funds employed.
- Value of firm $= \dfrac{\text{Earning before interest and taxes}}{\text{Weighted average cost of capital}}$
- The value of firm will increase for every decline in weighted average.
- Whereby, the debt content is reduced, the reverse will happen, *i.e.* weighted average cost of capital will increase thereby reducing the value of the firm. Thus, a firm can increase its value and lower the overall cost of capital by increasing the proportion of debt in the capital structure.
- The value of firm will be maximum at a point, where WACC is minimum. Thus, the theory of net income suggests total or maximum possible debt financing for minimising the cost of capital.

Application

- Determine Earning Before Interest and Taxes (EBIT).
- Compute EBT (Net Income) = Earning Before Interest and Taxes – Interest on debts funds
- Compute Market Value of Equity (E)

  EBT (Net Income)/Cost of Equity (K_e)
- Compute Market Value Debt (D) = Interest/Cost of Debt (K_d)
- Market Value of Firm (V) = E + D

  = Market Value of Equity + Market Value of Debt
- Compute Overall Cost of Capital (K_0)

  = EBIT/Value of Firm (V)

where, there is tax then (EBIT–Tax Rate)

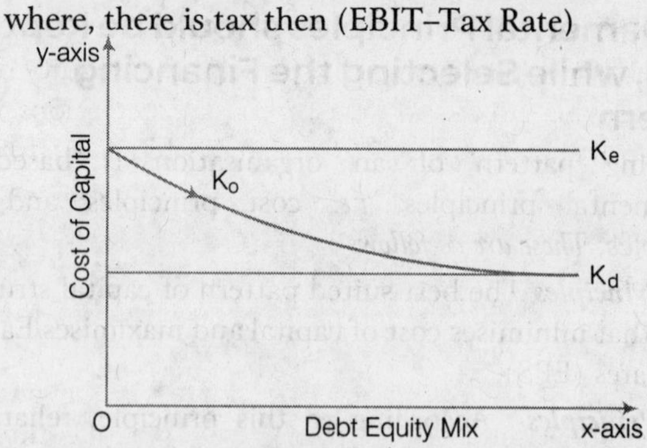

Relationship Between Debt Equity Mix and Cost of Capital

Illustration If X Ltd provides the following information for determination of value of firm and overall cost of capital.

Solution 10% Debenture = ₹ 9,00,000

EBIT = 20% of Total assets

Total assets = ₹ 15,00,000

Tax rate = 50%

Equity capitalisation rate = 15%

Net Income Approach

Earning Before Interest and Tax ₹ 3,00,000 [20% of Total Assets 20% × ₹ 15,00,000]	
(–) Interest (₹ 9,00,000 × 10%)	₹ 90,000
Earning before Tax	₹ 2,10,000
(–) Tax @ 50%	(₹ 1,05,000)
Earning after Tax	₹ 1,05,000
Equity Capitalisation Rate (K_e)	15%
Value of Equity $\left(\dfrac{\text{Earning after tax}}{K_e}\right)$	₹ 7,00,000
Value of Debt	₹ 9,00,000
Value of Firm (Value of Equity + Value of Debt)	₹ 16,00,000
Overall Cost of Capital (EBIT – Tax)/Total Market Value of Firm	9.375%

Traditional Approach

Assumptions

Apart from the general assumptions, the following additional assumptions are made

- The Cost of Debt (K_d) is always less than the Cost of Equity (K_e).
- K_d and K_e vary with the change in debt equity mix.
- Increase in cost of equity is more steeper and higher than increase in cost of debt.

Theory

- Debt is a cheaper source of finance than equity due to tax saving effect and investor's risk expectations.
- Use of cheaper debt funds in total capital structure will reduce the overall or weighted average cost of capital.
- Hence, as the degree of financial leverage Broslect increases the Weighted Average Cost of Capital (WACC) will decline with every increase in the debt content in total funds employed.
- Hence, if financial leverage increases beyond the acceptable limit, the cost of debt and cost of equity start rising. This is because of high financial risk associated with the firm.
- The increasing cost of capital owing to increased financial risk and increasing cost of debt makes the overall cost of capital to increase.
- Therefore, the firm should strive to reach the optimal capital structure and maximise its total value through a judicious use of both debt and equity.
- At the optimal capital structure, the overall cost of capital will be minimum and the value of firm is maximum.
- As per traditional approach, the firm should try to achieve the optimal capital structure by minimising WACC and maximising its value.

Application of Theory

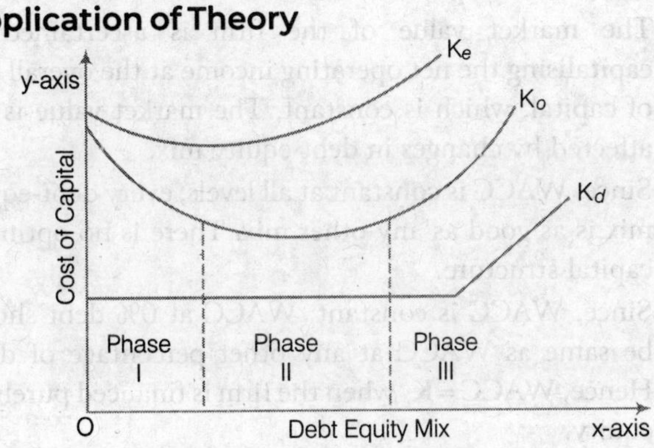

Application of Traditional Approach

Illustration Required to compute the optimal debt equity mix for the company by calculating the composite cost of capital.

Debt (% of Total Capital Employed)	Cost of Debt	Cost of Equity
0	7.0	15.0
10	7.0	15.0
20	7.0	16.0
30	8.0	17.0
40	9.0	18.0
50	10.0	21.0
60	11.0	24.0

Solution

Calculation of Optimal Debt-Equity Mix (%)

Debt (% of Total Capital Employed) (A)	Cost of Debt (B)	Weighted Cost of Debt (C) [A × B]	Equity (% of Total Capital Employed) (D)	Cost of Equity (E)	Weighted Cost of Equity (F) [D × E]	Cost of Capital [C + F]
0	7	0	100	15	15	15
10	7	0.7	90	15	13.5	14.20
20	7	1.4	80	16	12.80	14.20
30	8	2.4	70	17	11.90	14.30
40	9	3.6	60	18	10.80	14.40
50	10	5.0	50	21	10.50	15.50
60	11	6.6	40	24	9.60	16.20

At optimal, debt-equity mix of 20:80, the cost of capital is at minimum level of 14-20.

Net Operating Income Approach

Assumptions

- The Cost of Debt (K_d) is always less than Cost of Equity (K_e).
- K_d (debt capitalisation rate) remains constant at various levels of debt equity mix.
- K_e (equity capitalisation rate) increases as debt content increases due to higher financial risk and higher expectation of equity investors.
- The market capitalises the value of the firm as a whole, without giving importance to debt equity mix. Hence, overall cost of capital is constant.

Theory

- Debt may be cheaper than equity.
- Increase in financial risk causes the equity capitalisation rate to increase.
- Thus, the advantage of using low cost debt is set off exactly by increase in equity capitalisation rate.
- Therefore, the overall cost of capital remains constant for all degrees of debt equity mix.
- The market capitalises the value of firm as a whole.
- The market value of the firm is ascertained by capitalising the net operating income at the overall cost capital, which is constant. The market value is not affected by debt equity mix change.
- Since, Weighted Average Cost of Capital (WACC) is constant at all levels, every debt-equity mix is as goods as any other mix. There is no optimal capital structure. Every capital structure is optimal one.

Application

- Determine earning before interest and taxes (net operating income).
- Compute earning before tax.

[EBIT Interest on debt funds]

- Compute market Value of Firm (V)

$$= \frac{\text{EBIT (Net operating income)}}{\text{WACC } (K_o)}$$

- Compute market Value of Debt (D)

$$= \frac{\text{Interest}}{\text{Cost of Debt } (K_d)}$$

- Compute market value of equity

Value of Equity (E)

= Value of firm (V) – Value of Debt (D)

- Compute Cost of Equity Capital (K_e)

$$\text{Cost of Equity Capital } (K_e) = \frac{\text{Earning before taxes}}{\text{Value of Equity (E)}}$$

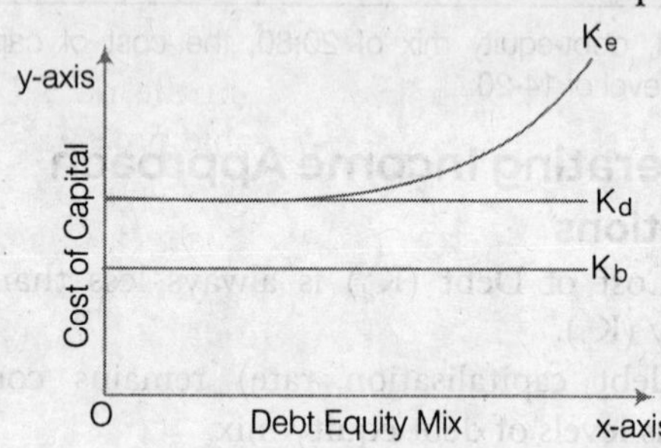

Diagrammatic representation of net operating income approach to capital structure

Illustration EBIT = ₹ 3,00,000

WACC = 15%

Interest = ₹ 90,000

Cost of debt = 10%

Solution

EBIT	₹ 3,00,000
(–) Interest	(₹ 90,000)
EBT	₹ 2,10,000
Market Value of Firm (EBIT/WACC)	₹ 20,00,000
Market Value of Debt (Interest/K_d)	₹ 9,00,000
Market Value of Equity (Value of Firm – Value of Debt)	₹ 11,00,000
Cost of Equity Capital (K_e) [Earning before taxes / Market value of equity]	19.09%

Modigliani and Miller Approach

This approach is a refinement of the net operating income approach.

Assumptions

- The Cost of Debt (K_d) is always less than Cost of Equity (K_e).
- The debt capitalisation rate remains constant at various level of debt equity mix.
- K_e increases as debt content increases due to higher financial risk and higher expectation of equity investors.
- The market capitalises the value of the firm as a whole, without giving importance to the debt equity mix. Hence, overall cost of capital is constant.
- The capital markets are perfect. Investors are free to buy and sell securities. They are well informed about the risk and return on all type of securities. There are transaction cost.
- Firms can be classified into 'homogenous risk class'. They belong to this class, if their expected earnings have identical risk characteristics.

Theory

- Debt may be cheaper than equity.
- Increases in financial risk causes the equity capitalisation rate to increase.
- Thus, the advantage of using low-cost debt is set off exactly by the increase in equity capitalisation rate.
- Therefore, the overall cost of capital remains constant for all degree of debt equity mix.
- The market capitalises the value of firm as a whole.
- The market value of the firm is ascertained by capitalising the net operating income at the overall cost of capital, which is constant. The market value is not affected by changes in debt-equity mix.
- Since, WACC is constant at all levels, every debt-equity mix is as good as any other mix. There is no optimum capital structure.
- Since, WACC is constant, WACC at 0% debt should be same as WACC at any other percentage of debt. Hence, WACC = K_e when the firm is financed purely by equity.

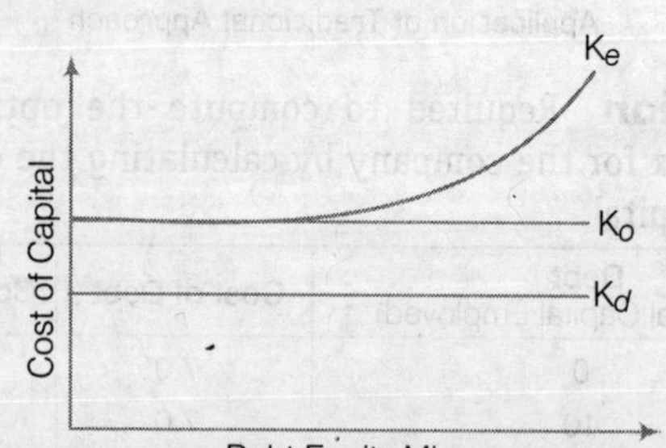

Diagrammatic Representation of Modigliani and Miller Approach to Capital Structure

Cost of Capital

The term 'cost of capital' may be defined as the required rate of return a firm must earn on his investment project, so that the market value of the firm's equity does not fall. It is the cost of obtaining funds, through debt or equity, in order to finance an investment. These funds can be procured from different types of investors.

The cost of capital of firms is a weighted average of the cost of each component of capital, *i.e.* combined cost of each type of source by which a firm raises funds. Thus, cost of capital is the rate which an organisation must pay to the suppliers of capital for the use of their funds.

According to **Solomon Ezra**, "Cost of capital is the minimum required rate of earning or the cut-off rate of capital expenditure."

According to **Hampton, John J**, "The rate of return the firm requires from investment in order to increase the value of the firm in the market place."

Cost of capital can be computed use formula

$$K = r_0 + b + f$$

Where, K = Cost of capital

r_0 = Normal rate of return at zero risk level

b = Premium for business risk

f = Premium for financial risk

Importance of Cost of Capital

The importance of cost of capital can be stated in terms of the contribution, it makes towards the achievement of the objectives of maximisation of the wealth of the shareholders. If the firm's return is more than its cost of capital, then the investors will no doubt be receiving their expected rate of return from the firm. The excess portion of the return will however be available to the firms and can be used in several ways. *e.g.*

- For distribution among the shareholders in the form of higher than expected dividends and
- For reinvestment within the firm for increasing further the subsequent returns.

The cost of capital, when used as a discount rate in capital budgeting, helps accepting only those proposals whose rate of return is more than the cost of capital of the firm and hence, results in increasing the value of the firm. Similarly, the firm's value is reduced, when the rate of return on the proposal falls below the cost of capital. Thus, the concept of cost of capital is consistent with the goal of maximisation of shareholder's wealth and it works as a tool to achieve this goal. Further, the cost of capital has a useful role to play in deciding the financial plan or capital structure of the firm. It may be noted that in order to maximise the value of the firm, the cost to all the different sources of funds must be minimised. The cost of capital of different sources usually varies and the firm will like to have a combination of these sources in such a way as to minimise the overall cost of capital of the firm.

Measurement of Cost of Capital

The measurement of cost of capital refers to the process of determining the cost of funds to the firms. Once, the cost has been determined, it is in the light of this cost that the capital budgeting proposal will be evaluated.

If there is a mistake in the determination of the cost of capital, then the investment decision as well as other decisions may be taken wrongly and thus, ultimately affecting the profitability and survival of the firm.

Thus, utmost care must be taken in the measurement of cost of capital otherwise unacceptable proposals might be selected and acceptable proposals might get rejected. Further, although the cost of capital is measured at a given point of time, it must reflect the cost of funds over the long run because the cost of capital is used in capital budgeting involving expenditures providing benefits in the long run.

Underlying Assumptions

- The basic assumption of the cost of capital concept is that the business risk of the firm is unaffected by the proposal being evaluated at the cost of capital.
- Another assumption required to be made is that the financial risk of the firm remains unchanged, whether a proposal is accepted or not.

The cost of capital is measured in two stages

- Computation of cost of each component (source) of capital.
- Computation of combined or composite cost termed as weighted average cost. In fact, this weighted average cost is used as cost of capital in investment decisions.

Classification of Cost of Capital

Explicit Cost The explicit cost of any source of capital may be defined as the discount rate equals tha present value of the cash inflows that are incremental to the taking of financing opportunity with the present value of its incremental cash outflow. In other words, explicit cost or direct cost refers to the interest rate adjusted for tax savings and the cost of raising funds.

Implicit Cost It is the rate of return associated with the best investment opportunity for the firm and its shareholders that will be foregone of the project presently under consideration by the firm was accepted.

➠ **Note** *The explicit cost arises when funds are raised and when funds are used, implicit cost arises. For capital budgeting decisions, cost of capital is nothing, but the explicit cost of capital.*

Marginal Cost of Capital It is the additional cost incurred to obtain additional funds required by a firm. It refers to the change in the total cost of capital resulting from the use of additional funds.

Average Cost/Composite/Overall **Cost** Average cost of capital is the weighted average cost of capital calculated on the basis of costs of the different components of equity, preference shares, debentures and retained earnings.

Historic Cost/ Book Cost Historical cost refers to the cost, which has already been incurred for financing a project.

Future Cost It refers to the expected cost of funds to be raised for financing a project. For all decision-making purposes, future cost is the relevant one than in comparison with the historic cost.

Spot Cost The cost that are prevailling in the market at a certain time.

Computation of Cost of Capital

Cost of Debentures

The cost of debentures and long-term loans is the contractual interest rate adjusted further for the tax liability of the company. When the firm employees debt, it must ensure that common shareholder's earning are not deducted. To keep the earning unchanged, the firm must earn a return equal to the interest rate of debt.

$$K_d = \frac{\text{Interest} \times [100\% - \text{Tax rate}]}{\text{Net proceeds of issue}}$$

Debentures

Irredeemable Debentures | Redeemable Debentures

$$K_d = \frac{\text{Interest} \times [100\% - \text{Tax rate}] + [\text{RV} - \text{Net proceeds}]/\text{N}}{[\text{RV} + \text{Net proceeds}]/2}$$

Where, RV = Redeemable value

N = Number of years

Illustration A company issued 10000, 10% Debentures of ₹ 100 each on 1st April, 2006 to be matured on 1st April, 2011. If the market price of the debentures is ₹ 80. Compute the cost of debt assuming 35% tax rate.

Solution $K_d = \frac{\text{Interest} \times [100\% - \text{Tax rate}] + [\text{Redeemable value} - \text{Net proceeds}]/\text{N}}{[\text{Redeemable value} + \text{Net proceeds}]/2}$

$$= \frac{10 \times [100\% - 35\%] + [100 - 80]/5}{[100 + 80]/2} = \frac{10 \times [65\%] + [20]/5}{[180]/2}$$

$$= \frac{10 \times 0.65 + 4}{90} = \frac{6.5 + 4}{90}$$

$$= \frac{10.5}{90} = 0.11667 = 0.12 \text{ or } 12\%$$

Cost of Preference Shares

The cost of preference share capital is the dividend expected by its holders. Though, payment of dividend is not mandatory, non-payment may result in exercise of voting lights by them. The payment of preference dividend is not adjusted for taxes as they are paid after taxes and is not deductible.

Preference Shares

Redeemable | Ireedemable

$$K_p = \frac{\text{Preference dividend} + [\text{RV} - \text{Net proceeds}]/\text{N}}{\left[\frac{\text{RV} + \text{Net proceeds}}{2}\right]}$$

$$Kp = \frac{\text{Preference dividend}}{\text{Net proceeds of issue}}$$

Where, RV = Redeemable value

N = Number of years

Illustration XYZ company issues 2000, 10% preference shares of ₹ 100 each at ₹ 95 each. Calculate the cost of preference shares.

Solution $K_p = \frac{\text{Preference dividend}}{\text{Net proceeds of issue}}$

$$= \frac{(₹ 100 \times 10\%)}{₹ 95} = \frac{10}{95} = 0.1053 \text{ or } 10.53\%$$

Illustration In the above illustration, if preference dividend are redeemable in 10 years.

Solution

$$K_p = \frac{\text{Preference dividend} + [\text{RV} - \text{Net proceeds}]/\text{N}}{\left[\frac{\text{RV} + \text{Net proceeds}}{2}\right]}$$

$$= \frac{10 + [100 - 95]/10}{[100 + 95]/2} = \frac{10.50}{97.50} = 0.1077 \text{ or } 10.77\%$$

Cost of Equity

Cost of equity capital represents the expectations of equity shareholders from a company. Based on investors behaviour and expectation, *the cost of equity capital can be determined by any of the following approach*

Dividend/Price Approach

The approach is based on the thinking that what the investors expect when they put in their savings in the company. It means that the investor arrives at the market price for a share by capitalising the expected dividend at a normal rate of return. Though, this approach is simple, but it suffers from two serious weaknesses *These are*

- It ignores the earnings on company's retained earnings, which increases the rate of dividend in equity share.

- It ignores the fact that price rise of shares may be due to the retained earnings also and not on account of only high rate of dividend.

$$K_e = \frac{\text{Dividend per share}}{\text{Market price per share}}$$

This approach applies where companies have stable dividend policy.

Earning/Price Approach

The E/P ratio assumes that shareholders capitalise a stream of uncharged earnings by the capitalisation rate of E/P ratio in order to evaluate their holdings. The advocates of this approach, however, differ on the earnings figure and market price.

This approach also has three main limitations

- All earnings are not distributed among the shareholders in the form of dividend
- Earnings per share cannot be assumed to be constant as this approach emphasises,
- Share price does not remain constant because investments in retained earnings result in market price of share.

$$K_e = \frac{\text{Earning per share}}{\text{Market price per share}}$$

Growth Approach

This approach emphasises what the investor actually receives, *i.e.* Dividend + The rate of growth in dividend.

The growth rate in dividend is assumed to be equal to the growth rate in earnings per share. In other words, if the earnings per share increased at a rate of 5%, of the dividend per share and market price per share should also be increased at a rate of 5%. This approach is considered to be the best conceptual measure of the cost of new capital that ensures the optimum capital budgeting decisions.

$$K_d = \frac{D}{P} + G$$

Where, D = Current dividend per share
P = Market price per share
G = Annual growth rate of earning of dividend.

$$K_e = \frac{E}{P} + G$$

Where, E = Current earnings per share
P = Market price per share
G = Annual growth rate of earnings

Realised Yield Approach

In case, where of future dividend and the sale price are uncertain, it is very difficult to estimate the rate of return on investment. In order to remove this difficulty, it is suggested the cost of capital. Under this approach, the realised yield is discounted at the present value factor and then compared with the value of investment.

$$Y_t = \frac{D_t + P_t}{P_{t-1}}$$

Where, Y_t = Yield for the year t
D_t = Dividend per share at the end of the year t
P_t = Price per share at the end of the year t
P_{t-1} = Price per share at the beginning

Cost of Retained Earnings

Cost of retained earnings or reserves are generally taken as the same as cost of equity. This is because, if earning are paid out as dividends without being retained and simultaneously a light issue is made, the investors would be subscribing to the issue based on some expected return. This is taken as the indicator of the cost of reserves or retained earnings.

The cost of retained earnings can be calculated as follows

Discounted Cash Flow Method

This method is also known as the 'dividend yield plus growth' model. Investors who buy stocks expect to receive two types of returns from those stocks dividends and capital gains. Firms payout profits in the form of dividends to their investors quarterly. The growth rate equates to the average, year-to-year growth of the dividend amount. *With these inputs, cost of retained earnings is calculated as*

$$K_r = \frac{D_1}{P_0} + G$$

Where, D_1 = Upcoming year's dividend
P_0 = Stock price
G = Growth

Captial Asset Pricing Model (CAPM) Method

This method requires three pieces of information to help determine the required rate of return on a stock or how much a stock should earn to justify its risk. This infromation includes, the risk free rate currently in the economy, the return on the market and the stock's Beta. *With these inputs, cost of retained earnings is calculated as*

$$K_r = R_f + B(R_m - R_f)$$

Where,

R_f = Risk free rate
B = Beta
R_m = Market rate of return
R_f = Risk free rate

Bond Yield Plus Risk Premium Method

This simple method of calculating the cost can provide a quick estimate. Take the interest rate on the firm's bonds and add on a risk premium. The risk premium would usually range from 3 to 5%, based on a judgement of the firm's riskiness.

Cost of Right Shares

The cost of right shares would, therefore be same as the cost of new equity capital issued to the public directly.

$$K_s = \frac{D_1}{P_0} + g$$

Where, K_s = Cost of right shares
D_1 = Dividend yield
P_0 = Market price of the share
g = Growth rate in dividend

Weighted Average Cost of Capital (WACC)

A firm obtains capital from various sources. Due to the risk differences and the contractual agreements between the entity and investor, the cost of capital of each source of capital differs. The cost of capital of each source of capital is known as component or specific cost of capital. The combined cost of all sources of capital is called overall or average cost of capital. The component costs are combined according to the weight of each component capital to obtain the average cost of capital. Thus, the overall cost is also called the Weighted Average Cost of Capital (WACC).

CIMA London defines weighted average cost of capital as, "the average cost of company's finance weighted according to the proportion of each element bears to the total pool of capital, weighting is usually based on market, valuations current yields and cost after tax."

The computation of the weighted average cost of capital involves the following steps

- Calculate the cost of specific sources of funds *e.g.* K_d, K_e, K_p, K_r.
- Assign weights to specific costs.
- Multiply the cost of each of the source by the appropriate weights.
- Compute the total weighted cost by adding the total of steps.

Hence, weighted average cost of capital = Sum of [Cost of individual components × Proportion in capital]

The following format may be adopted for computation of weighted average cost of capital

Component	Amt	Proportion	Individual Cost	Multiplication
Debt	...	W_1	K_d	$K_d \times W_1$
Preference capital	...	W_2	K_p	$K_p \times W_2$
Retained earnings	...	W_3	K_{re}	$K_{re} \times W_3$
Equity capital	...	W_4	K_e	$K_e \times W_4$
Total				K_o = Weighted Average Cost of Capital

Time Value of Money (TVM)

The Time Value of Money (TVM) is the important concept of financial management which refers to that money available at the present time is worth more than the identical sum in the future due to its potential earning capacity.

In simple words, time value of money means that the value of money is different in different time periods. The value of money received today is more than the value of same amount receivable at some other time in future. It can be used to compare investment alternatives and to solve problems involving loans, leases, savings etc.

Causes Due to Which Value of Money Decline

- Inflation in the economy
- Consumption
- Risks involved in delayed receipts of cash or financial transactions
- Opportunity cost of capital delayed

Importance of Time Value of Money

In Investment Decisions

Small businesses often have limited resources to invest in business operations, activities and expansion. One of the factors we have to look at is how to invest, is the time value of money.

In Capital Budgeting Decisions

When a business chooses to invest money in a project such as an expansion, a strategic acquisition or just the purchase of a new piece of equipment. It may be years before that project begins producing a positive cash flow. The business needs to know whether those future cash flows are worth the up-front investment. Companies apply the TVM in various ways to make yes-or-no decisions on capital projects as well as to decide between competing projects.

Techniques of Time Value of Money

Compounding Technique or Future Value Technique

Compounding technique is used to calculate the future value of present money (cash flows). In this concept, the interest earned on the initial principal amount becomes a part of the principal at the end of the compounding period.

Discounting Technique or Present Value Technique

Discounting technique is used to calculate the present value of cash flows.

The concept of this method is "what should be the amount, we need to invest today" to get a specific amount in future. This technique helps to ascertain the present value of future cash flows by applying a discount rate.

> Discounting converts future value amount into present value amount. Similarly, compounding converts present value amount into future value amount.

Important Terms related to Techniques

Future Value

Future value is also known as terminal value. The accrued amount FV_n on a principal *P* after *n* payment periods at *i* (in decimal) rate of interest per payment period is given by

$$FV_n = P_o(1+i)^n$$

Where,

$$i = \frac{\text{Annual rate of interest}}{\text{Number of payment periods per year}} = \frac{r}{k}$$

$(1+i)^n$ is known as future value factor or compound value factor.

Present Value

Present value is the current value of a 'Future Amount'. It can also be defined as the amount to be invested today at a given rate over specified period to equal the 'Future Amount'. Since, finding present value is simply the reverse of finding Future Value (FV), the formula for Future Value (FV) can be readily transformed into a present value formula. Therefore, the P_o (the present value) becomes

$$P_o = \frac{FV_n}{(1+i)^n} \text{ or } P_O = FV_n(1+i)^{-n}$$

Where, FV_n Future value *n* years hence

i = Rate of interest per annum

n = Number of years for which discounting is done

Simple Interest

Simple interest is calculated as a simple percentage of the original principal amount. *The formula for calculating simple interest is*

$$SI = P_o(i)(n)$$

Where,

SI = Simple interest in rupees

P_O = Original principal

i = Interest rate per time period

n = Number of time periods

If we add principal to the interest, *i.e.* $P_o + P_o(i)(n)$, we will get the total Future Value (FV).

Compound Interest

In compound interest, the interest is calculated on total of previously earned interest and the original principal. Naturally, the amount calculated on the basis of compound interest rate is higher than when calculated with the simple rate.

Capital Budgeting

Financing and investment of funds are two crucial financial functions. The investment of funds also termed as capital budgeting. It requires a number of decisions to be taken in a situation, in which funds are invested and benefits are expected over a long period.

Capital budgeting means planning for capital assets. The capital budgeting decision means a decision as to whether or not money should be invested in long-term projects such as the setting up of a factory or installing a machinery or creating additional capacities to manufacture a part, which at present may be purchased from outside. It includes a financial analysis of the various proposals regarding capital expenditure to evaluate their impact on financial condition of the company and to choose the best out of the various alternatives.

According to **EE Nemmers**, "Capital budgeting or capital management may be defined as the process of determining which investment or allocation of long-term funds are to be made by an enterprise."

According to **Charles T Horngreen**, "Capital budgeting is long-term planning for making and financing proposed capital outlays."

Need of Capital Budgeting

Relatively High Cost Almost, all the capital projects involve heavy investment of funds. Hence, their efficient budgeting becomes inevitable.

Permanent Commitment The funds invested in capital projects are more or less permanently blocked. These investments are of irreversible nature, *i.e.* they cannot be taken back quickly without any material loss. Hence, a careful planning of capital expenditures is essential.

Vitally affects Profitability and Financial Position The financial position and profitability of the concern are immediately and significantly affected by capital investments and the management becomes dependent on future event for the financial flexibility of their concern. Hence, such investments should be very carefully planned.

Long-run Effects Capital profits affect the earnings of the business of coming several years. *e.g.* Replacement of labour of machine increases the fixed costs of the business.

National Importance Investment decisions are of national importance too as they affect employment, economic activities and economic growth.

Importance of Capital Budgeting Decision

Capital budgeting decisions should be taken after careful analyse and review. *The importance of capital budgeting can be understood from the following points*

Cost Initial investment is substantial. Hence, commitment of resources should be made properly.

Time The effect of decision is known only in the near future and not immediately.

Irreversibility Decisions are irreversible and commitment should be made, on proper evaluation.

Complexity Decisions are based on forecasting of future events and inflows. Quantification of future events involves application of statistical and probalistic techniques careful judgement and application of mind is necessary.

Limitations of Capital Budgeting

- Capital budgeting has long-term implementation which can't be used in short-term. A wrong decision in the early stages can affect the long-term survival, of the company.
- Decisions in capital budgeting are not modifiable as it is hard to locate the market for capital goods.
- Inadequate investment makes it difficult for the company to increase its budget and the capital.
- It involves large number of funds so the decision has to be taken carefully.
- The estimation can be in respect of cash outflow and the revenues/saving and costs attached which are with projects.

Types of Capital Budgeting Decisions

Capital budgeting decisions are classified in two ways. One way is to classify them on the basis of 'firm's existence' and another way is to classify them on the basis of 'decision situation'.

Based on Firm's Existence

Cost Reduction Decision

These decisions focus on reduction of operating cost and improving efficiency.

They can be sub-classified into two parts

Replacement Decisions The main objective to replacement is to improve operating efficiency and reduce costs which lead to increased profit, but the firm's revenue may remain unchanged.

Modernisation Decisions As the time passes, assets become outdated and obsolete with technological changes. The firm must decide to replace these assets with new assets, so that firm may launch better product and operate more economically.

Revenue Expansion Decision

These decisions focus on improving sales product lines, improved versions of products etc.

These are sub-classified into two parts

Expansion Decisions To add capacity to existing product lines to meet increased demand. To improve production facilities and to increase market share of existing products.

Diversification Decisions To diversify and enter into new product lines, venture into new markets to reduce business risk by dealing in different products and operating in different markets.

Based on Nature of Decision

Mutually Exclusive Decisions

Decisions are said to be mutually exclusive, if two or more alternative proposals are such that the acceptance of one proposal will exclude acceptance of the other alternative proposals.

Accept-Reject Decisions

These are opposite to mutually exclusive decisions. The accept-reject decision occur when proposals are independent and do not compete with each other. The firm may accept or reject a proposal on the basis of a minimum return on the required investments.

Contingent Decisions

These are dependent proposals. The investment in one proposal require investment in one or more other proposals.

Process of Capital Budgeting

Project Generation

Under this phase, idea of new investment project generation is originated at different levels within a firm, *such as*

- To add new product to the product line.
- To expand capacity in existing product lines.
- To reduce the costs of the output.

Project Evaluation

Under second phase, various projects are evaluated envolving following two steps

- Estimation of benefits and costs. The benefits and costs must be measures in terms of cash flows.
- Selection of an appropriate criterion to judge the desirability of the project.

Project Selection

The third phase is screening and selecting the projects. Though, the final approval of the projects may be given by the top management, projects under consideration may be screened at various levels of management.

Project Execution

The last phase is of execution of project under this funds are appropriated for capital expenditure after the final selection of investment proposals. The formal planning for the appropriation of funds is called the capital budget. The project execution committee or the management must ensure that the funds are spent in accordance with appropriations made on the capital budget.

Conventional or Traditional Techniques of Capital Budgeting

Payback Period

Payback period represents the time period required for complete recovery of the initial investment in the project. It is the period within which the total cash inflows from the project equals to the cost of project. The lower the payback, the better it is, since initial investment is recouped faster.

Computation of Simple Payback Period

- Determine the total outflow of the project (Initial Investment).
- Determine the Cash Inflow After Taxes (CFAT) for each year.
- Determine the Cumulative CFAT at the end of every year.
- Determine the year in which cumulative CFAT exceeds initial investment.
- Compute payback period as under
  = Initial Investment/CFAT per annum.
- Accept, if payback period is less than maximum or bench mark period, else reject the project.

Illustration Project requires an outlay of ₹ 1,00,000 and yields annual cost help of ₹ 12,500 for 1 year. What is the payback period of the project?

Solution

$$\text{Payback period} = \frac{\text{Original investment}}{\text{Annual cost flow}} = \frac{1{,}00{,}000}{12{,}500} = 8 \text{ years}$$

Payback period in cost of unequal cost flows

$$= \text{Years before full recovery} + \frac{\text{Unreceivable amount investment}}{\text{Cash flow during year}}$$

Advantages of Payback Period

- This method is simple to understand and easy to operate.
- It clarifies the concept of profit or surplus. Surplus arises only, if the initial investment is fully recovered. Hence, there is no profit on any project unless the payback period is over.
- When funds are limited, projects having shorter payback periods should be selected. Since, they can be rotated more number of times.
- This method is suitable in the case of industries where the risk of technological obsolescence is very high and hence, only those project, which have a shorter payback period should be financed.
- The payback period can be compared to a break-even point, the point at which the costs are fully recovered, but profits are yet to commerce.

Limitations of Payback Period

- It stresses on capital recovery rather than profitability.
- It does not consider the post payback cash flows.
- This method becomes an inadequate measure evaluating two projects, where the cash inflows are even.
- This method ignores the time value of money.

Illustration Project requires a cash outlay of ₹ 30,000 and yield annual cash inflow of ₹ 10,000, ₹ 7,000, ₹ 6,000, ₹ 6,000; and ₹ 5,000 during the next 5 years respectively What is the payback period of the project?

Solution Payback Period (PbP)

$$= \text{Year before full recovery} + \left(\frac{\text{Unreceivable of investment}}{\text{Cash flow during the year}}\right)$$

$$= 4 + \frac{1{,}000}{5{,}000} = 4.2 \text{ years}$$

Discounted Payback Period

When the payback period is computed after discounting the cash flows by a predetermined rate, then it is called as the discounted payback period.

For calculating payback period, we need Cash Flow After Tax (CFAT).

Calculation of Cash Flows After Taxes (CFAT)

Cash Flow After Taxes

Particulars	Amt (₹)
Sales Revenue	...
(–) Variable Cost	(...)
Contribution	...
(–) Fixed Cost	(...)
Earning Before Depreciation and Taxes (EBDT)	...
(–) Depreciation	(...)
Earning Before Taxes (EBT)	...
(–) Taxes	(...)
Earning After Tax (EAT)	...
(–) Depreciation	(...)
Cash Flows After Tax (CFAT) or Earning After Taxes but Before Depreciation (EATBD)	

Computation of Discount Payback Period

- Determine the total outflow of the project.
- Determine the Cash Flow After Taxes (CFAT) for each year.
- Determine the PV factor for each year.
- Compute discounted CFAT by multiplying step 2 and step 3.
- Determine the cumulative discounted CFAT at the end of every year.
- Determine the year in which cumulative DCFAT exceeds initial investment.
- Compute discount payback period as the time at which cumulative DCFAT = Initial investment.
- Accept, if discounted payback period less than maximum/bench mark period, else reject the proposal.

Payback Reciprocal

Computed as

$$\text{Payback Reciprocal} = \frac{\text{Average annual cash inflows}}{\text{Initial investment}}$$

Utility

The payback reciprocal is considered to be an approximate of the internal rate of return, if

- the life of the project is at least twice the payback period.
- the project generates equal amount of the annual cash inflows.

Illustration Initial investment = ₹ 50 lakh

Life = 10 years

CFAT = ₹ 10 lakh per annum

Solution Payback Reciprocal

$$= \frac{\text{Average annual cash inflows}}{\text{Initial investment}} \times 100$$

$$= \frac{₹\,10\text{ lakh}}{₹\,50\text{ lakh}} \times 100 = 20\%$$

Average Rate of Return Method (ARR)

Average rate of return method means the average annual yield on the project.

Computation of Average Rate of Return

- Determine the net investment of the project.
- Determine the profit after tax for each year.
- Determine the cumulative PAT for N years, Where, N = Project life.
- Average PAT per annum = Cumulative PAT/N years.
- Average rate of return = $\dfrac{\text{Average PAT per annum}}{\text{Net investment}}$

Advantages of Average Rate of Return

- Simple to understand.
- Easy to operate and compute.
- It takes into consideration the total earnings from the project during its entire economic life.
- This method gives due weightage to the profitability of the project.
- This method can also be used for comparing inter se the projects of different nature.
- This method ignores the life of the project for determining the cost of investment. Hence, the amount of initial investment and average investment remain the same.

Limitations of Average Rate of Return

- It ignores time value of money, which is important in capital budgeting decision.
- It does not cash inflows (CFAT), which is important in project evaluation rather than PAT.
- It takes the rough average of profits of future years.
- It is an averaging technique, which does not take into account the impact of various external factors on overall profits of the firm.
- This method does not give consideration to the risk factor in respect of each project. Risk analysis should be the integral part of a project evaluation technique.

Scientific or Modern Techniques of Capital Budgeting

Net Present Value Method

The Net Present Value (NPV) of an investment proposal is defined as the sum of the present value of all future cash inflows less the sum of the present value of all cash outflows associated with the proposal.

Net present value = Discounted cash inflow – Discounted cash outflow

Computation of Net Present Value

- Determine the total cash outflow of the project and time period in which they occur.
- Compute the total discounted cash outflow. Total discounted cash outflow = Outflow × PV factor
- Determine the total cash inflows of the projects and the time period in which they arise.
- Compute the total discounted cash inflow. Total discounted cash inflow = Inflow × PV factor.
- Compute NPV = Discounted cash inflow – Discounted cash outflow
- Accept project, if NPV is positive, else reject.

Illustration A project requires an initial investment of ₹ 1,80,000 and is expected to generate the following net cash inflows

Year	1	2	3	4
Cash inflow	95,000	80,000	60,000	55,000

Compute net present value of the project if the minimum desired rate of return is 12%.

Solution The cash inflow generated by the project is uneven. Therefore, the present value would be computed for each year separately

Year	Present value of (₹) 1 at 12 %	Net cash flow (₹)	Present value of cash flow (₹)
1	0.893	95,000	84,835
2	0.797	80,000	63,760
3	0.712	60,000	42,720
4	0.636	55,000	34,,980
Total			2,26,295
Initial investment required			2,25,000
Net present value			1,295

Advantages of NPV Method

- All cash flows are considered.
- It focus on the basic objective of financial management, as NPV constitutes addition to the wealth of shareholders.
- It considers the time value of money.
- It takes care of the entire life of the project and its entire earnings including salvage of asset.
- It can be applied to both types of cash inflow patterns even and uneven cash inflows.

Limitations of NPV Method

- It involves complex calculations.
- It involves forecasting cash flows and application of discount rate.
- It ignores the difference in initial outflows, size of different proposals etc, while evaluating mutually exclusive project.
- It assumes that intermediate cash inflows are reinvested at the firm's cost of capital, which is not always true.
- The results from this method may contradict those under internal rate of return method, even in the case of alternative proposals, which are mutually exclusive.

Profitability Index or Desirability Factor

The profitability index is used where different investment proposals each involving different initial investments and cash inflows due, to be compared.

$$= \frac{\text{Total discounted cash inflows}}{\text{Total discounted cash outflows}}$$

Computation of Profitability Index

- Determine the total cash outflow of the project and the time period in which they occur.
- Computed the total discounted cash outflow = outflow × PV factor.
- Determine the total cash inflow of the projected the time period in which they arise.
- Compute the total discounted cash inflow = inflow × PV factor.
- Profitability Index (PI) = $\frac{\text{Total discounted cash inflow}}{\text{Total discounted cash outflow}}$

Illustration The initial cash outlays of a project is ₹ 2,50,000 and it generates cash inflows of ₹ 1,40,000, ₹ 90,000, ₹ 80,000 and ₹ 40,000. Assume a 10% rate of discount. Calculate profitability index.

Solution

Calculation of Profitability Index

Years	CFAT (₹)	DF 10%	Present Value (₹)
1	1,40,000	0.909	1,27,260
2	90,000	0.826	74,340
3	80,000	0.751	60,080
4	40,000	0.683	27,320
PV of Cash Inflows			2,89,000

Profitability Index = PV of cash inflows / Initial investment

= 2,89,000/2,50,000 = 1.156

Since, PI is > 1, hence it can be accepted.

Acceptance Rate

The project/proposal which have PI > 1 should be accepted.

Advantages of Profitability Index

- This method considers time value of money.
- This technique of project evaluation is better than NPV.
- It focuses on maximisation of return on per rupee investment.

Limitations of Profitability Index

- It fails to guide in resolving capital rationing, when projects are indivisible.
- Situations may arise, where project with lower profitability index selected may generate cash flows in such a way that another project can be taken up one or two years later, the total NPV. In such case, being more than one with a project with highest profitability index.

Internal Rate of Return (IRR)

Internal rate of return is the rate where the sum total of discounted cash outflow is equal to total of discounted cash inflow. At this point, the total NPV is zero.

Discounted cash inflows = Discount cash outflows.

Hence, NPV = 0

Computation of Internal Rate of Return

- Determine the total cash outflows and the time period in which they occur.
- Determine the total cash inflows of the project and the time in which they arise.
- Compute the NPV at an arbitrary discount rate.
- Choose another discount rate and compute NPV. The second discount rate is choosen in such a way that if first NPV is positive, then choose higher discount rate and if NPV is negative, then choose lower discount rate.
- Compute the change in NPV over the two selected discounted rates.
- Compute the discount rate on proportionate basic at which NPV is zero.

Illustration Project ALPHA costs ₹ 20,000 and is expected to generate cash inflow of ₹ 12,000, ₹ 8,000 and ₹ 6,000 at the end of each year for next 3 years. Find the IRR of a project.

Solution We know that IRR is the rate at which project will have a zero NPV. As a first step, we try a 20% discount rate. The project's NPV at 20% is ₹ 978, *i.e.* Total amount of present value of cash inflow is ₹ 19,022.

Now, we have to try at a lower rate let's try NPV at a discount rate of 17% it is ₹ 148, *i.e.* Total amount of present value of cash inflow is ₹ 19,852.

The NPV is still less than the present value of cash outflow, so, we will try it at still lower rate. Let's try NPV at a discount rate of 16% it is ₹ 134, *i.e.* total amount of present value of cash inflow is ₹ 20, ₹ 134 it means that the discount rate will fall somewhat in between 16% and 17%.

Now, *we will use interpolation formula*

$$IRR = A + \{(C - O)/(C - D)\} \times (B - D)$$

Where,

A = Discounted factor of low trial	16%
B = Discounted factor of high trial	17%
C = Present value of cash inflow in low trial	₹ 20,134
D = Present value of cash inflow in high trial	₹ 19,852
O = Original or initial outlay	₹ 20,000

$$IRR = 16\% + \{(20{,}134 - 20{,}000)/(20{,}134 - 19{,}852)\} \times (17\% - 16\%) = 16\% + 0.47\% = 16.47\%$$

Advantages of IRR Technique

- It considers time value of money.
- All cash inflows arising at different point of time are considered.
- Decisions are immediately taken by comparing IRR with cost of capital.

Limitations of IRR Technique

- It is tedious to compute in case of multiple cash outflows.
- It may conflicts with NPV, in case inflow/outflow patterns are different alternative proposals.

Modified Internal Rate of Return

The point in favour of internal rate of return is that it is expressed in terms of percentage, but IRR has also been critised on the grounds that it is a percentage that contains the implicit assumption that returns are invested at a rate equal to the IRR. It may not be possible for a firm to reinvest intermediate cash flow at a rate of return equal to the projects internal rate of return. The analysis favouring the use of IRR, but concerned about the impact of the reinvestment debate have provided a Modified Internal Rate of Return (MIRR) or terminal rate of return.

The MIRR of an investment is that rate of compounding, which if applied to the initial outlay produces the terminal value of project returns.

Various Phases of Capital Budgeting Decision-making Process

Capital budgeting is a complex and tedious process. It basically involves planning, availability and controlling allocation and expenditure of long-term investment funds.

Some of the important phases of capital budgeting process are discussed as under

Identification of Potential Investment Opportunities In this phase of budgeting process, financial managers/planners examine various investment opportunities available in the economy. For this purpose, a continuous study is made for new development. This helps the planners in identifying required investments opportunities.

Evaluating the Investment Proposals Identified investment proposals are evaluated and routed through several persons with a view to ensure that the proposals are viewed from different angles. This helps in interrelating and coordinating the diverse activities and selecting the right proposals.

Selecting the Project This is a crucial phase of capital budgeting process. Planners have to select among the available opportunities keeping in tune with the goals of the unit. Normally, planners are vested with the power to clear with investment proposals upto certain limits.

Preparation of Capital Budget and Appropriations Projects are covered by budget appropriation for expeditious. This phase ensures that the funds positions of the firms is sound enough at the time of implementations and it helps in reviewing the project at the time of implementation.

Implementations Investments proposals are put into action after the final selection. For expenditious implementations at a reasonable cost, techniques like CPM, PERT etc may be employed. Principle of responsibility accounting may help to reduces the cost of implementation.

Control and Performance Review This phase involves comparing of actual performance with projected performance. It is a feedback device. It helps in identifying deviations and making timely rectification, if needed.

The capital budgeting process ends with the auditing of expenditure incurred on the project based on the available data, using appropriate forecasting technique or a combination of techniques, the future demand will be estimated.

Technical Appraisal This is to ensure that all the technical aspects related to successful commissioning of projects have been taken care of. *The following issues are considered for technical appraisal*

- Availability of required quality and quantity of raw materials and other inputs.
- Availability of utilisations like power, water etc.
- Appropriateness of plant design and layout.
- The proposed technology *vis-a-vis* the alternative state-of-the-art technologies available.
- Optimality of the scale of operations.
- The technical specification of the plant and machinery in valuations to the proposed technology.
- Assembly line balancing.

Financial Appraisal It looks at the risk and the return, characterising the project and examines whether the risk adjusted return exceeds the cost of financing's the projects. It computes and analyses the data on the cost of the project, means of finance, the projected revenues and costs.

Economic Appraisal It is also called social cost-benefits analysis. This appraisal is done when the proposed project is a government sponsored one. It is to find whether the project is desirable from the social point of view or not.

The issues chiefly considered in this analysis are

- Impact of the projects on the distributions of income in the society.
- Impact of the projects on the level of savings and investments in the society.
- Contribution of the project towards socially desirable objectives like employment generation, self sufficiency etc.

EXAM BASED QUESTIONS

Capital Structure and Cost of Capital

1 ……… refers to make up of a firm's capitalisation.

(a) Capital (b) Capital structure
(c) Funds (d) None of these

2 Modigliani and Miller's dividend policy of a firm is

(a) relevant (b) irrelevant
(c) unrealistic (d) None of these

3 Patterns of capital structure include

(a) only equity shares
(b) Equity shares + Preference shares
(c) Equity shares + Debentures
(d) All of the above

4 Capital structure designing has nothing to do with

(a) profitability (b) solvency
(c) flexibility (d) transferability

5 Cost of depreciation fund is the

(a) explicit cost (b) average cost
(c) implicit cost (d) None of these

6 Retained earning is ……a cost free source of capital.

(a) not (b) sometimes
(c) compulsorily (d) consistently

7 Investment decision include

(a) expansion of existing business
(b) expansion of new business
(c) replacement
(d) All of the above

8 The concept of cost of capital can also be explained in terms of ……… cost.

(a) opportunity (b) variable
(c) fixed (d) capital

9 Cost of capital from all the sources of funds is called

(a) specific cost (b) composite cost
(c) implicit cost (d) simple average cost

10 Transaction costs include

(a) brokerage (b) commission
(c) printing (d) All of these

11 Interest rate risk is a type of

(a) credit risk
(b) market risk
(c) operational risk
(d) All of the above

12 After tax cost of debt capital is calculated by

(a) (1 – tax rate) × C_B (before tax)
(b) C_B (before tax) (1 – tax rate)
(c) (1 – tax rate × C_B (before tax)
(d) None of the above

13 Cost of capital does not mean

(a) cut-off rate decided by management
(b) rate of interest
(c) expectations of investors for dividend
(d) money paid to SEBI for permission to acquire capital

14 A firm's cost of capital is the

(a) overall cost of financing to the firm
(b) cost of bonds
(c) cost of issuing stock
(d) None of the above

15 The cost of issuing new stock is called

(a) the cost of equity
(b) marginal cost of capital
(c) floatation cost
(d) None of these

16 The total accounting value of the capital regularly empolyed in the business is called as

(a) capitalisation (b) overcapitalisation
(c) undercapitalisation (d) None of these

17 Which is not the technique of capital structure analysis?

(a) Trading on equity
(b) Capital gearing
(c) Capital budgeting
(d) Cost of capital

18 Which of the following statement(s) is/are incorrect?

(a) Capital budgeting is not the technique of capital structure analysis
(b) The term 'capital structure' includes also the financial structure
(c) Both (a) and (b)
(d) None of the above

19 Which of the following is/are included under causes of undercapitalisation?

(a) Under estimation of income
(b) Promotion during deflation
(c) Conservative dividend policy
(d) All the above

20 Over capitalisation may not be as a result of which one of the following?

(a) Promotion of a company with inflated assets
(b) Application of low capitalisation rate
(c) Shortage of capital
(d) Liberal dividend policy

21 Which of the following statement(s) is/are incorrect?

(a) Undercapitalisation leads to overcapitalisation
(b) 'Capital' and 'Capitalisation' are synonymous terms
(c) Both (a) and (b)
(d) None of the above

22 **Which of the following statement(s) is/are incorrect?**
(a) According to MM theory, the value of a firm is affected by the debt equity mix
(b) According to MM theory, 'the total value of the firm is static'
(c) Both (a) and (b)
(d) None of the above

23 **Which of the following is not a fundamental assumption made by Modigliani and Miller?**
(a) No taxes
(b) There is imperfect information
(c) Firms can be classified into distinct risk classes
(d) None of the above

24 **The main reasons for adjustments in capital structures include**
(a) to reduce the cost burden
(b) to capitalise the retained earnings
(c) to simplify the capital structure
(d) All of the above

25 **According to which of the following, the firm's market value is not affected by capital structure?**
(a) MM Hypothesis (b) Net Income Approach
(c) The Traditional View (d) None of these

26 **MM theory in perfect market suggests that dividend payment**
(a) has a positive impact on the value of a firm
(b) has no impact on the value of a firm
(c) has a negative impact on the value of a firm
(d) has negligible impact on the firm

27 **Which of the following factor(s) is/are responsible for overcapitalisation?**
(a) High promotion expenses
(b) Liberal dividend policy
(c) Both (a) and (b)
(d) None of the above

28 **The equity shareholders are the residual claimants of all earnings left after meeting all prior**
(a) claims (b) benefits
(c) losses (d) advantageous

29 **Which of the following statement(s) is/are correct?**
(a) The cost of retained earnings is always less than the cost of external equity
(b) The cost of external equity is always less than the cost of retained earnings
(c) The cost of retained earnings is power than the cost of external equity in presence of floatation costs
(d) None of the above

30 **Which of the following statement is correct regarding calculation of weighted cost of capital?**
(a) Retained earnings are always excluded
(b) Preference capital is given more weight
(c) Cost of issue is considered
(d) Weights are always based on the book values

31 **Which of the following statement(s) is/are incorrect?**
(a) Retained earnings have no cost because no interest or dividend is paid on them
(b) Cost of capital means the minimum rate of return, which a company should get on its investment
(c) Both (a) and (b)
(d) None of the above

32 **The concepts of cost of capital is/are very important from which point of view?**
(a) Capital expenditure decisions
(b) Capital structure decisions
(c) Both (a) and (b)
(d) None of the above

33 **The dividend paid on preference share is not deductible expenditure for**
(a) income tax (b) corporate tax
(c) gift tax (d) property tax

34 **Which of the following is not used to estimate cost of equity capital?**
(a) External yield criterion
(b) Dividend plus growth rate
(c) Equity capitalisation approach
(d) Capital asset pricing model

35 **The cost debt financing is generally .... the cost preferred or common equity financing.**
(a) less than
(b) equal to
(c) more than
(d) None of the above

36 **The explicit costs (in case of cost of debt capital) are measured by the interest rate only adjusted by the**
(a) tax rate (b) profit rate
(c) capital/net worth (d) None of these

37 **The overall capitalisation rate and the cost of debt remain constant for all degrees of financial leverage is advocated by**
(a) traditional approach
(b) net income approach
(c) net operating income approach
(d) MM approach

38 **When a company has surplus reserves but does not have adequate liquidity, then the company capitalises its reserves as**
(a) bonus share (b) equity shares
(c) preference shares (d) debt

39 **For calculating the cost of preference shares capital, the dividend of preference share is divided by .... and multiplied by 100.**
(a) net income
(b) net proceeds
(c) net sales
(d) net expenditure

40 Consider the following statements.
In case of overcapitalisation,
1. market value of shares come down from its face value.
2. organisation failed to earn sufficient profit.
Which of the statement(s) given above is/are correct?
Codes
(a) Only 1 (b) Both 1 and 2
(c) Only 2 (d) None of the above

41 "The cost of capital is the minimum rate of return which a firm requires as a condition for undertaking an investment." This definition is given by
(a) Soloman Ezra (b) Milton H Spencer
(c) RM Lynch (d) None of these

Capital Budgeting

42 Capital budgeting is also known as
(a) investments decision-making
(b) capital expenditure decisions
(c) planning capital expenditure
(d) All of the above

43 Which of the following statement is incorrect?
(a) Capital budgeting is the process of making investment decisions in the capital expenditure
(b) Capital budgeting is the process of making investment decisions in fixed assets
(c) Both (a) and (b)
(d) None of the above

44 Which of the following statement is/are correct?
(a) Payback period provides approximation of the rate of return
(b) Where revenues are unequal, discounted cash flow method is used
(c) Accounting rate of return method establishes ratio of average annual profits to total outlay
(d) None of the above

45 Which of the following statement is/are incorrect?
(a) Sometimes, IRR fails to indicate correct choice between mutually exclusive projects
(b) Payback period is widely used since it is a measure of profitability
(c) Both (a) and (b)
(d) None of the above

46 Need for budgeting arise due to
(a) relatively high cost (b) permanent commitment
(c) long-run effect (d) All of these

47 Net peresent value is equal to
(a) Total present value of cash inflow – Total present value of cash outflows
(b) Total present value of cash outflow – Total present value of cash inflows
(c) Total present value of cash outflows + Inflows
(d) None of the above

48 If NPV is positive, the IRR will be
(a) positive (b) K = R
(c) K < R (d) None of these

49 Which of the following statement(s) is/are incorrect?
(a) Cost of capital means the rate of interest at which the capital has been collected
(b) Payback is one of the methods of evaluating investment proposals
(c) Both (a) and (b)
(d) None of the above

50 Capital expenditure is one which is intended to benefits .... periods.
(a) future (b) past
(c) current (d) None of these

51 .... is long-term planning for making and financing proposed capital outlays.
(a) Capital budgeting
(b) Working capital management
(c) Planning for capital
(d) None of the above

52 Where desired rate of return is/are not known, which method of present value technique is adopted?
(a) TAR method
(b) Profitability index
(c) NPV method
(d) None of the above

53 Which of the following statement(s) is/are incorrect?
(a) The system of public deposits is economical
(b) Commercial banks do not grant long-term loans
(c) Both (a) and (b)
(d) All of the above

54 .... method is also known as time adjusted rate of return method.
(a) Account rate of return method
(b) Net present value method
(c) Internal rate of return method
(d) None of the above

55 Which one of the following is not a merit of net present value?
(a) Considers all cash flows
(b) True measures of profitability
(c) Based on the concepts of the time value of money
(d) Requires estimate of cash flows which is a tedious task

56 Which one of the following formulas used for calculating average rate of return?
(a) Average income ÷ Average investments
(b) Average investments ÷ Average income
(c) Income ÷ Capital employed
(d) None of the above

57 Which one of the following points is not a merit of payback period method?
(a) Easy to understand
(b) Emphasises liquidity
(c) Not a measure of probability
(d) Uses cash flow information

58 Which of the following methods does not consider the profitability of the whole life of the project?
(a) Payback period method
(b) Internal rate of return method
(c) Present value index method
(d) Net present value method

59 Which method is a 'crude rule thumb' of capital budgeting?
(a) NPV method
(b) Payback method
(c) Adjusted rate of return method
(d) None of the above

60 Discounted cash flow criteria for investment appraisal does not include
(a) net present value (b) benefit cost ratio
(c) accounting rate of return (d) internal rate of return

61 The forms of discounted cash flow technique for the appraisal of capital investments include
(a) TAR (b) NPV
(c) Both (a) and (b) (d) None of these

62 "Capital budgeting is long-term planning for making and financing proposed capital outlays." This definition is given by
(a) Milton H Spencer (b) RM Lynch
(c) Charles T Horngreen (d) Joel Dean

63 "Capital budgeting is concerned with designing and carrying through a systematic investment programme." Who said it?
(a) Charles T Horngreen
(b) TG Tokhey
(c) RM Lynch
(d) None of these

64 The capital budgeting technique that explicitly incorporates an estimated interest rate into its basic computations is the
(a) payback period method
(b) accounting rate of return method
(c) internal rate of return method
(d) NPV method

65 The capital budgeting generally refers to acquiring inputs with longer run returns. This definition is given by
(a) RM Lynch
(b) Charles T Horngreen
(c) Max D Richards and Paul S Green Law
(d) None of the above

66 The process of allocation or distribution of available capital funds over various capital projects according to their ranks and profitability is called
(a) capital rationing (b) capital budgeting
(c) capital planning (d) None of these

67 Arrange the following in chronological order about the steps of capital budgeting process.
1. Project selection 2. Project evaluation
3. Project generation 4. Project execution
Codes
(a) 3, 2, 1, 4 (b) 3, 1, 2, 4 (c) 2, 3, 4, 1 (d) 4, 3, 2, 1

68 Consider the following statements.
1. Payback period method measures the true profitability of a project.
2. Capital rationing and capital budgeting mean the same thing.
3. Internal rate of return and time adjusted rate of return mean the same thing.
4 Rate of return method takes into account the time value of money.

Which of the statement(s) given above is/are correct?
Codes
(a) 1, 2 and 3 (b) Both 2 and 3
(c) Only 3 (d) All of the above

Miscellaneous

Directions (Q. Nos. 69-78) *The following items consist of two statements, Statement I and Statement II. You have to examine these two statements carefully and select the answer to these items using the codes given below.*
Codes
(a) Both statements are correct
(b) Both statements are incorrect
(c) Statement I is correct, but Statement II is incorrect
(d) Statement I is incorrect, but Statement II is correct

69 **Statement** I Watered stock and overcapitalisation are synonymous.
Statement II Adopting defective depreciation policy causes watered stock.

70 **Statement** I The cost of equity capital is found by relating EPS with its market price.
Statement II Dividend yield method is also known as earnings/price ratio method.

71 **Statement** I Market Price per share ÷ EPS = Dividend ratio.
Statement II EPS ÷ Book value of assets = Normal rate of return.

72 **Statement** I Capital budgeting helps in long-term planning and formulation of policy.
Statement II Capital budgeting highlights the desirability of replacement of men by machines.

73 Statement I Payback period provides approximation of the rate of return.

Statement II Where revenues are unequal, discounted cash flow method is used.

74 Statement I Capital budgeting helps appraisal of the whole business operations.

Statement II Net annual flows can be estimated only when all relevant variables have been estimated.

75 Statement I Opportunity cost is not important in capital expenditure decisions.

Statement II The amount of income tax reduces the profitability and cash inflows of the project.

76 Statement I Capital budgeting is concerned with designing and carrying through a systematic investment program.

Statement II Capital budgeting is the most important in managerial decision-making.

77 Statement I Risk principle of capital structure is one that minimise cost of capital structure.

Statement II According to this principle, reliance is placed more on equity for financial purpose.

78 Statement I The capital structure should involve minimum risk of financial insolvency.

Statement II The use of excessive debt threatens the solvency of the company.

Directions (Q. Nos. 79-95) *In the questions given below are two statements labelled as Assertion (A) and Reason (R). In the context of the two statements, which one of the following is correct?*

Codes

(a) Both (A) and (R) are true and (R) is the correct explanation of (A)
(b) Both (A) and (R) are true, but (R) is not the correct explanation of (A)
(c) (A) is true, but (R) is false
(d) (A) is false, but (R) is true

79 Assertion (A) Businesses having more risks and unstable income should prefer equity shares.

Reason (R) Sales stability and debt ratios are directly related.

80 Assertion (A) The funds invested in capital projects are less permanently blocked.

Reason (R) These investments are of irreversible nature.

81 Assertion (A) Capital budgeting decisions are long-term investment decisions.

Reason (R) It includes expansion decisions, replacement decisions etc.

82 Assertion (A) Urgency method is a subjective technique of making investment decisions.

Reason (R) The projects are selected on the basis of subject matter under this method.

83 Assertion (A) The investment in capital assets is a very important but difficult problem.

Reason (R) Budgeting in itself an essential tool.

84 Assertion (A) Unadjusted rate of return method does not discount the future earnings to present values.

Reason (R) Unadjusted rate of return method considers the time value of earnings.

85 Assertion (A) Capital budgeting is important for the profitability of the concern.

Reason (R) It helps in long-term planning and formulation of policy.

86 Assertion (A) Unadjusted rate of return is a crude rule of thumb.

Reason (R) Payback period method over emphasises early recovery of invested funds.

87 Assertion (A) Trading on equity is a double-edged weapon.

Reason (R) If it is less, it will adversely effect the equity shareholders earnings.

88 Assertion (A) Unadjusted rate of return method ignores the salvage value of the asset.

Reason (R) It is not possible to calculate rate of return by this method.

89 Assertion (A) The risk involved in the business should not be discussed in the beginning.

Reason (R) The business having more risks should issue ownership securities only.

90 Assertion (A) Capitalisation is not an important constituent of the financial plan.

Reason (R) Capitalisation means the total amount of capital distributed.

91 Assertion (A) Overcapitalisation leads to loss of goodwill.

Reason (R) The market value of the shares falls down, which affects adversely the goodwill of the company.

92 Assertion (A) Overcapitalised company finds it difficult in obtaining loans.

Reason (R) It becomes very difficult to get loans at higher rate of interest.

93 Assertion (A) An undercapitalised company fails to pay a fair rate of dividend to its shareholders.

Reason (R) An undercapitalised company tends to neglect welfare facilities of the workers.

94 Assertion (A) Overcapitalisation is caused by over expansion.

Reason (R) Expanding of company more than its financial capacity results in overcapitalisation.

95 Assertion (A) Businesses having more risks and unstable income should not prefer equity shares.
Reason (R) Analysis of determinants of capital structure revolves around the adequacy and stability of earnings.

96 Match the following.

List I	List II
A. Net income approach	1. Also known as 'Intermediate Approach'
B. Net operating income approach	2. Change in the capital structure of a company does not affect the market value of the company and overall cost of capital
C. Traditional approach	3. It provide analytical sound and logically consistent behavioural justification for their hypothesis
D. Modigliani Miller approach	4. A firm can minimise the overall cost of capital by using debt financing to the maximum extent

Codes

	A	B	C	D		A	B	C	D
(a)	4	2	1	3	(b)	2	1	4	3
(c)	3	4	1	2	(d)	2	1	3	4

97 Match the following.

List I (Capital Structure Principles)	List II (Features)
A. Cost principle	1. Management chooses such combination of sources of financing, which can easily adapt to changes
B. Risk principle	2. While designing the structure, the finance manager remembers that existing management control and ownership remains undisturbed
C. Control principle	3. Reliance is placed more on equity for financing capital requirements than excessive use of debts
D. Flexibility principle	4. Cost of capital structure should be minimised and Earning Per Share (EPS) should be maximised

Codes

	A	B	C	D		A	B	C	D
(a)	2	1	4	3	(b)	3	2	4	1
(c)	3	4	1	2	(d)	4	3	2	1

98 Match the following.

List I (Measurements of Cost of Capital)	List II (Features)
A. Cost of debt	1. Its calculation is relatively difficult task
B. Cost of preference share capital	2. The amount of interest payment should be matched with the net cash proceeds of the debt
C. Cost of equity share capital	3. The shareholders have to incur some brokerage cost for investing the dividends received
D. Cost of retained earnings	4. The rate of dividend payable on these shares is fixed well in advance at the time of their issue

Codes

	A	B	C	D		A	B	C	D
(a)	4	3	1	2	(b)	2	3	4	1
(c)	3	4	2	1	(d)	2	4	1	3

99 Match the following.

List I	List II
A. Urgency method	1. It avoids in calculable risk and uncertainty in the long run
B. Payback method	2. Also known as net gain method
C. Unadjusted rate of return method	3. It is simple for the project with too large outlay
D. Net present value method	4. Also known as financial statement method

Codes

	A	B	C	D		A	B	C	D
(a)	4	3	2	1	(b)	3	1	4	2
(c)	2	3	4	1	(d)	3	4	1	2

100 Match the following.

List I	List II
A. Payback method	1. Give due weightage to the profitability of project
B. Unadjusted rate of return method	2. Predetermination of earnings is not necessary
C. NPV method	3. It avoids in calculable risk and uncertainty
D. IRR method	4. Its calculation is much simpler

Codes

	A	B	C	D		A	B	C	D
(a)	4	3	2	1	(b)	2	3	4	1
(c)	3	1	4	2	(d)	4	1	2	3

101 Match the following.

List I	List II
A. Capital budgeting	1. Time adjusted rate of return
B. Profitability index	2. Irreversible
C. Internal rate of return	3. Benefit/cost
D. Capital investment decisions	4. Planning capital expenditure

Codes

	A	B	C	D		A	B	C	D
(a)	4	3	2	1	(b)	1	4	2	3
(c)	4	3	1	2	(d)	2	1	3	4

102 Match the following.

	List I		List II
A.	Fixed capital	1.	........refers to make-up of a firm's capitalisation
B.	Normal rate of return	2.	.... is the cause of over-capitalisation
C.	Liberal dividend policy	3.	Earnings per share ÷ Market price per share = ...
D.	Capital structure	4.	.... is the funds required for a acquisition of assets that are to be used over and over a long period

Codes

	A	B	C	D		A	B	C	D
(a)	4	3	2	1	(b)	2	1	3	4
(c)	3	2	1	4	(d)	2	3	1	4

103 Match the following.

	List I (Concepts)		List II (Disadvantages)
A.	Undercapitalisation	1.	Ignores time patterns of returns
B.	Overcapitalisation	2.	Increase in speculative activities
C.	Profit maximisation	3.	Decline in value of securities

Codes

	A	B	C		A	B	C
(a)	3	1	2	(b)	1	2	3
(c)	3	2	1	(d)	2	3	1

PREVIOUS YEARS' QUESTIONS

December 2018

1 Which of the following sources of finance has an implicit cost of capital?
(a) Equity share capital
(b) Preference share capital
(c) Debentures
(d) Retained earnings

2 Which of the following variables is not known in internal rate of return method of capital budgeting?
(a) Amount of cash inflows
(b) Life of the project
(c) Amount of cash outflows
(d) Discount rate

July 2018

3 Which one of the following methods of capital budgeting assumes that cash inflows are reinvested at the project's rate of return?
(a) Net Present Value
(b) Accounting Rate of Return
(c) Internal Rate of Return
(d) Discounted Payback Period

4 Cost of equity share capital is more than cost of debt because
(a) equity shares are not easily saleable
(b) equity shares do not provide the fixed dividend rate
(c) generally the face value of equity shares is less than the face value of debentures
(d) equity shares have high risk than debts

5 Which of the following is an implicit cost of increasing proportion of debt of a company?
(a) PE ratio of the company would increase
(b) Rate of return of the company would decrease
(c) Tax shield would not be available on new debts
(d) Equity shareholders would demand higher return

6 Which of the following is not an approach to the capital structure?
(a) Gross Profit approach
(b) Net Operating Income approach
(c) Net Income approach
(d) Modigliani and Miller approach

November 2017

7 Which of the following statement is false ?
(a) The opportunity cost of an input is considered in capital budgeting
(b) Capital budgeting decisions are reversible in nature
(c) Cash flows and accounting profits are different
(d) An expansion decision is a capital budgeting decision

8 Which one of the following is not a method of calculating cost of equity capital ?
(a) Dividend yield method
(b) Dividend yield plus growth method
(c) Yield to maturity method
(d) Earnings yield method

9 Which one of the following equates the present value of cash out flows and the present value of expected cash inflows from a project ?
(a) Net Present Value
(b) Internal Rate of Return
(c) Payback Period
(d) Accounting Rate of Return

10 **Statement** I In payback period method, the risk of the project is adjusted by lessening the target payback period.

Statement II Sensitivity analysis helps in calculation of net present value of the proposal.

Codes
(a) Statement I is correct, but Statement II is wrong
(b) Statement I is wrong, but Statement II is correct
(c) Both statements are correct
(d) Both statement are wrong

January 2017

11 Which of the following statement is not correct ?

(a) The cost of capital is required rate of return to ascertain the value of the firm
(b) Different sources of funds have a specific cost of capital related to that source only
(c) Cost of capital does not comprise any risk premium
(d) Cost of capital is basic data for NPV technique

12 Which of the following is not true with reference to capital budgeting?

(a) Capital budgeting is related to asset replacement decisions
(b) Cost of capital is equal to minimum required rate of return
(c) Timing of cash flows is relevant
(d) Existing investment in a project is not treated as sunk cost

July 2016

13 From the following techniques of capital budgeting decision, indicate the correct combination of discounting techniques.

1. Profitability index
2. Net present value
3. Accounting rate of return
4. Internal rate of return

Codes

(a) 1, 2, 3 (b) 2, 3, 4
(c) 1, 2, 4 (d) 1, 3, 4

14 Which of the following is not a feature of payback period method?

(a) It is simply a method of cost recovery and not of profitability
(b) It does not consider the time value of money
(c) It does not consider the risk associated with the projects
(d) It is very difficult to calculate

December 2015

15 A company has issued 10% perpetual debt of ₹ 1,00,000 at 5% premium. If tax rate is 30%, then the cost of debt will be

(a) 10% (b) 15%
(c) 6.66% (d) 8.21%

16 The term 'capital structure' implies

(a) Share capital + Reserves + Long-term debts
(b) Share capital + Long and short-term debts
(c) Share capital+ Long-term debts
(d) Equity and preference share capital

17 From investor's point of view, the cost of capital is

(a) interest rate
(b) market value
(c) yield of capital sacrifice
(d) stock exchange value

18 Formula for net cash inflow of a project is

(a) Sales – Operating expenses – Interest – Tax
(b) Sales – Operating expenses
(c) Net profit after tax + Depreciation
(d) Gross profit + Depreciation

19 In case, cost of capital is 10%, EPS ₹ 10, IRR 8% and retention ratio is 60%, then the value of equity share as per Gordon's Model will be

(a) ₹ 100 (b) ₹ 87 (c) ₹ 90 (d) ₹ 77

June 2015

20 Which of the following techniques for appraisal of investment proposals are based on time value of money?

1. Accounting rate of return
2. Internal rate of return
3. Profitability index method
4. Earnings per share

Select the correct answer using the codes given below

Codes

(a) Both 1 and 2 (b) Both 2 and 3
(c) Both 1 and 4 (d) 1, 2 and 4

21 Which of the following is not true with reference to capital budgeting?

(a) Capital budgeting is related to asset replacement decisions
(b) Cost of capital is equal to minimum required return
(c) Existing investment in a project is not treated as sunk cost
(d) Timing of cash flows is relevant

22 In capital budgeting, the term 'capital rationing' implies

(a) that no retained earnings are available
(b) that limited funds are available for investment
(c) that no external funds can be raised
(d) that no fresh investment is required in current year

23 In certainty equivalent approach, adjusted cash flows are discounted at

(a) accounting rate of return (b) internal rate of return
(c) hurdle rate (d) risk free rate

December 2014

24 Match the following.

	List I		List II
A.	Payback rate of return	1.	Discounted cash flow technique
B.	Internal rate of return	2.	Compounded values of investments and returns
C.	Benefit cost ratio	3.	Crude method for project evaluation
D.	Net terminal value method	4.	Varying sized projects evaluation

Codes

	A	B	C	D		A	B	C	D
(a)	2	3	1	4	(b)	3	1	4	2
(c)	1	4	2	3	(d)	4	2	3	1

25 Match the following.

List I	List II
A. Realised yield method	1. Cost of equity share capital
B. Taxation	2. Cost of equity capital
C. Cost of total capital employed	3. Cost of debt capital
D. Dividend growth is a consideration	4. Weighted cost of capital

Codes

	A	B	C	D		A	B	C	D
(a)	4	3	2	1	(b)	2	4	1	3
(c)	2	3	4	1	(d)	1	2	3	4

26 **Assertion** (A) Arbitrage keeps the cost of capital constant despite change in the capital structure.

Reason (R) It ensures compensating inverse change in cost of equity capital with a change in the cost of debt capital.

Codes

(a) (A) and (R) both are true and (R) is the correct explanation of (A)
(b) (A) and (R) both are true, but (R) is not the correct explanation of (A)
(c) (A) is true, but (R) is false
(d) (A) is not true, but (R) is true

June 2014

27 Indicate the cost of equity capital based on capital asset pricing model with the following information. Beta coefficient 1.40 Risk free rate of interset 9% Expected rate of return on equity in the market 16%

(a) 98% (b)18% (c)18.8% (d) 16%

28 **Assertion** (A) When two or more investment proposals are mutually exclusive, ranking the proposals on the basis of IRR, NPV and PI methods may give contradictory results.

Reason (R) The contradictory results in the ranking are due to differing dimensions relating to the sacle of investments, cash flow patterns and project lives.

Codes

(a) Both (A) and (R) are true
(b) (A) is true, but (R) is a necessary condition, but not a sufficient condition
(c) Both (A) and (R) are false
(d) Both (A) and (R) are true and (R) is the correct explanation of (A)

29 Interim cash inflows are reinvested at a rate of return equal to the internal rate of return is the built-in mechanism for

(a) net present value method
(b) internal rate of return method
(c) profitablity index method
(d) None of the above

December 2013

30 Which one of the following is the most popular method for estimating the cost of equity?

(a) Capital asset pricing model
(b) Dividend yield method
(c) Gordon's dividend discount model
(d) Earnings yield method

31 Which one of the following is not the internal factor affecting the weighted average cost of capital of a firm?

(a) Investment policy of the firm
(b) Capital structure of the firm
(c) Dividend policy followed
(d) Market risk premium for the firm

32 **Assertion** (A) The IRR of a project is the discount rate which reduces its NPV to zero.

Reason (R) A project is worth accepting if the IRR exceeds the cost of capital.

Codes

(a) (A) is true, but (R) is false
(b) Both (A) and (R) are true
(c) (A) is false, but (R) is true
(d) Both (A) and (R) are false

June 2013

33 Positive NPV in project appraised by a firm may not occur an account of

(a) economics of scale (b) market research
(c) product differentiation (d) intangible benefits

34 In case, the projects are divided under capital rationing an appropriate project appraisal method is

(a) net present value method
(b) profitability index method
(c) internal rate of return method
(d) payback period method

June 2012

35 Which one refers to cash inflow under payback period method?

(a) Cash flow before depreciation and taxes
(b) Cash flow after depreciation and taxes
(c) Cash flow after depreciation, but before taxes
(d) Cash flow before depreciation and after taxes

36 The concept of present value is based on the

(a) principle of compounding (b) principle of discounting
(c) Both (a) and (b) (d) None of these

37 Cost of capital from all the sources of funds is called

(a) specific cost (b) composite cost
(c) implicit cost (d) simple average cost

38 The conflicts in project ranking in capital budgeting as per NPV and IRR may arise because of

(a) size disparity (b) time disparity
(c) life disparity (d) All of these

ANSWERS

Objective Questions

1 (b)	2 (b)	3 (d)	4 (b)	5 (d)	6 (a)	7 (d)	8 (a)	9 (a)	10 (a)
11 (b)	12 (c)	13 (d)	14 (a)	15 (c)	16 (b)	17 (c)	18 (b)	19 (d)	20 (c)
21 (a)	22 (a)	23 (b)	24 (d)	25 (a)	26 (b)	27 (c)	28 (a)	29 (c)	30 (c)
31 (b)	32 (c)	33 (b)	34 (d)	35 (a)	36 (a)	37 (c)	38 (a)	39 (b)	40 (d)
41 (b)	42 (d)	43 (c)	44 (c)	45 (b)	46 (d)	47 (a)	48 (c)	49 (a)	50 (a)
51 (a)	52 (a)	53 (b)	54 (c)	55 (d)	56 (a)	57 (c)	58 (a)	59 (b)	60 (b)
61 (c)	62 (c)	63 (a)	64 (d)	65 (c)	66 (a)	67 (a)	68 (b)	69 (d)	70 (c)
71 (d)	72 (a)	73 (b)	74 (a)	75 (d)	76 (c)	77 (d)	78 (a)	79 (a)	80 (d)
81 (a)	82 (b)	83 (a)	84 (c)	85 (a)	86 (d)	87 (a)	88 (b)	89 (d)	90 (c)
91 (a)	92 (c)	93 (b)	94 (a)	95 (d)	96 (a)	97 (d)	98 (d)	99 (b)	100 (c)
101 (c)	102 (a)	103 (d)							

Previous Years' Questions

1 (d)	2 (d)	3 (c)	4 (d)	5 (d)	6 (a)	7 (b)	8 (c)	9 (b)	10 (a)
11 (c)	12 (d)	13 (a)	14 (d)	15 (c)	16 (a)	17 (c)	18 (c)	19 (d)	20 (b)
21 (b)	22 (d)	23 (b)	24 (b)	25 (c)	26 (a)	27 (c)	28 (b)	29 (b)	30 (a)
31 (d)	32 (b)	33 (d)	34 (b)	35 (b)	36 (b)	37 (a)	38 (d)		

CHAPTER 15

Working Capital and Dividend Policy

The funds needed for short-term purposes for purchase of raw materials, payment of wages etc are known as working capital. Shareholders are the owners of the company which provide capital, bear the risk. Thus, they expect a fair return in the form of dividend from the management of the company.

Working Capital

Working capital is amount required to carry out in day-to-day operations.

It can be calculated as

Working capital = Current assets – Current liabilities

Current Assets are those, which can be converted into cash within short duration, *i.e.* generally less than 1 year. It includes inventory, debtors, cash and bank balances, prepaid expenses, loans and advances and marketable investments.

Current Liabilities are those, which fall due for payment or settlement within a short duration, *i.e.* generally less than 1 year. It includes creditors, outstanding expenses, tax provisions, proposed and unclaimed dividend, short-term loans, bank overdraft and cash credit.

In the broad sense, the term 'working capital' is used to denote the 'total current assets'.

According to **Weston** and **Brigham**, "Working capital refers to a firm's investment in short-term assets, cash, short-term securities, accounts receivable and inventories."

According to **Bonneville**, "Any acquisition of funds, which increases the current assets increases working capital also, for they are one and the same."

According to **JS Mill**, "The sum of the current assets is the working capital of a business."

In the narrow sense, the working capital is regarded as the excess of current assets over current liabilities.

In this Chapter

- *Working Capital*
- *Dividend Policy*
- *Dividend Theories*

Classification of Working Capital

Working capital can be classified either on the basis of its concept or on the basis of periodicity of its requirements. *These are as follows*

Based on Concept

On the basis of its concept, it may be either gross working capital or net working capital. *These are*

Gross Working **Capital** In the broad sense, the term working capital refers to the gross working capital and represents the amount of funds invested in current assets.

Gross working capital
= Only current assets of the enterprises

Net Working Capital In the narrow sense, the term working capital refers to the net working capital. Net working capital is the excess of current assets over current liabilities.

Net working capital = Current assets – Current liabilities

Based on Periodicity of Requirement

On the basis of time and requirement, working capital may be classified into two categories, *which are as follows*

Permanent Working Capital It is the minimum level of investment required in the business. Investment or minimum current asset such as inventory, book debts, cash balance should always be there to facilitate uninterrupted operation in a firm. Tondon Committee has referred this type of working capital as 'hardcore working capital'.

Temporary Working Capital Temporary or variable working capital is the amount of working capital which is required to meet the seasonal demands and some special exigencies. The capital required to meet the seasonal needs of the enterprise is called seasonal working capital. Special working capital which is required to meet special exigencies such as launching of extensive marketing campaigns for conducting research etc.

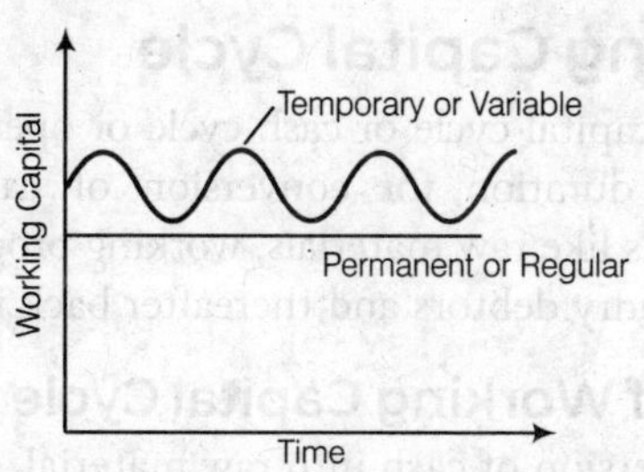

Working Capital for a Stable Operation Level

The above figure depicts the permanent or regular working capital that is stable over a period, whereas temporary or variable working capital is oscillating, or showing ups and down.

Factors Affecting Working Capital

Nature and Size of Business

The effect of the general nature of the business on working capital requirements cannot be exaggerated. Rail roads and other public utility services have large fixed investment, so they have the lower requirements for current assets. Industrial and manufacturing enterprises, on the other hand, generally require a large amount of working capital. The need of working capital for a large business are more than those of a small business.

Production Policies

If the production is evenly spreaded over the entire year, working capital requirements are greater because the inventories will be unnecessarily accumulated during off season period. But if production schedule favours a varying production plan as per seasonal requirements, working capital requirement will be high only in seasons.

Length of Period of Manufacturing Process

The time which elapses between the commencement and end of the manufacturing process has an important bearing upon the requirements of working capital. If it takes long to manufacture the finished product, naturally a large sum of money will have to be kept invested in the form of working capital.

Rapidity of Turnover

Turnover represents the speed with which the working capital is recovered by the sale of goods. In certain business, sales are made quickly so that stocks are soon exhausted and new purchases have to be made. In this manner, a small sum of money invested in stocks will result in sales of a much large amount. It will reduce the requirements of more working capital.

Credit Policy

If the company allows liberal credit to its customers, high amount would be invested in debtors. On the other hand, if no credit is allowed or the debt collection system is efficient, lesser working capital would be required.

Terms of Purchases

If continuous credit is allowed by suppliers, payment can be postponed for some time and can be made out of the sale proceeds of the goods produced. In such a case, the requirements of working capital will be reduced. If the company does not enjoy liberal credit facilities, large amount of working capital would be required.

Dividend Policy of Concern

If a conservative dividend policy is followed by the management, the needs of working capital can be met with the retained earnings. Often, variations in need of working capital bring about an adjustment in dividend policy. The relationship between dividend policy and working capital is well established and mostly company declare dividend after a careful study of their cash requirements.

Determinants of Working Capital

S.No.	Factors	High Working Capital	Low or Moderate Working Capital
1.	Production policy	High production during peak season requires high amount of working capital	Uniform production over the year
2.	Production process	Labour intensive process	Capital intensive process
3.	Nature of business	Manufacturing concerns	Trading concerns
4.	Credit policy	Liberal credit policy and low efforts for debtors follow-up	Strict credit policy and efficient credit collection mechanism
5.	Length of manufacturin g process	Long manufacturing process or production cycle	Short and quick manufacturing process, more bathrooms etc
6.	Inventory policy	High shortage period or stock holding period	Just in time inventory policy and moderate shareholding period
7.	Market condition	Fierce competition or Buyer's market	Seller's market - quick disposal of stocks and immediate collection of receivables
8.	Business cycle	During peak or boom conditions	During moderately active conditions
9.	Market standing	In case of highly inflationary conditions	For moderate and mild inflationary conditions
10.	Inflationary	Newly established concerns credit sales are made, but purchases are settled in cash	Reputed and established companies' better and advantageous credit term with debtors and supplies

Management of Working Capital

Working capital management is the functional area of finance that covers all the current accounts of its firm. It is a matter of balance.

A firm must have sufficient cash in hand to meet its immediate needs while ensuring that idle cash is invested to the organisations in the best possible advantage. Sound financial and statistical techniques, supported by judgement should be used to predict the quantum of working capital required at different times.

The various steps in the management of working capital involve

Cash Management Identify the cash balance, which allows for a business to meet day-to-day expenses, but reduces cash holding costs.

Inventory Management Identify the level inventory, which allows for uninterrupted production, but reduces the investment in raw materials and hence increases cash flow; the techniques like Just in Time (JIT) and economic order quantity are used for this.

Debtors Management Identify the appropriate credit policy. The tools like discounts and allowances are used for this.

Short-term Financing Inventory is ideally financed by credit granted by the suppliers dependent on the cash conversion cycle. It may however, be necessary to utilise a bank loan or to convert debtors to cash through factoring in order to finance working capital requirement.

Major Consideration in Working Capital Management and Policies

The three major considerations in working capital management are

- Profitability
- Liquidity
- Structural health

If amount of working capital is high, liquidity is high, but due to low capital turnover ratio, the return on investment or profitability will also be low.

Similarly, if the amount of working capital is less, a higher turnover indicates high profitability. But liquidity may be seriously affected causing loss of reputation in the short-term.

Also, the structural health of the firm on the long-term and short-term basis depends upon the optimum amount of working capital. Hence, the finance manager has to spike a balance between liquidity and profitability without affecting the structural health of the firm.

Working Capital Cycle

Working capital cycle or cash cycle or operating cycle is the time duration for conversion of cash into cash equivalents like raw materials, working progress, finished goods, sundry debtors and thereafter back into cash.

Steps of Working Capital Cycle

- Conversion of cash into raw material. ***Lead time***
- Conversion of raw material into work-in-progress and then to finished goods. ***Production/Process cycle***
- Conversion of finished goods into debtors through sales. ***Stock holding period***
- Conversion of receivables into cash. ***Average collection period***

Computation of Operating Cycle

Operating cycle is computed in terms of number of days (or sometimes in months).

Operating cycle = Raw material storage period + Work-in-progress holding period + Finished goods storage period + Debtors collection period – Creditors payment period.

Financing of Long-term Working Capital

The long-term working capital requirements include the initial working capital and the regular working capital.

This capital can be conveniently financed by the following sources

Issue of Shares A part of long-term working capital can be financed by issue of shares.

Issue of Debentures Debentures are also an important source of long-term working capital because they are fixed cost source.

Term Loans It is also an important source of working capital in which loans are raised for a period varying from 3 to 5-7 years.

Retained Profits Some part of the earned profits may be retained by the firm to meet its working capital requirements. This source does not involve any explicit cost of capital, so it is a regular and cheapest source of financing long-term working capital.

Sale of Idle Fixed Assets The sale proceeds of the idle fixed asset can be utilised for financing the working capital requirements.

Financing of Short-term Working Capital

This category of funds covers the need of working capital for financing day-to-day business requirements. The sources of short-term working capital may be internal as well as external, *which are as follows*

Internal Sources

Accrued Expenses It also constitutes an important source of working capital as the firm can postpone the payment of expenses for short periods.

Depreciation Funds It can also constitute an important source of working capital.

Provision for Taxation It can also be used by the companies as a source of working capital during the intermident period.

External Sources

Public Deposits Public deposits are also an important source of short-term and medium-term finance. They have been very popular among Indian companies.

Trade Credit It is one of the most important forms of short-term finance extended by one business enterprise to another on the purchase and sale of goods and equipment. It may also assume three forms, *i.e.* purchase on open account, purchase on furnishing a promote for specified period and purchase on trade acceptance.

Credit Papers In this source, bills of exchange and promissory notes of shorter duration varying between a month and six months are used. These papers are discounted with a bank or sold to commercial paper houses or can be endorsed to the creditors and capital can be arranged.

Bank Credit Commercial Banks provide working capital in a number of ways such as everdrafts, cash credit etc. So, they are considered as a principal source of working capital. This is the most flexible and widely used source because when the debt is no longer required it can be quickly and early reduced. It is also comparatively cheap.

Security of Employees If employees are required to make deposits with their employer companies, such companies can utilise those amounts in meeting their working capital needs.

Various Components of Working Capital

Component	Formula	Formula based on Turnover
Raw material storage period	$\frac{\text{Average stock of raw material}}{\text{Average cost of raw material per day}}$	$\frac{365}{\text{Raw material turnover ratio}}$
Work-in-progress holding period	$\frac{\text{Average stock of work-in-progress}}{\text{Average cost of production per day}}$	$\frac{365}{\text{Work-in-progress turnover ratio}}$
Finished goods storage period	$\frac{\text{Average of finished goods}}{\text{Average cost of goods sold per day}}$	$\frac{365}{\text{Finished goods turnover ratio}}$
Debtors collection period	$\frac{\text{Average account receivables}}{\text{Average credit sales per day}}$	$\frac{365}{\text{Debtors turnover ratio}}$
Creditors payment period	$\frac{\text{Average accounts payable}}{\text{Average credit purchases per day}}$	$\frac{365}{\text{Creditors turnover ratio}}$

Approaches of Financing Working Capital Requirements

	Name of Approach Basis	Matching Approach	Conservative Approach	Aggressive Approach
1.	Long-term funds	Fixed assets and permanent working capital	Fixed assets, permanent working capital and part of temporary working capital	Fixed asset and part of permanent working capital
2.	Short-term funds	Temporary working capital	Balance of temporary working capital	Balance of permanent working capital and entire temporary working capital
3.	Impact on liquidity	Comparatively well balanced	High liquidity	Low liquidity
4.	Impact on profitability	Comparatively well balanced	Low profitability and return on assets	High return on assets, but risky

MPBF

MPBF stands for Maximum Permissible Bank Finance, *i.e.* the maximum amount that bank can lend a borrower towards his working capital requirements.

The RBI had constituted various study groups/committee to study the trends of working capital financing by banks and recommend the norms to be followed in lending. The recommendations of the Tondon Committee (formed in July, 1974) have had far reaching impact in lending approach.

MPBF is based on Tondon's Committee's recommendations.

This committee suggested three different methods of computing the MPBF

Method I MPBF 75% of (Current assets – Current liabilities)

Method II MPBF (75% of Current assets) – (Current liabilities)

Method III MPBF = (75% of Fluctuating current assets) – Current liabilities

The comittee suggested gradual shift from *Method I* to *Method III* in order to make, the borrower more self-reliant in financing his working capital requirements.

Control over Working Capital

It goes without saying that the working capital quantum as well as its financing pattern are subject to constant monitoring and review by the financial manager. There are different analytical tools which can helps a financial manager in monitoring, reviewing and controlling the working capital.

Some of which are as follows

Monitoring the Operating Cycle

It is already noted that the total working capital need depends upon the length of the operating cycle. The longer the operating cycle, the greater would be the working capital need. The operating cycle of a firm is consisting of different for different elements of working capital. Therefore, the financial managers must monitor the duration of all these individual operating cycles for different elements in order to effectively control the working capital.

Working Capital Ratio

Another analytical tools that can be used to monitor the working capital is the accounting ratios, particularly the working capital ratios.

For this purpose, the following working capital ratios may be noted

- Current ratio, *i.e.* current assets to current liabilities ratio.
- Liquid ratio, *i.e.* quick assets to current liabilities ratio.
- Current assets to total assets ratio.
- Current assets to total sales ratio.

These ratio may be ascertained for a number of years to find out the emerging working capital position of the firm.

Dividend Policy

The term 'dividend' refers to that part of profits of a company, which is distributed by a company among its shareholders. It is reward of the shareholders for investment made by them in the shares of a company. The investors are interested in earning the maximum return on their investments and to maximise their wealth.

A company on the other hand, needs to provide funds to finance its long-term growth. If a company pay out as dividend most of what it earns then for business requirements and further expansion, it will have to depend upon outside resources such as issue of debt or new shares. Dividend policy affects both the long-term financing and wealth of shareholders.

Types of Dividend Policy

Regular Dividend Policy

Payment of dividend at the usual rate is termed as regular dividend. The investors such as retired persons, widows and other economically maker persons prefer to get regular dividends.

Stable Dividend Policy

The term stability of dividends means consistency or lack of variability in the stream of dividend payments.

It may be established in three forms

Constant Dividend Per Share Some companies follow a policy of paying fixed dividend per share irrespective of the level of earning year after year. Such firms usually create a reserve for dividend equalisation, to enable them pay the fixed dividend even in the year when the earning are not sufficient.

Constant PayOut Ratio It means payment of a fixed percentage of net earnings as dividend every year. The amount of dividends in such a policy. Fluctuates in direct proportion to the earnings of the company.

Stable Rupee Dividend Plus Extra Dividend Some companies follow a policy of paying constant low dividend per share plus an extra dividend in the years of high profits.

Irregular Dividends Policy

Some companies follow irregular dividend payment on account of the following

- Uncertainty of earnings.
- Unsuccessful business operations.
- Lack of liquid resources.
- Fear of adverse effects of regular dividends on the financial standing of the company.

No Dividend Policy

A company may follow a policy of paying no dividend presently because of its unfavourable working capital positions or an account of requirement of funds for future expansions and growth.

Dividend Models/Theories

Walters' Model

This model is given by **Prof Walter** in 1963. According to this, a company's dividend policy affects the wealth of the shareholders. As per Walter's model, the dividend policy of a company is based upon the Internal Rate of Return (IRR) and cost of capital thus, *the market price of a share can be determined as follows*

$$P = \frac{D}{K_e} + \frac{y(E-D)/K_e}{K_e}$$ Where,

P = Market price per share

y = IRR

K_e = Capitalisation rate

D = Dividend per share

E = Earning per share

Gordon's Model

This model is given by **Prof Gordon**. According to this, the dividend decisions of a firm affects its value and market value of a share is equal to the present value of its expected future divdends. Thus,

Market value of a share can be determined as follows

$$P = \frac{D}{K_e - g}$$

Or

$$= \frac{E(1-b)}{K_e - b_y}$$

Where,

P= Price per share

E = Earning per share

b = Retention ratio

g = Growth rate or rate of return on investment of all equity firms

D = Dividend per share

K_e = Cost of equity capital

Modigliani and Miller Model

According to this model, the value of the company remains unaffected by the dividend policy of the company. It is the earnings potential and the investment opportunities available to the company which affects its value and not the dividend policy. The market price of a share at the end of the year can be determined as follows

$$P_1 = P_0(1 + K_e) - D_1$$

Where,

P_1 = Market price per share at the end of the period

D_1 = Dividend to be received at the end of the period

K_e = Cost of equity capital or capitalisation rate

EXAM BASED QUESTIONS

Working Capital

1 The financial analysts says, working capital means the same things as
(a) current assets – current liabilities
(b) fixed assets
(c) total assets
(d) current assets

2 Which is not the long-term source of working capital?
(a) Retained earnings (b) Long-term debts
(c) Issue of shares (d) Provision for taxation

3 Total of all current assets is called
(a) gross working capital (b) net working capital
(c) fixed working capital (d) None of these

4 Net working capital is the excess of current assets over
(a) total liabilities (b) current liabilities
(c) intangible liabilities (d) None of these

5 The working capital ratio is
(a) Working capital + Sales
(b) Working capital + Total assets
(c) Current assets + Sales
(d) Current assets + Current liabilities

6 Which of the following is/are the source(s) of short-term finance?
(a) Trade credit (b) Bank credit
(c) Short-term borrowings (d) All of these

7 Which of the following is/are not a current asset?
(a) Land and building (b) B/R
(c) Debtors (d) All of these

8 When supplier extend credit to the buyer, it is called
(a) trade credit (b) instalment credit
(c) Both (a) and (b) (d) None of these

9 Investment in machines require
(a) short-term finance (b) long-term finance
(c) Both (a) and (b) (d) None of these

10 Long-term loans from the public is called
(a) debentures (b) retained earnings
(c) shares (d) public deposits

11 Working capital(s) is/are also called
(a) revolving capital (b) circulating capital
(c) Both (a) and (b) (d) None of these

12 A business concern should not have
(a) inadequate working capital
(b) excess working capital
(c) Both (a) and (b)
(d) None of the above

13 Three forms of trade credit include
(a) purchase on open account
(b) purchasing on furnishing a promote for specified period
(c) purchase on trade acceptance
(d) All of the above

14 "Hardcore working capital" is also called
(a) variable working capital
(b) permanent working capital
(c) gross working capital
(d) net working capital

15 Every business undertaking requires funds for
(a) investment in fixed assets
(b) investment in current assets
(c) Both (a) and (b)
(d) None of the above

16 Advantages of adequate working capital funds include
(a) cash discount (b) liquidity and solvency
(c) high morale (d) All of these

17 Net working capital = ... – Current liabilities
(a) Current assets (b) Fixed assets
(c) Stock (d) Bill receivable

18 The amount of current assets required to meet a firm's long-term minimum need is referred to as .... working capital.
(a) permanent (b) net
(c) temporary (d) gross

19 Which of the following would not be financed from working capital?
(a) Cash float
(b) A new personal computer for the office
(c) Credit sales
(d) Accounts receivable

20 Which of the following statements is/are incorrect?
(a) Retained earnings as a source of financing is most useful for a new company
(b) The terms 'permanent working capital' and 'core current assets' have synonymous meanings
(c) Both (a) and (b)
(d) None of the above

21 Arrange the following in chronological order about the events of operating cycle.
1. Conversion of accounts receivable into cash.
2. Conversion of finished goods into accounts receivable.
3. Conversion of raw materials into work-in-process.
4. Conversion of work-in-process into finished goods.

Codes
(a) 3,4,2,1 (b) 3,1,4,2
(c) 4,3,2,1 (d) 1,3,2,4

22 Operating cycle can be shortened by increasing
(a) manufacturing time
(b) duration of credit available
(c) stock held in stores shares
(d) credit period to the customers

23 Which is the most popular technique of working capital forecast?
(a) Cash forecasting method
(b) Adjusted profit and loss method
(c) Both (a) and (b)
(d) None of the above

24 Which of the following statement is incorrect?
(a) If the company allows liberal credit to its customers, high amount would be invested in debtors
(b) The needs of working capital for a large business is less than these of a small business
(c) Working capital requirement will be high only in seasons
(d) None of the above

25 Which of the following statement is/are correct?
(a) Public deposits have been very popular among Indian companies
(b) Central and State Governments provide short-term finance on easy terms
(c) Both (a) and (b)
(d) All of the above

26 Which of the following is not an application of working capital?
(a) Day-to-day expenditure of business
(b) Current obligations for payment
(c) Expenditure in the usual course of business
(d) Expenditure to acquire capital

27 Arrange the following terms of working capital cycle involves in correct sequence.
1. Acquisition of raw material
2. Finished goods
3. Receivables
4. Cash
5. Work-in-progress

Codes
(a) 4, 3, 1, 5, 2 (b) 1, 2, 3, 4, 5
(c) 1, 5, 2, 3, 4 (d) 4, 1, 2, 3, 5

28 Working capital represents the portion of current assets financed through long-term funds. This indicates
1. net working capital 2. gross working capital

Codes
(a) Only 1 (b) Only 2
(c) Both 1 and 2 (d) Neither 1 nor 2

29 Forecasting technique of working capital include
(a) cash forecasting method
(b) projected balance sheet method
(c) P/L adjustment method
(d) All of the above

30 Long-term sources of finance are also required for
(a) permanent part of working capital
(b) temporary part of working capital
(c) Both (a) and (b)
(d) None of the above

31 Under trade credit and instalment credit does not flow in
(a) trade credit (b) bank credit
(c) cash credit (d) None of these

32 Objectives of management of working capital include
(a) maintenance of satisfactory level of working capital
(b) availability of ample funds at the times of need
(c) Both (a) and (b)
(d) None of the above

33 Which of the following statements is true?
(a) The cost of work-in-progress includes raw materials, wages and factory overheads
(b) Cost of finished goods is estimated at profit amount
(c) Delay in payment of certain expenses provides long-term financing of working capital
(d) None of the above

34 Arrange the following steps of operation cycle in correct order
1. Conversion of a accounts receivables into cash.
2. Conversion of work-in-progress into finished goods.
3. Conversion of raw-material into work-in-progress.
4. Conversion of finished goods into accounts receivable.

Codes
(a) 2, 1, 4, 3 (b) 4, 3, 2, 1 (c) 3, 2, 4, 1 (d) 1, 4, 3, 2

Dividend Policy and Theories

35 Under rigid dividend policy, the rate of dividend is ....
(a) 0 (b) −1 (c) 1 (d) 2

36 The rate of dividend of preference shares is decided at the time of
(a) issue (b) dissolution of company
(c) payment (d) None of these

37 Dividend is the share of profit of company dividend amongst its
(a) shareholders (b) brokers
(c) debenture holders (d) None of these

38 Stock dividend .... the number of equity shares.
(a) increases (b) decreases
(c) neutralise (d) Both (a) and (b)

39 Maximum bonus ratio is
(a) 1 : 1 (b) 2 : 3 (c) 3 : 2 (d) 3 : 4

40 If the earnings of company are stable then it can easily follow
(a) stable dividend policy (b) flexible dividend policy
(c) lower rate dividend policy (d) None of these

41 According to Walter, a firm should pay 100% dividend, if

(a) r > k (b) r = k
(c) r < k (d) None of these

42 Dividend policy of a company mainly concerns with

1. Dividend payout and/or
2. Stability of dividend

Select the correct answer using the codes given below

Codes

(a) Only 1 (b) Only 2
(c) Both 1 and 2 (d) None of the above

43 Which of the following is not very much relevant in dividend decision?

(a) Availability of disposable profit
(b) Inventories expectations for dividend
(c) Capital market conditions
(d) Industry practice

44 Irregular dividend policy is followed due to

(a) uncertainty of earnings
(b) heavy fixed burden of interest
(c) shortage of liquid resources
(d) All of the above

45 Dividends are earnings for shareholders and they expect reasonable earnings from their

(a) profit (b) investments
(c) property (d) All of these

46 "Dividend policy determines the division of earnings between payments to shareholders and retained earnings." Who said this?

(a) Weston and Brigham (b) Gerstenberg
(c) Bonneville (d) None of these

47 Which of the following pairs is/are not correct?

(a) Payment of dividend at the usual rate is given under regular dividend policy
(b) Consistency or lack of variability in the stream of dividend payments describes that there is no dividend policy
(c) Both (a) and (b)
(d) None of the above

48 When a company gives an option to its shareholders to receive dividend either in cash or kind, then it is called

(a) option dividend (b) option currency
(c) option shareholders (d) None of these

49 XYZ Co earns ₹ 10 per share, capitalised at 10% and has a return on investment of 12%. What is the optimum dividend payout ratio as per Walter's dividend policy model?

(a) 0% (b) 2% (c) 10% (d) 12%

50 From the following information of ABC Ltd, determine the market price of a share using Gordon's model.

Total investment in assets = ₹ 10,00,000
Number of shares = 50,000
Total earnings = ₹ 2,00,000
Cost of capital = 16%
Payout ratio = 40%

(a) ₹ 20 (b) ₹ 40 (c) ₹ 60 (d) ₹ 80

Miscellaneous

Directions (Q. Nos. 51-58) *The following items consist of two statements, Statement I and Statement II. You have to examine these two statements carefully and select the correct answer by using the codes given below.*

Codes

(a) Both statements are correct
(b) Both statements are incorrect
(c) Statement I is correct, but Statement II is incorrect
(d) Statement I is incorrect, but Statement II is correct

51 **Statement** I "Working capital is the amount of funds necessary to cover the cost of operating the enterprise."

Statement II "Circulating capital means current assets of a company that are changed in the ordinary course of business from one form to another."

52 **Statement** I Gross working capital is the quantitative approach.

Statement II Net working capital is the qualitative approach.

53 **Statement** I Working capital is an index of the insolvency of a concern.

Statement II Working capital is just like the heart of business.

54 **Statement** I Number of operating cycles = Number of days in a year ÷ Period of operating cycle.

Statement II Operating cycle method is a method of sales forecast.

55 **Statement** I Optional dividend is paid partly in cash and partly in the form of property.

Statement II Interim dividend is declared by the company at the end of financial year.

56 **Statement** I 'Dividend policy' is a flexible and wide meaning word.

Statement II Dividend policy refers to the policy concerning quantum of profits distributed as dividend.

57 **Statement** I Future financial requirement of the company influence dividend decision.

Statement II During boom period, companies are usually in a race of increasing rate of dividend.

58 **Statement** I All companies follow irregular dividend policy.

Statement II Irregular dividend policy is most liked by retired persons etc.

Directions (Q. Nos. 59-67) *In the questions given below are two statements labelled as Assertion (A) and Reason (R). In the context of the two statements, which one of the following is correct?*

Codes

(a) Both (A) and (R) are true and (R) is the correct explanation of (A)
(b) Both (A) and (R) are true, but (R) is not the correct explanation of (A)
(c) (A) is true, but (R) is false
(d) (A) is false, but (R) is true

59 Assertion (A) The liquidity of funds is an important consideration in divided decisions.

Reason (R) If firm's liquidity position is weak, shareholders should be satisfied by stock dividends.

60 Assertion (A) Inflation act as a constraint in the payment of dividends.

Reason (R) Substantial part of current earnings cannot be retained.

61 Assertion (A) Corporate taxes do not affect dividends.

Reason (R) Due to high rate of income tax, Board of Directors declare cash dividend.

62 Assertion (A) Payment of dividend at usual rate is termed as irregular dividend policy.

Reason (R) Such policy is followed on account of uncertainty of earnings.

63 Assertion (A) Adequate working capital funds leads to availability of cash discounts.

Reason (R) If proper cash balance is maintained the business can offer cash discount facilities.

64 Assertion (A) Short-term working capital is needed to meet day to day business requirement.

Reason (R) The duration of such requirements exceeds beyond a year.

65 Assertion (A) Little working capital leads to speculation.

Reason (R) Little working capital increases the rate of return on the total investments.

66 Assertion (A) Little working capital leads to speculation.

Reason (R) Too much working capital leads to inefficiency.

67 Assertion (A) Management of working capital refers to the management of current assets and current liabilities.

Reason (R) But the major thrust of course, is on the management of current assets, because current liabilities arise in the context of current assets.

68 Match the following.

List I	List II
A. Gross working capital	1. Difference of current assets and current liabilities
B. Net working capital	2. It is referred to as "hardcore working capital"
C. Permanent working capital	3. It is the excess of working capital over permanent working capital
D. Variable working capital	4. Total current assets

Codes

	A	B	C	D		A	B	C	D
(a)	4	1	2	3	(b)	3	4	2	1
(c)	2	3	4	1	(d)	3	4	1	2

69 Match the following.

List I	List II
A. Depreciation funds	1. .... is comparatively cheap.
B. Public deposits	2. .... is the internal source of financing short-term working capital.
C. Term loans	3. .... have been very popular among Indian companies.
D. Bank credit	4. .... are resources raised for a period from 3 to 5-7 years.

Codes

	A	B	C	D		A	B	C	D
(a)	4	3	2	1	(b)	2	3	4	1
(c)	3	1	4	2	(d)	4	1	2	3

70 Match the following.

List I	List II
A. Depreciation funds	1. Its use has increased in recent years due to use of trade squeeze
B. Provision for taxation	2. Some authors do not accept them as a source of funds, but it is not reasonable
C. Accrued expenses	3. It can be used during the intermittent period
D. Trade credit	4. The firm can postpone the payment of expenses for short periods

Codes

	A	B	C	D		A	B	C	D
(a)	4	3	2	1	(b)	2	3	4	1
(c)	3	1	4	2	(d)	4	1	2	3

71 Match the following.

List I	List II
A. Qualitative	1. .... involves raising funds on the security of the company's.
B. Gross working capital	2. Gross working capital is the .... approach.

List I	List II
C. Commercial Banks	3. Total of current assets is called as ....
D. Factoring	4. .... are also principal sources of working capital.

Codes

	A	B	C	D
(a)	4	3	2	1
(b)	2	1	4	3
(c)	3	1	4	2
(d)	2	3	4	1

72 Match the following.

List I	List II
A. Shares	1. Fixed capital
B. Land and building	2. Period of medium-term finance
C. Public deposits	3. Source of long-term finance
D. 1-5 years	4. Short-term finance
E. Meeting day-to-day requirements	5. Source of medium-term finance

Codes

	A	B	C	D	E
(a)	4	2	3	1	5
(b)	4	1	5	2	4
(c)	2	3	5	1	4
(d)	5	3	2	4	1

73 Match the following.

List I (Forms of Dividend Payment)	List II (Features)
A. Cash dividend	1. The fair value of the additional shares issued is based on their fair market value when the dividend is declared
B. Stock dividend	2. On the date of payment, the company issues dividend payments
C. Property dividend	3. It creates a note payable
D. Scrip dividend	4. You record this distribution at the fair market value of the assets distributed

Codes

	A	B	C	D
(a)	4	3	1	2
(b)	2	1	4	3
(c)	2	3	4	1
(d)	3	2	4	1

74 Match the following.

List I (Concepts)	List II (Meanings)
A. Regular dividend policy	1. Part of divisible profits of a company, which is distributed among its shareholders
B. Dividend	2. Application of planning and control functions to the finance function
C. Capitalisation	3. Payment of dividend at usual rate
D. Financial management	4. Refers to the process of determining the quantum of funds required for a firm

Codes

	A	B	C	D
(a)	4	3	2	1
(b)	2	3	4	1
(c)	3	1	4	2
(d)	4	1	2	3

75 Match the following.

List I (Forms of Dividend Payment)	List II (Features)
A. Cash dividend	1. This type of dividend is rarely opted by companies
B. Stock dividend	2. The companies whose liquidity position is sound also prefer distribution of this dividend
C. Bond dividend	3. Companies which are short of cash resources for dividend payment can distribute this dividend
D. Property dividend	4. It is distributed only when the company is capable of bearing the increased burden of interest on bonds

Codes

	A	B	C	D
(a)	4	1	2	3
(b)	2	3	4	1
(c)	3	4	1	2
(d)	3	1	4	2

PREVIOUS YEARS' QUESTIONS

December 2018

1 Which of the following statement(s) is/are false?

1. Capital profits can never be distributed as dividends to the shareholders.
2. Dividends are paid out of profits and, therefore, do not affect the liquidity position of the firm.
3. Every company should follow the policy of low dividend payment.
4. Walter's model suggests that dividend payment dose not affect the market price of the share.

Choose the correct answer from the code given below

Codes

(a) 1, 2 and 3 (b) Both 3 and 4
(c) 2, 3 and 4 (d) All of the above

July 2018

2 Negative net working capital implies that

(a) long-term funds have been used for fixed assets
(b) short-term funds have been used for fixed assets
(c) long-term funds have been used for current assets
(d) short-term funds have been used for current assets

3 Profitability index of a project is the ratio of present value of cash inflows to

(a) total cash inflows
(b) total cash outflows
(c) present value of cash outflows
(d) initial cost minus depreciation

4 Which one of thc following statement is false?

(a) Effective dividend policy is an important tool to achieve the goal of wealth maximisation
(b) According to Walter, the optimal payout ratio for a growth firm is 100%
(c) MM model asserts that the value of the firm is not affected whether the firm pays dividend or not
(d) 'Bird-in-the-hand theory' in reference to dividend decision has been developed by Myron Gordon

November 2017

5 Match the items of List I with those of List II and indicate the correct code.

List I	List II
A. ABC analysis	1. Dividend decision
B. Walter model	2. Capital budgeting decision
C. Capital rationing	3. Capital structure decision
D. Net operating income approach	4. Working capital management decision

Codes

	A	B	C	D		A	B	C	D
(a)	1	3	2	4	(b)	2	1	4	2
(c)	4	1	2	3	(d)	3	1	2	4

6 Match the items of List I with those of List II and indicate the correct code.

List I	List II
A. Net income approach	1. Working capital management
B Profitability index	2. Over capitalisation
C. Concentration banking	3. Capital structure planning
D. Lower rate of return	4. Capital budgeting decision

Codes

	A	B	C	D		A	B	C	D
(a)	3	4	1	2	(b)	3	4	2	1
(c)	4	2	3	1	(d)	4	3	1	2

7 Dividend irrelevance argument of MM model is based on

(a) hedging
(b) issue of debentures
(c) liquidity
(d) arbitrage

January 2017

8 Which one of the following combination of rules stands true while preparing schedule of changes in working capital?

1. An increase in current assets increases working capital.
2. An increase in current assets decreases working capital.
3. An increase in current liabilities decreases working capital.
4. An increase in current liabilities increases working capital.

Codes

(a) Both 1 and 4 (b) Both 1 and 3
(c) Both 2 and 3 (d) Both 3 and 4

9 **Assertion** (A) The important aspect of dividend policy is to determine the amount of earnings to be distributed to shareholders and the amount to be retained in the firm.

Reason (R) Dividend policy of the firm has its effect on both the long term financing and the wealth of shareholders.

Codes

(a) Both (A) and (R) are correct and (R) is the correct explanation of (A)
(b) Both (A) and (R) are correct, but (R) is not the correct explanation of (A)
(c) (A) is correct, but (R) is incorrect
(d) (R) is correct, but (A) is incorrect

July 2016

10 Insufficient working capital may result into which combination of the following?

1. Failures to adapt to changes.
2. Enhancement in credit-worthiness of the firm.
3. Reduced availability of trade and cash discounts.
4. Reduced volume of sales.

Codes

(a) 1, 2 and 3 (b) 1, 3 and 4
(c) 1, 2 and 4 (d) All of the above

11 Which combination of the following represents the assumptions of the Walter's dividend model?

1. The company has a very long or perpetual life.
2. All earnings are either reinvested internally or distributed as dividend.
3. There is no floatation cost for the company.
4. Cost of capital of the company is constant.

Select the correct one from the codes given below

Codes

(a) 1, 2 and 3 (b) 2, 3 and 4
(c) 1, 2 and 4 (d) 1, 3 and 4

12 Which of the following is not a source of credit information of prospective customers?

(a) Letter of credit
(b) Bank reference
(c) Trade enquiry
(d) Credit bureau

13 The portion of earnings which is distributed among shareholders in the form of dividend is called

(a) Proprietary ratio
(b) Earnings-yield ratio
(c) Payout ratio
(d) Retention ratio

14 Select the correct code regarding motives for holding inventories by firms.

1. Transaction motive 2. Environmental motive
2. Precautionary motive 4. Speculative motive
5. Competitive motive

Codes

(a) 1, 2, 3 and 4 (b) 1, 2, 4 and 5
(c) 1, 4 and 5 (d) 1, 3 and 5

December 2015

15 'Dividend is not relevant in determining the value of the company'. Who among the following held this opinion?

(a) JE Walter
(b) Ezra Soloman
(c) Modigliani Miller
(d) MJ Gordon

16 Concentration banking is a method of

(a) decentralised collection
(b) centralised collection
(c) direct collection
(d) payment only through cheques

June 2015

17 Which one of the following assumptions is not included in the James E Walter Valuation model?

(a) All financing by retained earnings only
(b) No change in the key variables such as EPS and DPS
(c) The firm has finite life
(d) All earnings are either distributed as dividends or invested internally immediately

18 **Statement** I Working capital leverage measures the responsiveness of return on equity for changes in current assets.

Statement II When the annual demand for an item is 3,200 units, unit cost ₹ 6, inventory carrying charges 25% per annum and cost of one procurement ₹ 150, the economic ordering quantity would be 700 units.

Codes

(a) Both statements are true
(b) Both statements are false
(c) Statement I is true, but Statement II is false
(d) Statement I is false, but Statement II is true

December 2014

19 Cash flow management involves

1. Lock-box system
2. Marketable securities
3. Playing the float
4. Concentration bank account

Select the correct answer using the codes given below

Codes

(a) 1, 2 and 3 (b) 2, 3 and 4 (c) 1, 3 and 4 (d) 1, 2 and 4

20 Dividend capitalisation model was developed by

(a) Ezra Solomon
(b) Myron J Gordon
(c) James E Walter
(d) Merton H Miller and Franco Modigliani

21 Insufficient working capital in any enterprise may also result into

1. Failure to adapt to changes
2. Overcapitalisation
3. Reduced availability of trade and cash discounts
4. Reduced volume of production and sales

Select the correct answer using the codes given below

Codes

(a) 1, 2 and 3 (b) 1, 3 and 4
(c) Both 2 and 3 (d) Both 1 and 4

June 2014

22 Which one the following assumptions is not covered in the Walter's model of the Dividend Policy?

(a) All financing is done through ratained earnings
(b) Firm's business risk does not change due to additional investments
(c) The firm has an infinte life
(d) The key vanables like EPS and DPS keep on changing

23 Which one of the following emphasises the qualitative aspects of working capital maangement?
(a) Gross working capital (b) Quick working capital
(c) Net working capital (d) None of these

December 2013

24 **Assertion** (A) A company should pay dividend to its shareholders.
Reason (R) Dividends are heavilly taxed than capital gains.
Codes
(a) Both (A) and (R) are true
(b) Both (A) and (R) are false
(c) (A) is false, but (R) is true
(d) (A) is true, but (R) is false

25 Dividend irrelevance hypothesis implied in the
(a) Traditional model (b) Walter model
(c) Gordon model (d) MM model

June 2013

26 Permanent working capital is generally financed through
(a) long-term capital funds
(b) goverment assistance
(c) internal financing
(d) short-term loans from banks

27 The appropriate ratio for indicating liquidity crisis is
(a) operating ratio (b) sales turnover ratio
(c) current ratio (d) acid test ratio

28 Who proposed a model to apply economic order quantity concept of inventory mangement to determine the optimum cash holding in a firm?
(a) Keith V Smith (b) Miller and Off
(c) William J Baumol (d) JM keynes

June 2012

29 Match the following.

List I	List II
A. Modigliani Miller approach	1. Commercial papers
B. Net operating income approach	2. Working capital management
C. Short-term money market instrument	3. Capital structure
D. Factoring	4. Arbitrage

Codes

	A	B	C	D		A	B	C	D
(a)	4	3	1	2	(b)	3	4	1	2
(d)	4	3	1	2	(d)	3	2	4	1

ANSWERS

Objective Questions

1 (a)	2 (d)	3 (a)	4 (b)	5 (d)	6 (c)	7 (a)	8 (a)	9 (b)	10 (a)
11 (c)	12 (c)	13 (d)	14 (b)	15 (c)	16 (d)	17 (a)	18 (a)	19 (b)	20 (a)
21 (a)	22 (b)	23 (c)	24 (b)	25 (c)	26 (d)	27 (d)	28 (c)	29 (d)	30 (a)
31 (a)	32 (c)	33 (a)	34 (c)	35 (a)	36 (a)	37 (a)	38 (a)	39 (a)	40 (a)
41 (b)	42 (c)	43 (c)	44 (d)	45 (b)	46 (a)	47 (b)	48 (a)	49 (a)	50 (b)
51 (a)	52 (a)	53 (d)	54 (c)	55 (d)	56 (d)	57 (a)	58 (b)	59 (a)	60 (c)
61 (b)	62 (d)	63 (a)	64 (c)	65 (b)	66 (d)	67 (c)	68 (a)	69 (b)	70 (b)
71 (d)	72 (b)	73 (b)	74 (c)	75 (b)					

Previous Years' Questions

1 (d)	2 (b)	3 (c)	4 (b)	5 (c)	6 (a)	7 (d)	8 (b)	9 (a)	10 (b)
11 (a)	12 (a)	13 (c)	14 (d)	15 (c)	16 (a)	17 (c)	18 (b)	19 (c)	20 (b)
21 (b)	22 (d)	23 (c)	24 (a)	25 (d)	26 (a)	27 (d)	28 (c)	29 (b)	

CHAPTER 16

International Financial Market

International finance deals with the monetary transactions that occur between two or more countries. It is concerned with topics such as exchange rates of currencies, monetary systems of the world, foreign direct investment and other important issues associated with internationa financial management.

International Monetary System

International monetary system is a set of arrangements, rules, practices and institutions under which payments are made and received for international transactions across national boundaries. The international system is concerned not with the supply of international money but with the relationships among a hundred or so currencies of individual countries and with the pattern of balance of payments relationships and the manner in which they are adjusted and settled.

Thus, 'the system' is broader than 'monetary', in that it is concerned with trade relationships and fiscal and other national policies as well.

Eichengreen (2008) has defined the international monetary system, as "the glue that binds national economies together. Its role is to lend order and stability to foreign exchange markets, to encourage the elimination of balance of payments problems and to provide access to international credits in the event of disruptive shocks."

To sum up, the international monetary system is a set of rules and supporting institutions that facilitate international trade cross border investment and generally, the reallocation of capital between nation states. It provides means of payment acceptable between buyers and sellers of different nationality, including deferred payment. To operate successfully, the system need to inspire confidence, to provide sufficient liquidity for fluctuating levels of trade and to provide means by which global imbalances can be corrected. The system can grow organically as

In this Chapter

- *International Monetary System*
- *Foreign Exchange Market*
- *International Financial Markets*
- *International Arbitrage*
- *Multinational Capital Budgeting*

the collective result of numerous individual agreements between international economic actors spread over several decades.

Structure and Characteristics of International Monetary System

The international monetary system, a cooperative arrangement between sovereign nations, is composed of five main elements. *These are as follows*

- A set of rules for setting exchange rates.
- A lender or lenders of last resort.
- Instruments for providing liquidity and reserves, such as swap facilities among Central Banks and the special drawing right, an international reserve asset created by the IMF.
- Provisions for surveillance.
- A reserve currency or currencies.

In practice, the core components of an international monetary system should contain the following three aspects

- An international reserve standard, played as an anchor in the system.
- Arrangements such as an agreed foreign exchange regime to help adjust each participant's international balance of payment.
- Global collaboration mechanism.

Problems in the International Monetary System

- The persistent global imbalances has an adverse effect on the international monetary system.
- Large and volatile capital flows have been increased.
- Exchange rate gyrations have disconnected from fundamentals.
- Supply of safe global assets has been insufficient.

Remedies for the Problems in the International Monetary System

- Global policy collaboration should be increased in international monetary system.
- All the transactions that occur in this system, should have stronger surveillance.
- Systemetic financial safety net should be enhanced.
- There should be more focus on financial deepening in emerging markets.
- New reserve assets should be developed to bring stability to the capital market in global marketing.

Foreign Exchange Market

Foreign exchange market is a global online network where foreign currencies are bought and sold by traders. Here, traders include individuals, firms, foreign exchange brokers, commercial banks and the Central Bank. In foreign exchange market, there are large number of foreign currencies which are traded, converted and exchanged in the foreign exchange market. It has no physical location and operates 24 hours a day from 5 pm EST on Sunday until 4 pm. EST on Friday because currencies are in high demand. It sets the exchange rates for currencies with floating rates.

Functions of Foreign Exchange Market

Credit

It provides credit for foreign trade. Credit is required for this period in order to enable the importer to take possession of goods, sell them and obtain money to pay-off the bill. Bills of exchange with maturity period of three months are generally used for international payments.

Transfer

It transfers purchasing power between the countries involved in the transaction. This function is performed through credit instruments, *i.e.* bills of foreign exchange, bank drafts and telephonic transfers.

Hedging

When exporters and importers enter into an agreement to buy and sell goods on some future date at the current prices and exchange rate, it is called hedging. The purpose of hedging is to avoid losses that might be caused due to exchange rate variations in the future.

Kinds of Foreign Exchange Market

Broadly, the foreign exchange market is classified into two categories on the basis of the nature of transactions. *These are as follows*

Spot Market

A spot market is the immediate delivery market, representing that segment of the foreign exchange market wherein the transactions, *i.e.* sale or purchase of currency are settled within two days of the deal, *i.e.* when the seller and buyer close their deal for currency within two days of the deal, it is called as spot transactions. Spot market is of daily nature and deals only in spot transactions of foreign exchange. The rate of exchange, which prevails in the spot market, is termed as spot exchange rate or current rate of exchange.

Forward Market

The forward exchange market refers to the transactions sale and purchase of foreign exchange at some specified date in the future, usually after 90 days of the deal, *i.e.* when the buger and seller enter into a contract for the sale and purchase of foreign currency after 90 days of the deal at a fixed exchange rate agreed upon now, is called a forward transaction. The exchange rate quoted in forward transactions is known as the forward exchange rate. Generally, most of the international transactions are signed on one date and completed on a later date. Forward exchange rate becomes useful for both the parties involved in the transaction.

Thus, the spot and forward markets are the important kinds of foreign exchange market that often helps in stabilising the foreign exchange rate.

Exchange Rate Risk

Exchange rate risk is also known as currency risk or foreign exchange risk. It exists when a financial transaction is denominated in a currency other than that of the base currency of the company. Investors and multinational businesses exporting or importing goods and services or making foreign investments throughout the global economy are faced with an exchange rate risk which can have severe financial consequences, if not managed appropriately.

Thus, exchange rate risk or currency risk is the exposure faced by investors or companies that operate across different countries, in regard to unpredictable gains or losses due to changes in the value of one currency in relation to another currency.

Types of Foreign Exchange Exposures

Exposure is the sensitivity to fluctuations in the value of an asset, while risks refer to how much exposure can affect the asset or operation. Thus, an exposure can be defined as a contracted, projected or contingent cash flow whose magnitude is not certain at the moment. The magnitude depends on the value of variables such as foreign exchange rates and interest rates. *Following are the types of foreign exchange exposures*

Transaction Exposure

It involves the possible exchange of loss or gain on existing foreign currency-denominated transactions. The firm must exchange foreign currency for domestic currency to realise the domestic value of its foreign-denominated cash flows.

Economic Exposure

It is also known as operating exposure. It is the degree that the market value is influenced by unexpected exchange rate fluctuations. Such exchange rate adjustments can severely affect the firm's position with regards to its competitors, the firm's future cash flows and ultimately the firm's value.

Translation Exposure

A firm's translation exposure is the extent to which its financial reporting is affected by exchange rate movements. The exchange gain or loss occurring from the difference in the exchange rates at the beginning and the end of the accounting period. A firm is exposed to translation loss, it it uses current exchange rate to translate its assets and liabilities.

Hedging

Hedging refers to different strategies that reduce the risks and minimise the impact of eventual adverse movements in the market. It involves using financial instruments to increase protection against unforeseen fluctuations, thus making cash flows more stable and predictable. As a result, companies can estimate income, taxes and revenues more reliably.

A foreign exchange hedge is a method that is used by companies to eliminate or 'hedge' their foreign exchange risk resulting from transactions in foreign currencies. This is done using either the cash flow hedge or the fair value method. A foreign exchange hedge transfers the foreign exchange risk from the trading or investing company to a business that carries the risk, such as a bank. There is cost to the company for setting up a hedge.

Techniques of Hedging Currency Risk

Different assets and types of investments have different methods for hedging, so there is no specific set of tools for hedging. In foreign exchange, however, hedging methods mostly consist of specific contracts or agreements, meant to exchange currency at a fixed rate. Currency derivatives can reduce the risk in foreign exchange transactions. One can use forward transactions and options to hedge currency risk. *These are*

Currency Futures or Forward Contracts

Forward/futures are agreements that set today the price of the exchange rate in a given future date. The agreement specifies a given quality.

Currency Option

A currency option in its simplest form provides the buyer of the option with the right but not the obligation to buy or sell one currency amount at a specified exchange rate on a specified date. It insures the buyer against unfavourable changes in exchange rates. The buyer pays only for the right to exercise the option on expiry.

Debt Operations

Debt operations involve borrowing foreign currency. An investor borrows currency in the amount, they expect to receive in the future. Then they exchange it into local currency and deposit it, hedging exchange rate risk. When the investor receives foreign currency, they use it to pay the debt. However, local interest might not be enough to pay the loan's interest, so this can sometimes be an expensive method.

Swap Contracts

Swaps are contracts between two parties that need foreign currency, but don't want to borrow from a foreign bank. They exchange an initial amount and gradually swap back small amounts as interest. Finally they return the initial amounts. They usually borrow domestic currency as well, so the small amounts pay the loan's interest. Swaps are common among financial institutions.

International Financial Markets

The international financial market is the worldwide marketplace in which buyers and sellers trade financial assets, *i.e.* stocks, bonds, currencies, commodities and derivatives across national borders. It is a wide set of rules and institutions where assets are traded between agents in surplus and agents in deficit and where institutions lay down the rules. This market includes the market for foreign exchange, the Euro currency and related money markets, the international capital markets, the commodity market and the markets for forward contracts, options, swaps and other derivatives.

Motives for the Internationalisation of Financial Transactions

- Differences in interest rates
- International diversification
- Economic growth prospects
- Exchange rate fluctuations

Sources of International Funds

The flow of funds from providers to seekers of international funds takes place through different institutions or agencies and through different financial instruments. *The institutions or agencies that serve as the sources of international funds are*

- Multilateral development banks or agencies
- Government or governmental agencies
- International banks
- Securities market

Segments of International Financial Markets

International financial market facilitates the transfer of funds globally. The funds so transferred may be ownership funds or debt funds. The funds may be transferred for different maturity periods such as short-term, medium-term or long-term. *The segments of International financial markets are as follows*

Foreign Exchange Market

It is the market for the purchase and sale of foreign currencies. It is an important segment of the international financial markets. This market facilitates international trade and international transactions. Foreign exchange market is an over the counter market that means there is no physical location where traders get together to exchange currencies.

International Bond Market

It is the market where international bonds are brought and sold. Companies may raise long-term funds in foreign currencies through issue of international bonds. Foreign bonds and Euro bonds are the two types of international bonds. International bond market also includes straight bonds, global bonds, floating rate notes, convertible bonds, sinking fund bonds etc.

International Equity Market

Equity capital for a company is raised through the issue of shares. These shares are then traded in the stock exchange of the country. A multinational company would often like to raise equity capital from different countries by issuing shares in those countries. The shares would also be listed trading in stock exchanges of these countries. This may be done to raise foreign currency funds required for specific projects or for enhancing the prestige of the company in the global market, or sometimes the domestic market may not be large enough to absorb a large stock offering.

International Money Market

Money market is the place where short-term funds are transferred and traded. In international money market, transactions take place in a variety of different currencies. International banks and FIs across the world are the major suppliers of funds in these markets, while MNCs and governments of different countries are the major users of these funds.

International Credit Market

MNCs can obtain short-term funds in foreign currencies from the international money markets, and can obtain long-term funds in foreign currencies from the international bond markets. In this market, medium-term funds are exchanged between the suppliers and borrowers of such funds.

International Financial Market Instruments

Following are the important international financial market instruments

Euro Currency

The euro is the form of money for the 19 member countries of the eurozone. It is the second most widely used currency in forex trading after the US Dollar. It is also the second most widely held forex reserve used by Central Banks.

The euro was initially proposed to unify the entire European Union. All 28 member nations pledged to adopt the euro, when they joined the EU. But they must meet budget and other criteria before they can switch to the euro. As a result, nine EU members have not adopted the euro.

The euro symbol is £. Euros are divided into euro cents, each euro cent is one hundredth (1/100th) of a euro. *There are six denominations*

£ 5, £ 10, £ 20, £ 50, £ 100 and £ 500

Each bill and coin has a different size. The bills also have raised print, while the coins have distinct edges. These features allow the visually impaired to distinguish one denomination from another.

Advantages of Euro Currency

- Smaller countries have the advantage of being backed by Europe's powerhouse economies like Germany and France.
- Developed countries could produce more at a lower cost as euro allows to enjoy lower interest rates.
- Larger companies enjoys the benefit of high demand and production without paying the higher price.

Disadvantages of Euro Currency

- Adopting the euro means countries lose the ability to print their currency.
- Euro currency is shared by 19 countries that complicated its management.
- Each country sets its own fiscal policy that affects the euro's value.

American Depository Receipt (ADR)

An American Depository Receipt (ADR) is a physical certificate evidencing ownership of American Depository Shares (ADSs). The term is often used to refer to the ADSs themselves.

American Depository Share (ADS)

An American Depository Share (ADS) is a US Dollar denominated form of equity ownership in a non-US company. It represents the foreign shares of the company held on deposit by a custodian bank in the company's home country and carries the corporate and economic rights of the foreign shares, subject to the terms specified on the ADR certificate.

One or several ADSs can be represented by a physical ADR certificate. The terms ADR and ADS are often used interchangeably. ADSs provide US investors with a convenient way to invest in overseas securities and to trade non-US securities in the US.

ADSs are issued by a Depository Bank, such as JP Morgan Chase Bank. They are traded in the same manner as shares in US companies, on the New York Stock Exchange (NYSE) and the American Stock Exchange (AMEX) or quoted on NASDAQ and the Over The Counter (OTC) market.

Although, ADSs are US Dollar denominated securities and pay dividends in US Dollars, they do not eliminate the currency risk associated with an investment in a non-US company.

Types of American Depository Receipt

American depository receipt is a depository receipt representing one or more shares of a foreign company that is traded publicly in US markets. There are two types of ADR, *i.e.* unsponsored ADR and sponsored ADR.

Unsponsored ADR This is ADR, which involve no direct involvement of the foreign company (whose shares are involved). Custodian banks buy shares of the company, hold then and issues ADRs through a brokerage firm. The ADR holder may not receive all the benefits associated with the shares. Unsponsored ADRs are traded usually over-the-counter.

Sponsored ADR This is ADR, which involve direct involvement of foreign company. The company chooses a single depository bank and registers DRs with SEC. The ADR holder receives all shareholder benefits. Sponsored ADRs are usually traded through major exchanges like NYSE and AMEX.

Global Depository Receipts (GDRs)

Global Depository Receipts (GDRs) may be defined as a global finance vehicle that allows an issuer to raise capital simultaneously in two markets through a global offering. GDRs may be used in public or private markets inside or outside US. GDR, a negotiable certificate usually represents company's traded equity/debt. The underlying shares correspond to the GDRs in a fixed ratio say
1 GDR=10 shares.

A GDR is similar to ADR in the sense that it also represents shares of a foreign company, but is traded on the local exchange. Issued by global depository banks (like JP Morgan), GDRs are usually employed to invest in companies of emerging economies.

GDR is a negotiable instrument issued by a depository bank in international markets, typically in Europe and generally made available to institutional investors both outside and within the US that evidences ownership of shares in a non-US company, enabling the company (issuer) to access investors in capital markets outside its home country.

International Arbitrage

Arbitrage refers to the process of buying and selling of currencies. Arbitrage is not a method of hedging foreign exchange risk in a real sense. It is however, a method of making profits from foreign exchange transactions. In arbitrage, the sell or purchase of currencies takes place within an unstable market. The prices are affected by the supply and demand of currencies and it helps in adjusting the market to equilibrium.

Thus, the term 'International Arbitrage' refers to the practice of simultaneously buying and selling a foreign security on two different exchanges. International arbitrage is profitable when pricing inefficiencies occur due to factors such as timing and exchange rates. It is considered a low risk strategy, since the trades should only occur when the price differential between the two exchanges is large enough to cover the associated transaction fees.

Features of Arbitrage

- Arbitrage is the simultaneous purchase and sale of an asset to profit from an imbalance in the price.
- Arbitrage exploits short-term price differences of assets between markets in order to make a profit.
- Arbitrage exists only as a result of market inefficiencies and would therefore not exist if all markets were perfectly efficient.

Types of Arbitrage

Triangular Arbitrage

Triangular arbitrage is the result of a discrepancy between three foreign currencies that occurs when the currency's exchange rates do not exactly match up. This type of arbitrage is a riskless profit that exists when a quoted exchange rate does not equal the markets cross exchange rate.

Locational Arbitrage

Locational arbitrage is an arbitrage strategy in which one seeks to profit from differences in bid and asking exchange rates for the same currency at different banks. It is possible when a bank's buying or bid price is higher than another bank's selling price for the same currency.

Covered Interest Arbitrage

Covered interest arbitrage is the practice of using favourable interest rate differentials to invest in a higher yielding currency, and hedging the exchange risk through a forward currency contract. It occurs when exchange rate risk is hedged with a forward contract.

Multinational Capital Budgeting

Multinational Corporations (MNC's) evaluate international projects by using multinational capital budgeting, which compares the benefits and costs of these projects. Given that many MNC's spend more than $ 100 million per year on international projects. Multinational capital budgeting is a critical function. Many international projects are irreversible and cannot be easily sold to other corporations at a reasonable price. Proper use of multinational capital budgeting can identify the international projects worthy of implementation.

The most popular method of capital budgeting involves determining the projects net present value by estimating the present value of the projects future cash flows and subtracting the initial outlay required for the project. Multinational capital budgeting typically uses a similar process. However, special circumstances of international projects that affect the future cash flows or the discount rate used to discount cash flows make multinational capital budgeting more complex. Financial managers must understand how to apply capital budgeting to international projects, so that they can maximise the value of the MNC.

Inputs for Multinational Capital Budgeting

Regardless of the long-term projects to be considered, an MNC will normally require forecasts of the economic and financial characterstics related to the project. *Each of these characteristics is briefly described as follows*

Initial Investment

The parent's initial investment in a project may constitute the major source of fund to support a particular project. Funds initially invested in a project may include not only whatever is necessary to start a project, but also additional funds such as working capital, to support the project over time. Such funds are needed to finance inventory, wages and other expenses.

Price and Consumer Demand

The price at which the product could be sold can be forecasted using competitive products in the markets as a comparison. The future prices will most likely to be responsive to the future inflation rate in the host country (where project is to take place) but future inflation rate is not known.

Costs

Like the price estimate, variable cost forecasts can be developed from assessing prevailing comparative costs of the components. Such costs should normally move in tandem with the future inflation rate of the host country. On a periodic basis, fixed cost may be easier to predict than the variable cost, since normally it is not sensitive to changes in demand.

Tax Laws

The tax laws on earnings generated by a foreign subsidiary or remitted to MNC's parent vary among countries. Under some circumstances, the MNC receives tax deductions or credits for tax payments by a subsidiary to the host country.

Remitted Funds

In some cases, a host government will prevent a subsidiary from sending its earnings to the parent. The restrictions may reflect an attempt to encourage additional local spendings or to avoid excessive sales of the local currency in exchange for some other currency.

Exchange rates

An international project will be affected by exchange rate fluctuations during the life of the project, but these movements are often very difficult to forecast. There are methods of hedging against then, though most hedging techniques are used to cover short-term position. While it is possible to hedge over longer periods. Thus, the MNC may decide not to hedge the projected foreign currency net cash flows.

Salvage (Liquidation Value)

The after tax salvage value of most projects are difficult to forecast. It will depend on several factors including the success of the project and the attitude of the host government towards the project. It should be recognised that the MNC does not always have complete control over the life time decision.

Required Rate of Return

Once the relevant cash flows of a proposed project are estimated, they can be discounted at the project's required rate of return, which may differ form MNC's cost of capital because of that particular project's risk.

Calculation of NPV

Although several budgeting techniques are available, a commonly used technique is to estimate the cash flows and salvage value to be received by the parent and compute the NPV of the project as shown here

$$\text{NPV} = -IO + \sum_{t=1}^{n} \frac{cf_t}{(1+k)^t} + \frac{SV_n}{(1+k)^n}$$

Where,

IO = Initial Outlay (investment)

CF_t = Cash Flow in period t

SV_n = Salvage Value

k = Required rate of return on the project.

n = Lifetime of the project (number of periods)

Factor to be Considered in Multinational Capital Budgeting

The example of Spartan Inc, ignored a variety of factors that may affect the capital budgeting analysis *such as*

Exchange Rate Fluctuations Different scenarios should be considered together with their probability of occurrence.

Inflation Although price/cost forecasting implicitly considers inflation, inflation can be quite volatile from year to year for some countries.

Financing Arrangement Financing costs are usually captured by the discount rate. However, many foreign projects are partially financed by foreign subsidiaries.

Blocked Funds Some countries may require that the earnings be reinvested locally for a certain period of time before they can be remitted to the parent.

Uncertain Salvage Value The salvage value typically has a significant impact on the project's NPV and the MNC may want to compute the break-even salvage value.

Impact of Project on Prevailing Cash Flows The new investment may compete with the existing business for the same customers.

Host Government Incentives These should also be considered in the analysis.

EXAM BASED QUESTIONS

International Monetary System and Foreign Exchange Market

1 The core of the Brettonwoods system was the
(a) World Bank
(b) IMF
(c) United Nations
(d) Interstate Commerce Commission

2 For a foreign exchange of specific currency, the non-hedged position is classified as
(a) open position (b) close position
(c) currency long position (d) currency short position

3 Majority of retail forex trading happens in
(a) forward market (b) spot market
(c) futures market (d) swap market

4 The three different types of forex transactions are
(a) spot, forward, swaps (b) spot, cash, DTC
(c) spot, forwards, futures (d) spot, futures, options

5 The immediate (two days) exchange of one currency for another is a
(a) forward transaction (b) spot transaction
(c) money transaction (d) exchange transaction

6 An agreement to exchange of one currency for another in one month is a
(a) spot transaction (b) future transaction
(c) forward transaction (d) monthly transaction

7 For contingency exposure of foreign exchange, the best derivative that can be used to hedge is
(a) forwards (b) options
(c) futures (d) swaps

8 What is/are the effect(s) of speculation on exchange rate?
(a) It aggravates the market trends
(b) It causes violent fluctuations in exchange rate
(c) Both (a) and (b)
(d) Neither (a) nor (b)

9 Exchange rates are determined in the
(a) money market (b) foreign exchange market
(c) stock market (d) capital market

10 The potential effect of exchange rate fluctuations on FDI is expressed as
(a) translation
(b) transaction
(c) conversion
(d) economic

11 When domestic currency appreciates, it benefits .... and harms ....
(a) domestic exporters, domestic importers
(b) domestic exporter, foreign importer
(c) domestic importer, foreign exporter
(d) domestic importer, domestic exporter

12 Operational techniques include
(a) diversification of a company's operations
(b) purchasing of currency options
(c) exposure netting
(d) Both (a) and (c)

13 All of the following are types of financial instruments except
(a) currency forward contracts
(b) swap agreements
(c) currency futures contracts
(d) money market hedge

14 Which of the following is not a type of swap agreement?
(a) Currency (b) Credit
(c) Money market (d) Interest rate

15 Which of the following is not a means of diversified marketing?
(a) Economies of scale (b) Product strategy
(c) Pricing strategy (d) Market selection

16 A survey of Chief Financial Officers found that the most commonly used hedging technique is
(a) swaps (b) options
(c) forward contracts (d) future contracts

17 Hedging transaction is indicated by
(a) transactions in odd amounts
(b) presentation of documentary support
(c) frequency of such transactions
(d) None of the above

18 Hedging with options is best recommended for
(a) hedging receivables
(b) hedging contingency exposures
(c) hedging payables
(d) hedging foreign currency loans

19 A firm operating in India cannot hedge its foreign currency exposure through
(a) forwards (b) options
(c) futures (d) None of these

20 Translation exposure arises in respect of items translated at
(a) current rate (b) historical rate
(c) average rate (d) All of these

21 The following method cannot be used for managing translation exposure.
(a) Forward contract (b) Option contract
(c) Exposure netting (d) Leading and lagging

22 Economic exposure does not deal with
(a) change in real exchange rates
(b) future cash flow of the firm
(c) expected exchange rate changes
(d) None of the above

23 An operation in order to protect the domestic currency value of an asset or a liability that is denominated in foreign currency is called as

(a) Hedging (b) Hermes
(c) Indexation (d) Leading

24 .... means using short-term forward contracts to off set 'paper' gains and losses on the long-term assets and liabilities of foreign subsidiaries.

(a) Hedging transaction exposure
(b) Hedging balance sheet exposure
(c) Hedging economic exposure
(d) Hedging cost exposure

25 A multinational company that is faced with mild interference upto complete confiscation of all assets is encountering

(a) translation risk exposure
(b) transaction risk exposure
(c) political risk exposure
(d) economic risk exposure

26 The true cost of hedging transaction exposure by using forward market is

(a) difference between agreed rate and spot rate at the time of entering into contract
(b) difference between agreed rate and spot rate on the due date of contract
(c) forward premium
(d) discount annualised

27 A/An .... hedge protects the company from adverse exchange rate movements but allow the company to benefit from favoarable movements.

(a) balance sheet (b) forward market
(c) money market (d) options market

28 Which of the following is not one of the steps for currency exposure management?

(a) Forecast the degree of exposure
(b) Develop a reporting system to monitor exposure and exchange rate movements
(c) Buying additional foreign subsidiaries
(d) Assign responsibility for hedging exposure

29 The exchange rate is

(a) the price of one currency relative to gold
(b) the value of a currency relative to inflation
(c) the change in the value of money over time
(d) the price of one currency relative to another

30 Corporations today are operating in an environment in which exchange rate changes may adversely affect their competitive positions in the marketplace. This situation, in turn, makes it necessary for many firms to

(a) carefully manage their exchange risk exposure
(b) carefully measure their exchange risk exposure
(c) Both (a) and (b)
(d) Neither (a) nor (b)

31 In an agreement to exchange one currency for another in three months at a fixed price, the price is the ....

(a) spot exchange rate
(b) money exchange rate
(c) forward exchange rate
(d) monthly exchange rate

32 The larger fluctuations in portfolio value of foreign exchange of financial institutions leads to

(a) greater liquidity of assets
(b) greater volatility of rates
(c) lesser volatility of rates
(d) lesser liquidity of assets

33 In the foreign exchange market, the .... of one country is traded for the ....of another country.

(a) currency, currency
(b) currency, financial instruments
(c) currency, goods
(d) goods, goods

34 What prompted Brettonwoods Agreement?

(a) To set up a system that would maintain a stable exchange rate system
(b) To create a flexible exchange rate system
(c) To stop World War II
(d) Eradicate the economic difficulties brought in by World War II

35 The international monetary system can be defined as the institutional framework within which

(a) international payments are made
(b) movement of capital is accomodated
(c) exchange rates among currencies are determined
(d) All of the above

36 The international monetary system went through several distinct stages of evolution. These stages are summarised, in alphabetic order, as follows

1. Bimetallism
2. Brettonwoods system
3. Classical gold standard
4. Flexible exchange rate regime
5. Interwar period

The chronological order that they actually occurred is

Codes

(a) 3, 1, 4, 2, 5 (b) 1, 3, 5, 2, 4
(c) 4, 1, 3, 2, 5 (d) 5, 2, 1, 3, 4

37 Under the Brettonwoods system

(a) there was an explicit set of rules about the conduct of international monetary policies
(b) each country was responsible for maintaining its exchange rate within 1% of the adopted per value by buying or selling foreign exchanges as necessary
(c) the US dollar was the only currency that was fully convertible to gold
(d) All of the above

38 Special Drawing Right (SDR) are
(a) an artificial international reserve allotted to the members of the IMF, who can then use it for transactions among themselves or with the IMF
(b) a 'portfolio' of currencies and its value tends to be more stable than the currencies that it is comprised of
(c) used in addition to gold and foreign exchanges, to make international payments
(d) All of the above

39 Under a flexible exchange rate regime, governments can retain monetary policy independence because the external balance will be achieved by
(a) the exchange rate adjustments
(b) the price-specie flow mechanism
(c) the triffin paradox
(d) None of the above

40 Which of the following refers to the institutional arrangements countries adopt to govern exchange rates?
(a) International monetary fund
(b) International monetary system
(c) Global agreement on exchange rates
(d) Brettonwoods arrangement

41 Arbitrageurs in foreign exchange markets
(a) attempt to make profits by outguessing the market
(b) make their profits through the spread between bid and offer rates of exchange
(c) take advantages of the small inconsistencies that develop between markets
(d) need foreign exchange in order to buy foreign goods

42 It is very difficult to interpret news in foreign exchange markets because
(a) very little information is publicly available
(b) it is difficult to know which news is relevant to future exchange rates
(c) it is difficult to know whether the **news has** been obtained legally
(d) All of the above

43 The foreign exchange market is referred to as a market where one country's currency is exchanged for another currency. The currency exchange is usually made through the following methods
(a) buyers and sellers of foreign exchange meet at a physical location
(b) buyers and sellers of foreign exchange meet through a telephone network
(c) buyers and sellers of foreign exchange meet through computer communications
(d) Both (b) and (c)

44 The starting point for understanding how exchange rates are determined is a simple idea called ...., which states-if two countries produce an identical good, the price of the good should be the same throughout the world no matter which country produces it.
(a) Gresham's law
(b) the law of one price
(c) purchasing power parity
(d) arbitrage

45 In the foreign exchange market, factors that shift the expected return schedule for foreign deposits include
1. a change in the foreign interest rate.
2. a change in the expected future exchange rate.
3. a change in the current exchange rate.
Select the correct answer by using the codes given below
Codes
(a) Both 1 and 2
(b) Both 2 and 3
(c) Both 1 and 3
(d) All of the above

46 There are important differences between translation, transaction and economic exposure. Which of the following statements regarding these differences is true?
(a) Translation and economic exposure look to the future impact of an exchange rate change which has occurred or may occur
(b) Translation and transaction exposure involve actual or potential cash flow changes
(c) Economic exposure is essentially objective because it depends on outstanding obligations which existed before changes in exchange rates
(d) Economic exposure is essentially subjective because it depends on estimated future cash flows for an arbitrary

47 Which of the following are rules to use when choosing between forward contracts and currency options?
(a) When the quantity of a foreign-currency cash outflow is known, buy the currency forward
(b) When the quantity of a foreign currency cash outflow is unknown, buy the currency forward
(c) When the quantity of a foreign currency cash flow is partially known and partially uncertain, use a forward contract to hedge the known and unknown portions
(d) when the quantity of a foreign currency cash inflow is known, buy the currency forward

48 When assessing economic exposure, financial managers should consider how variations in exchange rates influence ....
(a) a company's sales prospects in foreign markets
(b) the product market, the factor market and the capital market
(c) the home-currency value of financial assets and liabilities denominated in foreign
(d) the costs of labor and other inputs to be used in overseas production

International Financial Markets, International Arbitrage and Multinational Capital Budgeting

49 Which of the following financial asset is/are traded in international financial market?

(a) Bonds
(b) Stocks
(c) Derivatives
(d) All of the above

50 The segments of international financial market include

1. Foreign Exchange Market
2. International Arbitrage Market
3. International Money Market
4. International Bond Market

Select the correct answer by using the codes given below

Codes

(a) Both 1 and 4 (b) 1, 3 and 4
(c) 2, 3 and 4 (d) All of the above

51 Global Depository Receipts (GDRs) are issued by successful corporations with a view to attracting

(a) overseas loan funds
(b) remittances from NRIs
(c) foreign equity capital
(d) foreign direct investment

52 The single European currency, the euro, was adopted by 11 member nations on 1st January, ...

(a) 1984 (b) 1991
(c) 1999 (d) 2001

53 Monetary policy for the countries using the euro as a currency is now conducted by

(a) the Federal Reserve
(b) the Bundes Bank
(c) European Central Bank
(d) RBI

54 The euro zone is remarkably comparable to the United States in terms of

(a) population size
(b) GDP
(c) international trade share
(d) All of the above

55 Which country is not using the euro?

(a) Greece (b) Italy
(c) Sweden (d) Portugal

56 An example of Euro currency is

(a) a dollar deposit outside the US
(b) a pound sterling deposit within UK
(c) a mark deposit with Germany
(d) All of the above

57 In which of the following stock exchanges, the GDRs are listed?

1. London Stock Exchange
2. New York Stock Exchange
3. Luxembourg Stock Exchange
4. Bombay Stock Exchange
5. Singapore Stock Exchange
6. Hong Kong Stock Exchange

Select the correct answer using the codes given below

Codes

(a) 1, 2 and 3 (b) 1, 4, and 6
(c) 3, 5 and 6 (d) 1, 3, 5 and 6

58 Once the changeover to the euro was completed by 1st July, 2002, the legal-tender status of national currencies in the euro zone

(a) was cancelled, leaving the euro as the sole legal tender in the euro zone countries
(b) was affirmed at the fixed exchange rate
(c) was tied to gold
(d) None of the above

59 Benefits from adopting a common European currency include

1. reduced transaction costs.
2. elimination of exchange rate risk.
3. increased price transparency that will promote Europe wide competition.

Select the correct answer by using the codes given below

Codes

(a) Only 2 (b) Both 1 and 3
(c) Both 2 and 3 (d) All of the above

60 The issues in international capital budgeting include

1. exchange rate risk
2. political risk
3. geographical risk
4. parent *vs* project cash flow

Codes

(a) Both 1 and 2 (b) Both 2 and 4
(c) 1, 2 and 4 (d) 1, 2 and 3

61 In multinational capital budgeting, the value of project is determined by

(a) discounted cash flow
(b) net present value of future cash flow
(c) net present value of present cash outflow
(d) risk factor cash flow

62 Which technique is common used to estimate the cash flow in multinational capital budgeting?

(a) Net present value method
(b) Internal rate of return method
(c) Exchange rate value method
(d) Discounted future value method

Miscellaneous

Directions (Q. Nos. 63-65) *The following questions consists of two statements, Statement I and Statement II. You have to examine these two statements carefully and select the correct answer to these by using the codes given below.*

Codes

(a) Both statements are true
(b) Both statements are false
(c) Only Statement I is true
(d) Only Statement II is true

63 **Statement** I A forward contract is an agreement between two entities to buy or sell the underlying asset, at a future date, at today's pre-agreed price.

Statement II Options trading in commodity take place in Indian commodity exchanges.

64 **Statement** I Forward contracts are bilateral contracts and hence, exposed to counter party risk.

Statement II A company that wants to sell an asset at particular time in the future can hedge by taking short futures position.

65 **Statement** I International financial market includes the market for forward, options and swaps.

Statement II ADRS stands for Australian Depository Receipts.

66 Match the following.

List I	List II
A. Certificate of deposits	1. 91 days, 182 days and 364 days
B. Debentures	2. 3 to 5 months
C. Treasury bills	3. 1 to 270 days
D. Commercial papers	4. Longer periods, i.e. *n* years

Codes

	A	B	C	D		A	B	C	D
(a)	2	4	3	1	(b)	2	4	1	3
(c)	4	3	1	2	(d)	3	4	2	1

ANSWERS

Objective Questions

1 (a)	2 (a)	3 (b)	4 (a)	5 (b)	6 (c)	7 (c)	8 (c)	9 (b)	10 (d)
11 (d)	12 (d)	13 (d)	14 (c)	15 (d)	16 (c)	17 (d)	18 (c)	19 (b)	20 (a)
21 (b)	22 (c)	23 (a)	24 (b)	25 (c)	26 (b)	27 (d)	28 (c)	29 (d)	30 (c)
31 (c)	32 (b)	33 (a)	34 (a)	35 (d)	36 (b)	37 (d)	38 (d)	39 (a)	40 (b)
41 (c)	42 (b)	43 (d)	44 (b)	45 (a)	46 (d)	47 (a)	48 (a)	49 (d)	50 (d)
51 (a)	52 (c)	53 (c)	54 (a)	55 (c)	56 (a)	57 (d)	58 (a)	59 (d)	60 (c)
61 (b)	62 (a)	63 (c)	64 (a)	65 (a)	66 (b)				

CHAPTER 17

Measures of Statistics

Common measures of statistics are mean, median, mode, variance, inter-quartile range, absolute deviation etc. The next step involves describing the characteristics of numerical data by finding various measures like average, dispersion, skewness, correlation coefficient etc.

In this Chapter

- Measures of Central Tendency
- Measues of Dispersion
- Skewness
- Correlation
- Regression Analysis

Statistics

The word 'Statistics' has been derived from the Latin word 'Status' or Italian word 'Statista' or the German word ' Statistik' or the French word 'Statistique' which means 'related to state'. In it, the methods of compilation, administration, classification, briefing, presentation, analysis and explanation of data have been developed to study the problems of any field of life.

Measures of Central Tendency

One of the most important objectives of statistical analysis is to get one single value that describes the characteristics of the entire data. This value is called the central value or average or central tendency. This value is the point around which all other values of the data cluster. Therefore, it is known as measure of central tendency.

Essentials of Average/Central Tendency

- It should be rigidly defined.
- It should be calculated based on all the observations.
- It should be capable of further algebaric treatment.
- It should be least affected by extreme fluctuations in sample.
- It should be easy to compute and understand.

Types of Average/Measures of Central Tendency

The following chart depicts the different types of averages or measures of central tendency

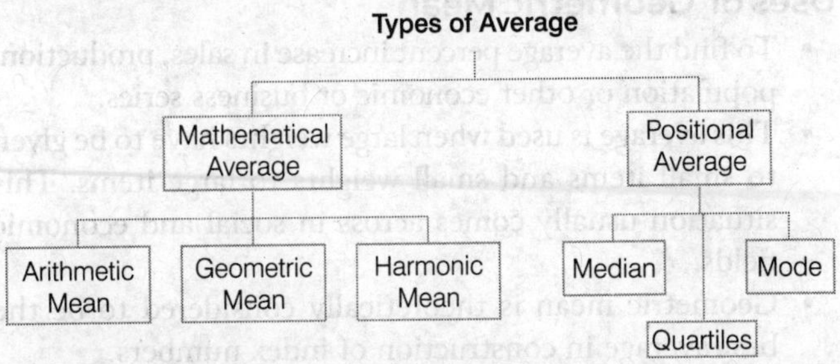

Mathematical Average

These are of three types *viz* arithmetic mean, geometric mean and harmonic mean, *which are as follows*

Arithmetic Mean

The Arithmetic Mean(AM) is the most simple and frequently used average. Arithmetic mean is represented by rotation $\overline{X}$.

Types of Arithmetic Mean

Arithmetic mean can be classified as

Simple Arithmetic Mean In simple arithmetic mean, all items of a series are taken as of equal importance.

Weighted Arithmetic Mean In weighted arithmetic mean, different items are taken as of different importance. Accordingly, weights are accorded to different items depending on their relative importance.

Calculation of Simple Arithmetic Mean

Arithmetic mean can be calculated in individual, discrete and continuous series, *which are as follows*

In Individual Series An individual series is one in which the items are listed separately and each item appears as an individual unit. It is also referred to as ungrouped data. *The arithmetic mean for this series can be computed by using the given formula*

$$\text{Arithmetic mean } (\overline{X}) = \frac{\Sigma X}{n}$$

Where, ΣX = Sum of all observations

$= X_1 + X_2 + X_3 \ldots\ldots + X_n$

n = Number of observations or terms

In Discrete and Continuous Series In these series, items are represented alongwith their respective frequencies. It is referred to as grouped data. *The arithmetic mean in these can be computed by the following formula*

$$\overline{X} = \frac{\Sigma fx}{\Sigma f} \text{ or } \frac{\Sigma fx}{n}$$

Where,

Σfx = Sum of the product of observations and corresponding frequencies.

Σf = Sum of frequencies (where, n is equal to Σf).

➠ **Note** *In continuous series, mid-value is taken as X. It is calculated as follows*

$$\text{Mid-value } (X) = \frac{\text{Lower Limit} + \text{Upper Limit}}{2}$$

If we use assumed mean or short-cut method, then following formula is used

$$\overline{X} = A + \frac{\Sigma fdx}{\Sigma f}$$

Where, A = Assumed mean

Σf = Sum of frequencies

Σfdx = Sum of the products of frequency and deviation from assumed mean

If we use step deviation method, then following formula is used

$$\overline{X} = A + \frac{\Sigma fd'x}{\Sigma f} \times c$$

Where, $\Sigma fd'x$ = Sum of product of step deviations with frequency

$$\text{Where, step deviation } (d'x) = \frac{X - A}{C}$$

C = Common factor, A = Assumed mean

Σf = Sum of frequencies

Calculation of Weighted Arithmetic Mean

Simple arithmetic mean gives equal importance to all the items while weighted mean takes into account the relative importance of each of the value to the total value.

Weighted arithmetic mean is obtained by assigning to the items weight as judged according to their relative importance in the group. Weights are assigned to different items according to their relative importance. *We use the following formula*

Weighted arithmetic mean $(\overline{X}_w) = \Sigma WX / \Sigma W$

Where, ΣWX = Sum of each weight multiplied by the element

ΣW = Sum of all the weights

Calculation of Combined Arithmetic Mean

If the mean of two or more groups are known, then combined mean of all the series can be calculated. *We use the following formula*

Combined mean ($X_{1,2,3,\ldots,n}$)

$$\overline{X}_{1,2,3,\ldots,n} = \frac{n_1 \cdot \overline{X}_1 + n_2 \cdot \overline{X}_2 + n_3 \cdot \overline{X}_3 + \ldots\ldots\ldots + n_n \cdot \overline{X}_n}{n_1 + n_2 + n_3 \ldots\ldots + n}$$

Where, $\overline{X}_{1,2,3,\ldots,n}$ = Combined arithmetic mean of n series

$\overline{X}_1$ = Arithmetic mean of series 1

$\overline{X}_2$ = Arithmetic mean of series 2

$\overline{X}_3$ = Arithmetic mean of series 3

$\overline{X}_n$ = Arithmetic mean of series n

n_1 = Number of items in series 1

n_2 = Number of items in series 2

n_3 = Number of items in series 3

n_n = Number of items in series n

Uses of Arithmetic Mean

- It is used to summarise large scale data as it is difficult to understand raw data.
- It is used to facilitate comparison or comparative study.
- Averages gives such values, which becomes a guideline for decision-making.
- Averages becomes very important when it is desired to establish relation between different groups.

Properties of Arithmetic Mean

- The sum of deviations of the observations from their arithmetic mean is always zero.
- The product of arithmetic mean and the number of values, on which the mean is based, is equal to the sum of all given values. Symbolically,

$$n\bar{x} = \Sigma X \qquad \left[\because \bar{x} = \frac{\Sigma X}{n}\right]$$

- It is affected by both *i.e.* by change in origin and change in scale.
- The sum of the squares of the deviation of a set of values is minimum when taken from mean.

Geometric Mean

Arithmetic mean is inaccurate to assess change in variables over a period of time. Hence, a new measure of central tendency is needed to calculate the changing rate, *i.e.* the geometric mean.

Geometric Mean(GM) is defined as the positive n^{th} root of product of finite set of values.

Formulae of geometric mean are as follows

$$GM = (X_1 \cdot X_2 \cdot X_3 \ldots\ldots\ldots, X_n)^{\frac{1}{n}}$$

Or $$= \sqrt[n]{X_1 \cdot X_2 \cdot X_3 \ldots\ldots\ldots, X_n}$$

Or $$= \text{Antilog}\left(\frac{1}{i=1}\Sigma^n \log X_i\right)$$

Where, 'n' is the number of variables

Uses of Geometric Mean

- To find the average percent increase in sales, production, population or other economic or business series.
- This average is used when large weights have to be given to small items and small weights to large items. This situation usually comes across in social and economic fields.
- Geometric mean is theoretically considered to be the best average in construction of index numbers.

Properties of Geometric Mean

- The geometric mean of the product of two variables is the product of their geometric means.
- The geometric mean of the ratio of two variables is the ratio of geometric means of the two variables.
- *Weighted geometric mean is calculated with the help of the following formula*

$$GM_W = \text{Antilog}\left[\frac{\Sigma W \cdot \log X}{\Sigma W}\right]$$

Harmonic Mean

Harmonic Mean(HM) is based on the reciprocals of the numbers averaged. It is defined as the reciprocal of the arithmetic mean of the reciprocal of the given individual observation.

It is calculated for individual series by using the given formula

$$\therefore \quad HM = \frac{n}{\frac{1}{x_1} + \frac{1}{x_2} + \ldots + \frac{1}{x_n}} \text{ or } \frac{n}{\Sigma \frac{1}{x}}$$

Where, 'n' is the number of items in the series $x_1, x_2, x_3 \ldots, x_n$.

For discrete and continuous series, the following formula is used

$$HM = \frac{\Sigma f}{\Sigma f / x}$$

Uses of Harmonic Mean

This mean is used to find averages involving rate, time and price.

Properties of Harmonic Mean

Its properties are as follows

- *If there are two groups with N_1 and N_2 observations and H_1 and H_2 as their respective harmonic means, then combined harmonic mean is given below*

$$HM_C = \frac{N_1 + N_2}{\frac{N_1}{H_1} + \frac{N_2}{H_2}}$$

- *Weighted harmonic mean could be calculated with the help of the following formula*

$$HM_W = \frac{\Sigma W}{\Sigma\left[\frac{W}{X}\right]}$$

Relationship between AM, GM and HM

- *For any set of positive observations the following relation is observed*

$$AM \geq GM \geq HM$$

- *For given two observations in a series, the following relation holds true*

$$AM \times HM = (GM)^2$$

Positional Average

Median, quartiles and mode are referred to as positional average which are as follows

Median

Median is another measure of central tendency. If a series of value is arranged either in ascending or in descending order of magnitude, then the middle term or the mean of the two middle terms according as the number of values is odd or even is called the median. This measure divides the series into two equal parts. Thus, the median is the size of the middle most item, if the items are arranged in ascending or descending order of magnitudes.

Calculation of Median

In Individual Series Arrange all the values of different items of given series in the ascending or descending order.

If number of items i.e. n is odd, then use the following formula to calculate median

$$\text{Median } (M) = \text{Size of } \left(\frac{n+1}{2}\right)\text{th item}$$

And if n is an even number, then use the following formula to calculate median

$$M = \frac{\text{Size of } \left(\frac{n}{2}\right)\text{th item} + \text{Size of } \left(\frac{n}{2}+1\right)\text{th item}}{2}$$

In Discrete Series To calculate median in discrete series First of all arrange the data in ascending or descending order and then calculate the cumulative frequencies (cf).

Find the position of the median by using following formula

$$\text{Position of median} = \left(\frac{n+1}{2}\right)\text{th item}$$

Where, n = Sum of frequency

The corresponding value at this position is the value of median.

In Continuous Series In case of continuous series, median cannot be located straight forward. In this case, median lies in between lower and upper limit of a class interval. To get the exact value of the median. Firstly, calculate the cumulative frequencies, then find the value of $\left(\frac{n}{2}\right)$th item and then by inspecting cumulative frequencies (cf) find out the cumulative frequency which is either equal to or just greater than it. The class interval corresponding to this value is called **median class.**

Now, apply the following formula to determine the actual median value

$$\text{Median } (M) = l_1 + \frac{\frac{n}{2} - cf}{f} \times c$$

Where, l_1 = Lower limit of the median class

cf = Cumulative frequency of the class preceding the median class

f = Frequency of the median class

c = Magnitude of the median class interval

n = Sum of frequencies

Properties of Median

- It is easy to calculate and simple to understand.
- It is well-defined, so it possesses the qualities of good average.
- We can determine median graphically with the help of ogives.
- In case of open-ended classification, it is specially useful because only the position is to be ascertained.
- It is useful for studying social phenomena, like wage, distribution of wealth, skill etc.
- It is a positional value and not a calculated value.

Quartiles

Quartiles are also positional averages which divide the data into four equal parts, each part containing equal number of observations.

There are three quartiles which are as follows

First Quartile It is also called lower quartile and is denoted by Q_1. First quartile has 25% of the items of the distribution below it and 75% of the items are greater than it.

Second Quartile It is the same as median and is denoted by Q_2. Second quartile has 50% of the items below it and 50% of the items above it.

Third Quartile It is also called upper quartile and is denoted by Q_3. Third quartile has 75% of the items of the distribution below it and 25% of the items above it.

Other Positional Averages

Deciles distribute the series into ten equal parts and is generally expressed as *D*. Accordingly, we have nine deciles $D_1, D_2, D_3, \ldots, D_9$ of a series.

Percentiles divide the series into hundred equal parts and is generally expressed as *P*. *There are 99 percentiles in a series denoted by*

$$P_1, P_2, P_3, \ldots, P_{99}$$

Also remember, $M = Q_2 = D_5 = P_{50}$

$Q_1 = P_{25}$

and $Q_3 = P_{75}$

Calculation of Quartiles

In Individual Series For calculating quartiles in individual series, check if the series is in the increasing order of magnitude or not. If it is not, then arrange it in ascending order.

Then, apply the following formulae to compute quartiles

$$Q_1 = \text{Size of}\left(\frac{n+1}{4}\right)\text{th item}$$

$$Q_2 = \text{Size of } 2\left(\frac{n+1}{4}\right)\text{th item or}$$

$$\text{Size of } \frac{(n+1)}{2}\text{ th item (same as median)}$$

$$Q_3 = \text{Size of } \frac{3(n+1)}{4}\text{th item}$$

Note

- *If on division, the result is a decimal number, then following formula should be applied to find quartiles*

  = Size of integral number + decimal part [size of next number–size of integral number]
- *While calculating median, series can be arranged either in ascending or in descending order, but while calculating quartile the series should be arranged in ascending order only, otherwise the value of* Q_1 *and* Q_3 *will get interchanged.*

In Discrete Series For calculating quartiles in discrete series, check if the series is in the increasing order of magnitude or not. If not, arrange it in ascending order. Then, find the cumulative frequencies and apply the same formulae as given in the case of individual series to find quartiles.

In Continuous Series For calculating quartiles in a continuous series, check if the series is a normal exclusive series arranged in ascending order. If more than, less than, inclusive or mid-value series is given, then it should first be converted into an exclusive series. Find the quartile numbers to find the quartile groups. *The formulae are*

$$q_1 \text{ number} = (n/4)\text{th item}$$

$$q_2 \text{ number} = 2\left(\frac{n}{4}\right)\text{th item}$$

$$q_3 \text{ number} = 3(n/4)\text{th item}$$

With the help of quartile numbers, locate the quartile groups. *Now, apply the following formulae to find the required quartiles*

$$Q_1 = l_1 + \frac{\left[\frac{n}{4}\right] - cf}{f} \times c$$

$$Q_2 = l_1 + \frac{2\left[\frac{n}{4}\right] - cf}{f} \times c$$

$$Q_3 = l_1 + \frac{3\left[\frac{n}{4}\right] - cf}{f} \times c$$

Where,

l_1 = Lower limit of class group

c = Width of the class group

cf = Cumulative frequency of the class preceding the class group

f = Frequency of class group

Note

- *The properties of quartiles are the same as that of the median.*
- *For the computation of quartiles, inclusive frequency distribution is required to be converted into exclusive frequency distribution.*
- *If mid-values are given, then exclusive frequency distribution should be formed before computing quartiles.*
- *Unequal class intervals need not be converted into equal class intervals.*

Mode

The word 'mode' has been derived from the French word 'La mode' which means the most fashionable. So, mode represents that value of a distribution which is repeated the maximum number of times, *i.e.* the most fashionable value. It is the most frequently observed data value. A series can have one mode or more than one mode.

Classification of Series on the Basis of Number of Modes

On the basis of number of modes, a series can be uni-modal, bi-modal or multi-modal.

Uni-modal Series is a series which has only one mode.

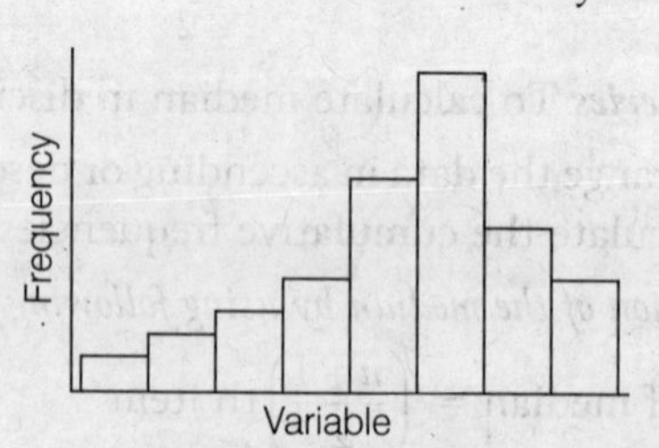

Uni-Modal Series

Bi-modal Series is a series which has two modes.

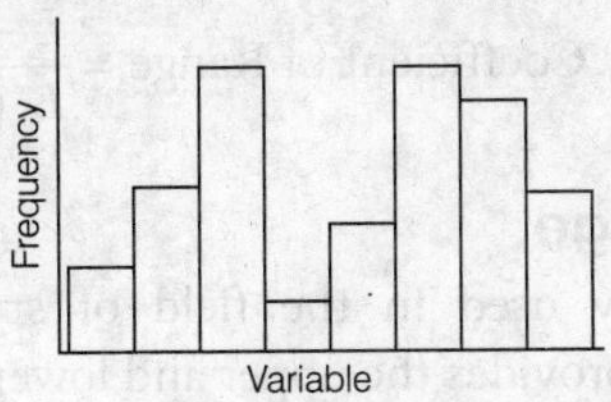

Bi-Modal Series

Multi-modal Series is a series which has more than two modes.

A series can also has no mode if no value appears more frequent than any other value in the distribution.

e.g. Series 4, 4, 5, 5, 6, 6 has no mode.

Calculation of Mode

In Individual Series In series of individual observation, mode is that value which occurs most frequently. That value is the mode of the series.

In Discrete Series In a discrete series, mode is the value corresponding to the highest frequency.

➠ **Note** *In certain cases, the items concentrate around more than one value, so it becomes difficult to observe the modal value. In such cases, the grouping method is used.*

In Continuous Series The distribution is observed and the class corresponding to the highest frequency is identified as the modal class.

Now, exact value of mode is calculated using the following formula

$$\text{Mode}\,(M_o) = l_1 + \frac{f_1 - f_0}{2f_1 - f_0 - f_2} \times c$$

Where,

l_1 = Lower limit of modal class

f_1 = Frequency of the modal class

f_0 = Frequency of the class preceding the modal class

f_2 = Frequency of class succeeding the modal class

c = Class interval of the modal class

➠ **Note** *For calculating mode, the continuous distribution should be exclusive with equal class intervals.*

Properties of Mode

- Mode is affected by change in origin as well as change in scale.
- It may be undefined in a series.
- It does not possess any mathematical properties.
- The value of mode is not based on each and every item of the series.
- As compared to mean, mode is affected to a great extent by sampling fluctuations.

Relationship between Mean, Median and Mode

The relationship between mean, median and mode depends upon the type of distribution, such as

- For a symmetrical distribution, mean, median and mode all coincide, *i.e.* all take the same mathematical value
- For a negatively skewed distribution
  Mode > Median > Mean
- For a positively skewed distribution
  Mean > Median > Mode
- The following empirical relationship is observed between mean, median and mode.
  Mode (M_0) = 3 Median (M) − 2 Mean $(\overline{X})$

In case, in a series, the mode is ill-defined, then the above formula can be used to compute mode.

Comparison among Mean, Median and Mode

- Mean and median are certain values but not the mode. It is not so precise and accurate.
- It is difficult to calculate mode as compared to mean and median.
- Mean is based on all the items in the series but median and mode are not based on all the items in the series.
- Algebraic treatment is possible with the help of mean. Median and mode are not useful for algebraic treatment.
- Mode is not affected by extremely small values. Median is slightly affected by extreme values, mean is affected by extreme values to a great extent.
- Median and mode can be computed graphically but not mean.

Measures of Dispersion

Measures of dispersion help to determine the spread or scatteredness of values from a measure of central tendency. They help to assess the extent to which values in a distribution differ from the average of the distribution.

Types of Measures of Dispersion

On the basis of the mode of expression, measures of dispersion can be classified as

Absolute Measures They are measures of dispersion which are expressed in terms of the original units of a series as rupees, kilogram etc. The various absolute measures of dispersion are range, inter-quartile range, quartile deviation, mean deviation and standard deviation *(These are discussed ahead).*

Relative Measures They are the measures of dispersion of a series expressed as a percentage or ratio of the average. These measures do not depend on the units of measurement. Relative measures of dispersion are coefficient of range, coefficient of quartile deviation, coefficient of mean deviation, coefficient of standard deviation and coefficient of variation.

Range

Range is defined as the difference between two extreme values, *i.e.* the largest and the smallest values in a distribution. Higher value of range implies higher dispersion and *vice-versa*. It is an absolute measure of dispersion and is computed on the basis of spread of values.

Coefficient of Range

It is a relative measure of dispersion. It is used to compare variation of two series expressed in different units. Generally, it is defined as the ratio of the difference between the largest value (L) and smallest value (S) to their sum.

➠ **Note** *Range is not affected by change in origin but is affected by change in scale.*

Calculation of Range and its Coefficient for Different Statistical Series

Calculation of range and its coefficient is discussed with respect to individual, discrete and continuous series.

These are as follows

In Individual Series To calculate range and its coefficient in an individual series, locate the largest and the smallest value of the series.

Compute range with the help of the following formula

$$\text{Range}\,(R) = \text{Largest Value}\,(L) - \text{Smallest Value}\,(S)$$

Compute coefficient of range with the help of the following formula

$$\text{Coefficient of Range} = \frac{L - S}{L + S}$$

In Discrete Series The steps for computation of range and its coefficient are the same as discussed in the case of individual series.

Frequencies corresponding to different values are not considered while computing range of the discrete series.

In Continuous Series Check if the given series is an exclusive distribution or not. If not, then it should be first converted into an exclusive distribution.

Calculate range with the help of given formula

Range = Upper Limit of the Highest Class Interval (L) − Lower Limit of the Lowest Class Interval (S)

Calculate coefficient of range with the help of following formula

$$\text{Coefficient of Range} = \frac{L - S}{L + S}$$

Uses of Range

- It is widely used in the field of statistical quality control. It provides the upper and lower limits in which the product quality should fall.
- It is also used by meteorological department, where the difference is used to forecast the weather of a particular day.

Inter-quartile Range and Quartile Deviation

Inter-quartile range and quartile deviation and its coefficient are also computed on the basis of spread of values. These measures of dispersion are computed with the help of quartiles.

These measures are explained below

Inter-quartile Range It is the difference between upper quartile and lower quartile. Thus,

$$\text{Inter-Quartile Range (IQR)} = Q_3 - Q_1$$

Where, Q_3 = Upper quartile
Q_1 = Lower quartile

It is based upon middle 50% of the value in a distribution and therefore, it is not affected by extreme values. It is an absolute measure of dispersion.

Quartile Deviation It is half the difference of upper quartile and lower quartile, *i.e.* half of inter-quartile range. It is also known as semi-inter-quartile range and denoted by QD. It is an absolute measure of dispersion. Thus,

$$\text{QD} = \frac{Q_3 - Q_1}{2}$$

Where, Q_3 = Upper quartile
Q_1 = Lower quartile

Coefficient of Quartile Deviation The relative measure corresponding to quartile deviation is known as the coefficient of quartile deviation. It is the ratio of the difference between upper and lower quartile to their sum. Thus,

$$\text{Coefficient of QD} = \frac{Q_3 - Q_1}{Q_3 + Q_1}$$

Coefficient of quartile deviation can be used to measure the degree of variation in two different distributions when both have different units of measurement.

An Interesting Relation

Quartile Deviation = Median − Lower Quartile and
Quartile Deviation = Upper Quartile − Median

Mean Deviation

Mean deviation is an absolute measure of dispersion which is assessed on the basis of the average of the distribution.

It is the sum of absolute deviations from an average divided by the number of items. It is also known as average deviation.

Coefficient of Mean Deviation

As we know that mean deviation is an absolute measure of dispersion, thus, in order to transform it into a relative measure, it is divided by the average, from which it has been calculated. It is then known as the coefficient of mean deviation. Thus,

$$\text{Coefficient of Mean Deviation from Arithmetic Mean} = \frac{\text{MD}}{\overline{X}}$$

and Coefficient of Mean Deviation from Median

$$= \frac{\text{MD}}{M\ (\text{Median})}$$

➠ **Note** *Mode is not a stable average so, it is not used to calculate mean deviation and coefficient of mean deviation.*

Calculation of Mean Deviation and its Coefficient

The calculation of mean deviation and its coefficient in different series is discussed below

In Individual Series Calculate the arithmetic mean of the values, *i.e.* $\overline{X} = \Sigma X / n$. Calculate the difference between each value and the arithmetic mean. All differences are considered to be positive. These differences are called deviations and denoted as $|D|$. We find sum of all deviations, *i.e.* $\Sigma|D|$

Now, mean deviation is calculated with the help of the following formula

$$\text{Mean Deviation from Mean } (\text{MD}_{\overline{X}}) = \frac{\Sigma|D|}{n}$$

Where,
$\Sigma|D|$ = Sum of absolute deviations
n = number of values

After that, to calculate coefficient of mean deviation, use the following formula

$$\text{Coefficient of MD} = \frac{\text{MD}_{\overline{X}}}{\overline{X}}$$

Where, $\text{MD}_{\overline{X}}$ = Mean Deviation from Mean,
$\overline{X}$ = Arithmetic Mean

➠ **Note** *If mean deviation is to be calculated from median, then deviations are to be taken from median.*

Why Plus and Minus Signs are Ignored

If algebraic signs are considered, then the sum of deviation from the mean should be zero and from the median would be nearly zero. So, to study the variation of items from a central value, plus and minus signs are ignored.

In Discrete Series First of all, calculate the arithmetic mean ($\overline{X}$). Find absolute deviations $|D|$ from the mean, *i.e.* ignoring the plus or minus signs of deviations. Then, multiply absolute deviation $|D|$ of each observation with the corresponding frequency (f) of the variable ($f|D|$) and find sum of these product, *i.e.* $\Sigma f|D|$.

Mean deviation is calculated with the help of the following given formula

Mean Deviation from Arithmetic Mean ($\text{MD}_{\overline{X}}$)

$$= \frac{\Sigma f|D|}{\Sigma f},$$

Where,

$\Sigma f|D|$ = Sum of the product of absolute deviations with frequency

Σf = Sum of frequencies

Now, coefficient of mean deviation is calculated with the help of following formula

$$\text{Coefficient of MD}_{\overline{X}} = \frac{\text{MD}_{\overline{X}}}{\overline{X}}$$

In Continuous Series Find the mid-values of the groups of the given frequency distribution.

Find the actual mean of the distribution and find the absolute deviations by subtracting the mean from the given values. Denote it as $|D|$.

Multiply frequency with deviation and then find the sum of their products, the formulae as discussed in discrete series are to be used.

Properties of Mean Deviation

- Mean deviation is not affected by change in origin but is affected by change in scale.
- It takes its minimum value when the deviations are taken from median.
- It is based on all the observations of the series.
- It is not much affected by extreme values.
- It is not an algebraic method, as plus and minus signs are ignored.
- It cannot be calculated for open-ended distributions.

Standard Deviation

Standard deviation is the positive square root of the sum of square of deviations of various values from their arithmetic mean divided by the sample size. It was first used by Karl Pearson in 1893. It is an absolute measure of dispersion and is assessed on the basis of average, *i.e.* mean.

Standard deviation is denoted by the small Greek letter σ (read as sigma).

Coefficient of Standard Deviation

To compare the variability in two series, relative measure of standard deviation is found out. It is known as coefficient of standard deviation. Symbolically,

$$\text{Coefficient of Standard Deviation} = \frac{\sigma}{\overline{X}}$$

Where,

σ = Standard Deviation and

$\overline{X}$ = Mean

Coefficient of Variation and Variance

Coefficient of variation represents the variation of a series in percentage. *It is computed as follows*

$$\text{Coefficient of Variation} = \frac{\text{Standard Deviation } (\sigma)}{\text{Mean } (\overline{X})} \times 100$$

Variance is the square of standard deviation.

Symbolically,

$$\text{Variance} = (\text{Standard Deviation})^2 = (\sigma)^2$$

Also, $\sqrt{\text{Variance}} = \text{Standard Deviation } (\sigma)$

Calculation of Standard Deviation and its Coefficient

In Individual Series First of all, obtain the sum of values and denote it by ΣX. Divide ΣX by n to find out actual mean $\overline{X}$. Then, calculate deviation of values from actual mean and denote it as d. Square up the deviation and obtain the sum of d^2 and denote it as Σd^2.

Obtain the standard deviation by applying the formula

$$\sigma = \sqrt{\frac{\Sigma d^2}{n}}$$

Where, Σd^2 = Sum of square of deviations from mean

n = Number of items

Calculate coefficient of standard deviation by applying the given formula

$$\text{Coefficient of Standard Deviation} = \frac{\sigma}{\overline{X}}$$

➠ **Note** *In addition to the above formula, the following formulae can also be used to compute standard deviation in this series*

- $\sigma = \sqrt{\frac{\Sigma X^2}{n} - (\overline{X})^2}$

Where, ΣX^2 = Sum of square of observations,

$\overline{X}$ = Arithmetic mean and n = Number of observations.

- $\sigma = \sqrt{\frac{\Sigma d^2}{n} - \left(\frac{\Sigma d}{n}\right)^2}$

Where, n = Number of observations,

Σd^2 = Sum of square of deviations from assumed mean

Σd = Sum of deviations from assumed mean

In Discrete Series *First of all, compute arithmetic mean by applying the following formula*

$$\overline{X} = \Sigma fX/\Sigma f$$

Where, Σfx = Product of X with frequency,

Σf = Sum of frequency

Then, calculate deviations of values from actual mean and denote it as d. Square the deviations to find d^2. Multiply f and d^2 to obtain fd^2. Find the sum of fd^2 and express it as Σfd^2. *Now, apply the given formula to compute standard deviation*

$\sigma = \sqrt{\frac{\Sigma fd^2}{\Sigma f}}$, where, symbols have their meanings as defined above.

Use the given formula to find the coefficient of standard deviation

$$\text{Coefficient of } \sigma = \frac{\sigma}{\overline{X}}$$

➠ **Note** *The following formulae can also be used to find standard deviation in this series*

$$\sigma = \sqrt{\frac{\Sigma fX^2}{\Sigma f} - (\overline{X})^2}$$

$$\sigma = \sqrt{\frac{\Sigma fd^2}{\Sigma f} - \left(\frac{\Sigma fd}{\Sigma f}\right)^2}$$

$$\sigma = \sqrt{\frac{\Sigma fd'^2}{\Sigma f} - \left(\frac{\Sigma fd'}{\Sigma f}\right)^2} \times C$$

In Continuous Series *Find the mid-values (m) of the class intervals and compute arithmetic mean by applying the following formula*

$$\overline{X} = \Sigma fm/\Sigma f$$

Calculate deviations of mid-values from actual mean and denote it as d.

Then proceed as discussed in case of discrete series.

Combined Standard Deviation

If there are two groups containing n_1 and n_2 observations, $\overline{X}_1$ and $\overline{X}_2$ as respective arithmetic means and s_1 and s_2 as respective standard deviations. *The combined standard deviation is given below*

$$\sigma_c = \sqrt{\frac{n_1s_1^2 + n_2s_2^2 + n_1d_1^2 + n_2d_2^2}{n_1 + n_2}}$$

Where, d_1 and d_2 are the differences between individual mean and combined mean of series 1 and series 2 respectively.

Properties of Standard Deviation

- Standard deviation is the most popular measure of dispersion.
- It is not affected by change in origin, but is affected by change in scale.
- A distribution with lesser coefficient of variation shows greater consistency, homogeneity and uniformity,

whereas a distribution with greater coefficient of variation is considered more scattered.

- For two or more groups, it is possible to measure the combined standard deviation.
- It is based on all values of the series.
- It is an exact and definite measure of dispersion.
- It is least affected by fluctuations in sampling because samples are based on all values of the series.
- It is suitable for further algebraic treatment.
- It is difficult to calculate as compared to other measures of dispersion.
- It is unduly affected by extreme values of the series as it is based on all the items.
- It cannot be used to compare two series expressed in 3 different units.

Lorenz Curve

It is measure of dispersion. It was derived by Dr. Max O Lorenz. This curve is used by him to measure the inequalities of income or wealth of a group as people, society or country.

Steps involved in constructing a Lorenz curve

Steps 1 Calculate cumulative values of size of items or mind-points.

Steps 2 Calculate percentage for these cumulative values.

Steps 3 Determine cumulative ferquencies.

Steps 4 Calculate the percentage for each cumulative frequency.

Steps 5 On the X-axis, start from 0 to 100 and take the percentage of cumulative frequencies.

Steps 6 On the Y-axis, start from 0 to 100 and take the percentage of variable.

Steps 7 Draw a diagonal line joining 0 to 100 known as 'line of perfect equality'.

Steps 8 Plot the various points corresponding to the values of the variable X and Y and then join these points with a smooth free hand curve. The curve so obtained is known as wrong curve.

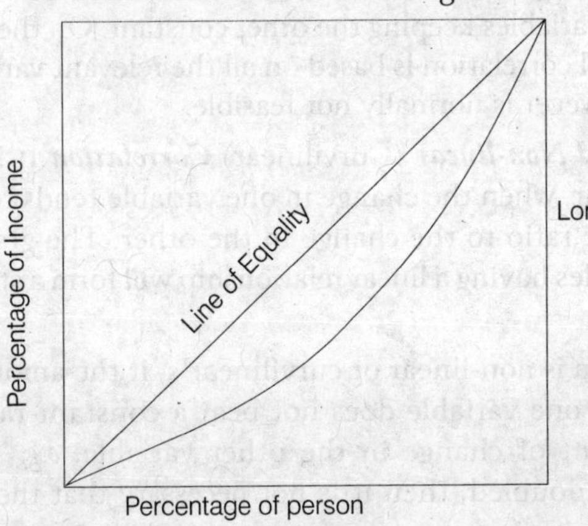

Relation between Various Measures of Dispersion

For a normal distribution, we have the following relations between the different measures of dispersion, which are as follows

- Mean ± QD covers 50% of the observations of the distribution.
- Mean ± MD covers 57.5% of the observations.
- Mean ± σ includes 68.27% of the observations.
- Mean ± 2σ includes 95.45% of the observations.
- Mean ± 3σ includes 99.73% of the observations.
- $QD = 0.6745\ \sigma \approx \frac{2}{3}\sigma$ (approx).
- $MD = \sqrt{\frac{2}{\pi}}.\sigma = 0.7979 \approx \frac{4}{5}\sigma$ (approx).
- $QD = 0.8459$ MD

  $QD \Rightarrow \frac{5}{6}$ MD (approx)

  Also,

  3 QD = 2 SD; 5 MD = 4 SD; 6 QD = 5 MD

  4 SD = 5; MD = 6 QD
- Range = 6 SD

Although the above results for various measures of dispersion hold true for normal distribution, but these results are approximately true even for symmetrical distributions or moderately skewed distributions.

Skewness

Literal meaning of skewness is 'lack of symmetry'. It helps us to determine the nature and extent of the concentration of the observations towards the higher or lower values of the variable.

A distribution is said to be skewed if

- the frequency curve of the distribution is not a symmetrically bell-shaped curve. A frequency distribution for which the curve has a longer tail towards the right is said to be positively skewed and if the longer tail lies towards the left, it is said to be negatively skewed.

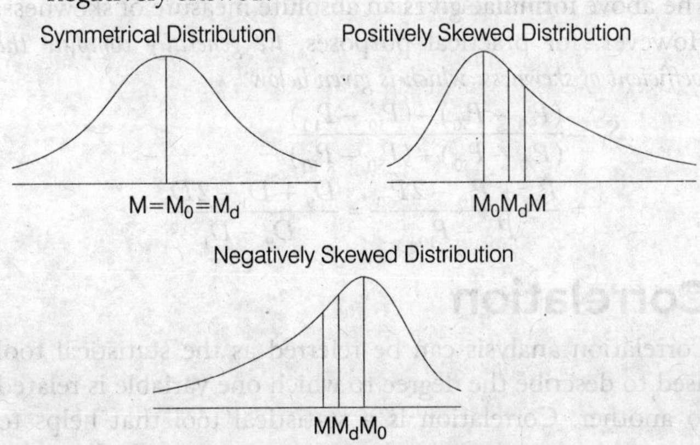

- The values of mean (M), median (M_d) and mode (M_0) do not coincide.
- Quartiles Q_1 and Q_3 are not equidistant from the median, *i.e.*

$$Q_3 - Md \neq Md - Q_1$$

- The sum of the positive deviations from the median is not equal to the sum of the negative deviations from the median.

Measures of Skewness

Karl Pearson's Coefficient of Skewness *This is given by the formula*

$$S_k = \frac{Mean - Mode}{s.d.} \text{ or } \frac{\overline{X} - Mo}{\sigma}$$

But quite often, mode is ill-defined and then following formula is used to find mode

$$\text{Mode } (Z) = 3M - 2\overline{X}$$

or *the following formula is used*

$$S_k = 3\frac{(Mean - Median)}{\sigma}$$

Bowley's Coefficient of Skewness *Prof. AL Bowley's coefficient of skewness is based on the quartiles and is given by*

$$S_k = \frac{(Q_3 - Md) - (Md - Q_1)}{(Q_3 - Md) + (Md - Q_1)}$$

$$\Rightarrow \quad S_k = \frac{Q_3 + Q_1 - 2Md}{Q_3 - Q_1}$$

Kelly's Measure of Skewness The drawback of Bowley's coefficient of skewness, (*viz* that it ignores the 50% of the data towards the extremes), can be partially removed by taking two deciles or percentiles equidistant from the median value.

The refinement was suggested by Kelly's percentile (or decile) measure of skewness is given by

$$S_k = (P_{90} - P_{50}) - (P_{50} - P_{10}) = P_{90} + P_{10} - 2P_{50}$$

But, $P_{90} = D_9$ and $P_{10} = D_1$

Hence, *it can be re-written as*

$$S_k = (D_9 - D_5) - (D_5 - D_1) = D_9 + D_1 - 2D_5$$

The above formulae gives an absolute measure of skewness. However, for practical purposes, *we generally compute the coefficient of skewness, which is given below*

$$S_k = \frac{(P_{90} - P_{50}) - (P_{50} - P_{10})}{(P_{90} - P_{50}) + (P_{50} - P_{10})} = \frac{P_{90} + P_{10} - 2P_{50}}{P_{90} - P_{10}} = \frac{D_9 + D_1 - 2D_5}{D_9 - D_1}$$

Correlation

Correlation analysis can be referred as the statistical tool used to describe the degree to which one variable is related to another. Correlation is a statistical tool that helps to measure and analyse the degree or extent to which two or more variables fluctuate with reference to one another. For correlating two phenomenon, it is essential that the two phenomenon should have a cause effect relationship and if such relationship does not exist then the two phenomenon cannot be correlated. *e.g.* When demand of a certain product or commodity increases, then its price goes up and when its demand decreases then its price come down. In this case, both the phenomena have a cause effect relationship and thus, can be correlated.

Thus, correlation is concerned with relationship between two related and quantifiable variables and can be positive or negative.

Uses of Correlation

- It aid decision-making.
- It also helps in understanding economic behaviour.
- It helps in research work.
- It establishes the relation between two variables.

Types of Correlation

Correlation is described or classified in several different ways. *They are as follows*

Positive or Negative Correlation Whether the correlation is positive (direct) or negative (inverse) would depend upon the direction of change of the variable. The correlation is said to be positive or direct in, when the variations in two variables take place in same direction, but when variations in two variables take place in opposite directions, the correlation is termed as negative.

Single and Multiple Correlation In single correlation, the relationship is confined to two variables and in multiple correlation the relationship between more than two variables. *e.g.* Study limited to two variables, saving and rate of interest is a case of simple correlation. When another variable inflation is considered then it is a case of multiple correlation.

Partial and Total Correlation In partial correlation, an analyst recognises more than two variables, but considers only two variables keeping the other constant. On the other hand, total correlation is based on all the relevant variables, which however is normally not feasible.

Linear and Non-linear (Curvilinear) ***Correlation*** It is said to be linear, when the change in one variable tends to bear a constant ratio to the change in the other. The graph of the variables having a linear relationship will form a straight line

Correlation is non-linear or curvilinear's, if the amount of change in one variable does not bear a constant ratio to the amount of change in the other variable. *e.g.* If the rainfall is doubled, then it is not necessary that the yield also doubles.

Method of Studying Correlation

Following is the important method to find the correlation between variables

Scatter Diagram Method

In this method, the given data is plotted on a graph paper in the form of dots, *i.e.* for each pair of variable. We mark dots and thus, obtain as many points as the number of observations. Generally, independent variables are plotted along the horizontal line (X-axis) and dependent variable along the vertical line (Y-axis). The picture, so obtained is called as scatter diagram.

Scatter Diagrams Depicting the Various Degrees of Correlation

Scatter diagram depicting the various degrees of correlation are as follows

Positive Correlation Points are scattered around an upward rising line indicating the movement of the variables in the same direction, *i.e.* when X rises, Y also rises and *vice-versa*.

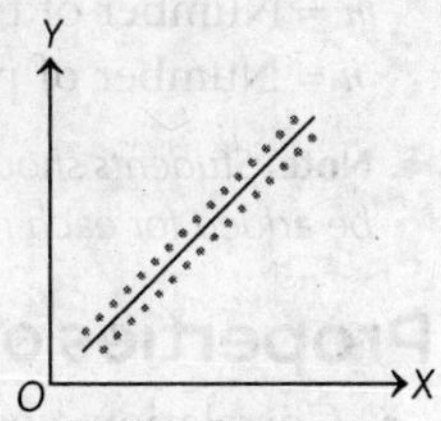

Positive Correlation

Negative Correlation Points are scattered around a downward sloping line indicating that variables are moving in opposite directions, *i.e.* when X rises, Y falls and *vice-versa*.

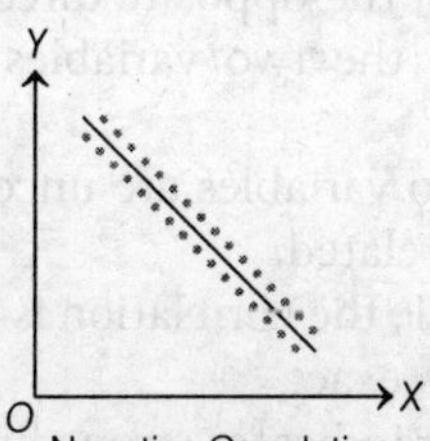

Negative Correlation

No Correlation There is no upward or downward movement in the points plotted, so variables show no correlation.

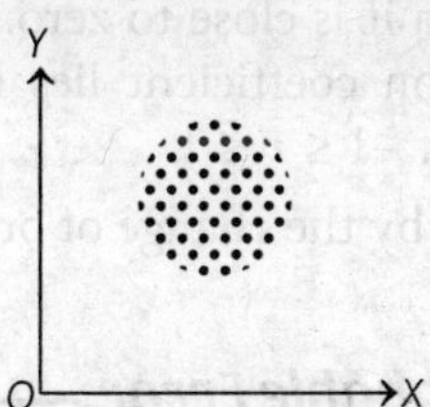

No Correlation

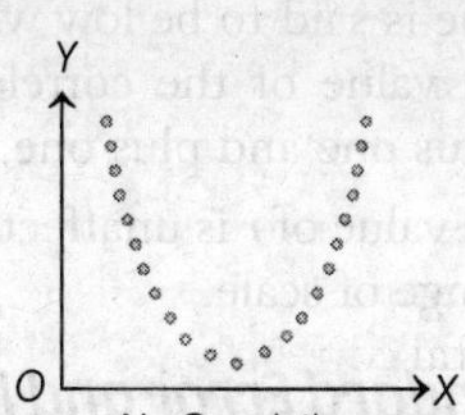

No Correlation

Perfect Positive Correlation Points are not scattered around the line rather, they are on the same upward sloping line, showing perfect positive correlation.

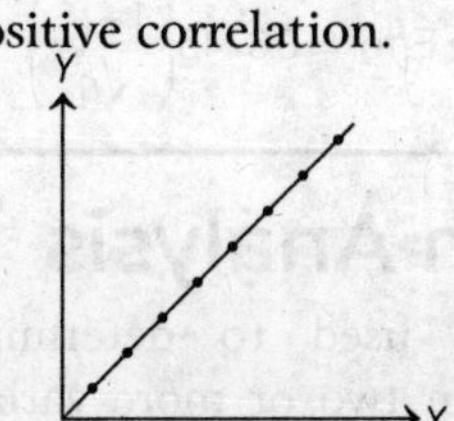

Perfect Positive Correlation

Perfect Negative Correlation Points are not scattered around the line rather, they are on the same downward sloping line, showing perfect negative correlation.

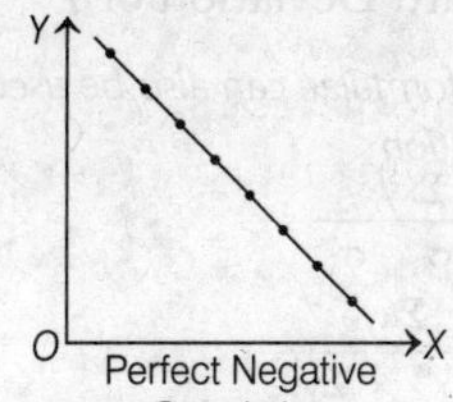

Perfect Negative Correlation

Points to be Remembered while Interpreting a Scatter Diagram

- If all the points lie on a line, the correlation is perfect and said to be unity, *i.e.* one.
- If the scatter points are widely dispersed around the line, the correlation is low.
- Correlation is said to be linear if the scatter points lie near a line or on a line.
- If the points move from left to right, upwards the correlation is said to be positive, whereas the movement of points from left to right, downwards indicates negative correlation.
- Points in a straight line indicate perfect correlation.
- Points falling close to each other in a straight line indicate high degree of correlation.
- If plotted points show no trend at all, then it shows absence of correlation or no correlation between the two variables.

Calculation of Coefficient of Correlation

Karl Pearson's Coefficient of Correlation

This is a mathematical method to calculate the coefficient of correlation. The coefficient of correlation is denoted by 'r', which is a measure of the degree of linear relationship or correlation between two variables say 'x' and 'y' one of which happens to be an independent variable and the other being a dependent variable.

According to British Statistician, Karl Pearson, "The correlation coefficient between two variables denotes as 'r_{xy}' is the ratio of the covariance between X and Y to the product of standard deviations of X and Y."

Symbolically,

$$\text{Correlation Coefficient } (r) = \frac{Cov(x,\ y)}{\sigma_x \times \sigma_y}$$

Where,

$Cov(x,\ y)$ = Covariance between X and Y and is computed as, $\dfrac{\Sigma xy}{n}$

Where,

$\Sigma x = \Sigma(X - \bar{X})$ and $\Sigma y = \Sigma(Y - \bar{Y})$,
σ_x = Standard Deviation of X,
σ_y = Standard Deviation of Y

➡ **Note** *The following formulae can also be used to find Karl Pearson's Coefficient of Correlation*

Or $$r = \frac{\Sigma xy}{n \cdot \sigma_x \cdot \sigma_y}$$

Or $$r = \frac{\Sigma xy}{\sqrt{\Sigma x^2 \times \Sigma y^2}}$$

Or $$r = \frac{\Sigma dxdy - \dfrac{\Sigma dx \times \Sigma dy}{n}}{\sqrt{\Sigma dx^2 - \dfrac{(\Sigma dx)^2}{n}} \times \sqrt{\Sigma dy^2 - \dfrac{(\Sigma dy)^2}{n}}}$$

Or $$\frac{\Sigma dxdy \cdot n - (\Sigma dx)(\Sigma dy)}{\sqrt{\Sigma dx^2 \cdot n - (\Sigma dx)^2} \times \sqrt{\Sigma dy^2 \cdot n - (\Sigma dy)^2}},$$

Or $$r = \frac{\Sigma XY}{\sqrt{\Sigma X^2 \times \Sigma Y^2}}$$

Where,
Σxy = Sum of products of values of series X and series Y
Σx^2 = Sum of squares of values of series X
Σy^2 = Sum of squares of values of series Y
$\Sigma d_x = \Sigma(X - A)$
$\Sigma d_y = \Sigma(Y - A)$

Where, A is assumed mean from series X and Y respectively.

Spearman's Rank Correlation Coefficient

In this method, a rank is assigned to each value of a variable. This method is especially useful, when quantitative measure of certain factors involving quantity or quality cannot be fixed. Thus, individuals belonging to a group can be arranged in order by assigning a number indicating a rank to each individual of the group. This method was developed by Charles Edward Spearman in 1904. *e.g.* Evaluation of leadership skills and ability of an individual may make use of this method.

Spearman's rank correlation coefficient is usually denoted by ρ (Rho). *It is computed with the help of the following formula*

$$\rho = 1 - \frac{6\Sigma D^2}{n^3 - n} \because \frac{6\Sigma D^2}{n(n^2 - 1)}$$

Where,
ΣD^2 is the sum of the square of the difference between ranks and n is the number of pairs.

When Ranks are given and there is Repetition in Ranks

Repetition of ranks imply that two or more contestants are given a similar rank by a judge. *e.g.* Judge, J can give 3rd rank to contestants M, Y and Z. When ranks are repeated, a correction factor $\frac{m(m^2 - 1)}{12}$ is applied.

The steps for computation are given below

Step 1 We represent the ranks of first series as R_1 and the ranks of second series as R_2.

Step 2 We find values of D, *i.e.* difference between two sets of ranks, $(R_1 - R_2)$.

Step 3 We find square of these differences and add them to obtain ΣD^2.

Step 4 Apply the given formula to compute rank correlation,

$$\rho = r_k = 1 - \frac{6\left[\Sigma D^2 + \dfrac{m(m^2 - 1)}{12} + \ldots\ldots \dfrac{m(m^2 - 1)}{12}\right]}{n^3 - n}$$

Where,
ΣD^2 = Sum of squared differences,
m = Number of times a rank is repeated,
n = Number of pairs

➡ **Note** *Students should remember that the correlation factor should be added for each repetition of rank in either of the series.*

Properties of Correlation Coefficient

- Correlation coefficient (r) has no unit. It is a pure number. It means units of measurement are not part of r.
- A negative value of r indicates an inverse relation. A change in one variable is associated with change in the other variable in the opposite direction.
- If r is positive, the two variables move in the same direction.
- If $r = 0$, the two variables are uncorrelated or they are not linearly correlated.
- If $r = 1$ or $r = -1$, the correlation is perfect. The relation between them is exact.
- A high value of r indicates strong linear relationship. Its value is said to be high when it is close to +1 or −1.
- A low value of r indicates a weak linear relation. Its value is said to be low when it is close to zero.
- The value of the correlation coefficient lies between minus one and plus one, *i.e.* $-1 \leq r \leq 1$.
- The value of r is unaffected by the change of origin and change of scale.

Standard Error and Probable Error

$$\text{Standard Error} = \frac{1 - r^2}{\sqrt{n}}$$

$$\text{Probable Error} = 0.6745\left(\frac{1 - r^2}{\sqrt{n}}\right)$$

Regression Analysis

This technique is used to determine the statistical relationship between two or more variables and to make prediction of one variable on the basis of one or more other variables. In regression analysis, the two types of variables, the dependent variable is known as regressed (or explained) and independent variable is known as regressor (or predictor or explanatory) variable.

Utility of Regression Analysis

- Regression analysis provides estimates of values of the regressed variables from the values of regressor variables.
- Regression analysis also help to obtain a measure of the error involved in using the regression line as a basis for estimation. For this purpose, standard error of estimate is calculated. An estimate can be good, if the regression line fits the data closely.
- Further, regression analysis also helps in obtaining a measure of the degree of association or correlation that exists between the two variables.

Types of Regression

Simple Regression Simple linear regression is, when you want to predict values of one variable on the basis of given values of another variable, *e.g.* You might want to predict a person's height (in inches) from his weight (in pounds). Imagine a sample of ten people for whom you know their height and weight. You could plot the values on a graph, with weight on the *X*-axis and height on the *Y*-axis. If there were a perfect linear relationship, then you could get a cluster of points on the graph, which slopes upward. In other words, people with good height should weigh more than people with short height.

Multiple Regression It estimates the relation between variables taking into account several additional (third) variables. *e.g.* Estimate the gain in weight due to quitting smoking, taking into account age, race, level of education, duration off follow-up, changes in physical activity and reproductive history.

Standard Multiple Regression It is the same idea as simple linear regression, except now you have several independent variables predicting the dependent variable. To continue with the previous example, imagine that you now wanted to predict a person's height from the gender of the person and from the weight. You would use standard multiple regression, in which gender and weight were the independent variables and height was the dependent variable. The resulting output would tell you a number of things. First, it would tell you how much of the variance of height was accounted for by the joint predictive power of knowing a person's weight and gender. This value is denoted by 'R_2'. The output would also tell you, if the model allows you to predict a person's height at a rate better than chance.

Assumptions in Regression Analysis

- There exists an actual relationship between the dependent and independent variable.
- The values of the dependent variable are random, but the values of the independent variable are fixed quantities without error and are chosen by the analyst.
- The regression analysis is used to estimate the value within the range, for which it is valid and not for values outside its range.
- The relationship that existed between the dependent and independent variable remains the same till the regression equation is calculated.
- In regression, we have only one dependent variable in our estimating equation. However, we can use more than one independent variable.

Regression Line

It is tool used for estimating the value of one variable from the value of the other. It is a line through the points drawn in such a manner as to represent the average relationship between the two variables.

Regression line gives the best estimate to the value of one variable for any specific value of the other variable.

There are two regression lines, which are as follows

Regression Line of X on Y This is used to find the value of *X*, when the value of *Y* is known.

It is represented in the following manner

$$X - \overline{X} = r \cdot \frac{\sigma x}{\sigma y}(Y - \overline{Y}) \quad \text{or} \quad X - \overline{X} = b_{xy}(Y - \overline{Y})$$

Regression Line of Y on X This is used to find the value of *Y*, when the value of *X* is known. *It is represented in the following manner*

$$Y - \overline{Y} = r \cdot \frac{\sigma y}{\sigma x}(X - \overline{X}) \quad \text{or} \quad Y - \overline{Y} = b_{yx}(X - \overline{X})$$

➠ **Note** b_{xy} *and* b_{yx} *are regression coefficients and*

$$r = \sqrt{b_{xy} \times b_{yx}}$$

Coefficient of Determination

The coefficient of determination is a parameter, by which we can measure the extent or strength of the association that exists between two variables 'X' and 'Y'.

Coefficient of determination is calculated by

$$r^2 = 1 - \frac{\Sigma(Y - Ye)^2}{\Sigma(Y - \overline{Y})^2}$$

Or
$$r^2 = \frac{\text{Explained Variance}}{\text{Total Variance}}$$

The value of R_2 is the proportion of the variation in the dependent variable by regression on the independent variable x.

Also, coefficient of non-determination is given by $(1 - r^2)$.

Regression Lines by Least Square Method

According to the principle of least squares, the normal equations for estimating '*a*' and '*b*', *i.e.* the '*Y*' intercept and slope of the best fitting 'Regression Line'. *These are as given below*

$$\Sigma Y = na + b\Sigma X$$

$$\Sigma XY = a\Sigma X + b\Sigma X^2$$

EXAM BASED QUESTIONS

Measures of Central Tendency

1 Important objective of statistical analysis is to get .... that describes the characteristics of the entire data.

(a) single value (b) average value
(c) central value (d) All of these

2 The modal class is a class with .... frequency.

(a) highest (b) lowest
(c) no (d) None of these

3 Calculation of arithmetic mean by short-cut and step-deviation method is based on assumed mean, which is taken/selected from

(a) given independent variable
(b) given frequency distribution
(c) estimated cumulative frequency distribution
(d) None of the above

4 The arithmetic mean of a series is the figure obtained by dividing the sum of values of all items by

(a) 2 (b) 3
(c) 4 (d) their number

5 Which of the following are the positional averages?

1. Mean 2. Median 3. Mode

Codes

(a) Both 1 and 2 (b) Both 2 and 3
(c) Both 1 and 3 (d) 1, 2 and 3

6 Which of the following is not a mathematical average?

(a) Median
(b) Arithmetic mean
(c) Geometric mean
(d) Harmonic mean

7 Arithmetic mean and harmonic mean includes all values of the data set in its calculation.

(a) True (b) False
(c) Partly true (d) None of these

8 A measure of central tendency means

(a) an average of a distribution
(b) a single figure which can be regarded as a representative of the whole distribution
(c) representative of a set of data
(d) All of the above

9 Weighted averages are considered when

(a) the data are not classified
(b) the data are put in the form of grouped frequency distribution
(c) all the observations are not of equal importance
(d) Both (a) and (c)

10 .... is particularly useful when we have to compute the mean of means.

(a) Arithmetic mean
(b) Geometric mean
(c) Weighted arithmetic mean
(d) None of the above

11 The less than and more than cumulative frequency plot should intersect at the .... of the data.

(a) mean (b) median
(c) mode (d) All of these

12 Mode is a positional average which is used to deal with which type of data?

1. Quantitative data
2. Qualitative data

Codes

(a) Only 1 (b) Only 2
(c) Both 1 and 2 (d) None of the above

13 Object of median is to

(a) fix a representative value
(b) establish a dividing line separating the higher from the lower values
(c) Both (a) and (b)
(d) Neither (a) nor (b)

14 The .... is less sensitive to extreme scores than the ....

(a) median, mean
(b) mean, median
(c) mode, median
(d) None of the above

15 Mode quantitatively describes

(a) standard behaviour
(b) abnormalities
(c) fashion or trend of the period
(d) None of the above

16 Find out the value of the median from the following frequency

Size of Items	8	10	12	14	16	18	20
Frequency	3	7	12	28	10	9	6

(a) 12 (b) 14
(c) 16 (d) 18

17 The following figures represent the number of book issued at the counter of a commerce library in 11 different ways. Calculate the median.
96, 180, 98, 75, 270, 20, 102, 100, 94, 75, 200

(a) 96 (b) 98
(c) 100 (d) 102

18 Statistical average has significance due to following sequence.

1. To present huge mass of data in a summarised form.
2. To facilitate comparison of different sets of data.
3. To help decision-making.

Select the correct answer using the codes given below

Codes

(a) 1, 2, 3 (b) 2, 3, 1
(c) 2, 1, 3 (d) 3, 2, 1

19 Which of the following statistical measures is based on all observations?

(a) Harmonic mean (b) Range
(c) Mode (d) None of these

20 Which of the following can be calculated from a cumulative frequency curve?

(a) Geometric mean (b) Harmonic mean
(c) Median (d) Mode

21 Which of the following can be calculated for grouped data with open-ended classes?

(a) Mean (b) Median
(c) Mode (d) Both (b) and (c)

22 How will the arithmetic mean be affected by adding a constant '*b*' to every item?

(a) $\overline{X}+b$ (b) $\overline{X}-b$
(c) $\overline{X}/b$ (d) None of these

23 It is appropriate to calculate the mean excluding the extreme value in order to make it more representative.

(a) True (b) False
(c) Partly true (d) None of these

24 In a series, the sum of all the observations is .... times the arithmetic mean.

(a) 2 (b) mean itself
(c) 5 (d) None of these

25 If first and third quartile is 40 and 80 respectively. The median is

(a) 60 (b) 50 (c) 45 (d) 70

26 Which of the following measure of central tendency may not be contained in the observation?

(a) Mean (b) Median
(c) Mode (d) All of these

27 Arithmetic mean of a group of 100 items is 50 and of another group of 150 items is 100. What will be the mean of all items?

(a) 75
(b) 100
(c) 80
(d) None of the abvoe

28 Given, mode = 22 and median = 21.4. Find out the average mean.

(a) 21.1 (b) 21.4
(c) 22.1 (d) 22.4

29 Calculate the mean of marks of 46 students from the following table.

Marks (X)	Frequency
9	1
10	2
11	3
12	4
13	5
14	6
15	7
16	8
17	9
18	10
Total	55

(a) 12.01 (b) 15
(c) 14.56 (d) None of these

30 In a moderately asymmetrical distribution, the mode and mean are 42 and 40, respectively. The median is

(a) 39 (b) 40.67 (c) 38 (d) 41.02

31 Calculate mean from the following data.

Age (X)	Frequency (f)
17	2
18	1
19	1
20	2
22	3
23	1

(a) 15 (b) 30 (c) 20 (d) 40

32 The mean age group of 100 persons was found to be 30.2. Later, it was discovered that age 57 was misread as 27. Find the corrected mean.

(a) 30.5 (b) 31.23 (c) 32.32 (d) 36.44

33 Arithmetic mean of 98 items is 50. Two items 60 and 70 were left out at the time of calculation. What will be the correct mean of all the items?

(a) AM = 50.2 (b) AM = 50.3 (c) AM = 49.9 (d) AM = 50.9

34 Find the median from the following data.

Gross Profit (Percent of Sales)	Number of Companies
0-10	21
10-20	32
20-30	43
30-40	34
40-50	23

(a) 23.40 (b) 25.46 (c) 40.40 (d) 38.53

Dispersion

35 Range limit can be expressed as

(a) R = L + S (b) R = L + S/2
(c) R = L – S (d) None of these

36 Which of the following is the tool of measures of the variation of items?

(a) Mean (b) Median
(c) Mode (d) Dispersion

37 The most commonly used measure of dispersion is ....

(a) range (b) standard deviation
(c) coefficient of variation (d) quartile deviation

38 Which measure of dispersion is square of standard deviation?

(a) Variance (b) Range
(c) Quartile deviation (d) Mean deviation

39 .... is a true measure of dispersion.

(a) Range (b) Mean deviation
(c) Inter-quartile range (d) None of these

40 Coefficient of range can be calculated as

(a) L + S/L × S (b) L + S/L − S
(c) L − S/L + S (d) L × S/L + S

41 Standard deviation can be expressed as

(a) $\frac{\Sigma|\bar{x} - x|}{N}$ (b) $\frac{\Sigma|x - \bar{x}|}{N}$

(c) $\sigma = \sqrt{\frac{\Sigma(x - \bar{x})^2}{N}}$ (d) None of these

42 Which of the following is correct formula to calculate 'width of the class'?

(a) Class range ÷ Number of classes
(b) Class range × Number of classes
(c) Class range ÷ Total number of sample
(d) None of the above

43 Which of the statement(s) are true about 'measures of dispersion'?

1. The divergence of a set of observation
2. The concentration of a set of observation

Codes

(a) Only 1 (b) Only 2
(c) Both 1 and 2 (d) None of the above

44 For a continuous frequency distribution, range is defined as

(a) difference between the upper limit of the first class and lower limit of last class
(b) difference between the upper limit of the highest class and the lower limit of the smallest class
(c) difference between the upper limit of the highest class and lower limit of the highest class
(d) None of the above

45 Range is the measure of dispersion which is used for the following purpose.

1. Quality control of products.
2. Studying the fluctuation in financial and share market.

Codes

(a) Only 1 (b) Only 2
(c) Both 1 and 2 (d) None of the above

46 The range based on middle 50% of the observations is called ....

(a) quartile deviation
(b) inter-quartile deviation
(c) inter-quartile range
(d) None of the above

47 A small quartile deviation denotes .... in the central 50% of the observations.

(a) high variation (b) low variation
(c) highest value (d) None of these

48 Calculate the value of variance if median = 23, mode = 29 and coefficient of variation is 50%.

(a) 100 (b) 10
(c) 90 (d) 80

49 Compute the coefficient of range from the following data 91, 54, 44, 56, 71, 25, 09, 27, 72, 62.

(a) 0.79 (b) 0.82
(c) 0.85 (d) 0.76

50 Following is the information about the employees in an organisation in various age groups. Compute range and coefficient of range.

Class (Years)	Number of Employees
56-60	7
61-65	16
66-70	39
71-75	28
76-80	10

(a) 22, 1.02 (b) 23, 0.12
(c) 24, 0.1765 (d) None of these

51 In case of .... distribution mean, median, mode coincide.

(a) symmetrical
(b) asymmetrical
(c) moderately asymmetrical
(d) None of the above

52 For symmetrical distribution which of the following is true?

(a) Median − Q_1 = Q_3 − Median
(b) Mode − Q_1 = Q_3 − Median
(c) Mean − Q_1 = Q_3 − Mode
(d) None of the above

53 In a unimodal and symmetric distribution, the relationship between average is like this.

(a) Mean > Median > Mode (b) Mean < Median > Mode
(c) Mean = Median = Mode (d) Mean > Median < Mode

Skewness

54 Karl Pearson's coefficient of skewness is calculated by following formula.

(a) $\frac{\bar{X} - Z}{\sigma}$ (b) $\frac{\bar{X} - M}{\sigma}$

(c) $\frac{Z - \bar{X}}{\sigma}$ (d) $\frac{\bar{X} - \sigma}{Z}$

55 Bowley's Coefficient of skewness is calculated by following formula.

(a) $\frac{Q_3+Q_1-M}{Q_3-Q_1}$ (b) $\frac{Q_3+Q_1-2M}{Q_3+Q_1}$

(c) $\frac{Q_3+Q_1-2M}{Q_3-Q_1}$ (d) $\frac{Q_3+Q_1-3M}{Q_3-Q_1}$

56 Skewness will be negative, when

(a) $\overline{X}>Z$ (b) $\overline{X}<Z$

(c) $\overline{X}=Z$ (d) None of these

57 In a series, the difference of the two quartiles is 10, their sum is 25 and the median is 6.5, then the coefficient of skewness will be

(a) 0.12 (b) 1.2 (c) 12 (d) 2.5

58 In a frequency distribution, Bowley's coefficient of skewness is 0.6, if the sum of two quartiles is 100 and median is 38, the value of third quartile will be

(a) 70 (b) 30 (c) 60 (d) 40

59 If mean $=45$, median $=48$ and coefficient of skewness $=-0.4$, then the value of standard deviation will be

(a) 20.5 (b) 15.9 (c) 22.5 (d) 25.8

Correlation and Regression

60 The theory by means of which quantitative connections between two sets of phenomena are determined is called the ....

(a) theory of correlation (b) theory of regression

(c) theory of determination (d) None of these

61 Which one of the following is a formula of Karl Pearson's coefficient correlation?

(a) $r=\sqrt{\frac{\Sigma XY}{\Sigma X^2\,\Sigma Y^2}}$ (b) $r=\frac{\Sigma XY}{\sqrt{Y^2-\Sigma X^2}}$

(c) $r=\frac{\Sigma XY}{\sqrt{X^2-\Sigma Y^2}}$ (d) None of these

62 In the Spearman's rank correlation coefficient, when the ranks are equal, the formula is

(a) $1-\frac{\left[6\,\Sigma D^2+\frac{1}{2}(m^2-m)+\frac{1}{2}(m^2-m)+....\right]}{N^3-N}$

(b) $1-\frac{6\left[\Sigma D^2+\frac{1}{12}(m^3-m_1)+\frac{1}{12}(m^3-m_2)+....\right]}{N^3-N}$

(c) $1-\frac{\frac{1}{2}\left[(m^3-m)+\frac{1}{2}(m^3-m)+....\right]}{N^3-N}$

(d) None of the above

63 Correlation is said to be linear, when the

(a) increase in one variable results decrease in the other

(b) decrease in one variable results an increase in the other

(c) change in one variable does not affect the other

(d) change in one variable tend to bear constant ratio of change in the other

64 Correlation obtained by concurrent deviation method indicate only following result.

(a) Direction of co-changes

(b) Degree of co-changes

(c) Direction and degree of co-changes

(d) None of the above

65 Coefficient of correlation between X and Y is directly proportional to

(a) standard deviation of X (b) standard deviation of Y

(c) covariance of X and Y (d) Both (a) and (b)

66 While drawing a scatter diagram if all the points appear to form a straight line going downward from left to right, then it is inferred that there is a

(a) perfect positive correlation

(b) simple positive correlation

(c) perfect negative correlation

(d) No correlation

67 Coefficient of determination is defined as

(a) r^3 (b) $1-r^2$

(c) $1+r^3$ (d) r^2

68 There will be positive correlation in X and Y, if

(a) both the variables are varying in the same direction

(b) variables are varying in opposite direction

(c) there is no certain trend of changes in both variables

(d) None of the above

69 Concurrent deviation correlation coefficient is obtained by the following formula.

(a) $\pm\sqrt{\pm\left(\frac{2c-n}{n}\right)}$ (b) $\pm\sqrt{\pm\left(\frac{2c+n}{n}\right)}$

(c) $\pm\sqrt{\pm 2\left(\frac{c-n}{n}\right)}$ (d) $\pm\sqrt{\pm 2\left(\frac{2c-n}{n}\right)}$

70 Rank correlation coefficient is obtained by following the formula.

(a) $1-\frac{\Sigma D^2}{N^3-N}$ (b) $\frac{6\Sigma D^2}{N(N^3-N)}$

(c) $1-\frac{6\Sigma D^2}{N(N^2-1)}$ (d) $1+\frac{6\Sigma D^2}{N(N^3-N)}$

71 Proportion of changes in y due to changes in x is denoted by the following measure.

(a) Standard error of estimate

(b) Coefficient of correlation

(c) Coefficient of determination

(d) Probable error

72 Correlation coefficient by least square method is obtained by the following formula.

(a) $1-\frac{S_y}{\sigma_y}$ (b) $\sqrt{1-\frac{S^2y}{\sigma^2y}}$ (c) $\sqrt{1-\frac{\sigma^2y}{S^2y}}$ (d) $\frac{S^2y}{\sigma^2y}$

73 Probable error in statistics is obtained by

(a) $\frac{1-r^2}{\sqrt{N}}$ (b) $0.6475\,\frac{1-r^2}{\sqrt{N}}$

(c) $0.6745\,\frac{1-r^2}{\sqrt{N}}$ (d) $0.6475\,\frac{1-r^3}{\sqrt{N}}$

74 Standard error of estimate is obtained by the following formula.

(a) $\frac{\Sigma(Y-\bar{Y})^2}{N}$ (b) $\frac{\Sigma(Y-Y_c)^2}{N}$

(c) $\sqrt{\frac{\Sigma(Y-Y_c)^2}{N}}$ (d) $\sqrt{\frac{\Sigma(Y-\bar{Y})^2}{N}}$

75 If in two series the change occurs in same direction (either increase or decrease) then correlation is

(a) negative (b) positive
(c) zero (d) None of these

76 Which of the following is/are related with the utility of correlation?

(a) Help in decision-making
(b) Useful in research work
(c) Relation between two variables
(d) All of the above

77 Which of the following is a causes of correlation?

(a) Direct relationship
(b) Correlation due to any other common cause
(c) Mutual reaction
(d) None of the above

78 If two entries are assigned the average of rank 5 and it's next rank 6, then the next rank after 5.5 is

(a) 5 (b) 6
(c) 7 (d) 8

79 In the formula $R = 1 - \frac{6\Sigma D^2}{N(N^2-1)}$, '$D$' stands for

(a) deviation (b) difference of two ranks
(c) coefficient of correlation (d) None of these

80 Arrange the following steps in sequence for finding the correlation between variable.

1. Determine the two variables 'X' and 'Y'.
2. Variables 'X' and 'Y' are plotted on X-axis and Y-axis in the XY-plane.
3. Then correlation is determined by seeing the scatter diagram.

Codes

(a) 1, 2 and 3 (b) 2, 3 and 1
(c) 1, 3 and 2 (d) 3, 2 and 1

81 Karl Pearson's coefficient of correlation between two variables x and y is equal to

(a) covariance between two variables
(b) product of their standard deviation
(c) square root of the product of two regression coefficient
(d) None of the above

82 From the following data, calculate coefficient of correlation.

X	1	2	3	4	5
Y	10	20	30	40	50

(a) 0.9 (b) 0.8
(c) 0.6 (d) 10.1

83 Calculate rank correlation coefficient from the following data.

X	59	69	39	49	29
Y	79	69	39	49	39

(a) 0.2 (b) 0.8
(c) 0.7 (d) 0.9

84 If the coefficient of correlation between x and y is 0.28, covariance between x and y is 7.6 and the variance of x is 9, then the standard deviation of y series is

(a) 9.0 (b) 9.1
(c) 9.05 (d) 10

85 What type of correlation exists in the following two variates?

X	1	2	3	4	5	6
Y	10	12	14	16	18	20

(a) − 1 (b) 0 (c) + 1 (d) ± 1

86 Correlation coefficient is taken to be significant, if

(a) $r > 5$ P.E. (b) $r > 6$ P.E.
(c) $r < 6$ P.E. (d) $r = 6$ P.E.

87 The product moment coefficient correlation (r) is obtained by

(a) $\Sigma XY / xy$ (b) $\Sigma xy / N.\sigma_x\sigma_y$
(c) $\Sigma XY / N.\sigma_y$ (d) $\Sigma X\Sigma Y / \sigma_x.\sigma_y$

88 The limits of the population correlation is

(a) $r \pm$ P.E. (b) $r \pm 3$ S.E.
(c) $r \pm 3$ P.E. (d) None of these

89 If sum of the product of deviations of x and y series from their means is zero, the coefficient of correlation shall be

(a) + 1 (b) 0
(c) − 1 (d) None of these

90 High degree of correlation is assumed, when

(a) $r = 0.52$ (b) $r = 0.45$
(c) $r = 0.9$ (d) $r = 0.65$

91 In regression analysis, it is assumed that there is an actual relationship between the .... and independent variable.

(a) dependent (b) another variable
(c) given variable (d) None of these

92 Least Square Method of fitting a line (the line of best fit or the regression line) through the scatter diagram is a method, which .... the sum of the squared vertical deviations from the fitted line.

(a) maximises
(b) minimises
(c) Neither (a) nor (b)
(d) All of the above

93 The intersecting point of two regression lines is

(a) 0, 0 (b) $\bar{x}, \bar{y}$
(c) b_{xy}, b_{yx} (d) None of these

94 The larger the standard error of estimate the .... happens to be the dispersion of given observations around the regression line.

(a) lower
(b) greater
(c) Both (a) and (b)
(d) None of the above

95 If 'x' and 'y' are independent variables, then the two lines of regression are

(a) $x = 0, y = 0$ (b) $x =$ constant, $y =$ constant
(c) $x = 0, y =$ constant (d) None of these

96 If the regression coefficient of Y on X is 4/3, then the regression coefficient of X on is

(a) more than 1 (b) less than 1
(c) less than 0 (d) None of these

97 When there is either perfect positive correlation and either perfect negative correlation between the two variables the two regression lines will ....

(a) overlap (b) coincide
(c) Both (a) and (b) (d) None of these

Miscellaneous

98 Which of the following measures are unit free?

1. Correlation coefficient
2. Covariance
3. Coefficient of variation
4. Index numbers

Select the correct answer using the codes given below

Codes

(a) 1, 2 and 3 (b) 1, 3 and 4
(c) Both 1 and 4 (d) None of the above

99 **Assertion** (A) Median is simply the middle value when the data have been arranged in ascending or descending order.
Reason (R) Median refers to middle value in the distribution.

Codes

(a) Both (A) and (R) are true
(b) (A) is true, but (R) is false
(c) (A) is false, but (R) is true
(d) Both (A) and (R) are false

100 **Assertion** (A) Median of a distribution is that value of the variant which divides it in two equal parts.
Reason (R) Median is a positional average.

Codes

(a) Both (A) and (R) are true
(b) Both (A) and (R) are true, but (R) is not the correct explanation of (A)
(c) Both (A) and (R) are false
(d) (A) is true, but (R) is false

101 **Assertion** (A) The simple arithmetic mean will be equal to the weighted arithmetic mean, when all items are assigned equal weights.
Reason (R) The simple arithmetic mean will be less than the weighted arithmetic mean when items of small values are given less weights and items of big values are give more weights.

Codes

(a) Both (A) and (R) are true
(b) Both (A) and (R) are true, but (R) is not the correct explanation of (A)
(c) Both (A) and (R) are false
(d) (A) is true, but (R) is false

102 **Assertion** (A) Range is not useful to manager for comparison, if the observations are in different units.
Reason (R) For the purpose of comparison a relative measure of range is required which is called coefficient of range.

Codes

(a) Both (A) and (R) are true
(b) (A) is true, but (R) is false
(c) (A) is false, but (R) is true
(d) Both (A) and (R) are false

103 **Assertion** (A) Standard deviation is independent of change of origin.
Reason (R) The value of standard deviation remains the same, if in a series each the observation is increased or decreased by a constant quantity.

Codes

(a) Both (A) and (R) are true
(b) Both (A) and (R) are true, but (R) is not the correct explanation of (A)
(c) Both (A) and (R) are false
(d) (A) is true, but (R) is false

104 **Assertion** (A) In mean deviation, everything is considered positive.
Reason (R) Sum of the deviations of the value of items in a series from arithmetic mean is zero and from other averages it is nearly zero.

Codes

(a) Both (A) and (R) are true
(b) Both (A) and (R) are true, but (R) is not the correct explanation of (A)
(c) Both (A) and (R) are false
(d) (A) is true, but R is false

105 **Assertion** (A) The value of coefficient of correlation shall always lie between $-1 < r < +1$.
Reason (R) When the value or $r = +1$ the correlation between the variable is perfect and positive and when $r = -1$, correlation is said to be perfect and negative.

Codes

(a) Both (A) and (R) are true
(b) (A) is true, but (R) is false
(c) (R) is true, but (A) is false
(d) Both (A) and (R) are false

106 Assertion (A) The two lines of regression can never be parallel.

Reason (R) The two lines of regression always pass through common point $(x \cdot y)$. Therefore, they can never be parallel.

Codes
(a) Both (A) and (R) are true and (R) is the correct explanation of (A)
(b) (A) is true, but (R) is false
(c) (R) is true, but (A) is false
(d) Both (A) and (R) are false

107 Assertion (A) In regression analysis, the values of the dependent variable are random, but the values of the independent variable are fixed quantities without error and are chosen by the analyst.

Reason (R) Regression analysis provides value of the regressed variables (dependent) from the value of the regressor variables (independent variable).

Codes
(a) Both (A) and (R) are true and (R) is the correct explanation of (A)
(b) Both (A) and (R) are true, but (R) is not the correct explanation of (A)
(c) Both (A) and (R) are false
(d) (A) is false, but (R) is true

108 Match the following.

List I	List II
A. Range	1. Not based on all observation in data
B. Mode	2. Middle value of a series arranged in any order of magnitude
C. Mean	3. It can be used even when classes are open-ended
D. Median	4. Is the most simple and frequently used average

Codes

	A	B	C	D		A	B	C	D
(a)	1	3	4	2	(b)	1	2	3	4
(c)	2	1	4	3	(d)	3	2	1	4

109 The mean and standard deviation of 10 observations are 35 and 2 respectively.

List I	List II
A. Changed mean if each observation is increased by 4	1. 39
B. Standard deviation if each observation is increased by 4	2. 2
C. Changed mean if each observation is multiplied by 5	3. 175
D. Changed standard deviation if each observation is multiplied by 5	4. 10

Codes

	A	B	C	D		A	B	C	D
(a)	1	2	3	4	(b)	2	1	3	4
(c)	3	2	4	1	(d)	4	3	2	1

110 From the given table match the following.

Class Interval	350-369	370-389	390-409	410-429	430-449	450-469
Frequency	15	27	31	19	13	6

List I	List II
A. Mid-value of class interval 370-389	1. 379.5
B. Σf	2. 111
C. Σfx	3. 44464.5
D. Arithmetic mean	4. 400.58

Codes

	A	B	C	D		A	B	C	D
(a)	2	1	3	4	(b)	1	2	3	4
(c)	3	4	2	1	(d)	4	3	2	1

111 Match the following from the given observations 15, 20, 25.

List I	List II
A. Arithmetic mean	1. 30
B. Sum of deviations from their arithmetic mean	2. 20
C. Range	3. 10

Codes

	A	B	C		A	B	C
(a)	1	2	3	(b)	2	1	3
(c)	1	3	2	(d)	3	2	1

112 Match the following.

16,17,22,16,14

List I	List II
A. Arithmetic mean	1. 16
B. Median	2. 16.63
C. Mode	3. 17
D. Harmonic mean	4. 16

Codes

	A	B	C	D
(a)	1	2	3	4
(b)	3	4	1	2
(c)	4	2	3	1
(d)	4	3	2	1

113 Match the following.

List I	List II
A. Quartile deviation	1. Obtained by calculating the absolute deviation of each observation from mean
B. Standard deviation	2. Is one-half of the inter-quartile range
C. Mean deviation	3. Is the square root of the average of the squared distances of the observation from the mean

Codes

	A	B	C		A	B	C
(a)	2	3	1	(b)	1	2	3
(c)	2	1	3	(d)	3	2	1

114 Match the following.

List I (In Case of Correlation)	List II (Value of 'r')
A. Perfect positive	1. 0
B. Perfect negative	2. +1
C. No correlation	3. – 1

Codes

	A	B	C		A	B	C
(a)	1	2	3	(b)	2	1	3
(c)	3	1	2	(d)	2	3	1

115 Match the following.

List I	List II
A. Positive correlation	1. When two or more variables are involved and they are to be studied in relation to their relationship with one another
B. Multiple correlation	2. When ratio of change between two variables is uniform
C. Linear correlation	3. When relationship of two variables is studied by eliminating the effect of other variables from both
D. Partial correlation	4. When movement of variables take place in same direction

Codes

	A	B	C	D
(a)	4	1	2	3
(b)	1	2	3	4
(c)	3	2	4	1
(d)	2	3	1	4

116 Match the following.

List I (Terms)	List II (Definitions)
A. Simple regression	1. Process of predicting one variable from another
B. Multiple regression	2. Single variable is used to predict another variable on the assumption of linear relationship between the given variables
C. Simple linear regression analysis	3. Involves two or more independent variables and one dependent variable

Codes

	A	B	C
(a)	1	2	3
(b)	1	3	2
(c)	3	1	2
(d)	3	2	1

PREVIOUS YEARS' QUESTIONS

December 2018

1 If a perpendicular on X-axis from the point of intersection of both 'less than' and 'more than' frequency curves is drawn, it gives the value of

(a) arithmetic mean (b) third quartile
(c) mode (d) median

2 The probable error of the coefficient of correlation(r) is calculated by which one of the following formula?

(a) $0.6745\sqrt{\frac{1-r^2}{n}}$ (b) $0.6745\frac{(1-r^2)}{\sqrt{n}}$

(c) $0.6745\frac{1+r^2}{\sqrt{n}}$ (d) $0.6745\frac{(1+r^2)}{n}$

July 2018

3 There is a very high inverse relationship between measures of 'overweight' and 'life expectancy'. Which one of the following value of the coefficient of correlation is consistent with the statement?

(a) 0.80 (b) 0.20 (c) – 0.20 (d) – 0.80

November 2017

4 Which of the following statements are true? Select the correct code.

1. The coefficient of rank correlation has the same limits as the Karl Pearson's coefficient of correlation.
2. The coefficient of correlation is independent of the change of origin but not of scale.
3. The covariance between X and Y is defined as $\frac{\Sigma xy}{n}$ where, $x = (X - \bar{X})$, $y = (Y - \bar{Y})$ and n = no. of paired observations.
4. b_{xy} is called regression coefficient of X variable on Y variable.
5. If b_{xy} is 0.4 and b_{yx} is 1.6, coefficient of determination would be 0.8.

Select the correct answer using the codes given below

Codes

(a) 1, 2 and 3
(b) 1, 3 and 4
(c) 3, 4 and 5
(d) 2, 3 and 5

January 2017

5 Which one of the following is a false statement?

(a) The signs of the regression coefficients are always the same
(b) Correlation coefficient is the geometric mean of the two regression coefficients
(c) The covariance between two variables divided by the product of their standard deviations produces the value of coefficient of correlation
(d) Coefficient of correlation is independent of origin but not of scale

6 If the two regression coefficients are 0.8 and 0.2, then the value of coefficient of correlation is

(a) – 0.16
(b) + 0.50
(c) + 0.40
(d) – 0.40

7 If unexplained variation between variables X and Y is 36%, what is the coefficient of correlation between the variables?

(a) 0.36 (b) 0.64
(c) 0.60 (d) 0.80

July 2016

8 Which one of the following is a false description?

(a) In a moderately asymmetrical distribution, the empirical relationship between mean, mode and median suggested by Karl Pearson is Mean – Mode = 3 (Mean – Median)
(b) Coefficient of variation is an absolute measure of dispersion
(c) Measure of skewness indicates the direction and extent of skewness in the distribution of numerical values in the data set
(d) Kurtosis refers to the degree of flatness or peakedness in the region around the mode of a frequency curve

9 Match the items of List I with the items of List II.

List I	List II
A. Coefficient of determination	1. $\gamma_{xy}\dfrac{\sigma_x}{\sigma_y}$
B. Spearman's rank correlation coefficient	2. $1-\dfrac{6\,\Sigma d^2}{n\,(n^2-1)}$
C. Regression coefficient of x on y variable	3. $\dfrac{\Sigma\, xy}{n\,\sigma_x\sigma_y}$
D. Karl Pearson's formula of calculating γ	4. γ^2

Codes

	A	B	C	D
(a)	1	2	3	4
(b)	1	4	2	3
(c)	4	3	2	1
(d)	3	2	4	1

10 Which one of the following formulas is used to calculate the standard error of coefficient of correlation between 25 paired observations of a sample?

(a) $\dfrac{(1-r^2)}{\sqrt{n}}$ (b) $\sqrt{\dfrac{(1-r^2)}{(n-2)}}$
(c) $0.6745\left(\dfrac{1-r^2}{\sqrt{n}}\right)$ (d) $\sqrt{\dfrac{(n-2)}{(1-r^2)}}$

December 2015

11 Select the methods of finding out correlation from the following.

1. Karl Pearson's Method 2. Spearman's Rank Method
3. Yule's Method
4. Coefficient of Contingency
5. Concurrent Deviation Method

Select the correct answer using the codes given below

Codes

(a) 1, 2 and 3 (b) 1, 2, 3 and 4
(c) 1, 2 and 5 (d) 3, 4 and 5

12 A set of data can be distinguished from other set of data by means of

(a) central value and dispersion
(b) central value, dispersion and skewness
(c) central value, dispersion, skewness and kurtosis
(d) None of the above

13 The following are the estimated regression equations for x and y variables.

$x = 0.85y$
$y = 0.89x$

With this information, the value of the coefficient of correlation would be

(a) 0.87 (b) 0.86 (c) 0.89 (d) 0.75

June 2015

14 Which one of the following formulas is used to calculate probable error of correlation coefficient between two variables of 'n' pairs of observations?

(a) $0.6745\left[\dfrac{1-r^2}{\sqrt{n}}\right]$ (b) $0.5758\left[\dfrac{1-r^2}{\sqrt{n}}\right]$
(c) $0.675\left[\dfrac{1-r^2}{n}\right]$ (d) $0.5758\left[\dfrac{1-r^2}{n}\right]$

15 Which one of the following statements is false?

(a) Both correlation and regression coefficients have same sign
(b) Arithmetic mean of the regression coefficients is always more than the correlation coefficient
(c) Regression coefficients are independent of both the origin and scale
(d) Correlation coefficient is the square root of two regression coefficients

June 2014

16 If the dependent variable increases as the independent variable increases in an estimation equation, the coefficient of correlation will be in the range

(a) 0 to – 1 (b) 0 to – 0
(c) 0 to – 0.05 (d) 0 to 1

17 **Assertion** (A) When there is an evidence of a linear relationship between two variables, it may not always mean an independent-dependent relationship between the two variables.

Reason (R) The casual relationship between the two variables may not imply a reasonable theoretical relationship between the two.

Codes

(a) Both (A) and (R) are true and (R) is the correct explanation of (A)
(b) Both (A) and (R) are true, but (R) is not the correct explanation of (A)
(c) (A) is true, but (R) is false
(d) (A) is false, but (R) is true

December 2013

18 A distribution, where the value of arithmetic mean is maximum as compared to median and mode, is

(a) normal distribution
(b) positively-skewed distribution
(c) negatively-skewed distribution
(d) None of the above

19 The most appropriate average to be used to compute the average rate of growth in population is

(a) arithmetic mean (b) median
(c) geometric mean (d) harmonic mean

20 **Assertion** (A) If regression coefficient of X on Y is greater than one, regression coefficient of Y on X must be less than one.

Reason (R) The geometric mean between two regression coefficients is the coefficient of correlation.

Codes

(a) Both (A) and (R) are true
(b) (A) is true, but (R) is false
(c) (A) is false, but (R) is true
(d) Both (A) and (R) are false

21 The regression equation of profits (X) on sales (Y) of a firm is given as: $3Y - 5X + 10 = 0$. If the sales of the firm is ₹ 44,000, the profit will be

(a) ₹ 23,370 (b) ₹ 26,422
(c) ₹ 24,422 (d) ₹ 21,370

22 Cricketer 'A' scores on an average 40 runs with a standard deviation of 5. Scores of players 'B' and 'C', on an average, are 75 and 90 with standard deviations 10 and 18 respectively. Arrange the players in the descending order of consistency.

(a) A, B and C (b) C, B and A
(c) B, A and C (d) C, A and B

December 2012

23 Which one of the following is not a measures of dispersion?

(a) Quartile
(b) Range
(c) Mean Deviation
(d) Standard Deviation

24 If $b_{xy} = 0.25$ and $b_{yx} = 0.64$ correlation coefficient is

(a) 0.16 (b) 0.40
(c) 0.89 (d) 0.30

25 If the value of coefficient of determination is 0.64, what is the value of coefficient of correlation?

(a) 0.40 (b) 0.80
(c) 0.08 (d) 0.04

June 2012

26 Karl Pearson's coefficient of correlation between two variables is

(a) the product of their standard deviations
(b) the square root of the product of their regression coefficients
(c) the covariance between the variables
(d) None of the above

27 If the two regression coefficients are 0.8 and 0.2, then the value of coefficient of correlation is

(a) +0.16 (b) – 0.40
(c) – 0.16 (d) +0.40

28 Which one of the following is a relative measures of dispersion?

(a) Standard deviation
(b) Variance
(c) Coefficient of variation
(d) None of the above

ANSWERS

Objective Questions

1 (c)	2 (a)	3 (a)	4 (d)	5 (b)	6 (a)	7 (a)	8 (d)	9 (c)	10 (d)
11 (b)	12 (a)	13 (c)	14 (a)	15 (c)	16 (b)	17 (a)	18 (a)	19 (a)	20 (c)
21 (b)	22 (a)	23 (a)	24 (d)	25 (a)	26 (d)	27 (b)	28 (a)	29 (b)	30 (b)
31 (c)	32 (a)	33 (b)	34 (b)	35 (c)	36 (d)	37 (b)	38 (a)	39 (d)	40 (c)
41 (c)	42 (a)	43 (c)	44 (b)	45 (c)	46 (a)	47 (b)	48 (a)	49 (b)	50 (d)
51 (a)	52 (a)	53 (a)	54 (a)	55 (c)	56 (b)	57 (b)	58 (a)	59 (c)	60 (a)
61 (c)	62 (b)	63 (d)	64 (a)	65 (c)	66 (c)	67 (d)	68 (a)	69 (a)	70 (c)
71 (c)	72 (b)	73 (c)	74 (c)	75 (b)	76 (d)	77 (a)	78 (c)	79 (b)	80 (a)
81 (d)	82 (a)	83 (b)	84 (c)	85 (c)	86 (b)	87 (b)	88 (a)	89 (b)	90 (c)
91 (a)	92 (b)	93 (b)	94 (b)	95 (b)	96 (b)	97 (b)	98 (b)	99 (a)	100 (a)
101 (a)	102 (a)	103 (a)	104 (a)	105 (a)	106 (a)	107 (b)	108 (a)	109 (a)	110 (b)
111 (b)	112 (b)	113 (d)	114 (d)	115 (a)	116 (b)				

Previous Years' Questions

1 (d)	2 (b)	3 (a)	4 (b)	5 (d)	6 (c)	7 (d)	8 (b)	9 (c)	10 (a)
11 (c)	12 (c)	13 (a)	14 (a)	15 (b)	16 (d)	17 (a)	18 (b)	19 (c)	20 (a)
21 (b)	22 (a)	23 (a)	24 (b)	25 (b)	26 (b)	27 (d)	28 (c)		

CHAPTER 18

Data Collection and Statistical Methods

Statistics is a branch of Mathematics, which deals with collection, organisation, analysis and interpretation of data. Statistical methods are Scientifically arranged to take out maximum possible outcome, so this chapter covers all such aspects about statistics and its methods.

Data

Data may be defined as information about some particular characteristics under consideration. *It can be classified as under*

Quantitative Data Data whose variables can be measured and expressed in numerical terms is referred to as quantitative data. Prices, income, height, weight etc are all examples of quantitative data. Statistics generally deals in quantitative data.

Qualitative Data Data whose variables cannot be measured and expressed in numerical terms is referred to as qualitative data. Good, bad, intelligence etc are examples of qualitative data.

Collection of Data

In every statistical investigation, the first thing is the collection of data.

Before collecting data for a given statistical enquiry, it is imperative to examine carefully the following points which may be termed as preliminaries to data collection

Objectives and Scope of the Enquiry

The first step in organising any statistical enquiry is to define in clear and concrete terms the objective of the enquiry. Deciding on the scope of the enquiry is also important. Scope of enquiry relates to the coverage with respect to the type of information, subject matter and geographical area.

In this Chapter

- Data
- Sampling Method of Collecting Data
- Classification of Data
- Data Presentation
- Statistical Estimation

Statistical Units to be Used

A well-defined and identifiable object or a group of objects with which the measurements or counts in a statistical investigation are associated is called a statistical unit. It can be an individual person, a family or physical units such as metres, kilograms etc.

A good statistical unit should have the following characteristics

- It should be unambiguous.
- It should be specific.
- It should be stable.
- It should be appropriate to the enquiry.
- It should be uniform.

Types of Statistical Units

Statistical units can be broadly classified as

Units of Collection *These can be further categorised as follows*

- ***Units of Enumeration*** It is the basic unit on which the observations are to be made. It may be a person, a household, a firm, a shop etc.
- ***Units of Recording*** These are the units in terms of which the data are recorded. *It may be further categorised as*
  (a) **Simple Units** The units which represent only one condition are called simple units. *e.g.*metre, rupee, ton, kilogram etc.
  (b) **Composite Unit** A simple unit with only one qualifying word is called a composite or compound unit. *e.g.* skilled workers, ton kilometre, man hours etc.

Units of Analysis and Interpretation These are the units in the form of which the statistical data are ultimately analysed and interpreted. These units facilitate comparison. Generally, the units of analysis and interpretation are rates, ratios, percentages and coefficients.

Sources of Information

Data can be collected by primary sources and secondary sources. These are discussed ahead in the chapter.

Method of Data Collection

If the data is to be collected from primary sources, then the method of data collection is to be decided. The method can be census or sampling. If census method is being used, then data is collected from each and every unit of statistical enquiry. In sampling, data is collected from a selected few. It is also discussed ahead.

Degree of Accuracy Aimed at in the Final Results

A decision regarding the degree of accuracy or precision desired by the investigator in his estimates or results is essential before starting statistical enquiry. If high degree of accuracy is required, then census method should be used.

Types of Enquiry

Another important point is to decide about the type of enquiry. *The statistical enquiries may be of the following different types*

- Official, semi-official or unofficial.
- Initial or repetitive.
- Confidential or non-confidential.
- Direct or indirect.
- Regular or ad-hoc.
- Census or sample.
- Primary or secondary.

Sources of Collection of Data

Data can be collected from primary and secondary sources. *These are as follows*

Primary Sources of Data

It refers to collection of data direct from its source of origin. The data collected from primary sources are referred to as primary data.

It is one which is collected directly from respondents using data collection method like survey, interviews, questionnaires, direct observation or tabulation. Here, researcher is directly involved in the collection of information required to answer research questions.

These are the following methods for collection of primary data

Telephone Survey Telephone survey elicit much higher response as, it is convenient, but excludes those who do not have a telephone and those, who have an unlisted number thus, making the sample unrepresentative to some degree.

Mailed Questionnaire Mailed questionnaire is more often used because of economy and practicability, especially if the population is widely dispersed geographically. Great care should be taken on the formulation of questionnaires. The language of the questionnaires should be specific and clear. The questions should be such that either they elicit clear yes or no answers or some other statement of facts.

Personal Interview The personal interview can usually result in more accurate responses, since the interviewer can probe more deeply into answers that show inconsistency in some form. Also, if questions are not properly understood by the respondent, then these can be clarified on the spot.

One of the major problem with personal interviews is the degree of bias that can be introduced because the answer can be highly exaggerated so, investigator must be thoroughly trained and psychologically aware of such possible exaggerations.

Indirect Oral Investigation This method is used in case, where informants are reluctant to give information or data and are of such complicated nature that it is difficult to get them directly. Merits of this method are wide coverage, economical, neutral etc. Demerits of this method are indirect information, bias of witnesses etc.

Information Through Correspondents Under this method, the investigator appoints local correspondents in different parts of the field of enquiry. They are instructed to send information on specific issues regularly to the investigator. This method is generally adopted by newspapers and periodicals, which require information regularly. This method is very cheap and yield results easily and promptly and a wide area can be covered.

Schedules to be Filled in by Informants Under this method, a schedule or questionnaire is prepared. The questionnaire contains a set of questions on problem under investigation. These questionnaire are addressed to individual informants and sent by post. They are requested to answer the questions and post back to the investigator. This method of data collection is simple and cheap, reliable, free from bias. But it suffer from demerits like non-response, limited scope and at times may be less accurate.

Advantages of Primary Data

- The data collected is original in character.
- Meet the required need of investigator without editing.
- Quality of data is better as have been collected by persons, who were specifically trained for that purpose. Thus, data is more accurate.
- The data collected is unbiased data.

Disadvantages of Primary Data

- Primary data is non-economical as it requires lot of money and time.
- Collected data is in raw form that cannot be used unless organised.
- Data collected and contains large volume.
- Direct and personal intervention has to be there.

Secondary Sources of Data

It refers to collection of data from one agency which has already collected the data and processed it. The data collected from this source is referred to as secondary data. It is the data that already exists which has been collected by some other person or organisation for their use and is generally made available to other researchers free or at concessional rate. Sources of secondary data are journals, reports, government publications or professional and research organisations. Collection of secondary data is less expensive in terms of money and time.

e.g. If a researcher wants to analyse the weather conditions of different regions, he can get the required information of data records from meteorology department. So, for the meteorology department, it is primary data and for the researcher same data becomes secondary data.

Secondary data may not always answer the specific questions of a researcher. Hence, a researcher should use a judicious mix of primary and secondary data to optimise the quality of research findings within allotted time and money.

The sources of secondary data can be broadly classified into the following groups

Published Sources *These comprise of the following*

- ***Official Publication of Central Government*** *The following government organisations collect, compile and publish statistical data on a number of topics such as prices, wages, population etc*
  (a) Office of the Registrar General and Census Commission of India, New Delhi (1949).
  (b) Directorate General of Commercial Intelligence and Statistics-Ministry of Commerce (1895).
  (c) Labour Bureau - Ministry of Labour (1946).
  In addition to the above organisations, a number of departments in State and Central Governments such as Income Tax Dept, Railways, Post Telegraphs etc publish statistical reports on current problems.

  ➟ **Note** *The year in bracket represents the year of establishment.*
- ***Publications of Semi-Government Statistical Organisations*** Important information is also provided by the publications of semi-government statistical organisations. Reserve Bank of India Bulletin (Monthly), statistical material published by Municipal and District Boards, Block and Panchayat Samiti etc are some examples of this source.
- ***Publications of Research Institutions*** An individual research scholars, various research organisations and institutes like Indian Statistical Institute, ICAR, NCERT, ISI etc publish the findings of their research which is a good source of secondary data.
- ***Publications of Commercial and Financial Institution*** A number of private commercial and financial institutions such as FICCI, ICAI, stock exchanges, trade unions etc also publish an important reports and statistical material on current economic and business scenario.
- ***Reports of Various Committees and Commissions appointed by the Government*** The government appoints committees and commissions to find their expert views of social and economic issues. *e.g.* Kothari Commission's report on educational reforms.

- ***Newspapers and Periodicals*** Secondary data can also be accessed from newspapers and journals such as Hindustan Times, The Financial Express, Statesman's Year Book etc.
- ***International Publication*** The publication of foreign agencies such as UNO, World Bank, IMF etc are also important sources of secondary data.

Unpublished Sources The statistical data need not always be published. There are various source of unpublished statistical material such as the records maintained by private firms, research papers of students etc.

Advantages of Secondary Data

- Secondary data can help to identify, clarify and redefine the research problem. In these situations, where the actual problem in a research study cannot be defined or is defined in an ambiguous way.
- Secondary data might also hold a solution to the problem. It happens when precise data regarding the current research is already available as secondary data.
- Secondary data may provide alternative methods that can be used for primary research. Every research situation has a custom made primary research designed for it.

Disadvantages of Secondary Data

- Lack of availability or relevance of available secondary data. Moreover, data available might be irrelevant because of the changes in competitive situation, changing trends and other variables from the time data was initially collected.
- Secondary data can be inaccurate data and insufficient data. Secondary data can be subject to doubt because of the errors that can occur in any of the steps or due to personal bias. Moreover, sometimes secondary data might be available, but might not possess all the required data for the research at hand.

Sampling Method of Collecting Data

Sampling is a technique, which helps us in understanding the parameters or characteristics of the universe or population by examining only a small part of it.

It is necessary to take a representative sample from the population, since it is extremely costly, time consuming and cumbersome to do a complete census. If the sample is truly representative of the population, then characteristics of the sample can be considered to be the same as those of the entire population.

The part of population which is chosen to study and make the inference is known as the sample and number of units in the sample is known as sample size.

e.g. A small amount of blood sample taken from a patient can determine whether the patient's sugar level is normal or not. This is so because the small sample of blood is truly representative of the entire blood in the body.

Need of Sampling

- It is not technically or economically feasible to take the entire population into consideration.
- Due to dynamic changes in business, industrial and social environment, it is necessary to make quick decision, so sample is necessary to save time.
- If data collection takes a long time, then values of some characteristics may change over the period of time thus, defeating the very purpose of data analysis. Therefore, due to importance of time element, sample is required.
- Sample, if representative, may yield more accurate results than the total census because samples can be more accurately supervised.
- Quality of some products can be tested only by destroying the products. So, in such a situation sampling is the only method.

  e.g. In testing cars for their ability to withstand accident, it is subjected to accidents. Naturally, the entire population of cars cannot be subjected to these accident tests and hence, a sample must be selected.

Characteristics of a Good Sample

While selecting a sample, one should look out for the following characteristics

- A sample should have all the characteristics of the population from where it is taken.
- Person collecting sample should not be biased in selecting sample.
- The findings or decisions taken based on the sample study should be applicable to the entire population.

Determination of Sample Size

For determining the sample size, a prior estimate of the standard deviation of the population and level of confidence is necessary. The confidence level is taken as 95%.

Following formula can be used to determine the minimum size of sample

$$\sqrt{n} = (1.96)(\sigma)/\text{precision}$$

$$n = [(1.96)(\sigma)/\text{precision}]^2$$

(Here, 2 is for square root so do it accordingly)

Where, n = Sample size, 1.96 = 95% confidence level,

σ = Population standard deviation

Precision = Estimated accuracy or difference between population mean and sample mean.

Methods of Sampling

Random or Probability Sampling

In random or probability sampling, the decision whether a particular element is included in the sample or not is governed by the chance alone.

It can be further categorised as

Simple Random Sampling It is one of the simplest sampling methods and can work well for relatively small populations. Under this, each element has an equal probability of getting included in the sample. It is imperative to have a list of all the members of the population before a simple random sample can be picked-up. Such a exhaustive list of all population members is called sampling frame or sample space.

Stratified Sampling Although, stratified sampling is more complex than simple random sampling, but it significantly increase the statistical efficiency of sampling. The basis for using stratified sampling is the existence of strata such that each stratum is more homogenous within and markedly different from another stratum. The higher the homogeneity within each stratum, the higher will be the gain in statistical efficiency due to stratification. A stratum can be conceived as sub-population, which is more homogeneous than complete population. The members of a stratum are similar to each other and are different from the members of another stratum in the characteristics that we are measuring.

Systematic Sampling Systematic sampling proceeds by picking-up one element after a fixed interval depending on the sampling ratio.

e.g. If we want to have a sample of size 10 from a population of size 100, our sampling ratio would ten/N=10/100=$\frac{1}{10}$ (where, n = Sample size, N = Population size). We would, therefore have to decide where to start from among the first 10 names in our frame. If this number happens to be 5, then sample would comprise of serial numbers 5, 15, 25, ..., 95 in the frame. It is to be noted that the random process establishes only the first member of the sample, the rest are determined automatically because of the known sampling ratio.

Cluster Sampling In cluster sampling, the population is divided into well defined groups or clusters. Then, few of these clusters are selected based on the assumptions that they represent the entire universe. All the units of the selected cluster are studied to arrive at a conclusion. The selection of these clusters is done by using anyone of the above discussed sampling methods.

e.g. When a pre-poll survey is conducted in an assembly segment, then the entire voting population is divided into clusters. Then, some clusters are selected as samples and every element of these clusters is studied to arrive at a final opinion regarding the entire population.

Multistage Sampling Sometimes, the population is too large and scattered, so collecting sample in practical sense make a list of the entire population from which we need to draw a sample. For instance, when we want to take a sample of 10,000 household in a state. At first stage, state will be divided into number of districts and then few districts are selected at random. At next stage, each district will be sub-divided into a number of villages and a sample of villages will be selected. In this way, at each stage the sample size price become smaller and our sample will be selected.

Non-Random or Non-Probability Sampling Methods

Any sampling process which does not ensure some non-zero probability for each element in the population to be included in the sample would belong to the category of non-probability sampling. In this case, samples may be picked-up based on the judgement or convenience of the enumerator.

Some of the non-probability sampling methods are as follows

Judgement Sampling In judgement sampling, the selection of the sample is based on the judgement of the manager, who is studying the situation. This method is also known as 'purpose sampling' or 'deliberate sampling'. This sampling method should be carried out by an expert in the field as his judgement which will influence the final outcome of the study.

Convenience Sampling This method is based on the convenience of the researcher. The researcher uses the sources available to him to come to the conclusion.

e.g. List of employees of an organisation available to him can be taken to study the employees.

Sequential Sampling Here, size of sample is not fixed in advance, but it is decided as the sampling process takes place depending on the results of the first sample. A number of sample lots are drawn in sequence one after another from the population depending on the results of the earlier sample.

e.g. A manager draws a lot from the inventory and tests it for acceptability. If it is acceptable, there will be no further samples required, but if it is found unacceptable, the entire stock will be rejected. So, when the results of the first sample fall in near to acceptable standard, the manager will go for another sample before deciding on the quality of the inventory.

Quota Sampling This is a method for selecting survey participants. In this, a population is first segmented into mutually exclusive sub-groups, just as in stratified sampling. Then, judgement is used to select the subjects or units from each segment based on a specified proportion.

e.g. An interviewer may be told to sample 400 females and 600 males between the age of 30 and 50. This means that individuals can specify, who they want to sample (targeting).

Sampling Distribution

If we draw a sample of size 'n' from a given finite population of size' N', then total number of possible samples is

$$N_{C_n} = \frac{N!}{n!(N-n)!} = k \text{ (say)}$$

So, for each of these k sample, we can compute some statistics $t = t(x_1, x_2 \ldots, x_n)$.

The set of the values of the statistics so obtained, one for each sample constitutes is called the sampling distribution of the statistics.

e.g. The values $t_1, t_2, t_3 \ldots, t_k$ determine the sampling distribution of the statistics 't'. *In other words, statistics 't' may be regarded as a random variable which take the values* $t_1, t_2 \ldots, t_k$ *and we compute the various statistical constants as*

$$\text{Mean} \Rightarrow \bar{t} = \frac{1}{k}(t_1 + t_2 + \ldots + t_k)\frac{1}{k}\sum_{i=1}^{n} t_i$$

Variance ⇒ Var

$$(t) = \frac{1}{k}[(t_1 - \bar{t})^2 + (t_2 - \bar{t})^2 + \ldots + (t_k - \bar{t})^2]$$

$$= \frac{1}{k}\sum_{i=1}^{k}(t_i - \bar{t})^2$$

Standard Error

The standard deviation of the sampling distribution of a statistics is known as Standard Error (SE). *Thus, the standard error of the statistics 't' is given below*

$$\text{S.E. } (t) = \sqrt{\text{Var } (t)} = \sqrt{\frac{1}{k}\sum_{i=1}^{k}(t_i - \bar{t})^2}$$

In particular, the SE of the sampling distribution of mean $\bar{x}$ is given by the standard deviation of the values $\bar{x}_1, \bar{x}_2, \ldots, \bar{x}_n$.

Basic Principles of Sample Survey

Sample survey is the study of the unknown population on the basis of a representative sample drawn from it.

The important principles of sample survey are

Law of Statistical Regularity According to this principle, if a sample of large size is drawn from the population under consideration, then on an average the sample would possess the characteristics of that population. So, larger the sample size, the better it would be in representing the characteristics of the population.

Principle of Inertia According to this principle, the larger the sample, the more the chances of it being reliable, accurate and precise. This is directly derived from the first principle.

Principle of Optimisation This principle ensures that an optimum level of efficiency at a minimum cost or maximum efficiency at a given level of cost can be achieved with the selection of an appropriate or suitable sample.

Principle of Validity This principle states that a sampling design is valid only if it is possible to obtain valid estimates and tests about population parameters. Probability sampling ensures this validity.

Principle of Persistence of Small Numbers If some of the items in a population possess markedly distinct characteristics from the remaining items, then this tendency would be revealed in the sample values also. Rather this tendency of persistence will be there even if the population size is increased in case of large sample. If a random sample of size 'n' from the group gives a fraction defective, then

$$p = \frac{1}{n} \times \text{(No. of defectives in the sample)}$$

Principle Steps in Sample Survey

- Objectives and scope of the survey should be clearly defined.
- Designing the population to be sampled.
- The framing of the sampling units.
- Collection of the data.
- Preparation of questionnaire or schedule.
- Deciding method of collecting information.
- Selecting proper sampling design.
- Organisation of field work.
- Pilot survey or pre-test.
- Summary and analysis of the data.

The Central Limit Theorem (CLT)

The CLT states that when the samples from the set of data with known mean and variance are summed, then their mean becomes roughly equal to the population mean. In other words, a given sufficiently large sample size from a universe with finite level of variance, the mean of all samples from same population will be approximately equal to the population mean. Also, all samples will follow normal distribution pattern approximately, with all variance being equal to the population variance divided by each sample size.

Also, according to the CLT, mean of the sample size will be equal to the mean of the population as the sample size increases. As a general rule, any sample size greater than or equal to 30 is considered as good for holding CLT.

Sample Mean of CLT

If random sample of size 'n' taken (*i.e.* $x_1, x_2 \ldots, x_n$) that are independent and identically distributed with mean 'μ' and standard deviation 'σ', therefore,

$$\text{Mean}(\overline{X}) = \frac{x_1 + x_2 + \ldots + x_n}{n} \text{ is sample mean}$$

We can show that

$$E(\overline{X}) = \mu \text{ and SD}(\overline{X}) = \frac{\sigma}{\sqrt{n}}$$

While CLT states that

$$\frac{\overline{X} - \mu}{\sigma/\sqrt{n}} \to N(0, 1) \text{ as sample size increase}$$

i.e. $n \to \infty$

We have, $\dfrac{\overline{X} - \mu}{\sigma/\sqrt{n}} \to N(0, 1);\ \overline{X} \to N(\mu, \dfrac{\sigma^2}{n})$

Lets say we have a population with probability 'p' of a certain characteristics ($q = 1 - p$). The mean and standard deviation will be 'p' and $\sqrt{pq/n}$ respectively.

Also, $x_1, x_2, \ldots, x_n$ are 'n' random variable that are independent and identically distributed with mean 'μ' and standard deviation 'σ', sample sum will be $S_n = x_1 + x_2 + \ldots + x_n$,

Here, CLT states that $\dfrac{S_n - n\mu}{\sigma/\sqrt{n}} \to N(0, 1)$ as sample size increase

i.e. $n \to \infty$

Application of Central Limit Theorem

Following are the steps to use CLT

- Write the random variable of interest Y as the sum of 'n' terms for random variable X_i

$$\therefore \quad Y = X_1 + X_2 + \ldots + X_n$$

- Find EY and Var (Y) by the following method

$$EY = n\mu \quad \text{Var}(Y) = n\sigma^2$$

Here, $\mu = EX_i$ and $\sigma^2 = \text{Var}(X_i)$

- According to the CLT, we conclude that $\dfrac{Y - EY}{\sqrt{(Y)}} = \dfrac{Y - n\mu}{\sqrt{n}\sigma}$ is approximately standard normal; thus to find $P(y_1 \le Y < y_2)$ we can write

$$P(y_1 \le \le y_2) = P\left(\frac{y_1 - n\mu}{\sqrt{n}\sigma} \le \frac{Y - n\mu}{\sqrt{n}\sigma} \le \frac{y_2 - n\mu}{\sqrt{n}\sigma}\right)$$

$$\approx \phi\left(\frac{y_2 - n\mu}{\sqrt{n}\,\sigma}\right) - \phi\left(\frac{y_1 - n\mu}{\sqrt{n}\,\sigma}\right)$$

Parameter and Statistics

The statistical constant of the population like mean (μ), variance (σ^2), skewness (β), Kurtosis (β_2) moments (μ_2), correlation coefficient (p) etc are known as parameters. One can compute similar statistical constants for the sample drawn from the given population. Prof. R.A. Fisher termed the statistical constants of the sample like mean ($\bar{x}$), variance (s^2), skewness (b_1), Kurtosis (b_2), moments (m_r), correlation (r) etc as statistics.

Let us consider a finite population of 'N' items and let $y_1, y_2, \ldots, y_n$ be the observations on the N units in the population. Suppose, we draw a sample of size 'n' from the given population. Let $x_1, x_2, \ldots, x_n$ be the observations on the sample units. *Then, we have by definition*

$$\mu = \frac{1}{N}(y_1 + y_2 + \ldots, y_N) = \frac{1}{N}\sum_{i=1}^{N} y_i$$

$$\sigma^2 = \frac{1}{N}[(y_1 - \mu)^2 + (y_2 - \mu)^2 + \ldots + (y_N - \mu)^2] = \frac{1}{N}\sum_{i=1}^{N}(y_i - \mu)^2$$

The sample mean ($\bar{x}$) and variance (s^2) are given below

$$\bar{x} = \frac{1}{n}(x_1 + x_2 + \ldots + x_n) = \frac{1}{n}\sum_{i=1}^{n} x_i$$

$$S^2 = \frac{1}{n}((x_1 - \bar{x})^2 + (x_2 - \bar{x})^2 + \ldots + (x_n - \bar{x})^2] = \frac{1}{n}\sum_{i=1}^{n}(x_i - \bar{x})^2$$

Generally, the population parameters are unknown and their estimates provided by the appropriate sample statistics are used. Obviously, the sample statistics are functions of the sample observations and vary from sample to sample. Thus, if 't' is any general statistics, then we may write 't' as a function of the sample observation $x_1, x_2 \ldots, x_n$ as $t = t(x_1, x_2 \ldots, x_n)$.

Errors in Sampling Process

An error in statistics is the difference between the value of a statistic and that of the corresponding parameter.

In the total process of statistical analysis by sampling, some are bound to be introduced.

These errors may be sampling errors or non-sampling errors

Sampling Errors

The sampling error arise due to drawing faulty inferences about the population based upon the results of the samples. The sampling error would be less, if the sample size is large relative to the population and *vice-versa*. The reason is that estimate is based on a part and not on the whole.

Causes of Sampling Errors

Some of the causes for errors in sampling are

- Error in selection of the sample.
- Bias in reporting of data.
- Diversity of population.
- Substitution of sampling units for convenience.
- Faulty demarcation of sampling universe.

However, the errors can be controlled. The modern sampling theory helps in designing the survey in such a manner that the sampling errors can be made small.

Types of Sampling Errors

Sampling errors are of two types

Biased Errors These errors arise from any bias in selection, estimation of the enumerators, investigators or the respondents.

e.g. If in place of simple random sampling, the investigator uses deliberate sampling, some bias is introduced in the result and hence, such errors are called biased sampling errors. If possibilities of bias exist, objective conclusions cannot be drawn. So, first essential of any sampling or census procedure must therefore be the elimination of all sources of bias.

Unbiased Errors These errors arise due to chance differences between the members of population included in the sample and those not included.

Non-sampling Errors

Non-sampling error occur at the time of observation, approximation and processing of data. This error is common to both the sampling and census survey. Non-sampling error can arise at any stage of the planning or execution of complete enumeration or sample survey.

Causes of Non-sampling Errors

Non-sampling errors may arise due to one or more of the following reasons

- Faulty sampling plan.
- Lack of trained and qualified investigators.
- Inaccuracy in response collected due to bias of the respondent or the researcher.
- Errors in design of the survey.
- Errors in compilation or publication.

➠ **Note** *In general, sampling errors decrease with increase in sample size, non-sampling error tend to increase with sample size. Non-sampling errors are required to be controlled and reduced to a level at which their presence does not vitiate the use of final results.*

Measurement of Errors

On the basis of method of calculation, errors can be classified as follows

Absolute Errors The difference between actual value or estimated value is called absolute errors.

$$\text{Absolute errors} = \text{Actual value} - \text{Estimated value}$$

- According to **Prof. Boddington,**

$$\text{Total absolute error} = \text{Average actual errors} \times N$$

- According to **Prof. Bowley,**

$$\text{Total absolute error} = \frac{2}{3} \times \frac{AE}{N}$$

Relative Errors The ratio between absolute errors and estimated errors are called relative errors.

$$\text{Relative errors} = \frac{\text{Absolute error}}{\text{Estimated value}}$$

$$RE = \frac{AE}{E} \times 100$$

Where, RE = Relative Error, AE = Absolute Error
E = Estimated Value

- According to **Prof. Boddington,**

$$\text{Relative error} = \frac{\text{Average AE} \times N}{E}$$

- According to **Prof. Bowley,**

$$\text{Total relative error} = \frac{\text{Total absolute error}}{\text{Estimated value}}$$

Classification of Data

Classification is the process of arranging data into different groups or classes on the basis of some common characteristics. Classification of data converts raw data into pure data.

Basis of Classification of Data

Data can be classified on the following basis

Geographical/Spatial Classification This classification of data is based on the geographical or locational (countries, states, cities etc) differences of the data. *The agricultural yield per hectare for different countries (as given below) is an example of geographical classification*

Agricultural Yield of Different Countries (in kg per hectare)

Country	Yield
China	269.2
India	123.7
Pakistan	257.5

Chronological Classification This classification is one in which the data are classified, preferably in ascending or in descending order, on the basis of difference in time.

Population of India in different years (as given below) is an example of chronological classification

Population of India (in crores)

Year	Population
1971	54.8
1981	68.3
1991	84.4

➠ **Note** *In the given example, the variable 'population' is a time series as it depicts a series of values in different years.*

Qualitative Classification When the data are classified according to qualities or attributes of data (such as honesty, beauty, intelligence etc), then the classification is referred to as qualitative or descriptive classification. Qualitative classification can be simple and manifold.

Quantitative Classification If the data are classified on the basis of phenomenon which is capable of quantitative measurement (such as age, height, weight, sales, profits etc), the classification is referred to as a quantitative classification.

It is also known as numerical classification. Earnings of different departmental stores (as stated below) is an example of quantitative classification.

Daily earnings of 40 departmental stores (in 000 rupees)

Daily Earning (in ₹)	Number of Stores
Upto 100	6
101 - 200	14
201 - 300	8
301 - 400	12

➠ **Note** *The quantitative phenomenon under study is known as variable and therefore quantitative classification is also referred to as 'classification by variables'.*

Variable

Variable is a characteristic or a phenomenon which is capable of being measured and generally changes its value over time.

It is broadly classified into two types

Discrete Variable A discrete variable can take only certain integral values. Its value changes only by finite 'jumps'. It jumps from one value to another but does not take any intermediate value, *i.e.* fractional value between them. *e.g.* Number of students in class XI could be 1, 2, 4, 10, 11, 15, 20 etc.

Continuous Variable A continuous variable is one which can take any value, *i.e.* integral value or fractional value in a specified interval.

e.g. The interval 0-10 can contain integral values such as 1, 4, 7 etc and fractional values such as 0.5, 4.6, 5.3 etc.

Minimum and maximum temperature of a city, height of an individual, weight of an individual are all examples of continuous variables.

Frequency Distribution

A frequency distribution is comprehensive way to classify raw data of a quantitative variable. It shows how the different values of a variable are distributed in different classes alongwith their corresponding class frequencies. It facilitates easy understanding of data. Frequency distribution is a type of statistical series.

➠ **Note** *A statistical series is one in which the data are arranged in a proper and systematic manner. There are two types of statistical series, viz individual series and frequency distribution.*

Terms Related to Frequency Distribution

The various terms related to frequency distribution are explained below

Frequency It refers to the number of times a given value appears in a series.

Class Frequency It means the number of values in a particular class.

Class Limits They are the two extreme ends of a class. The lower value is called lower class limit and higher value is called upper class limit. *e.g.* In the class interval 10-20, 10 is the lower class limit and 20 is the upper class limit.

Class Width (Class Interval) It is the difference between the upper class limit and lower class limit.

Class Width = Upper Class Limit – Lower Class Limit

Class Mid-Point The class mid-point is the middle value of class. It lies half way between the lower class limit and upper class limit of a class. It represents the class.

$$\text{Class Mid-point} = \frac{\text{Upper Class Limit} + \text{Lower Class Limit}}{2}$$

Class with Maximum Concentration of Data Class with maximum concentration of data represents the class which has the highest frequency.

Class with Minimum Concentration of Data Class with minimum concentration of data represents the class which has the lowest frequency.

Relative Frequency Relative frequency is the frequency of a group represented as a percentage of total frequency of the distribution.

$$\text{Relative Frequency} = \frac{\text{Frequency of a Group}}{\text{Frequency of Distribution}} \times 100$$

Types of Frequency Distribution

Discrete Frequency Distribution

A discrete frequency distribution is a distribution which is based on a discrete variable. A discrete variable is one which can take only specific integral values and jumps from one value to another. So, in a discrete frequency distribution, the integral values of the discrete variable alongwith their respective frequencies are represented in the form of a table.

Continuous Frequency Distribution

A continuous frequency distribution is a distribution which is based on a continuous variable. A continuous variable can take integral, as well as, fractional values between two specified limits. So, in a continuous frequency distribution, the groups alongwith their respective class frequencies are represented in the form of a table.

Some Specific Frequency Distributions

Some specific forms of frequency distribution are discussed below

Exclusive Frequency Distribution In exclusive frequency distribution, the classes are formed in such a way that the upper limit of one class equals the lower limit of next class. In this way, the continuity of the data is maintained.

This method is most suitable in case of data of a continuous variable. In this method, the upper class limit is excluded and lower class limit is included in the interval.

An example of exclusive frequency distribution is given below

Frequency Distribution of Income of 350 Employees of a Company

Income (₹)	Number of Employees
800–900	50
900–1000	100
1000–1100	200
Total	**350**

In the above example, it can be observed that the upper limit of one class becomes the lower limit of the succeeding class. Also, an employee earning ₹ 1,000 will not be included in the group 900-1000, but he will be a part of the group 1000-1100.

Inclusive Frequency Distribution In inclusive frequency distribution, the upper limit of one class does not become the lower limit of the succeeding class. Also, this distribution does not exclude the upper class limit in a class interval. Thus, both class limits are parts of the class interval.

An example of inclusive frequency distribution is given below

Frequency Distribution of Income of 350 Employees of a Company

Income (₹)	Number of Employees
800–899	50
900–999	100
1000–1099	200
Total	**350**

In the above example, it can be observed that the upper limit of one class is not equal to the lower limit of the succeeding class. Also in the class interval 800-899, all those employees have been included whose income is either ₹ 800 or between 800-899 or ₹ 899.

Preparation of a Frequency Distribution

To prepare the frequency distribution, following components of frequency distribution are required

Number of Classes To determine the number of classes, first of all the range of the values of variables is to be found. Range is the difference between the largest and the smallest values of a variable. Once the value of range is obtained, number of classes can be determined after finalising the class interval.

e.g. For the given observations 10, 31, 12, 15, 25, 30, 18, 13, 22 and 40, the range will be 30(40-10).

To find the number of classes, the range so computed is divided by the class interval. Symbolically,

$$\text{Number of Classes} = \frac{\text{Range}}{\text{Class Interval}}$$

For a given range, the number of classes would be large for small class intervals and *vice-versa*.

Sturge's Rule

It is also used to determine number of classes. According to this rule, Number of classes (K) $=1+3.322 \log_{10} N$ where, N is the total frequency.

Size of Class After finalising the number of classes, class intervals or size of the class is finalised.

The size of the class depends upon the range of data and the number of classes. Symbolically,

$$\text{Size of Class/Class Interval} = \frac{\text{Range}}{\text{Number of Classes}}$$

Normally, the size of class is kept equal for the whole distribution. However, a distribution with unequal class intervals can also be formed, if there are wide gaps in the observed data.

Data Presentation

The data collected are organised and presented in a narrative, tabular or a graphical/diagrammatic form. *These are as follows*

Textual Presentation of Data

In textual or descriptive presentation, data is presented in the form of text. The data to be presented is written in paragraphs.

Tabular Presentation of Data

In tabular presentation, data is presented in rows (horizontally) and columns (vertically) in the form of a table. This process is known as tabulation. A table is a systematic arrangement of the statistical data in rows or in columns.

A good table should have following features

Table Number Tables should be numbered so that they could be used for easy reference. Integral numbers (such as 1, 2, 3) or subscribed numbers (such as 3.1, 2.4).

Title of the Table It is a brief explanation of the contents of a table. A good title should be short, clear and complete in all respects.

Head Note If the need arises, a head note supplements the title by explaining the table or the parts of the table. It is given below the title.

Column Heading or Caption It is word or a phrase which explains the contents of a column in a table. Under caption, there may be sub-heads when information contained in the columns is divided in more than one class.

Stubs or Row Headings Stubs are title of the rows of a table. These titles indicate information contained in the row of the table. The complete left column is called the stub column.

Body of the Table Body of the table means sum total of the items in the table. It indicates value of various items in the table. Each item in the body is called 'cell'.

Unit of Measurement The unit of measurement of the figures in the table (actual data) should always be stated alongwith title, if unit does not change throughout the table.

Footnote It explains the specific feature of the data content of the table which is not self-explanatory.

Source Note When tables are based on secondary data, source of the data is to be given. Source of the data is specified below the foot note.

Types of Tables

The tables can be classified as follows

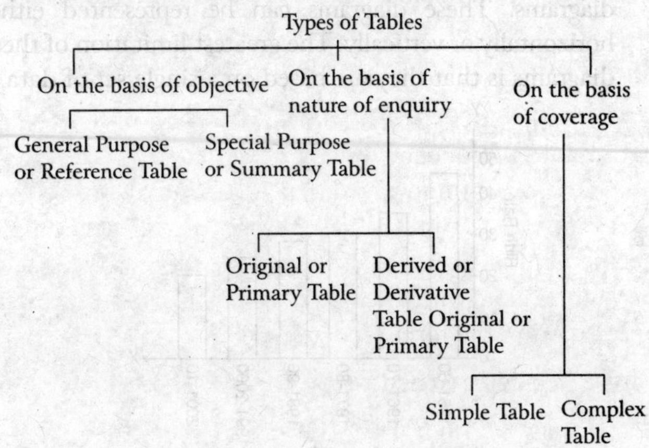

Diagrammatic or Graphical Presentation of Data

When data is presented in the form of diagrams, it is called diagrammatic presentation of data. Diagrams provide simple and attractive way of presenting the data.

Types of Diagrams

Geometric Diagram

It consists of following diagrams

Line Diagrams

It consists of drawing vertical lines, where each vertical line being equal to the frequency. *The line diagram is shown below*

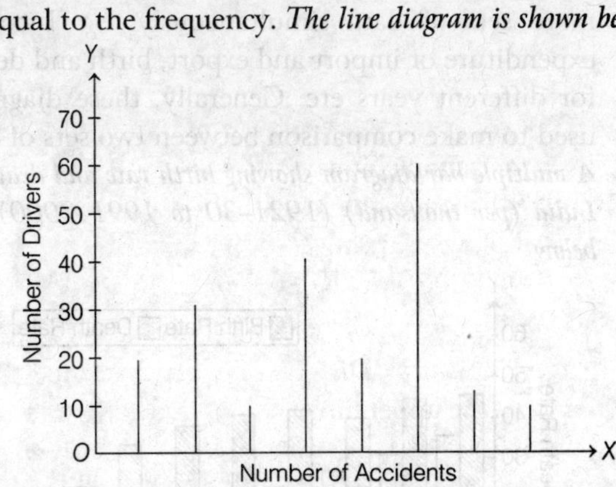

Bar Diagrams

Bar diagrams are those diagrams in which data is presented in the form of bars or rectangles. It comprises of a group of equispaced and equiwidth rectangular bars representing each class or category of data.

There are five types of bar diagrams

- ***Simple Bar Diagrams*** They are those diagrams which are based on a single set of numerical data. The different items or values are represented by different bars. Birth rate, weight of students, production of a commodity in different years etc are best represented through these diagrams. These diagrams can be represented either horizontally or vertically. The greatest limitation of these diagrams is that they are based on a single set of data.

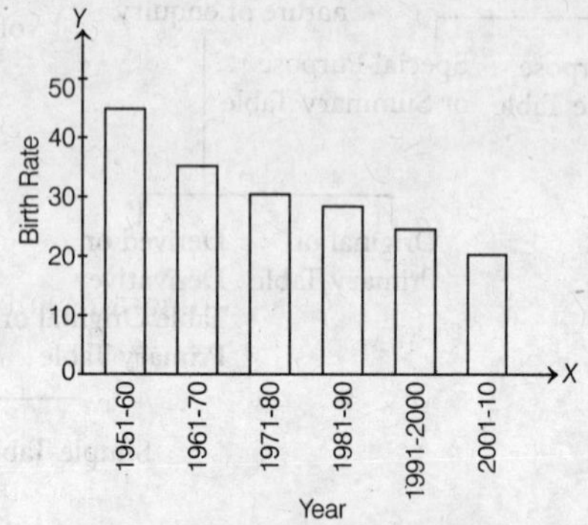

A horizontal bar diagram is given below

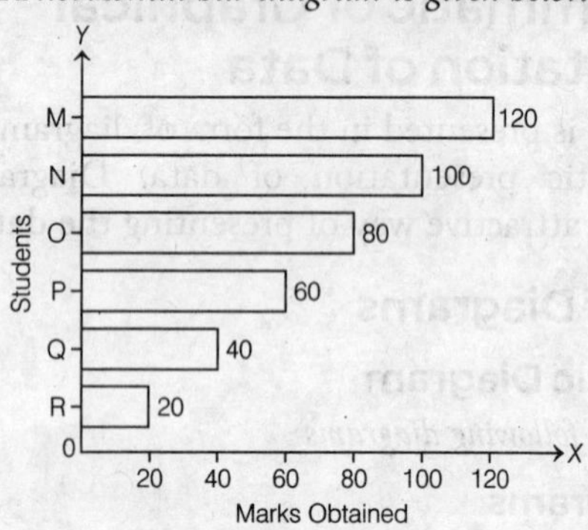

- ***Multiple Bar Diagrams*** These diagrams show two or more sets of data simultaneously. *e.g.* Income and expenditure or import and export, birth and death rate for different years etc. Generally, these diagrams are used to make comparison between two sets of series.

A multiple bar diagram showing birth rate and death rate in India (per thousand) (1921–30 to 1991–2000) is given below

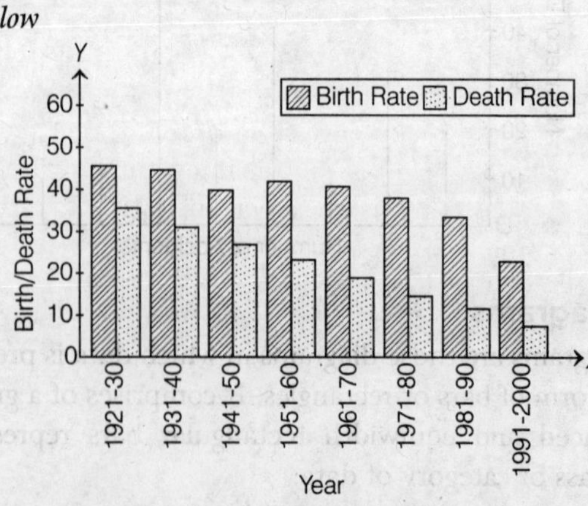

- ***Component Bar Diagrams*** A component bar diagram shows the bar and its sub-division into two or more components.

These diagrams simultaneously present total values as well as part values of a set of data. To indicate different parts of the bars, these are shaded with colours. Different parts of a bar must be shown in the same order for all the bars of a diagram.

A sub-divided bar diagram of the given data is shown below

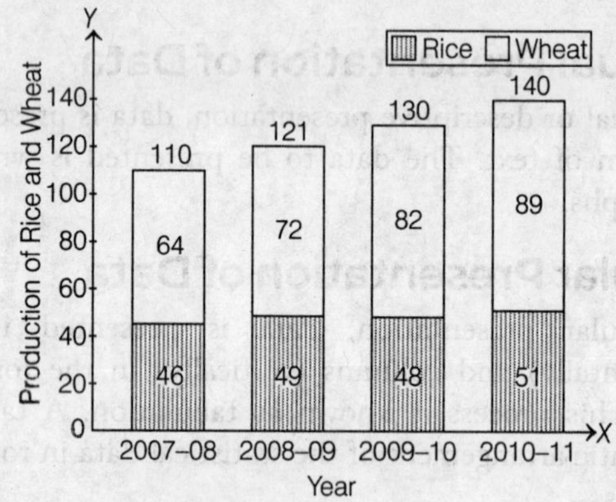

Note *In the first bar, the lower region represents the production of rice and the upper region represents the production of wheat. This sequence should be followed in all the bars.*

- ***Percentage Bar Diagrams*** These diagrams show simultaneously different parts of the values of a set of data in terms of percentages. Total value indicated by total length of bar is assumed to be 100.

Each part is first converted into a percentage and then shown as a part of the total length of the bar. The percentage bar diagrams are used generally when the values are of high magnitude.

Net Domestic Product by industry of origin in 2013–14 and 2014–15 depicted with the help of percentage bar diagram. *A percentage bar diagram is shown below*

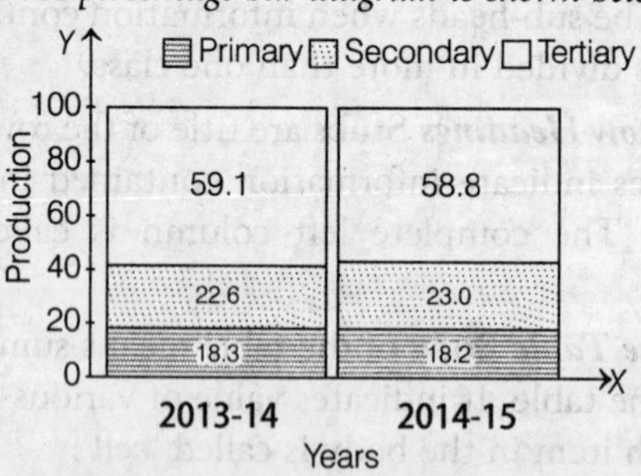

- ***Deviation Bar Diagrams*** The deviation bar diagrams are used to compare the net deviation in related variables with respect to time and location. Bars representing positive and negative deviations are drawn above and below the base line. This type of bar diagram is suitable for variable which can take positive as well as negative values, such as temperature, savings etc.

A deviation bar diagram is shown below

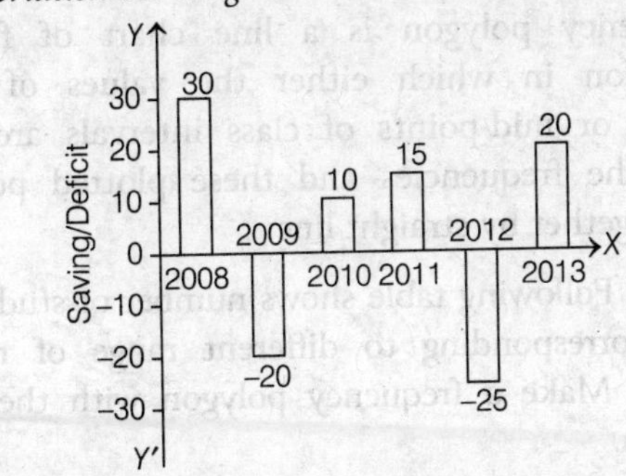

➡ **Note** *Students should remember that all types of bar diagrams can be represented either vertically or horizontally.*

Rectangle Diagrams

A rectangle is a two dimensional diagram since its areas is given by the product of its length and breadth. These diagrams are modified form of bar diagrams and give more detailed information.

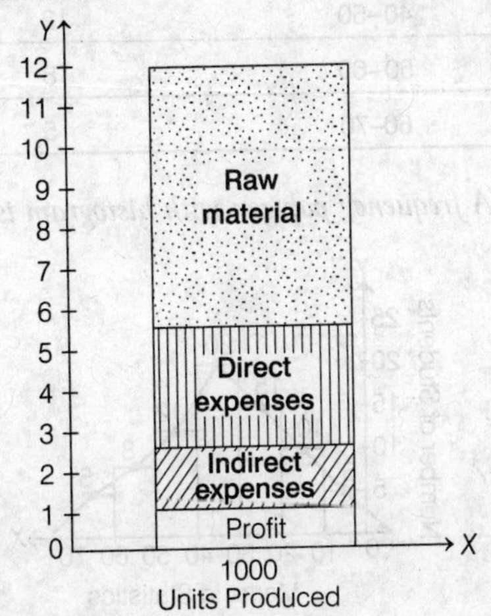

➡ **Note** *A rectangle diagram can be presented in the form of percentage and deviation diagrams also.*

Square Diagrams

A square diagram is a two dimensional diagram in which the given values are represented by the area of the square. Since, the area of the square is given by the square of its side, the side of the square diagram will be in proportion to the square root of the given observations.

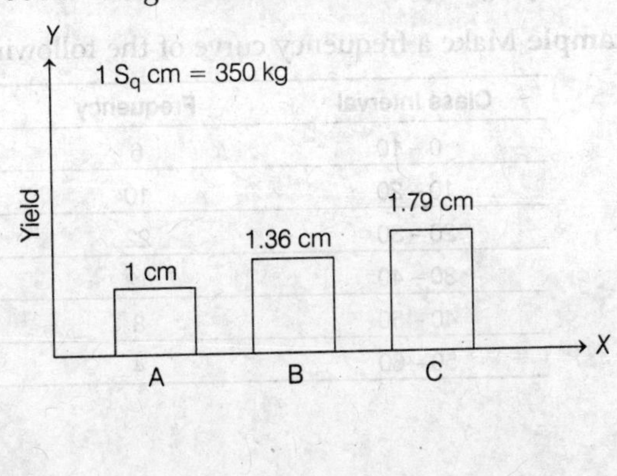

Circle Diagrams

Circles diagrams are also two dimensional figures which represents the given values by πr^2. In the construction of the circle diagram, the radius of the circle is proportional to the square root of the given magnitude.

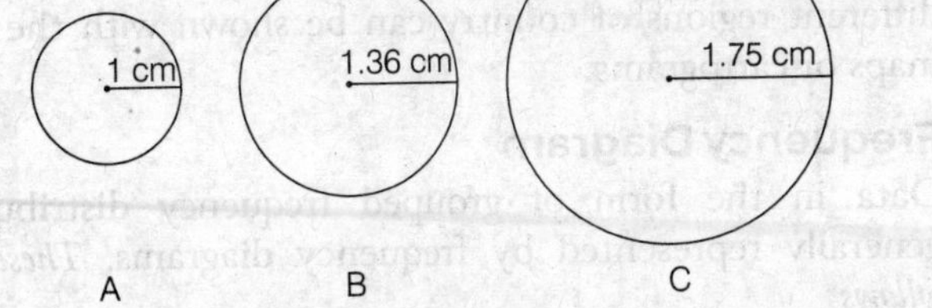

Yield in kg (per hectare)

Pie or Circular Diagrams

Pie diagram is a two dimensional diagram which represents the different values of a variable in a circle. These diagrams are very popular as they are an effective tool for representing different components of the aggregate data under study.

Following steps are taken for constructing a pie diagram

Step 1 Convert each component to degrees by using the following formula

$$\frac{\text{Value of the Component}}{\text{Total Value}} \times 360$$

Step 2 Draw the radius of the circle and then draw the largest sector angle.

Step 3 Draw the other angles, clockwise, in descending order of magnitude.

Step 4 Different segments of the circle should be shaded in different colours or patterns to distinguish amongst them.

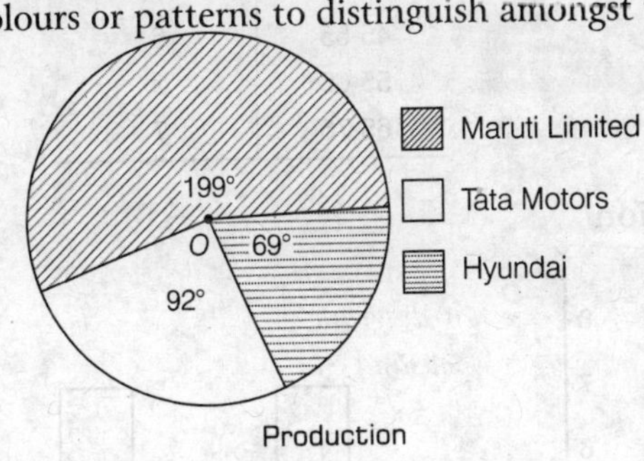

Production

Pictogram

Pictogram means presentation of data in the form of pictures, *i.e.* it conveys its meaning through its pictorial resemblance to a physical object. In statistics, it represents statistical data using statistical data using symbolic figures to match the frequencies. It is quite a popular method used by governments and other organisations for informational exhibition. Its main advantage is its attractive value. Pictograms stimulate interest in the information being presented.

Cartograms

In cartograms, statistical facts are presented through maps accompanied by various types of diagrammatic representation. They are specially used to depict the quantitative facts on a regional or geographical basis. *e.g.* The population density of different states in a country or different countries in the world or the distribution of the rainfall in different regions of country can be shown with the help of maps or cartograms.

Frequency Diagram

Data in the form of grouped frequency distribution is generally represented by frequency diagrams. *These are as follows*

Histogram

A histogram is the graphical description of data and is constructed from a frequency table. It displays the distribution method of a data set and is used for statistical as well as mathematical calculations.

It is constructed from a frequency distribution of a grouped data where the height of the rectangle is proportional to the respective frequency and the width represents the class interval. Each rectangle is joined with the other and any blank spaces between the rectangles would mean that the category is empty and that there are no values in that class interval.

Example From the following frequency distribution construct histogram.

Class Interval	Frequency (f)
15-25	5
25-35	3
35-45	7
45-55	5
55-65	3
65-75	7

Solution

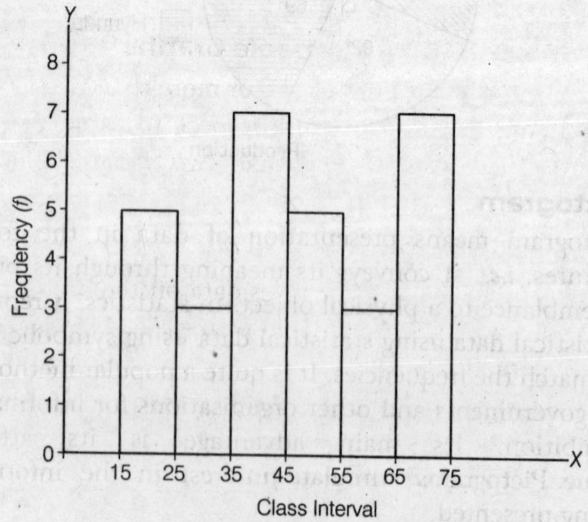

Frequency Polygon

A frequency polygon is a line chart of frequency distribution in which either the values of discrete variables or mid-points of class intervals are plotted against the frequencies and these plotted points are joined together by straight line.

Example Following table shows number of students of a college corresponding to different range of marks in statistics. Make a frequency polygon with the help of histogram.

Marks in Statistics	Number of Students
0–10	5
10–20	10
20–30	15
30–40	20
40–50	12
50–60	8
60–70	5

Solution *A frequency polygon with histogram is shown below*

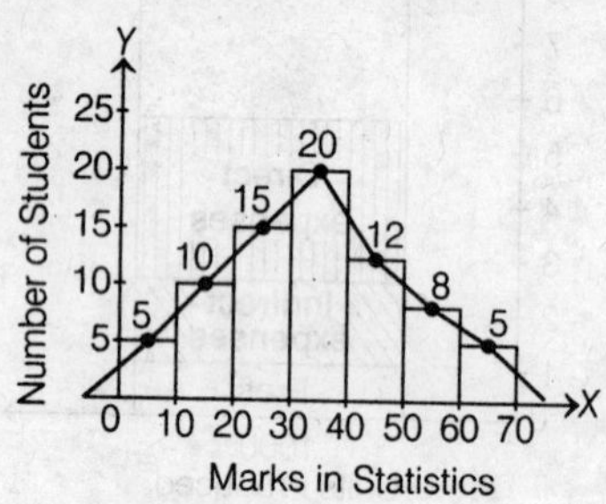

➡ **Note** *The end points of the polygon are extended to meet the mid values of preceding class and succeeding class.*

Frequency Curve

The frequency curve is obtained by drawing a smooth free hand curve passing through the points of the frequency polygon as closely as possible and extending it to meet the base line at hypothetical classes.

The example given below illustrates this case

Example Make a frequency curve of the following data.

Class Interval	Frequency
0 – 10	6
10 – 20	10
20 – 30	22
30 – 40	12
40 – 50	8
50 – 60	4

Soluiton *A frequency curve of given data is shown below*

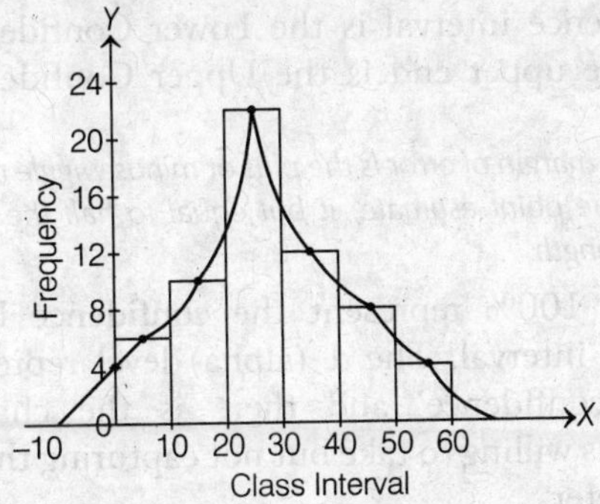

Cumulative Frequency Curves (Ogives)

The cumulative frequency curve or ogive is the graphic representation of a cumulative frequency distribution.

The uses of ogives are as follows

- To determine as well as to portray the number of proportions of cases above or below a given value.
- To compare two or more frequency distributions.
- Ogives are drawn for determining certain values graphically such as percentiles, quartiles etc.

Types of Ogives are as follows

- Less than ogive
- Greater than ogive

Marks	Number of Students
0–5	3
5–10	10
10–15	20
15–20	30
20–25	20
25–30	9
30–35	5
35–40	3

The graph showing both (more than and less than) ogives is given below

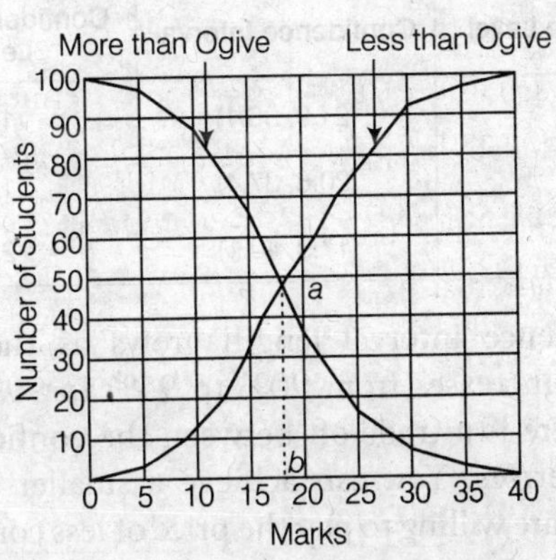

In the above graph, the curves intersect at '*a*'. A perpendicular is dropped from '*a*', which meets the *X*-axis at point '*b*'. Then '*b*' is the middle most value. For the given distribution, the value of *b* is 17.8 or 18 approx.

Graphs of Time Series

Graphs of time series are also referred to as 'arithmetic line graphs' or 'Histogram'. In this graph, time (hour, day/date, week, month, year) is plotted along *X*-axis and the corresponding value of variable along *Y*-axis. *Which are as follows*

There are two types of arithmetic line graph or time series graph

One Variable Graph

One variable graphs are those graphs in which values of only one variable are shown with respect to time period of equal duration.

The following example illustrates this case

Example Plot the following data of annual profits of a firm on a time series graph.

Year	2008	2009	2010	2011	2012
Profit (in thousand ₹)	50	62	65	55	70

Solution *The time series graph showing annual profits of a firm is given below*

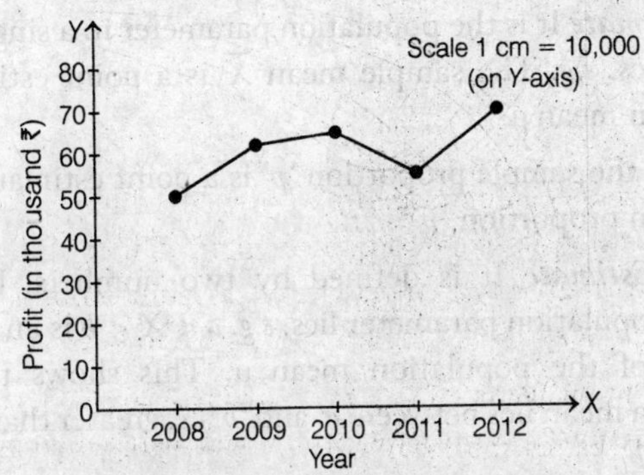

Two or More than Two Variable Graphs

The graphs in which values of two or more than two variables are simultaneously shown with respect to same period of time, are called two or more than two variable graphs or multiple time series graphs.

The example given below illustrates this case

Example The following table gives data on the production of wheat and rice between 2008 and 2013. Make a two variable time series graph.

Year	Wheat ('000 kg)	Rice ('000 kg)
2008	200	50
2009	250	100

Year	Wheat ('000 kg)	Rice ('000 kg)
2010	220	150
2011	300	90
2012	320	150
2013	330	200

Solution *The two variable graph with given data is shown below*

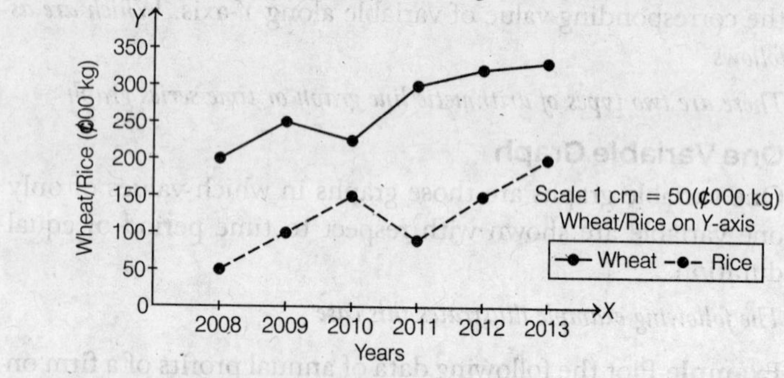

Statistical Estimation

According to statistics, estimation refers to the process of making inferences about a universe or population based on the information obtained from the samples.

Estimation can be done in two ways

Point Estimate It is the population parameter in a single value of statistics. *e.g.* The sample mean $\overline{X}$ is a point estimate of population mean μ.

Similarly, the sample proportion '*p*' is a point estimate of the population proportion '*p*'.

Interval Estimate It is defined by two numbers, between which a population parameter lies, *e.g.* $a < \overline{X} < b$ is an interval estimate of the population mean μ. This shows that the population mean lies between '*a*' and '*b*' *i.e.* greater than '*a*' but less than '*b*'.

Also, confidence interval is used to express the precision and uncertainty associated with a particular method of sampling. *A confidence level consists of three components i.e.* (i) confidence level (ii) a statistics (iii) a margin of error.

Confidence Interval for μ. When σ is known before hand.

To gain further insight into μ, we surround the point estimate with a margin of error

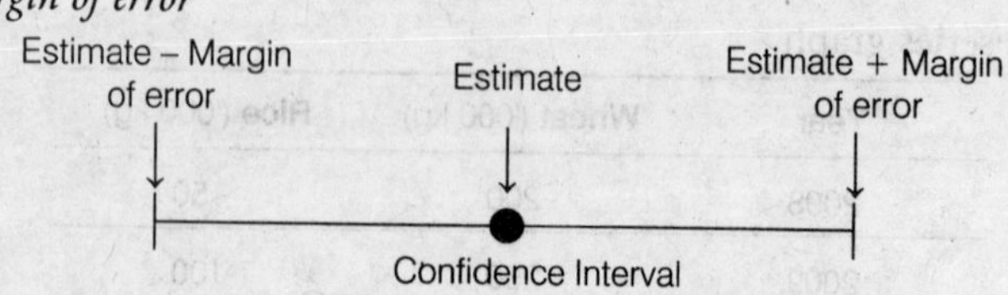

This forms a Confidence Interval (CI). The lower end of the confidence interval is the Lower Confidence Limit (LCL). The upper end is the Upper Confidence Limit (UCL).

➠ **Note** *The margin of error is the plus or minus wiggle room drawn around the point estimate; it but equal to half the confidence interval length.*

Let $(1-\alpha)$ 100% represent the confidence level of a confidence interval. The α (alpha) level represents the 'Lack of confidence' and there is the chance that researcher is willing to take but not capturing the value of the parameter.

$$A(1-\alpha)100\%$$

CI for μ is given below

$$\overline{X} \pm \left(Z_{1-\frac{\alpha}{2}}\right)(\text{SEM})$$

The $Z_{1-\alpha/2}$ in this formula is the Z quantile association with a $(1-\alpha)$ level of confidence. The reason we use $Z_{1-\alpha/2}$ instead of $Z_{1-\alpha}$ in this formula is because the random error is split between underestimates and overestimates. The confidence level $1-\alpha$ area lies between $-Z_{1-\alpha/2}$ and $Z_{1-\alpha/2}$.

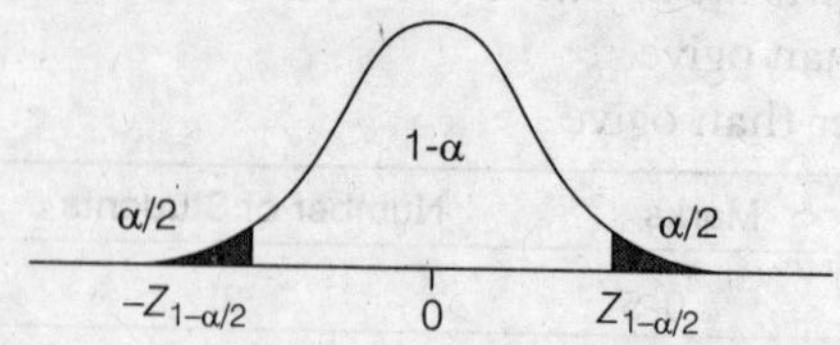

Here are common levels of confidence and their associated α level and z quantiles.

$(1-\alpha)$ 100%	α	$Z_{1-\alpha/2}$
90%	0.10	1.64
95%	0.05	1.96
99%	0.01	2.58

Here are confidence interval lengths (UCL – LCL) of the three intervals just calculated;

Confidence Level	Confidence Interval	Confidene Interval Length
90%	(21.9, 36.1)	14.2
95%	(20.6, 37.4)	16.8
99%	(17.9, 40.1)	22.2

The confidence interval length grows as the level of confidence increases from 90% to 95% to 99%. This is because there is a trade-off between the confidence and margin of errors. You can achieve a smaller margin of error if you are willing to pay the price of less confidence.

Sample Size Requirements for Estimating μ with Confidence

One of the questions we often faces is "How much data should be collected?" Collecting too much data is a waste of time and money. Also, by collecting fewer datȧ points, we can devote more time and energy into making these measurements accuracy. However, collecting two little data renders our estimate too imprecise to be useful. To address the question of sample size requirements, let m represent the desired margin of error of an estimate. This is equivalent to half the ultimate confidence interval length.

➠ **Note** Margin of error (m) = $z^2_{1-\frac{\alpha}{2}} \frac{\sigma}{\sqrt{n}}$

Solving this equation for *n* derives $n = z^2_{1-\frac{\alpha}{2}} \cdot \frac{\sigma^2}{m^2}$

We always round results from this formula upto the next integer to ensure that we have a margin of error not greater than m.

➠ **Note** *To determine the sample size requirement for estimating μ with a given level of confidence requires specification of the Z quantile based on the desired level of confidence* $\left(Z_{1-\frac{\alpha}{2}}\right)$, *population standard deviation (σ) and desired margin of error (m).*

Estimating *p* with Confidence Sampling Distrubution of the Proportion

Estimating parameter p is analogous to estimating parameter μ. However, instead of using $\overline{X}$ as an unbiased point estimate of μ, we use $\hat{p}$ as an unbiased estimate of p. The symbol $\hat{p}$ represents the sample proportion

$$\hat{p} = \frac{\text{Number of successes in the sample}}{n}$$

In samples that are large, the sampling distribution of $\hat{p}$ is approximately normal with a mean of p and standard error of the proportion $\text{SEP} = \sqrt{\frac{pq}{n}}$, Where, $q = 1 - p$. The SEP quantifies the precision of the sample proportion as an estimate of parameter p.

Confidence Interval for *p*

This approach should be used any in samples that are large, use this rule to determine if the sample is large enough.

If $npq \geq 5 \rightarrow$ Proceed with this method

An approximate (1 – α) 100%

$$\text{CI for } p \text{ is given by } \hat{p} \pm \left(Z_{1-\frac{\alpha}{2}}\right)(\text{SEP})$$

Where, the estimated $\text{SEP} = \sqrt{\frac{\hat{p}\hat{q}}{n}}$

Sample Size Requirement for Estimating *p* with Confidence

In planning a study, we want to collect enough data to stimate p with adequate precision. Earlier in the chapter, we determined the sample size requirements to estimate μ with confidence, we apply a similar method to determine the sample size requirements to estimate p. Let m represent the margin of error. This provides the 'wiggle room' around $\hat{p}$ for our confidence interval and is equal to half the confidence interval length. To achieve margin of error m,

$$n - \frac{Z^2_{1-\frac{\alpha}{2}} P^* q^*}{m^2}$$

Where, p^* represents the an educated guess for the proportion and $q^* = 1 - p^*$. When no reasonable guess of p is avaliable, use $p^* = 0.50$ to provide a 'worst case scenario' sample size that will provide more than enough data.

EXAM BASED QUESTIONS

Statistics and Collection of Data

1 The statistical study begins with collection of data and ends with

(a) organisation of data (b) analysis of data
(c) interpretation of data (d) None of these

2 Statistical data are used for knowing about the progress in the

(a) techniques of production
(b) volume of production
(c) imports and exports
(d) All of these

3 Consider the given statement, "the conclusions obtained statistically are universally true". This statement is

(a) true (b) false
(c) partly true (d) partly false

4 Which among the given statement is false?

(a) According to Boddington, "Statistics is the science of estimates and probabilities."
(b) According to Bowley, "Statistics may rightly be called the science of averages."
(c) According to Tippett, "Statistics is not a science, it is a scientific method."
(d) According to Seligman, "Statistics may be regarded as a body of methods for making wise decisions in the face of incertainty."

5 A statistical enquiry or investigation has to pass through in which of the following sequence?

1. Planning and statistical investigation
2. Editing and presenting data
3. Collection of data
4. Analysis of data
5. Interpretation and presentation of report

Select the correct answer using the codes given below

Codes

(a) 1, 2, 3, 5, 4 (b) 1, 2, 3, 4, 5
(c) 1, 2, 5, 4, 3 (d) 2, 4, 3, 1, 5

6 .... data is original in character and is generated by surveys conducted by individuals or research institutions.

(a) Primary (b) Secondary
(c) Tabulated (d) None of these

7 Which of the following statement(s) is/are true about a schedule?

1. If collects primary data.
2. If collects secondary data.
3. If collects qualitative data.

Codes

(a) Both 1 and 2 (b) Only 1
(c) Both 2 and 3 (d) Only 2

8 The data obtained from a newspaper called economic times is referred to as

(a) primary data (b) secondary data
(c) Both (a) and (b) (d) None of these

9 The unit of analysis and interpretation of statistical unit can be

(a) only rate (b) only ratio
(c) only coefficient (d) All of these

10 Questionnaire should have the following number of questions.

(a) 9 (b) 10
(c) 20
(d) According to the information required

11 Systematic sampling is used for which of the following?

1. Quota sampling
2. Non-probability sampling
3. Probability sampling

Codes

(a) Both 1 and 2 (b) Both 2 and 3
(c) Only 2 (d) Only 3

12 .... technique is employed when the complete and up to date list of the sampling units is available in some systematic order.

(a) Stratified sampling (b) Cluster sampling
(c) Systematic sampling (d) None of these

13 If the probability of inclusion of every unit of population in the sample is equal, it is called

(a) simple random sampling
(b) stratified random sampling
(c) systematic sampling
(d) None of the above

14 Sampling is simply the process of learning about the 'population' on the basis of a part of the universe or population called .... drawn from it.

(a) parameters (b) statistics
(c) sample (d) None of these

15 Which of the following characteristics a sampling unit must have?

(a) Must cover the entire population
(b) Non-overlapping
(c) Distinct and unambiguous
(d) All of the above

16 In ...., selection of sample items is independent of the person making the study.

(a) probability sampling
(b) non-probability sampling
(c) Both (a) and (b)
(d) Neither (a) nor (b)

17 **When a researcher uses a telephone directory to select the respondents for a opinion poll, he is following ....**
(a) sequential sampling (b) convenience sampling
(c) judgement sampling (d) None of these

18 **.............. method is used for statistical quality control.**
(a) Sequential sampling (b) Stratified sampling
(c) Cluster sampling (d) Simple random sampling

19 **Non-sampling error occur at the time of**
(a) observation (b) approximation
(c) processing of data (d) All of these

20 **According to sampling, as sample size increases, the error in sampling tends to ....**
(a) increase (b) decrease
(c) remains constant (d) be unstable

21 **Which of the following statements is/are true about a population in statistics?**
1. Population is the total number of items under observation.
2. Parameter is a characteristics of population.
3. Each unit in a population possess same characteristics.

Codes
(a) Both 1 and 2 (b) Both 2 and 3
(c) Both 1 and 3 (d) (i), (ii) and (iii)

22 **Sampling is the proces of learning about the**
(a) population (b) sample
(c) Both (a) and (b) (d) None of these

23 **The degree of confidence with, which it is asserted that a particular value of the population lies within the certain limits is known as the ....**
(a) parameter
(b) level of confidence
(c) level of significance
(d) level of standard error

24 **Statistics is a characteristic of a .... and parameter is a characteristic of a ....**
(a) sample, universe (b) universe, sample
(c) population, universe (d) None of these

25 **Sampling error is .... in incomplete enumeration.**
(a) existent (b) non-existent
(c) estimated (d) None of these

26 **Sample proportion taken from a population is equal to**
(a) X/n (b) X^2/n
(c) n/X (d) None of these

27 **Standard deviation of a binomial distribution is equal to**
(a) σp (b) $\sigma^2 p$
(c) $1-p$ (d) None of these

28 **According to central limit theorem, if the sample size increases, distribution is said to be...... .**
(a) binomial distribution (b) normal distribution
(c) posian distribution (d) None of these

29 **Two common forms of statistical inference are**
(a) estimation
(b) null hypothesis tests of significance
(c) Both (a) and (b)
(d) None of the above

30 **Variance of a sampling distribution with mean μ is**
(a) σ^2 / n (b) σ / n
(c) n / σ^2 (d) None of these

31 **Sampling distribution proportion $\hat{P}$ (hat) represent**
(a) number of successes in the sample
(b) number of successes in the sample/mean
(c) number of successes in the sample/n
(d) None of the above

32 **Which of the following qualities an investigator must possess in collection of primary data?**
1. Skill 2. Tact 3. Accuracy 4. Neutrality
5. Personal bias

Select the correct answer using the codes given below

Codes
(a) 1, 2, 3 and 4
(b) 2, 3, 4 and 5
(c) Both 4 and 5
(d) None of the above

33` **Schedule is a list of questions, which is filled in by .... while questionnaire is filled in by the .... themselves.**
(a) enumerators, informants
(b) informants, enumerators
(c) investigator, informants
(d) Both (a) and (c)

34 **In table, the wordings of stubs and captions should be ....**
(a) as detailed as possible
(b) as brief as possible
(c) to the point
(d) Both (b) and (c)

35 **Which amongst the following is not the source of secondary data?**
(a) Data published in journals
(b) Publications of Central and State Governments
(c) Data published by UNO
(d) The data obtained by firm in a market survey

36 **Non-sampling error may be caused by**
(a) inadequate data specification and inconsistency with respect to the objectives of the survey
(b) errors due to location of units, actual measurement of characteristics, ill designed questionnaire
(c) lack of trained and qualified investigators
(d) All of the above

37 .... state that other things being equal, as the sample size increases, the result tends to be more reliable and accurate.

(a) Principle of statistical regularity
(b) Law of inertia of large numbers
(c) Principle of representativeness
(d) None of the above

38 Sample results in order to provide reliable and accurate results must conform to which of the following requirements?

(a) Representativeness (b) Adequacy
(c) Homogeneity (d) All of these

39 Size of the sample is determined in terms of

(a) the margin of error permissible in the estimate
(b) the confidence coefficient with, which we want the estimate to be within the margin of error
(c) Both (a) and (b)
(d) Neither (a) nor (b)

40 Stratified random sampling is preferred when the parent population is found to be .... with respect to the characteristics under study.

(a) heterogeneous (b) homogeneous
(c) effective (d) None of these

41 The criterion which enables us to classify various sampling units into different strata is termed as ....

(a) probability factor (b) stratifying factor
(c) Both (a) and (b) (d) Neither (a) nor (b)

42 Under ...., only the first unit of the sample is selected at random and the remaining units are selected at fixed intervals.

(a) systematic sampling (b) multi-stage sampling
(c) sequential sampling (d) cluster sampling

43 .... error arise due to chance difference between the members of population included in the sample and those not included.

(a) Biased (b) Unbiased
(c) Relative (d) Absolute

44 When a population is heterogeneous, it is divided into groups, so that there is homogeneity within the group and heterogeneity between the groups and some items are selected at random from each group. It is a case of

(a) cluster random sampling
(b) systematic random sampling
(c) quota sampling
(d) stratified random sampling

45 Sampling method is prove to be a better method over census under which of the following condition?

1. When sample size is infinite.
2. When each unit of population is heterogenous.
3. When approximated results are required.

Codes
(a) Both 1 and 2 (b) Both 2 and 3
(c) Both 1 and 3 (d) 1, 2 and 3

46 Biased error, a type of sampling error, may arise due to

(a) faulty selection of sample
(b) faulty work during the collection
(c) faulty methods of analysis
(d) All of the above

47 The error present in both the complete enumeration survey and the sample survey............... .

(a) sampling error (b) non-sampling error
(c) Both (a) and (b) (d) None of these

48 Incorrect understandings, prestige bias, self interest, respondent's inability are the examples of

(a) compiling errors (b) response error
(c) non-response error (d) publication error

49 Sampling error .... with increase in sampling size while non-sampling error .... with increase in sample size.

(a) decrease, increase (b) increase, decrease
(c) decrease, decrease (d) increase, increase

50 The members of a stratum are .... to each other and are .... from the members of another stratum in the characteristics that is measured.

(a) similar,different (b) different, similar
(c) similar, similar (d) different, different

51 Any sampling process which does not ensure some for each element in the population to be included in the sample would be non-probability sampling or sampling.

(a) Zero probability (b) Non-zero probability
(c) Multiple probability (d) None of these

52 Which amongst the given statement is true?

(a) A well-sized random sample is not a good representative of the universe
(b) Sampling errors are present both in the census as well as sample survey
(c) Law of inertia of large numbers is a corollary of law of statistical regularity
(d) While taking a purposive sample, the items are seletcted at random

53 Number of people watching TV at a given point of time is an example of

(a) finite population (b) infinite population
(c) defined population (d) None of these

54 According to .... , "is a relatively large number of items be chosen at random from a group, such items are on average almost sure to have the characteristics of the group."

(a) WI King (b) CJ lyrohmann
(c) Connors (d) None of these

55 Which of the following is/are part of sampling distribution?

(a) Mean absolute value (b) Range
(c) Standard deviation (d) All of these

56 For a sampling theorem with mean μ, confidence interval should be

(a) $(X + Z - \alpha \text{ SEM})$ (b) $(X - Z - \alpha \text{ SEM})$
(c) $(X \pm Z - \alpha \text{ SEM})$ (d) None of these

57 In a general class interval, margin of error is equal to

(a) $m = Z^2_{1-\frac{\alpha}{2}} \cdot \frac{\sigma}{\sqrt{n}}$ (b) $m = Z^2_{1-\alpha/2} \cdot \frac{\sigma^2}{\sqrt{n}}$
(c) $m = Z^2_{1-\frac{\alpha}{2}} \cdot \frac{\sigma}{n}$ (d) $m = z_{1-\frac{\alpha}{2}} \cdot \frac{\sigma}{\sqrt{n}}$

58 In the margin of error, terms $n = \dfrac{Z^2_{1-\frac{\alpha}{2}} p * q *}{m^2}$ here, $P*$ stands for

(a) guess of proportion (b) probability of error
(c) population size (d) None of these

59 Statistical interference was the following forms.

1. Point estimation
2. Interval estimation

(a) Only 1 (b) Only 2
(c) Both 1 and 2 (d) None of these

60 In trees standard error of estimation '*n*' stands for

(a) $n = Z^2_{1-\frac{\alpha}{2}} \cdot \sigma^2 m^2$ (b) $n = Z_{1-\frac{\alpha}{2}} \frac{m^2}{\sigma^2}$
(c) $n = Z^2_{1-\frac{\alpha}{2}} \frac{\sigma}{m}$ (d) Both (a) and (c)

Classification and Presentation of Data

61 .... is the grouping of related facts into various classes.

(a) Classification (b) Tabulation
(c) Both (a) and (b) (d) None of these

62 The number of times each score occurs is called ....

(a) cumulation (b) frequency
(c) range (d) None of these

63 The difference between the lower limit and upper limit of a class is known as ....

(a) class limit (b) class interval
(c) mid-point of class (d) None of these

64 Which of the following are the methods of forming the class interval?

(a) Exclusive method
(b) Inclusive method
(c) Both (a) and (b)
(d) Neither (a) nor (b)

65 A graph of cumulative frequency distribution is called ....

(a) ogive (b) frequency polygon
(c) pie diagram (d) histogram

66 If the lower and upper limit of a class are 20 and 40, then the mid-point

(a) 20 (b) 30
(c) 40 (d) None of these

67 The .... can be formed by dividing the frequency distribution by the total number of observations.

(a) cumulative frequency distribution
(b) relative frequency distribution
(c) percentage frequency distribution
(d) None of the above

68 The income of 5 persons are as follows

Person	Income per month (₹)
Ram	1,500
Shyam	1,700
Mohan	2,000
Aryan	5,000
Krishna	6,000

Types of above series ....

(a) individual series (b) discrete series
(c) continuous series (d) time series

69 The weight of 50 students in pounds are given below

82	95	120	174	179	176	159	91	85	175
88	160	97	133	159	176	151	115	105	172
170	128	112	101	123	117	93	117	99	90
113	119	129	134	178	105	147	107	155	157
98	117	95	135	175	97	160	168	144	175

If the data are arranged in the form of frequency distribution with class interval as 81-100, 101-120, 121-140, 141-160, 161-180, then the frequencies for these five classes will be

Select the correct answer using the codes given below

Codes

(a) 6,9,10,11,14 (b) 12,11,6,9,11
(c) 6,9,12,12,11 (d) None of these

70 Arrange the following steps in sequence in constructing a frequency distribution.

1. The classes should be clearly defined and each observations should be included in only one of class interval.
2. Check that the number of classes should neither be too large nor too small.
3. Check that all class intervals are of same width.
4. List the value of the variable in different class interval.

Select the correct answer using the codes given below

Codes

(a) 1, 3, 2, 4 (b) 1, 2, 3, 4
(c) 1, 4, 3, 2 (d) 2, 1, 3, 4

71 In ...., size of the slice represents the proportion of the component out of the whole.
(a) percentage bar diagram
(b) pie chart
(c) multiple bar diagram
(d) Both (a) and (b)

72 Which of the following are the graphical representation of data?
(a) Histogram (b) Pictogram
(c) Frequency polygon (d) Both (a) and (c)

73 In 'Less than' cumulative frequency distribution, the omitted limit is
(a) lower (b) upper
(c) last (d) middle

74 For the discrete variables, more suitable class intervals are
(a) exclusive (b) inclusive
(c) Both (a) and (b) (d) None of these

75 In a chronological classification, data are classified on the basis of
(a) attributes (b) class-intervals
(c) time (d) location

76 Which of the following is used to compare two or more frequency distribution?
(a) Frequency polygon
(b) Histogram
(c) Cumulative frequency curves(ogives)
(d) None of the above

77 In an individual series, the frequency of each observation is
(a) equal (b) different
(c) Both (a) and (b) (d) None of these

78 When both lower and the upper limits are considered, such classes are called
(a) exclusive (b) inclusive
(c) open-end-classes (d) cumulative

79 .... is drawn by joining the mid-points of the upper widths of adjacent rectangles of the histogram, with straight lines.
(a) A frequency polygon (b) Histogram
(c) Ogive curve (d) None of these

80 The grouping of relating facts into classes is called
(a) diagram (b) graph
(c) classification (d) tabulation

81 Percentage bar diagram is similar to sub-divided bar diagrams.The only difference is
(a) in percentage bars diagram length of bar are equal while it is unequal in sub-divided bar diagram
(b) in percentage bars diagram width is equal while unequal in sub-divided bar diagram
(c) Both (a) and (b)
(d) None of the above

82 A histogram is constructed from a frequency distribution and is
(a) uni-dimensional (b) two dimensional
(c) three dimensional (d) None of these

83 Diagrams are more suitable to illustrate the data, which is .... while .... is better represented by graphs.
(a) discrete, continuous (b) continuous, discrete
(c) less than, more than (d) None of these

84 Arrange the following steps in sequence in constructing histogram.
1. Convert frequency table into equal class interval.
2. Check that class intervals are shown on X-axis and frequencies on the Y-axis.
3. Check that height of the rectangle is proportional to the respective frequency of grouped data.
4. Check that width of the rectangle represent the class interval.
5. Each rectangle is then joined.

Select the correct answer using the codes given below

Codes
(a) 1, 2, 3, 4, 5 (b) 1, 2, 4, 3, 5
(c) 1, 3, 4, 2, 5 (d) 1, 4, 3, 2, 5

Miscellaneous

Directions (Q. Nos. 85-93) *In the questions given below are two statements labelled as Assertion (A) and Reason (R). In the context of the two statements, which one of the following is correct?*

Codes
(a) Both (A) and (R) are true and (R) is the correct explanation of (A)
(b) Both (A) and R are true, but (R) is not the correct explanation of (A)
(c) Both (A) and (R) are false
(d) (A) is true, but (R) is false

85 **Assertion** (A) Applied statistics consists of application of statistical methods and techniques to the problems and facts as they exist.
Reason (R) Descriptive statistics is confined to treatment of data for the purpose of describing their characteristics.

86 **Assertion** (A) Personal interview usually result in more accurate responses.
Reason (R) In personal interview, interviewer can probe more deeply into answers and if questions are not properly understood by respondent it can be clarified by interviewer.

87 **Assertion** (A) Primary data is original in character.
Reason (R) Primary data is one which is collected by the investigator himself for the purpose of enquiry.

88 **Assertion** (A) In case of random sampling, law of inertia of large number and law of statistical regularity operate.

Reason (R) The greater is the number of items in the sample selected at random greater will be the chance of sample possessing the characteristics of the universe.

89 **Assertion** (A) In sequential sampling, the size of the sample is not fixed in advance.

Reason (R) Sample size is decided as the sampling process takes place depending on the results of the first sample.

90 **Assertion** (A) A sample is the representative of the entire population.

Reason (R) A sample should have all the characteristics of the population from where it is taken.

91 **Assertion** (A) Bar graphs are uni-dimensional.

Reason (R) For each category of data, one bar is constructed represented by lengths or height of rectangle whereas width of rectangle is immaterial.

92 **Assertion** (A) Purpose of a table is to simplify the presentation and facilitate comparison.

Reason (R) A table is a systematic arrangement of the statistical data in rows and columns.

93 **Assertion** (A) The data that we collect can often be more easily understood for interpretation, if it is presented graphically or pictorially.

Reason (R) Diagrams and graphs give visual indications of magnitudes, groupings, trends and patterns in the data.

94 **Assertion** (A) If a random sample of 'n' observations is taken from a binomial population with parameter as p, the sampling distributions will be a standard deviation which is normally distributed.

Reason (R) Standard deviation of binomial distribution $\sigma P = \sqrt{\frac{pq}{n}}$, where $q = 1 - p$

Codes

(a) (A) is true, but (R) is false
(b) (A) is false, but (R) is true
(c) Both are false (d) Both are true

95 **Assertion** (A) The mean of the sampling distribution of the mean is the same as the population mean.

Reason (R) As the sample size increases, samples tends to population.

Codes

(a) (A) is true, but (R) is false
(b) (A) is false, but (R) is true
(c) Both are true (d) Both are false

96 **Assertion** (A) The CLT is useful when examining returns for a stock or index because it simplifies many analysis procedures.

Reason (R) An appropriate sample size depends on the data available.

Codes

(a) (A) is true, but (R) is false
(b) (A) is false, but (R) is true
(c) Both are true
(d) Both are false

97 Match the following.

List I	List II
A. Range	1. Summing up the consecutive frequencies
B. Width of the interval	2. Range/ Number of classes
C. Open ended class	3. Highest value-lowest value in data
D. Cumulative frequency	4. No lower limit of first group or no upper limit of the last group

Codes

	A	B	C	D		A	B	C	D
(a)	1	2	3	4	(b)	3	2	4	1
(c)	2	3	4	1	(d)	4	3	2	1

98 Match the following.

List I	List II
A. Histogram	1. Line chart of frequency distribution
B. Bar diagram	2. Data is represented in form of series of rectangle and is two dimensional
C. Frequency polygon	3. Lengths of bars are proportional to their corresponding values
D. Cumulative frequency curve	4. Graphic representation of a cumulative frequency distribution

Codes

	A	B	C	D		A	B	C	D
(a)	2	3	1	4	(b)	1	2	3	4
(c)	4	2	3	1	(d)	3	1	2	4

99 Match the following.

List I	List II
A. Primary data	1. Representation of data in form of pictures
B. Secondary data	2. The totality of things under consideration
C. Pictogram	3. Data collected by the investigator himself
D. Population	4. Data used by the investigator, which has already been collected by others

Codes

	A	B	C	D		A	B	C	D
(a)	1	2	3	4	(b)	3	4	1	2
(c)	3	2	1	4	(d)	2	1	3	4

100 Match the following.

	List I		List II
A.	Diagrammatic representation	1.	Geographical, chronological, qualitative, quantitative
B.	Graphic representation	2.	Ungrouped, grouped
C.	Frequency distribution	3.	Bar diagram, pie chart, pictogram
D.	Classification of data	4.	Histogram, frequency polygon, ogive

Codes

	A	B	C	D		A	B	C	D
(a)	1	2	3	4	(b)	3	4	2	1
(c)	2	3	1	4	(d)	4	3	2	1

101 Match the following.

	List I		List II
A.	Statistical methods	1.	Technique used for collection, summarisation, analysis, comparison, classification and interpretation of huge and complex numerical data
B.	Branch of statistics	2.	Inductive and descriptive statistics
C.	Nature of statistics	3.	Science and art
D.	First user of statistics	4.	Hemlet

Codes

	A	B	C	D		A	B	C	D
(a)	1	2	3	4	(b)	2	3	4	1
(c)	1	3	2	4	(d)	3	4	2	1

PREVIOUS YEARS' QUESTIONS

December 2018

1 Which of the following statements relating to the sampling theory are correct?

1. The values of the statistical measures based on the sampled units are called values of statistics.
2. In the simple random sampling technique, the element of the population and the unit of the sample are different.
3. Snow-ball sampling technique is a probability based sampling technique.
4. The 'law of statistical regularity' and the 'law of inertia of large numbers' are the main bases of the sample to become representative of the population.

Choose the correct answer from the codes given below

Codes

(a) Both 2 and 3 (b) Both 1 and 4
(c) 1, 2 and 3 (d) 2, 3 and 4

July 2018

2 Assignment of numerals to the objects to represent their attributes is known as

(a) nominal data (b) ordinal data
(c) interval data (d) ratio data

3 A graph of a cumulative frequency distribution is called

(a) frequency polygon (b) frequency curve
(c) ogive (d) pie diagram

4 In the case of classification of data, the class having its upper limit is treated as the lower limit of its next class is called

(a) open ended class (b) close ended class
(c) exclusive class (d) inclusive class

November 2017

5 The formula to determine the number of classes given by Sturge's rule is which one of the following?

(a) $K = 1+3.322 (\log N)$ (b) $K = (\log N)1.322$
(c) $K = \dfrac{1+3.322}{(\log N)}$ (d) $K = \dfrac{3.322}{(\log N)+1}$

Where, K = Number of classes
N = Total number of observations
(log N) = Logarithm of the total number of observations

6 **Assertion** (A) A reasonably sized sample drawn randomly from large sized population contains almost all the characteristics which exist in the population.
Reason (R) The theory of sampling is based on the two important laws of statistics, *viz* law of statistical regularity and law of inertia of large numbers.

Codes

(a) Both (A) and (R) are correct and (R) is the correct explanation of (A)
(b) Both (A) and (R) are correct, but (R) is not the correct explanation of (A)
(c) (A) is not correct, while (R) is correct
(d) Both (A) and (R) are not correct

January 2017

7 **Statement** I The absolute value of the difference between an unbiased estimate and the corresponding population parameter is called sampling error.

Statement II Multi-stage sampling is a restricted non-probability based sampling technique.

Codes

(a) Both statements are correct
(b) Both statements are incorrect
(c) Statement I is correct, while Statement II is incorrect
(d) Statement I is incorrect, while Statement II is correct

8 Process of arranging data into a new order is called

(a) manipulation of data
(b) standardisation of data
(c) sequencing of data
(d) standardised input

December 2015

9 **Assertion** (A) A reasonably large sized sample drawn randomly from a given population contains almost all the characteristics of the population.

Reason (R) As per the sampling theory, the assertion is based only on the 'law of inertia of large numbers'.

Codes

(a) (A) is true and (R) as per the sampling theory is also fully true
(b) (A) is true, but the (R) as per the sampling theory is not fully true
(c) Both (A) and (R) are false
(d) (A) is false, but the (R) is sufficient as per the sampling theory

June 2015

10 If the population is heterogeneous, which one of the following probability sampling methods is more appropriate?

(a) Sequential sampling
(b) Quota sampling
(c) Double sampling
(d) Stratified sampling

11 The process of thoroughly checking the collected data to ensure optimal quality level is referred to as

(a) validation (b) editing
(c) classification (d) entry

December 2014

12 To show the trend for a variable, which one of the presentation method is used?

(a) Histogram (b) Frequency polygon
(c) Line graph (d) Scatter graph

13 Which one of the following objectives is not the objective of secondary data collection?

(a) Identify the problem
(b) Test the hypothesis of the relevant present problem
(c) Better define the problem
(d) Interpret primary data more insightfully

December 2013

14 The law of statistics, which says "Moderately large number of items chosen at random from a large group possess the characteristics of the large group", is referred to as

(a) the central limit theorem
(b) the law of statistical regularly
(c) the law of inertia of large numbers
(d) None of the above

June 2013

15 The difference between sample statistic and its corresponding population parameter is

(a) sampling error (b) measurement error
(c) coverage error (d) non-response error

December 2012

16 Sample design involves the following.

1. Sampling unit 2. Size of samples
3. Type of universe 4. Sources list
5. Sampling procedure

Which one of the following sequence is correct?

(a) 1, 2, 3, 4, 5 (b) 3, 4, 1, 2, 5
(c) 3, 1, 4, 2, 5 (d) 3, 5, 1, 4, 2

17 Sturge's rule is used to find out directly

(a) number of classes in a continuous distribution
(b) size of class limits
(c) direction of the classification
(d) None of the above

18 Sampling distribution of mean is very close to the standard normal distribution when

(a) population is normally distributed
(b) population is not normally distributed, but sample size is large
(c) Both (a) and (b)
(d) Neither (a) nor (b)

June 2012

19 Which of the following is not a restricted random sampling technique?

(a) Startified sampling
(b) Simple random sampling
(c) Systematic sampling
(d) Multi-stage sampling

20 Classification of respondents only on the basis of gender is an application of

(a) ordinal scale (b) nominal scale
(c) interval scale (d) ratio scale

21 Which of the following is the non-random method of selecting sampling from a population?

(a) Stratified sampling
(b) Quota sampling
(c) Systematic sampling
(d) Cluster sampling

✓ ANSWERS

Objective Questions

1	(c)	2	(d)	3	(b)	4	(d)	5	(b)	6	(c)	7	(b)	8	(b)	9	(d)	10	(d)
11	(d)	12	(c)	13	(d)	14	(a)	15	(d)	16	(b)	17	(b)	18	(d)	19	(d)	20	(a)
21	(a)	22	(a)	23	(b)	24	(a)	25	(a)	26	(a)	27	(a)	28	(b)	29	(c)	30	(a)
31	(c)	32	(a)	33	(b)	34	(b)	35	(d)	36	(d)	37	(b)	38	(d)	39	(c)	40	(a)
41	(b)	42	(c)	43	(a)	44	(d)	45	(c)	46	(d)	47	(b)	48	(c)	49	(b)	50	(a)
51	(b)	52	(c)	53	(b)	54	(b)	55	(d)	56	(c)	57	(a)	58	(c)	59	(c)	60	(a)
61	(a)	62	(b)	63	(b)	64	(c)	65	(a)	66	(b)	67	(b)	68	(a)	69	(c)	70	(a)
71	(d)	72	(d)	73	(a)	74	(b)	75	(c)	76	(d)	77	(d)	78	(b)	79	(a)	80	(c)
81	(a)	82	(b)	83	(a)	84	(b)	85	(b)	86	(a)	87	(a)	88	(b)	89	(b)	90	(a)
91	(b)	92	(b)	93	(b)	94	(b)	95	(c)	96	(c)	97	(b)	98	(a)	99	(b)	100	(b)
101	(a)																		

Previous Years' Questions

1	(b)	2	(b)	3	(c)	4	(c)	5	(a)	6	(b)	7	(a)	8	(c)	9	(a)	10	(d)
11	(b)	12	(c)	13	(d)	14	(c)	15	(a)	16	(c)	17	(a)	18	(a)	19	(b)	20	(a)
21	(a)																		

CHAPTER 19

Probability, Research and Hypothesis Testing

Probability is the measure of the likelihood of occurrence of an event, this helps in many other fields of study. Research is the systematic investigation into and study of materials and sources in order to establish facts and reach new conclusions while hypothesis testing is used to infer the result of a hypothesis performed on sample data from a larger population.

Probability

It refers to the quality or state of being probable the extent to which something is likely to happen. It is a random experiment which is an action or process that leads to one of many possible outcomes. The list of possible outcomes of a random experiment must be exhaustive and naturally exclusive.

Approaches to Probability

There are three ways to assign probabilities to events, *i.e.* classical approach, relative frequency approach and subjective approach. *These can be understood as follows*

Classical Approach

If an experiment has 'n' simple outcomes, this method would assign a probability of $\frac{1}{n}$ to each outcome. In other words, each outcome is assumed to have an equal probability of occurrence. This method is also called the 'Axiomatic' approach.

Relative Frequency Approach

Probabilities are assigned on the basis of experimentation or historical data. *This can be better explained with the help of following example*

Formally, let X be an event of interest and assume that you have performed the same experiment 'n' times, so that 'n' is the number of times X could have occurred.

In this Chapter

- Probability
- Research in Statistics
- Hypothesis Testing
- Small Sample Test
- Report Writing in Statistics

Further, let n_x be the number of times that X did occur. Now, consider the relative frequency n_x / n. Then, in this method, we 'attempt' to define $P(X)$ as $P(X) = \lim_{n\to\infty} \frac{n_x}{n}$

The above can only be viewed as an attempt because it is not physically feasible to repeat an experiment an infinite number of times. Another important thing is that two sets of 'n' experiments will typically result in two different ratios. However, we expect the discrepancy to converge to 0 for large 'n'. Hence, for large 'n' the ratio n_x / n may be taken as a reasonable approximation for $P(X)$.

Subjective Approach

In this approach, we define probability as the degree of belief that we hold in the occurrence of an event. Thus, judgement is used as the basis for assigning probabilities. What is different in this approach is that the use of the subjective approach is usually limited to experiments that are unrepeatable.

Bayes' Theorem

The concept of conditional probability is introduced in the elementary statistics.

A prior probability is an initial probability value originally obtained before any additional information is obtained. A posterior probability is a probability value that has been revised by using additional information that is obtained later. Bayes theorem comes into effect when multiple events E_i form an exhaustive set with another event A.

Working of Theorem

If an event 'A' can only occur in conjunction with one of the 'n' mutually exclusive and exhaustive events $E_1, E_2, \ldots\ldots, E_n$ and if 'A' actually happens, *then the probability that it was proceeded by the particular event E_i ($i = 1, 2, \ldots., n$) is given below*

$$P(E_i/A) = \frac{P(A \cap E_i)}{\sum_{i=1}^{n} P(E_i).P(A/E_i)} = \frac{P(E_i).P(A/E_i)}{\sum_{i=1}^{n} P(E_i).P(A/E_i)}$$

The probabilities $P(E_1), P(E_2), \ldots., P(E_n)$ which are already given or known conducting an experiment are termed as a prior probability. The conditional probabilities $P(E_1/A), P(E_2/A), \ldots, P(E_n/A)$ which are computed after conducting the experiment or occurrence of 'A' are termed as posteriori probabilities.

Probability Distributions

Theoretical probability distribution (univariate) are of three types which are as follows

Binomial Distribution

Binomial distribution is also called as 'Bernoulli Distribution'. *This distribution is used under following conditions*

- The random experiment is performed repeatedly by a finite and fixed number of times.
- The outcome of random experiment results in the classification of events.
- All traits are independent, *i.e.* the result of any trial is not affected by the previous trial.
- The probability of success in any trial is 'p' and is constant for each trial, while the probability of failure is '$q = 1 - p$' which is also constant.

Formation of Binomial Distribution

We are interested in finding the corresponding probabilities of $0, 1, 2, \ldots, n$ success. *The general expression for probability of 'r' successes is given below*

$$P(r) = P(X = r) = {}^nc_r.p^r q^{n-r} \quad (r = 0, 1, 2, \ldots., n)$$

Here, $${}^nc_r = \frac{n!}{r!\,(n-r)!}$$

All of which are mutually disjoint. The probability for each of these ${}^nc_r$ is mutually exclusive way which is same as $p^r q^{n-r}$. Putting $r = 0, 1, 2, \ldots, n$ in the above formula, we get probabilities of $0, 1, 2, \ldots, n$ successes respectively in 'n' trials. Since, these probabilities are successive terms in the binomial expansion $(q + p)^n$, it is called the binomial distribution. Mean of binomial distribution is equal to $n.p$ and variance $(\sigma^2) = n.p.q$

Where 'n' is number of trials, 'p' is probability of success and 'q' is probability of failure.

Poisson Distribution

This distribution was first derived in 1837. *Poisson distribution may be obtained as a limiting case of binomial probability distribution under the following conditions*

- n_1, the number of trials is indefinitely large, *i.e.* $n \to \infty$.
- p_1, the constant probability success for each trial is indefinitely small *i.e.* $P \to 0$.
- $np = m$, is finite

Under the above conditions, the binomial probability function tends to the probability function of the poisson distribution given below

$$P(r) = P(X = r) = \frac{e^{-m}.m^r}{r!}$$

$$r = 0, 1, 2, \ldots.$$

Where, X is the number of successes,

$m = np$

and $e = 2.71828$,

$r! = r(r-1)(r-2)\ldots.\times 3 \times 2 \times 1$

Formation of Poisson Distribution

We shall obtain the limiting form of the binomial probability function under following condition

$$n \to \infty \text{ and } np = m$$

$$\Rightarrow \quad p = \frac{m}{n} \text{ and } q = 1 - \frac{m}{n}$$

Probability function of binomial distribution is

$$^nc_r \cdot p^r q^{n-r} = \frac{n!}{r!\,(n-r)!}\, p^r q^{n-r}$$

Limiting this function for $n \to \infty$

we get $P(r) = P(X = r) = \dfrac{e^{-m} \cdot m^r}{r!}; r = 0, 1, 2, ...$

Properties of Poisson Distribution

- Poisson distribution is a discrete to probability distribution, since the variable X can take only integral values 0, 1, 2, ...∞.
- Putting $r = 0, 1, 2, ...$ in the above equation, we get the probabilities 0, 1, 2, 3.... successes respectively.
- The values of e^{-m} for some selected values of 'm' are given.
- If we know 'm', all the probabilities of the poisson distribution can be obtained, 'm' therefore is called parameter. Mean of poisson distribution is $np = m$ and variance $\sum r^2 p(r) - m^2$.

Normal Distribution

Among all the probability distributions, the normal probability distribution is by far the most important and frequently used continuous probability distribution. This is so because this distribution well fits in many types of problems. This distribution is of special significance in inferential statistics, since it describes probabilistically the link between a statistic and a parameter, *i.e.* between the sample results and the population, from which the sample is drawn.

Karl Gauss, a mathematician astronomer of 18th century, is associated with this distribution, so it's often known as Gaussian distribution. The normal distribution can be theoretically derived as the limiting form of many discrete distributions.

Equation of Normal Probability Curve or Normal Distribution

If X, a continuous random variable following normal probability distribution with mean μ and standard deviation σ, then its probability density function (p.d.f.) is given below

$$p(x) = \frac{1}{\sqrt{2\pi} \cdot \sigma} \cdot e^{-\frac{1}{2}\left(\frac{x-\mu}{\sigma}\right)^2}, \; -\infty < x < \infty$$

Or

$$p(x) = \frac{1}{\sqrt{2\pi} \cdot \sigma} \cdot e^{-\frac{(x-\mu)^2}{2\sigma^2}}, \; -\infty < x < \infty$$

Where, $\pi = \dfrac{22}{7}, \sqrt{2\pi} = 2.5066$, and $e = 2.71828$

Note

- *The base of the system of natural logarithms is e.*
- *The mean μ and standard deviation σ are called the parameters of the normal distribution.*

Standard Normal Distribution

- *If X is a random variable following normal distribution with mean μ and standard deviation σ, then the random variable Z is defined as follows*

$$Z = \frac{X - E(X)}{\sigma_X} = \frac{X - \mu}{\sigma}$$

- The Standard Normal Variate (SNV) 'Z' has mean 0 and standard deviation 1. *Hence, the probability density function (p.d.f.) of (S.N.V.) Z is given below*

$$\phi(z) = \frac{1}{\sqrt{2\pi}}\, e^{-\frac{z^2}{2}}, \; -\infty < z < \infty$$

Properties of Normal Distribution

- The graph of normal distribution is a bell shaped curve as shown in the figure. The top of the bell is directly above the mean (μ).
- *The curve is symmetrical about the line X = μ*

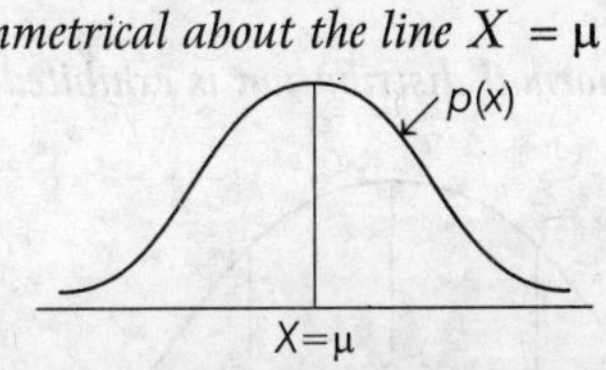

Normal Probability Curve

- Since, the distribution is symmetrical therefore, mean, median and mode coincide. Thus, in a normal distribution

  Mean = Median = Mode = μ
- The total area under normal probability curve is 1 and the area to the right of the ordinate as well as to the left of the ordinate at $X = \mu$ (or $Z = 0$) is 0.5.
- The quartiles are equidistant from median (μ), *i.e.*

$$Q_3 - M_d = M_d - Q_1 \text{ or } Q_1 + Q_3 = 2M_d = 2\mu$$

- In this distribution, the moment coefficient of skewness is given by

$$\beta_1 = 0 \text{ or } \gamma_1 = 0$$

- The coefficient of Kurtosis is given by

$$\beta_2 = 3 \text{ or } \gamma_2 = 0$$

- No portion of the curve lies below the X-axis.
- Theoretically, the range of the distribution is from $-\infty$ to ∞. But practically its range is equal to 6 σ.
- Normal distribution is unimodal and its mode occurs at $X = \mu$.
- For numerically large value of X (on either side of the line) ($X = \mu$), the curve becomes parallel to the X-axis and extends upto infinity.

- The sum of independent normal variates is also a normal variate. This is known as the 'Re-productive or Additive Property' of the normal distribution.
- Mean Deviation (MD) about mean or median or mode, is given by

$$\text{MD} = \frac{4}{5}\sigma$$

- Quartiles of a normal distribution are given as
  $Q_1 = \mu - 0.6745\ \sigma$ and $Q_3 = \mu + 0.6745\ \sigma$
- Quartile Deviation (QD) is given by
  $\text{QD} = \frac{2}{3}\sigma$ Also, $\text{QD} = \frac{5}{6}\text{MD}$
- In a normal distribution, the following ratio is observed between QD, MD and SD
  QD : MD : SD :: 10 :12 :15
- Points of inflexion of the normal curve are at $X = \mu \pm \sigma$ and they are equidistant from mean at a distance of σ and are given by

$$\left[x = \mu \pm \sigma,\ p(x) = \frac{1}{\sigma \cdot \sqrt{2\pi}} e^{-\frac{1}{2}}\right]$$

- The area under the normal probability curve between the ordinates at $X = \mu - \sigma$ and $X = \mu + \sigma$ is 0.6826. In other words, the range $\mu \pm \sigma$ covers 68.26% of the observations.

The area under normal distribution is exhibited in the graph below

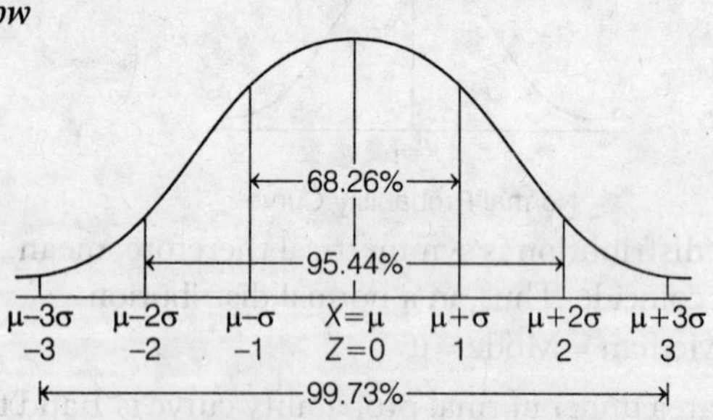

Areas Under Normal Probability Curve

Areas Under Standard Normal Curve

Distance from the Mean Ordinates in Terms of ± σ	Area Under the Curve
Z = ± 0.6745	50% = 0.50
Z = ± 1.00	68.26% = 0.6826
Z = ± 1.96	95% = 0.95
Z = ± 2.0	95.44% = 0.9544
Z = ± 2.58	99% = 0.99
Z = ± 3.0	99.73% = 0.9973

- The means and standard deviations of two or more normal distributions are independent of each other.

Areas Under Normal Probability Curve

Mathematically, the area bounded by the curve $p(x)$, X-axis and the ordinates at $X = a$ and $X = b$ is given by the definite integral.

$\int_a^b p(x)\,dx$ *and is shown in the figure given below*

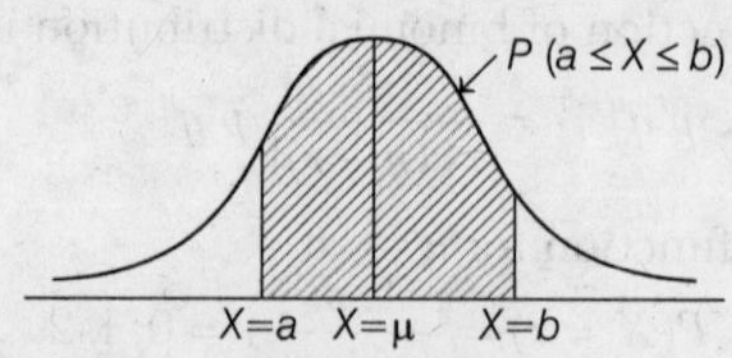

Critical Values of Standard Normal Probability Curve

In case of single tailed alternative, the critical values Z_α is determined so that the total area to the right of it (for right tailed test) is α and for left-tailed test, the total area to the left of $-Z_\alpha$ is α.

For right tailed test $= P(Z > Z_\alpha) = \alpha$

For left tailed test $= P(Z < -Z_\alpha) = \alpha$

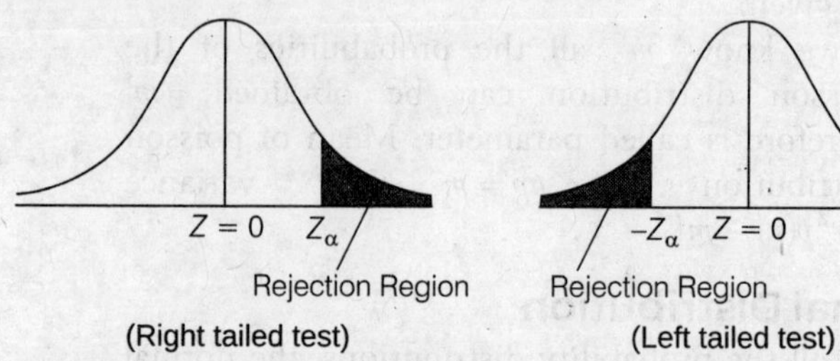

Let, Z_1 be the critical value of Z at level of significance α for a two tailed test so that

$$P(|Z| > Z_1) = \alpha$$
$$\Rightarrow P(Z > Z_1) + P(Z < -Z_1) = \alpha$$
$$\Rightarrow P(Z > Z_1) + P(Z > Z_1) = \alpha$$
$$\Rightarrow 2P(Z > Z_1) = \alpha$$
$$\Rightarrow P(Z > Z_1) = \frac{\alpha}{2}$$
$$Z_1 = Z_{\alpha/2}$$

Thus, the significant or critical value of Z for a single tailed test (left or right) at level of significance 'α' is same as the critical value of Z for a two tailed test at the level of significance '$Z\alpha$'.

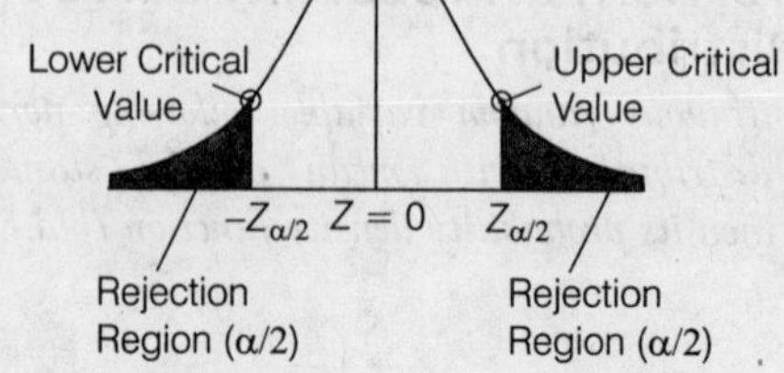

Research in Statistics

Research is a system of activity that involves finding out things which we don't know. In other words, research involves finding about things that no one else knew. Research methods, on the other hand, are the techniques we use to conduct research.

When there is a perception that more information and understanding is needed to advance the work or process of work, then ways are found that how research can be carried to meet this need.

Types of Research

Basic Research It is generally conducted in order to enhance knowledge. The main motive of this research is knowledge expansion. It is a non-commercial research which is not involved in creating or inventing anything.

Applied Research It focuses on solving and analysing problems related to real life situations. This type of research refers to the study that helps to solve practical problems using scientific methods.

Problem Oriented Research This research is conducted to understand the exact nature of the given problem and finding out relevant solution. In this type, the word 'problem' refers to having issues or two thoughts while making any decision.

Problem Solving Research This kind of research is conducted to understand and resolve one's own problems. It uses applied research to find out solutions to the existing problems.

Qualitative Research It is a process about an inquiry that helps indepth understanding of the given problem in their natural environment. This is a non-statistical research method. This method is heavily dependent on the experience of the researchers and the questions used to probe the sample. Under this research, sample size is generally restricted to 6-10 samples. This method comprises open-ended questions in which one question leads to another.

Methodology

Methodology simply refers to the methods which are used to conduct a research. *It includes following methods*

Systematic Research Research is not haphazard rather a psychology. This means that the psychologist deals a problem from theoretical prospective and they arrive at some question they want to answer which is known as hypothesis.

Naturalistic Observation This is the easiest way to study the behaviour of any observation in its natural environment. This is frequently informal and usually the first step which allows better understanding of the behaviour which further leads to in depth investigation.

Case Study This refers to gathering detailed information on a specific individual. It is the technique first used by Prof. Freud. It refers to the process of research into the development of a particular person, group or situation over a period of time.

Surveys Surveyer ask a large number of people questions related to their research and it is the most frequently used method to get an idea of the populations' attitudes towards something, such as who they are going to elect etc. In other words, it is a method used for collecting data from a pre-defined group of respondents to gain information on various topic of investigation.

Correlations This investigates the degree by which variables are related. The range is from –1 to +1 . Where –1 is perfect negative correlation, 0 is no-correlation and +1 is perfect positive correlation. Positive correlation represent high score of one variable with high score of another variable. However, correlation should not be confused with casuality.

Research Design

There are many types of research design, each of which depends upon nature of the problems posed by the research aims. Each type of research design has a range of research methods that are commonly used to collect and analyse investigations. *Following are the types of the research design*

Historical This aims at a systematic and objective evaluation and synthesis of evidence in order to establish facts and draw conclusion about past events. It uses primary historical data. It should be kept in mind that one need to carry out tests in order to sure about authenticity of the sources. It can also be used to find contemporary solution based on the past and to inform present and future trends.

Descriptive This design relies on observation as a means of collecting data. It attempts to examine situations in order to establish what is the norm, *i.e.* what can be predicated to happen again 'under the same circumstances', 'observation' can take many forms. Depending on the types of information sought, people can be interviewed, questionnaires distributed, visual records made, even sounds and smells recorded.

Correlation This design is used to examine a relationship between two concepts. There are two broad classifications of relational statements, *i.e.* an association between two concepts-where there is some kind of influence of one on the other; and a casual relationship-where one causes changes to occur in the other. Causal statements describe what is sometimes called a 'cause and effect' relationship. The cause is referred to as the 'independent variable', the variable that is affected is referred to as the 'dependent variable'.

Comparative This design is used to compare past and present or different parallel situations, particularly when the researcher has no control over events. It can look at situations at different scales, macro or micro. Analogy is used to identify similarities in order to predict results assuming that if two events are similar in certain characteristics, they could well be similar in others too.

Simulation Simulation involves devising a representation in a small and simplified form, of a system, which can be manipulated to gauge effects.

Evaluation This descriptive type of research is specifically designed to deal with complex social issues. It aims to move beyond 'just getting the facts' by trying to make sense of the myriad human, political, social, cultural and contextual elements involved.

Action Essentially, this is an 'on the spot' procedure, principally designed to deal with a specific problem found in a particular situation. There is no attempt made to separate the problem from its context in order to study it in isolation.

Ethnological It focuses on people. In this approach, the researcher is interested in how the subjects of the research interpret their own behaviour rather than imposing a theory from outside. It takes place in the undisturbed natural settings of the subject's environment.

Feminist This is more of a perspective than a research design that involves theory and analysis that highlight the differences between men's and women's lives. Researchers who ignore these differences can come to incorrect conclusions.

Cultural Many of the prevailing theoretical debates are concerned with the subjects of language and cultural interpretation. Cultural research provides methodology that allow a consistent analysis of cultural texts so that they can be compared, relicated disproved and generalised.

Hypothesis Testing

The branch of statistics which helps us in arriving at the criterion for taking business or other decisions is known as hypothesis testing. The theory of hypothesis testing was propagated by J. Neyman and E.S. Pearson.

Following are the concepts associated with hypothesis testing

Statistical Hypothesis

A statistical hypothesis is some assumption or statement, which may or may not be true. *It may be of the following types*

Simple Hypothesis A simple hypothesis completely specifies the population. *The following are examples of simple hypothesis from a normal population $N(\mu, \sigma^2)$*

$$H_0 : \mu = \mu_0 \text{ and } \sigma^2 = \sigma_0^2$$

Composite Hypothesis A composite hypothesis is the one which does not completely defines the population. *The following are its example*

$$H_0 : \mu \neq \mu_0 \text{ and } \sigma^2 \neq \sigma_0^2$$

Null Hypothesis

According to **Prof. AR Fisher**, "Null hypothesis is the hypothesis which is tested for possible rejection under the assumption that it is true." It is usually denoted by H_0. The first and the foremost problem in any testing procedure is the setting-up of the null hypothesis.

The following points may be borne in mind in setting the null hypothesis

- The claim or hypothesis to be tested should be expressed in symbolic form.
- Usually, the null hypothesis is expressed as an equality *e.g.*, $H_0 : \theta = \theta_0$, where, the parameter θ could be mean (μ), proportion (P), variance (σ^2) and so on.
- If we want to test the significance of the difference between a statistic and the parameter or between two sample statistics, then we set-up the null hypothesis H_0 that the difference is not significant. *e.g.* if we want to test if a particular medicine is effective, we shall set-up the hypothesis that it is not effective.
- If we want to test any statement about the population, then we set-up the null hypothesis that it is true. *e.g.* if we want to find if the population mean has specified value μ_0, then we set-up the null hypothesis as $H_0 : \mu = \mu_0$.
- To test the significance of any statistic t, we compute the standardised variate $Z = \frac{t - E(t)}{SE(t)}$

  Where, $E(t)$ = Estimated mean of 't'
  $SE(t)$ = Standard error of 't'

  For any statistic t, the values of $E(t)$ and $SE(t)$ are invariably in terms of the population parameters.

Alternative Hypothesis

Any hypothesis which is complementary to the null hypothesis is called an alternative hypothesis. It is usually denoted by H_1. It is very important to state the alternative hypothesis in respect of any null hypothesis H_0, because the acceptance or rejection of H_0 is meaningful only if it is tested against the alternative hypothesis.

Decisions in Hypothesis Testing

In hypothesis testing, the four possible mutually disjoint and exhaustive decisions are

- Reject H_0, when actually it is not true, *i.e.* when H_0, is false.
- Accept H_0, when it is true.

- Reject H_0, when it is true.
- Accept H_0, when it is false.

The decisions in first two points are correct decisions, while the decisions in last two points are wrong decisions.

Errors in Hypothesis Testing

In testing of hypothesis, we are likely to commit the following two types of errors

Type I Error We make type I error by rejecting a true null hypothesis. It is denoted by Greek letter alpha (α).

Type II Error We make type II error by accepting a wrong null hypothesis. This error is more serious. It is denoted by Greek letter beta (β).

Methods for Hypothesis Testing

The following are the methods for testing of hypothesis

Rejection Region Method *This method involves the following steps*

Step 1 Set-up the null hypothesis.

Step 2 Set-up the alternative hypothesis.

Step 3 Choose the appropriate level of significance (α) depending on the permissible risk.

Step 4 Identify the sample statistic to be used and its sampling distribution.

Step 5 Define and compute the test statistic under H_0.

Step 6 Obtain the critical value (or values) and the critical (rejection) region of the test statistic.

Step 7 If the computed value of the test statistic lies in the rejection region, we reject H_0 at level of significance 'α'.

Step 8 The result is written in simple language, *e.g.* if the calculated value of test statistic is greater than the tabulated value, then we write that it is significant and the null hypothesis H_0 is rejected at level of significance α, *i.e.* with confidence coefficient $(1 - \alpha)$.

P-Value Estimation Method *This method involves the following steps*

Step 1 to 5 are the same as discussed above.

Step 6 Find the P-value of the computed test statistic under H_0.

Step 7 If P-value $< \alpha$, we reject H_0 at 'α' level of significance.

If P-value $> \alpha$, we fail to reject H_0 at 'α' level of significance.

Step 8 Write conclusion of the test in simple language.

Small Sample Test

When samples are small, we cannot assume that random sampling distribution is approximately normal, *i.e.* sample values are approximately equal to those of the parent universe. In case of small samples, our main object is to test a given hypothesis.

In other words, we try to ascertain whether observed values could have arisen by sampling fluctuations. Various significance test have been developed for dealing with problems of small samples. *Some important tests are discussed ahead*

t-Test (t-Distribution)

t-test was developed by Sir William S. Cosset, which made significant contribution in the theory of sampling applicable in case of samples when population variance is not known. This test is also referred to as student's t-test as W.S. Cosset wrote under the pen name of student. If $x_1, x_2, \ldots, x_n$ is a random sample of size 'n' from a normal population with mean μ and variance σ^2, then student's t-statistic is defined as

$$t = \frac{\bar{x} - \mu}{s/\sqrt{n}}$$

Where, $\bar{x} = \frac{\Sigma x}{n}$ is the sample mean and 'S' $= \frac{1}{n-1} \Sigma (x - \bar{x})^2$ is an unbiased estimate of the population variance σ^2. 't' defined above, follows student's t-distribution with $\nu = (n - 1)$ d.f. and its probability density function is given as

$$p(t) = K \times \left[1 + \frac{t^2}{\nu}\right]^{-(\nu+1)/2}, \ -\infty < t < \infty \quad d_f = \text{degree of freedom}$$

Properties of t-Distribution

The important properties of t-distribution are

- Mean of t-distribution is zero.
- Standard deviation of t-distribution is $\sqrt{\frac{n}{(n-2)}}, n > 2$
- t-distribution is symmetrical about $t = 0$.
- For large n (> 30), t-distribution tends to the standard normal distribution. *A comparison between normal curve and t-curve is depicted in the below graph*

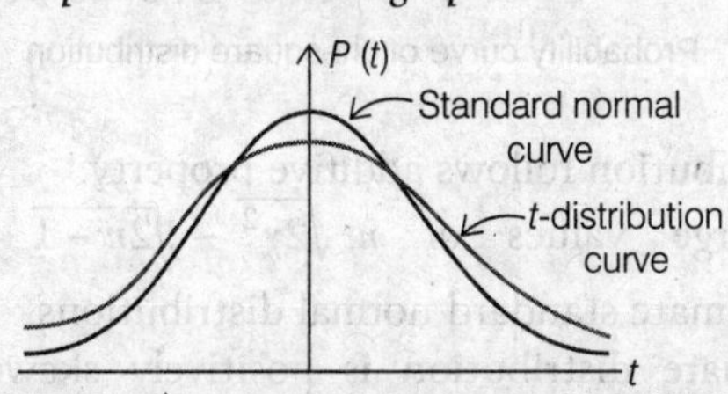

- An interesting property of this distribution is that, it does not depend on the population parameters, but depends only on $\nu = n - 1$, *i.e.* on the sample size.

Applications of T-Distribution

Some of the applications of t-distribution are

- *T*-test for the significance of single mean, population variance being unknown.
- *T*-test for the significance of the difference between two sample means, the population variances being equal but unknown.
- *T*-test for the significance of an observed sample correlation coefficient.

Chi-Square Test (χ^2- distribution)

The square of a standard normal variable is called a chi-square (Pronounced as ki, sky without s) variate with 1 degree of freedom, abbreviated as d.f. Thus, if 'x' is a random variable following normal distribution with mean μ and standard deviation σ, then, $\frac{x-\mu}{\sigma}$ is a standard normal variate and $\left[\frac{x-\mu}{\sigma}\right]^2$ is a chi-square represented by the letter χ^2 of the greek alphabet, variate with 1 d.f. This model was introduced by Prof. Yates.

Properties of Chi-square Distribution

The important properties of χ^2– distribution are mentioned below

- Mean of the χ^2-distribution is given by n.
- Standard deviation of χ^2-distribution is given by $\sqrt{2n}$.
- The probability density function of a χ^2-distribution is given by $f(x) = k.e^{-x/2}\, x^{n/2-1}$, where, k is a constant for $0 < x < \infty$.

After testing x^2-distribution, the result may be interpreted as shown in the figure

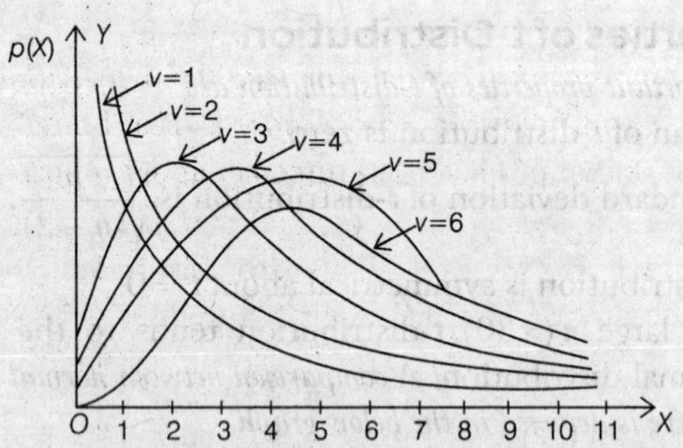

Probability curve of chi-square distribution

- χ^2-distribution follows additive property.
- For large values of n, $\sqrt{2\chi^2} - \sqrt{2n-1}$ follows as approximate standard normal distributions.
- Chi-square distribution is positively skewed, i.e. the probability curve of the χ^2-distribution is inclined more to the right, *which is represented in the figure given below*

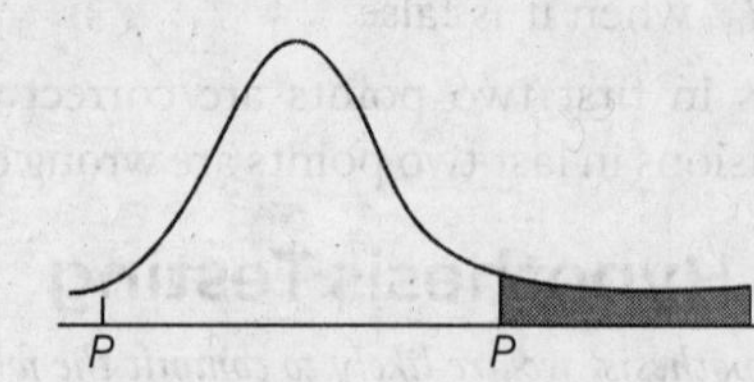

Showing the upper and lower p percent point of square distribution with n d.f.

Applications of the Chi-Square Distribution

Chi-square distribution has a number of applications, which are given below

- To test, if the population has a specified value of the variance (σ^2).
- To test the equality of several population proportions.
- Chi-square test of 'goodness of a fit'.
- Chi-square test for independence of attributes.

F-Distribution

It X is a χ^2-variate with n_1 d.f. and Y is an independent χ^2-variate with n_2 d.f, then F-statistic is defined as

$$F = \frac{X/n_1}{Y/n_2}$$

i.e. F-statistic is the ratio of two independent chi-square variates divided by their respective degrees of freedom. This statistic follows G.W. Snedecor's F-distribution with (n_1, n_2) d.f. with probability density function is given below

$$P(F) = y_0 \cdot \frac{F^{\frac{n_1}{2}-1}}{\left(1+\frac{n_1}{n_2}F\right)^{\frac{n_1+n_2}{2}}}, 0 \le F < \infty$$

Where, y_0 is a constant, so that the total area under the probability curve is 1.

Properties of F-Distribution

The important properties of F-distribution are as follows

- Mean of the F-distribution $= \frac{n_2}{n_2-2}$, $n_2 > 2$.
- Standard deviation of the F-distribution $= \frac{n_2}{n_2-2}\sqrt{\frac{2(n_1+n_2-2)}{n_1(n_2-4)}}$, $n_2 > 4$, and for large values of n_1 and n_2 SD$= \sqrt{\frac{2(n_1+n_2)}{n_1 n_2}}$

- *F*-distribution is positively skewed.
- For large values of n_1 and n_2, *F*-distribution tends to normal distribution with mean zero and SD $= \sqrt{\dfrac{2\,(n_1 + n_2)}{n_1\, n_2}}$
- The sampling distribution of *F*-statistic does not involve any population parameters and depends only on degrees of freedom n_1 and n_2.
- *A graphical representation of F-distribution is given below*

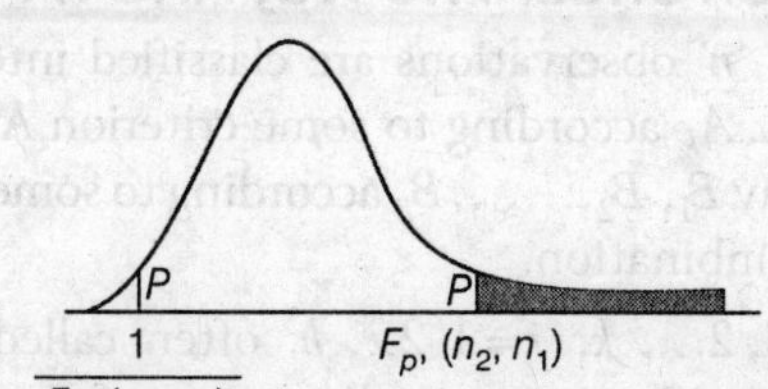

Showing the upper and lower '*p*' percent points of *F*-distribution with n_1 and n_2 degree of freedom.

Applications of F-Distribution

F-distribution has a number of applications in statistics. *Some of them are*

- *F*-test for testing the significance of an observed sample multiple correlation.
- *F*-test for testing the equality of several population means, *i.e.* for testing $H_0 : \mu_1 = \mu_2 = \ldots = \mu_n$, for *n* normal populations.
- *F*-test for equality of population variance.

Z-Distribution (Large Sample Test)

Z-distribution is generally used for large samples to test whether two population means are different when variance are known. Z-distribution assumes that the population is normally distributed with given variance. A one sample location test, two-sample location test, paired difference test are examples of Z-test. Z-test is closely related to t-test, but t-test is performed when sample size is small, *i.e.* less than or equal to 30. Also, t-test assumes standard deviation to be unknown, on the other hand, Z-test assumes it to be given or known. If SD of the population is unknown, the assumption of the sample variance equaling the population variance is made.

$$Z = \frac{X - \mu}{\sigma}$$

Hypothesis Testing in Relation to Z-Distribution

A statistical hypothesis is some assumption or statement, which may or may not be true, about a population or equivalently about the probability distribution characterising the given population, which we want to test on the basis of the evidence from a random sample. If the hypothesis completely specifies the population, then it is known as simple hypothesis. Otherwise it is known as composite hypothesis.

In sampling from normal population $N(\mu, \sigma^2)$ the hypothesis

$$H : \mu = \mu_0$$

and

$$\sigma^2 = \sigma_0^2$$

is a simple hypothesis since it completely specifies the distribution. *On the other hand, each of the following hypothesis is a composite hypothesis*

- $\mu = \mu_0$ (nothing known about σ^2)
- $\sigma^2 = \sigma_0^2$ (μ not specified)
- $\mu < \mu_0, \sigma^2 = \sigma_0^2$
- $\mu > \mu_0, \sigma^2 = \sigma_0^2$
- $\mu = \mu_0, \sigma^2 > \sigma_0^2$ and so on

A test of a statistical hypothesis is a two action decision after observing a random sample from the given population, the two actions being the acceptance or rejection of the hypothesis. *e.g.* Assume an investor wants to test whether the average daily return of a stock is greater than 1%.

A simple random sample of about 50 returns is calculated and has an average of 2%. Assuming the SD of 2.5% from returns. Thus, the null hypothesis is when the average is equal to 3%, *i.e.* H_0: $\mu = 3\%$.

Conversely, the alternative hypothesis is whether the mean return is greater than 3%. Assume an α of 0.05% is selected with two tailed test. Consequently, there is 0.025% of the samples in each tail and the α has a critical value of 1.96 or –1.96. If the value of *Z* is greater than 1.96 or less than –1.96, the null hypothesis is rejected.

It should be clearly borne in mind that the acceptance of a statistical hypothesis is due to insufficient evidence provided by the sample to reject and does not necessarily imply that it is true.

Analysis of Variance (ANOVA)

The analysis of variance is a powerful statistical tool for tests of significance. The test of significance based on t-distribution is an adequate procedure only for testing the significance difference between two sample means. The basic purpose of the analysis of variance is to test the 'homogeneity' of several means.

According to **Prof. RA Fisher**, "ANOVA is the separation of variance ascribable to one group of causes from the variance ascribable to the other group".

Assumptions of ANOVA Test

It has following assumptions

- The observations are independent.
- Parent populations from which observations are taken should be normally distributed.
- Various treatment and environmental effects are additive in nature.

ANOVA test can take two forms, *i.e.* one way classification and two way classification. *These are as follows*

One Way Classification of ANOVA

Let us suppose that '*n*' sample observations of a random variable *X* are divided into '*k*' classes on the basis of some criterion or factor of classification. Let the ith class consist of n_i observations and let

X_{ij} : i^{th} member of the *i* th class; $\{j = 1, 2, \dots n_j$

$i = 1, 2, \dots k\}$

$$n = n_1 + n_2 + \dots\dots + n_k = \sum_{i=1}^{n} n_i$$

Such scheme of classification according to a single criterion is called one way classification of variance.

Class	Sample	Total	Mean
1	$X_{11}\ X_{12} \dots X_{1n}$	T_1	$\bar{X}_1$
2	$X_{21}\ X_{22} \dots X_{2n}$	T_2	$\bar{X}_2$
⋮	⋮		⋮
i	$X_{i1}\ X_{i2} \dots X_{in}$	$T_i = \Sigma x_{ij}$	$\bar{X} = \frac{T_i}{ni}$
⋮	⋮		⋮
k	$X_{k1}\ X_{k2} \dots X_{kn}$	T_k	$\bar{X}_k$

The total variation in the observation X_{ij} can be divided into the following

- The variation between the classes or the variation due to difference in bases of classification.
- The variation within the classes, *i.e.* inherent variation of the random variable within the observation of a class.

The type of ANOVA depends upon multiple factors. It is applied when data needs to be experimented. Analysis of variance is employed if there is no access to statistical softwares. It is simple to use and best suited for small samples with many experimental designs, the sample sizes have to be the same for the various factor level combination.

Two Way Classification of ANOVA

A two way ANOVA is an extension of the one way ANOVA. With one way ANOVA, we have only one independent variable, while in this there are two independent variables.

e.g. a two way ANOVA allows a factory to compare worker's productivity based on two independent variables like wages and skill set. It is utilised to observe the interaction between the two factors. It tests the effect of two factors at one time.

Formulation Under Two Way ANOVA

Suppose the '*n*' observations are classified into '*k*' classes, say $A_1, A_2 \dots A_k$ according to some criterion A and into '*h*' categories, say $B_1, B_2, \dots\dots, B_h$ according to some criterion B, waving *kh* combination.

(A_i, B_j) $i = 1, 2 \dots k$, $j = 1, 2 \dots h$, often called cells. This scheme of classification according to two factors or criteria is called two way classification and its analysis is called two way ANOVA. The number of observations in each cell may be equal or different, but we shall consider the case of one observation per cell so that $n = hk$, *i.e.* the total number of cells is $n = hk$.

Two way ANOVA table is represented as shown below taking two variables say variety of goat and number of goats.

Treatments (Ratios)	Varieties of Goats 1, 2, … *j* … *h*	Row total	Row means
1	$X_{11}\ X_{12} \dots X_{ij} \dots X_{1h}$	R_1	$\bar{X}_1$
2	$X_{21}\ X_{22} \dots X_{2j} \dots X_{2h}$	R_2	$\bar{X}_2$
⋮	⋮	⋮	⋮
i	$X_{i1}\ X_{i2} \dots X_{ij} \dots X_{ih}$	R_j	$\bar{X}_i$
⋮	⋮	⋮	⋮
k	$X_{k1} \dots X_{k2} \dots X_{ki} \dots X_{kh}$	R_k	$\bar{X}_k$
Column total	$C_1\ C_2 \dots C_j \dots C_h$	$G = \sum X_{ij}$	
Column mean	$\bar{X}_1\ \bar{X}_2 \dots \bar{X}_{.j} \dots \bar{X}_{.n}$		

Two way ANOVA table

Let $R_i = \sum_{j=1}^{h} X_{ij}$ be the sum of the observations in the ith row; $(i = 1, 2, \dots\dots k)$

and $C_j = \sum_{i=1}^{R} X_{ij}$ be the sum of the observations in the jth column; $(j = 1, 2, \dots\dots h)$.

$$\bar{X}_{.i} = \text{mean yield of the } i^{th} \text{ treatment (ration)}$$

$$= \frac{1}{h} \sum_{j=1}^{h} X_{ij} = \frac{R_i}{h};$$

$(i = 1, 2 \dots\dots k)$.

$\overline{X}_j$ = mean yield of the jth variety of Goat

$$= \frac{1}{k} = \sum_{i=1}^{h} X_{ij} = \frac{C_j}{k};$$

$(j = 1, 2.....h)$

$$\overline{X}... = \text{The overall mean} = \frac{1}{hk}\sum_i\sum_j X_{ij} = \frac{G}{h}$$

$$= \frac{1}{k}\sum_{i=1}\overline{X}_i = \frac{1}{h}\sum_j \overline{X}_j$$

In two way classification, the total variation in the observation X_{ij} can be split into following components

- The variation between the classes due to one factor represented along the k rows of the table *i.e.* the variation between the treatments.
- The variation between the classes due to the other factor represented along the columns of the table.
- The inherent variation within the observation of each class due to a combination of a large number of uncontrolled or extraneous factors of random nature, termed as 'chance variation'.

Mann-Whitney U-Test

The Mann-Whitney U-test is a non-parametric test that can be used in place of an unpaired t-test. It is used to test the null hypothesis that two samples come from the same population, (*i.e.* have the same median) or alternatively, whether observation in one sample tend to be larger than observation in the other. Although, it is a non-parametric test which assume that the two distributions are similar in shape.

Suppose, we have a sample of n_x observations $\{x_1, x_2......x_n\}$ in one group, (*i.e.* from one population and α sample of n_y observations $\{y_1, y_2.......y_n\}$ in another group, (*i.e.* from another population).

The Mann-Whitney test is based on a comparison of every observation x_i in the first sample with every observation y_j in the other sample. The total number of pairwise comparison that can be made is $n_x n_y$.

If the samples have the same median, then each x_i has an equal chance, (*i.e.* probability $\frac{1}{2}$) of being greater or smaller than each y_j.

So, under the null hypothesis $H_0 : P(x_i > y_j) > \frac{1}{2}$

and under the alternative hypothesis $H_1 : P(x_i > y_j) \neq \frac{1}{2}$

We count the number of times an x_i from sample 1 is greater than y_j from sample 2. This number is denoted by u_x. Similarly, the number of times an x_i from sample 1 is smaller than *a* y_j from sample 2 is denoted by U_y. Under the null hypothesis, we would expect U_x and U_y to be approximately equal.

Procedure for Carrying out the Test

- Arrange all the observations in order of magnitude.
- Under each observation, write down X or Y to indicate which sample they are from.
- Under each x write down the number of y_s which are to the left of it, this indicates $x_i > y_j$, under each y write down the number of x_s which are to the left of it, this indicates $y_j > x_i$.
- Add up the total number of time $x_i > y_j$-denote by U_x. Add up the total number of times $y_i > x_i$ – denote by U_y. Check that $U_x + U_y = n_x n_y$
- Calculate $U = \min(U_x, U_y)$
- Use statistical tables for the Mann-Whitney U-test to find the probability of observation a value of U or lower. If the test is one sided, this is your p –value, if the test is a two sided, double this probability to obtain the p –value.

Note If the number of observations is such that $n_x n_y$ is large enough (> 20), a normal approximation can be used with $\mu_u = \frac{n_x n_y}{2}$, $\sigma_v = \sqrt{\frac{n_x n_y \ (N+1)}{12}}$, Where

$N = n_x + n_y$.

Dealing with Ties

It is possible that two or more observations may be the same. If this is the case, we can still calculate U by allocating half the tie to the X value and half the tie to the Y value. However, if this is the case then the normal approximation must be used with an adjustment to the standard deviation. *This becomes*

$$\sigma_U = \sqrt{\frac{n_x n_y}{N(N-1)} \times \left[\frac{N^3 - N}{12} - \sum_{j=1}^{g} \frac{t_j^3 - t_j}{12}\right]}$$

Where, $N = n_x + n_y$

g = the number of groups of ties

t_j = the number of tied ranks in group j

Kruskal-Wallis H-Test using SPSS Statistics

The Kruskal-Wallis H-test is a rank based test. Non-parametric in nature which can be used to determine if there are statistically significant difference between two or more groups of an independent variable on a continuous or ordinal dependent variable. It is considered the non-parametric alternative to the one way ANOVA and an extension of the Mann-Whitney U-test to allow the comparison of more than two independent groups.

It is important to realise that the Kruskal-Wallis H-test is an omnibus test statistic and cannot tell us which specific groups of the independent variable are statistically significantly different from each other, it only tells you that at least two groups were different. Since, we may have many groups in our study design, determining which of these groups differ from each other is important.

Assumptions of Kruskal-Walli: H-test

- Dependent variable should be measured at the ordinal or continuous level.
- Independent variable should consist of two or more categorical, independent groups.
- We should have independence of observations which means that there is no relationship between the observations in each group or between the groups themselves.
- We have to determine whether the distribution in each group, *i.e.* the distribution of scores for each group of the independent variable have the same shape.

The Kruskal-Wallis test is a non-parametric test, which means that if does not assume that the data come from a distribution that can be completely described by two parameters, mean and standard deviation.

Formulation of Kruskal-Wallis H-Test

Let n_j ($j = 1, 2, \ldots, k$) represent the sample sizes for each of the k groups, (*i.e.* samples) in the data. Next, rank the combined sample. Then compute R_j = the sum of the ranks for group j. Then, the Kruskal-Wallis test statistics is

$$H = \frac{12}{n(n+1)} \sum_{j=1}^{k} \frac{R_j^2}{n_j} - 3(n+1)$$

This statistics approximates a chi-square distribution with $(k - 1)$ degree of freedom, if the null hypothesis of equal population is true. Each of the n_j should be at least 5 for the approximately to be valid. We reject the null hypothesis of equal population means, if the test statistic H is greater than $(\alpha, k - 1)$.

Rank Test

The Wilcoxon signed-rank test is a non-parametric statistical hypothesis test. It is used to compare two related samples, matched samples, or repeated measurements on a single sample to assess whether their population mean ranks differ (i.e. it is a paired difference test). The Wilcoxon signed rank test should be used if differences between pairs of data are non-normally distributed.

Test procedure

Under the null hypothesis, the mean of W is zero. *The variance of W is given by the following*

$$Var(W) = \frac{1}{24}\left[N(N+1)(2N+1) - d_0(d_0+1)(2d_0+1) - \frac{1}{2}\sum_{i>0} d_i(d_i+1)(d_i-1)\right]$$

$$W = R^{+} - \frac{1}{4}[N(N+1) - d_0(d_0+1)]$$

The statistic t given by the following has an approximate t distribution with $N - 1$ degrees of freedom

$$t = W / \sqrt{Var(W)}$$

Report Writing in Statistics

Writing report is an important component of a statistician's work, which is concerned with presenting his results to 'customers' who are not usually much aware about statistics. These notes are aimed at helping you to present your statistical analysis more clearly. *We shall consider the following aspect of report writing*

Structure The report is made up of several components, like title, summary, methods, results, general discussions, references etc. Some reports may well be better split up into sections, while shorter reports will not require a full structure.

Content The decisions about the detailed contents are of extremely importance, but it is difficult to give much in the way of general guidelines. Nevertheless, a few things which are universally applicable may be said.

Presentation Reports should be attractive and easy to find one's way through. It follows that they should be neat, clean and tidy and must be legible, *i.e.* if they are handwritten, one should try to ensure that the handwriting is not a problem.

Style *Following points must be considered while writing a report*

- Be brief and to the point and use shorter rather than longer words.
- Try to avoid the use of the personal pronoun 'I', as it can get very irritating to the reader.
- Try to avoid using words in appropriately and get your spelling correct.
- Try to write grammatically whole sentences, each with its main verbs etc.

Detailed Preparation *There are two important things to be considered here which are as follows*

- It is essential to plan the report before you start writing.
- It is also essential to revise it.

EXAM BASED QUESTIONS

Probability and Research

1 **Which of the following are approaches of probability ?**

(a) Classical approach
(b) Relative frequency approach
(c) Objective approach
(d) Both (a) and (b)

2 **According to relative frequency approach $P(X)$ is equal to**

(a) $\lim_{n \to \infty} \frac{n_x}{n}$ (b) $\lim_{n \to \infty} \frac{n}{n_x}$
(c) $\lim_{n \to 0} \frac{n_x}{n}$ (d) None of these

3 **Which of the following approach of probability assumes 'degree of belief'?**

(a) Classical approach
(b) Relative frequency approach
(c) Subjective approach
(d) All of the above

4 **According to classical approach, if an experiment has 'n' simple outcome, each outcome will have probability equal to**

(a) n (b) $\frac{1}{n}$
(c) $\frac{1}{n^2}$ (d) None of these

5 **Which of the following is not a theoretical distribution of probability ?**

(a) Binomial distribution (b) Poisson distribution
(c) Bayes' theorem (d) Normal distribution

6 **Under binomial distribution, a random experiment performed repeatedly .... and .... number of times.**

(a) infinite, fixed (b) finite, fixed
(c) infinite, variable (d) finite, variable

7 **In binomial distribution, probability of 'not success' is equal to**

(a) p
(b) q
(c) $1 - p$
(d) Both (b) and (c)

8 **A prior probability is an .... probability value.**

(a) eventual (b) initial
(c) final (d) None of these

9 **A posterior probability is a .... probability value.**

(a) eventual
(b) initial
(c) revised
(d) None of the above

10 **Variance of binomial distribution is equal to**

(a) $n.p$ (b) $p.q$
(c) $n.p.q$ (d) None of these

11 **Which of the following statements are true for a standard normal curve?**

1. Standard normal curve is symmetrical.
2. Standard normal curve is non-symmetrical.

Codes

(a) Only 1 (b) Only 2
(c) Both 1 and 2 (d) None of the above

12 **The curve of normal distribution is .... the horizontal axis.**

(a) unimodal (b) bimodal
(c) multimodal (d) None of these

13 **The two tails of the normal distribution .... the horizontal axis.**

(a) touches (b) never touches
(c) sometimes touches (d) None of these

14 **Most business and economic variables are of continuous nature and their behaviour is best described by a .... continuous curve.**

(a) oval shaped (b) cylindrical shaped
(c) bell shaped (d) None of these

15 **Each normal distribution is defined by its two parameters *viz*.**

(a) mean and median
(b) standard deviation and mode
(c) mean and standard deviation
(d) None of the above

16 **The .... of the normal distribution occurs on the X-axis at a point, where the curve can reach the maximum height.**

(a) mean (b) median
(c) mode (d) standard deviation

17 **Arrange the following statements in chronological order.**

1. Normal distribution was discovered by English mathematician De Moivre.
2. Rediscovered and applied in Science, both natural and social and in parochial affairs by Laplace.
3. Normal distribution was extensively development and utilised by Carl Friedrich Gauss.

Codes

(a) 1, 2, 3 (b) 2, 3, 1
(c) 2, 1, 3 (d) 3, 1, 2

18 **The total area of a normal distribution between the average value ±1.96 of standard deviation is**

(a) 95.45% (b) 95% (c) 99% (d) 68.34%

19 Below figure shows which of the following?

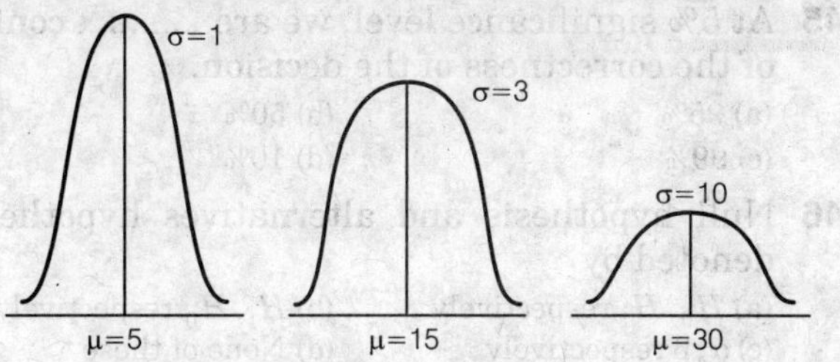

(a) Normal curves with identical means, but different standard deviation
(b) Normal curves identical standard deviation, but each with different means
(c) Normal curves with different standard deviation and different means
(d) None of the above

20 What proportion of area of a normal curve is included between (i) σ (ii) 2σ (iii) 3σ distances from the mean?
(a) 34.13%, 47.72%, 49.87%
(b) 60%, 70%, 90%
(c) 62.27%, 95.45%, 99.73%
(d) None of the above

21 The moment coefficient of skewness 'p_1' is equal to
(a) $\frac{p-q}{npq}$ (b) $\frac{q-p}{npq}$
(c) $\frac{(q-p)^2}{npq}$ (d) $\frac{(p-q)^2}{npq}$

22 The coefficient of Kurtosis under bionomial distribution 'β_2' is equal to
(a) $3+\frac{1-6pq}{npq}$ (b) $6+\frac{1-3pq}{npq}$
(c) $6+\frac{1-6p}{pq}$ (d) None of these

23 γ_2 coefficient is equal to
(a) $\beta_1 - 3$ (b) $\beta_2 - 6$
(c) $\beta_2 - 3$ (d) None of these

24 According to Bayes' theorem, conditional probability is equal to
(a) $\frac{P(E_i).P(A/E_i)}{\sum_{i=1}^{n} P(E_i)\,P(A/E_i)}$ (b) $\frac{P(A/E_i)}{\sum_{i=1}^{n} P(E_1).P(A/E_i)}$
(c) $\frac{P(E_i/A).P(E_i)}{\sum_{i=1}^{n} P(E_i)}$ (d) $\frac{P(E_i/A)}{\sum_{i=1}^{n} (E_i)}$

25 Mean and variance of poisson distribution is equal to
(a) $(m^2),(\Sigma r^2 p(r) - m^2)$ (b) $(m),(\Sigma r^2 P(r) - m^2)$
(c) $(m^2),\ (P(r) - m^2)$ (d) $(m),(P(r) - m^2)$

26 Which of the following not true for binomial distribution?
(a) The experiment is performed repeatedly
(b) Outcome of random experiment results in the dichotomous classification of events
(c) All trial are dependent
(d) None of the above

27 Which of the following are true for poisson distribution?
(a) The number of trials is indefinitely large
(b) Probability of success is indefinitely small
(c) Mean of poisson distribution is finite
(d) All of the above

28 Under poisson distribution, value of e^{-m} are derived from
(a) 'm' unknown values (b) 'm' given values
(c) 'm' calculated values (d) None of these

29 Poisson distribution is ....probability distribution.
(a) individual (b) discrete
(c) continuous (d) None of these

30 The shape of standard normal variate depends upon
1. mean 2. standard deviation
3. quartile deviation 4. mean deviation

Select the correct answer using the codes given below

Codes
(a) Both 1 and 2 (b) Both 2 and 3
(c) 1, 2 and 4 (d) 2, 3 and 4

31 Binomial distribution will be negatively skewed when
(a) $P > \frac{1}{2}$ (b) $P < \frac{1}{2}$ (c) $P = 0$ (d) $P = -\frac{1}{2}$

32 In a binomial distribution, if $n = 7$ and $P = 0.6$, then $P(x = 7)$ will be equal to
(a) $(0.6)^6$ (b) $(0.7)^6$
(c) $(0.6)^7$ (d) $(0.4)^7$

33 In which of the following distributions successive trials are taken without replacement?
(a) Normal distribution (b) Binomial distribution
(c) Poisson distribution (d) Both (a) and (c)

34 Variance of random variable X of γ (gamma) distribution can be calculated as
(a) $\text{var}(x) = n - 2/\mu\ \text{sup}^3$ (b) $\text{var}(x) = x\,n/\mu p^2$
(c) $\text{var}(x) = 2n/\mu p^2$ (d) $\text{var}(x) = n + 2/\mu p^2$

35 Which of the following distribution tends to standard normal distribution as the degree of freedom increases?
(a) Binomial distribution (b) Poisson distribution
(c) Normal distribution (d) T-statistics

36 In binomial distribution, if number of trials (n) is infinitely large, the probability of success (p) of occurrence of an event is close to .... and probability of failure (q) of occurrence of an event close to ....

(a) 0, 1 (b) 1, 1
(c) 1, 0 (d) None of these

37 Which of the following is/are types of research?

(a) Objective research
(b) Applied research
(c) Problem oriented research
(d) Both (b) and (c)

38 Which of the following is/are research methodology?

(a) Naturalistic observation
(b) Case study
(c) Survey
(d) All of the above

39 .... refers to devising a representation in a small and simplified form of a system, which can be manipulated to gauge effect.

(a) Simulation (b) Evaluation
(c) Comparative (d) None of these

40 Which kind of research is conducted to understand and resolve one's own problems?

(a) Qualitative research
(b) Problem solving research
(c) Both (a) and (b)
(d) None of the above

41 Which of the following are 'non-statistical' research?

1. Problem solving research
2. Qualitative research
3. Applied research

Select the correct answer using the codes given below

Codes

(a) Only 1 (b) Only 2
(c) Both 1 and 2 (d) Both 2 and 3

42 Research methodology refers to the ..... which are used to conduct an investigation.

(a) methods
(b) types
(c) designs
(d) All of the above

43 Comparative research design is used to compare .... and .... situation.

(a) prospective, applied (b) present, future
(c) past, present (d) known, unknown

44 Ethnological research design focuses on

(a) how individual interpret their own behaviour
(b) how researchers interpret behaviour of people
(c) how researcher and subject reacts to each others situation
(d) All of the above

Hypothesis Testing and Report

45 At 5% significance level, we are .... confident of the correctness of the decision.

(a) 95% (b) 50%
(c) 99% (d) 10%

46 Null hypothesis and alternatives hypothesis is denoted by

(a) H_0, H_1 respectively (b) H_1, H_0 respectively
(c) α, β respectively (d) None of these

47 Which of the following is more frequently used in statistical analysis of hypothesis?

1. Null hypothesis
2. Alternate hypothesis
3. Mixed hypothesis

(a) Both 3 and 2 (b) Both 2 and 3
(c) Both 1 and 3 (d) All of the above

48 The .... is a set of values for testing statistic, for which the null hypothesis is rejected in a hypothesis test.

(a) critical region (b) rejection region
(c) Either (a) or (b) (d) None of these

49 Not rejecting null hypothesis, when it is infact false is

(a) type I error
(b) type II error
(c) two tailed error
(d) None of the above

50 Which of the following is /are included under the characteristic of useful hypothesis?

(a) Clarity (b) Empiricism
(c) Specificity (d) All of these

51 Probability of rejecting the null hypothesis when it is true, is called

(a) type II error (b) type I error
(c) standard error (d) None of these

52 Which one among the following is a small sample?

(a) 5 (b) 35
(c) 29 (d) Both (a) and (c)

53 Goodness of fit of a distribution is tested by

(a) T-test (b) Chi-square test
(c) F-test (d) None of these

54 Z-list is used to know whether two population means are

(a) equal (b) different
(c) not defined (d) None of these

55 Z-test is closely related to which of the following test?

(a) T-test (b) Chi-square test
(c) F-test (d) None of these

56 Z-test is better used when sample size is

(a) less than 30 (b) equal to 30
(c) more than 30 (d) infinitely large

57 According to Kruskal-Wallis H-test, variable should be measured with

(a) discontinuous level (b) continuous level
(c) Both (a) and (b) (d) Neither (a) nor (b)

58 Which of the following is correct?

1. Large sample, $n > 30$
2. Small sample, $n < 20$
3. Probability of type I error (α) is also called significance level of least.
4. Accepting the null hypothesis, when it is false is called type II error.

Select the correct answer using the codes given below

Codes

(a) 1, 2 and 3 (b) 2, 3 and 4
(c) 1, 3 and 4 (d) All of the above

59 In ...., a hypothesis should explain all sufficient facts needed to understand the problem.

(a) empirical reference (b) logical reference
(c) Both (a) and (b) (d) Neither (a) nor (b)

60 If sample results fail to support the null hypothesis, we must conclude that something else is true, which is termed as

(a) type I error (b) type II error
(c) alternative hypothesis (d) None of these

61 Null hypothesis is always .... while alternate hypothesis gives a/an .... value.

(a) specific, approximate (b) specific, different
(c) approximate, specific (d) None of these

62 When the population mean is either lower or higher than some hypothesised value .... is considered to be appropriate.

(a) one tailed test (b) two tailed test
(c) Both (a) and (b) (d) None of these

63 Null hypothesis and alternate hypothesis is denoted by .... respectively.

(a) H_0, H1 (b) 0H, 1H
(c) H1, H_0 (d) None of these

64 Accepting the null hypothesis, when it is incorrect. This is known as

(a) error of data (b) error of statistics
(c) error of tools (d) None of these

65 The level of significance is the probability of committing

(a) type I error (b) type II error
(c) type III error (d) None of these

66 If the calculated value is equal or .... than the table value, the null hypothesis to be accepted but, if the calculated value is .... than the table value, the hypothesis is rejected.

(a) less, greater
(b) greater, less
(c) less, equal
(d) None of the above

67 Arrange the following steps in sequence for calculation of test of significance for large sample.

1. State the null hypothesis.
2. Compute the statistic.
3. Determine the level of significance.
4. Compute the critical value by testing the value of 'Z'.
5. Compare the value of test statistic 2 with the critical value to arrive at a decision.

Codes

(a) 1, 2, 3, 4, 5 (b) 2, 3, 4, 5, 1
(c) 1, 3, 2, 4, 5 (d) 5, 4, 3, 2, 1

68 The critical region of a test of hypothesis is equal to the

(a) probability of a correct decision
(b) probability of not making a correct decision
(c) probability of committing type I error
(d) probability of committing type II error

69 If a construction company claims that 40% of all residences being built are 2 bedroom homes, the null hypothesis is

(a) $H_0 / P = 0.4$ (b) $H_0 = P = 0.6$
(c) $H_0 = P = 60\%$ (d) None of these

70 If 'F' is quite large the null hypothesis of equal population means will have to be

(a) rejected (b) accepted
(c) Neither (a) nor (b) (d) Both (a) and (b)

71 To test the significant differences of two sets of related variables, we apply

(a) F-test (b) T-test
(c) Both (a) and (b) (d) None of these

72 In the application of chi-square,

1. no theoretical frequency should be small since in the derivation of chi-square continuity assumptions are made.
2. the constraint imposed on cell frequencies must be linear.
3. regroup the frequencies whenever some expected frequency was small.
4. the correction is needed, when some cell frequency was small, *i.e.* less than 5.

Which of the statements given above are correct?

(a) 1, 2 and 3 (b) 2, 3 and 4
(c) 1, 3 and 4 (d) None of these

73 If a number of chi-square values have been obtained from a number of samples similar data, then because of the additive nature of chi-square we can combine the various values of chi-square by just simply .... them.

(a) adding (b) subtracting
(c) multiplying (d) None of these

74 Yates has suggested a correction in chi-square value, when cell frequencies are

(a) large (b) small
(c) uniform (d) None of these

75 Chi-square is to be applied only, when the individual observations of sample are

(a) dependent
(b) independent
(c) Both (a) and (b)
(d) Neither (a) nor (b)

76 In small samples, we use relatively .... confidence intervals as the results of small samples usually vary widely from sample to sample.

(a) wide (b) small
(c) constant (d) None of these

77 Consider the following tests.

1. Z-test 2. T-test
3. F-test 4. Chi-square test

The concept of degree of freedom is associated with

(a) Both 1 and 2
(b) Both 2 and 3
(c) Both 3 and 4
(d) 2, 3 and 4

78 Which of the following test is used to test the significance of the coefficient of association?

(a) Z-test (b) T-test
(c) Chi-square test (d) F-test

79 Which of the following test are used for dealing with the problem of small samples?

(a) T-test
(b) Z-test
(c) Both (a) and (b)
(d) Neither (a) nor (b)

80 Shape of T-distribution loses its flatness when

(a) as the sample size gets larger
(b) as the sample size gets smaller
(c) with the passage of time
(d) None of the above

81 Which of the following statement(s) is/are correct?

(a) When n is small, the T-distribution is far from normal
(b) When n is infinite, it is identical with normal distribution
(c) Both (a) and (b)
(d) Neither (a) nor (b)

82 Find the value of x^2 (chi-square) for the following information.

Class	A	B	C	D	E
Observed Frequency	8	29	44	15	4
Expected Frequency	7	24	38	24	7

(a) 6.06 approx
(b) 6.76 approx
(c) 7.02 approx
(d) 5.05 approx

83 Arrange the following statements in sequence for applicability of Chi-square test.

1. Observations are recorded and samples are collected on a random basis.
2. Check whether all the members in the sample must be independent.
3. Check that no group contain items less than 10 otherwise regrouping needs to be done.
4. Check that are constraints are linear.

Codes

(a) 1, 2, 3, 4
(b) 4, 3, 2, 1
(c) 3, 2, 1, 4
(d) 4, 1, 3, 2

84 If expected frequency in a cell is less than 5, we combine adjacent cells, so that make it 5 or more than

(a) 5 (b) 10 (c) – 5 (d) 100

85 For 3X2 contingency table, the degree of freedom for testing the hypothesis is

(a) 6 (b) 2 (c) 3 (d) 4

86 Which of the following conditions need to be fulfilled for applicability of T- test?

(a) The sample size is less than 30
(b) The population standard deviation must be unknown
(c) Both (a) and (b)
(d) Neither (a) nor (b)

87 In using the T-test, we assume which of the following?

(a) Population is normal or approximately normal
(b) Observations are independent and samples are randomly drawn
(c) There is no measurement error
(d) All of the above

88 Mann-Whitney U-test uses which of the following function?

(a) $U = \min(u_y, u_y)$ (b) $U = \max(u_x, u_x)$
(c) $U = \max(u_x, u_y)$ (d) $U = \min(u_x, u_y)$

89 If the number of observations is such that $n_x\ n_y$ is large ($n > 20$), a normal approximation can be used with

(a) $\mu_\mu = n_x / n_y$ (b) $\mu_u = n_y / n_x$
(c) $\mu_\mu = \dfrac{n_x\ n_y}{2}$ (d) $\mu_u = \dfrac{n_x . n_y}{4}$

90 Which of the following statement is true about Kruskal-Wallis test?

(a) The alternative hypothesis of the Kruskal-Wallis test is the same as the mean
(b) The alternative hypothesis of the Kruskal-Wallis test is the same as variable
(c) The null hypothesis of the Kruskal-Wallis list is not that the means are the same
(d) The null hypothesis of the same as alternative hypothesis

91 The null hypothesis of Kruskal-Wallis test is that the mean ranks of the groups are the same. The expected mean rank depends upon

(a) $\frac{n}{2}$ (b) $\frac{n}{4}$
(c) $\frac{n+1}{4}$ (d) $\frac{n+1}{2}$

92 The most common use of Kruskal-Wallis test is
1. one nominal variable.
2. one measurement variable.

Select the correct answer using the codes given below

Codes
(a) Only 1 (b) Only 2
(c) Both 1 and 2 (d) None of these

93 Which of the following statement(s) is/are not true?
(a) Analysis of variance is helpful for test three or more variables.
(b) ANOVA leads to fewer errors
(c) ANOVA is based on emphrical evidences
(d) All statements are false

94 Normal approximation of Mann-Whitney 'U' stands at

(a) $\sigma_u = \sqrt{\frac{n_x n_y}{N(N-1)} \times \left[\frac{N^2 - N}{12} - \frac{\sum t_j^3 - t_j}{12}\right]}$

(b) $\sigma_u = \sqrt{\frac{n_x n_y}{N(N+1)} \times \left[\frac{N^2 - N}{12} - \frac{\sum t_j^3 - t_j}{12}\right]}$

(c) $\sigma_u = \sqrt{\frac{n_x n_y}{N(N-1)} \times \left[\frac{N^2 - N}{12} - \frac{\sum t_j^3 - t_j}{12}\right]}$

(d) None of the above

95 Which of the following are true for report writing under statistics?
1. A description explanation or development of the methodology tube used.
2. Analysis should be full scale analysis.
3. In the subsection containing the actual analysis it is important that you describe your analysis sufficiently clearly.

Codes
(a) Both 1 and 2 (b) Both 2 and 3
(c) Both 1 and 3 (d) All of these

96 Which of the following should be considered in report writing?
1. Structure 2. Content
3. Presentation 4. Use of english
5. Style 6. Detailed preparation

Select the correct answer using the codes given below

Codes
(a) 1, 2, 4 and 5 (b) 2, 3, 5 and 6
(c) 1, 3, 5 and 6 (d) All of these

Miscellaneous

Directions (Q. Nos. 97-111) *In the questions given below are two statements labelled as Assertion (A) and Reason (R). In the contex of the two statements, which one of the following is correct?*
(a) Both (A) and (R) are true
(b) (A) is true, but (R) is false
(c) (R) is true, but (A) is false
(d) Both (A) and (R) are false

97 **Assertion** (A) The parameters of the normal distribution are the mean and variance of the distribution.
Reason (R) The mean defines, where the peak of the curve occurs and the variance defines the spread of the curve.

98 **Assertion** (A) Normal distribution is a symmetric distribution.
Reason (R) The maximum ordinate divided the graph of normal curve into two equal parts.

99 **Assertion** (A) In a two tailed test there are two rejection region.
Reason (R) A two tailed test rejects the null hypothesis if the sample mean is either more or less than the hypothesised value of the mean of the population.

100 **Assertion** (A) The procedure, on which the basis of sample results enables to decide whether a hypothesis is to be accepted or rejected, is called hypothesis testing.
Reason (R) Hypothesis testing cannot prove the hypothesis to be correct.

101 **Assertion** (A) Sampling theory for large samples is not applicable in small sample.
Reason (R) When samples are small we cannot assume that the random sampling distribution is approximately normal or that the sample values are approximately equation to those of parent universe.

102 **Assertion** (A) The Critical Region (CR) is a set of values for testing statistic, for which the null hypothesis is rejected in a hypothesis test.
Reason (R) Critical Region corresponds to the range of values of the statistic, which according to the test requires the hypothesis to be rejected.

103 **Assertion** (A) Type I error are generally considered to be more serious than Type I error.
Reason (R) Type I error implies rejection of null hypothesis, when it is true.
This implies rejection of null hypothesis, which should have been accepted.

104 Assertion (A) ANOVA is an analysis tool used in statistics that splits the aggregate variability found inside a data set.

Reason (R) The systematic factor have a statistical influence an the given data set, but the random factors do not.

105 Assertion (A) Kruskal-Wallis H-test is an omnibus test statistics and cannot tell you specific group of independent variable is present.

Reason (R) As sample size increases Kruskal-Wallis test tends to Z-distribution.

106 Assertion (A) There is independence in the observation, *i.e.* no relationship between observation under each group of data under Z-test.

Reason (R) Kruskal-Wallis H-test is normally distributed with dependent variables.

107 Assertion (A) Under binomial distribution, probability of success remains constant.

Reason (R) Probability of failure also remains constant under binomial of distribution.

108 Assertion (A) Under poisson distribution, number of trials are infinitely small.

Reason (R) Success under each trial is also infinitely large under poisson distribution.

109 Assertion (A) Correlation research design is used to examine a relationship between two variables.

Reason (R) The interrelation is based on cause and effect relationship.

110 Assertion (A) Cultural research provides methodology that allows a consistent analysis of cultural texts.

Reason (R) Cultural research takes place in the undistributed natural setting of the subject's environment.

111 Assertion (A) Historical design aims at a systematic and objective evaluation and synthesis of evidence.

Reason (R) Historical design need not to be authenticated as the data obtained is truely original.

112 Assertion (A) Normal distribution curve is a bell shaped curve where mean, median and mode are equal to each other.

Reason (R) As the same size increases, all small-sample tests tends to merge with normal distribution.

Codes

(a) (A) is true, (R) is false
(b) (A) is false, (R) is true
(c) Both are true
(d) Both are false

113 Assertion (A) Parametric test are applied initially.

Reason (R) Non-parametric test are much less cumbersome to use and easy to compute.

Codes

(a) Both (A) and (R) are correct
(b) Both (A) and (R) are true, but (R) is the correct explanation of (A)
(c) (A) is true, but (R) is false
(d) (A) is false, but (R) is true

114 Match the following.

List I	List II
A. Contingency table	1. A statistical test in which the null hypothesis is true and the test statistics has F-distribution
B. Non-parametric statistics	2. Do not depend on the shape of the distribution of the population
C. Parametric statistics	3. Number and nature of parameters are fixed in advance
D. F-test	4. Used to record and analyse the relationship between two variables or more variables, basically categorical variables

Codes

	A	B	C	D		A	B	C	D
(a)	1	2	3	4	(b)	4	2	3	1
(c)	2	3	4	1	(d)	3	1	2	4

115 Match the following.

List I (Terms)	List II (Explanations)
A. Unimodal	1. The distribution that can take a limited number of values which can be listed
B. Discrete probability distribution	2. The curve has a single peak
C. Continuous probability distribution	3. Where variable is allowed to take any value within given range

Codes

	A	B	C		A	B	C
(a)	2	1	3	(b)	1	2	3
(c)	3	2	1	(d)	2	3	1

116 Match the following.

List I	List II
A. β_1	1. $\beta_2 - 3$
B. β_2	2. μ_3^2 / μ_2^3
C. γ_1	3. μ_4 / μ_2^2
D. γ_2	4. $\sqrt{\beta_1}$

Codes

	A	B	C	D		A	B	C	D
(a)	2	3	4	1	(b)	3	2	1	4
(c)	1	2	3	4	(d)	2	3	4	1

117 Match the following.

List I	List II
A. Research type	1. Problem solving
B. Research design	2. Feminist
C. Research method	3. Survey

Codes

	A	B	C
(a)	1	2	3
(b)	3	2	1
(c)	1	3	2
(d)	2	1	3

PREVIOUS YEARS' QUESTIONS

December 2018

1 Choose the correct code for the following statements being correct or incorrect.

Statement I If the value of β_2 *i.e.* $\frac{\mu_4}{\sigma_4}$, of a distribution gives the value more than 3, its curve is platykurtic.

Statement II In a moderately asymmetrical distribution, the standard deviation is 1.25 times of mean deviation.

Codes

(a) Both the statements are correct
(b) Both the statements are incorrect
(c) Statement I is correct, but Statement II is incorrect
(d) Statement II is correct, but Statement I is incorrect

2 Which one of the following is not the correct property of normal distribution?

(a) Continuous distribution
(b) Equality of central values (mean, mode and median)
(c) Standard deviation is the sole parameter of the distribution
(d) The model distribution

July 2018

3 For a standard normal probability distribution, the mean (μ) and the standard deviation (σ) are

(a) $\mu=0, \sigma=1$ (b) $\mu=16, \sigma=4$
(c) $\mu=25, \sigma=5$ (d) $\mu=100, \sigma=10$

4 Match the items of List II with the items of List I and select the code of correct matching.

List I	List II
A. Standard error of mean	1. Ha : $\mu_1 \neq \mu_2$
B. Base of point estimate of the mean of the population	2. Values based on all the observations of the population
C. Non-specific hypothesis	3. Mean of the sampling distribution of mean
D. Parameter value of descriptive statistics	4. Standard deviation of the sampling distribution of mean

Codes

	A	B	C	D
(a)	4	3	1	2
(b)	1	2	3	4
(c)	4	3	2	1
(d)	3	4	1	2

5 Match the items of List II with the items of List I and select the code of correct matching.

List I	List II
A. Chi-square test	1. Testing the significance of the differences of the mean values among more than two sample groups
B. ANOVA (F-test)	2. Testing the goodness of fit of a distribution
C. Z-test	3. Testing the significance of the difference of the mean values between two large sized samples
D. T-test	4. Testing the significance of the difference of the mean values between two small sized samples when population standard deviation is not available

Codes

	A	B	C	D
(a)	1	2	3	4
(b)	4	3	2	1
(c)	1	2	4	3
(d)	2	1	3	4

November 2017

6 Which one of the following is not the characteristics of normal distribution?

(a) Bell-shaped and symmetric
(b) Mean, median and mode of the distribution are equal
(c) The total area under the curve for the normal probability distribution is one
(d) The two tails of the distribution in both the directions touches the horizontal axis

7 In which one of the following situations is the application of T-test is most appropriate?

(a) Testing the significance of coefficient of correlation between paired observations of small sized sample
(b) Testing the significance of coefficient of correlation between paired observations of large sized sample
(c) Comparing variances of two small sized samples
(d) Testing the significance of the difference among mean values of more than two samples groups

8 **Statement** I If the alternative hypothesis is as Ha: $\mu \neq \mu_0$; a researcher requires two-tailed test in hypothesis-testing.

Statement II The mean of the sampling distribution of mean is not equal to the parametric value of mean.

Codes

(a) Both the statements are true
(b) Both the statements are false
(c) Statement I is true, while Statement II is false
(d) Statement I is false, while Statement II is true

9 The application of x^2-test as parametric test will be in which one of the following situations ?

(a) Test of independence of attributes
(b) Test of goodness of fit of a specific type of distribution
(c) Test for population variance on the basis of small sized sample variance
(d) Test of homogeneity of several populations with respect to some characteristic of interest

January 2017

10 Match the following items of List I and List II with regard to hypothesis-testing.

List I	List II
A. The ability of test to reject the null hypothesis when it is false	1. Level of significance
B. The probability of accepting a false null hypothesis	2. Type I error
C. The probability of rejecting a true null hypothesis due to sampling error	3. Type II error
D. The probability of rejecting a true null hypothesis	4. Power of a test

Codes

	A	B	C	D		A	B	C	D
(a)	4	2	1	3	(b)	4	3	1	2
(c)	1	2	3	4	(d)	2	3	1	4

11 Which one of the following statement is false regarding normal distribution?

(a) Mean, median and mode always coincide
(b) Within $\pm$ 1.96 σ limits from mean value, the area under the distribution is 99 percent of the total area
(c) The area under the normal curve represents probabilities for the normal random variable and the total area for the normal probability distribution is one
(d) For every pair of values of mean and standard deviation, the curve of the distribution is bell-shaped and symmetric

12 A researcher wants to test the significance of the difference between the average performance of the two small sized samples when the information of the population standard deviation is not available, which one of the following hypothesis-testing is suitably used?

(a) Z-test (b) Chi-square test
(c) F-test (d) T-test

July 2016

13 Read the following statement and indicate the correct codes from the alternative given below.

Statement I When the null hypothesis is true but as per the hypothesis-testing, it is rejected, it is known as beta type error in hypothesis testing.

Statement II Chi-square test is exclusively a non-parametric test.

Codes

(a) Both the statements are true
(b) Both the statements are false
(c) Statement I is true, while Statement II is false
(d) Statement I is false, while Statement II is true

14 Read the following statements and choose the correct code.

Statement I Non-parametric tests are based on some assumptions about the parent population from which the sample has been drawn.

Statement II The standard deviation of the sampling distribution of mean is called standard error of mean.

Codes

(a) Both the statements are correct
(b) Both the statements are incorrect
(c) Statement I is correct, while Statement II is incorrect
(d) Statement I is incorrect while Statement II is correct

15 Which one of the following is not the characteristic of normal distribution?

(a) Mean, median and mode for the normal distribution are equal
(b) The two tails of the normal curve extend to infinity in both directions but never touch the horizontal axis
(c) For different values of standard deviation, the height of the mean ordinate remains the same
(d) The number of independent constraints of normal distribution are N, –X and σ

16 Match the items of List I with the items of List II and indicate the code of correct matching.

List I	List II
A. Contingency coefficient for any size of contingency table	1. $\sqrt{\frac{N-n}{N-1}}$
B. Statistical approach to decide size of a sample	2. $\frac{\sigma_p}{\sqrt{n}}$
C. Finite population multiplier	3. $\sqrt{\frac{x^2}{x^2+n}}$
D. Standard error of mean	4. $\frac{z^2 \cdot \sigma_p^2}{e^2}$

Codes

	A	B	C	D
(a)	1	2	3	4
(b)	3	4	1	2
(c)	1	3	2	4
(d)	3	2	4	1

December 2015

17 Identify which of the following steps would be included in hypothesis testing.

1. State the null and alternative hypothesis.
2. Set the significance level before the research study.
3. Eliminate all outliers.
4. Obtain the probability value using a computer programme such as SPSS.
5. Compare the probability value to the significance level and make the statistical decision.

Select the correct answer using the codes given below

Codes

(a) 1, 3 and 4 (b) 3, 4 and 5
(c) 1, 2, 4 and 5 (d) 2, 3, 4 and 5

18 Statement I When a null hypothesis gets rejected in statistical hypothesis testing, it is known as II type error in hypothesis testing.

Statement II When a sample is small sized and parametric value of the standard deviation is not known, Z-test is the most appropriate test for hypothesis testing.

Codes

(a) Both statements are true
(b) Both statements are false
(c) Statement I is true, while Statement II is false
(d) Statement I is false, while Statement II is true

19 The power of the statistical hypothesis testing is denoted by

(a) α (alpha)
(b) β (beta)
(c) $1-\alpha$
(d) $1-\beta$

20 Match the following.

	List I (Terms)		List II (Explanations)
A.	$\frac{z^2\cdot\sigma_p^2}{e^2}$	1.	Measurement for Kurtosis
B.	$\frac{\lvert\bar{X}_1-\bar{X}_2\rvert}{\sqrt{\sigma_p^2\left(\frac{1}{n_1}+\frac{1}{n_2}\right)}}$	2.	Calculated value of F ratio
C.	$\frac{\mu_4}{\mu_2^2}$	3.	Statistical approach to find out the size of sample
D.	$\frac{\sigma_{s_1}^2}{\sigma_{s_2}^2}$	4.	Calculated z value of mean differences

Codes

	A	B	C	D
(a)	1	2	3	4
(b)	2	4	3	1
(c)	3	4	2	1
(d)	3	4	1	2

June 2015

21 Which of the following relating to normal distribution are not correct?

1. Coefficient of skewness is three.
2. It is mesokurtic.
3. Mean deviation for it is $\frac{2}{3}\sigma$.
4. $\mu\pm3\sigma$ covers 95.45% area.
5. Mean, median and mode are equal.
6. The standard normal variate z has mean one and SD zero.

Select the correct answer using the codes given below

Codes

(a) 1, 3 and 6 (b) 3, 4 and 5
(c) 1, 3 and 5 (d) 1, 3 and 4

22 Under which of the following situations, chi-square test is applicable?

1. Testing homogenity
2. Testing goodness of fit
3. Testing equality of two sample means
4. Testing equality of two sample proportions
5. Testing independence of attributes

Select the correct answer using the codes given below

Codes

(a) 1, 2 and 3 (b) 1, 2 and 5
(c) 3, 4 and 5 (d) 1, 3 and 5

23 Which one of the following is not the correct statement regarding sampling distribution of mean?

(a) Sampling distribution of mean is normally distributed for large sized samples
(b) Sampling distribution of mean is normally distributed for small sized samples drawn from not normally distributed population
(c) 'T' distribution is not nomally distributed
(d) Mean of the sampling distribution of mean is equal to the parametric value of mean

24 Consider the following statement and identify the wrong statements.

Statement I Accepting null hypothesis, when it is false, is called a level of significance.

Statement II 1-α is called power of a test.

Statement III Critical value of Z - static for two-tailed test at 5% level of significance is 1.96.

Codes

(a) Statements I, II and III (b) Statements I and III
(c) Statements II and III (d) Statements I and II

December 2014

25 In univariate data analysis, T-test is used when the data are in the form of

(a) metric data with one sample
(b) non-metric data
(c) non-metric data with independent variable
(d) metric data with independent two samples

26 In the hypothesis testing procedure, a researcher may commit type II error in which of the following conditions?
(a) When the true null hypothesis is rejected
(b) When the alternative hypothesis is accepted
(c) When the false null hypothesis is accepted
(d) When the true null hypothesis is accepted

June 2014

27 Which one of the following options deals with the process of making estimates, predictions and decisions?
(a) Descriptive statistics (b) Inferential statistics
(c) Probability theory (d) None of these

28 A hypothesis test is being performed for a process in which a type I error will be very costly, but a type II error will be relatively inexpensive and unimportant. Which of the following would be the best choice for alpha (α) in this test?
(a) 0.10 (b) 0.05 (c) 0.01 (d) 0.50

December 2013

29 Match the following.

	List I		List II
A.	Fisher	1.	Inverse probability
B.	Karl Pearson	2.	Normal distribution
C.	Thomas Baye's	3.	Correlation coefficient
D.	Kari Gaus	4.	Index number

Codes

	A	B	C	D		A	B	C	D
(a)	4	3	2	1	(b)	4	3	1	2
(c)	4	2	3	1	(d)	4	2	1	3

30 If a chi-square test is to be performed on a contingency table with 3 rows and 4 columns, how many degrees of freedom should be used?
(a) 6 (b) 12 (c) 8 (d) 9

31 If the sum of squares of deviations within sample is 140 with 12 degree of freedom and the sum of squares of deviations between sample is 190 with 2 degree of freedom the test statistic will be
(a) 81.4 (b) 12.28 (c) 8.14 (d) 1.22

32 Among the following choose the most suitable 'test' that can be applied to examine the influence of one factor on different groups.
(a) 'T' test (b) 'F' test
(c) 'Chi-square' test (d) None of these

33 A machine produced 20 defective articles in a batch of 400. After overhauling, it produced 10% defectives in a batch of 300. Which test of hypothesis can be applied to the above situation to examine whether the machine has improved?
(a) Test of significance of a sample proportion (two tail test)
(b) Test of significance of a sample proportion (one tail test)
(c) Test of significance of difference between two sample proportion (two tail test)
(d) Test of significance of difference between two sample proportion (one tail test)

June 2013

34 Consider the following statistical tests.
1. 'F' test 2. 'T' test
3. 'Z' test 4. 'Chi-square' test
Which of these are parametric tests?
(a) 1, 2 and 4 (b) 1, 3 and 4
(c) 1, 2 and 3 (d) 2, 3 and 4

35 Match the following.

	List I		List II
A.	Level of significance	1.	Sample mean is equal to population mean
B.	Standard deviation of sampling distribution	2.	Parameters
C.	Numerical value that describes the characteristics of the population	3.	Type I error
D.	Normally distributed population	4.	Standard error

Codes

	A	B	C	D		A	B	C	D
(a)	4	3	1	2	(b)	3	4	2	1
(c)	3	2	4	1	(d)	4	2	3	1

36 If there are 8 possible classes under consideration for a goodness of fit, the number of degrees of freedom will be
(a) 8 (b) 7 (c) 6
(d) Cannot be determined from the given information

37 Identify from the following, the test statistic for which the value of numerator should always be greater than that of denominator?
(a) 'Chi-square' (b) 'F' value
(c) 'Z' value (d) 'T' value

38 Which of the following tests can be applied to ordinal scale data?
1. Chi-square test 2. 'Z' test
3. Kruskal-Wallis test
4. Wilcoxon Mann-Whitney test
Codes
(a) 1, 2 and 3 (b) 2, 4 and 3
(c) 1, 3 and 4 (d) 1, 2 and 4

39 Which of the following test(s) can be based on the normal distribution?
(a) Difference between independent means
(b) Difference between dependent means
(c) Difference between proportions
(d) All of the above

40 From the following, identify one situation where 'F' test cannot be used.
(a) To compare more than two population means
(b) To test the hypothesis about a single population variance
(c) To test the hypothesis about two population variance
(d) To study about randomised block design

41 Which statistical test should be applied to test the effectiveness of 'special coaching' on the marks scored by the students?
(a) Paired 't' test (b) 'Chi-square' test
(c) 'Z' test (d) 'F' test

December 2012

42 The term (1-B) is called
(a) level of the test (b) power of the test
(c) size of the test (d) None of these

43 The area under normal distribution covered within $\mu \pm 3\sigma$ limit is
(a) 0.6827 (b) 0.9545
(c) 0.9973 (d) 1.0000

44 Sampling distribution of mean is very close to the standard normal distribution when
(a) population is normally distributed
(b) population is not normally distributed, but sample size is large
(c) Both (a) and (b)
(d) Neither (a) nor (b)

June 2012

45 F-test is used to test the significance of the difference between/among
(a) two sample mean
(b) more than two samples mean
(c) variance of two samples
(d) Both (b) and (c)

46 For testing of hypothesis $H_0 : M_1 = M_2$ and $H_1 : M_1 < M_2$, the critical value of Z at 5% level of significance when size of sample is more than 30 is
(a) 1.96 (b) 2.32
(c) 1.645 (d) 2.5758

ANSWERS

Objective Questions

1. (a)	2 (a)	3 (c)	4 (b)	5 (c)	6 (b)	7 (d)	8 (b)	9 (c)	10 (c)
11 (a)	12 (a)	13 (b)	14 (c)	15 (c)	16 (a)	17 (a)	18 (b)	19 (c)	20 (c)
21 (c)	22 (a)	23 (c)	24 (a)	25 (b)	26 (c)	27 (d)	28 (b)	29 (b)	30 (a)
31 (b)	32 (c)	33 (b)	34 (c)	35 (d)	36 (c)	37 (d)	38 (d)	39 (a)	40 (b)
41 (b)	42 (a)	43 (c)	44 (a)	45 (a)	46 (a)	47 (a)	48 (c)	49 (b)	50 (d)
51 (b)	52 (d)	53 (b)	54 (a)	55 (a)	56 (c)	57 (b)	58 (c)	59 (a)	60 (c)
61 (a)	62 (a)	63 (a)	64 (b)	65 (a)	66 (u)	67 (a)	68 (c)	69 (a)	70 (a)
71 (b)	72 (b)	73 (a)	74 (b)	75 (b)	76 (a)	77 (d)	78 (b)	79 (c)	80 (a)
81 (c)	82 (b)	83 (a)	84 (a)	85 (a)	86 (b)	87 (d)	88 (c)	89 (c)	90 (c)
91 (d)	92 (c)	93 (c)	94 (c)	95 (d)	96 (d)	97 (a)	98 (a)	99 (b)	100 (a)
101 (a)	102 (a)	103 (a)	104 (a)	105 (b)	106 (d)	107 (a)	108 (c)	109 (a)	110 (b)
111 (b)	112 (a)	113 (a)	114 (b)	115 (a)	116 (d)	117 (c)			

Previous Years' Questions

1 (d)	2 (c)	3 (a)	4 (a)	5 (d)	6 (d)	7 (a)	8 (c)	9 (c)	10 (b)
11 (b)	12 (d)	13 (b)	14 (d)	15 (c)	16 (b)	17 (c)	18 (b)	19 (d)	20 (d)
21 (c)	22 (b)	23 (b)	24 (d)	25 (d)	26 (c)	27 (b)	28 (c)	29 (b)	30 (a)
31 (c)	32 (b)	33 (d)	34 (c)	35 (b)	36 (d)	37 (b)	38 (c)	39 (d)	40 (b)
41 (a)	42 (b)	43 (c)	44 (c)	45 (d)	46 (c)				

CHAPTER 20

Principles and Functions of Management

Management is the art of getting work done by others. It is an important part of an organisation and basically it depends on different principles of management. It also consists of various functions such as planning, organising, directing, controlling etc. It is essential for achieving organisational goal with effective and efficient utilisation of resources.

Management

'Management' can be scanned as 'manage-men-t' (*i.e.* manage-men-tactfully). Therefore, management means managing men tactfully to get things done. In other words, management involves the art of getting things done through people. In modern approach, the term management may be defined as creating an internal environment of an enterprise, where individuals working together in groups can perform efficiently and effectively towards the attainment of group goals. Management influences behaviour in the sense that it affects the way people view their work and how they actually perform the work. It is the force that integrates human and non-human resources into an effective operative unit.

According to **FW Taylor**, "Management is the art of knowing exactly, what you want your men to do and then seeing that they do it in the best and cheapest way."

According to **Henry Fayol**, "To manage is to forecast to plan, to organise, to command, to coordinate and to control.

According to **Ralph C Davis**, ''Management is the function of executive leadership anywhere.''

Characteristics of Management

Human Activity Management is an human activity, it is only performed by human beings. Machines are used in managerial functions, but they cannot replace human beings.

In this Chapter

- *Management*
- *Principles of Management*
- *Taylor's Scientific Management*
- *Functions of Management*
- *Span of Control*

Goal Oriented Process It is a goal oriented process. Predetermined goals are decided by managers of the organisation according to which different types of functions are performed.

Combination of Art and Science Management is such type of work which is a combination of art and science, because knowledge and creativity matters a lot in management process.

Performed at All Levels It can be performed at all levels of organisation whether it is top level, middle level or lower level.

Creative Function It is a creative function. It manages human and physical resources in such a way that maximum production can be done at minimal cost.

Levels of Management

Top Level Management This level of management is responsible for direction and success of business. It involves directing committee, managerial directions and general managers. Main functions performed by top level management includes decision-making, planning, budgeting, advisory functions, controlling and directing etc.

Middle Level Management Different departments are made to perform functions of middle level management. Managers of these departments get work done by their subordinates. Some main functions of this level management includes categorised work according to ability, way of functioning and directions to subordinates etc.

Lower Level Management It is the lowest level of management, which includes supervisors, section leads, foreman etc. Main functions of this level management includes assigning employees tasks, ensuring the quality and quantity of production, up channeling employee problems etc.

Styles of Managers

Each managers have an individual approach to manage employees. A skilled manager has the ability to adopt the changes that occurs in an environment.

Various styles of managers are explained as under

Classic Leadership Styles It is also known as laissez-faire style. In laissez-faire style, the manager can simply communicate a message to employees and be assured that the employees will fulfil the goals of the department or organisation. This style is preferred for those employees, who require less supervision, attention or direction.

Autocratic Leadership Style An autocratic leadership style exerts complete control over the employees under the manager. This style may work in crisis situations, but for highly skilled and independent employees, this style is not effective.

Democratic Leadership Style It is the combination of the laissez-faire and the autocratic leader. This style works well for motivating employees while maintaining order in the work place.

Principles of Management

The principles of management are statements of fundamental truth, which can be used by managers as per guidelines for decision-making and action under different situations. Management principles are the basic elements of management theory.

A principle may be either descriptive (which merely describes the relationship between the variables) or prescriptive (which are stated to indicate what a manager should do). They are used to conduct in work places under certain situations. They help managers to take and implement decisions.

According to **George R Terry**, "A principle is a fundamental statement or truth providing guide to thought and action."

According to **Koontz** and **O' Donnell**, "Management principles are fundamental truth of general validity, which have value in predicting the result of management action."

Fayol's Principles of Management

Henry Fayol, the French industrialist and mining engineer, had the opportunity to search for sound management principles. Based on his experience, Fayol wrote a book entitled 'General and Industrial Administration'. He is known as the 'Father of General Management'.

On the basis of his long practical experience in the field of management, Henry Fayol listed and explained fourteen principles of management, *which are as under*

Division of Work

This principle is equally applicable to managerial work and technical work. This principle implies that the whole work should be divided into sub-works and each individual should be allotted sub-work according to his ability and aptitude, which bring about specialisation in every activity which increases the efficiency of individuals.

Fayol recommended that work of all kinds must be sub-divided and allotted to a number of persons. The reason being, when a particular individual performs the same job (work) repeatedly, he will attain proficiency in that job. It also helps to avoid waste of time and effort caused by changes from one work to another. But, when carried too far, it leads to loss of skill and craftsmanship of the employee and makes the job monotonous and less interesting.

Authority and Responsibility

Authority means the right to give orders and obtain obedience. Responsibility on the other hand, means obligation to perform the job assigned on time. There are two types of authority official authority *i.e.* authority to command and personal authority, which is the authority of the individual manager. Fayol suggested that there must be a balance between authority and responsibility.

One who exercises authority must accept responsibility for his work. Giving authority to a person without corresponding responsibility can lead to arbitrary and irresponsible use of authority. Therefore, sufficient authority should be delegated to a subordinate to enable him to discharge his duties. If authority is less, the subordinate will not be able to perform his duties well. If he is given excessive authority, he may misuse it.

Discipline

In the context of management, it means obedience, complying with the rules and regulations of the organisation, respect of authority and proper conduct in relation to others. Discipline is necessary for the smooth running of the organisation. Fayol insists that discipline requires good superiors at all level, clear and fair agreements and judicious application of penalties.

Discipline is required not only on the part of workers, but also on the part of management. Discipline facilitates smooth and systematic functioning of the business and also improves efficiency. Violation of this principle, leads to disobedience of the rules and regulations of the enterprise and creates unhealthy relations between management and employees.

Unity of Command

According to this principle, a subordinate should receive orders and instructions from one boss only and he should be accountable to him only. When each subordinate will receive clear cut orders from one boss only, this will improve his performance and there will be no confusion in the mind of subordinates regarding whose instructions he should follow.

Voilation of this principle leads to undermined authority, disturbed discipline and order, conflict among superiors and division of loyalty of employee. This principle helps to achieve harmonious relations between the superiors and the subordinates. Awkward situations will be difficult to avoid, if two bosses with the same powers and authority are allowed to control the same subordinates. In such situations, it may be very difficult to carry out the orders of two persons, when they are contradictory.

Unity of Direction

This principle implies that there should be 'One Head and One Plan' for a group of activities having the same objective. In other words, all the activities of a work unit or group should be directed towards its common objective. This will lead to better coordination and help in the effective management of the enterprise. Unity of direction is necessary for sound organisation whereas unity of command is necessary to fix responsibility of the subordinates and to avoid conflicts in the enterprise.

Fayol perceived unity of direction as related to the functioning of the business undertaking as a whole, while unity of command is related to the functioning of personnel. This principle facilitates unity of action and facilitates coordination. Violation of this principle leads to unnecessary duplication of efforts and wastage of resources. Secondly, efficiency of the organisation will also be adversely affected because of lack of unity of action.

Subordination of Individual Interest to General Interest

Here, general interest means interest of the organisation as a whole *i.e.* group interest whereas individual interest means personal interest of employees. According to this principle, the interest of the organisation as a whole must be given priority over the interest of the individuals/employees, in case of conflict between them.

There should be reconciliation ot individual and group interest. But in case of conflict, individuals must surrender or sacrifice in the larger interest of the organisation. Both, the employees and the management should subordinate their interests to the general interest of the concern, so that the goals of the concern are achieved.

Remuneration of Employees

According to **Fayol**, remuneration payable to employees should be fair and reasonable, so as to give maximum amount of satisfaction to both employees and employers. To be fair to the employees, wages should be determined on the basis of work assigned, cost of living, financial position of the business and average wage rates for similar work in the industry. While basic wages may be fixed according to the work done, there should be provision for allowance based on changes in cost of living.

This principle ensures good relations between workers and management. Through this principle, employees get motivated and their devotion and commitment improve. Working of the company would be smooth with the help of this principle. Violation of this principle leads to increase in labour turnover.

Centralisation and Decentralisation

According to **Fayol**, "Everything, which goes to increase the subordinate's role is decentralisation, everything which decreases it is centralisation." In other words, confinement of authorities in few hands is centralisation and dispersion of authorities to more persons is decentralisation. Fayol suggests that an organisation should strive to achieve a proper balance between centralisation and decentralisation. In small organisations, where the range of activities is generally small, greater centralisation is possible. But in large organisations, the degree of centralisation should be less.

Fayol feels that the superiors should keep the authority of taking important decisions in their own hands, while the authority to take day-to-day decisions should be delegated to the subordinates. Complete centralisation results in delay in decision-making. Complete decentralisation will lead to misuse of the authority by lower level managers. Therefore, there should be a balance between centralisation and decentralisation.

Scalar Chain

Fayol defines scalar chain as the chain of superiors ranging from the top management to the lowest rank. It serves as a chain of command as well as chain of communication. According to this principle, there is a scalar chain of authority and communication, which moves in a straight line from the superior most authority down to the lowest subordinate.

It is regarded as chain of command because orders and instructions issued at higher levels flow through intermediate managers before reaching lower levels. Similarly, reports on results achieved to be sent from lower to higher level.

As a chain of communication, it insists that all communications written or oral, upward or downward, should follow the hierarchy. This principle facilitates smooth flow of communication in the organisation and there will be no communication gap in the organisation as well as leads to unity of command in the organisation.

We consider a situation, where there is one head 'A' who has two lines of authority under him. One line consists of B-C-D-E. Another line of authority is L-M-N-O. If E has to communicate with O, who is at the same level of authority, then he has to tranverse the route E-D-C-B-A-L-M-N-O, *as shown in figure below*

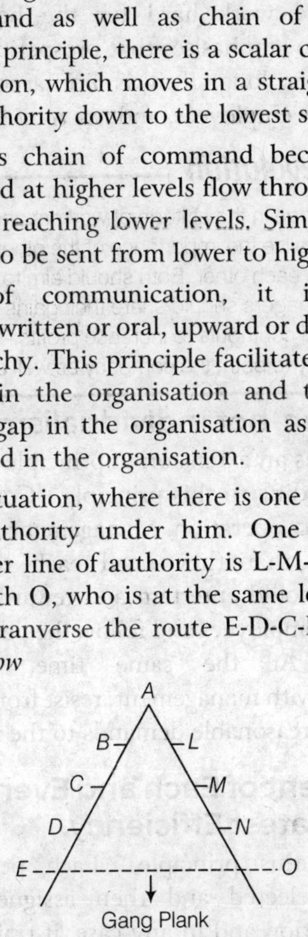

Scalar Chain and Gang Plank

If there is an emergency, then E can directly contact O through Gang Plank, which is a shorter route and has been provided, so that communication is not delayed. The idea of Gang Plank shows that Fayol's principles of management are not hard and fast rules. Rather, they are flexible guidelines, which can be modified to suit given situations.

Order

The principle of order applies to both material as well as men. Arrangement of things is known as material order and placement of men is called social or personnel order. Material order requires "a right place for everything and everything in the right place."

For personnel, it is "the right man in the right place." Fayol believed that this kind of order "demands precise knowledge of human requirements and resources of the concern and a constant balance between these requirements."

This balance is more difficult in bigger organisations. This principle will lead to increased productivity and efficiency. It also ensures effective utilisation of physical and human resources. Through this principle, there will be no wastage of time in search of men or material, which leads to smooth and systematic working of organisation. Violation of material order leads to wasteful movement of materials and tools. If social order is violated, it may be easy to contact the needed employee.

Equity

According to this principle, the manager should be fair and impartial, while dealing with their subordinates and there should be no room for favouritism, partisan etc. The principle of 'Equity' implies that similar treatment is assured to employees in similar positions. There should be no discrimination on the basis of sex, religion, caste, creed and colour. Equity does not exclude either forcefulness or sternness. This principle emphasises kindliness and justice in the behaviour of managers towards workers.

This principle will ensure loyalty and devotion of the employees and cordial relations between employers and employees. With the help of this principle, employees get satisfied and they are motivated as well as their morale increases. Violation of this principle will lead to unhealthy relations between managers and subordinates, which results in loss of their loyalty and devotion.

Stability of Tenure

According to this principle, employees should not be moved from their positions frequently. Management should remove the feeling of insecurity of job from the minds of personnel. The period of service in a position should be fixed. They should be given reasonable time to show results. If the job, of a person is not secure, he will be on look out for job, else where and will loose interest in his work. Too much transfers, shifting or promotions of employees will adversely affect the performance of employees. Fayol suggests that employee turnover should be minimised to maintain organisational efficiency. This principle provides a feeling of job security among the employees and their efficiency also increases, which results in their maximum contribution.

Initiative

Initiative implies freedom to propose and execute idea, plan or new techniques of work. According to **Fayol**, employees should be encouraged to develop and carry out their plans for improvements. In other words, it is the duty of the manager to encourage the feeling of initiative among the employees for doing some work or taking some decision, but within the limits of authority and discipline. This principle develops feeling of belongingness in employees or employees get satisfaction, when they are allowed to take initiative. Violation of this principle leads to frustration among the employees and employees will not work to the best of their ability, if they are not consulted while making plans.

Esprit De Corps

Esprit De Corps means 'Union is Strength'. Literally speaking, the phrase esprit de corps means the spirit of loyalty and devotion, which unites the members of the group. Strength of a business enterprise lies in the cooperation and harmony of its workers. 'Divide and Rule' should be replaced by 'Union is Strength'. Differences of opinions must be settled then and there.

Employees must work as a team for good result. Team spirit helps in developing an atmosphere of mutual trust and belongingness among team members. It also minimises the need to use penalties for defaulting persons. Violation of this principle will lead to loss of coordination and objectives would be difficult to realise.

Taylor's Scientific Management

Taylor is known as the 'Father of Scientific Management'. He made a significant contribution to the management of factory system of production. Scientific management means applying the standardised methods and tools to increase the output, its quality and to reduce costs and wastages.

According to **Taylor**, "Scientific management means knowing exactly what you want men to do and seeing that they do it in the best and the cheapest way." It emphasises replacement of 'rule of thumb' *i.e.* personal judgement, by scientific selected methods and tools.

Taylor's Principles of Scientific Management

The philosophy of scientific management is based upon the following principles

Science, not Rule of Thumb

According to **Taylor**, each job should be performed in an organisation as per the scientific approach, as there is always one best method to maximise efficiency. This method can be developed through study and analysis. Selecting 'one best method' for activities can result in saving time, effort, money and resources.

Harmony, not Discord

According to this principle, Taylor emphasised that there should be complete harmony between the management and workers and there should be transformation in thinking of both parties, called mental revolution. It implies that management should share the gains with workers and workers should work hard for the betterment of the business. It also emphasises that prosperity of the employer cannot exist for long, if it is not accompanied by the prosperity of its employees, and *vice-versa*.

> ***Mental Revolution***
>
> It involves change in the attitude of workers and management. Both should realise the importance of the other and should cooperate with each other. Both should aim to increase the size of surplus. Managers should share their gains with workers, while workers should contribute to increase profits. This attitude will bring prosperity to both, the company as well as the workers.

Cooperation, not Individualism

This principle is an extension of principle of 'harmony, not discord'. According to this principle, "Competition should be replaced by cooperation. Management and workers both should realise that they need each other". For this, management should entertain and reward the constructive suggestions of employees and follow the paternalistic style of management. At the same time, workers should also cooperate with management, resist from going on strikes and making unreasonable demands to the management.

Development of Each and Every Person to his/her Greatest Efficiency

According to this principle, "Each person should be scientifically selected and then assigned work as per their specialisation and in any case, if training is required, then impart training to them as efficient employees would produce more and earn more". Worker training is essential to learn the 'best method' developed as per the scientific approach. This would ensure greatest efficiency for both, workers and the organisation.

Functions of Management

Planning

It is the conscious determination of a future course of actions to achieve any desired result. It is the process of thinking before doing. Planning is an intellectual process of imagining and thinking of the possible alternative situations that may arise in future and to decide the line of action to achieve the desired results.

For proper planning, the following points should be decided in advance

- What is to be done in future?
- How it is to be done?
- Where it is to be done?
- When it is to be done?
- By whom it is to be done?

According to **Henry Fayol**, "Planning is deciding the best alternative to perform different managerial operations for achieving predetermined goals."

According to **Koontz** and **O'Donnell**, "Planning is an intellectual process of conscious determination of actions, decisions and considered estimates."

Objectives of Planning

"Planning keeps the organisation on the right path."

Following are the main objectives of planning

Economising Operations Planning of activities helps to reduce inefficiency and wastage, which leads to economy in operations. The main objective of planning is to realise the business activities in the cheapest and best possible manner. It avoids incorrect actions and reduces frequency of failures.

Providing Direction for Actions By stating in advance how work is to be done, planning provides direction for action. If goals are well defined, employees are aware of what the organisation has to do and what they must do to achieve those goals.

Reducing Overlapping and Wasteful Activities Since, planning ensures clarity in thought and action, work is carried on smoothly without interruptions. Useless and wasteful activities are minimised or eliminated. Through planning, it is easier to detect inefficiencies and take corrective measures to deals with them.

Promoting Innovative Ideas As planning is thinking in advance and therefore, there is scope of finding better ideas and better methods and procedures to reach the objectives/goals of the enterprise. This forces managers to think differently about the future of the organisations from the present. Thus, planning makes the managers more innovative and creative.

Establishing Standards for Controlling Planning provides the standards against which the actual performance can be measured and evaluated. It helps to identify the deviations and to take corrective action.'Controlling is blind without planning'. Thus, planning is the basis or pre-requisite for controlling.

Strategies of Planning

The term 'strategy' is a military term, which means countering the moves of the enemy forces. In other words, strategies are plans made in the light of the plans of the competitors because the modern business enterprise operates in a competitive environment.

According to **Glueck** and **Jauch**, "A strategy is a unified, comprehensive and integrated plan designed to ensure that the basic objectives of the enterprise are achieved." It ties all the parts of the enterprise together. Examples of strategies are choice of advertising media, sales promotion techniques, channel of distribution etc.

Strategy formulation covers three essential steps

- Determining long-term objectives.
- Adopting a particular course of action.
- Allocating resources necessary to achieve the objective.

The changes in the economic, political, social, legal and technological environment will affect an organisation's strategy.

Planning Process

Determination of Objectives of the Enterprise

This is the first step in the process of planning as planning starts with determination of objectives because all the policies, procedure and methods are framed for achieving objectives only. Objectives indicate the end points of what is to be done, where the emphasis is to be placed and what is to be accomplished. Hence, objectives are at the root of the planning process.

Developing the Planning Premises (Forecasting)

A business premise is an assumption on which the plans are based. Assumptions are made in the form of forecasts about the demand for a particular product, government policy, interest rates, tax rates etc. Therefore, accurate forecast becomes essential for successful plans.

Identifying Alternative Courses of Action

There may be numerous courses of action to achieve an objective. The management should find alternative ways and examine their effectiveness in the light of planning premises. Without resorting to a search for alternatives, a planner is likely to be guided by his limited imagination. Managers are required to apply their creative and innovative skills to develop alternative courses of action.

Evaluation of Alternatives

The positive and negative aspects of each proposal need to be evaluated in the light of the objective to be achieved, its feasibility and consequences.

Each of the alternatives is to be examined in relation to the following two tests

- To what extent is it in conformity with the basic objectives of the enterprise?
- To what extent each of these alternatives satisfies the cost, speed, quality and rate of return on investment requirements?

Selecting the Best Possible Alternative

This is the stage of decision-making. The techniques of decision-making are applied to select the appropriate course of action or plan. The manager must apply permutations and combinations and select the best possible course of action. Sometimes, a combination of plans may be selected instead of one best plan.

Implementation of the Plan

Once the plans are developed, they are put into action. For this, the managers communicate the plans to all the employees very clearly and allocate them resources (money, machinery etc).

Follow-up Action

Planning provides the future course of action. Future is uncertain. There may be situations, where we are not getting the expected results. For such situations there may be provision of review of the plans.

Decision-making

It is an essential aspect of modern management. It is a primary function of management. A manager's major job is sound or rational decision-making. Decision-making is a key part of manager's activities. A decision may be defined as a course of action which is consciously chosen from among a set of alternatives to achieve a desired result. It represents a well balanced judgement and a commitment to action. It is rightly said that the first important function of management is to take decisions on problems and situations. It pervades all managerial actions.

Means and ends are linked together through decision-making. The word 'decision' is derived from the Latin word deciso, which means a cutting away or a cutting off or in a practical sense to come to a conclusion. Decisions are made to achieve goals through suitable follow-up actions.

According to **RC Davis**, "Management is a decision-making process." Decision-making will be followed by second function of management called planning. Decision-making has priority over planning function.

According to Peter F Drucker, "It is the top management, which is responsible for all strategic decisions such as the objectives of the business, capital expenditure decisions and so on. Without such decisions, no action can take place and naturally the resources would remain idle and unproductive."

Characteristics of Decision-making

Decision-making Implies Choice It is the process of selection of one solution out of many available. Managers have to consider these alternatives and select the best one for actual execution. Here, planners/ decision-makers have to consider the business environment available and select the promising alternative plan to deal with the business problem effectively.

Continuous Activity/Process It is a continuous and dynamic process. It pervades all organisational activity. Managers have to take decisions on various policy and administrative matters. It is never ending activity in business management.

Mental/Intellectual Activity It is a mental as well as intellectual activity/process and requires knowledge, skills, experience and maturity on the part of decision maker. It is essentially a human activity.

Based on Reliable Information/Feedback Good decisions are always based on reliable information. The quality of decision-making at all levels of the organisation can be improved with the support of an effective and efficient Management Information System (MIS).

Goal Oriented Process It aims at providing a solution to a given problem/difficulty before a business enterprise. It is a goal oriented process and provides solutions to problems faced by a business unit.

Types of Decision-making

Decision-making is a fundamental element of the managerial process. In considering the types of decision-making, managers need to look at two aspects *i.e.* the five kinds of decisions that a manager might face or produce and the four processes or styles employed in making the decision, *which are as follows*

Irreversible The first kind of decision, a manager might face is an irreversible one. Such decisions cannot be undone or changed. Once NASA pushes the launch button, there is no turning back.

Reversible A reversible decision can be changed or totally revoked at any time, if it is deemed to be a mistake. *e.g.* Coca Cola discontinued 'New Coke' with a new formula and reintroduced classic coke to the market.

Experimental Experimental decisions cannot be finalised until the results of the preliminary data are in, *e.g.* NASA will not proceed with its plan to build a station on the Moon until early missions reveal, if scientists can find or make water there.

Trial and Error Through trial and error, the knowledge gained from mistakes is used to fine tune the proper course. Early choices might be blind or wild guesses, but eventually things become more clear.

Conditional A conditional decision remains effective as long as no external factors develop that make it unwise or no longer useful, at which point managers change the decision. *e.g.* Bank A may decide to close on Saturdays to save money, hoping Bank B will follow, if it doesn't, Bank A opens on Saturdays again.

Authoritative This style of decision-making comes from the top. In this, the decision comes from the top in a decisive way. *e.g.* When the CEO, the President or other leaders has all the facts and is the undisputed expert on the topic or situation, he can arrive at a decision effectively.

Facilitative The facilitative process is a joint collaboration of the leader and his subordinates. Often the department heads and employees may have first hand knowledge, experience and expertise that can enhance the decision-making process. The first phase involves a presentation of information, followed by a deliberative phase. Finally, a group arrives at a consensus jointly in the form of final decision.

Consultative It is similar to the first phase of the facilitative style, with the authoritative style coming in at the end. A leader may ask for advice from his subordinates or outside sources however, in the end, he is the sole decision maker.

Delegative Sometimes, a leader may use the delegative style of decision-making to pass off the responsibility for the decision to a subordinate or subordinates. This may be wise, if the subordinate or team of subordinates has the greater expertise, but managers normally reserve this for the lesser decisions involved with the everyday management of systems in a large organisation.

Importance of Decision-making

Primary Function of Management The functions of management start only when the top level management takes strategic decisions. Without decisions, actions will not be possible and the resources will not be put to use.

Facilitates the Entire Management Process of decision-making creates proper background for the first management activity called planning. Planning gives concrete shape to broad decisions about business objectives taken by the top level management.

Essential to Face New Problems and Challenges Decisions are required to be taken regularly as new problems, difficulties and challenges develop before a business enterprise. Such change leads to new problems and new decisions are needed.

Find Solution of Problems There are lots of problems faced by an organisation. Decision-making helps to find out solutions of those problems.

Risk Management Right decisions of management can manage risk of an organisation by minimising them. It is the process of identification, evaluation, analysis and acceptance of uncertainty in decisions.

Organising

Organising is one of the basic function of management. In the broadest sense, organising refers to the relationship between various factors present in a given enterprise. The purpose of organising is to relate organisational people to each other and to work for the achievement of organisational goals. Organising is the mechanism through which management directs, coordinates and controls business operation.

According to **Koontz** and **O'Donnell**, "Organising is the establishment of authority relationship with the provision for coordination both vertically and horizontally between positions in the enterprise structure."

According to **Henry Fayol**, "To organise a business is to provide it with everything useful to its functioning raw materials, machines and tools, capital and personnel."

Importance of Organising

Effective Administration It establishes coordination between different departments, which leads to unification of effort of harmony in work. It also governs the working of various departments.

Promotes Effective Communication It is an important means of creating communication among various departments. It specifies the channel and mode of communication among different members.

Creates Transparency Organising fixes the authority and responsibility among employees which brings clarity and transparency in the organisation.

Expansion and Growth When resources are optimally utilised and there exists a proper division of work among departments and employees, management can multiply its strength.

Resource Optimisation Organising ensure effective role-job-fit for every employee in the organisation. It helps in avoiding confusion and delays.

Organising Process

While organising, following steps must be followed

Identification of Activities

The manager should first identify the work that is essential to accomplish predetermined goals. The work must be divided into sub-parts that can be performed by single individuals. While exercising this step, the manager must ensure that no necessary activity is left out and no unnecessary activity is included.

Grouping of Activities

The activities so identified are to be grouped keeping in mind the available human and material resources and the best way of doing them. These activities may be grouped according to functions, geographical areas, types of products etc.

Assignment of Activities

After grouping the activities, these groups are assigned to various positions such as production manager, marketing manager, finance manager etc. This process is carried down to the operating level of management, thereby seeing that each individual knows exactly what work he is to do. The assignment of activities, thus creates responsibility and ensures certainty of work performance.

Delegation of Authority

An individual who has been assigned certain activities to perform requires some authority, rights and powers to carry out his assignment. It is important to remember that authority without responsibility is a dangerous thing and responsibility without authority is an empty vessel.

Establishment of Relationships

Organisational relationships between various members of the group are established on a permanent and continuing basis, so as to form a pattern to which people can be trained and developed, *i.e.* it means trying the various groups of activities together horizontally, vertically and through authority–responsibility relationships and providing for effective coordination of activities, authority and communication.

Staffing

It simply means 'putting people to jobs'. Staffing is concerned with filling various positions or jobs in the organisation with the suitable personnel. The staffing function focuses on maintaining and improving the competence and performance of the personnel in the organisation. In the existing enterprise, staffing is a continuous process because new jobs may be created and some of the existing employees may leave the organisation.

According to **Dalton E McFarland**, "Staffing is the function by which manager builds an organisation through the recruitment, selection and development of individuals as capable employees."

According to **Koontz** and **O'Donnell**, "The managerial function of staffing involves managing the organisational structure through the proper and effective selection, appraisal and development of personnel to fill the roles designed into the structure."

Importance of Staffing

An organisation can achieve its objectives only when it has the right persons in the right positions. The right people can help to take a business to the top, while the wrong people can break the business.

The following points highlight the importance of staffing to the organisation

Obtaining Competent Personnel It facilitates discovery of qualified and competent workers to take up various jobs in the business organisation.

Efficient Management of Personnel Management of personnel has become an integral part of every manager's job. Staffing leads to procurement of right type of people and also their training, remuneration and motivation.

Higher Performance Proper staffing ensures higher performance by putting right person on the right job.

Higher Productivity The staffing function must be performed efficiently by the managers to raise productivity.

Optimum Utilisation of Human Resources By avoiding overmanning, it prevents under utilisation of personnel and high labour costs. At the same time, it avoids disruption of work by indicating in advance the shortages of personnel.

Key to Other Functions No other function of management can be carried out without efficient staffing function because all the functions are performed by human beings and human beings join the organisation by staffing function only.

Staffing Process

Staffing consists of various interrelated activities, *i.e.* elements. *The elements or steps in the staffing process are as under*

Human Resource Planning

The primary concern of the staffing function is the timely fulfillment of the manpower requirements in an organisation. The process of manpower planning can be divided in two parts. One is an analysis for determining the quantitative needs of the organisation, *i.e.* how many people will be needed in the future. Another is an analysis for determining the qualitative needs, *i.e.* what qualities and characteristics are required for performing a job.

The qualitative aspect thus, involves job analysis. It is the study of job content to determine the human requirement. *It has two outcomes*

Job Description It is the study of job duties and responsibilities to determine human abilities required for execution.

Job Specification It is the study of the minimum acceptable qualities necessary to perform a job properly.

Recruitment

It is a positive process, which aims at attracting a number of candidates to apply for the given job.

The sources of recruitment of employees may be either internal or external. Internal sources of recruitment means the personnel already working in the organisation like transfer, promotion and reemployment of ex-employees. External sources denote recruitment from sources outside the organisation like direct recruitment, casual callers, advertising, placement agencies etc.

Interview is an essential part of external source of recruitment, *which can be of different types as follows*

Structured Interview It is useful for valid results, especially when dealing with large number of applicants.

Unstructured Interview It is useful when the interviewer tries to probe personal details of the candidate to analyse why they are not fit for the job.

Mixed Interview It is a realistic approach that yields comparable answers plus indepth in sight.

Behavioural Interview It is useful to understand aplicant's reasoning and analytical abilities under modest stress.

Selection

It is a negative process in which the candidates are required to take a series of employment tests and interviews. At each stage, many least promising candidates are eliminated and a few move on to the next stage, until the right type is found. It includes receiving of applications also. In other words, selection is the process of identifying and choosing the best person out of a number of prospective candidates, who have applied for a job.

Placements and Induction

When a new employee reports for a duty, he is to be placed on the job for which he is best suited. Placement is very important process as it can ensure 'right person doing the right job'. If a new employee is not able to adjust on his job, he may be given some training or transferred to some other job. Induction is concerned with the process of introducing or orienting a new employee to the organisation.

Training and Development

Every enterprise has some special jobs that need certain specialised skills. The staff appointed has to be trained and their existing abilities have to be developed further in order to accomplish the enterprise objectives.

Appraisal

It is concerned with rating the performance of each employee for the purpose of determining the need of training, transfer etc.

Promotion

It means advancement of employees to higher positions involving greater responsibilities, extra skills and carrying greater pay and prestige.

Compensation or Remuneration

It involves developing a system of fair and equitable remuneration of personnel commensurate with their contribution to the objectives of the organisation.

Directing

Directing as a function of management means instructing, guiding, supervising, motivating and leading the subordinates to contribute to the best of their capabilities for the achievement of group goals. Direction deals with the steps a manager takes to get subordinates to carry out plans.

This function of management is also called actuation because by performing this function, a manager is able to implement the plans by utilising the staff under the framework of organisation. Planning, organising and staffing are merely preparation for doing the work, but the work actually starts, when the manager performs the function of directing which literally means moving into action.

According to **Koontz** and **O' Donnell**, "Direction is the executive function of guiding and observing subordinates." According to **William Newman** and **E Kirby Warren**, "Direction deals with the steps a manager takes to get subordinates and others to carry out plans."

Features of Directing

Directing is Concerned with Human Element Directing function involves study and moulding of human behaviour. It improves interpersonal and intergroup relationship.

Directing Initiates Action A manager has to perform this function alongwith planning, organising, staffing and controlling while discharging his duties in the organisation.

Directing is Performance Oriented Performance is the essence of directing. This function of management directs the performance of individuals towards achievement of organisational goal.

Directing is a Continuous Process Directing takes place throughout the life of the organisation irrespective of people occupying managerial positions.

Directing Takes Place at Every Level of Management Every manager from top executive to supervisor performs the function of directing. Its takes place wherever superior-subordinate relations exist.

Elements of Directing

Supervision It is the process by which workers are guided and controlled to produce better results. Effective supervision ensures greater output of high quality. It teaches the subordinates the way their tasks are to be performed.

Motivation It is the function of a manager to motivate the people working under him to perform the work assigned. A successful manager has to make proper use of motivation to enthuse the people to work harmoniously for the attainment of desired objectives.

Leadership It is the process by which a manager guides and influences the work of others in choosing and attaining specified goals.

Communication A manager has to tell the workers what they are required to do, how to do and when to do it. He has to create an understanding in the minds of the subordinates of the work to be done. This is done by the process of communication.

➠ **Note** *Motivation and leadership are explained broadly in next chapter.*

Controlling

Managerial control is the function of constraining and regulating action in accordance with the plans for the achievement of specified objectives. Controlling is the process of checking, measuring and regulating the ongoing activities of the organisation to ensure that they are in conformity with the predetermined plans and produce the desired results.

In other words, controlling is the activity to see whether work is carried out according to schedule or plans laid down and taking corrective action, if necessary.

In this way, it is a comparison and verification process of the actual performance with the planned performance. It discovers deviations between the results achieved and the result expected, detects reasons responsible for the deviations and also employ corrective measures.

According to **Henry Fayol**, "Controlling consists of verifying whether everything occurs in conformity with the plans adopted, the instructions issued and the principles established . It has for its object to point out weaknesses and errors in order to rectify them and prevent recurrence."

According to **Philip Kotler**, "Control is the process of taking steps to bring actual results and desired results closer together."

Characteristics of Controlling

Controlling is a Fundamental Management Function Controlling is the most important of all the functions performed by management. Through this function, the management comes to know whether the activities are being performed according to plans or not.

Controlling is a Continuous Activity Control is a continuous or never ending activity throughout the life time of an organisation. The cycle of appraisal of work comparing with established standards, tracing deviations and ultimately taking corrective action goes on.

Controlling is Essential Function of Management Controlling is exercised at all levels of management from top to bottom though its nature and extent may differ according to the levels of management. *e.g.* Top management is responsible for administrative control, middle level management control is related to execution of policy and low level management control is related to execution of activities.

Controlling is a Pervasive Function Managers at all levels of management top, middle and lower need to perform controlling function to keep a control over activities in their areas.

Controlling is Forward Looking as well Backward Looking Effective control is said to be forward looking because past cannot be controlled. When deviations from the standards are pointed out, those serve as a guide to future improvements. Measures can be devised to control future on the basis of past.

Controlling seeks to improve future results on the basis of past weaknesses or short comings. Controlling will have to look backward to identify control points so as to remove and prevent the recurrence of mistakes.

Principles of Controlling

Effective controlling is necessary for success of an organisation. Controlling system must follow principles of controlling. *Some of them are as follows*

Principles of Assurance of Objectives This principle states that strong controlling system is a necessity of an organisation in which mistakes can be corrected and goals can be achieved easily.

Principle of Skill Controlling is related with identifying and solving the mistakes occurred in business activities.

Principle of Elasticity Controlling system should be flexible so that changes can be done according to situation.

Principle of Planning Controlling system should signify planning and its related activities of an organisation.

Future Oriented System Controlling system is not only relates with present, but it also relates with future and can be changed according to future situation.

Principle of Responsibility According to this principle, controlling is the responsibility of top level management of an organisation.

Controlling Process

Establishment of Performance Scale

It is the first stage of controlling process in which objectives, policies, planning and performance scales are determined according to which work of employees can be measured.

Measurement of Performance from Amputations

Measurement of actual performance is important step of controlling. Some standards of performance are decided by management, but it might be varied from actual performance. So, different types of techniques are adopted for measurement of performance such as direct observation and supervision, regular report, survey, statistical and mathematical techniques etc.

Identification of Variation and Analysis of its Causes

It is the third phase of controlling system in which actual performance is compared with standard performance. Variations between both are identified and reasons for the same are analysed.

Corrective Action

When reasons for variation in actual and standard performance are analysed in third stage, then in last stage corrective actions are taken to remove the variations in performance.

Span of Control

It is a span of supervision which shows the number of workers which can be effectively handled and controlled by a single manager. Simply, span of control refers to the number of subordinates under the manager's direct control. As an example, a manager with ten direct reports has a span of ten.

Importance of Span of Control

It is important for all business owners to think about the span of control in their organisation. *The reasons for the same are as follows*

Increased Managerial Effectiveness If the managers of an organisation has to oversee too many subordinates or make too many decisions, it creates problems. That's why span of control is important according to which limited subordinates comes under this span of control and it ultimately increased manager's effectiveness.

Increased Moral among Staff Business owners can avoid delays in decision-making of a manager by making sure managers direct a reasonable number of subordinates.

Improved Personal Contacts Managers can make better decisions, if they are familiar or well known about their subordinates. So, short span of control helps managers to be familiar with their subordinates, so that they can work more effectively for achieving organisational goal.

Better Supervision and Control If there is an appropriate span of control, then the superiors will have a limited number of subordinates under them. This will result in better supervision and control.

Good Communication and Coordination If there is an appropriate span of control, then managers will get time to communicate with every single subordinate. This will results in good coordination.

Types of Span of Control

Wider Span of Control It means a single manager oversees a large number of subordinates. This gives rise to a flat organisational structure.

Narrow Span of Control It means a single manager or supervisor oversees few subordinates. This gives rise to a tall organisational structure.

Factors Influencing Span of Control

Qualification and Qualities If the superiors and subordinates are well qualified, trained, experienced, then the span of control will be wide and *vice-versa*.

Level of Management If the superiors are working at the top level management, then they have more responsibilities. Therefore, their span of control will be narrow and *vice-versa*.

Nature of Work Nature of work decides span of control. If the work is difficult, then the span of control is narrow and *vice-versa*.

Degree of Centralisation/Decentralisation Under decentralisation, the superior has to take fewer decisions. Therefore, he can have a wide span of control. However, under centralisation, the superior has to take many decisions. Therefore, he should have a narrow span of control.

Use of Communication Technology If face-to-face communication is used, then the span of control will be narrow. If electronic devices are used for communicaiton, then the span of cosntrol will be wide.

EXAM BASED QUESTIONS

Management and its Principles

1 **"Management means forecasting, planning, organising, direction, coordinating and controlling". Who said this?**

(a) Peter F Drucker (b) Henry Fayol
(c) Parkins (d) FW Taylor

2 **"Management is an art of getting work done by others". The statement belongs to**

(a) Stainley Vense (b) Peter F Drucker
(c) Henry Fayol (d) Harold Koontz

3 **Management is pervasive in the sense that**

(a) it fulfills all purposes
(b) it uses all resources effectively
(c) it is relevant for all organisations
(d) All of the above

4 **......... can remove all the problems and can run the business on the right track.**

(a) Staffing (b) Management
(c) Administration (d) Coordination

5 **Which the following statement is incorrect?**

(a) Taylor disapproved the feeling of high handedness on the part of management
(b) Mental revolution in scientific management means total change in the attitude of workers only
(c) Mental revolution is the basis of scientific management propounded by Taylor
(d) None of the above

6 **Which of the following statement(s) is/are true?**

1. Management is a thinking function of top level management.
2. Management does not ensure utilisation of available resources to achieve some objectives.
3. Management means managing men tactfully to get things done.

Codes

(a) Both 1 and 2 (b) Only 3
(c) Both 1 and 3 (d) None of the above

7 **Which of the following statement(s) is/are true about Indian managers?**

(a) Many Indian top managements are relatively authoritarian in their relationship with lower managements and with labour
(b) Prevelance of low degree of control
(c) Management have faith in capacity of workers for taking initiative
(d) None of the above

8 **The fundamental components of management does not include**

(a) planning (b) organisation
(c) motivation (d) budgeting

9 **Management seeks to achieve which of the following results?**

1. Profits 2. Service 3. Style
4. Dynamism 5. Skills

Select the correct answer using the codes given below

Codes

(a) Both 1 and 3 (b) Only 1
(c) Both 1 and 2 (d) All of the above

10 **Which of the following statement(s) is/are correct?**

(a) Management cannot generate a favourable working environment
(b) An ideal management takes the right decisions on all matters at the right time
(c) Management activities need not to be result oriented
(d) None of the above

11 **Principle of management which implies that there should be 'One Head and One Plan' for a group of activities having the same objective is**

(a) unity of direction
(b) authority and responsibility
(c) unity of command
(d) None of the above

12 **Mohan, a manager, expects his colleagues to get work out of subordinates without giving them any powers. Here, principle of management over looked is**

(a) unity of command
(b) discipline
(c) order and equity
(d) authority and responsibility

13 **Which of the following statement is not true?**

(a) The principle of fair remuneration insists on adequate salary to employees
(b) The principle of management establish a relationship between cause and effect
(c) Management principles are developed overnight
(d) None of the above

14 **When the tools and/or raw materials are not found at the right place in the company, management principle violated is**

(a) scalar chain
(b) order
(c) authority and responsibility
(d) equity

15 **'Unity of objectives' principle states that there should be**

(a) only one objective
(b) predetermined objectives
(c) coordination among objectives
(d) None of the above

16 Consider the following statements.

1. Management principles are a set of rigid prescription on how to manage.
2. The principles of management establish a relationship between cause and effect.
3. Management principles are not used as a basis for management training, education and research.

Which of the statement(s) given above is/are correct?

Codes

(a) Both 1 and 2 (b) Only 3
(c) Only 1 (d) Only 2

17 Which of the following statement(s) is/are incorrect?

(a) The principle of 'Fair Remuneration' insists on adequate salary to employees
(b) Management principles are static or absolute in nature
(c) Management principles trained the managers to adopt the changes in technology in right direction
(d) All of the above

18 Which of the following statement is true?

(a) Order principle unifies the efforts of all the employees in common direction
(b) Management principles provide useful insights to managers
(c) Management principles provide readymade solution to all managerial problems
(d) All of the above

19 Consider the following statements.

1. Fayol believed that a single foreman is not competent to supervise all functional matters.
2. Gang boss helps in making arrangement of machines, materials etc for the jobs.
3. Taylor's principles are based on observation and experimentation.

Which of the statement(s) given above is/are correct?

Codes

(a) Only 1 (b) Only 3
(c) Both 2 and 3 (d) Both 1 and 3

20 Consider the following statements.

1. Taylor advocated unity of command so that each worker gets order from one boss only.
2. Taylor put his ideas through 'scientific management'.
3. Taylor's principles have universal application.

Which of the statement(s) given above is/are correct?

Codes

(a) Only 2 (b) Only 1
(c) Both 1 and 2 (d) None of the above

21 Which of the following is not a part of scientific management?

1. Harmony, not discord
2. Cooperation, not individualism
3. Subordination of individual interest to general interest
4. Science, not rule of thumb

Select the correct answer using the codes given below

Codes

(a) Only 3 (b) Both 1 and 2
(c) Only 4 (d) All of the above

22 Which of the following statement is correct?

1. Principles of scientific management are related to factory area.
2. General principles of management are applied universally.
3. Fayol's principles are scientific in nature.
4. Gang Plank is an excertion of 'scalar chain'.

Codes

(a) Both 1 and 2 (b) 1, 2 and 4
(c) 1, 3 and 4 (d) Both 3 and 4

23 Consider the following statements.

1. Management is a science because it uses certain principles.
2. Management is an art as it is based on practice and creativity.
3. Management can be accepted as a profession as it is a well defined body of knowledge of these statements.

Which of the statement(s) given above is/are correct?

Codes

(a) Both 1 and 2 (b) Only 2
(c) Only 3 (d) All of the above

24 A sales person is asked to finalise a deal with a customer. The marketing manager allows him to give a discount of upto 10% but the finance manager allows him to give discount of upto 25%. Which principle violated here management is?

(a) Unity of direction (b) Unity of command
(c) Initiative (d) None of these

25 The production manager of an automobile company asked a foreman to achieve a target production of 200 units (scooters) per day. But, he did not give him the authority to requisition tools and materials from the stores department. Principle relating to the situation is

(a) scalar chain (b) discipline
(c) equity
(d) authority and responsibility

26 Which of the following states the nature of management principles?

1. Universality
2. Evaluative
3. Dynamic
4. Alternative
5. Relative

Select the correct answer using the codes given below

Codes

(a) 1, 2 and 3 (b) Both 2 and 4
(c) Both 1 and 4 (d) Both 1 and 5

27 Which of the following statement is correct?

(a) Principles of management are broad and general guidelines for managerial decision-making and behaviour
(b) Techniques of management are something which are acceptable or desirable
(c) A person can perform managerial functions effectively without proper understanding of principles
(d) None of the above

Functions of Management

28 All managerial functions are settled by managers with the tool of

(a) planning (b) decision-making
(c) effective control (d) authority

29 Decisions which can be changed or totally revoked are called

(a) irreversible (b) trial and error
(c) experimental (d) reversible

30 The function of attracting, acquiring, retaining and developing human resources in an organisation is called

(a) recruitment
(b) induction
(c) training and development
(d) staffing

31 Techniques of managerial control are useful in

(a) selection of plant location
(b) identifying appropriate technology
(c) profit planning
(d) conducting shareholder's meeting

32 The number of subordinates who report directly to a manager is called that manager's

(a) work team
(b) informal organisation structure
(c) formal authority
(d) span of control

33 .... spans of management control create .... structures with many levels of management.

(a) Wide, tall (b) Wide, unpredictable
(c) Narrow, tall (d) Narrow, flat

34 To prepare plans regarding the work is performed by

(a) lower level management
(b) Board of Directors
(c) middle level management
(d) All of the above

35 Arrange the following functions of a manager in an organisation in correct sequence.

1. Motivation 2. Controlling
3. Organising 4. Planning

Codes

(a) 3, 4, 1, 2 (b) 3, 4, 2, 1
(c) 4, 3, 1, 2 (d) 4, 3, 2, 1

36 Consider the following statements.

1. Planning is the primary function of management.
2. Efficiencie means doing the right task, completing activities and achieving goals.
3. Management is not universally necessary in all organisation.

Which of the statement(s) given above is/are correct?

Codes

(a) Only 1 (b) Only 2
(c) Both 1 and 2 (d) None of the above

37 Which of the management functions are closely related?

(a) Planning and organisation
(b) Staffing and control
(c) Planning and control
(d) Planning and staffing

38 Which of the following is not an element of delegation?

(a) Accountability (b) Authority
(c) Responsibility (d) Informal organisation

39 Which of the following statement is correct?

(a) Directing converts plans into performance
(b) Planning is the process or pre-requesite for controlling
(c) Staffing is the basis of thinking before doing
(d) None of the above

40 Which of the following statement(s) are/is incorrect?

(a) Planning is a trap to capture the future
(b) Finding the right people for the right job is known as organising
(c) Teamwork divides the task and double the success
(d) None of the above

41 Consider the following statements.

1. Organising ensures resource optimisation.
2. Organising is an important means of communication.
3. Organising does not creates transparency.
4. Organising establish coordination between different departments of an organisation.

Which of the statement(s) given above is/are correct?

Codes

(a) 1, 2 and 4
(b) 3, 2 and 4
(c) Both 2 and 4
(d) None of the above

42 What is not an advantage of hierarchical structure?

(a) Clear chain of command (b) Quick response to change
(c) Discipline and stability (d) Small span of control

43 Which of the following statement is incorrect about span of control?

(a) It creates disputes between superior and subordinates
(b) It increased managerial effectiveness
(c) It enhance morale of the staff
(d) It accomplish a good communication

44 Which of the following factors does not affect span of control?
(a) Level of management
(b) Physical structure of organisation
(c) Nature of work
(d) Degree of centralisation

45 An electronic company is facing a problem of declining market share due to increased competition from other new and existing players in the market. Its competitiors are introducing lower price models for mass consumers who are price sensitive. For quality conscious consumers, company is introducing new model with added features and new technological advancements. The type of plan needed to be prepared under this situation is
(a) strategy
(b) policies
(c) objectives
(d) rules

46 Planning of the organisation with suitable personnel is known as
(a) organising function
(b) coordinating function
(c) directing function
(d) staffing function

47 A process of evaluating results against predetermined standards and correcting the deviation is known as
(a) directing (b) coordinating
(c) controlling (d) planning

48 Which of the following is not an element of planning?
(a) Programme (b) Procedure
(c) Policy (d) Information

49 Which of the following is not a technique of control?
(a) Budget (b) Disciplinary action
(c) Policy (d) Praise

50 An adequate control system does not need
(a) flexibility
(b) reporting deviations expeditiously
(c) reflected organisational pattern
(d) variability in directing

51 Which point is irrelevant while imposing strategic control system?
(a) Comprehensive coverage
(b) Balanced performance
(c) Delegation of authority
(d) Timeliness

52 Control denotes
(a) measurement of performance in accordance with objectives
(b) disciplinary action against employees
(c) curtailment in undesirable activities
(d) curtailment in expense

Miscellaneous

Directions (Q. Nos. 53-65) *In the questions given below are two statements labelled as Assertion (A) and Reason (R). In the context of the two statements, which one of the following is correct?*

Codes
(a) Both (A) and (R) are correct and (R) is the correct explanation of (A)
(b) Both (A) and (R) are incorrect, but (R) is not the correct explanation of (A)
(c) (A) is correct, but (R) is incorrect
(d) (A) is incorrect, but (R) is correct

53 **Assertion** (A) The span of management at the upper level is generally narrow while at lower level span is wide.
Reason (R) The tasks allocated to subordinates at the lower level of management are more specific and thus making supervision easy and simple.

54 **Assertion** (A) Management ensures maximum production at minimum cost.
Reason (R) Management eliminates wastes as far as practicable.

55 **Assertion** (A) Management is a dynamic function which is to be performed continuously.
Reason (R) Policies and procedures of management are quickly changed to cope with the changing business environment.

56 **Assertion** (A) Planning is required at all level of management as well as in all departments.
Reason (R) Planning is not a mental exercise.

57 **Assertion** (A) Authoritative style of decision-making comes from the top.
Reason (R) It is a joint collaboration of the leader and his subordinates.

58 **Assertion** (A) Decision-making is a fundamental element of the managerial process.
Reason (R) Irreversible decisions can be undone or changed.

59 **Assertion** (A) Management is not a decision-making function.
Reason (R) All managerial functions are settled by managers with the tool of decision-making.

60 **Assertion** (A) Controlling is based on the factors, which are prevailing in the organisation.
Reason (R) Controlling has nothing to do with external factors which are equally important.

61 **Assertion** (A) Proper staffing helps in obtaining competent personnel for various jobs.
Reason (R) Machineries and human resources are the principal assets of any organisation.

62 **Assertion** (A) Staffing avoids incorrect actions and reduces frequency of failures.

Reason (R) Staffing improves job satisfaction.

63 **Assertion** (A) Creation of jobs and departments is the third step in the process of organising.

Reason (R) Various jobs created are classified into specified categories.

64 **Assertion** (A) Induction is concerned with the process of introducing a new employee to the organisation.

Reason (R) Induction ensure 'right person doing the right job.'

65 **Assertion** (A) CPM provides the framework for treating a wide range of project management problems.

Reason (R) CPM is applied in those projects where activity timings are well known.

66 **Assertion** (A) Management principles increase managerial efficiency.

Reason (R) Management principles provide useful insights of managers.

Codes

(a) (R) is correct, but (A) is not correct
(b) (A) is correct, but (R) is not correct
(c) Both (A) and (R) are correct
(d) Both (A) and (R) are not correct

67 **Assertion** (A) Management principles are not developed overnight.

Reason (R) Principles are derived on the basis of observation and analysis of events which managers face in actual practice.

Codes

(a) (R) is correct, but (A) is not correct
(b) (A) is correct, but (R) is not correct
(c) Both (A) and (R) are correct
(d) Both (A) and (R) are not correct

68 Match the following.

List I (Concepts)	List II (Related Terms)
A. Authoritative, participative	1. Styles of managers
B. Classic, transformational	2. Objectives of management
C. Board of Directors, foremen	3. Types of decisions
D. Organisational, social	4. Levels of management

Codes

	A	B	C	D
(a)	4	3	2	1
(b)	3	4	1	2
(c)	3	1	4	2
(d)	2	1	4	3

69 Match the following.

List I (Styles of Manager)	List II (Features)
A. Classic style (Laissez-faire)	1. Require a strong vision or an inspirational leader
B. Autocratic leadership	2. Does not well in all situations
C. Transactional leadership	3. Exerts complete control over the employees
D. Transformational leadership	4. Preferred for those employees who require less supervision

Codes

	A	B	C	D
(a)	2	3	4	1
(b)	4	2	1	3
(c)	4	3	2	1
(d)	1	2	3	4

70 Match the following.

List I (Levels of Management)	List II (Functions)
A. Top level management	1. Collecting reports and forwarding them to top management
B. Middle level management	2. Represent worker's grievances before management
C. Lower level management	3. Assembling the required resources
D. Supervisory management	4. Maintain discipline among the workers

Codes

	A	B	C	D
(a)	4	3	2	1
(b)	3	2	1	4
(c)	2	1	4	3
(d)	3	1	2	4

71 Match the following.

List I (Types of Decisions)	List II (Features)
A. Experimental decisions	1. Pass off the responsibility for the decision to subordinate or subordinates
B. Trial and error decisions	2. First phase of the facilitative style, with the authoritative sytle coming in at the end
C. Delegative decisions	3. Cannot be finalised until the results of the preliminary data are in systematic manner
D. Consultative decisions	4. The knowledge gained from mistakes is used to fine tune the proper course

Codes

	A	B	C	D
(a)	4	3	1	2
(b)	4	3	2	1
(c)	3	1	4	2
(d)	3	4	1	2

72 Match the following.

List I (Nature of Principles)	List II (Description)
A. Contingent	1. Management principles enable a better understanding of the relationship between human and material resources
B. Universal applicability	2. Management principles are applicable to all types of organisation
C. Establish cause and effect relationship	3. Management principles are not static or absolute in nature
D. Behavioural	4. Tell the managers if a particular principle is applied in a particular situation, what may be its likely effect

Codes

	A	B	C	D		A	B	C	D
(a)	3	2	4	1	(b)	4	1	2	3
(c)	3	4	2	1	(d)	4	3	2	1

73 Match the following.

List I (Fayol's Principles)	List II (Examples)
A. Unity of command	1. The mission of a company is to provide quality goods at affordable prices of consumers. This should serve as a direction for all the departments
B. Remuneration of personnel	2. A worker is asked by the foreman to increase quantity but marketing management wants to improve quality
C. Unity of direction	3. A worker is asked to work extra time after his days work. He must be given adequate wages for the extra time
D. Division of work	4. Publication of a book involves several operations which should be performed by different persons

Codes

	A	B	C	D		A	B	C	D
(a)	4	3	2	1	(b)	3	4	1	2
(c)	2	3	1	4	(d)	2	3	4	1

74 Match the following.

List I (Scientific Management Principles)	List II (Features)
A. Science, not rule of thumb	1. Management should decide the method of work, working conditions etc instead of leaving these to the discretion of workers
B. Harmony, not discord	2. Enabled the management to innovate the best method of doing work, specify work standards and to provide the necessary incentives for motivation
C. Cooperation, not individualism	3. Management and workers must develop positive thinking for each other and work with harmony
D. Equal division of responsibility	4. This principle is an extension of principle of 'Harmony, not discord'

Codes

	A	B	C	D		A	B	C	D
(a)	2	3	4	1	(b)	4	3	2	1
(c)	3	4	1	2	(d)	3	2	4	1

75 Match the following.

List I (Scientific Management Principles)	List II (Features)
A. Science, not rule of thumb	1. Both workers and managers should realise that they need each other and there should be equal division of work and responsibility between workers and management
B. Harmony, not discord	2. Both the management and the workers should try to achieve maximum output in place of restricted output
C. Cooperation, not individualism	3. Highlights the need for mutual cooperation and humanious relationship between workers and management
D. Maximum, not restricted output	4. Also known as 'Trial and Error Method' is the established norm for guidance

Codes

	A	B	C	D		A	B	C	D
(a)	3	4	1	2	(b)	4	3	1	2
(c)	4	1	2	3	(d)	4	3	2	1

76 Match the following.

List I (Concepts)	List II (Meaning)
A. Centralisation	1. Right to give orders to the subordinates
B. Scalar chain	2. Concentration of authority at one place or at one level in the organisation
C. Esprit de corps	3. The chain of superiors ranging from the chief executive or ultimate authority to the lowest level in the organisation
D. Authority	4. The spirit of loyalty and devotion which unites the members of the group

Codes

	A	B	C	D		A	B	C	D
(a)	2	3	4	1	(b)	3	4	2	1
(c)	4	3	1	2	(d)	2	4	1	3

77 Match the following.

List I (Fayol's Principles)	List II (Features)
A. Remuneration of employees	1. Employees should be encouraged to develop and carry out their plans for improvements
B. Equity	2. Employees should not be moved from their positions frequently. The period of service in a position should be fixed
C. Stability of tenure of personnel	3. Managers should be fair and impartial while dealing with their subordinates and there should be no discrimination on the basis of sex, religion etc
D. Initiative	4. Wages, payable to employees should be fair, reasonable, just and equitable so as to give maximum satisfaction to both the employees and the organisation

Codes

	A	B	C	D
(a)	3	4	1	2
(b)	2	3	4	1
(c)	4	1	2	3
(d)	4	3	2	1

78 Match the following.

List I (Scientific Principles)	List II (Features)
A. Science, not rule of thumb	1. Management can earn higher profits, if workers perform their jobs efficiently and thus ensure better quality, lower costs and largest sales
B. Cooperation, not individualism	2. Maximum out will result in higher wages for the worker and greater profit for the management
C. Maximum, not restricted output	3. The management should assume responsibility for the work for which it is better suited
D. Equal division of responsibility between management and workers	4. To determine a fair's day's work for the workers

Codes

	A	B	C	D
(a)	4	3	2	1
(b)	3	1	2	4
(c)	2	3	4	1
(d)	4	1	2	3

79 Match the following.

List I (Fayol's Principles)	List II (Features)
A. Esprit de corps	1. Fayol said that there should be a place for everything and everyone
B. Stability of tenure	2. Unity among the personnel can be accomplished through proper communication and coordination
C. Order	3. It established the channels through which communication will pass
D. Scalar chain	4. If this principle is followed, the workers will feel secured and show higher productivity

Codes

	A	B	C	D
(a)	4	3	2	1
(b)	2	1	4	3
(c)	2	4	1	3
(d)	2	3	4	1

PREVIOUS YEARS' QUESTIONS

December 2018

1 Match the items of List I with the items of List II and choose the correct answer from the code given below.

List I (Types of Interview)	List II (Usual Application)
A. Structured	1. A realistic approach that yields comparable answers plus indepth insights
B. Unstructured	2. Useful to understand applicant's reasoning and analytical abilities under modest stress
C. Mixed	3. Useful for valid results, especially when dealing with large number of applicants
D. Behavioural	4. Useful when the interviewer tries to probe personal details of the candidate to analyse why they are not fit for the job

Codes

	A	B	C	D
(a)	3	1	2	4
(b)	4	2	1	3
(c)	1	4	2	3
(d)	3	4	1	2

November 2017

2 **Statement** I Management is not just a creature of the economy; it is a creator as well.

Statement II He who can manage, can manage anything.

Codes

(a) Statement I is correct, but Statement II is incorrect
(b) Statement II is correct, but Statement I is incorrect
(c) Both statements are incorrect
(d) Both statements are correct

3 **Statement** I Management control seeks to compel events to confirm to plans.

Statement II Controlling is determining, what is motivational to the employees of the organisation.

Codes

(a) Statement I is correct, but Statement II is incorrect
(b) Statement II is correct, but Statement I is incorrect
(c) Both statements are correct
(d) Both the statements are incorrect

4 **Assertion** (A) Sound planning is one of the essential elements for the success of corporate entities.

Reason (R) Planning is deciding in advance what is to be done. It involves the selection of objectives, policies, procedures and programmes from among alternatives.

Codes

(a) Both (A) and (R) are correct and (R) is the correct explanation of (A)
(b) Both (A) and (R) are correct, but (R) is not the correct explanation of (A)
(c) Both (A) and (R) are incorrect
(d) (A) is correct, but (R) is incorrect

December 2015

5 Who among the following is not related to the planning function given by Taylor?

(a) Route clerk (b) Time and cost clerk
(c) Inspector (d) Disciplinarian

June 2015

6 When the cost incurred on recruiting, training and developing the employees is considered for determining the value of employees, it is called

(a) the replacement cost approach
(b) the historical cost approach
(c) the opportunity cost approach
(d) None of the above

December 2014

7 **Assertion** (A) MBO is effective way of planning and organising the work.

Reason (R) Employees participate in setting the objectives.

Codes

(a) Both (A) and (R) are true
(b) Both (A) and (R) are false
(c) (A) is true, but (R) is false
(d) (A) is false, but (R) is true

December 2013

8 Strategies and policies

(a) are not closely related
(b) give direction
(c) are the framework for performance appraisal
(d) Both (a) and (b)

9 Arrange the following steps of management control.

1. Taking corrective action from standards
2. Establishing standards
3. Measuring actual performance
4. Comparing performance against standards

Codes

(a) 1, 2, 3, 4 (b) 2, 3, 4, 1
(c) 3, 4, 1, 2 (d) 2, 4, 1, 3

10 Consider the following statements.

1. Planning is today's action for tomorrow's decision.
2. Planning is forward looking while controlling is looking back.
3. Motivation is about getting voluntary willingness of subordinates for action.
4. Line and staff organisation is the oldest form of organisation.

Which of the statement(s) given above is/are correct?

Codes

(a) Both 2 and 3 (b) 1, 2 and 4
(c) 1, 3 and 4 (d) All of the above

June 2013

11 **Assertion** (A) When span of control is wide coordination and control becomes difficult.

Reason (R) In a narrow span, levels of authority reduces.

Codes

(a) Both (A) and (R) are true and (R) is the correct explanation of (A)
(b) Both (A) and (R) are true, but (R) is not the correct explanation of (A)
(c) (A) is true, but (R) is false
(d) (A) is false, but (R) is true

12 Which of the following is not a principle of management according to Henry Fayol?

(a) Subordination of individual interest over the organisational interest
(b) Esprit de crops
(c) Unity of managers
(d) Unity of direction

December 2012

13 **Assertion** (A) All decisions taken through mental process are rational.

Reason (R) Decision-making is a mental process.

Codes

(a) Both (A) and (R) are true and (R) is the correct explanation of (A)
(b) Both (A) and (R) are true, but (R) is not the correct explanation of (A)
(c) (A) is true, but (R) is false
(d) (A) is false, but (R) is true

14 Who is considered father of scientific management?

(a) Peter F Drucker (b) FW Taylor
(c) Victor Vroom (d) Henry Fayol

15 **Assertion** (A) Management is a continuous process.

Reason (R) Managers first plan, then organise and finally perform the function of controlling.

Codes

(a) Both (A) and (R) are true and (R) is the correct explanation of (A)
(b) Both (A) and (R) are true, but (R) is not the correct explanation of (A)
(c) (A) is true, but (R) is false
(d) (A) is false, but (R) is true

June 2012

16 Identify the true sequence of steps involved in planning.

1. Selecting the best course of action
2. Establishing the sequence of activities
3. Establishment of objectives
4. Evaluating alternative courses
5. Determining alternative courses

Select the correct answer using the codes given below

Codes

(a) 1, 2, 3, 4, 5 (b) 3, 5, 4, 2, 1
(c) 5, 4, 3, 2, 1 (d) 3, 5, 4, 1, 2

17 **Assertion** (A) One can be sure about future course of actions by making good plans.

Reasoning (R) Planning brings certainty in future course of actions of an organisation.

Codes

(a) (R) is true, but (A) is false
(b) (A) is true, but (R) is false
(c) Both (A) and (R) are true
(d) Both (A) and (R) are false

18 To manage a business well is to manage its future and to manage the future is to manage information is termed as

(a) management information system
(b) marketing information system
(c) future information system
(d) general information system

19 Who has given 'fourteen Principles of Management'?

(a) Barnard
(b) Henry Fayol
(c) FW Taylor
(d) Fleming

20 What is MBO?

(a) Management by Objective
(b) Multiple Business Organisation
(c) Management by Organisation
(d) Multiplicity of Business Operations

ANSWERS

Objective Questions

1 (b)	2 (d)	3 (c)	4 (b)	5 (b)	6 (b)	7 (a)	8 (d)	9 (b)	10 (b)
11 (a)	12 (d)	13 (c)	14 (b)	15 (a)	16 (d)	17 (b)	18 (b)	19 (c)	20 (a)
21 (a)	22 (b)	23 (d)	24 (b)	25 (d)	26 (a)	27 (a)	28 (b)	29 (d)	30 (d)
31 (b)	32 (d)	33 (a)	34 (a)	35 (d)	36 (a)	37 (c)	38 (d)	39 (c)	40 (b)
41 (a)	42 (b)	43 (a)	44 (b)	45 (a)	46 (d)	47 (c)	48 (d)	49 (d)	50 (a)
51 (d)	52 (d)	53 (d)	54 (a)	55 (a)	56 (c)	57 (c)	58 (c)	59 (d)	60 (a)
61 (c)	62 (d)	63 (c)	64 (c)	65 (d)	66 (c)	67 (b)	68 (c)	69 (c)	70 (d)
71 (d)	72 (a)	73 (c)	74 (a)	75 (b)	76 (a)	77 (d)	78 (d)	79. (c)	

Previous Years' Questions

1 (d)	2 (a)	3 (c)	4 (b)	5 (c)	6 (b)	7 (a)	8 (b)	9 (d)	10 (a)
11 (c)	12 (c)	13 (a)	14 (b)	15 (a)	16 (d)	17 (a)	18 (a)	19 (b)	20 (b)

CHAPTER 21

Organisational Structure and Its Culture

Organisations are of different types like formal and informal organisation. Responsibility and authority are two necessary components for proper functioning of an organisation, which includes delegation of authority and decentralisation. An organisational culture also affects development and change in an organisation.

Organisational Structure

Organisational structure is the framework of relationships of persons operating at various levels in an enterprise. It is a set of planned relationships between groups of related functions and between physical factors and personnel required for the achievement of organisational goals.

The main purpose of creating organisation structure is to explicitly allocate authority and responsibility among members of the organisation, so that each person knows who is responsible to whom and for what. Since, organisation structure represent authority-responsibility relationship, they are also referred to as 'forms of authority-responsibility relationships'.

According to **AW Wickesberg**, "Organisational structure is that set of relationships, which exists among individuals and groups."

According to **WH Newman**, "Organisational structure deals with the overall organisational arrangement in an enterprise."

According to **Hurley**, "Organisational structures are patterns of relationships among the various positions in a firm and among the various people occupying the positions."

In this Chapter

- *Organisational Structure*
- *Responsibility*
- *Authority*
- *Delegation of Authority*
- *Decentralisation*
- *Organisational Culture*

Types of Organisational Structure

Formal Organisational Structure

It refers to the structure of well defined jobs each bearing a definite measure of authority, responsibility and accountability. The structure in a formal organisation can be functional or divisional.

According to **JAC Brown**, "Formal organisation refers to the structure of well defined jobs, each bearing a definite measure of authority, responsibility and accountability."

According to **Chester Barnard**, "Formal organisation is a system of consciously coordinated activities of two or more persons towards a common objective."

Features of Formal Organisation

- Formal organisation is based on division of labour and specialisation.
- It is an action to achieve the objectives specified in the plans, as it lays down the rules and procedures essential for their achievement.
- The organisation does not take into consideration emotional aspect.
- It is deliberately designed by the top management to facilitate the smooth functioning of the organisation.
- It places more emphasis on work to be performed than interpersonal relationships among the employees.

Advantages of Formal Organisation

Easy Accomplishment of Goals It's in attainment of predetermined goals of the enterprise by providing framework for the operations to be performed.

Fixation of Responsibility It is easier to fix responsibility since mutual relationships are clearly defined.

Unity of Command is Possible It is possible to observe the principle of unity of command because of the presence of scalar chain of authority.

No Overlapping of Work There is a clear-cut division of work among the departments and individuals. Hence, there is no overlapping of work or any work being left out.

Stability in the Organisation It provides stability to the organisation. This is because, behaviour of employees can be fairly predicted since there are specific rules to guide them.

Disadvantages of Formal Organisation

Lack of Initiative In this type of organisation, rules, procedures etc are strictly followed. The employees have to abide by them. Thus, their initiative gets slackened.

Excessive Use of Authority Excessive and undue use of authority takes place in this type of organisation. Because of autocratic attitude of the officers, the employees are always under pressure, which adversely affect their efficiency.

Delay in Work Too much rigidity of rules and regulations cause unnecessary delay in work.

No Place for Human Feelings Formal organisation is impersonal, that is why human feelings have no place here.

Lack of Flexibility Rules and regulations in formal organisation are rigid in nature and cannot be changed easily.

Informal Organisational Structure

Interaction among people at work gives rise to a 'network of social relationships among employees', called informal organisation. Informal organisation emerges from within the formal organisation, when people interact beyond their officially defined roles.

According to **Keith Davis**, "Informal organisation is the network of personal and social relationships not established or required by formal organisation."

According to **Chester Barnard**, "That organisation is informal, where the mutual relations are established unconsciously for common objectives."

Features of Informal Organisation

- It originates from within the formal organisation as a result of personal interaction among employees.
- The standards of behaviour evolve from group norms rather than officially laid down rules and regulations.
- It does not have fixed lines of communication.
- It emerges spontaneously and is not deliberately created by the management.
- It has no definite structure or form because it is a complex network of social relationships among members.

Advantages of Informal Organisation

Faster Communication Prescribed lines of communication are not followed. Thus, the informal organisation leads to faster spread of information as well as quick feedback.

Fulfilment of Social Needs It helps to fulfil the social needs of the members. This enhances their job satisfaction since, it gives them a sense of belongingness in the organisation.

Fulfils Organisational Objectives Because of fellow feelings and brotherhood, it helps its members to solve their work problems through other members. Since, the problems are easily solved, it becomes easier to achieve the organisational objectives.

Correct Feedback Through informal structure, the top level management can know the real feedback of employees on various issues, policies and plans.

Disadvantages of Informal Organisation

Disruptive Force Informal organisation may become a disruptive force, when it spreads rumours. This may work against the interest of the formal organisation.

Resistance to Change The management may not be successful in implementing changes, if the informal organisation opposes them. Such resistance to change may delay or restrict growth.

Priority to Group Interests It pressurises members to confirm to group expectations. This can be harmful to the organisation, if the norms set by the groups are against organisational interests.

Danger to Formal Organisation In case informal organisation is over emphasised too much, formal organisation may be rendered ineffective.

Responsibility

It means the work or duties assigned to a person by virtue of his position in the organisation. It is the obligation of an individual, whether a manager or any other employee of the organisation, to carry out the task assigned to him.

According to **Koontz** and **O'Donnell**, "Responsibility is the obligation of a subordinate to carry out the duties assigned to him."

Features of Responsibility

- It always flows in upward direction, *i.e.* from juniors to seniors.
- It arises from duty assigned.
- It comes from superior-subordinate relationship.
- It cannot be delegated.
- It proves loyalty and dedication of an employee towards an organisation.

Kinds of Responsibility

When we talk of responsibility, there may be various kinds of responsibilities like responsibility may be legal, social or moral, *when we use the term in context of management, it implies the following kinds of responsibilities*

Specific Responsibility When a person is assigned a specific task or job, his responsibility is specific. As soon as the job is over, the responsibility is also over.

General Responsibility Ordinarily, responsibility is general unless some limit is specified.

Authority

Authority is defined as the legal and formal right of the manager or supervisor of the organisation to command subordinates, give them orders, instructions and directions.

According to **FG Moore**, "Authority means assigning work to others and giving them authority to do it."

According to **Louis A Allen** "Authority is the sum of powers and rights entrusted to make possible the performance of the work assigned."

Types of Authority

Line Authority It reflects existing superior-subordinate relationships. Line authority pertains to matters directly involving management system, production, sales, finance etc and as a result with the achievement of objectives.

Staff Authority It enables those who are responsible for improving the effectiveness of line personnel to perform their required tasks. It consists of the right to advise or assist those who possess line authority as well as other staff personnel.

Functional Authority This authority is usually assigned to individuals to complement the line or staff authority they already possess. It generally covers only specific task areas and is operational only for designated amounts of time.

Importance of Authority

- It creates a path of accountability for every project and activity within the organisation.
- It promotes employee development at all levels of an organisation.
- It establish efficient communication paths between employees, departments and divisions.

Comparison between Authority and Responsibility

Basis	Authority	Responsibility
Meaning	It refers to the power or right attached to a particular designation, to give orders, instructions and directions.	It denotes duty to accomplish a task assigned to any individual.
Requirement	Ability to give orders.	Ability to follow orders.
Flow	It flows in downward direction.	It flows in upward direction.
Objective	Its main objective is to make decisions and their proper implementation.	Its main objective is to execute duties assigned by superior.
Duration	It is a long time process.	It ends after the accomplishment of task.

Delegation of Authority

It means division of authority and power downwards to the subordinates. It can be defined as subdivision and sub-allocation of powers to the subordinates in order to achieve results.

It is a process through which a manager assigns responsibility to the subordinate to carry out the work on his behalf and also a certan authority is delegated to the subordinate to the extent, which is sufficient to accomplish the assigned responsibility.

Features of Delegation of Authority

- Delegation means giving power to the subordinate to act independently, but within the limits prescribed by the superior.
- Delegation does not mean that manager give up his authority, but certainly he shares some authority with the subordinate essential to complete the responsibility entrusted to him.
- Authority once delegated can be further expanded or withdrawn by the superior depending on the situation.
- The manager cannot delegate the authority which he himself does not possess. Also, he cannot delegate his full authority to a subordinate.
- The delegation of authority may be oral or written and may be specific or general.
- The delegation is an art and must comply with all the fundamental rules of an organisation.

Process of Delegation of Authority

Assignment of Duties First step of delegator is to define the task and duties to the subordinate. In this step, clarity of duty as well as result expectation has to be cleared.

Granting of Authority Subdivision of authority takes place when authority is divided among subordinates. The managers at all levels delegate authority and power which is attached to their job positions.

Creating Responsibility and Accountability It is the last phase of delegation of authority. Subordinates have to be obligatory towards the duties assigned to them. Accountability is the obligation of the individual to carry out his duties as per the standards of performance.

Therefore, it is said that authority is delegated, responsibility is created and accountability is imposed.

Elements of Delegation

Authority It can be defined as the power and right of a person to use and allocate the resource efficiently, to take decisions and give orders so as to achieve the organisational objectives.

Responsibility It is the duty of the person to complete the task assigned to him. Responsibility flows from bottom to top.

Accountability It means giving explanation for any variance in the actual performance from the expectations set. It cannot be delegated.

Advantages of Delegation of Authority

Gives Scope for Innovation To implement new ideas in the organisation, one needs to have certain powers and the right amount of freedom. If diserving individuals are given the right authorities, they may be able to bring innovation.

Builds Team Spirit Delegating authority to a group of individuals increases their bonding and mutual understanding. They get a chance to work together towards a common goal.

Motivate Employees Delegation of authority makes employees to feel important and more responsible.

Tests Employee Skills Authority added responsibilities. It requires one to work with greater focus and efficiency and to take initiatives.

Builds Trust and Understanding Delegation involves trusting in someone's abilities and relying on them. This helps to build a feeling of mutual understanding and trust.

Disadvantages of Delegation of Authority

Failure to Fulfil the Tasks The manager's instructions may not be well taken care of by the delegate. This may breed from unwillingners or incapacity of the delegate.

Business Risk An employcc may not perform the task in best manner. Therefore, delegating certain management tasks to employees does pose a risk to business.

Lack of Trust Many managers either lack trust or do not want to trust their subordinates. They try to do everything themselves, which creates obstacles in success of delegation of authority.

Misuse of Power In delegating authority, there is a risk of the delegate may misuse his power for personal gains.

Delay The delegate may take long to understand the new responsibility. A delay in planning or taking descisions may not be affordable for the organisation.

Decentralisation

When decision-making authority is dispersed throughout the organisation, so that decisions are made largely near the point of action, it is termed as decentralisation. It extends to the lowest level of the organisation. It can also be viewed as an extension of delegation.

According to **Louis A Allen**, "Decentralisation refers to tire systematic effort to delegate to the lowest levels of all authority expect that which can only be exercised at central points."

Advantages of Decentralisation

- The diversification of products, activities and markets is facilitated under decentralisation.
- When the authority is decentralised, executives in the organisation will get the opportunity to develop their talent by taking initiative.
- It stimulates the formation of small groups. Since, local managers are given a large degree of authority and local autonomy, they motivate their subordinates.
- It ensures better control and supervision as the subordinates at the lowest levels will have the authority to make independent decisions.
- It brings decision-making process closer to the scene of action. This leads to quicker decision- making at lower level.

Disadvantages of Decentralisation

- It creates problem of coordination as authority lies dispersed widely throughout the organisation.
- Under decentralisation, it is not possible to follow uniform policies and standardised procedures.
- It requires employment of trained personnel to accept authority and it involves more financial burden.
- It puts more pressure on divisional head and in meeting their new profit plans, bring conflicts among managers.

Comparison between Delegation of Authority and Decentralisation

Basis	Delegation of Authority	Decentralisation
Nature	It is a process of transferring authority and creation of responsibility between superior and subordinates.	It is delegation and dispersion or distribution of authority. It is not possible without delegation of authority.
Objective	Its main objective is to minimise the burden of managers.	It prepares the organisational participants of the organisation.
Relationship	It functions between superior and subordinates.	It functions between top level management and departments.
Responsibilities	Authority is only delegated.	In this, superior is relieved from responsibilities.
Withdrawal of Authority	It can be withdrawn by delegator at any time.	In decentralisation, withdrawal of authority is not possible.

Organisational Culture

The values and behaviours that contribute to the unique, social and psychological environment of an organisation are called as organisational culture.

It includes an organisation's expectation, experiences, philosophy and values that hold it together and is expressed in its self image, inner workings, interactions with the outside world and future expectations. It is based on shared attitudes, beliefs, customs, written and unwritten rules that have been developed overtime and are considered valid. It is also called corporate culture. *It is shown in*

- the ways the organisation conducts its business, treats its employees, customers and the wider community.
- the extent to which freedom is allowed in decision making, developing new ideas and personal expression.
- how power and information flow through its hierarchy.
- how committed employees are towards collective objectives.

Importance of Organisational Culture

Every organisation has its unique style of working, which often contributes to its culture. The beliefs, ideologies, principles and values of an organisation form its culture. The culture of the work place controls the way the employees behave amongst themselves as well as with people outside the organisation. *Following are the importance of organisational culture*

Employees Interact at the Workplace A healthy culture encourages the employees to stay motivated and loyal towards the management.

Promoting Healthy Competition at the Workplace Employees try their level best to perform better than their fellow workers and earn recognition and appreciation of the superiors. It is the culture of the work place, which actually motivates the employees to perform.

Represents Certain Predefined Policies Every individual is clear about his roles and responsibilities in the organisation and know how to accomplish the tasks ahead of the deadlines.

Brings all the Employees on a Common Platform The employees must be treated equally and no one should feel neglected or left out at the work place. It is essential for the employees to adjust well in the organisation culture for them to deliver their level best.

Unites the Employees from Different Backgrounds Families have varied attitudes and mentalities. The culture gives the employees a sense of unity at the work place.

Promotes Healthy Relationship Amongst the Employees No one treats work as a burden and moulds himself according to the culture.

Organisational Development

Organisational development is a field of study that addresses change and how it affects organisations and the individuals within the organisation. It assists organisations in coping with the turbulent environment, both internally and externally, frequently doing so by introducing planned change efforts.

According to **Middlenist** and **Hitt**, "Organisational development is a systematic means for planned change that involves the entire organisation and is intended to increase organisational effectiveness."

Objectives of Organisational Development

- It helps in improving the performance of the organisation.
- It improves the ability of the organisation to adapt to its environment.
- It improves inter-personal and inter-group behaviour to secure team work.

Characteristics of Organisational Development

- It is related to real problems of the organisation.
- These exists a close working relationship between change agents and the people who are being changed.
- It seeks to build problem solving capacity by improving group dynamics and problem confrontation.
- It is situational and contingency oriented.
- It is an educational strategy for bringing a planned change.
- It is a long-term approach and is meant to elevate the organisation to a higher level of functioning by improving the performance and satisfaction of organisation members.

Organisational Development Process

Organisation development is a planned approach to improve employee and organisational effectiveness. *An organisational development process can be phased in following manner*

Problem Identification The first step in organisational development process involves understanding and identification of the existing and potential problems in the organisation.

Data Collection After identification of problem the relevant data is collected through personal interview observations and questionnaires.

Diagnosis Organisational development begin with diagnosis of the current situation. *These are four steps in organisational diagnosis*

- ***Structural Analysis*** It determines how the different parts of the organisations are functioning in terms of laid down goals.
- ***Process Analysis*** Process implies the manner in which events take place in a sequence. It refers to pattern of decision-making, group dynamics and conflict management patterns within organisation.
- ***Function Analysis*** This includes strategic variables, performance variables, results, achievements and final outcome.
- ***Domain Analysis*** Domain refers to the area of the organisation for organisational diagnosis.

Planning and Implementation After diagnosing the problem, the next phase of organisational development involves the planning and implementation part of the change process.

Evaluation and Feedback Any organisational development activity is incomplete without proper feedback. Feedback is a process of relying evaluations by means of specific report or interaction.

Organisational Change

Organisational change is the process by which organisation move from their present state to some desired future state to increase effectiveness. When an organisation system is disturbed by some internal or external forces, changes frequently occur or any alteration, which occur in the overall work environment of an organisation.

Causes of Organisational Changes

Causes of organisational changes can be grouped as external pressures and internal pressures. *These are as follows*

External Pressures

Change in Technology and Equipment Advancements in technology are the major cause of change. Each technological alternative results in new forms of organisation to meet and match the needs.

Market Situation Changes in market situation include rapidly changing goals, needs and desires of consumers, suppliers, unions etc. If an organisation has to survive, it has to cope with changes in market situations.

Social and Political Changes Organisational units literally have no control over social and political changes in the country. Relations between government and business or drive for social equality are some factors which may compel for organisational change.

Internal Pressures

Changes in the Managerial Personnel One of the most frequent reason for major changes in the organisation is the change of executives at the top. Two managers cannot have the same style, skills or managerial philosophies.

Deficiencies in the Existing Organisation Many deficiencies are noticed in the organisations with the passage of time. A change is necessary to remove such deficiencies as lack of uniformity in the policies, obstacles in communication, any ambiguity etc.

Other Factors Certain other factors such as employee's desire to share in decision-making, employee's desire for higher wage rate, improvement in working conditions etc also demand a change in the organisation.

Process of Organisational Change

Unfreezing In this phase, the individual is made to realise that his beliefs, feelings and behaviour are no longer appropriate or relevant to the current situation in the organisation.

Changing Under this phase, after unfreezing an individual learn to behave in new ways. The individual is placed in a situation where new behaviour is demanded of him.

Refreezing During this phase, a person has to practice and experiment with the new method of behaviour and see that it effectively blends with his other behavioural attitudes. Reinforcement, for creating a permanent set in the individual, is provided through either continuous or intermittent schedules.

EXAM BASED QUESTIONS

Organisational Structure

1 Which of the following statements is/are true?
(a) The basis of staffing process is standards
(b) 'Unity of command' is a principle of planning
(c) The aim of organising is to enable people to work together for a common purpose
(d) All of the above

2 The main advantage of functional organisation is
(a) simplicity (b) specialisation
(c) experience (d) authority

3 Concept of functional organisation was given by
(a) FW Taylor (b) Elton Mayo
(c) Louis A Allen (d) Henry Fayol

4 In an electrical goods manufacturing company, there are four main activities marketing, production, finance and personnel. The general manager is planning to structure the organisation. Which type of organisation structure should he adopt?
(a) Formal organisation structure
(b) Functional organisation structure
(c) Informal organisation structure
(d) Divisional organisation structure

5 Ankit Limited is manufacturing chemicals and textiles. What type of organisational structure would suit the requirement of such an organisation?
(a) Divisional structure (b) Informal structure
(c) Formal structure (d) Functional structure

6 Anil runs a locks manufacturing factory. He wants to expand his business. For this, he wants to enter into the manufacturing of locks for cars as an ancillary company. By doing this, his company will be able to provide many products to car manufacturers. Type of organisational structure chosen by him for his factory is
(a) functional structure (b) formal structure
(c) divisional structure (d) None of these

7 Swapnil runs a factory, where he manufactures shoes. The business has been doing well and he intends to expand by diversifying into leather bags as well as Western formal wear, thereby making her company a complete provider of corporate wear. This will enable her to market his business unit as the one shop for working women. Type of structure recommended for the expanded organisation is
(a) functional structure (b) formal structure
(c) divisional structure (d) informal structure

Responsibility and Authority

8 The scalar principle of organisation implies
(a) a subordinate should have only one superior
(b) line of authority must be clearly defined
(c) manager should directly supervise only a limited number of subordinates
(d) None of the above

9 An organisation where the authority flows from top to bottom through various levels is called
(a) inter-unit administrative organisation
(b) line organisation
(c) project organisation
(d) line and staff organisation

10 Which of the following statement is correct?
(a) Authority and responsibility always flow upwards
(b) Authority and responsibility always flow downwards
(c) Authority flows downwards and responsibility flows upwards
(d) Authority flows upwards and responsibility flows downwards

11 The main advantage of decentralised organisation is
(a) top executive extends his central area
(b) coordination of activities becomes automatic
(c) top management can manage by 'exception'
(d) operation costs are lower

12 Which of the following statement is true?
(a) Authority can not be changed
(b) Authority and responsibility
(c) Responsibility can not be delegated
(d) None of the above

13 Principle of parity of authority and responsibility is related to
(a) decentralisation
(b) delegation
(c) divisionalisation
(d) autonomy

14 Delegation of authority may be effective, if
(a) delegation of rights with responsibility
(b) work load should be very low
(c) subordinate should be qualified and capable
(d) business has maximum staff

15 Under delegation of authority,
(a) authority is given to subordinates
(b) authority flows from top to bottom
(c) delegator of authority is not relieved
(d) All of the above

Organisational Culture

16 When an organisation becomes ...... it takes on a life of its own, apart from its founders or any of its members.

(a) institutionalised
(b) stablised
(c) cultured
(d) mature

17 Which of the following is not a characteristic of an organisation's culture?

(a) Outcome orientation
(b) Assertiveness
(c) Innovation and risk taking
(d) Attention to detail

18 Which of the following is not a function of culture?

(a) Enhances the stability of the social system
(b) Conveys a sense of identity
(c) Acceptance of diversity
(d) Generation of commitment

19 Which of the following statement is correct?

(a) Sprituality in organisation is inversely related to creativity
(b) Opportunities for sprituality have little impact on economic performance
(c) Sprituality in organisations is negatively associated with employee satisfaction and organisational commitment
(d) Sprituality based techniques improve productivity and significantly reduce turnover

20 Organisational development process is cyclical and ends when

(a) desired development result is obtained
(b) plan is implemented
(c) data is gathered
(d) problem is identified

21 Organisational development can also be called as a process

(a) for performance appraisal
(b) for change of people
(c) for teaching people how to solve the problem
(d) All of the above

22 Organisational development was founded on the belief that using behavioural science methods to increase collaborative problem solving would increase

(a) organisational effectiveness
(b) organisational turnover
(c) organisational reputation
(d) All of the above

23 It is proved that people can use their capabilities and creativity, if they are provided with

(a) adequate opportunities
(b) suitable work climate
(c) Both (a) and (b)
(d) None of the above

Miscellaneous

24 Which of the following statement(s) is/are not correct? Indicate the correct code.

Statement I Organisational culture means the general pattern of behaviour, belief and values that organisation members have in individuality.

Statement II As per contingency theory of leadership, people become leader only because of the demand of group members.

Statement III The group judgement can only be obtained through the formal committees,

Statement IV Ombudsperson in communication function is a person assigned to investigate employee concerns and providing valuable upward communication link.

Codes

(a) Statements I, II and IV (b) Statements I, II and III
(c) Statements I, III and IV (d) Statements II, III and IV

Directions (Q. Nos. 25 and 26) *In the questions given below are two statements labelled as Assertion (A) and Reason (R). In the context of the two statements, which one of the following is correct?*

Codes

(a) Both (A) and (R) are correct and (R) is the correct explanation of (A)
(b) Both (A) and (R) are correct, but (R) is incorrect explanation of (A)
(c) Both (A) and (R) are correct
(d) Both (A) and (R) are incorrect

25 **Assertion** (A) The organisation is a closed system that operates within and interacts with the external environment.

Reason (R) The system approach to management includes the outputs from the external environment on the basis of interactions between the management and employees.

26 **Assertion** (A) There is no place for human feelings in formal organisation.

Reason (R) Formal organisation is not impersonal.

27 Match the following.

List I	List II
A. Formal organisation	1. High degree of specialisation
B. Informal organisation	2. Rigid
C. Functional organisation	3. Product specialisation
D. Divisional organisation	4. Flexible

Codes

	A	B	C	D
(a)	2	4	1	3
(b)	4	2	3	1
(c)	2	1	4	3
(d)	3	1	2	4

28 Match the following.

List I	List II
A. Divisional structure	1. Groups similar or related jobs together
B. Functional structure	2. Friendly relationship exists
C. Formal structure	3. Each division is multi functional
D. Informal structure	4. Official relationship exists

Codes

	A	B	C	D
(a)	1	4	3	2
(b)	3	1	4	2
(c)	2	1	4	3
(d)	3	4	1	2

29 Match the following.

List I (Organisational Structures)	List II (Features)
A. Functional structure	1. Its purpose is to achieve planned organisational goals
B. Divisional structure	2. In this, authority flows vertically as well as horizontally
C. Formal organisation	3. Organisational design that groups similar or related jobs together
D. Informal organisation	4. Activities and personnel are grouped into a number of divisions on the basis of different products manufactured

Codes

	A	B	C	D
(a)	2	4	1	3
(b)	4	3	1	2
(c)	3	1	4	2
(d)	3	4	1	2

PREVIOUS YEARS' QUESTIONS

June 2014

1 Which of the following is incorrect about matrix organisation?
(a) It is relatively permanent
(b) Its project managers authority is distributed reasonably
(c) There is slow information processing
(d) Its project heads have to share resources with functional heads

2 **Assertion** (A) Classical organisations believed in the use of authority to achieve organisation.
Reason (R) Classical thinkers consider organisation is an open system.
Codes
(a) (A) is true, but (R) is false
(b) Both (A) and (R) are true
(c) (A) is false, but (R) is true
(d) Both (A) and (R) are false

3 Which of the following statements are true about informal organisation?
1. It arises spontaneously.
2. It reflects individual and group goals.
3. It tends to be permanent and stable.
4. It tends to be small and manageable.
5. Its basic purpose is to improve human relations.
6. Its basic purpose is to achieve organisation's goals.

Select the correct answer using the codes given below
Codes
(a) 1, 2, 3 and 5
(b) 1, 2, 4 and 6
(c) 1, 2, 4 and 5
(d) 2, 3, 5 and 6

December 2013

4 Another name for matrix organisation is
(a) flexible organisation
(b) geographic organisation
(c) project organisation
(d) None of the above

ANSWERS

Objective Questions

1 (c)	2 (b)	3 (b)	4 (b)	5 (a)	6 (c)	7 (c)	8 (b)	9 (b)	10 (c)
11 (c)	12 (b)	13 (b)	14 (c)	15 (c)	16 (c)	17 (b)	18 (a)	19 (a)	20 (a)
21 (c)	22 (a)	23 (c)	24 (b)	25 (d)	26 (c)	27 (a)	28 (b)	29 (d)	

Previous Years' Questions

1 (c)	2 (a)	3 (c)	4 (c)

CHAPTER 22

Motivation, Leadership and Corporate Governance

Efficient employees works as blood of an organisation. Management can make their employees more efficient with motivation and proper leadership. It enhances their performance and makes more easy to achieve organisational pre-decided goals. An organisation works with business ethics which are important for success of an organisation.

Motivation

Motivation has been derived from the word 'motive' which is defined as a need that requires satisfaction. Motivation has been considered as one of the most important reasons that inspires a person to move forward.

It means stimulating, inducing and inciting the employees to perform to their best capacity. In other words, motivation is a combination of forces inspiring a person at work to intensify his willingness to use his maximum capabilities for the achievement of pre-determined objectives. It involves arousing needs and desires in people to initiate and direct their behaviour in a purposive manner.

According to **MJ Jucius**, "Motivation is the art of stimulating someone or oneself to take desired course of action."

According to **Koontz** and **O' Donnell**, "To motivate is to induce people to act in a desired manner."

In this Chapter

Features of Motivation

Internal Instinct It is a psychological phenomenon, which generates from within an individual. It is a personal and internal feeling which arises from the needs and wants of a person. *e.g.* people may have urges or desires or aspirations for possessing a motorbike, comfortable house, reputation in the society. These urges are internal to an individual.

Produces Goal Directed Behaviour Motivations are directed towards the achievement of certain goals, which in turn determine the behaviour of individuals. Motivated person needs no supervision. He will always work in desired manner. *e.g.* if a person has a motive to get promotion, so he will work efficiently to get promotion.

Positive or Negative Motivation Positive motivation seeks to create an environment, which is wholly congenial for the employees to work more and better. It provides positive rewards like increment, bonus, promotion etc whereas negative motivation seeks to create a sense of fear and uncongenial atmosphere for the employee. It involves negative means like warning, cut in remuneration, demotion etc.

Complex Process It is a complex and difficult task because needs are mentally connected, which cannot be measured accurately. Moreover, human needs change from time to time. People satisfy their needs in different ways. Any type of motivation may not have uniform effect on all the people.

Dynamic and Continuous Process Human needs are unlimited and go on changing continuously. Satisfaction of one need gives rise to another. So, managers have to continuously perform the function of motivation.

Universal Managerial Function It is an universal managerial function, as it is used at every level of the organisation.

Inter-related Terms

While discussing about motivation, we need to understand three inter-related terms which are as follows

Motive It is an inner state that energises, activates and directs behaviour towards goals. Motives arise out of the needs of individuals *e.g.* the need for food. Such motives are hunger, thirst etc.

Motivation It is the process of stimulating people to action to accomplish desired goals. Motivation depends upon satisfying needs of people.

Motivator It is the technique used to motivate people in an organisation. Managers use diverse motivators like pay, bonus, promotion etc in the organisation to influence people to contribute their best.

Importance of Motivation

"Motivation is the Core of Management". It is through motivation that managers can inspire their subordinates to give their best to the organisation. It should be noted that a worker may be immensely capable of doing some work, nothing can be achieved, if he is not willing to do work.

The following points justify the importance of motivation in an organisation

Improves Performance Level Motivation helps to improve performance level of employees. Motivation builds the will to work among employees and enables the management to secure the best possible utilisation of all resources. Motivation bridges the gap between ability to work and willingness to work. By inducing people to work better, motivation helps in increasing productivity, reducing cost of operations and securing overall efficiency.

Development of Positive Attitude Motivation helps to change negative or indifferent attitude of employee to positive attitude so as to achieve organisational goals. Management offers various monetary and non- monetary rewards like promotional opportunities, recognition of efficient work, fringe benefits and involvement in decision-making. These bring about the need of satisfaction among employees, which leads to change in the attitude of the employees from negative or indifferent to positive.

Reduction in Employees Turnover Motivation helps to reduce employees turnover and thereby saves the cost of new recruitment and training. If managers identify motivational needs of employees and provide suitable financial and non-financial incentives, employees may not think of leaving the organisation.

Introduce Changes Smoothly Normally, for any change introduced in the organisation, there may be resistance for changes. Motivation helps managers to introduce changes smoothly without much resistance from employees. Motivated employees support all changes that are in the organisational interests because they identify their own advancement with the prosperity of the enterprise.

Reduce Absenteeism Motivation helps to reduce absenteeism in the organisation. Sound motivational system like increment, bonus, rewards, respect and recognition and good working conditions bring job satisfaction in the employees. Motivated employees feel pleasure in performing their work. They attend the work regularly and do not willingly keep themselves absent from the organisation.

Theories of Motivation

Maslow's Need Hierarchy Theory of Motivation

Needs are the starting point in motivation. Abraham Maslow, an eminent US Psychologist, offered a general theory of motivation called the Need Hierarchy Theory. He felt that people have a wide range of needs, which motivate them to strive for their fulfilment. Maslow highlighted two important characteristics of human needs. In the first place, man's needs depend completely on what he already has.

For this reason, satisfied needs do not motivate behaviour. It may be asserted that the manager has always be on the look out for the unsatisfied needs of the individuals in the organisation, so that he can take proper steps to motivate them by providing opportunities for the satisfaction of their needs. In the second place, human needs are arranged in a hierarchy of importance *i.e.* on the basis of a chain of sequence of needs. As soon as needs of a lower level are fulfilled or satisfied, those of a higher level emerge and demand satisfaction.

Maslow classified human needs into five categories in order of priority

Physiological Needs These needs concern the human body and are necessary to preserve human life, *e.g.* food, clothing, shelter, air, water and other necessities of life. These needs relate to the survival and maintenance of human life. Physiological needs are also known as survival needs.

Safety or Security Needs These needs are important for most of the people. Such needs include physical, economic and social safety. Physical safety includes protection against fire, accidents, diseases, crimes and other types of physical dangers. Economic safety means security of employment and making provision for old age. Social security comprises need for security in old age, state of illness or partial or total disablement.

Social Needs Man is a social being. He wants conversation, sociability, exchange of feelings, companionship, recognition, belongingness etc. Social needs include the desire for love, affection, belonging or association with family and for friendship. These needs are related to natural desire to socialise or to interact with others.

Esteem or Status Needs These needs are also called ego needs. These needs embrace such things as self-confidence, independence, achievement, competence, knowledge, initiative and success. These needs are concerned with prestige and respect of the individuals. In other words, these needs concern with the desire to prove one's worth in the eyes of others and self.

Self Actualisation Needs These are the needs of the highest order. They are generally found in persons whose first four needs have already been fulfilled. These needs are related with development of one's potential to the fullest possible extent.

They are concerned with achieving what a person considers to be his mission in life. *e.g.* getting India free from the British regime was the mission of Mahatma Gandhi.

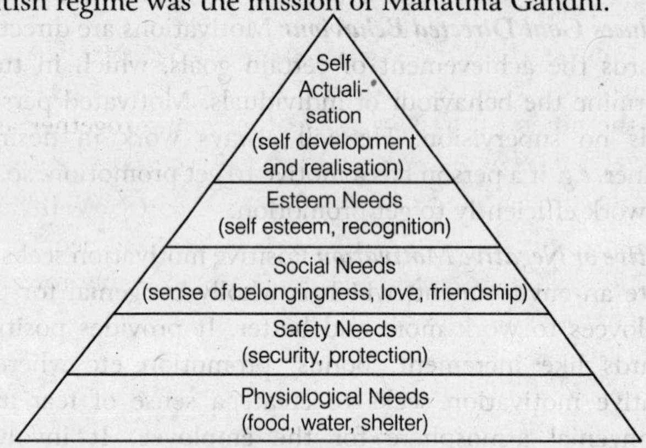

Maslow's Need Hierarchy Theory

Herzberg's Two Factor Theory

According to Herzberg, human needs can be classified into two parts-health and motivation. *These are*

Health Factor These factors are related with environment or situations of work and also with external environment.

Motivational Factor These factors are related with subject matters of work. These are those experience of people which provides satisfaction and related with internal environment.

'X' and 'Y' Theory of McGregor

McGregor propounded two types of philosophies related with human behaviour and motivation, which are known as 'X' and 'Y' theories. 'X' theory is known as negative theory and 'Y' theory is known as positive theory.

'X' theory states that everyone wants to save himself from work, so here motivation can be done by showing them fear. 'Y' theory states that if people get motivation, then they can work more effectively.

'Z' Theory of William Ouchi

It is a wide managerial philosophy which was propounded by William Ouchi, after studying and analysing the managerial behaviour.

According to Ouchi's Theory 'Z', management tends to promote stable employment, high productivity and high employee morale and satisfaction.

Leadership

Leadership is a quality whereby an individual is able to move a group towards specified goals normally without exerting force. In this way, leadership involves securing willing cooperation of others by influencing their behaviour. Whenever, we hear the success stories of an organisation, we are immediately reminded of their leaders.

According to **Keith Davis**, "Leadership is the ability to persuade others to seek defined objectives enthusiastically. It is the human factor, which binds a group together and motivates it towards goals".

According to **Harold Koontz** and **Heinz Weihrich**, "Leadership is the art or process of influencing people, so that they will strive willingly and enthusiastically towards the achievement of group goals".

Characteristics of Leadership

Personal Quality of Manager It is the personal ability, tact and competence of the leader who leads, directs, coordinates and channelises the group efforts towards desired goal of the business. To some extent, it is an inherent quality, but it can be developed also.

Influencing Process It is the process of influencing the behaviour and conduct of people in one direction.

Behaviour Changing Process Leadership has the power to change the behaviour of the followers (subordinates) and create an urge for higher performance among them.

Related to a Situation When we talk of leadership, it is always related to a particular situation, at a given point of time and under a specific set of circumstances.

Achieving Common Goal Leadership is exercised to persuade and motivate followers to strive willingly to achieve common goals of the organisation.

Continuous Process It is a continuous process, which never comes to an end. A leader always goes on influencing and directing the behaviour of the followers.

Importance of Leadership

Leadership is regarded as the most crucial quality of behaviour of the managers. *The importance of leadership can be discussed as follows*

Helps in Achieving Organisational Goals Leadership influences the behaviour of people and makes them to positively contribute their energies for the achievement of the organisational goals. Good leaders always produce good results through their followers. They are persuade employees to work enthusiastically and with confidence.

Creates Confidence among the Employees A leader maintains personal relations with the followers and helps them in fulfilling their needs. He creates confidence among them, when they fail to recognise their qualities and capabilities. He provides psychological support and infuses the spirit of enthusiasm in the followers by his conduct and expression.

Securing Cooperation The importance of leadership lies in the fact that it secures voluntary cooperation of the subordinates. He influences the behaviour of employees in such a way that, they readily work for organisational objectives. He makes them realise that by translating plans into action, they can earn adequate rewards. He thus, inculcates a sense of collectivism in the employees and forces them to work as a team.

Providing Conducive Environment Efficiency of performance depends on the work environment. Leadership aims at creating and maintaining a satisfactory environment for employees to contribute their maximum towards achieving the goals.

Helps in Introducing Required Changes In the dynamic requirement of today, rapid changes are taking place in the structure and working of an organisation. But people to resist change as change creates inconvenience and uncertainty. Leader plays a key role in introducing required changes in the organisation. He persuades, clarifies and inspires people to accept changes whole heartedly. Thus, he overcomes the problem of resistance to change and introduces it with minimum discontentment.

Management of Conflicts Effectively A good leader avoids conflicts between the employer and the employees. In case conflict arises, a leader handles it effectively and does not allow adverse effects resulting from the conflicts. A good leader always allows the followers to ventilate their feelings and disagreement, but persuades them by giving suitable clarifications.

Theories/Principles of Leadership

Qualitative Theory

According to this theory, leadership is an art. This theory is based on the philosophy that some people have leadership quality by birth. According to IV Teed, an individual can be a skilled labour, *if he had following features*

- Physical strength
- Courage and diligence
- Personality
- Instant decisions
- Capacity to teach
- Allegiance towards objectives
- Friendly behaviour
- Technological skills
- Ability
- Trust

Situational Theory

This theory assumes that, beside qualities situations also affects leadership. In other words, if the situations are favorable under which a leader guides his followers, then leader will succeed and if the situations are unfavorable then leader fails. In conclusion, we can say that leader can be by birth and can also be made according to situations. Because all situations are different from each other, therefore, leadership techniques can be adopted. Accordingly, *leadership depends on four situational based elements*

- Cultural environment
- Differences among people
- Different type of works
- Different type of organisation

Coincidental Theory

This theory emphasised that there is no leadership style which is appropriate for every situation. *There are three elements of this theory*

- If harmonious and peaceful relations are established between leader and his followers, then it can affect them in more better way.
- Leader can more efficiently control lower structural functions like teaching and research work rather than upper structural functions.
- Rights of leaders also affects control efficiency of a leader.

Follower Theory

Prof. FH Sanford propounded this theory. According to him, followers also enhances efficiency of leadership. The leaders who satisfies personal, social and physiological needs of his followers, they will depend on him. According to this theory, the leader who tries to fulfill needs of his followers is known as skilled leader.

Behavioural Theory

RA Million was propounded of this theory. According to him, whether a leader is a good decision maker, problem solver, a good advisor or good planner but he must present ideal behavior in front of his followers. *e.g.* If a leader play gambling and expect that his followers did not drink alcohol, then it is baseless.

Functional Theory

Hackman and Walton and McGrath were propounders of this theory. According to them, "as a leader is related with group of people, so it must be studied and analysed collectively rather than individually." This theory focused on philosophy of individual and group study.

Trait Theory

The trait theory of leadership is an early assumption that leaders are born and due to this belief, those that possess the correct qualities and traits are better suited to leadership. This theory is based on the characteristics of many leaders and is used to predict leadership effectiveness.

Styles of Leadership

Bureaucratic Leadership Under this leadership style, all the administrative powers are centralised in a leader. He does not believe in decentralisation. He self ordered his followers and wholesale responsible for everything. This style is also known as centralised style in which followers does know about their goals and depends on their leaders.

Democratic Leadership Under this leadership style, leaders make all the policies by group discussion. Rights are decentralised among followers, which make friendly relationship between a leader and his followers. This style is also known as decentralisation.

Free-rein or Laissez Faire Leadership It involves complete delegation of authority, so that subordinates themselves take decisions. The free-rein leader avoids holding power and surrenders the authority to subordinates. This is also known as laissez faire, which means no interference in the affairs of others.

Charismatic Leadership Charismatic leadership is basically the method of encouraging particular behaviours in others by way of eloquent communication, persuassion and force of personality. It is almost of divine origin. This is accomplished by conjuring up eagerness in others to achieve a stated goal or vision.

Responsibilities of a Leader

A leader plays many responsibilities, *some of them are as follows*

- A leader motivates his followers.
- A leader coordinates between management and employees.
- A leader maintains discipline.
- A leader is responsible for moral development of his followers.
- A leader provides suggestions and solutions for his followers.

Corporate Governance

Corporate governance refers to the way a corporation is governed. It is the technique by which companies are directed and managed. It means carrying the business as per the stakeholder's desires. It is actually conducted by the Board of Directors and the concerned committees for the company's stakeholders benefit. It is all about balancing individual and societal goals as well as economic and social goals.

Corporate governance is the interaction between various participants (shareholder's, Board of Directors' and company's management) in shaping corporation's performance and the way it is preceding towards. The relationship between the owners and the managers in an organisation must be healthy and there should be no conflict between the two. The owners must see that individual's actual performance is according to the standard performance. Corporate governance deals within the manner, the providers of finance guarantees themselves of getting a fair return on their investment. Corporate governance clearly distinguishes between the owners and the managers. The managers are the deciding authority. In modern corporations, the functions/tasks of owners and managers should be clearly defined, rather, harmonising.

Corporate governance deals with determining ways to take effective strategic decisions. It gives ultimate authority and complete responsibility to the Board of Directors. In today's market oriented economy, the need for corporate governance arises. Also, efficiency as well as globalisation are significant urging corporate governance. Corporate governance is essential to develop added value to the stakeholders.

Corporate governance ensures transparency, which ensures strong and balanced economic development. This also ensures that the interests of all shareholders are safeguarded. It ensures that all shareholders fully exercise their rights and that the organisation fully recognises their rights. Corporate governance has a broad scope. It includes both social and institutional aspects. Corporate governance encourages a trustworthy moral, as well as ethical environment.

Importance of Corporate Governance

Changing Ownership Structure In recent years, the ownership structure of companies has changed a lot. Public financial institutions, mutual funds etc are the only largest shareholders in most of the large companies. So, they have effective control on the management of the companies. They force the management to use corporate governance *i.e.* they put pressure on the management to become more efficient, transparent, accountable etc. They also ask the management to make consumer friendly policies, to protect all social groups and to protect the environment. So, the changing ownership has resulted in corporate governance.

Importance of Social Responsibility Today, social responsibility is given a lot of importance. The Board of Directors have to protect the rights of the customers, employees, shareholders, suppliers etc. This is possible only if they use corporate governance.

Protecting Investors from Scams In recent years, many frauds and corrupt practices have taken place. Misuse and misappropriation of public money are happening everyday in India and worldwide.

It is happening in the stock market, banks, financial institutions, companies and government offices. In order to avoid these scams and financial irregularities, may companies have started corporate governance.

Indifference on the Part of Shareholders In general, shareholders are inactive in the management of their companies. They only attend the annual general meeting. Postal ballot is still absent in India.

Proxies are not allowed to speak in the meetings. Shareholders associations are not strong. Therefore, directors misuse their power for their benefits. So, there is a need for corporate governance to protect all the stakeholders of the company.

Globalisation Today, most big companies are selling their goods in the global market. So, they have to attract foreign investors and foreign customers. They also have to follow foreign rules and regulations which requires corporate governance. Without corporate governance, it is impossible to enter, survive and succeed in the global market.

Takeovers and Mergers Today, there are many takeovers and mergers in the business world. Corporate governance is required to protect the interest of all the parties during takeovers and mergers.

SEBI It has made corporate governance compulsory for certain companies. This is done to protect the interest of the investors and other stakeholders.

Business Ethics

Ethics is a branch of Social Science. It deals with moral principles and social values. It helps us to classify, what is good and what is bad? It tells us to do good things and avoid doing bad things. So, ethics separate goods and bad, right and wrong, fair and unfair, moral and immoral and proper and improper human action. In short, ethics means a code of conduct. So, the businessman give a regular supply of good quality goods and services at reasonable prices to their customers.

They must avoid indulging in unfair trade practices like adulteration, promoting misleading advertisement, black marketing etc. They must give fair wages and provide good working conditions to their workers. They must not exploit the workers. They must encourage competition in the market. They must protect interest of small businessman.

They must avoid unfair competition. They must avoid monopolies. They must pay all their taxes regularly to the government. In short, business ethics means to conduct business with a human touch in order to give welfare to the society.

According to **Andrew Crane**, "Business ethics is the study of business situations, activities and decisions where issues of right and wrong are addressed".

According to **Raymond C Baumhart**, "The ethics of business is the ethics of responsibility. The businessman promise that he will not harm knowingly".

Features of Business Ethics

Code of Conduct Business ethics is a code of conduct. It tells what to do and what not to do for the welfare of the society. All businessmen must follow this code of conduct.

Based on Moral and Social Values Business ethics contains moral and social principles (rules) for doing business. This include self control, consumer protection and welfare service to society, fair treatment to social groups etc.

***Gives Protection to Social* Groups** Business ethics gives protection to different social groups such as consumers, employees, small businessmen, government shareholders etc.

Voluntary Business ethics must be voluntary. The businessmen must accept business ethics on their own. Business ethics must be like self-discipline. It must not be enforced by law.

Requires Education and Guidance Businessmen must be given proper education and guidance before introducing business ethics. The businessmen must be motivated to use business ethics. They must be informed about the advantages of using business ethics. Trade Associations and Chamber of Commerce must also play an active role in this matter.

Importance of Business Ethics

Stop Business Malpractices Some unscrupulous businessmen do business malpractice by indulging in unfair trade practices like back marketing, artificial high pricing, adulteration etc. These business malpractices are harmful to the consumers. Business ethics help to stop these business malpractice.

Improve Customer's Confidence Business ethics are needed to improve the customer's confidence about the quantity, quality etc of the products. The customers have more trust and confidence in the businessmen, who follow ethical rules. They feel that such businessmen will not cheat them.

Safeguarding Consumer's Rights The consumer has many rights such as right to health and safety, right to be informed, right to choose, right to be heard etc, but many businessmen do not respect and protect these rights. Businessmen ethics are must to safeguard these rights of the consumers.

Protecting Employees and Shareholders Business ethics are required to protect the interest of employees, shareholders and competitors, organisation will grow, expand and diversify easily and quickly. It will have more sales and more profits.

Consumer Satisfaction Today, the consumer is the king of the market. Any business simply cannot survive without the consumers. If the consumer is not satisfied, then there will be no sales and thus no profits too. Consumer will be satisfied only if the business follows all the business ethics and hence are highly needed.

Importance of Labour Labour *e.g.* employees and workers play a very crucial role in the success of a business. Therefore, businessman must use business ethics, while dealing with the employees. The business must give them proper wages and salaries and provide them with working conditions

EXAM BASED QUESTIONS

Motivation

1 Motivational process and not the motivators as such is associated with the

(a) need hierarchy theory
(b) two-factor theory
(c) ERG theory
(d) expectancy theory

2 Need Hierarchy Theory of motivation was given by

(a) WG Scott (b) AH Maslow
(c) Peter F Drucker (d) F Herzberg

3 Which of the following is not a 'non-financial incentive'?

(a) Pay
(b) Employee participation
(c) Bonus
(d) Commission

4 'Motivation Hygience Theory' was propounded by

(a) Herzberg (b) Maslow
(c) McGregor (d) Peter F Drucker

5 .... refer to those needs satisfaction of which leads of self-confidence and prestige.

(a) Self actualisation needs (b) Safety needs
(c) Esteem needs (d) Physiological needs

6 Which of the following is a 'financial incentive'?

(a) Status
(b) Job security
(c) Employee participation
(d) None of the above

7 Maslow defines one of the needs in the need hierarchy as the "desire to become everything one is capable of becoming". Identify the need.

(a) Security needs
(b) Esteem needs
(c) Physiological needs
(d) Self actualisation needs

8 According to need hierarchy theory of Maslow, human needs arise in which one of the following order?

(a) Physiological needs-Social needs-Safety needs-Ego needs-Self actualisation needs
(b) Physiological needs-Social needs-Ego needs-Safety needs-Self actualisation needs
(c) Physiological needs-Safety needs-Social needs-Ego needs-Self actualisation needs
(d) Physiological needs-Safety needs-Ego needs-Social needs-Self actualisation needs

Leadership

9 Good manager should possess many of the qualities of an effective

(a) candidate (b) employee
(c) superior (d) leader

10 "Leadership is the set of interpersonal behaviours designed to influence employees to cooperate in the achievement of objectives." Who said this?

(a) Glueck
(b) George Terry
(c) Keith Davis
(d) EB Flippo

11 Consider the following statements.

1. Leadership is a continuous process.
2. Leadership indicates interpersonal relations between managers and superiors.
3. The key to successful today is influence, not authority.

Which of the statement(s) given above is/are correct?

(a) Both 1 and 3 (b) Only 3
(c) Both 1 and 2 (d) Only 2

12 "Leadership is the activity of influencing people to strive willingly for group objectives". Who said this?

(a) Keith Davis
(b) George Terry
(c) Glueck
(d) None of these

13 Which of the following statements is/are incorrect?

(a) People oriented leadership is the opposite of task oriented leadership
(b) Autocratic leadership is an extreme form of charismatic leadership
(c) Laissez faire leadership works for team in which the individuals are very experienced
(d) All of the above

14 Which of the following statements is/are correct?

(a) Management directs the employees through formal authority
(b) All the managers are not leaders
(c) There is informal relationship between manager and the subordinates
(d) None of the above

15 Which of the following statements is/are correct?

(a) Motivation helps in reduction in resistance to change
(b) Leadership provides training to the employees
(c) Both (a) and (b)
(d) None of the above

16 Consider the following statements.

1. As per leadership theory (participative), leader retains the right to allow the input of others.
2. Faculty decoding is an example of feedback.
3. A satisfied need can no longer motivate a person.

Which of the statement(s) given above is/are correct?

(a) Only 1 (b) Only 2
(c) Both 1 and 2 (d) Both 1 and 3

17 Under democratic style, a leader

(a) keeps all the rights with him
(b) determines all the policies
(c) holds strict supervision and control
(d) delegates necessary rights to his subordinates

18 "Leadership qualities are inborn". This notion forms part of which of the following?

(a) The followership theory of leadership
(b) The behavioural theory of leadership
(c) The path goal theory of leadership
(d) The great men theory of leadership

Corporate Governance and Business Ethics

19 Which one of the following is not covered under Corporate Governance?

(a) Corporate social responsibility
(b) Business ethics
(c) Role of independent directors
(d) Government monitoring

20 Business ethics may be exposed in

(a) business code of conduct (b) business dealings
(c) Both (a) and (b) (d) None of these

21 Which one of the following is not involved in the characteristics of business ethics?

(a) It is a dynamic philosophy
(b) It is based on moral values
(c) It influenced by socio cultural values
(d) It is not inspired by social welfare

22 Consider the following statements.

1. Leadership is the ability to influence the behaviour of others.
2. Motivation increases the rate of labour turnover.

Which of the statement(s) given above is/are correct?

(a) Only 1 (b) Only 2
(c) Both 1 and 2 (d) None of the above

23 Consider the following statements.

1. Ethics is a branch of Social Science which deals with moral principles and social values.
2. Good decisiveness is not necessary for a good leader.
3. Pay and allowances is a non-financial incentive.

Which of the statement(s) given above is/are incorrect?

(a) Only 1 (b) Both 1 and 3
(c) Both 2 and 3 (d) All of the above

24 Which one is the most important theory of business ethics?

(a) Theory of unity of direction
(b) Theory of proportional judgement
(c) Theory of scalar chain
(d) Theory of span of control

25 Satisfaction or happiness is cosidered as ...... in business ethics.

(a) acceptor (b) controller
(c) guide (d) All of these

26 According to which business, ethics is related to the careful examination of the prevailing values in business society?

(a) Keith Devis
(b) George R Terry
(c) Bunteeg
(d) Koontz and Ont Donnel

27 Business ethics are based on

(a) emotions (b) facts
(c) reatity (d) All of these

28 Philosophy of business ethics is

(a) changeable
(b) unchangeable
(c) depend on management
(d) None of the above

29 Which of the following is emphasised in code of business conduct?

(a) Customer satisfaction
(b) Moral values
(c) Economic benefit
(d) All of the above

Miscellaneous

30 **Statement** I Maslow's theory conveys hygiene factors.

Statement II Maslow's theory conveys satisfied need is no more a motivator.

Codes

(a) Both statements are correct
(b) Both statements are incorrect
(c) Statement I is correct, but Statement II is incorrect
(d) Statement I is incorrect, but Statement II is correct

Directions (Q. Nos. 31-44) *In the questions given below are two statements labelled as Assertion (A) and Reason (R). In the context of the two statements, which one of the following is correct?*

Codes

(a) Both (A) and (R) are correct and (R) is the correct explanation of (A)
(b) Both (A) and (R) are correct, but (R) is not the correct explanation of (A)
(c) (A) is correct, but (R) is incorrect
(d) (A) is incorrect, but (R) is correct

31 **Assertion** (A) Motivation is an universal managerial function.
Reason (R) Motivation is used at every level of the organisation.

32 **Assertion** (A) Motivation increased efficiency of workers.
Reason (R) Motivational workers have more number of grievances against the management.

33 **Assertion** (A) External sources of motivation restricts infusion of fresh blood with new ideas into the enterprise.
Reason (R) External sources is a cheap process.

34 **Assertion** (A) Motivation is the core of management.
Reason (R) Through motivation, managers can inspire their subordinates to give their best to the organisation.

35 **Assertion** (A) Motivation creates good relations in the organisation.
Reason (R) Motivation provides a complex work environment.

36 **Assertion** (A) Laissez faire leadership describe a leader, who leaves his colleague to get on with their work.
Reason (R) 'Laissez faire' means 'Leave it be.'

37 **Assertion** (A) Leadership provides training to his subordinates only in special circumstances.
Reason (R) It helps in rough succession process.

38 **Assertion** (A) Charismatic leadership carries great responsibility.
Reason (R) Charismatic leadership needs long-term commitment from the leader.

39 **Assertion** (A) 'Good Corporate Governance' is simply 'good business'.
Reason (R) Corporate Governance ensures protection of manager's interests.

40 **Assertion** (A) Business ethics contains only social principles.
Reason (R) Business ethics are based on social values only.

41 **Assertion** (A) Corporate Governance is essential to develop added value to the stakekholders.
Reason (R) Corporate Governance is all about balancing individual and societal goals only.

42 **Assertion** (A) Regulation of good corporation means good business.
Reason (R) The corporation ensures the safety of the regulatory managers.

43 **Assertion** (A) Business code of conduct includes only social theory.
Reason (R) Business code of conduct depends only on social values.

44 **Assertion** (A) Business ethics is essential for the increase and development of shareholders.
Reason (R) Business ethics is the act of balancing personal goals.

45 Match the following.

List I (Monetary Incentives)	List II (Features)
A. Pay and allowances	1. Offer prices such as trips
B. Stock option	2. Amount of incentive linked to productivity
C. Bonus	3. Enhancement of basic salary
D. Productivity linked wage incentives	4. Employees are offered company shares

Codes

	A	B	C	D		A	B	C	D
(a)	3	2	4	1	(b)	4	3	1	2
(c)	3	4	1	2	(d)	3	1	2	4

46 Match the following.

List I (Type of Needs)	List II (Features)
A. Physiological needs	1. Provide protection from physical and emotional harm
B. Security needs	2. Survival and maintenance of human life
C. Esteem needs	3. Becoming, what a person is capable of becoming
D. Self actualisation needs	4. Satisfaction of which leads to self confidence and prestige

Codes

	A	B	C	D		A	B	C	D
(a)	4	3	1	2	(b)	3	4	2	1
(c)	2	1	4	3	(d)	4	3	2	1

47 Match the following.

List I (Theories of Leadership)	List II (Features)
A. Management theories	1. Also known as transformational theories
B. Relationship theories	2. People inherit certain qualities
C. Behavioural theories	3. Also known as transactional theories
D. Trait theories	4. Focus on the actions of leaders not on mental qualities

Codes

	A	B	C	D		A	B	C	D
(a)	4	1	3	2	(b)	2	4	3	1
(c)	3	1	4	2	(d)	4	3	2	1

48 Match the following.

List I (Authors)	List II (Definitions)
A. MJ Jucius	1. Motivation is the art of stimulating some one or oneself to take desired course of action
B. Theo Haimann	2. To motivate is to induce people to act in a desired manner
C. Koontz and O' Donnell	3. Leadership is the process by which an executive imaginatively directs, guides and influences the work of others in attaining and specified goals

Codes

	A	B	C		A	B	C
(a)	3	2	1	(b)	1	3	2
(c)	2	3	1	(d)	1	2	3

49 Match the following.

List I (Styles of Leadership)	List II (Features)
A. Autocratic leadership	1. The leader is totally focused on organising, supporting and developing the people in the team.
B. Bureaucratic leadership	2. It is used to describe a leader, who leaves his colleagues to get on with their work.
C. Laissez-faire leadership	3. Leaders work, by the book, ensuring that their staff follow procedures exactly.
D. People oriented leadership	4. Leader exerts high levels of power over his employees or team members.

Codes

	A	B	C	D		A	B	C	D
(a)	3	2	1	4	(b)	4	2	3	1
(c)	4	3	2	1	(d)	2	4	3	1

50 Match the following.

List I (Leadership Theories)	List II (Features)
A. Relationship theories	1. People can learn to become leaders through teaching and observation.
B. Management theories	2. The leader retains the right to allow the input of others.
C. Participative theories	3. Focuses on the role of supervision, organisation and group performance.
D. Behavioural theories	4. Focuses on the connections formed between leaders and followers.

Codes

	A	B	C	D		A	B	C	D
(a)	4	3	2	1	(b)	3	4	2	1
(c)	3	4	1	2	(d)	1	2	3	4

51 Match the following.

List I	List II
A. Koontz and O' Donnell	1. To motivate is to induce people to act in a desired manner
B. Alford and Beatty	2. Leadership is the ability to secure desired actions from a group of followers voluntarily, without achievement of objectives
C. EB Flippo	3. Communication is the act of inducing others to interpret an idea in the manner intended by the speaker or writer

Codes

	A	B	C		A	B	C
(a)	1	2	3	(b)	3	2	1
(c)	2	1	3	(d)	1	3	2

PREVIOUS YEARS' QUESTIONS

December 2018

1 Match the items of List I with the items of List II and choose the correct answer from the code given below.

List I (Propounder of Theory)	List II (Theory of Motivation)
A. Dr. William Ouchi	1. X Theory
B. Douglas McGregor	2. Need Hierarchy Theory
C. Frederick Herzberg	3. Z Theory
D. AH Maslow	4. Hygience Theory

Codes

	A	B	C	D		A	B	C	D
(a)	2	3	4	1	(b)	4	1	3	2
(c)	3	1	4	2	(d)	2	1	3	4

2 Corporations are controlled and directed by which of the following?

(a) Corporate ethics
(b) Corporate codes
(c) Corporate governance
(d) Corporate mechanism

July 2018

3 The popular statement, "if all you have is a hammer, everything looks like a nail", is given by

(a) AH Maslow (Hierarchy of Needs)
(b) Henry Fayol (Industrial and General Administration)
(c) FW Taylor (Scientific Management)
(d) Frederick Herzberg (Hygiene Theory)

4 Functional Leadership Theory is associated with
(a) Hackman and Walton and McGrath
(b) Barnard and Ordway Tead
(c) Koontz and O'Donnell
(d) Alford and Beatty

November 2017

5 Who among the following is not associated with theories of motivation?
(a) AH Maslow (b) Cris Argyris
(c) Frederick Herzberg (d) Peter F Drucker

6 As per the Herzberg's Hygiene Theory of motivation, which among the following is not a motivational factors?
(a) Recognition (b) Working Conditions
(c) Responsibility (d) Achievements

7 One of the techniques of stimulating creativity for developing new products where you start with an idea, then thinking of the next idea and link, then think of the next association and do this with all association that come up with each new idea, is known as
(a) attribute listing (b) forced relationship
(c) new contexts (d) mind mapping

8 **Statement** I We are motivated to re-evaluate our beliefs, attitudes, opinions or values occurred at two different time.

Statement II The difference due to some intervention occurred at either point of time motivates us to search a newer option and thus satisfies our mind/anxiety.

Codes
(a) Statement I is correct, but Statement II is not correct
(b) Statement II is correct, but Statement I is not correct
(c) Both statements are correct
(d) Both statements are incorrect

9 Which of the following statements are correct? Indicate the correct code.

Statement I Virtue ethics is a form of ethical approach associated with Aristotle which stresses the importance of developing virtuous principles, right character and the pursuit of a virtuous life.

Statement II Utilitarianism is an ethical approach where an action is right if, and only if, it conforms to the principle of utility, whereby utility is minimised and pain and unhappiness minimised more than any alternative.

Statement III 'Deontological Ethics' is an ethical approach where rightness or wrongness of an action or decision is not judged to be based exclusively on the consequences of that action or decision.

Codes
(a) Both II and III (b) Both I and II
(c) Both I and III (d) All of the above

January 2017

10 **Assertion** (A) Herzberg believes that today's motivators are tomorrow's hygiene factors.

Reason (R) Some job conditions operate primarily to dissatisfy employees when they are absent, but their presence does not motivate them in strong way.

Codes
(a) (A) and (R) both are correct and (R) is the correct explanation of (A)
(b) (A) and (R) both are correct, but (R) is not the correct explanation of (A)
(c) (A) is not correct while (R) is a correct
(d) Both (A) and (R) are incorrect

July 2016

11 Match List I and List II and indicate the correct code.

List I	List II
A. Equity theory	1. Motivation depends on ratios of inputs and outcomes of self and others.
B. Vroom's theory	2. People are motivated to achieve a goal to the extent that they expect that certain action will help them to reach the goal.
C. Porter and Lawler model	3. There exists a complex relationship among motivation, performance and satisfaction.
D. Herzberg's theory	4. A challenging job that has opportunities for achievement, recognition, responsibility and growth will motivate employees.

Codes

	A	B	C	D		A	B	C	D
(a)	1	2	3	4	(b)	2	1	3	4
(c)	3	2	1	4	(d)	1	3	2	4

12 Which of the following is related to the partical means of determining a moral course of action?
(a) Meta ethics (b) Virtue ethics
(c) Normative (d) Applied ethics

December 2015

13 According to Hersey and Blanchard's situational approach to leadership, the 'participating style' of leadership has
(a) high task and low relationship orientation
(b) high task and high relationship orientation
(c) low task and high relationship orientation
(d) low task and low relationship orientation

June 2015

14 Match the following.

List I	List II
A. Management of tomorrow	1. Chris Argyris
B. Motivation and personality	2. Frederick Herzberg
C. The motivation of work	3. LF Urwick
D. Personality and organisation	4. AH Maslow

Codes

	A	B	C	D		A	B	C	D
(a)	1	4	2	3	(b)	3	4	1	2
(c)	4	3	2	1	(d)	3	4	2	1

15 Narayan Murthy Committee revised its recommendations on Corporate Governance as on 29th October, 2004, which diluted the following areas?

1. Independence of directors
2. Whistle blower policy
3. Performance evaluation of non-executive directors
4. Mandatory training of non-executive directors

Select the correct answer using the codes given below

Codes

(a) 1,2 and 3 (b) Both 1 and 3
(c) 1,2 and 4 (d) All of these

16 In addition to motivation, learning and memory, which one of the following is included in the main psychological processes affecting consumer behaviour?

(a) Perception (b) Life cycle (c) Lifestyle (d) Social class

17 Find out the correct combination of statements with regards to business ethics.

1. Business ethics is the behaviour that a business adheres to in its daily dealings.
2. The ethics of a particular business can be diverse.
3. Business ethics has normative and descriptive dimensions.

Select the correct answer using the codes given below

Codes

(a) Both 1 and 2 (b) Both 1 and 3
(c) Both 2 and 3 (d) All of these

18 Which one of the following is not correct about business ethics?

(a) Business ethics reflects the philosophy of business
(b) Business ethics is a form of applied ethics
(c) Business ethics are governed by the government policies
(d) Ethics are the standards which governed decisions on daily basis

December 2014

19 According to which theory, people are motivated to the extent to which they expect that their actions will help in achievement of goals?

(a) Vroom's Vector Valence Theory
(b) Need Theory
(c) Z Theory (d) X Theory

20 Match the following.

List I	List II
A. Getting effective leadership in the industrial organisation	1. Dale Yoder
B. The nature of leadership, organisation and management	2. Alford and Beatty
C. Industrial management	3. Douglas McGregor
D. Personnel management	4. Chester I Barnard

Codes

	A	B	C	D		A	B	C	D
(a)	1	2	3	4	(b)	3	4	2	1
(c)	3	4	1	2	(d)	4	3	2	1

June 2014

21 Who has modified Maslow's hierarchical levels of needs and developed ERG model?

(a) Frederick Herzberg
(b) David C McClelland
(c) Douglas McGregor
(d) Clayton Alderfer

22 Where does recognition of an employee fall in Maslow's Hierarchy of Needs theory?

(a) Self actualisation needs (b) Security needs
(c) Social needs (d) Esteem needs

December 2013

23 Match the following.

List I	List II
A. Abraham Maslow	1. Achievement Motivation Theory
B. Herzberg	2. ERG Theory
C. Alderfer	3. Two Factor Theory
D. McClelland	4. Need Hierarchy Theory

Codes

	A	B	C	D		A	B	C	D
(a)	1	2	3	4	(b)	4	3	2	1
(c)	3	4	1	2	(d)	4	3	3	1

June 2013

24 Who has suggested that achievement motivation among individuals and nations can be developed through training courses?

(a) McClelland (b) Alderfer
(c) Maslow (d) Herzberg

25 Which of the following are sources of ethics?

1. Religion 2. Legal system
3. Economic system 4. Culture
5. Family system

Select the correct answer using the codes given below

Codes

(a) 1,2,3 and 5 (b) 1,2 and 4
(c) 1,4 and 5 (d) All of the above

December 2012

26 Who did give the concept of hierarchy of needs?
(a) Frederick Herzberg (b) Victor Vroom
(c) Douglas McGregor (d) AH Maslow

27 Appointment of independent directors is the part of corporate governance as per the
(a) SEBI (b) Indian Companies Act
(d) Government of India (d) RBI

28 While establishing relations between Maslow's and Herzberg's theories, which needs of hierarchy theory will fall under the hygiene factors?
(a) Self actualisation, esteem and social needs
(b) Esteem, social and safety needs
(c) Social, safety and physiological needs
(d) Only social needs

ANSWERS

Objective Questions

1 (d)	2 (b)	3 (b)	4 (a)	5 (c)	6 (d)	7 (d)	8 (c)	9 (d)	10 (a)
11 (a)	12 (b)	13 (b)	14 (a)	15 (c)	16 (d)	17 (d)	18 (d)	19 (b)	20 (c)
21 (d)	22 (a)	23 (c)	24 (b)	25 (c)	26 (c)	27 (d)	28 (b)	29 (b)	30 (d)
31 (a)	32 (b)	33 (b)	34 (a)	35 (b)	36 (a)	37 (b)	38 (a)	39 (c)	40 (b)
41 (d)	42 (c)	43 (b)	44 (d)	45 (c)	46 (c)	47 (a)	48 (b)	49 (c)	50 (a)
51 (a)									

Previous Years' Questions

1 (c)	2 (c)	3 (a)	4 (a)	5 (d)	6 (b)	7 (d)	8 (a)	9 (c)	10 (b)
11 (a)	12 (c)	13 (b)	14 (a)	15 (a)	16 (a)	17 (d)	18 (c)	19 (a)	20 (b)
21 (d)	22 (d)	23 (b)	24 (b)	25 (d)	26 (a)	27 (a)	28 (c)		

CHAPTER 23

Human Resource Management and Planning

Human resource work as a backbone of an organisation. So, it is a prime function of management to manage and plan human resources for high production and accomplishment of organisational goals. Human resource management process starts from recruitment and includes training and development. Succession planning encourages HR to hire from within and create a healthy environment where employees have career.

In this Chapter

- Human Resource
- Human Resource Planning
- Recruitment
- Selection
- Training
- Development
- Succession Planning
- Stress and its Management

Human Resource

Manpower is the most important resource of an organisation, without which organisation cannot exist. All the resources in an organisation are divided into two parts *i.e.* active and passive. Active means human beings, while land, machines, money and materials etc are passive means for production. An organisation may have large quantity of passive means for production, but have no use until the active means are effectively and efficiently used.

Human resource is concerned with the human beings in an organisation. It reflects a new philosophy, a new outlook, approach and strategy.

Concept of Human Resource Management

Human resource management refers to that part of management, which manages the people at work. HRM is the process, which coordinate people with organisation and helps both people and organisation to achieve each other goal.

In HRM, various policies and washing methods are designed to help both the parties to achieve their goal. An organisation is a group of people, so it is necessary to develop their skills, provide them motivation. HRM is responsible for the relationship between organisation and employees.

According to **Edwin Flippo**, "Planning, organising, directing, controlling of procurement, development, compensation, integration, maintenance and separation of human resources to the end that individual, organisational and social objectives are achieved."

Role of Human Resource Management

The role of Human Resource Management (HRM) is to hire, train and develop staff and maintain discipline or harmony in an organisation. They also provide effective training and their full potential. This reduces the need for external recruitment and makes maximum use of existing talent. This is a cost effective way for a business to manage its people.

Features of Human Resource Management

- It is one of the branches of management, where persons working in an organisation are treated as a resource.
- In HRM, employees' social and psychological needs are also taken care.
- It is quite different from personal management.
- It is the management of employees, abilities working skills, talents etc.

Functions of Human Resource Management

Managerial Function

Planning In regard to human development, planning is the process of setting-up of objectives and causes of action of transforming raw individuals on selection to highly motivated and empowered employees. Plan also carries out SWOT analysis and work out action plans to exploit Strength (S) and Opportunities (O) fully, while minimising effects of Weakness (W) and Threats (T).

Organising In regard to HRM, organising function is concerned with mobilising and planning human resources in an orderly manner in order to meet the objectives of the organisation.

Directing Function of directing involves three activities *viz* leading the team/group, motivating employees, communicating ideas, information and instructions.

Coordination It deals with the task of blending efforts in order to ensure a successful attainment of an objective. This is especially important in the area of HRM because lack of understanding and appreciation of each others' view points can conflict with clash of interests. This lease to low productivity and poor interpersonal and intergroup relationships.

Control It ensures that action plans are executed as effectively as possible within the time frame and cost frame envisaged in the plan.

It consists of the following three activities

- Setting-up standard for each objective or task.
- Measurement of deviations between actual output/ performance against the standard set.
- Initiate the corrective action, when deviations are beyond the limits specified.

Staffing Function

Acquisition and Absorption This function consists of activities like recruitment, selection and induction.

Development and Utilisation These function consists of activities like employees training, executive development programme and career growth plans.

Maintenance and Retention These activities provide conducive working condition, which promote high level of productivity and high state of physical and mental health.

Motivation and Empowerment This involves behaviour modification programme, whereby positive attitude is developed in the employees, so that they become innovatively competent, take genuine interest in their job and above all become strongly committed to the organisational objectives.

VRIO Framework

Every organisation goes through VRIO process which begins with a vision statement and continues on through objectives, internal and external analysis, strategic choices and strategic implementation. It is based on four questions, *which are as follows*

- ***Value*** Is the firm able to exploit on opportunity or neutralise an external threat with capability?
- ***Rarity*** Is control of the resource in the hands of a relative few?
- ***Imitability*** Is it difficult to imitate and will there be significant cost disadvantage to a firm trying to obtain, develop or duplicate?
- ***Organisation*** Is the firm organised, ready and able to exploit the resource capability?

Human Resource Planning

Human Resource Planning (HRP) is essentially the process of getting the right number of qualified people into the right job at the right time, so that an organisation can meet its objectives. It is a system of matching the supply of people with the demand the organisation expects over a given time frame. In order to realise company objectives, it is essential to have a human resource plan.

According to **Geisler**, "As a process of forecasting, developing and controlling human resources in an enterprise. This process helps the enterprise to ensure that it has right number of people and the right kind of people at the right place at the right time performing tasks for which they are most effective."

Characteristics of Human Resource Planning

The chief objective of human resource planning is to find out different categories of employees required by the organisation and choosing them for appropriate jobs in a cost effective way.

The following are its characteristics

- HR planning aims at achieving the organisational objectives by effective use of human resources.
- It includes effective decision-making related to human resource through systematic analysis of data/collected in a scientific objective manner.
- It not only fulfill the short-term HR requirement of an organisation, but also provide long-term strategies for the future HR needs.
- It is a continuous process, which includes of number related activities for HR planning.

Scope of Human Resource Planning

- Estimation of manpower requirement *i.e.* number and type of personnel required at different levels in organisation and recruitment and selection of right type of persons for various jobs in the organisation.
- Allocation of human resources to different departments as per the workload and needs of the department. Allocation of manpower is also made as per the qualification and qualities of persons selected.
- Manpower motivation, which depend on various factors such as wages and salaries, monetary and non-monetary incentives, leave, welfare and recreation facilities etc.

Recruitment

Every organisation need people with requisite skills, qualifications and experience to deliver outstanding results. Thus, recruiting becomes a demanding job and requires serious attention from top management.

Recruitment is the process of locating and encouraging potential applicants to apply for existing or anticipated job openings.

Thus, recruitment aims at

- attracting a large number of qualified applicants who are ready to take up the job.
- offering enough information for unqualified persons to self, select themselves out.
- creating a positive image of the firm in such a way that even unsuccessful applicants tend to develop positive attitudes towards the company and its products.

According to **Edwin B Flippo**, "Recruitment is defined as the process of searching for prospective employees and stimulating them to apply for jobs in the organisation."

The best results in recruitment would came only, when there is a fit between organisational recruitment efforts and a candidate's job search efforts.

Objectives of Recruitment

- To attract potential employees with necessary qualifications and skills for the vacant jobs.
- To search for fresh talent suitable for the vacant job.
- To stimulate more and more people for applying for vacant jobs in an organisation.
- To design entry process through which competent persons entered in an organisation to fulfill manpower requirement.

Need for Recruitment

- It is a process of searching for prospective employees and stimulating them to apply for vacant jobs in the organisation.
- *These vacancies may arise on account of the following*
  - (a) Creation of a new post in the organisation due to expention, diversification and increase in the work load of existing employees etc.
  - (b) Vacancies due to resignation/termination or retirement etc.

Sources of Recruitment

The sources of recruitment may be broadly divided into two categories, *i.e.* internal sources and external sources. Both have their own merits and demerits.

These are as follows

Internal Sources

Persons who are already working in an organisation constitute the internal sources. Retrenched employees, retired employees, dependents of deceased employees may also constitute the internal sources. Whenever any vacancy arises someone from within the organisation is upgraded, transferred, promoted or even demoted. *Internal sources of recruitment are as follows*

- Promotion
- Transfer
- Trainees
- Informal search
- Extension of services
- Lent services
- Internal advertisement

Advantages of Internal Sources of Recruitment

- The employees skill, capability and performance are already known and also the employee is familiar with the organisation's culture.
- As the employees are already familiar with the work culture, so time required to train them is reduced.
- Policy of preferring people from within motivate employees to earn promotion.
- Cost of recruiting internal candidates is minimal as no expenses are incurred on advertising.

Disadvantages of Internal Sources of Recruitment

- Option is limited in locating right talent.
- It discourages entry of talented people available outside an organisation.
- Promotions based on length of service rather than merit may demotivate efficient candidates.
- Recruitment from within may lead to infighting among employees aspiring for limited, higher level position in an organisation.

External Sources

External sources lie outside an organisation.

External sources of recruitment are as follows

- Employees working in other organisations.
- Job aspirants registered with employment exchange.
- Students from reputed educational institutions.
- Candidates referred by unions, friends and relatives.
- Candidates forwarded by search firms and contractors.

Advantages of External Sources of Recruitment

- Organisation has wide choice and freedom to select candidates from large pool.
- Improve knowledge and skill of the organisation by upgradation from external inputs.
- It helps in motivating internal employees to work hard and compete with external candidates, while seeking career growth.
- Long-term benefits for the organisation as talented people join the ranks.

Disadvantages of External Sources of Recruitment

- It is expensive.
- Time consuming as it takes time to advertise, screen and select suitable employees.
- Demotivate existing employees as they feel that their services have not been recognised by the organisation.
- Uncertainty in hiring the services of suitable candidates.

Procedure for Recruitment

Requisition

It is the first step, in which requisitioning of workers is done by the supervisor in whose department vacancies arise. It should state clearly the numbers of workers required and should be accompanied by the relevant job specification.

Advertising

The next step will be for the employment department to write to the employment exchange or advertise the vacancy in the newspapers asking the candidates to send applications giving their qualifications or tap some other source of labour. On receipt of applications from candidates or employment exchange, the recruitment office should eliminate the candidates who are unqualified for the job and prepare a list of candidates who are eligible for the job.

Application Blank

A competency based application form should be used for each vacancy, which identifies the main competencies specifies to that role. The application form can be shortened to include a limited number of competencies depending on the vacancy.

Some concerns have the practice of asking candidates to come for interview and fill up 'blanks' then and there. Filling up the application blank provides fair opportunity to those who do not feel at ease in the interview, but can write down their answers without any hesitation.

Trade Tests

It is generally required for those jobs, which involve technical work. For recruitment of a stenographer in an office, a test can be given to check up his speed both at dictation and typing.

Psychological Tests

Acting on the principle that individuals differ from one another by degree through not in kind, psychologists have devised certain tests, which seek to measure the psychological characteristics of individual applicants for a position. It consists in giving to the applicant a task, which is representative of the job for which he is being considered. His performance on the task is evaluated relative to that of the other candidates.

Interviewing

When being invited to interview, candidates should be asked to advise the authority in advance of any particular arrangements needed to accommodate them on arrival or during the interview. Its purpose is definitely not to confuse the candidate. Therefore, it must be conducted in a friendly atmosphere and the candidate must be made to feel at ease. Infact, in some concerns, it is the only tool of selection.

Medical Test

It is important to select a worker on the basis of medical test because a person of poor health may generally be absent and the training given to him may go waste and the disease may spread amongst other workers.

On-the-job Test and Selection

It is on the basis of the results of these various tests that the candidate would be finally selected, but before he is given a job on permanent basis, it would be better to try him out for a few weeks in a factory itself.

By observing a candidate at work it will be known whether he can do his job properly or not. Therefore, it is only after a trial for a few weeks that the person concerned should be treated as finally selected.

Selection

Selection involves a series of steps by which candidates are screened for choosing the most suitable persons for vacant jobs in the organisation. Selection leads to employment of personnel and is an integral part of staffing.

It facilitates selection of candidates, who possess the ability and qualifications to perform the jobs, which have fallen vacant in an organisation. It divides the candidates for employment into two categories, namely "those who will be offered employment and those who will not be".

Selection is a negative process as it involves rejection of unsuitable candidates. More candidates are rejected than are selected. Selection involves several steps to weed out the unsuitable candidates for the job under consideration. Criteria are laid down at each stage. Those who don't fulfil these criteria are rejected.

According to **Dale Yoder**, "Selection is the process of choosing among the candidates from within the organisation or from the outside, the most suitable person for the current position or for the future position."

Selection Process

Selection is a long process, commencing from the preliminary interview of the applicants and ending with the contract of employment. Selection is usually a series of handles or steps. Each one must be successfully cleared before the applicant proceeds to the next. The time and emphasis placed on each step will of course vary from job-to-job and organisation-to-organisation. The sequencing of steps may also vary from job-to-job and organisation-to-organisation. *e.g.* Some organisation may give importance to testing while, other may emphasise interviews and reference checks. *The process is as follows*

Preliminary Interview

The applicants received from job seekers would be subjected to scrutiny, so as to eliminate unqualified applicants. Preliminary interview helps to reject misfit applicants.

Selection Tests

Job seekers who pass the screening and the preliminary interview are called for test. Different types of tests may be administered depending on the job and the company. Generally, tests are used to determine the applicant's ability, aptitude and personality.

Ability test assist in determining, how well an individual can perform tasks related to the job. An aptitude tests determine a person's potential to learn in a given area. Personality test measure a prospective employee's motivation to function in a particular working environment.

Employment Interview

The next step in the selection process is employment interview. Interview is formal, in-depth conservation conducted to evaluate the applicant's acceptability. It allows two way exchange of information, the interviewer learns about the applicant and applicant learns about the employer. *Employment interview can be*

- One-to-one
- Sequential
- Panel

Reference and Background Checks

Although listed on the application form, references are not usually checked until an applicant has successfully reached the fourth stage of a sequential selection process. Reference and background checks gives additional information about the applicant. But when labour market is tight, organisations sometimes hire applicants before checking references. Previous employers, know public figures university professors, neighbours or friends can act as references. In several cases, references are a formality and are seldom verified by the employer.

Selection Decision

After obtaining information through the preceeding steps, selection decision is made from the pool of candidates who pass the test, interviews and reference checks. The views of the line manager will be generally considered in the final selection because he/she is responsible for the performance of the new employee. The HR manager plays crucial role in the final selection.

Physical Examination

After the selection decision and before the job offer is made, the candidate is required to undergo a physical fitness test. A job offer is, often contingent upon the candidate being declared fit after the physical examination. Objectives behind physical test is detected, if individual causes any infection disease and physical fit to perform the work. Such test also protect the employers from workers compensation claims.

Job Offer

It is the next step in selection process to those applicants who have crossed all the previous hurdles. Job offer is made through a letter of appointment. Such a letter generally contains a date by which the appointee must report on duty. Rejected application are informed about their non-selection and their applications are preserved for future use.

Contracts of Employment

After the job offer has been made and the candidates accept the offer, contract of employment is prepared. The basic information that is included in written contract of employment vary according to the level of job.

Selection process does not end with executing employment contract, but it ends with searching those candidates, who have not been selected. Rejected candidates must be told that they were not selected because of any series deficiencies in their personalities and their profile did not match the requirement of the organisation.

Training

After employees have been selected for various positions in an organisation, training given to them for the specific tasks to which they have been assigned and assumes great importance. Training is the act of increasing the knowledge and skills of an employee for performing a particular job. It enables an employee to do his present job more efficiently and prepare himself for a higher level job. Training is the act of increasing the knowledge and skill of an employee for doing a particular job.

According to **Flippo**, "Training is the process by which manpower is filled for the particular jobs to perform."

Types of Training

Training programmes can be categorised by industrial concerns for different specific purposes.

Accordingly training of workers may be of following types

Induction Training It refers to the initial training, provided to employees. Its basic objective is to introduce the employee to the business/department and its personnel/management structure of the organisation. Under it, employee is familiarise with layout of building (factory/offices), terms and conditions of employment, business rules and procedures and revelent personnel policies, such as training, promotion, health and safety etc. It provides general idea about the organisation to the employee.

Job Training The objective of job training is to increase the knowledge of workers about the jobs with which they are concerned, so that their efficiency and skill enhance. Job training enables the worker to learn correct methods of handling machines and equipments, which results in avoiding accidents, wastage and accumulation of work etc.

Promotional Training Many organisations have adopted a policy of filling some of the vacancies through promotion from existing employees. When existing employees are promoted in an organisation, they are required to bear additional responsibilities. For this, it is necessary to provide them proper training.

Refresher Training At the time of appointment, employees are formally trained, but with the passage of time, many of the methods and instructions may be forgotten or some of the methods or all of them may have become out-dated because of technological advancement. Hence, refresher training is arranged for existing employees in order to give them opportunity to refresh and improve their skills and knowledge.

Improvement in Adaptability Continuous training stimulates mental development of the worker which change their mind set and they become keen to learn about new technologies.

Training Methods

These are classified into two broad categories depending upon location of instruction. *These are as follows*

On-the-job Training Methods

On-the-job training is provided, when the workers are taught relevant knowledge, skills and abilities at the actual work place. *It includes*

Job Instruction Training (JIT) The JIT method is used primarily to teach workers how to do their current job. A trainer supervisor or co-worker acts as the coach. Here, trainee learns fast through practice and observation. It is economical as it does not require any special setting and the trainee gains confidence quickly as he does the work himself in actual setting with help from supervisor. Demerits of this method is that, while learning trainee may damage equipment, waste materials and can cause accidents frequently.

Coaching It is a kind of daily training and feedback given to employees by immediate supervisors. In coaching, supervisor explain things, answer questions and threw light on why things are done the way they are. Coaching method favours learning by doing. Its effectiveness depends on the capacity and the interest taken by the superior and also by the subordinate but trainee cannot develop much beyond the limits of his own superior abilities.

Mentoring It is a relationship, in which a senior manager in an organisation assumes the responsibility for grooming a junior person. The main objective of mentoring is to help an employee attain psychological maturity and effectiveness and get integrated with the organisation. In a work situation, such mentoring can take place at both formal and informal level, depending on the prevailing work culture and the commitment from the top management.

Job Rotation This kind of training involves the movement of trainee from one job to another. Purpose of job rotation is to provide trainees with a larger organisational perspective and a greater understanding of different functional areas. The cross-trained personnel offer a great amount of flexibility for organisations.

Apprenticeship Training Apprentices are trainees who spend a prescribed amount of time working with an experienced guide or trainer. Assistantships and internships are similar to apprenticeships. They also demand high levels of participation from the trainee. An internship is a kind of the on-the-job training that usually combines job training with classroom instruction in trade schools, colleges or universities.

Committee Assignments In this method, trainees are asked to solve an actual organisational problem. The trainees have to work together and offer solution to the problem.

Off-the-job Training Methods

Under this method of training, the trainee is seperated from the job situation and his attention is focused upon learning the material related to his future job performance. *Off-the-job training methods are as follows*

Vestibule Training In this method, actual work conditions are simulated in a classroom. Materials, files and equipment those that are used in actual job performance are also used in training. The duration of this training ranges from few days to a few weeks.

Role Playing It has been defined as a method of human interaction, which involves realistic behaviour in the imaginary situations. In the role playing training, a conflict situation is artificially created and two or more trainees are assigned different roles to play. Then both may be given a typical work situation and asked to respond as they expect others to do. Such role playing result in better understanding among individuals and helps to promote interpersonal, relations and attitude change.

Lecture Method The lecture is a traditional and direct method of instruction. The instructor organises the material and gives it to a group of trainees in the form of talk. Lecture method is direct and can be used for a large group of trainees, thus costs and time involved are reduced.

Conference/Discussion Approach In this method, the trainer delivers a lecture and involves the trainee in a discussion, so that his doubts about the job get classified. This gives additional information to participants and enables them to use the same in their daily routine.

Programmed Instruction In this method, subject matter to be learned is presented in a series of carefully planned sequential units. These units are arranged from simple to more complex level of instructions. The trainees goes through these units by answering questions or filling the blanks.

Virtual Organisation and E-learning Virtual organisation is a temporary network of companies that come together quickly to exploit fast changing opportunities. A virtual classroom employs special collaboration software to enable multiple remote learner, using their PCs or laptops to participate in live audio and visual discussions, communicate *via* written text and learn *via* content such as power point presentation.

E-learning methods include training delivered by CD-ROM, intranet or internet, satellite broadcasts and digital collaboration between partners willing to learn from each other.

Behaviourally Experienced Training In this method, employees learn about behaviour by role playing in which the role players attempt to act their part in respect of a case, as they would behave in real life situation. Business games, cases, incidents, group discussions and short assignments are also used in behaviourally experienced learning method.

Evaluation of a Training Programme The process of training evaluation has been defined as any attempt to obtain information on the effects of training performance and to assess the value of training in the light of that information. Thus, training evaluation checks whether training had the desired impact or not.

Development

Development is an education process as it tries to enhance ones ability to understand and interpret knowledge in a useful way. Development is different from training as it is often the result of experience and maturity that comes with it.

Features of Development

- It is a planned effort to improve executive's ability to handle a variety of assignments.
- It is long-term infact continuous and ongoing process.
- It aims at improving the total personality of an executive.
- It is proactive in nature as it focuses attention on the present as well as future requirements of both the organisation and the individual.

Methods of Management Development Programmes

Developing managers can opt for any of the following methods

Decision-making Skills

- In basket
- Business game
- Case study

Job Knowledge

- On-the-job experience
- Coaching and understudy

Inter-personal Skills

- Role play
- Sensitivity training
- Behaviour modelling

Off-the-job method includes

- Conferences
- Lectures
- Group discussion
- Programmed instruction

The sources of any management development programme largely depend on selection of the method. The objectives of the programme should be kept in mind, while choosing a particular method. In fact, no single technique is sufficient, so as suitable combination of techniques is selected to achieve good result.

Difference between Training and Development

Basis	Training	Development
Definition	Training means imparting skills and knowledge for doing a particular job.	Development means the growth of an employee in all respects.
Depth of Knowledge and Skills	It imparts job related technical skills. Training revolves around the job only.	It involves all round knowledge of present and future jobs. It shapes attitudes and imparts technical, human and conceptual skills.
Purpose	Training is concerned with maintaining and improving current job performance.	Executive development seeks to develop competence and skills for future performance.
Scope of Learning and Level of Trainees	The term 'Training' is used in the sense of imparting specific skills among operative workers and employees.	The term 'Development' is associated with the overall growth of the executives. Depth of knowledge gained is very wide.
Orientation or Focus	Training is job centred in nature. It seeks to make the workers proficient in their existing jobs.	Development is career centred in nature. It seeks to prepare the employees for handling higher level jobs.
Methods	It is imparted through on-the-job methods like coaching, job rotation etc.	It is based more on off-the-job methods such as lectures, conference etc.
Initiative	The boss takes initiative for imparting training to his subordinates. The role of the boss or trainer is very important in training.	The individual takes the initiative for self growth and development. He has to be internally motivated for self development.
Duration	Training programmes are organised for short-terms.	Development takes place over a larger period of time.

Succession Planning

The purpose of succession planning is to identify and develop people to replace current job holders in key positions. Through succession planning, companies assure a steady flow of internal talent to fill important vacancies. Succession planning encourages hiring from within and creates a healthy environment, where employees have careers and not merely jobs.

It helps in identifying human resource shortages and skill shortages before opening occur. Thereafter, it becomes easy to grasp qualified candidates for future vacancies. The organisation is, thus assured about continuity of operations and better qualified incumbents.

Succession planning increases the availability of experienced and capable employee that are prepared to assume these roles as they become available.

Objectives of Succession Planning

Research indicates that clear objectives are critical to establish effective succession planning. *These objectives tend to be core to many or most companies that have well established practices*

- Identify those with the potential to assume greater responsibility in the organisation.

- Provide critical development experiences to those that can move into key roles.
- Engage the leadership in supporting the development of high potential leaders.
- Build a data base that can be used to make better staffing decisions for key jobs.

Benefits of Succession Planning

- It enables the senior management to review the leadership talent available with in the organisation.
- It ensures the continuity of leadership in the organisation.
- It guides the promotion policies of the organisation. It eusures that the right people are promoted at the right time.
- It analyses human resource process like selection, appraisal and management development in the organisation.

Process of Succession Planning

Identify Critical Positions Critical positions are the focus of succession planning efforts. Without these roles, the department or agency would be unable to effectively meet its business objectives. Workforce projection data or demographic analysis is essential in identifying risk areas. A risk assessment may also be conducted and compared to current and future vacancies to identify critical positions within your organisation.

Identify Competencies A clear understanding of capabilities needed for successful performance in key areas and critical position is essential for guiding learning and development plans, setting clear performance expectations and for assessing performance. Through this process, current and future employees gain an understanding of the key responsibilities of the position including the qualifications and behavioural and technical competencies required to perform them successfully.

Identify Succession Management Strategies The next step here is to choose from a menu of several human resource strategies, including developing internal talent pools, on boarding and recruitment to address succession planning.

Document and Implement Succession Plans Once strategies have been identified, the next step is to document the strategies in an action plan. It provides a mechanism for clearly defining timelines and roles and responsibilities.

Evaluate Effectiveness To ensure that the department or agency's succession planning efforts are successful, it is important to systematically monitor workforce data, evaluate activities and make necessary adjustments.

Strategies for Successful Succession Planning

- It is important to customise succession planning to suit the company's needs. If an organisation cannot find a person, who can manage the company in the changed environment, an outsider might have to be brought in.
- Succession planning should develop key candidates through job rotation, mentoring and formal training programmes.
- Succession planning must take into account the organisational culture.
- It must be consistent with the company's strategic direction.

Career Planning and Succession Planning

The term 'career planning' and 'succession planning' are not synonymous, but they are similar. Succession planning is generally needed for key positions at higher levels. While career planning covers executives at all levels including high skilled employees and operatives.

Career planning includes succession planning. The career paths for executives are identified and how people can grow vertically is also indicated. In case of vacancy arising at any level, the career plan is well supported by a succession chart. Both are thus complimentary and interdependent.

Personality

Personality and personality development are one of the key concepts in human resource development. By personality, we mean the psyche and determine how an individual interact within its environment.

Personality is determined by a number of factors including the traits that one is endowed with as a result of genetic factors and characteristics that have been developed due to his interaction with the enviornment.

Types of Personality

Extrovert Personality This type has the tendency to live mostly outside the like to live with others. Those individuals are highly socialised and have contact with outside people in society.

Introvert Personality It is opposite to extrovert. These people always live alone and have their own imaginary world.

Ambivert Personality Beside extrovert and introvert personalities, there is a third type called ambivert. These people enjoy both the groups and attend them.

Importance of Personality

- It can help in motivating employees.
- It can reduce turnover because it utilise an employment assessment.
- It can decrease conflicts and improve collaboration.
- It can prevent burnouts.
- It can help in effective communication.

Perception

It means perceiving, *i.e.* giving meaning to the environment around us. It can be defined as a process which involves, seeing, receiving, selecting, organising, interpreting and giving meaning to the environment.

Nature of Perception

- It is the intellectual process.
- It is the basic cognitive or psychological process.
- It becomes a subjective process and different people may perceive the same event differently.

Factors Influencing Perception

Internal Factors *These are as follows*

Self Concept The way a person views the world depends a great deal on the concept or image he has about himself.

Beliefs A person's beliefs have profound influence on his perception. Thus, a fact is conceived not on what it is but what a person believes it to be.

Expectations These affect what a person perceives.

Response Disposition It refers to a person's tendency to perceive familiar stimuli rather than unfamiliar ones.

External Factors *These are as follows*

Size Bigger size attracts the attention of perceiver.

Intensity A loud, strong or bright light is noticed more as compared to a soft sound.

Repetition A repeated external stimulus is more attention getting than a single one.

Contrast It is a kind of uniqueness which can be used for attention like getting letters of bold types, person dressed differently than others get more attention.

Motion A moving object draws more attention as compared to a stationary object.

Attitudes

It is a predisposition or a tendency to respond positively or negatively towards a certain idea, object, person or situation. Attitude influences an individuals' choice of action and responses to challenges, incentives and rewards.

Components of Attitude

Affective Emotions or feelings.

Congnitive Belief or opinions held consciously.

Conative Inclination for action.

Evaluative Positive or negative response.

Role of Attitude in HRM

Attitude plays an important role in improving the relationship among the individuals. An individual should never ever have a negative attitude at workplace. One should not be too rigid and should not make issues out of small things. An individuals should always keep his personal life separate from his professional affairs.

Nature of Attitude

- Attitude is a complex combination of things, we tend to call personality, beliefs, values, behaviours and motivation.
- An attitude exists in every person's mind. It helps to define our identity, guide our actions and influence how we judge people.
- Attitude helps us define how we see situations as well as define how we behave toward the situation.
- It refers to the degree of likeliness or unlikeliness toward the incident.
- It refers to the amount of features creating the attitude and reach personal goals, developing others, leadership, conflict management and teamwork.

Emotions

The emotions of a human being can be love, hatred, anger and happiness. The manager has to control these emotions to a certain extent so that they can handle any situation.

According to **Dr Goleman**, "Emotional intelligence is defined as a set of skills or competencies, which provide human resource professionals, managers with a comprehensive tool to define, measure and develop emotional skills."

Dimensions of Emotions

There are five dimensions of emotions in HRM, *which are as follows*

- Knowing one's emotions.
- Controlling one's emotions.
- Recognising emotions in others.
- Controlling emotions in others.
- Improvement in emotional control.

Components of Emotions

Self-awareness The capacity for understanding one's emotions, strengths, weakness and self-confidence.

Self-management It is the capacity for efficiently managing one's motives and regulating one's behaviour, self-control, orientation and initiative.

Social Awareness It is the capacity for understanding what others are saying and feeling. And why they feel and act as they do.

Social Skill It is the capacity for acting in such a way that one is able to get the desired results from others and reach personal goals, developing others, leadership, conflict management and teamwork.

Benefits of Emotional Intelligence in HRM

Judicious applications of emotional intelligence can lead the following results

- It helps in understanding and enhancing emotional intelligence enhances management skills.
- It can provide team effectiveness.
- It assists managers to have flexible planning.
- Better decision-making comes from a balance between head and heart.
- It can help a person achieve a whole range of career development factors such as leadership, decision-making, open communication, trusting relationship and customer loyalty.

Group Dynamics

It deals with the attitudes and behavioural patterns of a group. It is concerned with the interactions and forces operating between groups.

Every organisation is a group into itself. A group refer to two or more people who share a common meaning and evaluation of themselves and come together to achieve common goals.

Characteristics of Group

Except size and purpose, every group has following features

- It consists two or more persons.
- It has formal social structure.
- It has common goal.
- All members are interdependent and compliment to each other.
- Face-to-face interaction takes place.

Stages of Group Development

Forming The first stage of a group is formation. In this stage, members seeking either a work assignment or other common benefit form a group.

Storming In this stage, members seek out familiar or similar individuals and begin a deeper sharing of self.

Norming The third stage of group development is marked by a more serious concern about task performance. Members begin to take greater responsibility for their own group and relationship while the authority figures become relaxed.

Performing This is a fully functional group where members see themselves as a group and get involved in the task.

Power

Power refers to the possession of authority and influence over others.

It is the ability to cause or prevent an action, make things happen. Power is an instrument transferring or vesting legal authorisation and alter the rights, duties, liabilities and other legal relations of himself or others.

Need of Power

- To provide direction.
- Get fast access to decision makers.
  Maintain regular, frequent contact with decision makers.
- Assisting in the management process.
- Assist employess in performing better.

Types of Power

Coercive Power It is the ability of a manager to force an employee to follow an order by threatning the employee with punishment, if the employee does not comply with the order.

Legitimate Power It is the power derived from formal position or office held in the organisation's hierarchy of authority.

Reward Power It is simply the power of a manager to give some type of reward to an employee as a means to influence the employee to act.

Referent Power It is the power of an individual over the team or followers, based on a high level of identification with admiration of or respect for the leader.

Expert Power This is the based upon employees perception that a manager or some other member of an organisation has a high level of knowledge or a specialised set of skills that other members of the organisation do not possess.

Positive Impacts of Power

- It enhances leadership responsibilities among managers.
- It helps in achieving personal and organisational goals.
- It inspire commitment.
- It enhances creativity in the organisation.
- It reduces bureaucratic obstacles.

Politics

Work place politics is the use of power and social networking within an organisation to achieve changes that benefit the organisation or individual within it. Influence by individuals may serve personal interests without regard to their effect on organisation itself.

Causes of Political Behaviour

- Never ending change is the cause of political behaviour, as a manager is faced with a constant barrage of initiatives.
- Rationing of resources are reason for political behaviour.
- Cuts in the cost base often reduce opportunities for promotion, so it needs political behaviour,
- Matrix structures and an orientation to project team often.

Types of Politics

Attacking and Blaming In this, others are targeted and blamed and faults are not accepted by individuals.

Controlling Information Maintaining secrets, incomplete information, wrong information or destroying information are the main features of this politics.

Forming Coalition In this, negative aspects are formed on others. Groupism and rationalism also comes in this category.

Effects of Politics

- It decreases job satisfaction.
- It increases anxiety and stress.
- It also decreases an overall productivity.
- It affects concentration and spoil the ambience.
- It changes the attitude of employees.

Conflict

It occurs whenever deviations exist in a social situation over issues of substances. Every aspect of organisational life that creates order and coordination of effort must overcome other tendencies to action and in that fact lies the potentiality for conflict.

Causes of Conflict

Filley recognised various main conditions which could cause conflict situations in an organisation. *These are as follows*

- Ambiguous jurisdiction, which occurs when two individuals have responsibilities which are interdependent but whose work boundaries and role definition are not clearly specified.
- Dependence on one party by another group or individual can also cause conflict among employees of an organisation.
- Communication barriers can cause conflict as difficulties in communicating can cause misunderstanding.
- Organisation have to make firm regulations for individual behaviour to ensure protection and safety. Individuals may perceive these regulations differently which can cause conflict.
- When individuals specialised in different areas work in a group, they may disagree amongst themselves because they have different goals, views and experience.

Consequences of Conflict

Positive Consequences *Positive consequences of conflict are as follows*

- It leads to new ideas.
- It stimulates creativity and innovation.
- It promotes organisational vitality.
- It helps individuals and groups to establish identities.
- It increases loyalty and performance within each of the groups.

Negative Consequences *Negative consequences of conflict are as follows*

- It diverts energy from work.
- It wastes resources.
- It reduces the organisation's capacity to complete in the marketplace.
- It can increase hostility and aggressive behaviours.
- It creates negative climate in the organisation.

Negotiation

Negotiation is an open process for two parties to find a satisfactory solution to a complex conflict. In an organisational context, negotiation may took place between two people, within a group or between the groups.

Types of Negotiation

Distributive Negotiation In it, the gain made by one person is loss incurred by the other person. Each person involved in the negotiation defines ultimate point where the settlement will be made. It creates win-lose situation.

Integrative Negotiation In this, the parties cooperate to achieve maximise benefits by integrating their interests. Both parties involved in negotiation process jointly look at the problem, try to search for alternatives and try to evaluate them and reach a mutually acceptable decision or solution, it creates win-win situation.

Factors Influencing Negotiation

There are many conditions that affects the success or failure of negotiations, which are as follows

Interdependence For prolific negotiations, the contributors must be dependent upon each other to have their needs met or interests satisfied.

Readiness to Negotiate Individuals must be ready to negotiate for conversation to begin. When participants are not mentally equipped to talk with the other parties or when a negotiation scheme has not been prepared, people may be unwilling to begin the process.

Agreement on Some Issues and Interests People must be able to agree upon some common issues and interests for good negotiations. Parties must have sufficient issues and interests in common to do themselves to a joint decision making process.

Will to Settle In order to have successful negotiations, contributors have to desire to settle. If conflict is continued instead of settlement, then negotiations are bound to failure.

Unpredictability of Outcome People bargain because they need something from another person. They also negotiate because the outcome of not negotiating is unpredictable.

Stress and its Management

Stress can have a big impact on human body in ways that are felt by an individual and in the way the world can see. Stress can also create a loss of apetite.

According to **Benjamin Franklin,** "Stress is often termed as a twentieth century syndrome, born out of man's race towards modern progress and its ensuing complexities."

Causes of Stress

There are different causes of stress, some of them are as follows

Financial Problems Financial problems like lack of money, debts, pending mortgage instalments creates stress. As human beings can fullfil their needs with the help of money only.

Workplace Stress An employee has lots of problems and tensions at his workplace such as worry about promotion, negative behaviour of boss, career goals and also because of office politics stress can caused.

Personal Problems Every individual have personal problems about studies of children, attitude of relatives, arguements with spouse or children or illness of a family member. All these can create stress.

Health Health can also be reason of stress. Heart diseases, hypertension, problems with eye sight and sugar affect many people becoming a major cause of life stress for them.

Irritants Problems in commuting to workplace, balance of work and family life can cause stress to an human being. Because of that some symptoms can be seen like visit to doctor, inadequate sleep, no time to relax etc.

Types of Stress

***Positive Stress** It has the following characteristics*

- It motivates employees and focuses on energy.
- It is short-term stress.
- It is perceived as within our coping abilities.
- People feels it exciting.
- It improves performance and enables concentration.

***Negative Stress** It has the following characteristics*

- It causes anxiety.
- It can be short or long term.
- It perceives outside of our coping abilities.
- People feels it unpleasant.
- It decreases performance and can lead to mental and physical problems.

Stress Management

It is the amelioration of stress and especially chronic stress often for the purpose of improving everyday functioning.

Stress produces numerous physical and mental symptoms which vary according to each individual's situational factors. These can include physical health decline as well as depression. The process of stress management is named as one of the keys to a happy and successful life in modern society. Although life provides numerous demands that can prove difficult to handle, stress management provides a number of ways to manage anxiety and maintain overall well being.

Advantages of Stress Management

- Less absenteeism due to stress related disorders.
- Less worker's compensation loss due to stress related illness or accidents.
- It improves job performance.
- More efficient workplace.
- Improved employee overall health.

EXAM BASED QUESTIONS

HRM and HR Planning

1 Human resource is the most important .... in an organisation.

(a) asset (b) liability
(c) capital (d) None of these

2 The ultimate responsibility for HRM activities rests with

(a) sales manager
(b) personnel manager
(c) each manager
(d) None of the above

3 Human relations theory focuses on

1. individuals
2. system
3. role of individual
4. organisational structure
5. informal groups

Select the correct answers using the codes given below

Codes

(a) 1, 2 and 5 (b) Both 4 and 5
(c) Only 3 (d) Both 2 and 4

4 Human relations approach to management was originate by

(a) Henry Fayol (b) FW Taylor
(c) Elton Mayo (d) Peter F Drucker

5 Which of the following does not consists in human relations?

(a) motivation (b) morale
(c) communication (d) competition

6 Mechanism of human resource development includes

(a) job redesign
(b) rewards
(c) human resource information system
(d) All of the above

Demand for workforce is not modified by which of the following factor?

(a) Retirements (b) Termination
(c) Resignations and deaths (d) Promotions

8 External challenges for forecasting the demand for human resources is/are

(a) economic development
(b) political, legal, social and technical changes
(c) Both (a) and (b)
(d) None of the above

9 Which of the following is/are an approach to employer-employee relations?

(a) Psychological approach (b) Critical approach
(c) Social approach (d) Both (a) and (b)

10 Human resource management emphasises

(a) development of people (b) punishment of people
(c) adoption of people (d) None of these

11 Which of the following statement(s) is/are correct?

1. Human resource management is a strategic management function.
2. Under human resource management, employee is treated as a resource.
3. Human resource management is the management of employee's skills, talents and abilities.

Select the correct answer using the codes given below

Codes

(a) Only 2 (b) Both 1 and 2
(c) Only 1 (d) All of the above

12 Which one of the following does not include under the function of human resource management?

(a) Planning (b) Organising
(c) Recruitment (d) Profitability

13 Which of the following statement(s) is/are correct?

1. Re-engineering implies a slow and steady change in an organisation.
2. The content, in which human resources are managed in today's organisations are constantly changing.
3. Employing contract labour is an example of proactive human resource management.

Select the correct answer using the codes given below

Codes

(a) Only 1 (b) Both 2 and 3
(c) Only 2 (d) All of the above

14 Human relations theory has been criticised on the ground that

1. the theory over emphasises the human aspects of the organisation.
2. it fails to take into consideration the inherent conflict between management and cowers.
3. it lacks in decision making.
4. it lacks in facilitating control.
5. it views organisation on a close system.

Which of following statements given above are correct?

Codes

(a) Both 1 and 3 (b) Both 2 and 4
(c) Both 1 and 4 (d) Both 1 and 2

15 Objective(s) of HR planning does not include
(a) forecast personnel requirement
(b) rigid with changes
(c) use existing manpower productively and promote employees in a systematic manner
(d) All of the above

16 Which of the following is not a typically used procedure to reduce the total number of employees?
(a) Lay off
(b) Terminations
(c) Dawn tuens
(d) Early retirement inducement

17 A commonly encountered stumbling block to successful HRP is
(a) a reliance on organisational goals as basic input to the process
(b) the incorporation of operating managers in the process
(c) the use of quantitative forecasting techniques
(d) an overly complicated initial efforts

18 HR needs can be estimated by examining past trends in
(a) trend analysis technique
(b) computer model technique
(c) mathematical model technique
(d) None of the above

19 ...... techniques uses historical rates of promotions, transfer and turnover to estimate future availabilities in the workforce.
(a) Trend analysis
(b) Markov analysis
(c) Staffing table
(d) None of the above

20 A chart showing future employment needs for each type of job is called
(a) staffing table
(b) replacement chart
(c) skill inventories
(d) None of the above

21 An executive inventory report showing which individuals are ready to move into higher positions in the company is called
(a) succession planning
(b) human resource planning
(c) replacement planning
(d) None of the above

22 "HRM is a managerial perspective which argues the need to establish an integrated series of personnel policies to support organisational strategy." Who said this?
(a) Bratton and Gold
(b) Buchanan and Huczynski
(c) Storey
(d) None of the above

23 Consider the following statements.
1. HRM views people as an important asset to be used for the benefit of the organisation.
2. HRP helps to communicate HR policies to all employees.
3. HRP is forward looking.

Which of the statement(s) given above is/are correct?

Codes
(a) Only 1
(b) Both 1 and 3
(c) Only 3
(d) All of the above

24 Consider the following statements.
1. The second step in HRP is supply forecasting.
2. Retention plan provide the scope for challenging, creative and innovative work.
3. Training is understanding and interpretations of knowledge.

Which of the statement(s) given above is/are correct?

Codes
(a) Only 1
(b) Only 2
(c) Both 1 and 2
(d) All of the above

25 Arrange the following steps of human resource planning in correct order.
1. Supply forecasting.
2. Analysing the organisational plans.
3. Estimating the net human resource requirement.
4. Forecasting the overall human resource requirement.

Codes
(a) 4, 3, 2, 1 (b) 2, 4, 1, 3
(c) 3, 1, 4, 2 (d) 1, 3, 2, 4

26 Arrange the following steps of human resource planning in correct order.
1. Action plan for recruitment, development etc.
2. Action plan for redeployment redundance retrinchment.
3. Modify the organisational plan.
4. Forecast future supply from all the sources.

Codes
(a) 3, 2, 1, 4 (b) 2, 4, 1, 3
(c) 4, 3, 2, 1 (d) 3, 1, 4, 2

27 Which of the following statement is correct?
(a) There is no restriction on the number of candidates in case of selection
(b) Internal sources of recruitment is costly
(c) HRM is a much broader concept and staffing is an inherent part of it
(d) All of the above

28 Which of the following statement is correct?
(a) The managerial functions and operating functions of human resource management are perfouned in conjunction with each other
(b) Operating function provides medical aid to employees
(c) Bonus can be given to an employer also
(d) All of the above

29 Which of the following statement is incorrect?
(a) Human resource planning aims at optimum utilisation of the resources
(b) Internal sources of recruitment facilitates boosting of employee's morale
(c) External sources of recruitment is a costly process
(d) None of the above

30 Which of the following statement is correct?
(a) HRM has replaced the traditional concept of labour welfare and personnel management
(b) Human resource personnel does not recruit the personnel
(c) The role of labour welfare officer was not limited to welfare activities of employees
(d) None of the above

Recruitment, Selection, Training and Development

31 The best way of recruiting is always
(a) walk-ins (b) advertisement
(c) variable (d) renewals

32 The primary source of information for recruiting is
(a) job analysis
(b) managerial interviews
(c) recruiter themselves
(d) None of the above

33 Aptitude tests measure
(a) an applicant's capacity and his potential for development
(b) the individual's learning ability
(c) the skills already acquired by the individuals
(d) None of the above

34 The most common constraints on recruiting include all but
(a) image of a firm (b) budgetary support
(c) interviewing (d) government policies

35 Internal sources of recruitment include
(a) direct recruitment
(b) re-employment of ex-employees
(c) casual callers
(d) All of the above

36 The external source of recuritment are
1. lay-off 2. casual callers
3. recommendations 4. campus recuritment

Select the correct answer using the codes given below

Codes
(a) Both 1 and 2 (b) 1, 2 and 3
(c) Both 1 and 4 (d) 2, 3 and 4

37 Recruitment is concerned with the process of
(a) selection of right candidate
(b) developing a pool of potential employees
(c) inviting applications for jobs
(d) None of the above

38 Ultimately, selection decisions are based on
(a) turnover potential (b) human resource plans
(c) performance issues (d) None of these

39 The most reliable and valid tests are generally
(a) attitude tests (b) intelligence tests
(c) performance tests (d) None of these

40 The test is reliable, if a person
(a) scores differently than others taking the same test
(b) scores the same at two or more different point in time
(c) scores the same as others taking the same test
(d) None of the above

41 .... are important sources of clerical and managerial personnel.
(a) Employment exchange (b) Search firms
(c) Vocational school (d) None of these

42 Which of the following is not the internal source of recruitment?
(a) Promotion (b) Transfer (c) Trainees (d) Placement

43 Which of the following challenges are faced by recruiters?
(a) Environmental conditions
(b) Affirmative action plans
(c) Both (a) and (b)
(d) None of the above

44 Which of the following are type of a selection test?
(a) Personality test (b) Aptitude test
(c) Mentality test (d) All of these

45 The advantages of the lecture method include
(a) economy (b) feedback
(c) participation (d) All of these

46 A frequently used analysis for determining training needs involves
(a) organisational analysis
(b) task or role analysis
(c) person analysis
(d) physical resource analysis

47 In creativity training, trainees often focus on
(a) breaking away
(b) generate new ideas
(c) delaying judgement
(d) rigidness

48 The human resource system does not cover under training and development.
(a) Recruit and select
(b) Job design and evaluation
(c) Train and develop
(d) Demotion

49 Objective of training does not include
(a) favourable reaction to change
(b) increased productivity
(c) increased morale
(d) increased competition

50 Transfer of executives from one location to another is called
(a) job rotation (b) job displacement
(c) mentoring (d) None of these

51 Which of the following is an on-the-job method of training?
(a) Internship
(b) Apprenticeship programmes
(c) Coaching
(d) Lecture

52 Method of training suitable for plumbers, electricians or iron-worker is
(a) coaching
(b) vestibule training
(c) apprenticeship programme
(d) None of the above

53 Which of the following relates to training workers?
(a) Job rotation (b) Induction
(c) Vestibule (d) Task

54 An interview conducted at the time of an employee leaving the organisation is called
(a) exit interview (b) feedback interview
(c) convincing interview (d) directed interview

55 Arrange the following steps involved in recruitment and selection procedure in correct order.
1. Application blank
2. Interviewing
3. Requisition
4. Medical test
5. On-the-job test and selection
6. Psychological test
7. Recruitment
8. Trade test

Codes
(a) 3, 1, 4, 2, 8, 5, 7, 6 (b) 2, 4, 6, 8, 1, 3, 5, 7
(c) 3, 7, 1, 8, 6, 2, 4, 5 (d) 1, 2, 3, 4, 5, 6, 7, 8

56 Which of the following statements is/are not correct?
(a) External sources of recruitment are time consuming
(b) Through external sources of recruitment existing staff, is motivated to improve their performance
(c) Both (a) and (b)
(d) None of the above

57 Input to the selection process include all except
(a) job analysis (b) job application
(c) human resource planning (d) supervision

58 Which of the following are true regarding internal sources of recruitment?
1. Economical
2. Suitable for picking the right candidate having requisite skill.
3. Wide choice.
4. Discourages entry of talented people.

Select the correct answer using the codes given below
Codes
(a) Both 1 and 2 (b) 1, 2 and 4
(c) Only 3 (d) All of the above

59 A private employment agency that maintains computerised list of qualified applicants and supplies, these to employers for a fee is called
(a) employment exchange
(b) search firms
(c) outsourcing
(d) None of the above

60 Which of the following statements is/are incorrect?
(a) Intelligence tests are used to evaluate occupational proficiency
(b) Employment tests are meant to screen out unsuitable condidates
(c) Both (a) and (b)
(d) None of the above

61 Consider the following statements.
1. External sources of recruitment offer wider choice of candidates.
2. Advertisement is an internal source of recruitment.
3. Transfer is an internal source of recruitment.

Which of the following statement(s) given above is/are correct?
Codes
(a) Both 2 and 3 (b) Only 3
(c) Both 1 and 3 (d) All of the above

62 The objective of the selection decision is to choose the individual who can most successfully perform the job from the pool of
(a) qualified candidates
(b) unqualified candidates
(c) qualified expert
(d) None of the above

63 Consider the following statements.
1. Selection is a positive process.
2. Selection ensures that the organisation gets the best among the available.
3. Selection leads to a contract of service between the employer and employee.

Which of the statement(s) given is/are correct?
Codes
(a) Only 1
(b) Both 2 and 3
(c) Both 1 and 3
(d) All of the above

64 Which of the following statements is/are incorrect?
(a) Interest tests are used to know the involvement of a person for the job
(b) Aptitude test measures the actual skills possessed
(c) Both (a) and (b)
(d) All of the above

65 Consider the following statements.
1. Invitation to interested people.
2. Preparing the list of deserving applicants.
3. Requisition of employees.
4. Identification of the sources of recruitment.
Which of the following statement(s) given is/are correct?
Codes
(a) 1, 3, 2 and 4 (b) 3, 2, 4 and 1
(c) 4, 3, 1and 2 (d) 3, 4, 1 and 2

66 Arrange the following steps of selection process in correct sequence.
1. Preliminary screening and interview.
2. Job offer and contract of employment.
3. Selection test and employment interview.
4. Selection decision and medical examination.
Codes
(a) 1, 2, 3, 4 (b) 1, 3, 4, 2
(c) 1, 3, 2, 4 (d) 1, 4, 3, 2

67 Which among the following is a part of psychological tests?
1. Aptitude test
2. General knowledge test
3. Personality test
4. Trade efficiency test
Select the correct answer using the codes given below
Codes
(a) Both 1 and 2 (b) Both 1 and 3
(c) Both 2 and 4 (d) 2, 3 and 4

68 Personality test aim at
1. measuring the basic make up of the individual.
2. measuring the candidate's skill and knowledge.
3. measuring the learning capacity of a candidate.
4. measuring the ability candidate how he/she interact with others, how much he/she influence and motivate them.
Which of the statement(s) given above is/are correct?
Codes
(a) Both 1 and 2 (b) Both 1 and 4
(c) 1, 2 and 4 (d) 2, 3 and 4

69 ……… involves a continuous flow of instructions, comments and suggestions from the manager to the subordinate.
(a) Coaching
(b) Understudy
(c) Behaviour modelling
(d) None of the above

70 ……… is employed to develop a situation that is close to reality, where people learn by doing things.
(a) Simulation method
(b) Understudy method
(c) In basket method
(d) None of the above

71 Training does not involves
(a) identification of training needs of the individuals and the company
(b) developing suitable training programmes
(c) evaluating the effectiveness of training programmes
(d) demoralisation of employees

72 The career planning and development process is also part of comprehensive organisation development
(a) process (b) project
(c) Both (a) and (b) (d) None of these

73 Training and development refers to the total structure of on-the-job and off-the-job training systems used by the
(a) candidates (b) organisation
(c) expert (d) None of these

74 Consider the following statements.
1. Training is required at different levels, namely, for unskilled worker, semi-skilled workers, skilled workers, office, staff, supervisory staff and managerial.
2. Semi-skilled workers are selected amongst the unskilled workers who have made themselves convergent with the handling of the machine.
3. Management training has become an essential activity of every firm.
4. Training programmes should not be periodically evaluated to determine its effectiveness.
Which of the following statement(s) given above is/are correct?
Codes
(a) Both 1 and 2
(b) 1, 2 and 3
(c) Only 2
(d) All of the above

75 The method and process of training should be ………. related to needs and objectives of an organisation.
(a) directly
(b) indirectly
(c) equally
(d) None of the above

76 A process by which participants provide their ideas on a stated problem during a free group discussion is called
(a) brain storming
(b) coaching
(c) business game
(d) behaviour modelling

77 Arrange the following steps involved in training programmes in correct order.
1. Presentation of operations and knowledge
2. Getting ready for the job
3. Follow-up
4. Performance try out
5. Preparation of the learner
6. Discovering training needs

Codes
(a) 6, 2, 5, 1, 4, 3 (b) 3, 1, 5, 6, 4, 2
(c) 6, 1, 5, 2, 3, 4 (d) 1, 2, 4, 5, 3, 6

78 Which of the following statement is incorrect?
(a) Development imports technical, human and conceptual skills
(b) Training is manager centred
(c) Development is a continuous activity
(d) None of the above

79 Which of the following are considered as development function of human resource development?
1. Training
2. Executive development
3. Career planning and development
4. Pay and allowance

Select the correct answer using the codes given below
Codes
(a) 1, 2 and 3 (b) 1, 3 and 5
(c) 2, 3 and 4 (d) Both 2 and 3

80 Which of the following statement is not true?
(a) Education is the process of increasing the knowledge and understanding of employees
(b) Education develops future managers
(c) Lectures, conferences etc are the methods used in development
(d) None of the above

81 Which of the following statement(s) is/are incorrect?
(a) Job rotation facilitates easy promotions, replacements or transfers
(b) Selection seeks to attract suitable applicants to apply for available jobs
(c) Training is job-oriented process
(d) All of the above

82 Which of the following statement(s) is/are correct?
1. Training imparting skills for doing a particular job.
2. Training and development involve all round knowledge of present and future.
3. Training and development programme are organised for short or larger period of time.
4. Development is associated with the overall growth of the executive.

Select the correct answer using the codes given below
Codes
(a) 1, 2 and 3 (b) Both 3 and 4
(c) Both 1 and 4 (d) Both 1 and 2

Succession Planning and Stress Management

83 Making progress in one's career through a series of right moves is called
(a) career progression
(b) career development
(c) career planning
(d) None of the above

84 A condition of stagnating in one's current job is called
(a) mid-career crisis (b) plateauing
(c) reality shock (d) None of these

85 Career progress largely depends on
(a) performance (b) experience
(c) qualifications (d) All of these

86 All employees have .... career goals.
(a) similar (b) dissimilar
(c) no (d) None of these

87 People pursue careers to satisfy deeply
(a) individual needs
(b) organisational needs
(c) leadership skills
(d) None of the above

88 Succession planning must be ...... with the future strategic direction of the company.
(a) consistent (b) inconsistent
(c) in accordance (d) Both (a) and (c)

89 Career planning is the responsibility of
(a) government (b) career counsellors
(c) the employer (d) the sponsor

90 Which of the following words does not describe perception?
(a) A passive process
(b) A psychological process
(c) No direct contact with the physical world
(d) Using sense organs

91 Groups are called ...., if jobs are similar.
(a) classes (b) grades
(c) scales (d) roles

92 The ability of one person to influence another is ....
(a) power (b) responsibility
(c) authority (d) None of these

93 Which of these suggestions is not an effective way to deal with stress?
(a) Meditation
(b) Aggressiveness
(c) Talking with others
(d) All of the above

94 A concern or value that employee will not give up, if a choice has to be made is called
(a) career path (b) career anchors
(c) career survival (d) career dynamics

95 The less of employees, who quit an organisation for various reasons?

(a) Downsizing
(b) Retrenchment
(c) Attrition
(d) None of the above

96 Succession management focuses attention on creating and stocking pool of candidates with ...... leadership potential.

(a) high (b) low
(c) no (d) different

97 A programme that encourages young managers with high potential to remain within an organisation by enabling them to advance more rapidly than those with less potential.

(a) Fast track programme
(b) Career development workshop
(c) Career mentoring
(d) None of the above

98 Which of the following statement(s) is/are correct?

(a) All employees have similiar career goals
(b) Good performance is always recognised by managers
(c) Career planning helps the managements of a diverse workforce
(d) All of the above

99 Consider the following statements.

1. Career planning helps the management of a diverse workforce.
2. All employees have similar career goals.

Which of the statement(s) given above is/are correct?

Codes

(a) Only 1 (b) Both 1 and 2
(c) Only 2 (d) None of the above

100 Arrange the following in chronological order about steps of succession planing process.

1. Document and implement succession plans.
2. Identify competencies.
3. Identify critical positions.
4. Identify succession management strategies.

Codes

(a) 4, 1, 2, 3 (b) 3, 2, 4, 1
(c) 2, 4, 1, 3 (d) 1, 3, 2, 4

101 Arrange the following in chronological order about steps of succession planning in a correct order.

1. Evaluate effectiveness.
2. Document and implement succession plans.
3. Identify succession management strategies.

Codes

(a) 3, 2, 1 (b) 1, 2, 3
(c) 2, 3, 1 (d) 3, 1, 2

102 Consider the following statements.

1. Employees only have themselves to blame for stalled careers.
2. All employees have similar career goals.
3. Career development aims at tracking career sponsors.

Which of the statement(s) given above is/are correct?

Codes

(a) Only 2 (b) Both 1 and 2
(c) Only 1 (d) None of the above

103 Which of the following personality characteristics are associated with people who are likely to exhibit violent behaviour on the job?

(a) Neurotic (b) Etraverted
(c) Optimistic (d) Type A

104 The field of organisational behaviour examines such questions as the nature of leadership, effective team development and

(a) inter-personal conflict resolution
(b) organisational control, conflict management
(c) motivation of individuals, planning
(d) planning development

105 We can define .... as activities people performs to acquire, enhance and use power and other resources to obtain their preferred outcomes in a situation of uncertainty or disagreement.

(a) organisational politics (b) executing authority
(c) collective bargaining (d) position power

106 Stress can affect not only your health but also other aspects of your life. What else can be affected by stress?

(a) Family relationships (b) Work performance
(c) Both (a) and (b) (d) None of these

107 Chronic stress is the stress that wears at people day after day. Which of these is an example of chronic stress?

(a) An unhappy marriage
(b) Ongoing money problems
(c) Both (a) and (b)
(d) None of the above

Miscellaneous

Directions (Q. Nos. 108-111) *In the questions given below are two statements labelled as Assertion (A) and Reason (R). In the context of two statements, which one of the following is correct?*

Codes

(a) Both (A) and (R) are true
(b) Both (A) and (R) are false
(c) (A) is true, but (R) is false
(d) (A) is false, but R is true

108 Assertion (A) HR planning is essential to determine the future manpower needs in an organisation.

Reason (R) It would be difficult to have the services of right kind of people at the right time in absence of HR planning.

109 Assertion (A) Promotion is time based rather than service based in case of recruitment from internal Sources.

Reason (R) Length of service based promotion is blessing for efficient candidates.

110 Assertion (A) Organisational policies set to achieve uniformity, economic public relation benefits or other objectives that are sometimes related to recruiting.

Reason (R) Promote from within policies are intended to give present employees the first opportunity for job openings.

111 Assertion (A) Succession planning is hiring from within.

Reason (R) Purpose of succession planning is to identify and develop people to replace current jobholders in key positions. It ensures steady flow of internal talent to fill important vacancies.

Directions (Q. Nos. 112-119) *In the questions given below are two statements labelled as Assertion (A) and Reason (R). In the context of two statements, which one of the following is correct?*

Codes

(a) Both (A) and (R) are true and (R) is the correct explanation of (A)

(b) Both (A) and (R) are true, but (R) is not the correct explanation of (A)

(c) (A) is true, but (R) is false

(d) (A) is false, but (R) is true

112 Assertion (A) Human resource help organisation to reach its goal.

Reason (R) Human resource manager need to get the right people into right place at the right time.

113 Assertion (A) Each role must have enough stressess which may help the role occupant to stretch himself to meet the challenge. In the role where the scope is limited to routine work, the role occupants do not perceive any challenge.

Reason (R) While every role has some routine elements, challenge can also be incorporated into every role. However, the challenge should not exceed an optional limit, otherwise it may produce dysfunctional stress, resulting in poor performance or damage to the health of the employee in the long run.

114 Assertion (A) Human resource management helps organisation to reach its goals.

Reason (R) Human resource management helps to communicate HR policies to all employees.

115 Assertion (A) Human resource planning helps to forecast personnel requirement.

Reason (R) Human resource planning is backward looking.

116 Assertion (A) Education is broader in scope than training.

Reason (R) Education is understanding and interpretations of knowledge.

117 Assertion (A) Development means mental growth of an employee.

Reason (R) Development is described as non-executive development.

118 Assertion (A) Selection is a comprehensive process, negative in nature.

Reason (R) Selection started from psychological test and end with medical examination.

119 Assertion (A) Recruitment is a negative process.

Reason (R) Large number of persons are attracted to submit their application in process of recruitment.

120 Match the following.

List I	List II
A. Productivity	1. Process of integrating the employee's needs and aspirations with organisational needs.
B. Effective	2. Using the minimum amount of resources to produce goods and services.
C. Efficient	3. Producing the right goods or services society which deem as appropriate.
D. Career planning	4. The ratio of an organisations output to its inputs.

Codes

	A	B	C	D		A	B	C	D
(a)	4	3	2	1	(b)	3	4	2	1
(c)	1	2	3	4	(d)	3	2	1	4

121 Match the following.

List I	List II
A. Markov analysis	1. Files of personnel education, experience, interest, skill etc that allow managers to quickly match job openings with employee backgrounds.
B. Replacement chart	2. Study of firm's past employment needs over a period of years to predict future needs.

List I	List II
C. Skill inventories	3. Method for tracking the pattern of employee movements through various jobs.
D. Trend analysis	4. A profile of jobholders department wise and offers a snapshot of who will replace, if there is a job opening.

Codes

	A	B	C	D		A	B	C	D
(a)	3	4	1	2	(b)	4	3	1	2
(c)	2	1	3	4	(d)	3	1	4	2

122 Match the following.

List I (Concepts)	List II (Meanings)
A. Human resource planning	1. Putting the right person to the right job
B. Aptitude test	2. A nominal amount which the candidates carrying internship get
C. Staffing	3. Knowing how many persons and of what type of organisation needs to perform various jobs and accomplishment of organisational goals
D. Stipend	4. Measure of individual's potential for learning new skills

Codes

	A	B	C	D		A	B	C	D
(a)	4	3	2	1	(b)	3	4	1	2
(c)	2	1	4	3	(d)	4	1	2	3

123 Match the following.

List I (Authors)	List II (Definitions)
A. Buchanan and Huczynski	1. Planning, organising, controlling of procurement, development, compensation, integration of human resources to the end that objectives are achieved.
B. Storey	2. HRM is the process by which management determines how the organisation should move from its current manpower position to its desired manpower position.
C. Flippo	3. HRM is a managerial perspective which argues the need to establish an integrated series of personnel policies to support organisational strategy.
D. Vetter	4. HRM is a distinctive approach to employment management, which seeks to achieve competitive advantage through the strategic development of a highly committed and capable workforce.

Codes

	A	B	C	D		A	B	C	D
(a)	4	3	2	1	(b)	3	4	1	2
(c)	2	3	4	1	(d)	4	1	2	3

124 Match the following.

List I (Concepts)	List II (Features)
A. Human resource management	1. Its objective is to create a pool of the prospective job candidates
B. Human resource planning	2. It involves growth of an employee in all respects
C. Development	3. Get qualified people at right time
D. Recruitment	4. It focuses on managing physical and emotional capital of employees

Codes

	A	B	C	D		A	B	C	D
(a)	4	3	2	1	(b)	2	3	4	1
(c)	3	1	4	2	(d)	4	3	1	2

125 Match the following.

List I	List II
A. Assessment centre	1. Informing applicants about all aspects of the job, including both its desirable and undesirable facts.
B. Test	2. A standard objective measure of a person's behaviour, performance or attitude.
C. Simulation exercise	3. A technique that evaluates employee potential through multiple type of group and individual exercises and multiple rates.
D. Realistic job/preview	4. A test that duplicates many of the activities and problems, an employee faces while at work.

Codes

	A	B	C	D		A	B	C	D
(a)	3	2	4	1	(b)	2	1	3	4
(c)	1	2	3	4	(d)	4	1	3	2

126 Match the following.

List I	List II
A. Recruitment	1. It is a recommendation from a current employee regarding a job applicant.
B. Employee referral	2. The process of picking individuals who have relevant qualifications to fill jobs in an organisation.
C. Selection	3. The process of finding and attracting capable applicants for employment.
D. Campus recruitment	4. It is a method of recruiting by visiting and participating in college campuses and placement centre.

Codes

	A	B	C	D		A	B	C	D
(a)	1	2	3	4	(b)	3	1	2	4
(c)	2	1	3	4	(d)	4	1	2	3

127 Match the following.

List I (Methods of Recruitment)	List II (Features)
A. Transfer	1. Internet is becoming a common source of recruitment.
B. Advertisement	2. It helps the organisations to recruit technical, professional and managerial personnel.
C. Web publishing	3. It gives the management a wider range of candidates from which to choose.
D. Management consultants	4. It can also be used for training of employees in learning different jobs.

Codes

	A	B	C	D		A	B	C	D
(a)	4	3	2	1	(b)	4	3	1	2
(c)	2	1	4	3	(d)	3	1	4	2

128 Match the following.

List I (Specific Training Methods)	List II (Their Qualities)
A. On-the-job training	1. Under this method, trainee is seperated focussed on learning the material related to his future performance.
B. Off-the-job training	2. Mostly, the executive training is done on-the-job. An executive is expected to learn his work while working.
C. Understudy method	3. The executive under this method is assigned an understudy or an assistant, who in addition to his regular duties, is expected to acquire some familiarity with the tasks and practices of his superior.
D. Role playing method	4. Under this method, an employee learn by playing a role in drammatic setting which corresponds to his work.

Codes

	A	B	C	D		A	B	C	D
(a)	1	2	3	4	(b)	2	1	3	4
(c)	2	3	4	1	(d)	4	2	3	1

129 Match the following.

List I	List II
A. Job rotation	1. The process of diagnosing present problems and future challenges to be met through training and development.
B. Needs assessment	2. Moving employees to various position in the organisation to expand their skills, knowledge and abilities.
C. Job instruction training	3. A broader long-term function educational programme offered to carry out non-technical functions more effectively.
D. Development	4. A systematic approach consisting of preparing the trainees presenting the instruction, having trainees try out the job and placing trainees on the job with a designated resource person.

Codes

	A	B	C	D		A	B	C	D
(a)	2	1	4	3	(b)	1	2	3	4
(c)	2	4	1	3	(d)	4	3	1	2

130 Match the following.

List I (Authors)	List II (Definitions)
A. Dale Yoder	1. The process by which management determines how the organisation should move from its current manpower position to its desired manpower position.
B. Beach	2. Training is the process by which manpower is filled for the particular jobs it is to perform.
C. Flippo	3. Training is the organised procedure by which people learn knowledge and skills for definite purpose.
D. Vetter	4. Training is the act of increasing the knowledge and skill of an employee for doing a particular job.

Codes

	A	B	C	D
(a)	4	3	2	1
(b)	2	3	4	1
(c)	3	1	4	2
(d)	4	3	1	2

PREVIOUS YEARS' QUESTIONS

December 2018

1 Which one of the following is not an advantage of external recruitment?
(a) Good performance is rewarded
(b) Scope for resentment, jealousies and heartburn are avoided
(c) Compliance with reservation policy becomes easy
(d) Benefits of new skills, new talents and new experiences to organisations are available

2 Which one of the following initiatives is not the strategy for managing shortage of employees in an organisation?
(a) Attempt to reduce turnover
(b) Offer incentives to postpone retirement
(c) Hire temporary employees
(d) Employee training

3 According to Donald Kirkpatrick, training programmes can be evaluated at four levels. Indicated the code of correct sequence from the following.
1. Result 2. Reaction
3. Learning 4. Behaviour
Choose the correct answer from the codes given below
Codes
(a) 1, 2, 3, 4 (b) 3, 4, 1, 2
(c) 2, 3, 4, 1 (d) 3, 1, 2, 4

4 **Assertion** (A) Training aids in encouraging and achieving self-development and self-confidence.
Reason (R) It helps a person handle stress, tension, frustration and conflict.
Codes
(a) Both (A) and (R) are correct and (R) is the right explanation of (A)
(b) Both (A) and (R) are correct, but (R) is not the right explanation of (A)
(c) Both (A) and (R) are incorrect
(d) (A) is correct, but (R) is not correct

July 2018

5 The VRIO Framework, used in HR function in today's era, refers to four criteria. Identify the correct code which stands as correct explanation to VRIO as proposed by Barney?
(a) Valence-Recruiting-Industrial relations-Opportunities
(b) Vision-Rewards-Improvements-Options
(c) Value-Rarity-Imitability-Organisation
(d) Versatile-Resource-Information-Outsourcing

6 **Assertion** (A) Induction is an informal information sharing session on miscellaneous issues in a organisation.
Reason (R) The rationale of induction is to ensure effective integration of staff into or across the organisation for their mutual benefit.
Codes
(a) Both (A) and (R) are correct and (R) is the correct explanation of (A)
(b) Both (A) and (R) are correct, but (R) is not the correct explanation of (A)
(c) (A) is correct, but (R) is incorrect
(d) (A) is incorrect, but (R) is correct

7 Select the correct code of the following statements being correct or incorrect.
1. Strategic HRM focuses on specific organisational intentions about what needs to be done while HR strategies focus on long-term issues only.
2. Strategic HRM focuses on macro concerns such as structure and culture while HR strategy focuses on specific issues assigned.
3. Human Resource strategy decisions are derived from strategic HRM.
Codes
(a) Statements I and II are correct while Statement III is incorrect
(b) Statements II and III are correct while Statement I is incorrect
(c) Statements I and III are correct while Statement II is incorrect
(d) All the statements are correct

November 2017

8 From the following two statements of Assertion (A) and Reason (R). Indicate the correct code.
Assertion (A) Development in HRM is a short-term educational process with temporary intervention.
Reason (R) It is an educational process utilising a systematic and organised procedure for development of operative employees performance in current jobs.
Codes
(a) (A) is correct and (R) is correct explanation of (A)
(b) (A) is correct, but (R) is not correct explanation of (A)
(c) (A) is not correct, but (R) is correct
(d) (A) and (R) both are not correct

9 Put the following steps of discrete selection process in correct sequence and select the correct code.

1. Preliminary interview
2. Completion of application blank
3. Background investigation
4. Physical examination
5. Employment tests
6. Comprehensive interview
7. Final employment decision

Codes

(a) 2, 1, 3, 4, 5, 6, 7 (b) 2, 1, 5, 6, 3, 4, 7
(c) 1, 2, 5, 6, 3, 4, 7 (d) 1, 2, 4, 3, 5, 6, 7

January 2017

10 Human resource planning benefits to an organisation are reflected in which of the combination of the following?

1. Balance between demand and supply of human resources.
2. Non-compulsion on management to assess critically and continuously the employees and personnel policies.
3. Duplication of efforts and conflicts are avoided.
4. Minimising the future returns on investment in human resources.

Codes

(a) Both 1 and 2 (b) Both 1 and 3
(c) 1, 2 and 3 (d) 1, 3 and 4

11 Match the List I with List II relating to human resource planning activities and indicate the code of correct matching.

List I	List II
A. Forecasting	1. Optimal employment
B. Inventorying	2. Development activities
C. Anticipation manpower problems	3. Mathematical projections of industrial trends
D. Planning programmes	4. Projecting present resources into future

Codes

	A	B	C	D		A	B	C	D
(a)	2	1	4	3	(b)	1	4	3	2
(c)	4	2	1	3	(d)	3	1	4	3

12 **Assertion** (A) Recruitment is positive while selection is negative in its application.

Reason (R) Recruitment aims at increasing the job seekers while selection rejects a large number of unqualified applicants.

Codes

(a) (A) is correct, but (R) is not correct
(b) (A) and (R) both are correct, but (R) is not the correct explanation of (A)
(c) (A) and (R) both are correct and (R) is the correct explanation of (A)
(d) (A) and (R) both are incorrect

July 2016

13 Examine the following statements and choose the correct code.

Assertion (A) Human resource planning must always be seen within the strategy making context.

Reason (R) Human resource planning process removed from the realities of the business will be a waste of time.

Codes

(a) Both (A) and (R) are correct
(b) Both (A) and (R) are incorrect
(c) (A) is correct, but (R) is incorrect
(d) (A) is not correct, but (R) is correct

December 2015

14 Which of the following is the most serious problem that might arise due to excessive reliance on internal recruitment?

(a) Reduced job performance (b) High labour turnover
(c) Lack of motivation (d) Internal resistance

15 **Assertion** (A) Human resource accounting is the measurement of the cost and value of people to the organisation.

Reason (R) Human resource accounting involves measuring costs incurred by the organisations to recruit, select, hire, train and develop employees and judge their economic value to the organisation.

Codes

(a) (A) and (R) are true and (R) is the correct explanation of (A)
(b) (A) and (R) are true, but (R) is not the correct explanation of (A)
(c) (A) is true, but (R) is false
(d) Both (A) and (R) are false

June 2015

16 Which of the following is not a basic objective of HRM?

(a) To attract HR into the organisation
(b) To develop and motivate HR for better performance
(c) To have the reward and punishment system for HR
(d) To integrate and maintain HR in the organisation

17 What is 'gate hiring'?

(a) To select people who approach on their own for employment in the organisation
(b) To select people who are recommended by the employees
(c) To select people from public employment exchanges
(d) To select people supplied by labour contractors

18 Which one of the following is a traditional method for selection of personnel?

(a) Interview
(b) Selection test
(c) Phrenology
(d) Aptitude test

19 The method of training in crafts, trades and technical areas is known as
(a) vestibule training (b) coaching
(c) mentoring (d) apprenticeship

20 Which of the following are not part of staffing process?
1. Human resource planning
2. Recruitment
3. Selection
4. Induction and Orientation
5. Training and development
6. Performance appraisal
7. Transfers
8. Separations

Select the correct answer using the codes given below
Codes
(a) 5, 6, 7 and 8 (b) Both 7 and 8
(c) Both 6 and 8 (d) None of the above

December 2014

21 The process of narrowing a large number of candidates to a smaller field is called
(a) rushing
(b) recruitment
(c) selection
(d) enrollment

June 2014

22 Which of the following is not included in the model of the systems approach to human resource management?
(a) Departmentation (b) Recruitment
(c) Performance appraisal (d) Promotion

December 2013

23 Which of the following are methods of on-the-job training?
1. Coaching 2. Vestibule training
3. Demonstration 4. Role playing
5. Apprenticeship training

Select the correct answer using the codes given below
Codes
(a) 1, 2, 3 and 4 (b) 1, 3 and 5
(c) 2, 3, and 4 (d) All of the above

June 2013

24 HRM is viewed as a management process, consisting of four functional activities.
1. Acquisition
2. Motivation
3. Development
4. Resolution of industrial disputes
5. Maintenance

Select the correct answer using the codes given below
Codes
(a) 1, 2, 3 and 4 (b) 1, 2, 3 and 5
(c) 1, 2, 4 and 5 (d) 1, 3, 4 and 5

December 2012

25 HRM does not include
(a) job evaluation (b) performance appraisal
(c) sales promotion (d) job enrichment

June 2012

26 Which of the following are covered under the scope of human resource management?
1. Forecasting human resource needs
2. Replacement planning
3. Human resource dynamics
4. Human resource development planning
5. Human resource audit

Select the correct answer using the codes given below
Codes
(a) 1, 3 and 5
(b) 1, 2, 3 and 4
(c) Both 3 and 5
(d) All of the above

27 Which one of the following is not the operative function of HRM?
(a) Development (b) Controlling
(c) Compensation (d) Integration

ANSWERS

Objective Questions

1 (a)	2 (c)	3 (b)	4 (d)	5 (d)	6 (a)	7 (d)	8 (c)	9 (d)	10 (a)
11 (a)	12 (d)	13 (b)	14 (d)	15 (b)	16 (c)	17 (d)	18 (a)	19 (b)	20 (a)
21 (a)	22 (b)	23 (b)	24 (a)	25 (b)	26 (b)	27 (c)	28 (a)	29 (d)	30 (a)
31 (c)	32 (a)	33 (a)	34 (c)	35 (b)	36 (b)	37 (b)	38 (c)	39 (c)	40 (b)
41 (b)	42 (d)	43 (c)	44 (b)	45 (a)	46 (d)	47 (d)	48 (d)	49 (d)	50 (d)
51 (a)	52 (c)	53 (c)	54 (a)	55 (c)	56 (b)	57 (d)	58 (c)	59 (b)	60 (a)
61 (c)	62 (a)	63 (b)	64 (b)	65 (d)	66 (c)	67 (b)	68 (b)	69 (a)	70 (a)
71 (d)	72 (a)	73 (b)	74 (b)	75 (a)	76 (a)	77 (a)	78 (b)	79 (a)	80 (b)
81 (b)	82 (c)	83 (a)	84 (b)	85 (a)	86 (b)	87 (a)	88 (d)	89 (c)	90 (a)
91 (a)	92 (a)	93 (b)	94 (a)	95 (c)	96 (a)	97 (a)	98 (c)	99 (a)	100 (b)
101 (a)	102 (d)	103 (a)	104 (a)	105 (a)	106 (c)	107 (c)	108 (a)	109 (c)	110 (a)
111 (a)	112 (a)	113 (a)	114 (a)	115 (c)	116 (a)	117 (b)	118 (c)	119 (d)	120 (a)
121 (a)	122 (b)	123 (b)	124 (a)	125 (a)	126 (b)	127 (b)	128 (b)	129 (a)	130 (b)

Previous Years' Questions

1 (a)	2 (d)	3 (c)	4 (b)	5 (c)	6 (d)	7 (b)	8 (d)	9 (c)	10 (b)
11 (d)	12 (c)	13 (a)	14 (c)	15 (a)	16 (c)	17 (a)	18 (d)	19 (c)	20 (d)
21 (a)	22 (a)	23 (b)	24 (b)	25 (c)	26 (d)	27 (b)			

CHAPTER

24

Compensation Management and Performance Appraisal

It is the nature of an human being to work with more efficiency if he get appraisal. In an organisation, management appraises their employees with different methods. Management also manage compensation of their employees so that they can develop their employees' performance to their full efficiency.

Compensation

It is the most important factor of employment relationship and is of critical importance to both employers and employees. Employees depend on salaries because it is their only source of income. For employees, compensation decisions influence their cost of doing the business.

Compensation is a systematic approach to provide monetary value to employees in exchange for work performed.

Compensation Management

Compensation management is the act of providing monetary value to an employee for the work they do by means of a company policy. The goal of compensation management is to find quality people who perform quality work and then compensate them in order to retain them and reduce turnover rates.

Importance of Compensation Management

A good compensation, as it gives an employee a reason to develop the organisation, is an important factor of an organisation due to following reasons

- It creates a base for happiness and satisfaction of the workers that limits the labour turnover and create stability in the organisation.
- It enhance the job evaluation process, which in return helps in setting-up more realistic and achievable standards.
- It enhance a positive control on the efficiency of employees and motivate them to work more efficiently.

In this Chapter

- *Compensation*
- *Job Analysis*
- *Performance Appraisal*
- *Collective Bargaining*
- *Worker's Participation in Management*
- *Industrial Relations in India*

- It excites an environment of morale, efficiency and cooperation among the workers and ensures satisfaction to the workers.
- It creates peaceful relationship between the employer and the employee.

Components of Compensation

Compensation as a whole is made up of different components that work as an aid for an employee after retirement or in case of some accident or injury. Major components of compensation includes wages, salary, incentives and fringe benefits.

Wage and Salary

Wage is defined as, "the remuneration paid by the employees for the services of hourly, daily, weekly and fortnightly employees." It also means the remuneration paid to production and maintenance or blue collar employees.

The term 'salary' means the remuneration paid to clerical and managerial personnel employed on monthly or annual basis.

Wage and Salary Administration

Wage and salary administration is essentially the application of a systematic approach to the problem of ensuring that employees are paid in a logical, equitable and fair manner.

Objectives of Wage and Salary Administration

- To acquire qualified and competent personnel.
- To retain the present employees.
- To serve internal and external equity.
- To keep labour and administrative costs in line with the ability of organisation to pay.
- To project in public as progressive employers and to comply with the wage legislations.
- To pay according to the content and difficulty of the job and in tune with the effort and merit of the employees.
- To facilitate pay roll administration of budgeting and wage and salary control.
- To improve motivation and morale of employees and to improve union-management relations.

Principles of Wage and Salary Administration

- Wage policies should be carefully developed having in mind the interests of management, the employees, the consumers and the community.
- There should be a definite plan to ensure that differences in pay for jobs are based upon variations in job requirements such as skill, effort, responsibility or job or working conditions, mental and physical requirements.
- The general level of wages and salaries should be reasonably in line with that prevailing in the labour market.
- The plan should be carefully distinguish between jobs and employees. A job carries a certain wage rate and a person is assigned to fill it at that rate.
- Wage policies should be clearly expressed in writing to ensure uniformity and stability.
- Wage decisions should be checked against formulated policies.
- Management should see to it that employees know and understand the wage policies.
- Wage policies should be evaluated from time to time to make certain that they are adequate for current need.
- Departmental performance should be checked periodical against the standards set in advance.
- Job descriptions and performance ratings should be periodically checked to keep them up-to-date.

Types of Wages

Minimum Wage It is that wage, which must invariably be paid whether the company, big or small, makes profit or not. It is the minimum amount that a worker can expect to get for services rendered by him. Minimum wage is defined as the remuneration, which may be sufficient to enable a worker to live in reasonable comfort, having regard to all obligations to which an average worker would ordinarily be subjected to.

Fair Wage It is that wage, which is above the minimum wage, but below the living wage. Fair wages are equal to that received by workers performing work of equal skill, difficulty or unpleasantness.

Fair wage is determined taking following factors into an account

- The productivity of labour.
- The prevailing rates of wages in the same or similar occupations in the same region or neighbouring regions.
- The level of national income and its distribution.
- The employer's capacity to pay.

Living Wage *It is the highest amount of remuneration and must include*

- Basic amenities of life.
- Efficiency of worker.
- Satisfy social needs of workers such as medical, education, retirement etc.

Methods of Wage Payment

Payment of wages can be made using any one of the following two methods

Time Wage System Under this method, wages are paid on the basis of time spent on the job irrespective of the amount of work done. The unit of time may be a day, a week, a fortnight or a month. In the past, daily wages have been the most common basis and therefore, it came to be known as the 'day wage system'.

Modified Time Rate

There are some other modified techniques of wage payment. This modified technique can motivate the high efficiency labour by offering them neccessary incentives. But it can be applied where work can be graded according to the skill. Another modification in the system is graduated time rate plan. Under such plan, new wage rate are adjusted, which suit different personal qualities in the workers.

Piece Wage System Under this system, remuneration is based on the amount of work done or output of a worker. One unit of output is considered as one piece and a specific rate of wage is paid per piece. Greater is the number of pieces produced by a worker, higher is his remuneration. Thus, a workman is paid in direct proportion to his output. It is called payment by results.

Incentive

Today, one of the important challenges in business is to attract and retain quality employees. Besides challenging work, good working conditions, fair wages and salaries, employer's benefit programme attract and retain quality employees.

Incentive plans envisage a basic rate usually on time basis applicable to all workers and incentive rates payable to more efficient among them as extra compensation for their meritorious performance in terms of time, costs and quality. The incentive rates may take the form of bonus or premium.

Features of Incentive Plan

Guaranteed Minimum Wages It must guarantee minimum wages irrespective of the performance of the worker.

Simple It must be simple to operate and easy to understand.

Equitable All workers should get an equal opportunity to earn the incentive pay. Equal pay for equal work should be the rule.

Economical The incentive plan should not be a costly affair. The benefits must exceed the costs.

Flexible It must be reasonably flexible, so as to take care of changes in technology, demand for and supply of skills, competitive rates in the industry etc.

Support The incentive plan should take workers and unions into confidence. It should be implemented after consulting the workers and their union.

Motivating The incentive should be large enough to motivate the worker to superior performance. At the same time, there should be checks and balances to ensure that the worker does not exert himself to painful levels, affecting the quality.

Prompt There should be very little time gap between performance and payment. As soon as the job is finished, the worker should get his earnings promptly.

Types of Incentive Plan

Individual Incentive Plans

Individual incentive plans are the most widely used pay for performance plans in industry. These pay plans attempt to relate individual effort to pay. *Different type of individual incentive plans are as follows*

Piece Rate Work Plans *These are as follows*

- ***Taylor's Differential Piece Rate System*** In this plan, two piece work rate, one is lower and other is higher is determined. If a worker finishes work within standard time or produces more than standard output within time, he will be given high piece rate. If the output of worker is less than standard output and does not complete his work within standard time, he is paid a low rate.

  So, this system penalises the slow worker by paying low rate because of low production, rewards on efficient worker by giving him high rate because of higher production.
- ***Merrick's Differential Piece Rate System*** Under this scheme, there are three piece rate. *The basic features of this scheme are as follows*
  - (a) Upto 83% of the standard output, workers are paid at the ordinary piece rate.
  - (b) 83% to 100% at 110% of the ordinary rate.
  - (c) Above 100% at 120% of ordinary piece rate.
- ***Gantt Task and Bonus Plan*** This plan combines time, piece and bonus system. Here, day wages are guaranteed. Standard time for task is fixed and both time wages as well as high rate per piece are determined. A worker, who cannot finish the work within the standard time is paid on time basis. If a worker reaches the standard, he will be paid time wage plus a bonus at a fixed per cent (20%) of normal time wage. If a worker exceeds the standards, he is paid a higher piece rate.
- ***Barth Variable Sharing Plan*** This plan is similar to Halsey and Rowan plans because it is also based on standard time set for the completion of a job. Unlike those plans, however, it does not guarantee a time rate.

  Wages under this plan are calculated according to the following formula

  $$\sqrt{\text{Standard hours} \times \text{Actual hours}} \times \text{Rate per hour}$$

Standard Hour Plan (Halsey Plan) *The main features of this plan are*

- Standard time is fixed for each job or operation.

- Time rate is guaranteed and the worker receives the guaranteed wages irrespective of whether he completes the work in the time allowed or takes more time to do the same.
- If the job is completed in less than the standard time, the worker is paid a bonus of 50% of time saved in addition to his normal wage.

Bonus = 50% of time saved.

Rowan Plan Under this plan, bonus is paid on the basis of time saved. So, bonus is that proportion of the wages of time taken, which the time saved bears to the time allowed or standard time.

Wages under this plan are calculated according to the following formula

$$\text{Bonus} = \frac{\text{Time saved}}{\text{Standard time or Time allowed}} \times \text{Time taken} \times \text{Hourly rate}$$

Total Earnings = Time taken× Hourly rate + Bonus

Performance Based Incentives Here, payment is dependent on individual employee's performance. Performance is evaluated in a subjective fashion. When high achievers are rewarded, they set benchmarks for others to follow.

Group Incentive Plans

Such plans reward all team members equally based on overall performance of the team members. Performance is evaluated using an objective standard.

As in individual plans, payments to team members may be made in the form of cash bonus or in the form of non-cash rewards. Such incentives foster cohesiveness among team members. They can motivate group members to behave and think as a unit rather than as competing individuals.

Also, it is easy to measure the overall performance of the entire team. *Group incentive plans, as research evidence indicates, seem to work best when the following criteria are present*

- When employees are committed to their work and are intrinsically motivated.
- Where it is possible to separate organisational work into self-contained independent groups.
- Where work tasks are so interconnected that it is not easy to single out who did what.
- Where there are few levels in the hierarchy and terms of individuals at the same level are expected to complete most of their work with little dependence on supervisors or upper management.

Organisation Incentive Plans

Reward to employees on the basis of the success of organisation over a specified time period. These plans promote a culture of ownership by developing a senses of belongingness, cooperation and teamwork among all employees. There are three basic types of organisation wide incentive plans; profit sharing, gain sharing and employees stock of ownership plans.

Besides above plans, others types of incentive plans are

Lumpsum Payments In this case, employees receive a single lumpsum payment at the time of review and this enable them to identify linkage between pay and performance.

Commission for Sales People Compensation plans for sales personnel generally consist of a straight salary plan, a straight commission plan or a combination of salary and commission plan.

Fringe Benefits

The term 'fringe benefits' refer to the extra benefits provided to employees in addition to the normal compensation paid in the form of wage or salary.

Features of Fringe Benefits

- Supplementary form of compensation.
- Paid to all employees unlike incentives.
- Indirect compensation because they are usually extended as a condition of employment and are not directly related to performance.
- Raise living condition of employees.
- It may be statutory or voluntary.

Objectives of Fringe Benefits

- To create and improve the industrial relation.
- To motivate the employees by identifying and satisfying their unsatisfied needs.
- To provide security to the employees against social risks like old age benefits and maternity benefits.
- To protect the health of the employees and to provide safety to the employees against accidents.
- To create a sense of belongingness among employees and to retain them.

Types of Fringe Benefits

Payment for Time not Worked *This category includes*

- ***Hours of Work*** No adult worker shall be required to work in a factory for more than 48 hours in any week. Rest of the hours are paid.

- ***Paid Holiday*** According to the Factories Act, 1948, an adult workers shall have weekly paid holidays preferably Sunday.
- ***Shift Premium*** Companies operating second and third shift. Pay a premium to the workers, who are required to work during the odd hours shift.
- ***Holiday Pay*** Generally, organisation offer double the normal rate of salary to those workers, who work on holidays.
- ***Paid Vacation*** Workers in manufacturing, mining and plantations, who worked for 240 days during a calender year are eligible for paid vacation at the rate of one day for every 20 days worked, in case of adult workers and at the rate of one day for every 15 days worked in case of child workers.

Workmen's Compensation Provision for payment of compensation has been made under Workmen's Compensation Act, 1923. The act is intended to meet the any contingency due to death of a worker, due to employment injury or on occupational disease specified under the act at the sole responsibility of the employer. Under the act, the amount of compensation depends on the nature of injury and monthly wages of the employee.

Health Benefits Today, various medical services like hospital, clinical and dispensary facilities are provided by organisations not only to employees, but also to their family members.

The Employees State Insurance Act, 1948 applies to all factories and establishments running with power and employing 10 or more persons and non-power using factories employing 20 or more persons.

Benefits under the act include the following

- Sickness benefit
- Medical benefit
- Temporary disablement benefit
- Permanent disablement benefit
- Maternity benefit

Voluntary Arrangements Most large organisations provide health services over and above the legal requirement to their employees free of cost by setting hospitals, clinics, dispensaries and homeopathic dispensaries.

Welfare and Recreational Facilities *It includes*

- Canteens
- Credit societies
- Legal aid
- Welfare organisations
- Educational facilities
- Parties and picnics
- Consumer stores
- Housing
- Employee counselling
- Holiday homes
- Transportation
- Miscellaneous

Job Analysis

It is a systematic way of gathering information about a job. It consists of two elements, *which are as follows*

Job Evaluation

It is a systematic way of determining the value or worth of a job in relation to other jobs in an organisation. It tries to make a systematic comparison between jobs to assess their relative worth for the purpose of establishing a rational pay structure.

Features of Job Evaluation

- It tries to assess job, not the people who are working.
- Its standards are relative.
- Job analysis is its base.
- It can be carried by group as it is a group activity.
- Degree of subjectivity is always present in this.

Process of Job Evaluation

- Gaining acceptance
- Creating job evaluation committee
- Finding the jobs to be evaluated
- Analysing and preparing job description
- Selecting the method of evaluation
- Classifying jobs
- Installing the programme
- Reviewing periodically

Guidelines for Job Evaluation

- Rate the job not the person or employ on the job.
- Strive to collect the facts accurately.
- Look especially for distinguishing features of jobs and relationship to other jobs.
- Job evaluation must be conducted systematically based on factual and accurate information.
- The result must be fair, rational and unbiased to the individuals being affected.

Job Specification

It specifies information about the skills or qualities required for doing the job. It is a statement which tells us minimum acceptable human qualities which helps to perform a job. It translate the job description into human qualification so that a job can be performed in a better manner. *The contents are as follows*

- Job title and designation
- Educational qualification for the title
- Physical and other related attributes
- Physique and mental health
- Special attributes and abilities

- Maturity and dependability
- Relationship of that job with other jobs in a concern

Objectives of Job Specification

- It helps in candidates analyse whether are eligible to apply for a particular job vacancy or not.
- It helps in recruiting team of an organisation to understand level of qualifications, qualities and set of characteristics should be present in a candidate to make him or her eligible for the job opening.
- It gives detailed information about any job including job responsibilities, desired technical and physical skills, conversational ability and much more.
- It is helpful in preliminary screening in the selection procedure.
- It helps the supervisors for counselling and monitoring performance of employees.
- It helps in giving due justification to each job.

Morale and Productivity

Morale is "a mental condition or attitude of an individual and groups, which determines their willingness to cooperate." Morale is not static, it changes depending on working condition, superiors, fellow workers, pay and so on. When a particular employee has a favourable attitude towards his work, he is said to have high morale. Poor morale is evidenced by surliness, insubordination, a feeling of discouragement and dislike of the job, company and associates.

Morale plays a vital role in the organisation success. High morale keep the employees loyal to job, profession and organisation. This leads to employee commitment and sincerity, which in turn leads to improved performance and productivity.

High morale leads to increased productivity due to following reasons

- Leads to employee satisfaction, which reduces employee turnover and absenteeism.
- Reduce employee grievances.
- Leads to employee commitment to industrial peace by avoiding the occurrence of industrial disputes.
- Increase in employee pride.
- Helps employees build team easily to maximise their contribution.

Morale and Productivity Relationship

Four combination of productivity and morale given by Miller and Form, which are as follows

High Productivity-High Morale

This situation is likely to occur, when group goals are satisfied leading to motivate employees to accomplish high standards of performance and where high productivity leads to high morale; which in turn reinforces high productivity.

Low Productivity-High Morale

This situation occur, when individual goals like good working condition, pleasant fellow workers etc. are satisfied, but supervisor lack technical and administrative skill lowering productivity of high morale group and workers lack adequate skill or training. This results in low productivity by high morale.

High Productivity-Low Morale

In this situation, supervisor is only able to increase productivity through his skills or planning ability rather than through motivation.

Low Productivity-Low Morale

This situation occurs when factors obtained in combination of high productivity-high morale are lacking.

Types of Morale

Individual Morale It involves knowing one's own expectations and living upto them. If we recognise our needs and how to satisfy them, our morale will be high. Here, morale refers to the feelings of an employee towards his work, it is a matter of work satisfaction.

Group Morale Group morale reflects the general tone, of a group of people. Each person either heightens the prospect of the team spirit or lowers the concept of cooperative effort. Morale emphasises social reactions and concentrates on attitudes towards group values.

Factors Affecting Morale

Organisation The goals of the organisation influence the attitudes of employees greatly. If the goals set by management are worthwhile, useful and acceptable, then workers develop a positive feelings towards the job and the organisation. Likewise, a clear structure with well defined duties and responsibilities encourages people to work with confidence.

Leadership The actions of managers exert a strong influence over the morale of the workforce. Fair treatment, equitable rewards and recognition for good work affect morale greatly. Workers feel comfortable when they work under a sympathetic, caring leader in place of one, who is authoritarian, dictatorial and dominating.

Co-worker Poor attitude of co-workers influence others, *e.g.* working with a person who talks about the negative points of an organisation all day long. Such a person can make each work day an unpleasant experience for others.

The Nature of Work Dull, monotonous, repetitive work affects employee morale adversely. On the other hand, if an employee is asked to do something interesting and challenging, his morale may be high.

Work Environment Morale is a direct function of the conditions in the work place. Clean, safe, comfortable and pleasant work conditions are morale boosters.

Performance Appraisal

Performance appraisal is the process of boosting the morale of new employees to do their jobs efficiently and effectively. It indicates how well an individual is fulfilling the job requirements.

In simple terms, performance appraisal may be understood as the assessment of an individual performance in a systematic way, the performance being measured against such factors as job knowledge, quality and quantity of output, initiative leadership abilities, supervision, cooperation, judgement etc.

Thus, it is a process that involves determining and communicating to an employee, how he or she is performing the job ideally and establishing a plan of improvement.

Performance appraisal is a formal structured system of measuring and evaluating an employee's job related behaviour and outcomes to discover how and why the employee is presently performing on the job and how the employee can perform more effectively in the future, so that the employee, organisation and society can be well developed.

Time of Appraisal

Informal appraisals are conducted whenever the supervisor or personnel manager feel it is necessary. Formal or systematic appraisal are conducted on regular basis, *i.e.* every six month or annually.

Appraiser

The appraiser may be any person who has through knowledge about the job content, contents to be appraised, standards of contents and who observes the employee, while performing a job.

Appraisers are

- Supervisors
- Peers
- Subordinates
- Self-appraisal
- Consultants
- Customers

Objectives of Performance Appraisal

- To effect promotion based on competence and performance.
- To confirm the services of probationary employees upon completing their probationary period.
- To assess training and development needs of employees.
- It can serve as a basis for pay raise.
- To let employee know where they stand as far as their performance is concerned and to assist them with constructive criticism and guidance for the purpose of their development.
- To improve communication between the superior and subordinates.
- To determine whether human resources programmes such as selection, training and transfers have been effective or not.

Advantages of Performance Appraisal

It is said that performance appraisal is an investment for the company. *It can be justified by following advantages which are as follows*

Promotion Performance appraisal helps the supervisors to chalk out the promotion programmes for efficient employees. In this regard, inefficient workers can be dismissed or demoted.

Compensation Performance appraisal helps in chalking out compensation packages for employees. Merit rating is possible through performance appraisal. It also tries to give worth to performance.

Employee's Development The systematic procedure of performance appraisal helps the supervisors to frame training policies and programmes, which in turn helps to analyse strengths and weaknesses of employees, so that new jobs can be designed for efficient employees.

Selection Validation Performance appraisal helps to supervisors to understand the validity and importance of the selection procedure. The supervisors come to know the validity and there by the strengths and weaknesses of selection procedure. Future changes in selection methods can be made in this regard.

Effective Communication *Through performance appraisal, communication can be sought for in the following ways*

- The employers can understand and accept skills of subordinates.
- The subordinates can also understand and create a trust and confidence in superiors.
- It also helps in maintaining cordial and congenial labour management relationship.
- It develops the spirit of work and boosts the morale of employees.

Motivation Performance appraisal serves as a motivation tool. Through evaluating performance of employees, a person's efficiency can be determined, if the targets are achieved. This very well motivates a person for better job and helps him to improve his performance in the future.

Process of Performance Appraisal

Performance appraisal is planned, developed and implemented through following as series of steps

Establishing Performance Standards

Appraisal systems require performance standards, which serve as benchmarks against, which performance is measured. So, the first step in the process of performance appraisal is the setting-up of standards, which will be used to as the base to compare the actual performance of the employees.

It requires setting the criteria to judge the performance of the employees as successful or unsuccessful and the degree of their contribution to the organisational goals and objectives. To be useful, standards should relate to the desired results of each job and should be clear, easily understandable as well as in measurable terms.

Communicating the Standards

Once set, it is the responsibility of the management to communicate the standards to all the employees of the organisation. The employees should be informed and the standards should be clearly explained to them. This will help them to understand their roles and to know what exactly is expected from them.

The standards should also be communicated to the appraisers or the evaluators and if required, the standards can also be modified at this stage itself according to the relevant feedback from the employees or the evaluators.

Measuring the Actual Performance

After the performance standards are set and accepted, the next step is to measure actual performance of the employees that is the work done by the employees during the specified period of time. It is the continuous process, which involves monitoring the performance through out the year.

It requires the careful selection of the appropriate techniques of measurement, taking care that personal bias does not affect the outcome of the process and providing assistance rather than interfering in an employee's work.

Comparing the Actual Performance with the Desired Performance

The actual performance is compared with the desired or the standard performance. Actual performance may be better than expected and sometimes it may go off the track. The comparison tells the deviations in the performance of the employees from the standards set. It includes recalling, evaluating and analysis of data related to the employee's performance.

Discussing Results

The result of the appraisal is communicated and discussed with the employees on one-to-one basis. The focus of the discussion is on communication and listening. The results, the problems and the possible solutions are discussed with the aim of problem solving and reaching consensus. The feedback should be given with a positive attitude as this can have an effect on the employee's future performance.

Decision

The last step of the process is to take decisions, which can be taken either to improve the performance of the employees, take the required corrective actions or the related human resource decisions like rewards, promotions, demotions etc.

Methods of Performance Appraisal

Critical Incident Technique

Under this method, the manager prepares lists of statements of every effective and ineffective behaviour of an employee. These critical incidents or events represent the outstanding or poor behaviour of employees on the job. The manager maintains logs on each employee, whereby he periodically records critical incidents of the worker's behaviour. This method is applied frequently to evaluate the performance of superiors.

Check Lists and Weighted Check Lists

A checklist represents, in its simplest form, a set of objectives or descriptive statements about the employee and his behaviour. If the rater believes strongly that the employee possess a particular listed trait, he checks the item otherwise he leaves the item blank.

Under the weighted checklist method, each question may be weighted equally or certain questions may be weighted more heavily than others.

Rating score from the checklist helps the manager in evaluation of the performance of the employee. This method suffer from serious limitation as rater may assign biased weights to the question.

Graphic Rating Scale

Under this method, a printed form is used to evaluate the performance of an employee. Rating scale consist of several numerical scales each representing a job related performance. Criterian such as dependability, initiative, output, attendance, attitude, cooperation etc.

Each rating scale ranges from excellent to poor rates, checks the appropriate performance level on each criterion and then computes the employee's total score.

Behaviourally Anchored Rating Scales

This method is a combination of rating scale and critical incident techniques of employee performance evaluation. The critical incidents serve as anchor statements on a scale and the rating form usually contains six to eight specifically defined performance dimensions.

Forced Choice Method

The primary purpose of the forced choice method is to correct the tendency of a rate to give consistently high or low ratings to all the employees. This method makes use of several sets of pair phrases, two of, which may be positive and two negative and the rater is asked to indicate, which of the four phrases is the most and least descriptive of a particular worker.

The favourable qualities earn a plus credit and unfavourable one earns the reverse. The worker gets on overall plus rating, when the positive factor over ride the negative ones or when one of the negative phrases is checked as being insignificantly rated.

Management by Objective (MBO)

It requires the management to set specific, measurable goals with each employee and then periodically discuss the latter's progress towards these goals. It is, thus a kind of goal setting and appraisal programme.

Ranking

Under this method, the ranking of an employee in a work group is done against that of another employee. The relative position of each employee is expressed in terms of his numerical rank. Employees are ranked according to their relative level of performance. While using this method, evaluator is asked to rate employees from highest to lowest on some overall criterion.

Forced Distribution Method

Under this method, an employee is appraised according to a predetermined distribution scale. Normally, the two criteria used here for rating are the job performance and promotability. Further, a five point performance scale is used without any details of descriptive statement. *e.g.* workers of outstanding merit may be placed at the top 10% of the scale. The rest placed as 20% good, 40% outstanding, 20% fair and 10% poor.

Apart from job performance as the criterion, another equally important factor in this method is promotability. Employees may be classified according to their promotional merits. The scale may consist of three points namely quite likely promotional material, may/may not be promotional material and quite unlikely promotional material.

Group Appraisal

Under this method, an employee is appraised by a group of appraisers. The group consists of the immediate supervisor of the employee, other supervisors who have close contact with the employee's work, manager or head of the department and consultants.

The head of the department or manager may be the chairman of the group and immediate supervisor may act as the coordinator for the group activities. This method eliminates 'personal bias' to a large extent, as performance is evaluated by multiple rates, but is a time consuming process.

Disadvantages of 360 Degree Performance Appraisal

- It is a time consuming process and being complex in administration.
- Feedback can be useless, if it is not carefully dealt.
- It will be very hard to figure out the results.
- Extension of exchange feedback can cause troubles and tensions to several staff.
- It can impose an environment of suspicion, if the information is not openly and honestly managed.

360 Degree Performance Appraisal

It is a type of employee performance review in which subordinates, co-workers and managers rate the employees. In this type of appraisal, an employee who receive rating from others is also required to make a self-assessment and rate himself. This information is then incorporated into that person's performance review.

Advantages of 360 Degree Performance Appraisal

- It offers a more comprehensive view towards the performance of employees.
- It improves credibility of performance appraisal.
- People who undervalue themselves are often motivated by feedback from others.
- It increases responsibility of employees to the customers.
- If more staff takes part in the process of performance appraisal, the organisational culture of the company will become more honest.

Collective Bargaining

It is a technique adopted by the organisation of workers and employers collectively to resolve their differences without the assistance of a third party.

"Collective bargaining is a process of discussion and negotiation between two parties, one or both of whom a group of persons is acting in consent."

Features of Collective Bargaining

Group Action It is a group action as opposed to individual action. Both the parties of settlement are represented by their groups.

Continuous Process It is a continuous process and does not end with one agreement. It provides a mechanism for continuing and organised relationship between management and trade union.

Bipartite Process It is a two party process. Both the parties-employers and employees collectively take some action. There is no intervention of any third party.

Flexible It has fluidity. There is no hard and fast rule for reaching an agreement. There is ample scope for compromise.

Complementary not Competitive It is not a competitive process, *i.e.* labour and management do not cooperate while negotiating for the same object. It is a complementary process, each party needs something which the other party have.

Worker's Participation in Management

Participation means sharing the decision-making power with the lower ranks of the organisation. It has motivation power and psychological value as workers participate in organisational decision.

According to **Davis**, "It is a mental and emotional involvement of a person in a group situation, which encourages him to contribute to goals and share responsibilities in them."

According to International Labour Organisation (ILO), "Worker's participation may broadly be taken to cover all terms of association of workers and their representatives with the decision-making process ranging from exchange of information, consultations, decisions and negotiations, to more institutionalised forms such as the presence of worker's member on management or supervisory boards or even management by workers themselves."

According to **Walpole**, "Participation in management gives the worker a sense of importance, pride and accomplishment, it gives him the freedom of opportunity for self-expression, a feeling of belongingness with the place of work and a sense of workmanship and creativity."

The concept of worker's participation in management is based on human relations approach to management, which brought about a new set of values to labour and management. Traditionally, the concept of worker's participation in management refers to participation of non-managerial employees in the decision-making of the organisation. It is also known as 'labour participation' or 'employee participation' in management. The international labour organisation has been encouraging member nations to promote the scheme of worker's participation in management.

Features of Worker's Participation in Management

- Participation means mental and emotional involvement rather than mere physical presence.
- Worker's participation in management not as individuals, but collectively as a group through their representatives.
- It may be formal or informal. In both the cases, it is a system of communication and consultation, whereby employees express their opinions and contribute to managerial decisions.
- It involves worker's participation in decision-making.
- It enhance possession of employee towards the organisation.

Objectives of Worker's Participation in Management

- To promote increased productivity for the advantage of the organisation; workers and society at large.
- To provide a better understanding to employees about their role and place in the process of attainment of organisational goals.
- To satisfy the worker's social and esteem needs.
- To strengthen labour management cooperation and thus, maintaining industrial peace and harmony.
- To build the most dynamic human resource.
- To build the nation through entrepreneurship and economic development.

Types of Participation

Worker's participation is possible at all levels of management, the only difference is that of degree and nature of application. For instance, it may be vigorous at lower level and faint at top level.

Broadly speaking, there are following five types of participation

Informative Participation It ensures that employees are able to receive information and express their views pertaining to the matter of general economic importance.

Consultative Participation Here, workers are consulted on the matters of employee welfare such as work, safety and health. However, final decision always rest with the top level management, as employee's view are only advisory in nature.

Associative Participation It is an extension of consultative participation as management here is under the moral obligation to accept and implement the unanimous decisions of the employees. Under this method, the managers and workers jointly take decisions.

Administrative Participation It ensures greater share of worker's participation in discharge of managerial functions. Here, decisions already taken by the management come to employees, preferably with alternatives for administration and employees have to select the best from those for implementation.

Decisive Participation Highest level of participation, where decisions are jointly taken on the matters relating to production, welfare etc.

Forms of Worker's Participation in Management

Works Committees (1947)

The Industrial Dispute Act, 1949 provides for the setting-up of works committee as a scheme of workers participation in management, which consists of representatives of employers and employees. The act provides for these committees in every undertaking employing 100 or more workmen. The workers directly elect their representatives, where there is no union.

These committees are consultative bodies and include discussion of conditions of work like lighting, ventilation, temperature, sanitation amenities like water supply for drinking purpose, provision of canteens, medical services etc. It shall be the duty of the works committee to promote measures for securing and preserving amenity and good relations between the employers and workmen and to comment upon matters of their common interest or concern and try to reconcile any difference of opinion.

The works committee have as office bearers a President, a Vice-President, a Secretary and a Joint Secretary. The President is the nominee of employer and the Vice-President is the representative of workers. The tenure of these bodies is two years. The total strength of these bodies should not exceed 20.

Joint Management Councils (JMCs) (1958)

The Government of India deputed a study group to study the schemes of worker's participation in management in countries like UK, France, Belgium etc.

This group made following recommendations

- Worker's participation in management schemes should be set-up in selected undertaking on a voluntary basis.
- A sub-committee consisting representative of employer, workers and government should be set-up for considering the details of worker's participation in management schemes.

Functions of JMCs

- To be consulted on matters like standing orders, retrenchment, rationalisation and closure reduction of operations.
- To receive information, to discuss and offer suggestions.
- To shoulder administrative responsibilities like maintaining welfare measures, safety measures, training schemes etc.

Worker Directors (1970)

Following recommendations of administrative reforms commission the government has accepted that representatives of workers be taken, Board of Directors of Public Sector Undertakings. The worker director was supposed to be elected by all the workers of the company through the secret ballot. After the nationalisation of banks, the government advised all nationalised banks to appoint employee directors to their board-one representing employees and other representing officers having a tenure of three years.

Shop and Joint Councils (1975 and 1977)

1975 scheme came into an existence after emergency was declared. The 1975 scheme envisaged the setting-up of shop councils at the shop/department level and joint councils at the enterprise level. These were to be introduced in manufacturing and mining units employing 500 or more workers whether in public, private or cooperative sector.

The actual number of shop councils in an enterprise was to be decided by employer after the consultation with the recognised union/workers. The chairman of the council is elected by management and vice-chairman by the workers representatives. The council would function for two years and meet regularly to discuss matters relating to safety, discipline, welfare measures etc.

The joint council having a tenure of two years would be constituted for the whole enterprise, comprising representative of both the management and the labour. The council was required to meet once in a quarter to discuss matters, which remained unsolved by shop councils. However, after the emergency was lifted most of the councils became defent.

The New Scheme (1984)

A new scheme of worker's participation in management was prepared and notified in 1984, after reviewing the progress of various schemes in industry. It was applicable to all central public sector enterprises. It was decided that workers would be allowed to participate at the shop level, plant level and the board level.

The 1990 Bill

Worker's participation scheme till date failed to give meaningful participation to workers at the enterprise level. To remedy the situation, the government introduced this bill.

This bill

- offered meaningful three tier participation to workers in management at three levels, shop floor, enterprise and board level.
- formulated schemes specifying detailed criteria regarding nomination of representatives from workers.
- provided for the principle of secret ballot for chasing representatives of workers.
- provided for rules for monitoring the programmes.
- extended the coverage of scheme to all corporate establishments.

Quality Circle

Quality circles are alternative approach to participation. It is a small group of employees, who meet periodically to identify, analyse and solve quality and other work related problem in their area. Members of a particular circle should be from the same work area or who perform similar work, so that the problems they select will be familiar to all of them. The ideal size of the group is 6 to 8 members.

Objectives of Quality Circle

- To improve quality of service/product.
- To meet the psychological needs of workers.
- To utilise human talents, skill and knowledge relating to a work area.
- To improve the quality of work life.
- To promote better understanding and thereby create cordial industrial relations.
- The organisational structure of a quality circle generally consists of four levels *viz.* (i) Members (ii) Leaders (iii) Facilitator (iv) Steering committee

Measures for Making Effective Participation

- Employer should adopt a progressive look. They should consider the industry as a joint endeavour, in which workers have an equal say. Workers should be provided enlightened about the benefits of their participation in the management.
- Employers and workers should agree on the objectives of the industry. They should recognise and respect the rights of each other.
- Workers and their representatives should be provided education and training in the philosophy and process of participative management. Workers should be made aware of the benefits of participative management.
- There should be effective communication between workers and management and effective consultation of workers by the management in decisions that have an impact on them.
- Participation should be a continuous process. To begin with, participation should start at the operating level of management.
- A mutual cooperation and commitment to participation must be developed by both management and labour.

Reasons for Failure of Worker's Participation Management in India

- Employers resist the participation of workers in decision-making because they feel that workers are not competent enough to take decisions.
- Worker's representatives, who participate in management have to perform the dual roles of worker's spokesman and a co-manager. Very few representatives are competent enough to assume the two incompatible roles.
- Generally, trade union leaders, who represent workers are also active members of various political parties. While participating in management, they tend to give priority to political interests rather than the worker's cause.
- In India, labour laws regulate virtually all terms and conditions of employment at the workplace. Workers do not feel the urge to participate in management, having an innate feeling that they are born to serve and not to rule.
- The focus has always been on participation at the higher levels, lower levels have never been allowed to participate much in the decision-making in the organisations.

Industrial Relations in India

The term 'industrial relations' refer to relationships between management and labour or among employees and their organisations that characterise or grow out of employment.

The subject therefore, includes individual relations and joint consultations between employers and work people at their work place, collective relations between employers and work people at their work place, collective relations between employers and their organisations and trade union and part played by the state in regulating these relations.

According to **Dale Yoder**, "A relationship between management and employees or among employees and their organisations, that characterise and grow out of employment."

In fact, industrial relation includes all such factors that influence behaviour of people at work.

Objectives of Industrial Relations

The fundamental objective of industrial relations is to maintain some relations between employees and employers.

Other objectives are

- To safeguard the interest of labour and management, who are participating in the process of production is being securing the highest level of mutual understanding and goodwill among all sections in the industry.
- To avoid industrial conflict or strike and develop harmonious relations, which is an essential factor in the productivity of workers and the industrial progress of a country.
- To raise productivity to a higher level in an era of full employment by lessening the tendancy to high turnover and frequency absenteeism.
- To establish and nurse the growth of an industrial democracy based on labour partnership in the sharing of profits and of managerial decisions, so that ban individuals personality may grow its full stature for the benefit of the industry and of the country as well.
- To established government control of such plants and units, which are running at a loss or in which productions has to be regulated in the public interest.

Functions of Industrial Relations

Functions of industrial relations include

- Communication is to be established between workers and the management in order to bridge the traditional gap.
- To establish a rapport between manager and the employee.
- To ensure creative contribution of trade unions to avoid industrial conflicts to safeguard the interest of workers on the one hand and the management on the other hand, to avoid unhealthy, unethical atmosphere in an industry.
- To lay down such considerations, which may promote understanding, creativity and cooperativeness to raise industrial productivity to ensure better workers participation.

Factors of Industrial Relations

Industrial relations are influenced by various factors.
They are

Institutional Factors These factors includes government policy, labour legislation, voluntary courts, collective agreements, employee courts, employer's federations, social institutions like community, caste, joint family and creed etc.

Economic Factors These factors includes economic organisations like capitalist, communist, mixed etc, the structure of labour force, demand for and supply of labour force etc.

Technological Factors These factors includes mechanisation, automation, rationalisation, computerisation etc.

Social and Cultural Factors These factors includes population, religion, customs and tradition of people race, etheric groups, cultures of various groups of people.

Political Factors These factors includes political system in the country, political parties and their ideologies, their growth, mode of achievement of their policies, involvement in trade unions etc.

Government Factors These factors includes government policies like industrial policy, economic policy, labour policy and export policy etc.

EXAM BASED QUESTIONS

Compensation and its Management

1 .... consists of various pay scales showing ranges of pay within each grade.

(a) Wage rate (b) Wage structure
(c) Wage curve (d) Compensation

2 Factors influencing compensation levels include

(a) job needs (b) productivity
(c) unions (d) All of these

3 Which of the following factor influence(s) employee compensation?

(a) Labour market (b) Labour union
(c) Both (a) and (b) (d) None of these

4 Factors influencing compensation levels does not include

(a) job needs (b) ability to pay
(c) cost of living (d) living standard

5 Institutions involved in payment of wages are

(a) employer
(b) collective bargaining
(c) legislation, wage board and pay commission
(d) All of the above

6 Rewards, one gets from the employer usually money, a promotion or benefits, are known as

(a) extrinsic rewards
(b) intrinsic rewards
(c) employee stock option plan
(d) None of the above

7 Group incentives would work best among

(a) assembly line workers (b) lawyers
(c) accountants (d) car sales people

8 Employee's high morale is favourable for implementation of

(a) enterprise resources planning
(b) business process reengineering
(c) Both (a) and (b)
(d) None of the above

9 Morale is an attitude of an employee towards his

(a) job (b) superior
(c) organisation (d) All of these

10 "Morale is a state of mind or a willingness to work which in turn affects individuals and organisational objectives". Who said this?

(a) Edwin B Flippo (b) Michael J Jucius
(c) Miller and Form (d) J Maslow

11 Productivity means

(a) an act of increasing the knowledge and skills of an employee for doing a particular job
(b) using the minimum amount of resources needed to produce goods and services
(c) one's skills, abilities in meeting the needs of the job which one is holding currently
(d) the ratio of an organisation's output to its inputs

12 Which of the following statement(s) is/are incorrect?

(a) An example of indirect compensation is 'pensions'
(b) Wage surveys determine point values for jobs
(c) Jobs with similar value are combined into pay ranges
(d) All of the above

13 An employee's perception that compensation received is equal to the value of work performed.

(a) Incentive (b) Pay grades
(c) Pay equity (d) None of these

14 A job that is used to anchor the employee's pay scale and around which other jobs are arranged in order of relative worth?

(a) Benchmark job (b) Job equity
(c) Job policy (d) None of these

15 Wage which must invariably be paid whether the company, big or small, makes profit or not is called

(a) minimum wage (b) fair wage
(c) living wage (d) None of these

16 .... serve as a cushion or sort of insurance against increase in price level of commodities.

(a) Compensatory allowance
(b) Dearness allowance
(c) Supplementary compensation
(d) None of the above

17 Wages and allowances of Central and State Governments employees are determined through the

(a) pay commission
(b) wage boards
(c) wage committee
(d) None of the above

18 The Payment of Wages Act, 1936 aims to

(a) provide for setting up a tripartite body consisting of employees, unions and the government
(b) provide for regular payment of wages without any unauthorised reductions
(c) Both (a) and (b)
(d) None of the above

19 Payment of Bonus Act, 1965 apply in factory or establishment in which ...... or more persons are employee in an accounting year.

(a) 10 (b) 15
(c) 20 (d) 25

20 Consider the following statements.
1. The Payment of Wages Act came into force in the year 1926.
2. Government wage surveys are often out of date.
3. Incentive systems are possible for all jobs.

Which of the statement(s) given above is/are correct?
Codes
(a) Both 1 and 2 (b) Only 1
(c) Only 2 (d) All of the above

21 Consider the following statements.
1. The Minimum Wages Act came into force in the year 1958.
2. Under incentive systems, worker pay is determined by performance.
3. Employee stock option plans are limited to executives.

Which of the statement(s) given above is/are correct?
Codes
(a) Only 1 (b) Only 2
(c) Both 1 and 2 (d) All of the above

22 Arrange the following state regulations of wages in the decreasing order of their year of implementation.
1. Payment of Wages Act 2. Minimum Wages Act
3. Payment of Bonus Act
Codes
(a) 3, 2, 1 (b) 1, 2, 3 (c) 3, 1, 2 (d) 2, 1, 3

23 Which of the following statement(s) is/are correct?
(a) Salary survey aimed at finding prevailing wages rates
(b) Motivational devices used to encourage special work effort is called an incentive
(c) Both (a) and (b)
(d) None of the above

24 Consider the following statements.
1. Unions oppose job enrichment.
2. Increased variety in the job adds to self-esteem.
3. The time needed to complete every task in the job is called 'job cycle'.

Which of the statement(s) given above is/are correct?
Codes
(a) Only 1 (b) Only 2
(c) Both 1 and 3 (d) Both 1 and 2

25 Which of the following statement(s) is/are incorrect?
(a) Under incentive systems, worker pay is determined by performance
(b) Subjective evaluation is a problem with merit pay systems
(c) Both (a) and (b)
(d) None of the above

26 Which of the following statement(s) is/are incorrect?
(a) Individual incentives offered to reward the effort and performance of individuals
(b) Organisation wide incentives reward team members with agreed standards met or exceeded
(c) Both (a) and (b)
(d) None of the above

27 Which of the following pair(s) is/are not correct?
(a) An incentive payment that is given to an employee beyond one's normal standard wage is known as bonuses
(b) These are extra payments given for superior performance are known as fringe benefits
(c) Both (a) and (b)
(d) None of the above

28 Which of the following statement(s) is/are incorrect?
(a) Fringe benefits helps to create and improve sound industrial relations
(b) Welfare and recreational facilities include canteens, consumer societies etc
(c) Provident fund is meant for social welfare of the employees
(d) All of the above

29 Which of the following statement(s) is/are correct?
(a) A condition of low morale is on the other hand, characterised by an attitude of indifference or hostility towards the work in hand and lack of a cooperative spirit
(b) Morale is basically a matter of human behaviour
(c) The Hawthrone experiment is related with morale
(d) All of the above

30 Which of the following statement(s) is/are incorrect?
(a) Living wage is the highest wage
(b) Minimum wage is a dynamic concept which grows in line with the growth of the national economy
(c) Fair wage is that which is above the minimum wage, but below the living wage
(d) All of the above

31 Which of the following statement(s) is/are correct?
(a) Subjective evaluation is a problem with merit pay systems
(b) Government wage surveys are often out of date
(c) Both (a) and (b)
(d) None of the above

Performance Appraisal and Collective Bargaining

32 Listing employees from best to worst is called
(a) comparison (b) ranking
(c) rating (d) None of these

33 Which one of the following is a future oriented appraisal technique?
(a) MBO (b) Rating
(c) Field review method (d) None of these

34 Performance appraisals serve as building block of
(a) recruiting (b) career planning
(c) manpower planning (d) job analysis

35 Future oriented appraisal technique is
(a) MBO (b) rating scale
(c) checklist (d) BARS

36 In 360 degree, feedback information is gathered from
(a) two sources (b) multiple sources
(c) employee himself only (d) None of these

37 The appraisal process is designed by
(a) personnel department (b) workshop
(c) factory (d) management

38 Arrange the following in correct order.
1. Promotion 2. Performance appraisal
3. Recruitment 4. Training and development
Codes
(a) 3, 4, 1, 2 (b) 3, 2, 1, 4
(c) 1, 2, 3, 4 (d) 3, 4, 2, 1

39 A systematic and objective way of evaluating both work related behaviour and potential of employees is
(a) evaluation (b) potential appraisal
(c) performance appraisal (d) None of these

40 A method requiring the rater to select the most descriptive statement in each pair of statements about the employee being rated is called
(a) graphic rating scale method
(b) forced choice method
(c) easy evaluation method
(d) None of the above

41 Which of the following technique is least susceptible to personal bias?
(a) Forced choice
(b) Behaviourally anchored rating scale
(c) Critical incident
(d) Checklist and weighted checklists

42 The reluctance to use the extremes of a rating scale and thereby fail to adequately differentiate employees being rated is called
(a) central tendency (b) paired comparison
(c) forced choice (d) None of these

43 Under this method, value of each question is weighted equally or certain questions are weighted more heavily than others
(a) checklist method
(b) graphic rating scale method
(c) weighted checklist method
(d) None of the above

44 Which of the following statement(s) is/are not true?
(a) Performance appraisal is carried out periodically
(b) Performance appraisal is linked to job specification
(c) Performance appraisal helps to assess training and development needs of employees
(d) None of the above

45 Arrange the following steps of working of MBO in correct order.
1. Comparison of the actual level of goal attainment with the goals agreed upon.
2. Establishing new goals and new strategies for goals not previously attained.
3. Setting the performance standards.
4. Establishing goals.
Codes
(a) 4, 3, 1, 2 (b) 3, 1, 4, 2
(c) 4, 3, 2, 1 (d) 2, 1, 4, 3

46 Consider the following statements.
1. Listing employees from best to worst is called central tendency.
2. BARS technique is least susceptible to personal bias.
3. Performance appraisal cannot serve as a useful basis for pay raises.

Which of the statement(s) given above is/are correct?
Codes
(a) Only 2 (b) Only 1
(c) Both 1 and 2 (d) None of the above

47 Which of the following statement is correct?
(a) Subjective measures in performance appraisal are most desirable
(b) Performance appraisal can reduce bias
(c) Employee self-appraisal are a good way to decide promotions
(d) None of the above

48 Name the method of performance appraisal, in which employees are evaluated one at a time without comparing them with other employees in the organisation?
(a) Management by objectives
(b) Checklists
(c) Essay evaluation
(d) Individual evaluation

49 Consider the following statements.
1. Using multiple raters improves evaluations.
2. Rating scales are particularly subject to bias.
3. Objective appraisal measures are always popular with employees.

Which of the statements given above is/are correct?
Codes
(a) Both 3 and 1 (b) Both 1 and 2
(c) Only 1 (d) All of the above

50 Arrange the following steps of performance appraisal process in a correct order.
1. Measuring the actual performance.
2. Establishing performance standards.
3. Comparing the actual performance with the desired performance.
4. Communicating the standards.
Codes
(a) 4, 3, 2, 1
(b) 2, 4, 1, 3
(c) 3, 1, 4, 2
(d) None of the above

51 Arrange the following steps of performance appraisal process in a correct order.
1. Discussing results.
2. Measuring the actual performance.
3. Taking decision.
4. Comparing the actual performance with the desired performance.

Codes
(a) 4, 3, 2, 1 (b) 3, 4, 1, 2
(c) 2, 4, 1, 3 (d) None of the above

52 The most important method to settle the dispute is
(a) arbitrations (b) mediation
(c) investigation (d) collective bargaining

53 Which of the following bargaining is based on worker's contribution to productivity?
(a) Coalition bargaining (b) Concession bargaining
(c) Productivity bargaining (d) None of theese

54 Which of the following is an outcome of collective bargaining?
(a) Award of labour court (b) Award of tribunal
(c) Arbitration award (d) Consent award

55 Which of the following is not a method of dealing with resistance to change?
(a) Education and communication
(b) Participation
(c) Facilitation and support
(d) Coercion and Punishment

56 Which of the following is a legal industrial action as per law?
(a) Mutual insurance (b) Collective bargaining
(c) Lock out (d) None of these

57 What is the role of the Arbitration Board in United Kingdom?
(a) Agreement
(b) Settlement
(c) Award
(d) Collective agreements non-legal

58 Consider the following statements.
1. Performance appraisals serve as building blocks of career planning.
2. A disadvantage of rating scales is time involved.

Which of the statement(s) given above is/are correct?

Codes
(a) Both 1 and 2 (b) Only 1
(c) Only 2 (d) All of the above

Worker's Participation in Management and Industrial Relations

59 Works committees/joint committees are ...... bodies.
(a) directive (b) consultative
(c) representative (d) Both (b) and (c)

60 The .... recommended the setting-up of joint councils of management.
(a) 1st Five Year Plan (b) 2nd Five Year Plan
(c) 3rd Five Year Plan (d) None of these

61 A quality circle is a small group of employees, who meet ....
(a) occasionally (b) quarterly
(c) periodically (d) None of these

62 Participation generally has a ...... impact on psychology of an individual.
(a) negative (b) positive
(c) no (d) None of these

63 The organisation structure of quality circle generally consists of ...... level.
(a) four (b) three
(c) two (d) multiple

64 Features of quality circle are
(a) voluntary group (b) manageable size
(c) regular meeting (d) All of these

65 Worker's participation in management in any organisation is
(a) voluntary (b) institutional
(c) democratic (d) All of these

66 Joint management councils are formed, where
(a) more than 100 workers are employed
(b) more than 500 workers are employed
(c) more than 200 workers are employed
(d) None of the above

67 Administration of standing order does not covers
(a) classification of employees
(b) attendance and late coming
(c) grievance machinery, stoppage and shutdown
(d) motivation of employees

68 Penalties for the misconduct is assigned in .... of the unit.
(a) standing order (b) low order
(c) fluctuating order (d) None of these

69 The scope of employee and employee relation is/are
(a) wide (b) narrow
(c) Both (a) and (b) (d) None of these

70 Which of the following statement(s) is/are true?
(a) Industrial relations reduces productivity
(b) Industrial relations helps to avoid industrial conflict
(c) Both (a) and (b)
(d) All of the above

71 Objectives of industrial relations does not include
(a) to raise productivity
(b) to enhance industrial conflict
(c) to establish government control
(d) All of the above

72 ……… refers to the collective relations between employers and employees as a group.

(a) Industrial relation (b) Employment relation
(c) Industrial conflict (d) None of these

73 Method of securing worker's participation in management involves

1. co-partnership
2. suggestions scheme
3. joint consultation
4. employees representations on the Board of Directors

Which of the statement(s) given above is/are correct?

Codes

(a) Only 1 (b) 2, 3 and 4
(c) 1, 3 and 4 (d) All of the above

74 The 1975 scheme envisaged the setting-up of shop councils at the ...... level and joint councils at the ....

(a) shop/department, enterprise
(b) enterprise, shop/department
(c) shop, department
(d) None of the above

75 A scheme for worker's participation in industry at the shop floor and plant levels was introduced in

(a) October 1970
(b) October 1975
(c) October 1985
(d) October 1978

76 The word 'participation' means sharing the decision-making power with ...... ranks of the organisation.

(a) higher (b) lower
(c) equivalent (d) None of these

77 According to ……… approach, industrial relations are attributable to the differences in the perceptions of labour and management.

(a) psychological (b) sociological
(c) human relation (d) None of these

78 Which of the following parties is/are directly involved in employer-employee relations?

1. Employers 2. Employees
3. Government 4. Central Parties
5. Trade Unions

Select the correct answer using the codes given below

Codes

(a) 1, 2 and 3 (b) 1, 2, 3 and 5
(c) 1, 3 and 5 (d) Both 2 and 4

79 Which of the following statement(s) is/are not true?

(a) Disputes arose, when employers failed to recognise a union as a bargaining agent
(b) Gherao means to surround
(c) Candidates should not exist for the maintenance of sound industrial relations
(d) None of the above

80 Which of the following statement(s) is/are not correct?

(a) The right to go on strike is not a fundamental right
(b) Lockout as a collective stoppage of work by a group of workers
(c) Partial stoppage of work amounts to strike
(d) All of the above

81 Consider the following statements.

1. Industrial relations are a 'web of rules' formed by the interactions of government the industry and the labour.
2. The industrial relations system, is not characterised by forces of conflict and compromise on either side.
3. Industrial relations are fairly multidimensional in nature.

Which of the statement(s) given above is/are correct?

(a) Only 1 (b) Both 2 and 3
(c) Both 1 and 3 (d) None of these

82 Three major schemes of worker's participation in management in India have been introduced which are

(a) works committees
(b) joint management councils
(c) shop councils
(d) All of the above

83 In the work committee, President is a nominee of the ...... and the Vice-President is the ...... representative.

(a) employer, worker's (b) worker's, employer
(c) government, employer (d) None of these

84 Various schemes of worker's participation in management have failed to live up to the expectation due to following reasons.

(a) Lack of understanding of the concept
(b) Rigid attitude of the employees
(c) Both (a) and (b)
(d) None of the above

85 Giving employees the authority to make decisions and providing them with financial resources to implement these decision is called

(a) empowerment (b) job sharing
(c) participation (d) None of these

Miscellaneous

Directions (Q. Nos. 86 and 87) *The following two items consist of two statements, Statement I and Statement II. You have to examine these two statements carefully and select the answers to these items using the codes given below.*

Codes

(a) Both statements are correct
(b) Both statements are incorrect
(c) Statement I is correct, but Statement II is incorrect
(d) Statement I is incorrect, but Statement II is correct

86 **Statement** I Time wage system is suitable when workers are new and learning the job. **Statement** II Piece wage system is suitable where quality and workmanship are not very important.

87 **Statement** I Fringe benefits, now a days are a significant component of 'compensation.'
Statement II Under piece rate plan, employees are paid at a stipulated rate per hour of work done by the employee.

Directions (Q. Nos. 88-90) *In the questions given below are two statements labelled as Assertion (A) and Reason (R). In the context of the two statements, which one of the following is correct?*

Codes
(a) Both (A) and (R) are true
(b) Both (A) and (R) are false
(c) Both (A) and (R) are true and (R) is the explanatory of (A)
(d) (A) is true but, (R) is false

88 **Assertion** (A) Wage boards are set-up by the Government of India for fixation and revision of wages.
Reason (R) Wage boards are not governed by any legislation, but are appointed on an adhoc basis by the government.

89 **Assertion** (A) Under performance base incentives, performance that is rewarded is likely to be repeated.
Reason (R) People tend to do thing that are rewarded.

90 **Assertion** (A) Performance appraisal is a critical activity of personnel management.
Reason (R) Its goal is to provide an accurate picture of past and future employee performance.

Directions (Q. Nos. 91-99) *In the questions given below are two statements labelled as Assertion (A) and Reason (R). In the context of the two statements, which one of the following is correct?*

Codes
(a) Both (A) and (R) are correct and (R) is the correct explanation of (A)
(b) Both (A) and (R) are incorrect, but (R) is not the correct explanation of (A)
(c) (A) is correct, but (R) is incorrect
(d) (A) is incorrect, but (R) is correct

91 **Assertion** (A) Performance appraisal cannot be done in isolation.
Reason (R) Performance appraisal is linked to job analysis.

92 **Assertion** (A) Industrial relations are fairly multidimensional in nature.
Reason (R) Industrial relations are not influenced by complex set of institutional, economic and technological factors.

93 **Assertion** (A) 360 degree technique is not a single handed technique.
Reason (R) Multiple raters are involved in evaluating performance.

94 **Assertion** (A) The size of quality circle should not be too big.
Reason (R) Size of quality circle should be small to enable members to interect actively and contribute meaningfully.

95 **Assertion** (A) Health promotion focuses on prevention rather than treatment or cure.
Reason (R) Promoting health consciousness is not an easy task.

96 **Assertion** (A) Welfare measures may be statutory only not voluntary.
Reason (R) Voluntary benefits are the result of employer's generosity, enlightenment feelings.

97 **Assertion** (A) Social security measures do not offer proper compensation.
Reason (R) Social security measures do not extend monetary assistance to workers.

98 **Assertion** (A) Worker's participation is possible at all levels of management.
Reason (R) Worker's participation may be faint at lower level and vigorous at top level.

99 **Assertion** (A) Employers resist the participation of workers in decision-making.
Reason (R) Employers feel that workers are not competent enough to take decisions.

100 Match the following.

List I	List II
A. Minimum wage	1. Wage above the minimum wage, but below the living wage.
B. Fair wage	2. Wage sufficient to sustain and preserve the efficiency of the worker and to provide him basic amenities.
C. Living wage	3. Consists of various pay scales showing ranges of pay within each grade.
D. Wage structure	4. Wages, which grows in line with the growth of the national economy.

Codes

	A	B	C	D
(a)	1	2	3	4
(b)	2	1	4	3
(c)	1	3	2	4
(d)	4	3	2	1

101 **Match the following.**

List I	List II
A. Wage curve	1. The perceived fairness of the relation.
B. Equity	2. Series of steps or levels within a pay grade, usually based on year's service.
C. Pay ranges	3. Pay programmes that are linked to profit and productivity gains.
D. Variable pay systems	4. Show the relationship between the value of the job and the average wage paid for this job.

Codes

	A	B	C	D		A	B	C	D
(a)	4	1	2	3	(b)	1	2	3	4
(c)	2	1	3	4	(d)	3	2	4	1

102 **Match the following.**

List I (Factors Influencing Wages and Salary Administration)	List II (Features)
A. State regulation	1. Projects determine the paying capacity of firm.
B. Productivity	2. Highly unorganised sectors have higher wages.
C. Unions	3. Good job performance lead to good wages.
D. Ability to pay	4. Determine the wage structure in an industry.

Codes

	A	B	C	D
(a)	3	1	4	2
(b)	3	1	2	4
(c)	2	1	4	3
(d)	4	3	2	1

103 **Match the following.**

List I (Concepts)	List II (Features)
A. Halsey plan	1. It assures minimum time wages.
B. Rowan plan	2. It is easy to follow and relatively simple to operate.
C. Gantt task plan	3. Earnings of workers increases with the improvement in their efficiency.
D. Accelerated premium bonus plan	4. Workers can easily understand its working.

Codes

	A	B	C	D
(a)	4	3	2	1
(b)	3	1	4	2
(c)	2	1	4	3
(d)	1	2	3	4

104 **Match the following.**

List I (Concepts)	List II (Demerits)
A. Time wage system	1. The earnings of workers are not stable.
B. Piece wage system	2. Does not encourage extraordinary efficiency.
C. Halsey plan	3. In this, cost of supervision are high.
D. Rowan plan	4. Fixation of standard is not easy.

Codes

	A	B	C	D		A	B	C	D
(a)	4	3	2	1	(b)	3	1	4	2
(c)	2	1	4	3	(d)	1	2	3	4

105 **Match the following.**

List I (Concepts)	List II (Merits)
A. Time wage system	1. It offers the necessary incentive to the high class labour, which is important for obtaining high production level.
B. Piece wage system	2. The rate of bonus increases gradually from 67% to 100% efficiency.
C. Modified time rate	3. Workers do not suffer from temporary loss of efficiency.
D. Emerson's efficiency plan	4. This method is just and fair to all.

Codes

	A	B	C	D		A	B	C	D
(a)	4	1	2	3	(b)	3	4	1	2
(c)	2	3	4	1	(d)	2	1	4	3

106 **Match the following.**

List I (Concepts)	List II (Meanings)
A. Merit pay	1. Extra benefits provided to employees in addition to the normal compensation paid in the form of wage or salary.
B. Fringe benefits	2. Financial and non-financial rewards to the employees for their services rendered to the company.
C. Compensation	3. Compensation plan where all team members receive an incentive bonus payment when production or services standards are met or exceeded.
D. Team incentive plan	4. Any salary increase awarded to an employee based on his or her individual performance.

Codes

	A	B	C	D		A	B	C	D
(a)	4	3	2	1	(b)	2	1	4	3
(c)	3	1	4	2	(d)	4	1	2	3

107 Match the following.

List I (Individual Incentive Plans)	List II (Features)
A. Halsey plan	1. If the worker exceeds the standards, he is paid a higher price rate.
B. Rowan plan	2. Every operation or job is expressed in terms of so many standard minutes.
C. Gantt task plan	3. It recognises individual efficiency and pays bonus on the basis of time saved.
D. Bedaux plan	4. Bonus is paid on the basis of time saved.

Codes

	A	B	C	D
(a)	4	3	2	1
(b)	3	4	1	2
(c)	2	1	4	3
(d)	4	3	1	2

108 Match the following.

List I (Types of Fringe Benefit)	List II (Features)
A. Safety and health	1. When the employee's services get confirmed, his job becomes secure.
B. Voluntary arrangements	2. Dependents of the employee are eligible for compensation in case of death of the employee.
C. Workmen's compensation	3. The Factories Act, 1948 stipulated certain requirements regarding working conditions with a view to provide safe working environment.
D. Employee security	4. Medical benefits are extended to employee family members.

Codes

	A	B	C	D
(a)	4	3	2	1
(b)	3	4	2	1
(c)	2	3	4	1
(d)	4	1	2	3

109 Match the following.

List I (Type of Incentive Plans)	List II (Examples)
A. Individual incentive plans	1. Profit sharing
B. Group incentive plans	2. Rucker plan
C. Organisation wide incentive plans	3. Rowan plan
D. Individual incentive plans	4. Gantt task and bonus plan

Codes

	A	B	C	D
(a)	4	2	1	3
(b)	2	1	4	3
(c)	3	1	4	2
(d)	4	3	2	1

110 Match the following.

List I (Group Incentives Plans)	List II (Features)
A. Priestman's production bonus	1. Employees receive a constant proportion of the 'added value'.
B. Scanlon plan	2. A standard is fixed in terms of units or points.
C. Co-partnership	3. Constant proportion of added value of output is paid to the workers, who are responsible for the addition of the value.
D. Rucker plan	4. Employees share the capital as well as profits.

Codes

	A	B	C	D
(a)	4	1	2	3
(b)	2	3	4	1
(c)	3	4	1	2
(d)	4	3	2	1

111 Match the following.

List I (Individual Incentive Plans)	List II (Features)
A. Taylor's differential piece rate system	1. Day wages are guaranteed.
B. Merrick's differential piece rate system	2. It penalises the slow worker by paying low rate.
C. Halsey plan	3. Under this, there are three piece rates instead of two.
D. Gantt task plan	4. Standard time is fixed for each job or operation.

Codes

	A	B	C	D
(a)	4	3	2	1
(b)	3	4	1	2
(c)	2	3	4	1
(d)	4	3	1	2

112 Match the following.

List I	List II
A. Motivation	1. A process of stimulating people to action to accomplish desired goals.
B. Morale	2. Capacity of a group of people to pull together persistently and consistently in pursuit of a common goal.
C. Effort	3. Outward action of individual directed towards some goals.
D. Apathy	4. Significant dysfunction tension resulting in no effort being made.

Codes

	A	B	C	D
(a)	1	2	3	4
(b)	2	1	3	4
(c)	4	1	2	3
(d)	4	2	3	1

113 Match the following.

List I (Methods of Performance Appraisal)	List II (Features)
A. Forced distribution method	1. The manager prepares lists of statements of behaviour of an employee.
B. Human resources accounting	2. Combination of rating scale and critical incident technique.
C. Critical incident technique	3. Tries to place a value on organisational human resources as assets and not as expenses.
D. Behaviourally anchored rating scales	4. Employee is appraised according to a predetermined distribution scale.

Codes

	A	B	C	D
(a)	2	3	4	1
(b)	4	3	1	2
(c)	3	1	4	2
(d)	2	1	4	3

114 Match the following.

List I (Factors of Industrial Relation)	List II (Features)
A. Technological factors	1. Population, religion, customs etc.
B. Economic factors	2. Mechanisation, automation etc.
C. Institutional factors	3. Economic organisations like labour force etc.
D. Social and cultural factors	4. Government policy, labour legislation etc.

Codes

	A	B	C	D
(a)	4	3	2	1
(b)	2	3	4	1
(c)	3	2	4	1
(d)	3	1	4	2

115 Match the following.

List I	List II
A. Autonomous work groups	1. A small group of employees, who monitor productivity and quality and suggest solutions to problem.
B. Flexi time	2. Employee groups with a high degree of decision-making responsibility and behavioural control for completing their work.
C. Quality of working life	3. Working hours that give employees the option of choosing starting and quitting times.
D. Quality circles	4. Work environment including factors like autonomy, recognition, belongingness, rewards etc.

Codes

	A	B	C	D
(a)	1	2	3	4
(b)	2	3	4	1
(c)	2	1	3	4
(d)	3	2	4	1

116 Match the following.

List I	List II
A. Empowerment	1. Granting employees power to initiate change.
B. Participation	2. Sharing the decision-making power with the lower ranks of the organisation.
C. Golden parachute	3. Agreement by a company to compensate executives with bonuses and benefits, if they are displaced by merger or acquisition.
D. Compressed work week	4. Reallocated work hours.

Codes

	A	B	C	D
(a)	1	2	3	4
(b)	2	1	4	3
(c)	4	3	2	1
(d)	3	2	4	1

PREVIOUS YEARS' QUESTIONS

December 2018

1. Arrange the following stages of staffing in correct sequence and indicate the code of correct sequence.

1. Performance appraisal 2. Recruitment
3. Transfers 4. Selection
5. Induction and orientation

Codes

(a) 2, 1, 4, 5, 3 (b) 2, 4, 5, 1, 3
(c) 4, 2, 5, 3, 1 (d) 1, 2, 4, 5, 3

2. Match the items of List I with the items of List II and choose the correct answer from the codes given below.

List I	List II
A. Behaviour referent	1. Wide ranging cultural, structural and personnel strategies
B. Focus of attention for interventions	2. Manage climate and culture
C. Conflict handling	3. Few
D. Job categories and grades	4. Values/mission

Codes

	A	B	C	D		A	B	C	D
(a)	4	2	1	3	(b)	3	1	2	4
(c)	4	1	2	3	(d)	1	2	4	3

3. Which one of the following items is not a part of job specification?

(a) Location
(b) Initiative
(c) Judgement
(d) Emotional characteristics

4. Match the items of List I with the items of List II and choose the correct answer from the codes given below.

List I	List II
A. Claims	1. Company car, club membership, paid holidays, furnished house
B. Fringe benefits	2. Telephone/mobile allowance, internet allowance, medical allowance
C. Perquisites	3. Canteen, uniform, accident relief

Codes

	A	B	C
(a)	1	2	3
(b)	2	3	1
(c)	3	2	1
(d)	2	1	3

5. Choose the correct code for the following statements being correct or incorrect.

Statement I Thousands of employees die everyday in factories due to accidents.

Statement II To make an accident free plant adds to cost and decreases productivity.

Codes

(a) Both statements are correct
(b) Both statements are incorrect
(c) Statement I is correct, but Statement II is incorrect
(d) Statement II is correct, but Statement I is incorrect

6. Match the items of List I with the items of List II and choose the correct answer from the codes given below.

List	List II
A. Job context	1. Procedures used
B. Job related tangibles and intangibles	2. Work schedule
C. Work activities	3. Work standards
D. Work performance	4. Services rendered

Codes

	A	B	C	D
(a)	3	4	2	1
(b)	2	4	1	3
(c)	4	3	1	2
(d)	1	4	2	3

7. In which one of the following forms of worker's participation in management is the role of the workers council not just advisory but the management is under a moral obligation to acknowledge, accept and implement the unanimous decision of the council?

(a) Consultative participation
(b) Associative participation
(c) Administrative participation
(d) Decisive participation

July 2018

8. **Assertion** (A) Compensation has two vital domains economic concept and psychological concept.

Reason (R) Compensation basically represents an employment contract.

Codes

(a) (A) is correct and (R) is the right explanation of (A)
(b) (A) is correct, but (R) is not the right explanation of (A)
(c) (A) is correct, but (R) is incorrect
(d) (A) is incorrect, but (R) is correct

9. Which of the following statements does not stand as a principle of compensation administration?

(a) An enterprise should have a clear cut plan to determine differential pay level in terms of divergent job requirements
(b) People and jobs should never be mingled
(c) The compensation system should be designed with subjectivity with respect to individual skill sets exercised from time to time
(d) There should be established wage grievance handling procedures

10. Match the items of List I with the items of List II pertaining to the ranking methods used in performance management systems and select the code of correct matching.

List I (Ranking Methods)	List-II (Methodology)
A. Simple ranking	1. Based on overall performance.
B. Alternation ranking	2. Ends up with predetermined number of people in each group.
C. Paired comparison	3. Based on particular trait only for quantity/quality of work.
D. Forced distribution	4. Based on a trait or a set of trait and avoids central tendency.

Codes

	A	B	C	D
(a)	2	3	4	1
(b)	1	4	3	2
(c)	4	2	1	3
(d)	3	1	2	4

11. Match the items of List I with the items of List II relating to industrial relationship and select the code of correct matching.

List I	List II
A. Healthy labour management relations	1. Industrial Disputes Act
B. Industrial peace law	2. Guiding principles for a grievance procedure
C. Industrial democracy	3. Worker's participation in management
D. National Commission on Labour, 1969	4. Voluntary arbitration and responsible trade union

Codes

	A	B	C	D
(a)	4	1	3	2
(b)	2	3	4	1
(c)	3	1	4	2
(d)	2	4	1	3

12. Which of the following is not the primary objective of industrial relations and labour laws?

(a) Maintaining social equity
(b) Providing credit facilities to industries
(c) International uniformity
(d) Promoting economic growth

13. Assertion (A) In real terms, worker's participation in management has failed in India.

Reason (R) There is lack of attitudinal change, multiplicity of unions and absence of a procedure to determine a sole bargaining agent in an organisation.

Codes

(a) (A) is correct and (R) is the correct explanation of (A)
(b) (A) is correct, but (R) is not the correct explanation of (A)
(c) (A) is correct, but (R) is incorrect
(d) (A) is incorrect, but (R) is correct

November 2017

14. Which of the statements are not correct? Indicate the correct code.

Statement I Social assistance is financed by tripartite or bipartite contributions.

Statement II Social insurance ignores the income and means of liable relation.

Statement III Social assistance makes the beneficiary a first charge on the liable relations.

Statement IV Social assistance aims at providing maximum subsistance to those who cannot make it on their own.

Codes

(a) Statements I and II
(b) Statements II and III
(c) Statements I and IV
(d) Statements III and IV

15. Which of the following statements relating to appraisal methods are not correct? Indicate the correct code.

Statement I The MBO programme is built on the assumption that individuals always need not to be responsible and self-directed and thus need to be motivated to work towards objectives.

Statement II Forced distribution method was developed by Karl Marx.

Statement III Peer evaluation and self-appraisal need to be done on well defined parameters in check-list method.

Statement IV Forced choice method consists of seven main factors on three point rating scale.

Codes

(a) Statements I and II
(b) Statements III and IV
(c) Statements I, II and III
(d) Statements I, II, III and IV

January 2017

16. Which council was established in India by Government of India in the year 1966 to promote safety consciousness among workers in industries ?

(a) Factory Advise Council
(b) National Safety Council
(c) National Industrial Council
(d) Safety Regulations Council

17. Match the items of List I with the items of List II relating to social security measures in India and indicate the code of correct matching.

List I	List II
A. Social assistance	1. Payable to workers in accidents and injuries during employment
B. Social insurance	2. Covers individual risks primarily
C. Commercial insurance	3. Maternity benefits
D. Workmen's compensation	4. Provident funds

Codes

	A	B	C	D		A	B	C	D
(a)	3	4	2	1	(c)	4	3	2	1
(c)	4	3	1	2	(d)	2	1	3	4

18. Which of the following statements relating to incentive payments is correct ?

(a) In Halsey incentive plan, bonus paid to a worker is equal to 50 per cent of time saved divided by rate per hour
(b) In Rowan incentive plan, bonus paid to employee is equal to the proportion of the time saved to the standard time
(c) In Taylor's differential piece rate system, a worker whose output exceeds standard output is paid 100 per cent of piece rate and a worker whose output falls short of standard is paid only 50 per cent of piece rate
(d) The Rowan incentive plan is the base of all other incentive payment plans

19. A statement containing items such as job title, location, summary, duties, materials used, working conditions etc is called

(a) job specification
(b) job evaluation
(c) job description
(d) job analysis

20. Match the items of List I with the items of List II regarding evaluation of project application.

List I	List II
A. Managerial appraisal	1. Analysis of working results
B. Economic appraisal	2. Disposal of factory effluents
C. Financial appraisal	3. Analysis about traits of an entrepreneur
D. Technical appraisal	4. Analysis on employment potential

Codes

	A	B	C	D		A	B	C	D
(a)	1	2	4	3	(b)	2	1	3	4
(c)	3	4	1	2	(d)	4	3	2	1

21. **Assertion** (A) Organisations are increasingly getting de-jobbed.

Reason (R) Jobs are becoming more amorphous and more difficult to define.

Codes

(a) (A) and (R) both are correct, but (R) is not the correct explanation of (A)
(b) (A) and (R) both are not correct
(c) (A) is correct, but (R) is incorrect
(d) (A) and (R) both are correct and (R) is the correct explanation of (A)

22. Match the most common rating errors made during performance appraisal with their right explanations. Indicate the code of correct matching.

List I (Common Rating Errors)	List II (Description)
A. Leniency	1. Subjective assessment
B. Halo error	2. One aspect of individual's performance influence his entire performance
C. Spillover effect	3. Past performance appraisal ratings unjustifiably influencing current ratings
D. Rater effect	4. Favoritism and stereotyping

Codes

	A	B	C	D		A	B	C	D
(a)	1	2	3	4	(b)	2	3	4	1
(c)	3	4	2	1	(d)	4	3	2	1

23. Which one of the following industrial relations approach believes in state intervention *via*. legislation and the creation of industrial tribunals as supporting management's interest rather than ensuring a balance between the competing groups?

(a) Unitary approach
(b) Pluralistic approach
(c) Marxist approach
(d) Judiciary approach

July 2016

24. Match the items of List I with the items of List II and indicate the correct code.

List I	List II
A. Job specifications	1. The procedure for determining the duties and skill requirements of a job and the kind of person who should be hired for it.
B. Job description	2. A list of human requirements.

List I	List II
C. Job analysis	3. A list of job's duties, responsibilities, reporting, relationships, working conditions and supervisory responsibilities.

Codes

	A	B	C		A	B	C
(a)	1	2	3	(b)	2	3	1
(c)	3	2	1	(d)	2	1	3

25. **Which of the following statement is correct about Wage Boards in India?**

1. A Wage Board is a tripartite body.
2. Labour and management representatives on a Wage Board can be selected from industries other than the one which is investigated.
3. Wage Boards are always statutory in nature.
4. Wage Boards work on the principle of living wage.

Select the correct answer using the codes given below

Codes

(a) Only 1 (b) Both 2 and 3
(c) Both 3 and 4 (d) All of the above

26. **Who gave the surplus value theory of wage?**

(a) David Ricardo (b) Karl Marx
(c) Adam Smith (d) FA Walker

December 2015

27. **Match the following.**

List I (Job Analysis)	List II (Examples)
A. Task	1. Payroll processing
B. Element	2. Compensation policy administrator
C. Duty	3. Compensation design manager
D. Position	4. Compensation specialist
E. Job	5. Preparing forms
F. Occupation	6. Signing pay cheques

Codes

	A	B	C	D	E	F
(a)	1	2	3	4	5	6
(b)	5	6	1	2	3	4
(c)	6	5	4	2	3	1
(d)	6	1	2	3	4	5

28. **The internal factors affecting the wage mix include**

1. relative worth of the job
2. area wage rates
3. employer's ability to pay
4. manpower market conditions

Select the correct answer using the codes given below

Codes

(a) 1, 2 and 3 (b) Both 1 and 3
(c) 2, 3 and 4 (d) All of the above

June 2015

29. **Matching essential managers and essential positions is a step in the process of**

(a) career cycle
(b) succession planning
(c) career planning
(d) career stages

30. **Areas of establishing objectives under MBO are**

1. market standing 2. innovation
3. industrial relations 4. public accountability
5. productivity 6. industrial policy

Select the correct answer using the codes given below

Codes

(a) 3, 4, 5 and 6 (b) 1, 2, 4 and 5
(c) 1, 2, 5 and 6 (d) 2, 3, 4 and 5

31. **The barriers to effective performance appraisal are**

1. psychological blocks of managers
2. faulty assumptions of the parties concerned
3. technical pitfalls
4. faulty written communications

Select the correct answer using the codes given below

Codes

(a) Both 2 and 3 (b) Both 1 and 2
(c) 1, 2 and 3 (d) All of the above

32. **Assertion** (A) Job evaluation is essentially a job rating process, not unlike the rating of employees.

Reason (R) Job evaluation is a practice which seeks to provide a degree of objectivity in measuring the comparative value of jobs within an organisation and among similar organisations.

Codes

(a) Both (A) and (R) are true
(b) Both (A) and (R) are false
(c) (A) is true, but (R) is false
(d) (A) is false, but (R) is true

December 2014

33. **Who has developed the 'systems approach' of industrial relations?**

(a) John Dunlop
(b) Gary S Becker
(c) Michael J Jucius
(d) Edwin B Flippo

34. **Assertion** (A) MBO is effective way of planning and organising the work.

Reason (R) Employees participate in setting the objectives.

Codes

(a) Both (A) and (R) are true
(b) Both (A) and (R) are false
(c) (A) is true, but (R) is false
(d) (A) is false, but (R) is true

35. Which one of the following is not the purpose of performance monitoring research?
(a) To provide feedback for evaluation and control
(b) To indicate things that are not going as planned
(c) To help the organisation to plan various activities
(d) It is required to explain why something went wrong

36. **Assertion** (A) Job design relates to the manner in which tasks are put together to form complete job.
Reason (R) The matrix organisation is a project organisation plus a functional organisation.
Codes
(a) Both (A) and (R) are true (b) (A) is true, but (R) is false
(c) (A) is false, but (R) is true (d) Both (A) and (R) are false

37. Which of the following is not a component of job analysis?
(a) Job description (b) Role analysis
(c) Job summary (d) Job specification

38. **Assertion** (A) High morale and high productivity go hand-in-hand.
Reason (R) Workers do not have their own ways for relief from fatigue and monotony.
Codes
(a) Both (A) and (R) are true
(b) (A) is true, but (R) is false
(c) (A) is false, but (R) is true
(d) Both (A) and (R) are false

39. Relationship at work is the source of
(a) status anxiety (b) managerial stress
(c) legitimate power (d) expert power

40. Match the following.

List I (Company Name)	List II (Brand)
A. Grievances	1. Profit sharing
B. Impact of technology	2. Effective planning
C. Adjustment to technology	3. Index of low morale
D. Morale improvement	4. Changes in occupation

Codes

	A	B	C	D		A	B	C	D
(a)	1	2	3	4	(b)	4	3	2	1
(c)	3	2	4	1	(d)	3	4	2	1

June 2014

41. An MBO programme usually involves the following steps
1. establishing unit's objectives
2. establishing organisational goals
3. negotiating or agreeing
4. reviewing the performance
5. creating action plans

Select the correct answer using the codes given below
Codes
(a) 1, 2, 3, 4, 5 (b) 2, 1, 3, 5, 4
(c) 2, 3, 1, 4, 5 (d) 5, 4, 3, 2, 1

42. Indicate the quantitative methods of job evaluation
(a) ranking methods and job comparison method
(b) point rating method and factor comparison method
(c) grading method and job classification method
(d) factor comparison method and ranking method

43. Match the following.

List I	List II
A. Career goals	1. The process goals where in an executive serves as a guide.
B. Career path	2. The future path positions one strives to reach as part of career.
C. Career counseling	3. The sequential pattern of jobs that form a career.
D. Mentoring	4. Guiding people on their possible career path.

Codes

	A	B	C	D		A	B	C	D
(a)	2	3	4	1	(b)	1	2	3	4
(c)	4	3	2	1	(d)	3	2	1	4

December 2013

44. Which one of the following does not serve the main objective of performance appraisal?
(a) Developmental uses (b) Administrative uses
(c) Ethical and moral values (d) Organisational objectives

45. **Statement** I Job evaluation is a technique of assessing the worth of each job in comparison with others throughout an organisation.
Statement II Job evaluation and job rating are one and the same for employees' appraisal purposes.
Codes
(a) Statement I is correct, but Statement II is incorrect
(b) Statement II is correct, but Statement I is incorrect
(c) Both statements are correct
(d) Both statements are incorrect

46. Match the following.

List I	List II
A. Job rotation	1. Involves conscious efforts to organise tasks, duties and responsibilities into a unit of work to achieve certain objectives.
B. Job design	2. Involves movement of employees from job to job.
C. Job evaluation	3. Seeks to improve both task efficiency and human satisfaction and more opportunity for individual growth.
D. Job enrichment	4. The formal procees by which the relative worth of various jobs in the organisation is determined for pay purpose.

Codes

	A	B	C	D
(a)	1	2	3	4
(b)	4	3	2	1
(c)	3	4	2	1
(d)	2	1	4	3

47. Assertion (A) Merit rating of an employee is the process of evaluating the employee's performance on the job in terms of the requirements of the job.

Reason (R) Employees' merit rating is a technique for fair and systematic evaluation of an employee's capacities, abilities and performance on the specific job.

Codes

(a) Both (A) and (R) are true and (R) is the correct explanation of (A)
(b) Both (A) and (R) are true, but (R) is not the correct explanation of (A)
(c) Both (A) and (R) are false
(d) (R) is true, but (A) is false

48. The major provisions for employees' health and safety are contained in

(a) The Industrial Disputes Act, 1947
(b) The Factories Act, 1948
(c) The Industrial Employment (Standing Orders) Act, 1946
(d) The Employees Compensation Act, 1923

49. Indicate your choice through the codes given below.

1. A club is an industry under the Industrial Disputes Act, 1947.
2. Factory as defined under the Factories Act, 1948 includes a mine.
3. For purpose of the payment of bonus to employees, the gross profits earned by a bank is to be calculated in the manner specified in Schedule I of the Payment of the Bonus Act, 1965.
4. Various labour laws do not apply to public sector undertakings.

Codes

(a) Only 1
(b) 2, 3, 4 and 5
(c) Both 1 and 2
(d) All of the above

50. Assertion (A) The emphasis in industrial psychology has shifted from the studies of the isolated individual and the physical environment to the consideration of motivation and morale.

Reason (R) A motivated employee with a high morale will always give high productivity.

Codes

(a) Both (A) and (R) are true and (R) is the correct explanation of (A)
(b) (A) is true, but (R) is false
(c) Both (A) and (R) are false
(d) Both (A) and (R) are true, but (R) is not the correct explanation of (A)

June 2013

51. According to D Katz, morale has four dimensions

1. jobs satisfaction
2. satisfaction with wages and promotional opportunities
3. identification with company
4. pride in the work group
5. top management support

Select the correct answer using the codes given below

Codes

(a) 1, 2, 3 and 4 (b) 1, 2, 3 and 5
(c) 1, 2, 4 and 5 (d) 1, 3, 4 and 5

52. Which of the following are the modern method of performance appraisal?

1. 360 degree performance appraisal
2. Graphic rating scale
3. Management by Objectives (MBO)
4. Forced distribution method
5. Behaviourally Anchored Rating Scales (BARS)

Select the correct answer using the codes given below

Codes

(a) 1, 2 and 3 (b) 2, 4 and 5 (c) 1, 3 and 5 (d) 4, 2 and 1

December 2012

53. Which among the following are parts of job description?

1. Duties performed 2. Job summary
3. Job identification 4. Supervision given
5. Delegation of authority

Select the correct answer using the codes given below

Codes

(a) 1, 2, 3 and 4 (b) 2, 3, 4 and 5
(c) 1, 3, 4 and 5 (d) 1, 2, 3 and 5

54. Which among the following is not a voluntary method for prevention and settlement of disputes?

(a) Collective bargaining (b) Standing orders
(c) Joint consultation (d) Works committee

55. Statement I It is no better to pay employees for little than to pay too much.

Statement II Competent employees will remain competent forever.

Codes

(a) Both statements are correct
(b) Both statements are incorrect
(c) Statement I is correct, but Statement II is incorrect
(d) Statement I is incorrect, but Statement II is correct

June 2012

56. Statement I Labour always get a major share of productivity gains.

Statement II Partial stoppage of work by workers amounts to strike.

(a) Statement I is correct, but II is incorrect
(b) Statement II is correct, but I is incorrect
(c) Both statements are correct
(d) Both statements are incorrect

57. What is MBO?
(a) Management by Objectives
(b) Multiple Business Organisation
(c) Management by Organisation
(d) Multiplicity of Business Operations

58. Under which method of performance appraisal, one person is compared with all others for the purpose of placing them in a simple order of work?
(a) Grading
(b) Person to person comparison
(c) Ranking
(d) None of the above

59. The purpose of job evaluation is
(a) fixation of responsibility
(b) promotion
(c) wage determination
(d) transfer to a better job

ANSWERS

Objective Questions

1 (b)	2 (d)	3 (c)	4 (d)	5 (d)	6 (a)	7 (a)	8 (c)	9 (d)	10 (b)
11 (d)	12 (b)	13 (c)	14 (a)	15 (a)	16 (b)	17 (a)	18 (b)	19 (c)	20 (c)
21 (c)	22 (a)	23 (c)	24 (d)	25 (b)	26 (b)	27 (b)	28 (c)	29 (d)	30 (b)
31 (b)	32 (b)	33 (a)	34 (b)	35 (a)	36 (b)	37 (a)	38 (d)	39 (c)	40 (b)
41 (b)	42 (a)	43 (c)	44 (b)	45 (a)	46 (a)	47 (b)	48 (d)	49 (b)	50 (b)
51 (c)	52 (d)	53 (c)	54 (d)	55 (d)	56 (b)	57 (d)	58 (b)	59 (d)	60 (b)
61 (c)	62 (a)	63 (a)	64 (c)	65 (a)	66 (b)	67 (d)	68 (a)	69 (a)	70 (b)
71 (b)	72 (a)	73 (a)	74 (a)	75 (b)	76 (a)	77 (a)	78 (c)	79 (c)	80 (c)
81 (c)	82 (d)	83 (a)	84 (c)	85 (a)	86 (a)	87 (d)	88 (a)	89 (b)	90 (c)
91 (a)	92 (c)	93 (a)	94 (c)	95 (a)	96 (d)	97 (b)	98 (c)	99 (a)	100 (b)
101 (a)	102 (d)	103 (b)	104 (b)	105 (b)	106 (d)	107 (b)	108 (b)	109 (a)	110 (b)
111 (c)	112 (a)	113 (b)	114 (b)	115 (b)	116 (a)				

Previous Years' Questions

1 (b)	2 (c)	3 (a)	4 (b)	5 (c)	6 (b)	7 (b)	8 (b)	9 (c)	10 (b)
11 (a)	12 (b)	13 (a)	14 (c)	15 (d)	16 (b)	17 (a)	18 (b)	19 (c)	20 (c)
21 (d)	22 (a)	23 (c)	24 (b)	25 (a)	26 (b)	27 (b)	28 (d)	29 (a)	30 (d)
31 (d)	32 (a)	33 (b)	34 (a)	35 (c)	36 (a)	37 (c)	38 (d)	39 (b)	40 (d)
41 (b)	42 (b)	43 (a)	41 (c)	45 (a)	46 (d)	47 (b)	48 (b)	49 (c)	50 (b)
51 (a)	52 (c)	53 (b)	54 (a)	55 (a)	56 (b)	57 (a)	58 (c)	59 (c)	

CHAPTER 25

Bank and its Types

Finance is the life blood of trade, commerce and industry. Now-a-days, banking sector act as the backbone of modern business. Development of any country mainly depends upon the banking system. There are different types of banks working for accomplishing financial and non-financial needs of people of the country.

Overview of Indian Financial System

The financial system is a system that allows the transfer of money between savers and borrowers. It is a set of institutional arrangement through which financial surplus are mobilised from unit generating surplus income to those who need such funds. It includes different financial markets, institutions, instruments, services and mechanisms which promote the generation of saving, investment, capital formation and growth and overall leads to growth of economy.

The economic development of any country depends upon the existence of a well organised financial system.

In short, the financial system is concerned about money, credit and finance. *It consist of*

- well established network of financial institutions.
- well developed financial markets.
- well developed system of financial assets.

So, the financial system provides the intermediation between savers and investors and promotes faster economic development.

According to **Gurusamy**, "Financial system is a set of complex and closely interconnected financial institutions, markets, instruments, services, practices and transactions".

In this Chapter

Banks

The word 'bank' was developed from the German word 'banck'. The word 'banck' means a joint stock firm.

A bank is an institution which accepts deposits from the general public and extends loans to the household, the firms and the government. In short, banks are those institution which deals in money and credit.

According to Indian Banking Regulation Act, 1949, "Banking company is one who do banking business." It means to accept deposits of money from public for the purpose of lending or investment and repayable on demand or otherwise and withdrawable by cheque, draft, order or otherwise.

History and Growth of Banking System in India

The Indian banking system traces sack its history to 1786, when the first bank general bank of India was established.

From that year till today, the journey of growth of the Indian banking system can be divided into three phases

Phase I *(Early Phase from 1786 to 1969 of Indian Banks)*

- In the mid 19th century, the East India Company established the Bank of Bengal in 1809, the Bank of Bombay in 1840 and the Bank of Madras in 1843. These were initially independent units and were referred as the Presidency Banks. These three were later merged in 1920, as Imperial Bank of India, which had European shareholders.
- Later in 1865, Allahabad Bank was established followed by Punjab National Bank in 1894. Between 1906 and 1913, Bank of India, Central Bank of India, Bank of Baroda, Canara Bank, Indian Bank and Bank of Mysore were set-up.
- Reserve Bank of India came into being in 1935.

Phase II *(Nationalisation of Indian Banks and upto 1991 prior to Indian Banking Sector Reforms)*

- In 1949, Banking Regulation Act enacted.
- After independence, the Imperial Bank of India was nationalised under the State Bank of India Act of 1955 and became known as the State Bank of India for handling Central and State Government Banking transactions and functioning as the principal agent of RBI.
- In 1959, seven subsidiaries of SBI were also nationalised.
- In1961, insurance cover extended to deposits.
- With effect from the midnight of 19th July, 1969, 14 major banks were nationalised.
- In 1971, credit guarantee corporation was created.
- Regional Rural Bank was introduced in 1975.
- In 1980, 6 banks with deposits over ₹ 200 crore were nationalised.

Phase III *(New Phase of Indian Banking System with the advent of Indian Financial and Banking Sector Reforms after, 1991)*

- Prior to 1991, all banks were state owned. In 1991, government opened the gate of liberalisation of banking practices as per the report of a banking committee set-up under the chairmanship of Mr. M. Narasimham.
- Later on, in the year 1993, the government merged New Bank of India with Punjab National Bank. It was the only merger between nationalised banks and resulted in the reduction of the number of nationalised banks from 20 to 19.
- Till now, banking industry has changed tremendously with retail banking shifting to universal banking, E-banking and has customer satisfaction as the highest priority.

Types of Banks

Banks are classified into two types *i.e.* commercial banks and cooperative banks

Commercial Banks

They are established with an objective of collecting money from general public and giving loans to general public by way of cash credit, overdrafts etc.

Structure of Commercial Banks

It can be classified by the following chart

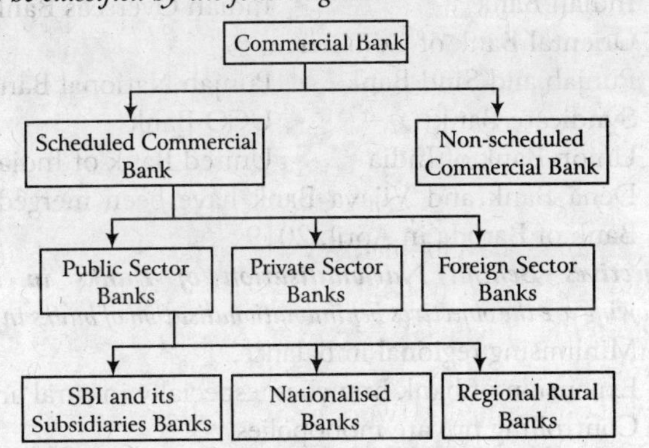

These are as follows

Scheduled Bank

These are those bank which are registered in the second schedule of the Reserve Bank of India, 1934. It includes those banks, which have a paid-up capital and reserves of an aggregate value of not less than ₹ 5 lakh and must satisfy the criteria laid down under Section 46(6)(a) of the Act and its economic condition must be sound.

Classification of Scheduled Banks

Scheduled banks can further be categorised as follows

Public Sector Banks

Public sector banks are banks, in which the government and RBI has major holding. They are managed and operated by the government. They can be further sub-divided into SBI and its associate banks, other nationalised banks and regional rural banks. *These are as follows*

SBI and Associate Banks

State Bank of India (SBI) is the country's largest commercial bank in terms of assets, deposits and employees. It is a government-owned corporation which offers a wide range of general banking services from loans and advances to corporates and individuals in India and abroad.

➠ **Note** *All subsidiary banks of SBI and Bhartiya Mahila Bank have been merged into SBI in April 2017.*

Nationalised Banks

In 1955, the Imperial Bank of India was nationalised and was given the name 'State Bank of India'. On 19th July, 1969, major 14 Indian commercial banks were nationalised. In 1980, another 6 banks were nationalised. Till the year 1980, approximately 80% of the banking segment in India was under government's ownership.

The following is the list of all nationalised banks

- Allahabad Bank
- Andhra Bank
- Bank of Baroda
- Bank of India
- Bank of Maharashtra
- Canara Bank
- Central Bank of India
- Corporation Bank
- Indian Bank
- Indian Overseas Bank
- Oriental Bank of Commerce
- Punjab and Sind Bank
- Punjab National Bank
- Syndicate Bank
- UCO Bank
- Union Bank of India
- United Bank of India
- Dena Bank and Vijaya Bank have been merged into Bank of Baroda in April, 2019

Objectives Behind Nationalisation of Banks in India

Following are the objectives behind nationalisation of banks in India

- Minimising regional imbalance.
- Expansion of bank branches, especially in rural areas.
- Controlling private monopolies.
- Speed-up economic growth.
- Priority sector lending.
- Developing banking habits.
- Provide better credit facility for agriculture.
- Using bank as tool of social welfare.

Regional Rural Banks

To liquidate rural indebtedness by stages and to dispense institutional credit facilities to farmers and artisans in rural areas, the Government of India promulgated on 26th September, 1975, the regional rural banks ordinance, 1975, to set-up regional rural banks throughout the country. Banks has started working from 2nd October, 1975. Regional rural banks came to be established under the Regional Rural Banks Act, 1976. Initially, 5 RRBs were set-up at Moradabad, Gorakhpur (UP), Bhiwani, Jaipur and Malda (W.B.). As on 31st March, 2019, there are 56 regional rural banks.

Regional rural banks in India penetrated every corner of the country and extended a helping hand in the growth process of the country.

These banks provide institutional credit to the weaker sections of the society at the concessional rate of interest, mobilise rural savings and channelise for supporting the productive activities in the rural areas.

The RRB is governed by a Board of Directors, who exercises all the powers and discharges all the functions of RRB. It consists of a chairman and 3 directors appointed by the Central Government for 5 years, 2 directors nominated by the concerned State Government and 3 directors nominated by the sponsor banks. Reserve Bank of India has brought RRB's under the ambit of priority sector lending on par with the commercial banks.

The National Bank for Agricultural and Rural Development (NABARD) is vested with powers of inspection of RRBs and to call for any data from them. It also provides refinance at concessional interest rate to the RRBs.

National Bank for Agricultural and Rural Development (NABARD)

It is an apex development financial institution of India. It was established on 12th July,1982 with an initial capital of ₹ 100 crore under National Bank for Agricultural and Rural Development Act, 1981.

Later, its capital was enhanced to ₹ 2,000 crore by the Government of India and RBI. It replaced the Agricultural Credit Department (ACD) and Rural Planning and Credit Cell (RPCC) of Reserve Bank of India and Agricultural Refinance and Development Corporation (ARDC). It is one of the premiere agencies to provide credit in rural areas. The amendment to NABARD Act in 2001, classify it as a 'Development Bank', which have permitted it to enhance its capital, subject to the minimum holding of 51% by the GOI and RBI. NABARD provides long-term refinance for minor irrigation, plantation, horticulture, land development, animal husbandry, fisheries etc. It also provide short-term loan assistance for financing of seasonal agricultural operations, marketing of crops etc. It also offers medium-term loan facilities for approved agricultural purposes.

Functions of NABARD

The functions of NABARD have been divided into three categories

Credit Distribution Take measures towards institutions building for improving capacity of the credit delivery system, including monitoring, formulation of rehabilitation schemes, restructuring of credit institutions, training of personnel etc.

Development Coordinates The rural financing activities of all institutions engaged in development work at the field level and maintain coordination with Government of India, State Governments, Reserve Bank of India and other national level institutions concerned with policy formations.

Regulatory It inspects the working of RRBs and cooperative banks of all types except the primary cooperative banks. All RRBs and cooperative banks submitting returns to the RBI are required to furnish a copy of return to the NABARD. It is empowered to obtain any information or statement from the RRBs and cooperative banks.

Private Sector Banks

After the nationalisation of 14 larger banks in 1969, no banks were allowed to be set-up in the private sector. Global Trust Bank was, thus, the first private bank after liberalisation; it was later amalgamated with Oriental Bank of Commerce (OBC). Then Housing Development Finance Corporation Limited (HDFC) became the first (still existing) to receive an 'in principle' approval from the Reserve Bank of India (RBI) to set-up a bank in the private sector. These banks are registered as companies with limited liability. They are formed as joint stock company under the Indian Companies Act and are governed by Banking Regulation Act, 1949.

The list of major private sector banks working in India are as follows

- Axis Bank
- HDFC Bank
- South Indian Bank
- City Union Bank
- ICICI Bank
- Yes Bank

Foreign Banks in India

Foreign banks are those banks which are registered in foreign country. They have set-up their branches in India and their headquarter is set-up in foreign country. Now, foreign banks in India are permitted to set-up local subsidiaries and they are treated equally under the Banking Regulation Act. The policy conveys that foreign banks in India may not acquire Indian ones (except for weak banks identified by the RBI, on its terms) and their Indian subsidiaries will not be able to open branches freely. It was made compulsory for these banks to deal in Indian currency.

Foreign Banks Operating in India

Few of these banks are as follows

- Abu Dhabi Commercial Bank
- American Express Banking Corp.
- Bank of America
- HSBC Ltd.

Non-scheduled Bank

It means a banking company as defined in clause (c) of Section 5 of the Banking Regulation Act, 1949 (10 of 1949), which is not a scheduled bank. Banks with reserve capital of less than ₹5 lakh qualify as non-scheduled banks, these banks are not governed according to the RBI Act and they receive no benefits from the RBI. These banks can avail remittance facilities from the RBI.

Cooperative Banks

Cooperative banks are registered under the Cooperative Societies Act and are governed by the Banking Regulations Act, 1949 and Banking Laws (Cooperative Societies) Act, 1955. People who come together to jointly serve their common interest often from a cooperative society under the Cooperative Societies Act.

When a cooperative society engages itself in banking business, it is called a cooperative bank. They generally give credit facilities to small farmers, salaried employees, small-scale industries etc. Cooperative banks are available in rural as well as in urban areas. Such banks can be categorised into Central Cooperative Banks and State Cooperative Banks. *These are as follows*

Central Cooperative Bank

These are the federations of primary credit societies in a district and are of two types, *i.e.* those having a membership of primary societies only and those having a membership of societies as well as individual. The funds of the banks consists of share capital, deposits, loan and overdrafts from State Cooperative Banks and joint stocks. These banks provide finance to member societies within the limits of borrowing capacity of societies. They also conduct all the business of a joint stock bank.

State Cooperative Bank

These banks, also known as apex banks, from the apex of the cooperative credit structure in each state. Its funds are obtained from their own share capital, deposits, loans and overdrafts from the Reserve Bank of India. 50-90% of working capital of SCBs are contributed by the Reserve Bank.

Functions of Commercial Banks

Following are the main function of a commercial banks

Primary Function

Following are the primary functions of commercial banks

Accepting Deposits

The main function of a commercial bank is to accept deposits from the public and grant loans.

The bank generally accept deposits by the *opening of following accounts*

Fixed Deposits Account This account is one in which a customer keep a fixed amount with a bank for a fixed period. The rate of interest is higher in comparison of other accounts.

Saving Account This type of account is generally opened by salary income group person. They deposit their saving and earn interest on this account. These deposits also help in capital formation. Bank gives cheque facility to withdrawal money from this account. The bank imposes a limit on the number and amount of withdrawals during a particular period.

Current Account Generally, this account is opened by businessmen, companies, institutions etc. Depositor can withdraw the money from this account several times in a day. The banks grants no interest on this account. Overdraft facilities are also available in this type of current account.

Other Accounts Banks are also providing deposit facility to different type of customer by opening different accounts like home deposit account, monthly income scheme, minor saving account etc.

Advancing of Loans

Bank receive deposit by various ways and grant loan from this deposited amount and charge higher interest rate.The difference between the interest rate (given on deposits and charge on loans) is the profit of the banks. *Generally, banks sanctions various types of loans and advances*

Cash Credit In this, bank grant loans and deposit in the borrower's account. The borrower can withdraw this amount at any time according to his convenience. The interest rate is charged only on the used amount.

Overdraft Bank allow a customer to draw amount which is greater than the balance lying in his account. This is known as overdraft facility. This facility is provided only for current account holder. In the case of overdraft, a customer pays interest on the amount by which is actually overdrawn.

Loans and Advances In this, the loan money is credited to the account of the borrower and he/she can withdraw amount anytime as per his/her requirement. The borrower has to pay interest on the entire amount of loan from the data of sanctioning of loan to the data of repayment.

Discounting of Bills of Exchange Bank can lend money by discounting bill of exchange. The banks charges a commission for discounting of bill of exchange.

Agency Function

- The bank collects the payment of cheques, bill of exchange or the credit instrument on behalf of its customer.
- The bank collects dividends and interest paid by the companies on behalf of their customer.
- Bank helps in transferring funds from one place to another.
- Bank purchases and sells securities on behalf of its customer.
- Bank also acts as on trustee, executor, administrator.

General Utility Function

- Banks provides lockers facilities to its customer for safe keeping of their valuables.
- Banks can provide reliable information about their customer which reduce risk and help in explanation of their customer's trade and business.
- Banks collect statistics about money, banking trade and commerce and publishes them.
- Banks give useful advice to its customer on financial matters.
- Banks grant consumer loan to their customer for purchasing of consumer article such as T.V., fridge, scooter etc.

Arrangement for Foreign Trade

Banks make available short-term credit to the traders engaged in foreign trade. Banks accepts discounting of bill, hundies, letter of credit to make international trade easier and convenient.

Credit Creation

Commercial banks undertake the function of credit creation according to the credit policy of Reserve Bank of India. Whenever, a bank grants a loan, it creates deposit since the deposits of the bank circulate as money. The creation of such deposits leads to increase money in the economy. This is known as credit creation by banks. Credit creation indirectly increase the supply of money and make transaction convenient.

Reserve Bank of India (RBI)

The Reserve Bank of India (RBI) is the Central Bank of the country. It was established in April 1935 on the basis of the recommendation of the Hilton Young Commission with a share capital of ₹ 5 crore divided into shares of ₹ 100 each. Private shareholders subscribed ₹ 4,97,80,000 and ₹ 20,000 were subscribed by the Central Government for disposal of 2,200 shares at par to the directors of bank (including members of the local boards) seeking the minimum share qualification. Thus, the Reserve Bank of India started working since 1st April, 1935, in accordance with the provisions of the Reserve Bank of India Act, 1934. RBI was nationalised with the passing of the Reserve Bank of India (transfer to public ownership) Act in 1948. Since,

1st January, 1949 the Reserve Bank of India is functioning as a (nationalised) bank.

RBI controls the entire banking system of our country. It is the sole agency of note issuing in our country. It secures as a banker to the government and controls the supply of money in our country. The Reserve Bank of India is the central and apex banking institution in India. It is a state owned organisation that functions as a corporate body with special powers and obligations for serving the national interest.

Organisation and Management of RBI

The general superintendence and direction of the bank is entrusted to Central Board of Directors of 20 members, as

- The Governor, for the term of 5 years, is the highest authority of RBI. He is appointed by the Government of India.
- Four Deputy Governors, for the term of 5 years.
- One government official from the Ministry of Finance.
- Ten nominated directors by the Government of India for the term of 4 years.
- Four nominated directors by the Central Government for the term of 4 years, to represent the four local boards with the headquarters at Mumbai, Kolkata, Chennai and New Delhi.

Local boards consist of 5 members, each appointed by the Central Government for a term of four years to represent territorial and economic interest and the interest of cooperative and indigenous banks. Central Board of Directors must hold atleast 6 meetings in a year and atleast one meeting in 3 months. Bank's head office is located in **Mumbai.** The bank has 14 branch offices. In places where there are no offices of the bank, it is represented by the State Bank of India.

Objectives of RBI

- To regulate the issue of bank notes.
- To maintain reserves with a view to secure monetary stability.
- To operate the credit and currency system of the country to its advantage.
- To stablise internal and external value of money.
- To manage public debt.
- To develop organised money market in the country.

Functions of RBI

Central Banking Functions

Issuing Note The Reserve Bank of India has the monopoly to issue currency notes of all denominations (except one rupee note which are issued only by the Government of India). As on 8th November, 2016, the RBI had denominations ₹ 500, ₹ 1,000 notes and issued new notes of ₹ 200, ₹ 500 and ₹ 2,000.

Bankers' Bank and Lender of the Last Resort As the bankers' bank, RBI holds a part of the cash reserves of banks, lends the funds to bank for short periods and provides them with centralised clearing, cheap and quick remittance facilities. Banks are supposed to meet their shortfalls of cash from sources other than RBI and approach RBI only as a matter of last resort, because RBI as the Central Bank is supposed to function as only the 'lender of last resort'.

Banker to Government The RBI works as an agent of the Central and State Government. It accepts money for the account of Union and State Government in India, makes payment on their behalf, carries out their exchange, remittance and other banking operations and manages public debt.

Controller of Credit As a Central Bank of the nation, the RBI has to look for growth with price stability. RBI regulates the credit creation capacity of commercial banks by using various credit control tools, such as each scheduled bank must send a weekly return to the Reserve Bank, showing in detail, its assets and liabilities.

RBI can inspect the account of any commercial bank. New branch of any commercial bank can be opened with due permission of RBI.

Custodian of Foreign Exchange Reserves RBI has to maintain the official rate of exchange and has the responsibility of maintaining fixed exchange rates with all other member countries of the IMF. RBI act as the custodian of India's reserve of international currencies. It also has the responsibility of administering the exchange controls of the country. There is separate department for this purpose in RBI known as "Exchange Control Department."

Regulatory Functions

Provide License Every bank wishing to commence banking business in India is required to obtain a license from the Reserve Bank of India. License is also given for opening extension counters, new branches, even to close down existing branches. RBI has the power to cancel the license, if a bank work against the interest of depositor.

Periodical Inspections The RBI is authorised to carry out periodical inspections of the bank and to call for returns and necessary information from them.

Improving Standard The RBI have helped a great deal in improving the standard of banking in India to develop on sound lines and to improve the method of their operations.

Liquidation of Weak Banks The RBI is empowered to order the compulsory liquidation of weak banks or their merger with stronger one. According to Section 38, RBI is empowered to request to High Court for winding-up the bank which has no hope.

Promotional Functions

Performs Development Programme The RBI performs variety of developmental and promotional functions to support national objectives which, at one time, were regarded as outside the normal scope of central banking.

Promoting Banking Habit The RBI promote banking habit, extend banking facilities to rural and semi-rural areas and establishes and promotes new specialised financing agencies.

Promoting National Housing Bank The RBI promoted in July 1988, the National Housing Bank, as its wholly owned subsidiary to organise and augment resources for housing.

Promoting Finance to Farmers The RBI has set-up the agricultural refinance and development corporation to provide long-term finance to farmers. Now, all functions relating to agriculture are performed by NABARD.

Promotes Research The RBI also encourages and promotes research in the areas of banking.

Expansion of Banking Facilities RBI has played an important role in expansion of banking facilities in rural area of the country.

Prohibitory Functions of RBIs

- RBI cannot provide any direct financial assistance to any industry, trade or business.
- It can't purchase shares of any commercial and industrial undertaking.
- It can't buy its own or other banking company's shares.
- It can't purchase any immovable property.
- It can't give loans on the security of shares and property.
- It can't participate in business/trade/industry.

Subsidiaries of the RBI

The Reserve Bank has the following fully-owned subsidiaries

- Deposit Insurance and Credit Guarantee Corporation (DICGC)
- National Housing Bank (NHB)
- Bharatiya Reserve Bank Note Mudran Private Limited (BRBNMPL)
- National Bank for Agriculture and Rural Development (NABARD)

Monetary Policy of the RBI

Monetary policy controls the supply of money in the economy by exercising its control over interest rates in order to maintain price stability and achieve high economic growth.

According to **Prof. Harry Johnson**, "A policy employing the Central Banks' control of the supply of money as an instrument for achieving the objectives of general economic policy is a monetary policy". Monetary policy regulates both volume and value of currency and credit.

Objectives of Monetary Policy

- Adjusting equilibrating mechanism for demand and supply of money market.
- Encouraging sectoral and overall development by influencing the cost, volume and direction of credit.
- To enable borrowers and lenders of short-term funds to fulfill their borrowing and investment requirements at an efficient market clearing price.
- To maintain price stability.
- To maintain Balance of Payments (BoP) equilibrium.
- Formulating equitable distribution of credit.
- To reduce the rigidities.
- To promote fixed investment.
- To promote more competitive environment.
- To promote exports.
- To impart greater discipline and prudence in the operations of the financial system.
- To generate full employment.

Techniques/Instruments of Monetary Policy

The techniques or instruments of monetary policy may be broadly divided into quantitative techniques and qualitative techniques, which are as follows

Quantitative Techniques

The detailed description of quantitative techniques are as follows

Open Market Operations OMO is an actively used technique of monetary control. This method is used to influence the flow of credit. Through the open market sales and purchases of government securities. The RBI can effect the reserves position of banks, yields on government securities, volume and cost of bank credit.

Bank Rate It is the basic cost of refinance and rediscounting facilities. According to the definition of RBI Act, bank rate is the standard rate at which the bank is prepared to buy or rediscount bill of exchange or other eligible commercial paper.

Discretionary Control of Refinance and Rediscounting This technique is used to regulate the cost and availability of refinance and to change the volume of lendable resources of banks and other financial institutions. The refinance policy has to take care of seasonal needs of funds also.

Direct Regulation of Interest Rates The weakening of the bank rate technique till 1991, had compelled the RBI to directly regulate interest rates on bank deposits and credits. Normal change in the bank rate is expected to lead to appropriate changes in all market rates of interest and help to achieve the given objective of monetary action. When the bank rate lost its significance as a cost factors and signal value, the RBI used to salvage the situation by regulating market rates of interest directly.

Fractional Reserve System The present banking system is called a "fractional reserve banking system" because the banks need to keep only a fraction of their deposit liabilities in the form of liquid cash. The authorities earlier used to change this fraction mainly for the purpose of ensuring the safety and liquidity of deposits. However, it has become an important and effective tool for directly regulating the lending capacity of banks. In this context, the RBI has been using two ratios—CRR (Cash Reserve Ratio) and SLR (Statutory Liquidity Ratio).

These are as follows

- ***Cash Reserve Ratio** (CRR)* The CRR refers to the cash which banks have to maintain with the RBI as a certain percentage of their demand and time liabilities. This ratio can be varied from 3% to 15% as directed by Reserve Bank.
- ***Statutory Liquidity Ratio** (SLR)* It is the ratio of cash in hand. The SLR enables it to impose secondary and supplementary reserve requirements on the banking system. Three objectives behind the use of SLR is to restrict expansion of bank credit, to augment banks investment in government securities and to ensure solvency of banks. RBI is empowered to change this ratio.

Qualitative Techniques

Selective Credit Control The objective of this tool is to control and discourage some forms of activities which are subject to speculative hoarding and wide price fluctuation. The seasonal nature of the Indian economy and the nature of inflation, SCCs particularly useful in this context. SCCs seek to change the composition of credit, they all used to reduce the supply of credit in certain directions and to encourage it in desired directions. They have been used particularly to prevent speculative hoarding of sensitive commodities such as paddy, rice, wheat, cotton, sugar etc.

Customer Credit Regulation The RBI has been, through the appointment of various committees, continuously reviewing and studying the working of commercial banks in respect of different functional areas. RBI issued certain guidelines to banks in respect of credit regulations. Now, the banks are required to advance credit for working capital to different industries in the light of inventory norms led down by committee of direction and it's sub-committee.

Fixing of Margin Requirements RBI fixes the margin upto which the purchaser of securities may borrow against securities. It is the most important qualitative method of regulating or controlling of the credit. The margin requirements against specific securities are determined by the RBI.

Moral Persuasion This is another most actively and consistently used technique of monetary control. It takes the form of written letters and holding discussion between the RBI and the banks about trends in the economy in general and in money, credit and finance in particular and about the measures which ought to be taken from time to time in light of national objectives.

Types of Banking System

Unit Banking It is a system where the operations of a bank are confined to a single office located in a particular area. Local area banks and regional rural banks in India are the replica of unit banking. Unit banking functioned in small town or cities and these are called country banks and city banks.

Branch Banking It is a multi-office banking spread over to a vast geographical area. A branch is an office where acceptance of money for the purposes of lending or investment and any or all the banking services are carried out.

Local Area Banking It provide institutional mechanisms for promoting rural savings and provisions of credit for viable economic activities in the local areas. This is expected to bridge the gaps in credit availability and enhance the institutional credit framework in the rural and semi-urban areas.

Group Banking It is a system where two or more banks are controlled by holding company. This company may be banking or non-banking company.

Chain Banking It refers to a situation, in which informal groups own or control more than one bank.

Corresponding Banking It has a limited access to certain financial markets, thus uses the services of another bank to conduct certain transactions. Such banking system provide necessary services to account holders by other banks, thus not required for setting-up a branch in another city or country. New York city is the centre of correspondent banking.

Deposit Banking Such banking system involves only in acceptance of deposits repayable on demand and lending money to trade and industry for short period not exceeding a year.

Investment Banking It is a system where banks arrange long-term funds for business and industry. They work both as financiers as well as under writers.

Offshore Banking Unit An Offshore Banking Unit (OBU) of a bank is a deemed foreign branch of the parent bank situated within India. It is the bank located outside the country of residence of the depositor, typically in a low tax jurisdiction that provides financial and legal advantages.

Universal Banking It offers entire range of financial services such as term finance, working capital, project advisory services, investment banking and insurance, issuing, underwriting and trading in securities, treasury consultancy etc.

Merchant Banking It means those banking and financial institutions who provide their services to industrial project, establishment of new entrepreneur, sponsoring, planning and execution of new projects. It provides a wide range of services from starting until running a business. There are 135 merchant bankers who are registered with SEBI in India.

Relationship Banking It means relationship and mutual trust between the banker and the customer. It starts the moment an account is opened and ends immediately on the closer of the account.

Indigenous Banking The indigenous banking are individuals or private firms who receive deposits and grant loan. They operate as banks dealing in hundies and mostly in urban areas, especially in Western and Southern regions of the country. Borrowers are small manufacturers and traders.

Development Banking It includes the discovery of investment projects, undertaking the preparation of project reports, provision of technical advice and assisting in the management of industrial units.

EXAM BASED QUESTIONS

Banks, its Types and Functions

1 **In the early stages, commercial banks were**

(a) in private sector
(b) in public sector
(c) government agency
(d) quasi-autonomous National Government Organisation

2 **After independence, the Imperial Bank of India was nationalised and became known as**

(a) Reserve Bank of India (b) State Bank of India
(c) Punjab National Bank (d) Central Bank of India

3 **UCO bank is a**

(a) private sector bank (b) public sector bank
(c) non-scheduled bank (d) None of these

4 **Which of the following is not the fund based business of commercial banks?**

(a) DP Operations (b) Loans
(c) Deposits (d) Discounting of Bills

5 **Bank show provision for income tax under the head**

(a) contingent liabilities
(b) other liabilities and provisions
(c) contingent account
(d) other accounts

6 **Which of the following is the latest buzzword among bankers?**

(a) Social banking (b) Financial inclusion
(c) Mass banking (d) None of these

7 **Which one of the following statement is corrrect?**

(a) The Governor is the Reserve Bank's chief executive
(b) IFCI can grant long-term loans to partnership firms
(c) Money market is a market for stock market operations
(d) The Export-Import Bank of India is a subsidiary of IDBI

8 **Which one of the following statement is incorrect?**

(a) Only 14 banks were nationalised in the first stage of nationalisation of commercial banks
(b) The second dose of nationalisation came in April 1980, when banks were nationalised
(c) RBI started its operation with a paid-up capital of ₹ 5 crore
(d) Safe deposit vaults are made available by bank only to fixed deposit account holders

9 **Rural Infrastructure Development Fund (RIDF) is maintained by**

(a) RRB
(b) NABARD
(c) Cooperative Bank
(d) None of the above

10 **The only merger between nationalised banks was between New Bank of India and Punjab National Bank in**

(a) 2003 (b) 1993 (c) 1997 (d) 2000

11 **Which bank was incorporated as one of the Public Sector Banks in India during 2004-05?**

(a) ICICI Bank Ltd (b) Yes Bank Ltd
(c) IDBI Bank Ltd (d) UTI Bank Ltd

12 **All banking institutions are**

(a) intermediaries (b) non-intermediaries
(c) specialised institutions (d) term lending institutions

13 **Credit creation is a .... of a bank.**

(a) primary function (b) agency function
(c) general utility function (d) None of these

14 **Universal banking is the combination of commercial banking with**

(a) investment banking (b) insurance company
(c) Both (a) and (b) (d) None of these

15 **Credit gaps can be eliminated by reducing**

(a) information asymmetry (b) size of the firm
(c) Both (a) and (b) (d) None of these

16 **Which of the following is not an instrument of credit control in the banking system?**

(a) Open market operations (b) Moral per suasion
(c) Cash reserve ratio (d) Tax rates

17 **Which of the following is not a function of a Rural Bank?**

(a) To accept deposit
(b) To waive loans
(c) To grant advances
(d) To supply inputs to farmers

18 **The commercial banks in India are governed by**

(a) Reserve Bank of India Act, 1934
(b) Indian Company Act, 1956
(c) Indian Banking Regulation Act, 1949
(d) Securities and Exchange Board of India Act, 1992

19 **Bank rate is also known as**

(a) discount rate (b) penalty rate
(c) interest rate (d) None of these

20 **When a drawer draws a cheque without keeping sufficient balance and if the cheque is bounced for insufficient funds, the drawer is punishable with imprisonment which may extend to ...... and/or a fine.**

(a) two months (b) one year
(c) four months (d) six months

21 **Paid-up capital of a bank should not be less than the following percentage of subscribed capital.**

(a) 25% (b) 50% (c) 75% (d) 100%

22 **Nationalisation of banks aimed at all of the following except**
(a) removal of control by a few
(b) provision of control by a few
(c) provision of adequate credit for agriculture, small industry and export units
(d) encouragement of a new class of entrepreneur

23 **The powers of the Board of Directors to borrow from the bank are mentioned in**
(a) Article of Association
(b) Memorandum of Association
(c) Special Resolution
(d) Both (a) and (b)

24 **The chief promoter of 'Clearing Corporation' is**
(a) SBI (b) RBI
(c) Financial Ministry (d) None of these

25 **Bank deposit refers to**
(a) the amount of money standing to the credit of a customer of a bank
(b) a term used by the federal reserve to refer to the total deposits of member banks
(c) the amount of money standing to the debit of a customer of a bank
(d) All of the above

26 **Which one of the following statement is correct?**
(a) Granting loan to the borrowers is not the main function of a bank
(b) Bank cannot buy and sell shares and debentures on behalf of customers
(c) Narasimham Committee recommended making banking structure of the counting three tier
(d) Banks have the same function as development bank

27 **Which one of the following statement is incorrect?**
(a) A bank interacts directly with customers, but NBFI interacts with banks and governments
(b) Credit creation is one of the primary functions of commercial bank in India
(c) Banks generally grant long-term loans to industries
(d) To purchase and sell securities is also one of the function of scheduled bank

28 **Banks lend money by**
1. Loan 2. Cash credit
3. Overdraft 4. Discounting of bill
Select the correct answer using the codes given below
Codes
(a) Both 1 and 2 (b) 1, 2 and 4
(c) 2, 3 and 4 (d) All of these

29 **Which one of the following statement is incorrect?**
(a) NABARD acts as regulator for Cooperative Banks and Regional Rural Banks (RRBs)
(b) NABARD promotes research in the fields of rural banking, agriculture and rural development
(c) Development bank helps an enterprise from planning to operational level
(d) The chairman of the RRB is nominated by the State Government

30 **Which one of the following statement is incorrect?**
(a) NABARD Consultancy Services (NABCONS) is a subsidiary of NABARD
(b) In 1947, the Reserve Bank stopped acting as banker to the Government of Burma
(c) Every NBFC should not be registered with RBI
(d) RBI uses CRR either to drain excess liquidity or to release funds needed for the growth of the economy

31 **Which of the following statement(s) is/are correct?**
1. Corporative Banks are governed by the banking Regulations Act, 1951.
2. State Bank of India Act was enacted in the year 1955.
3. After nationalisation of 24 major commercial banks, they become the important instrument for advancement of rural banking.
4. NABARD was established on 12th July, 1992 with an initial capital of ₹ 200 crore.
Select the correct answer using the codes given below
Codes
(a) Only 1
(b) Only 2
(c) 1, 2 and 3
(d) Only 4

32 **Which of the following can be described as involving indirect finance?**
(a) A corporation take out loans from bank
(b) People buy shares in a mutual fund
(c) A corporation buys commercial paper in a secondary market
(d) All of the above

33 **Nationalised banks have been permitted to offer their equity shares to the public to the extent of 49% of their capital as per amendments made in 1994 in**
(a) Banking Regulation Act, 1949
(b) Banking Companies (Acquisition and Transfer of Undertakings) Acts, 1970/1980
(c) Both (a) and (b)
(d) None of the above

34 **Which of the following is not the liabilty of commercial banks?**
(a) Security holdings
(b) Treasury deposits at banks
(c) Demand deposits and time deposits
(d) Borrowing from Central Banks

35 Which is the oldest bank in existence in India, originated in the Bank of Calcutta in June 1806, which almost immediately became the Bank of Bengal?
(a) State Bank of India (b) Punjab National Bank
(c) Syndicate Bank (d) Vijaya Bank

36 Which of the following limits the power of credit creation by commercial banks?
(a) Fiscal Policy (b) Banking Laws
(c) Business Pessimism (d) None of these

37 Consortium lending is a lending facility, defined by a single loan agreement, in which ..... participate.
(a) several or many banks (b) two banks
(c) RBI (d) development bank

38 Which bank has become the first foreign bank to open a branch in Israel's diamond exchange?
(a) American Express Bank
(b) Citi Bank
(c) Standard Chartered Bank
(d) State Bank of India

39 Which Indian PSU Bank in tune with its plans to expand its retail division in the UK entered the mortgage market in the country for the first time?
(a) Punjab National Bank
(b) Oriental Bank of Commerce
(c) State Bank of India
(d) Indian Overseas Bank

40 Which bank had its office in Anarkali Bazaar, Lahore when registered on 19th May, 1894 under Indian Companies Act?
(a) Punjab and Sind Bank
(b) Syndicate Bank
(c) Punjab National Bank
(d) United Bank of India

41 Which one of the following statement is correct?
(a) A bank can also exercise the right of set-off in respect of the future or contingent debts
(b) Minimum paid-up capital for entry of new private sector banks is ₹ 200 crore
(c) Ancillary services are also known as supplementary functions of a commercial banks
(d) Provisions of Banking Regulation Act are not applicable to cooperative banks

42 Which of the following statements are correct?
1. The Central Bank is usually control and quite often owned by the government of a country.
2. Export-Import Bank of India took over the export finance function of the IDBI.
3. Unit Bank has virtually one or two branches.
4. Citi Bank and ING Bank are universal banks.
Select the correct answer using the codes given below
Codes
(a) Both 1 and 2 (b) 1, 2 and 4
(c) 1, 2 and 3 (d) 2, 3 and 4

43 Which of the following statement is incorrect?
(a) Using bank as tool of social welfare was the objective behind nationalisation of banks in India
(b) Expansion of bank branch specially in rural area was the objectly behind nationalisation of bank in India
(c) Non-priority sector lending was the objective behind nationalisation of banks in India
(d) Speed up economic growth was the objective behind nationalisation of banks in India

44 Which one of the following statement is correct?
(a) General insurance corporation provides cover for life risks
(b) NBFC take deposits from the public
(c) NABARD was established on the recommendations of Narasimham Committee-I (1991)
(d) IDBI, NABARD have been notified as Public Financial Institutions (PFIs) under Companies Act, 1956

RBI

45 RBI was established with a share capital of ₹ ....
(a) 10 crore (b) 5 crore
(c) 50 crore (d) 100 crore

46 Who is the custodian of monetary reserves in India?
(a) SBI (b) SIDBI
(c) NABARD (d) RBI

47 Who is the fiscal agent and advisor to government in monetary and financial matters in India?
(a) SBI
(b) NABARD
(c) Corporative Banks
(d) None of the above

48 Before issuance of currency notes, RBI held .... securities.
(a) gold coins and bullion
(b) foreign securities
(c) government of India's securities
(d) All of the above

49 Which of the rate is not determined by RBI?
(a) CRR (b) PLR
(c) Bank Rate (d) SLR

50 Who is authorised to issue coins of smaller denomination in India?
(a) RBI
(b) Ministry of Finance
(c) SBI
(d) None of the above

51 Open market operations, one of the measures taken by RBI in order to control credit expansion in the economy means as
(a) sale or purchase of government securities
(b) issuance of different types of bonds
(c) auction of gold
(d) None of the above

52 Which of the following statement is true?
(a) The currency notes issued by RBI are legal tender throughout the world
(b) All commercial banks including those owned by government do not need a licence from the RBI to do banking business
(c) The treasury bills are sold by the RBI for raising its working capital
(d) The RBI is a banker to both Central and State Government

53 On which of the following banks the Reserve Bank of India depends?
(a) Cooperative Banks (b) Regional Rural Banks
(c) Commercial Banks (d) Development Banks

54 Which bank is called the 'Bank of Issue'?
(a) RBI (b) SBI
(c) IDBI (d) ICICI

55 RBI controls the commercial banks through ....
(a) periodic inspection of banks
(b) follow-up action
(c) calling for returns and other information
(d) All of the above

56 Annual report on currency and finance is published by
(a) SIDBI (b) RBI
(c) Ministry of Finance (d) None of these

57 Fully-owned subsidiary of RBI
(a) National Housing Bank (NHB)
(b) NABARD
(c) Both (a) and (b)
(d) None of the above

58 Differential rate of interest scheme was introduced in which year?
(a) 1962 (b) 1982 (c) 1972 (d) 1980

59 Which of the following bodies tightened the norms for foreign exchange risk cover in India mentioning that only companies with a net worth of ₹ 200 crore can use derivatives to hedge against risk of volatility in currency rates?
(a) IMF
(b) SEBI
(c) Reserve Bank of India
(d) Union Ministry of Finance

60 During the depression, it is advisable to
(a) lower bank rate and purchase securities in the open market
(b) increase bank rate and purchase securities in the open market
(c) decrease bank rate and sell securities in the open market
(d) increase bank rate and sell securities in the open market

61 Which of the following is restricted fund of RBI?
(a) Credit control
(b) Interest on debt
(c) Bank note issue
(d) Lending to bank

62 The bank rate means
(a) rate at which RBI purchases or rediscounts bills of exchange of commercial banks
(b) rate of interest allowed by commercial banks on their deposits
(c) rate of interest charged by commercial banks from borrowers
(d) rate of interest at which commercial banks discounted bills of their borrowers

63 Credit creation capacity of a bank depends on the cash reserve ratio and statutory liquidity ratio. If the initial deposit (O) is ₹ 1,000 and the Cash Reserve Ratio (CRR) and Statutory Liquidity Ratio (SLR) is 5% and 20%, then the credit creation capacity will be as follows
(a) ₹ 3,000 (b) ₹ 5,000 (c) ₹ 6,000 (d) ₹ 2,000

64 Reserve Bank of India is
(a) an extension wing of Ministry of Finance, Government of India
(b) a body corporate, having perpetual succession and a common seal
(c) an institution owned by Indian Banks Association
(d) a private sector bank

65 In order to control credit in the country, the RBI may
(a) buy securities in the open market
(b) sell securities in the open market
(c) reduce CRR
(d) reduce bank rate

66 In order to encourage investment in the country, the RBI may
(a) reduce CRR
(b) increase CRR
(c) sell securities in the open market
(d) increase bank rate

67 One of the major challenges, banking industry is facing these days is money laundering. Which of the following acts/norms are launched by the banks to prevent money laundering in general?
(a) Know Your Customer Norms
(b) Banking Regulation Act
(c) Negotiable Instrument Act
(d) None of the above

68 Governmental economic policy which deals with taxation, expenditure, borrowing and the management of public debt in an economy is ....
(a) monetary policy (b) credit policy
(c) fiscal policy (d) taxation policy

69 RBI's open market operation transactions are carried with a view to regulate
(a) liquidity in the economy
(b) prices of an essential commodities
(c) inflation
(d) All of the above

70 Currency chest balance will be periodically verified by
(a) Bank's own officials (b) RBI officials
(c) Both (a) and (b) (d) Officials of AG's office

71 From which date, banks were allowed free to fix base rates by RBI?
(a) 1st April, 2011 (b) 1st April, 2012
(c) 1st April, 2013 (d) None of these

72 Arrange the following in correct order according to the year of establishment and occurrence of the event.
1. Establishment of Regional Rural Bank.
2. Establishment of Reserve Bank of India.
3. Nationalisation of 6 Commercial Banks.
4. Nationalisation of 14 major Commercial Banks.
Codes
(a) 2, 4, 1, 3 (b) 2, 4, 1, 3
(c) 1, 4, 3, 2 (d) 3, 1, 2, 4

73 Which one of the following statement is incorrect?
(a) Till 1942, RBI was the currency issuing authority of Burma (now Myanmar)
(b) National Housing Bank (NHB) is the fully owned subsidiary of RBI
(c) RBI is the king pin of the Indian gold market
(d) RBI can provide any direct financial assistance to any industry, trade or business

74 Which one of the following statement is incorrect?
(a) The secondary market, also known as the aftermarket
(b) The non-fulfillment of PO and C entail penalty in the form of higher CRR/SLR
(c) Over The Counter Exchange of India (OTCEI) is non-corporate body
(d) The non-fulfillment of PO and C entail penalty in the form of higher CRR/SLR

Miscellaneous

Directions (Q. Nos. 75-79) *In the questions given below are two statements labelled as Statement I and Statement II. You have to examine these two statements carefully and select the answer to these items using the codes given below.*
Codes
(a) Statement I is correct, but Statement II is incorrect
(b) Both statements are correct
(c) Statement I is incorrect, but Statement II is correct
(d) Both statements are incorrect

75 **Statement** I In 1959, 7 subsidiaries of SBI were also nationalised.
Statement II In 1980, 6 banks with deposits over ₹ 200 crore were nationalised.

76 **Statement** I Making advances is the primary function of commercial banks.
Statement II Credit creation is the secondary function of commercial banks.

77 **Statement** I Central Cooperative Banks provide finance to member of societies within the limits of borrowings capacity of societies.
Statement II The funds of district cooperative banks consists of shares capital, deposits, loans and overdrafts from state cooperative banks and joint stocks.

78 **Statement** I Commercial banks provide mainly short-term credit to the industrial sector.
Statement II Modern banking become an effective force only after 1910.

79 **Statement** I Small savings are considered as the oldest media for community saving.
Statement II The first stock exchange was established at Pune in 1857.

Directions (Q. Nos. 80-88) *In the questions given below are two statements labelled as Assertion (A) and Reason (R). In the context of the two statements, which one of the following is correct?*
Codes
(a) Both (A) and (R) are true and (R) is the correct explanation of (A)
(b) Both (A) and (R) are true, but (R) is not the correct explanation of (A)
(c) (A) is true, but (R) is false
(d) (A) is false, but (R) is true

80 **Assertion** (A) The Indian banking system is of the branch-banking type and it is characterised by excessive concentration of business in a small number of big public sector banks.
Reason (R) The relatively small unit banks are perhaps more suitable for our environment and objectives.

81 **Assertion** (A) New business can expect to pay higher interest rate than older one, those are more established companies.
Reason (R) Lending institutions may feel that lending to newer companies presents a higher degree of risk.

82 **Assertion** (A) The scheduled banks are required to maintain a certain minimum balance in their accounts with RBI.

Reason (R) The scheduled banks are entitled to borrowings and rediscounting facilities from the RBI.

83 **Assertion** (A) Banks generally grants no interest on current account.

Reason (R) Interest is not regarded as the payment of the use or service of capital.

84 **Assertion** (A) The present banking system is called a fractional reserve banking system.

Reason (R) The banks need to keep only a fraction as their deposits and liabilities in the form of liquid cash.

85 **Assertion** (A) CRR refers to the cash which banks have to maintain with the RBI as a certain percentage of their demand and time liabilities.

Reason (R) Statutory liquidity ratio is the ratio of cash in hand.

86 **Assertion** (A) Bank have control over a large part of the supply of money in circulation.

Reason (R) They cannot influence the nature and character of production in any country.

87 **Assertion** (A) Custodian of foreign exchange reserve is one of the main function of RBI.

Reason (R) Periodical inspections of various banks is also the main function of RBI.

88 **Assertion** (A) NABARD produce long-term refinance for minor irrigation, plantation, horticulture, land development, animal husbandry, fisheres etc.

Reason (R) NABARD is one of the premiere agencies to provide credit in rural areas.

89 Match the following.

List I	List II
A. RBI	1. Private Bank
B. SBI	2. Foreign Bank
C. Citi Bank	3. Regulator
D. Catholic Syrian Bank	4. Public Bank

Codes

	A	B	C	D
(a)	4	3	2	1
(b)	3	4	1	2
(c)	1	4	3	2
(d)	1	2	3	4

90 Match the following.

List I	List II
A. Hawala	1. Clearing of cheques
B. RBI	2. Illegal transactions of foreign exchange
C. SEBI	3. Regulator body
D. Commercial Bank	4. Central Bank

Codes

	A	B	C	D		A	B	C	D
(a)	1	3	2	4	(b)	2	3	4	1
(c)	3	2	1	4	(d)	1	2	3	4

91 Match the following.

List I	List II
A. Financial instruments	1. Organised and unorganised
B. Financial market	2. Intermediaries and non-intermediaries
C. Financial institutions	3. Unorganised financial system
D. Indigenous bankers	4. Facilitate transfer of funds

Codes

	A	B	C	D		A	B	C	D
(a)	4	1	2	3	(b)	2	1	4	3
(c)	1	2	4	3	(d)	3	2	1	4

92 Match the following.

List I (Institutions)	List II (Head Offices)
A. RBI	1. New Delhi
B. PNB	2. Mumbai
C. Vijaya Bank	3. Vadodara
D. ICICI	4. Bengaluru

Codes

	A	B	C	D		A	B	C	D
(a)	1	2	3	4	(b)	2	4	1	3
(c)	1	2	4	3	(d)	3	2		4

93 Match the following.

List I	List II
A. Bank of Hindustan	1. 1843
B. General Bank of India	2. 1840
C. Bank of Bombay	3. 1786
D. Bank of Madras	4. 1770

Codes

	A	B	C	D
(a)	4	3	2	1
(b)	3	4	1	2
(c)	1	4	3	2
(d)	3	2	1	4

94 Match the following.

List I	List II
A. Reserve Bank of India	1. 1975
B. Nationalisation of 14 major commercial banks	2. 1935
C. Nationalisation of 6 commercial banks	3. 1969
D. Regional Rural Banks	4. 1980

Codes

	A	B	C	D		A	B	C	D
(a)	1	3	2	4	(b)	3	2	4	1
(c)	4	3	1	2	(d)	2	3	4	1

95 Match the following.

List I	List II
A. State Cooperative Banks	1. Government has a major holdings.
B. Indigenous Banks	2. 50%-90% of the working capital is contributed by RBI.
C. Public Sector Banks	3. Comes under the ambit of the RBI control.
D. Non-scheduled Banks	4. Operated by seths, sahukars, mahajans, sardars etc.

Codes

	A	B	C	D		A	B	C	D
(a)	4	3	2	1	(b)	2	4	1	3
(c)	3	4	2	1	(d)	4	3	1	2

96 Match the following.

List I	List II
A. Rate at which RBI gives loans to commercial banks by discounting bills	1. Reverse Repo rate
B. Rate at which RBI borrows from commercial banks	2. Repo rate
	3. Prime lending rate

Codes

	A	B		A	B
(a)	3	1	(b)	2	1
(c)	1	2	(d)	3	2

97 Match the following.

List I	List II
A. CRR	1. Maximum expected rate
B. Fiscal policy	2. Government of India
C. Monetary policy	3. RBI
D. RRR	4. Rate of interest

Codes

	A	B	C	D
(a)	3	2	1	4
(b)	1	3	2	4
(c)	2	4	1	3
(d)	4	1	2	3

98 Match the following.

List I	List II
A. Monetary policy	1. Instrument for regulation of money and credit
B. Bank rate	2. Instrument of fiscal policy
C. Taxation policy	3. Instrument of monetary policy
D. Repo rate	4. Quantitative instrument of monetary policy

Codes

	A	B	C	D
(a)	1	3	2	4
(b)	3	1	2	4
(c)	1	2	4	3
(d)	4	1	2	3

PREVIOUS YEARS' QUESTIONS

December 2018

1 Which one of the following is not the fund based business of commercial banks?

(a) Overdraft facility
(b) Issuance of letters of credit
(c) Acceptance of deposits
(d) RTGS/NEFT transactions

2 Match the items of List I with the items of List II and choose the correct answer from the code given below.

List I	List II
A. NPA	1. The percentage of deposits to be kept with RBI in the form of cash.
B. SLR	2. The rate at which RBI lends money to commercial banks.
C. Repo rate	3. Loans and advances not paid for more than 90 days.
D. CRR	4. The percentage of net demand and time liabilities to be kept in the form of liquid assets.

Codes

	A	B	C	D
(a)	3	4	1	2
(b)	3	4	2	1
(c)	2	3	4	1
(d)	3	2	4	1

3 When RBI reduces CRR, it results into

(a) increase in lendable resources
(b) decrease in lendable resources
(c) decrease in deposits
(d) increase in deposits

4 Which one of the following is not the function of the Reserve Bank of India?

(a) Issue of bank notes
(b) Custodian of cash reserves of commercial banks
(c) Accepting deposits and advancing loans to public
(d) Controller of credit

July 2018

5 **Assertion** (A) The Reserve Bank of India is entrusted with the management of the public debt and issue of new loans and treasury bills on behalf of the Central and State Governments.

Reason (R) The Governor and the Deputy Governors of Reserve Bank of India are appointed by the Central Government.

Codes

(a) (A) is correct, but (R) is not correct
(b) (A) and (R) are correct, but (R) is not the right explanation of (A)
(c) (A) and (R) both are correct and (R) is the right explanation of (A)
(d) (A) and (R) both are not correct

6 Which one of the following is not the function of NABARD?

(a) To provide refinance assistance by way of short-term credit to state cooperative banks and sectoral rural banks etc, approved by the RBI for some specific purposes
(b) To undertake inspection of cooperative societies other than primary cooperative societies and RRBs
(c) To promote research in various aspects of the problems of urban development
(d) To subscribe to share capital or invest in securities of any institution concerned with agricultural and rural development

7 .... refers to the process of removing or stripping the legal status of a currency.

(a) Digitisation
(b) Financial inclusion
(c) Demonetisation
(d) Micro finance

January 2017

8 Match the items of List I with the items of List II and suggest the correct code.

List I	List II
A. Relationship banking	1. Dealing in hundis and acceptance of deposits.
B. Merchant banking	2. Widening the entrepreneurial base and assist in a rapid rate of industrial growth.
C. Indigenous banking	3. Engaged in the business of issue management.
D. Development banking	4. Creating, maintaining and enhancing strong relationship with customers.

Codes

	A	B	C	D
(a)	1	2	4	3
(b)	2	4	3	1
(c)	4	3	1	2
(d)	2	1	4	3

July 2016

9 Identify the correct combination of statements with regard to banking in India.

1. For many years the presidency banks had acted as quasi-central banks.
2. The Bank of Hindustan was liquidated during 1829-32.

3. General Bank of India was an unsuccessful bank and was dissolved in 1791.
4. Bank of Calcutta was renamed as Bank of Bengal in 1921.

Codes

(a) 1, 2 and 3 (b) 2, 3 and 4
(c) 1, 2 and 4 (d) 1, 2, 3 and 4

10 Assertion (A) "Banks globally are facing more challenges now and macro sustainability is a necessity but not sufficient for sustainable economic growth."

Reason (R) "Putting regulations in place is only one part and their implementation is equally important for achieving growth and sustainability."

Codes

(a) Both (A) and (R) are correct and (R) is the correct explanation of (A)
(b) Both (A) and (R) are true, but (R) is not the correct explanation of (A)
(c) (A) is true, but (R) is incorrect
(d) (A) is incorrect, but (R) is correct

11 Which combination of the following methods indicates quantitative methods of control of credit creation practiced by the Reserve Bank of India?

1. Bank Rate
2. Open Market Operations
3. Variable Reserve Ratio
4. Credit Rationing

Codes

(a) 1, 2 and 3 (b) 1, 2 and 4
(c) 2, 3 and 4 (d) 1, 3 and 4

December 2015

12 Identify the years in which different phases of bank nationalisation took place in India.

1. 1950
2. 1955
3. 1969
4. 1949
5. 1980

Select the correct answer using the codes given below

Codes

(a) 1, 2, 3 and 4 (b) 2, 3 and 5
(c) 2, 4 and 5 (d) 3, 4 and 5

13 Assertion (A) Taking of deposits and granting of loans single out banks.

Reason (R) Banks act as intermediaries when they mobilise savings from surplus units to shortage units in order to finance productive activities.

Codes

(a) (A) is true and (R) is the correct explanation of (A)
(b) Both (A) and (R) are true, but (R) is not the correct explanation of (A)
(c) (A)is true, but (R) is false
(d) (R) is true, but (A) is false

14 Match the following.

List I (Activities)	List II (Functions)
A. Underwriting	1. Primary functions
B. Transfer of funds	2. Granting advances
C. Overdraft	3. Utility functions
D. Recurring deposits	4. Agency functions

Codes

	A	B	C	D		A	B	C	D
(a)	1	2	4	3	(b)	4	3	2	1
(c)	3	4	2	1	(d)	2	4	3	1

15 Which among the following is not a subsidiary of Reserve Bank of India?

1. Deposit Insurance and Credit Guarantee Corporation of India.
2. Bharatiya Reserve Bank Note Mudran Private Limited.

Select the correct answer using the codes given below

Codes

(a) Only 1 (b) Only 2
(c) Both 1 and 2 (d) Neither 1 nor 2

16 Which among the following is not associated with NABARD?

1. NIEAF 2. BIRD 3. RIDF 4. SHPI

Select the correct answer using the codes given below

Codes

(a) Only 1 (b) Only 2
(c) Both 2 and 3 (d) None of these

17 Select the techniques of monetary control adopted by RBI from the following.

1. Cash reserve ratio
2. Statutory liquidity ratio
3. Bank rate
4. Currency rate

Select the correct answer using the codes given below

Codes

(a)1,2,3 and 4 (b) 2,3 and 4
(c) 1,3 and 4 (d) 1,2 and 3

June 2015

18 The operations of banks and financial institutions are regulated by

(a) The RBI Act, 1934
(b) The Banking Regulation Act, 1949
(c) Information Technology Act, 2000
(d) All of the above

19 **Interest earned by a depositor against a deposit with a commercial bank for custodial service**

(a) is a fund based income
(b) is a fee based income
(c) is a combination of fund and fee based gain
(d) is a commitment based gain

20 **For the purpose of extending rural banking and agro finance, the NABARD**

(a) directly lends and monitors the rural borrowers
(b) refinances the banks extending rural finance
(c) refinances the rural borrowers obtaining credit from banks
(d) directly finances the rural borrowers and gets refinance from government

21 **When RBI grants loan to commercial banks and charges interest on it, it is called**

(a) repo rate
(b) reverse repo rate
(c) sweep stack rate, basic rate
(d) bank rate

December 2014

22 **Match the following.**

	List I	List II
A.	RBI nationalisation	1. 1964
B.	Imperial bank nationalisation	2. 1949
C.	Nationalisation of 14 commercial banks	3. 1955
D.	Establishment of IDBI	4. 1969

Codes

	A	B	C	D		A	B	C	D
(a)	1	2	3	4	(b)	2	3	1	4
(c)	3	2	4	1	(d)	2	3	4	1

23 **Under the cooperative bank structure, the apex institution is**

(a) National Cooperative Bank
(b) State Cooperative Bank
(c) District Cooperative Bank
(d) IDBI Bank

24 **The regulatory authority of Regional Rural Banks is**

(a) NABARD
(b) Central Government
(c) State Government
(d) Sponsor Bank

25 **As per the RBI Act, 1934, the following functions are described as the functions of a Central Bank.**

1. Banking functions
2. Advisory functions
3. Supervisory functions
4. Promotional functions

Select the correct answer using the codes given below

Codes

(a) 1, 3 and 4
(b) 1, 2 and 4
(c) 2, 3 and 4
(d) Both 1 and 3

26 **What is true about the Basel Committee on Banking Supervision (BCBS)?**

1. BCBS is an Indian National Committee of banking supervisory authority.
2. BCBS was established by a group of 19 nationalised commercial banks.
3. BCBS was established in 1996.
4. It provides a forum for regular cooperation on banking supervisory matters.

Select the correct answer using the codes given below

Codes

(a) Both 1 and 2
(b) Both 2 and 3
(c) Both 3 and 4
(d) Only 4

27 **What is SLR ratio of a bank?**

(a) Ratio of total deposits against total investments
(b) Amount deposited by the bank with the Central Bank in the form of cash, gold and securities
(c) Amount that commercial banks are required to maintain before providing credit to customers
(d) Amount that commercial banks deposit with the foreign banks

June 2014

28 **The profitability of public sector banks is low due to**

1. over-cautions approach to lending
2. Reserve Bank policies
3. high overhead costs
4. social sector lending

Codes

(a) Both 1 and 2
(b) Both 1 and 4
(c) 1, 3 and 4
(d) Both 2 and 3

29 **Which of the following financial institutions is not with in the supervisory purview of Reserve Bank of India?**

(a) Foreign Commercial Banks Operating in India
(b) Regional Rural Banks
(c) Mutual Funds
(d) State Cooperative Banks

30 **The repo and reverse repo rate are resorted to by the RBI as a tool of**

(a) credit control
(b) settlement systems
(c) currency management
(d) liquidity control

31 **Which of the following committees is intended to review the working of the monetary system in India?**

(a) Narasimham Committee
(b) Tandon Committee
(c) Sukhamoy Chakravarty Committee
(d) Dehejia Committee

32 Match the following.

	List I	List II
A.	Bank rate policy	1. Involving the shortening of the currency of bills eligible for rediscount.
B.	Credit rationing	2. Involving the purchase and sale of securities in the open market.
C.	Variable reserve system	3. Involving the alteration of discount rate.
D.	Open market operations	4. Involving the variation of the minimum reserves.

Codes

	A	B	C	D		A	B	C	D
(a)	1	4	2	3	(b)	2	1	3	4
(c)	4	2	1	3	(d)	3	1	4	2

33 According to the recent guidelines (2013) of the Reserve Bank of India, the private sector banks are required to have a minimum paid-up equity capital of

(a) ₹ 300 crore (b) ₹ 200 crore (c) ₹ 400 crore (d) ₹ 500 crore

December 2013

34 Match the following.

	List I	List II
A.	Letter of reference	1. Advancing loans
B.	Sale of gold coins	2. Receiving deposits
C.	Recurring account	3. Non-banking function
D.	Overdrafts	4. Agency function

Codes

	A	B	C	D		A	B	C	D
(a)	1	2	3	4	(b)	4	3	2	1
(c)	4	2	3	1	(d)	1	3	2	4

35 Which of the following are included under representation functions of a bank?

1. Payment of cheques and bills
2. Providing remittance facilities
3. Underwriting of securities
4. Advancing clean credit
5. Allowing overdrafts on current account
6. Purchase and sale of securities

Codes

(a) 1, 2, 3 and 4 (b) 3, 4, 5 and 6
(c) 1, 2, 3 and 6 (d) 2, 3, 5 and 6

36 **Assertion** (A) The Central Bank of the country is responsible to maintain stability of the monetary standard which involves currency circulation.

Reason (R) The Central Bank is the only authorised entity to do so.

Codes

(a) Both (A) and (R) are true
(b) Both (A) and (R) are false
(c) (A) is true, but (R) is false
(d) (R) is true, but (A) is false

37 Identify the quantitative credit control methods among the following.

1. Bank Rate
2. Credit Rationing
3. Open Market Operations
4. Variable Reserve Ratio
5. Selective Credit Control
6. Liquidity Ratio

Codes

(a) 1,2,3 and 4 (b) 2,3,4 and 5
(c) 1,2,5 and 6 (d) 1,3,4 and 6

38 Reserve Bank of India was nationalised on

(a) 26th January, 1948 (b) 1st January, 1949
(c) 26th January, 1950 (d) 1st January, 1956

39 When a banking company is placed under moratorium under Section 45 of the Banking Regulation Act, 1949, the RBI must prepare a scheme of

(a) VRS for staff
(b) Capital Buy Back
(c) Reconstruction of the company or amalgamation with any other bank
(d) IPO of the bank

40 Reserve Bank of India controls the activities of which of the following banks in India?

1. Commercial banks
2. Cooperative banks
3. Foreign banks
4. Rural banks

Codes

(a) 1,2 and 3 (b) 1,3 and 4
(c) 2,3 and 4 (d) All of the above

June 2013

41 RBI ensures that banks operate within the set norms by conducting .... inspections and .... monitoring.

(a) on site, off site (b) off site, on site
(c) on site, field (d) field, on site

42 Under Section 37 of the Banking (Regulation) Act, a moratorium order can be issued by the High Court for a maximum total period of

(a) one month (b) six months
(c) one year (d) one and a half year

43 **Assertion** (A) "The problem of rural credit is not primarily one of rural credit, it may be said to be one of rural minded credit."

Reason (R) The Indian economy has yet to come out of rural mentality.

Codes

(a) Both (A) and (R) are correct
(b) Both (A) and (R) are incorrect
(c) (A) is correct, but (R) is incorrect
(d) (R) is correct, but (A) is incorrect

December 2012

44 Match the following.

	List I		List II
A.	Selective credit control	1.	Consumer credit recusation
B.	Encourage credit for desirable use	2.	Cash reserve
C.	Quantitative credit control	3.	Variation in margin
D.	Bank rate	4.	Rediscounting rate

Codes

	A	B	C	D		A	B	C	D
(a)	4	2	3	1	(b)	3	1	2	4
(c)	1	3	2	4	(d)	2	1	3	4

June 2012

45 In India, the commercial banks are given license of operation by

(a) the Government of India
(b) the Ministry of Finance
(c) Reserve Bank of India
(d) Banking Companies Regulation Act, 1949

46 The commercial banks do not perform one function out of the following

(a) Mobilisation of savings
(b) Giving loans and advances
(c) Issuing currency notes
(d) Financing priority sectors

47 Imperial Bank was established on 27th January, 1921 on the advise of

(a) JM Keynes
(b) Lord Illingworth
(c) King George V
(d) Winston Churchill

48 The provisions of general reserve in banking companies are made keeping in view the provisions of

(a) Indian Companies Act, 1956
(b) Banking Companies Act, 1949
(c) SEBI Act, 1992
(d) Statutory Auditor

ANSWERS

Objective Questions

1 (a)	2 (b)	3 (b)	4 (a)	5 (b)	6 (c)	7 (a)	8 (d)	9 (b)	10 (b)
11 (c)	12 (a)	13 (a)	14 (c)	15 (a)	16 (d)	17 (d)	18 (c)	19 (a)	20 (b)
21 (b)	22 (a)	23 (b)	24 (a)	25 (d)	26 (c)	27 (c)	28 (d)	29 (d)	30 (c)
31 (b)	32 (d)	33 (b)	34 (a)	35 (d)	36 (d)	37 (a)	38 (d)	39 (c)	40 (c)
41 (c)	42 (b)	43 (c)	44 (d)	45 (b)	46 (d)	47 (d)	48 (d)	49 (b)	50 (b)
51 (a)	52 (d)	53 (c)	54 (a)	55 (d)	56 (b)	57 (c)	58 (c)	59 (c)	60 (a)
61 (b)	62 (a)	63 (a)	64 (b)	65 (b)	66 (a)	67 (d)	68 (c)	69 (d)	70 (c)
71 (a)	72 (b)	73 (c)	74 (c)	75 (b)	76 (a)	77 (b)	78 (b)	79 (a)	80 (a)
81 (a)	82 (b)	83 (b)	84 (a)	85 (b)	86 (b)	87 (c)	88 (b)	89 (c)	90 (b)
91 (a)	92 (b)	93 (a)	94 (d)	95 (b)	96 (b)	97 (a)	98 (a)		

Previous Years' Questions

1 (b)	2 (b)	3 (a)	4 (c)	5 (b)	6 (c)	7 (c)	8 (c)	9 (a)	10 (a)
11 (a)	12 (b)	13 (a)	14 (c)	15 (d)	16 (d)	17 (d)	18 (a)	19 (a)	20 (c)
21 (b)	22 (d)	23 (b)	24 (a)	25 (a)	26 (d)	27 (c)	28 (c)	29 (c)	30 (d)
31 (c)	32 (d)	33 (d)	34 (b)	35 (c)	36 (c)	37 (d)	38 (b)	39 (c)	40 (d)
41 (a)	42 (b)	43 (b)	44 (b)	45 (c)	46 (c)	47 (a)	48 (c)		

CHAPTER

26

Banking Sector Reforms in India

Banking sector reforms are needed to increase the efficiency of financial resource mobilisations and generate higher levels of growth. The main objective of banking sector reforms was to promote a diversified, efficient and competitive financial system with the ultimate goal of improving the allocative efficiency of resources.

Banking Sector Reforms

Indian banking sector has undergone major changes and reforms from 1991, since then India has grown significantly in terms of economic development, so has its banking sector. To make banking sector stronger, the Finance Ministry of Government of India set-up various committees in which Narasimham Committee-I Report, (1991) and the Narasimham Committee-II, Report (1998) were the prominent one, Government of India accepted all the major recommendations of Narasimham Committee (1991). *Below mention are the points of banking sector reforms in India, which include major recommendations of Narasimham Committee (1991) as well*

- Interest rate on deposits and advances of all cooperative banks including urban cooperative banks deregulated. Similarly, interest rate on bank loans above ₹ 2 lakh and on domestic term deposits above 2 years and non-resident (External) rupee accounts have been fully decontrolled. Interest on all deposits are determined by banks except on saving deposits.
- Banks allowed to set their own interest rate on post shipment export credit in rupees for over 90 days.
- The State Bank of India and other nationalised banks enabled to access the capital market for debt and equity.

In this Chapter

- The Cash Reserve Ratio (CRR) and Statutory Liquidity Ratio (SLR) are gradually reduced during the economic reforms period in India. By law in India, the CRR remains between 3-20% of the net demand and time liabilities.
- Capital to Risk (Weighted) Assets Ratio (CRAR) was introduced in 1992. It resulted in an improvement in the capital position of commercial bank, almost all the banks in India has reached the Capital Adequacy Ratio (CAR) above the statutory level of 9%.
- Prudential norms for income recognition, classification of assets and provisioning for bad debts for commercial banks, including regional rural banks and financial institutions introduced.
- The Performance Obligations and Commitments (PO and C) obtained by RBI from each bank is meant to ensure a high level of portfolio quality so that problems such as heavy losses, low profits, erosion of equity do not recur.
- Banks required to make their balance sheet fully transparent and make full disclosures in keeping with International Accounts Standards Committee.
- Banking Ombudsman Scheme 1995 introduced to appoint 15 Ombudsmen (by RBI) to look into and resolve customer's grievances in a quick and inexpensive manner.
- Bank set free to fix their own foreign exchange open position limit subject to RBI approval.
- Scheduled commercial banks have now been given freedom to open new branches and upgrade extension counters, after obtaining capital adequacy norms and prudential accounting standards.

Second Phase

Narasimham Committee-II Report, 1998

- Committee suggested the merger of strong banks with weak banks.
- It suggested that 2 or 3 larger banks should be given international orientation and global character.
- It suggested new and higher norms for capital adequacy.
- To take over the bad debts of banks, committee suggested setting-up of assets reconstruction fund.
- A Board for Financial Regulation and Supervision (BFRS) can be set-up to supervise the activities of bank and financial institution.
- Net non-performing assets for all banks were to be brought down to 3% by 2002.
- Rationalisation of bank branches and staff emphasised licensing policy for new private banks.
- Foreign banks may be allowed to set-up subsidiaries and joint ventures.

Capital Adequacy

Capital adequacy reflects the

- overall soundness of the individual bank.
- risk exposure of the individual bank.

Thus, it is the optimum amount of capital that would require to ensure the confidence of all stakeholders, investors, depositors, creditors and regulators.

Capital Adequacy Norms (Basel Norms)

Bank capital plays a very important role in the safety and soundness of individual banks and the banking system. Basel Committee for Bank Supervision (BCBS) has prescribed a set of norms for the capital requirement for the banks in 1988 known as Basel-I accord. These norms ensure that capital should be adequate to absorb unexpected losses or risks involved. The minimum capital requirement was fixed at 8% of risk weighted assets. All these considerations suggest the need to review new and the minimum prescription for capital adequacy with a view to their possible enhancement.

India and Capital Adequacy Norms

Basel committee had released the guidelines on capital measures and capital standards in July 1988, which were been accepted by Central Bank in various countries including RBI. In India, it has been implemented by RBI with effect from 1st April, 1992. All the 27 Public Sector Banks in India (except UCO and Indian Bank) had achieved the capital adequacy norm of 8% by March 1997.

Capital Adequacy Ratio (CAR)

Capital Adequacy Ratio (CAR) is defined as the ratio of bank's capital to its risk assets. CAR is also known as Capital to Risk (Weighted) Assets Ratio (CRAR).

$$\text{CAR} = \frac{\text{Tier one capital} + \text{Tier two capital}}{\text{Risk weighted assets}}$$

Capital Fund

Capital fund has two tiers

Tier I or Core Capital This capital is considered the most permanent and readily available support against unexpected losses. It includes paid-up capital, statutory reserves, other disclosed free reserves, capital reserves representing surplus arising out of sale proceeds of assets.

Tier II Capital This capital is second readily available capital to protect the unexpected losses. It includes undisclosed reserves and paid-up capital, perpetual preference shares, revaluation reserves (at discount of 55%), hybrid (debt/equity) capital, subordinated debt and general provisions and loss reserves.

Subordinated Debt

These are bonds issued by banks for raising Tier II capital

- They should be fully paid-up instruments.
- They should be unsecured debt.
- They should be subordinated to the claims of other creditors.
- The bonds should not be redeemable at the option of the holders.

Minimum Requirements of Capital Fund in India

- Existing banks-9%
- New private sector banks-10%
- Banks undertaking insurance business-10%
- Local area banks-15%

Tier I capital should at no point of time be less than 50% of the total capital. This implies that Tier II cannot be more than 50% of the total capital.

Risk Weighted Assets Risk weighted assets means fund based assets such as cash, loans, investments and other assets. The value of bank's assets are not taken according to the book value, but according to the risk factor involved. Degrees of credit risk expressed as percentage weights have been assigned by RBI to each such assets.

Basel-II Norms

In 2004, BCBS published Basel-II guidelines, which were considered to be the refined and reformed versions of Basel-I accord. *The guidelines were based on three parameters which are as follows*

- Banks should maintain a minimum capital adequacy requirement of 8% of risk assets.
- Banks were needed to develop and use better risk management techniques in monitoring and managing all the three types of risks that is credit and increased disclosure requirements. *The three types of risk are* - operational risk, market risk and capital risk.
- Banks need to mandatory disclose their risk exposure etc to the Central Bank.

Basel-III Norms

In 2010, BCBS released Basel-III guidelines. These, guidelines were introduced in response to the financial crisis of 2008. *These are as follows*

- Basel-III norms aim at making most banking activities such as their trading book activities more capital intensive.
- The guidelines aim to promote a more resilient banking system by focusing on four vital banking parameters *viz.* capital, leverage, funding and liquidity.
- The Reserve Bank of India has extended the timeline for full implementation of the Basel-III capital regulations by a year to 31st March, 2020.

Risk and its Management

Banks have started specialised committees to measure and monitor various risk.

A risk can be defined as an unplanned event with financial consequences resulting in loss or reduced earnings.

In investment analysis, risk refers to the likelihood that the actual return on an investment received is different from the expected return. In other words, risk can be referred as the volatility in the return with respect to expected return.

Types of Risk

Risks are classified into two types, which are as follows

- Systematic Risk and
- Non-systematic Risk

∴ Total Risk = Systematic Risk + Non-systematic Risk

Systematic Risk

Risks, which are caused due to uncontrollable factors that tend to affect all sectors of business, government and any other entity and leads to unavoidable affects for the investor, are systematic risk. These risks are practically impossible to protect and influences large number of assets.

There are basically three types of systematic risks

Market risk, purchasing power risk and interest rate risk.

Systematic Risk = Market Risk + Purchasing Power Risk + Interest Rate Risk

Market Risk Risk caused due to market cycles, *i.e.* demand and supply pressures, sudden movements in the market and change in public fashions among investment alternatives leading to uncertainty of return is market risk. Factors that leads to market risks are recessions, wars and structural changes in the economy, tax law changes, even changes in consumer preferences.

Purchasing Power Risk/Inflation Risk The purchasing power risk is also called as inflation risk. It refers to exchange in real value of return as a result of inflation. Inflation leads to rise in cost of production, lower margins, lesser profits etc. These risks are inherent in all the investments and are beyond the control of an investor.

Interest Rate Risk The interest rate risk refers to uncertain returns caused by the uncertain market rates of interest. The return on an investment depends upon the interest rates promised on it and changes in market rate of interest from time to time adversely affects the investor's return. Interest rate risk affects bonds more directly than common stocks and is a major risk faced by all bondholders. As interest rates change, bond prices change in the opposite direction.

Non-systematic Risk

Risks are firm specific risks, caused due to known or controllable factors and can be eliminated or reduced through diversification. Non-systematic risk can be further divided into business risk, financial risk, liquidity risk, credit risk etc.

i.e. Non-systematic Risk = Business Risk + Liquidity Risk + Credit Risk

Business Risk The risk of doing business in a particular industry or environment is called business risk. This risk refers to uncertain return to the investor caused due to uncertain business environment, in which it operates. These risks may arise due to both internal and external factors. Business risk caused due to internal factors leads to poor performance of the company, but can be reduced or avoided by some changes in the company's policies.

Financial Risk Risk caused due to inability of the organisation to meet its financial obligations is referred to as financial risk. *e.g.* Obligations such as interest and principal payment of the funds borrowed. Investment in an organisation that is heavily into debt may leads to greater uncertainty of return because of financial risk to their owners.

Default Risk It is also called as insolvency risk or credit risk. This is the risk that a company or individual will be unable to pay the contractual interest or principal on its debt obligations. This type of risk is particularly a concern to investors, who hold bonds within their portfolio. Government bonds, especially those issued by the Federal Government, have the least amount of default risk and least amount of returns, while corporate bonds tend to have the highest amount of default risk, but also the higher interest rates.

Liquidity Risk It refers to the risk of liquidating the assets as and when required. Liquidity here means both ability of converting assets into cash and doing it without compromising on price levels. The more uncertainty about the time element and the price concession, the greater is the liquidity risk. A treasury bill has little or no liquidity risk, whereas a small OTC stock may have substantial liquidity risk.

Risk Management

It is important in an organisation because without it, a firm cannot possibly define its objectives for the future. If a company defines objectives without taking the risks into consideration, then on the occurrence of any risk, the company may lose its strength.

Risk management is the process of identifying assessing and controlling threats to an organisations capital and earnings. These threats or risk could stem from a wide variety of sources including financial uncertainty, legal liabilities, strategic management errors accidents and natural disasters.

A risk management plan increasingly includes company's process for indentifying and controlling threats to its digital assets, including proprietary corporate data, a customers personal identifiable information and intellectual property.

Risk Management Strategies and Processes

All risk management plans follow the same steps that combine to make up the overall risk management process.

Risk Identification The company identifies and defines potential risks that may negatively influence a specific company process on project.

Risk Analysis The goal of the analysis is to further understand each specific instance of risk and how it could influence the company's project and objetive.

Risk Reduction Companies are sometimes able to reduce the amount of effect certain risks can have on company process. This is achieved by adjusting certain aspects of an overall project plan.

Risk Sharing Sometimes a risk is shared on distributed among several of the project's participants or business department.

Risk Retaining Sometimes, companies decided a risk is worth it from a business standpoint and decided to retain the risk and deal with any potential fallout.

Risk Mitigation During this steps, companies assess their highest ranked risks and develop a plan to alleviate them using specific risk controls.

Risk Monitoring Part of the mitigation plan includes following up on both the risks and the overall plan to continuously monitor and track new and existing risks.

Non-Performing Assets (NPAs)

The Securitisation Reconstruction of Financial Assets and Enforcement of Security Interest Act, 2002 defined Non-Performing Assets (NPAs) as "an asset or account of a borrower, which has been classified by a bank or financial institute as sub-standard, doubtful or loss assets, in accordance with the directions or guidelines relating to asset classification issued by RBI". If any advance or credit facilities granted by bank to a borrower become non-performing, then the bank will have to treat all the advances/credit facilities granted to that borrower as non-performing without having any regard to that fact that there may still exist certain advances/credit facilities having performing status. As per RBI's guidelines, income on loans is to be recognised on receipt basis (as against accrual basis) and if it has not been received for a specified period, the same asset is to be treated as non-performing.

With effect from 31st March, 2004, Non-Performing Assets (NPAs) shall be a loan or an advance where

- Interest and/or installment of principal remains overdue for a period of more than 90 days in respect of a term loan.
- The account remain 'out of order' for a period of more than 90 days, in respect of an Overdraft/Cash Credit (OD/CC).
- The bill remains overdue for a period of more than 90 days in the case of bills purchased and discounted.
- Interest and/or installment of principal remains overdue for two harvest seasons, but for a period not exceeding two-half years, in the case of an advance granted for agricultural purpose.
- Any amount to be received remains overdue for a period of more than 90 days in respect of other.

Causes of NPAs

Willful Defaults The Indian Public Sector Banks are worst hit by these defaults. It is a default in repayment obligation.

Insustrial Crisis Industries depend on banks to fulfill their projects. If industry is in crisis, it is bound to hit the banking sector and their NPA will rise.

Credit Distribution Mis-management Often, illminded borrowers bribe bank official to get loans with an intention of default.

Lenient Lending Norms One of the main reasons of rising NPAs is the Lenient Lending Norms especially for corporate honchos where their financial status and credit rating is not analysed property.

Speculation Investing in high risk assets to earn high income.

Impact of NPA

- Banks profit will come down which they earn in the form of interest.
- Banks will become reluctant to lend thus affecting their borrowers.
- It affects the liquidity position of banks.
- The service to good customers may get affected.
- It adversely affected the bank balance sheet.

Types of NPAs

Following are the types of NPAs, which are as follows

Standard Assets/Performing Assets These are the assets (advances), which continue to generate income and repayments as and when they fall due without any default or risk. Such assets carry a normal risk and are not NPA in the real sense.

Sub-standard Assets All those assets (loans and advances), which are considered as non-performing for a period of 12 months are called as sub-standard assets.

Doubtful Assets All those assets, which are considered as non-performing for period of more than 12 months are called as doubtful assets, earlier this period was of 18 months.

Loss Assets All those assets, which cannot be recovered are termed as loss assets.

NPA Mangement

An NPA mangement is a tool which identifies risks and gives early warning signals to take proactive action against NPA. There are some provisions under certain guidelines for NPA or future loss. As it is mentioned earlier that the assets can be classified in four main categories, *the below mentioned table give a brief introduction of various degree of provision required in each case*

Provisions on Types of Assets

S. No.	Types of Assets	Provisions
1.	Standard assets	0.25% for all types of standard advances
2.	Sub-standard assets	10% for all types of standard advances
3.	Doubtful assets	
	Upto 1 year	100% of unsecured advances and 20% of secured advances
	One to 3 years	100% of unsecured advances and 30% of secured advances
	More than 3 years	100% of unsecured advances and 100% of secured advances
4.	Loss assets	100% of unsecured advances and 100% of secured advances

Digitisation of Banking and other Financial Services

Stiff competition has started prevailing in the banking sector, as a result of policy of liberalisation. Several Indian and foreign banks, established in the private sector, have started providing various new services, through innovative banking, which includes e-banking also. Banking and its related services are also being provided to the customer even without going to the bank, with the help of wider use of information technology through ATMs, credit and debit cards, internet banking, core banking solutions etc.

E-banking

It refers to electronic banking, also known as Electronic Funds Transfer (EFT), is simply the use of electronic means to transfer funds directly from one account to another, rather than by cheque or cash. This covers both computer and telephone banking. It is like e-business in banking industry. E-banking is also called as 'Virtual Banking' or 'Online Banking'.

E-banking Services

To accesss electronic banking feature, customers are required to provide their Know Your Customer (KYC) information. A customer is issued a Personal Identification Number (PIN) and access details once his internet account is verified.

Forms of E-banking/Digital Payment Systems

Internet Banking Through its website, a bank may offer its customers online access to account information, payment and fund transfer facilities. The range of services offered differs from bank to bank depending mainly on the type and size of the bank.

Automated Teller Machines (ATMs) These are electronic machines, which are operated by a customer to deposit or to withdraw cash from bank. For using an ATM, a customer has to obtain an ATM card from his bank. The ATM card is a plastic card, which is magnetically coded. It can be easily read by the machine.

Mobile Banking The RBI has adopted bank led model, in which mobile phone banking is promoted through business correspondents of banks. The operative guidelines for banks on 'Mobile Banking Transactions' in India were issued on 8th October, 2008. Cellular phone operators are now moving towards the new age technology *i.e.* Wireless Application Protocol (WAP). WAP is the latest technology which also enables banking transaction through mobile phone.

Smart Card A smart card, chip card or Integrated Circuit Card (ICC) is a plastic card of pocket-sized with embedded integrated circuits. It contains micro processor. The chip in these cards is capable of many kinds of transactions. *e.g.* A person could make purchases from their credit account, debit account or from a stored account value that is reloadable.

Debit Card A debit card is basically an ATM card which bank clients can access to their account to withdraw cash or pay for goods and services. Whenever a debit card is used to make a payment, the total amount charged is instantly reduced from the bank balance. Debit cards are also known as 'check cards'.

Credit Card A credit card is a plastic card bearing an account number assigned to a cardholder with a credit limit that can be used to purchase goods and services and to obtain cash disbursements on credit, for which cardholder is subsequently billed by an issuer for repayment of the credit extended at once or on an instalment basis. Credit card is a way to 'pay later,' a debit card is a way to 'pay now'. With increasing regularity, banks offer services at times and locations that are more convenient for customer.

E-Cheque An e-cheque work the same way a cheque does, the cheque writer 'writes' the e-cheque, using one of many types of electronic devices and 'gives' the e-cheque to the payee electronically.

The payee 'deposits' the electronic cheque, receives credit and the payee's bank 'clears' the e-cheque to the paying bank. The paying bank validates the e-cheque and then 'charges' the check writer's account for the check.

Other Forms of E-banking

Direct Deposit It allow to authorise specific payment are expecting or a regular basis to be deposited in coustomer's account automatically. The fund will be automatically withdrawn from customers account to pay the bill on the date which they choose. Direct Withdrawl should only be authorised with parties or companies.

Electric Bill Payment Bill pay is a service that banks offer to help you pay your bills on time at the same time every month. You collect the bills that you want to included in the bill pay service and set-up your bank account to pay a certain amount each month to each biller.

Skimming Skimming is a method of stealing credit card information by using a small electronic device that scans and stores card data from the magnetic stripe. It can be done manually by a corrupt retail store employee who surreptitiously skims customer's card or by criminals who place a skimming device on top of a regular credit card reader (usually at ATM machines) stolen credit card information can be used to make fraudulent purchases online or to close new cards.

E-wallet An e-wallet, sometimes called a digital wallet, is a secure place that contains one or more currency purses. Your shoppers can fund and e-wallet in several different ways. Once funded, shoppers can use e-wallet online to buy goods or services. A shopper must register with the provider and may have to complete a full KYC process before they're allowed to use an e-wallet. Some payment serivce providers have the concept of a verified and unverified e-wallet account for usess who have completed KYC and those who have not varified shoppers normally have a higher spending limit.

UPI The Unified Payment Interface (UPI) is a payment system that allows you to transfer money between any two parties. It allows you to pay directly from your bank account to different merchants without the hassle of typing your card detail, or net banking/wallet password.

Various Methods of Transfer of Funds Electronically

***Electronic Clearing System** (ECS)* ECS is a retail funds transfer system to effect payments like utility bills, dividend interest etc.

***Real Time Gross Settlement** (RTGS)* It is an electronic payment system where payment instructions are processed on a 'Continuous' or 'Real Time Base' and settled on a 'Gross' or individual basis without netting the debit against credit.

***National Electronic Funds Transfer** (NEFT)* It is a system similar to RTGS with some difference. Transfer of funds through NEFT is safe quick. It reduce the paper work and cost effective.

***Core Banking Solutions** (CBS)* Core banking solutions helped banks to offer better customer service. It is mainly work on the support of effective communication and good information technology

Advantages of E-banking

- Funds can be easily transferred by the customer.
- The operating cost per unit services is lower for the banks.
- The customers can obtain money at anywhere and any time from ATM machines.
- No requirement of going the bank's premises.
- Incidence of errors is very low.
- The credit cards and debit cards enables the customers to obtain discounts from retail outlets.

EXAM BASED QUESTIONS

Banking Sector Reforms

1 **Tier II capital should not be more than .... of Tier I capital.**

(a) 150% (b) 100%
(c) 50% (d) None of these

2 **Renewal charges for all advance accounts to be recovered on**

(a) 31st March of every Financial Year
(b) 1st April of every Financial Year
(c) the date of sanction for renewal
(d) the date of application for renewal

3 **Advance, which remain NPA upto a period of 12 months is called**

(a) sub-standard advance
(b) doubtful advance
(c) loss advance
(d) All of the above

4 **Which of the following public sector banks in November 2011, froze its lending to the power sector?**

(a) State Bank of India
(b) Allahabad Bank
(c) Punjab National Bank
(d) United Bank of India

5 **FDI upto 49% in private banking sector of India is allowed through**

(a) automatic route (b) government route
(c) Both (a) and (b) (d) None of these

6 **FDI beyond 49%, but upto 74% in private banking sector of India is allowed through**

(a) automatic route (b) government route
(c) Both (a) and (b) (d) None of these

7 **The .... advance is an advance where payment of interest and/or repayment of installment of principal remain unpaid for a period of two quarters or more.**

(a) loss (b) doubtful
(c) non-performing (d) All of these

8 **The minimum capital adequacy ratio currently fixed by RBI for banks is**

(a) 12% (b) 10%
(c) 9% (d) 11%

9 **Non-performing advances means**

(a) non-functional assets
(b) obsolete assets
(c) assets transferred to company liquidator
(d) loans becoming overdue beyond 90 days

10 **In regard to assigning risk weight to NPAs, which one of the following is incorrect?**

(a) 150% risk weight, when specific provisions are less than 20% of the outstanding amount of the NPA
(b) 100% risk weight, when specific provisions are atleast 20% of the outstanding amount of the NPA
(c) 50% risk weight, when specific provisions are more than 50% of the outstanding amount of the NPA
(d) 50% risk weight, when specific provisions are atleast 50% of the outstanding amount of the NPA

11 **Loans upto ₹ 1 lakh against gold and silver ornaments will attract a risk weight of**

(a) 20% (b) 30%
(c) 50% (d) 75%

12 **Revaluation reserves are considered as a discount, while determining their value for inclusion in Tier II capital. What is that discount?**

(a) 40% (b) 50%
(c) 60% (d) 55%

13 **Credit risk is defined as**

(a) probability of default by the counter party
(b) probability of worsening of credit quality of a borrowal account
(c) Either (a) or (b)
(d) Both (a) and (b)

14 **Unsecured exposure will attract the following provision**

(a) 20% for assets in sub-standard category
(b) 100% for assets in doubtful and loss category
(c) Both (a) and (b)
(d) None of the above

15 **Which one of the following statement is incorrect?**

(a) Doubtful advance is an advance which remains NPA for more than 12 months
(b) The account remain 'out of order' for a period of more than 100 days, in respect of an Overdraft/Cash Credit (OD/CC)
(c) Net NPA is having provisions for bad debts
(d) Net NPAs = Gross NPAs – Provision for NPAs

16 **Which Indian PSU bank in tune with its plans to expand its retail division in the UK entered the mortgage market in the country for the first time?**

(a) Punjab National Bank
(b) Oriental Bank of Commerce
(c) State Bank of India
(d) Indian Overseas Bank

17 **The increase in foreign investment limit in the banking sector to 74% includes portfolio investment.**
(a) Foreign Institutional Investors (FIIs)
(b) Non-Resident Indians (NRIs)
(c) Private placement
(d) All of the above

18 **If all the banks in an economy are nationalised and converted into a monopoly bank, the total deposits**
(a) will decrease
(b) will increase
(c) will neither increase nor decrease
(d) None of the above

19 **Under which pillar of RBI's new capital adequacy framework (Basel-II guidelines), minimum 8% capital adequacy for credit risk, market risk and operational risk has been prescribed?**
(a) Pillar-I (b) Pillar-II
(c) Pillar-III (d) None of these

20 **Pillar-II of RBI's new capital adequacy framework (Basel-II guidelines) prescribes that**
(a) banks are required to adhere to market discipline by furnishing a set of disclosure requirements, which will enable market participants to assess key pieces of information on the scope of application, capital, risk exposure and risk assessment processes and hence, the capital adequacy of the institution
(b) banks will come under supervisory review process of RBI in regard to efficacy of their risk management system and will have to adhere to "Internal capital adequacy assessment process" to capture risks such as liquidity risks, reputational risks etc. Other than those prescribed under Pillar-I to convince RBI that adequate capital is maintained for various risks they are exposed to
(c) banks are required to maintain minimum 9% capital adequacy for credit risk, market risk and operational risk
(d) None of the above

21 **Which one of the following statement(s) is/are incorrect?**
(a) For computation of Tier I capital, intangible assets and losses in the current period and those brought forward from previous year, should be deducted from Tier I capital
(b) Any gain or loss arising at the time of securitisation of standard assets, if recognised, should be deducted from Tier I capital.
(c) Securitisation exposures shall be deducted from regulatory capital and the deduction must be made 50% from Tier I and 50% from Tier II capital.
(d) All of the above

22 **The methods used for computation of capital for credit risk under Basel-II are**
(a) standardised approach
(b) internal rating based approach-foundation
(c) internal rating based approach-advanced
(d) All of the above

23 **The idea behind a capital adequacy ratio is that banking risk should be borne by**
(a) borrowers (b) shareholders
(c) directors (d) creditors

24 **As a consortium leader, the Lead Bank would**
1. coordinate with government office's, banks and other stakeholders.
2. undertake planning and formulation of annual district credit plans through block and district consultative committees.
3. help in synergising all efforts to fulfill plan priorities and district specific requirements.

Select the correct answer using the codes given below
Codes
(a) Both 1 and 2 (b) Only 1
(c) Only 2 (d) All of the above

25 **Which of the following statement is incorrect?**
1. NPAs = [(Gross or Net NPAs)/Total advances] × 100
2. Net NPAs = Gross NPAs − Provision for NPA's
3. $\text{CAR} = \dfrac{\text{Tier two capital + Tier three capital}}{\text{Risk weighted assets}}$
4. Capital fund has two tiers-Tier I or core capital Tier II

Codes
(a) Only 4 (b) Only 1
(c) 1, 2 and 4 (d) Only 3

26 **Consider the following statements.**
1. In case of standard assets, provision for NPA must be 25% for all types of standard assets.
2. In case of sub-standard assets, provision for NPA must be 10% for all types of standard assets.
3. In case of doubtful assets, 100% provision is required for unsecured and secured advances.
4. In case of loss assets, 10% of unsecured and 100% of secured advance must be kept as provision for NPAs.

Which of the statement(s) given above is/are correct?
Codes
(a) Only 3 (b) 1, 2 and 4
(c) Only 4 (d) Both 1 and 3

Digitisation of Banking

27 **Lot of banks in India, these days are offering M-Banking facility to their customers. What is the full form of 'M' in 'M-Banking'?**
(a) Money (b) Mobile Phone
(c) Marginal (d) Message

28 **For tele banking, banks required approval from RBI**
(a) time to time as per licensing policy
(b) at the end of every financial year
(c) one time
(d) at the end of five financial years

29 E- banking is synonymous with
(a) tele banking (b) internet banking
(c) euro banking (d) None of these

30 Real Time Gross Settlement (RTGS) is managed by
(a) State Bank of India
(b) Reserve Bank of India
(c) Indian Banks' Association
(d) Government of India

31 Which one of the following statement is incorrect?
(a) ATMs are part of virtual banking
(b) A smart card is also known as Integrated Circuit Card (ICC)
(c) Credit card is a way to 'pay now', a debit card is a way to 'pay later'
(d) Debit cards are known as check cards

32 A ...... card is basically a payment mechanism which allows the holder of the card to make purchase without any immediate cash payment.
(a) ATM (b) credit
(c) debit (d) Kisan credit land

33 ATM was first introduced in India by Hongkong and Singapore Banking Corporation (HSBC) in the year
(a) 1984 (b) 1989
(c) 1982 (d) 1987

34 Which bank has introduced 'Prepaid Card' first?
(a) OBC (b) BoB
(c) Corporation Bank (d) SBI

Miscellaneous

35 **Statement** I For strengthening capital base of banks.

Statement II For sanctioning more loans.

Codes
(a) Both statements are correct
(b) Both statements are incorrect
(c) Statement I is correct, but Statement II is incorrect
(d) Statement I is incorrect, but Statement II is correct

Directions (Q. Nos. 36-39) *In the questions given below are two statements labelled as Assertion (A) and Reason (R). In the context of the two statements, which one of the following is correct?*

Codes
(a) Both (A) and (R) are true and (R) is the correct explanation of (A)
(b) Both (A) and (R) are true, but (R) is not the correct explanation of (A)
(c) (A) is true, but (R) is false
(d) (A) is false, but (R) is true

36 **Assertion** (A) The banks predominantly follow the 'liquidation approach' or 'real bills' doctrine rather than the 'going concern approach' in their lending, their unsecured loans are hardly one-fourth of the total laons.

Reason (R) Banks provide advances primarily on a secured basis.

37 **Assertion** (A) The banks have moved towards the best international practice with regard to capital adequacy, supervisory standards, transparency and disclosure, risk management and settlement of dues.

Reason (R) The private sector banks are more aggressive and want to capture more market and earn more profit.

38 **Assertion** (A) As per directives of RBI, all scheduled commercial banks are required to maintain NPA both on gross and net basis and generally expressed in the percentage term.

Reason (R)

NPAs = [(Gross or Net NPAs)/Total advances] × 100

39 **Assertion** (A) Capital to Risk (Weighted) Assets Ratio (CRAR) was introduced in 1992.

Reason (R) Capital Adequacy Ratio (CAR) is also known as Capital to Risk (Weighted) Assets Ratio (CRAR).

40 Match the following.

List I	List II
A. Performing assets	1. Investments
B. Loss assets	2. Standard assets
C. Cash balance	3. Non-performing assets
D. Government securities	4. Liquid assets

Codes

	A	B	C	D
(a)	2	3	4	1
(b)	2	1	3	4
(c)	3	4	2	1
(d)	4	3	2	1

PREVIOUS YEARS' QUESTIONS

December 2018

1 Banks are required to classify non-performing assets into option
(a) sub-standard assets, doubtful assets and loss assets
(b) standard assets and sub-standard assets
(c) doubtful assets and bad debts
(d) doubtful assets, bad debts and loss assets

2 'Skimming' in e-banking is a method of
(a) converting debit card into credit card
(b) transferring cash from one account to another account
(c) stealing credit card information
(d) intimating the customer about his heavy with drawals

3 Second generation reforms in our country do not comprise of which one of the following?
(a) Exploiting the knowledge based global economy
(b) Growing Indian transnational corporations
(c) Population control measures
(d) Clean environment

November 2017

4 **Assertion**(A) The future will see mostly the electronic money clearance through satellite networking.
Reason (R) RBI is encouraging e-banking.
Codes
(a) (A) is true, (R) is false
(b) (A) is false, but (R) is true
(c) Both (A) and (R) are true and (R) is the correct explanation of (A)
(d) Both (A) and (R) are true, but (R) does not support (A)

5 Which of the following are the forms of e-banking? Select the correct code.
1. Internet banking
2. Telephone banking
3. Electronic cheque conversion
4. Electronic bill payment
5. Direct fund transfer through RTGS

Codes
(a) 1, 3 and 4 (b) 1, 2, 3 and 4
(c) 2, 3 and 4 (d) 1, 2, 3, 4 and 5

6 'RWA' with regard to capital adequacy stands for which one of the following?
(a) Risk Withdrawal Adjustments
(b) Risk Withdrawal Arrangements
(c) Risk Weighted Assets
(d) Risk free Weighted Assets

July 2016

7 Banking on telephone service includes
1. automatic balance voice out
2. inquiry all term deposit account
3. direct cash withdrawal
4. utility bill payment
5. voice out last five transactions

Codes
(a) 1, 2, 3 and 5 (b) 1, 2, 4 and 5
(c) 2, 3, 4 and 5 (d) All of the above

8 Match the items of List I with List II with regard to the Basel-III norms.

List I	List II
A. Pillar 1	1. Supervisory review process
B. Pillar 2	2. Market discipline
C. Pillar 3	3. Minimum regulatory capital requirements based on Risk Weighted Assets (RWAs)

Codes

	A	B	C
(a)	1	2	3
(b)	1	3	2
(c)	3	2	1
(d)	3	1	2

9 'Skimming' in e-banking refers to
(a) identifying fraudsters copying vital information from credit cards
(b) multiple transactions by one credit card
(c) conversion of a debit card into credit card
(d) None of the above

June 2015

10 E-banking business is essentially regulated by the Information Technology Act, 2000, under which personal signature is replaced by
(a) encrypted signature (b) image signature
(c) digital signature (d) online signature

11 Match the following.

List I	List II
A. ATM card	1. NPA
B. Debts due for more than 30 days	2. John Shephard Barron
C. Micro finance	3. State Finance Corporations Act
D. State level finance corporations	4. NABARD

Codes

	A	B	C	D
(a)	1	3	2	4
(b)	2	1	4	3
(c)	4	3	2	1
(d)	2	1	3	4

12 To operationalise online, internet, mobile banking, debit card and credit card tools, some of the essential ingredients are
(a) compliance with the Information Technology Act, 2000
(b) satellite connection
(c) selection of a portal and server
(d) All of the above

13 In 1992, the banking sector reforms were introduced as per
(a) C Rangarajan Committee Report
(b) M Narasimham Committee Report
(c) Suresh Tendulkar Committee Report
(d) Sukhamoy Chakraborty Committee Report

June 2014

14 Match the following.

	List I		List II
A.	Narasimham Committee	1.	Lending under consortium arrangement
B.	Shetty Committee	2.	Frauds and malpractices in banks
C.	Ghosh Committee	3.	Securities operations of bank and financial institutions
D.	Janakiraman Committee	4.	Financial system in India

Codes

	A	B	C	D		A	B	C	D
(a)	3	4	2	1	(b)	2	3	4	1
(c)	4	2	3	1	(d)	3	4	1	2

December 2013

15 PIN in banking transaction is known as
(a) Postal Index Number
(b) Permanent Identification Number
(c) Personal Identification Number
(d) Public Interlocking Numeric

June 2013

16 Transaction of internet banking excludes
(a) withdrawal of cash anywhere in India
(b) statement of account for a specific period
(c) transfer of funds from one account to another account
(d) balance enquiry

17 Match the following.

	List I		List II
A.	Debit card	1.	Several storage
B.	Credit card	2.	Online recovery of amount
C.	Electronic purse	3.	Image processing use
D.	Cheque function	4.	Revolving credit

Codes

	A	B	C	D		A	B	C	D
(a)	3	1	4	2	(b)	1	2	4	3
(c)	4	3	1	2	(d)	4	3	2	1

18 Which among the following is not a category of non-performing assets?
(a) Sub-standard assets (b) Doubtful debts
(c) Loss assets (d) Devaluated assets

19 When a loan will be NPA?
(a) Interest and/or loan instalments overdue for more than 90 days
(b) The account is out of order for more than 90 days in case of overdraft/cash credit
(c) Bill remains overdue for more than 90 days
(d) All of the above

December 2012

20 What is OTP in credit card transactions?
(a) Odd Transaction Passward
(b) Owner's Trading Passcode
(c) One Time Password
(d) One Time Pincode

21 The powers of Controller of Capital Issues of India is now shifted of
(a) Ministry of Finance
(b) SEBI
(c) AMFI
(d) Ministry of Corporate Affairs

22 The success of e-banking depends upon
1. Multi-layer Security System
2. Risk and Surveillance Management
3. Updated Flawless Softwares
4. Stringent Legal Frame work

Select the correct answer using the codes given below
Codes
(a) Both 1 and 2 (b) 1, 2 and 3
(c) 2, 3 and 4 (d) All of the above

June 2012

23 One of the items is not related with e-banking.
(a) Demand draft (b) SPNS
(c) ECS (d) ATM

ANSWERS

Objective Questions

1 (c)	2 (c)	3 (c)	4 (c)	5 (b)	6 (a)	7 (b)	8 (a)	9 (b)	10 (c)
11 (c)	12 (d)	13 (c)	14 (c)	15 (d)	16 (d)	17 (c)	18 (b)	19 (c)	20 (d)
21 (c)	22 (a)	23 (b)	24 (d)	25 (d)	26 (b)	27 (d)	28 (d)	29 (a)	30 (b)
31 (c)	32 (b)	33 (b)	34 (d)	35 (b)	36 (d)	37 (a)	38 (c)	39 (a)	40 (b)

Previous Years' Questions

1 (a)	2 (c)	3 (c)	4 (c)	5 (d)	6 (c)	7 (b)	8 (d)	9 (a)	10 (a)
11 (b)	12 (d)	13 (c)	14 (b)	15 (c)	16 (a)	17 (a)	18 (d)	19 (d)	20 (c)
21 (b)	22 (b)	23 (a)							

CHAPTER 27

Financial Markets and Institutions

Financial markets are the most necessary place in the modern era, such as money market and capital market. Government provide securities to these markets and also regulates them. Different financial institutions works to maintain finance in the market like DFIs, NBFIs, etc. These institutions fulfill needs of investors by providing them their services like mutual and pension funds.

In this Chapter

- Financial Market
- Stock Exchanges in India
- Government Security Market
- Development Financial Institutions
- Non-banking Financial Institutions
- Mutual Funds
- Pension Fund
- Financial Sector Reforms in India

Financial Market

A financial market is a market where financial instruments are exchanged or traded. A financial market is a mechanism that allows people to buy and sell financial securities and commodities at efficient market prices. In broad term, financial market is the market place where buyers and sellers participate in the trade of assets such as equities, bonds, currencies and derivatives.

Financial markets are one of the important components of the financial system. They create a mechanism for the exchange trading of financial products guided by a policy framework. The borrowers (issuers of securities), lenders (buyers of securities) and financial intermediaries are the participants in the financial markets.

Financial markets perform various functions such as risk diversification and reduction, efficient payment mechanism, providing information about companies, transformation of financial claims to suit the preferences of both savers and borrowers and enhancing liquidity of financial claims through trading.

Characteristics of Financial Markets

- Financial markets have a large volume of transactions and the speed with which financial resources move in this market is very high.

- There are various segments of financial markets such as money market and capital market, primary and secondary segments, stock markets, bond markets etc.
- There is scope for instant arbitrage among various markets and types of instruments.
- Financial markets are highly volatile. Panic and distress selling by a limited group of operators can spread as a general tendency.
- Financial intermediaries are the dominant participants in the financial markets and they take investment decisions as well as risks on behalf of their depositors.
- Financial market provides a channel through which new saving helps to aid capital formation of a country.
- There is need for regulation of financial markets in order to safeguardthe interest of the investors.

Classification of Financial Market

It can be classified into organised market and unorganised market

- Organised market can be further divided as money market and capital market, which are discussed ahead.
- Unorganised market includes money lenders, indigeneous bankers etc

Money Market

Money market is a place where short-term money borrowing/lending is arranged between the various parties across the country.

Types of Money Market

Organised Money Market

It is dominated by commercial banks. The other major participants are the Reserve Bank of India, Life Insurance Corporation, General Insurance Corporation, Unit Trust of India, Securities Trading Corporation of India Limited, Discount and Finance House of India, other primary dealers, commercial banks and mutual funds.

The core of the money market is the interbank call money market whereby short-term money borrowing/lending is effected to manage temporary liquidity mismatches. The Reserve Bank of India occupies a strategic position of managing market liquidity through open market operations of government securities, access to its accommodation, cost (interest rates), availability of credit and other monetary management tools.

Unorganised Money Market

There is still an active unorganised market inspite rapid expansion of the organised money market through a large network of banking institutions that have extended their reach even to the rural areas. It consists of indigenous bankers and money lenders.

In the unorganised market, there is no clear destination between short-term and long-term finance and even between the purposes of finance. The unorganised sector provides finance for trade as well as personal consumption.

Money Market Instruments

Money market instruments provide the tools, by which one can operate in the money market. Money market instruments meets short-term requirements of the borrowers and provides liquidity to the lenders. *The most common money market instruments are*

Treasury Bills (T-bills) Treasury bills are issued by Central Government and are one of the safe money market instruments. In T-bills, returns are not that attractive. They are zero risk instruments. These T-bills are circulated by both primary as well as the secondary markets. They come with the maturities of 3 months, 6 months and 1 year. It is highly liquid because its repayment by the government. At present, the Government of India issues three types of treasury bills through auctions, namely; 91 days, 182 days and 364 days.

Certificate of Deposits (CDs) Certificate of deposit is issued by a bank in form of a certificate authorising the bearer to receive interest. It is similar to bank term deposit account. The certificate bears the maturity date, fixed rate of interest and the value. These certificates are available in the tenure of 3 months to 5 years. The returns on certificate of deposits are higher than T-bills because they carry high level of risk. These certificate of deposits may be for a maximum amount of ₹ 25 lakh in multiples of ₹ 5 lakh.

Commercial Papers (CPs) Commercial papers are short-term unsecured promissory notes issued by corporates and financial institutions at a discounted value. They come with fixed maturity period, ranging from 1 day to 270 days.

Bill of Exchange This is the most prevalent and popular instrument of the money market. This is an order written by the lender, on the borrower that the borrower to market payment of the amount mentioned in the bill on the due date.

Call Money/Notice Money/Term Money This is an interbank market for short-term funds. Call money is for 1 day, notice money is for 1 day to 14 days and term money is for more than 14 days. It is highly liquid.

Capital Market

It is a market, in which instruments with maturity of more than one year (long-term maturity) are bonded. The capital market consists of the primary (new issues) market and the secondary market. The primary market provides the channel for sale of new securities while the secondary market deals in securities previously issued.

Types of Capital Market

Primary Market

The primary market provides the channel for sale of new securities. Primary market provides opportunity to issuers of securities, government as well as corporates, to raise funds to meet their requirements of investment and/or discharging some obligations.

The primary market deals with the issue of new instruments such as equity shares, preference shares and debt instruments by the Corporate Sector, Central and State Governments, various Public Sector Industrial Units (PSUs), statutory and other authorities such as state electricity boards and port trusts also issue bonds/debt instruments. Therefore, it is also called the New Issue Market (NIM).

The primary market is one in which public issue of securities is made through a prospectus in a retail market and there is no physical location.

Secondary Market

It is a market for trading and settlement of securities that have already been issued. It is a market where securities are traded after being initially offered to the public in the primary market and/or listed on the stock exchange. Secondary market comprises of equity and the debt markets.

In secondary market or stock exchange, the investors holding securities, sell securities through registered brokers of the stock exchange. Investors, who are interested in buying securities, purchase securities through registered brokers of the stock exchange. It may have a physical location like a stock exchange or a trading floor. The secondary market consists of 22 stock exchanges. The secondary market provides a trading place for the securities already issued, to be bought and sold.

Capital Market /Instruments

The broad types of capital *viz,* equity, debt and preference shares were introduced earlier. *Some capital market/ instruments are listed below*

***Global Depository Receipt** (GDR)/**American Depository Receipt** (ADR)* Foreign investors investing in the Indian stock markets need to comply with various regulations of the securities market regulator, the Securities and Exchange Board of India (SEBI) and the Central Bank, the Reserve Bank of India (RBI). Further, their investments are settled through the Indian settlement system, where receipts and payments are made in Indian rupees.

Convertible Preference Shares The preference shares that are convertible into equity shares are called convertible preference shares. Depending on the terms of issue, they are either compulsorily convertible or optionally convertible.

Debentures/Bonds These are a form of debt security, which are issued by companies. They may be secured against fixed assets, in that case these are called secured debentures others are unsecured. As with preference shares, they may be convertible (compulsorily or optionally) or they may be non-convertible.

Foreign Currency Convertible Bonds These are debt securities issued by companies and denominated in foreign currency. Further, they are compulsorily or optionally convertible into equity shares of the company.

Government Securities They are issued by the Government of India for government's requirement of funds. Further, the yield on government securities in the market sets the benchmark for yields on other debt securities. It is totally secure financial instrument ensuring safety of both capital and income.

Difference between Capital Market and Money Market

Basis	Money Market	Capital Market
Meaning	It is a market for short term loanable funds for a period of not exceeding one year.	It is a market for long-term funds exceeding a period of one year.
Regulatory Body	It is regulated and executed by RBI.	Capital market is regulated and executed by SEBI.
Transactions	Transactions have to be conducted without the help of brokers.	Transactions have to be conducted only through authorised dealers.
Institutions	The central bank and commercial banks are the major institutions in the money market.	Development banks and insurance company play a dominant role in the capital market.
Instruments	The Instruments of money market are bill of exchange, treasury bills, commercial paper, certificate of deposits etc.	This market deals in instruments like share, debenture, government bonds etc.

Financial Market Participants

The major players in the primary market include the merchant bankers, mutual funds, financial institutions, Foreign Institutional Investors (FIIs) and individual investors. In the secondary market, there are the stock exchanges, stock brokers, mutual funds, financial institutions, Foreign Institutional Investors (FIIs) and individual investors.

Registrars and transfer agents, custodians and depositories are capital market intermediaries that provides infrastructure services for both primary and secondary.

Stock Exchanges in India

The Securities Contract (Regulation) Act, 1956 [SCRA] defines Stock Exchange as "any body of individuals, whether incorporated or not, constituted for the purpose of assisting, regulating or controlling the business of buying, selling or dealing in securities". Stock exchange could be a regional stock exchange whose area of operation is specified at the time of its recognition or national exchanges, which are permitted to have nationwide trading since, their commencement.

Stock exchange plays an important role as it act as a free market for securities, where prices are determined by the forces of supply and demand. Stock exchanges also assists in mobilising funds for the government and the industry. In India, the stock exchanges have been assigned with the primary responsibility of undertaking market surveillance. Information relating to price and volume movements in the market, broker positions, risk management, settlement process and compliance pertaining to listing agreement are monitored by the exchanges on a real time basis as part of their self-regulatory function.

Among the various stock exchanges, the National Stock Exchange (NSE) and the Bombay Stock Exchange (BSE) are the leading ones in India.

The stock exchanges offers a wide range of products including equity shares, Exchange Traded Funds (ETF), mutual funds, debt instruments, index futures and options, stock futures and options and currency futures and options, interest rate futures etc.

National Stock Exchange (NSE)

The national stock exchange commenced its operations in 1994 as a first step in reforming the securities market through improved technology and introduction of best practices in management. It started with the concept of an independent governing body without any broker representation thus, ensuring that the operators' interests were not allowed to dominate the governance of the exchange.

Before the NSE was setup, trading on the stock exchanges in India used to take place through open outcry without use of information technology for immediate matching or recording of trades. To obviate this, the NSE introduced Screen Based Trading System (SBTS), where a member can punch into the computer the quantities of shares and the prices at which he wants to transact.

With SBTS, it becomes possible for market participants to see the full market, which helps to make the market more transparent, leading to increased investor confidence.

The NSE started nation wide SBTS, which have provided a completely transparent trading mechanism. The NSE has set-up a clearing corporation to provide legal counterparty guarantee to each trade thereby eliminating counterparty risk. The National Securities Clearing Corporation Limited. (NSCCL) commenced operations in April 1996. Counterparty risk is guaranteed through finetuned risk management systems and an innovative method of online position monitoring and automatic disablement. Principle of 'novation' is implemented by NSE capital market segment.

Bombay Stock Exchange (BSE)

The Bombay Stock Exchange (BSE) is the first and longest securities market in India and was established in 1875 as the native share and stock broker's association. Based in Mumbai, India, the BSE lists close to 6,000 companies and is one of the largest exchange in the world, alongwith the New York Stock Exchange (NYSE), NASDAQ, London Stock Exchange Group, Japan Exchange Group and Shanghai Stock exchange.

In 1995, the BSE switched from an open floor to an electronic trading system. There are more than a dozen electronic exchange in US alone. Securities that the BSE lists includes stock's, stock future, stock options, index futures, index options and weekly options. The BSE's overall performance is measured by the sensex an index of 30 of the BSE's largest stocks covering 12 sectors.

Securities and Exchange Board of India (SEBI)

SEBI is one of the regulatory authority on capital and derivative market in India.

The SEBI Act of 1992 vests it with wide ranging powers to regulate the stock exchanges and securities industry to promote their orderly functioning. It can frame or issue rules, regulations, directives, guidelines and norms in respect of primary markets and secondary markets intermediaries operating in the market and certain financial institutions. The role of SEBI is to create conditions for efficient mobilisation and allocation of resources through the securities markets, stimulating competition and encouraging innovations.

SEBI provides a high degree of protection to investors with regard to their rights and interests through adequate, accurate and authentic information and disclosure of such information on a continuous basis. In short, the SEBI endeavours to create an effective surveillance mechanism and encourage responsible and accountable autonomy on the part of all players in the market.

Role of SEBI in the Development of Stock and Capital Markets

SEBI and the Primary Market

- Companies need not obtain prior permission for raising of capital from the market.
- SEBI has issued guidelines for all companies for disclosure of information and protection of investor's interest.
- Book building requirement has been introduced for issues above ₹100 crore.
- Bankers to the issue and portfolio managers have to be registered with SEBI.

SEBI and the Secondary Market

- The governing bodies of stock exchange have been recognised, restructured and broad based.
- SEBI has drawn up a comprehensive plan of inspecting all stock exchanges to determine the extent of compliance with SEBI guidelines.
- Computerised screen based trading has been introduced on all major stock exchanges.
- All Stock Exchanges (SEs) have been directed to set-up a clearing house or clearing corporation.
- Brokers, sub-brokers have been brought under the regulatory framework of SEBI. Penal action is taken by SEBI against any member for violation of SEBI Act.
- Registers to issues and share transfer agents have been brought under SEBI.
- SEBI has issued guidelines pertaining to buy-back of shares.

SEBI and Mutual Funds

All mutual funds have to be registered with the SEBI. UTI has also been brought under SEBI. SEBI has issued guidelines to provide for portfolio disclosure, standardisation of accounting policies, valuation norms for determining net asset value and pricing. SEBI is the regulator for the securities market in India.

SEBI can conduct enquiries, audits and inspection of all concerned and adjudicate offences under the act. It has powers to register and regulate all market intermediaries and also to penalise them in case of violations of the provisions of the act, rules and regulations made there under. SEBI has full autonomy and authority to regulate and develop an orderly securities.

Functions of SEBI/Working of SEBI

SEBI has been obligated to protect the interests of the investors in securities and to promote the development of and to regulate the securities market by such measures as it thinks fit.

The measures referred to therein may provide for

- regulating the business in stock exchanges and any other securities markets.
- registering and regulating the working of the depositories, participants, custodians of securities, foreign institutional investors, credit rating agencies and such other intermediaries as specified by SEBI.
- registering and regulating the working of venture capital funds and collective investment schemes including mutual funds.
- promoting and regulating self-regulatory organisations.
- prohibiting fraudulent and unfair trade practices relating to securities markets.
- promoting investors' education and training of intermediaries of securities markets.
- prohibiting insider trading in securities.
- regulating substantial acquisition of shares and take over of companies.
- calling for information from, undertaking inspection, conducting inquiries and audits of the stock exchanges, mutual funds, other persons associated with the securities market, intermediaries and self-regulatory organisations in the securities market.

Powers of Securities and Exchange Board of India

- SEBI has powers to call information or explanation from recognised stock exchanges or their members and intermediaries regarding their business transactions for inspection or scrutiny purpose.
- SEBI has powers to compel listing of securities by public companies.
- SEBI has powers to levy fees or to impose monetary penalties or other charges on intermediaries and other participants for a range of violations or for carrying out the purposes of regulation. It can even impose suspension of their registration for a short period.
- SEBI has a power to initiate actions in regard to assigned functions.
- SEBI is empowered to grant approval to bye-laws and also to make or amend bye-laws of recognised stock exchanges.

Government Security Market

It is also called 'Gilt-edged securities market'. It is a market where government securities are traded. In India, there are many kinds of government securities for short-term and long-term. In these securities, the return is guaranteed and there is no scope for speculation and manipulation of market. As the value of the securities remain stable, these securities are always demanded by banks and other financial institutions.

The government securities do not suffer from risk of default and are highly liquid. The open market operations of the RBI are also conducted in such securities. *These securities are issued by*

- Centeral government
- State government
- Semi-government authorities
- Autonomous institutions, such as metropolitan authorities
- State electricity boards
- Public sector corporations
- Other governmental agencies, such as SFCs, NABARD, LDBs, SIDCs, housing boards etc.

Characteristics of Government Security Market

- It is risk free market and returns are guaranteed.
- These securities are most liquid debt instruments.
- Government securities are held by RBI which uses them as an important instrument of monetary control.
- These securities bear a fixed rate of interest which is generally lower than interest rate on other securities.
- These securities have a fixed maturity period.

Government Security Market Instruments

Zero Coupon Bonds These are bonds issued at discount and repaid at face value, the difference between the issue price and the redemption price represents the return to the investor.

Floating Rate Bonds These bonds were introduced by Government of India on 29th September, 1995, linking it to 364 days treasury bill rate. These instruments give a variable rate, a characteristic that allows both issuer and investor to share the risk in changing interest rate.

Tap Stock Short taps are short dated stocks and long taps are long dated stocks. These stocks were introduced by Government of India on 29th July, 1994. These forms has not been fully subscribed and is released into the market slowly when its market price reaches predetermined levels.

Partly Paid Stock This is an innovative instruments (15th November, 1994) for which the payment is made in installments. These bonds are of four years maturity and carry a coupon rate of 6 per cent.

Strips It stands for Separately Traded Registered Interest and Principal of Securities. Strips are created by separating the coupon from the principal and trading them independently.

Development of Government Securities Market

Government securities and treasury bill market was underdeveloped in India, before the beginning of the age of reform in banking and financial sectors. RBI has taken some steps in mid 1991 to remove drawbacks and the develop government securities market. *These are as follows*

Treasury Bills of Various Time Period Earlier, treasury bill of 81 days was the main instrument among the government securities. Now-a-days, various types of treasury bills have been introduced like treasury bill of 14 days, 91 days, 182 days, 364 days etc.

Determination of Rates of Interest on Government Securities Now, attention is paid on near market rates, to determine interest rates, while issuing the loans to attract the investors towards government securities.

Development of Primary and Secondary Market In primary market of government securities, now include commercial banks, life insurance corporation, financial companies, mutual fund etc. Besides, a secondary market also exists for government securities, within which transaction are undertaken through subsidiary general ledger accounts.

Beginning of Delivery Vs Payment System RBI has started delivery v/s payment system in Mumbai for transactions of government securities.

Beginning of New Instruments Some new instruments have been introduced in government securities market, like conversion of auction treasury bills in term securities, zero coupon and capital indicator bonds, tap stocks and partly paid stocks etc.

Liquidity Support to Mutual Funds RBI has started giving liquidity support to those mutual funds, who make investment only in government securities.

Development Financial Institutions/Development Banks

These are the financial agencies engaged in the promotion and development of industry, agriculture and other key sectors. These are national or regional financial institutions to provide medium and long-term capital for productive investment.

Some development institutions are government-owned, while others are private. These banks also provide development services that can aid in the accelerated growth of an economy.

Features/Characteristics of Development Banks

- To serve as an agent of development in various sectors like, industries, agriculture and international trade.
- To allocate resources to high priority areas.
- To promote the development of rural areas.
- Lay foundations for industrialisation.
- To finance housing, small scale industries, infrastructure and social utilities.
- Help small and medium sectors.
- Provide financial assistance to both public and private undertakings.

History of Development Banks in India

- The recommendation for setting-up industrial financing institutions was made in 1931 by Central Banking Enquiry Committee, but no concrete steps were taken.
- It was in 1948, that the first development bank, *i.e.* Industrial Finance Corporation of India (IFCI) was established.
- In 1951, Parliament passed State Financial Corporation Act. Under this act, State Governments could establish financial corporations for their respective regions.
- The Industrial Credit and Investment Corporation of India (ICICI) was established in 1955, as a Joint Stock Company.
- In 1964, Industrial Development Bank of India (IDBI) was setup as an apex institution in the area of industrial finance, RCI was merged with IDBI.
- The State Industrial Development Corporations (SIDCs) were established in the sixties to promote medium scale industrial units.

The various development financial institutions working in India are discussed ahead.

Industrial Development Bank of India (IDBI)

It has been a leading development bank with the mission of promoting industrial growth by financing of medium and long-term projects in accordance with national plans and priorities. IDBI was set-up on 1st July, 1964 vide Government of India notification dated 22nd June, 1964 under Industrial Development Bank of India Act. In July, 1995, IDBI made the first public issue of equity shares which was the largest issue on the Indian capital market.

Some of the institutions built by IDBI are as follows

- The National Stock Exchange of India (NSE)
- The National Securities Depository Limited (NSDL)
- The Exim Bank
- The Small Industries Development Bank of India (SIDBI)
- The Entrepreneurship Development Institute of India
- IDBI Bank, which today is owned by the Indian Government, though for a brief period, it was a private scheduled bank.

Services/Functions of IDBI

Merchant Banking Merchant banking is a combination of banking and consultancy services. It provides consultancy to its clients for financial, marketing, managerial and legal matters. IDBI leading as a merchant banker, encompass professional advice and service to industry for issue management, loan syndication project concealing etc.

Debenture Trusteeship IDBI act as a debenture trustee for holders of debentures issued by companies and also to the non-convertible debentures issues subscribed by financial institutions, banks and mutual funds on private placement basis.

Forex Services IDBI offers a variety of foreign exchange services namely spot and forward purchase of currencies for letter of credit and debts servicing, placement of deposits abroad, swaps, forward rate agreements and derivative products.

Industrial Finance Corporation of India (IFCI)

The Industrial Finance Corporation of India was established on 1st July, 1948 under the Industrial Finance Corporation Act, 1948 to provide financial assistance, (medium and long-term) to large scale industries all over the country. After 1993, it was changed from a statutory corporation to a company under the India Companies Act, 1956 and was named as IFCI limited with effect from October, 1999.

Functions of IFCI

- Granting loans or advances to or subscribing to debentures of industrial concerns repayable within 25 years.
- Underwriting the issue of industrial securities, *i.e.* shares, stock, bonds or debentures to be disposed off within 7 years.
- Subscribing directly to the shares and debentures of public limited companies.
- Guaranteeing of deferred payments for the purchase of capital goods from abroad or within India.

- Working as an agent of the Central Government or the World Bank in respect of loans sanctioned to the industrial concerns.
- Guidance to new, tiny, small scale and medium scale entrepreneurs.

State Level Institutions

Several financial institutions have been set-up at the state level, which supplement the financial assistance provided by the all India institutions. They act as a catalyst for promotion of investment and industrial development in the respective states. They broadly consist of 'state financial corporations' and 'state industrial development corporations'. *These are as follows*

State Financial Corporations (SFCs)

SFCs are the state level financial institutions, which play a crucial role in the development of small and medium enterprises in the concerned state. Central Government passed the State Financial Corporation Act of 28th September, 1951, which empowered the State Government to establish financial corporation to operate within the state.

Functions of SFCs

- Project Advisory and Finance.
- Industry Research/Information Services.
- Legal Advisory Services.
- Grant loans or advances to industrial concern repayable within a period not exceeding 20 years.
- To give guarantee to loans taken by industrial units from Commercial Banks and State Cooperative Banks for a period not exceeding 20 years.
- To subscribe to the share capital of the industrial units, in case they wish to raise additional capital.
- To underwrite the issue of shares, bonds and debentures of industrial concerns.
- Provide loans in foreign currency for the import of machinery and technical expertise or assistance.

State Industrial Development Corporations (SIDCs)

SIDCs have been established under the Companies Act,1956, as wholly-owned underta-kings of State Governments. They have been set-up with the aim of promoting industrial development in the respective states and providing financial assistance to small enterprises.

Functions of SIDCs

- Providing term finance to the small, medium and large Industries those set-up in the state.
- Underwriting and subscribing the shares and the debentures of industrial set-up in the state.
- Collaborating with the private industry in the state.
- Conducting market survey and motivating private entrepreneurs.
- Implementing IDBI's schemes of seed capital in the state.

Unit Trust of India (UTI)

The formation of Unit Trust of India on 1st February, 1963. Under the Act of Unit Trust of India Act, marked the evolution of the Indian mutual fund industry and UTI enjoyed complete monopoly. It was set-up by the Reserve Bank of India and it continued to operate under the regulatory control of the RBI until the two were de-linked in 1978 and the entire control was transferred in the hands of Industrial Development Bank of India (IDBI). UTI launched its first scheme in 1964, named as Unit Scheme, 1964 (US-64), which attracted the largest number of investors in any single investment scheme over the years.

In November 1987, SBI Mutual Fund from the State Bank of India became the first Non-UTI Mutual Fund in India. SBI Mutual Fund was later followed by LIC Mutual Fund, Indian Bank Mutual Fund, Bank of India Mutual Fund, GIC Mutual Fund and PNB Mutual Fund. UTI maintained its pre-eminent place till 2001. In February 2003, the UTI Act was repealed and UTI was stripped of its special legal status as a trust formed by an Act of Parliament.

Functions of UTI

- To cover the small savings into industrial finance.
- To encourage savings of lower and middle-class people.
- To sell units to investors in different parts of the country.
- To give them an opportunity to share the benefits and fruits of industrialisation in the country.
- To provide liquidity to units.

Small Industries Development Bank of India (SIDBI)

Small Industries Development Bank of India (SIDBI), set-up on 2nd April, 1990 under an Act of Indian Parliament, it was incorporated initially as a wholly-owned subsidiary of Industrial Development Bank of India. Current shareholding is widely spread among various state-owned banks, insurance companies and financial institutions. SIDBI is the principal financial institution for the promotion, financing and development of the Micro, Small and Medium Enterprise (MSME) sector.

SIDBI has provided assistance, so the entire SSI's sector including tiny village and cottage industries through suitable schemes tailored to meet the requirement of setting-up new projects, expansion, diversification, modernisation and rehabilitation.

Functions of SIDBI

- SIDBI refinances loans extended by the primary lending institutions to small scale industrial units and also provide resources to support them.
- It provides services like leasing, factoring etc to industrial concerns in the small scale sector.
- To initiate steps for technological upgradation and modernisation of existing units.
- It facilitates timely flow of credit for both term loans and working capital to SSI in collaboration with commercial banks.
- It grants direct assistance and refinance loans extended by primary lending institution for financing exports of products manufactured by small scale units.

Infrastructure Development Finance Company (IDFC)

The IDFC a new financial institution, has been set-up for providing long-term finance for infrastructure development with an authorised share capital of ₹ 5,000 crore to be contributed by Government of India (GoI), RBI banks, and FIs.

It was incorporated on 30th January, 1997 in Chennai as a specialised institution to facilitate the flow of private finance to commercially riable infrastructure projects in the areas such as telecom, power, roads, ports railways, urban infrastructure, environment friendly infrastructure, food and agriculture related infrastructure, urban water etc.

The IDFC produces debt and equity support and advisory services. It helps promoters in raising resources from international markets. By offering financial guarantees. It's enitial paid-up capital ₹ 1,000 crore. The government and RBI have provided ₹650 crore as subordinate debt. Thus, the total capital or IDFC at present is ₹ 1,650 crore.

Functions of IDFC

- It helped mid cap companies to strengthen their business.
- Providing legal support.
- Financing projects to helping companies go public through IPOs.

Non-banking Financial Institutions

Non-banking Financial Institutions (NBFIs) are financial institutions that provide financial services without meeting the legal definition of a bank, *i.e.* one that does not hold a banking license. NBFCs are incorporated under the Companies Act, 1956.

These include

- A financial institution, which is a company.
- A non-banking institution which is a company and which has, as its principal business, the receiving of deposits under any scheme or arrangement or in any other manner or lending in any manner.
- Such other non-banking institution or class of such institutions as the RBI may with the previous approval of the Central Government specify.

Features of NBFIs

Small Size NBFIs are generally small in terms of size and scope except a few NBFIs like provident fund, pension fund etc which are large in size. The structure of these institutions is simple and management cost is low.

Low Capital Intensity These institutions have a very low amount of owned capital. They collect larger sum of money from the people by offering attractive returns. They have to do this as they find it difficult to collect deposits.

Easy Availability of Loans Borrowers turned down by the commercial banks and development banks, approach these NBFIs for loans as they make it available easily with very few documentation requirement.

Unsecured Loans The loans offered by NBFIs involve more risk as these are offered without or with inadequate mortgage or security. This results in recovery of loans becoming difficult.

Rescheduling of Loans NBFIs convert the loans offered for short and medium-term into long-term loans when they are not recovered. As a result, amount of loan term and rate of interest increase.

Support for Economic Needs NBFIs provide loan assistance for several economic activities like agriculture, industry, trade, service sector and also finance to household sector for consumption, education, home construction, purchase of vehicle, health etc.

Independent Policy NBFIs in the organised sector are required to follow certain regulation imposed by the RBI but capital limitation, profit provisioning, maintaining reserves, auditing of accounts and publication of balance sheet etc are not binding on them. As a result, most NBFIs conduct their business independently.

Types of Non-Banking Financial Institutions

The Reserve Bank of India categorises the NBFIs into following categories on the basis of their nature and activities

Equipment Leasing Company Equipment leasing company means any company, principal business of which is leasing of equipment or the financing of such activity.

Hire Purchase Company Hire purchase companies are those whose principal business is hire purchase or financing such transactions. The goods are let on hire by the hire purchase company with a condition to pay the instalments by the hirer and after all the instalments are paid by the hirer will have with an option to purchase them later.

Housing Finance Company Housing finance company is a company which provides finance for acquisition and/or construction of houses, acquisition of land and development of land.

Investment Company The investment company acquires securities from security issuers and resales it later to the investing public.

Loan Company Loan company is a company which provides finance by making loans or advances for any activity other than its own. These activities exclude leasing and hire purchase.

Mutual Benefit Financial Companies Mutual benefit financial companies are usually the Nidhi which are notified by the Central Government under Section 620A of the Companies Act, 1956. These companies provide finance to the members of the companies and accept deposits from them.

Role of Non-banking Financial Institutions

The role and importance of non-banking financial institutions is clear from the various functions performed by these institutions.

Major role or functions of the NBFIs are as follows

Financial Intermediation The most important function of the non-banking financial institutions is the mobilisation of funds from the savers to the investors.

Such financial intermediation is economical to both small business and small savers in the following ways

- It provides funds to small businesses which find it difficult to raise funds by selling stocks and bonds because of high transaction costs.
- It is also advantageous to small savers as it diversifies their investments by pooling their funds.

Economies of Scale Large size of assets in portfolios enables the NBFIs to take advantage of economies of scale in portfolio management. *The main economies are*

- Reduction in risk through portfolio diversification.
- Employment of professional managers to manage funds.
- Low administrative cost of disbursing large loans.
- Low costs of establishment, information and transactions.

Inducement to Save Non-banking financial institutions play an important role in promoting savings in the country. These institutions provide a wide range of financial assets as store of value for savers where they can park their funds. Financial assets have an edge over the physical assets as stores of value because they can be stored easily and are more liquid, easily divisible and less risky.

Mobilisation of Saving Mobilisation of savings takes place when the savers hold savings in the form of bank deposits, post office savings deposits, life insurance policies, bills, bond's equity shares etc. NBFIs provide an efficient mechanism for mobilisation of savings.

Investment of Funds The main objective of NBFIs is to earn profits by investing the mobilised savings. Different types of non-banking financial institutions follow different investment policies. *e.g.* Savings and loan associations usually invest in mortgages, while insurance companies invest in bonds and securities.

Stability in Capital Market Different financial instruments are made available by the NBFIs. The credit needs of different entities are fulfilled. As a result, the mismatch between demand and supply for funds is avoided and stability is maintained in capital market.

Providing Specialised Services NBFIs work in specific area providing specialised services to people. *e.g.* LIC in life insurance, GIC in general insurance, UTI mutual fund for investment in stock market, HDFC in housing finance and so on.

Accelerating the Rate of Economic Development NBFIs work efficiently throughout the country supported by financial reforms. They help in mobilising savings and increase the rate of capital formation which is the basis of economic development of a country.

Balanced Growth NBFIs provide easy availability of loans at moderate rate of interest providing benefits to different regions and sections of society. Small and large, old and new, all types of businesses or individual entities can access loan assistance.

Providing Liquidity NBFIs offer different types of investment opportunities and saving options suiting the liquidity requirements of different types of savers and investors in the economy.

Mutual Funds

Mutual fund is a body corporate registered with Securities Exchange Board of India (SEBI) that pools money from individuals/corporate investors and invests the same in a variety of different financial instruments or securities such as equity shares, government securities, bonds, debentures etc. Mutual funds can thus, be considered as financial intermediaries in the investment business that collect funds from the public and invest on behalf of the investors. Mutual funds issue units to the investors.

The appreciation of the portfolio or securities, in which the mutual fund has invested the money leads to an appreciation in the value of the units held by investors. The investment objectives outlined by a mutual fund in its prospectus are binding on the mutual fund scheme. The investment objectives specify the class of securities a mutual fund can invest in.

Mutual funds invest in various asset classes like equity, bonds, debentures, commercial paper and government securities. The schemes offered by mutual funds vary from fund to fund. Some are pure equity schemes others are a mix of equity and bonds. Investors are also given the option of getting dividends, which are declared periodically by the mutual fund or to participate only in the capital appreciation of the scheme.

Risks Involved in Investing in Mutual Funds

Mutual funds do not provide assured returns and their returns are linked to their performance. They invest in shares, debentures, bonds etc. All these investments involve an element of risk. The unit value may vary depending upon the performance of the company and if a company defaults in payment of interest/principal on their debentures/bonds the performance of the fund may get affected. Besides in case, there is a sudden downturn in an industry or the government comes up with new a regulation, which affects a particular industry or company the fund can again be adversely affected. All these factors influence the performance of mutual funds.

Some of the risk to which mutual funds are exposed to is given below

Market Risk If the overall stock or bond markets fall on account of overall economic factors, the value of stock or bond holdings in the fund's portfolio can drop, thereby impacting the fund performance.

Non-market Risk Bad news about an individual company can pull down its stock price, which can negatively affect fund holdings. This risk can be reduced by having a diversified portfolio that consists of a wide variety of stocks drawn from different industries.

Interest Rate Risk Bond prices and interest rates move in opposite directions. When interest rates rise, bond prices fall and this decline in underlying securities affects the fund negatively.

Credit Risk Bonds are debt obligations. So, when the funds invest in corporate bonds, they run the risk of the corporate defaulting on their interest and principal payment obligations and when that risk crystallises, it leads to a fall in the value of the bond causing the NAV of the fund to take a beating.

Different Types of Mutual Funds

Mutual funds are classified in the following manner

On the Basis of Objectives

Equity Funds/Growth Funds Funds investing in equity shares are called equity funds. They carry the principal objective of capital appreciation of the investment over medium to long-term. They are best suited for investors who are seeking capital appreciation.

Diversified Funds Investment is made in companies spread across the sectors. They are generally meant for risk-averse investors, who want a diversified portfolio across sectors.

Sector Funds These funds invest primarily in equity shares of companies in a particular business sector or industry. These funds are targeted at investors, who are bullish or fancy the prospects of a particular sector.

Index Funds These funds invest in the same manner as popular market indices like S and P CNX Nifty or S and P CNX 500. The money collected from the investors is invested only in the stocks, which represent the index. The objective of such funds is not to beat the market, but to give a return equivalent to the market returns.

Tax Saving Funds These are those funds, which offer tax benefits to investors under the Income Tax Act. Opportunities provided under this scheme are in the form of tax rebates under the Income Tax Act.

Debt/Income Funds Investment made in high rated fixed income bearing instruments like bonds, debentures, government securities, commercial papers and other money market instruments. They provide a regular income to the investor and best suited for medium to long-term investors, who are averse to risk and seek capital preservation.

Liquid Funds/Money Market Funds Investment is made in highly liquid money market instruments. The period of investment could be as short as a day. They provide easy liquidity. They act as an alternative for savings and short-term fixed deposit accounts with comparatively higher returns.

Gilt Funds These funds invest in Central and State Government Securities. Since, they are backed by government they give a secured return and also ensure safety of the principal amount. They are best suited for medium to long-term investors, who are averse to risk.

Balanced Funds Investment is made in some proportion both in equity shares and fixed income bearing instruments (debt). They provide a steady return and reduce the volatility of the fund while providing some upside for capital appreciation. They are ideal for medium to long-term investors, who are willing to take moderate risks.

On the Basis of Flexibility

Open-Ended Funds Funds, which do not have a fixed date of redemption are open-ended funds. Generally, they are open for subscription and redemption throughout the year. Their prices are linked to the daily Net Asset Value (NAV). From the investors perspective, they are much more liquid than closed-ended funds.

Close-Ended Funds Funds, which are open initially for entry during the Initial Public Offering (IPO) and thereafter closed for entry as well as exit are close-ended funds. These funds have a fixed date of redemption. Close-ended schemes are generally traded at a discount to NAV, but the discount narrows as maturity nears. These funds are open for subscription only once and can be redeemed only on the fixed date of redemption. The units of these funds are listed on stock exchanges (with certain exceptions), are tradable and the subscribers to the fund would be able to exit from the fund at any time through the secondary market.

Advantages of Investing in Mutual Funds

Small Investments Mutual funds help in reaping the benefit of returns by a portfolio, which is spread across a wide range of companies with small investments.

Professional Fund Management Professionals having considerable expertise, experience and resources manage the pool of money collected by a mutual fund. They thoroughly analyse the markets and economy to pick good investment opportunities.

Spreading Risk An investor with limited funds might be able to invest in only one or two stocks/bonds, thus increasing his or her risk.

Transparency Mutual funds regularly provide investors with information on the value of their investments.

Regulations All the mutual funds are registered with SEBI and they function within the provisions of strict regulation designed to protect the interests of the investors.

Disadvantages of Mutual Funds

Risks and Costs Changing market conditions can create fluctuations in the value of a mutual fund investment.

No Guarantees There are no sure returns. As mutual funds invest in debts as well as equities. Returns depends on the market conditions.

No Control As all the decisions are taken by the fund manager. Investor does not have control on investment. Investor can just join or leave the show.

Fees and Commission All funds charge administrative fees to cover their day-to-day expenses. Some funds also charge sales commissions or 'loads' to compensate brokers, financial consultants or financial planners.

Taxes During a typical year, most actively managed mutual funds sell anywhere from 20 to 70% of the securities in their portfolios.

Selecting Right Financial Securities is not Easy It's difficult task for a mutual fund manager to select appropriate and suitable financial securities for investment to generate higher returns.

Unethical Practices may Creep Mutual fund managers may follow unethical (corrupt) practices to boost the performance of the various fund related schemes.

Pension Fund

Pension fund is a financial institution which specialises in the management and administration of personal and corporate pension schemes. Pension funds collect regular contributions from individuals, employees and employers in the case of occupational pension scheme and make payments to retired beneficiaries. Pension funds use the money they receive not only to make day-to-day disbursement to pensioners but also to generate additional income and profit by investing their funds in financial securities.

Types of Pension Funds in India

Employees Provident Fund Scheme EPF Scheme was introduced to promote retirement savings. EPF is only applicable to salaried people. Both the employee and employer contribute to EPF account. EPF is governed by the Employees Provident Fund and Miscellaneous Provision Act, 1952. *There are three scheme under this act*

- **EPF** (Employee's Provident Fund) Its aims at promoting retirement savings.
- **EPS** (Employees Pension Scheme) Its aims at providing a post retirement pension.

- EDLI (Employees Deposit Linked Insurance Scheme) Its aims at providing relief to family members in case of subscriber's untimely death.

Voluntary Provident Fund VPF is a voluntary contribution that you make towards your Employee Provident Fund (EPF). A VPF account can be opened even in the middle of a financial year.

Public Provident Fund PPF is a long-term saving instrument to provide income security in retirement years. PPF was introduced for the benefit of self-employed and workers in the unorganised sector. Any resident Indian and minors can open a PPF account.

Financial Sector Reforms in India

While presenting the budget of 2010-11, the Finance Minister of Government of India had announced to constitute a commission to bring reforms in various law of financial sector, in accordance with the process of presently continuing economic reforms and requirements of the economy. Commission for law related reforms in financial sectors was constituted, under the Chairmanship of retired Justice Shri N. Shrikrishna.

The commission submitted its report to the government in March 2013 presenting recommendations through several committees/working groups. With this report, the commission also prepared a form of expansion and overall law.

Legal Reforms in Financial Sector

Existing and Proposed Legal Provisions The commission proposed legal provision relating to important aspects like consumer protection, capital control, monetary policy, misuse of business and markets.

Suggestion to Convert as a Company The commission has made the suggestion of convert government bodies like Life Insurance Corporation of India, State Bank of India etc. Working in the financial sector as a company, under Companies Act.

Recommendation of Regulatory Bodies The commission recommended to establish regulatory bodies for financial sectors.

Constitution of Financial Data Management Centre Financial data management centre may be constituted who may reliably maintain datas received from all regulatory bodies.

Judicial Review Boundary All regulators may be brought within judicial review boundary who presently out of it.

Constitution of Monetary Policy Committee The commission made recommendation to constituted monetary policy committee, under finance ministry.

Financial Inclusion Financial inclusion means that individuals and businesses have access to useful and affordable financial products and services that meet their needs *i.e.* transactions, payments, savings, credit and insurance delivered in a responsible and sustainable way. Financial inclusion is defined as the availability and equality of opportunities to access financial services. *e.g.* Jan dhan yojana.

Forex Market Reforms

In 1991, the first important reform in the external sector was done in the area of foreign exchange, in order to quell the crisis of the balance of payments, the rupees was devalued against foreign currency. This brought in a greater inflow of foreign currency into our nation and also was the first step trying to free the determination of the value of rupee from the hands of the government. Now-a-days, the market demand and supply determines the value of rupee.

- Brokers play a significant role in the foreign exchange market in India.
- The RBI has permitted licensed hotels and individuals to deal in foreign exchange business.
- The FEMA helps to smoothen the flow of foreign currency and to prevent any misuse of foreign exchange which is a scare commodity.

Capital Market Reforms

- After setting up of SEBI, it has been vested with the powers to regulate and control the capital market.
- Indian companies have been granted permission to enter into international capital market, through euro share capital.
- Share market intermediaries have been brought under the control of SEBI.
- National stock exchange has been set up at Mumbai, which will substantially contribute towards proper development of stock market.
- Effective powers has been granted to SEBI for regulation and control over stock exchanges and SEBI have implemented them.
- Appointment of registrar has been made compulsory for the issues.
- Provision has been made for buying back of their own shares by the companies and also for buying back of other special securities.
- Depository system has been introduced.

EXAM BASED QUESTIONS

Financial Market

1 The holders of which instrument are members of the company and have voting rights?

(a) Treasury Bill (b) Commercial Paper
(c) Debenture (d) Equity

2 The well established and well-organised market where the sale-purchase of different securities takes place according to certain laws, is known as

(a) production exchange (b) stock exchange
(c) commodity exchange (d) None of these

3 In stock exchange operations, when the speculator buys the right to sell a certain number of shares on an agreed amount at a specified time it is known as

(a) no option (b) put option
(c) call option (d) double option

4 Interest rate futures trading in India is available on

(a) 91 days, T-bills
(b) 10 years, National Government of India Security
(c) Both (a) and (b)
(d) None of the above

5 Treasury bills are short-term debt instruments (less than .... year to maturity) issued at a discount.

(a) 2 (b) 3 (c) 4 (d) 1

6 Which of the following are an important source of information about companies for investors?

(a) Research reports (b) Advertisements
(c) Market rumours (d) Market tips

7 The features of the commercial papers are

(a) it is an unsecured money market instrument issued in the form of promissory note
(b) the highly rated corporate borrowers can raise short-term funds through this instrument
(c) it is an additional instrument to the investing community
(d) All of the above

8 An option which gives the holder the right to sell a stock at a specified price at some time in the future is called a

(a) naked option (b) call option
(c) out of the money option (d) put option

9 QFI is defined to means a person (not resident in India), who is resident in a country that is compliant with which standards?

(a) Financial Task Force
(b) Financial Action Audit Force
(c) Financial Action Enforcement Force
(d) Financial Action Task Force

10 The financial market for securities with maturities of less than one year is known as

(a) derivatives market
(b) cash market
(c) money market
(d) rupee market

11 How are the market borrowings of State Government managed?

(a) Bonds are privately placed with PDs
(b) Bonds are issued by the State Government
(c) Bonds are issued by the RBI as well as the respective State Government
(d) Bonds are issued by the RBI

12 Which of the following statement is correct about daily volumes in the call money market?

(a) These volumes are usually lower than the volumes in the repo markets
(b) These volumes are comparable with volumes in the ICD and CP markets
(c) They register the largest transaction value after government securities
(d) Call money markets record the highest daily transaction value amongst all segments of debt markets

13 Which of the following are the means of marketing new issues of securities?

1. By listing of securities
2. Through jobbers and brokers
3. By private placing of securities
4. Through privileged subscription

Select the correct answer using the codes given below

Codes

(a) Both 1 and 2 (b) 1, 2 and 3
(c) Both 3 and 4 (d) All of the above

14 The comprehensive meaning of an efficient stock market is that it is market which

(a) allocates resources efficiently
(b) reflects the effective use of information in the price of the shares traded therein
(c) signals the changes in the listed company's performance
(d) safeguards the investors money

15 Arrange the following institutions in chronology order.

1. SEBI (Securities Exchange Board of India), 1988
2. Board for Industrial and Financial Reconstruction (BIFR)
3. EXIM Bank
4. National Stock Exchange

Codes

(a) 4, 1, 2, 3 (b) 3, 1, 2, 4
(c) 3, 2, 1, 4 (d) 4, 2, 1, 3

16 Consider the following statements.

1. Transfer and transmission of shares are the same thing.
2. 'Stag' is a speculative person who applies for shares in a new issue expected to be over subscribed to make profit by selling such shares at a premium.
3. Stock is a bundle of fully paid shares put together for convenience.

Which of the statement(s) given above is/are correct?

Codes

(a) Both 1 and 2 (b) Both 2 and 3
(c) Only 3 (d) Only 2

17 Which one of the following best supports the theory that the stock exchange is a secondary market? In a stock exchange

(a) securities are bought and sold by way of transfer
(b) an existing holder of securities can dispose of the holdings to another investor who intends to buy them
(c) no new investment is created
(d) securities are dealt in for dual purposes investment and speculation

18 If in a year, the company does not have adequate profits, the dividend will not be payable in the case of which shares?

(a) Non-cumulative preference
(b) Cumulative preference
(c) Both (a) and (b)
(d) None of the above

19 Who are professionals who offer independent advice on financial matters to their clients and recommend suitable financial products or products that are traded and settled like financial products?

(a) Independent commercial advisors
(b) Independent investment advisors
(c) Independent product advisors
(d) Independent financial advisors

20 Since, investors can diversify away their .... risks, they have to be compensated only for .... risk.

(a) systematic, non-systematic
(b) non-systematic, systematic
(c) Both (a) and (b)
(d) None of the above

Stock Exchanges and Government Security Market

21 SEBI regulations require that there should be atleast .... trustees (or directors in the trustee company) in a mutual fund.

(a) 7 (b) 5 (c) 6 (d) 4

22 Recognised stock exchange means a stock exchange which is for the time being recognised by

(a) State Government (b) Parliament
(c) Central Government (d) State Legislatures

23 The pay-in and pay-out dates for the settlement calendar is declared

(a) by SEBI
(b) as per the Securities Contract Regulation Act, 1957
(c) by NSDL
(d) by the respective stock exchange

24 To operate in the derivative segment of NSE, the dealer/broker and sales persons are required to pass .... examination.

(a) Certified Financial Analyst
(b) MBA (Finance)
(c) NCFM
(d) Chartered Accountancy

25 A January month Nifty futures contract will expire on the last .... of January.

(a) monday (b) thursday
(c) tuesday (d) wednesday

26 The F and O segment of NSE provides trading facilities for the following derivative instruments, except

(a) individual warrant options
(b) index based futures
(c) index based options
(d) individual stock options

27 Verification and upload of client details has to be done on SEBI website every

(a) one week (b) two week
(c) 15 days (d) None of these

28 Who can nominate members on the governing body of a recognised stock exchange?

(a) The SEBI (b) The State Government
(c) The SAT (d) None of these

29 NSE's Certification in Financial Markets (NCFM) is a necessary qualification for becoming a trading member.

(a) Yes (b) No
(c) Both (a) and (b) (d) None of these

30 As per the SEBI (Substantial Acquisition of Shares and Takeovers) Regulations, 1997, no acquirer who has acquired 15% or more, but less than 55% of the shares of a company shall acquire additional shares of the percentage specified below unless a public announcement is made.

(a) 2% (b) 15%
(c) 10% (d) 5%

31 Every listed company is required to submit to the stock exchange the shareholding pattern of the company on a

(a) quarterly basis
(b) monthly basis
(c) yearly basis
(d) half yearly basis

32 Under the member constituent agreement, trading members are required to make the clients aware of which of the following?

1. Trading segment in which the trading member is admitted.
2. SEBI registration number.
3. Basic risks involved in trading on the exchange.

Select the correct answer using the codes given below

Codes

(a) Both 2 and 3 (b) Both 1 and 2
(c) Both 1 and 3 (d) All of the above

33 Which of the following is maintained by NSE to make good investor claims, which may arise out of non-settlement of obligations by the trading member, who has been declared defaulter, in respect of trades executed on the exchange.

(a) Investor Education and Reimbursement Fund (IERF)
(b) Investor Reimbursement Fund (IRF)
(c) Investor Education and Protection Fund (IEPF)
(d) Investor Protection Fund (IPF)

34 Demutualisation of stock exchanges refers to

(a) the legal structure of an exchange whereby the ownership, the management and the trading rights at the exchange are segregated from one another
(b) the legal structure of an exchange whereby the ownership and the management at the exchange are segregated from one another
(c) the legal structure of an exchange whereby the ownership, the management and the trading rights at the exchange vests in one person
(d) None of the above

35 Prospectus issued by a company is to be vetted and approved by the SEBI. This, however, does not mean that

(a) disclosures are adequate as per it guidelines
(b) project proposal has been presented in conformity with its guidelines
(c) disclosures are adequate to take an informed decision by investors
(d) project proposal is sound or satisfactory

36 Consider the following statements.

1. Foreign institutional investors have been allowed to invest in mutual funds.
2. The main objective of SEBI is to protect the investors.
3. Private placement is the route, through which promoters' contribution is mobilised by a public company.
4. RBI lays down the guidelines governing the capital market operation.

Which of the statement(s) given above is/are correct?

Codes

(a) Both 1 and 2
(b) 2, 3 and 4
(c) 1, 2 and 3
(d) 1, 3 and 4

37 SEBI, in recent times, has made it mandatory for listed companies to disclose to the public the number of 'Encumbered Shares'. What do such shares mean?

(a) Shares held by promoters
(b) Promoter's holding pledged with lenders
(c) Shares not issued by the company
(d) Preference shares

38 The committee constituted by SEBI under the Chairmanship of Justice Dr. Dhanuka had which of the following terms of reference?

1. Review of inter-alia, the SEBI Act, SCR Act, Depositories Act and the provisions of the Companies Act pertaining to the capital market.
2. To review, the penal provisions contained in the Sections 15(A) to 15(J) of the Securities Laws (Amendment) Act.

Select the correct answer using the codes given below

Codes

(a) Only 1 (b) Only 2
(c) Both 1 and 2 (d) Neither 1 nor 2

39 What is the maximum brokerage that can be charged by an NSE trading member for a deal in government securities for ₹ 20 million?

(a) ₹ 30,000 (b) ₹ 22,000 (c) ₹ 20,000 (d) ₹ 25,000

40 Which of the following statement is true about the NSE MIBOR polling process?

(a) NSE disseminates information about the rates and participants, but not the amount associated with each quote
(b) NSE does not reveal the identity of the participants, but discloses the rates of each participant
(c) NSE keeps both participant identity and polled rate confidential
(d) NSE disseminates information on rates quoted by each participant and the amounts associated with those rates

41 Which of the following statements is true?

(a) A SEBI registered stock broker having a minimum networth of ₹ 1 crore is eligible to join NSDL as a DP
(b) A stock broker having a minimum networth of ₹ 50 lakh is eligible to join NSDL as a DP irrespective of whether it is registered with SEBI
(c) A SEBI registered stock broker is eligible to join NSDL as a DP. There is no minimum networth requirement
(d) A SEBI registered stock broker having a minimum networth of ₹ 50 lakh is eligible to join NSDL as a DP

42 An investor owns one thousand shares of Reliance. Around budget time, he gets uncomfortable with the price movements. One contract on Reliance is equivalent to 100 shares. Which of the following will give him the hedge he desires?

(a) Buy 5 Reliance futures contracts
(b) Sell 10 Reliance futures contracts
(c) Sell 5 Reliance futures contracts
(d) Buy 10 Reliance futures contracts

43 Any person or persons acting in concert, who together own .... or more of the open interest in index derivatives are required to disclose the same to the clearing corporation.

(a) 35% (b) 15% (c) 5% (d) 1%

44 Who under Section 13 of the SEBI Act, 1992, may make grants to the SEBI?

(a) No grants are made to the SEBI
(b) The Central Government
(c) The Reserve Bank of India
(d) Any one who desires

45 The Central Government has powers to supersede the SEBI, if it is of the opinion that

(a) the members of the SEBI make an application to the Central Government to do so
(b) the SEBI is unable to discharge its functions and duties imposed on it under the provisions of the SEBI Act, 1992 or it is necessary to do so in the public interest
(c) the SEBI on its own makes an application to the Central Government to do so
(d) the SEBI does not have the required number of members for performing the functions entrusted to it

46 If the chairman is unable to attend any meeting of the SEBI then

(a) the meeting shall be adjourned till the chairman is able to attend the meeting
(b) the meeting shall continue without anyone chairing it and the chairman shall be informed about the proceedings of the same
(c) the chairman has to leave a message appointing some other person to be in the chair in his absence
(d) any other member chosen by the members present from amongst themselves shall preside at the meeting

47 Who have to compensate any loss occasioned to any investor or to the scheme and/or plan on account of non-compliance by the fund?

(a) RTAs (b) Stock Exchanges
(c) Custodians (d) AMCs

48 Which of the following entities provide 'Take out Finance' to banks engaged in financing of infrastructure projects?

(b) ICICI (b) SIDBI (c) IDFC (d) RBI

Development Financial Institutions and NBFIs

49 Consider the following statements.

1. UTI is established by an Act of Parliament in 1964. So, UTI does not come under the SEBI regulations for mutual funds.
2. Mutual fund organisations can invest their mobilised funds abroad.

Which of the statement(s) given above is/are correct?

Codes

(a) Only 1 (b) Only 2
(c) Both 1 and 2 (d) Neither 1 nor 2

50 The first development financial institution of India was

(a) IDBI (b) IFCI
(c) ICICI (d) UT

51 Arrange the following banks in order, in which they were established.

1. IDBI 2. IFCI 3. SIDBI 4. IIBI

Codes

(a) 2, 1, 3, 4 (b) 2, 1, 4, 3
(c) 1, 2, 3, 4 (d) 1, 2, 4, 3

52 IFCI is authorised to borrow from

(a) Central Government
(b) Reserve Bank of India
(c) Industrial Development Bank of India
(d) All of the above

53 IFCI can accept deposits from the public, State Government and local authorities for a period of less than

(a) 10 years (b) 1 year
(c) 5 years (d) None of these

54 One of the functions of IDBI is to assist other financial institutions by .... of loans granted for exports.

(a) planning
(b) refinancing
(c) Both (a) and (b)
(d) None of the above

55 .... acquired United Western Bank in a rescue in 2006.

(a) ICICI (b) IDBI
(c) AXIS Bank (d) SBI

56 Which one of the following is the main objective of Unit Trust of India?

(a) To mobilise the savings of high income groups
(b) To mobilise the savings of low and high income groups
(c) To mobilise the savings of corporate
(d) To mobilise the savings of low and middle income groups

57 Which one of the following statements is incorrect?

(a) The LIC and GIC are non-banking financial intermediaries in India
(b) LIC, UTI are non-banking financial institutions
(c) ICICI was promoted as a Private Sector Development Bank at the initiative of the World Bank in 1955
(d) Unit Trust of India is a mutual fund in private sector

58 Contribution towards Rural Infrastructure Development Fund is made by

(a) NABARD and Commercial Banks jointly
(b) State Government and Government of India
(c) only those commercial banks, who fail to achieve the stipulated benchmark of agricultural advances and/or priority sector advances
(d) Infrastructure Development Finance Company

59 The IDBI underwriters and .... the shares and debentures of industrial concern.
(a) imposes on (b) subscribes to
(c) targets (d) None of these

60 Which one of the following statement is correct?
(a) Small scale industries are not financed by any SFI
(b) IDBI is wholly-owned subsidiary of the Reserve Bank of India
(c) Non-banking financial institutions can also act as intermediaries
(d) Financial institutions are mainly banking institutions

61 Which one of the following statement is incorrect?
(a) Development banks provide financial assistance to both private as well as public sector institutions
(b) Development banks react to the socio-economic needs of development
(c) The National Securities Depository Limited (NSDL) is the institute which is built by IDBI
(d) The Securities Trading Corporation of India (STCI) was promoted by SEBI jointly with the public sector banks

62 Which one of the following statement is incorrect?
(a) ICRA is a credit rating agency promoted by the Industrial Finance Corporation of India
(b) Loan Company (LC) NBFCs are registered with RBI
(c) GIC was incorporated on 22nd November, 1972 under the Companies Act, 1956 as a private company limited by shares
(d) An endowment policy is a life insurance contract designed to pay a lumpsum after a specified term (on its maturity) or on earlier death

63 Which one of the following statement is incorrect?
(a) The National Securities Depository Limited (NSDL) is the institute, which is built by IDBI
(b) Insurance is the collective bearing of risk
(c) LIC was founded in 1956
(d) The IFCI is the first universal bank in India

64 Which one of the following statement is incorrect?
(a) In a developed economy, there is usually direct supply of capital
(b) In 1976, the IDBI was restructured and separated from the control of the RBI
(c) Due date of bill is also known as date of maturity
(d) SIDBI is the subsidiary of IDBI, which was set-up in 1990

Mutual Funds, Pension Funds and Financial Sector Reforms

65 The first Mutual Fund Scheme in India was introduced by
(a) Government of India
(b) Reserve Bank of India
(c) Unit Trust of India
(d) State Bank of India

66 In a mutual fund, the trust acts through ...., who are appointed by the sponsor.
(a) lawyers
(b) investors
(c) trustees
(d) auditors

67 Which option gives the holder the right, but not the obligation to buy an asset by a certain date for a certain price?
(a) Put (b) ITM
(c) OTM (d) Call

68 Mutual funds need to calculate NAV for each calendar .... for their liquid fund schemes and plans.
(a) day (b) week (c) month (d) year

69 ETFs are .... ended funds that can be bought at prices, which vary during the day and operate with low tracking error.
(a) close
(b) open
(c) Both (a) and (b)
(d) None of the above

70 Consider the following statements regarding mutual funds.
1. Mutual funds can participate in options trading and carrying forward transactions in securities.
2. Mutual funds can invest in transferable securities in the money and capital markets.

Which of the statement(s) given above is/are correct?
Codes
(a) Only 1 (b) Only 2
(c) Both 1 and 2 (d) Neither 1 nor 2

71 An investor sold 100 nifty futures at ₹ 4,500 future. He bought them back at ₹ 5,000 per future total profit/loss is ₹
(a) (+) 4,000
(b) (–) 4,000
(c) (–) 5,000
(d) (+) 5,000

72 Suppose Party A has a right to buy USD 6,000 from Party B, 1 month down the line, at ₹ 46 = 1USD (US Dollar). However, after 1 month Party A does not exercise the right. This is possible in which contract?
(a) Swap (b) Futures
(c) Forward (d) Options

73 .... schemes are seen as riskier than .... schemes.
(a) Debt, equity
(b) Equity, debt
(c) Both (a) and (b)
(d) None of the abvoe

74 .... capital investors are long-term investors who are prepared to take the risk that the entrepreneurial project can fail.
(a) Mega (b) Progress
(c) Multiple (d) Venture

75 Which option is an option that would lead to a zero cash flow to the holder if it were exercised immediately?
(a) In the money (b) At the money
(c) Out of the money (d) Put the money

76 Application from investors are to be received by mutual funds only at the
(a) head office or branch offices of the mutual fund
(b) designated RTAs
(c) official points of acceptance
(d) designated banks

77 RTA carries out the redemption processing at its end and provides final redemption information to the exchange on
(a) T+2 (b) T+1
(c) T+3 (d) T+4

78 The investment management activity of a mutual fund is managed by the
(a) sponsors (b) AMC
(c) custodians (d) RTA

79 Short-term deposits by mutual funds can only be placed with
(a) public sector banks
(b) scheduled banks
(c) public sector banks or cooperative banks
(d) cooperative banks

80 Which of the following sets out concisely the information about the scheme that a prospective investor ought to know before investing?
(a) Scheme source document
(b) Scheme information book
(c) Scheme document
(d) Scheme information document

81 An Indian investor investing in a US equity stock mutual fund, would be worried about what happens to the exchange rate of
(a) US Dollar : Euro
(b) Euro : Indian Rupee
(c) US Dollar : Indian Rupee
(d) British Pound : Indian Rupee

82 Investments by holders of Overseas Citizen of India (OCI) cards, in mutual fund schemes, is repatriable provided the original investment came into India in .... currency.
(a) local
(b) foreign
(c) Both (a) and (b)
(d) None of the above

Miscellaneous

Directions (Q. Nos. 83-92) *In the question given below are two statements labelled as Assertion (A) and Reason (R). In the context of two statements, which one of the following is correct?*

Codes
(a) Both statements are true
(b) Both statements are false
(c) Statement I is true, but Statement II is false
(d) Statement II is true, but Statement I is false

83 **Statement** I SEBI (Intermediaries) Regulations, 2008 are not applicable for foreign venture capital investor.
Statement II The securities market has two segments primary and secondary.

84 **Statement** I Investors are mutual, beneficial and proportional owners of the scheme's assets.
Statement II Investors have a right to be informed about changes in the fundamental attributes of a scheme.

85 **Statement** I Trading member at NSE can choose to become a member of only the CD segment.
Statement II For mutual fund investments through Power of Attorney, both the investor and power of attorney holder need to comply with the KYC documentation.

86 **Statement** I For any body to start a mutual fund, relevant experience in financial services is mandatory.
Statement II Mutual funds in India follow a three tier structure.

87 **Statement** I A passively managed fund charges a higher fee than the actively managed fund since, it has higher expenses of research and analysis.
Statement II Short-term capital gains tax are not applicable for equity oriented mutual fund schemes.

88 **Statement** I Equity mutual fund investors have to bear Securities Transaction Tax (STT).
Statement II Growth option is for those investors who are looking for capital appreciation.

89 **Statement** I All trading members are required to pay turnover fees to SEBI.
Statement II Compliance of SEBI rules is required by the constituents of a trading member.

90 **Statement** I Forward contracts are bilateral contracts and hence, exposed to counter party risk.
Statement II A company that wants to sell an asset at a particular time in the future can hedge by taking short futures position.

91 **Statement** I An active fund manager will try and give a return to the investor as close as possible to the Nifty Index returns.

Statement II The maximum amount that a single investor can invest in a PMS scheme offered by a mutual fund is set at ₹ 500 crore.

92 **Statement** I Mutual funds are allowed to lend money to investment grade rated corporates and banks.

Statement II When on a particular valuation day, a security has not been traded on the selected stock exchange, the value at which it is traded is taken as zero.

Directions (Q. Nos. 93-103) *In the question given below are two statements labelled as Assertion (A) and Reason (R). In the context of the two statements, which one of the following is correct?*

Codes

(a) Both (A) and (R) are true and (R) is the correct explanation of (A)
(b) Both (A) and (R) are true, but (R) is not the correct explanation of (A)
(c) (A) is true, but (R) is false
(d) (R) is true, but (A) is false

93 **Assertion** (A) SEBI issues guidelines for all companies for disclousure of information and protection of investor's interest.

Reason (R) Computerised screen based trading has been introduced on all major stock exchanges.

94 **Assertion** (A) SEBI cannot conduct enquiries, audit and inspection for the offences under the act.

Reason (R) Bankers to the issue and portfolio managers have to be registered with SEBI.

95 **Assertion** (A) SEBI has power to compel listing of securities by public companies.

Reason (R) SEBI has power to regulate insider trading or can regulate the functions of merchant bankers.

96 **Assertion** (A) An ADR is not a US dollar denominated form of equity ownership in a non-US company.

Reason (R) An ADR is a physical certificate evidencing ownership of American Depository Shares (ADSs).

97 **Assertion** (A) Development banks serve as an agent of development in various sectors like industries, agriculture and international trade.

Reason (R) First industrial develop, i.e. Industrial Finance Corporation of India (IFCI) was established in 1949.

98 **Assertion** (A) Granting loans or advances to or subscribing to debentures of industrial concerns repayable within 25 years is one of the functions of IFCI.

Reason (R) IFCI was established to provide financial assistance (medium and long-term) to large scale industries all over the country.

99 **Assertion** (A) A fund fact sheet is published by mutual funds.

Reason (R) Fund fact sheet gives comparison of performance of each scheme with its benchmark.

100 **Assertion** (A) All the mutual funds must get registered with SEBI.

Reason (R) Securities Exchange Board of India (SEBI) is the regulatory body for all the mutual funds.

101 **Assertion** (A) With mutual fund investment, the risk factor gets minimised.

Reason (R) Investors money gets diversified in a lot of things, with mutual fund investment.

102 **Assertion** (A) Mutual funds are good if you want to invest in something, which you can liquidate easily.

Reason (R) Mutual funds are very simple to buy and sell.

103 **Assertion** (A) Screen based trading system cuts down on time, cost and risk of error as well as on the chances of fraud.

Reason (R) Screen based trading system electronically matches the buyer and seller in an order driven system.

104 Match the following.

List I	List II
A. Certificate of deposits	1. 91 days, 182 days and 346 days
B. Debentures	2. 3 to 5 months
C. Treasury bills	3. 1 day to 270 days
D. Commercial papers	4. Longer period in years

Codes

	A	B	C	D		A	B	C	D
(a)	2	4	1	3	(b)	2	4	3	1
(c)	4	3	1	2	(d)	3	4	2	1

105 Match the following.

List I (Mutual Fund Schemes)	List II (Characteristics)
A. Open-ended mutual fund scheme	1. It offers capital appreciation of the underlying investment.
B. Close-ended mutual fund scheme	2. It is a fund accepted and liquidated on a continuous basis by a mutual fund manager.
C. Growth fund scheme	3. It is also known as regional or country fund.
D. Off-shore mutual fund	4. No exit possible till the closure of the scheme.

Codes

	A	B	C	D		A	B	C	D
(a)	2	1	4	3	(b)	3	4	1	2
(c)	2	4	1	3	(d)	3	1	4	2

106 Match the following.

List I	List II
A. When one company purchases another one	1. Conglomerate merger
B. Merger between two companies having no common business areas	2. Consolidation merger
C. Merger between two companies that sell the same products in different markets	3. Purchase merger
D. Two companies are bought and combined under new entity	4. Market extension merger

Codes

	A	B	C	D		A	B	C	D
(a)	1	2	3	4	(b)	2	3	1	4
(c)	3	1	4	2	(d)	3	4	1	2

107 Match the following.

List I	List II
A. RBI	1. To provide medium and long-term credit to industrial concerns
B. ICICI	2. Banker' bank
C. IFCI	3. To provide term finance to industry
D. IDBI	4. Underwriting institution

Codes

	A	B	C	D		A	B	C	D
(a)	2	3	4	1	(b)	2	1	4	3
(c)	1	2	4	3	(d)	4	3	2	1

PREVIOUS YEARS' QUESTIONS

July 2018

1 Which one of the following financial institutions coordinates the functions and operations of all the financial institutions into a single integrated financial structure so that each may contribute to the growth of the economy ?

(a) IFCI (b) UTI (c) IDBI (d) SIDBI

2 Which one of the following is not the objective of UTI ?

(a) To mobilise savings of the community by offering savers the triple benefits of safety, liquidity and profitability of investments
(b) To channelise the pooled savings into productive outlets
(c) To provide finance under hire purchase finance and housing finance to its members
(d) To give everyone a chance to indirectly own shares and securities in a large number of select companies

3 Which one of the following is the main objective of IFCI ?

(a) To offer both small and large investors the means of acquiring shares in the widening prosperity resulting from the steady industrial growth of the country
(b) To upgrade technology, modernisation and to promote marketing of products of small scale sector
(c) To serve as the apex institution for term finance for industry with coordination, regulation and supervision of the working of other financial institutions
(d) To provide medium and long-term financial assistance to industrial undertakings, particularly in those circumstances in which banking accommodation is in appropriate or resource to capital market is impracticable.

November 2017

4 Match the following items of List I with the items of List II and indicate the code of correct matching.

List I (Name of Organisation)	List II (Year of Establishment)
A. IDBI	1. 1956
B. ICICI	2. 1955
C. LIC of India	3. 1990
D. SIDBI	4. 1964

Codes

	A	B	C	D		A	B	C	D
(a)	3	1	2	4	(b)	3	1	4	2
(c)	4	2	1	3	(d)	1	2	3	4

January 2017

5 Match the items of List I with List II and denote the code of correct matching.

List I	List II
A. International Bank for Reconstruction and Development	1. 1945
B. International Finance Corporation	2. 1956
C. Asian Development Bank	3. 1966
D. Export-Import Bank of India	4. 1981

Codes

	A	B	C	D
(a)	1	2	3	4
(b)	4	3	2	1
(c)	1	3	2	4
(d)	2	1	4	3

6 **Assertion** (A) International Finance Corporation (IFC) contributes to increase sustainable agriculture opportunities, improve health and education and increase access to financing for micro finance and business client.

Reason (R) The IFC has focused on a set of development goals to ensure that its projects are expected to achieve the target.

Codes

(a) Both (A) and (R) are correct, but (R) is not the correct explanation of (A)
(b) Both (A) and (R) are correct and (R) is the correct explanation of (A)
(c) (A) is correct, but (R) is incorrect
(d) Both (A) and (R) are incorrect

7 SIDBI was set-up as a subsidiary of IDBI to

(a) takeover the functions of small business financing of IDBI
(b) takeover the venture capital operations of ICICI
(c) reconstruct and rehabilitate the sick and closed industrial units financed by IDBI
(d) facilitate, finance and promote India's foreign trade

8 Match the following items of List I with the items of List II and indicate the code of correct matching.

List I (Name of Bank)		List II (Year of Establishment)	
A.	IFCI	1.	1981
B.	SIDBI	2.	1982
C.	NABARD	3.	1948
D.	EXIM	4.	1990

Codes

	A	B	C	D		A	B	C	D
(a)	3	1	2	4	(b)	4	2	3	1
(c)	4	3	2	1	(d)	3	4	2	1

9 With a view to encourage newer classes of entrepreneurs and bringing about wider dispersal of ownership and control of industrial undertakings, IDBI operates a special scheme for supplementing the equity contribution to projects made by small and new entrepreneurs. This scheme is known as

(a) Bridge Loan Scheme
(b) Soft Loan Scheme for Modernisation
(c) Technical Development Fund Scheme
(d) Seed Capital Assistance Scheme

10 Which one of the following is not the objective of UTI ?

(a) To give everyone a chance to indirectly own shares and securities in a large number of select companies
(b) To maximise mobilisation of people's savings by making insurance linked savings adequately attractive
(c) To channelise the pooled savings into productive outlets
(d) To mobilise savings of the community by offering savers the triple benefits of safety, liquidity and profitability of investments

July 2016

11 Which one of the following banks currently ranks number one in India in terms of market capitalisation?

(a) State Bank of India (b) ICICI Bank
(c) UTI Bank (d) IDBI Bank

12 Which one of the following development financial institutions in India has started the special refinance scheme for the resettlement and rehabilitation of voluntary retired workers of the National Textile Corporation of India?

(a) IDBI (b) SIDBI
(c) ICICI (d) None of these

13 Read the following statements and choose the correct code.

Statement I Small Industry Development Bank of India (SIDBI) was set-up as a wholly owned subsidiary of RBI.

Statement II SIDBI has taken over the responsibility of administering small indutry development fund managed by IDBI.

Codes

(a) Only I is correct (b) Only II is correct
(c) Both I and II are correct (d) Both I and II are incorrect

December 2015

14 Which of the following is not a development banking institutions?

(a) IDBI (b) IFCI (c) EXIM bank (d) ICICI

December 2014

15 Which of the following is not provided by EXIM bank, for financing overseas investments?

(a) Term loans to Indian companies upto 80% of their equity investment in overseas JV/WOS
(b) Term loans to Indian companies towards upto 100% of loan extended by them to the overseas JV/WOS
(c) Term loan to overseas JV/WOS towards part financing
(d) Guarantee facility to the overseas JV/WOS for raising term loan/working capital

December 2013

16 The following activities are mainly related to which organisation?

1. Micro Finance 2. Rural Finance
3. Self Help Groups 4. Cooperative Banks Finance

Codes

(a) Industrial Finance Corporation of India
(b) Ministry of Finance
(c) Reserve Bank of India
(d) National Bank for Agriculture and Rural Development

June 2013

17 **Assertion** (A) Most of the development bank in India have setup private commercial banks after the introduction of capital adequacy norms.
Reason (R) Development banks in India have not adhered to their basic objectives.

Codes

(a) (A) and (R) both are correct and (R) is correct explanation of (A)
(b) (A) and (R) both are correct but (R) is not a correct explanation of (A)
(c) (A) is correct, but (R) is incorrect
(d) (R) is correct, but (A) is incorrect

December 2012

18 Which one among the following has not started commercial banking?

(a) SIDBI (b) IDBI
(c) ICICI (d) UTI

June 2012

19 Arrange the events in the ascending order of their occurrence.

1. Allowing convertibility of rupee at the market rate in the current account.
2. Nationalisation of general insurance business.
3. Establishment of IDBI.
4. Nationalisation of life insurance business.
5. Capital adequacy norms for commercial banks.

Codes

(a) 4, 3, 2, 1, 5 (b) 5, 4, 3, 2, 1
(c) 1, 2, 3, 5, 4 (d) 1, 5, 2, 4, 3

20 Which among the following is not true with regard to merchant banker?

1. It can accept deposits.
2. It can advance loans.
3. It can do other banking activities.
4. It can be managed to a public issue.

Select the correct answer using the codes given below

Codes

(a) 1, 2 and 3 (b) 2, 3 and 4
(c) 1, 3 and 4 (d) Both 2 and 4

21 Match the following.

List I	List II
A. Reserve Bank of India	1. NPA
B. EXIM Bank	2. Facilitating small scale industries
C. SIDBI	3. Credit control
D. Capital Adequacy	4. Export/Import financing

Codes

	A	B	C	D		A	B	C	D
(a)	1	2	3	4	(b)	4	3	2	1
(c)	2	3	4	1	(d)	3	4	2	1

ANSWERS

Objective Questions

1 (d)	2 (b)	3 (b)	4 (c)	5 (d)	6 (a)	7 (d)	8 (d)	9 (d)	10 (c)
11 (c)	12 (d)	13 (d)	14 (b)	15 (c)	16 (b)	17 (b)	18 (a)	19 (b)	20 (b)
21 (d)	22 (c)	23 (d)	24 (c)	25 (b)	26 (a)	27 (d)	28 (a)	29 (a)	30 (d)
31 (a)	32 (d)	33 (d)	34 (a)	35 (b)	36 (b)	37 (b)	38 (c)	39 (a)	40 (c)
41 (a)	42 (b)	43 (b)	44 (b)	45 (b)	46 (d)	47 (d)	48 (d)	49 (d)	50 (b)
51 (a)	52 (d)	53 (c)	54 (b)	55 (b)	56 (d)	57 (d)	58 (c)	59 (b)	60 (c)
61 (c)	62 (b)	63 (b)	64 (a)	65 (c)	66 (c)	67 (d)	68 (a)	69 (b)	70 (b)
71 (c)	72 (a)	73 (d)	74 (d)	75 (b)	76 (c)	77 (b)	78 (b)	79 (b)	80 (d)
81 (c)	82 (b)	83 (a)	84 (a)	85 (a)	86 (a)	87 (b)	88 (a)	89 (a)	90 (a)
91 (b)	92 (b)	93 (b)	94 (d)	95 (a)	96 (d)	97 (b)	98 (b)	99 (a)	100 (a)
101 (a)	102 (a)	103 (a)	104 (b)	105 (c)	106 (c)	107 (b)			

Previous Years' Questions

1 (c)	2 (c)	3 (d)	4 (c)	5 (a)	6 (b)	7 (a)	8 (d)	9 (d)	10 (b)
11 (a)	12 (a)	13 (b)	14 (c)	15 (b)	16 (d)	17 (c)	18 (a)	19 (a)	20 (a)
21 (d)									

CHAPTER 28

Insurance

In today's dynamic environment, life and business is subject to innumerable risks. A man needs protection against such risks and insurance is one such tool which indemnifies a man against losses incurred due to such risks.

Concept of Insurance

Insurance is a form of contract which provides protection against possible eventual loss of goods or life.

It is an arrangement by which the insurer undertakes to cover risks by providing compensation for specified loss, damage, illness or death in return for payment of a specified premium.

According to **Disnadle**, "Insurance is an instrument of distributing the loss of few among many."

According to **Encyclopedia Britannica**, "Insurance may be described as a social device whereby a large group of individuals, through a system of equitable contributions, may reduce or eliminate certain measurable risks of economic loss common to all members of the group".

Characteristics of Insurance

- It is a cooperative device for sharing and valuation of risks.
- Insurance is a device to share the financial losses which might be fall on an individual on the happening of a specified event.
- In the contract of insurance, the risk is evaluated before insuring to determine the premium.
- It is a contract for compensating losses.
- The loss is compensated as per the terms of agreement.
- It is a future contract based on good faith and mutual benefit.
- It is an instrument of distributing the loss of few among many.

In this Chapter

- *Insurance*
- *Reinsurance*
- *Risk Classification and Management*
- *Insurance Regulatory and Development Authority (IRDA)*

Important Terms related to Insurance

Insurer The agency or firm who insures the risk of loss.

Insured The person who gets his life/property insured.

Insurance Policy The document carrying written agreement or contract between insurers and the insured, alongwith terms and conditions of insurance.

Insurance Premium A small periodic payment for a risk of large possible loss.

Sum Assured This is the amount for which the insurance policy is taken.

Reinsurance It can be defined as 'insurance of insurance'. In this type of insurance, the insurer transfers the insurance taken by a insured to another insurer.

Double Insurance In this form of insurance, the insured gets covered for the same risk by two or more insurers.

Surrender Value It is an amount that a policyholder receives from the insurer in case he plans to terminate the policy before maturity.

Under Insurance It is a type of insurance (health. a property) that does not offer complete financial protection.

Over Insurance Over insurance can be defined as a situation where an insured as brought so much coverage that exceeds the actual cash value of the risk or property insured.

Insurable Interest Insurable interest exists when an insured person derives a financial or other kind a benefit from the continuous existence, without impairment or damage of the insured object. It is the reasonable concern of a person to obtain insurance for any individual or property against unforseen events such as death, loss etc. *It can be divided into two types*

- Insurable interest in own's life.
- Insurable interest in other's life.

This insurable interest is estimated on the basis of the amount of risk involved, responsibilities of the insured and the age of the insured. In simple words, it is considered as an estimated value of one's life and business and his interest to safeguard it.

Assurance It is a term used for death claims. Death is a certain risk and if an insured purchases the life insurance policy, it is assured that the beneficiary will get claim after the death of insured.

Warranties A warranty is a promise or assurance given by the insurer to the insured to fulfill the claim settlement with full responsibility and faith. The insured must disclose all the facts to the best of his knowledge. On the other hand, the promisory warranty states the possibility of the future risk and subsequently promises to avoid such an uncertain act.

FDI Policy in Insurance Sector

Seeking to increase investment in insurance sector. on 18th March, 2016 government allowed FDI upto 49% in insurance sector from 26% in domestic insurance companies by overseas companies without prior approval.

Earlier 26% FDI was approved through automatic route. For FDI upto 49% approval of Foreign Investment Promotion Board is required subject to the verification of insurance regularity authority of India. There are 52 insurance companies in India out of which 24 are life insurance companies and 28 are general insurance companies.

Types of Insurance

There are two types of insurance, which are as follows

Life Insurance

The term 'life insurance' implies the type of insurance, that covers the risk of life and provides a guarantee to compensate by paying the specified sum, either on the death of the insured or after the specified period.

It is a contract by which the insurer, in consideration of a certain premium, undertakes to pay to the person, for whose benefit the insurance is made, a certain sum of money on the death of the person whose life is insured or on his attaining a certain age. Life insurance encourage savings as the amount of premium has to be paid regularly. It thus, provides a sense of security to the insured and his dependents.

In India, life insurane is defined under Section 2 (11) of Insurance Act, 1938. It states that, "life insurance means the business of effecting contracts of insurance upon human life including any contract whereby the payment of money is assured on death (except death by accident only) on the happening of any contigency dependent upon human life any contract which is subject to payment of premium for a term dependent on human life."

Features/Characteristics of Life Insurance Contract

Following are the important features/characteristics of life insurance contract

- It is a contract which is related to human life.
- The contract provides payment for lumpsum money.
- The amount is paid at the expiration of a certain period or on the death of a person.
- The rules of the policy are set according to the requirements of the insurer.
- The policy may include accidental and disability clause. It may include accidental death as a cause of death on which life insurance benefits are payable.

- It also includes special clauses for the persons who undertake risky work such as security personnel etc called the superannuation clause which is exclusively made to provide extra protection to the family of the professionals who undertake difficult tasks.

Important Elements of Life Insurance Contract

Life insurance contract can be described as an effective social tool to reduce or eliminate the risk of loss to life and property. *The essential elements of life insurance contract are as follows*

It should Contain Elements of a Valid Contract For a valid contract of life insurance between the parties, one party makes a proposal and the other party accepts the proposal. The agreement must contain all the rules and regulations to be followed by both the parties with full responsibility. *Other essential elements of valid contract are as follows*

- ***Free Constent*** The parties who are entering in an agreement should enter by their free will and consent. The contract or agreement made under undue influence, coercion, fraud, misrepresentation, hiding the facts and mis-interpretations is not a legal contract.
- ***Competency to Contract*** The parties to the contract should be competent of contracting. This means that the parties must be at the age of majority. He/she must have a sound mind. He/she should be mentally fit so that he/she can understand the laws of the contract and can act accordingly.
- ***Legal Consideration*** Consideration is the value that each party gives to the other party. In the contract of insurance, the consideration should be legal and real.
- ***Certainty*** The terms and conditions of a contract should be clearly stated and certain. It should be well understood by both the parties. The insurance company provides a printed copy of the policy which contains all the terms and conditions of the policy.
- ***Compliance with Legal Formalities*** In the contract of insurance, the contract between parties must be in a written form and signed by both the parties. It must be properly tested by the witness and registered, otherwise it will not be enforced by the court.

Principle of Utmost Good Faith Life insurance is based utmost good faith principle. Both the parties must have trust or faith upon each other. The insured must not hide any information or give fake documents about his economic status, age and permanent residence. These issues could lead to cancellation of the policy. The insurer must pay the claim amount to the insured at the time of maturity without any delay.

Principle of Proximate Cause Proximate cause is the cause which led to the loss. It is the actual cause of loss. If the cause of the loss is listed in the policy, then the insurer will pay for the loss and if it is not listed then the insurer can deny for the claim settlement. The policy holder must ensure the insurer that the loss has been caused by the insured peril.

Assignment and Nomination The contract of life insurance is incomplete without specifying the terms of assignment and nomination. The life insurance contract can be assigned freely for a legal consideration or for love and affection. Also, the holder of the policy should name a nominee to whom the money should be paid on the death of the insured.

General or Non-life Insurance

It is a contract that covers any risk apart from the risk of life. *It includes the following insurances*

Social Welfare Insurance

The development of the welfare state and its systems of social welfare, social insurance and social security is significant for the social history of the modern west in a number of ways. These programmes affect the standard of living and quality of life of a large section of the population both, *i.e.* directly through the monetary assistance and services they provide and indirectly through their impact on the dynamics of the labour market.

The main purpose of such insurance is to provide social security to the weaker and the dependent/unproductive sections of society. Pension schemes, unemployment allowances, disability benefits, old age allowances, compensation in case of accidents, natural calamities etc are some of the examples of social security schemes. It is the responsibility of the government to look after the basic fundamental rights of the weaker sections of the society and provide them with basic necessities like food, shelter, clothing, health and education. The government pays the premium on behalf of the people and the people get the benefit of it.

Following are the features of social welfare insurance

- The benefits, eligibility requirements and other aspects of the program are defined by statute.
- Explicit provision is made to account for the income and expenses, generally through a trust fund.
- It is funded by taxes.
- The program serves a defined population and participation is either compulsory or heavily subsidised, so that most eligible individuals choose to participate.

Mortgage Insurance

Mortgage insurance is an insurance policy which compensates lenders or investors for losses due to the default of a mortgage loan. Mortgage insurance can be either public or private depending upon the insurer.

The following are the features of mortgage insurance

- Lenders and investors are protected from losses in the event, if borrowers are unable to repay the mortgages.
- Borrowers have the flexibility of paying in multiple ways. There is the option of borrower-paid, lender-paid and split insurance plans.

Fire Insurance

Under a fire insurance contract, the insurer undertakes, payment of the premium and subject to the conditions of the contract, to pay any loss or damage by fire, which may happen to the property insured during the period covered by the policy upto the amount specified in the policy. Normally, the fire insurance policy is for a period of one year after which it is to be renewed from time-to-time. The premium may be paid either in lumpsum or instalments.

The following are the features of fire insurance

- The insured party must contain insurable interest in the property which he/she wants to insure and it should exist both at the time of taking the policy and also at the time of claiming loss.
- The contract of fire insurance is also based on the principle of utmost good faith. The insured should provide information regarding construction of house, environment, possibility of catching fire etc. If all the facts are not disclosed, then the insurance company can cancel the contract.
- A fire insurance contract is a personal contract and therefore the insurance policy cannot be transferred without the permission of the insuer.
- Average clause is applicable, if the sum insured is less than the actual value of the goods or the property.

Marine Insurance

A marine insurance contract is an agreement, whereby the insurers undertakes to indemnify the insured, in the manner and to the extent thereby agreed, against marine losses caused by ferils of the sea, such as collision of ship with the rock or ship attacked by the enemies or captured by pirates and any loss due to the actions of the captain and crew of the ship.

The following are the features of marine insurance

- In contract of marine insurance, there are two parties. One party is insurance company and another party is insurance holder.
- The insurable interest is the interest whereby the policy holder is benefited by the existence of the subject matter and is adversely affected by the death or damage of the subject matter. The insured should have insurable interest in the policy.
- The marine insurance contract exist only on the basis of good faith.
- Marine insurance contract is a contract of indemnity under which insurance company agrees to pay a certain sum of money to compensate loss cuased by the perils of sea.
- The proximate cause of loss should be covered by the marine insurance policy.
- In marine insurance ships, ship products, ship rent etc should be the subject matter or insurance.
- There are two kinds of marine insurance policy. One of specific sea journey base and other one is on the basis of time.
- *The marine insurance contract can contain the following warranties*
  - (a) Ship neutrality
  - (b) Journeys time
  - (c) Safety time
  - (c) Properties neutrality
  - (d) Ability to ships journey
  - (e) Legality of sea journey
  - (f) No late journey

Other Insurances

Motor Vehicle Insurance In motor insurance, the owner's liability to compensate people who are killed or injured through negligence of drivers, is passed on the insurance company.

Burglary Insurance In case of burglary policy, the loss of damages of household goods and properties and personal effects due to theft, larceny, burglary, house-breaking etc are covered.

Cattle Insurance A contract of cattle insurance is a contract, whereby a sum of money is secured to the assured in the event of death of animals like Bulls, Buffaloes, Cow and heifers.

Cattle Insurance A contract of crop insurance is a contract to provide a measure of financial support to farmers in the event of a crop failure due to drought or flood.

Sports Insurance This policy assures a comprehensive cover available to amateur sportsmen covering their sporting equipment, personal effects, legal liabilities and personal accident risks.

Reinsurance

Reinsurance is a form of insurance. A reinsurance contract is legally an insurance contract. The reinsurer agrees to indemnify the cedant insurer for a specified share of specified type of insurance claims paid by the cedant for a single insurance policy or for a specified set of policies.

The nature and purpose of reinsurance is to reduce the financial cost to insurance companies arising from the potential occurrence of specified insurance claims, thus further enhancing innovation, competition and efficiency in the market place. The cession of shares of liability spreads risk further throughout the insurance system. Just as an individual or company purchases an insurance policy from an insurer, an insurance company may purchase fairly comprehensive reinsurance from one or more reinsurers.

Characteristics of Reinsurance

- Reinsurance is a contract between the two insurance companies.
- The original insurer agrees to transfer part of his risk to other insurance company on the same terms and conditions.
- The fundamental principles of insurance such as insurable interest utmost good faith, indemnity, subragation and proximate cause also apply to reinsurance.
- In the event of fire, the insured is entitled to get the amount of claim only from the original insurer and not from reinsurer.
- Original insurer cannot insure the risk with a reinsurer, more than the sum assured, originally by the insured.
- The original insurer should intimate to the reinsurer about the alternation, if any, made in terms and conditions with the insured.

Objectives of Reinsurance

- Wide distribution of risk to secure the full advantages of the law of averages.
- Limitation of liability of an amount which is with in the financial capacity of the insurers.
- Stability in underwriting over a period.
- A safeguard against serious effects of conflagrations.

Apart from these, sometimes an insurer may undertake the insurance of certain risks at a higher rate of premium and may reinsure part of these or the whole of it with some other insurers at a lower rate with the objective of earning of profit out of it, *i.e.* making profits by way of retaining the difference between the two premiums.

Risk Classification and Management

Risk

Risk is a probability or threat of damage, injury, liability, loss or any other negative occurrence, *i.e.* caused by external or internal vulnerabilities and that may be avoided through preemptive action.

In insurance, a risk is a situation where the probability of a variable (such as a burning of a building) is known but when a mode of occurrence or the actual value of the occurrence is not.

Types of Risk

Financial and Non-financial Risks

Financial risks are the risk where the outcome of an events can be measured in monetary terms. The losses can be assessed and a proper money value can be given to those losses. *e.g.* Financial risks are material damage, theft of a property, personal injuries, loss of profit etc.

Non-financial risks are the risk, the outcome of which cannot be measured in monetary terms. There may be a wrong choice or a wrong decision giving risk to possible discomfort but not being capable of valuation in monetary terms. *e.g.* Non-financial risks are choice of a car, selection of a thing, career selection etc.

Pure and Speculative Risks

Pure risk are those risk where the outcome shall result into loss only or at best a break even situation. We cannot think about a gain situation, the result is always unfavorable. *e.g.* Pure risk are fire damage, machinery breakdown possibility, theft possibility etc.

Speculative risk is a category of risk that can be taken an voluntarily and will either result in a profit or loss. All specnlative risks are undertaken as a result of a conscious choice. Almost all financial investment activities are examples of speculative risk.

Fundamental and Particular Risks

Fundamental risk are the risks mostly emanating from nature. These are the risks which arise from causes that are beyond the control of an individual or a group of individuals. Common examples are Earthquake, Tsunami, Famine, Draught etc.

Particular risk are as opposed to what has been narrated here-in-before. There are risks which usually arise from actions of individuals or even group of individuals. These may be identified as cause arising from personal behaviour and effects not being of that magnitude. These are mostly man created because of their negligence and error of judgement. *e.g* Particular risk are fire, explosion, burglary, motor accidents etc.

Factors Limiting the Insurability of Risk

A risk that conforms to the norms and specifications of the insurance policy in such a way that the criterion for insurance is fulfilled is called insurable risk.

There are various essential conditions that need to be fulfilled before acceptance of insurability of any risk. In case of a scenario, where the loss is too huge that no insurer would want to pay for it, the risk is said to be uninsurable.

These are as follows

Premium Loading In premium loading, the amount of an insurance need to cover its expenses and generate profit. Fair premium is determines using premium loading and pure premium.

Parameter Uncertainty It includes uncertainty in a parameter due to lack of reasonable knowledge of its relationship or due to lack of accuracy with which it can be described or estimated.

Moral Hazard It is a situation in which one party gets involved in a risky event knowing that it is protected against the risk and the other party will incur the cost. It occurs when both party have incomplete information about each other.

Risk Management

The risk management is nothing but a method to prejudge the risk that may occur sometime in future. It is not prediction but a process of reducing the risk to a minimum level. Risk management involves a number of measures that are used to keep the risk at possible minimum level.

Risk Management Process

Step 1 **Risk Assessment and Analysis**

This is the first step of risk management. Risk assessment helps to evaluate an organisation's exposure to uncertain events that could impact its day-to-day operations. Effectively assessing and analysing an organisation's risks helps protect assets, improve decision-making and optimise operational efficiency.

Step 2 **Risk Evaluation**

After assessing and analysing risk, the next step is risk evaluation. In this step, estimated risks are compared against established risk criteria. Risk criteria can include associated costs and benefits, socio-economic factors etc.

Step 3 **Risk Treatment and Response**

It is the last step in risk management process. In this step, policies and procedures are implemented to help avoid or minimise risks.

Insurance Regulatory and Development Authority (IRDAI)

IRDAI is an autonomous statutory body tasked with regulating and promoting the insurance and reinsurance industries in India. It was constituted by the Insurance Regulatory and Development Authority Act, 1999, an Act of Parliament passed by the Government of India. The agency's headquarters are in Hyderabad, Telangana, where it moved fair Delhi in 2001.

IRDAI is a 10 member body including the Chairman, five full time and four part-time members appointed by the Government of India.

Functions of IRDAI

The functions of the IRDAI are defined in Section 14 of the IRDAI Act, 1999 and include

- issuing, renewing, modifying, withdrawing, suspending or cancelling registrations.
- protecting policyholder interests.
- specifying qualifications, the code of conduct and training for intermediaries and agents.
- specifying the code of conduct for surveyors and loss assessors.
- promoting efficiency in the conduct of insurance businesses.
- promoting and regulating professional organisation connected with the insurance and insurance industry.
- levying fees and other charges.
- inspecting and investigating insurers, intermediaries and other relevant organisations.
- specifying how books should be kept.
- regulating company investment of funds.
- regulating a margin of solvency.
- adjudicating disputes between insurers and intermediaries or insurance intermediaries.
- supervising the Tariff Advisory Committee.
- specifying the percentage of premium income to finance schemes for promoting and regulating professional organisations.
- specifying the percentage of life and general insurance business undertaken in the rural or social sector.
- specifying the form and the manner in which books of accounts shall be maintained and statement of accounts shall be rendered by insurers and other insurer intermediaries.

Role of IRDAI

- To protect the interest of and ensure just treatment to insurance policyholder.
- To encourage and ensure the systematic growth of the insurance industry so as to benefit the common man and help in bringing economic growth.
- To set, promote, monitor, apply high standard of integrity, fair, dealing financial viability and capability of those it regulates.
- To provide dispute resolution mechanism and ensure speedy settlement of genuine claims.
- To take suitable steps against circumstances, where set standards do not prevail or inappropriately enforced.
- To bring about the optimal amount of self-regulation in day-to-day activities of the industry reliable with the requirement of the prudential regulation.

EXAM BASED QUESTIONS

Insurance

1 **Which of the following is the best description of what insurance is?**

(a) Insurance – Paying for other mistake
(b) Insurance – Collective bearing of risk
(c) Insurance – Paying for something with will never happen
(d) All of the above

2 **Which of the following term is not used in the world of finance, banking and insurance?**

(a) Hard currency (b) Amnesty
(c) Devaluation (d) Sinking fund

3 **The insurance companies collect a fixed amount from its customers at a fixed interval of time, what is it called?**

(a) Premium (b) EMI
(c) Contribution (d) Instalment

4 **"Insurance is a plan by which large number of people associate themselves and transfer to the shareholders of all, risk that attach to the individual." Who said these words.**

(a) AH Willed (b) John H Magee
(c) Sprigller (d) Lewis

5 **By which scholar insurance defined as "insurance is a social device for making accumulation to meet uncertain losses of capital which is carried out through the transfer of risk of many individual to one person or to a group of persons"?**

(a) Lewis (b) Willset
(c) AH Willed (d) Magee

6 **A person or company that underwrites an insurance risk or the party in an insurance contract undertaking to pay compensation is known as**

(a) insured (b) insurer
(c) assured (d) insurant

7 **The amount of money an insurance policy guarantees to pay before any bonuses are added is known as**

(a) sum assured (b) return
(c) premium (d) None of these

8 **Inadequate insurance coverage held by a policy holder is known as**

(a) insurance (b) underinsurance
(c) max insurance (d) premium

9 **When the insurance paper is not deposit on time, then it is known as**

(a) underinsurance paper (b) timeless insurance
(c) max insurance paper (d) All of these

10 **Which type of insurance usually requires higher premium?**

(a) Broad form insurance (b) Whole life insurance
(c) Health insurance (d) Term insurance

11 **Which of the following form is designed to be used by many different insurers and has exactly the same provisions?**

(a) Guaranteed replacement form
(b) Standard insurance form
(c) Standard endorsement form
(d) Standard policy form

12 **Limit of FDI in insurance sector**

(a) 47% (b) 50%
(c) 49% (d) 51%

13 **Insurance is listed in the Constitution of India in .... schedule as union list subject.**

(a) eighth (b) ninth
(c) seventh (d) tenth

14 **Insurance is legislated by**

(a) Insurance Company (b) State Government
(c) Central Government (d) Government of India

15 **Which of the following is not the principle of insurance?**

(a) Utmost good faith (b) Principle of contribution
(c) Maximisation of profit (d) Causa proxima

16 **As per the news published in various newspapers, life insurance policies may become paperless in the near future. This means**

(a) LIC will not insure any person hereafter as it has already reached its peak
(b) all policy related documents and policy certificates will henceforth be available in electronic form and not in their persent physical form
(c) LIC henceforth will not entertain any claim or complaint in written form or on paper. Things should be in electronic condition
(d) None of the above

17 **Which of the following correctly describes, what the Bancassurance is**

1. It is an arrangement whereby the branches of a bank sell/distribute insurance products of an insurance company.
2. It is a new product developed/launched by the banks in which the risks of the high value customers are covered for any losses to their property and/or lives through an insurance cover.
3. It is a new product launched by the banks by which they are providing insurance cover to exporters/ importers for the losses, if any due to high fluctuations in the exchange rates of dollars and other major currencies.

Select the correct answer using the codes given below

Codes

(a) Only 2 (b) Only 1
(c) Both 1 and 2 (d) None of the above

18 Which is not an objective of insurance from amongst the following?

(a) Security of risk (b) Limited area
(c) Insurance is a contract (d) Risk transfer method

19 The written insurance contract that may include all clauses, riders and endorsements, it is called?

(a) Instalment (b) Premium
(c) Policy (d) Assets

20 A seller's market in which insurance is expensive and in short supply is termed as ....

(a) hard market (b) soft market
(c) alternative market (d) None of these

21 Which of the following statement is correct?

(a) An insurance agent has fixed working hours
(b) An insurance agent has to mark his attendance in office every day
(c) An insurance agent works according to his schedule
(d) An insurance agent cannot do any other work

22 Which of the following statement is correct?

(a) A policy reported to be lost, may actually have been assigned
(b) A policy has no value after the payment of survival benefits
(c) Both (a) and (b)
(d) None of the above

Life Insurance and General Insurance

23 The central office of the Life Insurance Corporation of India (LIC) is located to

(a) Kolkata (b) New Delhi
(c) Pune (d) Mumbai

24 A contract that pledges payment of an agreed amount to the person on the happening of an event covered against, is technically known as

(a) life insurance (b) death coverage
(c) saving for future (d) provident fund

25 Largest life insurance company in India is

(a) The New India Assurance Company Limited
(b) Life Insurance Corporation of India (LIC)
(c) United India Insurance Company Limited
(d) National Insurance Company Limited

26 Which was an oldest insurance company found in 1906?

(a) LIC
(b) National Insurance Company
(c) Agriculture Insurance Company of India
(d) United India Insurance Company

27 What is the CRISIL rating for New India Assurance Company Limited?

(a) AA/Stable (b) AAA/Stable
(c) AA/Negative (d) AAA/Negative

28 Which one of the following does not belong to the main products of life insurance?

(a) Term
(b) Whole life
(c) Endowment
(d) Personal accident insurance

29 A type of insurance that combines protection with investment plan is called

(a) whole life (b) limited pay
(c) universal (d) endowment

30 Which of the following was the parent company of New India Insurance?

(a) LIC (b) GIC
(c) United India Insurance (d) None of these

31 Which of the following insurance companies was launched with NABARD as one of its promoter's with 30% stake in it?

(a) General Insurance Corporation Ltd
(b) SBI Life Insurance Company Ltd
(c) National Insurance Company Ltd
(d) None of the above

32 Oldest operating general insurance company in India

(a) NIACL (b) NICL
(c) LIC (d) OICL

33 Which of the following public sector companies organisations provides insurance cover to exporters?

(a) NABARD (b) ECGC
(c) SIDBI (d) IRDA

34 When the general insurance business nationalised?

(a) 1970 (b) 1971
(c) 1972 (d) 1973

35 A single policy covering a group of individuals, usually employees of the same company or members of the same association and their dependants is called ....

(a) hospital insurance (b) hull insurance
(c) group insurance (d) identity theft insurance

36 A state law requires individuals suffering injury or loss from an automobiles accidents to be reimbursed by their own insurance companies. What type of insurance is this?

(a) No fault auto insurance
(b) Public liability insurance
(c) Automobile physical damage insurance
(d) Comprehensive insurance

37 Which type of insurance policy will protect a business from theft and forgery by its employees?

(a) Burglary insurance
(b) Facility bond
(c) Indemnity insurance
(d) Liability insurance

38 Which type of insurance covers damage or injury caused by a vechile with no liability insurance coverage?
(a) Comprehensive insurance
(b) Uninsured motorists insurance
(c) Public liability insurance
(d) No-fault automobile insurance

39 Insurance company transfers the risk insured to another company. This is known as
(a) Reinsurance (b) TPAs
(c) Bancassurance (d) Actuaries

40 An insurance that is purchased by an insurance company to remain solvent after major claims is known as
(a) insurance (b) under insurance
(c) max insurance (d) reinsurance

41 Most firms shift their risks by
(a) buying an insurance policy
(b) establishing a self-insurance fund
(c) establishing a safety programme
(d) stopping the questionable activity

Reinsurance, Risk Classification, Management and IRDA

42 Which of the following statements is the best explanation of how insurance allows a company to manage risk?
(a) By avoiding risk (b) Modifying risk
(c) By preventing risk (d) Transferring risk

43 Risks that insurance firms will not assume are called
(a) uninsurable risk (b) insurable risk
(c) pure risk (d) avoidable risk

44 Which risk management technique does self-insurance satisfy?
(a) Risk reduction (b) Risk assumption
(c) Risk avoidance (d) Shifting risk

45 The main role of an underwriter in a non-life insurance company is normally to
(a) assess the acceptability of particular risk
(b) certify loss when claims are submitted
(c) design the structure of the products to be offered
(d) negotiate with the industry regulator

46 Which of the following is not an example of a method of protection of risk?
(a) Group insurance plans
(b) Employee benefits
(c) Social insurance
(d) Humanitarian aid

47 Defective electrical wiring that may lead to fire is an example of
(a) pure risk (b) non-diversifiable risk
(c) speculative risk (d) physical hazard

48 Risk pooling is an example of
(a) a catastrophic loss event
(b) diversifying risk
(c) a speculate risk
(d) applying the risk return trade-off

49 A pure risk is defined as
(a) an event that offer no opportunity for financial gain
(b) the chance a loss will occur
(c) a diversifiable risk
(d) a contingency that increase the chance of loss

50 Which of the following statement is false?
(a) Risk averse people will pay an insurance premium that is greater than the mathematically fair chance of loss in order to relieve themselves of uncertainty
(b) A risk seeker is willing to assume risk
(c) The mathematically fair price for insurance is the objective risk for the insurer multiplied by the maximum possible loss
(d) Insurance is never a mathematically fair trade because the insurer adds several operating and other costs to loss costs when it calculates the premium

51 Insurance business in India is regulated by which of the following authorities?
(a) IRDA (b) CII
(c) FICCI (d) All of these

52 IRDA has the power to frame the regulations under .... of the Insurance Act, 1938.
(a) Section 114(B) (b) Section 112(B)
(c) Section 118(C) (d) None of these

53 IBAI was incorporated as a company under Section 25 of the Companies Act, 1956. What is the meaning of 'B' in IBAI?
(a) Basel (b) Broadcasting
(c) Brokers (d) Board

54 Registering the nomination or cancellation or change of nomination shall be regarded as important policy holder services as observed by IRDA. Recently it has taken steps regarding this registration that
(a) no charge for late payment of premium
(b) no charge for reimbursement
(c) no charge for change of nomination
(d) None of the above

Miscellaneous

Directions (Q. Nos. 55-57) *In the questions given below are two statements labelled as Assertion (A) and Reason (R). In the context of the two statements, which one of the following is correct?*
(a) Both (A) and (R) are true and (R) is the correct explanation of (A)
(b) Both (A) and (R) are true, but (R) is not the correct explanation of (A)
(c) (A) is true, but (R) is false
(d) (R) is true, but (A) is false

55 **Assertion** (A) Insurance is not known as a gambling.
Reason (R) Under insurance, the insurer provides contributions to various insured persons and controls the risk.

56 **Assertion** (A) The sum insured is that amount which the insured person has to pay to the insurer as a premium.
Reason (R) When insurance value is more than the value of assets, then it is called term insurance.

57 **Assertion** (A) Artistic insurance is subject to the conditions of a contract according to the terms of insurance.
Reason (R) Under the artistic insurance, when the insured person fails to pay insurance premium at the right time, he ceases to receive the leverage benefit.

58 Match List I from List II.

List I	List II
A. Life insurance	1. Used to avoid fire related risks
B. Simple insurance	2. Harvest insurance, aircraft insurance etc
C. Fire insurance	3. It is an insurance that is done for the protection of life
D. Marine insurance	4. Insurance to be done to avoid marine risks

Codes

	A	B	C	D		A	B	C	D
(a)	1	2	3	4	(b)	3	2	1	4
(c)	2	1	4	3	(d)	4	3	2	1

59 Match List I from List II.

List I	List II
A. Assets, liabilities and personal risks	1. Property damage due to hurricane, fire, increased risk
B. Physical, social and economical risks	2. Damage of assets and liability of business and family
C. Hypothesis risks	3. These are those risk in which, a person is likely to suffer or not
D. Net risks	4. It has the potential of both profit and loss

Codes

	A	B	C	D		A	B	C	D
(a)	2	4	1	3	(b)	1	2	3	4
(c)	2	1	4	3	(d)	3	1	2	4

ANSWERS

Objective Questions

1 (b)	2 (b)	3 (a)	4 (b)	5 (c)	6 (b)	7 (a)	8 (b)	9 (b)	10 (a)
11 (d)	12 (c)	13 (c)	14 (c)	15 (c)	16 (b)	17 (b)	18 (b)	19 (c)	20 (c)
21 (c)	22 (c)	23 (d)	24 (a)	25 (b)	26 (b)	27 (b)	28 (d)	29 (c)	30 (b)
31 (a)	32 (b)	33 (b)	34 (d)	35 (c)	36 (a)	37 (a)	38 (b)	39 (a)	40 (d)
41 (a)	42 (d)	43 (a)	44 (b)	45 (a)	46 (d)	47 (d)	48 (b)	49 (a)	50 (d)
51 (a)	52 (a)	53 (d)	54 (c)	55 (a)	56 (d)	57 (a)	58 (b)	59 (a)	

CHAPTER 29

Marketing and Market Segmentation

Marketing and market segmentation are essential elements of a product, which directly relates with consumer behaviour. We have to understand the criteria for targeting selected segments effectively and also the relationship between market segmentation and consumer behaviour.

Marketing

Marketing is the management process responsible for identifying, anticipating and satisfying customer requirements profitably. According to American Marketing Association (AMA), marketing is the process of planning and executing the conception, pricing, promotion and distribution of ideas, goods and services to create exchanges that satisfy individual and organisational goals.

Thus, marketing consists of all those activities designed to create exchanges, which satisfy human or organisational needs or wants in a way that brings profit for the firm. It performs the task of both identifying and satisfying customer needs. This helps business enterprises in anticipating customer demand and creating satisfied customers through conception, production, promotion and physical distribution of goods and services. Marketing deals with products. A product can be a good, service or an idea. A good is a physical entity, *i.e.* it is a tangible product, which can be felt or touched. A service created, when human efforts are clubbed with mechanical efforts to provide intangible benefits to the customer. While ideas provide intellectual or spiritual benefit to customers.

On the whole, a marketing transaction is one in which the buyer and the seller, irrespective of the nature of the product, experience mutual satisfaction, the seller

In this Chapter

on selling the product and making a profit and buyer on purchase and subsequent consumption of the product.

According to **Bartles**,"Marketing is the process, whereby society, to supply its consumption needs, evolves distributive systems composed of participants, who interacting under constraints, technical (economic) and ethical (social), create the transaction and flows, which resolve market separations and results in exchange and consumption."

Evolution of Marketing

Although, the concept of marketing emerged after the Industrial Revolution, but the change in business in terms of adapting to the concept come about gradually. It took many years for businesses to realise that satisfying customers is the key for making sales and profits in the long run. Businesses have gone through different phases or stages of marketing over the years.

These four stages (era) can be classified as follows

Production Era The Industrial Revolution of the 17th century brought about the production era, which continued till the late 1920. Before Industrial Revolution, markets existed without much competition, producers and consumers were not closely knit. As such, demand and supply remained passive and distribution activities were ignored.

Sales Era The sales era began in the late 1920s and lasted till mid 1950s. The economic depression of the late 1920s proved that producing the goods was not everything, a company had to sell them also. By that time, most companies had made their production processes efficient, which paved the way for competition. In this era, marketers focused their efforts only on selling their products to the customers.

Marketing Era During the sales era, companies ignored consumer wants and needs. They focused simply on selling their products. So, products in sales era were sold without looking at the consumer needs and wants. Later, companies began to realise that they would fail, if they did not satisfy consumer needs.

Societal Marketing Era (*Relationship Marketing Era*) In this era, it was emphasised that the key task of the company is not only to determine the needs and wants of the target markets and deliver the desired satisfaction, but also to preserve and enhance the consumers and societies overall well being. It is also called relationship marketing era.

Concepts of Marketing

Firm vary in their perception about business and their orientation to the market place. This has led to the emergence of many different concepts of marketing.

These are as follows

Exchange Concept

The exchange concept of marketing holds that exchange of a product between seller and the buyer is the central idea of marketing. Although, exchange forms a significant part of marketing, but to view marketing as mere exchange will result in missing out the essence of marketing. Marketing is much broader than exchange. Exchange only covers the distribution aspect and price mechanism, but other important aspects like concern for customer, generation of value satisfaction etc are left out.

Production Concept

This concept is based on the belief that marketing can be managed by managing production and so, all the effort should be focussed on production.

According to this concept, consumer would support those products that are produced in great volume at a low unit cost. But in reality, customers are motivated by a variety of considerations in their purchases besides price. So, production concept failed to serve as the right marketing philosophy for an enterprise.

Product Concept

It is different from the production concept. Production concept seeks to win markets and profits by high volume of production and low unit cost, while product concept seeks to achieve the same result by product excellence, improved products, new products and ideally designed and engineered products. In general, product concept tries to achieve marketing success through product attributes.

Sales Concept

According to sales concept, the company has to aggressively promote and push its products, it cannot expect its products to get picked-up automatically by the customers. Heavy advertising, high power personal selling, large scale sales promotion, heavy price discounts are the normal tools used by organisations.

Companies practicising the sales concept assume that selling is synonymous with marketing. In reality, there is great deal of difference between selling and marketing.

Marketing Concept

It is a customer oriented philosophy that is implemented and integrated throughout an organisation to serve customers better than competitors and to achieve specified goals.

Marketing starts with identifying customer needs and wants and ends with satisfying them through a coordinated set of activities that also allows a firm to achieve its own goals. Awareness of this fact gave rise to the marketing concept. The marketing concept embraces all the activities of a firm. It aims at matching the company's offering with customer needs, to achieve desired level of customer satisfaction and generate profits for the company.

Marketing concept is based on the following assumptions

- Company's planning and operations are customer oriented.
- The goals of the company should be profitable sales volume and not just volume.
- All marketing activities should be coordinated effectively.

Elements or Tools of Marketing

Marketing encompasses a number of different activities such as product design, pricing strategies, advertising and others. However, these are just activities, which have to be done in the process of marketing. There are also some crucial elements of marketing, which are very necessary for the success of marketing and they form the backbone of marketing. *These four elements are as follows*

Research

The first thing to be done before the launch of a company or product is market research to determine, what the market actually wants. Similarly, during marketing too, market research is needed to determine what message should be the company adopt and which medium will be best, what positioning needs to be achieved to target the right segment.

Strategy

Once you have your data ready, you know where your product stands and also the standing of your company in the market in terms of strengths and weaknesses. You also have an idea of what strategies will need to be implemented and what factors will need to be adopted by the company to beat competitors and succeed in the market.

Planning

The marketing plan involves sales forecasting, financial planning, communications strategy and many such benchmarks, which define how the company is going to achieve its strategic goals in the future. The planning department also keeps a track of the timeline, so that time to time we can determine whether we are on track with the strategic plan or not.

Tactics

Where planning happens at the top most level, tactics are the street smart, short-term plans implemented to attract customers, beat your competitors, increase sales, provide a better value for your customers as for any other short-term objective, which needs to be achieved.

Marketing Approaches

Product Approach The study relates to the flow of a certain commodity and its movement from the producer to the ultimate customer, comes under this approach. The system claims that it is simple and gives good result over the marketing of each product, but at the same time this approach is time consuming and repetitive process.

Institutional Approach This approach is also known as middleman approach. In this approach, emphasise is given to understand and analyse the functions of institutions, who are discharging their marketing functions.

Functional Approach In this approach, marketing splits into many functions like buying, selling, pricing, standardisation, advertising, packing etc. Here, each function is studied in detail in order to understand and analyse the nature, need and importance of each function.

Management Approach This approach is mainly concerned with, how managers handle specific problems and situations. It aims through evaluation of current market practices to achieve specific marketing objectives.

System Approach Systems focus on inter-relations and interconnections among the functions of marketing. The system examines marketing connections inside as well as outside the firm.

Societal Approach This system gives no importance as to how the business meets the consumer's needs. Therefore, attention is paid to ecological factors like sociological, cultural, legal etc and marketing decisions and their impact on the society's well being.

Legal Approach Under this approach, the study is concentrated only on legal aspects, leaving other important aspects. This approach does not benefit in giving any idea of marketing.

Economical Approach This approach deals with only the problems of supply, demand and price which are important from the economic point of view.

Marketing Channels

Physical distribution has become more dynamic. The aim of marketing channel is to maximise customer satisfaction. It can be referred to any firm or individuals who participate in the flow of goods and services as they move from producer to an ultimate user.

Organised network of interconnected organisations and agencies involved in the process of making a product or service available to the customers are called marketing channels.

According to **Philip Kotler**, "Marketing channels are set of interdependent organisations involved in the process of making products or services available for use or consumption."

Types of Marketing Channels

Non-integrated Channel

In this channel, each enterprise is separately owned and operated concern. Manufacturers, wholesalers and retailers bargain with each other, negotiate over terms of sale and otherwise behave autonomously. The other name for non-integrated channel is individualistic or conventional market channel. *In this marketing channel, there are following two types of channels*

Direct Channel

When the manufacturer instead of selling the goods to the intermediary, sells it directly to the consumer, then it is known as direct channel or zero level channel. Retail outlets, mail order selling and internet selling are some of its examples.

Following are the main types of indirect channel

One Level Channel In this method, an intermediary is used. Here, a manufacturer sells the goods directly to the retailer, instead of selling it to agents or wholesalers. This method is used for expensive products.

Two Level Channel In this method, a manufacturer sells the material to a wholesaler, the wholesaler to the retailer and then, the retailer to the consumer. This medium is mainly used to sell soap, tea, salt etc.

Three Level Channel Under this, one more level is added to two level channel in the form of agent. An agent facilitates to reduce the distance between the manufacturer and the wholesaler. Some big companies do not directly contact the wholesaler, they take the help of agents.

Indirect Channel

When the manufacturer gets the help of one or more middlemen to move goods from the production place to the place of consumption, then the distribution channel is called indirect channel.

Integrated Channel

Integrated channels are the networks in which channel components participate in a coordinated manner. *Integrated channel is classified into following two types*

Vertical Distribution Channel

These channels are professionally managed and centrally programmed networks, pre-engineered to achieve operating economies and maximum market impact.

Its main types are as follows

Administered Vertical Channel In administered vertical channels, one of a limited number of firms use developed programmes to achieve the coordination of marketing activities. A manufacturer controls the marketing of a particular line of merchandise.

Contractual Vertical Channel Under contractual vertical distribution channel, independent firms are employed on a voluntary basis to develop a more efficient system on a contractual basis, be as to achieve systematic economies and increased market impact.

Corporate Vertical Channel Under corporate vertical distribution channel, channel components are owned and operated by one organisation. The firms own both production and distribution facilities. *e.g.* Bata, Tata etc.

Horizontal Distribution Channel

A horizontal marketing system is a distribution channel arrangement, whereby two or more organisations at the same level join together for marketing purposes to capitalise on a new dictionary. In other words, horizontal marketing system is the merger of two unrelated companies who have come together to exploit the market opportunities. Generally, this type of marketing system is followed by companies who lack in capital, human resources, production techniques, marketing programmes and are afraid of incurring the huge losses.

Functions of Marketing Channels

Helps in Production Function The producer can concentrate on the production function leaving the marketing problem to middlemen, who is specialised in the profession.

Promotion Promoting the products in their territories is another function that middlemen perform. Many of them design their own sales incentive programmes, aimed at building customers traffic at the other outlets.

Information Provider Middlemen have a role in providing information about the market to the manufacturer. Developments like change in customer demography, psychography, media, habits and the entry of a new competitor etc are some of the information that all maufacturers want.

Pricing The middlemen can give suggestions to the producer, regarding paying habits of different users. Pricing may be different for different markets or products depending upon the distribution channel.

Price Stability Maintaining price stability in the market is the main function of the middlemen. In many situations, the middlemen absorb an increase in the price of the products and try to charge old price from the users. This helps in maintaining price stability.

Financing Middlemen provide necessary working capital in the form of advance payments for goods and services for financing manufacturer's operation.

Matching Demand and Supply Intermediaries assemble the goods from many producers, in such a manner that a customer can affect purchases with ease. The goal of marketing is the matching of segments of supply and demand.

Matching the Needs of Buyers and Sellers Marketing channel members helps to match the needs of buyers and sellers. Normally, most sellers want to reach the potential buyers and in the same way, buyers also want to know about the potential sellers.

Standardisation of Transactions By standardising transactions, marketing channel automate most of the stages in the flow of products from the manufacturer to the customers.

Consolidation and Distribution Consumers often prefer to buy a wide variety of consumer goods at one time and place. Retail stores enable consumers to do just that because they stock and display a great number of different products.

Marketing Mix

It describes the specific combination of marketing elements used to achieve an organisation's/ individual's objectives and satisfy the target market.

Conditions of Marketing Mix

To create the right marketing mix, businesses have to meet the following conditions

- The product has to have the right features, *e.g.* it must look good and work well.
- The price must be right. Consumer will need to buy in large numbers to produce a healthy profit.
- The goods must be in the right place at the right time. Making sure that the goods arrive, when and where they are wanted is an important operation.
- The target group needs to be made aware of the existence and availability of the product through promotion. Successful promotion helps a firm to spread cost over a larger output.
- The fair elements product, distribution/place, price and promotion constitute the marketing mix of the firm. The marketing mix is the sole vehicle for creating and delivering customer value.

The Four Ps of Marketing

James Culliten, a noted marketing expert coined the expression 'marketing mix' and described the marketing manager as a minor of ingredients.

McCarthy, an American Professor of marketing, first described the marketing mix in terms of four Ps.

It is customary to accept that marketing is made up of four Ps

- Price
- Product
- Place
- Promotion

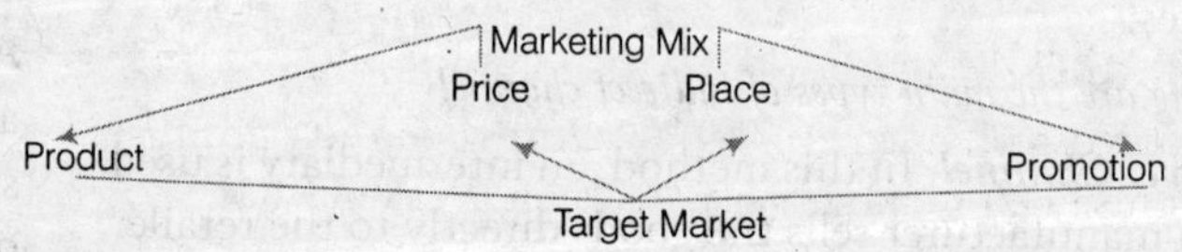

Product

It is a good, service and idea, ***i.e.*** offered to a customer to satisfy his/her need. The attributes of a product are variety, quality, warranty, design, packaging, after sale service etc. Products need to be modified over time to retain the interest of the consumer. A lot of work goes behind the scene before a product is brought to the market.

Price

It is the value at which a marketer offers the product/service to a customer. The actual price at which the exchange may take place between the offerer and the customer may be different than the initial offer. Efforts are made to find out ways by which costs can be reduced, so that price offered can be competitive.

Place

It refers to the distribution of goods from the point of production to the target consumer. It may include distributors/wholesalers, stockiest, retailers, who are together refer to as middlemen or as channel partners.

Promotion

Communicating product features and its benefits to target customers through different mediums is known as promotion. Advertising, personal selling, public relations, sales promotion etc are some of the promotional tools being used.

Modern Components of the Mix, Additional 3 Ps

Three additional P's have been added to the marketing mix *viz.* people, processes and physical evidence. *These are as follows*

People

In the service industry, people play most important role, *e.g.* in hotel or wellness care centre people become the real differentiator.

Processes

This term is commonly used for manufacturing concerns, where the products would go through processes. Due to adoption of total quality management, marketers are not merely satisfied with quality in the final product, but are deeply involved in the entire processes that an enterprise puts into practice throughout the organisation.

Physical Evidence

Marketers use offer experimental learning on their products as a test use before a purchase decision is taken.

The other key marketing elements associated with the concept of marketing mix are

Target Marketing The process of aiming marketing efforts to meet more precisely the needs and wants of customers.

Segmentation The breakdown of customers into segments that will respond to more precisely targeted marketing mixes.

Positioning Distinguishing a brand from its competitors, so that it becomes the preferred brand defined market segments.

Assembling and managing the marketing mix is the crux of the marketing task. And, it is through the marketing mix that the marketing manager achieves the marketing objectives. Besides the marketing mix variables, the marketing manager has to tackle another set of variables that lie outside the control of the firm.

These relate to the environment, competition, consumer, government etc, constitute the environmental variables of marketing. A marketing manager can choose, alter and control the marketing mix variables, he cannot choose or alter the environment variables against, which he markets his product. This is why, environment variables are referred as non-controllable variables of marketing, while the marketing mix variables are referred to as the controllable variables of marketing. Marketing can basically be looked upon as the interaction between marketing mix variables and environment variables. Using the marketing mix variables, the marketing manager tackles the environmental variables.

Marketing mix elements can be combined in an infinite number of ways. Marketing manager consider a number of combinations and select the best out of them. Without considering several alternatives, the objective of optimisation cannot be realised. Depending on the objective and the content, relevant weightage has to be assigned to each of the elements.

Marketing Mix for Various Kinds of Consumer Goods

Convenience Goods These are the goods which consumer expects to find almost everywhere. These are generally low unit price goods bought frequently and consumed rapidly. *e.g.* Food items.

Shopping Goods These are purchased after comparison for price, style, quality, colour and the like. *e.g.* Readymade garments, shoes etc.

Speciality Goods These may or may not be generally available and for which brand preferences influence buying. *e.g.* Car, refrigerator, mobiles etc.

Strategic Marketing Planning

Strategic marketing planning is an ongoing process through which the company creates marketing strategies and plans its implementation in the target market. It is a process of analysing one or more potentially interesting market places in order to determine how a business can optimally compete in them. The market planning process typically results in a marketing strategy that can be used to enhance sales for the business producing it. Marketing planning is concerned with the identification of resources that are available and their allocation to meet specified objectives. The American Marketing Association (AMA) has defined the marketing planning as the work of setting-up objectives for marketing activity and of determining and scheduling the steps necessary to achieve such objectives.

Marketing planning is done by the marketing department. Various sub-divisions or sections under the marketing department submit their proposals to the marketing department and then, the marketing department prepare the plan for the whole marketing division.

Elements of Marketing Planning

It involves the work of setting-up objectives for marketing activity and of determining the steps to achieve such objectives. All the activities to be performed in the process of marketing planning are known as elements of marketing planning.

The main elements of marketing planning are

Determination of Objectives Setting-up of objectives is the first step of planning. It is the responsibility of the marketing executive not only to set the objectives, but also to explain them clearly to the members of his staff and inspire them to achieve those objectives. The objective must be certain and clearly defined to the staff.

Forecasts It is an art of drawing conclusions about the future. Marketing planning is based on these forecasts for the future. It gives an idea of the possible risk, so that firm gets prepared to meet any eventuality. It helps in taking right decisions at the appropriate time, so that the chances of loss are minimised.

Policies The policies guide the manager, administrator and the subordinates of the company as what is to be done in a particular situation. The basic principles through which the objectives are attempted to be achieved are called policies.

Procedures It is a part of marketing planning. Procedures are laid down to serve as guidelines to the actual marketing activity or manner in which work is to be performed and actions to take place. Once the procedure is laid down, it serves to carry out the programmes of the company.

Programmes It is a special kind of planning, which helps the solution of some problems.

Schedules In the field of marketing, schedule shows the actual time of starting a particular programme with a view to achieve the overall objectives of the firm.

Rules They are specific guide to actions and permit no discretion or judgement. Rules must be decided well in advance and all efforts should be made to ensure that these are followed strictly.

Strategies It is a specific plan, which is prepared to meet certain specific problems.

Budgets Budgeting forms an important part of marketing planning. It helps in the control of marketing operations.

Factors Affecting Marketing Planning

Internal Factors They are those factors, which arise in the enterprise itself. *e.g.* Size of the company, risk bearing capacity, financial resources of the enterprise, product line channels of distribution etc.

Industry Factors It include technological changes in the industry, severity of competition in the industry, relations between the enterprise and the industry etc.

National Factors It include population of the country and its distribution, national income of the country, distribution of wealth, price trends in the country, trade policy of the country etc.

International Factors It include international stability and peace, international monetry system, scientific and technical developments in the world.

Importance of Marketing Planning

- It helps to offset future uncertainties.
- It helps in management by objectives.
- It is helpful in coordination.
- It is helpful in controlling process.
- It analyse customer's wants satisfaction.
- It improves performance standards.

Marketing Control

Marketing control is a tool for ensuring that the marketing programmes and activities of the firm are always directed towards its marketing objectives. Marketing control provides the means of testing, whether the desired goals and results are being achieved or not.

Role and Scope of Marketing Control

It involves gathering information on marketing performance and comparing the achieved performance against the planned or budgeted performance using pre-determined standards and year sticks. It provides feedback, it regulates and it exercises a restraint or redirecting influence. Marketing control is a part of management control.

Key result areas of marketing monitored by marketing control are

- Market share
- Sales volume
- Marketing costs
- Market standing
- Profits
- Productivity in each marketing activity

Types of Marketing Control

Business firms use several marketing control. *These are as follows*

Credit Control Most business firms are forced to extend to increase sales. So, it is essential for any business firm to evolve a policy on credit and exercise proper control on it.

Budgetary Control Budgetary control is yet another marketing control device. Budgetary control essentially involves preparation of control statement at specified intervals of time, showing the budgeted figures, the achieved figures and the variance. Review and remedial steps are other parts of budgetary control.

Strategic Control It is one of the technique of marketing control which involves identifying the marketing objectives and developing and implementing marketing programmes.

Ratio Analysis Most firms use ratio analysis also as a control device in marketing as well as other areas. Ratio analysis seeks to measure the effectiveness and profitability of the various marketing functions. While budgetary control reveals absolute figures, ratio analysis focuses attention on relative figures.

Annual Plan Control Annual plan control consists of many tools all of which are used to establish whether the targets set in the company's annual plan have been achieved or not. Plan performance are regularly checked using the five tools like sales analysis, market share analysis, marketing expense analysis, financial analysis and customer attitude tracking.

Profitability Control Profitability control allow a company to closely monitor its sales, profits and expenditures. It demonstrates the relative profit earning capacity of a company's different products and consumer groups. This control is to determine the actual profitability of the firms products, territories, market segments and intermediaries.

Efficiency Control Efficiency control involves micro level analysis of the various elements of the marketing mix, including sales, force, advertising, sales promotion and distribution. It is of different types like sales force efficiency control, advertising efficiency control, sales promotion efficiency control, distribution efficiency control and marketing research efficiency control.

Market Segmentation

Dividing the market by grouping the customers with similar tastes and preferences into one segment is called segmentation. Segmentation helps marketers understand the need of different customers better and serve them with better value propositions.

Market segmentation is the first step in applying the marketing strategy. In this process, the marketers divide the market into homogeneous sub-markets. On the basis of segmentation, the company prepare and follow different marketing programmes for different segments to ensure better customer relationship.

According to **Philip Kotler**, "Whenever a market for a product or service consists of two or more buyers, the market is capable of being segmented, *i.e.* divided into meaningful buyer groups." The purpose of segmentation is to determine differences among buyers, which may be consequential in choosing away them or marketing to them.

Requirements for an Effective Segmentation

The five main requirements of a market segment to ensure that it is effective are that they must be measurable, actionable, accessible, substantial and differential. If each of these requirements are met in a market segment, market segmentation is likely to occur in a successful and effective way. *These are as follows*

Measurable A market segment must be measurable in terms of its size in purchasing power and profiles. While there are some aspects of segmentation that are difficult to measure, wherever possible it is a process that should be double.

Actionable In order for effective segmentation to occur, a market segment must also be actionable. This means that effective programmes can be designed for serving and attracting the segments.

Accessible A market segment should also be accessible, *i.e.* they should be easy to reach and serve.

Substantial For effective segmentation, a market segment should be large or profitable enough to serve. They should be the largest possible homogeneous group, *i.e.* is worth pursuing with a marketing programme that has been tailored.

Differential Market segments need to be distinguishable conceptually and must respond in different ways to the different marketing mix programmes and elements.

Benefits of Market Segmentation

- Understanding the needs of consumers.
- To adopt better positioning strategies.
- Proper allocation of marketing budget.
- Helps in preparing a better competitive strategy.
- Provides guidelines in preparing media plan of the company.
- Different offerings in different segment enhance the sales.
- Customer gets more customised product.
- Helps company to identify niche markets.
- Provides opportunities to expand markets.
- Encourages innovation.

Process of Market Segmentation

Identify Existing and Future Wants in the Current Market Marketers must examine the changing needs of the customer. This process provides opportunity to examine, whether customers are satisfied with the existing product or not. If customers are not satisfied, additional features should be added.

Examine the Attributes that Distinguish Segments In this process, marketers segregate different types of wants into homogeneous categories. This may be on the basis of product features, life style or behaviour.

Evaluate the Proposed Segments Segments selected in the above steps should be evaluated against the requisites, i.e. measurability, accessibility, substantial, actionable and differentiability. Company's further programmes will depend on the outcome of this process.

Bases for Market Segmentation

There are several ways or methods to segment a market. Such ways or methods depends upon consumer characteristics and their responses to the products or services.

Variables used for segmentation include

Psychographic Segmentation

Segmenting people according to their lifestyles and values and how they translate into consumption or purchases of products or services is what psychographic segmentation is all about. How ones' interest, opinions, values, attitude and the activities they perform, affect their choices and why a group of people would lean towards one product more than others. A high status would translate into an expensive flying habit, while a thrift value will translate into an economy flight.

Geographical Segmentation

It is done by dividing people (markets) into different geographical locations. The country, state or neighbourhood, climate, size of a place segmented into size of its age wise population etc, all play a vital role in devising market strategies. This helps the producer and the marketers to understand what to sell and what won't.

Demographic Segmentation

It refers to wide study of potential customers. While marketing a product, many variables like age, gender, education, income, family size, occupation, socio-economic status, culture, region, language and nationality are taken into account. There are many instances where such a segmentation has worked very profitably. This segmentation plays a vital role in determining, whether a product can be mass marketed or designed for a specific clientele.

Behavioural Segmentation

It is based on the customer's needs and subsequent reaction to those who needs or towards the purchase of intended products and/or services. This study is conducted on all variables that are closely related to the product itself like loyalty to a particular brand, cost effectiveness in terms of benefits and usage, circumstances responsible for the purchase, whether the customer is a regular, a first timer or has the potential to become a customer and whether the readiness to buy is linked to status.

Segmenting Consumer Markets

Market can be segmented in many ways. Segmentation variables are the criteria that are used for dividing a market into segments. *There are three broad groups of consumer segmentation criteria, which are as follows*

Behavioural Variables

Such as benefit sought from the product and buying patterns such as frequency and volume of purchase may be considered the fundamental basis. *Some behavioural segmentation variables are as follows*

Benefits Sought People may seek different benefits from a product like benefits sought in the fruit drink market are extra energy, vitamins, being natural, low calories, low price etc.

Purchase Occasions Products like tyres may be purchased as a result of an emergency or as a routine unpressurised buy. Price sensitivity is likely to be lower, when products are bought in emergency situation.

Purchase Behaviour Difference in purchase behaviour can be based on the time of purchase relative to the launch of the product or on patterns of purchase. When a new product is launched, a key task is to identify the innovator segment of the market.

Brand Loyalty The degree of brand loyalty can be the basis for segmenting customers. Some buyers are totally brand loyal, buying only one brand in a product group. Most buyers switch brands.

Usage Customers can be segmented on the basis of heavy users, light users and non-users of a product category. Profiling of heavy users allow this group to receive most marketing attention because creating brand loyalty among these people will pay heavy dividends.

Perception and Beliefs They are strongly linked to behaviour. Consumers are grouped by identifying these people, who view the products in a market in a similar way (perceptual segmentation) and have similar beliefs (belief segmentation).

Psychographic Variables

These are used when purchasing behaviour correlates with the personality or life styles of consumers.

Some psychographic segmentation variables are as follows

Life Style A company groups people according to their way of living as reflected in their activities, interests and opinions. The company identifies groups of people with similar pattern of living.

Personality In some product categories, there is relationship between brand personality and the personality of the buyer. Buyer and brand personalities are likely to match, where brand choice is a direct manifestation of personal values.

Profiling Variable

It is not essentially a criteria for segmentation. After finding these differences, marketers need to describe the people, who exhibit them. Profile variables such as socio-economic group or geographic locations are valuable in describing the customers of the identified segment. But in practice, segmentation may not follow this logical sequence. Often profile variables will be identified first and then the segments, so described will be examined to see if they show different behavioural responses.

Some other groups of consumer segmentation, which are as follows

Demographic Variables

These are classified into three parts

Age It is used to segment many consumer markets like food and clothing.

Gender Differing tastes and customs between men and women are reflected in specialist products aimed at these market segments.

Life Cycle Disposable income and purchase requirement vary according to life cycle stage (young singles *vs* married).

Socio-economic Variables

Social class a predictor of buyer behaviour has been open to question. Many people, who hold similar occupations have dissimilar lifestyles and purchasing patterns.

Educational qualification and income are also used as variables for segmentation.

Geographic Variables

A marketer can use pure geographic segmentation or a hybrid of geographic and demographic variables to segment the market. It is useful, when there are geographic locational differences in consumption patterns and preferences. Variations in food preferences may form the basis of geographic segmentation.

Evaluating Market Segments and Target Market Selection

Segmentation is a mean to target marketing. Target marketing is the choice of specific segments to serve. A firm needs to evaluate the segments and decide, which one to serve.

For evaluation of market segments, company should examine two broad issues

Market Attractiveness

For finding out that whether a particular market segment is worth pursuing, following factors should be evaluated

Market Factors

- Segment size
- Segment growth rate
- Price sensitivity
- Bargaining power of customers
- Bargaining power of suppliers
- Barriers to market segment entry
- Barriers to market segment exit

Competitive Factors

- Nature of competition
- New entrants
- Competitive differentiation

Political, Social and Environmental Factors

- Political issues
- Social trends
- Environmental issues

Firms Capability to Serve Segments

A market segment may be attractive, but it may be beyond the resources and competencies of the company to serve it profitability. However, attractive segment may look to be a company should not venture to serve it, unless it is certain that it has the required resources and competencies. *Following points should be considered while assessing firms' capability*

Exploitable Market Assets The target market segment should allow the firm to exploit its current technological manufacturing and marketing strengths. Where new segment entry is inconsistent with its current image, a new brand name may be considered or created.

Cost Advantage Companies which can exploit cheaper material, labour or technological cost advantages to achieve a low cost position compared to competition will be in a strong position particularly, if the segment is price sensitive.

Technological Edge Superior technology may be a source of differential advantage in the market segment. If the companies has patent protection, it can form the basis of a strong entry. If the company possess resources, it can invest in building technological leadership.

Managerial Capabilities and Commitment The technological capabilities of the company and its superior products may be insufficient to compete against strong competitors. The segment needs to be assessed from the view point of managerial skills that will be required to develop and maintain the marketing mix.

Target Market Strategies The purpose of evaluating market segments is to choose one or more segments to enter. Target market selection is the choice of which and how many segments the company will compete in.

Strategies of Target Marketing

Undifferentiated Marketing

There may be no strong differences in customer characteristics. Alternatively, the cost of developing a separate marketing mix for separate segments may outweigh the potential gains of meeting customer needs more exactly. Under these circumstances, a company will decide to develop a single marketing mix for the whole mare. There is absence of segmentation.

This strategy can occur by default. Companies which lack an orientation may practice this strategy because of lack of customer knowledge. It is convenient, since a single product has to be developed.

Differential Marketing

This strategy exploits the differences between marketing segments by designing a specific marketing mix for each segment. Specific marketing mixes would be developed to target cross border segments of consumers and organisations and reap high profits through customer satisfaction and economies of scale. One potential disadvantage of differential marketing strategy is loss of cost economics.

Focus Marketing

Focused marketing allows research and development expenditure to be concentrated on meeting the needs of one set of customers and managerial activities are devoted for understanding and catering to these needs.

Large organisations may not be interested in serving the needs of this one segment or their energies may be so dissipated across the whole market that they pay insufficient attention to the requirement of this small segment.

One danger that such niche marketers face is attracting competition from larger organisations in the industry, if they are very successful.

Customised Marketing

In some markets, the requirements of individual customers are unique and their purchasing power is sufficient to make designing a separate marketing mix for each customer a viable option. Customised marketing is also found within organisational markets because of high value of orders and special needs of customers.

Customised marketing is associated with close relationships between the supplier and customer because the high value of an order justifies large marketing and sales effort being focused on each buyer.

Market Positioning

It is the process of portraying a picture of company's product and its customer relation in the minds of customers. It is the act of designing the company's offering and image to occupy a distinct place in the target's mind.

Consumer Behaviour

Consumer behaviour is the process through which the ultimate buyer makes the purchasing decisions. The study of consumer behaviour is the study of how individuals make decisions to spend their available resources on consumption related items. It includes the study of what they buy, why they buy it, when they buy it, from where they buy it, how often they buy it and how often they use it.

Consumer behaviour may be defined as, "The decision process and physical activity individuals engage in when evaluating, acquiring and using or disposing of goods and services."

According to **Jacobs**, "Consumer behaviour reflects the totality of consumer's decisions with respect to the acquisition, usage and disposition of goods, services, time and ideas by human decision-making units."

Buying Decision Process

Consumer passes through different stages while purchasing the product which are as follows

Need Recognition The process of buying starts when a person realises that he has a problem or an unsatisfied need. A need can be arised internally or by an external stimulus. Internal stimuli are customer's desire attitude or perception and external stimuli are advertising etc.

Information Search A consumer, who realises the need for a product will try to gather information regarding the product. Information search helps the customer understand the feature of a product and competing brands better.

Evaluation of Alternatives In this stage, a customer analyses the information available with him to select the right brand or product. The criteria to evaluate a product may differ depending either on the buying situation or on the level of involvement required. Sales personnel can help customer evaluate the product or brand features *vis-a-vis* other products.

Purchase Decision and Purchase Selection or purchase of a particular brand is dependent on the evaluation criteria and ratings. The purchase decision also depends on the availability of the brand as consumer buy the most preferred brand. Affordability also play an important role at this stage.

Post Purchase Evaluation of Decision A customer evaluates the performance of a product after buying it. The consumer will either be satisfied or dissatisfied after this evaluation. Buyer's post purchase feelings are important to marketers. The post purchase evaluation might either lead to repeat purchase and the buyer talking favourably about the product to others or the buyer may talk negative about firm's product.

Factors Influencing Consumer Buying Decisions

The factors that influence the consumer buying decisions include cultural, social, personal and psychological factors which are as follows

Cultural Factors

Culture It is considered as a set of rules, values, beliefs, behaviour and concepts, *i.e.* is common to and binds together the member of a society.

The diversity of cultures across the world calls for marketers to adopt different approaches and use variations in their marketing mix to cater to the needs of those markets.

Sub-culture Every culture has its own set of sub-culture. A sub-culture is a culture followed by a group of people within a culture, *i.e.* distinctly identified within a larger society. To tackle the problems created by sub-cultural differences, marketers need to understand the requirements of the sub-cultural groups and adopt strategies like altering the product, promotion, packaging or price suitable to these groups.

Social Class It refers to the classification of members of the society into a hierarchy of distinct classes, so that every individual in a class has approximately same position in the society. Social class can be sub-divided into four categories *viz.* upper class, upper-middle class, middle class and lower class.

Every social class prefer to buy distinct products and exhibit brand preferences in categories like clothes, home appliances, furnishings, leisure, food, automobiles etc.

Social Factors

Family, friends, formal social groups, colleagues at work influence the consumer's buying behaviour significantly.

These are as follows

Family Individual's family greatly influence the buying patterns of the individual. Family go through various stages of life cycle, each stage creates different demand for different products and the buying behaviour of the members is greatly influenced by the stage of family life cycle.

Friends It is the next important social group that influences the buying behaviour of the individual. A friendship group is an informal and unstructured group. The influence of this group is significant on individual buying process because things that are not normally discussed with the family member are discussed with friends. Suggestions offered by friends influence an individual's buying behaviour.

Formal Social Groups Members of formal social groups like Lion's Club, Rotary Club etc influence the individual buying behaviour. The members in such groups influence other member during informal discussions or by becoming a role model to other members.

Personal Factors

There are different personal factors, which affect the buying decision process. *These factors are as follows*

Age and Life Cycle Stage Over the life cycle stages, people use different products and their demand for goods and services keep changing. People at different ages will have different tastes in food, clothes, furniture and recreation.

Occupation and Financial Status Occupation and income level of a person have a major impact on his savings and buying behaviour. The financial condition of an individual such as his disposable income, savings, his ability to buy costly products and services on instalments and bear the interest rates etc will have a significant influence on his buying behaviour.

Lifestyle An individual's way of leading his life will determine his lifestyle and this influences his buying behaviour.

Psychological Factors

Psychological factors that influence consumer buying behaviour are

Motivation Customers are influenced by a motive or set of motives, when they have unfulfilled needs. Thus, needs are the motivational elements behind the purchasing decision of customers.

*According to **Maslow**, needs can be classified as*

(a) Physiological (b) Security
(c) Social (d) Esteem
(e) Self-actualisation

Customers tend to satisfy their needs on the basis of the intensity or requirement of the needs.

Perception It is the process by which an individual selects, organises and interprets stimuli into meaningful thoughts and pictures. Customers base their perception on their needs, wants, past experiences and something that they consider to be true. Understanding the customer's perception helps the marketers position their product better than that of competitors.

Learning It is learned behaviour of the consumer, here it changes the behaviour of the consumer, which he gained from his past experiences (after using same or similar products).

Beliefs and Attitude The beliefs and attitude held by people influence their buying behaviour.

Buyer Behaviour Models

The more rational part of a consumer's behaviour or his evaluation of the choices before him has been expressed in several models. *These are as follows*

Conjunctive Model Here, the consumer finds minimum levels for each attribute of a product or service, he considers desirable. He eliminates those products/services that fall short on any of these attributes.

Disjunctive Model Here, the consumer considers what meets atleast one minimum attribute level.

Expectancy Value Here, the consumer assigns weights to each attribute according to its importance and calculate the expectancy value of each product/service. He then chooses the one with maximum expectancy value.

Lexicographic Model Here, the attributes are ranked in order of their importance. The consumer will compare the objects on the first rank attribute and choose the superior one.

EXAM BASED QUESTIONS

Marketing, it's Channels, Marketing Mix and Planning

1 Which concept of marketing is/are customer oriented?
(a) Old concept of marketing
(b) Modern concept of marketing
(c) Entity concept of business
(d) All of the above

2 Marketing is often considered synonymous with
(a) selling
(b) advertising
(c) Both (a) and (b)
(d) None of the above

3 .... is the process of planning and executing the conception, pricing, promotion and distribution of ideas, goods and services to create exchanges that satisfy individual and organisational objectives.
(a) Marketing (b) Selling
(c) Advertising (d) Planning

4 The first objective in marketing is
(a) brainstorming
(b) discovering the needs of perspective consumers
(c) promotion of product to make consumers aware of its existence
(d) None of the above

5 According to the societal marketing concept, who is most important in deciding what needs and wants are good for consumers in the long run?
(a) The organisation itself
(b) The individual consumers
(c) Regulatory bodies
(d) None of the above

6 Marketing concept is based on the belief that
(a) the company's planning and operations are customer oriented
(b) the goals of the company should be profitable sales volume and not just volume
(c) all the marketing activities need not be coordinated effectively
(d) Both (a) and (b)

7 Organisations must strive to alter, adopt and develop their products to keep pace with ever changing customer preferences and desire. This is important feature of
(a) marketing concept
(b) exchange concept
(c) production concept
(d) None of the above

8 Marketing deals with .... and meeting human and social needs.
(a) identifying (b) rejecting
(c) Both (a) and (b) (d) None of these

9 The major instruments of marketing in the hands of management are
(a) product (b) promotion
(c) price (d) All of these

10 The .... is the idea that an organisation should seek to satisfy the wants of consumers, while also trying to achieve the organisations goals.
(a) selling concept (b) production concept
(c) marketing concept (d) None of these

11 The exchange concept of marketing takes place between .... and ....
(a) seller, buyer (b) customer, consumer
(c) consumer, buyer (d) buyer, purchaser

12 Marketing stresses on needs of the buyer, whereas selling stress on the need of
(a) market (b) seller
(c) product (d) consumer

13 Find the true statement?
(a) Marketing is waste of the employees' time
(b) Marketing is not required in India due to its vast population
(c) Marketing involves additional work
(d) Marketing involves team work

14 How do you distinguish marketing and selling?
(a) They are one and same
(b) Marketing is a part of selling
(c) Selling is a part of marketing
(d) None of the above

15 Which one is not a function of marketing?
(a) Identification of customer needs and wants
(b) Product planning and development
(c) Guiding the funding agencies
(d) Communicating

16 In marketing, selling and buying would be called the
(a) primary function (b) secondary function
(c) exchange function (d) profit function

17 According to Peter Drucker, the focus of a business is not .... but ....
(a) customers, profits
(b) profits, customers
(c) profits, new markets
(d) new markets, customers

18 The need or want for a particular product becomes a demand, when
(a) the product/service is available
(b) it is backed by buying power
(c) a product represents that particular need
(d) All of the above

19 Social marketing concept is based upon
(a) large target market with active buyers
(b) customer satisfaction and customer welfare
(c) realisation of maximum profit through service of society
(d) None of the above

20 Which of the following is/are objective(s) of marketing?
(a) Satisfying customers and increasing demand
(b) Creating goodwill for the organisation
(c) Providing better quality products
(d) All of the above

21 Exchange concept of marketing deals with
(a) exchange of products between sellers and buyers covering distribution and price aspects
(b) mere appendage to production
(c) achieving marketing success through product attributes
(d) aggressively promote and push the products

22 Which one of the following contains the three elements of service marketing triangle?
(a) Management, Marketing Agency and Consumer
(b) Marketing Agency, Government and Consumer
(c) Management, Employees and Marketing Agency
(d) Management, Employees and Consumer

23 In this stage of business cycle, employment rate is high, interest rates are low, inflation is low and income is high.
(a) Growth/prosperity (b) Recession
(c) Depression (d) Recovery

24 Which of the following channels of distribution is correct?
(a) Manufacturer → Agents → Wholesalers → Retailers → Consumer
(b) Manufacturer → Agents → Retailers → Consumers
(c) Both (a) and (b)
(d) None of the above

25 Which one of the following element is not in the marketing mix?
(a) Price (b) Product
(c) Storage (d) Promotion

26 The concept of marketing mix involves a deliberate and careful choice of organisation, product, price, promotion and place strategies and
(a) policies
(b) concept
(c) planning
(d) All of the above

27 Which one of the following is controllable variable of marketing management?
(a) Environment (b) Competition
(c) Consumer (d) Price

28 The choice of marketing mix does not depends upon
(a) the marketing environment of the organisation
(b) employee objectives
(c) marketing organisation structure and information system
(d) All of the above

29 Promotion mix is the particular combination of promotional tools used by a company to .... with its audiences.
(a) plan (b) communicate
(c) decide (d) None of these

30 Among the four P's of marketing, 'place' includes
(a) types of intermediaries (b) public relation
(c) location of cutlets (d) Both (a) and (c)

31 Conditions necessary for exchange are
(a) atleast two parties must be involved
(b) each party must have something that interests the other
(c) Both (a) and (b)
(d) None of the above

32 .... reduce the demand for a product or service on a temporary or permanent basis.
(a) Counter marketing (b) Mega marketing
(c) Demarketing (d) None of these

33 Convenience goods are those which are
(a) consumed easily (b) distributed easily
(c) purchased frequently (d) None of these

34 Grading is an important process in the functions of
(a) standardisation (b) specialisation
(c) Both (a) and (b) (d) Neither (a) nor (b)

35 Promotion media are the various vehicles that corporation can use to carry their promotion.
(a) Audience (b) Managers
(c) Owners (d) None of these

36 Which of the following will not lead to change in the marketing mix of a product?
(a) Change in corporate/competitive strategy of the firm
(b) Change in the organisation or resource level of the firm
(c) Rigidness in the product lines of the firm
(d) All of the above

37 .... occurs when a marketer is excessively pre-occupied with product development, manufacturing or selling and ignores customer needs, wants and interests.
(a) Customisation (b) Target marketing
(c) Marketing myopia (d) None of these

38 .... is/are the ways to overcome marketing myopia.

(a) Be customer led not product oriented
(b) Market orientation should be permitted through out the organisation
(c) Managers need to be proactive and visionary
(d) All of the above

39 Of the following, the item that is most likely to be a shopping good to most people is

(a) a TV set (b) health food
(c) toothpaste (d) None of these

40 Goods purchased by individuals for their own personal use rather than for business or industrial use is called ....

(a) convenience goods (b) capital goods
(c) consumer goods (d) None of these

41 .... places the customer at the beginning as well as at the end of the business cycle.

(a) Functional integration (b) Customer orientation
(c) Marketing myopia (d) None of these

42 .... shows the actual time of starting a particular programme.

(a) Programmes (b) Schedules
(c) Procedures (d) Policies

43 .... indicates that if company's future seems to be bright, its present policies should be continued.

(a) Diagnosis (b) Prognosis
(c) Strategy (d) None of these

44 .... suggest how to use the company's strategies to achieve its objectives.

(a) Tactics (b) Programmes
(c) Schedules (d) None of these

45 Internal factors affecting marketing planning are

(a) size of the company
(b) risk bearing capacity of the company
(c) price trends in the country
(d) Both (a) and (b)

46 Customer orientation is .... to development and someone within the organisation must have the foresight to see that there are .... prospects for what has been developed.

(a) not important, immediate
(b) critical, commercial
(c) non-important, commercial
(d) critical, non-commercial

47 Which of the following is not a part of strategic planning?

(a) Purposes and mission (b) Objectives
(c) Choice of businesses (d) Social responsibility

48 The strategy of introducing a product with high introductory price is called

(a) penetration strategy (b) skimming strategy
(c) pull strategy (d) push strategy

49 In the first stage of the new product development process, the company determines which markets it wants to enter, this is known as ....

(a) opportunity identification
(b) testing
(c) introduction
(d) life cycle management

50 All of the following factors are correlated with successful new product introductions except

(a) a superior product with throughout product benefits
(b) a strong market orientation unouged the new product development process
(c) the appropriate organisational structure
(d) strong retailiation by competitors

51 .... assess whether the marketing policies, programmes, systems and methods established in the distant past are valid for today.

(a) Ratio analysis
(b) Marketing audit
(c) Credit control
(d) None of the above

52 Of the following, the statement that best expresses the basic idea behind the marketing concepts is

(a) produce the best possible product
(b) produce the cheapest possible product
(c) try to reduce the cost of marketing
(d) keep the consumer foremost in mind

53 The price of a product must be relevant to the

(a) utility or satisfaction it delivers to buyers
(b) amount of profit the sellers can obtain
(c) availability of substitutes
(d) None of the above

54 Marketing concept involves following ideas.

(a) Marketing department becomes the main management force in a company
(b) The company becomes completely consumer oriented
(c) Both (a) and (b)
(d) Neither (a) nor (b)

55 "The marketing concept is a customer orientation backed by integrated marketing aimed at generating customer satisfaction as the key to satisfying organisational goals." Who said it?

(a) P Kataler
(b) Kotler
(c) LG Peter
(d) None of the above

56 Arrange the following elements of marketing in their correct order.

1. Planning 2. Strategy
3. Tactics 4. Research

Codes

(a) 1, 2, 3, 4 (b) 4, 2, 1, 3
(c) 2, 3, 4, 1 (d) 3, 2, 1, 4

57 Marketing can be viewed as an activity that takes the basic physical characteristics of a product, adds value to it and makes it attractive targeted segments of the buying population. This value added activity could be

(a) brand (b) customer service
(c) packaging (d) All of these

58 Traditional marketing focused on .... while today's marketers must focus on .... as the end result of a successful marketing strategy.

(a) transactions, relationships
(b) customer, profits
(c) profits, products
(d) relationships, transactions

59 All of the following are true regarding marketing except

(a) only those, who work in the traditional marketing department are charged with performing marketing activities
(b) any individual inside of an organisation, who can potentially win or lose customers is in marketing
(c) marketing is involved whenever individuals or organisations have a choice to make
(d) any set of activities attemting to influence consumer choice is marketing

60 Which of the following factors affects the choice of channel of distribution?

1. Size of manufacturer
2. Desire to control the channel
3. Perishability of product
4. Weight of product
5. Number of customers

Select the correct answer using the codes given below

Codes

(a) Only 2 (b) Both 4 and 5
(c) Both 3 and 4 (d) None of the above

61 Which of the following statement is true about 'production era'?

(a) Supply creates its own demand
(b) Consumer is king
(c) Focus only on selling products to consumers
(d) None of the above

62 All of the following statements are true except.

(a) It costs more to get a new customer than to keep an existing one
(b) Marketers that can retain more customers by satisfying them better than competitors will have profitable products in the long-run not just the short-run
(c) A product with low brand loyalty will have a higher lifetime customer value than a product with high brand loyalty
(d) Marketing managers will have to focus on the relationship between the organisation and the customer as the end result of a successful marketing strategy

63 Consider the following statements.

1. Assembling and managing the marketing mix is the crux of the marketing task.
2. Assembling the marketing mix is a continuous task.
3. Public relation is a key ingredient in the marketing mix.

Which of the statement(s) given above is/are correct?

Codes

(a) Only 1
(b) Only 2
(c) Only 3
(d) All of the above

64 Accordingly marketing managers, in developing a product line strategy, do not address the following issue.

(a) How many products should be in the line?
(b) How should the products in the line be targeted and differentiated?
(c) How should the products be manufactured?
(d) How should resources be allocated across the line to maximise profits or market share?

65 Which of the following are the merits of marketing planning?

1. Identification of future development.
2. Consideration of opportunities and problems.
3. Focus on objectives.
4. Profitable employment of resources.

Select the correct answer using the codes given below

Codes

(a) Only 1
(b) Both 1 and 2
(c) 1, 2 and 3
(d) All of the above

66 .... is the new product introduction factor that refers to knowing the target market, specifying the benefits to be delivered to the target customers, having a basic idea of how the product will be positioned and finalising the features and attributed.

(a) Strong market orientation
(b) Careful launch planning
(c) Sharp product definition
(d) Detailed new product development process

67 Which of the following characterisitics of a technology driven organisation is incorrect?

(a) The philosophy is 'what we make, we sell'
(b) Focus is on the research and development groups as well as sales
(c) Much money is spent on marketing research and test marketing until the product is finally made
(d) Understand that customers buy products that the product features provide and do not inherently want to buy products

68 When the ideal selling price is first determined and the feasibility of meeting that price is assessed and costs are controlled in order to produce product that can be sold at the target price, this is called

(a) market development (b) price determination
(c) target costing (d) product development

69 Which of the following is the main reason, many experts believe that relying on customers for new products, particularly true innovations, is doomed to failure?

(a) Customers' limited ability to see into the future and conceptualise what could be
(b) Customers could be biased and purchase only expension products
(c) Customers don't have the time to think about new products
(d) Customers not wanting the submit new ideas to the organisation

Market Segmentation

70 In ...., companies attempt to give customers the perception that they are being lived as unique segments.

(a) mass customisation (b) mass marketing
(c) global marketing (d) international marketing

71 One criterion that should always be applied to market segmentation is

(a) parsimony (b) homogeneity
(c) mass marketing (d) image appeal

72 Which of the following levels of market segmentation typically entails marketing to a small market whose needs are not well served?

(a) Segment marketing
(b) Niche marketing
(c) Local marketing
(d) Individual marketing

73 Market segments can be built-up in many ways, such as preference segments .... preferences occur, when the market reveals distinct preference groups, called natural market segments.

(a) clustered (b) natural
(c) homogeneous (d) diffused

74 A segmentation approach would develop .... advertising campaigns focusing on each benefit purchased by the members of each segment.

(a) general (b) separate
(c) price oriented (d) cost efficient

75 Market segmentation provides a focused approach to winning the game by answering the issues.

(a) Which groups of users should we serve?
(b) With whom we will complete?
(c) Neither (a) nor (b)
(d) Both (a) and (b)

76 A marketing manager's task is to identify variables that describe customers in terms of their own particular characteristics. These variables are called

(a) demographic (b) descriptors
(c) geographic (d) behavioural

77 .... is the process of dividing a potential market into distinct sub-markets of consumers with common needs and characteristics.

(a) Target marketing (b) Differentiation
(c) Market segmentation (d) None of these

78 In .... segmentation, buyers are divided into different groups on the basis of life style or personality and values.

(a) demographic (b) psychographic
(c) behavioural (d) None of these

79 .... is a market average strategy, in which company follows' one product one segment' drupe.

(a) Concentrated marketing (b) Market positioning
(c) Target marketing (d) None of these

80 When buyers have too narrow image of the brand, this error is

(a) under positioning (b) over positioning
(c) doubtful positioning (d) confused positioning

81 When product is positioned as offering the best value, it is called?

(a) User positioning
(b) Quality or price positioning
(c) Product category positioning
(d) None of the above

82 .... involves concentrating on the different needs of a customer group.

(a) Market specialisation (b) Selective specialisation
(c) Product specialisation (d) None of these

83 In ...., company position itself on an attribute such as size or number of years in existence.

(a) benefit positioning
(b) attribute positioning
(c) quality or price positioning
(d) None of the above

84 .... is the out of designing the company's offering and image to occupy a distinctive plan in the target customers.

(a) Positioning
(b) Image differentiation
(c) Product differentiation
(d) None of the above

85 Generally, a niche is a small segment of the market that has some specific

(a) satisfied need (b) unsatisfied need
(c) basic need (d) None of these

86 What type of major segmentation variable for business markets would be applicable to business customers that buy products or services based on urgency of need?

(a) Operating approaches (b) Purchasing approaches
(c) Situational factors (d) Personal characteristics

87 When marketing managers select, which segments to pursue, it is called

(a) analysing the competition
(b) selecting the target market
(c) promoting the product
(d) consumer behaviour analysis

88 The concept of segmentation is important because it implies an understanding that customers are

(a) the same (b) do not offer
(c) homogeneous (d) heterogeneous

89 Why do a segmentation approach to the market is more efficient than a mass market approach?

(a) Because money is spent only on those whom the manager has determined are potential customers
(b) Because money is spent on both customers and non-customers evenly
(c) Because customers are homogeneous
(d) Because consumer's tasters are all the same

90 Consider the following statement about segmentation?

1. Help in understanding needs of consumer.
2. Customer gets more customised product.
3. Does not enlavage innovation.
4. Helps in preparing a better competitive strategy.

Which of the statement(s) given above is/are correct?

Codes

(a) Both 1 and 2 (b) 1, 2 and 4
(c) 1, 2 and 3 (d) None of the above

91 When companies try to create brand awareness among customers even before positioning the brand clearly in the market, it is called

(a) doubtful positioning (b) over positioning
(c) confused positioning (d) under positioning

92 The requisite of segmentation, which is different on 4 Ps and programme is

(a) substantial (b) allersible
(c) differentiable (d) actionable

93 Which variable is related to the marketing decision taken by an enterprise?

1. Internal variable 2. Marketing decision variable
3. Sole variables 4. Demand variables

Select the correct answer using the codes given below

Codes

(a) Both 1 and 4
(b) Both 1 and 2
(c) Both 1 and 3
(d) Both 3 and 4

94 To which of the following categories of business are cycle defined in years most related as an evaluation?

(a) Fast food, utilities and long distance telephone services
(b) Retail shopping and movies
(c) Ice cream, soft drinks and cold remedies
(d) Durably goods replacement cycles

95 All of the issues below help to determine whether a particular segmentation scheme is useful except

(a) do the people in different segments behave differently towards the product or service
(b) would we use different marketing elements with the different segments
(c) would the different segments behave differently of different marketing elements were used
(d) if the different segments do not behave differently, then we would apply market segmentation

96 Which of the following are three important criteria on which a firm should base its segmentation strategy decisions?

(a) Measurable, substantial, differentiable
(b) Measurable, geographic, marketable
(c) Measurable, meaningful, marketable
(d) None of the above

97 One of the criteria for a variable segment, is that it must be sustantial. The means

(a) that the segment is one that is large enough to have sufficient sales and growth potential to offer long-run profits for the firm
(b) the segment is one that be easily reached
(c) the size, profile and other relevant characteristics must be measurable
(d) All of the above

98 The 'Times of India' publish local editors for different regions such as 'The Hyderabad Times' for its Hyderabad editors. Here, consumer market is segmented on the basis of

(a) geographic features
(b) psychographic features
(c) demographic features
(d) None of the above

99 The .... and .... are the two elements of marketing strategy that determine the success of a product in the market place.

(a) target market, price
(b) target market, product
(c) product, price
(d) None of the above

Consumer Behaviour

100 Religion is one of the .... factor that influence consumer behaviour.

(a) social (b) personal
(c) cultural (d) psychological

101 The habit of the people to analyse the information completely and interpreting, it is called as
(a) self-actualisation (b) selective attention
(c) selective distortion (d) selective retention

102 The process of acquiring, interpreting, selecting and organising sensory information is called as
(a) perception (b) self-actualisation
(c) selective retention (d) selective distortion

103 Which of these are related with Maslow's basic need theory?
(a) Esteemed need (b) Seller's need
(c) Distributor's need (d) None of these

104 In the buying decision process, what is the term used for a person, who first suggests buying the product?
(a) Consumer (b) Initiator
(c) Decider (d) Influence

105 Which of the following influences consumer's buying behaviour?
(a) Consumer's identity
(b) Consumer's beliefs and needs
(c) Altitudes and kind of product
(d) All of the above

106 .... is a culture followed by a group of people within a culture that is definitely identified within a larger society.
(a) Values (b) Beliefs
(c) Sub-culture (d) None of these

107 Which type of customers should be analysed to help understand weakness in your product or service operations?
(a) Competitors customers
(b) Former customers
(c) People who have never purchased the product
(d) Current customers

108 Analysing................. helps you to understand how to expand the market and achieve sales level closer to market potential?
(a) competition customers
(b) former customers
(c) current customers
(d) people who never purchased the product

109 Under which method, product is launched in a particular area of market?
(a) Test method (b) Product test method
(c) Market test method (d) Trend analysis

110 Values affect customer behaviour in the
(a) short run (b) long run
(c) Both (a) and (b) (d) None of these

111 Variables for segmenting market on the basis of the purchase behaviour of customers are
(a) obansions (b) benefits
(c) loyalty (d) All of these

112 The experimental product positioning includes
(a) provide sensory stimulation
(b) provide cognitive stimulation
(c) Both (a) and (b)
(d) social meaningfulness

113 There is a close link between .... and brand loyality.
(a) social class (b) habits
(c) perception (d) None of these

114 .... are consumers, who buy one brand all the time.
(a) Shifting loyals (b) Switchers
(c) Hand-care loyals (d) None of these

115 .... are those customers who are not brand specific.
(a) Switchers (b) Split loyals
(c) Both (a) and (b) (d) Neither (a) nor (b)

116 .... is the term that describes the actions, a person takes in purchasing and using products and services.
(a) Consumer behaviour
(b) Consumer management
(c) Consumer sovereignty
(d) None of the above

117 By studying about ...., a company can pin point, which brands are most competitive with its air?
(a) switchers (b) shifting loyals
(c) split loyals (d) None of these

118 Which of the following attitudes and behaviour are influenced by culture?
(a) Sense of self and space
(b) Dress and appearance
(c) Both (a) and (b)
(d) None of the above

119 In case of ...., individual tries to resent the values and beliefs of such a group.
(a) disclaiment reference group
(b) avoidance group
(c) aspiration reference group
(d) None of the above

120 The third stage in buyer decision process for new products is
(a) awareness (b) evaluation
(c) interest (d) trial

121 The customer group who adopt the new product at the end are called as
(a) laggards (b) seekers
(c) strivers (d) None of these

122 Customer satisfaction or dissatisfaction is determined in .... stage of consumer decision process.
(a) information search (b) evaluation of alternative
(c) purchase (d) past purchase

123 Customers .... be able to tell you what products they want and need, but they .... be able to tell you what problems they are having with current products and the benefits they would like to be obtain from new ones.
(a) will not always, will always
(b) will always, will not always
(c) never, sometimes
(d) sometimes, never

124 Which of the following methods is best for developing a complete picture of customer behaviour in the relevant product category on market?
(a) Co-joint analysis
(b) Customer analysis
(c) Perpetual map
(d) Segmentation research

125 Which of the following types of variables characterises the psychological differences between people in terms of lifestyles, personalities and social class?
(a) Geographic (b) Demographic
(c) Psychographic (d) Behavioural

126 Which of the following examples is not a demographic variable?
(a) Age (b) Gender
(c) Lifestyle (d) Income

127 Which of the following best describes the first step any kind of purchasing behaviour or reasons why people purchase what they do?
(a) Need recognition (b) Purchase anticipation
(c) Alternative evaluation (d) Post-purchase dissonance

128 .... sources of information are those that are retrieved from memory.
(a) Internal (b) External
(c) Permanent (d) Temporary

129 .... memory can be stimulated by any kind of information.
(a) Short-term (b) Immediate term
(c) Long- term (d) Temporary

130 For frequently purchased products, ... is critical to success because of the lack of new, untapped buyers.
(a) trial (b) repeat buying
(c) brand awareness (d) brand equity

131 Dissonance reducing behaviour is
(a) significant difference between brands and high involvement
(b) significant difference between brands and low involvement
(c) few differences between brands and high involvement
(d) few differences between the brands and low involvement

132 What is one of the theories in regard to buying behaviour?
1. Inherent and learned buying motives
2. Emotional buying
3. Rational buying motives
4. Confessional buying motives
Select the correct answer using codes given below
(a) 1, 2 and 4 (b) 2, 3 and 4
(c) 1, 2 and 3 (d) 1, 3 and 4

133 Which of the following is an uncontrollable variable(s)?
1. Consumer variable
2. Environmental variable
3. Common variable
4. Competitive variable
Select the correct answer using codes given below
Codes
(a) 1, 2 and 3 (b) 1, 2 and 4
(c) 2, 3 and 4 (d) 3, 4 and 1

134 Which of the following buying process sequence is correct?
1. Adoption 2. Legitimisation
3. Attitude 4. Awareness
Select the correct answer using the codes given below
Codes
(a) 4, 3, 2, 1 (b) 2, 3, 4, 1 (c) 1, 2, 3, 4 (d) 3, 4, 2, 1

135 Making connections between two or more ideas or simply observing the outcomes of others behaviours and adjusting one's own behaviour accordingly is what type of learning?
(a) Behavioural learning (b) Lognitive learning
(c) Brand loyalty (d) None of the above

136 Buying situations may be caused by
(a) awareness about competing brands in a product group
(b) customer has a decision criteria
(c) customer is able to evaluate and decide on his choice
(d) All of the above

137 Economic theory suggests that rational customers will collect information only to the point at which
(a) the marginal benefit of obtaining the information in terms of incremental value to making a choice equals the marginal cost
(b) they are exhausted
(c) they can no longer pay for syndicated information
(d) the marginal benefit of obtaining the information in terms of incremental value to making a choice is less than the marginal cost

138 Which of the following listed terms best describes the set of products that the customer has no intension of buying?
(a) Evoked or consideration set
(b) Inert set
(c) Purchase set
(d) Positive set

Miscellaneous

139 **Statement** I Lead means a prospect, who is more likely to avail of the banker's product.

Statement II Market information means knowledge of customer profile and product mix.

Codes

(a) Both statements are true
(b) Both statements are false
(c) Statement I is true, but Statement II is false
(d) Statement I is false, but Statement II is true

Directions (Q. Nos. 140-148) *In the questions given below are two statements labelled as Assertion (A) and Reason (R). In the context of the two statements, which one of the following is correct?*

Codes

(a) Both (A) and (R) are true and (R) is the correct explanation of (A)
(b) Both (A) and (R) are true, but (R) is not the correct explanation of (A)
(c) (A) is true, but (R) is false
(d) (A) is false, but (R) is true

140 **Assertion** (A) Customer becomes the focal point in marketing concept.

Reason (R) In marketing concept, customer orientation places the customer at the beginning as well as at the end of the business cycle.

141 **Assertion** (A) The marketing concept is a way of thinking or a management philosophy that affects most efforts of the organisation.

Reason (R) Marketing concept is based on product orientation.

142 **Assertion** (A) Marketing adds value to the product by storing it from the time of its manufacture to the time it is needed.

Reason (R) It is place utility. In order to have value an item must be in the right place.

143 **Assertion** (A) Marketing mix is a mix of markets for optimum sales.

Reason (R) Marketing mix can notes four P's-product, price, promotion and physical distribution of goods.

144 **Assertion** (A) Marketing mix refer to all or a particular combination of activities a firm uses in marketing its products.

Reason (R) It consists of the product itself, channels of distribution, pricing and promotion and a firm must decide which combination of these elements will best accomplish its marketing objectives.

145 **Assertion** (A) A product may be both a consumer good and an industrial good at the same time.

Reason (R) A product that is a convenience good to one person may be shopping good or speciality good to another person.

146 **Assertion** (A) Standardising and grading mean the same thing.

Reason (R) Standardising and grading are basic marketing functions, but while assigned grades attest the quality of products such as eggs, milk, wheat etc, standardising aims at maintenance of uniform size and quality standards.

147 **Assertion** (A) To an extent, social class determines the type, quality and quantity of products that a person buys or uses.

Reason (R) Every social class prefer to buy distinct products and exhibits brand preferences in categories likes clothes, home appliances, furnishing its.

148 **Assertion** (A) Generation plays a major role in segmenting markets.

Reason (R) Every generation is deeply influenced by various activities of its time like movies, politics, society, music etc.

Directions (Q. No. 149-151) *In the questions given below are two statements labelled as Assertion (A) and Reason (R). In the context of the two statements, which one of the following is correct?*

Codes

(a) Both (A) and (R) are true
(b) Both (A) and (R) are false
(c) (A) is true, but (R) is false
(d) (A) is false, but (R) is true

149 **Assertion** (A) Customer is the centre point of marketing concept.

Reason (R) Customer orientation is called as the pillar of marketing concept.

150 **Assertion** (A) Consumer purchases are influenced by the internal psychological and personal characteristics and external social and environmental influences.

Reason (R) The role and status of a person does not influence buying behaviour.

151 **Assertion** (A) Customers base their perception on their needs, wants, past experience and something that they consider to be true.

Reason (R) Perception helps marketers to position their product better than that of competitors.

152 Match the following.

List I	List II
A. Product concept	1. Marketing myopia
B. Production concept	2. Mass production and distribution
C. Marketing concept	3. Customer satisfaction
D. Societal marketing concept	4. Ethical marketing practices

Codes

	A	B	C	D
(a)	1	2	3	4
(b)	2	3	4	1
(c)	4	1	2	3
(d)	4	3	2	1

153 Match the following.

List I (Concepts of Marketing)	List II (Features)
A. Exchange concept	1. The company has to aggressively promote and push its products
B. Production concept	2. It holds that exchange of a product between seller and the buyer is the central idea of marketing
C. Product concept	3. Marketing can be managed by managing production
D. Sales concept	4. It tries to achieve marketing success through product attributes

Codes

	A	B	C	D
(a)	4	3	2	1
(b)	2	3	4	1
(c)	3	2	4	1
(d)	4	1	2	3

154 Match the following.

List I (Concepts)	List II (Meanings)
A. Marketing	1. State of felt deprivation of some basic satisfaction in a person
B. Needs	2. The systematic gathering, recording and analysing of marketing data
C. Marketing research	3. All or a particular combination of activities a firm uses in marketing its products
D. Marketing mix	4. The performance of business activities that direct the flow of goods and services from producer to consumers

Codes

	A	B	C	D
(a)	4	3	2	1
(b)	2	3	4	1
(c)	3	2	4	1
(d)	4	1	2	3

155 Match the following.

List I (Era's of Marketing)	List II (Features)
A. Production era	1. Marketers focused their efforts only on selling their products to the customers
B. Sales era	2. It calls upon the marketers to build social, ethical and environmental considerations into marketing process
C. Marketing era	3. Companies focused on mere manufacturing processes
D. Societal marketing era	4. It focused on setting their products

Codes

	A	B	C	D
(a)	3	1	4	2
(b)	4	1	2	3
(c)	2	3	1	4
(d)	2	3	4	1

156 Match the following.

List I	List II
A. Method of market monitoring	1. Finance
B. Aim of successful marketing	2. Needs, wants and demands
C. Basic concept of marketing	3. To monitor media outlets
D. Blood of business	4. To increase sale, profit and output of sellers

Codes

	A	B	C	D
(a)	1	2	3	4
(b)	3	4	2	1
(c)	4	3	2	1
(d)	2	3	1	4

157 Match the following.

List I	List II
A. "Marketing is the delivery of standard of living."	1. Peter F Drucker
B. "Marketing comprises both buying and selling activities."	2. Philip Kotler
C. "Marketing is human activity directed at satisfying needs and wants through exchange process."	3. Paul Mazur
D. "Marketing is a process, which converts a resource, distinct knowledge into a contribution of economic value in the market place."	4. Pyle

Codes

	A	B	C	D
(a)	4	3	1	2
(b)	4	2	3	1
(c)	3	4	2	1
(d)	1	2	4	3

158 Match the following.

List I	List II
A. "Marketing mix is a pack of four sets of variables, namely product variables, price variables, promotion variables and place variables".	1. Wheeler
B. "The marketing mix is the set of marketing tools the firm uses to pursue its marketing objectives in the target market."	2. Cundiff, Still and Govoni
C. "Marketing is the managerial process by which products are matched with markets and through which transfers of ownership are affected."	3. McCarthy
D. "Marketing is concerned with all the resources and activities involved in the flow of goods and services from producer to consumer."	4. Philip Kotler

Codes

	A	B	C	D		A	B	C	D
(a)	2	4	1	3	(b)	1	2	4	3
(c)	4	3	1	2	(d)	3	4	2	1

159 Match the following.

List I	List II
A. Re-marketing	1. .... involves the creation of place utility.
B. Customer satisfaction	2. ....is rebuilding interest in a stable or declining product or service.
C. Transporting	3. Marketers must focus on customer needs and wants to ensure.
D. Storing	4. ....creates time utility because marketers after maintain excessive inventories.

Codes

	A	B	C	D		A	B	C	D
(a)	4	3	2	1	(b)	3	4	1	2
(c)	2	3	1	4	(d)	4	3	1	2

160 Match the following.

List I (Classification of Products)	List II (Explanations)
A. Consumer product	1. Products which are designed for use by ultimate consumers or households
B. Durable product	2. Product which a consumer usually purchase frequently, immediately and with minimum effort
C. Convenience product	3. Products with unique characteristics and/or brand identification for which a significant group of buyers are habitually willing to make a special purchasing effect
D. Speciality product	4. Products which normally survive many use

Codes

	A	B	C	D
(a)	1	2	3	4
(b)	1	4	2	3
(c)	2	1	3	4
(d)	4	3	2	1

161 Match the following.

List I	List II
A. Supply chain	1. Putting the management product in the mind of the prospective buyer
B. Product	2. The process of positioning gathering, filtering and analysing information relating to the marketing environment
C. Marketing	3. Improving the environment performance of analysis dealers through sharpening of their sales skills and product knowledge
D Dealer	4. Larger in scope training than both physical and marketing logistics

Codes

	A	B	C	D		A	B	C	D
(a)	1	2	3	4	(b)	4	1	2	3
(c)	2	4	3	1	(d)	3	4	1	2

162 Match the following.

List I	List II
A. Market segmentation	1. Pricing high of a new product initially.
B. Skimming price	2. Process of disagreegating a market into a number of sub-markets.
C. Multilevel marketing	3. Translation of the marketing plan into marketing performance.
D. Sales management	4. Modified version of direct marketing.

Codes

	A	B	C	D		A	B	C	D
(a)	2	1	4	3	(b)	3	1	2	4
(c)	1	2	3	4	(d)	4	2	3	1

PREVIOUS YEARS' QUESTIONS

December 2018

1 **Assertion** (A) Databases assist in market segmentation, especially behavioural segmentation such as developing loyalty segments.

Reason (R) Customer Relationship Management (CRM) databases have become an asset for the analysis of customer behaviour.

Codes

(a) Both (A) and (R) are correct and (R) is the right explanation of (A)

(b) Both (A) and (R) are correct, but (R) is not the right explanation of (A)

(c) Both (A) and (R) are incorrect

(d) (A) is correct and (R) is incorrect

2 Choose the correct code for the following statements being correct or incorrect.

Statement I A well-chosen marketing channel must be aligned to company's marketing strategy with respect to segmentation, targeting and positioning.

Statement II Marketing channels are set of interdependent organisations participating in the process of making the product available for the use of consumption.

Codes

(a) Both statements are correct

(b) Both statements are incorrect

(c) Statement I is correct, but Statement II is incorrect

(d) Statement II is correct, but Statement I is incorrect

3 To examine whether the company is pursuing its best opportunities with respect to markets, products and channels is the purpose of which one of the following types of marketing control?

Codes

(a) Annual plan control

(b) Profitability control

(c) Efficiency control

(d) Strategic control

4 Match the items of List I with the items of List II and choose the correct answer from the code given below.

List I	List II
A. The economy was characterised by small regional suppliers who sold goods on a local basis	1. Mass marketing
B. Standardised, branded goods were sold at national level	2. Hyper segmentation
C. Era of market differentiation based on demographic, socio-economic and life style factors	3. Segmentation
D. Technological advancements, especially in the area of digital communication allow marketers to communicate with individual consumers or very small groups	4. Fragmentation

Codes

	A	B	C	D
(a)	1	4	2	3
(b)	4	1	3	2
(c)	4	1	2	3
(d)	1	2	3	4

5 Which among the following is not included in seven Ps of marketing mix given by Booms and Bitner?

(a) Process
(b) People
(c) Physical evidence
(d) Politics

July 2018

6 **Statement** I A form of non-store retailing that uses advertising to contact consumers who, in turn, purchase products without visiting a retail store is called direct selling.

Statement II A form of non-store retailing in which personal contact between a sales person and a consumer occurs away from a retail store is called direct marketing.

In the light of above statements, identify the correct code of statements being correct or incorrect.

Codes

(a) Statement I is correct, but Statement II is not correct

(b) Statement I is not correct, but Statement II is correct

(c) Both statements are correct

(d) Both statements are not correct

7 34% of the customers who fall in one of the categories of diffusion process who are deliberate customers to accept an innovation just before the average adopter in a social system. Such customers who are above average in social and economic measures, rely quite a bit on advertisements and salesmen are known as

(a) early adopters
(b) early majority
(c) late majority
(d) late adopters

8 When a company treats each single customer as a separate segment, this is called

(a) niche marketing
(b) nano marketing
(c) single marketing
(d) micro marketing

9 A reduction from the list price that is offered by a seller to buyers in payment for marketing functions, the buyers will perform is known as

(a) trade discount (b) functional discount
(c) cash discount (d) Both (a) and (b)

November 2017

10 When Walt Disney World's Magic kingdom lets customers visit a fairy kingdom, a pirate ship, or a haunted house, then what is marketed in this example?

(a) Services (b) Events
(c) Experiences (d) Ideas

11 Which one of the following statements is true according to VALS framework of psychographic segmentation?

(a) The consumers who are primarily motivated by ideals are guided by knowledge and principles
(b) The consumers who are motivated by achievement look for knowledge and principles
(c) The consumers who are motivated by self expression don't desire social or physical activity, variety and risk
(d) The consumers who are motivated by achievement desire social or physical activity, variety and risk

July 2016

12 Which one of the following is the most likely result of a marketing strategy that attempts to serve all potential customers?

(a) All customers will be delighted
(b) Customer perceived value will be increased
(c) The company will need to follow up with a demarketing campaign
(d) None of the above

December 2015

13 When the consumers favour those products which offer the most quality, performance or innovative features, then it is called as

(a) production concept (b) product concept
(c) sales concept (d) marketing concept

14 A person's distinguishing psychological characteristics that lead of relatively consistent and enduring responses to his or her environment is called

(a) life style (b) self-concept
(c) personality (d) attitude

15 In which of the following types of collective bargaining, one party gains at the expense of the other?

(a) Distributive bargaining (b) Integrative bargaining
(c) Centralised bargaining (d) None of these

June 2015

16 The service marketing mix is an extended marketing mix and includes

1. people 2. process
3. service 4. physical evidence

Select the correct answer using the codes given below

Codes

(a) 2, 3 and 4 (b) 1, 2 and 3
(c) 1, 2 and 4 (d) 1, 3 and 4

17 A common market is one where

(a) all the trading nations agree commonly to levy a common and uniform tariff rate for all goods
(b) all the trading nations agree commonly to rationalise tariff and non-tariff barriers mutually to promote intra-region trade
(c) there is a customs union alongwith free intra-union movement of factors of production
(d) there is an economic union along with free intra-union movement of residents

18 Which of the following can be used by a company as communication mix to reach the target customers?

1. Advertising 2. Sales promotion
3. Events and experiences 4. Public relations
5. Direct marketing 6. Personal selling

Select the correct answer using the codes given below

Codes

(a) 1, 2, 4 and 6 (b) 1 , 2, 5 and 6
(c) 1, 2, 4, 5 and 6 (d) All of the above

19 A marketing network consists of

(a) the tasks to devise marketing activities
(b) the tasks of hiring, training and motivating employees
(c) the activities that help in designing and implementing the marketing programmes
(d) the company and its supporting stakeholders with whom it has built mutually profitable business relationships

20 Target marketing involves which of the following activities?

1. Market positioning 2. Market targeting
3. Market behaviour 4. Market segmentation

Select the correct answer using the codes given below

Codes

(a) Both 1 and 2 (b) Both 2 and 4
(c) 1, 2 and 4 (d) 2, 3 and 4

21 Black box model in marketing relates to

(a) marketing planning (b) marketing mix
(c) marketing control (d) consumer behaviour

22 Items, considered part of the augmented product, do not include

(a) guarantee
(b) warranty
(c) complementary products
(d) channels of distribution

23 **Horizontal marketing system comprises of**
(a) the producer, wholesaler and retailer acting in a unified system
(b) multichannel marketing
(c) two or more marketing channels to reach one or more customer segments
(d) two or more unrelated companies put together resources to exploit an emerging market

24 **Which of the following is not a type of direct marketing?**
(a) Direct mail marketing (b) Retail marketing
(c) Telemarketing (d) Email direct marketing

December 2014

25 **Marketing strategy development is also known as**
(a) marketing control (b) marketing exercise
(c) marketing planning (d) situation analysis

26 **Which of the following is not a method of segmenting a market?**
(a) Behavioural segmentation
(b) Psychographic segmentation
(c) Benefits segmentation
(d) Customer segmentation

December 2013

27 **Which of the following is not the major component of holistic marketing?**
(a) Relationship marketing
(b) Integrated marketing
(c) Customer satisfaction
(d) Sociality responsible marketing

28 **Which of the legislations listed below do not form part of the marketing environment of India?**
(a) The Drugs and Cosmetics Act, 1940
(b) The Prevention of Food and Adulteration Act, 1954
(c) The Monopolies and Restrictive Trade Practices Act, 1969
(d) Both (b) and (c)

29 **In the model of consumer behaviour given by Philip Kotler, what constitutes the marketing stimuli?**
(a) Marketing environment
(b) Four P's of marketing
(c) Consumer needs and wants
(d) None of the above

June 2013

30 **Which of the following concepts is based on development, design and implementation of marketing programmes, processes and activities that recognise their breadth and interdependence?**
(a) Product concept
(b) Sales concept
(c) Societal marketing concept
(d) Holistic marketing concept

31 **The concept of marketing mix, consisting of the four P's of marketing, was developed by**
(a) E Jerome McCarthy (b) Peter F Drucker
(c) Philip Kotler (d) William J Stonton

December 2012

32 **In marketing mix, which four P's are covered?**
(a) Product, Price, Place, Promotion
(b) Product, Price, Power, Promotion
(c) Product, Price, Penetration, Promotion
(d) Product, Price, Positioning, Promotion

33 **Which subject is relevant to the study of consumer behaviour?**
(a) Economics (b) Psychology
(c) Sociology (d) All of these

34 **Which research includes all types of researches into human motives, when it refers to qualitative research designed to uncover the consumer's sub-consciousness or hidden motivations?**
(a) Motivational research (b) Marketing research
(c) Managerial research (d) Price research

June 2012

35 **Which concept of marketing is based on the assumption that superior products sell themselves?**
(a) Production (b) Marketing
(c) Societal (d) Product

36 **Market sub-divided on the basis of behavioural characteristics is called**
(a) segmentation
(b) aggregation
(c) precision
(d) None of the above

37 **Which one of the following is incorrect?**
(a) Marketers arouse emotional motives
(b) Marketers satisfy rational motives
(c) Marketers formulate different sales promotions for different motives
(d) None of the above

38 **Non-store marketing includes**
(a) home selling (b) VPP
(c) vending machines (d) All of these

39 **What is customer delight?**
(a) Performance equal to expectation
(b) Performance less than expectation
(c) Performance more than expectation
(d) Expectation more than performance

40 **Which terms are often used interchangeably in marketing literature?**
(a) Concept, method, philosophy
(b) Concept, approach, technique
(c) Orientation, concept, philosophy
(d) Philosophy, system, concept

41 Which one of the following is not the fundamental procedure that should be considered for the collective bargaining?

(a) Prenegotiation phase
(b) Selection of negotiators
(c) Tactic and strategy bargaining
(d) None of the above

42 'VSAT' technology is first followed for online trading by

(a) BSE (b) OTCEI (c) NSE (d) ISE

43 What is mass marketing?

(a) Offering the same products and marketing mix to all consumers
(b) Offering variety of products to the entire market
(c) Offering differentiated products to all customers
(d) Following concentrated marketing strategy

44 In broader sense, marketing communication includes

(a) product
(c) place
(b) price
(d) All of the above

45 What is relevant to place variable of marketing mix?

(a) Branding
(b) Price penetration
(c) Sales personnel motivation
(d) None of the above

46 Physical distribution provides

(a) place utility
(b) time utility
(c) place and time utility
(d) form utility

ANSWERS

Objective Questions

1 (b)	2 (c)	3 (a)	4 (b)	5 (a)	6 (d)	7 (a)	8 (a)	9 (d)	10 (c)
11 (a)	12 (b)	13 (d)	14 (c)	15 (c)	16 (c)	17 (b)	18 (b)	19 (b)	20 (d)
21 (a)	22 (d)	23 (a)	24 (c)	25 (c)	26 (a)	27 (d)	28 (b)	29 (b)	30 (d)
31 (c)	32 (c)	33 (a)	34 (a)	35 (a)	36 (c)	37 (c)	38 (d)	39 (a)	40 (c)
41 (b)	42 (b)	43 (b)	44 (a)	45 (d)	46 (b)	47 (b)	48 (b)	49 (a)	50 (d)
51 (b)	52 (d)	53 (a)	54 (c)	55 (a)	56 (b)	57 (d)	58 (a)	59 (a)	60 (d)
61 (a)	62 (c)	63 (d)	64 (c)	65 (d)	66 (c)	67 (b)	68 (c)	69 (a)	70 (a)
71 (a)	72 (b)	73 (a)	74 (b)	75 (d)	76 (b)	77 (c)	78 (b)	79 (a)	80 (b)
81 (b)	82 (a)	83 (b)	84 (a)	85 (d)	86 (d)	87 (b)	88 (d)	89 (a)	90 (b)
91 (a)	92 (c)	93 (b)	94 (d)	95 (d)	96 (a)	97 (a)	98 (a)	99 (d)	100 (c)
101 (d)	102 (a)	103 (a)	104 (b)	105 (d)	106 (c)	107 (b)	108 (d)	109 (c)	110 (b)
111 (d)	112 (c)	113 (b)	114 (c)	115 (a)	116 (a)	117 (c)	118 (c)	119 (b)	120 (c)
121 (a)	122 (d)	123 (a)	124 (b)	125 (c)	126 (c)	127 (a)	128 (a)	129 (c)	130 (b)
131 (c)	132 (c)	133 (b)	134 (a)	135 (b)	136 (d)	137 (a)	138 (b)	139 (a)	140 (a)
141 (d)	142 (c)	143 (d)	144 (a)	145 (b)	146 (d)	147 (a)	148 (a)	149 (a)	150 (b)
151 (a)	152 (a)	153 (b)	154 (d)	155 (a)	156 (b)	157 (c)	158 (c)	159 (c)	160 (b)
161 (b)	162 (b)								

Previous Years' Questions

1 (a)	2 (a)	3 (d)	4 (b)	5 (d)	6 (d)	7 (a)	8 (d)	9 (d)	10 (c)
11 (a)	12 (d)	13 (b)	14 (b)	15 (b)	16 (a)	17 (c)	18 (d)	19 (d)	20 (c)
21 (c)	22 (b)	23 (d)	24 (c)	25 (c)	26 (d)	27 (c)	28 (d)	29 (b)	30 (d)
31 (a)	32 (a)	33 (d)	34 (a)	35 (c)	36 (b)	37 (d)	38 (d)	39 (a)	40 (c)
41 (d)	42 (c)	43 (c)	44 (d)	45 (c)	46 (c)				

CHAPTER 30

Service Marketing and Trends in Marketing

Service marketing is a part of marketing which is used to market a service or good. Modern marketing includes social marketing, online marketing and green marketing. Customers are the king of market, so, CRM has an important place in marketing. Logistic management helps an organisation to manage the flow of raw materials and finished goods from the source to the user.

Service Marketing

It is a marketing based on relationship and value. It may be used to market a service or a product. Marketing a service based business is different from marketing a product.

Service marketing is a sub-field of marketing which can be split into the two main areas of goods marketing and services marketing.

It is defined as "the integrated system of business activities designed to plan, price, promote and distribute appropriate services for the benefit of existing and potential consumers to achieve organisational objectives."

Objectives of Service Marketing

Building Trust Building trust in customer's eyes through tangible signs of quality is one of the principle objectives of service marketing.

Establish Uniform Process The provision of services is inherently variable as each instance is different from all others, varying by service delivery personnel, the circumstances of delivery and service environment. Service marketers establish uniform processes to provide consistent delivery service.

Empowering Personnel Service marketing should focus on empowering key players to ensure that they are able to communicate effectively with customers, respond appropriately while giving feedback and in still confidence throughout the service delivery process.

In this Chapter

- *Service Marketing*
- *Social Marketing*
- *Online Marketing*
- *Direct Marketing*
- *Green Marketing*
- *Rural Marketing*
- *Customer Relationship Management*
- *Logistic Management*

Promoting Customer Satisfaction The transient nature of services requires service marketers to manage the peaks and valleys of supply and demand to ensure optimal business performance.

Significance of Service Marketing

Generation of Employment Opportunities The organised and systematic development of the service sector would create enormous employment opportunities. If the service sector is properly developed, it will solve the problem of unemployment.

Optimum Utilisation of Resources The human resources of a country helps in the growth of service sector. The growth of this kind of service firms conserve natural resources which helps in conserving the valuable resources for future generations.

Increasing the Standard of Living The standard of living is determined by the availability of goods and services for people and a wise spending on them. The development of service industry is sure to promote the living standard of people.

Capital Formation There are indications that services will grow more rapidly in the near future. Economic, social and political factors signal an expansion of service sector. If investments are made in the service sector, it will contribute to the nation building process.

Trends in Marketing

Recent developments in manufacturing technologies have made significant changes possible in the way firms respond to market opportunities. There are, however clear trends in the way in which markets are developing that point to the need for further developments in manufacturing technologies and for marketing management. Recent trends in marketing have been emerged significantly. *These have been discussed ahead*

Social Marketing

It emphasises, on social responsibilities and suggests to sustain long-term success. It helps in making good marketing decisions by considering consumer's want's, company's requirements and societies long-term interests.

Social marketing is a marketing of such goods that serve the society. It always aims to promote society's well being as a whole and convince people to adopt a behaviour or product that will improve their quality of life. In India, social marketing is spreading its wings as many corporate houses and government of India is quite keen in such marketing, campaign relating to tobacco is injurious to health is one of the example of it. It is apparent that marketing of goods and services are bounded within the legal framework of the respective country and sometimes they have to follow international standards as well. In marketing arena, there are many issues of which no readily solution is available from the legal domain which shows that company has to follow laws, regulations and ethics simultaneously not anyone part of it. Marketing campaigns in India are governed by government and private bodies and many times, they have adopted strict measures.

Objectives of Social Marketing

- To create a better image in the society for the company than its competitors.
- To maintain long-term relationship with customers.
- To carry out social responsibilities.
- To develop community awareness towards its brands.
- To carry out its social responsibilities.

Advantages of Social Marketing

- It gives a competitive advantage over the competitors.
- It is useful in customer retention and long-term relationship.
- Economic resources are properly used.
- It raises the living standard of the people in society.
- It ensures the economic planning more significant and more fruitful to society.

Disadvantages of Social Marketing

- It exposes strategies to customers.
- It needs qualified personnel.
- It provide slow returns on investment.
- It is time consuming process.

Online Marketing

Online marketing or internet marketing, refers to advertising and marketing efforts that use the web and email to drive direct sales *via* e-commerce as well as sales leads from websites or emails. Internet marketing and online advertising efforts are typically used in conjunction with traditional types of advertising like television, radio, newspapers and magazines.

Types of Online Marketing

Internet marketing can be broken down into more specialised areas such as

Web Marketing It includes e-commerce websites, affiliate marketing websites, promotional or informative websites, online advertising on search engines and organic search engines results *via* Search Engine Optimisation (SEO).

Email Marketing It involves both advertising and promotional marketing efforts *via* email messages to current and prospective customers.

Social Media Marketing It involves both advertising and marketing efforts *via* social networking sites like Facebook, Twitter etc.

Advantages of Online Marketing

Trackable You can measure the number of clicks and impressions your advertisement receives and also measure the amount of traffic it brings to your website. Check out your google analytics guide to find out how you can use it to track the visitors to your website and understand their behaviour.

Targeted You can really pinpoint your target market and reach them in cost effective ways. If you are an online shoe retailer, placing an ad on a fashion or shoe blog is a great way to reach your audience.

Cost Effective The cost of placing an ad online is far less than placing an ad in a newspaper or billboard.

Personalised Internet marketing allows you to tailor your message and ads based on your customer's previous purchase history or preferences. Sending customer personalised email has a far greater impact than sending a generic message to all your email subscribers.

Build Relationships Social media is a great platform for engaging our customers in a two way conversation. You are not just talking to your customers but you are talking with them.

Disadvantages of Online Marketing

Involves High Competition Promoting your business online offers international reach, but it also means that you are competing with other international competitors.

Limited Use Everyone does not use the internet. Consider your target market, do they have access to the internet? Do they use it regularly? You need to truly understand your target audience before you decide to market yourself online.

Lot to Learn There is a lot to learn and the internet is constantly evolving. You might never know everything there is to know about internet marketing, but you can certainly try.

Online Marketing Process

An online marketing process is a broad term to explain. *Generally, it contains following steps*

Research In the first step, the companies/organisation learn what customers want and how they behave/interact with their brand. To a large extent they understand the market forces.

Planning In next step, the companies align research with business goals and capabilities to attract leads into a paying customer.

Implement After planning, companies identify and create content offers and promotion strategies that will get their message out to a qualified audience.

Measure In this step, they prove to leadership that the investments made are yielding incremental results towards their goals.

Optimise Finally, the companies report on goals and refine their strategies that increase the productivity of input > output. Then double down on investment in areas that show promising results.

Direct Marketing

Direct marketing is a type of advertising campaign that seeks to elicit an action (such as an order, a visit to a store or website or a request for further information) from a selected group of consumers in response to a communication from the marketer. The communication itself may be in any of a variety of formats including postal mail, telemarketing, direct email marketing and point of sale interaction. In other words, direct marketing, is just what it sounds like directly reaching a market (customers and potential customers) on a personal basis (phone calls, private mailing) or mass media basis (infomercials, magazine ads etc.)

Direct marketing is often distinguished by aggressive tactics that attempt to reach new customers usually by means of unsolicited direct communication. But it can also reach out to existing or past customers. A key factor in direct marketing is a 'call to action', *i.e.* direct marketing campaigns should offer an incentive or enticing message to get customer to respond (act).

Types of Direct Marketing

Telemarketing Direct marketing that involves calling people at home or work to ask for donations, an opinion or for sales purposes.

Email Direct Marketing This form of direct marketing targets consumers through their email accounts. Email addresses can be harvested from websites, forums or purchased. Some companies require you to receive announcements to use their websites.

Direct Mail Marketing Advertising material sent directly to home and business addresses.

Advantages of Direct Marketing

Selective Reach Direct marketing lets the advertiser reach a large number of people and reduces or eliminates waste coverage. Intensive coverage may be obtained through broadcast advertising or through the mail.

Flexibility Direct marketing can take on a variety of creative forms, *i.e.* the discovery network sent 17inch TV sets to media buyers through the mail.

Timing While many media require long range planning and have long closing dates, direct response advertising can be much more timely. Direct mail, *i.e.* can be put together very quickly and distributed to the target population.

Personalisation No other advertising medium can personalise the message as well as direct media. Parents with children at different age levels can be approached with their child's name included in the appeal.

Measures of Effectiveness No other medium can measure the effectiveness of its advertising efforts as well as direct response. Feedback is after immediate and always accurate.

Disadvantages of Direct Marketing

Accuracy On the advantages cited for direct mail and telemarketing was targeting potential customers specifically. But the effectiveness of these methods depends on the accuracy of the lists used.

Content Support In direct response advertising, mood creation is limited to the surroundings programme and/or editorial content. Direct mail and online services are unlikely to create a desirable mood.

Rising Costs As postal rates increase direct mail profits are immediately and directly impacted.

Green Marketing

Green marketing refers to the process of selling products or services based on their environmental benefits. Such a product or service may by environmental friendly or produced or packaged in an environmental friendly way.

It is the marketing of products that are presumed to be environmentally preferable to others. Thus, green marketing incorporates a broad range of activities, including product modification, changes to the production process. It involves developing and promoting products and services that satisfy customer wants and needs for quality, performance, affordable pricing and convenience, all without a detrimental impact on the environment.

Evolution of Green Marketing

First Phase It was termed as 'ecological' green marketing and during this period, all marketing activities were concerned to help environment problems and provide remedies for environmental problems.

Second Phase It was 'environmental' green marketing and the focus shifted on clean technology that involved designing of innovative new products, which take care of water and pollution issues.

Third Phase It was 'sustainable' green marketing. This was the result of the term sustainable development which is defined as, "meeting the needs of the present without compromising the ability of future generation to meet their own needs."

Advantages/Benefits of Green Marketing

- It ensures sustained long-term growth alongwith profitability.
- It saves money in the long run, through initially the cost is more.
- It helps companies market their products and services keeping the environment aspects in mind.
- It helps in accessing the new markets and enjoying competitive advantage.
- Most of the employees also feel proud and responsible to be working for an environment friendly company.

Disadvantages of Green Marketing

- It change leads to costs as when a company puts effort into changing their brand to be more environmentally friendly, those changes can have expensive upfront costs.
- It is a long and pricely process to obtain the environmental certifications. Particularly because without these official standards customers and industries will have no way of measuring the facts of green 'claims'.
- Majority of the people are not aware of green products and their uses, *i.e.* a big challenge of green marketing.
- Deceptive advertising and false claims are also a major problem for green marketing.
- Green products requires a technology, which requires huge investments in research are development.

Rural Marketing

Rural marketing is promotion of company's products in the rural markets by using strategies which are different from that of urban market. The rural market is more 'price' sensitive but it has preferences for both quantity and quality.

Rural marketing can be defined as a function which manages all those activities in asserting, stimulating and converting the purchasing power of rural people into an effective demand for specific products and services and thereby achieving the goals of the organisation.

Nature of Rural Marketing

Larger Diverse and Scattered Market Rural marketing is large and scattered into a number of regions. There may be less number of shops available to market products.

Major Income of Rural Customers from Agriculture Rural prosperity is tied with agricultural prosperity. In the event of crop failure, the income of masses is directly affected.

Diverse Socio-economic Background Due to difference in geographical areas and uneven land fertility, rural people have different socio-economic background which ultimately affects the rural markets.

Infrastructure Facilities The infrastructure facilities like warehouses, communication system and financial facilities in rural areas, physical distribution are challenge to marketers who has found innovative ways to market their products.

Significance of Rural Marketing

- A market increase in the rural income due to agrarian prosperity.
- Large inflow of investment for rural development programmes from government and other resources.
- Increased contact of rural people with their urban counterparts due to development of transport and a wide communication network.
- Increase in literacy and educational level among rural folks and the resultant inclination to lead sophisticated life.
- Inflow of foreign remittances and foreign made goods in rural areas.

Customer Relationship Management (CRM)

CRM is the development and maintenance of mutually beneficial long-term relationships with strategically significant customers. It is concerned with the creation, development and enhancement of individual customer relationship.

"CRM is the strategic use of information, process, technology and people to manage customer and company's relation."

Benefits of CRM

- It increased sales through better timing due to anticipating needs.
- It focused on effective target marketing communication aimed at customer needs.
- It enhanced customer statisfaction and retention.
- It improved profitability by focusing on the most profitable customers.
- It focused on more personal approach and the development of new or improved products and services.

Objectives of CRM

To Simplify Marketing and Sales Process CRM ensures that the right lead is distributed to the right sales person at the right time.

Increases Sales Effectiveness With the help of CRM, sales department can have instant access to customer information when they need it, without being connected to a computer, which helps them in increased and effective sales.

Reduced Customer Support Cost CRM enables service agents to answer all customers inquiries quickly, accurately and consistently by phone, email chat or in person. Due to maximum offload customer interaction, customer support cost reduced.

Implementation of CRM

To implement CRM, following factors need to be given due consideration

- Easy interaction between customers and company.
- Easy access to information about company like content of customisation , advantages of the company, benefits to the customers.
- Abundant supply of customers.
- Customer's information should be updated.
- Have cordial relationship with other companies targeting the same customer segment.

CRM Techniques

Some techniques which CRM aid in customer retention are as follows

Builds up a Comprehensive Viewing of 'Customer Journey Map' Mapping the customer journey helps in jotting down focal points of customer's experience, from initial contact, through the process of engagement and into a long-term relationship. This will help to asses the strengths and weakness of marketing strategy and also provide guidelines to re-engage the customer, if the rate of engagement has been less.

Targets Customers through Tailor made Offers Identifying ways to convert customer interest into an actual purchase is the main point here, which can be achieved through providing discounts and offers to add value to the experience.

Helps to Create Loyalty Programs Information gathered in CRM software can bring out the varied levels of engagement by the customers, revealing which of the accounts are responsible for the most revenue. This information helps to create loyalty programs for those valued customers.

Personalising the Interactions CRM software helps to see customer beyond the rotes of revenue. The effect of personalisation is of great impact to not only purchase but post purchase relationship, where it is equally essential.

Helps Assess Performances CRM can be utilised through dashboards to review service execution and pinpoint areas for improvement. It assess to develop incentive schemes that reward staff for outstanding performance.

Logistic Management

The word logistics is derieved from French word 'loger' which means art of war pertaining to movement and supply of armies. It means the art of managing the flow of raw materials and finished goods from the source to the user.

According to Council of Logistics Management, "Logistics is the process of planning, implementing and controlling the efficient, effective flow and storage of goods and services and related information from point of origin to point of consumption for the purpose of conforming the customer requirement."

Concept of Logistics

- It is the designing and managing a system in order to control the flow of material throughout an organisation.
- It is similar to a particular organisation's supply chain to the complete value chain of a product.
- In nutshell, logistics is a key to the success of supply chain in management.

Objectives of Logistics

Rapid Response It is concerned with a firm's ability to satisfy customer service requirements in a timely manner. It emphasis to customer requirement on a shipment.

Minimum Variance Variance is an unexpected event that disrupts performance of the system. operational areas of logistics are subject to potential variance. With the use of IT, logistics tries to minimise variance in operations.

Consolidated Movement The most important logistical cost is transportation. Decreasing the transportation cost is desirable to achieve the movement consolidation.

Quality Commitment to 'Total Quality Management' (TQM) is one of the major forces which contributes to logistics. Logistics is a main part of developing and maintaining continuous total quality management improvements.

Create Visibility Logistic management creates visibility into a company's supply chain.

Role of Logistic Management

Logistic management is a key component of the supply chain process that facilitates the strategy, planning and implementation thereby reducing cost significantly and enhancing customer satisfaction. *There are six key functional areas of logistic management, which are as follows*

Inventory Control Inventory management is to keep enough inventories to smooth running of business. The major issue in this function is to keep a complicated balance between carrying less inventory and carry too much of it.

The management of the organisation makes an effective inventory decision to maintain it.

Warehousing An organisation must determine about the important aspects of the functions of warehousing like how many warehouses are required? Which kinds of warehouses are needed? etc. In modern technological age, new, highly automated warehousing replaces the older warehousing system.

Order Processing When an order has been recieved, it should be quickly and accurately processed by the organisation. Now-a-days sophisticated computerised order processing system is used by most of the companies that speeds up the cycle of order, shipping and billing.

Transportation Major logistic function also include the transportation in which certain decisions about the transportation of goods are made in the light of the interest of the organisation.

Customer Service Customer service has been defined as, "a customer oriented philosophy which integrates and manage all elements of the customer interlace within a predetermined optimum cost service mix. It is the output of the logistic system. It involves getting the right product to the right customer at right place.

EXAM BASED QUESTIONS

Service Marketing

1 Service marketing become difficult because of
(a) intangibility
(b) no demand
(c) more complex market
(d) difficult to enter the market

2 Which of the following statements about the pricing of services is false?
(a) The demand for services tends to be more elastic than the demand for goods
(b) Cost oriented pricing is more difficult for services
(c) Comparing prices of competitors is more difficult for service consumers
(d) Customers are less able to stockpile services by taking advantage of discount prices

3 A buyer's perception of value is considered a trade-off between
(a) product value and psychic cost
(b) total customer value and total customer cost
(c) image value and energy cost
(d) service value and monetary cost

4 Services are characterised by all of the following characteristics except for
(a) intangibility
(b) homogeneity
(c) perishability
(d) inseparability

5 Which of the following statement can be considered as false?
(a) Services cannot be touched or seen in the same manner as goods
(b) Consumer judgements about services tends to be more subjective than objectives
(c) Customers involvement affects service quality
(d) None of the above

6 Solutions used to minimise the marketing problems attributed to heterogeneity include
(a) standardising the service
(b) using multi-site locations
(c) stressing tangible clues
(d) appealing to different market segments with different demand patterns

7 Customer satisfaction can be defined by comparing
(a) predicted service and perceived service
(b) predicted service and desired service
(c) desired service and perceived service
(d) adequate service and perceived service

8 Which of the following statement(s) is/are not true?
(a) Service purchases are perceived as riskier than goods purchases
(b) The participation of the consumer in the service process increases the amount of perceived risk
(c) The variability in services increases the perceived risk associated with the purchase
(d) Consumers of services have less purchase information versus goods

Trends in Marketing

9 Email marketing involves
(a) advertising (b) promotional marketing
(c) Both (a) and (b) (d) None of these

10 Which of the following is not the example of social networking sites?
(a) Facebook (b) Twitter (c) Instagram (d) Amazon

11 Which of the following is/are benefit(s) of online marketing?
(a) It helps in tracking (b) It build relationships
(c) Both (a) and (b) (d) Neither (a) nor (b)

12 Which of the following is not considered as types of direct marketing?
(a) Web marketing (b) Telemarketing
(c) Email direct marketing (d) Direct mail marketing

13 Advantages of direct marketing is/are
(a) it can take on a variety of creative forms
(b) it is time saving
(c) Both (a) and (b)
(d) None of the above

14 Which of the following is not included in types of online marketing?
(a) Web marketing (b) Email marketing
(c) Social media marketing (d) Direct marketing

15 .... is the subset of e-business focused on transactions.
(a) E-commerce
(b) E-marketing
(c) Digital technology
(d) Environment, strategy and performance

16 Green marketing is a part of
(a) social marketing (b) service marketing
(c) relationship marketing (d) rural marketing

17 A major way to reverse the cultural pollution caused by marketing is to adjust ....
(a) product selection (b) consumer attitudes
(c) product positioning (d) advertising levels

18 Sustainable marketing can also be characterised as the third age of
(a) planned obsolescence
(b) green marketing
(c) pollution
(d) recycling

19 Rural markets and rural marketing involves a number of strategies, which include
(a) management of demand
(b) unique selling proposition
(c) Both (a) and (b)
(d) None of the above

20 Scattered market is the feature of
(a) rural market (b) urban market
(c) Both (a) and (b) (d) None of these

21 Companies emphasising .... are developing 'green marketing' programmes that develop ecologically safer products, recyclable and biodegradable packaging, more energy efficient operations and better pollution controls.
(a) sustainability vision (b) new clean technology
(c) beyond greening (d) pollution prevention

22 The .... holds that the organisation's task is to determine the needs, wants and interests of target markets and to deliver the desired satisfactions more effectively and efficiently than competitors in a way that preserve the consumer's and society's well-being.
(a) customer centered business
(b) focused business model
(c) social marketing concept
(d) ethically responsible marketing

23 Under which strategy "Companies will enter the rural markets with a lot of skepticism, after being successful in the urban markets for a long time, they finally decides to enter rural markets?"
(a) A new entrant
(b) A mid entrant
(c) A late entrant
(d) None of the above

24 Which of the following would be leveraging both social network and traditional marketing?
(a) Handing out print advertisements with a coupon for a store
(b) A print advertisement in a magazine which drives people to a website where there is a free trial of offer
(c) Posting an advertisement on a message board
(d) Hosting a video ad on youtube not otherwise

25 Which of the following statement(s) is/are correct?
1. Direct marketing campaigns should offer an incentive or enticiting message to get customer to respond.
2. Direct marketing is a process of directly reaching a market on a personal or mass media basic.
3. 'Call to action' is not the feature of direct marketing.
4. Telemarketing and email direct marketing are the types of direct marketing.

Codes
(a) 1, 2, 4
(b) 2, 3, 4
(c) All of the above
(d) None of the above

Customer Relationship Management and Logistic Management

26 Customer relationship management technology can help in
(a) designing direct marketing efforts
(b) processing transaction faster
(c) Both (a) and (b)
(d) None of the above

27 The main drawback of CRM is
(a) implementing CRM before creating a customer strategy
(b) developing new prices model
(c) processing transaction faster
(d) All of the above

28 Process of managing information about customers to maximise loyalty is said to be
(a) company relationship management
(b) supplier management
(c) retailers management
(d) customer relationship management

29 Third step of customer's value analysis
(a) assessing attributes importance
(b) assessing company's performance
(c) monitoring competitors performance
(d) Both (b) and (c)

30 Percentage or number of customers who move from one level to next level in buying decision process is called
(a) conversion rates (b) marketing rates
(c) shopping rates (d) loyalty rates

31 Customised products and services for customers and interaction to individual customers are part of
(a) retailers management
(b) customer relationship management
(c) company relationship management
(d) supplier management

32 Company's 'customer relationship capital' is another name of
(a) satisfied customers
(b) dissatisfied customers
(c) customer retention
(d) customer conversion

33 A person or company that yields a revenue more than incurred cost of selling and serving is called
(a) customer life time value
(b) customer purchases value
(c) customer cost incurred
(d) customer relationship

34 Program designed for customers which is limited to any affinity group are classified as

(a) club membership program (b) royalty program
(c) loyalty program (d) All of these

35 Difference between customers evaluation including all costs incurred and benefit is called

(a) customer perceived value (b) company market value
(c) customer affordability (d) customer reliability

36 This is an arrangement in which a company outsources some or all of its customer relationship management functions to an application service provider. Name that arrangement.

(a) Spend management
(b) Supplier relationship management
(c) Hosted CRM
(d) Customer information control system

37 "Zero defects in manufacturing ...."

(a) is a relevant goal only in electronic assembly
(b) is readily achievable in all areas
(c) is the goal of TQM
(d) is an unobtainable and misleading idea

38 Total quality management emphasises

(a) the responsibility of the quality control staff to identify and solve all quality related problems
(b) a commitment to quality that goes beyond internal company issues to supplier and customers
(c) a system where strong managers are the only decision makers
(d) a process where mostly statistician get involved

39 Among the tools of TQM, the tool ordinarily used to aid in understanding the sequence of events through which a product travel is a ....

(a) pareto chart (b) flow chart
(c) check sheet (d) taguchi chart

40 Which one of the following would not generally be considered as an aspect of operations management?

(a) Work methods
(b) Secure financial resources
(c) Maintain quality
(d) Product or service design

41 The inputs to a transformation process include all of the following except

(a) material (b) people
(c) information (d) assembly

42 Which came last in the development of manufacturing techniques?

(a) Learn production
(b) Division of labour
(c) Mass production
(d) Interchangeable parts

43 Which of the following is not an area of responsibility for a logistics manager?

(a) Inventory (b) Purchasing
(c) Warehousing (d) Marketing

44 A supply chain which includes the distribution of finished products and services?

(a) Outbound logistics
(b) Inbound logistics
(c) Supply of goods
(d) Transportation

45 What additional factor does overall equipment effectiveness takes into account which makes it more meaningful than efficiency or utilisation?

(a) Flexibility (b) Speed (c) Cost (d) Quality

Miscellaneous

Directions (Q. Nos. 46-48) *In the questions given below two statements are labelled as Statement I and Statement II. You have to examine these two statements, select the correct code.*

Codes

(a) Only Statement I is correct
(b) Only Statement II is correct
(c) Both statements are correct
(d) Both statements are incorrect

46 **Statement** I Service marketing may be used to market a service or product.

Statement II The organised and systematic development of the service sector does not create employment opportunities.

47 **Statement** I Social marketing is not related with the goods that serve the society.

Statement II Social marketing focused to carry out social responsibilities.

48 **Statement** I Direct marketing is a type of advertising compaign that seeks to elicit an action.

Statement II 'Call to action' is a key factor in direct marketing.

Directions (Q. Nos. 49-52) *In the questions given below two statements labelled as Assertion (A) and Reason (R). In the context of the two statements, which one of the following is correct?*

Codes

(a) (A) is correct and (R) is the correct explanation of (A)
(b) (A) is correct, but (R) is not the correct explanation of (A)
(c) (A) is not correct, but (R) is correct
(d) (A) and (R) both are not correct

49 **Assertion** (A) Green marketing refers to the process of selling products or services based on their environmental benefits.

Reason (R) Green marketing is more price sensitive.

50 **Assertion** (A) A market increase in the rural income due to agrarian prosperity.

Reason (R) Rural marketing decrease contact of rural people with urban counterparts.

51 **Assertion** (A) CRM is the development and maintainence of mutually beneficial long-term relationship with strategically significant customers.

Reason (R) CRM increased sales through better timing due to anticipating nuds.

52 **Assertion** (A) Easy interaction between customer and company needed for implementation of CRM.

Reason (R) Abundant supply of customers is needed for implementation of CRM.

53 Match the following.

List I	List II
A. Stock away	1. Incorporates weight and space consideration
B. Density	2. Cost which does not change with the service or volume
C. Variable cost	3. Product dimension and impact of the same on vehicle space utilisation
D. Fixed cost	4. Cost which changes with the service

Codes

	A	B	C	D
(a)	1	2	3	4
(b)	4	2	1	3
(c)	2	1	4	3
(d)	3	1	2	4

PREVIOUS YEARS' QUESTIONS

December 2018

1 Which one of the following modes is not an example of direct and database marketing communication?

(a) Social media marketing (b) Catalogues
(c) Mailings (d) Telemarketing

November 2017

2 Which of the following is not a major aspect of digital marketing?

(a) Jurisdiction (b) Ownership
(c) Security (d) Entertainment

December 2015

3 In the course of converting to a marketing oriented company, a company may face which of the following hurdles?

(a) Organised resistance (b) Slow learning
(c) Fast forgetting (d) All of these

July 2014

4 Which one of the following stages of the marketing research process is most expensive?

(a) Data analysis
(b) Data collection
(c) Developing the research plan
(d) Report writing

June 2013

5 Consider the following statements and find out the correct alternative from the codes given below.

1. A firm's marketing information system is a component of its marketing research system.
2. The most common forms of marketing researches conducted in most of the firms are the measurement of market potential and the analysis of market share.
3. Survey research is seldom used for studying consumer's perception and attitudes.
4. The concept of cognitive dissonance is relevant to study consumer's post purchase behaviour.

Which of the statement(s) given above is/are correct?

Codes

(a) All the statements are true
(b) All the statements are false
(c) Statement 1 is false and the rest are true
(d) Both Statements 2 and 4 are true and the rest are false

ANSWERS

Objective Questions

1 (a)	2 (b)	3 (d)	4 (b)	5 (c)	6 (a)	7 (c)	8 (b)	9 (c)	10 (d)
11 (c)	12 (a)	13 (c)	14 (d)	15 (a)	16 (c)	17 (a)	18 (b)	19 (c)	20 (a)
21 (a)	22 (c)	23 (b)	24 (b)	25 (a)	26 (c)	27 (a)	28 (d)	29 (d)	30 (a)
31 (b)	32 (a)	33 (a)	34 (a)	35 (a)	36 (c)	37 (c)	38 (b)	39 (b)	40 (b)
41 (d)	42 (d)	43 (b)	44 (a)	45 (a)	46 (a)	47 (b)	48 (c)	49 (a)	50 (b)
51 (a)	52 (b)	53 (d)							

Previous Years' Questions

1 (a)	2 (d)	3 (d)	4 (b)	5 (d)

CHAPTER 31

Marketing Decisions

Market is a key element for a business because its whole profit is based on it. Thus, a business management must take marketing decisions carefully such as product, price, distribution, promotion etc.

Concept of Marketing Decisions

The marketing manager has to take many decisions that affect the day to day activities of the organisation. Its main objective is to achieve the predetermined marketing ojectives. It defines the scope of marketing activities of the organisation.

Types of Marketing Decisions

There are four categories or areas, which are always kept in mind, while making different sorts of marketing plans for different products and services. *These are as follows*

- Product decision
- Pricing decision
- Distribution decision (Place decision)
- Promotion decision

Product Decisions

The product is one of the important elements of the 4Ps of the marketing mix. It consists of a bundle of tangible and intangible attributes that satisfies consumers. A product can be a good, a service, an idea or a combination of all these.

Product Personality

Products carry meaning with them and project distinctive images. These meanings and images arise out of many components that make up the product personality.

Following are the components of a product

Core Feature A core feature is a basic component of a product. A marketer needs to define the core benefits offered by the product to the customers. All other components are super imposed on the core product to form the personality of the product. *e.g.* In case of car, care feature is the core benefit that car offers.

In this Chapter

Associated Feature Every product contains several associated features besides the core constituent. In case of car, shape of the car, size and capacity, brand name etc constitute the associated feature. Firms selling the similar product compete on the basis of the associated features as the core feature is the same for all.

Brand Name Brand name of the product is one of the most important of its associated features. It helps in identifying the product offered by one seller from that of the other. A brand includes a name, symbol, design or a combination of all these.

Package and Label Packaging and labelling are another associated features. The main purpose of packaging is to protect the product from damage and to facilitate smooth handling during the distribution stage. The size, colour, design and labelling of the package helps in attracting customers attention. Every product has its unique label. A label contains written information about the attributes of the product. It helps the buyer in understanding the features and composition of the product. It also gives other information like the date of manufacture, date of expiry, bar codes, batch number etc.

Nature of the Product

According to Levitt, a product offer can be conceived at four levels

Generic Product The generic product is the unbranded and undifferentiated commodity like rice, bread or cloth. Here, the product does not have an identity through a name and is not linked to anyone maker or owner.

Expected Product After developing the basic product, the marketers add attributes to transform the product into the expected product. Expected product represents the basic requirement, a customer finds essential to buy a product. Marketers try to identify attributes and conditions required by customers and try to build these into their products.

Augmented Product When additional features are added to expected product, it is converted into an augmented product. Companies do not limit the attributes of a product to what the customer expects in the product. They try to put in additional attributes in the product to differentiate it from their competitor's products. This leads to augmented product. The aim here is to go beyond the expectations of the customers and to delight them.

Potential Product When more augmentation and transformations are made to augmented product, it is converted into potential product. Thus, potential products are the products which include all the improvements that are possible under given technological, economic and competitive conditions. Potential products help in attracting and retaining customers.

Product Mix and Product Line

The product mix is the set of all the products that an organisation offers to its customers. It consists of all the product mix, lines and categories. It has certain characteristics/features like product width, length, depth and consistency. *These are as follows*

Width This is the total number of product lines a company carries.

Length It is the total number of items in the mix.

Depth It is the assortment of sizes, colours and variations offered for each product in the product line.

Consistency It refers to closeness exhibited by the products lines in production requirement, distribution and usage etc.

Product Mix Strategies/ Modifications

Several strategies used to manage product mix effectively are as follows

Expansion of Product Mix Existing product mix can be expanded by increasing its product lines. New product lines may be either related or unrelated to the existing product lines.

Contraction of Product Mix Organisations contract their product mix either by eliminating the entire product line or by simplifying the assortments within the lines. The product mix is contracted to eliminate low profit yielding products and to get a better profit margin from few products.

Altering Existing Products Redesigning or adding new features to the existing products can be more lucrative. Packaging is an important tool in altering the look and usage of the product. *e.g.* tetra pack of milk/juices increases the ease of handling and storage.

Positioning the Product Product positioning is the image projected by the product against the competitor's product and other products of the same firm.

Trading Up Companies offer higher priced, prestigious products to their existing product line in an effort to increase the sales of their low priced products and enhance the company's image.

Trading Down Marketers, who adopt the trading down strategy add low priced items to their existing line of speciality products. Trading down is used in order to provide a new product to customers, who cannot afford the original product.

Product Life Cycle

A typical product goes through four stages in its life, *i.e.* introduction, growth, maturity and decline. It gives marketers a better understanding in managing their profitable products and eliminating the unprofitable ones. As the product moves from one stage to another, marketers try to evaluate and adjust strategies for promoting, pricing and distributing the product. *These stages can be further understood as follows*

Introduction Stage

In this stage, the product is introduced to the customer. As the product is new to the market, consumer awareness is usually very low. Here, company adopts heavy sales promotion and product awareness programmes. The cost of the product is very high and sales are very low. At this stage, company charges high price to the customers.

Growth Stage

This stage is crucial for the product's survival in the market because the reactions of the competitors to the product success will affect the product's life expectancy. This stage is characterised by increase in sales, heavy demand for the product and peaking of profits.

Companies increase their level of promotional expenditure to meet the competition. Initially, the profit of the firm increases because promotional costs are spread over a larger volume and unit manufacturing cost falls. But at a later phase in growth stage, the profits begin to decline as competition increases, forcing the lowering of prices and heavy spending on promotion.

Maturity Stage

This stage is marked by a steady decline in profits. The sales tends to grow, stabilise and then start to decline. The sales growth rate slows down as the distribution channels get exhausted. Then, the sales tend to flatter or stabilise on a per capita basis as the market reaches its saturation. And finally, the sales start declining and customers try out new products and substitutes. Competition is fierce at this stage.

Decline Stage

In this stage, product sales and profit decline. Company should phase out weak items from their product mix and may even lower the prices of the existing products. The advertisement budget of the company come down and the company struggle to meet its costs.

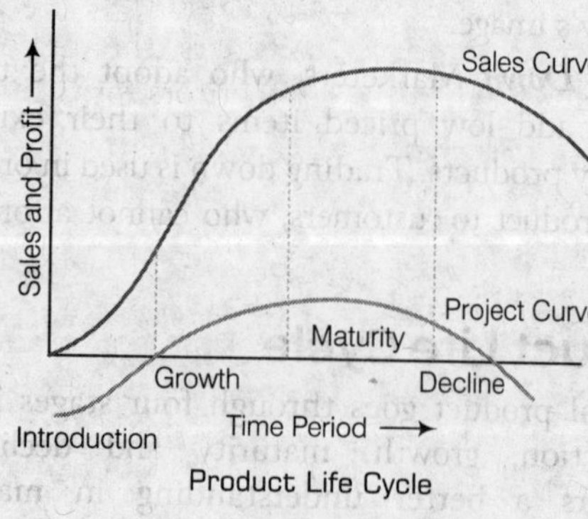

Product Life Cycle

Product Development

It is the process of finding out the possibility of producing a product keeping in view the customer's needs and wants. It may include addition of a new product line, elimination of an existing product or a product line and changes in the colour, size, design, packing, price and discontinuation of unprofitable item of product line.

According to **William J. Stanton**, "Product development encompasses the technical activities of product research, engineering and design."

According to **Lipson** and **Darling**, "Product development involves the adding, dropping and modification of item specifications in the product line for a given period of time, usually one year."

Scope of Product Development

Product development has a much wider scope. *Some of the important areas of product development are discussed as under*

Price of Product It plays a vital role in the proper planning of a product. Failure in proper price planning results in failure of the whole business.

Designing and Size of the Product There exists different consumer wants of a particular product in terms of its size and design. Such size and design depends upon purchasing power, branding, packaging, utilities etc.

Quality It is one of the most important characteristics of the product. It includes various components like shape, hardness, colour, nature and various other contents of the product. If the product is of good quality, then its demand will automatically boost up in the market.

Stage of the Product It refers to the nature of the product suited to specified industry, *i.e.* instrument industry, mechanical industry, cloth industry etc.

Guarantee and Service of the Product The concept of product development should specifically cover the guarantee and varied services related to product. In the present scenario, satisfactory and high utility based products are successfully sold in the market.

Other Areas Covered *Some of the other areas covered under it are discussed as under*

- Branding and packaging of the product.
- Updated knowledge of various innovative uses of product.
- Name of the product which should be attractive and descriptive in nature.

Stages of Product Development

Product development process is a crucial process for the success and survival of any business. The product development process starts from idea generation and ends with product development and its commercialisation.

Following are the steps in the process of product development

Idea Generation The first step of product development is idea generation, *i.e.* identification of new products required to be developed considering consumer needs and demands. Idea generation is done through research of market sources like consumer liking, disliking and competitor policies.

Idea Screening The second step in the process of product development is idea screening, *i.e.* selecting the best idea among the ideas generated at the first step. As the resources are limited, therefore, all the ideas cannot convert into products. Most promising idea is kept for the next stage.

Concept Development At this step, the selected idea is moved towards development process. For the selected idea, different product concepts are developed. Out of several product concepts, the most suitable concept is selected and introduced to a focus group of customers to understand their reaction.

Market Strategy Development At this step, market strategies are developed to evaluate market size, product demand, growth potential and profit estimation for initial years. Further, it includes launch of product, selection of distribution channel, budgetary requirements etc.

Business Analysis At this step, business analysis of the new product is done. Business analysis includes *viz* estimation of sales, frequency of purchase, nature of business, production and distribution related cost and expenses and estimation of profit.

Product Development At this step, the concept moves towards production. Decisions are taken from operational point of view, whether the product is technically and commercially feasible to the market. Here, the research and development department develop a sample product.

Test Marketing Now, the product is ready to be launched in market with brand name, packaging and pricing. Initially, the product is launched in a small market. Before full scale launching, the product is exposed to a carefully chosen sample of the population, called test market. If the product is found acceptable in test market, the product is ready to be launched in target market.

Commercialisation Here, the product is launched across target market with a proper market strategy and plan. This is called commercialisation phase of product development.

Pricing Decisions

The price of a product or service is the number of monetary units, a person pays to obtain one unit of the product or service.

Pricing is the method used by a company to fix or change its price with respect to costs, sales and profit targets, the pricing policies of competitors and the perceived value of the product by customers.

To sustain and achieve its objectives in the competitive market, a company should adopt the most effective pricing mechanism.

A marketer should bear in mind the following factors before adopting a pricing strategy

- The demand for the product/service in the market.
- Customer's perception.
- How much margin is adequate to sustain in the market?
- Image of the company in the market.
- Expenditure incurred for producing the goods.
- Intensity of competition.

Setting the prices of products should be a coordinated effort between the various departments of an organisation. If a coordinated effort is made, the organisation will be able to estimate the total cost of a product accurately. After that organisation can adopt the right pricing strategy.

Factors Influencing Pricing Decisions

Objectives of the Business There may be various objectives of the firm such as getting a reasonable rate of return, to capture the market etc. A pricing policy, thus should be established only after proper consideration of the objectives of the firm.

Cost of the Product Cost and price of a product are closely related. Normally, the price cannot or shall not fixed below its cost. Price also determines the cost.

Market Position The prices of the products of different producers are different either because of difference in quality or because of the goodwill of the firm. A reputed concern may fix higher prices for its products. On the other hand, a new producer may fix lower prices for its products.

Competitor's Prices Competitive conditions affect the pricing decisions. The company considers the prices fixed and quality maintained by the competitors for their products.

Distribution Channels Policy The nature of distribution channels used and trade discounts which have to be allowed to distributors and the distribution expenses also affect the pricing decisions.

Government Policy Price discreation is also affected by the government's price control through enactment of legislation, when it is thought proper to arrest the inflationary trend in prices of certain commodities.

Buying Patterns of the Consumers If the purchase frequency of the product is higher, lower prices should be fixed to have a low profit margin. It will facilitate increasing the sale volume and the total profits of the firm.

Product Differentiation The price of the product also depends upon the characteristics of the product. In order to attract the customers, different characteristics are added to the product such as quantity, size, colour etc.

Selection of Pricing Policy

The selection of a pricing policy is vital for an organisation, since, it is the single most important factor on which the existence of the organisation depend. The selection of a pricing policy is dependent on its external and internal environment.

Some of these pricing policies are

Psychological Pricing Consumers generally fridge a product quality by its price, they feel that a higher priced product normally indicates good quality. This perception is more apparent, when pricing patterns of certain goods like perfumes and higher-end automobiles is considered. If no other information is available to the customers about the quality of the product, then price becomes a major factor in judging its quality.

Transfer Pricing When one division of an organisation transfers or sells goods or services to another division, the price charged for the goods is called transfer pricing.

Companies normally adopt a pricing pattern on the basis of several aspects like geographic factors, demand patterns of the customer etc.

Methods of Pricing

Popular methods adopted by marketers to fix the price of their products and services are as follows

Value Pricing In this method, marketers offer low prices for high quality products or services. The idea is to help customers perceive that they are getting a high quality product at low price.

Market Skimming This method is useful in the pricing of new product, especially those that have a luxury or speciality element. Here, company aims at high price and high profits in the early stage of the marketing of the product. This is done, if marketers feel that the product being developed or technology being utilised has a short life cycle.

Geographical Pricing When customers are geographically scattered in different locations, marketers adopt different pricing for different regions using a pricing method that adequately covers their delivery process. This form of pricing is known as geographic pricing, since it is based on the geographic location of the customer.

Promotional Pricing A general perception among marketers is that a price reduction or any other promotional deal will attract customers to try the product or service. So, promotional price is offered to increase sales to the maximum extent possible.

Discriminatory Pricing In the discriminatory pricing, companies charge different customers differently for the same product on the basis of their paying capacity and the value of the customers.

Discounts and Allowances Discounts and allowances are the pricing techniques, marketers adopt to increase the stock movement and thus, increase the sales volume. Various types of discounts and allowances that marketers resort are seasonal discounts, cash discounts, quantity discounts, trade discounts etc.

Experience Curve Pricing In experience curve pricing, new products are introduced at a low price. This is strategically done to attract price sensitive customers to purchase these products. Although, the company loses revenue initially by setting the prices low, it should be able to recover it as the experience of employees increases and the cost of production comes down.

Product Mix Pricing Setting appropriate prices for the product mix variables is very difficult, since the demand patterns and the market segments vary significantly from product to product.

Distribution Decisions/ Place Decisions

Distribution is related with the 'P' for place in the 'four Ps' of the marketing mix. It covers the channels, through which goods are sold *viz* wholesalers, retailers, agents and so forth, as well as physical distribution (logistics).

A distribution channel is the chain of individuals and organisations involved in getting a product or service from the producer to the consumer. Distribution channels are also known as marketing channels or marketing distribution channels.

Marketing is understood to be an exchange process. Marketing channel helps this exchange process to take place. A marketing channel is defined as a group of exchange relationships, which create customer value in acquiring, consuming and disposing of products and services. The marketing channel right from the producer to the final consumer is designed in such a way, that it provides sufficient value to the customer and creates a competitive advantage to the producer.

Functions of Distribution Channels

Helps in Physical Distribution Transporting goods and storing them in the assigned warehouses or godowns.

Promotes Communication Marketing intermediaries promote the company's products. Here, channel member provides the information regarding the products and pushes it to the customers.

Provides Information Retailers and wholesalers collect the information or feedbacks from customers and provide the same to the company or manufacturer.

Plays a Key Role in Title Transferring Marketing intermediaries purchase the goods from the company and transform the title of goods or ownership to the next channel intermediary or customer.

Supports Relationship Management Here, marketing intermediaries try to understand the needs of consumers, try to match his needs and satisfy them.

Types of Distribution Channels

Industrial channels tends to be shorter than consumer channels because of a small number of ultimate customers, the greater geographical concentration of industrial customers and greater complexity of the product, which requires close manufacturer-customer liaison. The consumer channels are normally longer and buy in small quantities. *The channels can be understood as follows*

Consumer Channels *These are*

- Manufacturer to consumer
- Manufacturer to retailer to consumer
- Manufacturer to wholesaler to retailer to consumer
- Manufacturer to agent to wholesaler to retailer to consumer.

Industrial Channels *These are*

- Manufacturer to industrial customers
- Manufacturer to agent to industrial customer
- Manufacturer to distributor to industrial customer
- Manufacturer to agent to distributor to industrial customer

Service Channels *These are*

- Service provider to consumer or industrial consumer
- Service provider to agent to consumer or industrial consumer
- Service provider *via* internet to consumer or industrial customer.

Factors affecting Channels of Distribution

Important factors affecting the choice of channels of distribution by the manufacturer are

Considerations Related to Product

When a manufacturer selects some channel of distribution he/she should take care of such factors, which are related to the quality and nature of the product. *These are as follows*

Unit Value of the Product When the product is very costly, it is best to use small distribution channel. On the other hand, for less costly products, long distribution channel is used.

Standardised V/s Customised Product Standardised products are predetermined and there has no scope for alteration. To sell this, long distribution channel is used.

On the other hand, customised products are those which are made according to the discretion of the customer and also there is a scope for alteration. For such products, face-to-face interaction between the manufacturer and the consumer is essential.

Perishability A manufacturer should choose minimum or no middlemen as channel of distribution for such an item or a product, which is of highly perishable nature. On the contrary, a long distribution channel can be selected for durable goods.

Technical Nature If a product is of a technical nature, then it is better to supply it directly to the consumer. This will help the user to know the necessary technicalities of the product.

Considerations Related to Market

Market consideration is a necessary process in business. *It includes various components, which are as follows*

Number of Buyers If the number of buyer is large, then it is better to take the services of middlemen for the distribution of the goods. On the contrary, the distribution should be done by the manufacturer directly, if the number of buyers is less.

Types of Buyers If the more buyers of the product belong to general category, then there can be more middlemen. But in case of industrial buyers, there can be less middlemen.

Buying Habits A manufacturer should take the services of middlemen, if his financial position does not permit him to sell goods on credit to those consumers, who are in the habit of purchasing goods on credit.

Buying Quantity It is useful for the manufacturer to rely on the services of the middlemen, if the goods are bought in smaller quantity.

Size of the Market If the market area of the product is scattered fairly, then the producer must take the help of middlemen.

Channel Management

It is the process by which a producer or supplier directs marketing activity by involving and motivating parties comprising its channel of distribution. It is defined as the management of all activities which facilitate movement and coordination of supply and demand in creation of time, place utility in goods.

Importance of Channel Management

- It helps in developing a programme for selling and servicing customers within a specific channel.
- Its aim is to streamline communication between business and the customer.
- Its goal is to create utility and facilitate exchange efficiencies.
- It matches the segment of supply and demand.
- It is also helpful in standardising transactions.
- It can offer promotion and financial support.

Promotion Decisions

Promotion activities are a key component of marketing mix. Their aim is to present product and services in an attractive light to customers to encourage them to buy.

They consist of

- selling, which is concerned with direct contact with customers.
- advertising, which is non-personal man communication, paid for by a sponsor. It is sometimes referred to as above the line, which is an advertising term that refers to the line above, which the agency receives a commission for placing the sponsor's advertising.
- sales promotion, which refers to short-term activities like free samples and competitions that encourage quick action by buyers. This is referred to as below the line, as agencies do not receive commission here and a direct change is made to the sponsor for the work performed.
- public relation, which also covers publicity and is not promotion that is paid for directly by a company to the media. It relies for its coverage on news or editorial about a company's products/services.

Role/Importance of Promotion in Marketing

Wider Gap between Producers and Consumers This is because of the widening of today's market. The various tools of promotion like advertising, sales promotion etc reduces this gap.

Increase in Potential Consumers The number of potential customers has increased considerably and they are highly scattered.

Large Number of Middlemen The number of middlemen in the channel have risen due to widening of the markets and the producer is required to provide relevant marketing information to these middlemen as well.

Rising Competition The inter-industry and inter-firm competition has been stiffening day by day. This requires greater attention from marketing manager towards promotional activities.

Dormant Demand Today's customer demand is largely dormant, it must be awakened and stimulated by promotional efforts.

Large Scale Production The large scale production of today necessitates large scale promotional efforts too.

Promotion Mix

The manufacturer has to take effective steps in meeting the consumer in the market after taking the decision relating to the nature of product, its price and distribution.

The customers are attracted to buy the products on the basis of promotional activities. The promotion mix is the integration of advertising, personal selling, sales promotion, publicity and public relations.

These are as follows

Advertising

Advertising is the means of providing the most persuasive possible selling message to the right prospects at the lowest possible cost. Simply, advertising is a paid form of non-personal presentation of goods or services by an identified sponsor to reach out to maximum number of audiences.

Benefits of Advertising

- Advertising create awareness, interest and desire for products and services in customers to buy them.
- It is cost efficient as it reaches vast number of audiences.
- It create impact on minds of customer as it is repeated several times.
- It helps in boosting the sales of the company.
- It helps in changing the customer's perception of a product.
- It helps in building a strong image of a product or brand, apart from increasing its sales.

Developing an Advertisement Programme

Identify the Target Audience The first step in developing an advertisement campaign is to identify the target audience. The target audience is a market segment to which a marketer wants to communicate a product or brand message. The composition of the target audience and their specific needs must be identified before developing an advertising programme. *e.g.* Advertisement of food item is targeted at the mass market, while the advertisement of luxury car is targeted at a niche market of status conscious and high income group customers.

Define the Objectives of Advertising Campaign The objectives of advertisement should be determined in the initial phase of the programme. The objectives should be laid down in clear, precise and measurable terms, so that the marketers can evaluate whether it has been accomplished by the end of campaign.

Objectives of advertisements are as follows

- Provide information about advertisement and create awareness about the product.
- Highlight the uniqueness of company's product over competitors.
- Reminding about the product that it will yield benefits in the future and retain a product in customer's mind during the off season.

Determine the Advertisement Budget Advertising budget is the amount of money allocated by a firm for its advertising campaigns for a specific period of time. It is influenced by various factors like the type of products advertised, the size of the market, the geographic distribution of customers within the market and the sales volume as compared to the competitor's sales volume.

The amount of money spent on an advertising campaign should be in accordance with the sales it generate. The budget of an advertisement varies depending on the stage of life cycle of the product. A new product may need a larger share of the advertising budget, as the advertising has to create awareness about the product and encourage the potential in customers to buy it.

Developing the Advertisement Message Clarity of an advertising message is more important than the amount spent on it. Factors that affect the advertisement message can be both product related and customer related. Product related factors are its features, usage and benefits. Further characteristics of target customers such as age, gender, their likes and dislikes, their habits, education affect the content and form of advertisements. An advertisement message should be meaningful, distinctive and believable.

Selecting the Right Media *Before selecting an appropriate medium, firm must take care of the following*

- Who are the target audience?
- Where are they located?
- What is the message that has to be delivered?
- When do we run the advertising campaign?

To select the right type of medium, media planners need to have a good knowledge of the different media that are available to reach the target audience.

Evaluation of Advertising Effectiveness Since, there is heavy expenditure on advertisement, advertisers primarily evaluate the effectiveness of an advertisement. To measure the effectiveness of an advertisement, marketers use intermediate measures. They are called intermediate measures because the target audiences are tested after they are exposed to the ad and before they take any action. Some of these methods are recognition method, *i.e.* showing the advertisement and asking whether they have seen it before, aided recall, *i.e.* asking people to tell the brand they remember and unaided recall, *i.e.* asking people what they have seen recently without showing them any copy of the advertising message.

Major Media for Advertisement

Broadcast Advertising Media
- Radio
- Television

Print Advertising Media
- Newspaper
- Magazines

Outdoor Advertising Media
- Bill boards
- Painted bulletins
- Displays
- Electric boards

Online Advertising Media
- E-mail

Other Advertising Media
- Transit advertisement
- Movie advertising
- Yellow pages and pamphlets

Personal Selling

Personal selling is a personal form of communication where direct face to face conversation takes place between the buyer and the seller for the purpose of exchanging goods and services. Sales persons are appointed by the companies to create awareness and develop preference among the customers about their products with the eventual aim of making sale.

In other words, personal selling is the most traditional method, devised by manufacturers, for promotion of the sales of their products. Prior to the development of the advertising technique, personal selling was used to be the only method used by manufacturers for promotion of sales.

According to **Philip Kotler,** "Personal selling is personal presentation by the firm's sales force for the purpose of making sales and building customer relationship."

According to **Cundiff** and **Still,** "Personal selling is basically a method of communication. It involves not only individual but social behaviour, each of the person in face to face contrast salesman and prospect influence the other."

Importance/Functions of Personal Selling in Business

Following points explain the importance or functions of personal selling

Two-way Communication It is the best tool for two- way communication. Salesman can provide necessary information to customer about company's offer and also collect information from customer. Customer can actively involve with salesman to solve his doubts and objections. It is not possible in any other methods of market promotion.

Personal Attention An advertising and publicity are among mass communication tools. They do not cater individual needs. Personal selling focuses on personal problems of customers. It is comparatively more effective and result oriented.

Detailed Demonstration Expect television advertisements, demonstration is not possible. However, television demonstration is much limited. Salesman can provide a detailed demonstration and can supervise the customer in making the actual use of products. For technical products, it has more relevance.

Complementary to Other Promotional Tools Personal selling can support advertising, sales promotion and publicity. It removes the drawbacks of advertising and sales promotion. Advertising increases awareness while personal selling reinforces the advertising message. Similarly, it can make sales promotion tools more effective by personal guidance or conviction.

Immediate Feedback This is the only market promotion technique that provides an immediate feedback. At the end of every call/visit, a salesman can easily judge whether the customer is interested or intended to buy.

Individual Services It offers individual services. It can meet personal expectations of buyers. It leads to customer satisfaction.

Flexibility Sales talks and presentation can be adjusted according to situation to suit individual nature, motives and problems.

Customer Confidence By systematic sales talk and presentation, a capable salesman can remove all doubts, queries, objections and misunderstandings and can win customer's confidence. It increases customer's faith in company and its offers.

Triple Reward Salesmanship offers triple rewards. It benefits all parties, including customer, salesman and company. Customer is satisfied with products and services. Salesman can achieve his targets and companies can improve its market share and profits.

Improving Image The detailed explanation about company and its products removes all doubts and misunderstandings, which helps in restoring company's image and reputation in market.

Sales Promotion

Sales promotion is incentive to consumers or trade that is designed to stimulate purchase. A customer has to be made to believe that he is getting more value for the money he is spending than he would have otherwise got, if the sales promotion was not in operation.

Sales promotion scheme serve to signal the arrival of a time period in which customers will get the value that they were getting earlier by spending less. In typical consumer promotions, companies reduce the price for a limited period of time or after more quantity for the same price, or offer extra items or gifts or prizes with the purchase. Discounts and incentives are some of the trade promotions. Companies have to operate sales promotion scheme in a way that customers do not start equating the product with low priced brands.

Effects of Sales Promotion

Sales promotion is used to provide short, sharp impetus to sales. In this sense, it is a short-term tactical device. Sales promotion boosts the sales during the promotion period because of the incentive effect. This is followed by a fall in sales to below normal level because some consumers will have stocked-up on the product during the promotion.

The long-term sales effect of the sales promotion could be positive, neutral or negative. If the promotion has attracted new buyers, who find that they like the brand, repeat purchases from them give rise to a positive long-term effect. Alternatively, if the promotion has devalued the brand in the eyes of consumers, the effect may be negative. Where the promotion has caused consumers to buy the brand only because of its incentive value with no effect on underlying preferences, the long-term effect may be neutral.

Sales Promotion Tools and Techniques

The two types of sales promotion tools and techniques are as follows

Consumer-oriented Promotion Tools and Techniques

Consumer sales promotion is a marketing technique that is used to entice customers to purchase a product. The promotions typically last for a set period of time and are used to achieve a specific purpose, such as increasing market share or unveiling a new product. A number of promotional techniques are commonly used by product manufacturers and sellers, *which are as follows*

Providing Free Samples Providing free samples is a technique used to introduce new products to the marketplace.

Offering a Free Trial A free trial is a way for a consumer to try a new product while eliminating risk. It may be used when a product is unique to the marketplace, which can make consumers leery of trying it out.

Giving Free Gifts Free gifts entice consumers to make a purchase by including a bonus along with the product. The gift may be included in the outer part of the product packaging to serve as a visual attraction.

Offering Customer Contests Contests offer the customer a chance to win prizes like cash or store merchandise.

Social Media and Influencer Marketing Social media and the continued popularity of blogging and vlogging have created a new generation of influence marketers who regularly promote products in a particular field to their established audience.

Using Digital Marketing Digital marketing folds directly into other promotional strategies by providing a different avenue, online display ads or direct marketing, to advertise other consumer-centric efforts.

Coupons This involves offering price reduction or saving to customers on the purchase of a specific product. The coupons may be mailed or enclosed alongwith other products, or inserted in a magazine or newspaper advertisement.

Premium Offers These can be extra quantities of the same product at the regular price. Premium offers are used by several firms selling FMCG goods such as detergents, soaps and food items.

Personality Promotions This type of promotion is used to attract the greater number of customers in a store and to promote sale of a particular item.

Trade-oriented Sales Promotion

Stock Return Some firms take back partly or wholly the unsold stocks lying with the retailers, and distribute it to other dealers, where there is a demand for such stocks.

Credit Terms Special credit terms may provide to encourage bulk orders from retailers or dealers.

Dealer Conferences A firm may organise dealer conferences. The dealers may be given information of the company's performance, future plans, and so on.

Dealer Trophies Some firms may institute a special trophy to the highest performing dealer in a particular period of time.

Public Relations

Public relations involves with the management of internal and external communications of an organisation to create and maintain a positive image.

According to the Institute of Public Relations (UK), "Public relations is the planned and sustained effort to establish and maintain goodwill and mutual understanding between an organisation and its public." A firm's public includes its employees, stakeholders, trade unions, general public, customers (past, present and future), charities, media, government and politicians etc. An organisation needs to communicate with the public, both internally as well as externally. As the attitude of the public influences, the sales of an organisation, enhanced public relations work to enhance the overall image and create goodwill for the company.

The role of public relations is to

- identify the relevant public.
- influence the opinions of the public by reinforcing the favourable opinion, transforming neutral opinions of the public into positive opinions and changing or neutralising the hostile opinions.

Publicity and Public Relations

Publicity, a function of public relations is a communication about an organisation and/or its products to the public.

It is usually carried out in the forms of

- news item, a press release or an article in a newspaper or a mass medium like the TV.
- an interview or speech delivered by the company executive at a press conference.
- one-to-one communication with the target audience.

Publicity may have both positive or negative impacts. Organisation can minimise the effects of bad publicity by providing people with accurate information and giving clarifications, taking safety measures, effective quality control measures, inspections etc.

Benefits of Public Relations

- It helps in building and maintaining relations with local community.
- It helps in keeping better relations with the investors.
- It helps in reducing the conflicts and misconception about company or its products.
- It helps in publicising the products.

Like any other marketing activity, public relations needs to follow a systematic approach of setting objectives, selecting the message and media vehicle, plan implementation and finally conduct evaluation.

EXAM BASED QUESTIONS

Product Decision

1 When a product is viewed as the tangible characteristics alongwith the whole cluster of services that accompany it, this is called?

(a) Tangible product (b) Extended product
(c) Generic product (d) None of these

2 Which of the following is not one of the three primary dimensions of a firm's product mix?

(a) Width (b) Benefits
(c) Depth (d) Consistency

3 Which of the following is not one of the stages of the product life cycle?

(a) Introduction (b) Revive
(c) Decline (d) Growth

4 In .... stage, a product is well established in the market.

(a) decline (b) growth
(c) maturity (d) None of these

5 The number of versions offered of each product in the line is known as

(a) product line depth (b) product line length
(c) product line width (d) None of these

6 Maximising the market share is the objective of company in .... stage of product life cycle.

(a) growth (b) maturity
(c) introduction (d) None of these

7 Which of the following is not a factor that serves to increase the brand image strength?

(a) Product quality (b) Consistent advertising
(c) Distribution intensity (d) All of these

8 Which of the following contribute to the formation of product personality?

(a) Core features (b) Associated features
(c) Both (a) and (b) (d) Neither (a) nor (b)

9 Label of the product contains written statement about the following attributes of the product.

(a) Features
(b) Composition
(c) Date of expiry and manufacture
(d) All of the above

10 Who differentiated products on the basis of the value, they provide to customers?

(a) WH Newman (b) P Kotler
(c) Theodore Levitt (d) LG Peter

11 .... represents the basic requirement, a customer finds essential to buy a product.

(a) Expected product (b) Potential product
(c) Generic product (d) None of these

12 After developing the basic product, the marketer add attributes to transform the product into

(a) augmented product (b) expected product
(c) Both (a) and (b) (d) Neither (a) nor (b)

13 .... are products that a customer purchases, when he is faced with sudden problem.

(a) Industrial products
(b) Convenience products
(c) Unsought products
(d) None of the above

14 Marketers who adopt .... strategy add low priced items to their existing line of speciality products.

(a) trading down (b) trading up
(c) expansion (d) contraction

15 .... products are consumed during production and delivery of the product, but they do not become part of the final product.

(a) Capital equipment
(b) Consumable supplies
(c) Component part
(d) None of the above

16 In which stage of product life cycle, the company takes decision, whether to maintain, harvest or drop the product?

(a) Introduction (b) Growth
(c) Maturity (d) Decline

17 In general, products can be classified according to two basic criteria. They are

(a) vertical market and horizontal market
(b) product mix and product line
(c) end use and degree of positioning
(d) None of the above

18 According to the concept of product life cycle, profits are likely to be highest during the period of

(a) introduction (b) growth
(c) maturity (d) decline

19 When a product is in the growth stage of its life cycle, a firm should most likely expect

(a) competition entering the market
(b) decrease in the cost of production
(c) increase in the cost of production
(d) None of the above

20 One key of the management of a product's life cycle is/are to

(a) try to control the length of a product's life cycle
(b) constantly search for new products and product improvements
(c) eliminate advertising in the decline stage
(d) All of the above

21 Which of the following are strategies for growth stage of product life cycle?
1. Price cuts to attract price sensitive customers.
2. Enter new markets.
3. Abandon weaker product.
4. Increase advertising and sales promotion.
Select the correct answer using the codes given below
(a) Both 1 and 2 (b) Both 3 and 4
(c) 1, 2 and 3 (d) All of the above

Pricing Decision

22 Slow skimming is feasible, when
(a) market is aware of the product
(b) market size is limited
(c) customers are ready to pay a higher price for the product
(d) All of the above

23 Most consumers want
(a) small quantities of many products
(b) small quantities of few products
(c) large quantities of few products
(d) large quantities of many products

24 Which of the following is not one of the most common pricing objective?
(a) Target return (b) Survival
(c) Cost per thousand (d) Product quality

25 Skimming price relate to
(a) charging competitive price
(b) charge initially high price
(c) charge initially low price
(d) None of the above

26 Which of the following is/are pricing objectives?
(a) Competition (b) Market share
(c) Market penetration (d) All of these

27 Which of the following is one of four more important legal restraints on pricing?
(a) Less leader pricing (b) Deceptive pricing
(c) Price discrimination (d) Promotional pricing

28 Which of the following cost may be used for pricing decision?
(a) Fixed cost (b) Variable cost
(c) Average cost (d) All of these

29 Which of the following factor affects pricing decision?
(a) Demand of the product
(b) Product characteristics
(c) Cost of the product
(d) All of the above

30 In non-price competition, marketer focus on factors such as
(a) product features
(b) quality of the product/services
(c) packaging and promotions
(d) All of the above

31 Competitiors react to price changes in following ways.
(a) Maintain status quo
(b) Set the price equal to that of the company
(c) Setting price lower than that of the company
(d) All of the above

32 Under ...., marketers launch the product at a higher price and higher promotional level to skim the market rapidly.
(a) slow skimming
(b) rapid skimming
(c) maturity
(d) None of the above

33 .... includes all activities directly related to the sale of goods or services to the ultimate consumer for personal non-business use.
(a) Retailing (b) Producing
(c) Manufacturing (d) Wholesaler

34 Which of the following is not one of the three primary considerations in how demand influences pricing decisions?
(a) Demographic factors (b) Rate of return
(c) Psychological factors (d) Price elasticity

35 Sometimes, several products are sold together at a single price to suggest a good value. This is an example of which product mix pricing strategy?
(a) Product bundle pricing
(b) Mark-up pricing
(c) Odd pricing
(d) None of the above

36 A seller charges a relatively low price on a new product in order to obtain economies of scale and rapid creation of Mass Market. This is an example of which kind of pricing strategy?
(a) Cost plus (b) Mark-up
(c) Penetration (d) Skimming

37 "Price policies provide the guidelines within, which pricing strategy is formulated and implemented," who said it ?
(a) Cundiff and Still (b) Kotler
(c) Adam Smith (d) Levitt

38 In price competition, marketer who can sell his product at the .... cost will usually win a large part of the market share.
(a) highest (b) lowest
(c) right (d) None of these

39 In .... marketers, adopt different prices for the same product at different locations or for different types of customers.
(a) differentiated pricing
(b) market skimming
(c) Both (a) and (b)
(d) Neither (a) nor (b)

Distribution Decision

40 .... mode of transport is used to transport goods like oil.
(a) Pipeline (b) Air transport
(c) Water transport (d) None of these

41 Process selection of salesman consist
(a) selection test (b) advertisement
(c) interview (d) All of these

42 Full time wholesalers are most likely to be used in the marketing of
(a) clothing (b) vegetables
(c) steel (d) All of these

43 Retailing consists of all those activities involved in selling directly to ultimate
(a) wholesaler (b) consumer
(c) agents (d) All of these

44 Which one of the following is not the mode of direct distribution system?
(a) Trading mediators (b) Vending machines
(c) Own sales depot (d) Franchise shops

45 Middleman take credit risk that a manufacturer would
(a) rather not assume (b) be unable to assume
(c) like to assume (d) None of these

46 Which out of the following is not a type of non-store retailing?
(a) Limited line stores (b) Automatic vending
(c) Direct selling (d) Telemarketing

47 Channel design is a .... marketing tool.
(a) strategic (b) fixed
(c) stable (d) permanent

48 In ...., exact requirement of the customer is ascertained for a target groups of customers.
(a) allocating (b) assorting
(c) sorting (d) accumulation

49 One type of wholesaler that never handles the item physically is known as the
(a) merchant wholesaler
(b) drop shopper
(c) cash and carry wholesaler
(d) All of the above

50 A strategy, in which company stores goods in maximum numbers of retail outlet is
(a) intensive distribution
(b) exclusive distribution
(c) selective distribution
(d) None of the above

51 Super markets are retail stores, which handle relatively a large volume of goods, service at .... cost, high margin principle of retailing.
(a) high cost (b) no profit-no loss
(c) low cost (d) Both (a) and (c)

52 Manufacturers, who sell to wholesalers rather than directly to retailers can
(a) dispense with advertising their products
(b) dispense with personal selling
(c) operate with small amount of capital
(d) None of the above

53 A type of merchant wholesaler typically used, where prompter of delivery or fresheners is an important factor is known as
(a) rack jobber
(b) cash and carry wholesaler
(c) truck wholesaler
(d) All of the above

54 A type of agent middleman who is likely to sell all the manufacturer's output is a
(a) manufacturer's agent (b) commission agent
(c) selling agent (d) rack jobber

55 In order to close the gaps that arise between producers and customers, there representing marketing channels perform which one of the following task?
(a) Possession and ownership
(b) Financial flow
(c) Risk flow
(d) All of the above

56 The .... of the channel represents the number of intermediary level that exits between the producer and the final user.
(a) length (b) breadth
(c) height (d) None of these

57 .... refers to the ease of location or the case with which customers can acquire the products.
(a) Convenience utility (b) Spatial convenience
(c) Temporal convenience (d) None of these

58 .... act as a temporary part for transfer of goods from one location to another.
(a) Storage warehousing
(b) Distribution warehousing
(c) Neither (a) nor (b)
(d) Both (a) and (b)

59 Classification of wholesaler and retailers is done on the basis of who the .... are and not on the .... that has to be made.
(a) purchasers, amount of purchase
(b) sellers, amount of purchase
(c) purchasers, amount of stock
(d) None of the above

60 Which of the following offer wide selection of products to consumers?
1. Speciality stores 2. Departmental stores
3. Super markets 4. Hyper markets

Select the correct answer using the codes given below
(a) Both 1 and 2 (b) 1, 2 and 3
(c) 2, 3 and 4 (d) All of these

61 Which of the following factors affects to the choice of channel of distribution?

1. Size of manufacture 2. Desire to control the channel
3. Perishability of product
4. Weight of product

Select the correct answer using the codes given below

(a) Only 1 (b) Both 3 and 4
(c) Both 2 and 3 (d) All of the above

Promotion Decision

62 Institutional advertising is

(a) aimed only at people in institutions
(b) run only by institutions
(c) designed to promote a type of product rather than a particular brand
(d) designed simply to show that the firm is a good place to do business

63 A planned, coordinated, unified series of ads is called a

(a) campaign (b) tactic
(c) promotional survey (d) None of these

64 .... advertisements are used to create awareness.

(a) Pioneer (b) Comparative
(c) Competitive (d) None of these

65 In ...., price of a product is reduced in an exchange of an old product.

(a) exchange promotion (b) combination promotion
(c) multiple promotion (d) None of these

66 Which of the following is not a tool of sales promotion?

(a) Sales contests (b) Free gifts
(c) Point of purchase display (d) Public relations

67 To develop marketing communication programmes, so that the organisation presents a consistent message is the goal of

(a) advertising (b) personal selling
(c) non-personal selling (d) None of these

68 Which of the following is not one of the methods by which firms decide how much to spend on advertising?

(a) Percentage of sales (b) Task approach
(c) Check and balance (d) All you can afford

69 Some firms set their advertising budget as a predetermined share of profits or financial resources. This would be an example of which budgeting method?

(a) Percentage of sales (b) Per unit expenditure
(c) Task approach (d) All you can afford

70 Translating the product idea or marketing message into an effective ad is termed

(a) motivation
(b) encoding
(c) decoding
(d) customer psychology

71 When competing firms in the same industry unit promote their product as a whole, their advertising is best described as

(a) primary demand advertising
(b) institutional advertising
(c) trade advertising
(d) indirect demand advertising

72 The biggest disadvantage of using outdoor advertising as a medium is

(a) difficulty in obtaining good locations
(b) high cost
(c) poor quality of reproduction in that size
(d) limited copy

73 The most important advertising medium today, at least in total advertising monetary terms is

(a) newspapers (b) magazines
(c) television (d) direct mail

74 Advertising budget is influenced by which of the following factors?

1. Type of product advertised
2. Size of the market
3. Demographic condition
4. Sales volume

Select the correct answer using the codes given below

(a) 1, 2 and 3 (b) 1, 2 and 4
(c) Only 3 (d) All of the above

75 Road blocking advertisement is

(a) advertising a product by blocking a road
(b) putting an advertisement on a blocked road
(c) a technique of gathering potential customers on the road
(d) advertising a product on all similar TV/Radio channels at the same time

76 A product line strategy where in a company adds a higher priced product to a line, in order to attract a broader market which helps the sale of its existing lower priced products is called

(a) trading up
(b) trading down
(c) life cycle extension
(d) product line extension

Miscellaneous

77 **Assertion** (A) According to the concept of product life cycle, a company should begin a search for new products during stage.

Reason (R) The growth stage is the time in which a company should begin to search for new products.

Codes

(a) Both (A) and (R) are true
(b) Both (A) and (R) are false
(c) (A) is true, but (R) is false
(d) (R) is true, but (A) is false

Directions (Q. Nos. 78-82) *In the questions given below are two statements lablelled as (A) Assertion and (R) Reason. In the context of the two statements, which one of the following is correct?*

Codes

(a) Both (A) and (R) are true and (R) is the correct explanation of (A)
(b) Both (A) and (R) are true, but (R) is not the correct explanation of (A)
(c) (A) is true, but (R) is false
(d) (A) is false, but (R) is true

78 **Assertion** (A) Advertising involves impersonal communication and persuasion.
Reason (R) It pays to advertise. Money spent on advertising is investment and not a waste.

79 **Assertion** (A) The marketing manager has to take many decisions that affect the day-to-day activities of the organisation.
Reason (R) Main objective of marketing manager is to achieve the predetermined marketing objectives.

80 **Assertion** (A) The product is one of the important element of the 4Ps of the marketing mix.
Reason (R) A typical product goes through four stages in its life.

81 **Assertion** (A) The product mix is the set of all the products that an organisation offers to its customers.
Reason (R) Width is the total number of product lines a company carries.

82 **Assertion** (A) Product development is the process of finding out the possibility of producing a product keeping in view the customers needs and wants.
Reason (R) Pricing strategy does not depend on customer perception.

83 Match the following.

List I (Features of Product Mix)	List II (Explanations)
A. Width	1. Varieties offered for each product in the product line.
B. Length	2. Total number of product lines a company carries.
C. Depth	3. Total number of items in product mix.
D. Consistency	4. Closeness exhibited by product lines.

Codes

	A	B	C	D
(a)	2	3	1	4
(b)	1	2	3	4
(c)	3	2	1	4
(d)	1	4	3	2

84 Match the following.

List I (Pricing Methods)	List II (Explanations)
A. Mark-up pricing	1. Set high price and recover the cost as early as possible
B. Target return pricing	2. Cost of the product + Mark-up (desired profit)
C. Going rate pricing	3. Specified rate of return on investment
D. Market skimming	4. Prevailing pricing matters

Codes

	A	B	C	D		A	B	C	D
(a)	2	3	4	1	(b)	1	2	3	4
(c)	2	4	3	1	(d)	4	3	2	1

85 Match the following.

List I	List II
A. Scrambled lines	1. Super markets selling non-food items.
B. Pipelines	2. A major means of transporting goods to market.
C. Wholesalers	3. Marketing institutions buying goods and reselling them to retailers other wholesaler or industrial users.
D. Brokers	4. Bringing buyer and seller together, but do not take title of goods.

Codes

	A	B	C	D		A	B	C	D
(a)	2	1	3	4	(b)	1	2	3	4
(c)	4	2	3	1	(d)	3	2	4	1

86 Match the following.

List I	List II
A. Grading	1. Facilitates selling
B. Packaging	2. Naming the product for identification and distinguishing it from others
C. Branding	3. Art of informing customers
D. Advertising	4. Classification, wins more confidence of customers

Codes

	A	B	C	D		A	B	C	D
(a)	4	1	2	3	(b)	1	2	3	4
(c)	2	1	4	3	(d)	4	3	2	1

87 Match the following.

List I	List II
A. Personal selling	1. Stimulates demand for a whole type of product.
B. Geographic selectivity	2. Personal presentation and promotion of ideas, goods or services.
C. Qualitative selectivity	3. Ability of an advertising medium to reach almost everyone in given area.
D. Primary demand advertising	4. Ability of an advertising medium to reach only certain types of people.

Codes

	A	B	C	D		A	B	C	D
(a)	2	3	4	1	(b)	1	2	3	4
(c)	2	4	3	1	(d)	4	3	2	1

PREVIOUS YEARS' QUESTIONS

December 2018

1 Advertising method in which a commercial is broadcast simultaneously on several radio stations and/or television channels is known as

(a) Exclusive drive (b) Intensified campaign
(c) Road side (d) Road block

2 Which among the following is not an internal factor of pricing decision?

(a) Price elasticity as per sales of product
(b) Consumer's expectation from company by past pricing
(c) Position of product in product cycle
(d) Consumer behaviour for given product

3 *Given below are two statements, one labelled as Assertion (A) and the other labelled as Reason (R). Read the statements and choose the correct answer using the code given below.*

Assertion (A) Purchase decisions are not based on how customers perceive prices but on the marketer's stated price.

Reason (R) Customers may have a lower price threshold, below which prices signal inferior or unacceptable quality, and an upper price threshold where the product appears not worth the money.

(a) Both (A) and (R) are correct and (R) is the right explanation of (A)
(b) Both (A) and (R) are correct, but (R) is not the right explanation of (A)
(c) Both (A) and (R) are incorrect
(d) (A) is incorrect, but (R) is correct

July 2016

4 Product line pricing strategy includes which combination of the following ?

A. Public utility pricing
B. Complementary goods pricing
C. Spare parts pricing
D. Load factor pricing

Select the correct answer using the codes given below

Codes

(a) A, B and C (b) B, C and D
(c) A, B and D (d) A, C and D

5 Production function for a product is based on certain assumptions. Indicate the correct code from the following.

A. Complementarity B. Substitutability
C. Product elasticity D. Specificity

Select the correct answer using the codes given below

Codes

(a) A, B, C (b) B, C, D
(c) A, C, D (d) A, B, D

December 2015

6 Match the following.

List I	List II
A. Product category	1. One of several variant shapes
B. Product forms	2. Longest PLC
C. Products	3. Standard PLC
D. Branded products	4. Short or long PLC

Codes

	A	B	C	D
(a)	3	4	2	1
(b)	1	2	4	3
(c)	4	2	1	3
(d)	2	3	1	4

June 2015

7 Match the following.

List I (Strategies)	List II (Examples)
A. Differential pricing	1. Customer lounges to sit in while waiting for a table at service centres etc
B. Complimentary service	2. Breakfast service by McDonald's and mini vacation and weekends by hotels
C. Reservation system	3. Low prices for early and evening movies, weekend discounts for car parking rentals
D. Non-peak demand cultivation	4. Airlines, hotels and physicians employ extensively

Codes

	A	B	C	D
(a)	1	3	2	4
(b)	4	2	1	3
(c)	2	1	4	3
(d)	3	1	4	2

8 The pricing strategy which adjusts the basic price to accommodate differences in customers, products and locations is called

(a) differentiated pricing
(b) promotional pricing
(c) geographical pricing
(d) price discounts and allowances

December 2014

9 Which of the following is not a product mix strategy?

(a) Trading up (b) Alteration
(c) Simplification (d) Value addition

10 'Relationship' in marketing means

(a) relation between buyer and seller
(b) relation between sales person
(c) relation between company and consumers
(d) All of the above

June 2014

11 Match the following.

List I	List II
A. Skimming pricing	1. A market having high price elasticity
B. Differential pricing	2. A market having high price inelasticity
C. Penetrating pricing	3. A market having several segments differing prominently with regard to price elasticities of their demand

Codes

	A	B	C
(a)	1	2	3
(b)	3	1	2
(c)	2	3	1
(d)	3	2	1

June 2012

12 Match the following.

List I	List II
A. Mega marketing	1. Advertising
B. Penetration price	2. Kotler
C. Promotion mix	3. Low price
D. Customer satisfaction	4. Post purchase behaviour

Codes

	A	B	C	D		A	B	C	D
(a)	1	2	3	4	(b)	3	1	2	4
(c)	4	3	2	1	(d)	3	4	1	2

13 **Statement** I Sales promotion has a strong impact on consumer behaviour in rural India.
Statement II Rural people in India give utmost significance to sales promotion schemes.

Codes

(a) Statement I is correct, but Statement II is incorrect
(b) Statement I is incorrect, but Statement II is correct
(c) Both statements are correct
(d) Both statements are incorrect

ANSWERS

Objective Questions

1 (b)	2 (b)	3 (b)	4 (c)	5 (a)	6 (a)	7 (d)	8 (c)	9 (d)	10 (c)
11 (a)	12 (b)	13 (c)	14 (a)	15 (b)	16 (d)	17 (c)	18 (a)	19 (a)	20 (b)
21 (a)	22 (d)	23 (a)	24 (c)	25 (b)	26 (c)	27 (a)	28 (d)	29 (d)	30 (d)
31 (d)	32 (b)	33 (b)	34 (a)	35 (a)	36 (c)	37 (a)	38 (b)	39 (a)	40 (a)
41 (d)	42 (b)	43 (b)	44 (a)	45 (b)	46 (a)	47 (a)	48 (b)	49 (b)	50 (a)
51 (b)	52 (c)	53 (c)	54 (c)	55 (a)	56 (a)	57 (b)	58 (b)	59 (a)	60 (c)
61 (a)	62 (d)	63 (a)	64 (a)	65 (a)	66 (b)	67 (a)	68 (c)	69 (d)	70 (b)
71 (a)	72 (d)	73 (a)	74 (b)	75 (d)	76 (d)	77 (d)	78 (b)	79 (a)	80 (b)
81 (b)	82 (c)	83 (a)	84 (a)	85 (b)	86 (a)	87 (a)			

Previous Years' Questions

1 (d)	2 (d)	3 (d)	4 (b)	5 (d)	6 (d)	7 (d)	8 (a)	9 (d)	10 (c)
11 (c)	12 (b)	13 (a)							

CHAPTER 32

Indian Contract Act

The contracts or agreements between various parties are framed and validated by the Indian Contract Act. Contract act is one of the most central laws that regulates and oversees all the business wherever a deal or an agreement is to be reached at. Without contract act, it would have been difficult to carry on trade or any other business activity.

Indian Contract Act, 1872

Indian Contract Act came into force on 1st September, 1872. It extends to the whole of India except the state of Jammu and Kashmir. This act mostly deals with the general principles and rules governing contracts.

According to **Anson**, "A contract is an agreement enforceable at law, made between two or more persons, by which rights are acquired by one or more to acts or forbearances on the part of the other or others."

According to **Salmond**, "A contract is an agreement creating and defining obligations between the parties."

As per Section 2(h) of Indian Contract Act, "A contract is an agreement enforceable by law."

These definitions indicate that a contract essentially consists to two distinct parts, *i.e.*

- there must be an agreement.
- such an agreement must be enforceable by law.

A contract therefore, is a combination of the two elements, *i.e.*

- an agreement
- a obligation

In this Chapter

Important Terms related to Contract

Offer or Proposal A proposal is also termed as an offer. An offer is a proposal by one person, whereby he expresses his willingness to enter into a contractual obligation in return for a promise, act or forbearance. As per Section 2 (a) of the Indian Contract Act, when one person signifies to another his willingness to do or abstain from doing anything with a view to obtaining the assent of that other to such act or abstinence, he is said to make a proposal or offer. The person making the proposal/offer is called the proposer or offeror and the person to whom the proposal is made, is called the offeree.

Acceptance A contract emerges from the acceptance of an offer. Acceptance is the act of assenting by the offeree to an offer. Under Section 2 (b) of the Contract Act, "When a person to whom the proposal is made, signifies his assent thereto, the proposal is said to be accepted".

Promise A proposal, when accepted becomes a promise.

Elements of a Valid Contract

As per Section 10 of the Indian Contract Act, 1872, "All agreements are contracts if they are made by the free consent of parties competent to contract, for a lawful consideration and with a lawful object and are not hereby expressly declared to be void."

The essential elements of a vaild contract are

- An offer or proposal by one party and acceptance of that offer by another party resulting in an agreement.
- An intention to create legal relations or an intent to have legal consequences.
- The agreement is supported by a lawful consideration.
- The parties to the contract are legally capable of contracting.
- Genuine consent between the parties.
- The object and consideration of the contract is legal and is not opposed to public policy.
- The terms of the contract are certain.
- The agreement is capable of being performed, *i.e.* it is not impossible of being performed.

Therefore, to form a valid contract, there must be

- an agreement.
- based on the genuine consent of the parties.
- supported by a lawful consideration.
- made for a lawful object.
- between the competent parties.

Capacity of Parties to Contract

For a contract to be valid, the parties of a contract must have capacity, *i.e* competence to enter into a contract. Every person is presumed to have capacity to contract but there are certain person whose age, condition or mental status renders them incapable of binding themselves by a contract. This incapacity must be proved by the party claiming the benefit of it.

As per Section 11 of the Act, it deals with the competency of parties and provides that "every person in competent of contract who is of the age of majority according to the law to which he is subject and who is of sound mind and is not disqualified from contracting by any law to which he is subject."

Therefore, the following persons are incompetent to contract

- Minor
- Person of unsound mind
- Person disqualified by any law to which they are subject

Thus, any contract entered into by the persons mentioned above, are void.

Free Consent

For a contract to be valid, the consent of the parties must be genuine *i.e.* free. The principle of consensus-ad-idem is followed which means that the parties entering into the contract, must mean the same thing in the same sense. The parties to the contract must have the same understanding in regards to subject matter of the contract.

As per the Act, free consent is consent, *i.e.* free from coercion, undue influence, fraud, misrepresentation or mistake. When the given consent is affected by these elements, it calls into question whether the consent given was free and voluntary.

Discharge of a Contract

A contract is said to be discharged or terminated when the rights and obligations arising out of a contract are extinguished.

Contracts may be discharged by any of the following modes

Performance of Contracts

As per Section 37 of the Act, provides that the parties to a contract must either perform or offer to perform their respective promises, unless such performance is dispensed with or excused under the provision of this act or any other law. In case of death of the promisor before performance, the representatives of the promisor are bound to perform the promise unless a contrary intention appears from the contract.

e.g. A promises to deliver a house to B on a certain day on payment of ₹ 8,000. A dies before that day. A's representatives are bound to deliver the horse to B and B is bound to pay ₹ 8,000 to A's representatives.

Discharge by Mutual Agreement or Consent

A contract may be discharged by the agreement of all parties to the contract or by waiver or release by the party entitled to performance. As per Section 62 and Section 63 of the Act, *following are the methods for discharging a contract by mutual consent*

Novation A new contract is substituted for existing contract.

Alteration Change in one or more of the material terms of a contract.

Rescission By agreement between the parties at any time before it is discharged.

Remission Acceptance of a lesser sum that what was contracted for.

Waiver Deliberate abandonment or giving up of a right which a party is entitled to under a contract.

Discharge by Lapse of Time

The Limitation Act, in certaion circumstance, affords a good defence to suits for breach of contract and terminates the contract by depriving the party of his remedy to law.

Discharge by Operation of the Law

- By merger, *i.e.* when the parties embody the inferior contract in a superior contract.
- By the unauthorised alteration of items of a written document.
- By insolvency, *i.e.* where the court passes an order discharging the insolvent.

Discharge by Impossibility of Frustration

A contract which is entered into, to perform something, *i.e.* clearly impossible, is void. If the impossibility is not obvious and the promisor alone knows of the impossibility, such promisor is bound to compensate the promisor for any loss, he may suffer through the non-performance of the promise inspite to the agreement being void ab initio.

Breach of Contract

Where the promisor neither performs his contract nor does he tenders performance or where the performance is defective, there is a breach of contract. The breach of contract may be actual or anticipatory. The actual breach may take place either at the time of the performance is due or when actually performing the contract. Anticipatory breach means a breach before the time for the performance has arrived.

Anticipatory breach may take place either by the promisor doing an act which makes the performance of his promise impossible or by the promisor in some other way showing his intention not to perform it.

Breach of contract may occur where one of the parties definitely renounces the contract and shows his intention not to perform it or does some act which makes performance impossible. On such a breach, the other party has a right of action for damages.

Remedies for Breach

Where a contract is broken, the injured party has several courses of action open to him. The appropriate remedy in any case will depend upon the subject-matter of the contract and the nature of the breach.

Remedies against Breach of Contract

When a contract is broken, the injured party has several courses of action open to him, *which are as follows*

- The injured party may rescind the contract and refuse further performance of the contract.
- The injured party may sue for damages.
- The injured party may sue for specific performance.

As per Section 65 of the Act, "When a party treats the contract or rescinded he makes himself liable to restore any benefits, he has received under the contract to the party from whom such benefits were received."

As per Section 75 of the Act, "If a person rightfully rescinds a contract, he is entitled to a compensation for nay damage which he has sustained through the non-fulfilment of the contract by the other party."

Damages for Breach of Contract

As per Section 73 of the Act, "When a contract has been broken, a party who suffers by such breach is entitled to receive, from the party who has broken the contract, compensation for any loss or damage, caused to him."

Specific Performance

Where a party fails to perform the contract, the court may at its discretion, order the defendant to carry out his undertaking according to the terms of the contract. A decree for specific performance may be granted in addition to or instead of damages.

Injuction

An injuction is an order of a court restraining a person from doing a particular act. It restrains continuance of a wrongful commission.

Quasi-Contracts

A valid contract must contain certain essential element, *i.e.* offer and acceptance, consideration, free consent etc. But sometimes the law implies a promise which imposes obligations on one, party and confers right in favour of the other one, when there is neither agreement nor promise. Such cases are not contracts in the strict sense but law recognises them as relations resembling those of contracts and enforces them as if they were contracts. These contracts are known as quasi-contracts. A quasi-contract is not a contract at all but it is an obligation which the law creates, in the absence of any agreement.

The following kinds of quasi-contracts have been dealt within the Indian Contract Act

- Necessaries supplied to person incapable of contracting such as minors and persons of unsound mind etc or to anyone whom he is illegally bound to support.
- Suit for money had and received.
- ***Quantum Meruit*** means 'as much as earned' or reasonable remuneration. It is used where a person claims reasonable remuneration for the services rendered by him when there was no express promise to pay the definite remuneration.
- Obligations of a finder of goods.
- Obligation of person enjoying benefit of a non-gratuitous act.

Special Contracts

Special contracts include the contract of indemnity, contract of guarantee, contract of bailment and contract of agency, *which are as follows*

Contract of Indemnity

As per Section 124 of the Act, a contract of indemnity is a contract by which one party promises to save the other party from loss caused to him by the conduct of the promisor himself or by the conduct of any other person. The person who promises to indemnify or make good the loss is called the indeminifier and the person whose loss is made good is called the indeminified or the indemnity holder.

Under the Indian Contract Act, the contract of indemnity is restricted to such cases only where the loss promised to be reimbursed, is caused by the conduct of the promisor or of any other person. The loss caused by events or accidents which do not depend on the conduct of any person it seems, can not be sought to be reimbursed under a contract of indemnity.

e.g. A contracts to indemnify B against the consequence of any proceedings which C may take against B in respect of a certain sum of ₹ 500.

Essential Elements of Contract of Indemnity

Existence of All Elements of a Valid Contract It is essential for a contract of indemnity that all the essential elements of a valid contract must present otherwise indemnity would not be valid. It means there must be offer, acceptance, consideration, capacity of parties to contract etc.

Promise to Save from Loss It is essential for a valid contract of indemnity that there must be a promise by the indemnified to save the indemnity holder from the loss. The loss may be caused by the conduct of the promisor himself or by the conduct of any other person.

It means, loss must be caused by a human agency. The losses caused by accidents are not covered under the contract of indemnity that's why contract of insurance is not a contract of indemnity.

Contract may be Express or Implied Contract of indemnity may be express (by words oral or written) or implied. Implied means contract of indemnity is inferred from the conduct of parties or from the circumstances of the case.

Commencement of Liability of Indemnifier Liability of the idemnifier commences when the indemnity holder had really incurred a liability and the liability is absolute. The indemnity holder can claim damages for only actual amount of liability which the indemnity holder had incurred.

Contract of Guarantee

As per Section 126 of the Act, a contract of guarantee is a contract to perform the promise or discharge the liability of a third person in case of his default. The person who gives the guarantee is called the surety, the person for whom the guarantee is given is called the principle debtor and the person to whom the guarantee is given is called the creditor. A guarantee may be either oral or written, although in the English law, it must be in writing.

Like a contract of indemnity, a guarantee must also satisfy all the essential elements of a valid contract. Section 127 provides that anything done or any promise made for the benefit of the principle debtor may be a sufficient consideration to the surety for giving the guarantee.

e.g. A sells and delivers goods to B. C afterwards requests A to forbear to sue B for the debt for a year and promises that if he does so, C will pay for them in default of payment by B. A agrees to forbear as requested. This is sufficient consideration for C's promise.

Essential Elements of Guarantee

Three Parties There are three parties in every contract of guarantee. *They are*

- ***Principle Debtor*** The person for whom guarantee is given is called principle debtor.
- ***Creditors*** The person to whom guarantee is given is called creditor.
- ***Surety*** The person who gives guarantee is called surety.

Three Contracts There are three contract in every contract of guarantee first one is between principal debtor and creditor, second one is between principal debtor and surety and third one is between creditor and surety.

Guarantee may be Expressed or Implied Contract of guarantee may be express or implied by words whether written or oral. Implied guarantee means which is inferred from the conduct of the parties or from the circumstances of the case.

Consideration It is essential for a valid contract of guarantee that it must be supported by consideration but it is not necessary that, there should be a direct consideration between surety and creditor. According to Section 127 of the Indian Contract Act, "Anything done or any promise made for the benefit of the principal debtor, may be a sufficient consideration to the surety for given guarantee. So, the consideration received by the principal debtor is sufficient consideration for the surety and surely need not be benefited.

Liability of Surety In contract of guarantee, the liability of surety is secondary, not primary. It means surety becomes liable only when the principal fails to discharge his liability.

Liability or Debt must be Lawful In contract of guarantee, the liability or debt for which guarantee is given, must be lawful. It means they should not be time barred under the law of limitation.

Disclosure of Facts by Creditor It is essential for a valid guarantee that the creditor must disclose all the material facts to the creditor before entering into the contract otherwise guarantee is not valid. Scction 142 provides that a guarantee, obtained by misrepresentation or concealment of fact is not valid.

Essential Elements of a Valid Contract In the contract of guarantee, there must trust all the essential elements of a valid contract like offer, acceptance, consideration, capacity of parties to contract.

Contract of Bailment

As per Section 148 of the Act, a bailment is a transaction whereby one person delivers goods to another person for some purpose, upon a contract that they are, when the purpose is accomplished, to be returned or otherwise disposed of according to the directions of the person delivering them. The person who delivers the goods is called the bailor and the person to whom they are delivered is called the bailee. The ownership of the goods remains with the bailor, the bailee, getting only the possession delivery of goods may be actual or constructive.

Rights of Bailor

Right to Claim Damages *(Section 151)* The bailor has a right to claim damages from the bailee, if due to the negligence of the bailee goods bailed are destroyed or get damaged and bailor suffers loss.

Right to Terminate the Contract *(Section 153)* If the bailee close any act with regard to the goods bailed which inconsistent with the terms of the contract. Then the bailor becomes entitle to terminate the contract of bailment.

Right to Claim, Compensation for Unauthorised Use of Goods Bailed *(Section 154)* If the bailee makes unauthorised use of the goods bailed and due to this, bailee suffers loss regarding the goods bailed, bailor can claim compensation for the loss suffered.

Right to Terminate Gratuitous Bailment *(Section 159)* In case of gratuitous bailment, the bailor may, at any time, terminate the bailment. It means, he can take back the goods bailed. Even before the accomplishment of purpose of bailment.

Right to Return Back the Goods *(Section 160)* It is one of the essential elements of the bailment that after the accomplishment of the purpose of the bailment, goods shall be returned to the bailor. Hence, the bailor has right to return back the goods after accomplishment of the purpose of bailment.

Right of Compensation, if Goods Bailed are not Returned *(Section 161)* If after the accomplishment of the purpose of the bailment, the bailee does not return the goods to bailor and thereby the bailor suffers some loss. The bailor can claim compensation for the loss.

To Received Increase or Profit from Bailed Goods *(Section 163)* The bailor is entitled to any increase or profit which may have accrued to the bailee from the goods bailed.

Right to Separate the Goods *(Section 155,156,157)* It is the duty of the bailee not to mix the bailed goods with his own goods. But, if he mixes the both goods, *then following are the rights of bailor*

- If the bailee mixes the goods with the consent of the bailor, the bailor and the bailee shall how an interest in proportion to their respective shares in the mixed goods.
- If the bailee mixed the goods without the consent of the bailor and the goods can be separated. Then the bailee shall bear the expenses of separation of mixed goods.

- If the bailee mixes the goods without the consent of the bailor and the mixed goods cannot be separated, then the bailee is bound to compensate the bailor for the loss of goods.

Duties of Bailor

To Deliver the Goods to Bailee It is the duty of bailor to deliver the goods bailed to the bailee under the contract of bailment.

To Disclose Faults of Goods *(Section 150)* It is the duty of the bailor to disclose the material faults in the goods of which he is aware. If he does not disclose such faults, he shall be responsible for damages arising to the bailee from such faults. But in case of non-gratuitous bailment, the bailor is responsible for the loss to the bailee arising from any fault of goods whether he was aware or not of such faults.

To Pay Necessary Expenses *(Section 158)* In gratuitous bailment, it is the duty of bailor to pay to bailee all the necessary expenses incurred by him for the purpose of bailment.

To Pay Extra Ordinary Expenses *(Section 158)* In case of non-gratuitous bailment, if the bailee has incurred some extra ordinary expenses regarding the goods bailed. It is the duty of the bailor to pay extra ordinary expenses to the bailee.

To Indemnify Bailee for Excess Loss *(Section 159)* In case of gratuitous bailment, if the bailor compels the bailee to return the goods before the accomplishment of purpose or before the specified time of bailment. The bailor shall indemnify the bailee for the loss which results from such premature return of goods.

To Compensate for Loss due to Defective Title of Goods *(Section 164)* If the title of bailor over the goods bailed is defective and due to this the bailee suffers loss, it is the duty of the bailor to compensate the bailee for the loss.

To Pay Remuneration to Bailor It is the duty of bailor to pay bailee his agreed remuneration or if not agreed to pay a reasonable remuneration for bailment of goods.

To Receive Back the Goods Bailed It is the duty of bailor to receive back the goods when they are returned by the bailee after the accomplishment of the purpose of bailment or after the expiry of specified period of bailment.

Rights of Bailee

Right to Damages for Non-disclosure of Faults *(Section 150)* If the bailor does not disclose the material faults in the goods bailed and the bailee suffers loss due to such faults or defects, the bailee has right to claim damages for the loss.

Right to Receive Necessary Expenses *(Section 158)* In case of gratuitous bailment, if the bailee is not received any remuneration under the bailment, he is entitled to recover from the bailor, all the necessary expenses incurred by him for the purpose of bailment.

Right to Receive Extra Ordinary Expenses If the bailee has incurred any extra ordinary expenses regarding the goods bailed, he is entitled to recover all such expenses.

Right to Damages for Defective Title of Bailor *(Section 164)* If the bailee suffers any loss due to the defective title of bailor over the goods bailed, he can claim damages for such loss from the bailor.

Right to Deliver the Goods to any one of the Joint Bailors *(Section 165)* If there are more then one bailor in the contract of bailment, the bailee has right to deliver back the goods to any one of the joint bailor.

To Stop Delivery of Goods to Decide Title of Goods Bailed *(Section 171)* If a third person claims titles over the goods bailed, the bailee has rights to stop the delivery of goods and apply the court to decide the title to the goods.

Right of Lien *(Section 170)* Lien means rights to retain the possession of goods till the claims regarding the goods are fulfilled. As per Section 170, where the bailee has rendered any service involving the exercise of labour or skill, he has right to retain the goods until he receives the due remuneration for the service he has rendered.

Duties of Bailee

Duty to take Reasonable Care of Goods Bailed *(Section 151)* It is the duty of bailee in all kinds of bailment to take as much care of the goods bailed to him as a man of ordinary prudence would take of his own goods.

Duty to Compensate for Loss due to his Negligence *(Section 152)* If the goods bailed are destroyed or damaged due to the negligence of bailee, he is responsible to compensate the bailor for the loss, he has suffered due to the negligence of bailee.

Duty not to Act Inconsistent with the Terms of Bailment *(Section 153)* It is the duty of the bailee not to act inconsistent with the terms of the bailment otherwise the bailor will get the right to terminate the bailment.

To Pay Compensation for Loss due to Unauthorised use of Goods Bailed *(Section 154)* It is the duty of bailee to use the goods according to the terms of the bailment. If make any unauthorised use that against the terms of bailment and due to this use, the goods are damaged, he is responsible to compensate the bailor for the loss.

Duty not to Mix Bailed Goods with his own Goods *(Section 155,157,158)* It is the duty of bailee not to mix his own goods with bailed goods. If he mixes both the goods without the consent of the bailor. *Following rules will apply*

- If the bailee mixes the goods without the consent of the bailor and goods can be separated, the bailee shall bear the expenses of separation of goods.
- If the bailee mixes the goods without the consent of the bailor and goods cannot be separated, the bailee is bound to compensate the bailor for the loss of whole goods.

Duty to Return Bailed Goods *(Section 160)* It is the duty of the bailee to return the goods bailed according to the direction of the bailor when the time for which they were bailed has expired or the purpose for which they were bailed has fulfilled.

To Compensate for Loss arising due to Non-return of Goods *(Section 161)* If the bailee faults to return over offer before the expiry of the time for which goods were bailed or the purpose of bailment has fulfilled and due to this the bailor suffers some loss, bailee is liable to compensate the bailor for the loss.

To Return any Increase or Profit in the Goods Bailed *(Section 163)* If there is any increase or profit in the goods bailed to bailee, it is the duty of the bailee to return the increase or profit according to the direction of the bailor.

Duty not to Establish Adverse Title *(Section 117)* It is the duty of the bailee that he will not establish his title over the goods bailed to him.

Termination of Bailment

As per Section 153 of the Act, where the bailee wrongfully uses or dispose of the goods bailed, the bailor may determine the bailment. As soon as the period of bailment expires or the object of the bailment has been achieved, the bailment comes to an end and the bailee must return the goods to the bailor. Bailment is terminated when the subject matter of bailment is destroyed or by reason of change in its nature, becomes incapable of use for the purpose of bailment.

Contract of Pledge

As per Section 172 of the Act, pledge (pawn) in a contract whereby an article is deposited with a lender of money or promisee as security for the repayment of a loan or performance of a promise. The bailor or depositor is called the 'pawnor' and the bailee or depositee is called the 'Pawnee'. Since, pledge is a branch of bailment, the pawnee is bound to take reasonable care of the goods pledged with him.

Following are the essentials of a pledge

- The pledged property should be delivered to the pawnee.
- Delivery should be in pursuance of a contract.
- Delivery should be for the purpose of security.
- Delivery should be upon a condition to return.

Rights of Pawnee

Right of Lien *(Section 173)* The pawnee has right of lien over the goods pledged. According to Section 173, *the pawnee may retain the goods for the following payments*

- For the payment of debt or performance of the promise.
- For the interest of the debt.
- For all necessary expenses incurred by the pawnee in respect of the possession of the pledged goods.
- The lien of the pawnee is in the nature of particular lien.

Right to Retain the Goods for Subsequent Debt *(Section 174)* If after the date of the pledge the pawnee lends money to the same pawnor without any other security, then the pawnee can return the goods for subsequent debt also.

Right to Extra Ordinary Expenses *(Section 175)* If the pawnee has incurred extra ordinary expenses for the preservation of pledged goods. The pawnee is entitled to receive from the pawnor such expenses.

Right to Sue against Pawnor *(Section 176)* If the pawnor makes a default in the payment of debt or performance of the promise at the time fixed in the contract, the pawnee may file a suit against the pawnee for the recovery of the debt or performance of the promise and at the same time retained the goods pledged as collateral security.

Sale of Pledged Goods *(Section 176)* If the pawnor makes a default in payment of debt or the performance of the promise, the pawnee may sell the pledged goods but he has to give a reasonable nature of the sale.

Right to Receive the Balance Amount If the pawnee sells the goods for the recovery of his debt but the proceeds of such sale is less than the amount due in respect of the debt, the pawnee has a right to claim the balance.

Duties of Pawnee

Duty to Take Reasonable Care of Goods It is the duty of the pawnee to take reasonable care of the goods pledged to him.

Duty not to Use the Pledged Goods for Personal Purpose It is the duty of the pawnee that he must not the goods pledged to him for the personal purpose. If the pawnee uses such goods, he may be hold liable for damages for any loss caused to the goods by such use.

Duty to Return the Surplus Amount If the pawnee sells the goods for the recovery of his debt in case pawnor makes a default and the proceeds of sale are greater than the amount of debt, the pawnee shall pay the surplus to the pawnor.

Duty to Return the Pledged Goods When the amount of debt is paid by the pawnor, it is the duty of the pawnee to return the pledged goods to the pawnor.

Duty not to Mix Pledged Goods It is the duty of the pawnee that he must not mix pledged goods with his own goods.

Duty to Return Increase of Profit If there is any increase or profit in the pledged goods, it is the duty of the pawnee to return such increase of profit to the pawnor.

Duty not to Act against the Terms of Pledge It is the duty of pawnee that he shall not use the goods pledged against the terms of the contract of pledge.

Duty not to Retain Goods for Extra Ordinary Expenses It is the duty if the pawnee not to retain the goods for any extra ordinary expenses incurred him regarding the goods pledged.

Rights of Pawnor

Right to Redeem the Goods (Section 171) The pawnor may redeem (get back) the pledged goods by paying, the debt interest on debt and all other necessary expenses incurred by the pawnee in respect of pledged goods.

Right to Damages If any damage incurred to the pledged goods due to the negligence of the pawnee, the pawnor can claim damages for the loss suffered by him.

Right to Receive Surplus When the pawnor makes a default in payment of debt and pawnee sell the pledged goods for the recovery of his debt, if the proceeds of sale of goods are greater than the amount of debt, the pawnor has right to receive the surplus.

Right to Receive Increase or Profit in Goods If there is any increase or profit in the pledged goods after the pledge is made, the pawnor has right to receive such increase of profit.

Duties of Pawnor

Duty to Disclose Defects in Goods It is the duty of the pawnor to disclose all material defects in goods which are to be pledged to the pawnee.

Duty to Pay Debt at Fixed Time It is the duty of the pawnor to pay, at the fixed time, the debtor or perform the promise under the pledge.

Duty to Pay Extra Ordinary Expenses If the pawnee has incurred some extra ordinary expenses for the preservation of the pledged goods, it is the duty of the pawnor to pay such expenses to the pawnee.

Duty to Pay the Balance Amount When the pawnor makes a default in payment of debt and pawnee sell the pledged goods, if the proceeds of the sale is less than the amount of debt, it is the duty of the pawnor to pay the balance amount to the pawnee.

Duty to Compensate for Defective Title If the title of the pawnor is defective over the pledged goods and due to this pawnor suffers loss, the pawnee is liable to compensate the loss to the pawnee.

Contract of Agency

A contract of agency may be expressed or implied but consideration is not an essential element in this contract. *Contract of agency are as follows*

Express Agency

A contract of agency may be made orally or in wirting. The power of attorney is the usual form of written contract of agency, that gives him the authority to act on behalf of his principale in accordacne with the terms and conditions therein. A power of attorney may be general (giving several powers to the agent) or special (giving authority to the agent for transacting a single act).

Implied Agency

Implied agency may arise by estoppel, necessity or ratification. *It includes*

Agency by Estoppel Estoppel arises when you are precluded from denying the truth of anything which you have represented as a fact, although it is not a fact.

Agency of Necessity In certain circumstances, a person who has been entrusted with anothers's property, may have to incur unauthorised expenses to protect or preserve it, such an agency is called an agency of necessity.

Agency by Ratification Where a person having no authority purports to act as agent or a duly appointed agent exceeds his authority, the principale is not bound by the contract but he may ratify the agents transaction and so accept liability.

Thus, an agency by retification arises. This is also known as ex-post facto agency, *i.e.* an agency arising after the event.

Agent and Agency

According to Section 182, "Agent is a person employed to do act for another or to represent another in dealing with third persons."

The person for whom such act is done or who is so represented is called the principal. The relationship between agent and principal is called agency. Thus, the agency is a relation between agent and the principal under which the agent acts for or represents the principal in dealing with other persons.

Duties of an Agent to Principal

To Follow the Direction of Principal *(Section 211)* It is the duty of an agent to conduct the business of agency according to the direction of his principal. If there are no direction from the principal, he must follow the custom which prevails in the same kind of business. If the agent does not follow the direction of the principal and principal suffers losses, the agent is liable to compensate the loss.

To Act with Reasonable Skill and Diligence *(Section 212)* It is the duty of an agent to conduct the business of agency with reasonable skill and diligence. He is bound to carry on the business with as much skill as is possessed by persons engaged in the similar business. If the agent acts negligently and principal suffers loss, the agent must compensate the principal for the loss.

To Maintain and Render Proper Accounts *(Section 213)* It is the duty of an agent to maintain the proper accounts of business of agency and renders them when demanded by the principal.

To Communicate with Principal in Difficulties *(Section 214)* It is the duty of an agent that in cases of difficulty, he must use all reasonable diligence in communicating with principal and obtain his instructions.

Not to Deal in his own Account *(Section 215)* It is the duty of the agent that he shall not deal in his account in the business of agency. He can deal in his own account with the permission of the principal. If he deals in his own account without obtaining the consent of the principal, the principal may repudiate the act done.

To Disclose Secret Profits *(Section 216)* If the agent deals on his own account in the business of agency and earned profit, agent is bound to disclose the profit. The principal can claim the profit, so earned.

To Pay the Amount Received for the Principal *(Section 218)* It is the duty of an agent to pay to his principale all sums received on his account. However, he may deduct from them his lawful remuneration and all expenses properly incurred by him for the business of the agency.

Not to Use Any Information Against Principal If during the conduct of the business of agency, agent comes to know some information relating to agency, it is the duty of the agent not to use such information against the interests of the principal.

Not to Establish Adverse Title It is the duty of the agent that he shall not establish adverse title over the goods of the principal of which he got the possession during the business of the agency.

Not to Delegate his Authority *(Section 190)* It is the duty of the agent that he must act personally which he has undertaken to perform personally. Thus, he must not delegate the authority given to him by the principal without the permission of the principal or when its permitted to close.

Rights of an Agent against Principal

Right to Retain Money Received on Principal Account *(Section 217)* An agent has right to retain his principal's money until his claim in respect of his remuneration and other expenses incurred by him in conducting the business of agency are satisfied.

Right to Receive Remuneration An agent has right to receive such remuneration as fixed by the terms of the agency. If remuneration is not so fixed, he is entitled to receive a reasonable remuneration. The agent is entitled to remuneration only when he has completed his work.

Right of Lien An agent has right to retain goods and other properties of the principal received by him until the amount due to himself for commission, disbursements and service in respect of the same has been paid.

Right to be Indemnified *(Section 222, 224)* An agent has right to be indemnified where the lossses and expenses have resulted as a consequence of any lawful act done by him in exercise of the authority conferred upon him by the principal. The right to be indemnified is not available against criminal acts.

Right to be Indemnified for Acts Done in Good Faith *(Section 223)* Where an agent does an act in the good faith which causes an injury to a third person, the employer is liable to indemnify the agent for the injury to third person.

Right to Compensation for Injury caused by Principal's Negligence *(Section 225)* An agent has right to be compensated by the principal for an injury caused to him by the principal's negligence.

Right to Stoppage in Transit If the agent purchased goods with his own funds or on his personal liability for price, he can stop the goods in transit if the principal has become insolvent.

Right to Appoint Sub-agent An agent has right to appoint sub-agent or substituted agent, if he is authorised by the principal.

Right of Compensation for Premature Revocation of Agency *(Section 205)* If the principal revokes the agency before its fixed time and agent suffers loss by such revocation, he can claim compensation for such loss from the principal.

Termination of Agency

An agency comes to an end or terminates

- By the performance of the contract of agency (Section 201).
- By an agreement between the principal and the agent.
- By expiration of the period fixed for the contract of agency.
- By the death of the principal or the agency (Section 201).
- By the insanity of either the principal or the agent (Section 201).
- By the insolvency of the principal and in some cases that of the agent (Section 201).
- Where the principal or agent is an incorporated company, by its dissolution.
- By the destruction of the subject matter (Section 56).
- By the revocation of authority by the principal (Section 201).

Termination of an agency takes effect or is complete, as regards the agent when it becomes known to the agent. As regards the third party, the termination takes effect when it comes to their knowledge.

EXAM BASED QUESTIONS

Indian Contract Act, 1872

1 Which of the following is correct?

(a) Indian Contract Act, 1882
(b) Indian Contract Act, 1972
(c) Indian Contract Act, 1872
(d) Indian Contract Act, 1888

2 The law of contract is nothing but

(a) a child of religion
(b) a child of commercial dealing
(c) a child of economics
(d) a child of day to day politics

3 The Indian Contract Act, 1872 extends to

(a) whole of India
(b) whole of India excluding Jammu and Kashmir
(c) North India
(d) South India

4 To form a valid contract, there should be atleast

(a) two parties
(b) three parties
(c) four parties
(d) five parties

5 Contractual rights and duties are created by

(a) state
(b) statue
(c) parties
(d) custom or usage

6 A contract is

(a) agreement + offer
(b) agreement + consideration
(c) agreement + enforceable by law
(d) None of the above

7 The correct sequence in formation of a contract is

(a) offer, acceptance, consideration, agreement
(b) offer, consideration, acceptance, agreement
(c) agreement, consideration, offer, acceptance
(d) offer, acceptance, agreement, consideration

8 A contract creates

(a) rights in personam
(b) rights in rem
(c) only rights and no obligations
(d) only obligations and no rights

9 Which of the following feature is not essential for a contract?

(a) It should be in writing only
(b) Free consent of parties competent of contract
(c) Lawful consideration and with a lawful object
(d) It should not be declared void expressly

10 When one person signifies to another his willingness to do or to abstain from doing anything with a view to obtaining the assent of that other person to such act or abstinence, he is said to make a

(a) proposal
(b) promise
(c) contract
(d) None of these

11 A offers to sell B his car for ₹ 2,00,000. C standing nearby says, "I will take it if B does not take it." B is not interested in the car. What will be the position if C says to A, "here is the money, I take the car."

(a) There is a contract between A and C
(b) There is no contract between A and C
(c) A may or may not accept the offer
(d) Both (b) and (c)

12 An agreement is a voidable contract when it is

(a) enforceable
(b) enforceable by law at the option of the aggrieved party
(c) enforceable by both the parties
(d) Not enforceable at all

13 Which one of the following statement is true?

(a) Offer and acceptance are revocable
(b) Offer and acceptance are irrevocable
(c) An offer can be revoked, but acceptance can not
(d) An offer can not be revoked, but acceptance can be revoked

14 Which one of the following falls into the category of offer?

(a) Newspaper advertisement regarding sale
(b) Display of goods by a shopkeeper in his window with prices marked on them
(c) An advertisement for a concert
(d) Announcement of reward to the public

15 Which of the following circumstances is undue influence not exercised?

(a) Where one person holds a real or apparent authority over the other
(b) Where he stands in a fiduciary relation with the other
(c) Where he makes a contract with a person whose mental capacity is temporarily or permanently affected by reason of age, illness or mental distress
(d) When something is said or done in a dishonest way to trick people

16 Where the parties to a contract are under the mistake as to matter of fact essential to the agreement, the agreement is
(a) voidable at the option of the party making the proposal
(b) voidable at the option of the party accepting the proposal
(c) considered valid
(d) void

17 Who among the following is not competent to contract?
(a) Person who has acquired the age of 18
(b) Person who has acquired the age of 16
(c) Person is of sound mind
(d) Person who is disqualified from contracting by any law

18 What is consent under the Indian Contract Act, 1872?
(a) When acceptance of proposal is made by the party to whom the proposal is made
(b) When the acceptance is made by another person other than the person to whom the proposal is made
(c) When they agree upon the same thing in the same sense
(d) When both the parties agree upon a thing in the way, it is understood by them

19 Which of the following is not a necessary feature for free consent?
(a) When the consent is not caused by coercion
(b) When the consent is not caused by undue influence
(c) When the consent is not caused by mistake
(d) When the consent is not caused by misunderstanding

20 What is the meaning of novation?
(a) Rescinding of a contract
(b) Alteration of a contract
(c) Change in provisions of a contract
(d) Substituting an old contract for a new one

21 A contract is discharged on account of change of circumstances where the performance becomes
(a) virtually impossible
(b) extremely difficult or hazardous
(c) temporarily impossibility
(d) Both (a) and (b)

22 When after the formation of a valid contract, an event happens which makes the performance of contract impossible, the contract becomes
(a) voidable (b) void
(c) valid (d) illegal

23 The discharge of contract means the
(a) enforcement of obligations of parties
(b) coming to end of obligations of parties
(c) starting of obligation
(d) payment of carriages and penalty

24 The legal provisions relating to discharge of contract by impossibility of performance are contained in
(a) Section 55 (b) Section 56 (c) Section 58 (d) Section 59

25 Which of the following impossibility is the ground for discharge of contract?
(a) Initial impossibility
(b) Supervening impossibility
(c) Both (a) and (b)
(d) None of the above

26 A contract containing an undertaking to do an impossible act, is
(a) void ab initio (b) voidable
(c) valid (d) illegal

27 Which of the following is a made of discharge of contract?
(a) By performance of contract
(b) By agreement
(c) By impossibility of performance
(d) All of the above

28 In which of the following modes, the contract is discharge?
(a) By operation of law (b) By lapse of law
(c) By breach of contract (d) All of these

29 If a person who is incapable of entering into a contract is supplied with necessaries by another person, then the latter shall
(a) be reimbursed for such supplies by a relative of the incapable person and that relative must be capable of contracting
(b) be reimbursed for such supplies' from the property of such incapable person
(c) be reimbursed for such supplies' from the property of such incapable person
(d) not entitled to be reimbursed at all

30 A owes ₹ 10,000 to B under a contract. It is agreed between A, B and C that B shall henceforth accept C as his debtor instead of A for the same amount. Old debt of A is discharged and a new debt from C to B is contracted. This is
(a) alteration of contract
(b) rescission of contract
(c) novation of contract
(d) charge in contract

31 In which of the following cases, the contract is not discharged on the ground of subsequent impossibility?
(a) Death of promisor
(b) Change of law
(c) Commercial hardships
(d) Destruction of subject matter

32 A agreed to let a room to B for holding music shows on a certain dates. Before any show wars organised the room has destroyed in an accidental fire. In this case, the contract becomes
(a) void and is discharged
(b) voidable at A's option
(c) void, but not discharged
(d) voidable at B's option

33 **A owes B ₹ 5,000. C pays to B ₹ 100 and B accepts them, in satisfaction of his claim on A. What is the status of payment?**

(a) This payment is a partial discharge of the whole claim
(b) This payment is a discharge of the whole claim
(c) This payment is not a discharge of the whole claim
(d) None of the above

34 **A contract is void on the ground of initial impossibility**

(a) only where it is unknown to the parties
(b) only where it is known to the parties
(c) whether it is known or unknown to the parties at the time of agreement
(d) whether it is known to the third parties

35 **A agreed to sell his horse to B, but unknown to both the parties, the horse was dead at the time of agreement, in this case, the contract is**

(a) void and the parties are discharged from performance
(b) void but the parties are not discharged from performance
(c) voidable at the option of either party
(d) voidable at the option of A only

36 **In which of the following cases, a contract is discharged on the ground of frustration or subsequent impossibility?**

(a) Outbreak of war
(b) Change of law or government policy
(c) Both of (a) and (b)
(d) None of the above

37 **A agreed to supply certain goods to B which to be procured from C's factory. Due to strike is C's factory, A could not supply the goods. The contract**

(a) becomes void on account of impossibility
(b) becomes voidable on account of difficulty
(c) is discharged on account of impossibility
(d) is not discharged on account of impossibility

Breach of Contract and Quasi-contracts

38 **Generally, the following damages are not recoverable?**

(a) Ordinary damages (b) Special damages
(c) Remote damages (d) Nominal damages

39 **When there is breach of contract, the party which aggrieved by breach is entitled for**

(a) compensation against the breacher
(b) nothing
(c) registration of criminal case against the breacher
(d) None of the above

40 **Consideration should not be ...... but is should be natural.**

(a) quasi (b) complete
(c) party (d) legal

41 **Quasi-contract is a**

(a) contract (b) legal obligation
(c) agreement (d) conlingent contract

42 **The term quasi-contract is used in Indian Contract Act in**

(a) Section 68 to 72 (b) Section 69
(c) Section 71 (d) None of these

43 **In case of breach of contract, which of the following remedy is available to the aggrieved party?**

(a) Suit for rescission
(b) Suit for damages
(c) Suit for specific performance
(d) All of the above

44 **In case of breach of contract of sale of some rare article or thing for which there is no substitute in the market, the court may grant**

(a) quantum Meruit (b) rescission
(c) injuction (d) specific performance

45 **When a contract is breached, the party who suffers such breach shall**

(a) be indemnified for the loss or damage caused to him
(b) receive compensation for any loss or damage caused to him
(c) be remunerated for the loss or damage caused to him
(d) Not have any right under the act

46 **Which of the following is/are true in the context of quasi-contract?**

1. There is no real contract in existence.
2. There is no offer and acceptance.
3. There is no intention to create contract.

Select the correct answer by using the codes given below

Codes

(a) Only 1 (b) Both 1 and 2
(c) Both 1 and 3 (d) All of the above

47 **The basis of quasi-contractual relation is the**

(a) existence of a valid contract between the parties
(b) existence of a voidable contract between the parties
(c) prevention of unjust enrichment at the expenses of others
(d) provisions contained in Section 10 of the Contract Act

48 **The quasi-contractual obligations arise where a person**

(a) supplies necessaries to an incompetent person
(b) makes payment of money or delivery of goods or under coercion
(c) Both (a) and (b)
(d) None of the above

49 **A person supplying necessaries to an incompetent person (such as a minor or lunatic), is entitled to be reimbursed from the property of such person on the basis of**

(a) valid contract (b) quasi-contract
(c) vaidable contract (d) contingent contract

50 **In which of the following circumstances, the quasi contractual obligations arise?**

(a) Liability of a finder of goods
(b) Compensation for non-gratiuitous acts
(c) Recovery of payments made by interested persons
(d) All of the above

51 A person supplying 'necessaries' to an incompetent person is entitled to be reimbursed from the
(a) incompetent person personally
(b) parents of incompetent person
(c) property of incompetent person
(d) funds with the State Government

52 A supplies to B, a lunatic, the 'necessaries' suitable to his condition in life. In this case
(a) B is personally liable to pay
(b) B's property is liable
(c) B's parents are personally liable
(d) if B's property is not sufficient to reimburse, than he is personally liable

53 Mr A's property was wrongfully advertised for sale for recovery of government revenue due from B. In order to save his property, Mr A paid the government dues. In this case, Mr A is entitled to recover the amount of dues paid by him from Mr B on the basis of
(a) government contract (b) valid contract
(c) quasi-contract (d) None of these

54 Which of the following expression is used in the Indian Contract Act in the part dealing with quasi-contracts?
(a) Quasi contractual obligations
(b) Certain relations of quasi contractual obligations
(c) Certain relations resembling those created by contract
(d) Obligations in the absence of actual contract

55 When a party of the contract fails to perform a contract within the fixed time
(a) such contract remains valid provided the promise is fulfilled whether at the time of performance or later
(b) such a contract becomes void
(c) such contract becomes voidable at the option of the promise if the intention of the parties was that time should be of essence of the contract
(d) such a contract becomes voidable at the option of the promises or promise and the intention of the parties does not matter

56 A, a singer, enters into a contract with B, the manager of a theatre, to sing at his theatre two nights in every week during the next two months and B engages to pay her ₹ 1,000 for each night's performance. On the sixth night, A willfully absent herself from the theatre.
(a) B is at liberty to put an end to the contract
(b) B cannot put an end to the contract
(c) Either (a) and (b)
(d) None of the above

57 A season article marked "price ₹ 50" in Neha's shop, Sonal offers Neha ₹ 50 for the article. Neha refuses to sell saying the article is not for sale. Advice Sonal.
(a) Sonal cannot force Neha to sell the article at ₹ 50
(b) Sonal can force Neha to sell the article at ₹ 50
(c) Sonal can claim damages
(d) Sonal can sue Neha in the court

58 Mr X, a tradesman, left certain goods at Mr Y's house by mistake, in this case, Mr Y
(a) is bound to return the goods under quasi-contratual obligations
(b) is not bound to return the goods as there is no agreement between the two
(c) can use the goods as his own and can also claim compensation from Mr X
(d) is under obligation to make a fresh contract with Mr X for the use of these goods

59 Mr X, a builder, contracts to erect and finish a house by the 1st January, in order that Mr B may give possession of it at that time to Mr C, to whom Mr B has contracted to let it. Mr A is informed of the contract between Mr B and Mr C. Mr A builds the house so badly that, before the 1st January, it falls down and has to be rebuild by Mr B, who in consequence, loses the rent which he have received from Mr C and is obliged to make compensation to Mr C for the breach of his contract.
(a) Mr A must make compensation to Mr B for the cost of rebuilding the house
(b) Mr A must take compensation to Mr B for the rent lost
(c) Mr A must make compensation to Mr B for the compensation made to Mr C
(d) All of the above

60 Mr A advertises in a daily newspaper that he will give a prize of ₹ 90,000 to the first person to swim the English channel and back during the month of August. F, who has read the advertisement, sets off from Dower on Ist August and reaches the coast of Fracne on 2nd August. On that day, a further advertisement appears in the same newspaper stating that the offer of the prize has been withdrawn. On 3rd August, F completes the return swim to England can F recover the prize.
(a) Yes, as the second advertisement is ineffective so for as F is concerned
(b) No, as the offer was revocated
(c) F can only claim for damages
(d) None of the above

Special Contracts

61 Which of these contracts has three parties consisting of creditor, principle debtor and surety?
(a) Contract of indemnity
(b) Contract of surety
(c) Contract of pledge
(d) Contract of guarantee

62 Any guarantee which the creditor has obtained by means of keeping silence as to material circumstances is
(a) valid
(b) considered to be his approval
(c) invalid
(d) considered to be his denial

63 Where a person pledge goods in which he has only a limited interest, the pledge is
(a) invalid to the extent of that interest
(b) entire contract is invalid
(c) valid to the extent of that interest
(d) entire contract is valid

64 What is the minimum consideration required to create an agency?
(a) Minimum of ₹ 1,00,000
(b) Minimum of ₹ 1,000
(c) No consideration at all is required
(d) Minimum of ₹ 10,000

65 What are the essentials for a person to employ an agent?
(a) The person should not be of sound mind
(b) The person should be a major (not minor), according to the law to which the agent is subject
(c) The person should be a major (not minor), according to the law to which he is subject and should also be of sound mind
(d) The person should have executed a contract of indemnity before employing an agent

66 A contracts to pay B a sum of money when B marries C. C dies without being married to B.
(a) The contract still can be forced
(b) The contract becomes void
(c) Either (a) or (b)
(d) None of the above

67 The extent of the liability under an indemnity depends on
(a) the nature and terms of the contract
(b) the case which must be governed by his own facts and circumstances
(c) Both (a) and (b)
(d) None of the above

68 .... contract is made by spoken words.
(a) Implied (b) Express
(c) Void (d) Special

69 A guarantee with extend to a series of transaction is called
(a) special guarantee
(b) continuing guarantee
(c) specific guarantee
(d) None of the above

70 A sub-bailee is a person to whom the actual possession of goods is transferred by someone
(a) who is not himself not an owner of goods
(b) who has a present right to possession of them as bailee of the owner
(c) Both (a) and (b)
(d) None of the above

71 What is a continuing guarantee?
(a) A guarantee which continues even after the contract comes to an end
(b) A guarantee which shall be applicable to any other person who becomes a party to the contract
(c) A guarantee which extends to a series of transaction
(d) A guarantee which continues till the contract does not come to an end

72 What happens to a continuing guarantee in case of surety's death?
(a) Indemnification from the property of the surety with regard to future transactions
(b) Revocation of the continuing guarantee with regard to future transactions
(c) The continuing guarantee shall continue in the name of the surety's heirs
(d) The continuing guarantee shall be continued by any other person

73 A transfers possession or custody of the farmland to his son 'P'. P shall pay rent or a lease fee in return P only receives custody and control of the property, but A still owns it. A is, thus responsible for paying the property taxes and is liable for what happens on the land. This kind of contract or arrangement is called
(a) guarantee (b) bailment
(c) pledge (d) set off

74 An agent's authority can be created
(a) only by expressly writing the terms thereof
(b) only by implication
(c) only by expressly writing the terms thereof and registering the same with sub -registrar
(d) either expressly or impliedly

75 A sub-agent is a person employed by and acting under the control of
(a) the principal
(b) the original agent in the business of agency
(c) Both (a) and (b)
(d) Neither (a) nor (b)

76 Which of the following statement is correct with regard to the termination of agency in which the agent himself has an interest in the subject matter?
(a) Such an agency can be terminated by the principal at his will
(b) Such an agency can be terminated on the death or insanity of the principal
(c) Such an agency cannot be terminated at all
(d) Such an agency can be terminated only upon an express contract to the said effect

77 A contracts to indemnify B against the consequences of any proceedings which C may take against B in respect of a certain sum of ₹ 500.
(a) This is contract of indemnity
(b) This is not a valid contract of indemnity
(c) This is contract of stipulation
(d) None of the above

78 A employs B to beat C and agree to indemnify him against all consequence of the act. B thereupon beats C and to pay damages to C for so doing.

(a) A is liable to indemnify B for those damages
(b) A is partially liable to indemnify B for those damages
(c) A is not liable to indemnify B for those damages
(d) None of the above

79 A engages B as clerk to collect money for him. B fails to account for some of his receipts and A in consequence calls upon him to furnish security for his duly accounting. A does not acquaint C with B's previous conduct. B afterwards makes default.

(a) The guarantee is not invalid
(b) The guarantee is partly invalid
(c) The guarantee is invalid
(d) None of the above

80 The extent of an agent's authority, whether express or implied, depends upon

(a) the nature of act or business for which he has been appointed
(b) things which are incidental to the business or are usually done in carrying it out
(c) the usual customs and usages of the trade
(d) All of the above

81 Subject to a contract between the partners, the firm shall indemnify a partner is respect to payments made and liabilities incurred by him.

(a) In the ordinary and proper conduct of the business
(b) In doing such act, in an emergency, for the purpose of protecting the firm form loss, as would be done by a person of ordinary prudence, in his won case, under similar circumstances.
(c) Both (a) and (b)
(d) None of the above

82 Termination of an agency with public authority or a public body may attract judicial intervention in writ petition

(a) if the termination be unreasonable
(b) if the termination be arbitrary
(c) if the termination be unconscionable
(d) All of the above

83 A directs B, his solicitor, to sell his estate by auction and so employ an auctioneer for the purpose. B names C, an auctineer to conduct the sale.

(a) C is a sub agent, and A's sub agent for the conduct to the sale
(b) C is not sub-agent, but B's agent for the conduct for the sale
(c) C is not a sub-agent, but A's agent for the conduct of the sale
(d) None of the above

84 A contracts with B to grow a crop of indigo on A's land and to deliver it to B at a fixed rate and C guarantee A's performance of this contract. B diverts a stream of water which is necessary for irrigation of A's land and thereby prevents him from raising the indigo.

(a) A is liable on his guarantee
(b) A is partly liable on his guarantee
(c) A is no longer liable on his guarantee
(d) None of the above

Miscellaneous

85 **Statement** I Every contract in an agreement but every agreement is not a contract.

Statement II All agreements are contracts, if they are made by the free consent of parties.

Codes

(a) Statement I is correct, but Statement II is incorrect
(b) Statement II is correct, but Statement I is incorrect
(c) Both statements are correct
(d) Both statements are incorrect

Directions (Q. Nos. 86-90) *In the questions given below are two statements labelled as Statement I and Statement II. In the context of two statements, which one of the following is correct?*

Codes

(a) Only Statement I is true
(b) Only Statement II is true
(c) Both statements are true
(d) Both statements are false

86 **Statement** I Acceptance must be communicated.

Statement II Acceptance may not be in the prescribed manner.

87 **Statement** I Oral acceptance is valid acceptance.

Statement II Mere silence in not acceptance.

88 **Statement** I On the valid performance of contract, the contracts is said to be discharged.

Statement II The discharge of contracts means that the parties are no more liable under the contract.

89 **Statement** I The breach of contract may be actual or anticipatory.

Statement II On breach of contract, the injured party may sue for damages.

90 **Statement** I A quasi-contract is an obligation which the law creaters in the absence of any agreement.

Statement II The term Quantum Meruit means unfavorable remuneration.

91 The agency extends to receiving notice on behalf of whatever in material to be stated in the course of the proceedings. For this rule to operate

1. the agent must be under a duty to communicate.
2. the information must be material.

3. it must have been obtained in the course of business. for which the agent has been engaged.
4. the agent is not privy to a fraud on the principal.

Codes

(a) Statement 1 and 2 are true
(b) Statement 2 and 4 are true
(c) Statement 3 and 4 are true
(d) All statements are true

92 The guarantor's right to indemnifications a right to be reimbursed.

Statement I The amount which is actually paid for the principal debtor with interest.

Statement II Because, he is entitled to full indemnification from the principal debtor.

Codes

(a) Statement I is true, but Statement II is false
(b) Statement I is false, but Statement II is true
(c) Both statements are true
(d) Both statements are false

Directions (Q. Nos. 93-98) *In the questions given below are two statements, labelled as Assertion (A) and Reason (R). In the context of two statements, which one of the following is correct?*

(a) Both (A) and (R) are true and (R) is the correct explanation of (A)
(b) Both (A) and (R) are true, but (R) is not the correct explanation of (A)
(c) (A) is true, but (R) is false
(d) (A) is false, but (R) is true

93 **Assertion** (A) Quasi-contractual relationships are not based on the intentions of the parties.

Reason (R) In quasi-contracts, this relation is imposed upon the parties by the law.

94 **Assertion** (A) Quasi-contract are enforceable even, if the essential elements of contract are not there.

Reason (R) Quasi contractual obligations have specifically made enforceable.

95 **Assertion** (A) A quasi-contract in not a contract in the strict sense of the term.

Reason (R) In quasi-contract, there is no contract in existence.

96 **Assertion** (A) The agreement is supported by a lawful considerations.

Reason (R) There must be an agreement to form a valid contract.

97 **Assertion** (A) Contract of indemnity is a special contract.

Reason (R) A contract of agency is the contract of indemnity.

98 **Assertion** (A) A proposal emerges from the acceptance of a contract.

Reason (R) A proposal, when accepted becomes a promise

99 Match the following.

List I (Sections)	List II (Explanation)
A. Section 68	1. Liability of finder of goods
B. Section 69	2. Supply of necessaries to incompetent person
C. Section 70	3. Payment made by interested persons
D. Section 71	4. Compensation for non-gratuitous acts

Codes

	A	B	C	D		A	B	C	D
(a)	1	2	3	4	(b)	2	3	4	1
(c)	3	2	1	3	(d)	3	4	2	1

100 Match the following.

List I (Term)	List II (Explanation)
A. Contract	1. Accepted proposal
B. Offer	2. Agreement enforceable by law
C. Promise	3. Proposal

Codes

	A	B	C		A	B	C
(a)	2	3	1	(b)	1	3	2
(c)	1	2	3	(d)	3	2	1

ANSWERS

1 (c)	2 (b)	3 (b)	4 (a)	5 (c)	6 (c)	7 (a)	8 (a)	9 (a)	10 (a)
11 (d)	12 (b)	13 (a)	14 (c)	15 (d)	16 (d)	17 (b)	18 (c)	19 (d)	20 (d)
21 (d)	22 (b)	23 (b)	24 (b)	25 (c)	26 (a)	27 (d)	28 (d)	29 (b)	30 (c)
31 (c)	32 (a)	33 (b)	34 (c)	35 (a)	36 (c)	37 (b)	38 (c)	39 (a)	40 (a)
41 (b)	42 (d)	43 (d)	44 (d)	45 (b)	46 (d)	47 (c)	48 (c)	49 (b)	50 (d)
51 (c)	52 (b)	53 (c)	54 (c)	55 (c)	56 (a)	57 (a)	58 (a)	59 (d)	60 (a)
61 (d)	62 (c)	63 (c)	64 (c)	65 (c)	66 (b)	67 (c)	68 (b)	69 (c)	70 (c)
71 (c)	72 (b)	73 (b)	74 (d)	75 (b)	76 (d)	77 (a)	78 (c)	79 (c)	80 (d)
81 (c)	82 (d)	83 (c)	84 (c)	85 (c)	86 (a)	87 (c)	88 (c)	89 (c)	90 (a)
91 (c)	92 (c)	93 (a)	94 (a)	95 (a)	96 (b)	97 (c)	98 (d)	99 (b)	100 (a)

CHAPTER 33

Legal Aspects of Companies and Firms-I

(Companies Act, LLP, Competition Act)

The Companies Act, 2013 makes comprehensive provisions to govern all listed and unlisted companies in the country. The Limited Liability Partnership Act, 2008 was introduced to make provision for the formation and regulation of limited liability partnerships and for matters connected therewith or incidental thereto. The Competition Act, 2002 intends to promote and sustain competition in the market to protect the interests of consumers.

The Companies Act, 2013

Company

A company is an incorporated association which is an artificial person, created by law, having separate legal entity, with a perpetual succession and a common seal.

As per Section 2(20) of the Companies Act, 2013, "Company means a company incorporated under this act or under any previous company law."

According to **Chief Justice Marshall**, "A company is a person artificial, invisible, intangible and existing only in the eyes of law. Being a mere creation of law, it possesses only the properties which the charter of its creation confers upon either expressly or as incidental to its very existence."

According to **Haney**, "A company is an incorporated association, which is an artificial person created by law, having separate entity, with a perpetual succession and a common seal."

In this Chapter

- *The Companies Act, 2013*
- *Limited Liability Partnership*
- *Competition Act, 2002*

Features of Company

Incorporated Association A company is an artificial person which comes into existence through the process of law, *i.e.* after being registered under the Companies Act, 2013.

Voluntary Association Persons who are willing to carry on a business, come together voluntarily to form a company.

Separate Legal Entity A company has a separate legal entity distinct from that of its members who have formed it. Thus, it can enter into contract, own property, conduct business, sue or be sued. The business undertaken and the working of a company is regulated by its Articles of Association, Memorandum of Association and provisions of the Companies Act.

Limited Liability Liability of the members of a company is limited to the amount outstanding on the shares subscribed by each of them. *e.g.* If on a share of ₹ 100, a shareholder has paid ₹ 60, then he will be liable to pay only ₹ 40.

Perpetual Succession Since, company has a separate legal entity distinct from its shareholders, therefore it is not affected by the death, lunacy or bankruptcy of its members or shareholders. As it is very appropriately observed, "Members may come and go, but the company remains forever."

Common Seal Company, being an artificial person cannot sign the documents. So, for this, a company is provided with a legal tool, called common seal. The common seal is affixed on all legal documents and is bonafide treated as the sign of the company.

Transferability of Shares Shares of a company are freely transferable, without restriction in the case of public companies and with restriction in case of private companies.

May Sue or be Sued A company being a legal person can sue and be sued, if there is a breach of contract.

Management and Ownership are Separate A company is not managed by all the members but by their elected representatives called directors.

Kinds of Companies

Companies can be classified on the following basis

Incorporation

It refers to the mode of formation of a company.

The different categories of companies under this head are

Chartered Companies These companies are formed by a special charter by the King or a sovereign, *e.g.* East India Company.

Statutory Companies These companies are formed by the special acts of the legislatures, *e.g.* RBI.

Registered Companies These companies are formed by registering under the Companies Act, 2013 or any other previous applicable acts, *e.g.* Reliance Company, Tata Motors etc.

Liability

It refers to the personal liability of members to pay for the debts incurred by the company. *The different categories of companies under this head are*

Limited Liability Company or Company Limited by Shares According to Section 2(22) of the Companies Act, 2013, "A company having the liability of its members limited by the memorandum to the amount, if any, unpaid on shares respectively held by them, is termed as a company limited by shares".

Unlimited Liability Company According to Section 2(92) of the Companies Act, 2013, "It is a company where the liability of its members is unlimited". It means, in the event of winding-up, the debts of the company shall be met from the private property of the members.

Company Limited by Guarantee According to Section 2(21) of the Companies Act, 2013, "It is a company having the liability of its members limited by the memorandum to such amount as the members may respectively undertake to contribute to the assets of the company in the event of its being wound-up".

Note *All companies do not have share capital. Only companies limited by shares have share capital.*

Number of Members

It refers to the right of the members to transfer the shares held by them. *The different forms of companies under this head are*

Private Company As per Section 2(68) of Companies Act, 2013, a private company is one which has a minimum paid-up capital as may be prescribed and which by its Articles of Association

- Restricts the right to transfer its shares, if any.
- Except in one person company, limits the number of its members excluding its present and past employee members to 200. (If any share is held jointly by two or more persons, they shall be treated as a single member).
- Prohibits any invitation to the public to subscribe for any securities of the company.

The name of a private company ends with the words, 'Private Limited'.

***Public Company** As per Section 2(71) of Companies Act, 2013, public company is a company which*

- is not a private company.
- has minimum capital of as may be prescribed.

- is a private company, being a subsidiary of a company which is not a private company.

The name of the public company ends with the word 'Limited.'

One Person Company According to Section 2(62) of the Companies Act, 2013 defines one person company as a company which has only one person as a member. It is a company incorporated as a private company which has only one member.

➠ **Note** *Minimum paid-up capital is not prescribed. Private or public companies can have share capital as the promoters decide.*

Ownership

It refers to the legal right to the possession of a thing, *i.e.* share capital in a company. *The different forms of companies under this head are*

Government Companies According to Companies Act, 2013, "It refers to those companies in which 51% or more of the paid-up share capital is held by the Central Government or by one or more State Government or partly by Central Government or partly by one or more State Government."

Holding Companies Where one company holds the majority of shares in another company, then the former becomes the holding company and a later a subsidiary company. The term 'majority shares' means more than half (50%) of the total share capital of the company. Thus, the company becomes a holding company if it holds more than 50% of the total shares of another company.

Subsidiary Companies *A company is deemed to subsidiary of another if*

- the other company controls its management.
- the other company holds more than 50% of the total shares or voting rights,
- one company is the subsidiary of another company, which itself is a subsidiary company of some other company.

Nationality

It refers to the company's status of belonging to a particular nation. *The different forms of company under this head are*

Indian Companies It refers to those companies which are incorporated in India under the companies act and is operating under the provision of the act.

Foreign Companies It refers to those companies which are incorporated outside India. As per Section 2 (42) of Companies Act, 2013, "A foreign company means any company or body incorporated outside India, which has a place in India of business, whether by itself or through an agent, physically or through electronic mode and conducts any business activity in India in other manner."

Company Formation

The whole process of formation of a company may be divided into four parts. *These are*

Promotion

It refers to the sum total of activities by which a business enterprise is bought into existence. It involves the discovery of business idea, investigation and assembling necessary resources to set-up a profitable concern. The promotion is the first stage in the formation of a company.

According to **GW Gerstenberg**, "Promotion may be defined as the discovery of business opportunities and subsequent organisation of funds, property and managerial ability into a business concern for the purpose of making profits there from."

The person or a group of persons who performs the work of promotion and forms a company is known as promoter. *Following are the functions of promoter*

Discovery of Idea Promotion stage begins with the discovery of the idea to set up a business. Promoter analyses the amount of capital required and the degree of risk involved.

Detailed Investigation A detailed investigation regarding cost, profitability production process, demand of the product etc is undertaken which in turn helps the promoter to take decision regarding the size of the business, location of the plant and amount of capital etc.

Assembling of Resources Promoter makes contract for purchase of material, land, machinery, recruitment of staff etc.

Preparing Preliminary Documents *The important documents prepared by the promoters are*

- Memorandum of Association
- Articles of Association
- Prospectus

Entering into Preliminary Contracts The promoter signs a contract with different parties before incorporation of the company.

Naming a Company While naming, promoter keeps in mind that the name should not be identical to the name of any other company.

Incorporation of a Company

Under Section 3, any seven or more persons (2 or more in the case of a private company and 1 person in case of a one person company) may form an incorporated company for a lawful purpose. *Such an incorporated company may be a company*

- limited by shares
- limited by guarantee
- an unlimited company

The purpose for which a company is going to be incorporated must be lawful.

Following formalities are required to be fulfiled before applying for incorporation certificate

- DIN (Directors Identification Number) has to be obtained.
- Digital signature of the promoters have to be obtained.
- Both DIN and digital signature are to be registered with the MCA (Ministry of Corporate Affairs) portal.
- It must be ensured that the minimum paid up capital of the company ₹ 5 lakh, in case of public company and ₹ 1 lakh, in case of private company, has been arranged.

Formalities to Obtain Certificate of Incorporation

- *Application form shall be filed with ROC in*

(a) Form no. INC 2 (for one person company)

(b) Form no. INC 7 (other than one person company)

Documents to be filed with the registrar to incorporate a company

- Memorandum of association duly stamped.
- Articles of association, if any, duly stamped.
- If company proposes to appoint a person as managing director or whole time director or manager a copy of agreement is to be enclosed.
- Statutory declaration of compliance.
- Power of attorney to correct memorandum and articles.
- If articles of public company having share capital specify name of directors their written consent as attachment.
- Original letter approving name of the company.
- Notice of registered office.
- Proof of payment of filing fees.

The documents are to be submitted electronically as scanned attachment to e-form no. 1. After submission a SRN (Service Request Number) will be generated by system. The original memorandum of association and articles of association duly stampted signed should be submitted to ROC giving reference to SRN.

A declaration is to be filled in form INC-8 with the registrar of companies. This statutory declaration is then filed with the registrar for the registration.

On registration the registrar will issue a certificate of incorporation in form INC-11 bearing a Corporate Identity Number (CIN) consisting of 21 digits whereby he certifies that the company is incorporated.

Capital Subscription

The following formalities are required to be fulfiled

- When a company has been registered and has received certificate of incorporation, it is ready for floatation means raising capital to commence business and carry on its operations.
- Private company is prohibited from inviting public to subscribe to its share capital.
- Promoters of public company raise their capital by inviting public to subscribe to its share capital. *Either of the following two steps can be taken in this connection*

(a) Issue of prospectus, if public is to be invited to subscribe to its share capital.

(b) File a statement in lieu of prospectus. In case capital has been arranged privately.

Classification of Capital

Authorised Share Capital According to Section 2(8) of Companies Act, 2013, 'authorised capital' or 'nominal capital' means such capital as is authorised by the memorandum of a company to be the maximum amount of share capital of a company.

Issued Capital According to Section 2 (50) of the Companies Act, 2013, 'issued capital' means such capital as the company issues from time-to-time for subscription. It is that part of the authorised capital which is actually issued to the public for subscription.

Subscribed Capital According to Section 2 (86) of the Companies Act, 2013, 'subscribed capital' means such part of the issued capital which has been subscribed by the members of a company.

Called-up Capital According to Section 2 (15) of the Companies Act, 2013, 'called-up capital' means such part of the capital, which has been called for payment.

Paid-up Capital According to Section 2 (64) of the Companies Act, 2013, 'paid-up share capital' means such part of the capital, which has been called for payment.

Reserve Capital It is that portion of subscribed share capital, remaining uncalled, which shall not be capable of being called-up except in the event and for the purpose of the company being wound up.

Commencement of Business

Under Section 11 of Companies Act, 2013, if the company has share capital it shall not commence business until

- a declaration is filed by a director in the form INC-21 and its content shall be verified by a company secretary or chartered accountant or a cost accountant in practice with the registrar that every subscriber to the memorandum has paid the value of the shares agreed to be taken by him.
- On receipt of declaration in the Form INC-21 and verification of the registered office in the Form INC-22 the registrar of companies shall then issue the certificate of commencement of business.

Management of Company

A company management includes board of directors which consists of managing director, whole time director and manager etc.

Directors

A company being an artificial person cannot act by itself. The persons by whom the business of the company is carried on are termed as directors.

According to Section 2(34) of the Companies Act, 2013, "Director means a director appointed to the Board of a Company".

Types of Directors

Managing Director 'Managing Director' means a director who, by virtue of the articles of a company or an agreement with the company or a resolution passed in its general meeting, or by its Board of Directors, is entrusted with substantial powers of management of the affairs of the company and includes a director occupying the position of managing director, by whatever name called.

Whole-time/Executive Directors Whole-time Directors/ Executive Directors includes a director in the whole-time employment of the company. A company can have one or more whole time directors but it can have only one managing director or manager.

Qualification of Directors

The Companies Act does not lay down any specified academic qualification for appointment as a company director, not even qualification shares. So far as the act is concerned a director need not hold any shares and need not be a member of a company.

The articles of association generally requires that the qualification of director shall be the holding of a specified number of shares known as qualification shares. A director must hold atleast one share in company.

Power of the Directors

General Powers of the Board

Section 179 defines the general powers of the board and lays down that the Board of Directors of a company shall be entitled to exercise all such powers and undertake all such acts and things as the company is authorised to exercise and do.

However, the board shall not exercise any power or do any act or thing which is directed or required to be exercised or done by the company in general meeting.

Powers to be Exercised by the Board at Meeting

According to Section 179(3) the Board of Directors of a company shall exercise the following powers on behalf of the company and it shall do so only by means of resolutions passed at meeting of the board, *which are as follows*

- The power to make calls on shareholders in respect of money unpaid on their shares.
- The power to issue debentures.
- The power to borrow money otherwise than on debentures.
- The power to invest the company's funds.
- The power to make loans.

Powers under Rule 8

Rule 8 of the Companies (Meeting of the board and its powers), 2014 provides that in additions to be matters specified under Section 179(3) *the following powers shall be exercised only by means of resolutions passed at meeting of the Board, namely*

- To make political contributions.
- To appoint or remove Key Managerial Personnel (KMP).
- To take note of appointment(s) or removal(s) of one level below the key management personnel.
- To appoint internal auditors and secretarial auditors.
- To take note of the disclosure of director's interest and shareholding
- To buy, sell investments held by the company (other than trade investments), constituting five per cent or more of the paid-up share capital and free reserves' of the investee company.
- To accept or accept or renew public deposits and related matters.
- To review or change the terms and conditions of public deposits.
- To approve quarterly, half-yearly and annual financial statements or financial results as the case may be.

Other Matters

In addition to the items referred to above, there are various other matters, as illustrated below in the routine working of a company which are considered by the board at board meetings

- Issuance of shares.
- Allotment of shares and debentures.
- Appointment of directors and Managing Director/ Whole-time Director.
- Consideration of annual accounts.
- Approval of interim dividend and recommendation of final dividend.
- Appointment of sole selling/buying agents.
- Merger and amalgamation of companies.
- Capitalisation of reserves and issuance of bonus shares.
- Appointment of auditors in casual vacancy caused otherwise than by resignation.
- Appointment of whole-time secretary for issuance of compliance certificate.

Manager

As per Section 2 (24) of the Act, a manager means "An individual who has the management of the whole or substantially the whole of the affairs of a company, and includes a director or any other person occupying the position of a manager, by whatever name called." To be deemed as the manager of a company, the individual must be incharge of the whole business of the company. A mere head of a department or a branch manager is not a manager.

Company Meetings

A meeting is defined as assembly of people for a lawful purpose or coming together of atleast two persons for the same reason.

According to **Sharp V Dawes**, "There must be atleast two perons to constitute a meeting."

Kinds of Meetings

Meetings of the Members

These meetings can further be categorised as follows

General Meetings These meetings can be attended by all the members of a company who have a right to vote.

These meetings can further be classified as

- Annual general meeting (U/S 96)
- Extraordinary general meeting (U/S 100)

Class Meetings These meetings relate to a specific group of members who hold a particular class of shares.

Meetings of Directors

The directors have to meet regularly to conduct the affairs of the company. *Their meetings can be classified as follows*

- Board meetings
- Committee

Meeting of Creditors

The creditors of a company can call meeting, if their interests are being threatened. *Their meetings can be classified as under*

- Debentureholders meeting.
- Creditors and contributories meeting at the time of winding-up.

Final Meeting at Dissolution

A final meeting is called at the time of winding-up of a company.

➠ **Note** *As per Companies Act, 2013, a company is no longer required to hold statutory meeting.*

Winding-up of a Joint Stock Company

Winding-up of a company is the process whereby its life is ended and its property administered for the benefit of its creditors and members. An administrator, called a 'liquidator' is appointed and he takes control of the company, collects its assets, pays its debts and finally distributes and surplus among the members in accordance with their rights.

According to **Perrins** and **Jeffiys**, "Winding-up means applying assets of a company in the discharge of its liabilities returning any surplus to those entitled to it, subject to the cost of doing so."

According to **Prof Grower**, "Winding-up of a company is a process whereby its life is ended and its property administered for the benefit of its creditors and members."

Modes of Winding-up

Compulsory Winding-up by Tribunal (NCLT)

A company may be wound up by an order of the tribunal. This is called compulsory winding-up. The tribunal will make an order for winding-up on an application by any of the person enlisted in Section 272.

Section 271 lays down the following grounds where a company may be wound up by the tribunal

Special Resolution of the Company [Section 271 (b)]

If the company has by a special resolution resolved that it may be wound up by the tribunal, the tribunal may pass a winding-up orders.

The power of the tribunal in such a case is discretionary and should be exercised only where a bonafide case is made out. The tribunal may refuse to order winding-up where it is opposed to public or company's interest.

Inability to Pay Debts [Section 271 (2)]

The tribunal may order for the winding-up of a company if it is unable to pay its debts. The basis of an order for winding-up under this clause is that the company has ceased to be commercially solvent, *i.e.* it is unable to meet its current demands, although the assets when realised may exceed its liabilities.

According to Section 271 of the act, a company shall be deemed to be unable to pay its debts in the following cases

Statutory Notice If a creditor to whom the company owes a sum of ₹ 1,00,000 or more has served on the company a notice at the registerar office for payment and the company has, for three weeks, neglected to pay or otherwise satisfy him.

Decreed Debt If execution or other process issued on a decree or order of any Civil court in favour of a creditor is returned unsatisfied in whole or in part.

Commercial Insolvency If company is unable to meet its current liabilities, it is commercially insolvent and liable to be wound up.

Just and Equitable [Section 271(g)]

The another ground on which the Tribunal can order the winding-up of a company is when the Tribunal is of the opinion that it is just and equitable that the company should be wound up. This clause gives the tribunal a very wide power to order winding-up wherever the tribunal considers it just and equitable to do, what is just and equitable will depend upon the facts of each particular case.

Following are the instances where the tribunals have dissolved the companies under the just and equitable clause

Loss of Substratum It is just and equitable to wind-up a company where the company's main object or substratum is gone. The substratum of a company is deemed to be gone when

- the subject matter of the company is gone, or
- the object for which it was incorporated has substantially failed, or
- it is impossible to carry on the business of the company except at a loss, or
- the existing and the possible assets are insufficient to meet the existing liabilities of the company.

Deadlock in Management When there is a deadlock in the management of a company, it is a proper case for winding-up under the just and equitable clause.

Oppression of Minority Where the majority shareholders have adopted an aggressive or oppressive policy towards the minority, it is a sufficient ground for winding-up of the company under this clause.

Fraudulent Purpose Where the company was conceived and brought forth in fraud, or for illegal purposes, it is just and equitable to wind-up a company.

Incorporated or Quasi Partnership Where a private company consisting of members of one or more families or a group of friends, is really in nature of partnership business, any circumstances justifying the dissolution of a partnership (such as misconduct of one or more partners) will constitute just and equitable ground for winding-up of the company though they may not consitute sufficient grounds for winding-up under the provision of the Companies Act.

Company is a Bubble Where the company is a bubble and has no business to carry on, it was wound up.

Company being Run to Benefit Debentureholders Where the company was insolvent and was being carried on for the benefit of the debentureholders, who had taken possession, a winding-up order was made.

Non-filing of Financial Statements or Annual Returns with the Register

If the company has made a default in filing with the Registrar its balance sheet and profit and loss account or annual return for five consecutive financial years. [Section 271(f)]

If Company Acts against Sovereignity and Integrity of India

If the company has acted against the interests of the sovereignity and integrity of India, the security of the state, friendly relations with foreign states, public order, decency or morality.

Provided that the tribunal shall make an order for winding-up of a company an application made by the Central Government or a State Government. [Section 271 (c)]

Sick Company

If Tribunal is of the opinion that the company should be wound up under chapter XIX, *i.e.* where a sick industrial company is not likely to become viable in future and that it is just and equitable that the company should be wound up.

Voluntary Winding-up

A voluntary winding-up of a company is entirely different from a compulsory winding-up. Voluntary winding-up is winding-up by the members or creditors of a company without interference by the Tribunal.

A company may be wound up voluntarily when

- the period fixed by the articles for the company has expired or an event upon which the company is to be wound up, has happened and the company in general meeting has passed oridinary resolution.
- the company has for any cause whatever passed a special resolution to wind up voluntarily (Section 304). The company may be wound up by special resolution even if it is prosperous. No articles of the company can prevent the exercise of this statutory right.

The voluntary winding-up may be of the following types

Members's Voluntary Winding-up A member's voluntary winding-up takes place only when the company is solvent. It is initiated by the members and is entirely managed by them. The liquidator is appointed by the members.

No meeting of creditors is held and no committee of inspection is appointed. To obtain the benefit of this form of winding-up, a declaration of solvency must be filed.

Creditor's Voluntary Winding-up Where a company proposes to wind up voluntarily and the directors are not in a position to make the statutory declaration of solvency, the winding-up is a creditor's voluntary winding-up.

The provisions for creditors voluntary winding-up are similar to those applicable to the member's voluntary winding-up except that in the former, it is the creditors who appoint the liquidator, fix his remuneration and generally conduct the winding-up.

Limited Liability Partnership

A limited liability partnership is popularly known as 'LLP' and has become an alternative business vehicle to carry out business as it combines the characteristics of a private company and a conventional partnership.

As per Clause (n) of Section 2(1) of the Limited Liability Partnership Act, 2008, a limited liability partnership means a partnership formed and registered under this act.

As per Section 3 of the Act, a *limited liability partnership has the following characteristics*

- It is a body corporate formed and incorporated under this Act.
- It is a legal entity separate from that of its partners.
- It shall have perpetual succession.
- Any change in the partners of a limited liability partnership shall not affect the existence, rights or liabilities of the LLP.
- It must have atleast two partners and atleast two individuals as designated partners.
- The rights and duties of all partners are governed by an agreement between them.

Difference between Limited Liability Partnership and General Partnership

A limited liability partnership is a legal entity separate from its partners and therefore, offers limited liability to its partners whereby any debts and obligations of the LLP will be borne by the assets of the LLP. In the case of a conventional partnership, the partners arc jointly and severally liable for each debt and obligation of the partnership firm.

Structure of LLP in India

The formation and regulation of LLP is governed by Limited Liability Partnership Act, 2008 and the rules made thereunder, *i.e.* Limited Liability Partnership Rules, 2009. It must have atleast two individuals as designated partners. LLP provides limited liability status to its partners and offers the flexibility of internal arrangement through an agreement between the partners.

Who can be a Partner of Limited Liability Partnership?

As per Clause (q) Section 2(1) of the Act, a 'Partner' in relation to a limited liability partnership, means any person who becomes a partner in the LLP in accordance with the limited liability partnership agreement.

As per Section 5 of the Limited Liability Partnership Act, 2008, any individual or body corporate can be a partner in a limited liability partnership.

Procedure of Formation of LLP in India

Application for DSC

Every individual proposed to be appointed as the partner and designated partner of the LLP, shall obtain a Digital Signature Certificate.

Application for DPIN

- Every LLP shall have atleast two partners. Every LLP shall have atleast two individual as designated partners out of which atleast one of them shall be a resident in India.
- The designated partners of the proposed LLP are required to apply for DIN in Form DIR-3 by attaching prescribed documents.
- The designated partner Identification No./DIN is valid for lifetime of applicant.
- Every designated partner shall alongwith his consent to be designated partner, intimate his DPIN to LLP in form 9.
- If the proposed designated partner already having DIN/DPIN, he need not apply for another DIN/DPIN.
- If the proposed designated partner already having DIN, he need not require to apply for another DPIN, the DIN will be treated as DPIN.

Incorporation of LLP

Application for Reservation of Name

The application for the reservation of the name of the LLP is to be filed in Form 1. Such name shall be availablc for reservation for a period of three months from the data of intimation by the Registrar. Every limited liability partnership shall have either the words 'limited liability partnership' or the acronym 'LLP' as the last words of its name.

Criteria for Name Approval The name of LLP should not be one prohibited under Emblems and Names (prevention of improper use) Act, 1950. The proposed name is not generally reserved in case it includes the words as provided in Section 15 (2) of the Act read with Rule 18 (2).

Filing of Incorporated Document

- Two or more persons associated for carrying on a lawful business with a view to profit shall subscribe their names to an incorporation document.
- The incorporation document is required to be filed in Form 2 with the Registrar of the state in which the registered office of the limited liability partnership is to be situated.
- *The incorporation document shall state*

  (a) Name of the limited liability partnership.

(b) Proposed business of the limited liability partnership.
(c) Address of the registered office of the limited liability partnership.
(d) Name and address of each of the persons who are to be partners of the limited liability partnership on incorporation.
(e) Name and address of the persons who are to be designated partners and partners of the limited liability partnership on incorporation.
(f) Contain such other information concerning the proposed limited liability partnership as may be prescribed.

- Alongwith the incorporation document there shall be filed, a statement in Part B of Form 2, made by either an advocate, or a Company Secretary or a Chartered Accountant or a Cost Accountant who is engaged in the formation of the limited liability partnership and by anyone who subscribed his name to the incorporation document, that all the requirements of this act and the rules made thereunder have been complied with, in respect of incorporation and matters precedent and incidental thereto.
- In case of incorporation, the individual who has given consent to act as partner or designated partner shall file consent in Form 2 alongwith fees.
- When the requirements imposed by Clauses (b) and (c) of Sub-section (1) of Section 11 have been complied with, the Registrar shall retain the incorporation document and he shall, within a period of 14 days.
  (a) Register the incorporation document and
  (b) give a certificate that the limited liability partnership is incorporated by the name specified therein.
- The Registrar may accept the statement (made by an advocate/Company Secretary/Chartered Accountant/Cost Accountant) who is engaged in the formation of the limited liability partnership and by any one who subscribed his name to the incorporation document, that all the requirement of this Act and the rules made thereunder have been complied with, in respect of incorporation and matters precedent and incidental thereto as sufficient evidence that the requirement has been complied with.
- The certificate shall be signed by the Registrar and authenticated by his official seal.
- The certificate shall be conclusive evidence that the limited liability partnership incorporated by the name specified therein.
- Every LLP so registered shall be assigned a LLP Identification Number (LLPN) in one consecutive series (Rule 14).
- Where the intending partner is a body corporate, *the following is required to be attached with incorporation document*
  (a) A copy of resolution on the letterhead of such body corporate to become a partner in the proposed LLP.
  (b) A copy of resolution or authorisation of such body corporate also on letterhead mentioning the name and address of an individual nominated to act as nominee or nominee and designated partner on its behalf.
  (c) In the case of foreign nationals residing outside India or foreign body corporates registered outside India, seeking to register a LLP in India, the name, address and signature of an individual or nominee and designated partner of a body corporate on the incorporation document, proof of identity. Where required and documents referred in this rule shall be duly certified and the provisions of Sub-rule (2) of Rule 34, shall apply mutatis mutandis for this purpose.

Filing of LLP Agreement

LLP shall file its LLP agreement with the Registrar in Form-3 within 30 days of its incorporation of the LLP (Rule 21).

➠ **Note** *Any change made in the limited liability partnership agreement shall be filed in Form 3 within 30 days of such change alongwith the fee as provided in Annexure 'A'.*

The Competition Act, 2002

On 16th December, 2002 the Lok Sabha passed a bill to replace the MRTP (Monopolies and Restrictive Trade Practices) Act, 1969 which was enacted to curb the tendency to create monopoly in commerce, trade and industry. This act is known as Competition Act, 2002. This act was passed on the basis of recommendation of committee on 'Competition policy and law' under the chairmanship of Sri SVS Raghavan. This act was enforced on 13th January, 2003. Later on, the government made some amendments through passing of Competition (Amendment) Bill, 2007. This act covers whole of India except Jammu and Kashmir.

Objectives of Competition Act, 2002

- To eliminate practices having adverse effect on competition.
- To promote and sustain competition in markets.
- To protect consumers interests.
- To ensure freedom of trade carried on by other participants in markets in India.

Main Provisions of this Act

Anti-competitive Agreements

An anti-competitive agreement is an agreement having appreciable adverse effect on competition. *Anti-competitive agreements include, but are not limited to*

- Agreement to limit production and/or supply.
- Agreement to allocate markets
- Agreement to fix price
- Bid rigging or collusive bidding
- Conditional purchase/sale (tie-in-arrangement)
- Exclusive supply/distribution arrangement
- Resale price maintenance
- Refusal to deal

As per Section 3(1) of the Act, provides that no enterprise or association of enterprises or person or association of persons shall enter into any agreement in respect of production, supply, distribution, storage, acquisition or control of goods or provision of services, which causes or is likely to cause an appreciable adverse effect on competition. Section 3(2) further declares that any anti-competitive agreement within the meaning of Sub-section 3(1) shall be void.

Prohibition of Abuse of Dominant Position

Dominance refers to a position of strength which enables an enterprise to operate independently of competitive forces or to affect its competitors or consumers or the market in its favour. Abuse of dominant position impedes fair competition between firms, exploits consumers and makes it difficult for the other players to compete with the dominant undertaking or merit.

Abuse of dominant position includes

- Imposing unfair conditions or price
- Predatory pricing
- Limiting production/market or technical development
- Creating barriers to entry
- Denying market access
- Using dominant position in one market to gain advantages in another market.

As Section 4 of the Act, prohibits any enterprise or group from abusing its dominant position, meaning thereby a position of strength, enjoyed by an enterprise or group, in the relevant market, in India, *which enables it to*

- Operate independently of competitive forces prevailing in the relevant market.
- Affects its competitors or consumers or the relevant market in its favour.

Combination

Combination under the Act means acquisition of control, shares, voting rights or assets, acquisition of control by a person over an enterprise where such person has direct or indirect control over another enterprise engaged in competing businesses and mergers and amalgamations between or amongst enterprises when the combining parties exceed the thresholds set in the act. The thresholds are specified in the Act in terms of assets or turnover in India and outside India. Entering into a combination which causes or likely to cause an appreciable adverse effect on competition within the relevant market in India is prohibited and such combination shall be void.

Competition Commission of India

The Central Government under Section 7 has been empowered to establish a commission to be called 'Competition Commission of India' by issue of a notification. The commission is a body corporate having perpetual succession and a common seal. The commission has power to acquire, hold movable or immovable property and to enter into contract in its name and by the said name, sue or be sued. This is a corporate body with quasi-judicial powers. The order of this commission can be challenged only in the Supreme Court. The commission shall be headed by a chairman and there would not be more than 10 members of the commission to be appointed by the Government of India.

Duties, Powers and Functions of Commission

As per Section 18 of the Act, duties of CCI are

- To eliminate practices having adverse effect on competition.
- To promote and sustain competition.
- To protect interests of consumers.
- To ensure freedom of trade carried on by other participants, in markets in India.

Section 18 empowers the commission to enter into any memorandum or arrangement, with the prior approval of the Central Government for the purpose of discharging the duties and functions under this Act with any agency of any foreign country.

The commission may inquire into any alleged contravention of Section 3 (1) or 4(1) on its own motion or on receipt of any information in such manner and accompanied by such fee, from any person, consumer or consumer association or trade association.

Miscellaneous Provisions

- Under Section 20 of the Act, the commission may inquire into the appreciable adverse effect caused or likely to be caused on competition in India.
- Section 22 provides that the commission shall meet at such times and places and shall observe such rules and procedure in regard to the transaction of business at its meetings as may be provided by regulations.

- Section 19 provides that, if the commission is of the opinion that there exists a prima facie case, on receipt of an information from any person, consumer, their association or trade association or on a reference free Central Government or State Government.
- Section 32 extends the jurisdiction of Competition Commission of India to inquire and pass orders in accordance with the provisions of the act into an agreement or dominant position or combination, which is likely to have, an appreciable adverse effect on competition in relevant market in India.
- The Competition Commission of India has been empowered to lay down its own procedure and regulations.
- The commission may amend any order passed by it under the provisions of this act with a view to rectifying any mistake apparent from the record.
- Section 39 provides that if a person fails to pay any monetary penalty imposed on him under the act, the commission shall proceed to recover such penalty, in such manner as may be specified by the regulations.
- The act provides that the Director General when so directed by the commission, is to assist the commission in investigation into any contravention of the provisions of this act. The director general is bound to comply with such a direction to render requisite assistance to the commission.
- The act prescribes penalties for contravention of orders of the commission. As per Section 42, the commission may cause an inquiry to be made into compliance of its orders or directions.
  (a) If any person, without any reasonable cause, fails to comply with any order of the commission or condition or restriction subject to which any approval, sanction, direction or exemption in relation to any matter has been accorded, given, made or granted under this act.
  (b) If any person fails to pay the penalty imposed under the act.
- The Central Government may make to the commission grants of such sums of money as it may thinks fit for being utilised for the purposes of the act. Such grant is to be made after due appropriation made by the Parliament.

  The act provides for the constitution of a fund called the 'Competition Fund' for meeting the establishment and other expenses of the competition commission in connection with the discharge of its functions and for the purpose of this act. Proper accounts and other relevant records shall be maintained by the commission and an annual statement of accounts shall be prepared by it in prescribed form in consultation with the Comptroller and Auditor General of India (CAG).

EXAM BASED QUESTIONS

The Companies Act, 2013

1 The term company is defined under which section of the Act?

(a) Section 3(1) (b) Section 4(2)
(c) Section 2(4) (d) Section 1(3)

2 Minimum number of members in case of public company.

(a) 1 (b) 2 (c) 5 (d) 7

3 Minimum number of members in case of private company.

(a) 2 (b) 3 (c) 5 (d) 7

4 Maximum number of members in case of public company.

(a) 10 (b) 50
(c) 70 (d) Unlimited

5 Maximum number of members in case of private company.

(a) 10 (b) 50
(c) 70 (d) 200

6 Who stands in the fiduciary position of the company?

(a) Directors (b) Promoters
(c) Auditors (d) Shareholders

7 The first meeting of the company after incorporation is

(a) AGM
(b) extra ordinary meeting
(c) statutory meeting
(d) class meeting

8 Who orders to call a EGM even though one member present in person or by proxy?

(a) Registrar of Companies
(b) Central Government
(c) NCLT
(d) Department of Company Affairs

9 Copy of the financial statement is to be filed with registrar within how many days of date of Annual General Meeting?

(a) 30 days (b) 60 days
(c) 90 days (d) 120 days

10 Time gap between two AGM should not exceed ...... months.

(a) 12 (b) 15
(c) 18 (d) 21

11 The first AGM should be conducted within ...... months from the date of incorporation.

(a) 12 (b) 15
(c) 18 (d) 6

12 How many day's clear notice should be given to hold a AGM?

(a) 7 days (b) 14 days (c) 21 days (d) 28 days

13 According to Companies Act, 2013 the resolution passed in the general meeting are of ......types.

(a) three (b) four (c) five (d) two

14 Written record of the business done at a meeting is known as

(a) agenda (b) reports
(c) minutes (d) quorum

15 What is the duration to file the consent of a newly nominated director?

(a) 7 days (b) 10 days (c) 15 days (d) 30 days

16 What is the term for an independent director to hold office?

(a) 2 years (b) 3 years
(c) 5 years (d) 7 years

17 The power of the company to borrow is exercised by its

(a) directors (b) members
(c) shareholders (d) manager

18 Every listed public company must have atleast ...... of total number of directors as independent directors.

(a) 1/3 (b) 2/3 (c) 1/5 (d) 1/2

19 A person can not act as a managing director of more than how many company/companies at a time?

(a) One (b) Two (c) Four (d) Five

20 Who is not key managerial personnel in the company?

(a) The Company Secretary
(b) The Whole time Director
(c) The Chief Financial Officer
(d) Accountant

21 Who constitute the top administrative organ of the company?

(a) General Manager (b) Shareholders
(c) Board of Directors (d) Advisory panel

22 What is Quorum for general meeting for private and public companies?

(a) Both 2 and 5 (b) Both 3 and 6
(c) Both 5 and 7 (d) None of these

23 The minutes book can be inspected by the

(a) shareholders free of charge
(b) debenture holders on payment
(c) any one on payment
(d) None of the above

24 Quorum for a board meeting is
(a) 1/3 of total number of directors or 2 directors, whichever is higher
(b) 1/2 of total number of directors or 3 directors, whichever is higher
(c) 1/2 of total number of directors or 3 directors, whichever is lower
(d) None of the above

25 A company can be wound-up
(a) voluntarily by members
(b) voluntarily by creditors
(c) by the order of the Tribunal
(d) All of the above

26 Compulsory winding-up means winding-up by
(a) the Tribunal (b) the members
(c) the creditors (d) All of these

27 As per the act, who can file a petition to the Tribunal for winding-up?
(a) The Registrar (b) Company
(c) Contributory (d) All of these

28 In the event of company being wound up, the Tribunal shall prepare list of contributories into
(a) List A (b) List B
(c) Either (a) or (b) (d) Both (a) and (b)

29 A voluntary winding-up means winding-up by
(a) members or creditors
(b) members or contributors
(c) creditors or contributors
(d) shareholders or Tribunal

30 A company may be wound up by the Tribunal by passing
(a) special resolution (b) extra-ordinary resolution
(c) ordinary resolution (d) no resolution

31 On a winding-up order being made, the company's property comes under the custody of
(a) liquidator (b) Tribunal
(c) Central Government (d) shareholders

32 A voluntary winding-up is deemed to commence from the date when the declaration of solvency is made by the
(a) manager
(b) a court of competent jurisdiction
(c) Board of Directors
(d) Central Government

33 A person liable to contribute towards the assets of the company on the event of its being wound-up is a....... .
(a) liquidator (b) solicitor
(c) contributory (d) Tribunal

34 On a winding-up, order being made in respect of a company, the official liquidator shall become the ...... of the company.
(a) liquidator (b) solicitor
(c) contributory (d) Tribunal

35 Official liquidators are appointed from a panel of
(a) professional firms of Chartered Accountants
(b) advocates
(c) Company Secretaries
(d) All of the above

36 Tribunal may appoint the official liquidator to be the liquidator provisionally at any time
(a) after the presentation of petition for winding-up
(b) after making the winding-up order
(c) after dissolution
(d) before the statutory meeting

37 The official liquidator after receipt of statement of affairs of the company must submit a preliminary report to the tribunal not later than ...... of the order.
(a) 6 months (b) one year
(c) two weeks (d) one month

38 One of the following is the instance where the just and equitable clause for winding-up can be adopted by the Tribunal.
(a) Oppression of minority by the majority
(b) Inability to pay debts
(c) Commercial insolvency
(d) Reduction of members below minimum

39 The object of winding-up of a company by the tribunal is
(a) to facilitate the protection of its assets
(b) to convert the company into private company, if it is a public company
(c) to convert the company into public company, if it is a private company
(d) to change the Memorandum and Articles

40 If the guarantee company having share capital, the liability of shareholders will be upto
(a) guarantee amount
(b) unpaid value of shares
(c) unlimited
(d) Both (a) and (b)

41 The prospectus, issued in order to test the market before finalising issue size/price is known as
(a) deemed prospectus
(b) shelf prospectus
(c) red herring prospectus
(d) None of the above

42 The companies which are formed under special act, are known as
(a) statutory companies (b) chartered companies
(c) registered companies (d) government companies

43 XYZ company is a government company and X company is a subsidiary of XYZ company. Then X company will be
(a) public company
(b) private company
(c) government company
(d) one person company

44 The companies which are formed under special charter granted by the king or queen of England, are called

(a) statutory companies (b) registered companies
(c) chartered companies (d) None of these

45 Which term refers to a company in which that other company has a significant influence?

(a) Subsidiary company (b) Associate company
(c) Branch office (d) holding company

46 Consider the following statements regarding New Companies Act, 2013.

1. It replaced the Companies Act, 1956.
2. It has introduced concept of one person company.
3. It mandates corporate social responsibility for select class of companies.

Identify the correct statement.

Codes

(a) Both 1 and 2 (b) Both 2 and 3
(c) Both 1 and 3 (d) All of the above

47 Which of the following are characteristics of a company?

(a) It has unlimited liability
(b) It exists only in contemplation of law
(c) It has not a perpetual succession
(d) It comes to an end on the death of all its members

48 The contracts, entered into by promoters on behalf of a prospectus company are known as

(a) post incorporation contracts
(b) pre-incorporation contracts
(c) provisional contracts
(d) Both (b) and (c)

49 Contracts made after incorporation but before the grant of certificate of commencement of business are known as

1. provisional contracts
2. pre-incorporation contracts
3. preliminary contract

Select the correct answer by using the codes given below

Codes

(a) Only 1 (b) Both 1 and 2
(c) Only 3 (d) Both 2 and 3

50 Who is authorised to convene extra-ordinary general meeting?

(a) The Board of Directors
(b) The board on requisition of members
(c) Tribunal
(d) All of the above

51 An act ultra virus the directors can be rectified, if it does not ultra virus

(a) the articles
(b) the memorandum
(c) Company Act
(d) None of the above

52 Which of the following is not the specific powers of the director?

(a) To make calls on shares
(b) To borrow money
(c) To issue debentures
(d) To sell part of the undertaking

53 Which of the following company must have atleast one woman director in their board?

(a) Every listed company
(b) A public company having paid-up capital of ₹ 100 crore or more
(c) A public company having turnover of ₹ 300 crore or more
(d) All of the above

54 How many directors of a public company, unless the articles provide otherwise, must be appointed by the company in general meeting?

(a) All the directors
(b) One-half of the directors
(c) Two-third of the director
(d) Three-fourth of the directors

55 Which of the following is beyond the powers of the Board of Directors?

(a) To issue debentures
(b) To make loans
(c) To remit the payment of any debt due by a director
(d) To issue prospectus

56 Which of the following methods can be used to pass resolution?

(a) Voting by show of hands
(b) Voting through electronic means
(c) Poll
(d) All of the above

57 A company may be wound up by the Tribunal, if

(a) the company passes an ordinary resolution to this effect
(b) the company does not commence its business within 6 months of its incorporation
(c) number of members reduced below 7 in the case of a private company
(d) company is unable to pay its debts

Limited Liability Partnership

58 Limited liability partnership is the combination of

1. partnership
2. joint Stock company
3. public and Company
4. private Company
5. conventional partnership

Select the correct answer by using the codes given below

Codes

(a) Only 1
(b) 1, 2 and 4
(c) Both 4 and 5
(d) All of the above

59 The formation and regulation of LLP is governed by
(a) Partnership Act, 1932
(b) Companies Act, 2013
(c) Limited Liability Partnership Act, 2008
(d) Limited Liability Partnership Act, 2010

60 Who can be a partner in a limited liability partnership?
(a) An individual
(b) A body corporate
(c) A HUF
(d) Both (a) and (b)

61 To whom the LLP files its LLP agreement?
(a) To Central Government
(b) To its partners
(c) To Registrar
(d) To State Government

62 Which form is used by the LLP to file its LLP agreement with the Registrar?
(a) Form 2 (b) Form 3
(c) Form 5 (d) Form 7

63 LLP shall file its LLP agreement with the registrar within ...... of its incorporation.
(a) 15 days (b) 30 days (c) 45 days (d) 90 days

64 Arrange the steps of incorporation of an LLP in sequence.
1. Application for DPIN
2. Filing of LLP agreement
3. Application for DSC
4. Incorporation of LLP

Codes
(a) 1, 3, 2, 4 (b) 3, 1, 4, 2
(c) 2, 1, 3, 4 (d) 1, 2, 3, 4

65 Consider the following statements regarding Limited Liability Partnership (LLP).
1. It provides an alternative to the traditional partnership with unlimited personal liability on the one hand and the statue based company on the other.
2. Unlike company, it does not allow individual partners to be protected from the joint and several liabilities of partners in a partnership firm.

Identify the correct statement.
Codes
(a) Only 1 (b) Only 2
(c) Both (a) and (b) (d) None of the above

66 DPIN stands for
(a) Designated Partner Identification Number
(b) Director Personal Identification Number
(c) Director and Partner Identification Number
(d) Direct Partner Identification Number

67 Minimum number of partner(s) in LLP
(a) 1 (b) 2
(c) 3 (d) 4

68 Who cannot become partner in LLP?
(a) Person who has been found of unsound mind
(b) Person who is an undischarged insolvent
(c) Person who has applied to be adjudicated as an insolvent
(d) All of the above

69 A person shall cease to be a partner of LLP
(a) on receiving advance from LLP
(b) on giving advance to LLP
(c) on his death
(d) after completing age of 60 years

70 Partner of LLP is personally liable in case of
(a) liabilities of LLP
(b) personal liability of other partner
(c) his own personal liability
(d) wrongful act or omission of any other partner

71 Document which is defining the role and obligations of partner in LLP?
(a) Partnership deed
(b) LLP agreement
(c) MoA
(d) AoA

72 Incorporation documents shall be filed by LLP with
(a) Tribunal (b) SEBI
(c) Registrar (d) Central Government

Competition Act, 2002

73 In the year 2002, the Competition Act was enacted replacing
(a) Contract Act (b) Trademark Act
(c) MRTP Act (d) Copyright Act

74 CCI stands for
(a) Competition Commission of India
(b) Cricket Council of India
(c) Contract Commission of India
(d) Container Corporation of India

75 When was CCI established?
(a) 2nd October, 2003
(b) 14th March, 2003
(c) 14th May, 2003
(d) 14th October, 2003

76 Competition Act, 2002, bill got presidential assent in
(a) December 2003 (b) January 2003
(c) March 2003 (d) November 2003

77 Whose association can be taken as an cartel?
(a) Supplier (b) Distributor
(c) Trader (d) All of these

78 What is the minimum number of members to be appointed by Central Government in CCI, as per the Competition Act, 2002?
(a) 1 (b) 2 (c) 3 (d) 4

79 What is the maximum number of members to be appointed by the Central Government in CCI, as per the Competition Act, 2002?
(a) 4 (b) 5
(c) 6 (d) 7

80 Which section of the Competition Act, 2002 enlists abuse of dominant position?
(a) Section 2 (b) Section 3
(c) Section 4 (d) Section 5

81 Which section of the Competition Act, 2002 enlists anti-competitive agreements?
(a) Section 2 (b) Section 3
(c) Section 4 (d) Section 5

82 Which section of the Competition Act, 2002 details combinations?
(a) Section 2 (b) Section 3
(c) Section 4 (d) Section 5

83 What can not be acquired as per the Competition Act, 2002?
(a) Share (b) Voting right
(c) Management control (d) None of these

84 Which of the following as per the Competition Act, 2002 is exempted as anti-competitive agreement?
(a) Patent (b) Trademark
(c) Copyright (d) All of these

85 As per the Competition Act, 2002, what is the tenure of the chairman of the CCI?
(a) 2 years (b) 3 years
(c) 4 years (d) 5 years

86 What is the number of days, after giving notice to CCI, an enterprise can enter into a combination, as per the Competition Act, 2002?
(a) 60 days (b) 180 days
(c) 210 days (d) 240 days

87 How many number of days for notice is to be given to CCI while an enterprise proposes to enter into a combination, as per the Competition Act, 2002.
(a) 7 days (b) 15 days
(c) 30 days (d) 45 days

88 ...... is horizontal agreement.
(a) Cartel (b) Exclusive distribution
(c) Resale price maintenance (d) Tie-in-arrangement

89 Competition Commission of India (CCI) consists of a ...... appointed by the Central Government.
(a) chairperson and four members
(b) chairperson and six members
(c) director and four members
(d) director and six members

90 What is the most crucial component of the Competition Act, 2002?
(a) Abuse of dominance
(b) Anti-competition agreement
(c) Combination regulations
(d) Competition advocacy

91 CCI shall not initiate an inquiry into a combination after the expiry of ...... year(s) from the date on which the combination has taken effect.
(a) one (b) two (c) three (d) five

92 Which of the following is a vertical agreements?
(a) Bid rigging (b) Market share
(c) Price fixation (d) Refusal to deal

93 Section 32 of the Competition Act, deals with
(a) international cartel
(b) power to impose lesser penalty
(c) establishment of commission
(d) composition of commission

94 For consumers, ... results in higher price, poor quality and less choice.
(a) cartelisation (b) bid rigging
(c) tie-in-arrangement (d) refusal to deal

95 Consider the following statements regarding Competition Commission of India (CCI).
1. It is a constitutional body.
2. It has objective of eliminating practices having an adverse effect on competition.

Identify the correct statements.

Codes
(a) Only 1 (b) Only 2
(c) Both (a) and (b) (d) None of the above

96 Which of the following is not regulated by the Competition Act, 2002?
(a) Anti-competitive agreements
(b) Medical negligence
(c) Abuse of dominant position
(d) Predatory pricing

97 What as per the Competition Act, 2002, refers to the sale of goods or provision of services, at a price which is below the cost to eliminate the competitors?
(a) Prepatory price (b) Predatory price
(c) MRP (d) GST price

98 Which of the following as per the Competition Act, 2002, refers to any agreement requiring a purchaser of goods, as a condition of such purchase, to purchase some other goods?
(a) Tie-in-arrangement
(b) Exclusive supply agreement
(c) Exclusive distribution agreement
(d) Refusal to deal

99 Which of the following as per the Competition Act, 2002, refers to any agreement to limit, restrict or withhold the output or supply of any goods or allocate any area or market for the disposal or sale of the goods?
(a) Tie-in-arrangement
(b) Exclusive supply agreement
(c) Exclusive distribution agreement
(d) Refusal to deal

100 Which of the following as per the Competition Act, 2002, refers to any agreements restricting in any manner the purchaser in the course of his trade from acquiring or otherwise dealing in any goods other than those of the seller or any other person?
(a) Tie-in-arrangement
(b) Exclusive supply agreement
(c) Exclusive distribution agreement
(d) Refusal to deal

101 Which of the following as per the Competition Act, 2002 refers to any agreement to sell goods on condition that the prices to be charged on the resale by the purchaser shall be the prices stipulated by the seller unless it is clearly stated that prices lower than those prices may be charged?
(a) Tie-in-arrangement
(b) Exclusive supply agreement
(c) Exclusive distribution agreement
(d) Resale price maintenance

102 Which of the following as per the Competition Act, 2002, refers to any agreement which restricts or is likely to restrict, by any method the persons or classes of persons to whom goods are sold or from whom goods are bought?
(a) Tie-in-arrangement
(b) Exclusive supply agreement
(c) Exclusive distribution agreement
(d) Refusal to deal

103 To achieve its objectives, the CCI endeavours to do the following functions.
1. Develop and nurture effective relations and interactions with sectoral regulators.
2. Ensure fair and healthy competition.
3. Implement competition policies aiming for the most efficient utilisation of economic resources.
4. Make the markets work for the benefit and welfare of politicians.

Identify the correct statements.

Codes
(a) Both 1 and 4 (b) 2, 3 and 4
(c) 1, 2 and 3 (d) 1, 3 and 4

104 Which of the following acts are administered by ministry of corporate affairs?
1. Companies Act, 2013
2. Limited Liability Partnership Act, 2008
3. Competition Act, 2002

Identify the correct statementsl.

Codes
(a) Only 1
(b) Only 2
(c) Both 1 and 3
(d) All of the above

Miscellaneous

Directions (Q. Nos. 105-109) *In the questions given below are two statements labelled as Statement I and Statement II. In the context of two statements, which one of the following is correct?*

Codes
(a) Only Statement I is true
(b) Only Statement II is true
(c) Both statements are true
(d) Both statements are false

105 **Statement** I Company's owners are shareholders. So the company property belongs to the shareholders.

Statement II XYZ company's shares are totally held by government. The company will be government.

106 **Statement** I In case of a private company, statutory meeting need not to be held.

Statement II In a one person company, one member must be a woman.

107 **Statement** I LLP is a body corporate, which is formed and incorporate under LLP Act, 2008.

Statement II LLP does not have perpetual succession.

108 **Statement** I The designated partners of the proposed LLP are required to apply for DIN in Form DIR 3.

Statement II Every individual proposed to be appointed as a partner of LLP need to obtain DSC.

109 **Statement** I One of the objectives of Competition Act, 2002 is to protect the interests of organisations.

Statement II Abuse of dominance is a term which contemplates acquisitions, mergers or amalgamations.

Directions (Q. Nos. 110-114) *In the questions given below are two statements labelled as Assertion (A) and Reason (R). In the context of two statements which one of the following is correct?*

Codes
(a) Both (A) and (R) are true and (R) is the correct explanation of (A)
(b) Both (A) and (R) are true, but (R) is not the correct explanation of (A)
(c) (A) is true, but (R) is false
(d) (A) is false, but (R) is true

110 **Assertion** (A) Every government company may be a public company but every public company need not be government company.

Reason (R) Public company and government company are same.

111 Assertion (A) A company is a juristic person with a perpetual succession.

Reason (R) It is created by a process of law and can be put to an end only by a process of law.

112 Assertion (A) An LLP offers limited liability to its partners.

Reason (R) A LLP is a legal entity separate from its partners.

113 Assertion (A) Competition Commission of India is a corporate body with quasi-judicial powers.

Reason (R) CCI is a body corporate having perpetual succession.

114 Assertion (A) An official liquidator is appointed by the Central Government.

Reason (R) Official liquidator is liable to contribute towards the assets of the company on the event of its being wound up.

115 Match the following.

List I (Section)	List II (Explanation)
A. Section 3	1. Annual general meeting
B. Section 103	2. Extra-ordinary general meeting
C. Section 96	3. Formation of company
D. Section 100	4. Quorum for meeting

Codes

	A	B	C	D		A	B	C	D
(a)	1	2	3	4	(b)	3	4	1	2
(c)	2	3	4	1	(d)	4	1	2	3

116 Match the following.

List I (Form)	List II (Explanation)
A. Form 1	1. Clarification about incorporation document
B. Form 2	2. Application for reservation of name
C. Form 3	3. LLP agreement

Codes

	A	B	C		A	B	C
(a)	1	3	2	(b)	2	3	1
(c)	2	1	3	(d)	1	2	3

117 Match the following.

List I	List II
A. Void agreement	1. Subcontracting
B. Form of bid rigging	2. Perfect competition
C. Free entry and exit in the market	3. Agreement having appreciable adverse effect on competition
D. Cartel	4. Horizontal agreement

Codes

	A	B	C	D		A	B	C	D
(a)	3	1	2	4	(b)	1	2	3	4
(c)	4	3	1	2	(d)	2	1	4	3

PREVIOUS YEARS' QUESTIONS

July 2018

1 Which of the following does not form the part of the important information to be incorporated in the Memorandum of Association as specified in the Companies Act, 2013?

(a) The name of the company and the state in which it is situated
(b) The objects for which the company is proposed to be incorporated
(c) The rules, regulations and bye-laws for the internal management of the company
(d) The liability of the members of the company, whether limited or unlimited

November 2017

2 Which one of the following is not correct relating to competition policy and law?

(a) Collusion and dominance have potential for unfair competition
(b) The appeal against decisions of competition commission of India can be made to the competition Appellate Tribunal
(c) State monopolies, government's business policies and functioning of regulatory authorities cannot be scrutinised under this law
(d) Abuse of dominance rather than dominance should be the key for competition policy law

January 2017

3 Which of the following is not the objective of the Competition Act, 2002?

(a) Prohibition of Restrictive Trade Practices
(b) Prohibition of Dominant Position
(c) Prohibition of Anti-competitive Agreements
(d) Regulation of Combinations

June 2014

4 The Competition Act, 2002 seeks to regulate

(a) anti-competitive agreements
(b) mergers and amalgamation
(c) unfair trade practices
(d) Both (a) and (b)

5 Indicate the true statement.

(a) Large industrial houses are outside the purview of the Competition Act, 2002

(b) There is no provision for curbing frivolous complains under the CPA

(c) The Trademark Act, 1999 does not apply to services

(d) All of the above

December 2013

6 Which of the following is not regulated by the Competition Act, 2002?

(a) Abuse of dominant position

(b) Anti-competitive agreements

(c) Medical negligence

(d) Predatory pricing

ANSWERS

Objective Questions

1 (a)	2 (d)	3 (a)	4 (d)	5 (d)	6 (b)	7 (c)	8 (b)	9 (a)	10 (b)
11 (c)	12 (c)	13 (a)	14 (c)	15 (d)	16 (c)	17 (a)	18 (a)	19 (b)	20 (d)
21 (c)	22 (a)	23 (a)	24 (a)	25 (d)	26 (a)	27 (d)	28 (d)	29 (a)	30 (a)
31 (a)	32 (c)	33 (c)	34 (a)	35 (d)	36 (a)	37 (a)	38 (a)	39 (d)	40 (d)
41 (c)	42 (a)	43 (c)	44 (c)	45 (b)	46 (d)	47 (b)	48 (d)	49 (c)	50 (b)
51 (c)	52 (d)	53 (a)	54 (c)	55 (c)	56 (d)	57 (d)	58 (c)	59 (c)	60 (d)
61 (c)	62 (b)	63 (b)	64 (b)	65 (a)	66 (a)	67 (b)	68 (d)	69 (c)	70 (c)
71 (b)	72 (c)	73 (c)	74 (a)	75 (b)	76 (b)	77 (d)	78 (b)	79 (c)	80 (c)
81 (b)	82 (d)	83 (d)	84 (d)	85 (d)	86 (c)	87 (c)	88 (a)	89 (b)	90 (d)
91 (a)	92 (d)	93 (a)	94 (a)	95 (b)	96 (b)	97 (b)	98 (a)	99 (c)	100 (b)
101 (d)	102 (d)	103 (c)	104 (d)	105 (d)	106 (a)	107 (a)	108 (c)	109 (d)	110 (c)
111 (a)	112 (a)	113 (b)	114 (c)	115 (b)	116 (c)	117 (a)			

Previous Years' Questions

1 (c)	2 (c)	3 (a)	4 (d)	5 (c)	6 (c)

CHAPTER 34

Legal Aspects of Companies and Firms-II

(IT Act, RTI Act, IPRs)

The focus of Information Technology Act, 2000 was recognition of electronic records and facilitation of e-commerce. Right to information act provides for setting out the practical regime of the right to information for citizens. Intellectual property rights have become significantly conspicuous on the legal horizon of India both in terms of new status and judicial pronouncement.

The Information Technology Act, 2000

Information Technology Act was primarily based on Uncitral Model law on e-commerce. Attempts were made in year 1998 for introducing law pertaining to information technology in India but the Information Technology Act was passed only in June, 2000. The Government of India has brought major amendments to IT Act, 2000 in form of the Information Technology Amendment Act, 2008. ITA Act, 2008 as the new version of Information Technology Act, 2000, has provided additional focus on information security. It has added several new sections on offences including cyber terrorism and data protection. IT Act, 2000 extends to the whole of India and save as otherwise provided in this act, it also applies to any offence or contravention there under committed outside India by any person. According to Information Technology Act, 2000, any company can store their data in electronic storage.

Non-applicability of the Act

IT Act, 2000 does not apply to

- A negotiable instrument as defined in Section 13 of the Negotiable Instruments Act, 1881.
- A power of attorney as defined in Section 1(A) of the Powers of Attorney Act, 1882.

In this Chapter

- *Information Technology Act, 2000*
- *Right to Information Act, 2005*
- *Intellectual Property Rights*

- A trust as defined in Section 3 of the Indian Trust Act, 1882.
- A will as defined in clause (n) of Section 2 of the Indian Succession Act, 1925 including any other testamentary disposition by whatever name called.
- Any contract for the sale or conveyance of immovable property or any interest in such property.

Objectives of IT Act, 2000

- To give legal recognition to any transaction which is done electronically or use of internet.
- To give legal recognition to digital signature for accepting any agreement *via* computer.
- To provide facility of filling document online relating to school admission or registration in employment exchange.
- To stop cyber crime and protect privacy of internet users.
- To give legal recognition for keeping books of accounts by bankers and other companies in electronic form.
- To make more power to IPO, RBI and Indian Evidence Act for restricting electronic crime.

Main Provisions of IT Act, 2000

Digital Signature

As per Section 3 of IT Act, 2000 as amended, any subscriber may authenticate an electronic record by affixing his digital signatures. The authentication of electronic records shall be effected by the use of asymmetric Crypto System and hash function which envelops and transform the electronic records into another record.

Electronic Signature

As per Section 3(A) of the Amended Act, notwithstanding anything contained in Section 3, but subject to the provisions of Sub-section 2, a subscriber may authenticate any electronic record by such electronic signature or electronic authentication technique which is considered reliable and may be specified in the second schedule. The government has yet not notified the electronic signature or electronic authentication technique.

Authentication and use of Electronic Records

As per Section 3 of IT Act, 2000, as amended, any subscriber may authenticate an electronic record by affixing his digital signature. Here, electronic record means data, record or stored or sound stored, received or sent in an electronic form or micro film or computer generated microfiche.

As per Section 6 of IT Act, 2000, as amended, where any law provides for the filing of any form application or any other document with any office, authority, body or agency owned or controlled by the appropriate government in a particular manner and the receipt or payment of money in a particular manner, then, notwithstanding anything contained in any other law for the time being is force, such requirement shall be deemed to have been satisfied if such filing issue, grant, receipt or payment, as the case may be, is effected by means of such electronic form as may be prescribed by the appropriate government.

Retention of Electronic Records

As per Section 7 of the IT Act, 2000, documents, records or information shall be retained for any specific period, then, that requirement shall be deemed to have been satisfied, if such documents, records or information are rationed in the electronic form if,

- the information contained therein remains accessible so as to be usable for a subsequent reference.
- the details which will facilitate the identification of the origin, destination, date and time of dispatch or receipt of such electronic record are available in the electronic record.

Audit of Electronic Records

As per Section 7(A) of IT Act, 2000 as amended, there is a provision of audit of documents, records or information maintained in electronic form.

Attribution of Electronic Records

Section 11 of IT Act, 2000 as amended, provides that an electronic record shall be attributed to the originator, if it was sent by the originator himself or by a person who had the authority to act on behalf of originator.

Time and Place of Dispatch and Receipt of Electronic Records

Section 13 of IT Act, 2000, as amended provides that unless otherwise agreed between the originator and the addressee, the dispatch of an electronic record occurs when it enters a computer resource outside the control of the originator and the time of receipt of an electronic record shall be at the time when the electronic record enters the designated computer resource and at the time when the electronic record is retrieved by the addressee.

Certifying Authority

A 'certifying authority' means a person who has been granted a licence to issue 'Electronic Signature Certificate'. Any person may make an application to the controller, for a licence to issue Electronic Signature Certificates provided he fulfills the Central Government prescribed requirements with respect to qualification, expertise, manpower, financial resources and other infrastructure facilities, which are necessary to issue Electronic Signature Certificates.

Renewal of Licence

A certifying authority can apply for renewal of license not less then 45 days before the date of expiry of the period of validity of licence and comply all the rules of Information Technology (certifying authorities) Rules, 2000, which are applied in case of fresh application for becoming certifying authority.

Electronic Signature Certificates

Section 35-39 of IT Act, 2000 provides that certifying authority will issue Electronic Signature Certificates on an application by a person in the form prescribed by the Central Government. The application should be accompanied by a fee not exceeding ₹ 25,000 and a certificate practices statement or where there is no such statement, a statement containing such particulars, as may be specified by regulations.

Suspension of Digital Signature Certificate

The provisions, relating to suspension of digital signature certificate are contained in Section 37 of IT Act, 2000 as amended. This provides that the certifying authority which has issued a digital signature certificate may suspend it on receipt of are request.

Revocation of Digital Signature Certificate

A certifying authority may revoke a digital signature certificate issued by it

- where the subscriber or any other person authorised by him makes a request to that effect, or
- upon the death of the subscriber
- upon the dissolution of the firm or winding-up of the company where the subscriber is a firm or a company.

When a digital signature certificate is suspended or revoked under Section 37 or 38, the certifying authority shall publish a notice of such suspension or revocation, as the case may be, in the repository specified in the digital signature certificate for publication of such notice.

Offences and Penalties under IT Act, 2000

Computer related Offence

(Section 66 read with Section 43)

Section 66 of IT Act, 2000, as amended deals with computer related offences. Computer related offences have been defined in Section 43 of IT Act, 2000, as amended. Section 43 of IT Act, provides that if any person without permission of the owner or any other person, who is incharge of a computer, computer system or computer network

- accesses or secures access to such computer, computer system or computer network or computer resource.
- download, copies or extracts any data, computer database or information from such computer, computer system or computer network including information or data held or stored in any removable storage medium.
- introduced or causes to be introduced any computer contaminant or computer virus into any computer, computer system or computer network.
- damage's or causes to be damaged any computer, computer system or computer network, data, computer database or any other programmes residing in such computer, computer system or computer network.
- disrupts or causes disruption of any computer, computer system or computer network.
- denies or causes the denial of access to any person authorised to access any computer, computer system or computer network by any means.
- provides any assistance to any person to facilitate access to a computer, computer system or computer network in contravention of the provisions of this act, rules or regulations made there-indus.
- charges the service availed of by a person to the account of another person by tempering with or manipulating any computer, computer system or computer network,
- destroys, deletes or alters any information residing in a computer resource or diminishes its value or utility or affects it injuriously by any means.
- steal, conceals, destroys or alters or causes any person to steal, conceal, destroy or any other computer course code used for a computer resource with an intention to cause damage.

Then, he shall be liable to pay damages by way of compensation not exceeding one crore rupees to the person so affected.

Penalties

Compensation for Failure to Protect Data

As per Section 43(A) of IT Act, 2000 as amended, where a body corporate, possessing, dealing or handling any sensitive personal data or information in a computer resource which it owns, controls or operates, is negligent in implementing and maintaining reasonable security practices and procedures and thereby causes wrongful, loss or wrongful gain to any person, such body corporate shall be liable to pay damages by way of compensation to the person so affected.

Penalty for Failure to Furnish Information, Return etc

As per Section 44 of IT Act, 2000 as amended, *if any person who is required under this act or any rules or regulations made there under to*

- furnish any document, return or report to the controller or the certifying authority. If, fails to furnish the same he shall be liable to a penalty not exceeding one lakh and fifty thousand rupees each such failure.
- file any return or furnish any information, books or other documents within the time specified therefore in the regulations, fails to file return or furnish the same within the time specified therefore in the regulations, he shall be liable to a penalty not exceeding five thousand rupees for everyday during which such failure continues.
- maintain books of account or records, fails to maintain the same, he shall be liable to a penalty not exceeding ten thousand rupees for everyday during which the failure continues.

Residuary Penalty

Section 45 of IT Act, 2000, as amended, provides that whoever contravenes any rules or regulations made under this act, for the contravention of which no penalty has been separately provided, shall be liable to pay a compensation not exceeding twenty five thousand rupees to the person affected by such contravention or a penalty not exceeding twenty five thousand rupees.

Punishment for Tampering with Computer Source Documents

This section provides for punishment upto three years or with a fine which may extend upto rupees two lakh or with both to a person who knowingly or intentionally tampers with the computer code source documents. Computer source code means the listing of programmes, computer commands, design and layout and programme analysis of computer resource in any form.

Punishment for Sending Message through Communication Service etc

As per Section 66A of the IT Act, 2000, *if any person who sends*

- any information that is grossly offensive or has meaning character, or
- any information which he knows to be false, but for the purpose of causing annoyance, inconvenience, danger, obstruction, insult, injury, criminal intimidation, enmity, hatred or ill will, persistently by making use of such computer resource or a communication device, or
- any electronic mail or electronic mail message for the purpose of causing annoyance or inconvenience or to deceive or to mislead the addressee or recipient about the origin of such messages, by means of a computer it resource or a communication device,
- then, she/he shall be punishable with imprisonment for a term which may extend to three years and with fine.

Punishment for Dishonestly Receiving or Retaining any Stolen Computer Resource or Communication Device

As per Section 66(B) of the IT Act, 2000 as amended, whoever dishonestly received or retains any stolen computer resources or communication device knowing or having reason to believe the same to be stolen computer resource or communication device, shall be punished with imprisonment of either description for a term which may extend to three years or with fine which may extend to rupees one lakh or with both.

Punishment for Identity Theft

As per Section 66(C) of the IT Act, 2000 as amended, whoever fraudulently or dishonestly make use of the electronic signature, password or any other unique identification feature of any other person, shall be punished with imprisonment of either description for a term which may extend to three years and shall also be liable to fine which may extend to rupees one lakh.

Punishment for Cheating by Personation by using Computer Resource

As per Section 66(D) of the IT Act, 2000 as amended, whoever intentionally or knowingly captures, publishes or transmits the image of a private area of any person without his or her consent, under circumstances violating the privacy of that person, shall be punished with imprisonment which may extend to three years or with fine not exceeding rupees two lakh, or with both.

Punishment for Cyber Terrorism

As per Section 66(F) of the IT Act, 2000 as amended, whenever

- with intent to threaten the unity, integrity, security or sovereignty of India or to strike terror in the people or any section of the people by
  - (a) denying or cause the denial of access to any person authorised to access computer resource, or
  - (b) attempting to penetrate or access a computer resource without authorisation or exceeding authorised access, or
  - (c) introducing or causing to introduce any computer contaminant and by means of such conduct causes or is likely to cause death or injuries to persons or damage or destruction of property or disrupts or knowing that is likely to cause damage or disruption of supplies or services essential to the

life of the community or adversely affect the critical information infrastructure specified under Section 70, or

- knowingly or intentionally penetrates or accesses a computer resource without authorisation or exceeding authorised access and by means of such conduct obtains access to information, data or computer database that is restricted for reasons for the security of the state or foreign relations, or any restricted information, data or computer database, with reasons to believe that such information, data or computer database so obtained may be used to cause or likely to cause injury to the interests of the sovereignty and integrity of India, the security of the state, friendly relations with foreign states, public order, decency or morality, or in relation to contempt of court, defamation or incitement to an offence, or to the advantage of any foreign nation, group of individual or otherwise, commits the offence of cyber terrorism, shall be punishable with imprisonment which may extend to imprisonment for life.

Punishment for Publishing or Transmitting of Obscene Material in Electronic Form

As per section 67 of the IT Act, 2000 as amended, whoever published or transmits or causes to be published or transmitted in the electronic form, any material which is lascivious or appeals to the prurient interest or if its effect is such as to tend to deplane and corrupt persons who are likely, having regard to all relevant circumstances, to read, see or hear the matter contained or embodied in it, shall be punished on first conviction with imprisonment of either description for a term which may extend to three years and with fine which may extend to five lakh rupees and in the event of second or subsequent conviction with imprisonment of either description for a term which may extend to five years and also with fine which may external to ten lakh rupees.

Punishment for Publishing or Transmitting Material containing Sexually Explicit Act, etc in Electronic Form

As per Section 67(A) of the IT Act, whoever publishes or transmits or causes to be published or transmitted in the electronic form any material which contains sexually explicit act or conduct shall be punished on first conviction with imprisonment of either description for a term which may extend to five years and with fine which may extend to ten lakh rupees and in the event of second or subsequent conviction with imprisonment of either description for a term which may extend to seven years and also with fine which may extend to ten lakh rupees.

The Right to Information Act, 2005

Right to information is derived from our fundamental right of freedom of speech and expression under Article 19 of the Constitution. The Right to Information Act, 2005 came into force on the 12th October, 2005. The act extends to the whole of India except the State of Jammu and Kashmir. The act applies both to Central and State Governments and all public authorities.

As per Section 2(F) of the Act, 'Information' means any material in any form including records, documents, memos, emails, opinions, advices, press-releases, circulars, orders, logbooks, contracts, reports, papers, samples, models, data material held in any electronic form and information, relating to any private body which can be accessed by a public authority under other law for the time being in force.

Right to Information

As per Section 2 (J) of the Act, 'Right to information' means the information held by a public authority as accessible under the act and includes the right to

- inspect works, documents and records.
- take notes, extracts or certified copies of documents or records.
- take certified samples of material.
- obtain information in form of printouts, diskettes, floppies, tapes, video cassettes or in any other electronic mode or through printouts.

Objectives of RTI Act

- To empower the citizens to access the information that is under the control of public authorities.
- To promote transparency and accountability in the working of the government.
- To make our democracy work for the people in real sense.
- To curtail corruption and to hold government and their instrumentalities accountable to the governed.
- To ensure less expensive and time bound information.
- To ensure informed citizenry and transparency in governance.

Main Provisions of the Act

Obligations of Public Authority

AS per Section 4(1)(b) of the Act, *every public authority is required to publish*

- the particulars of its organisation, functions and duties.
- the powers and duties of its officers and employees.
- the procedure followed in its decision making process, including channels of supervision and accountability.
- the norms set by it for the discharge of its functions.

- the rules, regulations, instructions, manuals and records used by its employees for discharging its functions.
- A statement of the categories of the documents held by it or under its control.
- the particulars of any arrangement that exists for consultation with, or representation by the formulation of policy or implementation thereof.
- a directory of its officers and employees.
- particulars of recipients of monthly remunerations and concessions, permits or authorisations granted by it.
- the names, designations and other particulars of the Public Information Officers etc.

Exempt from Disclosure

As per Section 8 of the Act, *some informations are exempt from disclosure which are as follows*

- Information, disclosure of which would prejudicially affect the sovereignty and integrity of India, the security, strategic, scientific or economic interests of the state, relation with foreign state and lead to incitement of an offence.
- Information which has been expressly forbidden to be published by any court of law or tribunal or the disclosure of which may constitute contempt of court.
- Information, the disclosure of which would cause a breach of privilege of parliament or the state legislature.
- Information including commercial confidence, trade secrets or intellectual property, the disclosure of which would harm the competitive position of a third party, unless the competent authority is satisfied that larger public interest warrants the disclosure of such information.
- Information received in confidence from Foreign Government.
- Information, the disclosure of which would endanger the life or physical safety of any person or identify the source of information or assistance given in confidence for law enforcement or security purpose etc.

Procedure for Seeking Information

- The citizen desirous of seeking information should apply in writing or through electronic means in English or Hindi or in the official language of the area, to the PIO, specifying the particulars of the information sought for.
- Reason for seeking information are not required to be given.
- Pay fees as may be prescribed (if not belonging to the below poverty line category).

Time Limit for Providing Information

- 30 days from the date of application.
- 48 hours for information concerning the life and liberty of a person.
- 5 days shall be added to the above response time, in case the application for information is given to Assistant Public Information Officer.
- If the interests of a third party are involved, then time limit will be 40 days.
- Failure to provide information within the specified period is a deemed refusal.

Payment of Fees for Information

- Application fees to be prescribed which must be reasonable. If further fees are required, then the same must be intimated in writing with calculation details of how the figure was arrived at.
- Applicant can seek review of the decision on fees charged by the PIO by applying to the appropriate Appellate Authority.
- No fees can be charged from people living below the poverty line.
- Applicant must be provided information free of cost, if the PIO fails to comply with the prescribed time limit.

Grounds of Refusal to Provide Information

- If it is covered by exemption from disclosure (Section 8).
- If it infringes copyright of any person other than the state (Section 9).

Authorities Excluded from Providing Information

Central intelligence and security agencies specified in the second schedule like IB, R and AW, Directorate of Revenue Intelligence, Central Economic Intelligence Bureau, Aviation Research Centre, BSF, CRPF, CISF, NSG, Special Service Bureau, CID etc are excluded from providing information.

Appellate Authorities

First Appeal First appeal to the officer senior in rank-to the PIO in the concerned public authority within 30 days from the expiry of the prescribed time limit or form the receipt of the decision. However, delay may be condoned by the Appellate Authority, if sufficient cause is shown. First appeal shall be disposed of within 30 days from the date of its receipt. Such period is extendable by 15 days, if necessary (Section 19).

Second Appeal Second appeal to the Central Information Commission or the State Information Commission as the case may be, within 90 days of the date on which the decision was given or should have been made by the first Appellate Authority. However, delay may be condoned by the commission, if sufficient cause is shown.

Third Appeal Third party appeal against PIO's decision must be filed within 30 days before first Appellate Authority and within 90 days of the decision on the first appeal, before the appropriate information commission which is the second Appellate Authority. Burden of proving that denial of information was justified lies with the PIO.

Penal Provisions

Every PIO will be liable for fine of ₹ 250 per day, upto a maximum of ₹ 25,000 for

- not accepting an application.
- delaying information release without reasonable cause.
- malafidely denying information.
- knowingly giving incomplete, incorrect, misleading information.
- destroying information that has been requested and
- obstructing furnishing of information in any manner.

As per Section 20, the information commission at the centre and the state levels have the power to impose this penalty. The information commission can also recommend disciplinary action for violation of the law against an erring PIO.

Reporting Procedure

As per Section 25, Central Information Commission will send an annual report to the Central Government on the implementation of the provisions of this law at the end of the year. The State Information Commission will send a report to the State Government. Each Ministry has a duty to compile reports from its public authorities and send them to the Central or State Information Commission, as the case may be.

Rule Making Power

As per Section 27 and 28, Central Government, State Government and the Competent Authority [as defined in Section 2 (e)] are vested with powers to make rules to carry out the provisions of the Right to Information Act, 2005.

Power to Deal with the Difficulties While Implementing this act

As per Section 30, If any difficulty arises in giving effect to the provisions in the act, the Central Government may, by order published in the official Gazette, make provisions necessary for removing the difficulty.

Intellectual Property Rights (IPRs)

Intellectual Property (IP) refers to the creations of the human mind like inventions, literary and artistic works and symbols, names, images and designs used in commerce. *Intellectual property is divided into two categories*

- Industrial property, which includes inventions (patents), trademarks, industrial designs and geographic indications of source.
- Copyrights, which includes literary and artistic works such as novels, poems and plays, films, musical works, artistic works.

Creators are given the right to prevent others from using their inventions. These rights are known as intellectual property rights. Thus, it protects the interests of creators by giving them property rights over their creations.

With the establishment of the World Trade Organisation (WTO), the importance and role of the intellectual property protection has been crystallised in the Trade Related Intellectual Property Systems (TRIPS) Agreement. The TRIPS Agreement, which come into effect on 1st January, 1995, is to date the most comprehensive multilateral agreement on intellectual property. *The area of intellectual property that it covers, are*

- Copyright and related rights (*i.e.* the rights of performers, producers of sound recordings and broadcasting organisations).
- Trade marks including service marks.
- Geographical indications including appellations of origin.
- Industrial designs.
- Patents including protection of new varieties of plants.
- The lay-out designs (topographies) of integrated circuits.
- The undisclosed information including trade secrets and test data.

Patents

Patent is a monopoly grant and it enables the inventor to control the output and within the limits set by demand, the price of the patented products. A patent is an exclusive right granted by a country to the owner of an invention to make, use, manufacture and market the invention, provided the invention satisfies certain conditions stipulated in the law. Exclusivity of right implies that no one else can make, use, manufacture or market the invention without the consent of the patent holder. This right is available only for a limited period of time.

Thus, a patent is an official document given to an inventor by the government allowing him to exclude anyone else from commercially exploiting his invention for a limited period which is 20 years at present.

Provisions of Patent Act

They main provisions of Patent Act, 1970 are as follows

- A patent is granted for an invention which may be related to any process or product.
- Section 6 of the Act, provides that an application for a patent for an invention may be made by any of the following persons either alone or jointly with another.
  (a) By any person claiming to be the true and first inventor of the invention.
  (b) By any person being the assignee of the person claiming to be the true and first inventor in respect of the right to make such an application.
- As per Rule 4 of the Patents Rules, 2003 [as amended by Patents (Amendment) Rules, 2005], application for the patent has to be filed in the respective patent office, as mentioned below, *where the territorial jurisdiction is decided based on whether any of the following occurrences falls within the territory*
  (a) Place of residence, domicile or business of the applicant.
  (b) Place from where the invention actually originated.
  (c) Address for service in India given by the applicant when he has no place of business or domicile in India.
- A patent application shall be filled on Form-1 alongwith provisional/complete specification, with the prescribed fee as given in first schedule at an appropriate office.
- The patent office provides the facility to file a patent application online from the native place of the agent of the applicant or applicant through e-filing. For e-filing, applicant or agent must have a digital signature.
- As per Section 11B, an application for a patent will not be examined unless the applicant or any other person interested, makes a request for examination in the prescribed manner.
- Section 14 provides that in case the report of the examiner is adverse to the applicant or requires any amendment of the application, specification or other documents, the controller shall, before proceeding to dispose of the application, communicate the gist of obligations to the applicant as expeditiously as possible and give him an opportunity of being heard.
- Section 15 empowers the controller to refuse the application or direct to amend the application, specification or other documents.
- Section 17 provides that at any time after the filing of an application and before the grant of the patent, the controller may at the request of the applicant direct that the application shall be post dated to such date as may be specified in the request and proceed with the application accordingly.
- Section 21 provides that an application for a patent shall be deemed to have been abandoned unless, the applicant has complied within the prescribed period with all the requirements imposed on him by or under the act.
- Section 43-dealing with grant of patents provides that where an application for a patent has been found to be in order for grant of the patent and either the application has not been refused by the controller by virtue of any power vested in him by the act, or the application has not been found to be in contravention of any of the provisions of the act, the patent shall be granted as expeditiously as possible to the applicant.
- Section 63 entitles the patentee to offer to surrender his patent, at any time by giving notice to the controller.
- Any interested person including the government can file a petition on any of the grounds specified for revocation of a patent under Section 64 of the Patent Act.
- Section 70 of The Patents Act, 1970 gives the person(s), persons registered as grantee or proprietor of a patent, power to assign, gant licences under, or otherwise deal with, the patent and to give effectual receipts for any consideration for any such assignment, licence or dealing.
- The work relating to drafting of specifications, making of application for a patent, subsequent correspondence with the patent office on the objections raised, representing the applicant's case at the hearing, filing opposition and defending application against opposition, is entrusted to a qualified patent agent.

Trademarks

A trade mark is a visual symbol which may be a word to indicate the source of the goods, a signature, name, device, label, numerals or combination of colours used, or services, or other articles of commerce to distinguish it from other similar goods or services originating from another. It is a distinctive sign which identifies certain goods or services as those produced or provided by a specific person or enterprise. The current law of trade marks contained in the Trademarks Act, 1999.

Provisions of Trademarks

The main provisions of the act are as follows

- Under Section 3 of the Act, the Central Government appoints Controller–General of Patents, Designs, and Trademarks, as the Registrar of Trademarks for the purposes of the act.
- Section 6 contains provisions relating to maintenance of a single register of trademarks at the Head Office of the Trademarks Registry and allows the maintenance of records in computer floppies or diskettes or in any other electronic form subject to the prescribed safeguards.
- As per Section 18 of the Act, any person "claiming to be the proprietor" of the trademark 'used' or 'proposed to be used' by him may make an application in the prescribed manner for registration of his trademarks.
- Section 24 enables registration of two or more persons to be registered as joint proprietors of the trademarks, where the mark is used or proposed to be used in relation to goods or services connected with the joint applicants.
- As per rule 4, an application for registration of a trademark may be made on form TM-1 with prescribed fee of ₹ 2,500/- at one of the five offices of the Trademarks Registry located at Mumbai, Delhi, Kolkata, Chennai and Ahmedabad, depending on the place where the applicant resides or has his principal place of business.
- Trademark protection in India is perpetual subject to renewal of the registration after every 10 years. The application for renewal can be filed six months before the expiry of the validity period of the trademark.
- Section 21 provides that 'any person' may give a notice of opposition to the application for registration of a trademark whether he has or has not any commercial or personal interest in the matter.
- The registration of a trademark confers on the registered proprietor of the trade mark the exclusive right to use the trademark in relation to the goods or services in respect of which the trademark is registered. While registration of a trademark is not compulsory, it offers better legal protection for an action for infringement.
- An unregistered trademark may be assigned or transmitted with or without the goodwill of the business concern.
- Section 37 entitles the registered proprietor of a trademark and to give effectual receipts for any consideration for such assignment.
- Section 39 of the Act, has simplified the provisions in relation to assignment of unregistered trademark without goodwill. It lays down that an unregistered trademark may also be assigned with or without goodwill.
- Section 50 empowers the Registrar to vary or cancel registration as registered uses on the ground that the registered user has used the trademark.
- Section 51 empowers the Registrar to require the proprietor to confirm, at any time during the continuation of registration as registered user, whether the agreement on the basis of which registered user was registered is still in force and if such confirmation is not received within a period of three months, the Registrar shall remove the entry thereof from the register in the prescribed manner.
- Section 54 provides that the registered user will not have a right of assignment or transmission.
- Section 61 to 68 contain provisions relating to the registration of collective trademarks. These provisions provide for registration of a collective mark which belongs to a group or association of persons and the use thereof is reserved for members of the group or association of persons.
- Section 101 to 121 deals with the matters relating to offences, penalties and procedure. *These are*
  - (a) Section 103 deals with the penalty for applying false trademark, trade description, etc and imposes punishment with imprisonment for a term which shall not be less than six months but which may extend to three years and with fine which shall not be less than ₹ 50,000/- but which may extend to ₹ 2,00,000.
  - (b) Section 105 prescribes enhanced penalty on second and subsequent conviction for offences committed under Section 103 and 104 and imposes punishment with imprisonment which shall not be less than one year but which may extend to three years and with fine which shall not be less than ₹ 1,00,000 but which may extend to ₹ 2,00,000.
  - (c) Section 106 provides penalty for removing piece goods etc, in violation of the provisions of Section 81 dealing with stamping of piece goods, cotton yarn and thread. This section provides for forfeiture of goods to the government and fine upto ₹ 1,000.
  - (d) Section 107 makes it an offence if a person falsely represents a trademark as registered. It has been clarified that use of symbols like 'R' in circle in relation to unregistered trademark would constitute an offence. The punishment for such offences is imprisonment for a term which may extend to three years or with five or with both.

It is also clarified that where the mark in question is registered under the law of the country outside India, the use of the word or other expression to denote such registration in foreign country is permissible.

(e) According to Section 108, the use of any words which would lead to the belief that a person's place of business is officially connected with the trademark office shall be treated as offence and be punishable with imprisonment for a term which may extend to two years or with fine or both.

(f) Section 109 contains provisions for penalty for falsification of entries in the register. The offence is punishable with imprisonment not exceeding two years or with fine or both.

- A suit can be initiated either under the law of passing off or for infringement under the Trademarks Act, 1999 depending on whether the trademark is unregistered, pending registration or registered respectively.
- Section 135 expressly stipulates that the relief which a court may grant in any suit for infringement or for passing off referred to in Section 134 includes injunction and at the option of the plaintiff, either damages or an account of profits, together with or without any order for the delivery up to the infringing labels and marks for destruction or erasure.

Copyright

Copyright is a right given by the law to creators of literary, dramatic, musical and artistic works and producers of cinematograph, films and sound recoding. In fact, it is a bundle of rights including, inter alia, rights of reproduction communication to the public, adaptation and translation of the work. Section 14 of the Act, defines the term copyright as to mean the exclusive right to do or authorise the doing of the following acts in respect of a work or any substantial part thereof.

The main objective of the act is to give protection to the owner of the copyright from the dishonest manufacturers, who try to confuse public and make them believe that the infringed products are the products of the owner.

Provisions of Copyright

The main provisions of copyright are as follows

- Section 13 of the Copyright Act, provides that copyright shall subsist throughout India in certain classes of works which are enumerated in the section.

Copyright subsists throughout India in the following classes of works

(a) Original literary, dramatic, musical and artistic works.

(b) Cinematograph films.

(c) Sound recording.

- Copyright protects the rights of authors, *i.e.* creators of intellectual property in the form of literary, musical, dramatic and artistic works and cinematograph films and sound recordings. Generally, the author is the first owner of copyright in a work.
- Section 22 to 29 deal with term of copyrights, *which are as follows*

(a) Literary, dramatic, musical or artistic works enjoy copyright protection for the life time of the author plus 60 years beyond, *i.e.* 60 years after his death.

(b) In the case of joint authorship, the term of copyright is to be construed as a reference to the author who dies last.

(c) In the case of copyright in posthumous, anonymous and pseudonymous works, photographs, cinematograph films, sound recordings, work of government public undertaking and international organisations, the term of protection is 60 years from the beginning of the calendar year next following the year which the work has been first published.

- Section 9 of the Copyright Act, requires for establishment of an office to be called the copyright office for the purpose of the act.
- Section 11 of the Act, provides for the establishment of the copyright board and empowers the Central Government to constitute the same consisting of a Chairman and not less than two, but not more than 14 members.
- Section 18 of the Copyright Act, provides for the assignment of copyright in an existing work as well as future work. In the case of assignment of copyright in any future work, the assignment has the real effect only when the work comes into existence.
- Section 19 of the Act, provides that an assignment of copyright should be in writing signed by the owner of the copyright.
- Section 30 of the Act, empowers the owner of the copyright in any existing work or the prospective owner of the copyright in any future work to grant any interest in the right by licence in writing by him or by his duty authorised agent.
- Section 32 entitles any person to apply to the copyright board for a licence to produce and publish a translation of a literary or dramatic work in any language after a period of seven years from the first publication of the work.
- Section 32 (B) of the Act, deals with termination of licences and provides that if at any time after the granting of a licence, the owner of the copyright in the work or any person authorised by him publishes a translation of such

work in the same language and which is substantially the same in content at a price reasonably related to the price normally charged in India for the translation of works of the same standard on the same or similar subject, the licence so granted shall be terminated.

- Section 40 of the Act, empowers the Government of India to extend the benefits of all or any of the provisions of the act to works first published in any foreign country.
- Chapter X of the Act containing Section 44 to 50 (A) deal with various aspects of registration of copyright. It is evident from the provisions of the aforesaid section that registration of the work under the act is not compulsory and is not a condition precedent for maintaining a suit for damages, if somebody infringes the copyright.
- Act contemplates situations where copyright in a work is deemed to be infringed and provides for civil remedies, administrative remedies and criminal to the owner of the copyright in the event of infringement.
- Apart from remedies for infringement of copyright, the act, expressly provides for the protection of special rights of the author known as moral rights.

Emerging Issues in Intellectual Property

- Restrictive trade practices under the guise of intellectual property licensing can always be corrected by competition authorities.
- A number of multilateral agreements in the field of intellectual property deal with unfair competition in intellectual property transactions.
- Most sophisticated business enterprises recognise the need to protect the confidential information/trade secrets/known-how, but little real attention is paid by protecting or securing the confidential information.
- Proper consideration and handling of the intellectual property matter greatly in the sale of a business, as failure to consider or handle them properly can cause problems for the seller at the front and back end of a sale transaction.
- The transfer of ownership in intellectual property is usually effected by a formal assignment.
- Assignment agreements are of considerable importance in intellectual property rights, since they allow the intellectual property owners to transfer their intellectual property for commercial returns, ensuring that the intellectual property can be used for monetary gain. Intellectual property that is created, is utilised and exploited by the assignment agreement, where the purchaser or assignee takes benefit of the assignment right that are created. These assignment agreement give rise to legal and equitable rights in law and purport many issues, if they are not carefully constructed as required by law.

EXAM BASED QUESTIONS

The IT Act, 2000

1 Which of the following the act provides legal framework for e-governance in India?

(a) Indian Penal Code (b) E-governance Act, 2000
(c) IT Act, 2000 (d) IT Act, 2002

2 Which among the following act, is not amended in Information Technology Act, 2000?

(a) The Bankers's Books Evidence Act, 1891
(b) BSNL IT Policy
(c) RBI Act, 1934
(d) The Indian Evidence Act, 1872

3 How many schedules are there in IT Act, 2000?

(a) 2 (b) 3 (c) 4 (d) 6

4 Which section of IT Act deals with hacking of computer systems and its penalties?

(a) Section 62 (b) Section 63
(c) Section 64 (d) Section 66

5 Which section of IT Act deals with cyber terrorism?

(a) Section 66 A (b) Section 66 B
(c) Section 66 D (d) Section 66 F

6 Which section of IT Act deals with the legal recognition of electronic records?

(a) Section 4 (b) Section 5
(c) Section 6 (d) Section 7

7 E-records and digital signatures are used to

(a) filling of any form in government
(b) issue of grant
(c) making payment
(d) All of the above

8 Verification of electronic record is possible through

(a) digital signature (b) e-commerce
(c) public key (d) e-governance

9 Digital signature is created and verified using

(a) HTML (b) programme
(c) cryptography (d) graphical coding

10 Private key is used to

(a) sign digitally (b) verify the sign
(c) verify the documents (d) make payments

11 Public key is used to

(a) sign digitally (b) verify the sign
(c) verify the documents (d) make payment

12 .... is a person in whose name the digital signature certificate is issued.

(a) Certified authority (b) Subscriber
(c) Holder (d) Controller

13 Who has the power to suspend or revoke digital signature certificate?

(a) Certifying authority (b) Commissioner
(c) Subscriber (d) Controller

14 The components of IT Act, 2000 includes

1. Legal recognition of digital signatures.
2. Regulation of certification authorities.
3. Digital certificates

Codes

(a) Only 1 (b) Both 1 and 2
(c) Both 2 and 3 (d) All of the above

15 Which section of IT Act deals with the appointment of Controller of certifying authorities?

(a) Section 5 (b) Section 10
(c) Section 14 (d) Section 17

16 What is the maximum term given for publishing electronic obscene information?

(a) 2 years (b) 5 years
(c) 10 years (d) 15 years

17 As per IT Act, 2000, those who fails to furnish documents will be penalised upto

(a) ₹ 5,000 (b) ₹ 25,000
(c) ₹ 50,000 (d) ₹ 1,50,000

18 What is the penalty for hacking of computers?

(a) Three years imprisonment or ₹ 5,00,000
(b) Three years imprisonment or ₹ 3,00,000
(c) Two years imprisonment or ₹ 2,00,000
(d) Ten years of imprisonment or ₹ 10,00,000

19 The authentication to be affected by use of asymmetric Crypto system and hash function is known as

(a) public key (b) private key
(c) digital key (d) e-governance

20 The Central Government may appoint a ...... of certifying authority who shall exercise supervision over the activities of certifying authorities.

(a) commissioner (b) controller
(c) executive (d) president

21 A person who has been granted a license to issue a Digital Signature Certificate, is

(a) controller (b) certifying authority
(c) licensed authority (d) director general

22 As per Information Technology Act 2000, if you fails to maintain books of account, then you will be penalised upto

(a) ₹ 5,000 per day (b) ₹ 50,000
(c) ₹ 25,000 (d) ₹ 1,50,000

23 As per the IT Act, what is the maximum penalty for damage to computer, computer systems, unauthorised access, download of data, infecting with virus, denial of access etc.
(a) ₹ 50 lakh (b) ₹ 75 lakh (c) ₹ 1 crore (d) ₹ 5 crore

The RTI Act, 2005

24 What is the time limit to get the information under RTI Act, 2005?
(a) 15 days (b) 30 days (c) 45 days (d) 60 days

25 What is the fee for getting information under RTI Act?
(a) ₹ 10 (b) ₹ 20 (c) ₹ 50 (d) ₹ 100

26 Central Chief Information Commissioner (CIC) is appointed by
(a) President (b) Vice-President
(c) Prime Minister (d) Home Minister

27 Which section of RTI Act 2005 deals with obligations of public authorities?
(a) Section 6 (b) Section 7
(c) Section 4(1) (d) Section 8

28 Which section of RTI Act, 2005 deals with 'Constitution of Central Information Commission'?
(a) Section 11 (b) Section 16
(c) Section 14 and 15 (d) Section 12 and 13

29 Time limit for disposal of first appeal by the first Appellate Authority is
(a) 10-15 days (b) 30-45 days
(c) 50-65 days (d) 70-90 days

30 'Right to Information' includes the right to obtaining information in the form of
(a) diskettes (b) floppies
(c) tapes (d) All of these

31 The preamble to the RTI Act, states that transparency of information is vital to
(a) eradicate corruption (b) contain corruption
(c) promote corruption (d) measure corruption

32 Which section of RTI Act deals with 'exemption from disclosures of information'?
(a) Section 7 (b) Section 8 (c) Section 9 (d) Section 11

33 The officer designated by the public authorities in all administrative units or offices under it to provide information to the citizens requesting for information under the act is known as
(a) Appellate Authority
(b) Chief Information Commissioner
(c) Public Information Officer
(d) Assistant Public Information Officer

34 If the interests of a third party are involved in information sought for, the maximum time limit to get the information will be
(a) 30 days (b) 40 days (c) 45 days (d) 60 days

35 If information sought has been supplied by third party or is treated as confidential by that third party, the third party must be given a representation before the PIO in reply to the notice issued to him within .... days from the date of receipt of such notice.
(a) 5 (b) 15 (c) 10 (d) 7

36 First appeal to the first Appellate authority can be preferred by the applicant within .... days from the expiry of the prescribed time limit or from the receipt of the decision from the PIO
(a) 30 (b) 45
(c) 60 (d) 90

37 First appeal shall be disposed of by the first appellate authority within .... days from the date of its receipt.
(a) 30 (b) 40
(c) 50 (d) 60

38 Period for disposing first appeal can be expand by .... days from 30 days, if necessary.
(a) 10 (b) 30
(c) 15 (d) 25

39 Second appeal to the Central Information Commission or the State Information Commission can be preferred by the applicant within .... days from the date on which the decision was given or should have been made by the first Appellate Authority.
(a) 30 (b) 45
(c) 60 (d) 90

40 The long title of the RTI Act, seeks to promote the following quality (qualities) in the working of every public authority
(a) transparency (b) efficiency
(c) punctuality (d) All of these

41 Appointment Committee of Central Chief Information Commissioner (CIC) includes
(a) Prime Minister
(b) leader of the opposition in the Lok Sabha
(c) one Union Cabinet Minister to be nominated by the Prime Minister
(d) All of the above

42 Consider the following statements about the Right to Information (RTI) Act, 2005 and select one which is not provided for or specially exempted?
(a) It is not applicable in the state of Jammu and Kashmir
(b) An applicant making request for information will have to give reasons for seeking information
(c) Removal of Chief Information Officer
(d) Every Information Commissioner shall hold office for a term of 5 years or till the age of 65 years whichever is earlier

43 **The RTI Act gives right to seek information from the following.**

(a) Private companies (b) Public authorities
(c) MNCs (d) Associations

44 **Chief Information Commissioner (CIC) shall be appointed for a term of .... years from date on which he enters upon his office or till he attains the age of .... years, whichever is earlier.**

(a) 6 years, 66 years (b) 5 years, 70 years
(c) 5 years, 65 years (d) 5 years, 60 years

45 **Under the RTI Act, the grounds for a complaint could be**

1. being asked to pay an unreasonable amount of fee.
2. being given incomplete or false information.
3. any matter relating to requesting or obtaining access to records.

Select the correct answers by using the codes given below

Codes

(a) Only 3 (b) Both 1 and 3
(c) Both 2 and 3 (d) All of the above

46 **How much time does an APIO, at the most, have to forward the RTI application/appeal to the Public Information Officer/first Appellate Authority?**

(a) 5 days (b) 30 days (c) 35 days (d) 45 days

47 **"There is an upper limit for the number of PIOs and APIOs to be appointed by a Public Authority (PA) as per the 'RTI Act, 2005'.**

(a) Yes
(b) No, there is no such limit, whatsoever, as per the 'RTI Act, 2005'
(c) Yes, but only for state PAs
(d) Yes, because, the number of PIOs should be in a definite proposition to the total number of APIOs

48 **As per Section 2(H), public authority means any authority or body or institution of self-government established or constituted**

1. by or under the Constitution.
2. by any other law made by Parliament.
3. by any other law made by State Legislature.
4. by notification issued or order made by the appropriate government.

Choose the correct answer from the codes given below

Codes

(a) 1, 2 and 3
(b) 1, 2 and 4
(c) 1, 3 and 4
(d) All of the above

49 **Assistant Public Information Officer (APIO) has to forward first appeals to**

(a) Public Information Officer (PIO)
(b) the head of the authority
(c) first Appellate Authority
(d) None of the above

50 **"The RTI Act, 2005 stipulates that a public authority should transfer an RTI application or a part thereof to another public authority, if the application or a part of it pertains to information."**

(a) Held by another public authority
(b) The subject matter of which is more closely connected with the functions of another public authority
(c) Both (a) and (b)
(d) Neither (a) nor (b)

51 **Assistant Public Information Officer (APIO) has to receive the following from the citizens.**

(a) Applications for information
(b) First appeal
(c) Second appeal
(d) All of the above

52 **RTI Act is not applicable to**

(a) all non-government organisation substantially financed by political parties
(b) all body owned, controller or substantially financed by the appropriate government
(c) all non-government organisation substantially financed by the appropriate government
(d) All of the above

53 **Which of the following are true about an inquiry carried out by an Information Commission?**

1. It may examine any record to which the RTI Act, 2005 applies.
2. No such record can be withheld from it (irrespective of any provision of any act passed by the Parliament or the State Legislature).
3. Information commission has the powers of a Civil Court trying a suit under the code of civil procedure.

Choose the correct answer from the codes given below

Codes

(a) Both 1 and 2 (b) Both 1 and 3
(c) Both 2 and 3 (d) All of the above

54 **The preamble argues that revelation of information in actual practice is likely to conflict with**

(a) pther private interests (b) other financial interests
(c) other public Interests (d) None of these

55 **Right to information includes the right to**

1. inspect works, documents, records
2. take notes, extracts or certified copies of documents or records.
3. take certified samples of material.
4. obtain information in form of printouts, diskettes, floppies, tapes, video cassettes or in any other electronic mode or through printouts.

Choose the correct answer from the codes given below

Codes

(a) 1, 2 and 3
(b) 1, 2 and 4
(c) 1, 3 and 4
(d) All of the above

56 The obligations of public authorities under RTI Act, 2005 includes

1. It shall publish the powers and duties of its officers and employees.
2. It shall publish the norms set by it for the discharge of its functions.
3. It shall not publish the statement of the categories of the documents held by it or under its control.

Choose the correct answer from the codes given below

Codes

(a) Only 1 (b) Both 1 and 2
(c) Both 2 and 3 (d) All of the above

57 Who receives applications under the RTI Act, 2005?

(a) Public Information Officer at the administrative unit level
(b) Assistant Public Information Officer at the sub district, sub-divisional levels
(c) Any officer of a public authority who is available in the authority's office when the application is made.
(d) Both (a) and (b)

58 An applicant making request for information

(a) shall be given the reason why the information sought for
(b) shall be given the personal details of the applicant
(c) shall not be given any reason for requesting the information or any other personal details except those that may be necessary for contacting him
(d) None of the above

59 How could a Public Information Officer receive applications?

1. Those submitted by a requesters in hand.
2. Those sent by an applicant by email.
3. Transferred by another public authority.
4. Forwarded by an Assistant Public Information Officer.

Choose the correct answer from the following codes

Codes

(a) 1, 2 and 3 (b) 1, 3 and 4
(c) 1, 2 and 4 (d) All of the above

60 The second schedule of the RTI Act 2005 lists

(a) The intelligence and security organisations established by the Central Government that are exempted from the purview of the 'RTI Act, 2005'
(b) All the government organisations come under the purview of RTI Act
(c) All departmental information of Central and State Government
(d) None of the above

61 A first appeal against the decision of a PIO can be preferred by

(a) an applicant
(b) a person from within the public authority
(c) a person outside the public authority to whom the information pertains
(d) All of the above

62 A Public Information Officer will be liable to be imposed a monetary penalty for

(a) refusal to receive an information application
(b) not providing information within specified time limits
(c) destroying information
(d) All of the above

63 "While inquiring into a complaint, Information commission have the power to"

1. summon and enforce attendance of persons.
2. compel them to give evidence on oath and produce documents or things
3. require discovery and inspection of documents.

Choose the correct answer from the codes given below

Codes

(a) Only 1 (b) Only 2
(c) Only 3 (d) All of the above

64 While inquiring into a complaint, information commissions have the power to

(a) receive evidence on affidavit
(b) requisition record or copies thereof from any court or office
(c) issue summons for examination of witnesses or documents
(d) All of the above

65 Indian citizens have the right to information because of

(a) judgement of Supreme Court
(b) implementation of international laws by Indian Government
(c) all states adopted agree to implement the act
(d) a law passed the Parliament of India

66 Rules can be made by appropriate governments or competent authorities by notifying the rules

(a) in the official gazette
(b) by publishing them on the website of the appropriate government
(c) by publishing them on the websites of Information Commissions–as applicable
(d) None of the above

Intellectual Property Rights (IPRs)

67 Which of the following is an intellectual property?

(a) Patents
(b) Copyright
(c) Trademarks
(d) All of the above

68 The area of intellectual property includes

1. copyrights and related rights.
2. trademarks including service marks.
3. industrial designs
4. the lay-out designs of integrated circuits.

Select the correct answer from the codes given below

Codes

(a) Only 1
(b) Both 1 and 2
(c) 1, 2 and 3
(d) All of the above

69 Patent ability criteria includes
1. novelty 2. inventive step
3. capable of Industrial application
Select the correct answer from the codes given below
Codes
(a) Only 2 (b) Both 1 and 3
(c) Both 2 and 3 (d) All of the above

70 Invention means
(a) new product having inventive step and capable industrial application
(b) new process
(c) new product or process having inventive step and capable industrial application
(d) None of the above

71 Which of the following is the oldest convention for patent protection?
(a) TRIPs (b) Rome convention
(c) Berne convention (d) Paris convention

72 What is the maximum duration allowed under right to priority for patent filing?
(a) One year
(b) Two years
(c) Five years
(d) Depends on legal jurisdiction and patentable product

73 Which article of TRIPs deals with patentability?
(a) 25 (b) 27
(c) 28 (d) 29

74 Patent is a form of
(a) tangible property
(b) intellectual property
(c) industrial property
(d) Both (b) and (c)

75 Which of the following constitute an important consideration for grant of patent for an invention?
(a) Novelty (b) Exclusivity
(c) Disclosure (d) Process complexity

76 Which characteristic of a patentable product is emphasised by Article 54 of the EPC?
(a) Exclusivity (b) Grant
(c) Commercial Value (d) Novelty

77 What aspect of a patented product is tested by PCT?
(a) Priority (b) Novelty
(c) Exclusivity (d) Commercial value

78 A patent application is filed on
(a) Form-1 (b) Form-2
(c) Form-3 (d) Form-4

79 Patent application can be filed in India by
(a) true and first inventor
(b) assignee of the inventor
(c) legal representative of the inventor
(d) All of the above

80 Which section of Copyright Act defines copyright?
(a) Section 14 (b) Section 15
(c) Section 16 (d) Section 17

81 What is the default period of copyright assignment, if not specified?
(a) 1 year (b) 2 years
(c) 5 years (d) 7 years

82 How is a copyright assigned?
(a) By copyright board (b) By appellate authority
(c) By court of law (d) By assignor

83 How long before an item loses its copyright?
(a) 25 years (b) 50 years
(c) 75 years (d) 100 years

84 Which of the following does not constitute infringement under Section 52 of Copyright Act?
(a) Back up copy (b) Review
(c) Reading extract in public (d) All of these

85 What is public domain?
(a) Work belonging to the public as a whole
(b) Work that people know about
(c) Work that is in public
(d) All of the above

86 What needs to be done before a copyrighted book may be printed?
(a) The book must be registered with the copyright office
(b) Consent of the copyright owner must be obtained
(c) The copyright symbol must be affixed to the book
(d) None of the above

87 What is the characteristics of something being an original work under copyright law?
(a) Must be new or novel
(b) Must not based upon another work
(c) Must contain factual information
(d) None of the above

88 Which section of the Trademarks Act, illustrates refusal of trademark registration?
(a) Section 8 (b) Section 9
(c) Section 10 (d) Section 11

89 What is the duration of a trademark registration as defined by Trademarks Act, 1999?
(a) 2 years
(b) 5 years
(c) 10 years
(d) Depends on the commercial value of infringement

90 The following cannot be exploited by assigning or by licensing the rights to others.
(a) Patents (b) Copyrights
(c) Trademarks (d) All of these

91 Which organisation attends to cyber squatting related cases?
(a) ITO (b) ITA
(c) WIPO (d) PCT

92 What is the role of Section 135 of the Trademarks Act, 1999?
(a) Injunction relief
(b) Evidence preservation
(c) Infringement relief
(d) Real of infringement suit

93 A complete patent specification shall disclose
(a) the best method of performing the invention
(b) all the methods of performing the invention
(c) all anticipated uses of the invention
(d) All of the above

94 As per the Indian Patent Act, a resident in India can
(a) free to file a patent in a foreign country without first filing the said patent in India.
(b) file a patent in a foreign country without first filing the said patent in India, only under certain special circumstances.
(c) file a patent in a foreign country only after filing a PCT application on the same subject matter
(d) All of the above

95 Which of the following is an exclusive right of copyright owner?
(a) Right to public distribution of the work
(b) Right to reproduction of the work
(c) Right of public performance
(d) All of the above

96 What should be done to prevent copying of product by copyright protection?
(a) The claimant's product must be represented in an artistic work
(b) Articles made to the design must have marketed
(c) The defendant's product must be a substantial copy of the claimant's product
(d) The claimant's designer must have created the design for the clamant's product in the form of a drawing or a model that is an artistic work

97 In India, the literary work is protected until
(a) lifetime of author
(b) 25 years after the death of author
(c) 40 years after the death of author
(d) 60 years after the death of author

98 To qualify for copyright protection, what must the work be?
(a) Original, creative to a minimal degree and in a fixed or tangible form of expression
(b) Something that is deemed useful by the public
(c) Anything
(d) All of the above

99 Which of the following will qualify for a copyright?
(a) New song tune hummed by a musician
(b) New song words told to a musician
(c) New song tune tweaked by a musician
(d) New song recorded by a musician

100 What element does copyright law protects?
(a) Tangible property
(b) Intangible property
(c) The name of a particular goods or service
(d) Ideas contained in varied forms of expression

101 What is the distinctive feature of plagiarism against copyright violation even though both are similar?
(a) Using someone else
(b) Distributing someone copyright
(c) Reproducing someone else
(d) All of the above

102 What element does trademark law protects?
(a) Only brand names
(b) Names of specific people and places
(c) Words, symbols or devices that differentiate goods or services from one another
(d) Inventions that feature some sort of utility function

103 Who is responsible to prove the infringement of registered trademark U/S 29 of Trademarks Act, 1999?
(a) Plaintiff
(b) Accused
(c) Depends on the commercial value of infringement
(d) Depends on the legal viability of trademark registration

104 What happens where two or more persons are registered proprietors of trademarks, which are identical with or nearly resemble each other?
(a) Depends on the commercial value of trademark
(b) Depends on the legal viability of trademark registration
(c) Sole ownership is given to party which registered the trademark earlier
(d) No one holds the trademark as being sole registered proprietor

Miscellaneous

Directions (Q. Nos. 105-110) *In the following question, two statements are given, labelled as Statement I and Statement II. Which of the following statement(s) is/are correct or incorrect?*

Codes
(a) Only Statement I is correct
(b) Only Statement II is correct
(c) Both statements are correct
(d) Both statements are incorrect

105 **Statement** I Controller of certifying authorities works under Ministry of Communication and IT.
Statement II IT Act, 2000 came into force on 10th October, 2000.

106 **Statement** I Data material held in any electronic form is 'information' under RTI Act, 2005.
Statement II The time limit to get the information concerning the life and liberty of a person is 48 hours.

107 **Statement** I A PIO has to offer reasonable assistance to an applicant to reduce an oral application into writing.
Statement II A PIO is under a no obligation to provide requested information to non-BPL category persons without the payment of application/initial fees.

108 **Statement** I Patent right is an exclusive right.
Statement II The naturally occuring micro-organism is patentable in India.

109 **Statement** I Movies are copyrighted.
Statement II Using copyright material without the creator's consent considered stealing.

110 **Statement** I "I can legally upload scenes from my favorite hollywood movies to Youtube.com."
Statement II "Even, if I pay a subscription fee to an online movie distribution site, I am still not protected from being accused of copyright infringement."

111 Which of the following statement(s) is/are true?
Statement I Trademark is represented graphically.
Statement II Trademark is capable of distinguishing the goods or services of one person from those of others.
Statement III Trademark may includes shapes of goods or combination of colours.
(a) Only Statement I
(b) Both Statements I and III
(c) Both II and III
(d) All of the above

Directions (Q. Nos. 112-114) *In the questions given below are two statements labelled as Assertion (A) and Reason (R). In the context of two statements, which one of the following is correct?*

Codes
(a) Both (A) and (R) are true and (R) is the correct explanation of (A)
(b) Both (A) and (R) are true, but (R) is not the correct explanation of (A)
(c) (A) is true, but (R) is false
(d) (A) is false, but (R) is true

112 **Assertion** (A) Patent right is limited period right.
Reason (R) A patent right is available to patentee for 20 years from date of filling on that jurisdiction.

113 **Assertion** (A) Trademark registrations can be renewed for an unlimited number of ten periods.
Reason (R) The registered user will not have a right of assignment or transmission.

114 **Assertion** (A) Trademark law is intended to protect the owners original work.
Reason (R) To qualify for a trademark, one must be graduated.

115 Match the following.

List I	List II
A. Patent	1. Berne convention
B. Trademark	2. Paris convention
C. Copyright	3. Madrid

Codes

	A	B	C		A	B	C
(a)	1	2	3	(b)	2	3	1
(c)	3	1	2	(d)	1	3	2

116 Match the following in respect of IT Act, 2000.

List I (Offeree)	List II (Penalty/Punishment)
A. Punishment for identity theft	1. ₹ 5,000 per day
B. Residuary penalty	2. Imprisonment of 3 years and fine of ₹ 1 lakh
C. Penalty for failure to furnish information	3. Imprisonment for life
D. Punishment for cyber terrorism	4. ₹ 25,000

Codes

	A	B	C	D		A	B	C	D
(a)	2	4	1	3	(b)	1	2	3	4
(c)	4	2	3	4	(d)	3	4	2	1

117 Match the following in respect of RTI Act, 2005.

List I (Appeal)	List II (To whom)
A. First appeal	1. First Appellate Authority
B. Second appeal	2. To the officer senior in rank to the PIO
C. Third appeal	3. Central/State Information Commission

Codes

	A	B	C		A	B	C
(a)	1	2	3	(b)	2	1	3
(c)	2	3	1	(d)	3	2	1

118 Match the following.

List I	List II
A. Patent	1. An exclusive right to do or authorise the doing the literary, dramatic and artistic works.
B. Trademark	2. An exclusive right granted to the owner of an invention to make, use manufacture and market it.
C. Copyright	3. A visual symbol which may be a word to indicate the source of the goods, signature, name etc.

Codes

	A	B	C		A	B	C
(a)	1	3	2	(b)	2	3	1
(c)	3	2	1	(d)	1	2	3

ANSWERS

Objective Questions

1 (c)	2 (b)	3 (c)	4 (c)	5 (d)	6 (a)	7 (d)	8 (a)	9 (c)	10 (a)
11 (b)	12 (b)	13 (a)	14 (d)	15 (d)	16 (c)	17 (c)	18 (a)	19 (c)	20 (b)
21 (b)	22 (c)	23 (c)	24 (b)	25 (a)	26 (a)	27 (c)	28 (d)	29 (b)	30 (d)
31 (b)	32 (b)	33 (c)	34 (b)	35 (c)	36 (a)	37 (a)	38 (c)	39 (d)	40 (a)
41 (d)	42 (c)	43 (b)	44 (c)	45 (d)	46 (a)	47 (b)	48 (d)	49 (c)	50 (c)
51 (a)	52 (a)	53 (d)	54 (c)	55 (d)	56 (b)	57 (d)	58 (c)	59 (d)	60 (a)
61 (d)	62 (d)	63 (b)	64 (d)	65 (d)	66 (a)	67 (d)	68 (c)	69 (d)	70 (c)
71 (c)	72 (a)	73 (b)	74 (d)	75 (a)	76 (d)	77 (a)	78 (d)	79 (d)	80 (a)
81 (c)	82 (d)	83 (c)	84 (b)	85 (a)	86 (b)	87 (d)	88 (b)	89 (c)	90 (c)
91 (c)	92 (b)	93 (a)	94 (b)	95 (d)	96 (d)	97 (d)	98 (a)	99 (d)	100 (b)
101 (a)	102 (c)	103 (a)	104 (d)	105 (a)	106 (c)	107 (c)	108 (a)	109 (c)	110 (b)
111 (d)	112 (a)	113 (b)	114 (c)	115 (b)	116 (a)	117 (c)	118 (b)		

CHAPTER 35

Legal Aspects of Goods and Services

India is one of the largest economies and also a great country where and thus has adequate checks and measures to ensure the safety and prosperity of its business and commerce community. Sale of commodities, Goods and Service Tax (GST) and Negotiable Instruments Act etc constitute important types of contracts under the law in India.

Sale of Goods Act, 1930

The law relating to sale of goods is contained in the Sale of Goods Act, 1930. According to Section 4 of the Act, a contract of sale of goods is a contract, whereby the seller transfers or agrees to transfer the property in goods to the buyer for a money consideration called the price.

It shows that the expression 'contract of sale' includes both a sale, where the seller transfers the ownership of the goods to the buyer and an agreement to sell, where the ownership of goods is to be transferred at a future time or subject to some conditions to be fulfilled later on.

Important Terms Related to Act

Buyer As per Section 2 (1) of the Act, "a buyer is someone who buys or has agreed to buy goods."

Seller As per Section 2 (13) of the Act, "a seller is someone who sells or has agreed to sell goods."

Goods As per Section 2 (7) of the Act, "Every kind of movable property other than actionable claims and money, and includes stock and shares, growing crops, grass, and things attached to or forming part of the land which are agreed to be served

In this Chapter

before sale or under the contract of sale will be considered goods."

Delivery The delivery of goods signifies the voluntary transfer of possession from one person to another. It can be in various forms, *i.e.* actual delivery, constructive delivery, symbolic delivery etc.

The Document of Title of Goods It includes "the bill of lading, dock-warrant, warehouse keeper's certificate, railway receipt, multimodal transport document, warrant or order for the delivery of goods and any other document used in the ordinary course of business as proof of the possession or control of goods or authorising or purporting to authorise, either by endorsement or by delivery, the possessor of the document to transfer or receive goods thereby represented."

Sale and Agreement to Sell

Sale Where the property immediately transfers from the seller to buyer, it is called sale. Sale can be defined as "transfer of ownership in the goods by the seller to buyer in exchange of price paid or promised or partly paid and partly promised."

Agreement to Sell Where the transfer of property in goods is to take place in future, from seller to buyer is called 'agreement to sell'. Agreement to sell can be defined as "the condition when the seller agrees with the buyer to transfer the title of ownership on a future date upon satisfying certain condition."

The following points will bring out the distinction between sale and an agreement to sell

- In a sale, the property in the goods sold passes to the buyer at the time of contract, so that he becomes the owner of the goods. In an agreement to sell, the ownership does not pass to the buyers at the time of the contract, but it passes only when it becomes sale on the expiry of certain time or the fulfilment of certain conditions subject to which the property in the goods is to be transferred.
- An agreement to sell is an executory contract, but a sale is an executed contract.
- An agreement to sell is a contract pure and simple, but a sale is contract plus conveyance.
- If there is an agreement to sell and goods are destroyed by accident, the loss falls on the seller. In a sale, the loss falls on the buyer, even though the goods are with the seller.
- If there is an agreement to sell and the seller commits a breach, the buyer has only a personal remedy against the seller, namely, a claim for damages. But if there has been a sale and the seller commits a breach by refusing to deliver the goods, the buyer has not only a personal remedy against him but also the other remedies which an owner has in respect of goods themselves such as a suit for conversion or detinue etc.

Doctrine of Caveat Emptor

The term 'caveat emptor' is a latin word which means "Let the buyer beware". This principle states that it is for the buyer to satisfy himself that the goods which he is purchasing are of the quality which he requires. If he buys goods for a particular purpose, he must satisfy himself that they are fit for that purpose.

The doctrine of caveat emptor is embodied in Section 16 of the act which states that "Subject to the provisions of this act and of any other law for the time being in force, there is no implied warranty or condition as to the quality or fitness for any particular purpose of goods supplied under a contract of sale."

In simple words, it is not the seller's duty to give to the buyer, the goods which are fit for a suitable purpose of the buyer. If he makes a wrong selection, he cannot blame the seller, if the goods turn out to be defective or do not serve his purpose. The principle was applied in the case of Ward *vs* Hobbs, (1878) 4 AC 13, where certain pigs were sold by auction and no warranty was given by seller in respect of any fault or error of description.

The buyer paid the price for healthy pigs but they were ill and all but one died of typhoid fever. They also infected some of the buyer's own pigs. It was held that there was no implied condition or warranty that the pigs were of good health. It was the buyer's duty to satisfy himself regarding the health of the pigs.

Exceptions to the Doctrine of Caveat Emptor

Section 16 lays down the following exceptions to the doctrine of caveat emptor

- Where the seller makes a false representation and the buyer relies on it.
- When the seller actively conceals a defect in the goods which is not visible on a reasonable examination of the same.
- When the buyer, relying upon the skill and judgement of the seller, has expressly or impliedly communicated to him the purpose for which the goods are required.
- Where goods are bought by description from a seller who deals in goods of that description.

Unpaid Seller

Meaning of Unpaid Seller

AS per Section 45 of the Act, the seller of goods is deemed to be unpaid seller,

- when the whole of the price has not been paid or tendered, or

- when a conditional payment was made by a bill of exchange or other negotiable instrument and the instrument has been dishonoured.

Rights of Unpaid Seller against the Goods

Right of Lien An unpaid seller in possession of goods sold, may exercise his lie on the goods, *i.e.* keep the goods in his possession and refuse to deliver them to the buyer until the fulfilment or tender of the price in cases, where

- the goods have been sold without stipulation as to credit; or
- the goods have been sold on credit, but the term of credit has expired; or
- the buyer becomes insolvent.

Right of Stoppage in Transit The right of stoppage in transit is a right of stopping the goods while they are in transit, resuming possession of them and retaining possession until payment of the price. *The right to stop goods is available to an unpaid seller*

- when the buyer becomes insolvent and
- the goods are in transit.

The right to stop in transit may be exercised by the unpaid seller either by taking actual possession of the goods or by giving notice of the seller's claim to the carrier or other person having control of the goods.

Right of Re-sale *The unpaid seller may re-sell,*

- where the goods are perishable.
- where the right is expressly reserved in the contract.
- where in exercise of right of lien or stoppage in transit, the seller gives notice to the buyer of his intention to re-sell, and the buyer, does not pay or tender the price within a reasonable time.

If on a re-sale, there is a deficiency between the price due and amount realised, he is entitled to recover it from the buyer. If there, is surplus, he can keep it. He will not have these rights, if he has not given any notice and he will have to pay the buyer profit, if any, on the re-sale.

Right to Withhold Delivery If the property in the goods has passed, the unpaid seller has right as described above. If, however, the property has not passed, the unpaid seller has a right of withholding delivery similar to and co-extensive with his rights of lien and stoppage in transit.

Rights of Unpaid Seller against the Buyer

An unpaid seller may sue the buyer for the price of the goods in case of breach of contract, where the property in the goods has passed to the buyer or he has wrongfully refused to pay the price according to the terms of the contract. The seller may sue the buyer even if the property in the goods has not passed where the price is payable on a certain day.

Under Section 56, the seller may sue the buyer for damages on breach of contract, where the buyer wrongfully neglects or refuses to accept and pay for the goods. *Thus, an unpaid seller's rights against the buyer personally are*

- A suit for the price.
- A suit for damages.

Rights of Buyer

The rights of buyer under Sale of Goods Act, 1930 are discussed below

- To have delivery of the goods as per contract (Section 31 and 32).
- To reject the goods when they are not of the description, quality or quantity as specified in the contract (Section 37).
- To repudiate the contract when goods are delivered in installments without any agreement to that effects [Section 38(1)].
- To be informed by the seller, when the goods are to be sent by sea route, so that he may arrange for their insurance [Section 39 (30)].
- To sue the seller for recovery of the price, if already paid, when the seller fails to deliver the goods.
- To sue the seller for damages, if the seller wrongfully neglects or refuses to deliver the goods to the buyer (Section 57).
- To sue the seller for damages for breach of warranty or for breach of a condition treated as breach of a warranty (Section 59).
- To have a reasonable opportunity to examine the goods for ascertaining whether they are in conformity with the contract (Section 41).
- To sue the seller for specific performance.

Goods and Service Tax (GST)

GST, *i.e.* Goods and Service Tax is a major milestone in indirect tax reforms in independent India. GST is a common and unified tax on goods and services which was rolled out in India with effect from 1st July, 2017. It transforms the system of taxation and tax administration into a digital world by adopting the latest information technology. It is a destination based consumption tax. It is applicable all over India including Jammu and Kashmir. It adorns dual taxation model where union and states levy and collect taxes simultaneously. The tax rates, rules and regulations of GST are governed by the GST council which consists of the finance ministers of centre and all the states.

Objectives of GST

- To eliminate classification dispute between goods and services.

- To ensure the availability of input tax credit across the value chain.
- To ensure the uniformity of tax rates and automated compliances.
- To simplify the process of registration, filing of return, tax administration and compliance.
- To minimise tax rate slabs to avoid classification issues.
- To prevent the unhealthy competition among states.
- To increase the tax base and raising compliance.
- To remove the cascading effect.
- To make free movement of goods across the country without any additional tax.

Main Provisions of GST

- GST is applicable on 'Supply' of goods or services as against the present concept of tax on the manufacture of goods or on sale of goods or on provision of services.
- GST is based on the principle of destination based consumption taxation or against the present principle of origin based taxation.
- It is a dual GST with the Centre and the States simultaneously levying it on a common base. The GST to be levied by the Centre would be called Central GST (Central tax-CGST) and that to be levied by the States (including union territories with legislature) would be called State GST. Union territories without legislature would levy union territory GST.
- An integrated GST is levied on inter-state supply (including stock transfers) of goods or services. This would be collected by the Centre, so that the credit chain is not disrupted.
- Import of goods are treated as Inter-state supplies and would be leaded subject to IGST in addition to the applicable customer duties.
- Import of services are treated as inter-state supplies and would be subject to IGST.
- CGST, SGST/UTGST and IGST are levied at rates to be mutually agreed upon by the Centre and the States under the aegis of the GST.
- *GST has replaced the following taxes, currently levied and collected by the Centre*
  - (a) Central Excise Duty
  - (b) Duties of Excise (Medicinal and Toilet Preparations)
  - (c) Additional Duties of Excise (Goods of Special Importance)
  - (d) Additional Duties of Excise (Textiles and Textile Products)
  - (e) Additional Duties of Customs (Commonly known as CVD)
  - (f) Special Additional Duties of Customs (SAD)
  - (g) Service Tax
  - (h) Cesses and surcharges in so far as they relate to supply of goods or services
- *State taxes that has been subsumed within the GST are*
  - (a) State VAT
  - (b) Central Sales Tax
  - (c) Purchase Tax
  - (d) Luxury Tax
  - (e) Entry Tax (all forms)
  - (f) Entertainment Tax (except those levied by the local bodies)
  - (g) Taxes on advertisements
  - (h) Taxes on lotteries, betting and gambling
  - (i) State cesses and surcharges in so far as they relate to supply of goods and services
- GST is applied to all goods and services except alcohol for human consumption.
- GST on five specified petroleum products (Crude, Petrol, Diesel, ATF and Natural Gas) would be applicable from a date to be recommended by the GSTC.
- Tobacco and product related to it are subject to GST. In addition, the Centre would continue to levy Central excise duty.
- A common threshold exemption is applied to both CGST and SGST. Taxpayers with an annual turnover of ₹ 20 lakh (except Jammu and Kashmir) would be exempt from GST. A compounding option (*i.e.* to pay tax at a flat rate without credits) would be available to small taxpayers (including the manufactures other than specific category of manufacturers and service providers) having an annual turnover of upto ₹ 75 Lakh (₹ 50 lakh for special category states except Jammu and Kashmir and Uttarakhand enumerated in Article 279A of the Constitution). The threshold exemption and compounding scheme would be optional.
- All exports and supplies to SEZs and SEZ units would be zero-rated.
- Credit of CGST paid on inputs may be used only for paying CGST on the output and the credit of SGST/UTGST paid on inputs may be used only for paying SGST/UTGST. In other words, the two streams of input tax credit can not be cross utilised.
- Accounts would be settled periodically between the Centre and the State to ensure that the credit of SGST used for payment of IGST is transferred by the originating state to the centre. Similarly, the IGST used for payment of SGST would be transferred by Centre to the destination State.
- Various modes of payment of tax available to the taxpayer including internet banking, debit/credit card and NEFT/RTGS.

- Obligation on certain persons including government departments, local authorities and government agencies, who are recipients of supply, to deduct tax @1% from the payment made or credited to the supplier where total value of supply, under a contract, exceeds ₹ 2,50,000.
- Refund of tax to be sought by taxpayer or by any other person who has borne the incidence of tax within two years from the relevant date.
- Audit of registered persons to be conducted in order to verify compliance with the provisions of act.
- Arrears of tax to be recovered using various modes including detaining and sale of good, movable and immovable property of defaulting taxable person.
- Goods and Services Tax Appellate Tribunal would be constituted by the Central Government for hearing appeals against the orders passed by the Appellate Authority or the Revisional Authority. States would adopt the provisions relating to Tribunal in respective SGST Act.

GST Registration

Requirement for Registration

- A business entity that is currently registered under any of the existing tax regimes including Central Excise Duty, Service Tax, State VAT, Central Sales Tax.
- If a business doesn't have any existing registration, then it needs to get registered if aggregate turnover in any financial year exceeds the threshold limit, *i.e.* ₹ 20 lakh.
- Every person who makes a supply from the territorial waters of India.

➠ **Note** *GST registration will be a single PAN-based registration in one State or Union Territory, but a person having multiple business verticals in one state or businesses in multiple states has to get a separate registration for each such business.*

Process of Registration

- The applicant needs to submit his PAN, mobile number and email address in Part-A of form GST REG–01 on GSTN portal.
- The PAN is then verified on the GSTN portal while the mobile number and the email address are verified through on OTP. An acknowledgement will be issued to the applicant in the form GST REG–02.
- The applicant then needs to fill the Part-B of form GST REG-01 and specify the application reference number. The form can be submitted after attaching the required documents. The authentication would be done by signature through DSC or e-signature.
- If any additional information is required, form GST REG–03 will be issued. The applicant needs to respond in form GST REG–04 with the required information within 7 working days from the date of the receipt of form GST REG–03.
- If applicant has provided all the required information *via* form GST REG–01 or form GST REG–04, the registration certificate in form GST REG–06 for the principal place of the business as well as for every additional place of business will be issued. If, however, the details submitted are not satisfactorily, the registration application will be rejected using form GST REG–05.
- The applicant who is required to deduct TDS or collect TCS shall, however, submit an application in form GST REG–07 for the purpose of registration.

Various GST Tax Slabs in India

No Tax

Goods No taxes will be levied on goods like sanitary napkins, deities made of stone, marbles or wood, rakhis without any precious metals, raw material used in brooms, saal leaves and forfeited milk, fruits, vegetables, bread, salt, bindi, curd, sindoor, natural honey, bangles, handloom, besan, flour, eggs, stamp, printed books etc.

Services All hotels and lodges who carry a tariff below ₹ 1,000, bank charges on saving account, Jan Dhan Yojana etc.

GST Tax Slab of 5%

Goods Skimmed milk powder, frozen vegetables, coffee, coal, fertilizers, tea, spices, pizza bread, kerosene, insulin, cashew nuts, agarbatti, ayurvedic medicines, lifeboats etc.

Services Restaurant in hotels with a room tariff less than ₹ 7,500, small restaurants alongwith transport services like railways and airways, special flights for pilgrims etc.

GST Tax Slab of 12%

Goods Frozen meat products, butter, cheese, ghee, pickles, fruit juices, namkeen, tooth powder, medicine, umbrella, instant food mix, cell phones, sewing machine, handbags, jewellery box etc.

Services Business class air tickets, movie tickets priced under ₹100.

GST Tax Slab of 18%

Goods Flavored refined sugar, cornflakes, pasta, pastries and cakes, detergents, washing and cleaning preparations, safety glass, mirror, sheets, pumps, fans, light fitting, chocolated, sauces, soups, suitcase, shampoo, oil powder, washing powders, T. V, fridge, heaters, washing machines and many more items.

(Most of the items are part of this tax slab)

Services Restaurants located inside hotels with tariffs of ₹ 7,500 and above, outdoor catering, IT and telecom services etc.

GST Tax Slab of 28%

Goods Over 200 goods are taxed at this rate that includes sunscreen, pan masala, dishwasher, cement, paint, vacuum cleaner, automobiles, hair clippers, motorcycle etc.

Services Five star hotels, movie tickets, betting on casinos and racing etc.

Benefits of GST

GST is very beneficial for all stakeholders *viz* industries, government and citizens. *Some of these benefits are listed below*

- It facilitates seamless credit across all states under a common tax base.
- It eliminates the cascading effects of taxes on production and distribution cost of goods and services.
- Revenue increases under GST regime because of widening of the dealer base by capturing value addition in the distributive trade and increased compliance.
- It enhances transparency in the indirect tax framework and is expected to bring down the rate of inflation.
- It promotes Indian exports, thereby improving the balance of payments position.
- Uniform GST rates reduces the incentive for evasion by eliminating rate arbitrage between neighbouring states and that between intra and inter-state sales.
- It is largely technology driven, thus reduces the human interface between the taxpayer and the tax administration, leading to speedy decisions.

Implementation Mechanism

GST is a destination base indirect tax collected by Central as well as State Government to meet the public expenditure as a part of important mechanism of fiscal system of a nation. Unlike other prevailing indirect taxes, GST is proposed to be a comprehensive indirect tax leviable on manufacture, sale and consumption of goods as well as services with a input tax credit facility on output tax liability at the national and state level in an uniform modus. India is a federal country, where both the Centre and the States have been assigned the powers to levy and collect taxes through respective legislations. Alongwith the amendment in the constitution to empower, the Centre and the States to levy and collect the GST, four legislations were given assent by the President on 12th April, 2017, *which include*

- The Central GST Act, 2017
- The Integrated GST Act, 2017
- The GST (Compensation to States) Act, 2017
- The Union Territory GST Act, 2017

Working of Dual GST

In India, both Centre and States have been assigned the powers to levy and collect taxes through appropriate legislation. Both the Centre and State Government have distinct responsibilities to perform according to the division of powers as prescribed in the Constitution that needs resources for implementation. A dual GST is therefore, appropriately aligned with the constitutional requirement of fiscal federalism.

Features of Dual GST Model

- GST shall have two components; one levied by the Centre (referred to as Central GST) and the other levied by the States (referred to as State GST).
- Central GST and the state GST would be applicable to all transactions of goods and services.
- Central GST and the State GST are to be paid to the accounts of the Centre and the State individually.
- Central GST and State GST are to be treated individually, therefore taxes paid against the Central GST shall be allowed to be taken as Input Tax Credit (ITC).
- Cross utilisation of ITC between the Central GST and the State GST would not be permitted except in the case of inter-state supply of goods and services cross utilisation of ITC between the Central GST and the State GST would not be permitted except in the case of inter-state supply of goods and services.
- Credit accumulation on account of refund of GST should be avoided by both the Centre and the States except in the cases such as exports, purchase of capital goods, input tax at higher rate than output tax etc.
- Uniform procedure for collection of both Central GST and State GST would be prescribed in the respective legislation for Central GST and State GST.
- Composition compounding scheme for the purpose of GST should have an upper ceiling on gross annual turnover and a floor tax rate with respect to gross annual turnover.
- The taxpayer would need to submit periodical returns, in common format as far as possible, to both the Central GST authority and to the concerned State GST authorities.

- Each taxpayer would be allotted a PAN-linked taxpayer identification number with a total of 14/15 digits.

Negotiable Instrument Act, 1881

The Negotiable Instrument Act, 1881 defines and amends the law relating to promissory notes, bills of exchange and cheques. The term 'negotiable instrument' means a document transferable from one person to another. However, the act has not defined the term. It merely says that "a negotiable instrument means a promissory note, bill of exchange or cheque payable either to order or to bearer" [Section 13 (1)]. According to the act, negotiability involves two elements namely, transferability free from equities and transferability by delivery or endorsement. However, the act recognises only three types of instruments *viz* a promissory note, a bill of exchange and a cheque as negotiable instruments. *But it does not mean that other instruments are not negotiable instruments provided that they satisfy the following conditions of negotiability*

- The instrument should be freely transferable by the custom of trade. Transferability may be by delivery or endorsement and delivery.
- The person who obtains it in good faith and for consideration gets it free from all defects and can sue upon it in his own name.
- The holder has the right to transfer. The negotiability continues till the maturity.

Types of Negotiable Instruments

The act recognises only three kinds of negotiable instruments under Section 13 but it does not exclude any other negotiable instruments, provided the instrument entitles a person to a sum of money and is transferable by delivery. Instruments written in oriental languages, *i.e.* hundies are negotiable instruments. *These instruments are as follows*

Promissory Notes

A 'promissory note' is an instrument in writing containing an unconditional undertaking, signed by the maker to pay a certain sum of money to, or to the order of, a certain person, or only to bearer of the instrument (Section 4).

Essentials of a Promissory Note

To be a promissory note, an instrument must possess the following essentials

- It must be in writing. An oral promise to pay will not do.
- It must contain an express promise or clear undertaking to pay.
- The promise or undertaking to pay must be unconditional.
- The maker must sign the promissory note in token of an undertaking to pay to the payee or his order.
- It must be properly stamped in accordance with the provisions of the Indian Stamp Act. Each stamp must be duly cancelled by maker's signature or initials.
- It must contain the name of place, number and the date on which it is made.

Bills of Exchange

A 'bill of exchange' is an instrument in writing containing an unconditional order, signed by the maker, directing a certain person to pay a certain sum of money only to or to the order of a certain person or to the bearer of the instrument (Section 5).

Essentials of a Bills of Exchange

To be a bill of exchange, an instrument must possess the following essentials

- It must be in writing.
- It must contain an unconditional order to pay money only and not merely a request.
- It must be signed by the drawer.
- The parties must be certain.
- The sum payable must also be certain.
- It must comply with other formalities, *e.g.* stamps, date etc.

Forms of Bills of Exchange

- Inland bill
- Foreign bill
- Trade bill
- Accommodation bill

Cheques

A 'cheque' is a bill of exchange drawn on a specified banker and not expressed to be payable otherwise than on demand and it includes the electronic image of a truncated cheque and a chegue in the electronic form (Section 6).

The Negotiable Instruments (Amendment and Miscellaneous Provisions) Act, 2002 has broadened the definition of cheque to include the electronic image of a truncated cheque and a cheque in the electronic form.

Thus, a cheque is a bill of exchange drawn on a bank payable always on demand.

Essentials of a Cheque

To be a cheque, an instrument must possess the following essentials

- It is always drawn on a banker.
- It is always payable on demand.
- It does not require acceptance.
- A cheque can be drawn on bank where the drawer has an account.
- Cheques may be payable to the drawer himself.

- The banker is liable only to the drawer. A holder has no remedy against the banker, if a cheque is dishonoured.
- A cheque is usually valid for six months.
- No stamp is required to be affixed on cheques.

Negotiation and Assignment

As per Section 14 of the Act, a negotiable instrument may be transferred by negotiation or assignment. Negotiation is the transfer of an instrument (a note, bill or cheque) for one person to another in such a manner as to convey title and to constitute the transferee the holder thereof. When a negotiable instrument is transferred by negotiation, the rights of the transferee may rise higher than those of the transferor, depending upon the circumstances attending the negotiation.

When the transfer is made by assignment, the assignee has only those rights which the assignor possessed. In case of assignment, there is a transfer of ownership by means of a written and registered document.

A transfer of negotiation differs from transfer by assignment in the following respects

- Negotiation requires mere delivery of a bearer instrument and endorsement and delivery of an order instrument to effectuate a transfer. Assignment requires a written document signed by the transferor.
- Notice of transfer of debt (actionable claim) must be given by the assignee to the debtor in order to complete his title, no such notice is necessary in a transfer by negotiation.
- On assignment, the transferee of an actionable claim takes it subject to all the defects in the title of, and subject to all the equities and defences available against the assignor, even though he took the assignment for value and in good faith. In case of negotiation the transferee, as holder-in-due course, takes the instrument free from any defects in the title of the transferor.

Dishonour of Negotiable Instruments

When the negotiable instrument is violated, the holder must given a sign of dishonour to all the earlier parties to make them accountable. A negotiable instrument can be violated either by non-acceptance or by non-payment. A cheque and a promissory note can only be violated by non-payment but a bill of exchange can be violated any by non-acceptance or by non-payment.

These are as follows

Dishonour by Non-acceptance

Section 91 provides that a bill is said to be dishonoured by non-acceptance

- When the drawee does not accept it within 48 hours from the time of presentment for acceptance.
- When presentment for acceptance is excused and the bill remains unaccepted.
- When the drawee is incompetent to contract.
- When the drawee is a fictitious person or after reasonable search cannot be found.
- When the acceptance is a qualified one.

Dishonour by Non-payment

Section 92 provides that an instrument is said to be dishonoured by non-payment when the maker of the note, acceptor of the bill or drawee of the cheque makes default in payment upon being duly required to pay the same. Also, a negotiable instrument is dishonoured by non-payment when presentment for payment is excused and the instrument when overdue remains unpaid.

If the bill is dishonoured either of non-acceptance or by non-payment, the drawer and all the endorsers of the bill are liable to the holder, provided he gives notice of such dishonour. The drawee is liable only when there is dishonour by non-payment.

Discharge of Negotiable Instrument

The discharge in relation to negotiable instrument may be either (i) discharge of the instrument or (ii) discharge of one or more parties to the instrument from liability.

A negotiable instrument is discharged

- by payment in due course.
- when the principal debtor becomes the holder.
- by an act that would discharge simple contract.
- by renunciation and
- by cancellation.

EXAM BASED QUESTIONS

Sale of Goods Act, 1930

1 Which of the following section of Sale of Goods Act defines contract of sale?
(a) Section 4 (b) Section 5
(c) Section 6 (d) Section 2 (7)

2 A contract of sale of goods includes
(a) sale (b) agreement to sell
(c) Both (a) and (b) (d) Neither (a) nor (b)

3 Which of the following is an essential of contract of sale?
(a) Two parties (b) Sale of goods only
(c) Transfer of ownership (d) All of these

4 The term 'caveat emptor' is a/an
(a) Greek word (b) Indian word
(c) Latin word (d) British word

5 Caveat emptor means
(a) buyer has the right to inspect goods
(b) seller has the right to sell goods
(c) let the buyer beware
(d) None of the above

6 The doctrine of the Caveat Emptor is embodied in which section of Sale of Goods Act, 1930?
(a) Section 14 (b) Section 16
(c) Section 18 (d) Section 20

7 In case of sale, if goods are destroyed loss will be of
(a) buyer (b) seller
(c) third party (d) None of these

8 In a case of sale of car, the defects relating to engine are
(a) patent defects (b) latent defects
(c) technical defects (d) None of these

9 Right against goods include
(a) right of rem (b) right of personam
(c) Both (a) and (b) (d) None of these

10 Which of the following section of sale of goods act deals with right of stoppage in transit?
(a) Section 50 (b) Section 47
(c) Section 48 (d) Section 49

11 A contract where the seller transfers or agrees to transfer property in goods to buyer for a price is called.
(a) contract of sale
(b) contract of purchase
(c) contract of lease
(d) None of the above

12 Doctrine of caveat emptor does not apply, when
(a) there is an usage of trade
(b) goods have latent defects
(c) contract is induced by fraud
(d) in all the above situations

13 The rule of caveat emptor does not apply in case of
(a) fitness for buyer's purpose
(b) sale under a patent or trade name
(c) usage of trade or consent by fraud
(d) All of the above

14 Which of the following is/are an exception to the doctrine of caveat emptor?
(a) Usage of trade
(b) Sale by sample
(c) Seller commits fraud
(d) All of the above

15 Doctrine of caveat emptor provides that it is the duty of .... to see that goods are fit for his purpose.
(a) seller (b) buyer
(c) owner (d) All of these

16 Which of the following section defines unpaid seller?
(a) Section 45 (b) Section 46
(c) Section 47 (d) Section 48

17 Unpaid seller is a seller who has not been
(a) paid whole of the price
(b) tendered whole of the price
(c) Both (a) and (b)
(d) Neither (a) nor (b)

18 When buyer pays some part of the price of goods to the seller, the seller is called
(a) unpaid seller (b) partly paid-up seller
(c) short paid seller (d) None of these

19 Where a seller has been paid by cheque and cheque has been dishonoured by bank, seller is called
(a) fully paid seller (b) unpaid seller
(c) only seller (d) None of these

20 An unpaid seller may have right(s) against
1. goods 2. buyer
3. government

Which of the following code is true?
Codes
(a) Only 1 (b) Only 2
(c) Both 1 and 2 (d) All of the above

21 An unpaid seller has right to retain the goods until price of the goods is paid. This right is called
(a) lien
(b) stoppage in transit
(c) pledge
(d) None of the above

22 When the goods are sold on credit and credit period is not expired, the seller of goods is
(a) called unpaid seller
(b) is not the seller at all
(c) not called an unpaid seller
(d) None of the above

23 When goods have been delivered to a carrier, right of lien
(a) terminates (b) starts
(c) exists (d) All of these

24 Which of the following is/are a condition(s) of right of stoppage in transit?
(a) Goods must be in transit
(b) Buyer becomes insolvent
(c) Both (a) and (b)
(d) Neither (a) nor (b)

25 Right of stoppage in transit means right of stopping the goods while they are
(a) on the way to buyer's place
(b) on the way to seller's place
(c) on the way to place of goods
(d) All of the above

26 Which of the following section of sale of goods act deals with right of resale of unpaid seller?
(a) Section 50 (b) Section 51
(c) Section 54 (d) Section 58

27 Right of resale can be exercised by unpaid seller when right to resale is expressly reserved by
(a) agreement (b) seller
(c) buyer (d) None of these

28 Unpaid seller can exercise the right of resale of goods when
(a) goods are of perishable nature
(b) unpaid seller gives notice of his intention to resell
(c) Both (a) and (b)
(d) Neither (a) nor (b)

29 Termination of right of stoppage takes place when
(a) buyer or his agent obtains delivery
(b) when goods are rejected by buyer
(c) carrier wrongfully refuses to deliver goods to buyer
(d) All of the above

30 Goods are deemed to be in .... from the time when they are delivered to a carrier or bailee until delivery is taken by buyer.
(a) transit
(b) way
(c) possession
(d) None of the above

31 Which of the following is a right of unpaid seller against buyer?
(a) Suit for price (b) Suit for interest
(c) Both (a) and (b) (d) Neither (a) nor (b)

32 Which of the following right is not available personally against the buyer?
(a) Right of lien (b) Right of resale
(c) Suit for price (d) Both (a) and (b)

33 Under which of the following section, buyer can file a suit against seller for breach of warranty ?
(a) Section 57
(b) Section 58
(c) Section 59
(d) Section 60

34 Where seller wrongfully neglects or refuses to deliver goods to buyer, the buyer may sue for
(a) non-delivery of goods (b) possession of goods
(c) compensation (d) All of these

35 Which of the following is not a right of buyer against seller?
(a) Suit for price
(b) Suit for non-acceptance of delivery
(c) Suit for breach of warranty
(d) Both (a) and (b)

36 A, contracts to buy from B 1000 bags of cement. B sends 1000 bags through truck. When cement arrives it becomes stone by the contact of rainwater. Can A reject the goods?
(a) Yes, breach of condition as to wholesomeness
(b) Yes, conditions as to merchantability
(c) No, B never knew himself
(d) No, A should have seen it

37 In which of the following cases, right of lien can be exercised?
(a) Where goods have not been sold on credit
(b) Goods have been sold on credit and period of credit has expired
(c) Both (a) and (b)
(d) Neither (a) nor (b)

38 If the goods are rejected by the buyer, and the carrier or other bailee continues in possession of them, then the transit .... even if the seller has refused to receive them back.
(a) is deemed to be at an end
(b) is not deemed to be at an end
(c) in nobody's hand
(d) None of the above

39 Where the seller expressly reserves the right of resale in case the buyer makes a default. If there are losses to the seller, on a resale, the seller ....
(a) can not claim the same from the buyer as damages
(b) can claim the same from the buyer as damages
(c) sue the buyer for not purchasing
(d) None of the above

40 **Which is not the condition fulfilled before a seller is deemed to be an unpaid seller?**
(a) He must be unpaid either wholly or partly
(b) He must have not refused payment when tendered
(c) He must have sold goods against cash or in exchange of other things
(d) He must have an immediate right of action for the price

41 **In which of the following case(s), right of lien comes to an end?**
(a) Buyer or his agent lawfully obtains delivery
(b) Seller has waived his right of lien
(c) Goods delivered to carrier
(d) All of the above

42 **Which of the following suit(s) can be filed by the unpaid seller against buyer?**
(a) Suit for damages for non-acceptance of delivery
(b) Suit for damages for repudiation of contract
(c) Suit for interest
(d) All of the above

Goods and Services Tax (GST)

43 **GST stands for**
(a) Goods and Supply Tax (b) Government Sales Tax
(c) Goods and Services Tax (d) General Sales Tax

44 **In India, GST become effective from**
(a) 1st April, 2017 (b) 1st January, 2017
(c) 1st July, 2017 (d) 1st March, 2017

45 **Which of the following tax is not subsumed in GST?**
(a) VAT (b) Stamp Duty
(c) Entry Tax (d) Entertainment Tax

46 **GST is levied on**
(a) manufacturers (b) retailers
(c) Consumers (d) All of these

47 **Which form is to be used for registration of GST?**
(a) Form GSTR-1A (b) Form GSTR-2
(c) Form GST REG (d) Form GST REG-01

48 **For an e-commerce operator, GST registration threshold limit is**
(a) ₹ 20 lakh (b) ₹ 50 lakh
(c) ₹ 75 lakh (d) None of these

49 **Which of the subsequent taxes have subsumed in GST?**
(a) Central excise duty (b) Central sales tax
(c) VAT (d) All of these

50 **The first committee to outline a GST model was sustained by**
(a) Dr. Manmohan Singh (b) Vijay Kelkar
(c) Asim Das Gupta (d) None of these

51 **First Discussion Paper (FDP) which formed the basis for GST in 2009 was released by?**
(a) Union Finance Ministry (b) GST Council
(c) Empowered Committee (d) Dr Manmohan Singh

52 **IGST deals with**
(a) composition scheme
(b) time of supply
(c) service tax on imported services
(d) All of the above

53 **IGST tax levy means**
(a) within state (b) between two states
(c) between two countries (d) None of these

54 **What are the taxes levied on an intra-state supply?**
(a) CGST (b) SGST
(c) IGST (d) CGST and IGST

55 **What is the maximum rate prescribed under CGST?**
(a) 12% (b) 20%
(c) 28% (d) 18%

56 **Which of the following taxes will be levied on imports of goods and services?**
(a) CGST (b) SGST (c) IGST (d) Exempt

57 **How will the goods and services be classified under GST regime?**
(a) SAC/HSN code (b) HSN code
(c) SAC code (d) GST code

58 **The Tax IGST is charged by .... Government.**
(a) Central (b) State
(c) concerned department (d) All of these

59 **India has chosen .... model of dual GST.**
(a) Canadian (b) Cuba
(c) Belize (d) Nicaragua

60 **The main objective of GST to .... excessive taxation.**
(a) exempt (b) exclude (c) eliminate (d) None

61 **A person is having multiple business requires GST registration**
(a) single only (b) two times only
(c) five times only (d) each business separately

62 **First return filed under GST is**
(a) GSTR-1 (b) GSTR-2
(c) GSTR-3A (d) GSTR-3B

63 **The details of outward supplies of goods or services shall be submitted by**
(a) 10th of the succeeding month
(b) 15th of the succeeding month
(c) 18th of the succeeding month
(d) 20th of the succeeding month

64 **Which of the following statement is not correct about GST?**
(a) GST is like a last point retail tax, it is going to be collected at point of sale
(b) GST will abolish all the direct tax levied in India
(c) It is implemented from 1st July, 2017 throughout the country
(d) It will unified the tax structure in India

65 Who will notify the rate of tax to be levied under CGST?

(a) GST council suo moto
(b) Central Government suo moto
(c) State Government suo moto
(d) Central Government as per the recommendations of the GST council

66 Which of the following is an intra-state supply?

(a) Supplier of goods located in Nagpur and place of supply of goods SEZ located in Mumbai
(b) Supplier of good located in Kolkata and place of supply of goods in Bengaluru
(c) Supplier of goods located in Goa and place of supply of goods in Goa
(d) All of the above

67 In India, the GST council has come out with a four-rate structure. They are

(a) 5%, 12%, 18% and 24%
(b) 5%, 12%, 18% and 26%
(c) 5%, 12%, 18% and 28%
(d) 5%, 12%, 16% and 28%

68 Which Article of the Constitution as amended by 101st Constitutional Amendment Act, 2016 defines the Goods and Service tax (GST) as a tax on supply of goods or services or both?

(a) Article 366 (12 A)
(b) Article 366 (1 A)
(c) Article 366 (14 A)
(d) Article 366 (18 A)

Negotiable Instrument Act, 1881

69 The Negotiable Instrument Act came into force on

(a) 1st June, 1881
(b) 1st May, 1881
(c) 1st March, 1882
(d) 1st January, 1881

70 According to Section 13, negotiable instrument means

(a) promissory Note
(b) bill of exchange
(c) cheque
(d) All of these

71 Which of the following is not a promissory note?

(a) Bank note
(b) Currency note
(c) Both (a) and (b)
(d) Neither (a) nor (b)

72 How many parties are there to a promissory note?

(a) 2
(b) 3
(c) 1
(d) 4

73 The person who writes a promissory note, is called

(a) payee
(b) maker
(c) drawer
(d) None of these

74 Which of the following is an essential of promissory note?

(a) Written
(b) Certain Sum
(c) Unconditional promise to pay
(d) All of the above

75 'A orally promises to pay to B' ₹ 1000. This promise amount to

(a) bill of exchange
(b) promissory note
(c) cheque
(d) None of these

76 An instrument containing an unconditional promise to pay a certain sum, is called

(a) bill of exchange
(b) Cheque
(c) promissory note
(d) All of these

77 Mr. X writes, "I promise to pay 'Mr. Y' ₹ 5,000, 7 days after the death of Mr. Z." This is

(a) invalid
(b) valid
(c) illegal
(d) void

78 How many parties are there in a bill of exchange?

(a) 2
(b) 3
(c) 4
(d) 1

79 The person who makes a bill of exchange, is called

(a) writer
(b) drawer
(c) maker
(d) None of these

80 An instrument in writing containing an unconditional order to pay a certain sum, is called

(a) promissory note
(b) bill of exchange
(c) cheque
(d) All of these

81 Which of the following section of Negotiable Instrument Act defines cheque?

(a) Section 4
(b) Section 5
(c) Section 6
(d) Section 7

82 A cheque is a bill of exchange which is drawn on a

(a) specified banker
(b) specified person
(c) special party
(d) None of the above

83 A cheque includes

(a) electronic cheque
(b) electronic image of a truncated cheque
(c) Both (a) and (b)
(d) Neither (a) nor (b)

84 A bill of exchange must be .... by the drawee before it is presented for payment.

(a) permitted
(b) accepted
(c) refused
(d) None of these

85 Which of the following is an essential(s) of bill of exchange?

(a) Unconditional order
(b) Certain sum of money
(c) Three parties
(d) All of these

86 A cheque is always payable

(a) on demand
(b) on request
(c) after specified time
(d) All of the above

87 Which of the following is a type of cheque?

(a) Bearer cheque
(b) Order cheque
(c) Crossed cheque
(d) All of these

88 A negotiable instrument may be dishonoured

(a) by non-acceptance
(b) by non-payment
(c) Both (a) and (b)
(d) Neither (a) nor (b)

89 Which of the following section deals with dishonour by non-acceptance?
(a) Section 90 (b) Section 91
(c) Section 92 (d) Section 97

90 Which of the following section deals with dishonour by non-payment?
(a) Section 92 (b) Section 91
(c) Section 138 (d) Section 140

91 Notice of dishonour is given by holder to .... liable under instrument.
(a) drawer (b) all parties
(c) maker (d) payee only

92 When a party liable under a negotiable instrument, makes payment in due course, the instrument is
(a) discharged (b) released
(c) altered (d) None of these

93 When liability of a party under an instrument comes to an end, he is said to be
(a) discharged (b) released
(c) waived (d) None of these

94 When a party makes material alternations in an instrument, then instrument is
(a) discharged (b) altered
(c) not discharged (d) completed

95 A party to a negotiable instrument is discharged when
(a) there is a delay in presenting the cheque
(b) there is a material alternation in instrument
(c) payment is made
(d) All of the above

96 Which of the following law contains law relating to promissory note, bill of exchange and cheque?
(a) Negotiable Instrument Act
(b) Reserve Bank of India Act
(c) Contract Act
(d) All of the above

97 Which statement(s) does/do not apply on bill of exchange?
(a) It should be in writing (b) It should be accepted
(c) It should be stamped (d) It should be registered

98 When a party to instrument refuses to accept or pay the instrument, it is called .... of negotiable instrument.
(a) dishonour (b) release
(c) alteration (d) All of these

99 When all the rights under a negotiable instrument are extinguished and instrument cannot be further negotiated, it is called .... of instrument.
(a) release (b) completion
(c) discharge (d) All of these

100 Which of the following is a mode of discharge of a negotiable instrument?
(a) Payment in due course
(b) Party liable becomes holder
(c) Material alteration in instrument
(d) All of the above

Miscellaneous

Directions (Q. Nos. 101-105) *In the questions given below are two statements labelled as Statement I and Statement II. You have to examine these two statements carefully, select the correct code.*

Codes
(a) Only Statement I is true
(b) Only Statement II is true
(c) Both statements are true
(d) Both statements are false

101 **Statement** I A sale has the immediate effect of transferring property, where as in an agreement to sell the property is to pass at some future time.
Statement II A sale makes the buyer the owner of goods but agreement to sale does not make the buyer the owner of goods.

102 **Statement** I According to doctrine of caveat emptor seller is not bound to supply the goods that serves a particular purpose of buyer.
Statement II When the buyer trusts on the skill and judgement of seller, the seller cannot take the defense of doctrine of Caveat Emptor.

103 **Statement** I Right of lien of an unpaid seller is a right against goods.
Statement II An unpaid seller has rights against the buyer.

104 **Statement** I GST is a destination based tax on consumption of goods and services.
Statement II 'I' stands for integrated in IGST.

105 **Statement** I A negotiable instrument may be made payable to two or more persons jointly.
Statement II 'I' promise to pay Mr. A ₹ 1,000 and all other sums which shall be due. It is not a valid promissory note.

106 **Statement** I It is a pre-condition of right of stoppage in transit that seller must have parted with possession of goods.
Statement II Unpaid seller can exercise his rights of resale when goods are in his possession.
Statement III Where property in goods has been passed to the buyer, seller can file a suit against buyer for recovery of price.
Which of the above statement(s) is/are true?
Codes
(a) Only I (b) Only III
(c) Both I and II (d) All of the above

107 **Statement** I A cheque is an unconditional order to a specified banker to pay the sum mentioned in the cheque.
Statement II A cheque can be drawn only by a person who has his account with bank while a bill can be drawn by any person.
Statement III A cheque may be crossed but a bill of exchange can not be crossed.
Which of the following statement(s) is/are true?
Codes
(a) Only Statement I is true
(b) Only Statement III is true
(c) Both statements II and III are true
(d) All statements are true

Directions (Q. Nos. 108-112) *In the questions given below are two statements labelled as Assertion (A) and Reason (R). In the context of two statements, which one of the following is correct?*
Codes
(a) Both (A) and (R) are true and (R) is the correct explanation of (A)
(b) Both (A) and (R) are true, but (R) is not the correct explanation of (A)
(c) (A) is true, but (R) is false
(d) (A) is false, but (R) is true

108 **Assertion** (A) It is for buyer to satisfy himself that the goods which he is purchasing, are of the quality, which are requires.
Reason (R) There is no implied warranty or condition as to the quality or fitness for any particular purpose of goods supplied under a contract of sale.

109 **Assertion** (A) An unpaid seller may sue the buyer for the price of the goods in case of breach of contract.
Reason (R) The unpaid seller may resell the goods if it is perishable in nature.

110 **Assertion** (A) GST eliminates the cascading effects of taxes on production and distribution cost of goods and services.
Reason (R) GST is a common and unitified tax, *i.e.* "one nation, one tax", on goods and services.

111 **Assertion** (A) Cheque is dishonoured by non-payment.
Reason (R) Cheque is always payable on demand.

112 **Assertion** (A) A bill of exchange is an instrument in writing containing an unconditional order.
Reason (R) Bill of exchange must contain five parties.

113 Match the following.

List I	List II
A. Unpaid seller	1. Section 45
B. Right of lien	2. Section 47
C. Right of stoppage in transit	3. Section 50
D. Right of resale	4. Section 54

Codes

	A	B	C	D		A	B	C	D
(a)	1	2	3	4	(b)	4	3	2	1
(c)	2	3	4	1	(d)	4	1	3	2

114 Match the following.

List I	List II
A. Definition of Negotiable Instrument	1. Section 4
B. Promissory Note	2. Section 5
C. Bill of Exchange	3. Section 6
D. Cheque	4. Section 13

Codes

	A	B	C	D		A	B	C	D
(a)	1	2	3	4	(b)	4	1	2	3
(c)	4	3	2	1	(d)	2	3	1	4

115 Match the following.

List I (Form)	List II (Explanation)
A. GSTR–1	1. Gross tax liabilities, total description of payment
B. GSTR–2	2. Details of supply/sales
C. GSTR–3	3. Details of purchases
D. GSTR–4	4. Quarterly statement

Codes

	A	B	C	D		A	B	C	D
(a)	4	3	1	2	(b)	2	3	1	4
(c)	2	1	4	3	(d)	3	4	1	2

116 Match the following.

List I (Form)	List II (Explanation)
A. Cheque	1. must be signed by the drawer
B. Bill of exchange	2. is always drawn on a banker
C. Promissory note	3. must contain an express promise to pay

Codes

	A	B	C		A	B	C
(a)	1	2	3	(b)	3	2	1
(c)	2	1	3	(d)	1	3	2

ANSWERS

Objective Questions

1 (a)	2 (c)	3 (d)	4 (c)	5 (c)	6 (b)	7 (b)	8 (c)	9 (a)	10 (a)
11 (a)	12 (d)	13 (d)	14 (d)	15 (b)	16 (a)	17 (c)	18 (a)	19 (b)	20 (d)
21 (a)	22 (c)	23 (a)	24 (c)	25 (a)	26 (c)	27 (a)	28 (c)	29 (d)	30 (a)
31 (c)	32 (d)	33 (c)	34 (a)	35 (d)	36 (b)	37 (c)	38 (b)	39 (b)	40 (c)
41 (d)	42 (d)	43 (c)	44 (c)	45 (b)	46 (d)	47 (d)	48 (c)	49 (d)	50 (c)
51 (c)	52 (c)	53 (b)	54 (d)	55 (b)	56 (c)	57 (a)	58 (d)	59 (a)	60 (c)
61 (d)	62 (d)	63 (a)	64 (b)	65 (d)	66 (c)	67 (c)	68 (a)	69 (c)	70 (d)
71 (c)	72 (a)	73 (b)	74 (d)	75 (d)	76 (c)	77 (b)	78 (b)	79 (b)	80 (b)
81 (c)	82 (a)	83 (c)	84 (b)	85 (d)	86 (a)	87 (d)	88 (c)	89 (b)	90 (a)
91 (b)	92 (a)	93 (a)	94 (a)	95 (d)	96 (a)	97 (d)	98 (a)	99 (c)	100 (d)
101 (c)	102 (b)	103 (c)	104 (d)	105 (c)	106 (c)	107 (d)	108 (a)	109 (b)	110 (a)
111 (a)	112 (c)	113 (a)	114 (b)	115 (b)	116 (c)				

UNIT 10 : Income-tax and Corporate Tax Planning

CHAPTER 36

Basic Concepts of Income Tax

According to Law of India, any Central Act enacts that income tax shall be charged for any assessment year at any rate or rates, income tax at that rate or those rates shall be charged for that year in accordance with, and subject to the provisions of this Act in respect to the total income of the previous year of every person.

Tax

Tax is the imposition of financial charges upon an individual or a company by the government or their respective state or similar other functional equivalents in a state. In India, taxes are levied by the Central Government, State Governments and by the local authorities such as the municipality. A tax is not a voluntary payment or donation, but an enforced contribution, exacted pursuant to legislative authority.

Types of Taxes

Direct Taxes Direct tax is the tax paid to the government directly by the assessee like income tax, capital gains tax, corporate tax, securities transaction tax, banking cash transaction tax, fringe benefit tax etc.

Indirect Taxes An indirect tax is a tax collected by an intermediary from the person, who bears the ultimate economic burden of the tax. An indirect tax is one that can be shifted by the taxpayer to someone else. *e.g.* Service tax, central excise, VAT etc.

Income Tax

Income tax is a direct tax, which is imposed upon the income of a person. It is computed on accrued or received net taxable incomes by a person during a previous year according to prescribed rates of income tax in current assessment year. It is an important source of income of Central Government.

In this Chapter

Features of Income Tax

- It is a direct tax.
- It is levied and collected by the Central Government.
- It is computed upon net taxable income of previous year.
- Certain amount of income is exempted from income tax according to Income Tax Act.
- It is computed on the basis of rates of income tax applicable in current assessment year.
- Income is grouped in various slabs which is charged on progressive rates on increasing slabs of income.
- Various activities relating to income tax *viz* proceedings of tax, assessment, recovery of tax etc. administrative activities are performed by Income Tax Department.

Liability to Pay Income Tax

Every individual and Hindu Undivided Family (HUF), whose total income of the previous financial year exceeds the exempted limit of income according to Income Tax Act, shall be liable to pay income tax. Besides this, a firm, a company, a cooperative society and association of person etc are also liable to pay income tax.

Important Terms related to Income Tax

Assessment Year (AY)

According to Income Tax Act, assessment year is the period of 12 months, which starts from 1st April of every year and ends on 31st March of next year.

Previous Year (PY)

Income earned in a year is taxable in the next year. The year, in which income is earned is known as previous year and the next year, in which income is taxable is known as assessment year. Previous year is the financial year immediately preceding the assessment year.

Previous Year in the Case of Newly Setup Business/Profession

The first previous year commences on the date of setting up of the business/profession or the date, on which the source of income newly comes into existence and ends with 31st March of the financial year.

Thus, in the case of a newly set-up business /profession or new source of income, the first previous year is a period of 12 months or less than 12 months.

Exception to the Rule

Income of a previous year is taxable in the immediately following assessment year.

In the following cases, income of previous year is taxable in the previous year itself

- Income of non-resident from shipping.
- Income of person leaving India either permanently or for a long period of time.
- Income of bodies formed for a short duration.
- Income of a discontinued business.

Person [Section 2 (31)]

Person includes

- an individual
- a Hindu Undivided Family (HUF)
- a company
- a firm
- an Association of Persons (AoPs) or a Body of Individuals (BoIs), whether incorporated or not
- a local authority
- every artificial juridical person not falling within any of the preceding sub-clauses.

Assessee [Section 2 (7)]

Assessee means a person, by whom income tax or any other sum of money is payable under the act. It includes every person in respect of whom any proceeding under the act has been taken for the assessment of his income or loss or the amount of refund due to him. *It includes following*

Deemed Assessee A deemed assessee is liable to pay income tax on income of another person.

Assessee in Default A person has to fulfil the legal obligation under Income Tax Act to pay income tax on behalf of others.

If a person fails to fulfil the obligation due to which Income Tax Department suffers a loss of revenue, then such person has to compensate this loss. For this loss, he is called assessee in default.

Income [Section 2 (24)]

The term 'income' specifically includes the following

- Profits and gains
- Dividend
- Voluntary contributions received by a trust
- Perquisites in the hands of employee
- Any special allowance benefit
- City compensatory allowance/dearness allowancce
- Any benefit or perquisite to a representative assessee
- Capital gains
- Insurance profit
- Banking income of a cooperative society
- Winning from lottery
- Amount received under Keyman insurance policy

Gross Total Income [Section 14]

Income of a person is computed under the following five heads

- Salaries
- Income from house property
- Profits and gains of business or profession
- Capital gains
- Income from other sources

The aggregate income under these heads is termed as gross total income.

Total Income [Section 2 (45)]

Total income means the amount left after making the deductions under Section 80C to 80U from gross total Income. It is also known as net taxables income. Net taxable income is rounded-off for calculating income tax in multiple of ₹ 10.

Agricultural Income [Section 10(1)]

Section 10(1) provides that agricultural income is not be included in the total income of the assessee. However, a method has been laid down to levy tax on agricultural income in an indirect way. It is applicable to individuals, HUF, unregistered firms, AoP, BoI and artificial persons.

Two conditions, which need to be satisfied for partial integration are

- Net agricultural income exceeds ₹ 5,000 p.a.
- Non-agricultural income exceeds basic exemption limit.

Computation of Tax on Agricultural Income in India

Step 1 Compute tax on non-agricultural income plus agricultural income.

Step 2 Compute tax on agricultural income plus basic exemption limit.

Step 3 Tax payable by the assessee=Step 1– Step 2.

Step 4 Add surcharge/deduct rebate under Section 87 A, if applicable.

Step 5 Add education cess @2% and SHEC@1%.

Taxability in Case of Non-agricultural and Agricultural Income

Rule	Particulars	Non-agricultural Income	Agricultural Income
		Taxable	Exempt
7A	Income from the manufacture of rubber in India	35%	65%
7B	Income from the manufacture of coffee		
	(i) Sale of coffee grown and cured in India	25%	75%
	(ii) Sale of coffee grown, cured, roasted and grounded in India	40%	60%
8	Income from the manufacture of tea in India	40%	60%

Residential Status and Incidence of Tax

Total income of an assessee cannot be computed unless we know his residential status in India during the previous year *i.e.* an assessee may earn his income in India or outside India or at both the places. Which income is assessable in India depends on the residential status of an assessee. There are separate rules for determining the residence of different kinds of assesses.

Residential Status of Individual [Section 6]

There are two types of individuals

Individual is Resident in India [Section 6(1)]

An individual is said to be resident in India, *if he satisfy any of the following two basic conditions*

- He is in India for a period of 182 days or more in the relevant previous year.
- He has been in India for atleast 365 days during the 4 years immediately preceding the previous year and is in India for atleast 60 days during the previous year.

Exceptions to the above [Rule (b)]

- An individual, who is a citizen of India and leaves India in any previous year for purpose of employment or as a member of the crew of an Indian ship, shall be called resident only, when he satisfies the condition number (i) mentioned above.
- In case of an individual, who is a citizen of India, or is a person of Indian origin, who being outside India, come on a visit to India in any previous year, the condition number (ii) mentioned above in his case shall not be applicable.

Types of Residents

Individual is Resident and Ordinarily Resident in India

[Section 6 (6) (a)] Individual to become ordinarily resident in India, he is to satisfy both the following additional conditions besides satisfying any one of the basic conditions.

Additional conditions are

- He has been resident in India in atleast 2 out of the 10 previous years preceding the relevant previous year.
- He has been in India for atleast 730 days in all during the 7 previous years preceding the relevant previous year.

Individual is not Ordinarily Resident in India [Section 6 (6) (a)] If an individual satisfies any one of the basic condition, but does not satisfy the two additional conditions, he is said to be 'not ordinarily resident'.

Individual is Non-resident

If an individual satisfies none of the aforesaid basic conditions stated under Section 6 (i), he is said to be non-resident. In this case, additional conditions are irrelevant.

Residential Status of a Hindu Undivided Family [Section 6 (2)]

A Hindu undivided Family (HUF) is either resident in India or non-resident in India.

When HUF is Resident

A Hindu undivided family is said to be resident in India, if control and management of its affairs is wholly or partly situated in India. A resident Hindu Undivided Family (HUF) is either ordinarily resident or not ordinarily resident.

Residential Hindu Undivided Family is Ordinarily Resident in India

A resident Hindu undivided family is ordinarily resident in India, if the Karta or manager of the family satisfies the following two additional conditions as laid down by Section 6(6)(b).

Additional conditions are

- He has been resident in India in 2 out of the 10 previous years preceding the relevant previous year *i.e.* he fulfilled atleast 1 of the basic condition to become resident for atleast 2 years.
- He has been in India for atleast 730 days in all during the 7 previous years preceding the relevant previous years.

Hindu Undivided Family (HUF) is not Ordinarily Resident in India

If the Karta or manager of a resident, Hindu Undivided Family (HUF) does not satisfy the two additional conditions, the family is treated as resident, but not ordinarily resident in India.

When HUF is Non-resident

A Hindu undivided family is non-resident in India, if control and management of its affairs is wholly situated outside India.

In order to determine whether a Hindu undivided family is resident or non-resident, the residential status of the Karta of the family during the previous year is not relevant.

Residential Status of the Firm and Association of Persons [Section 6(2)]

A partnership firm and an association of persons are said to be resident in India, if control and management of their affairs are wholly or partly situated within India during the relevant previous year, *i.e* if even a part of their control and management is situated in India during previous year, they will be called resident in India, if control and management of their affairs are situated wholly outside India.

A firm/an association of persons cannot be ordinarily or not ordinarily resident. The residential status of the partners/ members of the firm/association is not relevant in determining the status of the firm/association.

Residential Status of a Company [Section 6 (3)]

A company is said to be resident in India in any previous year, if it is an Indian company, *i.e.* Indian company is always resident in India. But, in case of other than Indian company, it is resident in India only, if during the previous year, control and management of its affairs is situated wholly in India.

A company can never be 'ordinarily' or 'not ordinary resident' in India.

Residential Status of Every other Person [Section 6 (4)]

Every other person (local authority, artificial juridical person) is resident in India, if control and management of his affairs is wholly or partly situated within India during the relevant previous year. On the other hand, every other person is non-resident in India, if control and management of his affairs is wholly situated outside India.

Incidence of Tax on the Basis of Residence

No.	Types of Income	Incidence of Tax		
		Resident	Not-ordinarily Resident	Non-resident
1.	Income received or deemed to be received in India whether accrued in India or outside India.	Taxable	Taxable	Taxable
2.	Income accrued or arise and deemed to be accrued or arise in India whether received in India or outside India.	Taxable	Taxable	Taxable
3.	Income accrued and received outside India from a business controlled or a profession set-up in India.	Taxable	Taxable	No

No.	Types of Income	Incidence of Tax		
		Resident	Not-ordinarily Resident	Non-resident
4.	Income accrued and received outside India from a business controlled or a profession set-up outside India.	Taxable	No	No
5.	Foreign income relating to years preceding to the previous year brought to India during the previous year.	No	No	No

Exempted Incomes

Incomes not to be included in Total Income of Any Person [Section 10]

There are many incomes, which are exempt as per Section 10. Some of them are as under

- Agriculture income is totally exempt, provided it falls within the definition of agriculture income under Section 2 (1A). Agricultural income, though exempt, is to be aggregated in case of certain assesses for the purpose of determining the rate of tax on non-agricultural income.
- Sum received by a member from HUF [Section 10 (2)].
- Share of profit of a partner from a firm [Section 10 (2A)].
- Remuneration received by a foreign national as employee of a foreign enterprises [Section 10 (6) (vi)].
- Non-resident employed on a foreignship.
- Remuneration of employee of foreign government during his training in India [Section 10(6) (xi)].
- Allowances or perquisites outside India [Section 10 (7)].
- Death-cum-retirement gratuity received by an employee [Section 10 (10)].
- Payment in commutation of pension received by the employees [Section 10 (10) A].
- Leave encashment [Section 10 (10 AA)].
- Compensation on retrenchment [Section 10 (10 B)].
- Exemption for compensation received or receivable on account of any disaster [Section 10 (10BC)].
- Amount received on voluntary retirement [Section 10 (10C)].
- Amount received under a life insurance policy [Section 10 (10D)].
- Provident fund [Section 10 (11)].
- Payments from recognised provident fund [Section 10 (12)].
- Interest, premium or bonus on specified investments [Section 10 (15)].
- Exemption of the family pension received by the family members of armed forces personnel killed in action in certain circumstances [Section 10 (19)].
- Scholarship granted to meet the cost of education [Section 10 (16)].
- Pension received by certain awardees/any member of their families [Section 10 (18)].
- Income of local authority [Section 10 (20)].
- Income of an approved research association [Section 10 (21)].
- Income of specified news agency [Section 10 (22B)].
- Income of professional association/institution [Section 10 (23A)].
- Income of notified mutual funds [Section 10 (23D)].
- Income of minor clubbed in the hands of a parent [Section 10 (32)].
- Dividend to be exempt in the hands of the shareholder [Section 10 (34)].
- Income from units to be exempt in the hands of the unit holders [Section 10 (35)].
- Exemption of capital gains on compensation received on compulsory acquisition of agricultural land situated within specified urban limits [Section 10 (37)].
- Capital gain arising from sale of shares and units [Section 10 (38)].
- Amount received by an individual as loan under reverse mortgage [Section 10 (43)].
- Income received by any person or on behalf of new pension system trust [Section 10 (44)].
- Income of an infrastructure debt fund [Section 10 (47)].

Income of Newly Established Units in Special Economic Zones [Section 10 AA]

Assessees eligible for deduction available to all categories of assessees being entrepreneurs *viz* individuals, firms, companies etc who derive any profits or gains from an undertaking being a unit engaged in the export of articles or things or providing any service.

Conditions to Claim Deduction

- It has begun or begins to manufacturing or produce articles or things or provide any service during the previous year thereafter in any special economic zone.
- It should not be formed by splitting up or reconstruction of a business already in existence. However, deduction is provided, if the unit is formed as a result of the re-establishment, re-construction or revival by the assessee of the business of the undertaking as is referred to and satisfying the conditions in Section 33B.
- It should also not be formed by the transfer of machinery or plant, previously used for any purpose, to a new business, however there are certain exceptions also relating to it.

- The assessee should furnish in the prescribed form [Form No. 56 F] alongwith the return of income, the report of a Chartered Accountant certifying that the deduction has been correctly claimed in accordance with the provisions of this section.

Income from Property Held for Charitable or Religious Purposes

The income of charitable or religious trusts is exempt from tax under Section 11 subject to the fulfillment of certain conditions

Income Exempt under Section 11

- Income from property held under trust wholly for charitable or religious purposes [Section 11 (1) (a)].
- Income from property held under trust which is applied in part only for charitable or religious purposes [Section 11 (1) (b)].
- Income from property held under trust which is applied for charitable purposes outside India [Section 11 (1) (c)].
- Voluntary contributions forming part of corpus [Section 11 (1) (d)].

Income of Political Parties [Section 13A]

- Income, which is chargeable under the head income from house property.
- Income chargeable under the head income from other sources.
- Any income by way of voluntary contribution from any person.
- Any income by way of capital gains.

The exemption of the above incomes shall be available only, when the following conditions are satisfied

- The political party keeps and maintains such books of accounts and other documents as will enable the assessing officer to assess properly its income.
- Where the voluntary contribution from a person exceeds ₹ 20,000, it keeps and maintains a record of such contribution and the name and address of the person has made such contribution.
- The accounts of the political party are audited by a Chartered Accountant.
- The treasure of such political party or any person authorised by the political party in this behalf must submit a report under Section 29 C (3) of the Representation of People Act, 1951 for the relevant financial year.

Income of a Electoral Trust [Section 13 B]

Any voluntary contributed received by an electoral trust shall be treated as income of the electoral trust.

However, such income shall be exempt if the following conditions are satisfied

- The electoral trust distributes to any political party, registered under Section 29 A of the Representation of the People Act, 1951, during previous year 95% of the aggregate donations received by it during the said previous year alongwith the surplus, if any, brought forward from any earlier previous year.
- Such electoral trust functions in accordance with the rules made in this regard by the Central Government.

Computation of Taxable Income under Various Heads

As per Section 14, all incomes, for purposes of charge of income tax and computation of total income, are classified under the following 5 heads

- Salaries [Section 15 to 17]
- Income from house property [Section 22 to 27]
- Profits and gains of business and profession [Section 28 to 44 DA]
- Capital gains [Section 45-55A]
- Income from other sources [Section 56-59]

Salaries

The meaning of the term 'Salary' for purposes of income tax is much wider than what is normally understood. The term 'Salary' for the purposes of Income Tax Act, 1961, will include both monetary payments (*e.g.* basic salary, bonus, commission, allowances etc) as well as non-monetary facilities (*e.g.* housing accommodation, medical facility, interest free loans etc). Section 17 (1) defined the term 'Salary'. It is an inclusive definition and includes monetary as well as non-monetary items.

Computation of Income under the Head 'Salaries'

Particulars		Amount (₹)
(i) Basic Salary		...
(ii) Commission		...
(iii) Bonus		...
(iv) Taxable Allowances		...
(v) Taxable Perquisites		...
(vi) Profits in Lieu of Salary		...
Gross Salary		...
Less Deduction under Section 16		
Standard deduction U/S 16(ia) upto ₹ 40,000		(...)
Entertainment allowance U/S 16 (ii) (only for government employees)		(...)
Least of the following is allowable as deduction		
(a) ₹ 5,000	...	
(b) 1/5th of basic salary	...	
(c) Actual entertainment allowance received	...	(...)
Professional Tax (paid by employer/employee) under Section 16 (iii)		(...)
Income under the Head Salary		...

Allowances

Different types of allowances are given to employees by their employers. Generally, allowances are given to employees to meet some particular requirements like house rent, expenses on uniform, conveyance etc. Under the Income Tax Act, 1916, allowance is taxable on due or receipt basis, whichever is earlier.

Various types of allowances normally in vogue are discussed below

Allowance which are Fully Taxable

- Entertainment allowance
- Dearness allowance
- Overtime allowance
- Fixed medical allowance
- City compensatory allowance (to meet increased cost of living in cities)
- Interim allowance
- Servant allowance
- Project allowance
- Tiffin/Lunch/Dinner allowance
- Any other cash allowance
- Warden allowance
- Non-practicing allowance
- Transport allowance to employee other than blind/ deaf and dumb/orthopedically handicapped employee.

Allowances which are Fully Exempt

- Allowances to High Court Judges.
- Allowance paid by the United Nations Organisation.
- Compensatory allowance received by a Judge.
- Sumptuary allowance granted to High Court or Supreme Court Judges.
- Allowance granted to government employees outside India.

Allowances which are Partly Taxable

- House Rent Allowance (HRA)–payment of rent for residence of the employee.

  Least of the following is exempt [Section 10 (13A)]

  (a) HRA actually received.

  (b) Rent paid –10% of salary of the relevant period.

  (c) 50% of salary, if accommodation is located in Mumbai, Kolkata, Delhi or Chennai or 40% of salary in any other city for the relevant period.

- Allowances prescribed for the purposes of Section 10(14)(ii)

  (a) special compensatory (hilly areas) allowance ₹ 800 or ₹ 300 per month depending upon the specified locations.
  ₹ 7,000 p.m. in Siachen area of Jammu and Kashmir.

  (b) special compensatory (tribal areas/scheduled areas/agency areas) allowance – ₹ 200 p.m.

  (c) allowance granted to an employee working in any transport system 70% of such allowance upto a maximum of ₹ 10,000 p.m.

  (d) children education allowance – ₹ 100 per month per child upto a maximum of two children.

  (e) allowance granted to an employee to meet the hostel expenditure of his child – ₹ 300 p.m. per child upto a maximum of two children etc.

Taxable Perquisites

Valuation of Rent Free Accommodation

- Where the accommodation is provided by the government to its employees

License fee determined by the government	...
Less Rent actually paid by the employee	(...)
	...

- Where the accommodation is provided by any other employer

If the accommodation is owned by the employer

(a) Cities having population > 25 lakh as per 2001 census

15% of salary in respect of the period of occupation	...
Less Rent actually paid by the employee	(...)
	...

(b) Cities having population > 10 lakh ≤ 25 lakh as per 2001 census 10% salary in respect of the

period of occupation	...
Less Rent actually paid by the employee	(...)
	...

In other cities

7.5% of salary in respect of the period of occupation	...
Less Rent actually paid by the employee	(...)
	...

If the accommodation is taken on lease by the employer

Lower of lease rental paid or payable by the employer (or) 15% of salary	...
Less Rent actually paid by the employee	(...)
	...

➠ **Note** *In case of furnished accommodations, the value will be increased by 10% p. a. of the cost of furniture or hire charges, as the case may be less amount recovered from the employee.*

Value of Use of Motor Car

S. No.	Car owned/ hired by	Expenses met by	Wholly official use	Partly personal use	
1.	Employer	Employer	No value	CC of Engine	Perquisite Value
				upto 1.6 litres	₹ 1,800 p. m.
				above 1.6 litres	₹ 2,400 p. m.
				If chauffeur is also provided, ₹900 p.m. should be added to the above value.	
2.	Employee	Employer	No value	Actual amount of expenditure incurred by the employer as reduced by the perquisite value arrived at in (1) above.	
3.	Employer	Employee	–	CC of Engine	Perquisite Value
				Upto 1.6 litres	₹ 600 p.m.
				above 1.6 litres	₹ 900 p.m.
				If chauffeur is also provided, ₹ 900 p. m. should be added to the above value.	

Profit in Lieu of Salary

Gratuity

It is exempt U/S 10(10)

(i) Death-cum-retirement gratuity received by Central Government employees/members of civil services/local authority employees etc is fully exempt U/S 10 (10)(i).

(ii) Other employees

(a) Covered under the Payment of Gratuity Act, 1972
- ₹ 10 lakh
- Actual gratuity received
- 15 days salary for every completed year of service or part thereof in excess of 6 months (No. of days taken in a month is 26).

Whichever is less is exempt U/S 10 (10)(ii).

(b) Not covered under the Payment of Gratuity Act, 1972
- ₹ 10 lakh
- Actual gratuity received
- Half month salary (based on the average of last 10 months) (No. of days taken in a month is 30).

Whichever is less is exempt U/S 10 (10) (iii).

Commuted Pension

Exempt U/S 10 (10A)

- Employees of Central Government/local authority/statutory corporation/members of civil services/Defence services etc is fully exempt U/S 10 (10A) (i).
- Other employees

(a) if the employee receives gratuity $1/3 \times$ (commuted pension received ÷ commutation %) $\times 100$ would be exempt U/S 10 (10A) (ii) (a).

(b) if the employee does not receive gratuity $1/2 \times$ (commuted pension received ÷ commutation %) $\times 100$ would be exempt U/S 10 (10 A) (ii) (b).

Leave Encashment

Exempt U/S 10 (10AA)

Leave encashment received on retirement, whether on superannuation or otherwise

- By a government employee fully exempt U/S 10 (10AA) (i).
- By any other employee

(a) ₹ 3,00,000.

(b) leave encashment actually received.

(c) 10 months salary (on the basis of average salary of last 10 months preceding retirement).

(d) Cash equivalent of unavailed leave (based on last 10 months average salary) to his credit at the time of retirement cannot exceed 30 days every year of actual service.

Whichever is less would be exempt U/S 10 (10 AA) (ii).

Provident Funds

Particulars	Recognised PF	Unrecognised PF	Statutory PF
Employer's Contribution	Amount in excess of 12% of salary is taxable	Not taxable yearly	Fully exempt
Employee's Contribution	Eligible for deduction U/S 80 C	Not eligible for deduction	Eligible for deduction U/S 80 C
Interest Credited	Amount in excess of 9.5% p. a. is taxable	Not taxable yearly	Fully exempt
Amount received on retirement etc.	Exempt from tax, if employee served a continuous period of 5 years or more or retires before 5 years of service because of ill, health or reason beyond the control of the employee. In other case, it is taxable.	Employer's contribution and interest thereon is taxable as salary. Interest on employees contribution is taxable under income from other sources.	Fully exempt U/S 10 (11)

Income from House Property

Income from house property is taxable on the basis of annual value of house property. House means any building used for residential or commercial purposes.

Conditions for Chargeability

- *Property should consist of any building or land appurtenant thereto*

(a) Buildings include not only residential buildings, but also factory buildings, offices, shops, godowns and other commercial premises.

(b) Land appurtenant means land connected with the building like garden, garage etc.

- *Assessee must be the owner of the property*
  (a) Owner is the person who is entitled to receive income from the property in his own right.
  (b) The requirement of registration of the sale deed is not warranted.
  (c) Ownership includes both free-hold and lease-hold rights.
  (d) Ownership includes deemed ownership.
  (e) The person who owns the building need not also be the owner of the land upon which it stands.
  (f) The assessee must be the owner of the house property during the previous year.
  (g) If the title of the ownership of the property is under dispute in a court of law, the decision as to who will be the owner chargeable to income tax under Section 22 will be of the income tax department till the court gives its decision.
- The property may be used for any purpose, but it should not be used by the owner for the purpose of any business or profession carried on by him, the profit of which is chargeable to tax.
- The income earned by an assessee engaged in the business of letting out of properties on rent would be taxable as business income.
- Annual value of house property will be charged under the head "Income from house property", where it is held by the assessee as stock-in-trade of a business also.
- However, the annual value of property being held as stock-in-trade would be treated as NIL for a period of one year from the end of the financial year in which certificate of completion of construction of the property is obtained from the competent authority.

Determination of Annual Value (Section 23)

Particulars	Amount (₹)
Determination of Gross Annual Value (GAV) (WN1)	...
Less Municipal tax paid by the owner during the previous year	(...)
Net Annual Value (NAV)	...

Working Note

1. Determination of gross annual value

Step 1 [Section 23 (1) (a)]
(a) municipal valuation
(b) fair rent
(whichever is higher, but)
(c) not more than standard rent.

Step 2 [Section 23 (1) (b)]
Rent received or receivable as reduced by the unrealised rent, or the amount computed as per Step I (Whichever is higher, shall be GAV)

Step 3 [Section 23 (1) (c)]
If the property was vacant during the whole or any part of the previous year, the actual rent received by the owner is less than the sum referred to in Step I, then the amount received is GAV.

Deductions from Annual Value [Section 24]

Deduction from Annual Value (in respect of self-occupied house)

Interest on borrowed capital

Conditions

- Where loan is taken for repair, renewal or reconstruction of house property–maximum ₹ 30,000.
- Where loan is taken for acquisition or construction of house property
  (a) Loan borrowed before 01-04-1999 maximum interest payable ₹ 30,000.
  (b) Loan borrowed on or after 01-04-1999, where acquisition or construction is completed within 5 years from the end of the FY in which capital was borrowed, then actual interest payable to maximum of ₹ 2,00,000.
  But if it is used for repair and reconstruction, then the actual interest payable to a maximum of ₹ 30,000.

Deduction from Annual Value (in respect of let out house)
(i) Standard deduction under Section 24 (a) @ 30% of NAV.
(ii) Interest on borrowed capital under Section 24 (b) is fully allowed.

Profits and Gains of Business or Profession

Income from business and profession is an important head of income because government is receiving maximum revenue from it. This third head of income includes income from business, profession, vocation and speculation.

Computation of income under the head "Profits and gains of business and profession"

Particulars	Amount (₹)
Net Profit as per Statement of Profit and Loss	...
Add *Expenses debited in statement of profit and loss but not allowable*	
• Depreciation as per books of accounts	...
• Income tax [disallowed U/S 40 (a) (ii)]	...
• 30% of sum payable to residents on which tax is not deducted at source or has not been remitted on or before the due date U/S 139 (1)	...
• Any expenditure incurred, in respect of which payment is made for goods, services or facilities to a related person, having regards to its FMV [disallowed U/S 40 A (2)]	...
• Any payment to partner by way of salary, interest, bonus, commission or remuneration in excess of prescribed limits U/S 40 (b)	...
• Any expenditure incurred in respect of which payment or aggregate of payments to person exceeding ₹ 10,000	...
• Certain sums payable by the assessee which has not been paid during relevant P.Y.	...
• Personal expenses [not allowable as per Section 37]	...
• Capital expenditure [not allowable as per Section 37]	...
• Repairs of capital nature [not allowable as per Section 30 and 31]	...
• Amortization of preliminary expenditure U/S 35 D/expenditure incurred under voluntary retirement scheme U/S 35 DDA	...
• Fine or penalty paid for infringement or breach of law	...
• All expenses related to income which is not taxable	...
	...
Less *Expenditure allowable as deduction but not debited to statement of profit and loss*	
• Depreciation computed as per Rule 5 of Income Tax Rules, 1962	...
• Additional depreciation @20% actual cost of new P and M	...
• Deduction @ 15% of actual cost of new P and M U/S 32 AD	...
• Weighted deduction for expenditure on/contribution for research U/S 35 (1) (ii), 35 (2AA), 35 (2AB) in excess of the amount already debited to statement of profit and loss	...
• Investment-linked tax deduction in respect of specified businesses U/S 35 AD	(...)
	...
Less *Income credited in statement of profit and loss but not taxable/taxable under any other head*	(...)
Add *Deemed income*	
• Bad debts allowed as deduction U/S 36 (1) (vii) in an earlier PY	...
• Remission or cessation of a trading liability	...
Profit and Gains from Business or Profession	...

Special Provisions for Computing Profits and Gains on Presumptive Basis

S. No.	Particulars	Section 44 AD	Section 44 ADA	Section 44 AE
1.	Eligible Assessee	Resident individual, HUF or Partnership firm engaged in eligible business and who has not claimed deduction U/S 10AA. **Deductions in Respect of Certain Incomes** *Non-applicability of Section 44 AD in respect of the following persons* • Carrying on profession U/S 44 AA (1). • Earning income in the nature of commission or brokerage. • Carrying on any agency business.	Resident assessee engaged in any profession specified U/S 44 AA (1), namely legal, medical, engineering, architectural profession or profession of accountancy or technical consultancy or interior decoration or notified profession.	An assessee owning not more than 10 goods carriages at any time during the P.Y.
2.	Eligible Business/ Profession	Any business, other than business referred to in Section 44 AE, whose total turnover/gross receipts in the P.Y. ≤ ₹ 200 lakh.	Any profession specified under section 44 AA (1), whose total gross receipts ≤ ₹ 50 lakh in the relevant P.Y.	Playing, hiring or leasing goods carriages.
3.	Presumptive Income	8% of total turnover/gross receipts or a sum higher than the aforesaid sum claimed to have been earned by the assessee 6% of total turnover/gross receipts received by A/c payee cheque/bank draft/ECS during the P.Y. or before due date of filing of return U/S 139(1).	50% of total gross receipts or a sum higher than the aforesaid sum claimed to have been earned by the assessee.	₹ 7,500 for every month or part of the month during which such goods carriage is owned or a higher amount claimed to have been actually earned from the vehicle.

Capitals Gains

Any profit or gain arising from the transfer of capital assets affected in the Previous Year are chargeable to income tax if such gains are not exempted under the Income Tax Act. [Section 45(1)]

Modes of Computation of Capital Gains [Section 48]

Computation of Taxable Short-term Capital Gain

Particulars		Amt (₹)
Full value of consideration received or occurring as a result of transfer		...
Less Exp. incurred wholly and exclusively in connection with such transfer (*e.g.* brokerage on sale)		(...)
Net Sale Consideration		...
Less Cost of acquisition	(...)	
Cost of improvement	(...)	(...)
Short-term Capital Gain (STCG)		...
Less Exemption U/S 54 B/54 D		(...)
Taxable STCG		...

Computation of Taxable Long-term Capital Gain

Particulars	Amt (₹)
Full value of consideration received or occurring as a result of transfer	...
Less Expense incurred wholly and exclusively in connection with such transfer	(...)
Net Sale Consideration	...
Less Indexed Cost of Acquisition (ICoA)	
Cost of acquisition × $\frac{\text{CII for the year in which the asset is transferred}}{\text{CII for the year in which the asset was first held by the assessee or PY 2001-02, whichever is later}}$	(...)
Less Indexed Cost of Improvement (ICoI)	
Cost of improvement × $\frac{\text{CII for the year in which the asset is transferred}}{\text{CII for the year in which improvement took place}}$	(...)
Long-term Capital Gains (LTCG)	...
Less Exemption U/S 54/54 B/54D/54EC/54EE/54 F	(...)
Taxable LTCG	...

Capital Gain Exempted from Tax

As per provisions of income tax capital gain exempt U/S 10 (33), 10 (36), 10 (37), 10 (38), 54, 54B, 54D, 54EC, 54EE, 54F, 54G, 54GA and 54GB. *Capital gain exempt from tax is following*

- Capital Gain on transfer of Unit Scheme 64 [Section 10(33)].
- Long-term Capital Gain on transfer of Listed Equity Shares [Section 10 (36)].
- Capital Gain on compulsory acquisition of Urban Agricultural Land [Section 10(37)].
- Long-term Capital Gain on transfer of Securities [Section 10(38)].
- Transfer of assets by undertaking engaged in generation, transmission and distribution of power [Section 10(41)].
- Exemption of Long-term Capital Gain from Residential House Property [Section 54].
- Exemption of Capital Gain on transfer of Urban Agricultural Land [Section 54B].
- Exemption of Capital Gain on compulsory acquisition of Industrial Land and Building [Section 54D].
- Exemption of Long-term Capital Gain on transfer of any Long-term Capital Asset [Section 54EC].
- Exemption of Long-term Capital Gain on transfer of any Long-term Capital Asset [Section 54 EE].
- Exemption of Long-term Capital Gain other than Residential House Property [Section 54F].
- Exemption of Capital Gain on shifting of Industrial Undertaking from Urban Area [Section 54G].
- Exemption of Capital Gain from Industrial Land, Building, Plant and Machinery from Urban Area to Specified Economic Zone (SEZ) [Section 54GA].
- Exemption of long-term capital Gain from Residential Land and Building [Section 54GB].

Income from Other Sources

Income from other sources is the last head of income. The incomes which are not chargeable to tax under the first four heads of incomes and not declared exempted, is chargeable to tax under the head "Income from Other Sources." [Section 56(1)]

Computation of Income from Other Sources

S. No.	Particulars	Amt (₹)
(i)	Dividend Income	...
(ii)	Casual Income (Winning from lotteries, crossword puzzles, races including horse races, card games and other games, gambling betting etc.)	...
(iii)	Consideration received in excess of FMV of shares of a closely held company, where such shares are issued at a premium [Section 56 (2) (vii b)]	...
(iv)	Interest received on compensation/enhanced compensation deemed to be income in the year of receipt [Section 56 (2) viii]	...
(v)	Advance forfeited due to failure of negotiations for transfer of a capital assets [Section 56 (2) (ix)]	...
(vi)	Sum of money or property received by any person [Section 56 (2) (x)]	...
(vii)	Compensation or other payment, due to or received by any person, in connection with termination of his employment or the modification of the terms and conditions relating thereto [Section 56 (2) (xi)]	...
(viii)	Any income chargeable to tax under the Act, but not falling under any other lead of income	...
(ix)	Deemed income U/S 59-Remission or cessation of a trading liability or receipt of any amount in respect of loss or expenditure allowed as deduction in an earlier P.Y	...
	Less Deductions Allowable [Section 57]	(...)
(a)	Income from letting on hire of machinery, plant and furniture, with or without building	
	• current repairs to the machinery, plant, furniture or building	(...)
	• insurance premium	(...)
	• depreciation/unabsorbed depreciation	(...)
(b)	Family Pension–$33\frac{1}{3}$% of such income, or ₹ 15,000, whichever is less	(...)
(c)	Interest on compensation/enhanced compensation received-50% of such interest	(...)
(d)	Any other expenditure not in the nature of capital expenditure incurred wholly and exclusively for earning such income.	(...)
	Income from Other Sources	...

Sum of Money or Property Received by any Person [Section 56 (2) (x)]

S. No.	Nature of Asset	Particulars	Taxable Value
1.	Money	Without Consideration	The whole amount, if same exceeds ₹ 50,000.
2.	Movable Property	Without Consideration	The aggregate fair market value of the property, if it exceeds ₹ 50,000.
3.	Movable Property	Inadequate Consideration	The difference between the aggregate fair market value and consideration, if such difference exceeds ₹ 50,000.
4.	Immovable Property	Without Consideration	The stamp value of the property, if it exceeds ₹ 50,000.
5.	Immovable Property	Inadequate Consideration	The difference between the stamp duty value and the consideration, if such difference exceeds the higher of ₹ 50,000 and 5% of consideration.

Clubbing of Incomes

Under the Income Tax Act, 1961, an assessee is generally taxed in respect of his own income. However, there are certain cases where an assessee has to pay tax in respect of income of another person. The provisions for the same are contained in Section 60 to 64 of the act. These provisions have been enacted to counteract the tendency on the part of the tax payers to dispose of their property or transfer their income in such away that their tax liability can be avoided or reduced.

These are as follows

Section 60 Income transferred without transfer asset, when a person transfers the income occurring to an asset, without the transfer of the asset itself, such income is to be included in the total income of the transferor, whether the transfer is revocable or irrevocable.

Section 61 Income arising from revocable transfer of assets such income is to be included in the hands of the transferor.

A transfer is deemed to be revocable if it

- contains any provision for re-transfer of the whole or any part of the income or assets to the transferor; or
- gives right to re-assume power over the whole or any part of the income or the asset.

Section 64 (1) (ii) Income arising to spouse by way of remuneration from a concern in which the individual has substantial interest.

Such income arising to spouse is to be included in the total income of the individual.

However, if remuneration received is attributable to the application of technical or professional knowledge and experience of spouse, then, such income is not to be clubbed.

Section 64 (1) (iv) Income arising to spouse from assets transferred without adequate consideration

Income arising from an asset (other than house property) transferred otherwise than for adequate consideration or in connection with an agreement to live apart from one spouse to another shall be included in the total income of the transferor.

However, this provision will not apply in the case of transfer of house property, since the transferor-spouse would be the deemed owner as per Section 27.

Section 64 (1) (vi) Income arising to son's wife from an asset transferred without adequate consideration.

Income arising from an asset transferred otherwise than for adequate consideration, by an individual to his or her son's wife shall be included in the total income of the transferor.

Section 64 (1) (vii)/(viii) Income arising from transfer of assets for the benefit of spouse or son's wife.

All income arising to any person or association of persons from assets transferred without adequate consideration is includible in the income of the transferor, to the extent such income is used by the transferee for the immediate or deferred benefit of the transferor's spouse or son's wife.

Section 64 (1A) All income arising or occurring to a minor child (including a minor married daughter) shall be included in the total income of his or her parent.

The income of the minor child shall be included with the income of that parent, whose total income, before including minors's income, is higher. The parent in whose total income, the income of the minor child or children are included, shall be entitled to exemption of such income subject to a maximum of ₹ 1,500 per child under Section 10 (32).

Section 64 (2) Conversion of self-acquired property into the property of a Hindu Undivided Family.

Where an individual, who is a member of the HUF, converts his individual property into property of the HUF of which he is a member, directly or indirectly, to the family otherwise than for adequate consideration, the income from such property shall continue to be included in the total income of the individual.

Set-off and Carry Forwards of Losses

Inter-source and Inter-head Set-off of Losses

Inter-source Set-off of Losses under the Same Head of Income (Section 70) Any loss in respect of one source shall be set-off against income from any other source under the same head of income.

Exceptions

- Loss from speculation business can be set-off only against profits from another speculation business.
- Loss from specified business under Section 35 AD can be set-off only against profits from any other specified business.
- Long-Term Capital Loss (LTCL) can be set-off only against income from the activity of owning and maintain race horses.
- Loss from the activity of owning and maintaining race horses.

Inter-head Adjustment (Section 71) Loss under one head of income can be set-off against income assessable under any other head of income.

Exceptions

- Loss under the head 'Profits and gains of business or profession' cannot be set-off against income under the head 'Salaries'.
- Loss under the head 'Capital gains' cannot be set-off only against income under any other head.
- Speculation loss, losses from Specified business under Section 35 AD and loss from the activity of owning and maintaining race horses cannot be set-off against income under any other head.
- Loss from house property can be set-off against income under any other head only to the extent of ₹ 2 lakh. The remaining loss can be carried forward for set-off against income from house property of the succeeding years.

Losses which cannot be Set-off or Carried Forward

- Loss from gambling, betting, card games etc.
- Loss from an exempt source (*e.g.* share of loss of partnership firm cannot be set-off).

Maximum Period of Carry Forward of Losses and Manner of Set-off of Brought Forward Losses

Section	Nature of loss to be carried forward	Income against which the brought forward loss can be set-off	Maximum period (from the end of the relevant assessment year) for carry forward of losses
32 (2)	Unabsorbed depreciation	Income under any head other than salaries	Indefinite period
71 B	Unabsorbed loss from house property	Income from house property	8 assessment years
72	Unabsorbed business loss	Profits and gains from business or profession	8 assessment years
73	Loss from speculation business	Income from any speculation business	4 assessment years
73 A	Loss from specified business U/S 35 AD	Profit from any specified business.	Indefinite period
74	Long-term capital loss Short-Term capital loss	Long-term capital gains/Short-term/ long-term capital gains	8 assessment years 8 assessment years
74 A	Loss from the activity of owning and maintaining race horses	Income from the activity of owning and maintaining race horses	4 assessment years

Deductions from Gross Total Income

Deductions in Respect of Certain Payments

Section	Eligible Assessee	Eligible Payments	Permissible Deduction
80 C	Individual or HUF	Deduction in respect of life insurance premium, contribution to provident fund, repayment of housing loan, tution fees of any two children, post office time deposit etc.	Amount of payment or ₹ 1,50,000 (whichever is less).
80 CCC	Individual	Contribution to certain pension funds	Amount of contribution or ₹ 1,50,000 (whichever is less).
80 CCD	Individuals employed by the Central Government or any other employer, any other individual assessee	Contribution to Pension Scheme of Central Government.	In case of a salaried, individual deduction of own contribution U/S 80 CCD (1) is restricted to 10% of his salary. In any other case, deduction U/S 80 CCD (1) is restricted to 20% of GTI. Further, additional deduction of upto ₹ 50,000 is available U/S80 CCD (1B). Deduction of employers contribution U/S 80 CCD(2) restricted to 10% of salary. However, the limit ₹ 1.50 lakh U/S 80 CCE does not apply to deduction U/S 80 CCD (2) and 80 CCD (1 B).
80 CCG	Individual	Deduction in respect of investment made under equity investment scheme.	50% of amount of investment or ₹ 25,000 (whichever is less).
80 D	Individual and HUF	Medical Insurance Premium 1. Deduction in respect of insurance premium paid for family (self, spouse and dependent children). 2. Deduction in respect of insurance premium for parents. 3. Contribution to Central Government Health Scheme (CGHS). Any premium paid, otherwise than by way of cash, to keep in force an insurance on the health. Payments, including cash payment, for preventive health check up himself, spouse, dependent children and parents.	Deduction to the extent of ₹ 25,000. Deduction of ₹ 25,000 (₹ 50,000, in case the person insured is a senior citizen). ₹ 25,000 (₹ 50,000, in case the person insured is a senior citizen). Amount paid subject to a cap of ₹ 5,000 in aggregate [subject to the overall individual limit of ₹ 25,000/50,000 as the case may be].

Section	Eligible Assessee	Eligible Payments	Permissible Deduction
80 DD	Resident Individual and HUF	Medical treatment and maintenance of dependent disabled : expenses and deposits	Deduction of ₹ 75,000 [in case of severe disability ₹ 1,25,000].
80 DDB	Resident Individual and HUF	Deduction for medical treatment of specified diseases or ailments.	Deduction upto ₹ 40,000 and [in case of senior citizen 60,000 and in case of very senior citizen ₹ 80,000], whichever is less. Minus the amount received from the insurance company.
80 E	Individual	Deduction in respect of interest of loan taken for higher education of himself or the spouse or the children.	For 7 assessment year or upto payment of entire interest (whichever is earlier).
80 EE	Individual	*Deduction for interest on loan taken for residential house conditions* 1. Loan should be sanctioned during P.Y. 2. Loan sanctioned ≤ ₹ 35 lakh. 3. Value of house ≤ ₹ 50 lakh. 4. The assessee should not own any other residential house.	Deduction of upto ₹ 50,000 would be allowed in respect of interest on loan.
80 G	All Assessees	Deduction in respect of donations to certain funds, charitable institutions etc. (100% deductions for donations to family planning to government or to certain specified donations to provide relief to the victims of certain disasters and 50% on others)	Maximum deduction of 10% of adjusted GTI, but this restriction does not apply to donations to funds. No deduction shall be allowed for donation paid in cash in excess of ₹ 2,000 and donation in kind.
80 GG	Individual not in receipt of house rent allowance	Rent paid for residential accommodations **Conditions** 1. Should not have house in name of self/wife/ and minor child. 2. No house rent allowance is received.	• 25% of total income. • Rent paid-10% of total income. • ≤ ₹ 5,000 p.m. (whichever is less).
80 GGB	Indian Company	Contributions to political parties	Actual contributions (otherwise than by way of cash)
80 GGC	Any person other than local authority	Contributions to political parties	Actual contributions (otherwise than by way of cash)

Deductions in Respect of Certain Incomes

Section	Eligible Assessee	Eligible Payments	Permissible Deduction
80 IA	All Assessee	Profit from industrial undertaking engaged in infrastructure development.	Upto 10 assessment year 100%
80 IAB	Developer	Profit of an undertaking engaged in the development of Special Economic Zones.	Upto 10 assessment year 100%
80 IB	All Assessee	Profit from industrial undertaking other than infrastructure and building projects.	Upto 10 assessment year 100%
80 IC	All Assessee	Certain industrial undertaking in certain states.	1. In some cases, upto 10 assessment year 100% 2. In some cases, upto 5 assessment year 100%, next 5 years 30% (company) or 25% (others)
80 JJAA	All Assessee	In respect of new employment.	30% of additional employment cost
80 P	Cooperative society	Deduction in respect of income of cooperative society	1. 100% (Agriculture, marketing, banking activities 2. ₹ 50,000 (Income from other activities)
80 QQB	Resident individual being an author	Royalty incomes etc of authors of certain books other than text books.	100% of royalty or ₹ 3,00,000 (whichever is less).
80 RRB	Resident individual, being a patentee	Royalty on patents.	100% of royalty or ₹ 3,00,000 (whichever is less).
80 TTA	Individual or HUF	Amount of interest credited in Savings Bank Account or Post Office.	Amount of interest or ₹ 10,000 (whichever is less).
80U	Resident Individual	Deduction in respect of disabled person.	Deduction of ₹ 75,000 in case of severe disability deduction of ₹ 1,25,000.

Assessment of Individual and Tax Rate

Assessment of Individual

Every assessee has to furnish his income tax return regarding the details of his income tax department. The income tax department examines the return of income for its correctness. This process of examining the return is called as Assessment.

Types of Assessment

Self Assessment

Self assessment refers a system under which an assessee computes his taxable income himself as well as tax on it while submitting return of income (Section 140 A).

Regular Assessment

Such assessment can be made by the assessing officer in the following ways

- Assessment on basis of return under Section 143 (1).
- Assessment on basis of evidence produced under Section 143 (3).

Best Judgement Assessment

If any person fails to furnish return of income or fails to respond or comply with notice issued, the information which he has gathered and giving the assessee an opportunity of being heard, shall make the assessment of total income or loss to the best of his judgement and determine the sum payable by the assessee (Section 144).

Re-assessment

It is also known as assessment of escaping income where assessing officer has sufficient reason to believe that any income chargeable to tax has escaped assessment for any assessment year, then he can assess or re-assess income U/S 148 to 153 (Section 147).

Tax Rate

Tax has to be computed by applying the rates of tax mentioned in the annual finance act and the rate specified under the Income Tax Act, 1961, *as the case may be*

Persons	Rates of taxes	
Individual	**Total Income** (in ₹)	**Rate of Tax**
	(a) (i) Upto ₹ 2,50,000 (below 60 years)	Nil
	(ii) Upto ₹ 3,00,000 (60 years or above but less than 80 years and resident in India)	Nil
	(iii) Upto ₹ 5,00,000 (above 80 years and resident in India)	Nil
	(b) ₹ 2,50,001/₹ 3,00,001, as the case may be, to ₹ 5,00,000 [in case (i) and (ii) above, respectively]	5%
	(c) ₹ 5,00,001 to ₹ 10,00,000	20%
	(d) Above ₹ 10,00,000	30%
Hindu Undivided Family (HUF)/Association of Persons (AoP) / Body of Individuals (BoI)/ Artificial Juridical Person	**Total Income** (in ₹)	**Rate of Tax**
	Upto ₹ 2,50,000	Nil
	₹ 2,50,001 to ₹ 5,00,000	5%
	₹ 5,00,001 to ₹ 10,00,000	20%
	Above ₹ 10,00,000	30%
Firm /LLP/Local Authority		30%
Cooperative Society	**Total Income** (₹)	**Rate of Tax**
	Upto ₹ 10,000	10%
	₹ 10,001 to ₹ 20,000	20%
	Above ₹ 20,000	30%
Company	Domestic Company	
	(i) Total turnover or gross receipts in the P.Y. ≤ ₹ 250 crore	25%
	(ii) Other domestic companies	30%
	Foreign Company	40%

Surcharge

1.	**Individual /HUF/AoP/BoI/Artificial Juridical Person**	
	Where the total income > ₹ 50 lakh but is ≤ ₹ 1 crore	10%
	Where the total income > ₹ 1 crore	15%
2.	**Firm/Limited Liability Partnership/Local Authorities/Co-operative Societies**	
	Where the total income > ₹ 1 crore	12%
3.	**Domestic Company**	
	Total income > ₹ 1 crore, but is ≤ ₹ 10 crore	7%
	Total income is > ₹ 10 crore	12%
4.	**Foreign Company**	
	Total income > ₹ 1 crore, but is ≤ ₹ 10 crore	2%
	Total income is > ₹ 10 crore	5%

Rebate (U/S 87A) Rebate of upto ₹ 2,500 for resident individuals having total income of upto ₹ 3.5 lakh.

Health and Education Cess on Income Tax 4 % of income tax and surcharge, if applicable.

Deduction and Collection of Tax at Source

Deduction of Tax at Source and Advance Payment [Section 190]

The total income of an assessee for the previous year is taxable in the relevant assessment year. *However, income tax is recovered from the assessee in the previous year itself through*

- Tax Deduction at Source (TDS)
- Tax Collection at Source (TCS)
- Payment of Advance Tax

Another mode of recovery of tax is from the employer through tax paid by him [U/S 192 (1A)] on the non-monetary perquisites provided to the employee.

These taxes are deductible from the total tax due from the assessee. The assessee, while filing his return of income has to pay self-assessment tax (U/S 140 A) if tax is due on the total income as per his return of income after adjusting, inter alia, TDS, TCS and advance tax.

Tax Collection at Source [Section 206 C]

Sellers of certain goods are required to collect tax from the buyers at the specified rates. *The specified percentage for collection of tax at source is as follows*

Nature of Goods	Percentage
• Alcoholic liquor for human consumption	1%
• Tendu leaves	5%
• Timber obtained under a forest lease	2.5%
• Timber obtained by any mode other than (iii)	2.5%
• Any other forest produce not being timber or tendu leaves	2.5%
• Scrap	1%
• Minerals, being coal or lignite or iron ore	1%

However, no collection of tax shall be made in the case of a resident buyer, if such buyer furnishes a declaration in writing in duplicate to the effect that goods are to be utilised for the purpose of manufacturing, processing or producing articles or things or for the purposes of generation of power and not for trading purposes.

Advance Payment of Tax

Liability for Payment of Advance Tax [Section 207 and 208]

Tax shall be payable in advance during any F.Y. in respect of the total income of the assessee which would be chargeable to tax for A.Y. immediately following that F.Y.

Advance tax is payable during a F. Y. in every case, where the amount of such tax payable by the assessee (after reducing TDS/TCS) during the year is ₹ 10,000 or more.

However, an individual resident in India of the age of 60 years or more at any time during the P. Y., who does not have any income chargeable under the head "Profits and gains of business or profession", is not liable to pay advance tax.

Installments of Advance Tax and Due Dates [Section 211]

Advance tax payment schedule for corporates and non-corporates (other than an assessee computing profits on presumptive basis U/S 44 AD or 44 ADA)-four instalments

Due Date of Instalment	Amount Payable
On or before 15th June	Not less than 15% of advance tax liability
On or before 15th September	Not less than 45% of advance tax liability (–) amount paid in earlier instalment
On or before15th December	Not less than 75% of advance tax liability (–) amount paid in earlier instalment
On or before 15th March	The whole amount of advance tax liability (–) amount paid in earlier instalment

Assessee Computing Profits on Presumptive Basis

U/S 44 AD (1) or 44 ADA (1) to pay advance tax by 15th March.

An eligible assessee, opting for computation of profits or gains of business or profession or presumption basis in respect of eligible business referred to in Section 44 AD (1) or in respect of eligible profession referred to in Section 44 AD A (1), shall be required to pay advance tax of the whole amount on or before 15th March of the F. Y.

However, any amount paid by way of advance tax on or before 31st March shall also be treated as advanced tax paid during the F. Y. ending on that day.

Interest for Defaults in Payment of Advance Tax U/S 234 B

- Interest U/S 234 B is attracted for non-payment of advance tax or payment of advance tax of an amount less than 90% of assessed tax.
- The interest liability would be 1% per month or part of the month from 1st April following the F. Y. upto the date of determination of total income U/S 143 (1) and where regular assessment is made, upto the date of such regular assessment.
- Such interest is calculated on the amount of differences between the assessed tax and the advance tax paid.
- Assessed tax means the tax on total income determined U/S 143 (1) under regular assessment, as the case may be, less TDS and TCS.

Interest for Deferment of Advance Tax U/S 234 C

Manner of Computation of Iinterest U/S 234 C for Determent of Advance tax by Corporate and Non-corporate Assesses

In case an assessee, other than an assessee who declares profits and gains in accordance with the provisions of Section 44 AD (1) or 44 ADA (1), who is liable to pay advance tax U/S 208 has failed to pay such tax or the advance tax paid by such assessee on its current income on or before the dates specified in column (1) below is less than the specified percentage of tax due on returned income, then simple interest @1% per month for the period specified in column (4) on the amount of shortfall as per column (3) is leviable U/S 243 C.

Specified date (1)	Specified (2)	Shortfall in advance tax (3)	Period (4)
15th June	15%	15% of tax due on returned income – advance tax paid upto 15th June	3 months
15th September	45%	45% of tax due on returned income – advance tax paid upto 15th September	3 months
15th December	75%	75% of tax due on returned income – advance tax paid upto 15th December	3 months
15th March	100%	100% of tax due on returned income – advance tax paid upto 15th March	1 month

➠ **Note** *However, if the advance tax paid by the assessee on the current income, on or before 15th June or 15th September, is not less than 12% or, as the case may be, 36% of the tax due on the returned income, then, the assessee shall not be liable to pay any interest on the amount of the shortfall on those dates. Tax due on returned income = Tax chargeable on total income declared in the return of income – TDS – TCS.*

Computation of Interest U/S 234 C in Case of an Assessee who Declares Profits and Gains in Accordance with the Provisions of Section 44 AD (1) or 44 ADA (1)

In case, an assessee who declares profits and gains in accordance with the provisions of Section 44 AD (1) or 44 ADA (1), who is liable to pay advance tax U/S 208 has failed to pay such tax or the advance tax paid by the assessee on its current income on or before 15th March is less than the tax due on the returned income, then, the assessee shall be liable to pay simple interest at the rate of 1% on the amount of the shortfall from the tax due on the returned income.

Non-applicability of Interest U/S 234 C in certain Cases

Interest U/S 234 C shall not be leviable in respect of any shortfall in payment of tax due on returned income, *where such shortfall is an account of under-estimate or failure to estimate*

- the amount of capital gains.
- income of nature referred to in Section 2 (24) (ix), winnings from lotteries, crossword puzzles, etc.
- Income under the head "PGBP" in cases where the income accrues or arises under the said head for the first time.
- Income of the nature referred to in Section 115 BBDA (1), *i.e.* dividend in aggregate exceeding ₹ 10 lakh included in the assessee's TI.

However, the assessee should have paid the whole of the amount of tax payable in respect of such income referred to in (i),(ii),(iii) and (iv), as the case may be, had such income been a part of the total income, as part of the remaining instalments of advance tax which are due or where no such instalments are due, by 31st March of the F. Y.

E-Filing of Income Tax Returns

Return of Income

The Income Tax Act, 1961 contains provisions for filing of return of income. Return of income is the format in which the assessee furnishes information as to his total income and tax payable. The format for filing of returns by different assessees is notified by the CBDT.

Assessees Required to File Return of Income Compulsorily [Section 139 (1)]

- Companies and firms (whether having profit or loss or nil income).
- A person, being a resident other than not ordinarily resident, having an asset (including any financial interest in any entity) located outside India or signing authority in any account located outside India, whether or not having income chargeable to tax.
- Individuals, HUF, AoPs or BoIs and artificial juridical persons whose total income before giving effect to the provisions of Chapter VI-A exceeds the basic exemption limit.

Due Date of Filing Return of Income

30th September of the assessment year, in case the assessee is

- a company;
- a person (other than company) whose accounts are required to be audited; or
- a working partner of a firm whose accounts are required to be audited.

31st July of the assessment year, in case of any other assessee (other than assessees who are required to furnish report under Section 92 E, for whom the due date is 30th November of the assessment year).

Loss Return U/S 139 (3)

To be filed on or before the due date U/S 139 (1) for carry forward of

- business loss U/S 72 (1).
- loss from speculation business U/S 73 (2).
- loss from specified business U/S 73 A (2).
- loss under the head "Capital gains" U/S 74 (1).
- loss from the activity of owning and maintaining race horses U/S 74 A (3).

Belated Return under Section 139 (4)

If return is not filed within the time specified U/S 139 (1), a belated return U/S 139 (4) can be filed at any time before

- the completion of the assessment .

Or

- the end of the relevant A.Y., whichever is earlier.

Revised Return under Section 139 (5)

Return filed U/S 139 (1) or a belated return filed U/S 139 (4) can be revised U/S 139 (5)

- at any time before the end of the relevant A. Y.

Or

- before the completion of assessment, whichever is earlier.

If any omission or any wrong statement therein is discovered by the person.

Quoting of PAN under Section 139A (5)

Mandatory quoting of PAN

- In all returns to, and correspondence with, any income tax authority.
- In all challans for the payment of any sum due under the Income Tax Act, 1961.
- In all document pertaining to such transactions entered into by him as may be prescribed by CBDT in the interests of the revenue.

Quoting of Aadhar Number under Section 139 AA

- To be quoted on or after 01/07/2017 by every person eligible to obtain Aadhar No. in the application form for allotment of PAN and in the RoI.
- If he does not possess Aadhar No., the enrolment ID of Aadhar application form issued to him at the time of enrolment shall be quoted.

- Aadhar No. to be intimated to prescribed authority on or before the notified date, by every person who has been allotted PAN as on 01/07/2017 and who is eligible to obtain Aadhar No.

ITR Forms

ITR–1 [SAHAJ] An individual, who has income from salary, pension or interest.

ITR–2 An individual or HUF, who does not have income from business or profession.

ITR–2A An individual or HUF, who has income from one or more house property and other sources.

ITR–3 An individual or HUF, who is partner in a firm but does not have any income from his own business or profession.

ITR–4 S (SUGAM) An individual, HUF or firm, who has income under Section 44 or 44 AE.

ITR–4 An individual or HUF, who has income from his own business or profession.

ITR–5 For firm, AoP or BoI.

ITR–6 For companies

ITR–7 Assessee, who is required to submit his return U/S 139 (4) to 139 (4b).

Interest for Default in Furnishing Return of Income U/S 234 A

Interest U/S 234 A is payable, where an assessee furnishes the return of income after the due date or does not furnish the return of income.

Assessee shall be liable to pay simple interest @1% per month or part of the month for the period commencing from the date immediately following the due date and ending on the following dates

Circumstances	Ending on the Following Dates
Where the return is furnished after due date	the date of furnishing of the return
Where no return is furnished	the date of completion of assessment

However, where the assessee has paid taxes in full on or before the due date, interest U/S 234 A is not leviable.

EXAM BASED QUESTIONS

Basic Concepts of Income Tax

1 Income tax was levied in India first by the following

(a) Sir Lucas Paciolo (b) Sir Newton
(c) Sir James (d) Sir James Wilson

2 Out of the following, which expense is not an admissible expense?

(a) Bad debts (b) Sales tax
(c) Income tax (d) Excise duty

3 If any agriculture land is sold it is covered under the head

(a) capital gain
(b) income from house property
(c) agricultural income
(d) not under any head

4 Any profit earned from purchasing and selling standing crop is

(a) house property income (b) agriculture income
(c) non-agriculture income (d) All of these

5 The daily allowance received by a Member of Parliament is

(a) exempted
(b) to be included in total income for tax purposes
(c) taxable
(d) None of the above

6 The income of an educational institution on non-profit motive is exempt under which section?

(a) 10 (23C) (b) 10 (80G)
(c) 10 (10B) (d) 10 (23D)

7 Scholarship received by a student to meet the cost of education is

(a) fully taxable (b) fully exempt
(c) casual income (d) None of these

8 State, which of the following income is exempted from text?

(a) Share in income of HUF
(b) Interest on government securities
(c) Income from salaries
(d) Capital gains

9 Rate of income tax on different slabs of income in case of an individual assessee are

(a) decreasing (b) increasing
(c) constant (d) None of these

10 Tax is computed on agricultural income, when

(a) agricultural income is more than ₹ 5,000
(b) total non-agricultural income is more than exemption limit
(c) on happening of both (a) and (b)
(d) None of the above

11 Which of the following will be considered as agricultural income?

(a) Income from live stock breeding
(b) Income from cattle breeding
(c) Income from juice centre
(d) Rent received from agricultural land

12 Which of the following is non-agricultural income?

(a) Income from agriculture in Nepal
(b) Reward received from higher yield
(c) Income from letting out agricultural machinery
(d) All of the above

13 Any individual, who is resident in any previous year, in the next previous year, he shall be

(a) not-ordinarily resident (b) non-resident
(c) resident (d) Any one of the three

14 The basis of determination of total income of a person is

(a) his citizenship in India
(b) his residential status in India
(c) Both (a) and (b)
(d) None of the above

15 Income which accrue or arise outside India from a business controlled from India is taxable in case of

(a) resident only
(b) both ordinarily resident and not ordinarily resident
(c) non-resident
(d) All of the above

16 A citizen of India, who goes abroad for the purpose of employment, must stay in India to become resident at least

(a) 182 days (b) 90 days
(c) 60 days (d) 180 days

17 Income tax is levied on those individuals

(a) whose income is less than exempted limit in any previous year
(b) whose income is more than exempted limit in any previous year
(c) whose income is upto ₹ 1,00,000 in any previous year
(d) None of the above

18 Which of the following receipt is revenue in nature as per Income Tax Act?

1. When any contract is entered into in the ordinary course of business, any compensation received for its termination would be a revenue receipt.
2. A receipt under a general insurance policy may be a revenue receipt, if the policy relates to circulation asset.
3. Forfeited security deposits would be revenue receipts, where they are related to the assessee's trading activity.

Select the correct answer using the codes given below

Codes

(a) Both 1 and 2 (b) Only 3
(c) Both 2 and 3 (d) All of the above

19 Which of the following is/are agricultural income?

1. Income from growing flowers and creepers.
2. Income from dairy farming.
3. Rent for agricultural land received from sub- tenants by mortgagee in possession.

Select the correct answer using the codes given below

Codes

(a) Only 1 (b) Both 1 and 3
(c) Both 2 and 3 (d) All of the above

20 Which of the following is non-agricultural income?

(a) Income from leasing out tea estates
(b) Income from sale by the assessee of plants grown in pots
(c) Amount received in reward by a farmer for growing more crops on his field
(d) Income from sale of tobacco after drying it

21 According to Section 5 of Income Tax Act, 1961, Incomes, which accrue arise outside India, but are received directly into India are taxable in case of

(a) resident only
(b) both ordinarily resident and not ordinarily resident
(c) non-resident
(d) All of the above

22 X Ltd is an Indian company. It carries own business in Mumbai and London. The entire control and management of X Ltd is situated outside India. Three-fourth of total income of the company is from the business in London, what is the residential status of X Ltd?

(a) Resident (b) Non-resident
(c) Ordinarily resident (d) Not ordinarily resident

23 Mr P was born on 18th April, 1986 in India and later on he took the citizenship of USA. Neither his parents nor his grandparents were born in undivided India. In this Mr P shall be

(a) a person of Indian origin (b) a citizen of India
(c) a foreign national (d) None of these

24 According to Section 5 of Income Tax Act 1961, income deemed to accrue arise in India is taxable in case of

(a) resident only
(b) both ordinarily resident and not ordinarily resident
(c) non-resident
(d) All of the above

25 Which of the following statements is/are correct?

1. An assessee may enjoy different residential status for different assessment year.
2. It is not necessary that a person, who is resident in India, cannot become resident in any other country for the same assessment year.
3. Where a person is in India only for a part of a day, it will be calculated as one complete day.

Select the correct answer using the codes given below

Codes

(a) Only 1 (b) Both 1 and 2
(c) Both 1 and 3 (d) All of the above

26 Which of the following statements is/are correct?

1. Any income, which is received in India, during the previous year by any assessee, is liable to tax in India, irrespective of the residential status of the assessee and the place of accrual of such income.
2. The day the individual enters India and the day he leaves India should both be treated as stay in India for calculating residential status of a person.
3. Presence in territorial water of India would also be regarded as presence in India.

Select the correct answer using the codes given below

Codes

(a) Only 1 (b) Both 1 and 2
(c) Both 2 and 3 (d) All of the above

27 Which of the following statements is/are correct?

1. A foreign company can be a domestic company.
2. There is no difference between an Indian company and a domestic company.
3. The control and management of a company should be examined for each previous year as the company many change the place of its control and management and consequently its residential status may also change.

Select the correct answer using the codes given below

Codes

(a) Both 1 and 3 (b) Only 3
(c) Both 2 and 3 (d) All of the above

28 R Ltd, a German company, which is non-resident in India, earned the following income by way of fee for technical services. Advice about the taxability of such income in the hands of R Ltd in India.

1. Government of India paid ₹ 20,00,000 under an agreement, to be used for a project in India.
2. S Ltd, an Indian company, paid ₹ 30,00,000 for the know-how to be used in India.
3. Y Ltd, an Indian company, paid ₹ 40,00,000 for know-how acquired in Germany to be used in China.
4. Z Ltd, a non-resident company paid ₹ 24,00,000 for acquiring a know-how to be used in India for carrying on certain manufacturing business.

Select the correct answer using the codes given below

Codes

(a) 1 and 2 Taxable (b) Only 1 Taxable
(c) 1, 2 and 4 Taxable (d) 1, 2 and 3 Taxable

29 Which one of the following incomes is/are taxable?

1. A local authority has earned income from the supply of water or electricity outside its own jurisdictional area.
2. An income under the head capital gain to a local authority.
3. A daily allowance received by a Member of Parliament.
4. Income arising from the transfer of units of the Unit Trust of India or of mutual fund covered under Section 10 (23 D).

Select the correct answer using the codes given below

Codes

(a) 1 and 2 Taxable (b) Only 3 Taxable
(c) 1, 2 and 4 Taxable (d) 1, 2 and 3 Taxable

30 **Which one of the following statement is true?**

(a) Different residential status in respect of different previous years of the same assessment year not possible
(b) A resident in India cannot become resident in any other country for the same A.Y.
(c) Any sum received by an individual, as a member of a Hindu undivided family, shall be taxable in the hands of the member
(d) All of the above

31 **Dividend paid by an Indian company outside India is**

(a) taxable in india in the hands of the recipient
(b) taxable in the hands of the company and exempt in the hands of the recipient
(c) taxable outside India
(d) exempt in the hands of the recipient

32 **Which of the following incomes are exempt from tax?**

1. Dividend received from foreign company.
2. Agricultural income.
3. Income received by a foreigner in outside India.
4. Capital gain income.
5. Dividend received from Indian company.
6. Rental income of house property.

Codes

(a) 2, 3 and 4 (b) 1, 3, 5 and 6
(c) 3, 4 and 6 (d) None of the above

Computation of Taxable Income, Clubbing of Income, Deduction from Gross Total Income and Assessment

33 **Which of the following is fully taxable allowance?**

(a) Overseas allowance (b) Tribal area allowance
(c) House rent allowance (d) Dearness allowance

34 **Any profit or facility received by an employee is called**

(a) perquisites (b) gratuity
(c) wages (d) pension

35 **Amount received from unrecognised provident fund is**

(a) taxable
(b) exempted
(c) 50% taxable and 50% exempted
(d) None of the above

36 **Salary received by a partner from partnership firm will be included in income from**

(a) salary
(b) business and profession
(c) house property
(d) None of the above

37 **Which of the following is not taxable under the head salaries?**

(a) Commission received by an employee director of a company
(b) Salary received by member of the Parliament
(c) Remuneration paid to the lecturer of a college for setting a question paper by university
(d) Both (b) and (c)

38 **Due to some dispute, the salary of a person is retained by an order of the court. Then, such salary will be**

(a) included in income under the head salaries
(b) not included in income under the head salaries
(c) exempted
(d) None of the above

39 **Income from house property owned by trade union is exempt under**

(a) Section 10 (24) (b) Section 10 (10)
(c) Section 10 (20 A) (d) Section 10 (AA)

40 **On which value assessee has to pay income tax on building or land appurtenant?**

(a) Actual value (b) Actual income
(c) Annual value (d) None of these

41 **House used for self-residence comes under**

(a) Section 24 (b) Section 24 (1)
(c) Section 23 (d) Section 23 (1)

42 **Paying guest's accommodation is chargeable under**

(a) income from house property
(b) profit and gains of business and profession
(c) income from other sources
(d) None of the above

43 **Time limit to set-off the losses from house property is**

(a) 2 years (b) 6 years (c) 8 years (d) 9 years

44 **Income from house property which is owned by political party is exempt under?**

(a) Section 12 C (b) Section 13 A
(c) Section 10 (10) (d) Section 10 (24)

45 **Compulsory audit of account books is covered**

(a) Section 10 (b) Section 44 AB
(c) Section 21 (d) Section 21 AA

46 **Which of the following capital expenditure is not allowed deduction?**

(a) Purchase of machinery
(b) Purchase of furniture
(c) Purchase of land
(d) Repairing

47 **If payment of royalty is paid outside India and no tax at source has been deducted, then such expenses will be**

(a) allowed as deduction (b) disallowed
(c) exempt (d) None of these

48 For persons carrying on profession, tax audit is compulsory, if the gross receipts of the PY exceed
(a) ₹ 1 crore (b) ₹ 50 crore
(c) ₹ 25 lakh (d) ₹ 10 lakh

49 A company sold a residential house. Under which Section, the company can get exemption on long-term capital gains?
(a) Section 54 (b) Section 54D
(c) Section 54EC (d) Section 54F

50 For capital gain being long-term capital gain, an assessee should retain the asset for a period of
(a) 24 months (b) 36 months
(c) more than 36 months (d) 12 months

51 Which of the following would attract capital gains tax?
(a) Special Bearer Bond, 1991
(b) 6½% Gold Bond, 1977
(c) Stock-in-trade
(d) None of the above

52 Capital gain on shifting of industrial undertaking from urban area to any special economic zone is
(a) taxable (b) exempt
(c) partly taxable (d) partly exempt

53 The conversion of preference share into equity share
(a) does not give rise to capital gain
(b) give rise to capital gain
(c) gives rise to capital gain only, if it is LTCG
(d) None of the above

54 Bond washing transaction is done
(a) to reduce the tax liability (b) to make poor happy
(c) to give money to wife (d) None of these

55 Dividend paid by Indian company outside India as per Section 9 (1) (iv) is deemed as
(a) paid in India (b) accrued in India
(c) received in India (d) None of these

56 Family pension is taxable under the head
(a) salary
(b) income from other sources
(c) capital gain
(d) None of the above

57 Dividend from an Indian company is not taxable. It is exempt under Section.
(a) 10 (10) (b) 10 (34)
(c) 10 (2A) (d) 2 (AA)

58 Deduction in respect of contribution to pension scheme of Central Government is covered under Section
(a) 80 C (b) 80 CCC
(c) 80 CCD (d) 80 D

59 Deduction in respect of medical insurance premium is covered under Section
(a) 80 C (b) 80 D (c) 80 E (d) 80 F

60 Which of the following are allowed as 100% deduction?
(a) Prime Minister National Relief Fund
(b) Africa (Public contribution India) Fund
(c) National Defence Fund and National Children Fund
(d) Indira Gandhi Memorial Trust

61 Deduction, which are permissible from gross total income are from
(a) Section 80C to 80IA (b) Section 80C to 80IC
(c) Section 80C to 80U (d) Section 80C to 80P

62 The income arrived after deductions under Section 80C to 80U from gross total income is known as
(a) total income (b) taxable income
(c) Both (a) and (b) (d) None of these

63 The maximum amount of deduction allowed under Section 80C
(a) ₹ 80,000 (b) ₹ 90,000
(c) ₹ 1,50,000 (d) ₹ 1,10,000

64 Preliminary expenses incurred are allowed deduction in
(a) 10 equal installments
(b) 8 equal installments
(c) 5 equal installments
(d) fund

65 Deduction in respect of contribution to certain pension fund under Section 80 CCC is available
(a) only to individual, even to non-resident individual
(b) only to members of HUF
(c) only to members of AOP/BOI
(d) All of the above

66 Which assesses are allowed deduction under Section 80C?
(a) An individual or a HUF
(b) An individual and a company
(c) An individual; HUF or AOP/BOI
(d) An individual; HUF; AOP/BOI or a company

67 Deduction allowed under Section 80C, towards any sum paid an individual to effect or to keep an insurance on the life of
(a) an individual
(b) an individual spouse
(c) any child of such individual, children may be married/unmarried, dependent/not dependent
(d) All of the above

68 Deduction under Section 40(b) shall be allowed on account of salary/remuneration paid to
(a) any partner (b) major partner only
(c) working partner only (d) sleeping partner only

69 Deduction under Section 36(1) shall be allowed of those expenditure which are of
(a) capital nature
(b) revenue nature
(c) Both (a) and (b)
(d) deferred revenue nature

70 Salary, bonus, commission or remuneration due or received by a working partner from the firm is taxable under the head
(a) income from salaries
(b) income from other sources
(c) income from business and profession
(d) None of the above

71 Rent from vacant plot of land is assessable under the head
(a) income from business and profession
(b) income from other sources
(c) income from house property
(d) income from capital gain

72 If any of income from house property is received in previous year, then it is chargeable to tax under lead
(a) income from capital gain
(b) income from business and profession
(c) income from house property
(d) will not be chargeable

73 In which of the following cases, the house property income is exempt from tax?
(a) House property of university
(b) House property of registered trade union
(c) House property of local authority
(d) All of the above

74 Which of the following expense/loss is not admissible as deduction while computing income from business and profession?
(a) Stock-in-trade lost in fire ₹ 20,000
(b) Entertainment expenses ₹ 10,000
(c) Commission of ₹ 2,000 paid in order to receive business
(d) Gift on the marriage of an employee

75 Which of the following statements are correct?
1. 30% depreciation is allowed on neon sign board.
2. Animals are used for business purposes. Hence, depreciation shall be allowed on them.
3. For the purpose of taxation, there should not be and indeed there is no distinction made between legal and illegal business.

Select the correct answer using the codes given below
Codes
(a) Only 1 (b) Both 1 and 2
(c) Only 3 (d) Both 1 and 3

76 In which of the cases the amount withdraw form Site Restoration Account shall not be taxable?
1. Amount withdrawn for the purpose specified in the scheme
2. Closure of business
3. Death of an assessee
4. Partition of HUF
5. Dissolution of a firm
6. Liquidation of a company

Select the correct answer using the codes given below
Codes
(a) Only 1 (b) 1,2, 3 and 5
(c) 1, 3, 4 and 6 (d) 1, 4, 5 and 6

77 Which of the following statements are correct?
1. Provision made for sales tax is admissible deduction.
2. Wealth tax paid by a company is a deductible expense.
3. Contribution to a political party is a deductible expense.

Select the correct answer using the codes given below
Codes
(a) Only 1 (b) Both 1 and 2
(c) Only 2 (d) None of the above

78 Which of the following statements are correct?
1. Charity received from customers is not business income
2. In connection with the statutory income tax preceding, expenses upto ₹ 20, 000 are admissible
3. Expenses incurred for issuing share are deductible

Select the correct answer using the codes given below
Codes
(a) Only 1 (b) Both 1 and 2
(c) Both 1 and 3 (d) All of the above

79 Deduction under Section 80C to 80U are not allowed from the following incomes, although these incomes are part of gross total income.
1. Salary income
2. Long-term capital gains
3. Winnings of lotteries, race etc
4. Income by way of interest on safe deposit
5. Short-term capital gain on transfer of equity shares and units of equity oriented fund through a recognised stock exchange

Select the correct answer using the codes given below
Codes
(a) Only 1 (b) Both 1 and 2
(c) 2, 3, 4 and 5 (d) 2, 3 and 5

80 Consider the following statements.
1. The aggregate amount of deduction under Sections 8oC to 8oU can exceed gross total income.
2. If a deduction is allowed under the above sections to the AoP or BoI, then deductions for the same payment/income will not be allowed to the members of the AoP/BoI.
3. Deduction is allowed only when it is claimed in his return under the heading "C Deductions in respect of certain incomes."

Which of the statement(s) given above is/are correct?
Codes
(a) Only 1 (b) Both 1 and 2
(c) Both 1 and 3 (d) Both 2 and 3

81 Donation made to following are eligible for 100% deduction without any qualifying limit.
1. National Defence Fund set-up by the Central Government
2. National Sports Fund set-up by the Central Government
3. Jawaharlal Nehru Memorial Fund

4. National Illness Assistance Fund
5. National Children's Fund

Select the correct answer using the codes given below

Codes

(a) 1, 2 and 4 (b) 1, 2, 3 and 4
(c) 1, 2, 4 and 5 (d) All of the above

82 Which of the expenses on scientific research related to the business are allowed a deduction in the PY of commencement of the business, although incurred within 2 years immediately before the commencement of the business?

1. Any revenue expense on scientific research.
2. Payment of salary to employee engaged in scientific research.
3. Purchase of material used in scientific research.
4. Repair and maintenance expense on the asset acquired for scientific research.
5. Land acquired for scientific research.
6. Building constructed for scientific research.
7. Plant and machinery acquired for scientific research.

Select the correct answer using the codes given below

Codes

(a) 1, 3, 4 and 7 (b) 3, 4, 5 and 6
(c) 2, 3, 7 and 6 (d) 3, 4, 5 and 7

83 According to Section 80G, donations made to, which of the following are eligible for 100% deduction without any qualifying limit?

1. National Defence Fund set-up by the Central Government
2. Prime Minister's National Relief Fund
3. Prime Minister's Armenia Earthquake Relief Fund
4. Africa (Public Contributions-India) Fund
5. National Foundation for Communal Harmony
6. Prime Minister's Drought Relief Fund
7. National Children's Fund
8. Indira Gandhi Memorial Trust

Select the correct answer using the codes given below

Codes

(a) 1, 4, 6 and 8 (b) 4, 5, 7 and 8
(c) 1,2, 3, 4 and 5 (d) 6,7 and 8

84 Gross total income includes

(a) 3 heads of income (b) 4 heads of income
(c) 5 heads of income (d) 6 heads of income

85 Education cess and secondary higher education cess is liable on

(a) individual (b) company (c) all assessee (d) HUF

86 Age of senior citizen as per income tax

(a) 80 years or more (b) 55 years or more
(c) 65 years or more (d) 60 years or more

87 The total income of the assessee has been computed at ₹ 1,53,494.90 after rounding off, the total income will be taken as

(a) ₹ 1,53,500 (b) ₹ 1,53,490
(c) ₹ 1,53,495 (d) ₹ 1,53,400

88 Income tax or demand notice or refund order is rounded off to

(a) nearest ten rupees
(b) nearest on rupee
(c) no rounding off of tax is done
(d) nearest hundred rupees

89 The aggregate of income computed under each head, after giving effect to the provision for clubbing of income and set off of losses is known as

(a) gross total income (b) net total income
(c) taxable income (d) net taxable income

90 Tax rates on the basis of slab system are applicable for the following assessee.

(a) Company
(b) Partnership firm
(c) Limited liability partnership firm
(d) Hindu Undivided Family

91 Which of the following is true for reverse merger?

(a) Profits making company merges into loss making company
(b) The sick company retains its same
(c) Losses could be carried forward
(d) All of the above

92 Regular assessment means assessment made under Section

(a) 143(3)
(b) 144
(c) Both (a) and (b)
(d) None of the above

93 Interest under Section 234B is payable by an assessee due to the following reason

(a) defaults in furnishing return of income
(b) defaults in payable of advance tax
(c) defaults in installment of advance tax
(d) defaults due to non-deduction tax at source

94 Interest under Section 234A is payable by an assessee due to the following reason

(a) defaults in furnishing return of income
(b) defaults in payable of advance tax
(c) defaults in installments of advance tax
(d) defaults due to non-deduction tax at source

95 Which of the following is the type of assessment?

(a) Self-assessment
(b) Regular assessment
(c) Best judgement assessment
(d) All of the above

96 In which of the following assessment procedure, assessees compute his taxable income as well as tax on it?

(a) Best judgement assessment
(b) Re-assessment
(c) Self-assessment
(d) Regular assessment

97 Assessment of escaping income in known as
(a) re-assessment
(b) best judgement assessment
(c) self-assessment
(d) regular assessment

98 Which of the following reason shall be deemed as the income has escaped assessment?
(a) Less income in the return
(b) Taxable income has been assessed less
(c) Shown more deductions and rebates for which he is entitled
(d) All of the above

99 Any mistake apparent from record passed by the authority can be rectified within
(a) 3 years (b) 4 years (c) 5 years (d) 6 years

100 Rectification of mistake is covered under Section
(a) 144 (b) 154
(c) 164 (d) 174

101 Which authority has right to rectify the mistakes?
(a) Lower authority
(b) The authority which has passed the order
(c) Higher authority
(d) Any of the above

102 Revision of assessment ordered is covered under Section
(a) 145 (b) 155 (c) 263 (d) 175

103 Intimation of loss is covered under Section
(a) 150 (b) 155 (c) 157 (d) 159

104 Application for applying a PAN is given in form no.
(a) 48C (b) 49A
(c) 42B (d) 54

105 Regular assessment in respect of any income is to be made in a later assessment year, but .... on such income is payable in the previous year itself.
(a) interest (b) tax
(c) penalty (d) sucharge

106 Return of income is submitted under which of the following sections?
(a) U/S 139(3) (b) U/S 139(1)
(c) U/S 145 (d) U/S 143

107 Notice of demand is served under which Section?
(a) 139(1) (b) 154 (c) 139(3) (d) 156

108 The best judgement assessment is done under which of the following sections?
(a) U/S 144 (b) U/S 139(A)
(c) U/S 45 (d) U/S 143

109 Interest under Section 201(1A) is payable by an assessee due to the following reason
(a) defaults in furnishing return of income
(b) defaults in payable of advance tax
(c) defaults in installment of advance tax
(d) defaults due to non-deduction tax at source

110 Quoting of Permanent Account Number is mandatory is case of a contract for sale or purchase of securities exceeding value of
(a) ₹ 50,000 (b) ₹ 1,00,000
(c) ₹ 1,50,000 (d) ₹ 2,00,000

111 Quoting of Permanent Account Number is mandatory in case of sale or purchase of any immovable property valued at
(a) ₹ 2,00,000 or more (b) ₹ 3,00,000 or more
(c) ₹ 4,00,000 or more (d) ₹ 5,00,000 or more

112 Quoting of PAN is compulsory in case of sale/purchase of any immovable property valued at
(a) ₹ 5 lakh or more (b) ₹ 10 lakh or more
(c) ₹ 15 lakh or more (d) ₹ 20 lakh or more

113 In case of issuance of PAN and card, the maximum period should be .... from the date of application.
(a) 2 months (b) 3 months (c) 4 months (d) 5 months

114 Income arising to a minor daughter shall be
(a) clubbed with income of that person whose total income is higher
(b) clubbed with the income of her spouse
(c) exempt from tax
(d) assessed in lands of minor married daughter

115 Following income of the member of AoP/BoI will be deemed to income of AoP/BoI
(a) profit (b) remuneration
(c) interest (d) All of these

116 Loss from speculation business can be set-off against
(a) speculation business income
(b) any business income
(c) cannot be set-off
(d) only 20% loss can be set-off

117 Loss from lottery can be set-off against
(a) income from lottery (b) any other business
(c) cannot be set-off (d) None of these

118 Set-off of losses of the firms is covered under Section
(a) 72 (b) 75 (c) 77 (d) 78

119 For how many assessment years unabsorbed depreciation can be carried forward for set-off?
(a) 5 years (b) 7 years
(c) 8 years (d) Unspecified period

120 Unabsorbed speculation business loss can be carried forward only for a period of
(a) 4 assessment years (b) 6 assessment years
(c) 7 assessment years (d) 8 assessment years

121 Losses can be carried forward by
(a) successors, if he had purchased the business
(b) heirs, if they got the business from inheritance
(c) Both (a) and (b)
(d) None of the above

122 Which of the losses cannot be carried forward, if the return of loss is not submitted in time?
(a) Capital loss
(b) Business loss (speculative or otherwise)
(c) Loss from the activity of owing and maintaining race horses
(d) All of the above

123 Total income of an assessee is
(a) gross total income
(b) computed by deducting from the gross total income, all deductions under Section 80 C to 80 U
(c) computed by deducting from the gross total income, all deductions permissible under Chapter VIA of the Income Tax Act
(d) Both (b) and (c)

124 The following income is included in the total income of an individual, but a rebate of income tax is allowed thereon
(a) profit of a firm
(b) profit of HUF
(c) agriculture income
(d) long-term capital gains

125 Which of the following statement is true?
1. The tax rate on STCG is 10%.
2. The tax rate on LTCG is 15%.
3. The tax rate on casual income is 30%.
4. The tax rate on dividend received from domestic company is 10%.

Codes
(a) 1 and 2 are true
(b) 2 and 4 are true
(c) 3 and 4 are true
(d) All statements are true

126 Which of the following statements are incorrect?
1. Income tax is grouped in various slabs.
2. Income tax is not charged to progressive rate on increasing slabs of income.
3. A deemed assessee is liable to pay tax on behalf of another person.
4. Assessment year begins as on 1st January of every year.
5. Certain amount of income tax is exempt from income tax.

Select the correct answer using the codes given below
Codes
(a) Both 1 and 3
(b) Both 2 and 4
(c) Both 1, 3 and 5
(d) All of the above

127 Which of the following statement's are correct?
1. Assessment year is a period of 12 months.
2. Income tax is distributed between State and Central Government.
3. There are 6 heads of income under Income Tax Act.
4. Income earned in a year is taxable in that year only.
5. Total income of an assessee cannot be computed unless his residential status is known.

Select the correct answer using the codes given below
Codes
(a) Both 1 and 5
(b) Both 2, 3 and 5
(c) Both 1, 3 and 5
(d) All of the above

128 Which of the following income are taxable under income tax?
1. Short-term capital gain
2. Providend fund receipt
3. Capital gain on sale of shares under Section 10(38)
4. Income of local authority
5. Interest received on government securities
6. Money found on the road

Select the correct answer using the codes given below
Codes
(a) 1, 3 and 5
(b) 1, 5 and 6
(c) 2, 4, 5 and 6
(d) Both 4 and 5

129 Which of the following statement(s) is/are true?
1. Section 147 is related to re-assessment.
2. Section 148 is related to regular assessment.
3. Section 145 is related to best judgement assessment.
4. Section 140A is related to self-assessment.
(a) Both 1 and 3 are true
(b) Both 1 and 4 are true
(c) Both 2 and 3 are true
(d) Both 3 and 4 are true

130 If the amount paid by the assessee falls short of the aggregate of tax and interest, the amount, so paid shall be adjusted towards
(a) firstly by interest payable, then the balance, if any
(b) firstly by balance and then the interest payable, if any
(c) proportioned amount of interest and balance
(d) interest first and then with balance or *vice versa* rest at the discretion of the assessing officer

131 Income of minor is clubbed however the clubbing provision is not applicable if
(a) minor is handicapped as specified under Section 80U
(b) minor is a married daughter
(c) parents are separated
(d) minor is a married son

132 According to Section 60, income is clubbed if
(a) asset is transferred without transferring income
(b) asset yielding income is transferred as revocable transfer
(c) asset yielding income is transferred as irrevocable transfer
(d) income is transferred without transferring asset yielding income

133 In case where profits are insufficient to absorb brought forward losses, current depreciation and current business losses, the same should be deducted in the order
1. Current scientific research expenditure [Section 35(1)].
2. Current depreciation [Section 32(1)].
3. Brought forward business losses [Section 72(1)].
4. Unabsorbed depreciation [Section 32(2)].
5. Unabsorbed investment allowance [Section 32A(3) (b)].
6. Unabsorbed development allowance [Section 33A(2)(b)].

7. Unabsorbed family planning promotion expenditure [Section 36(1)(I)].
8. Unabsorbed scientific research capital expenditure [Section 35(4)].

Codes

(a) 1, 3, 2, 7, 4, 6, 5, 8 (b) 1, 2, 3, 7, 4, 8, 6, 5
(c) 1, 2, 3, 4, 7, 5, 6, 8 (d) 3, 2, 7, 1, 8, 4, 5, 6

TDS, Advance Payment of Tax and E-Filing of IT Return

134 TDS on payments to contractor is covered under Section
(a) 194 B (b) 194 D
(c) 194 C (d) 188

135 Specified person shall measure as per Section 194C
(a) Central Government (b) Company
(c) Trust (d) All of these

136 Rate of deduction of tax for winning of lottery is
(a) 10% (b) 20% (c) 30% (d) 40%

137 A person is liable to pay interest, if advance tax paid by him is less than
(a) 99% or less (b) 92% or less
(c) 95% or less (d) 90%

138 Signing of return is covered under Section
(a) 130 (b) 140 (c) 150 (d) 170

139 Form issued for TDS on salary is
(a) Form 16 (b) Form 16A
(c) Form 12BA (d) Form 10E

140 First instalment of advance tax payable falls due on or before
(a) 15th June (b) 15th July
(c) 18th June (d) 16th April

141 Second instalment of advance tax payable falls due on or before
(a) 15th October (b) 31st March
(c) 15th September (d) None of these

142 Third instalment of advance tax payable falls due on or before
(a) 15th October (b) 31st March
(c) 15th September (d) 15th December

143 Interest for default in payment of advance tax is covered under Section
(a) 324 A (b) 234 B
(c) 166 C (d) 254 C

144 Rate of interest on advance tax, if it is paid less than 90%
(a) 2% per month (b) 1% per month
(c) 3% per month (d) 5% per month

145 Interest for deferment of advance tax is covered under Section
(a) 248 B (b) 264 C (c) 234 C (d) 228 A

146 For an individual, having income from salary or family pension and interest prescribed form
(a) ITR-1 (b) ITR-2 (c) ITR-3 (d) ITR-4

147 Assessee who is 62 years old, has to file a return of income if his gross total income is in excess of
(a) ₹ 2,00,000 (b) ₹ 2,50,000
(c) ₹ 3,00,000 (d) ₹ 10,00,000

148 Due date for filing return of in case of firm, whose accounts are required to be audited is
(a) 31st July (b) 31st August
(c) 30th September (d) 31st October

149 Assessment U/S 143 shall be computed from the end of relevant assessment year
(a) within 18 months (b) within 21 months
(c) within 12 months (d) within 30 months

150 Getting permanent account number is compulsory for
(a) income tax assessee (b) importer
(c) assessee under section tax (d) All of these

151 Who is empowered to exempt any class or classes of person from the requirement of furnishing a return?
(a) State Government (b) Central Government
(c) Both (a) and (b) (d) None of these

152 Revised return is covered under Section
(a) 140 (b) 139(5) (c) 139(2) (d) 140(4)

153 Who will sign return of income of HUF?
(a) Any member (b) Karta
(c) Chartered Accountant (d) None of these

154 Who will sign return of income in case of political party?
(a) Chief Executive Officer (b) Any Member
(c) Prime Minister (d) None of these

155 The due date for filing return of income of the trust would be
(a) 30th October (b) 30th September
(c) 31st December (d) 31st March

156 Which of the following will make return defective, if not attached?
(a) Audit report
(b) Cost audit report under Section 233B of Companies Act
(c) Proprietor business (Personal account)
(d) All of the above

157 Assessee other than companies having income under PGBP are required of file return in
(a) ITR-I (b) ITR-4 or IRR-5
(c) ITR-2 (d) ITR-7 or ITR-8

158 The person under statutory obligation to file return
(a) company or firm
(b) any university/college
(c) chief executive officer of every political party
(d) All of the above

159 Due date of furnishing return of income in case of a company is
(a) 31st July of the assessment year
(b) 30th November of the assessment year
(c) 30th October of the assessment year
(d) 30th September of the assessment year

160 The time to rectify the defect in return given by assessing officer, after given intimation of such defect by him is
(a) 10 days (b) 15 days
(c) 20 days (d) 1 month

161 Due date of furnishing return of income in case of a non-working partner shall be .... of the assessment year, whether the account of the firm are required to be audited or not.
(a) 31st July (b) 30th September
(c) 30th October (d) 30th November

162 Which of the following statement is true?
1. The due date of first instalment of advance tax is 15th July.
2. The due date of second instalment of advance tax is 15th September.
3. The due date of third instalment of advance tax is 15th January.
4. The due date of final instalment of advance tax is 15th March.

Codes
(a) Both 1 and 2 are true
(b) Both 2 and 4 are true
(c) 1, 2 and 4 are true
(d) 2, 3 and 4 are true

163 In case of salary, the liability to deduct tax at source arise
(a) when employees account is credited with the salary due to him, which due to some reason not paid
(b) only at the time of payment
(c) when it is due or at the time of payment
(d) only in the last three months of the financial year

164 No tax shall be deducted where the amount of winning from each lottery, crossword puzzle, card game etc does not exceed
(a) ₹ 50,000 (b) ₹ 20,000
(c) ₹ 10,000 (d) ₹ 5,000

165 The rate of TDS on income from winning from lottery, crossword puzzle, card game is
(a) 15% + Education cess + SHEC
(b) 20% + Education cess + SHEC
(c) 25% + Surcharge + Education cess + SHEC
(d) 30%

166 No tax is to be deducted at source, where the aggregate amount of such interest to be paid or credited to the account of payee during the financial year does not exceed
(a) ₹ 20,000 (b) ₹ 15,000
(c) ₹ 40,000 (d) ₹ 5,000

167 Tax is .... at source by the seller from the buyer at the time of debiting the amount to account of the buyer or the receipt of payment whichever is earlier.
(a) deducted (b) deposited (c) payable (d) collected

168 If assessee is a government servant or an employee in company, cooperative society or university etc, and entitled for relief under Section 89, then he may furnish to his employer such particular in form.
(a) 15G (b) 15H (c) 10E (d) 12BA

169 Form 15G or 15H shall not be valid if it does not contain the PAN of the declarant. In case any declaration becomes invalid, the deductor shall deduct the tax
(a) @ 10% (b) @ 15% (c) @ 20% (d) @ 25%

170 Amount of advance tax paid on due date on or before December 15th by assessee is
(a) 75% of advance tax payable
(b) 30% of advance tax payable
(c) 10% of advance tax payable
(d) 5% of advance tax payable

171 Fourth instalment of advance tax payable falls due on or before
(a) 15th October (b) 15th March
(c) 15th September (d) None of these

172 Advance tax shall be payable during the financial year, only when the amount of such advance tax payable by the assessee during that year is
(a) ₹ 10,000 or more (b) ₹ 20,000 or more
(c) ₹ 30,000 or more (d) ₹ 50,000 or more

173 Form for filing the returns of income for individuals having income from salary/pension/income from house property is
(a) ITR-1 SAHAJ (b) ITR-2
(c) ITR-3 (d) ITR-4S SUGAM

174 The 5th character of the PAN indicate
(a) first letter of the first name of the assessee
(b) first letter of the middle name of the assessee
(c) last letter of the first name of the assessee
(d) first letter of the last name of the assessee

175 Consider the following statements.
1. From 1st June, 2006 onwards, the assessing officer has the power, inter alia, to allot PAN to any person by whom no tax is payable.
2. A tax return preparer can be an individual.
3. CBDT conducts various courses at different computer centres of the department to build up/in house expertise in the field of computers at various operational levels.

Which of the statements given above is/are correct

Codes
(a) Both 1 and 3 (b) Only 3
(c) Both 2 and 3 (d) All of the above

176 Consider the following statements.

1. E-filing of return can filed without digital signature as well.
2. PAN can be used to pay the TDS deducted into government account.
3. IN 1972, system of Permanent Account Number was introduced.

Which of the statement(s) given above is/are correct?

Codes

(a) Both 1 and 3
(b) Only 3
(c) Both 2 and 3
(d) All of the above

177 A tax return preparer can be an individual, other than

1. any officer of a scheduled bank with which the assessee maintains a current account or has other regular dealings.
2. any legal practitioner, who is entitled to practice in any Civil Court in India.
3. a Chartered Accountant.
4. an employee of the 'specified class or classes of persons'.

Select the correct answer using the codes given below

Codes

(a) 1, 2 and 3
(b) Only 3
(c) Both 2 and 3
(d) All of the above

178 Which of the following are the types of E-filing of return?

1. E-filing through e-return intermediary.
2. E-file without digital signature.
3. E-file with digital signature.

Select the correct answer using the codes given below

Codes

(a) Both 1 and 2
(b) Only 3
(c) Both 2 and 3
(d) All of the above

179 What is the time limit for filing revised return at present year?

(a) With in the assessment
(b) Before the expired of one year from the end of the relevant assessment year
(c) Before the expiry of two years from the end of the relevant assessment year
(d) Before the completion of assessment even if it takes more than one year from the end of the relevant assessment year

180 Intimation for assessment on the basis of return U/S 143(1) cannot be sent after the expiry of

(a) one year from the end of the relevant assessment year
(b) one year from the end of financial year in which return is made
(c) two years from the end of relevant assessment year
(d) two years from the end of financial year in which the return in made

181 If recipient of income fails to furnish his Permanent Account Number to deductor of tax, the tax shall be deducted

(a) at the rate specified in the relevant section
(b) at the rate or rates in forces
(c) at the rate of 20%
(d) higher of the above rate

182 Losses can be set-off and carry forward only if

(a) return of loss is filed under Section 139(1)
(b) a person has informed to income tax department on phone
(c) a person has huge loss
(d) None of the above

Miscellaneous

Directions (Q. Nos. 183-189) *Following questions consists of two statements, Statement I and Statement II. You have to examine these two statements carefully and select the correct answer by using the codes given below.*

Codes

(a) Statement I is correct, but Statement II is incorrect
(b) Both statements are correct
(c) Statement I is incorrect, but Statement II is correct
(d) Both statements are incorrect

183 **Statement** I The maximum deduction for Site restoration fund under Section 33 ABA shall be 20% of the profits from such business.

Statement II The maximum deduction for site restoration fund under Section 33 ABA shall be 20% of the amount deposited in the scheme.

184 **Statement** I Capital receipts are exempts from tax unless they are expressly taxable.

Statement II Revenue receipts are taxable unless they are expressly exempt from tax.

185 **Statement** I Receipt under general insurance policy may be a capital receipt, if the policy relates to a capital asset.

Statement II Profits from capital, which is exhausted or consumed during the process of realisation are chargeable to tax.

186 **Statement** I As per Section 194C of the Income tax Act, 1961, all association of persons and body of individuals are liable to deduct tax at source from specified payments made to resident contractors.

Statement II The rate of TDS applicable for payment made on 28.02.2011 to non-individual sub-contractor, as per Section 194C, is 2%.

187 **Statement** I In case of firm (if audit is required under Section 44AB) and companies, return should be submitted in electronic format with or without digital signature.

Statement II ITR-7 form is required for person including companies to furnish return under Section 139(4A)/(4B)/(4C)/(4D) and can be submitted only in paper format.

188 **Statement** I Individual, who is not in India, can sigh the return of income from outside India.

Statement II An individual, who is not in India, his return can be signed any person holding a valid power of attorney and duly authorised by such individual.

189 **Statement** I Belated return of income for the assessment year 2018-19 can be filed on or before 31st March, 2020, where no assessment has been made.

Statement II Electronic furnishing of income tax return in approved computer readable media can be furnished under Sub-section (1B) of Section 139 of the Income Tax Act, 1961.

Directions (Q. Nos. 190-195) *In the questions given below are two statements labelled as Assertion (A) and Reason (R). In the context of the two statements, which of the following is correct?*

Codes

(a) Both (A) and (R) are true and (R) is the correct explanation of (A)

(b) Both (A) and (R) are true, but (R) is not the correct explanation of (A)

(c) (A) is true, but (R) is false

(d) (A) is false, but (R) is true

190 **Assertion** (A) The amount of tax deducted should be deposited by the deduction in the government treasury within the time limit.

Reason (R) Form 16 and 16 A can be prepared without valid PAN number.

191 **Assertion** (A) An assessee can pay his tax on the basis of his self assessment.

Reason (R) Only 20 to 3% returns are went for scrutiny for the detailed checking of self assessment returns.

192 **Assertion** (A) Expension of business in always profitable than outsourcing.

Reason (R) Expension of business helps the companies to keep the trade secrates intact.

193 **Assertion** (A) Companies can save taxes by replacing its old machines with the new ones.

Reason (R) There is a provision of additional depreciation in Income Tax Act on purchase of new machines.

194 **Assertion** (A) Income tax is computed upon net taxable income of the current year.

Reason (R) Income tax is paid in current assessment year.

195 **Assertion** (A) Distribution of income from income tax is done among central and different states based on the recommendations of Finance Commission.

Reason (R) Income tax is levied and collected by the Central Government.

196 **Assertion** (A) A person can not be liable to pay income tax for the income earned by the another person.

Reason (R) Income tax department is governed by the CBDT.

Which of the following is correct?

Codes

(a) Both (A) and (R) are true

(b) Both (A) and (R) are false

(c) (A) is true, but (R) is false

(d) (R) is true, but (A) is false

197 Match the following.

	List I		List II
A.	.... means accumulated wealth	1.	Flow
B.	Capital is	2.	Capital
C.	.... is one, which is turned over, and in the process of being turned over yields income or loss.	3.	Fund
D.	Revenue is	4.	Circulating Capital

Codes

	A	B	C	D		A	B	C	D
(a)	2	3	4	1	(b)	4	3	2	1
(c)	2	4	3	1	(d)	4	2	3	1

198 Match the following.

	List I		List II
A.	Deduction in respect of income of cooperative societies	1.	100% of such income or ₹ 3,00,000, whichever is less
B.	Deduction in respect of royalty on patent	2.	Maximum of ₹ 10,000
C.	Deduction in respect of interest on deposits in saving account	3.	100% of profit, but in some case amount is fixed at ₹ 50,000/₹ 1,00,000
D.	Deduction in respect of contribution to certain provident funds	4.	Maximum ₹ 1,50,000

Codes

	A	B	C	D		A	B	C	D
(a)	3	1	2	4	(b)	1	3	2	4
(c)	3	1	2	4	(d)	1	3	4	2

199 Match the following.

List I	List II
A. House rent allowance	1. Taxable income
B. Casual income	2. A perquisite
C. Collection charges on interest on securities	3. A deduction from income
D. Best judgement assessment capital gain	4. A step taken by 'ex authorities'
	5. Is taxable income
	6. Party taxable income

Codes

	A	B	C	D		A	B	C	D
(a)	6	5	1	3	(b)	4	5	3	1
(c)	2	5	3	4	(d)	6	5	3	4

200 Match the following.

List I	List II
A. Individual more than 80 years age	1. ₹ 2,50,000
B. Individual ago between 60 to 80	2. Nil
C. Other individual	3. ₹ 3,00,000
D. Cooperative society	4. ₹ 5,00,00

Codes

	A	B	C	D		A	B	C	D
(a)	4	1	3	2	(b)	4	3	1	2
(c)	3	4	2	1	(d)	1	2	4	3

201 Match the following.

List I	List II
A. Self assessment	1. Section 143(3)
B. Scrutiny assessment	2. Section 147
C. Best judgement assessment	3. Section 144
D. Income escaping assessment	4. Section 140A

Codes

	A	B	C	D		A	B	C	D
(a)	4	1	2	3	(b)	3	1	4	2
(c)	1	4	2	3	(d)	3	4	2	1

202 Match the following.

List I	List II
A. ITR-2	1. For a company other than a company claiming exemption under Section 11
B. ITR-6	2. For presumptive business income covered under Section 44AD and 44AE
C. ITR-7	3. For a person including a company whether or not registered under Section 25 of the Companies Act, 1956
D. ITR-4S SUGAM	4. For individual and HUF not having income from business of profession

Codes

	A	B	C	D		A	B	C	D
(a)	4	1	2	3	(b)	4	1	3	2
(c)	3	2	4	1	(d)	2	1	4	3

PREVIOUS YEARS' QUESTIONS

December 2018

1 Given below are two statements, one labelled as Assertion (A) and the other labelled as Reason (R). Read the statements and choose the correct answer using the code given below.

Assertion (A) Among all methods of charging depreciation on fixed assets, diminishing balance method is the best method.

Reason (R) Diminishing balance method of charging depreciation has been permitted under the Income Tax Act, 1961 for claiming deduction for depreciation.

Codes

(a) Both (A) and (R) are correct and (R) is the correct explanation of (A)
(b) Both (A) and (R) are correct, but (R) is not the correct explanation of (A)
(c) (A) is correct, but (R) is not correct
(d) (A) is incorrect, but (R) is correct

2 Match the items of List I with the items of List II and choose the correct answer from the code given below.

List I	List II
A. Compensation received by an employee from his employer on termination of job	1. Exemption upto specified limit
B. Pension received by the widow of an employee	2. Profits in lieu of salary
C. Foreign allowance for rendering services abroad	3. Income from other sources
D. Children hostel allowance	4. Fully exempt from tax

Codes

	A	B	C	D
(a)	3	4	2	1
(b)	2	3	4	1
(c)	2	4	3	1
(d)	4	3	1	2

3 Under Section 194 IB of the Income Tax Act, 1961 an individual or HUF (who is not required to get his accounts audited U/S 44 AB) who is responsible for paying to a resident any rent, shall deduct income tax, for the use of any land and building or both, if the rent exceeds

(a) ₹ 50,000 per month (b) ₹ 40,000 per month
(c) ₹ 25,000 per month (d) ₹ 15,000 per month

4 Which one of the following is agricultural income under Income Tax Act?

(a) Income from the land used for storing agricultural produce
(b) Dividend from a company engaged in agriculture
(c) Income from dairy farm, poultry farm etc
(d) Income from the sale of replanted trees where denuded parts of the forest are replanted and subsequent operations in forestry are carried out

5 On fulfilling certain conditions, for an undertaking set up in special economic zones, deduction under Section 10 AA of the Income Tax Act is allowed for

(a) 5 years (b) 10 years
(c) 15 years (d) unlimited period

6 Given is the information related to a house :

Municipal Value (M. V.)	₹ 1,50,000
Fair Rent	₹ 1,80,000
Standard Rent	₹ 1,60,000
Actual Rent	₹ 20,000 p.m.

Municipal tax paid by owner is 20% of M.V. Unrealised rent ₹ 40,000 (conditions of rule 4 satisfied). What is the annual value of the house?

(a) ₹ 1,50,000 (b) ₹ 1,60,000
(c) ₹ 1,70,000 (d) ₹ 2,10,000

July 2018

7 Which one of the following is agricultural income under the Income Tax Act, 1961 ?

(a) Interest on arrears of rent in respect of agricultural land
(b) Interest received by a money-lender in the form of agricultural produce
(c) Income from sale of trees of forest which are of spontaneous growth and in relation to which forestry operations alone are performed
(d) Interest on capital received by a partner from the firm engaged in agricultural operations

8 Under the Income Tax Act, 1961 "block of assets" for the purpose of charging depreciation means

(a) value of all the assets after depreciation
(b) value of all tangible assets after charging depreciation
(c) value of all those assets to which one rate of depreciation is applicable
(d) gross value of machinery and plant less accumulated depreciation

9 The maximum amount of exemption of compensation received at the time of voluntary retirement U/S 10(10C) of the Income Tax Act, 1961, is

(a) ₹ 1,00,000
(b) ₹ 2,50,000
(c) ₹ 5,00,000
(d) ₹ 10,00,000

10 Which one of the following statements is not correct with reference to the assessment of firms?

(a) All partnership firms formed under the Indian Partnership Act, 1932, are assessed as firms under the Income Tax Act, 1961
(b) Income of a firm is taxable at a flat rate of 30% without any exemption
(c) Partners' share in the income of a firm is not chargeable to tax in the hands of partners
(d) Remuneration paid to partners of a firm (assessed as such) is allowed as deduction subject to statutory limit

11 The due date of first instalment of advance tax by assessees other than companies is

(a) 15th April (b) 15th June
(c) 15th September (d) 15th December

12 Which one of the following items is not allowed as deduction while computing income from business and profession?

(a) Fees paid to the lawyer for drafting partnership deed
(b) Loss due to embezzlement by an employee
(c) Legal expenses paid to protect the building of the business
(d) Cost of installing a new telephone

November 2017

13 Dividends declared by Unit Trust of India or by mutual fund is

(a) fully exempt in the hands of unit holders
(b) fully taxable in the hands of unit holders
(c) fully exempt in the hands of individual unit holders and fully taxable in the hands of institutional unit holders
(d) Included in the gross total income but a deduction is allowed under Section 80 L

14 Match the items of List I with the items of List II and choose the correct answer from the code given below

List I (Types of Income)	List II (Heads of Income)
A. Salary, bonus, commission etc received by a working partner from the firm	1. Income from other Sources
B. Pension received by the widow of a government employee	2. Income from (short-term) Capital Gains

List I (Types of Income)	List II (Heads of Income)
C. Profits on the sale of machinery used in business	3. Income from Capital Gains
D. Compensation received from the government on compulsory acquisition of land and profit earned	4. Income from Business and Profession
	5. Income from Salaries

Select the correct answer using the codes given below

Codes

	A	B	C	D		A	B	C	D
(a)	5	2	1	3	(b)	4	2	3	5
(c)	5	4	3	2	(d)	4	1	2	3

15 Which of the following will be considered as tax planning effort?

1. Mr. A purchased a house for self-residence of ₹80 lakh by taking a loan of ₹60 lakh from SBI at 10% interest, instead of using his own funds.
2. Mr. A made investment in purchasing 12% redeemable debentures of TISCO worth ₹ 1.50 lakh
3. Mr. A purchased 100 gram gold biscuits of ₹ 2.5 lakh from SBI on the occasion of Diwali.
4. Mr. A invested ₹ 1 crore in purchasing 5 acres of agricultural land in his native village in Gaya.

Secect the correct answer using the codes given below

Codes

(a) Both 1 and 2 (b) Both 2 and 3
(c) Both 1 and 4 (d) Both 3 and 4

16 Assertion (A) If the interest is payable outside India, tax must be deducted at source.

Reason (R) If tax has not been deducted at source, the amount paid as interest will not be allowed as a deduction in computing business income.

Codes

(a) Both (A) and (R) are correct and (R) is the correct explanation of (A)
(b) Both (A) and (R) are correct, but (R) is not the correct explanation of (A)
(c) (A) is correct, but (R) is wrong
(d) (A) is wrong, but (R) is correct

17 Under the Income Tax Act, 1961 the education cess of (2% + 1%) is calculated on the amount of

(a) Income Tax
(b) Income Tax Plus Surcharge (if any)
(c) Gross Total Income
(d) Taxable Income

18 Exemption, under Section 54F of the Income Tax Act, 1961, shall not be allowed if the assessee, on the date of transfer owns

(a) any residential house
(b) a residential house which is let out
(c) a house which is self occupied
(d) more than one residential house

19 The income from the sale of a machinery used in business is treated as

(a) income from business and profession
(b) short-term capital gain
(c) long-term capital gain
(d) income from other sources

January 2017

20 An equipment was acquired at a cost of ₹ 10 lakh and was put to use in Scientific Research. After one year of research the equipment was brought into another business of the assessee. For charging depreciation, block of assets shall be increased by

(a) ₹ 10 lakh
(b) market value of the equipment on the date it was brought into another business
(c) cost or market value of the equipment, whichever is less
(d) Nil

21 If an assessee is engaged in the business of growing and manufacturing tea in India, the portion of agricultural income in that case shall be

(a) 100% (b) 60%
(c) 50% (d) 40%

22 Which of the following statement is not correct ?

(a) X is an individual assessee. He pays a monthly rent of portion of ₹ 10,000 pm. He cannot deduct tax at source
(b) On salaries, tax is deducted at source according to provisions of Section 192
(c) No tax is deducted at source in respect of interest on securities issued by a domestic company
(d) Bank will deduct tax at source @ 10% if bank fixed deposit's interest credit is more than ₹ 10,000 in a year

23 X donated ₹ 20,000 to a charitable institution, which is eligible for deduction U/S 80 G, during the financial year 2018-19. His total income during the period was ₹ 1,50,000. How much deduction he can claims U/S 80 G ?

(a) ₹ 7,500 (b) ₹ 10,000
(c) ₹ 15,000 (d) ₹ 20,000

24 X is employed in a private company at a salary of ₹ 70,000 per month and ₹ 10,000 per month as dearness pay. He received ₹ 2,000 per month as house rent allowance. He paid ₹ 2,500 per month as house rent. What is the exempted portion of house rent allowance?

(a) ₹ 2,500 (b) ₹ 2,000
(c) ₹ 1,000 (d) Nil

25 Surcharge is payable by an individual where the total income exceeds

(a) ₹ 10 lakh (b) ₹ 25 lakh
(c) ₹ 50 lakh (d) ₹ 1 crore

26 Which one of the following statement is not correct?
(a) A person may not have assessable income but still be an assessee
(b) In some cases, the assessment year and the previous year can be same
(c) An Indian company is always resident assessee
(d) Surcharge is additional tax calculated on total income

July 2016

27 As per the Income Tax Act, 1961 for the assessment year 2019-20, a deduction U/S 80 QQB for authors of books of literacy, artistic or scientific nature is allowed upto
(a) ₹ 1,00,000 (b) ₹ 2,00,000
(c) ₹ 2,40,000 (d) ₹ 3,00,000

28 Gratuity received by a government employee is
(a) exempted upto ₹ 3,50,000
(b) exempted upto ₹ 10,00,000
(c) fully exempted
(d) fully taxable

29 Match the items of the List I with those of the List II.

List I	List II
A. Residential status of an individual	1. Section 10 (13A)
B. Agricultural income	2. Section 10 (10)
C. House rent allowance	3. Section 6
D. Gratuity	4. Section 10 (1)

Codes

	A	B	C	D		A	B	C	D
(a)	1	3	2	4	(b)	3	4	1	2
(c)	2	1	3	4	(d)	4	2	1	3

30 Match the items of the List I with List II.

List I	List II
A. House rent allowance	1. A deduction from income
B. Casual income	2. A step taken by tax authorities
C. Collection charges of interest on securities	3. Taxable income
D. Best judgement assessment	4. Partly taxable allowance

Codes

	A	B	C	D		A	B	C	D
(a)	4	3	2	1	(b)	4	3	1	2
(c)	3	4	1	2	(d)	2	4	1	3

31 The statutory limit for deduction U/S 80 GG of Income Tax Act, 1961, for the assessment year 2019-20 is
(a) ₹ 2,000 per month
(b) ₹ 3,000 per month
(c) ₹ 2,500 per month
(d) ₹ 5,000 per month

32 For the purpose of assessment under Income Tax Act, 1961, which combination of the following represent income?
1. Tax-free salary from the private sector employer
2. Pin money received by a family member
3. Awards received by the sports person
4. Loss incurred by the assessee
5. Perquisites received by employees

Select the correct one from the codes given below

Codes
(a) 1, 2, 3 and 4 (b) 2, 3, 4 and 5
(c) 1, 3, 4 and 5 (d) 1, 2, 4 and 5

33 Indicate the correct code for forms for filing income tax return from the following income tax return forms.
1. ITR-4S 2. ITR-2
3. ITR-2B 4. ITR-3

Codes
(a) 1, 2 and 3 (b) 2, 3 and 4 (c) 1, 2 and 4 (d) 1, 3 and 4

December 2015

34 Consider the following conditions.
1. An individual is in India for a period of 182 days in the financial year in which he is getting his salary income.
2. An individual is in India for a period of 60 days or more during financial year in which he gets his salary and 365 days or more during 4 years immediately preceding to that financial year.
3. If one of the above conditions is satisfied, as per the provisions of Income Tax Act, 1961, he is

Select the correct answer using the codes given below

Codes
(a) resident but not ordinarily resident of India
(b) non-resident citizen of India
(c) resident and categorised citizen of India under Section 29
(d) ordinary resident of India

35 Agriculture income is exempted from income tax under the following section of Income Tax Act, 1961
(a) 2(1A) (b) 10 (1) (c) 10 (2) (d) 10 (4)

36 Match the following.

List I	List II
A. When the assessee is in default or is deemed to be in default in making payment of tax, including the tax deducted at source	1. Section 271 (1) C
B. Failure to pay the advance tax as directed by the assessing officer	2. Section 273 (1)
C. Concealment of particulars of income or furnishing of inaccurate particulars of income	3. Section 201 (1)

Codes

	A	B	C		A	B	C
(a)	1	2	3	(b)	3	2	1
(c)	3	1	2	(d)	2	1	3

37 Which among the following are necessary documents to file Income Tax Return for an employed person in India?

1. Aadhar Card
2. PAN Card
3. Form No. 16 issued by employer

Select the correct answer using the codes given below

Codes

(a) Only 1 (b) Both 1 and 2
(c) Both 2 and 3 (d) All of the above

June 2015

38 In which of the following cases, assessing officer has the discretion to assess the income of the previous year in the previous year or in the subsequent assessment year?

(a) Shipping business of non-residents
(b) Association of Persons (AoP) or Body of Individuals (BoI) formed for a particular event or purpose
(c) Assessment of persons likely to transfer property to avoid tax
(d) Discontinued business

39 Rental income received by a foreign individual, from another foreign individual, in respect of the property situated in Delhi is taxable in the hands of

(a) Resident and Ordinarily Resident (OR)
(b) Ordinarily Resident (OR) and Not Ordinarily Resident (NOR)
(c) Non-Resident (NR)
(d) Ordinarily Resident (OR), Not Ordinarily Resident (NOR) and Non-Resident (NR)

40 Which of the following income is not chargeable under the head 'income from business and profession'?

(a) Profits and gains carried on by an assessee during the previous year
(b) Income derived by a trade professional or similar association from specific services performed for its members
(c) Income from the activity of owning or owning and maintaining race horses
(d) Salary received by a partner of a firm from the same firm

41 Mr A earned a capital gain of ₹ 100 lakh on 31st February, 2019 from the sale of a long-term capital asset (land) within the limits of Jaipur corporation. If he invests ₹ 60 lakh, out of ₹ 100 lakh, in Rural electricity corporation bonds approved under Section 54 EC in 20th February, 2019, what is the amount of exemption he can claim under Section 54 EC of Income Tax Act for the AY 2019-20?

(a) ₹ 60 lakh (b) ₹ 50 lakh
(c) ₹ 100 lakh (d) ₹ 30 lakh

42 Under which of the following situations, the appellate tribunal can rectify the mistake in the order passed by it Under Section 254 (2) of Income Tax Act?

1. If subsequent decision of the Supreme Court/High Court is available on the subject after the appellate tribunal's order.
2. If an assessee apply for rectification of the tribunal's order by raising fresh grounds before the tribunal.
3. If the omission or mistake is on the part of appellate tribunal.
4. If the order is passed by the appellate tribunal under an erroneous impression of fact or law.

Select the correct answer using the codes given below

Codes

(a) 1, 2 and 3
(b) 2, 3 and 4
(c) 1, 3 and 4
(d) Both 3 and 4

December 2014

43 Under Section 271 C of the Income Tax Act, 1961, the amount of penalty for failure to deduct tax at source is

(a) 10% of tax which is otherwise deductible under Section 194 C
(b) 100% of tax which is otherwise deductible under Section 194 C
(c) 200% of tax which is otherwise deductible under Section 194 C
(d) 300% of tax which is otherwise deductible under Section 194 C

44 Match the following.

List I (Sections)	List II (Maximum Deduction)
A. Section 80 C of IT Act	1. ₹ 10,000
B. Section 80D of IT Act	2. ₹ 40,000
C. Section 80 DDB of IT Act	3. ₹ 1,50,000
D. Section 80 TTA of IT Act	4. ₹ 25,000

Codes

	A	B	C	D
(a)	3	1	4	2
(b)	3	4	2	1
(c)	4	3	2	1
(d)	2	3	1	4

45 In which of the following cases, income of previous year is assessable in the previous year itself?

(a) A person in employment
(b) A person engaged in illegal business
(c) A person who is running charitable business
(d) A person leaving India permanently

46 Long-term capital loss can be set-off from which of the following?

(a) Short-term capital gain only
(b) Long-term capital gain only
(c) Income from business and profession
(d) Capital gain head of income

47 In which of the following long-term assets, cost indexation benefit is allowed ?

(a) Debentures issued by a company
(b) Self generated goodwill of a business
(c) Bonus shares allotted on 01-04-2000
(d) Jewellery

48 Calculate the gross annual value from the following details.

Municipal value	-	₹ 45,000
Fair rental value	-	₹ 50,000
Standard rent	-	₹ 48,000
Actual rent	-	₹ 42,000

(a) ₹ 50,000 (b) ₹ 48,000
(c) ₹ 45,000 (d) ₹ 42,000

49 Minimum Alternate Tax (MAT) is imposed on

(a) all companies
(b) public limited companies only
(c) private limited companies only
(d) partnership firms and companies

June 2014

50 Mr X, a non-resident, earned ₹ 36,000 as interest on German Development Bonds. Of this, he received 1/6th in India.The amount to be included as interest for the computation of his gross total income is

(a) ₹ 36,000
(b) ₹ 30,000
(c) ₹ 6,000
(d) Nil

51 Consider the following problem relating to a let-out house property

Municipal value	- ₹ 60,000
fair rent	- ₹ 68,000
Standard rent under the Rent Control Act	- ₹ 62000
Annual rent received	- ₹ 65,000

The gross annual value of the property will be

(a) ₹ 68,000
(b) ₹ 62,000
(c) ₹ 65,000
(d) ₹ 60,000

52 The benefits of debt financing over equity financing are likely to be highest in which of the following situations?

(a) High marginal tax rates and low non-interest tax benefits
(b) Low marginal tax rates and low non-interest tax benefits
(c) High marginal tax rates and high non-interest tax benefits
(d) Low marginal tax rates and high non-interest tax benefits

December 2013

53 Match the following.

	List I		List II
A.	Amount deposited in PPF	1.	80-IA
B.	Profits and gains from undertakings engaged in infrastructure development	2.	80-G
C.	Contribution to National Defence Fund	3.	80-IAB
D.	Profits and gains by an undertaking engaged in the development of special economic zone	4.	80-C

Codes

	A	B	C	D
(a)	4	3	2	1
(b)	4	1	2	3
(c)	4	1	3	2
(d)	2	1	3	4

54 Which one of the following deductions will not come under Section 80 of the Income Tax Act?

(a) Deduction in the case of a person with disability
(b) Deduction for interest paid on loan taken for pursuing higher education
(c) Deduction for interest on loan taken for the construction/ purchase of house property
(d) Deduction for repayment of any instalment of principal amout borrowed for the purchase/constuction of house property

55 X purchased a land in th PY 1997-98 for ₹ 50,000 . This land was sold by him during the PY 2018-19 for ₹ 8,00,000. The fair market value of this land on 01-04-01 was ₹ 1,20,000. It the cost inflation index for the AY 2019-20 is his capital gain for the AY 2019-20 will be

(a) ₹ 4,64,000 (b) ₹ 7,50,000
(c) ₹ 6,80,000 (d) ₹ 41,600

56 Any amount of money received in excess of ₹ 50,000 without consideration is fully taxable in the hands of

(a) individuals
(b) individuals and HUF
(c) individuals, HUF and Comany
(d) All of the above

57 Given that fair rent of a let out house property is ₹ 75,000. Its municipal value is ₹ 60,000, standard rent is ₹ 72,000 and actual rent received is ₹ 63,000. What is the gross annual value of this house property?

(a) ₹ 60,000 (b) ₹ 63,000
(c) ₹ 72,000 (d) ₹ 75,000

June 2013

58 Donation to National Children's Fund will come in which of the following deduction under Section 80G of Income Tax Act, 1961?
(a) 100% deduction without any qualifying limit
(b) 50% deduction without any qualifying limit
(c) 100% deduction subject to qualifying limit
(d) 50% deduction subject to qualifying limit

59 If the taxable income of a domestic company for the assessment year 2019-20 is ₹ 9,00,000, its tax liability will be
(a) ₹ 2,76,800 (b) ₹ 2,78,100
(c) ₹ 3,70,800 (d) ₹ 3,70,880

60 Unabsorbed depreciation which could not be setoff in the same assessment year, can be carried forward upto
(a) 4 years
(b) 8 years
(c) 10 years
(d) indefinite period

61 If the book profits of a partnership firm is ₹ 1,10,000, the remuneration admissible to working partners under Section 40(b) of the Income Tax Act, 1961 is
(a) ₹ 1,10,000 (b) ₹ 1,50,000
(c) ₹ 99,000 (d) None of these

62 Which of the following expenses is in admissible while computing income from other sources?
(a) Interest paid on amounts borrowed to meet tax liabilities
(b) Collection charges paid to the banker or any other person to collect interest/dividend
(c) Interest on loan taken to invest in securities
(d) Depreciation on let out machinery and plant

December 2012

63 Minimum Alternative Tax (MAT) under Section 115 JB of the Income Tax Act is applicable on
(a) partnership firm (b) association of persons
(c) certain companies (d) all types of companies

64 For the assessment year 2019-20, deduction under Section 80G is available without any limit, but at the rate of 50% on
(a) Prime Minister's National Relief Fund
(b) National Foundation for Communal Harmany
(c) Jawahar Lal Nehru Memorial Fund
(d) Chief Minister Relief Fund

65 Interest on capital paid by a firm to its partners, under the Income Tax Act, 1961, is allowed
(a) 6% (b) 12%
(c) 15% (d) 18%

66 Under capital gains head of the Income Tax Act, the income from sale of household furniture is
(a) taxable income
(b) capital gain
(c) revenue gain
(d) exempted income

67 Under Section, ... of the Income Tax Act, 1961 deduction in respect of payment of interest on loan taken for higher education shall be allowed.
(a) 80E (b) 80EE
(c) 80DD (d) 80DDB

June 2012

68 Mr James, a citizen of US, arrived in India for the first time on 1st July, 2018 and left for Nepal on 15th December, 2018. He arrived to India again on 1st January, 2019 and stayed till the end of the financial year 2018-19. His residential status for the assessment year 2019-20 is
(a) resident (ordinarily resident)
(b) not ordinarily resident
(c) non-resident
(d) None of the above

69 The value of free accommodation in Delhi provided by employer in the private sector is
(a) 10% of salary
(b) 15% of salary
(c) 20% of salary
(d) 25% of salary

70 Which of the following is not a capital asset under capital gains head of income ?
(a) Stock in trade
(b) Goodwill of business
(c) Agricultural land in Delhi
(d) Jewellery

71 Under the Income Tax Act, 1961 unabsorbed depreciation can be carried forward for set-off purpose
(a) for 4 years
(b) for 5 years
(c) for 8 years
(d) for unspecified period

ANSWERS

Objective Questions

1 (d)	2 (c)	3 (c)	4 (b)	5 (a)	6 (a)	7 (b)	8 (a)	9 (b)	10 (c)
11 (d)	12 (d)	13 (d)	14 (b)	15 (b)	16 (a)	17 (b)	18 (d)	19 (b)	20 (b)
21 (d)	22 (a)	23 (a)	24 (d)	25 (b)	26 (d)	27 (a)	28 (c)	29 (b)	30 (a)
31 (b)	32 (a)	33 (d)	34 (a)	35 (d)	36 (b)	37 (d)	38 (b)	39 (a)	40 (c)
41 (c)	42 (b)	43 (c)	44 (b)	45 (b)	46 (c)	47 (b)	48 (b)	49 (c)	50 (c)
51 (d)	52 (b)	53 (b)	54 (a)	55 (b)	56 (b)	57 (b)	58 (c)	59 (b)	60 (d)
61 (c)	62 (b)	63 (c)	64 (c)	65 (a)	66 (a)	67 (d)	68 (c)	69 (b)	70 (c)
71 (b)	72 (c)	73 (c)	74 (d)	75 (c)	76 (a)	77 (a)	78 (a)	79 (d)	80 (d)
81 (a)	82 (c)	83 (c)	84 (c)	85 (c)	86 (d)	87 (b)	88 (a)	89 (a)	90 (d)
91 (d)	92 (a)	93 (b)	94 (a)	95 (d)	96 (c)	97 (a)	98 (d)	99 (b)	100 (b)
101 (b)	102 (c)	103 (c)	104 (b)	105 (b)	106 (b)	107 (d)	108 (a)	109 (d)	110 (b)
111 (d)	112 (a)	113 (b)	114 (a)	115 (d)	116 (a)	117 (c)	118 (b)	119 (d)	120 (a)
121 (b)	122 (d)	123 (d)	124 (d)	125 (c)	126 (b)	127 (c)	128 (b)	129 (b)	130 (a)
131 (a)	132 (d)	133 (b)	134 (c)	135 (d)	136 (c)	137 (d)	138 (b)	139 (a)	140 (a)
141 (c)	142 (d)	143 (b)	144 (b)	145 (c)	146 (a)	147 (c)	148 (c)	149 (c)	150 (d)
151 (d)	152 (b)	153 (b)	154 (a)	155 (b)	156 (d)	157 (b)	158 (d)	159 (d)	160 (b)
161 (a)	162 (b)	163 (b)	164 (c)	165 (d)	166 (d)	167 (d)	168 (c)	169 (c)	170 (a)
171 (b)	172 (a)	173 (a)	174 (a)	175 (d)	176 (c)	177 (d)	178 (d)	179 (b)	180 (b)
181 (d)	182 (a)	183 (c)	184 (b)	185 (b)	186 (b)	187 (b)	188 (b)	189 (c)	190 (c)
191 (a)	192 (d)	193 (a)	194 (b)	195 (a)	196 (a)	197 (a)	198 (a)	199 (d)	200 (b)
201 (a)	202 (b)								

Previous Years' Questions

1 (d)	2 (b)	3 (a)	4 (d)	5 (c)	6 (c)	7 (d)	8 (c)	9 (c)	10 (a)
11 (b)	12 (a)	13 (a)	14 (d)	15 (c)	16 (a)	17 (b)	18 (d)	19 (b)	20 (d)
21 (b)	22 (c)	23 (a)	24 (d)	25 (c)	26 (d)	27 (d)	28 (c)	29 (b)	30 (b)
31 (d)	32 (c)	33 (c)	34 (d)	35 (b)	36 (b)	37 (c)	38 (d)	39 (d)	40 (c)
41 (b)	42 (c)	43 (b)	44 (b)	45 (d)	46 (b)	47 (d)	48 (b)	49 (a)	50 (c)
51 (c)	52 (a)	53 (b)	54 (c)	55 (a)	56 (b)	57 (c)	58 (a)	59 (b)	60 (d)
61 (b)	62 (a)	63 (c)	64 (c)	65 (b)	66 (d)	67 (a)	68 (b)	69 (b)	70 (a)
71 (d)									

CHAPTER 37

Corporate Tax Planning and International Taxation

Corporate tax planning activities generally seek to avoid legally triggering tax costs rather than illegally evading an existing obligation to pay taxes. International taxation refers to treaty provisions relieving international double taxation. In broader terms, it includes domestic legislation covering foreign income of residents and domestic income of non-residents.

Concept of Corporate Tax Planning

Corporate tax planning is the arrangement of financial activities in such a way that maximum tax benefits are enjoyed by making use of all beneficial provisions in the tax laws.

It entitles the assessee to avail certain exemptions, deductions, rebates and reliefs, so as to minimise his tax liability.

Corporate tax planning provides strategies that are significant in minimising taxes.

Some valuable ways to save include

- Sponsoring a retirement plan
- Writing-off company assets
- Claiming depreciation expense
- Taking deductions on business automobiles
- Office expenses and self-employment health insurance

Business tax planning includes taking advantage of opportunities to provide

- Tax relief, when possible.
- Tax exemption, like charitable contributions are a great way for a company to save on taxes and help those in the community.

In this Chapter

Objectives of Corporate Tax Planning

- An assessee can save the maximum amount of tax.
- A proper tax planning aims at conforming to the provisions of the tax law.
- Tax planning is channelisation of taxable income to different investment plans.
- It involve generating white money that flows freely and results in the sound progress of the economy.
- Proper tax planning brings economic stability.

Points to be Remembered

- Corporate tax planning is not avoidance to payment of taxes.
- Tax planning should not be done with an intent to defraud the revenue.
- All transactions with respect to tax planning should be in correct form and substance.
- Tax planning work should be done within the framework of law and its not illegal.

Significance of Corporate Tax Planning

Tax planning strategies are typically employed to help a business achieve their financial and business goals. *There are benefits of tax planning for both large and small businesses and planning plays an important role in*

- lowering the amount of taxable income.
- reducing the tax rate.
- allowing greater control of when taxes get paid.
- maximising tax relief available.

Common Practices to Save Taxes

Tax payer generally plan their affairs so as to attract the least incidence of tax. Tax payer spares no efforts in maximising his profits and attracting the least incidence. The tax gatherer, on the other hand try to break the plan whose sole objective is to save taxes. *Three common practice to save taxes*

- Tax planning
- Tax avoidance
- Tax evasion

Tax Planning

Tax planning is an activity conducted by the tax payer to reduce the tax liable upon him by making maximum use of all available deductions, allowances, exclusions etc feasible under law. In other words, it is the analysis of a financial situation from the taxation point of view. The objective behind tax planning is assurance of tax efficiency. Tax planning allows all elements of the financial plan to function in sync to deliver maximum tax efficieny.

Objectives of Tax Planning

- Increase in disposable income.
- Shield against high taxation.
- Inequity in tax burden.
- Maximum deductions allowed to business persons, minimal to others.
- Avoidance of litigation.
- Curb on tax evasion.

Methods of Tax Planning

Short-term Tax Planning

Short range tax planning means the planning thought of and executed at the end of the income year to reduce taxable income in a legal way.

e.g. Suppose, at the end of the income year, an assessee finds taxes have been too high in comparison with last year and he intends to reduce it. Now, he may do that, to a great extent by making proper arrangements to get the maximum tax rebate under Section 88. Such plan does not involve any long-term commitment, yet it results in substantial savings in tax.

Long-term Tax Planning

Long-term tax planning means a plan charted out at the beginning of the income year to be followed around the year. This type of planning does not help immediately as in the case of short range planning but is likely to help in the long run.

e.g. If an assessee transferred shares held by him to his minor son or spouse, though the income from such transferred shares will be clubbed with his income under Section 64, yet is the income is invested by the son or spouse, then the income from such investment will be treated as income of the son or spouse. Moreover, if the company issue any bonus shares for the shares transferred, that will also be treated as income in the hands of the son or spouse.

Permissive Tax Planning

Permissive tax planning means making plans which are permissible under different provisions of the law. Such as planning of earning income covered by Section 10(1), planning of taking advantage of different incentives and deductions etc.

Purposive Tax Planning

It means making plans with specific purpose to ensure the availability of maximum benefits to the assessee through correct selection of investment, making suitable programme for replacement of assets, varying the residential status and diversifying business activities and income etc.

Tax Planning vs Tax Management

Basis	Tax Planning	Tax Management
Objective	The objective of tax planning is to reduce the tax liability to the minimum.	The objective of tax management is to comply with the provisions of law.
Nature	Tax planning is futuristic in its approach.	Tax management relates to past (assessment proceedings, rectification, revision, appeals) present (filing of return of income on time on the basis of updated records) and future (corrective action).
Scope	Tax planning is very wide in its coverage and includes tax management.	Tax management has a limited scope, *i.e.* it deals with specific activities such as filing of returns of income on time, drafting appeals, deduction of tax at source on time, updating records from time-to-time etc.
Result	The benefits arising from tax planning are substantial particularly in the long run.	As a result of effective tax management, penalty, penal interest, prosecution etc can be avoided.

Comparison between Tax Avoidance and Tax Evasion

Basis	Tax Avoidance	Tax Evasion
Meaning	Minimisation of tax liability by taking such means which do not violate the tax rules, is tax avoidance.	Reducing tax liability by using illegal ways is known as tax evasion.
What is it?	Hedging of tax	Concealment of tax
Attributes	Immoral in nature, which involves bending the law without breaking it.	Illegal and objectionable, both in script and moral.
Concept	Taking unfair advantage of the shortcomings in the tax laws.	Deliberate manipulations accounts resulting in fraud.
Legal implication	Use of justified means.	Use of such means that are forbidden by law.
Time of occurrence	Before the occurrence of tax liability.	After tax liability arises.
Type of act	Legal	Criminal
Consequences	Deferment of tax liability	Penalty or imprisonment
Objective	To reduce tax liability by applying the script of law.	To reduce tax liability by exercising unfair means.

Tax Avoidance vs Tax Evasion

Tax Avoidance

An arrangement made to beat the intent of the law by taking unfair advantage of the shortcoming in the tax rules is known as tax avoidance. It refers to finding out new methods or tools to avoid the payment of taxes which are within the limits of the law.

The only purpose of tax avoidance is to postpone or shift or eliminate the tax liability. This can be done by investing in government schemes and offers like the tax credit, tax privileges, deductions, exemptions etc which will result in the reduction in the tax liability without making any offence or breach of law.

Tax Evasion

An illegal act, made to escape from paying taxes is known as tax evasion. Such illegal practices can be deliberate concealment of income, manipulation in accounts, disclosure of unreal expenses for deductions, showing personal expenditure as business expenses, overstatement of tax credits or exemptions suppression of profits and capital gains etc. This will result in the disclosure of income which is not the actual income earned by the entity.

Tax evasion is a criminal activity for which the assessee is subject to punishment under the law. *It includes acts like*

- Deliberate misrepresentation of material facts.
- Hiding relevant documents.
- Not maintaining complete records of all the transactions.
- Making false statements.

Techniques of Corporate Tax Planning

Tax Planning in respect of Employee's Remuneration

- One has to ensure that while calculating business income of the employer, remuneration paid to employee are fully deductable.
- One has to see that remuneration received by the employee is taxable in their hands at concessional rates.

Deductions of remuneration in hand of employer

- Remuneration to employees engaged in carrying on scientific research.
- Insurance premium on health of employees.
- Bonus and commission to employees.
- Employers contribution towards PF and gratuity fund.
- Employees contribution to staff welfare scheme.
- Family planning expenditure.
- Payment of salary, allowances, perquisites.
- Salary payable outside India.
- Payment of salaries to relatives.
- Payment of salaries exceeding ₹ 20,000 in cash or bearer cheque.

Tax Planning in respect of Amalgamation

As per the Income Tax Act [Section 2 (1B)] *'Amalgamation' in relation to companies means*

- one or more companies with another company; or
- the merger of two or more companies to from one company.

Tax Concessions

Tax concessions are available if an amalgamation satisfies the condition of Section 2 (1B) and the amalgamated company is an Indian Company. *These conditions are*

- Non-chargeability of capital gain on the transfer of a capital asset including shares held by a shareholder at the time of amalgamation.
- Eligibility of amalgamated company for the deduction in respect of any asset representing expenditure of a capital nature on scientific research.
- Eligibility of the amalgamated company for the deduction in respect of acquisitions of patent rights or copyrights.
- Similar deduction in respect of expenditure on know-how as provided in.
- Amortisation of expenditure for obtaining telecom licence fees.
- Amortisation of certain preliminary expenses.
- Amortisation of expenditure on amalgamation.
- Amortisation of expenditure on prospecting etc for certain minerals.
- Writing-off bad debts.
- Computation of written down value of the transferred fixed assets in the case of amalgamated company.
- Continuance of deduction available.
- Benefit of carry forward and set-off of accumulated losses and unabsorbed depreciation.

Deduction of Tax at Source

In certain specified cases of income, tax at source should be deducted by the person responsible for making payment of such income. Income tax act provides that such tax must be deducted from the amounts of both residents and non-residents according to the rates prescribed in Finance Act of that year.

Tax Consideration on Capital Structure

A company's capital structure is the method of a company uses to finance its operation and growth utilising various sources of funding. Capital structure is a mix of a company's long-term debt, specific short-term debt, common equity and preferred equity.

There are two options for capital i.e. debt and equity

- Debt receives a tax break but increases the financial risk of a company.
- Equity does not share those same qualities.

Cost of Capital and its Tax Treatment for Debentures

The cost of capital for loans and debentures refers to interest payable to lender or debenture holder. An interest rate is the rate at which interest is paid by borrowers for the use of money that they borrow from a lender.

Tax Treatment of Interest

Interest on loans or debentures is 100% tax deductible while calculating business income. *In following cases, interest will be allowed as deduction*

- Paid during the previous year itself.
- If not paid, it must be paid on or before due date of furnishing of return of income.
- Interest on any loan from any public financial institutions like IDBI, ICICI, SFC.
- Interest on any loan taken from a scheduled bank including a cooperative bank.

Cost of Capital and its Tax Treatment for Equity and Preference Shares

Dividend signifies cost of capital for owned capital.

Tax Treatment of Dividend

- Dividend paid to shareholders is not deductible as business expenditure. It has to be paid out profits after tax.
- Such dividend distribution tax shall be payable @15% +surcharge @5% + education cess @2%+SHES @1% of amount so declared, distribution or paid.

Tax Planning in respect of Bonus Shares

- When bonus shares are issued to the equity shareholders, the value of the share is not taxed as such issue is deemed to be dividend distributed to them.
- When bonus shares are issued to preference shareholders, on their issue it is deemed to be dividend and liable to tax.
- Redeemable preference shares are issued as bonus share on their redemptions, the amount shall be taxed distributed.
- Expenses on issue of bonus shares allowed as deduction as per Supreme Court judgement.

C Corporate Tax Management Managerial and Financial Decisions

- Location and nature of business [New].
- Deemed dividend.
- Lease or buy decisions.
- Repair, replace and make or buy decisions.
- Capital gains on distribution of assets by companies in liquidation.
- Sale of scientific research asset.
- Tax management with reference to capital structure.
- Conversion of firm/sole proprietorship to company.

Tax Considerations in Specific Business Situations

The scope of tax planning is wider. The decisions taken by the managers or owners in the interest of business affects the tax liability of the organisation. Thus, management has to see the effect of the decisions taken by them on the taxation. They have to see the different provisions of tax laws before taking decisions. The decisions taken by them should attract either nil tax liability or reduce the tax liability.

Make or Buy Decisions

A component is required by manufacturer for its production. Such component is readily available in the market but this can be manufactured by the manufacturer in its own factory. To take the decision whether such component should be purchased or to produce, several factors like financial, costing and tax planning are to be considered.

If items are to be manufactured, then following decisions will be taken

- Is licence required to manufacture?
- What capacity is required to produce?
- Whether this component can be produced by existing plant or an extra plant is required?
- What would be technical qualities of the component?
- What capital or finance be required to install new plant?
- How will such finance be managed?
- What additional working capital will be required?
- Whether sufficient raw material and labour will be available or not?
- What would be the fixed and variable cost of manufacturing?
- If new unit is to be installed, *then following points will also be considered*
    (a) Benefit of Section 10 (A) or 10 (B) or 10 (C) of Income Tax Act should be received.
    (b) Deduction under Section 80 (IA) or 80 IB or 80 (IC) or 80 (ID) or 80 (IE) of Income Tax Act should be availed.
    (c) Maximum benefit of excise duty, sales tax etc must be received.
    (d) Maximum rate of depreciation under Section 32 of Income Tax Act must be availed.
    (e) If new employees are admitted, then deduction under Section 80(JJAA) must be availed.

If component is to be purchased from the open market, then following must be decided

- Is desired quality and technique of goods available in the open market?
- What is the market rate of item required?
- Is supplier a bonafide?
- Will desired item be continuously supplied?
- Will desired quantity of item be available?

Generally, this type of decision is taken by assembling industry. By adding one or two components, they develop a new product.

Own or Lease an Asset

Leasing is a financial arrangement whereby an organisation is vested with the use and control over assets without a title of ownership in consideration of a lease rent for a period of time. The person who leases, *i.e.* the owner is called the lessor, while the person who takes the asset on lease is called the lessee.

The decision to lease or buy an asset can only be made after considering the following key factors

Asset to be Arranged by Own or Borrowed Funds or on Lease If the asset is purchased through owned funds, there will be heavy initial outlay and the funds will be locked up being denied of other investment opportunities. If the asset is purchased through borrowed funds, then apart from interest payments, provisions would have to be made for payment of loan instalments. However, in lease option, there is significant recurring expenditure in the form of annual rentals.

Tax Implications The full amount of lease rentals is deductible for income tax purposes as operating expenses of the concern. In case, assets are purchased with owned funds, the assessee will be entitled to deduction of depreciation. In case of purchase of asset with borrowed funds, the interest payment will also be deductible. The overall tax effects will have to be calculated for selecting appropriate alternative.

Operating Expenses The costs of operating the asset are irrelevant since it is same irrespective of mode of acquiring the asset. If the operating costs are different in case of own or lease, then only they should be considered.

Consideration of Residual Value In case, the firm owns the asset it has full right over the residual value at the end of useful life of the asset while in case of lease, the residual value doesn't belong to the firm.

Advantages of Lease Finance

- The lessee need not pay immediate cash as the leasing companies provide 100 per cent of the equipment cost. The lessee can utilise his cash in a beneficial manner.
- Lessee lends medium-term finance for 3-6 years.
- The lease rentals are fixed after accomodating the cash flow situation of the lessee.

- Budget planning can be done in lease financing because the annual rental and period, both are fixed.
- Since lease has to pay current prices for the equipment in future currency, leasing provides a safeguard against inflation.

Disadvantages of Lease Finance

- Lease assets are not owned assets and therefore the fixed assets to equity ratio comes down with increased dependence on lease finance.
- Due to lighter dependence on lease, the financial ratios reveal distorted picture of the organisation.
- Since lease rentals are paid out of working capital, this results in negative position of financing of fixed assets out of short-term funds.
- The salvage value of asset belongs to lease.

Retain, Renewal or Replacement of Asset

Retain

Expenses incurred to keep the asset in usable or operating situation is known as repair. If an organisation spent on repair of asset, such expenditures are allowed under Section 30 and 31 of the Income Tax Act. If expenditure is deductible as revenue expenditure, the cost of financing such expenditure is reduced to the extent of the amount of tax saved.

Replacement

When an asset is not in condition to use effectively for commercial purposes and either asset is replaced or any important part of the asset is replaced is known as replacement. Because of such expenses the efficiency of asset is also known as renovation. Because of such expenses the efficiency of asset is increased permanently or organisation gets additional capacity. Such expenses are treated as capital expenditure and not deductible directly from the incomes but indirectly, the depreciation is allowed under Section 32 of the Income Tax Act.

At the time of taking the decision regarding replacement of asset, organisation must think about the increase in profitability because of increase in efficiency. The profit will be analysed for tax point of view.

Renewal

When a part of asset is changed to keep the asset in operating or useable situation is known as renewal. Sometimes, these expenses are treated as revenue expenses and sometimes it is treated as capital expenses. If capacity of asset is increased because of renewals, then it will be a capital expenditure ans such expenses are disallowed under Section 31 of the Income Tax Act and not deductible directly from the income. But on such expenses, the depreciation will be allowed as deduction under Section 32 of the Income Tax Act. In case, because of renewal, the capacity is not increased, the expenditure will be treated as revenue expenditure and allowed as routine repair expenses under Section 30 and 31 of the Income Tax Act.

Thus, the expenses incurred to get capacity of asset back is a revenue nature expenses but if the existing capacity is increased, it is a capital nature expenditure.

Generally, following expenses incurred on the asset is known as routing repair expenses and allowed under the provisions of Income Tax Act

- Periodical expenses incurred to maintain the asset.
- Colouring, painting of asset.
- Petty repair of asset
- Replacement of parts to keep the asset in the same capacity.

Shutdown or Continue Operations

Whenever, there is a situation of industrial sickness, the management may have to think whether to shutdown the unit or continue to carry on with it. *The reasons of industrial sickness may be*

Reduction in Demand This may be because of competition, changes in the fashion etc.

Financial Problems Sickness may be because of inadequate finance or poor financial management. This may impede replacement of worn-out plant and machinery.

High Rates of Taxation Heavy sales tax, excise duty, custom duty increase the cost of production. The product may prove to be uncompetitive and the result is loss.

Changes in Technology Rapid changes in technology often introduces new dimensions like fall in demand. Manufacturer is to keep pace with such development otherwise there will be heavy loss because of heavy dead stock.

Pressure of Commercial Banks Industry generally depends on banks for finance. When there is default in payment of interest and instalment bank charges penal interest and put restriction on further loan. Sometimes, bank may resort to litigation. All such causes pressure in operation of business.

Tax Provisions

The tax aspects may be too significant in moulding the situation. *The relevant tax provisions are*

- The organisation may carry forward the business loss and amount of unabsorbed depreciation, even such business is discontinued. The business loss can be set off in next 8 assessment years from the business income while the unabsorbed depreciation can be set-off from any income of assesse without any restriction of time period.

- Few deductions which were allowed earlier for profit of foreign project, profit of hotel project, profit of shipping companies etc will be reverted and will be treated as income of that year in which such business is discontinued.
- The capital expenses incurred on scientific research and family planning programme in deductible as expenses according to the provisions of Income Tax Act. If such assets is sold at the time of discontinuation of business, then selling value of the extent of amount deducted will be treated as business income and in case selling price exceeds the amount of deduction, then such excess will be treated as capital gains.
- At the time of closure of business, if depreciable assets are sold and selling price is more than the written down value of block of assets, then such difference will be short-term capital gain and in adverse case, short-term capital loss.
- In case of sale of non-depreciation assets there may be long-term or short-term capital gain or loss. Accordingly tax liability shall be calculated.
- The bad debts of discontinued business cannot be allowed as deduction according to Section 36(i) (vii) of the Income Tax Act.
- Interest on loan taken for discontinue the business cannot be allowed as deduction according to the provision of Section 36(i) (iii) of the Income Tax Act.

In case, organisation is continued even if there is a loss, there are following benefits with regard to tax

- As there is no sale of asset, hence the short-term or long-term capital gain will not be arisen.
- No violation of sections mentioned in provision above.
- Bad debts and interest on loan taken for continued business is treated as allowable expense.
- Interest on loan taken for business suffering losses can be charged from other heads of income.

International Taxation

International taxation is the study or determination of tax on a person or business subject to the law of different countries. Goverments usually limit the scope of their income tax in same manner territorially or provide for offsets to taxation relating to extraterritorial income. Many governments tax individuals and/or enterprises on income.

Concept of Double Taxation and its Avoidance Mechanism

Where a taxpayer is resident in one country but has a source of income situated in another country, it give rise to possible double taxation. This arises from the two basic rules that enables the country of residence as well as the country where the source of income exists, to impose tax namely,

- the source rule and • the residence rule

The source rule holds that income is to be taxed in the country in which it originates irrespective of whether the income accrues to a resident or a non-resident, whereas the residence rule stipulates that the power to tax should rest with the country in which the taxpayer resides.

If both rules apply simultaneously to a business entity and it were to suffer tax at both ends, the cost of operating on an international scale would become prohibitive and would deter the process of globalisation. It is from this point of view that Double Taxation Avoidance Agreements (DTAA) become very significant.

Double taxation means taxing the same income twice in the hands of an assessee. In India, a person is taxed on the basis of his residential status. Likewise, it may so happen that he is taxed on this basis or some other basis in another country on the same income. However, it is a universally accepted principle that the same income should not be subjected to tax twice. In order to take care of such situations, the Income Tax Act, 1961 has provided for double taxation relief.

Types of Relief/Avoidance Mechanism

Bilateral Relief

Under this method, the government of two countries can enter into an agreement to provide relief against double taxation by mutually working out the basis on which the relief is to be granted. *Bilateral relief may be granted in either one of the following methods*

Exemption Method A particular income is taxed in only one of the two countries.

Tax Credit Method Income is taxable in both countries in accordance with their respective tax laws read with double taxation avoidance agreement.

The country of resident of the tax payer, however, allows him credit for the tax charged thereon in the country of source.

In India, double taxation relief is provided by a combination of the two methods.

Unilateral Relief

This method provides for relief of some kind by the home country even where no mutual agreement has been entered into by the two countries.

Double Taxation Relief Provisions Under the Income Tax Act, 1961

1. Agreement with foreign countries or specified territories-bilateral relief (Section 90). *It includes*
   (i) Section 90(1) provides that the Central Government may enter into an agreement with the government of any country outside India or specified territory outside India.
   (a) For granting of relief in respect of
   - income on which income tax has been paid both in India and in that country or specified territory; or
   - income tax chargeable under this act and under the corresponding law in force in that country or specified territory to promote mutual economic relations, trade and investment; or

   (b) For the avoidance of double taxation of income under this act and under the corresponding law in force in that country or specified territory; or
   (c) For exchange of information for the prevention of evasion or avoidance of income tax chargeable under this act or under the corresponding law in force in that country or specified territory or investigation of cases such evasion or avoidance; or
   (d) For recovery of income tax under this act and under the corresponding law in force in that country or specified territory.

   (ii) Where the Central Government has entered into such an agreement with the government of any country outside India or specified territory outside India for granting relief of tax, or for avoidance of double taxation, then, in relation to the assessee to whom such agreement applies, the provisions of this act shall apply to the extent they are more beneficial to that assessee.
   (iii) However, the provisions of Chapter X-A, general anti-avoidance rule, shall apply to the assessee even if such provisions are not beneficial to him.
   (iv) Section 90 (4) provides that the non-resident to whom the agreement referral to in Section 90 (1) applies, shall be allowed to claim the relief under such agreement if a Tax Residence Certificate (TRC) obtained by him from the government of that country or specified territory, is furnished declaring his residence of the country outside India or the specified territory outside India, as the case may be.
   (v) Therefore, a certificate issued by the government of a foreign country would constitute proof of tax residency, without any further conditions regarding furnishing of 'prescribed particulars' therein.
   (vi) The charge of tax in respect of a foreign company at a rate higher than the rate at which a domestic company is chargeable, shall not be regarded as less favourable charge or levy of tax in respect of such foreign company.
   (vii) DTAA provides for a particular mode of computation of income, this mode will take precedence over the Income Tax Act, 1961. However, where there is no specific provision in the treaty, then the Income Tax Act will apply.

2. Double taxation relief to be extended to agreements between specified associations adopted by the Central Government (Section 90A). *It includes*
   (i) Section 90A provides that any specified association in India may enter into an agreement with any specified association in the specified territory outside India and the Central Government may, by notification in the official gazette, make the necessary provisions for adopting and implementing such agreement for
   (a) grant of double taxation relief.
   (b) avoidance of double taxation of income.
   (c) exchange of information for the prevention of evasion or avoidance of income tax.
   (d) recovery of income tax.

   Section 90A (1) provides that an agreement may be entered into by any specified association in India with any specified association in the specified territory outside India which may be adopted by the Central Government by way of notification in the official gazatte, for granting relief of tax or, as the case may be, for avoidance of double taxation.
   (ii) In relation to any assessee to whom the said agreement applies, the provisions of the Income Tax Act, 1961 shall apply to the extent they are more beneficial to that assessee.
   (iii) However, the provisions of Chapter X-A, general anti-avoidance rule, shall apply to the assessee even if such provisions are not beneficial to him.
   (iv) Section 90A (4) provides that the non-resident to whom the agreement, referred to the Section 90A (1) applies shall be allowed to claim the relief under such agreement, if a Tax Residence Certificate (TRC) obtained by him from the

government of that country or specified territory is furnished, declaring his residence of the country outside India or the specified territory outside India, as the case may be.

(v) Therefore, a certificate issued by the government of a foreign country would constitute proof of tax residency, without any further conditions regarding furnishing of 'prescribed particulars' therein. In addition to such certificate by the foreign government, Section 90A (5) requires the assessee to provide such other documents and information.

(vi) The charge of tax at a higher rate for a company incorporated in the specified territory outside India as compared to a domestic company would not be considered as less favourable charge or levy of tax in respect of such company.

(vii) For the purpose of this section, the 'specified association' means any institution, association or body, whether incorporated or not, functioning under any law for the time being in force in India or the laws of the specified territory outside India and which may be notified as such by the Central Government and 'specified territory' means any area outside India which may be notified by the Central Government.

3. Countries with which no agreement exits-unilateral agreements (Section 91).

In the case of income arising to an assessee in countries with which India does not have any double taxation agreement, *relief would be granted under Section 91 provided all the following conditions are fulfilled*

(i) The assessee is a resident in India during the previous year in respect of which the income is taxable.

(ii) The income accrues or arises to him outside India.

(iii) The income is not deemed to accrue or arise in India during the previous year.

(iv) The income in question has been subjected to income tax in the foreign country in the hands of the assessee.

(v) The assessee has paid tax on the income in the foreign country.

(vi) There is no agreement for relief from double taxation between India and the other country where the income has accrued or arisen.

In such a case, the assessee shall be entitled to a deduction from the India income tax payable by him. The deduction would be a sum calculated as such doubly taxed income at the Indian rate of tax or the rate of tax in the said country, whichever is lower, or at the Indian rate of tax, if both the rates are equal.

Transfer Pricing

Transfer pricing as a concept traditionally began with the amount charged by one segment of an enterprise for a product or service that it supplied to another segment of the same enterprises. With the evolution of MNC concept, segments of the enterprises started spreading as independent entities operating in various parts of the globe. Accordingly, the term has evolved to mean price which is charged between two or more entities of a MNC [Associated Enterprises (AE)] operating in different countries. Thus, the tax administrators believe is unjust. Therefore, to protect each country's fair share in an MNC's total profit, the tax authorities have established principles under which, it can be assumed that related parties deal with each other as if they are independent and this principle is called the arm's length principle.

Arm's Length Principle

The Arm's Length Price (ALP) of a transaction between two associated enterprises is the price that would be paid, if the transactions had taken place between two comparable independent and unrelated parties, where the consideration is only commercial.

The arm's length, in the context of taxation, is explained in the Organisation for Economy Cooperation and Development (OECD) model tax convention as under, "Where conditions are made or imposed between two associated enterprises in their commercial or financial relations which differ from those which would be made between independent enterprises, then any profits which would, but for those conditions, have accrued to one of the enterprises, but by reason of those conditions, have not so accrued, may be included in the profits of that enterprises and taxed accordingly."

The OECD transfer pricing guidelines provided guidance on the application of the arm's length principle in order to arrive at the proper transfer pricing range between associated enterprises. Market forces determine business relations between independent parties. The arm's length principle seeks to adjust the profits between two independent enterprises. It treats each enterprises as a separate independent entity rather than as inseparable parts of a single business.

Significance of Arm's Length Principle

- Party between MNC's and independent enterprises.
- Determines real taxable profits.
- Reduction of artificial price distortion.
- Minimisation of double taxation.
- Accurate measurement of economic contribution.

Practical Difficulties in Application of ALP

- True comparison difficult in certain cases.
- Availability of data and reliability of available data.
- There must be a reasonably reliable and comparable uncontrolled market price.
- There must be a administrative burden on tax payer.
- Enterprise establishes the conditions for a transaction at the time it is undertaken.

The Indian Scenario related to Transfer Pricing

Transfer Pricing in relation to International Transactions

In order to provide a statutory framework empowering the tax authorities to determine reasonable, fair and equitable profits and tax in respect of cross-border transactions, Section 92 to 92 F had been included in Chapter X of the Income Tax Act, 1961, through the Finance Act, 2001, providing for a transfer pricing mechanism based on computation of income from cross-border transactions. *The following conditions must be satisfied in order to attract the special provisions of Chapter X relating to avoidance of tax*

- There must be an international transaction.
- Such international transaction should be between two or more associated enterprises, either or both of whom are non-residents.
- *Such international transaction should be in the nature of*
  - (a) purchase, sale or lease of tangible or intangible property; or
  - (b) provision of service; or
  - (c) lending or borrowing money; or
  - (d) any other transactions having a bearing on the profits, income, losses or assets of such enterprise.
- Further, such transactions may also involve allocation and apportionment of, or any contribution to any cost or expenses incurred or to be incurred in connection with a benefit, service or facility provided to anyone or more of the associated enterprises on the basis of mutual agreement or arrangement between such associated enterprises.
- Such international transaction must be done at arm's length price and if such international transaction has been done at less than the arm's length price, it shall require determination of income or apportionment of cost or expense on the basis of arm's length price.
- The above adjustment should either result in an increase of income or decrease of loss returned by the assessee. In other words, the adjustment should not have the effect of reducing the income chargeable to tax or increasing the loss.

Computation of Income from Transaction with Non-resident (Section 92)

Section 92 provides that any income arising from an 'international transaction' shall be computed having regard to the 'arm's length price'. For this purpose, the allowance for any expense or interest shall be determined on the basis of arm's length price. The section further provides that in an international transaction between two or more associated enterprises. when there is a mutual agreement or arrangement for the allocation or apportionment of, or any contribution to any cost or expenses in connection with a benefit, service or facility provided to anyone or more of such enterprises, the allocation of cost, expenses etc shall be determined having regard to arm's length price of such benefit, service or facility. Similarly, the price received for exports and amounts received for services rendered to associated enterprise will be determined on the basis of arm's length price. It will be noticed that in the international transaction. The income or expense will have to be at arm's length price, if the transaction is between associated enterprises.

While determining arm's length price under the provisions of transfer pricing regulations, if the income works out to a figure lower than the income shown in the books of accounts, the provision of transfer pricing regulations will not apply.

The assessing officer will have wide powers to determine what is an arm's length price for such transactions and make adjustments for computation of income.

Associated Enterprises (Section 92 A)

The term 'associated enterprise' in relation to another enterprise is defined in Section 92A (1). *It means an enterprise*

- which participates, directly or indirectly, or through one or more intermediaries, in the management or control or capital of the other enterprise; or
- in respect of which one or more persons who participate, directly or indirectly, or through one or more intermediaries, in its management or control or capital, are the same persons who participate, directly or indirectly, or through one or more intermediaries, in the management or control or capital of the other enterprise.

Arm's Length Price

Arm's length price is defined in Section 92F (ii) to mean price which is applied or proposed to be applied in a transaction between persons other than associated enterprises in uncontrolled conditions. Section 92C deals with the method for determining arm's length price and the factors which are to be considered for applicability or non-applicability of a particular method to a given situation. The factors as well as methods incorporated in this section are not exhaustive and the CBDT may prescribe further factors and methods. Section 92C provides that the arm's length price in relation to an international transaction shall be determined by any of the following methods, being the most appropriate method, having regard to the nature of transaction or class of transaction or class of associated persons or functions performed by such persons or such other relevant factors as the board may prescribe.

Comparable Uncontrolled Price Method

- Under this method, the price charged or paid for property transferred or services provided under any comparable uncontrolled transaction or transactions should be identifiable.
- Adjustment to account for differences between the international transaction and comparable uncontrolled transactions or between the enterprises entering into such transactions which could materially affect the price in the open market can be made.
- The adjusted price as worked out under (ii) will be considered as an arm's length price in respect of the property transferred or services provided in the international transaction.

Resale Price Method

- Under this method, the price at which property purchased or services contained by the enterprise from an associated enterprise is resold or are provided to an unrelated enterprise should be identifiable.
- *The following adjustments can be made to such resale price*
  - (a) for normal gross profit margin.
  - (b) for expenses incurred in connection with the purchase of property or obtaining of services.
  - (c) for functional and other differences, including differences in accounting practices which could materially affect the gross profit margin in the open market.
- The adjusted price as stated in (ii) above will be considered as the arm's length price.

Cost Plus Method

- Under this method, the direct and indirect costs of production incurred by the enterprise in respect of property transferred or services provided to an associated enterprise should be determined.
- The amount of a normal gross profit mark-up to such costs arising from the transfer or provision of the same or similar property or services by the enterprise, or by an unrelated enterprise in comparable uncontrolled transaction or transactions should be determined.
- The above normal gross profit mark-up can be adjusted to take into account, the functional and other differences which could materially affect such profit mark-up in the open market.
- Costs referred to in (ii) above should be increased by the adjusted profit mark-up as stated in (iii) above and the price so arrived at will be considered as the arm's length price.

Profit Split Method

- This is a method which may be applicable mainly in international transactions involving transfer of unique in tangibles or in multiple international transactions which are so inter-related that they cannot be evaluated separately for the purpose of determining the arm's length price of any one transaction.
- Under this method, combined net profit of the associated enterprises arising from the international transactions in which they are engaged in first determined.
- The relative contribution of each associated enterprises to the earning of such combined net profit is then evaluated on the basis of the functions performed, assets employed and risks assumed by each enterprise. This evaluation is to be made on the basis of reliable external market data which can indicate how such contribution would be evaluated by unrelated enterprises performing comparable functions in similar circumstances.
- The combined net profit is then split amongst the enterprises in proportion to their relative contributions. The profit, thus apportioned to the assessee is taken into consideration to arrive at an arm's length price in relation to the international transaction.

Transactional Net Margin Method

- In this method, the net profit margin realised by the enterprise from an international transaction with an associated enterprise is computed having regard to costs incurred or sales effected or assets employed or having regard to any other relevant base.
- The net profit margin realised by the enterprise or by an unrelated enterprise from a comparable uncontrolled transaction by applying the same base as in (i) above is computed. This profit margin is adjusted to take into account, the differences which could materially affect the net profit margin in the open market having regard to international transaction and comparable uncontrolled transactions or having regard to the enterprise entering into such transactions.
- If the net profit margin realised by the enterprise as in (i) above is established to be the same as the net profit margin as in (ii) above, then the same is taken into consideration to arrive at an arm's length price in relation to the international transaction.

EXAM BASED QUESTIONS

Concept of Corporate Tax Planning

1 Tax……… is tax hedging within the frame of law.
(a) planning (b) management
(c) evasion (d) avoidance

2 Tax ……… takes into account the loopholes of law.
(a) planning (b) management
(c) evasion (d) avoidance

3 Nature of tax planning includes
(a) legal (b) moral
(c) honest effort (d) All of these

4 Objective of tax planning is
(a) avoidance of tax (b) minimise of tax liability
(c) payment of tax at time (d) different of tax

5 In the tax avoidance, the provisions law
(a) not abided (b) misused
(c) wrong interpretation (d) All of these

6 Causes of tax evasion is/are
(a) higher tax rates (b) complex of provisions
(c) corruption (d) All of these

7 Better way of reducing tax liability is
(a) tax evasion (b) tax avoidance
(c) tax planning (d) Both (a) and (b)

8 Tax planning is done
(a) before tax management (b) after tax management
(c) during tax management (d) never

9 Tax planning is
(a) ethical (b) legal
(c) Both (a) and (b) (d) None of these

10 Which of the following is not a punishable?
(a) Tax management (b) Tax planning
(c) Both (a) and (b) (d) None of these

11 Medium of tax planning are
(a) incentives (b) deductions
(c) rebates (d) All of these

12 An art of lodging tax without actually breaking the law is
(a) tax planning (b) tax evasion
(c) tax avoidance (d) tax management

13 Methods of the tax planning are
(a) capital gain
(b) income from property
(c) income from other source
(d) All of the above

14 Tax planning brings reduction in tax liability of the following
(a) a company
(b) an individual
(c) a Hindu Undivided Family
(d) an assessee

15 To reduce tax burden of the assessee by following the provisions of the income tax law is called
(a) tax planning (b) tax avoidance
(c) tax evasion (d) tax management

16 An exercise undertaken to minimise tax liability through the best use of all available allowances, deductions, exclusions, exemptions etc to reduce income tax liability is known as
(a) tax evasion (b) tax planning
(c) tax avoidance (d) tax lodging

17 The technique of keeping the tax liability at the minimum level without violating tax laws and without defeating the main intention of law is called
(a) tax evasion (b) tax avoidance
(c) tax planning (d) None of these

18 Taking full advantage of loopholes of law so as to attract least incidence of tax is known as
(a) tax evasion (b) tax avoidance
(c) tax planning (d) tax management

19 Which of the following is based on the measures which circumvent law?
(a) Short range planning (b) Purposive tax planning
(c) Permissive tax planning (d) Long-range tax planning

20 Tax planning opportunities arise due to difference in …… amongst various countries.
(a) tax rates (b) tax exemptions
(c) Both (a) and (b) (d) Neither (a) nor (b)

21 Who do people often define to tax evasion?
(a) As a victimless crime
(b) As a pointless battle that waste resources
(c) As a crusade against the rich
(d) As a crime against the taxpayer

22 What is expected to cut out tax avoidance?
(a) A change in law to make it illegal
(b) An amnesty for those involved in avoidance
(c) The government introducing more resources to fight the problem
(d) The introduction of professional conduct in relation to taxation code

23 What is the difference between tax avoidance and evasion?
(a) Avoidance is done by corporates
(b) There is no difference in law
(c) Avoidance is legal and evasion is illegal
(d) Evasion is done by individuals

24 "Tax planning is a moral way of tax saving, in it a tax payer reduce tax liability honestly and it's a long-term process." This definition is given by
(a) Prof Colder (b) Prof Dalton
(c) Alderson (d) Andrew

25 Consider the following statements.
1. Legal provisions are not followed in tax-planning.
2. The advantage due to loopholes of tax laws are taking in tax avoidance.
3. Tax evasion is punishable crime.

Which of the statement(s) given above is/are correct?
Codes
(a) Both 1 and 2 (b) Only 3
(c) Both 2 and 3 (d) All of the above

26 Consider the following statements.
1. To file return of income on prescribed date is covered under tax management.
2. Tax planning is always possible without tax management.
3. Tax management is done prior to tax planning.

Which of the statement(s) given above is/are correct?
Codes
(a) Both 1 and 2 (b) Only 3
(c) Both 2 and 3 (d) All of the above

27 Consider the following statements.
1. Concealment of income is a step of tax evasion.
2. Tax evasion is a immoral process.
3. Tax planning is long and short-term.

Which of the statement(s) given above is/are correct?
Codes
(a) Both 1 and 2 (b) Only 3
(c) Both 2 and 3 (d) All of the above

28 Consider the following statements.
1. Tax avoidance is temporary.
2. Tax planning is temporary in nature, while tax avoidance is permanent.
3. Certain conditions relating to Sections of Act are to be complained in tax management.

Which of the statement(s) given above is/are correct?
Codes
(a) Only 1 (b) Both 1 and 3
(c) Only 2 (d) All of the above

29 X is an individual. For the assessment year 2012-13 his gross total income is ₹ 3,40,000. Tax on it is ₹ 16,480. To reduce his tax liability, he deposits ₹ 50,000 in public provident fund account. Consequently, his taxable income and tax liability will be reduced to ₹ 1,10,000 and ₹ 11,330 respectively.
(a) Tax evasion (b) Tax planning
(c) Tax avoidance (d) Tax management

30 If a sum of money is gifted by a husband to his wife, income generated there from is taxable in the hands of husband under the clubbing provisions of Section 64 (1). Section 64 (1) is not applicable, if gift is made by the same person out of the funds of his Hindu Undivided Family in capacity as karta of the family. In such a case it is
(a) tax evasion (b) tax planning
(c) tax avoidance (d) tax management

31 Consider the following statements.
1. Tax planning is not essential for every assessee, while tax management is essential for every person, otherwise he may be liable for penal interest, penalty and prosecution.
2. In tax planning alternative economic activities are studied and an activity with least incidence of tax is selected. Whereas tax management includes maintenance of accounts in prescribed form. Get these audited, filling the required forms and returns, payment of taxes etc.
3. Tax planning always done in isolation.
4. Tax planning is guide in decision making, while tax management is a regular feature of an undertaking.

Which of the statement(s) given above is/are correct?
Codes
(a) Both 1 and 2 (b) Only 1
(c) 1, 2 and 4 (d) 2, 3 and 4

Tax Considerations in Specific Business Situations

32 The replacement may be of
(a) defective parts
(b) entire machinery
(c) substantial part of the entire machinery
(d) All of the above

33 An expenditure incurred to preserve and maintain an existing asset is
(a) maintenance (b) repairs
(c) current repairs (d) current maintenance

34 When expenses incurred on replacement of an asset are capitalised, it will
(a) decrease tax liability
(b) increase tax liability
(c) have no impact on tax liability
(d) decrease block of asset

35 A loss in business suffer due to
(a) fall in demand (b) high rate of taxes
(c) change in technology (d) All of these

36 To reduce tax liability, in case of income is high in relevant years, the pace of repair and renewal can be
(a) neutral (b) slower
(c) faster (d) None of these

37 Cost of issue of share is allowed as deduction in
(a) the same year of issue under Section 32(D)
(b) 3 years under Section 33(D)
(c) 5 years under Section 35(D)
(d) 7 years under Section 36

38 If the business or profession has been discontinued, unabsorbed depreciation can be
(a) set-off against income from business or profession
(b) set-off against income from any head
(c) carried forward and set-off for indefinite period
(d) All of the above

39 The cost of own asset is .... in computing the income.
(a) deductible (b) not deductible
(c) capitalised (d) None of these

40 Non-availability of depreciation to the lessee will .... his tax liability.
(a) decrease (b) increase
(c) have no impact on (d) None of these

41 The interest on borrowed fund or under hire-purchase/instalment system is .... in computing the income.
(a) deductible (b) not deductible
(c) added back (d) None of these

42 When the asset is purchased or acquired under hire-purchase/instalment system, the depreciation is......... in computing income.
(a) allowed (b) not allowed
(c) added back (d) None of these

43 In a case of asset with large residual value, it is better to .... it rather than taken on......... .
(a) fire-purchase, lease
(b) purchase, hire-purchase
(c) purchase, lease
(d) purchase, instalment

44 In case of......, the profit of the ...... will be the loss to the.......... .
(a) lease, lessor, lessee
(b) lease, lessee, lessor
(c) hire-purchase, seller, financer
(d) hire-purchase, hirer, seller

45 In case of replacement of a part only, the expenditure for such replacement is .... in computing the income.
(a) deductible (b) not deductible
(c) added back (d) None of these

46 In case of make or buy decision, the product is consumable one, raw material or required to replace a worn out part at the time of repair, its cost will be treated as......... expense and deductible in computing the income.
(a) capital (b) revenue
(c) deferred revenue (d) abnormal

47 Where an expenditure is incurred to bring new asset into existence or to obtain a new or fresh advantage, it is considered as a
(a) replacement (b) renewal
(c) Both (a) and (b) (d) None of these

48 .... neither refers to petty repairs nor the repairs carried out year to year, but it refers to the repairs carried out presently, whatever its cost may be
(a) Maintenance (b) Current maintenance
(c) Current repairs (d) Repairs

49 The amount paid on account or repairs of current repairs shall not include any expenditure in the nature of
(a) revenue expenditure
(b) capital expenditure
(c) deferred revenue expenditure
(d) Both (a) and (b)

50 .... is an arrangement that provides a person with the use and control over an asset, for a price payable periodically, without having a title of ownership.
(a) Lease (b) Royalty
(c) Hire purchase (d) Indirect sale

51 If a concern has surplus capacity and even decide to buy a product, it may require to sell a part of its plant and machinery. In such a case, it may be liable to
(a) income tax (b) capital gain tax
(c) deduct depreciation (d) None of these

52 If an asset is used for scientific research related to the business of assessee, is used in business for sometime and then sold, the selling price is deducted from the WDV of the block of asset. This will reduce
(a) profit for that year (b) loss for that year
(c) tax liability for that year (d) None of the above

53 If an asset used for scientific research related to the business of assessee, is used in business for sometime and then sold, the selling price is deducted from the
(a) profit
(b) written down value of the block of asset
(c) cost of the asset
(d) scrap value

54 If an asset used for scientific research related to the business of assessee is used in business for sometime and then sold, the selling price is deducted from the WDV of the block of asset. This will bring more cash in hand and tax liability will
(a) decrease in future (b) increase in future
(c) same in future (d) None of these

55 If the product, either manufactured or purchased, is a capital asset, its cost will not be allowed as a deduction in computing the income. However, if the asset is such, on which depreciation is allowed, it will be allowed in case(s) of
(a) manufactured (b) purchased
(c) hire-purchased (d) Both (a) and (b)

56 **In which of the following cases, dividend tax is not charged?**

1. With effect from 1st April, 2009, the amount of dividend paid to any person for, on behalf of the New Pension System Trust.
2. When the dividend is interim.
3. If such dividend is paid by accumulated profit.
4. If dividend distributed on or after 1st April, 2005 out of income generated from special economic zone.

Select the correct answer using the codes given below

Codes

(a) Only 1
(b) Both 1 and 4
(c) Only 2
(d) None of the above

57 **In the following cases, it cannot be said that the business has been discontinued**

1. Where the business of the assessee has been shifted from one premises to another.
2. Where the business of the assessee has been shifted from one market to another.
3. Where one or the other department of the business had been closed down.
4. Where the business of an industrial undertaking carried on in India is discontinued in any previous year, due to extensive damage and such business is reestablished within 3 years.

Select the correct answer using the codes given below

Codes

(a) Only 1 (b) Both 2 and 4
(c) Both 1 and 3 (d) All of the above

58 **Which of the following conditions are satisfied in case of sale of depreciable assets, in which assessee has claimed depreciation and sale was in even of discontinuance of business?**

1. The difference between the net consideration and WDV shall be treated as short-term capital gain/loss.
2. If the difference between the net consideration and WDV results in gain, then it will be liable to tax.
3. If the difference between the net consideration and WDV results in loss, then it will set-off against any head.

Select the correct answer using the codes given below

Codes

(a) Only 1
(b) Both 1 and 2
(c) Both 1 and 3
(d) Both 2 and 3

Double Taxation and its Avoidance Mechanism

59 **Double taxation relief could be**

(a) bilateral relief
(b) unilateral relief
(c) multilateral relief
(d) Both (a) and (b)

60 **Bilateral relief could be provided by way of**

(a) credit method
(b) exemption method
(c) Both (a) and (b)
(d) None of the above

61 **Residence rule provides that income is to be taxed in the country**

(a) where the recipient of income is a resident
(b) where it originates
(c) Both (a) and (b)
(d) None of the above

62 **Source rule of taxation provides that income is to be taxed**

(a) in the country of residence of taxpayer
(b) in the country in which such income originates
(c) Both (a) and (b)
(d) None of the above

63 **Where an assessee is eligible to claim the the DTAA benefit**

(a) provisions of DTAA shall apply to the assessee
(b) provisions of Income Tax Act shall apply to the assessee
(c) provisions of DTAA or Income Tax Act, whichever is more beneficial, shall apply to the assessee
(d) None of the above

64 **Which one of the following statements concerning double taxation is correct?**

(a) If there is a double taxation agreement, then relief will never be available
(b) If there is a double taxation agreement, then relief will always be available
(c) It there is no double taxation agreement, then relief will never be available
(d) If there is no double taxation agreement, then relief will often not be available

65 **Central Government may enter into an agreement, with the government of any country outside India under Section 90 for granting relief in respect of**

(a) income, where income tax has been paid both in India and in country of residence of taxpayer
(b) income on which income tax is chargeable under the IT Act and under the corresponding law in force in that country
(c) Both (a) and (b)
(d) None of the above

66 **Bilateral relief means a relief in which**

(a) home country of the taxpayer provides tax relief, where no mutual agreement has been entered into by the two countries for providing relief from double taxation
(b) government of two countries, enter into an agreement to provide relief against double taxation on mutually agreed basis
(c) Both (a) and (b)
(d) None of the above

67 Unilateral relief means a method of providing relief from double taxation in which
(a) home country of the taxpayer provides tax relief, where no mutual agreement has been entered into by the two countries for providing relief from double taxation
(b) government of two countries, enter into an agreement to provide relief against double taxation on mutually agreed basis
(c) Both (a) and (b)
(d) None of the above

68 In exemption method,
(a) income is taxed in the country of source and country of residence and deduction is provided in other country
(b) income is taxed in one country and exempt from tax in the other country
(c) Both (a) and (b)
(d) None of the above

69 In Tax credit method,
(a) income is taxed in country of source and country of residence deduction is provided in other country
(b) income is taxed in one country and exempt from tax in the other country
(c) Both (a) and (b)
(d) None of the above

70 What is the main reason for shifting profits from one country to another country?
(a) To avoid double taxation
(b) To benefit from investment opportunities
(c) To increase overall pre-tax profits
(d) To benefit from a difference in tax rates

71 Advance ruling can resolve complex issues arising under .... where a difference of opinion may exist.
(a) Income Tax Act, 1961 (b) DTAA
(c) Both (a) and (b) (d) None of these

72 Any term used in DTAA with a foreign country and not defined in the agreement or the act but assigned a meaning in the notification issued by the Central Government in the official gazette, shall have the meaning assigned in such notification and shall be effective from the
(a) date of the DTAA
(b) date of the notification
(c) date of publication of the official gazette
(d) None of the above

73 In case of conflict between the provisions of the DTAA and the Income Tax Act, 1961, then
(a) the provision of the act will always prevail over the DTAA
(b) the provision of the DTAA will always prevail over the act
(c) the provision of the act will apply to the extent, they are more beneficial to the assessee
(d) the issue will be resolved by mutual consent of the contracting states

74 Where a person derives income from a nation with which India does not have a DTAA, such person is given credit in India in the following manner.
(a) Entire tax paid in the foreign country is allowed as deduction
(b) Tax paid in the foreign country on income which is doubly taxed, is allowed as deduction
(c) Tax paid on income which is doubly taxed, is allowed as deduction, at the Indian rate of tax only
(d) Tax paid on income which is doubly taxed, is allowed as deduction, at the Indian rate of tax or rate of tax of the foreign country, whichever is lower

75 Assume that Arjun has earned an income of ₹ 4 lakh by way of lumpsum consideration for copyright of book from a publisher in Country Y, with which India does not have a DTAA. The same has been taxed at a flat rate of 5% in Country Y. In India, his gross total income is ₹ 7 lakh. The double taxation relief available is
(a) ₹ 20,000 (b) ₹ 5,000 (c) ₹ 12,000 (d) ₹ 1,932

76 Taxes on income and on capital imposed on behalf of a contracting State or of its political subdivisions or local authorities, irrespective of the manner in which they are levied, are covered in the following model convention(s)
(a) only in the OECD model convention
(b) only in the UN model convention
(c) only in the US model convention
(d) Both (a) and (b)

77 In the tax treaties based on OECD and UN model tax conventions, where capital gains arises on alienation of an immovable property, such gains derived
(a) will always be taxed only in the place of residence of the taxpayer
(b) will always be taxed only in the place of location of the immovable property
(c) can be taxed in both States and appropriate relief allowed as per the terms of the DTAA in the place of residence
(d) None of the above

78 A separate article on 'Independent Personal Service' is present
(a) only in the OECD model convention
(b) only in the UN model convention
(c) only in the US model convention
(d) Both (a) and (b)

79 Which of the following factors is not considered under the OECD model convention to determine the residence of an individual?
(a) Habitual abode
(b) Centre of vital interests
(c) Own house in Calcutta given on rent for the last ten years
(d) Flat taken on rent in Pune, where he is living for the last ten years

80 If a company is resident of two contracting states, namely, Country X, being the place of incorporation, and Country Y, being the place of effective management, then the company would be resident of Country Y, being the place of effective management as per

(a) only the OECD model convention
(b) only the UN model convention
(c) only the US mode convention
(d) Both (a) and (b)

81 As per the OECD model convention, the term 'Permanent Establishment' would not include

(a) branch
(b) an office for carrying out routine administrative work
(c) a factory for manufacture of goods
(d) a warehouse for storage of goods

82 The provisions relating to taxation of indirect transfer of shares of an Indian company were introduced Vide Finance Act, 2012 as a consequence of which of the following decisions of the Supreme Court?

(a) McDowell and Co Ltd *vs* CTO
(b) Vodafone International Holding BV *vs* UOI
(c) Union of India *vs* Azadi Bachao Andolan
(d) CIT *vs* Yokogawa India Limited

83 Which of the following incomes is not deemed to accrue or arise in India under Section 9 (1) (i) of the Income Tax Act, 1961?

(a) Income from any business connection in India
(b) Income through or from any property in India
(c) Income arising from transfer of a capital asset situate in India
(d) Income relating to operations which are confined to purchase of goods in India for the purpose of export

84 The provisions relating to limitation of interest deduction in respect of debt issued by a non-resident associated enterprises are not applicable to an Indian company engaged in the business of

(a) information technology
(b) banking and insurance business
(c) bio-technology
(d) aviation

85 The provisions relating to limitation of interest deduction in respect of debt issued by a non-resident associated enterprise would not apply, where the expenditure by way of interest or similar nature is

(a) ₹ 2.10 crore (b) ₹ 2 crore
(c) ₹ 1.50 crore (d) ₹ 1 crore

86 A Ltd has a wholly owned subsidiary in Sri Lanka and it extends corporate guarantee to the said non-resident subsidiary. If the amount guaranteed is ₹ 95 crore, the assessing officer has to accept the guarantee fee declared by A Ltd for financial year 2018-19, if the guarantee fee declares is

(a) ₹ 47. 50 lakh (b) ₹ 90 lakh
(c) ₹ 95 lakh (d) Either (a) or (b)

87 Which of the following approaches does India follow in relation to secondary adjustments?

(a) Deemed equity approach
(b) Deemed dividend approach
(c) Deemed loan approach
(d) Either (a) or (c)

88 Which of the following statements reflects the incorrect position?

(a) Domestic tax laws are irrelevant while considering application of the provisions of a DTAA
(b) Provisions of Income Tax Act, 1961 empower the Union Government to enter into tax treaties for relieving double taxation
(c) Provisions of a DTAA overrides the provisions of domestic laws unless the latter are more beneficial for a taxpayer
(d) In the absence of a DTAA, domestic tax laws provide unilateral relief to tackle double taxation

89 Which of the following would not be considered as a permanent home in context of tie-breaker rule for dual residency?

(a) Accommodation taken on rent for occupation
(b) Hotel accommodation provided for the purpose of prolonged employment
(c) Self-occupied house co-owned with spouse
(d) None of the above

90 Tax treaty is part of international law; hence its interpretation should be based on a certain set of principles and rules of interpretation. Which convention is used globally for interpretation of tax treaties?

(a) The UN model convention
(b) The OECD model convention
(c) Either (a) or (b)
(d) The Vienna convention

91 In order to claim relief under the tax treaty in India, a non-resident

(a) should have a business presence in India
(b) should produce his permanent account number
(c) should produce Tax Residency Certificate (TRC)
(d) should produce his income tax return filed in the home country

92 As per the provisions of the Income Tax Act, 1961, which of the following is not an objective of the Central Government to enter into tax treaty with another country?

(a) For granting relief in respect of income tax chargeable to tax in India and other country
(b) For enabling round tripping of unaccounted money in India
(c) For recovery of income tax
(d) For exchange or information for prevention of evasion or avoidance of income tax

93 In order to invoke the tax treaty for a person who is a dual resident, *i.e.* tax resident in both the countries, which rule may be applied under the relevant article of the tax treaties to resolve the issue?
(a) Force of attraction
(b) Tie-breaker
(c) Equivalent beneficiary
(d) Non-discrimination

Transfer Pricing

94 The purpose of transfer pricing was to ensure that the profit of a non-tax holiday segment were not
(a) overstated
(b) understated
(c) Either (a) or (b)
(d) Neither (a) nor (b)

95 Transfer pricing is, arriving at the price for goods and services, which are transacted between
(a) controlled legal entities within an enterprise
(b) independent entities within an enterprise
(c) Both (a) and (b)
(d) Neither (a) nor (b)

96 Transactions between unrelated entities are carried out at
(a) arm's length price (b) control price
(c) Both (a) and (b) (d) Either (a) or (b)

97 The objective of transfer pricing is to .... within an organisation.
(a) minimise cost
(b) achieve economic efficiency
(c) maximise benefit
(d) None of the above

98 The monetary amount used to record inter-company transactions is called
(a) exchange rate
(b) transfer price
(c) conversion rate
(d) incremental cost

99 When compared to a multilateral transfer pricing agreement. What is the main advantage of a unilateral agreement?
(a) It will eliminate the need to keep transfer pricing documentation
(b) It is quicker to negotiate
(c) It will enhance a company's profitability
(d) It will ensure no transfer pricing disputes arise

100 Which one of the following does not describe a type of transfer pricing?
(a) Cost based (b) Negotiated
(c) Administered (d) Target based

101 How many traditional methods are there for calculating a transfer price?
(a) 2 (b) 4
(c) 5 (d) 3

102 Which is the most useful method for setting a transfer price when very little value is added by the company that sells the product outside the group?
(a) Resale price method
(b) Transactional net margin method
(c) Cost plus method
(d) Profit split method

103 What is the overriding problem with the three traditional methods when trying to set a transfer price?
(a) They are too time-consuming
(b) External data may not be available
(c) They are too expensive
(d) Internal data may not be available

104 Which of the following statements correctly the approach of customs authorities and direct taxation authorities, when it comes to setting a transfer price?
(a) Both authorities will want to set the lowest possible transfer price
(b) The customs authorities will want to set a high transfer price while the direct taxation authorities will want to set a low price
(c) Both authorities will want to set the highest possible transfer price
(d) The customs authorities will want to set a low transfer price while the direct taxation authorities will want to set a high price

105 Which of the following is a limitation of cost-based transfer pricing?
(a) Determining which cost to use
(b) Lack of incentive for selling division to control cost
(c) inefficiencies in one unit may be transferred to another unit
(d) All of the above

106 A price on goods and services sold by one member of a corporate family to another, such as from a parent to its subsidiary in a foreign country, is known as
(a) arm's length price (b) export price
(c) import price (d) transfer prices

107 What can the worst-case scenario be for a firm that has subsidiaries that use cost-based transfer pricing?
(a) Failure of those businesses
(b) Prison for managers
(c) Nothing
(d) Failure of one business

108 What is the process by which subsidiaries transfer goods and assign prices?
(a) Transfer pricing
(b) Cost plus transfer pricing
(c) There is no name for this
(d) Trading resources

109 If ABC Ltd has two units, Unit 1 is engaged in power generation business and Unit 2 is engaged in manufacture of wires. Both the units were set-up in Karnataka in the year 2014. In the year 2018-19, twenty lakh metres of wire are transferred from Unit 2 to Unit 1 at ₹ 125 per metre when the market price per metre was ₹ 180, which of the following statements is correct?

(a) Transfer pricing provisions would be attracted in this case
(b) Transfer pricing provisions would not be attracted in this case since Unit 1 and Unit 2 belong to the same company and are not associated enterprises
(c) Transfer pricing provisions would not be attracted in this case as it is not an international transaction since both units are in India. However, for the purpose of Chapter VI A deduction, the profits of power generation business shall, however, be computed as if the transfer has been made at the market value of ₹ 180 per.
(d) Transfer pricing provisions would not be attracted in this case due to reasons mentioned in both (b) and (c) above

110 Alpha Ltd's total income of A.Y. 2019-20 has increased by ₹ 34 lakh due to application of arm's length price by the assessing officer on transactions of purchase of goods from its foreign holding company in respect of a retail trade business carried on by it, and the same has been accepted by S Ltd, then

(a) business loss of A.Y. 2015-16 cannot be set-off against the enhanced income
(b) deductions under Chapter VI-A cannot be claimed in respect of the enhanced income
(c) unabsorbed depreciation of A.Y. 2010-11 cannot be set-off against the enhanced income
(d) Business loss referred to in (a), deductions referred to in (b) and unabsorbed depreciation referred to in (c) cannot be set-off against the enhanced income

Miscellaneous

Directions (Q. Nos. 111 and 112) *In the questions given below two statements are labelled as Statement I and Statement II. You have to examine these two statements carefully and select the correct codes.*

Codes
(a) Statement I is correct, but Statement II is incorrect
(b) Both statements are correct
(c) Statement I is incorrect, but Statement II is correct
(d) Both statements are correct

111 **Statement** I Tax planning is very wide in its coverage and includes tax management.
Statement II Tax management is futuristic in its approach.

112 **Statement** I Tax avoidance is international tax planning before the actual tax liability arises.
Statement II The object of tax management is to comply with the provisions of law.

Directions (Q. Nos. 113-117) *In the questions given below two statements are labelled as Assertion (A) and Reason (R). In the context of the two statements, which of the following is correct?*

Codes
(a) Both (A) and (R) are true and (R) is the correct explanation of (A)
(b) Both (A) and (R) are true, but (R) is not the correct explanation of (A)
(c) (A) is true, but (R) is false
(d) (A) is false, but (R) is true

113 **Assertion** (A) When asset is taken on lease, the depreciation is not allowed to the lessor.
Reason (R) Lessor is the owner of the asset.

114 **Assertion** (A) In case of replacement of whole machinery with a view to bring a new asset into existence, the expenditure will not be deductible.
Reason (R) Expenditure to bring new asset is of capital nature.

115 **Assertion** (A) In India, tax evadors are not a bad persons. If he is rich, he is respectable person in the society.
Reason (R) This encourage assessee to tax evasion.

116 **Assertion** (A) Tax planning is possible without tax management.
Reason (R) The concept of tax planning is related to future.

117 **Assertion** (A) When a reason reduce his total income by making false claims to reduce its tax liability.
Reason (R) Tax evasion is illegal in India and may result to penalty and prosecution.

118 Match the following.

List I	List II
A. Tax evasion	1. Is done a financial activity, which a person proposes to carry out in near future
B. Tax avoidance	2. Unrecorded sales
C. Tax planning	3. Is a device, which technically satisfies the requirement of the law, but in fact it is not in accordance with the legislative intent
D. Tax management	4. Takes steps to avail various tax incentives

Codes

	A	B	C	D		A	B	C	D
(a)	2	1	3	4	(b)	2	3	1	4
(c)	2	1	4	3	(d)	2	4	1	3

PREVIOUS YEARS' QUESTIONS

November 2017

1 Which of the following will be considered as tax planning effort?

1. Mr A purchased a house for self-residence of ₹ 8 lakh by taking a loan of ₹ 60 lakh from SBI at 10% interest, instead of using his own funds.
2. Mr A made investment in purchasing 12% redeemable debentures of TISCO worth ₹ 1.50 lakh.
3. Mr A purchased 100 gm gold biscuits of ₹ 2.5 lakh from SBI on the occasion of Diwali.
4. Mr A invested ₹ 1 crore in purchasing 5 acres of agricultural land in his native village in Gaya.

Codes

(a) Both 1 and 2 (b) Both 2 and 3
(c) Both 1 and 4 (d) Both 3 and 4

December 2015

2 Assertion (A) Tax evasion is undertaken by employing unfair means.

Reason (R) Payment of tax is avoided through illegal means or fraud for tax evasion.

Codes

(a) (A) is true and (R) is the correct explanation of (A)
(b) (A) is true, but (R) is not the correct explanation of (A)
(c) Both (A) and (R) are true independently and (R) may be considered as an explanation of (A)
(d) Both (A) and (R) are false

July 2014

3 Which of the following are true in tax planning?

1. It is futuristic in its approach.
2. It has limited scope compared to tax management.
3. The benefits arising from it are limited particularly in the short-run.
4. Its main objective is to reduce the tax liability.

Codes

(a) 1, 2 and 3 (b) Both 1 and 2
(c) Both 1 and 4 (d) 2, 3 and 4

June 2012

4 Match the following.

	List I		List II
A.	Tax planning	1.	Making suitable arrangement of TDS
B.	Tax avoidance	2.	Understatement of income
C.	Tax evasion	3.	Availing deduction under Section 10 (A) of IT Act
D.	Tax administration	4.	Misinterpreting the provisions of the IT Act

Codes

	A	B	C	D		A	B	C	D
(a)	2	1	4	3	(b)	1	4	3	2
(c)	3	4	2	1	(d)	4	1	3	2

ANSWERS

Objective Questions

1 (d)	2 (b)	3 (d)	4 (b)	5 (b)	6 (d)	7 (c)	8 (b)	9 (c)	10 (c)
11 (d)	12 (a)	13 (d)	14 (d)	15 (a)	16 (b)	17 (c)	18 (b)	19 (b)	20 (c)
21 (d)	22 (b)	23 (c)	24 (a)	25 (c)	26 (a)	27 (d)	28 (b)	29 (b)	30 (c)
31 (c)	32 (d)	33 (b)	34 (b)	35 (d)	36 (c)	37 (c)	38 (d)	39 (b)	40 (b)
41 (a)	42 (a)	43 (a)	44 (a)	45 (a)	46 (b)	47 (c)	48 (c)	49 (b)	50 (a)
51 (b)	52 (c)	53 (b)	54 (b)	55 (d)	56 (b)	57 (d)	58 (b)	59 (d)	60 (c)
61 (a)	62 (b)	63 (c)	64 (b)	65 (c)	66 (b)	67 (a)	68 (b)	69 (a)	70 (d)
71 (c)	72 (a)	73 (c)	74 (d)	75 (d)	76 (d)	77 (c)	78 (b)	79 (c)	80 (d)
81 (d)	82 (b)	83 (d)	84 (b)	85 (d)	86 (c)	87 (c)	88 (a)	89 (b)	90 (d)
91 (c)	92 (b)	93 (b)	94 (a)	95 (a)	96 (a)	97 (b)	98 (b)	99 (a)	100 (d)
101 (d)	102 (a)	103 (b)	104 (b)	105 (d)	106 (d)	107 (d)	108 (a)	109 (a)	110 (b)
111 (a)	112 (c)	113 (d)	114 (a)	115 (a)	116 (d)	117 (a)	118 (b)		

Previous Years' Questions

1 (c)	2 (a)	3 (c)	4 (c)

NTA

UGC

NET/JRF/SET

MODEL PAPERS (1-3)

UGC NET/JRF/SET

COMMERCE (Paper-2)

Model Paper-1

General Instructions

1. There are total one hundred questions in this paper. Each question carries 2 marks.
2. All questions are compulsory.

1 Which of the following is an element of internal environment?

(a) Financial institution (b) Customers
(c) Policies and objectives (d) All of these

2 Foreign exchange reserves include

(a) gold stock (b) US Dollar
(c) Both (a) and (b) (d) Neither (a) nor (b)

3 Which of the following is not Balance of Payment?

(a) Capital Account (b) Loss Account
(c) Current Account (d) None of these

4 The quotas of all the member countries with the IMF are valued in terms of

(a) SDR (b) GDR
(c) Dollar (d) Swaps

5 In which of the following year, the Articles of Agreement of IMF were changed for the first time?

(a) 1967 (b) 1958
(c) 1969 (d) None of these

6 Statement I Business environment always changes.

Statement II Society exchanges business for production.

Codes

(a) Statement I is correct
(b) Statement II is correct
(c) Both statements are correct
(d) Both statements are incorrect

7 Match the following.

	List I		List II
A.	Micro environment	1.	Interest rate
B.	Macro environment	2.	Restrictions of WTO
C.	Political environment	3.	Suppliers
D.	Globalisation environment	4.	Planning Commission

Codes

	A	B	C	D		A	B	C	D
(a)	3	1	4	2	(b)	2	4	1	3
(c)	1	3	2	4	(d)	3	2	4	1

8 Match the following.

	List I		List II
A.	Foreign trade	1.	It is in undertaking by its issue that the bills of exchange drawn by the foreign dealer on the importer will be honoured on presentation upon a specified amount.
B.	Bill of lading	2.	It is a document of title to the goods.
C.	Quotation	3.	Trade between two or more nations.
D.	Letter of credit	4.	It is reply by the seller to the prospective buyer.

Codes

	A	B	C	D		A	B	C	D
(a)	4	1	3	2	(b)	3	2	4	1
(c)	2	3	4	1	(d)	4	3	2	1

9 **Assertion** (A) In BoP, every transaction has two aspects.

Reason (R) Since, for every credit there is corresponding debit and for every debit there is corresponding debit is explanatory.

Codes

(a) Both (A) and (R) are true and (R) is the correct explanation of (A)
(b) Both (A) and (R) are true, but (R) is not the correct explanation of (A)
(c) (A) is true, but (R) is false
(d) (A) is false, but (R) is true

10 **Assertion** (A) International trade enables a country to consume things which it can not produce.

Reason (R) International trade fosters trade.

Codes

(a) Both (A) and (R) are true and (R) is the correct explanation of (A)
(b) Both (A) and (R) are true, but (R) is not the correct explanation of (A)
(c) (A) is true, but (R) is false
(d) (A) is false, but (R) is true

11 Which of the following practices is not in consonance with the convention of conservatism?

(a) Creating provision for bad debts
(b) Creating provision for discount on creditors
(c) Creating provision for discount on debtors
(d) Creating provision for tax

12 **Assertion** (A) Human resource accounting is the measurement of the cost and value of people to the organisation.

Reason (R) Human resource accounting involves measuring costs incurred by the organisations to recruit, select, hire, train and develop employees and judge their economic value to the organisation.

Codes

(a) Both (A) and (R) are true and (R) is the correct explanation of (A)
(b) Both (A) and (R) true, but (R) is not the correct explanation of (A)
(c) Both (A) is true, but (R) is false
(d) Both (A) and (R) are false

13 A, B and C are three equal partners. D is admitted for $\frac{1}{4}$th share. What is the sacrificing ratio?

(a) 1 : 1 : 1 (b) 1 : 2 : 1
(c) 2 : 1 : 1 (d) 1 : 1 : 2

14 If cost of goods sold is ₹ 1,00,000; other operating expenses are ₹ 20,000 and total net sales are ₹ 1,50,000 the operating ratio will be equal to

(a) 70% (b) 80% (c) 90% (d) 100%

15 **Statement** I The scope of valuation is wider than verification.

Statement II Valuation is done after vouching but before verification.

Codes

(a) Statement I is true, but Statement II is false
(b) Statement II is true, but Statement I is false
(c) Both statements are true
(d) Both statements are false

16 Match the following.

	List I		List II
A.	Operating profit	1.	Capital employed = ... + Preference share capital
B.	Liquid liabilities	2.	......= Gross profit – Operating expenses
C.	Capital employed	3.	Quick assets = Quick ratio × ...
D.	Equity share capital	4.	Fixed assets ratio = Fixed assets ÷ ......

Codes

	A	B	C	D		A	B	C	D
(a)	2	3	4	1	(b)	3	4	1	2
(c)	4	3	2	1	(d)	2	1	4	3

17 A company forfeited 1,000 shares of ₹ 10 each fully called, on which ₹ 6,000 has been paid. Out of these 800 shares were re-issued upon payment of ₹ 6,600. What is the amount to be transferred to capital reserve?

(a) ₹ 4,800 (b) ₹ 6,000
(c) ₹ 4,600 (d) ₹ 3,400

18 Which of the following statement is correct?

(a) Whenever there is inflow of cash there will definitely be inflow of funds though reverse is not true
(b) Cash from operations and funds from operations mean the same thing
(c) Cash flow statement is a substitute of cash account
(d) Cash generated from trading operations is equal to the net profit as reported in the profit and loss account

19 If BEP sales is 60% of current sales and profit is ₹ 4,000, then what is contribution?

(a) ₹ 10,000 (b) ₹ 15,000
(c) ₹ 8,000 (d) ₹ 20,000

20 The costing method in which fixed factory overheads are added to inventory is

(a) process costing (b) activity based costing
(c) marginal costing (d) standard costing

21 Price discrimination will always lead to

(a) increase in output
(b) decrease in output
(c) no change in output
(d) None of the above

22 Which of the following is the best general definition of the study of economics?
(a) Inflation and unemployment in a growing economy
(b) The best way to invest in the stock market
(c) Business decision-making under foreign competition
(d) Individual and social choice in the face of scarcity

23 A shift in supply will have a bigger effect on price than output, if demand is
(a) income elastic (b) income inelastic
(c) price elastic (d) price inelastic

24 When total utility increases, marginal utility is
(a) negative and increasing (b) negative and declining
(c) positive and increasing (d) positive and declining

25 The normal LAC curve is influenced by
(a) principle of constant returns to scale
(b) economies and diseconomies of large scale production
(c) principle of diminishing returns
(d) All of the above

26 Match the following.

List I	List II
A. Utility	1. MU tends to decline as consumption of the commodity increases
B. Total utility	2. It is a want satisfying power of a good
C. Marginal utility	3. Sum total of utility derived from the consumption of all the units of a commodity
D. Law of diminishing marginal utility	4. Additional utility and account of the consumption of an additional unit of a commodity

Codes

	A	B	C	D		A	B	C	D
(a)	4	1	2	3	(b)	2	4	1	3
(c)	2	3	4	1	(d)	1	2	3	4

27 Match the following.

List I	List II
A. Perfectly elastic demand	1. $e_D = 1$
B. Elastic demand	2. $e_0 > 1$
C. Inelastic demand	3. $e_D = 0$
D. Perfectly inelastic demand	4. $e_D = \infty$
E. Unitary elastic demand	5. $e_D < 1$

Codes

	A	B	C	D	E
(a)	2	5	3	1	4
(b)	4	2	5	3	1
(c)	3	1	5	2	4
(d)	1	2	3	4	5

28 **Assertion** (A) Giffen goods face negative price effect.

Reason (R) Giffen goods has a low demand with rise in its price.

Codes
(a) Both (A) and (R) are true and (R) is the correct explanation of (A)
(b) Both (A) and (R) are true, but (R) is not the correct explanation of (A)
(c) (A) is true, but (R) is false
(d) (A) is false, but (R) is true

29 **Statement** I The objective of finance function is wealth maximisation.

Statement II The objective of finance function is profit maximisation.

Codes
(a) Both statements are correct
(b) Both statements are incorrect
(c) Statement I is correct, but Statement II is incorrect
(d) Statement I is incorrect, but Statement II is correct

30 Arrange the following in chronological order.
1. Diminishing returns 2. Negative returns
3. Increasing returns

Codes
(a) 1, 2, 3 (b) 3, 2, 1
(c) 2, 3, 1 (d) 3, 1, 2

31 Under the factoring arrangement, the factor
(a) produces and distributes the goods or services
(b) makes the payment on behalf of the client
(c) collects the client's debt or account receivables
(d) transfer the goods from one place to another

32 Match the following.

List I	List II
A. Regular dividend policy	1. Part of divisible profits of a company, which is distributed among its shareholders
B. Dividend	2. Application of planning and control functions to the finance function
C. Capitalisation	3. Payment of dividend at usual rate
D. Financial management	4. Refers to the process of determining the quantum of funds required for a firm

Codes

	A	B	C	D		A	B	C	D
(a)	4	3	2	1	(b)	2	3	4	1
(c)	3	1	4	2	(d)	4	1	2	3

33 Which of the following is not a capital budgeting decision?
(a) Expansion programme (b) Inventory level
(c) Replacement of an asset (d) Merger

34 Cost of capital from all the sources of funds is called
(a) specific cost (b) composite cost
(c) implicit cost (d) simple average cost

35 **Assertion** (A) A company should pay dividend to its shareholders.

Reason (R) Dividends are heavilly taxed than capital gains.

Codes
(a) Both (A) and (R) are true (b) Both (A) and (R) are false
(c) (A) is false, but (R) is true (d) (A) is true, but (R) is false

36 Under the Brettonwoods system,
(a) there was an explicit set of rules about the conduct of international monetary policies
(b) each country was responsible for maintaining its exchange rate within 1% of the adopted per value by buying or selling foreign exchanges as necessary
(c) The US dollar was the only currency that was fully convertible to gold
(d) All of the above

37 **Assertion** (A) Business having more risks and unstable income should prefer equity shares.
Reason (R) Sales stability and debt ratios are directly related.
Codes
(a) Both (A) and (R) are true and (R) is the correct explanation of (A)
(b) Both (A) and (R) are true, but (R) is not the correct explanation of (A)
(c) (A) is true, but (R) is false
(d) (A) is false, but (R) is true

38 Benefits from adopting a common European currency include
1. reduced transaction costs.
2. elimination of exchange rate risk
3. increased price transparency that will promote Europe wide competition.

Select the correct answer by using the codes given below
Codes
(a) Only 2 (b) Both 1 and 3
(c) Both 2 and 3 (d) All of the above

39 Which risk arises, if a party discharges his obligations, but the counterparty defaults?
(a) Replacement cost risk
(b) Principal risk
(c) Systematic risk
(d) Unsystematic risk

40 Match the following.

List I	List II
A. Payback method	1. Give due weightage to the profitability of project
B. Unadjusted rate of return method	2. Pre-determination of earnings is not necessary
C. NPV method	3. It avoids in calculable risk and uncertainty
D. IRR method	4. Its calculation is much simpler

Codes

	A	B	C	D
(a)	4	3	2	1
(b)	2	3	4	1
(c)	3	1	4	2
(d)	4	1	2	3

41 Match the following.

List I	List II
A. Range	1. Summing up the consecutive frequencies
B. Width of the interval	2. Range/Number of classes
C. Open-ended class	3. Highest value-lowest value in data
D. Cumulative frequency	4. No lower limit of first group or no upper limit of the last group

Codes

	A	B	C	D		A	B	C	D
(a)	1	2	3	4	(b)	3	2	4	1
(c)	2	3	4	1	(d)	4	3	2	1

42 ...... data is original in character and is generated by surveys conducted by individuals or research institutions.
(a) Primary (b) Secondary
(c) Tabulated (d) None of these

43 **Assertion** (A) A reasonably sized sample drawn randomly from large sized population contains almost all the characteristics which exist in the population.
Reason (R) The theory of sampling is based on the two important laws of statistics, *viz* law of statistical regularity and law of inertia of large numbers.
Codes
(a) Both (A) and (R) are correct and (R) is the correct exphanation of (A)
(b) Both (A) and (R) are correct, but (R) is not the correct explanation of (A)
(c) (A) is not correct, while (R) is correct
(d) Both (A) and (R) are not correct

44 Null hypothesis and alternatives hypothesis is denoted by
(a) H_0, H_1 respectively (b) H_1, H_0 respectively
(c) α, β respectively (d) None of these

45 Choose the correct code for the following statements being correct or incorrect.
Statement I If the value of β_2, *i.e.* $\frac{\mu_4}{\sigma_4}$, of a distribution gives the value more than 3, its curve is platykurtic.
Statement II In a moderately asymmetrical distribution, the standard deviation is 1.25 times of mean deviation.
Codes
(a) Both statements are correct
(b) Both statements are incorrect
(c) Statement I is correct, but Statement II is incorrect
(d) Statement II is correct, but Statement I is incorrect

46 Coefficient of correlation between X and Y is directly proportional to

(a) standard deviation of X (b) standard deviation of Y
(c) covariance of X and Y (d) Both (a) and (b)

47 Read the following statement and indicate the correct code from the alternative given below.

Statement I When the null hypothesis is true but as per the hypothesis testing, it is rejected, it is known as beta type error in hypothesis testing.

Statement II Chi-square test is exclusively a non-parametric test.

Codes

(a) Both statements are true
(b) Both statements are false
(c) Statement I is true, while Statement II is false
(d) Statement I is false, while Statement II is true

48 Under which of the following situations, chi-square test is applicable?

1. Testing homogenity
2. Testing goodness of fit
3. Testing equality of two sample means
4. Testing equality of two sample proportions
5. Testing indepndence of attributes

Select the correct answer using the codes given below

Codes

(a) 1, 2 and 3 (b) 1, 2 and 5
(c) 3, 4 and 5 (d) 1, 3 and 5

49 The area under normal distribution covered within $\mu \pm 3\sigma$ limit is

(a) 0.6827 (b) 0.9545
(c) 0.9973 (d) 1.0000

50 Match the following.

List I	List II
A. Level of significance	1. Sample mean is equal to population mean
B. Standard deviation of sampling distribution	2. Parameters
C. Numerical value that describes the characteristics of the population	3. Type I error
D. Normally distributed population	4. Standard error

Codes

	A	B	C	D		A	B	C	D
(a)	4	3	1	2	(b)	3	4	2	1
(c)	3	2	4	1	(d)	4	2	3	1

51 "Management means forecasting, planning, organising, direction, coordinating and controlling". Who said this?

(a) Peter F Drucker (b) Henry Fayol
(c) Parkins (d) FW Taylor

52 The main advantage of decentralised organisation is

(a) top executive extends his central area
(b) coordination of activities becomes automatic
(c) top management can manage by 'exception'
(d) operation costs are lower

53 Motivational process and not the motivators as such is associated with the

(a) need hiearchy theory (b) two factor theory
(c) ERG theory (d) expectancy theory

54 The primary source of information for recruiting is

(a) job analysis (b) managerial interviews
(c) recruiter themselves (d) None of these

55 Factors influencing compensation levels does not include

(a) job needs (b) ability to pay
(c) cost of living (d) living standard

56 Match the following.

List I (Concepts)	List II (Demerits)
A. Time wage system	1. The earnings of workers are not stable
B. Piece wage system	2. Does not encourage extraordinary efficiency
C. Halsey plan	3. In this, cost of supervision are high
D. Rowan plan	4. Fixation of standard is not easy

Codes

	A	B	C	D		A	B	C	D
(a)	4	3	2	1	(b)	3	1	4	2
(c)	2	1	4	3	(d)	1	2	3	4

57 Match the following.

List I	List II
A. Formal organisation	1. High degree of specialisation
B. Informal organisation	2. Rigid
C. Functional organisation	3. Product specialisation
D. Divisional	4. Flexible

Codes

	A	B	C	D		A	B	C	D
(a)	2	4	1	3	(b)	4	2	3	1
(c)	2	1	4	3	(d)	3	1	2	4

58 **Assertion** (A) Management principles increase managerial efficiency.

Reason (R) Management principles provide useful insights of managers.

Codes

(a) (R) is correct, but (A) is not correct
(b) (A) is correct, but (R) is not correct
(c) Both (A) and (R) are correct
(d) Both (A) and (R) are not correct

59 Consider the following statements.

1. As per leadership theory (participative), leader retains the right to allow the input of others.
2. Faculty decoding is an example of feedback.
3. A satisfied need can no longer motivate a person.

Which of the statement(s) given above is/are correct?

(a) Only 1 (b) Only 2
(c) Both 1 and 2 (d) Both 1 and 3

60 Arrange the following in chronological order about steps of succession planning process.

1. Document and implement succession plans
2. Identify competencies
3. Identify critical positions
4. Identify succession management strategies

Codes

(a) 4, 1, 2, 3 (b) 3, 2, 4, 1 (c) 2, 4, 1, 3 (d) 1, 3, 2, 4

61 The features of the commercial papers are

(a) it is an unsecured money market instrument issued in the form of promissory note
(b) the highly rated corporate borrowers can raise short-term funds through this instrument
(c) it is an additional instrument to the investing community
(d) All of the above

62 E-banking is synonymous with

(a) tele banking (b) internet banking
(c) euro banking (d) None of these

63 The chief promoter of 'Clearing Corporation'is

(a) SBI (b) RBI
(c) Finacial Ministry (d) None of these

64 Real Time Gross Settlement (RTGS) is managed by

(a) State Bank of India (b) Reserve Bank of India
(c) Indian Banks' Association (d) Government of India

65 Which of the following term is not used in the world of finance, banking and insurance?

(a) Hard currency (b) Amnesty
(c) Devaluation (d) Sinking fund

66 Match the following.

List I	List II
A. Performing assets	1. Investments
B. Loss assets	2. Standard assets
C. Cash balance	3. Non-performing assets
D. Government securities	4. Liquid assets

Codes

	A	B	C	D		A	B	C	D
(a)	2	3	4	1	(b)	2	1	3	4
(c)	3	4	2	1	(d)	4	3	2	1

67 Match the following.

List I	List II
A. Financial Instruments	1. Organised and unorganised
B. Financial market	2. Intermediaries and non-intermediaries
C. Financial institutions	3. Unorganised financial system
D. Indigenous bankers	4. Facilitate transfer of funds

Codes

	A	B	C	D		A	B	C	D
(a)	4	1	2	3	(b)	2	1	4	3
(c)	1	2	4	3	(d)	3	2	1	4

68 Which one of the following statement is correct?

(a) General insurance corporation provides cover for life risks
(b) NBFC take deposits from the public
(c) NABARD was established on the recommendations of Narashimham Committee-I (1991)
(d) IDBI, NABARD have been notified as Public Financial Institutions (PFIs) under Companies Act, 1956.

69 **Assertion** (A) The Central Bank of the country is responsible to maintain stability of the monetary standard which involves currency circulation.

Reason (R) The Central Bank is the only authorised entity to do so.

(a) Both (A) and (R) are true (b) Both (A) and (R) are false
(c) (A) is true, but (R) is false (d) (R) is true, but (A) is false

70 The profitability of public sector banks is low due to

1. over-cautions approach to lending
2. Reserve Bank policies 3. High overhead costs
4. Social sector lending

Codes

(a) Both 1 and 2 (b) Both 1 and 4
(c) 1, 3 and 4 (d) Both 2 and 3

71 Social marketing concept is based upon

(a) large target market with active buyers
(b) customer satisfaction and customer welfare
(c) realisation of maximum profit through service of society
(d) None of the above

72 Email marketing involves

(a) advertising (b) promotional marketing
(c) Both (a) and (b) (d) None of these

73 Customer relationship management technolgoy can help in

(a) designing direct marketing efforts
(b) processing transaction faster
(c) Both (a) and (b)
(d) None of the above

74 Which of the following is not the example of social networking sites?

(a) Facebook (b) Twitter (c) Instagram (d) Amazon

75 Institutional advertising is

(a) aimed only at people in institutions
(b) run only by institutions
(c) designed to promote a type of product rather than a particular brand
(d) designed simply to show that the firm is a good place to do business

76 Match the following.

List I	List II
A. Personal selling	1. Stimulates demand for a whole type of product
B. Geographic selectivity	2. Personal presentation and promotion of ideas, goods or services
C. Qualitative selectivity	3. Ability of an advertising medium to reach almost everyone in given area
D. Primary demand advertising	4. Ability of an advertising medium to reach only certain types of people.

Codes

	A	B	C	D		A	B	C	D
(a)	2	3	4	1	(b)	1	2	3	4
(c)	2	4	3	1	(d)	4	3	2	1

77 Match the following.

List I	List II
A. Product concept	1. Marketing myopia
B. Production concept	2. Mass production and distribution
C. Marketing concept	3. Customer satisfaction
D. Societal marketing concept	4. Ethical marketing practices

Codes

	A	B	C	D		A	B	C	D
(a)	1	2	3	4	(b)	2	3	4	1
(c)	4	1	2	3	(d)	4	3	2	1

78 Assertion (A) "Advertising plays a vital role in selling products/services."

Reason (R) "Sales promotion is incomplete without a good advertising plan."

Codes

(a) Both (A) and (R) are true
(b) Both (A) and (R) are false
(c) (A) is true, but (R) is false
(d) (A) is false, but (R) is true

79 Statement I Lead means a prospect, who is more likely to avail of the banker's product.

Statement II Market information means knowledge of customer profile and product mix.

Codes

(a) Both statements are true
(b) Both statements are false
(c) Statement I is true, but Statement II is false
(d) Statement I is false, but Statement II is true

80 Which of the following buying process sequence is correct?

1. Adoption
2. Legitimisation
3. Attitude
4. Awareness

Codes

(a) 4, 3, 2, 1 (b) 2, 3, 4, 1 (c) 1, 2, 3, 4 (d) 3, 4, 2, 1

81 A contract where the seller transfers or agrees to transfer property in goods to buyer for a price is called

(a) contract of sale (b) contract of purchase
(c) contract of lease (d) None of these

82 To qualify for copyright protection, what must the work be?

(a) Original, creative to a minimal degree and in a fixed or tangible or of expression
(b) Something, *i.e.* deemed useful by the public
(c) Anything
(d) All of the above

83 Verification of electronic record is possible through

(a) digital signature (b) e-commerce
(c) public key (d) e-governance

84 Maximum number of members in case of private company

(a) 10 (b) 50
(c) 70 (d) 200

85 The Indian Contract Act, 1872 extends to

(a) whole of India
(b) whole of India excluding Jammu and Kashmir
(c) North India
(d) South India

86 Match the following.

List I (Sections)	List II (Explanation)
A. Section 3	1. Annual general meeting
B. Section 103	2. Extraordinary general meeting
C. Section 96	3. Formation of company
D. Section 100	4. Quorum for meeting

Codes

	A	B	C	D		A	B	C	D
(a)	1	2	3	4	(b)	3	4	1	2
(c)	2	3	4	1	(d)	4	1	2	3

87 Match the following.

List I	List II
A. Patent	1. Berne convention
B. Trademark	2. Paris convention
C. Copyright	3. Madrid

Codes

	A	B	C		A	B	C
(a)	1	2	3	(b)	2	3	1
(c)	3	1	2	(d)	1	3	2

88 Statement I Every contract is an agreement but every agreement is not a contract.

Statement II All agreements are contracts, if they are made by the free consent of parties.

Codes

(a) Statement I is correct, but Statement II is incorrect

(b) Statement II is correct, but Statement I is incorrect
(c) Both statements are correct
(d) Both statements are incorrect

89 Arrange the steps of incorporation of LLP in sequence.
1. Application for DPIN 2. Filing of LLP agreement
3. Application for DSC 4. Incorporation of LLP

Codes
(a) 1, 3, 2, 4 (b) 3, 1, 4, 2 (c) 2, 1, 3, 4 (d) 1, 2, 3, 4

90 Limited liability partnership is the combination of
1. partnership 2. joint stock company
3. public and company 4. private company
5. conventional partnership

Select the correct answer by using the codes given below

Codes
(a) Only 1 (b) 1, 2 and 4
(c) Both 4 and 5 (d) All of these

91 In exemption method,
(a) income is taxed in the country of source and country of residence and deduction is provided in other country
(b) income is taxed in one country and exempt from tax in the other country
(c) Both (a) and (b)
(d) None of the above

92 Match the items of the List I with those of the List II.

	List I		List II
A.	Residential status of an individual	1.	Section 10 (13A)
B.	Agricultural income	2.	Section 10 (10)
C.	House rent allowance	3.	Section 6
D.	Gratuity	4.	Section 10 (1)

Codes

	A	B	C	D		A	B	C	D
(a)	1	3	2	4	(b)	3	4	1	2
(c)	2	1	3	4	(d)	4	2	1	3

93 Donation to National Children's Fund will come in which of the following deduction under Section 80G of Income Tax Act, 1961?
(a) 100% deduction without any qualifying limit
(b) 50% deduction without any qualifying limit
(c) 100% deduction subject to qualifying limit
(d) 50% deduction subject to qualifying limit

94 Which of the following will be considered as agricultural income?
(a) Income from live stock breeding
(b) Income from cattle breeding
(c) Income from juice centre
(d) Rent received from agricultural land

95 Which of the following statements are correct?
1. Charity received from customers is not business income.
2. In connection with the statutory income tax preceding, expenses upto ₹ 20,000 are admissible.
3. Expenses incurred for issuing share are deductible.

Select the correct answer using the codes given below

Codes
(a) Only 1 (b) Both 1 and 2
(c) Both 1 and 3 (d) All of the above

96 Which of the following factors is not considered under the OECD model convention to determine the residence of an individual?
(a) Habitual abode
(b) Centre of vital interests
(c) Own house in Calcutta given on rent for the last ten years
(d) Flat taken on rent in Pune, where he is living for the last ten years

97 Transactions between unrelated entities are carried out at
(a) arm's length price (b) control price
(c) Both (a) and (b) (d) Either (a) or (b)

98 Dividend from an Indian company is not taxable It is exempt under Section
(a) 10 (10) (b) 10 (34) (c) 10 (2A) (d) 2 (AA)

99 Applicaiton for applying a PAN is given in form no.
(a) 48C (b) 49A (c) 42B (d) 54

100 In order to claim relief under the tax treaty in India, a non-resident
(a) should have a business presence in India
(b) should produce his permanent account number
(c) should produce Tax Residency Certificate (TRC)
(d) should produce his income tax return filed in the home country

ANSWERS

1 (c)	2 (c)	3 (b)	4 (a)	5 (c)	6 (c)	7 (a)	8 (b)	9 (a)	10 (a)
11 (b)	12 (c)	13 (b)	14 (b)	15 (b)	16 (a)	17 (d)	18 (c)	19 (a)	20 (b)
21 (c)	22 (d)	23 (d)	24 (d)	25 (b)	26 (c)	27 (b)	28 (b)	29 (a)	30 (d)
31 (c)	32 (c)	33 (b)	34 (b)	35 (a)	36 (d)	37 (a)	38 (d)	39 (b)	40 (c)
41 (b)	42 (b)	43 (b)	44 (a)	45 (d)	46 (c)	47 (b)	48 (b)	49 (c)	50 (b)
51 (b)	52 (c)	53 (d)	54 (a)	55 (d)	56 (b)	57 (a)	58 (c)	59 (d)	60 (b)
61 (d)	62 (b)	63 (a)	64 (b)	65 (b)	66 (a)	67 (a)	68 (d)	69 (c)	70 (c)
71 (b)	72 (c)	73 (c)	74 (d)	75 (d)	76 (a)	77 (a)	78 (a)	79 (a)	80 (a)
81 (a)	82 (a)	83 (a)	84 (d)	85 (b)	86 (b)	87 (b)	88 (c)	89 (b)	90 (c)
91 (b)	92 (b)	93 (a)	94 (d)	95 (a)	96 (c)	97 (a)	98 (b)	99 (b)	100 (c)

UGC NET/JRF/SET

COMMERCE (Paper-2)

Model Paper-2

General Instructions

1. There are total one hundred questions in this paper. Each question carries 2 marks.
2. All questions are compulsory.

1 Reason of decline of monetary policy is

(a) wide non-monetary region (b) flow of black money
(c) measuring credit money (d) All of the above

2 Which of the following are engaged in external influence?

(a) Political policies (b) Legal practices
(c) Both (a) and (b) (d) Neither (a) nor (b)

3 Mercantilism was known as ...... in France.

(a) colbertism (b) physiocratism
(c) cameralism (d) None of these

4 The quotas of all the member countries with IMF are valued in terms of

(a) SDR (b) Dollar
(c) Both (a) and (b) (d) None of these

5 One of the characteristics of the economic environment is

(a) tradition (b) society
(c) life (d) public policies

6 Match the following.

List I	List II
A. Social factors	1. Increment and reduction in price of fuel
B. Political factors	2. Primary function of business
C. Economic factors	3. Customs, traditions and assumptions
D. Analysis of needs and interest of customers	4. Industrial policy of government

Codes

	A	B	C	D
(a)	4	2	1	3
(b)	3	4	1	2
(c)	1	2	3	4
(d)	4	3	2	1

7 Match the following.

List I	List II
A. Merchandise exports	1. Purchase of foreign goods
B. Merchandise imports	2. Sales of goods abroad
C. Investment income	3. Largely caused by excess of imports over exports in merchandise
D. Balance of payment deficits	4. Dividends, interest etc received from abroad

Codes

	A	B	C	D
(a)	1	2	3	4
(b)	2	3	4	1
(c)	2	1	4	3
(d)	3	4	2	1

8 Consider the following statements in context of WTO.

1. WTO is a permanent body with its over dispute settlement mechanism.
2. Scope of WTO has been broadened by inclusion of services, intellectual property rights and investment measures.
3. WTO promote international trade.
4. WTO banned the foreign currency.

5. WTO managed the hybrid system of clean floating, currency block etc.

Which of the statement(s) given above is/are correct?
(a) Both 1 and 2
(b) Both 2 and 5
(c) 1, 2 and 3
(d) Both 3 and 4

9 **Assertion** (A) Business is responsible for whole society rather than businessman.

Reason (R) As business converts into independent from its responsibility maximise.

Codes
(a) Both (A) and (R) are true and (R) is the correct explanation of (A)
(b) Both (A) and (R) are true, but (R) is not the correct explanation of (A)
(c) (A) is correct, but (R) is incorrect
(d) (A) is incorrect, but (R) is correct

10 **Arrange the following concepts/acts in the order in which they came into force.**
1. Competition Act
2. Foreign Exchange Management Act
3. Consumer Protection Act
4. Securities and Exchange Board of India Act

Codes
(a) 3, 4, 2, 1 (b) 4, 3, 2, 1
(c) 1, 2, 4, 3 (d) 2, 1, 3, 4

11 **As per revenue recognition concept, revenue is deemed to be realised**
(a) when purchase order is received from the purchaser
(b) when goods are delivered to the purchaser
(c) when the title of the goods has been transferred to the purchaser
(d) when cash is received from the purchaser

12 **Match the following.**

List I	List II
A. Materiality concept	1. The same accounting method used by a firm from one period to another
B. Going concern concept	2. An inappropriate assumption of a firm being bankrupt
C. Historical cost concept	3. A normal basis used for accounting assets
D. Consistency concept	4. Relates to the importance of an item or event

Codes

	A	B	C	D
(a)	4	2	3	1
(b)	1	2	3	4
(c)	2	3	4	1
(d)	4	2	1	3

13 **A and B are partners in a firm sharing profit and loss in the ratio of 3:2. They admit C into partnership for $\frac{1}{4}$th share and the new ratio between A and B is 2 : 1. The sacrificing ratio is**
(a) 1 : 1 (b) 2 : 1 (c) 3 : 1 (d) 2 : 3

14 **Consider the following information.**
1. Gross sales ₹ 20,00,000
2. Sales tax 7% on gross sales
3. Income tax 40%
4. Profit before tax ₹ 4,00,000

What is net profit before tax ratio?
(a) 21.5% (b) 22.5% (c) 23.5% (d) 24.5%

15 **Statement** I Management audit is a part of financial audit.

Statement II Management audit is not compulsory under any law.

Codes
(a) Only Statement I is true (b) Only Statement II is true
(c) Both statements are true (d) Both statements are false

16 **Match the following.**

List I	List II
A. Excess of actual sales over the break-even sales volume	1. Contribution
B. Sum of fixed cost and profit	2. Cost volume profit analysis
C. Break-even chart	3. Unaffected by change in output
D. Break-even point	4. Margin of safety

Codes

	A	B	C	D
(a)	4	1	2	3
(b)	4	3	2	1
(c)	4	3	1	2
(d)	3	1	4	2

17 **If a share of ₹ 100 on which ₹ 60 has been paid, is forfeited, it can be re-issued at the minimum price of**
(a) ₹ 60 (b) ₹ 100 (c) ₹ 40 (d) ₹ 140

18 **Which of the following cash flows is not a cash flow from operating activity?**
(a) Cash receipts from royalties, fees, commissions and other revenue
(b) Cash payments to suppliers for goods and services
(c) Cash payment to and on behalf of employees
(d) Payment of dividend

19 **If sales is ₹ 1,00,000 in 2018 and ₹ 4,00,000 in 2019 and loss ₹ 10,000 in 2018 and profit ₹ 50,000 in 2019, P/V ratio will be**
(a) 50% (b) 20% (c) 30% (d) 40%

20 **Kaizen costing is applied to a product that is**
(a) produced (b) under production
(c) targeted to produce (d) sold to customer

21 In the case of giffen goods like Bajara, a fall in its price tends to
(a) reduce the demand
(b) increase the demand
(c) demand will remain constant
(d) None of the above

22 Demand curve for a firm facing perfect competition is

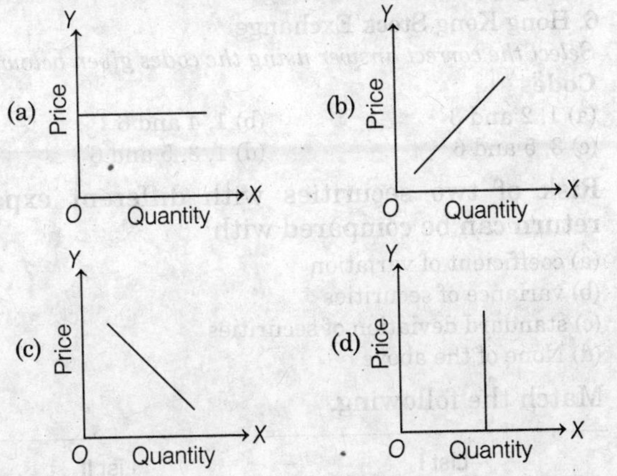

23 Which one is not the characteristics of oligopoly firm?
(a) Conflicting attitude of firms
(b) Advertising and sales promotion
(c) One firm
(d) Few sellers

24 The area which lies under the demand curve for a given good measures
(a) marginal utility (b) marginal cost
(c) marginal profit (d) total utility

25 The basic nature of average fixed cost is that it
(a) increases as output increases
(b) remain same at all levels of output
(c) decreases with increase in output
(d) All of the above

26 Match the following.

List I	List II
A. $AP \times L$	1. Marginal product
B. $TU_n - TU_{n-1}$	2. Marginal utility
C. $TP - TP_{n-1}$	3. Total product

Codes

	A	B	C		A	B	C
(a)	1	2	3	(b)	3	2	1
(c)	2	3	1	(d)	2	1	3

27 Match the following.

List I	List II
A. Substitute goods	1. Income effect is positive
B. Complementary goods	2. Tea and coffee
C. Normal goods	3. Car and petrol
D. Inferior goods	4. Income effect is negative

Codes

	A	B	C	D		A	B	C	D
(a)	2	3	1	4	(b)	1	2	3	4
(c)	1	4	3	2	(d)	4	3	2	1

28 **Assertion** (A) Negative MR is not possible in case of perfect competition.
Reason (R) Price remains constant for a perfectly competitive firm.
Codes
(a) Both (A) and (R) are true and (R) is the correct explanation of (A)
(b) Both (A) and (R) are true, but (R) is not the correct explanation of (A)
(c) (A) is true, but (R) is false
(d) (A) is false, but (R) is true

29 **Statement** I The important difference between our assumptions for monopolistic competition and those for perfect competition is that monopolistic competitors sell similar, but not identical products.
Statement II In monopolistic competition, we have many firms selling a differentiated product.
Codes
(a) Both statements are correct
(b) Both statements are incorrect
(c) Statement I is correct, but Statement II is incorrect
(d) Statement I is incorrect, but Statement II is correct

30 Returns to scale involve variations in the quantities of the various factors of production
1. Simultaneously 2. Proportionately
Codes
(a) Both 1 and 2 are correct
(b) 1 is correct, but 2 is incorrect
(c) 1 is incorrect, but 2 is correct
(d) Neither 1 nor 2

31 Financing a long lived assets with short-term financing would be
(a) an example of 'moderate risk-moderate (potential) profitability' assets financing
(b) an example of 'low risk-low (potential) profitability' assets financing
(c) an example of 'high risk-high (potential) profitability' assets financing
(d) an example of the 'hedging approach' for financing

32 Match the following.

List I (Forms of Dividend Payment)	List II (Features)
A. Cash dividend	1. This type of dividend is rarely opted by companies
B. Stock dividend	2. The companies whose liquidity position is sound also prefer distribution of this dividend

List I (Forms of Dividend Payment)	List II (Features)
C. Bond dividend	3. Companies which are short of cash resources for dividend payment can distribute this dividend
D. Property dividend	4. It is distributed only when the company is capable of bearing the increased burden of interest on bonds

Codes

	A	B	C	D		A	B	C	D
(a)	4	1	2	3	(b)	2	3	4	1
(c)	3	4	1	2	(d)	3	1	4	2

33 Which of the following is not followed in capital budgeting?

(a) Cash flows principle
(b) Interest exclusion principle
(c) Accrual principle
(d) Post-tax principle

34 Which one of the following is not used to estimate cost of equity capital?

(a) External yield criterion
(b) Dividend plus growth rate
(c) Equity capitalisation approach
(d) Capital asset pricing model

35 **Statement** I In payback period method, the risk of the project is adjusted by lessening the target payback period.

Statement II Sensitivity analysis helps in calculation of net present value of the proposal.

Codes

(a) Statement I is correct, but Statement II is wrong
(b) Statement II is wrong, but Statement II is correct
(c) Statement I and Statement II, both are correct
(d) Statement I and Statement II, both are wrong

36 What prompted Brettonwoods Agreement?

(a) To set up a system that would maintain a stable exchange rate system
(b) To create a flexible exchange rate system
(c) To stop World War II
(d) Eradicate the economic difficulties brought in by World War II

37 **Assertion** (A) Arbitrage keeps the cost of capital constant despite change in the capital structure.

Reason (R) It ensures compensating inverse change in cost of equity capital with a change in the cost of debt capital.

Codes

(a) (A) and (R) both are true and (R) is the correct explanation of (A)
(b) (A) and (R) both are true, but (R) is not the correct explanation of (A)
(c) (A) is true, but (R) is false
(d) (A) is not true, but (R) is true

38 In which of the following stock exchanges, the GDRs are listed?

1. London Stock Exchange
2. New York Stock Exchange
3. Luxembourg Stock Exchange
4. Bombay Stock Exchange
5. Singapore Stock Exchange
6. Hong Kong Stock Exchange

Select the correct answer using the codes given below

Codes

(a) 1, 2 and 3 (b) 1, 4 and 6
(c) 3, 5 and 6 (d) 1, 3, 5 and 6

39 Risk of two securities with different expected return can be compared with

(a) coefficient of variation
(b) variance of securities
(c) standard deviation of securities
(d) None of the above

40 Match the following.

List I	List II
A. Realised yield method	1. Cost of equity share capital
B. Taxation	2. Cost of equity capital
C. Cost of total capital employed	3. Cost of debt capital
D. Dividend growth is a consideration	4. Weighted cost of capital

Codes

	A	B	C	D
(a)	4	3	2	1
(b)	2	4	1	3
(c)	2	3	4	1
(d)	1	2	3	4

41 Match the following.

List I	List II
A. Statistical methods	1. Technique used for collection, summarisation, analysis, comparison, classification and interpretation of huge and complex numerical data
B. Branch of statistics	2. Inductive and descriptive statistics
C. Nature of statistics	3. Science and art
D. First user of statistics	4. Hemlet

Codes

	A	B	C	D
(a)	1	2	3	4
(b)	2	3	4	1
(c)	1	3	2	4
(d)	3	4	2	1

42 **Assertion** (A) In mean deviation, everything is considered positive.

Reason (R) Sum of the deviations of the value of items in a series from arithmetic mean is zero and from other averages it is nearly zero.

Codes
(a) Both (A) and (R) are true
(b) Both (A) and (R) are true, but (R) is not the correct explanation of (A)
(c) Both (A) and (R) are false
(d) (A) is true, but (R) is false

43 Identify which of the following steps would be included in hypothesis testing.
1. State the null and alternative hypothesis.
2. Set the significance level before the research study.
3. Eliminate all outliers.
4. Obtain the probability value using a computer programme such as SPSS.
5. Compare the probability value to the significance level and make the statistical decision.

Select the correct answer using the codes given below

Codes
(a) 1, 3 and 4 (b) 3, 4 and 5
(c) 1, 2, 4 and 5 (d) 2, 3, 4 and 5

44 The ...... is a set of values for testing statistic, for which the null hypothesis is rejected in a hypothesis test.
(a) critical region (b) rejection region
(c) Either (a) or (b) (d) None of these

45 Match the following.

	List I		List II
A	Quartile deviation	1.	obtained by calculating the absolute deviation of each observation from mean.
B.	Standard deviation	2.	is one-half of the inter-quartile range.
C.	Mean deviation	3.	is the square root of the average of the squared distances of the observation from the mean.

Codes

	A	B	C		A	B	C
(a)	2	3	1	(b)	1	2	3
(c)	2	1	3	(d)	3	2	1

46 If the value of coefficient of determination is 0.64, what is the value of coefficient of correlation?
(a) 0.40 (b) 0.80 (c) 0.08 (d) 0.04

47 The statistical study begins with collection of data and ends with
(a) organisation of data (b) analysis of data
(c) interpretation of data (d) None of these

48 **Assertion** (A) Median is simply the middle value when the data have been arranged in ascending or descending order.

Reason (R) Median refers to middle value in the distribution.

Codes
(a) Both (A) and (R) are true (b) (A) is true, but (R) is false
(c) (A) is false, but (R) is true (d) Both (A) and (R) are false

49 While drawing a scatter diagram, if all the points appear to form a straight line going downward from left to right, then it is inferred that there is a
(a) perfect positive correlation
(b) simple positive correlation
(c) perfect negative correlation
(d) No correlation

50 Which one of the following is not a measures of dispersion?
(a) Quartile (b) Range
(c) Mean Deviation (d) Standard Deviation

51 Decisions which can be changed or totally revoked are called
(a) irreversible (b) trial and error
(c) experimental (d) reversible

52 Under delegation of authority,
(a) authority is given to subordinates
(b) authority flows from top to bottom
(c) delegator of authority is not relieved
(d) All of the above

53 'Motivation Hygience Theory' was propounded by
(a) Herzberg (b) Maslow
(c) McGregor (d) Peter F Drucker

54 Which of the following is an on-the-job method of training?
(a) Internship
(b) Apprenticeship programmes
(c) Coaching
(d) Lecture

55 Rewards, one gets from the employer usually money, a promotion or benefits, are known as
(a) extrinsic rewards
(b) intrinsic rewards
(c) employee stock option plan
(d) None of the above

56 Match the following.

	List I (Concepts)		List II (Features)
A.	Human resource management	1.	Its objective is to create a pool of the prospective job candidates
B.	Human resource planning	2.	It involves growth of an employee in all respects
C.	Development	3.	Get qualified people at right time
D.	Recruitment	4.	It focuses on managing physical and emotional capital of employees

Codes

	A	B	C	D		A	B	C	D
(a)	4	3	2	1	(b)	2	3	4	1
(c)	3	1	4	2	(d)	4	3	1	2

57 Match the following.

List I (Concepts)	List II (Meaning)
A. Centralisation	1. Right to give orders to the subordinates.
B. Scalar chain	2. Concentration of authority at one place or at one level in the organisation.
C. Esprit de corps	3. The chain of superiors ranging from the chief executive or ultimate authority to the lowest level in the organisation.
D. Authority	4. The spirit of loyalty and devotion which unites the members of the group.

Codes

	A	B	C	D		A	B	C	D
(a)	2	3	4	1	(b)	3	4	2	1
(c)	4	3	1	2	(d)	2	4	1	3

58 **Assertion** (A) There is no place for human feelings in formal organisation.

Reason (R) Formal organisation is not impersonal.

Codes

(a) Both (A) and (R) are correct and (R) is the correct explanation of (A)
(b) Both (A) and (R) are correct, but (R) is not the correct explanation of (A)
(c) (A) is correct, but (R) is incorrect
(d) (A) is incorrect, but (R) is correct

59 Consider the following statements.

1. Leadership is the ability to influence the behaviour of others.
2. Motivation increases the rate of labour turnover.

Which of the statment(s) given above is/are correct?

(a) Only 1
(b) Only 2
(c) Both 1 and 2
(d) None of the above

60 **Assertion** (A) Under performance base incentives, performance that is rewarded is likely to be repeated.

Reason (R) People tend to do thing that are rewarded.

Codes

(a) Both (A) and (R) are true
(b) Both (A) and (R) are true and (R) is the correct explanation of (A)
(c) Both (A) and (R) are false
(d) (A) is true, but (R) is false

61 Interest rate futures trading in India is available on

(a) 91 days, T-bills
(b) 10 years, National Government of India Security
(c) Both (a) and (b)
(d) None of the above

62 Bank show provision for income tax under the head

(a) contingent liabilities
(b) other liabilities and provisions
(c) contingent account
(d) other accounts

63 Under which pillar of RBI's new capital adequacy framework (Basel-II guidelines), minimum 8% capital adequacy for credit risk, market risk and operational risk has been prescribed?

(a) Pillar-I
(b) Pillar-II
(c) Pillar-III
(d) None of these

64 Which bank had its office in Anarkali Bazar, Lahore when registered on 19th May, 1894 under Indian Companies Act?

(a) Punjab and Sind Bank
(b) Syndicate Bank
(c) Punjab National Bank
(d) United Bank of India

65 A type of insurance that combines protection investment plan is called

(a) whole life
(b) limited pay
(c) universal
(d) endowment

66 Match the following.

List I (Mutual Fund Schemes)	List II (Characteristics)
A. Open-ended mutual fund scheme	1. It offers capital appreciation of the underlying investment.
B. Close-ended mutual fund scheme	2. It is a fund accepted and liquidated on a continuous basis by a mutual fund manager.
C. Growth fund scheme	3. It is also known as regional or country fund.
D. Off-shore mutual fund	4. No exist possible till the closure of the scheme.

Codes

	A	B	C	D		A	B	C	D
(a)	2	1	4	3	(b)	3	4	1	2
(c)	2	4	1	3	(d)	3	1	4	2

67 Match the following.

List I	List II
A. Hawala	1. Clearing of cheques
B. RBI	2. Illegal transactions of foreign exchange
C. SEBI	3. Regulator body
D. Commercial Bank	4. Central Bank

Codes

	A	B	C	D		A	B	C	D
(a)	1	3	2	4	(b)	2	3	4	1
(c)	3	2	1	4	(d)	1	2	3	4

68 Arrange the events in the ascending order of their occurrence.

1. Allowing convertibility of rupee at the market rate in the current account.
2. Nationalisation of general insurance business.
3. Establishment of IDBI.
4. Nationalisation of life insurance business.
5. Capital adequacy norms for commercial banks.

Codes

(a) 4, 3, 2, 1, 5 (b) 5, 4, 3, 2, 1
(c) 1, 2, 3, 5, 4 (d) 1, 5, 2, 4, 3

69 Identify the quantitative credit control methods among the following.

1. Bank Rate 2. Credit Rationing
3. Open Market Operations 4. Variable Reserve Ratio
5. Selective Credit Control 6. Liquidity Ratio

Codes

(a) 1, 2, 3 and 4 (b) 2, 3, 4 and 5
(c) 1, 2, 5 and 6 (d) 1, 3, 4 and 6

70 Assertion (A) SEBI issues guidelines for all companies for disclosure of information and protection of investor's interest.

Reason (R) Computerised screen based trading has been introduced on all major stock exchanges.

(a) Both (A) and (R) are true and (R) is the correct explanation of (A)
(b) Both (A) and (R) are true, but (R) is not the correct explanation of (A)
(c) (A) is true, but (R) is false
(d) (R) is true, but (A) is false

71 Which one of the following contains the three elements of service marketing triangle?

(a) Management, Marketing Agency and Consumer
(b) Marketing Agency, Government and Consumer
(c) Management, Employees and Marketing Agency
(d) Management, Employees and Consumer

72 Service marketing become difficult because of

(a) intangibility
(b) no demand
(c) more complex market
(d) difficult to enter the market

73 Which of the following is/are benefit(s) of online marketing?

(a) It helps in tracking (b) It build relationship
(c) Both (a) and (b) (d) Neither (a) nor (b)

74 Which of the following is not one of the most common pricing objecitve?

(a) Target return (b) Survival
(c) Cost per thousand (d) Product quality

75 Which of the following influences consumer's buying behaviour?

(a) Consumer's identity
(b) Consumer's beliefs and needs
(c) Altitudes and kind of product
(d) All of the above

76 Match the following.

List I	List II
A. Market segmentation	1. Pricing high of a new product initially.
B. Skimming price	2. Process of disagreegating a market into a number of sub-markets.
C. Multilevel marketing	3. Translation of the marketing plan into marketing performance.
D. Sales management	4. Modified version of direct marketing

Codes

	A	B	C	D
(a)	2	1	4	3
(b)	3	1	2	4
(c)	1	2	3	4
(d)	4	2	3	1

77 Match the following.

List I (Pricing Methods)	List II (Explanations)
A. Mark-up pricing	1. Set high price and recover the cost as early as possible
B. Target return pricing	2. Cost of the product + Mark-up (desired profit)
C. Going rate pricing	3. Specified rate of return on investment
D. Market skimming	4. Prevailing pricing matters

Codes

	A	B	C	D		A	B	C	D
(a)	2	3	4	1	(b)	1	2	3	4
(c)	2	4	3	1	(d)	4	3	2	1

78 Assertion (A) According to the concept of product life cycle, a company should begin a search for new products during stage.

Reason (R) The growth stage is the time in which a company should begin to search for new products.

Codes

(a) Both (A) and (R) are true
(b) Both (A) and (R) are false
(c) (A) is true, but (R) is false
(d) (R) is true, but (A) is false

79 Which of the following are the merits of marketing planning?

1. Identification of future development.
2. Consideration of opportunities and problems.
3. Focus on objectives.
4. Profitable employment of resources.

Which of the statement(s) given above is/are correct?

Codes

(a) Only 1 (b) Both 1 and 2
(c) 1, 2 and 3 (d) All of the above

80 Which of the following is an uncontrollable variable(s)?

1. Consumer variable
2. Environmental variable
3. Common variable
4. Competitive variable

Select the correct answer using the codes given below

Codes

(a) 1, 2 and 3 (b) 1, 2 and 4
(c) 2, 3 and 4 (d) 3, 4 and 1

81 Which of the following is an intra-state supply?

(a) Supplier of goods located in Nagpur and place of supply of goods SEZ located in Mumbai
(b) Supplier of goods located in Kolkata and place of supply of goods in Bengaluru
(c) Supplier of goods located in Goa and place of supply of goods in Goa
(d) All of the above

82 Any gurantee which the creditor has obtained by means of keeping silence as to material circumstances is

(a) valid
(b) considered to be his approval
(c) invaild
(d) considered to be his denial

83 What is public domain?

(a) Work belonging to the public as a whole
(b) Work that people know about
(c) Work that is in public
(d) All of the above

84 What is a continuing guarantee?

(a) A guarantee which continues even after the contract comes to an end
(b) A guarantee which shall be applicable to any other person who becomes a party to the contract
(c) A guarantee which extends to a series of transaction
(d) A guarantee which continues till the contract does not come to an end

85 Section 32 of the Competition Act, deals with

(a) international cartel
(b) power to impose lesser penalty
(c) establishment of commission
(d) composition of commission

86 Match the following.

	List I		List II
A.	Definition of negotiable instrument	1.	Section 4
B.	Promissory note	2.	Section 5
C.	Bill of exchange	3.	Section 6
D.	Cheque	4.	Section 13

Codes

	A	B	C	D		A	B	C	D
(a)	1	2	3	4	(b)	4	1	2	3
(c)	4	3	2	1	(d)	2	3	1	4

87 **Assertion** (A) Patent right is limited period right.

Reason (R) A patent right is available to patentee for 20 years from the date of filling on that jurisdiction.

(a) Both (A) and (R) are true and (R) is the correct explanation of (A)
(b) Both (A) and (R) are true, but (R) is not the correct explanation of (A)
(c) (A) is true, but (R) is false
(d) (A) is false, but (R) is true

88 **Assertion** (A) Trademark registrations can be renewed for an unlimited number of ten periods.

Reason (R) The registered user will not have a right of assignment or transmission.

(a) Both (A) and (R) are true and (R) is the correct explanation of (A)
(b) Both (A) and (R) are true, but (R) is not the correct explanation of (A)
(c) (A) is true, but (R) is false
(d) (A) is false, but (R) is true

89 **Statement** I Right of lien of an unpaid seller is a right against goods.

Statement II An unpaid seller has rights against the buyer.

Which of the following statement(s) is/are true?

(a) Only I (b) Only II
(c) Both I and II (d) Neither I nor II

90 **Statement** I GST is a destination based tax on consumption of goods and services.

Statement II 'I' stands for integrated in IGST.

(a) Only Statement I is true
(b) Only Statement II is true
(c) Both statements are true
(d) Both statements are false

91 Advance rulling can resolve complex issues arising under...... where a difference of opinion may exist.

(a) Income Tax Act, 1961 (b) DTAA
(c) Both (a) and (b) (d) None of these

92 Match the following.

	List I		List II
A.	Whe the assessee is in default or is deemed to be in default in making payment of tax, including the tax deducted at source	1.	Section 271 (1) C
B.	Failure to pay the advance tax as directed by the assessing officer	2.	Section 273(1)
C.	Concealment of particulars of income or furnishing of inaccurate particulars of income	3.	Section 201(1)

Codes

	A	B	C		A	B	C
(a)	1	2	3	(b)	3	2	1
(c)	3	1	2	(d)	2	1	3

29 Consider the following statements.

1. Point of inflexion exists where Ist state of law of variable proportions ends.
2. TP increases even when MP is decreasing.
3. Producer will stop only at IInd stage of variable proportions.

Which of the statement(s) given above is/are correct?

Codes

(a) Both 1 and 2 (b) 1, 2 and 3
(c) Only 1 (d) None of the above

30 Consider the following statements.

1. Cartel is an informal agreement among the firms to avoid competition.
2. There is a free entry of firms in monopoly market.
3. There is a full control over price in perfect competition.

Which of the statement(s) given above is/are correct?

Codes

(a) Only 1 (b) Both 1 and 2
(c) Only 2 (d) All of the above

31 Which of the following is the most appropriate form for financing a new capital investment in plant and equipment?

(a) Trade credit (b) Six months bank notes
(c) Account payable (d) Common stock equity

32 Match the following.

List I	List II
A. Share	1. Fixed capital
B. Land and building	2. Period of medium-term finance
C. Public deposits	3. Source of long-term finance
D. 1-5 years	4. Short-term finance
E. Meeting day-to-day requirements	5. Source of medium-term finance

Codes

	A	B	C	D	E		A	B	C	D	E
(a)	4	2	3	1	5	(b)	4	1	5	2	4
(c)	[illegible]	3	5	1	4	(d)	5	3	2	4	1

33 What is the advantage of 'NPV Method'?

(a) This method considers the entire economic life of the project
(b) It takes into account the objective of maximum profitability
(c) This method can be allied where cash inflows are even
(d) All of the above

34 Which one of the following is not a sources of conflict in project ranking in capital budgeting geting decision as per NPV and IRR?

(a) Independent investment project
(b) No capital budget constraints
(c) No time disparity
(d) None of the above

93 Which of the following expenses is in admissible while computing income from other sources?

(a) Interest paid on amounts borrowed to meet tax liabilities
(b) Collection charges paid to the banker or any other person to collect interest/dividend
(c) Interest on loan taken to invest in securities
(d) Depreciation on let out machinery and plant

94 Which of the following is non-agricultural income?

(a) Income from agriculture in Nepal
(b) Reward received from higher yield
(c) Income from letting out agricultural machinery
(d) All of the above

95 Which of the following statement(s) is/are correct?

1. An assessee may enjoy different residential status for different assessment year.
2. It is not necessary that a person, who is resident in India, cannot become resident in any other country for the same assessment year.
3. Where a person is in India only for a part of a day, it will be calculated as one complete day.

Select the correct answer using the codes given below

(a) Only 1
(b) Both 1 and 2
(c) Both 1 and 3
(d) All of the above

96 As per the OECD model convention, the term 'Permanent Establishment' would not include

(a) branch
(b) an office for carrying out routine administrative work
(c) a factory for manufacture of goods
(d) a warehouse for storage of goods

97 The purpose of transfer pricing was to ensure that the profit of a non-tax holiday segment were not

(a) overstated (b) understated
(c) Either (a) or (b) (d) Neither (a) nor (b)

98 Deduction in respect of contribution to pension scheme of Central Government is covered under section

(a) 80 C (b) 80 CCC (c) 80 CCD (d) 80 D

99 Return of income is submitted under which of the following sections?

(a) U/S 139 (3) (b) U/S 139 (1) (c) U/S 145 (d) U/S 143

100 The provisions relating to limitation of interest deduction in respect of debt issued by a non-resident associated enterprises are not applicable to an Indian company engaged in the business of

(a) information technology
(b) banking and insurance business
(c) bio-technology
(d) aviation

ANSWERS

1 (b)	2 (c)	3 (a)	4 (a)	5 (d)	6 (b)	7 (c)	8 (b)	9 (a)	10 (a)
11 (c)	12 (c)	13 (d)	14 (a)	15 (b)	16 (a)	17 (c)	18 (d)	19 (b)	20 (b)
21 (a)	22 (a)	23 (c)	24 (d)	25 (c)	26 (b)	27 (a)	28 (a)	29 (a)	30 (c)
31 (c)	32 (b)	33 (c)	34 (a)	35 (a)	36 (a)	37 (a)	38 (d)	39 (a)	40 (c)
41 (a)	42 (a)	43 (c)	44 (c)	45 (d)	46 (b)	47 (c)	48 (a)	49 (c)	50 (a)
51 (d)	52 (c)	53 (a)	54 (a)	55 (a)	56 (a)	57 (a)	58 (c)	59 (a)	60 (b)
61 (c)	62 (b)	63 (a)	64 (c)	65 (c)	66 (c)	67 (b)	68 (a)	69 (d)	70 (b)
71 (d)	72 (a)	73 (c)	74 (c)	75 (d)	76 (b)	77 (a)	78 (d)	79 (d)	80 (b)
81 (c)	82 (c)	83 (a)	84 (c)	85 (a)	86 (b)	87 (a)	88 (b)	89 (c)	90 (c)
91 (c)	92 (b)	93 (a)	94 (d)	95 (b)	96 (d)	97 (a)	98 (c)	99 (b)	100 (b)

UGC

NET/JRF/SET

COMMERCE (Paper-2)

Model Paper-3

General Instructions

1. There are total one hundred questions in this paper. Each question carries 2 marks.
2. All questions are compulsory.

1 Which function is not performed by the government for promotion of economic environment?
(a) Nurture the mentality of country's development
(b) Exploitation of environment
(c) Effects proper utilisation of resources
(d) All of the above

2 A global company is sometimes called
(a) a joint stock company (b) a corporation
(c) a globally integrated company
(d) None of the above

3 The effects of foreign trade on the domestic economy may be at
(a) micro level (b) macro level
(c) Both (a) and (b) (d) Neither (a) nor (b)

4 Board of executive director of IMF may be appointed for
(a) 6 years (b) 2 years
(c) 8 years (d) None of these

5 International trade brings developing countries in contact with
(a) developed nations (b) underdeveloped countries
(c) low developed countries (d) All of these

6 Match the following.

	List I		List II
A.	Importing	1.	Modes of international business
B.	Marketing	2.	Functions of international business
C.	Sales expansion	3.	Objectives of international business
D.	Economic forces	4.	External influence

Codes

	A	B	C	D		A	B	C	D
(a)	1	2	3	4	(b)	3	1	4	2
(c)	4	1	3	4	(d)	4	3	2	1

7 Match the following.

	List I		List II
A.	SAARC	1.	To promote cooperative peace and shared prosperity
B.	NAFTA	2.	To provide protection and enforcement of intellectual property rights
C.	ASEAN	3.	To promote the welfare of the people of South Asia and to improve their quality of life

Codes

	A	B	C		A	B	C
(a)	3	2	1	(b)	2	1	3
(c)	2	3	1	(d)	1	2	3

8 **Statement** I A bill of lading is a document of title to the goods.

Statement II A bill of lading contains all the terms and conditions agreed upon between the ship owner and the charterer.

Codes
(a) Both statements are correct

(b) Bots statements are
(c) Statement I is
(d) Stateme

9 A
ch
1. O
2. Or
3. Goo
4. Good
Codes
(a) 4, 3, 2,
(c) 3, 1, 4,

10 **Assertion**
serves as a
India and ov
Reason (R)
several countri
Codes
(a) (A) and (R) bo explanation of (A
(b) (A) and (R) both a explanation of (A)
(c) (A) is correct, but (R
(d) (R) is correct, but (A)

11 Which of the following
(a) Accounting principles respective governments
(b) Accounting principles accounting expert
(c) Accounting principles repres by a legal board
(d) Accounting principles represe particular time to the reco transactions

12 Match the following.

	List I		List II
A.	Intangible assets	1.	Ind AS-
B.	Impairment of assets	2.	Ind AS-3
C.	Interim financial reporting	3.	Ind AS-36
D.	Interests in joint ventures	4.	Ind AS-38

Codes

	A	B	C	D		A	B	C	D
(a)	1	2	3	4	(b)	4	3	2	1
(c)	4	1	2	3	(d)	4	2	1	3

13 X and Y are partners in a firm sharing profits the ratio of 3 : 1. They admit Z as a partner wi new profit sharing ratio of 2 : 1 : 1. The amount o goodwill brought in by new partner will be credited to
(a) X and Y equally
(b) Only X
(c) Only Y
(d) None of the above

22 When the income elasticity of demand is gre than unity, the commodity is
(a) a necessity (b) a luxury
(c) inferior good (d) non-related good

23 In the long-run, for all monopolistic firms
(a) MR = AR (b) Price = MR = MC
(c) MR = MC = Price = AC (d) None of these

24 Assuming a downward sloping demand cu upward sloping supply curve, a equilibrium price may be caused by
(a) a fall in demand
(b) an increase in supply
(c) improvements in production technology
(d) an increase in demand

25 The equilibrium level of output fo monopolist is where
(a) MR = MC (b) P < AC
(c) MR < MC (d) MR > MC

26 Match the following

	List I		List II
A.	Total cost	1.	TR ÷ Q
B.	Average revenue	2.	ΔTC ÷
C.	Marginal cost	3.	AR ×
D.	Total revenue	4.	TFC +

Codes

	A	B	C	D		A
(a)	4	3	2	1	(b)	3
(c)	2	3	4	1	(d)	4

27 Match the following.

	List I		List II
A.	Total revenue	1.	Price
B.	Average revenue	2.	Tota
C.	Marginal revenue	3.	%
D.	Profit	4.	T

Codes

	A	B	C	D
(a)	1	2	3	4
(c)	4	3	1	2

28 **Assertion** (A) Under demand and supply, by the government.
Reason (R) Mark proves to be ineffici
Codes
(a) (A) is true, but (R)
(b) (A) is false, but (R)
(c) Both are true
(d) are false

35 **Assertion** (A) The IRR of a project is the discount rate which reduces its NPV to zero.

Reason (R) A project is worth accepting if the IRR exceeds the cost of capital.

Codes

(a) (A) is true, but (R) is false
(b) Both (A) and (R) are true
(c) (A) is false, but (R) is true
(d) Both (A) and (R) are false

36 The international monetary system went through several distinct stages of evolution. These stages are summarised, in alphabetic order, as follows

1. Bimetallism
2. Brettonwoods system
3. Classical gold standard
4. Flexible exchange rate regime
5. Interwar period

The chronological order that they actually occurred is

Codes

(a) 3, 1, 4, 2 and 5
(b) 1, 3, 5, 2 and 4
(c) 4, 1, 3, 2 and 5
(d) 5, 2, 1, 3 and 4

37 **Assertion** (A) The important aspect of dividend policy is to determine the amount of earnings to be distributed to shareholders and the amount to be retained in the firm.

Reason (R) Dividend policy of the firm has its effect on both the long-term financing and the wealth of shareholders.

Codes

(a) (A) and (R) both are correct and (R) is the correct explanation of (A)
(b) (A) and (R) both are correct, but (R) is not the correct explanation of (A)
(c) (A) is correct, but (R) is wrong
(d) (R) is correct, but (A) is wrong

38 Once the changeover to the euro was completed by 1st July, 2002, the legal-tender status of national currencies in the euro zone

(a) was cancelled, leaving the euro as the sole legal tender in the euro zone countries
(b) was affirmed at the fixed exchange rate
(c) was tied to gold
(d) None of the above

39 Efficient portfolios can be defined as those portfolios which for a given level of risk provides

(a) maximum return
(b) average return
(c) minimum return
(d) None of the above

40 Match the following.

List I (Measurements of Cost of Capital)	List II (Features)
A. Cost of debt	1. Its calculation is relatively difficult task
B. Cost of preference share capital	2. The amount of interest payment should be matched with the net cash proceeds of the debt
C. Cost of equity share capital	3. The shareholders have to incur some brokerage cost for investing the dividends received
D. Cost of retained earnings	4. The rate of dividend payable on these shares is fixed well in advance at the time of their issue

Codes

	A	B	C	D		A	B	C	D
(a)	4	3	1	2	(b)	2	3	4	1
(c)	3	4	2	1	(d)	2	4	1	3

41 Match the following.

List I	List II
A. Primary data	1. Representation of data in form of pictures
B. Secondary data	2. The totality of things under consideration
C. Pictogram	3. Data collected by the investigator himself
D. Population	4. Data used by the investigator, which has already been collected by others

Codes

	A	B	C	D		A	B	C	D
(a)	1	2	3	4	(b)	3	4	1	2
(c)	3	2	1	4	(d)	2	1	3	4

42 Which among the given statement is false?

(a) According to Boddington, "Statistics is the science of estimates and probabilities."
(b) According to Bowley, "Statistics may rightly be called the science of averages."
(c) According to Tippett, "Statistics is not a science, it is a scientific method."
(d) According to Seligman, "Statistics may be regarded as a body of methods for making wise decisions in the face of incertainty."

43 At 5% significance level, we are .... confident of the correctness of the decision.

(a) 95% (b) 50% (c) 99% (d) 10%

44 F-test is used to test the significance of the difference between/among

(a) two sample mean
(b) more than two samples mean
(c) variance of two samples
(d) Both (b) and (c)

92 Match the following.

	List I		List II
A.	Amount deposited in PPF	1.	Section 80-IA
B.	Profits and gains from undertakings engaged in infrastructure development	2.	Section 80-G
C.	Contribution to National Defence Fund	3.	Section 80-IA
D.	Profits and gains by an undertakings engaged in the development of special economic zone	4.	Section 80-C

Codes

	A	B	C	D
(a)	1	3	2	1
(b)	4	1	2	3
(c)	4	1	3	2
(d)	2	1	3	4

93 For the assessment year 2019-20, deduction under Section 80G is available without any limit, but at the rate of 50% on

(a) Prime Minister's National Relief Fund
(b) National Foundation for Communal Harmany
(c) Jawahar Lal Nehru Memorial Fund
(d) Chief Minister Relief Fund

94 The basis of determination of total income of a person is

(a) his citizenship in India
(b) his residential status in India
(c) Both (a) and (b)
(d) None of the above

95 Which of the following statements is/are correct?

1. A foreign company can be a domestic company.
2. There is no difference between an Indian company and a domestic company.
3. The control and management of a company should be examined for each previous year as the company many change the place of its control and management and consequently its residential status may also change.

Select the correct answer using the codes given below

(a) Both 1 and 3 (b) Only 3
(c) Both 2 and 3 (d) All of these

96 A separate article on 'Independent Personal Services' is present

(a) only in the OECD model convention
(b) only in the UN model convention
(c) only in the US model convention
(d) Both (a) and (b)

97 The objective of transfer pricing is to ……… within an organisation.

(a) minimise cost
(b) achieve economic efficiency
(c) maximise benefit
(d) None of the above

98 Deduction, which are permissible from gross total income are from

(a) Section 80C to 80IA (b) Section 80C to 80IC
(c) Section 80C to 80U (d) Section 80C to 80P

99 Notice of demand is served under which section?

(a) Section [illegible] (b) Section 154
(c) Section [illegible](3) (d) Section 156

100 When compared to a multilateral transfer pricing agreement. What is the main advantage of a unilateral agreement?

(a) It will eliminate the need to keep transfer pricing documentation
(b) It is quicker to negotiate
(c) It will enhance a company's profitability
(d) It will ensure no transfer pricing disputes arise

ANSWERS

1 (a)	2 (b)	3 (c)	4 (b)	5 (c)	6 (a)	7 (a)	8 (c)	9 (b)	10 (c)
11 (d)	12 (a)	13 (b)	14 (d)	15 (a)	16 (c)	17 (d)	18 (d)	19 (c)	20 [illegible]
21 (a)	22 (b)	23 (d)	24 (d)	25 (a)	26 (d)	27 (a)	28 (d)	29 (b)	30 [illegible]
31 (d)	32 (b)	33 (d)	34 (d)	35 (b)	36 (b)	37 (a)	38 (d)	39 [illegible]	40 [illegible]
41 (b)	42 (d)	43 (d)	44 (d)	45 (d)	46 (a)	47 (b)	48 (c)	49 [illegible]	50 [illegible]
51 (b)	52 (b)	53 (b)	54 [illegible]	55 (a)	56 (a)	57 (d)	58 (b)	59 [illegible]	60 [illegible]
61 (d)	62 (b)	63 (a)	64 (c)	65 [illegible]	66 (a)	67 (b)	68 (b)	69 [illegible]	70 [illegible]
71 (b)	72 (d)	73 (c)	74 (b)	75 (a)	76 (b)	77 (d)	78 (a)	79 [illegible]	80 [illegible]
81 (c)	82 (c)	83 (d)	84 [illegible]	85 (c)	86 (c)	87 (c)	88 (a)	89 [illegible]	90 [illegible]
91 (d)	92 [illegible]	93 (c)	94 [illegible]	95 (c)	96 (b)	97 (b)	98 (c)	99 [illegible]	100 [illegible]